Dictionary of
British Women
Writers

Dictionary of British Women Writers

Edited by Janet Todd

London

First published in 1989 by Routledge
11 New Fetter Lane, London EC4P 4EE
by arrangement with The Continuum Publishing Company

First published in paperback in 1991

British Library Cataloguing in Publication Data available

ISBN 0 415 07261 1

Printed and bound in Great Britain by
Biddles Ltd, Guildford and King's Lynn

Contents

List of Writers

Acton, Eliza (1799–1859)
Adams, Jane (1710–65)
Adams, Sarah Flower (1805–48)
Adcock, Fleur (1934–   )
Aguilar, Grace (1816–47)
Aiken, Joan (1924–   )
Aiken, Lucy (1781–1864)
Allingham, Margery (1904–66)
Anger, Jane (fl. 1589)
Arnim, Elizabeth von (1866–1941)
Ashford, Daisy (1881–1972)
Askew, Anne (1521–46)
Astell, Mary (1666–1731)
Audley, Lady *see* Douglas, Lady
    Eleanor
Aubin, Penelope (1679–1731)
Austen, Jane (1775–1817)
Ayres, Ruby (1883–1955)
Bacon, Anne, Lady (1528–1610)
Bagnold, Enid (1889–1981)
Baillie, Lady Grisell (1665–1746)
Baillie, Joanna (1762–1851)
Bainbridge, Beryl (1934–   )
Banks, Isabella (1821–87)
Bannerman, Helen (1862–1946)
Barbauld, Anna Laetitia (1743–1825)
Barker, A. L. (1918–   )
Barker, Jane (1652–c. 1727)
Barnard, Lady Anne (1750–1825)
Bawden, Nina (1925–   )
Bayly, Ada Ellen *see* Lyall, Edna

Bedford, Sybille (1911–   )
Beer, Patricia (1924–   )
Beeton, Isabella (1836–65)
Behn, Aphra (1640–89)
Bell, Gertrude (1868–1926)
Belloc-Lowndes, Marie (1868–1947)
Bennett, Anna Maria (?–1808)
Benson, Stella (1892–1933)
Bentley, Phyllis (1894–1977)
Berridge, Elizabeth (1921–   )
Betham-Edwards, Matilda
    (1836–1919)
Bishop, Isabella Bird (1831–1904)
Blessington, Marguerite, Countess
    of (1789–1849)
Blind, Mathilde (1841–96)
Blyton, Enid (1897–1968)
Bodichon, Barbara (1827–91)
Bonhote, Elizabeth (1744–1818)
Bonner, Hypatia Bradlaugh
    (1858–1935)
Boston, Lucy (1892–   )
Bottome, Phyllis (1882–1963)
Bowen, Elizabeth (1899–1973)
Braddon, Mary (1835–1915)
Bray, Anne Eliza (1790–1883)
Brazil, Angela (1869–1947)
Bridge, Anne (1889–1974)
Brittain, Vera (1893–1970)
Brontë, Anne (1820–49)
Brontë, Charlotte (1816–55)

Ewing, Juliana Horatia (1841–85)
Fainlight, Ruth (1931–   )
Fairless, Michael (1869–1901)
Falkland, Elizabeth Cary, Lady (1585?6–1639)
Fanshawe, Ann, Lady (1625–80)
Farjeon, Eleanor (1881–1965)
Farrell, M. J. *see* Keane, Molly
Feinstein, Elaine (1930–   )
Fell, Margaret (1614–1702)
Fenwick, Eliza (?–1840)
Ferrier, Susan (1782–1854)
'Field, Michael' (1846–1914)
Fielding, Sarah (1710–68)
Fiennes, Celia (1662–1741)
Figes, Eva (1932–   )
Findlater, Mary (1865–1963) and Jane (1866–1946)
Fitzgerald, Penelope (1916–   )
Forbes, Rosita (1890–1967)
Forest, Antonia (?)
Forster, Margaret (1938–   )
Fothergill, Jessie (1851–91)
Frankau, Pamela (1908–67)
Fox, Margaret *see* Fell, Margaret
Fraser, Antonia (1932–   )
Fullerton, Lady Georgina (1812–85)
Fyge, Sarah *see* Egerton, Sarah
Gardam, Jane (1928–   )
Gardner, Helen (1908–86)
Garnett, Constance (1861–1946)
Gaskell, Elizabeth (1810–65)
Gatty, Margaret (1809–73)
Gems, Pam (1925–   )
Gibbons, Stella (1902–   )
Gilliatt, Penelope (1932–   )
Glasse, Hannah (1708–70)
Glyn, Elinor (1864–1943)
Godden, Rumer (1907–   )
Gore, Catherine (1799–1861)
Goudge, Elizabeth (1900–84)
Grand, Sarah (1854–1943)
Greenwell, Dora (1821–82)
Greer, Germaine (1939–   )
Gregory, Augusta, Lady (1852–1932)
Greville, Frances (1726–89)
Grierson, Constantia (1706–33)
Griffith, Elizabeth (1727?–93)
Grymeston, Elizabeth (?1563–?1604)
Gunning, Susannah (1740?–1800)
Halkett, Anne, Lady (1622–99)
Hall, Radclyffe (1880–1943)

Hall, Mrs S. C. (1800–81)
Hamilton, Cicely (1872–1952)
Hamilton, Elizabeth (1758–1816)
Harraden, Beatrice (1864–1936)
Harrison, Jane (1850–1928)
Havergal, Frances Ridley (1836–79)
Hawkes, Jacquetta (1910–   )
Hawkins, Laetitia Matilda (1759–1835)
Hays, Mary (1760–1843)
Haywood, Eliza (1693–1756)
Hemans, Felicia (1795–1835)
Heyer, Georgette (1902–74)
Hobbes, John Oliver (1867–1906)
Holden, Molly (1927–   )
Holme, Constance (1880–1955)
Holtby, Winifred (1898–1935)
Howard, Elizabeth Jane (1923–   )
Howitt, Mary (1799–1888)
Hughes, M. V. (Molly) (1867–1956)
Hungerford, Margaret (c. 1854–97)
Hunt, Violet (1862–1942)
Hutchinson, Lucy (1620–70s)
Huxley, Elspeth (1907–   )
Inchbald, Elizabeth (1753–1821)
Ingelow, Jean (1820–97)
Jacob, Naomi (1884–1964)
James, P. D. (1920–   )
Jameson, Anna (1794–1860)
Jameson, Storm (1891–1986)
Jellicoe, Ann (1927–   )
Jenkins, Elizabeth (1907–   )
Jennings, Elizabeth (1926–   )
Jesse, F. Tennyson (1888–1958)
Jewsbury, Geraldine (1812–80)
Jewsbury, Maria Jane (1800–33)
Jhabvala, Ruth Prawer (1927–   )
Jocelin, Elizabeth (1595?6–1622)
Johnson, Pamela Hansford (1912–81)
Johnston, Jennifer (1930–   )
Julian of Norwich (c. 1343–?)
Katherine of Sutton (?–1376)
Kavan, Anna (1901–67)
Kavanagh, Julia (1824–77)
Kaye-Smith, Sheila (1887–1956)
Keane, Molly (1904–   )
Kelly, Isabella (?)
Kemble, Adelaide (1814?–79)
Kemble, Fanny (1809–93)
Kempe, Anna Eliza *see* Bray, Anna Eliza
Kempe, Margery (c. 1373–c. 1439)

Introduction

According to temperament and the fashion of the times, men have hurled satiric abuse or showered gallant praise on women in all literary periods. Pursuing the latter aim, they have compiled lists of exemplary or highly placed ladies, famous for virtuous lives or appropriate talents. As early as the eighth century BC Hesiod was collecting heroines and goddesses, while a thousand years later the historian Plutarch displayed heroic and artistic women to show that 'man's virtues and woman's virtues are one and the same'. In the medieval period men like Boccaccio turned mythical and biblical females into moral exemplars, while a similar aim in part inspired eighteenth-century compilers like George Ballard, whose monumental *Memoirs of Several Ladies of Great Britain Who Have Been Celebrated for their Writing or Skill in the Learned Languages, Arts, and Sciences* of 1752 was a clear step towards the modern biographical dictionary. Many compilations followed Ballard, such as the *Feminiad* of the Reverend John Duncombe, a friend of the literary ladies who surrounded the novelist Samuel Richardson, and the *Biographium Femineum. The Female Warriors: or Memoirs of the Most Illustrious Ladies of All Ages and Nations.*

Ballard compiled his work to encourage women to scholarship and creativity by example, as well as to prove to men that female education was a worthwhile cause. He had discovered the early fame and subsequent neglect of the Anglo-Saxon scholar Elizabeth Elstob, and in passing he wanted to suggest one reason for the apparent paucity of achieving women, a paucity noted as well by women writers throughout the seventeenth and eighteenth centuries: the short memory of a culture that did not expect female achievement. 'Many ingenious women of this nation who were really possess'd of a great share of learning and have, no doubt, in their time been famous for it, are not only unknown to the publick in general, but have been passed by in silence by our greatest biographers,' he remarked. In the late seventeenth century the Duchess of Newcastle, the first extensively publishing woman in English, found hardly any heroic literary women before herself – although, since she greatly desired pre-eminence, she perhaps did not search very diligently.

On the whole women made lists, memoirs, and dictionaries for more political reasons than men. Most of the male compilations stressed worthy personal qualities rather than art or skill, celebrating women within the current ideology of femininity. Female compilers, however, were frequently taking part in an argument about the status of women and about established inequalities of power in the culture; in the medieval period, for example, Christine de Pisan countered male misogyny with a list of virtuous and worthy ladies. But it is when women truly entered literature in large numbers as professional writers in the eighteenth century that they began compiling the modern sort of biographical dictionary suggesting the extent of women's activity as well as the repeated obliteration of its memory, at the same time both accepting certain ideological assumptions about female achievement and making the polemical point that women have done much and could, with fairer conditions, do more.

In 1774 Mary Scott published her praise poem on women which used both poetry and copious footnotes to present a history of famous women and reveal the brevity of cultural memory. Aware of the work of Ballard and Duncombe, she wanted to build upon their achievement; so she selected many of the same women whom they had praised, while also adding the less conventional. Her aim was, in her own words, to show

> What bright daughters *Britain* once could boast,
> What daughters now adorn *Her* happy coast.

Women should use their talents, she argued – and men should welcome them when they do. If men could understand that women were able to achieve as much as men, they would in time allow them equal educational opportunities; they would no longer 'regard the woman who suffers her faculties to rust in a state of listless indolence, with a more favourable eye, than her who engages in a dispassionate search after truth'.

After the heady radicalism of the 1790s the period of Mary Wollstonecraft's *Vindication of the Rights of Woman*, a clarion call for a female future in education but showing very little interest in past women's achievements, there was a period of consolidation in the face of renewed misogyny, and women again suggested the need for progress through rehearsing the achievement of the past. In 1803 Wollstonecraft's friend Mary Hays compiled six volumes of 'female worthies' entitled *Female Biography*, as counterblast to many scurrilous listings of radical and liberal writing women, 'the blasphemous band' as they were termed. One such listing was the Reverend Polwhele's *Unsex'd Females* in which Hays herself, along with Wollstonecraft, was included.

In the nineteenth century there was another upsurge of compiling for similar informative and polemical reasons. Josepha Hale's *Woman's Record, or Sketches of All Distinguished Women from the Creation to AD 1854* and Charlotte Yonge's *Biographies of Good Women* gave examples of pious female self-sacrifice and exemplary womanhood. Neither volume concentrated on writers but instead chose women who had, in Hale's words, exhibited 'Strength of Character, Piety, Benevolence or Moral Virtues'. Compensation for the bias was provided by Julia Kavanagh's *English Women of Letters*, which squarely aimed to redefine literature so as to include women in the tradition. But it was a difficult task since Kavanagh accepted the hierarchy of genres that ensured male pre-eminence and, however admiring of female literary talent she declared herself to be, she did require her female writers of the past to come up to the standards of womanhood demanded by her own Victorian period. Consequently an extremely important and innovative writer like Aphra Behn from the Restoration received harsh treatment for her 'grossness', 'indelicacy' and 'corrupt mind'.

As we move up to the feminist movement of our own times, there is another spate of works, some making claims for a particular emphasis or selection, all no doubt as embedded in the issues of their times and as revealing of current prejudices as the earlier efforts. The present dictionary of writers, the most comprehensive to date, is still selective, including many women who have achieved in the main literary areas of patriarchal culture, as well as some who have worked in less prestigious areas such as poetry for children or the public letter of advice. The selection is not systematic; some women are included because they are innovative in subject matter or method, some because they are popular with readers, and others because they represent small groups like working-class women writers from particular regions; inevitably those are privileged who have educational advantages and access to the main organs of publication. But however idiosyncratic the selection may appear to some, it is based on much the same desire as most of the early compilations: to rehearse women's achievement rather than lament their absence from culture.

The making of biographical dictionaries is always begun in enthusiasm and ended in weariness. It is a thankless task, no one is satisfied, and the end is always arbitrary and less complete and consistent than the editor would have wished. Mary Scott concluded her catalogue by writing in herself as an ill, tired lady, probably summing up the state and attitude of most compilers of such works. Yet she managed to end on an inspirational note, rallying sufficiently to call her effort at recording the female past her 'glorious toils'. In my particular 'toils' I am especially grateful to Simon Jarvis, Lucy Sloan, Elizabeth Spearing, and Anne Fernihough for their lengthy and generous aid and to many of the contributors for their patience and co-operation. My final thanks must go to Alison Hennegan who, having warned me against such a project, yet gave graciously and unstintingly of her time; without her library and expertise there would be many more errors than there are.

Janet Todd

Abbreviations of Reference Works

Allibone: S. Austin Allibone, *A Critical Dictionary of English Literature, and British and American Authors Living and Deceased from the Earliest Accounts to the Middle of the Nineteenth Century*, Philadelphia, Childs & Peterson; London, N. Trubner & Co., 1859. John Foster Kirk, *A Supplement to A Critical Dictionary . . .* , Philadelphia, J. B. Lippincott Co.; London, 10 Henrietta Street, Covent Garden, 1891.

BA **(18)**: Stanley J. Kunitz and Howard Haycraft (eds), *British Authors Before 1800*, New York, H. W. Wilson Co., 1952.

BA **(19)**: Stanley J. Kunitz and Howard Haycraft (eds), *British Authors of the Nineteenth Century*, New York, H. W. Wilson Co., 1936.

Ballard: George Ballard, *Memoirs of Several Ladies of Great Britain who have been celebrated for their writings . . .* , Oxford, W. Jackson, 1752.

BDRPD: John Whiteside Saunders (ed.), *A Biographical Dictionary of Renaissance Poets and Dramatists 1520–1650*, Brighton, Harvester, 1983.

CA: Hal May (ed.), *Contemporary Authors*; Ann Evory and Linda Metzger (eds), *Contemporary Authors New Revision Series*, Detroit, Gale Research Company, 1962–88.

CD: James Vinson and D. L. Kirpatrick (eds), *Contemporary Dramatists*, 2nd edn, London, St James Press, 1977.

CMW: John M. Reilly (ed.), *Twentieth Century Crime and Mystery Writers*, 2nd edn, London, St James Press, 1985.

CN: D. L. Kirkpatrick and James Vinson (eds), *Contemporary Novelists*, 4th edn, London, St James Press, 1986.

CP: James Vinson and D. L. Kirkpatrick (eds), *Contemporary Poets*, 4th edn, London, St James Press, 1985.

Crawford: Anne Crawford *et al.* (eds), *The Europa Biographical Dictionary of British Women*, London, Europa, 1983.

DLB: *Dictionary of Literary Biography*, Detroit, Gale Research Company, 1978–86.

DNB: *Dictionary of National Biography*, London, 1885–1901; supplements, 1901–60.

Drabble: Margaret Drabble (ed.), *The Oxford Companion to English Literature*, 5th edn, Oxford, Oxford University Press, 1985.

Hogan: Robert Hogan (ed.), *The Macmillan Dictionary of Irish Literature*, London, Macmillan, 1979.

Kunitz: Stanley J. Kunitz and Howard Haycraft (eds), *Twentieth Century Authors*, 6th edn, New York, H. W. Wilson Co., 1966; *Twentieth Century Authors, First Supplement*, 4th edn, 1967.

NWAD: Helen C. Black, *Notable Women Authors of the Day: Biographical Sketches*, Glasgow, David Bryce & Son, 1893.

OCCL: Humphrey Carpenter and Mari Pritchard (eds), *The Oxford Companion to Children's Literature*, Oxford, Oxford University Press, 1984.

RGW: James Vinson and D. L. Kirkpatrick (eds), *Twentieth Century Romance and Gothic Writers*, London, Macmillan, 1982.

Todd: Janet Todd (ed.), *Dictionary of British and American Women Writers 1660–1800*, Totowa, New Jersey, Rowman & Allanheld; London, Methuen, 1985.

Uglow: Jennifer S. Uglow and Frances Hinton (eds), *The Macmillan Dictionary of Women's Biography*, London, Macmillan, 1982; published in the US as *The Continuum Dictionary of Women's Biography*, New York, Continuum, 1989.

A small part of the material used also appears in Todd and in Katherine M. Wilson (ed.), *Women Writers of the Renaissance and Reformation*, Athens, Georgia, University of Georgia Press, 1987.

Dictionary of British Women Writers

Acton, Eliza
b. 1799, Sussex; d. 1859, London
Cookery writer
EA was the daughter of John Acton, an Ipswich brewer. Her health in her youth was poor, and as a result she spent a year in Paris. There she became engaged to an officer in the French army, but the marriage did not take place. She returned to Ipswich, and in 1826 published by subscription a small volume of conventional poetry, which ran to a second edition. After moving to Tonbridge, Kent, she continued to write occasional verse, including in 1842 'Voice of the North', a Loyal Address to the young Queen Victoria, celebrating her first visit to Scotland. By this time, however, EA had already had the famous interview with Thomas Longman at which she asked him to publish another volume of her poems. 'Madam,' he replied, 'it is no good bringing me poetry. Bring me a cookery book and we might come to terms.' Cookery writing also had the advantage of being considered a respectable occupation for an unmarried woman.

Four years later, after testing virtually every 'receipt' in it in her own kitchen in Tonbridge, she brought him *Modern Cookery* (1845). 'The young housekeepers of England', to whom it was dedicated, bought it in such large numbers that two further editions were published in the same year. A revised edition in 1855, with an Introduction attacking those who had plagiarized her, reflected a new awareness of the needs of families on lower incomes, and of the science of nutrition, as represented by Liebig's *The Chemistry of Food*.

By then EA had set up a household in Hampstead, London, where she was frequently visited by a young woman described – some were sceptical – as her niece. In 1857, distressed by the practices of commercial bakeries, she produced *The English Bread Book*, which advocated that every woman in England, mistress or servant, should know how to bake her own bread.

She died in Hampstead in 1859 after a long illness.

Modern Cookery is unquestionably the most important English work in its field in the nineteenth century. The young Mrs Beeton, in *Household Management* (1861), besides making uncredited use of several of EA's recipes, extended the latter's project of a guide in economy for the expanding middle class to the whole domestic domain, and her book has become more famous. Yet EA was more advanced in the rigour of her approach, and in her interests in continental cuisine and nutrition. She was an innovator in the presentation of recipes – the modern list of ingredients originates with her – and by far the superior writer. Her influence is evident in the work of Elizabeth David, who has often paid tribute to 'this peerless writer'.   JOHN DUGDALE
Works: *Poems* (1826); *Modern Cookery* (1845; revised edn, 1855); *The English Bread Book* (1857).
References: Allibone; David, E., 'Introduction' to *The Best of Eliza Acton* (1974); *DNB*.

Adams, Jane
b. 1710, Crawfordsdyke, Renfrewshire; d. 3 April 1765, Glasgow
Poet
JA, daughter of a shipmaster, was orphaned when young and employed as a nursery governess and housemaid by Mr Turner, a minister, and educated herself from his library. Here she wrote religious poems which were collected

by Mrs Drummond of Greenock as *Miscellany Poems, by Mrs Jane Adams, in Crawfordsdyke* (1734). JA dedicated the collection to Thomas Crawford of Crawfordburn, and Archibald Crawford wrote a preface.

The poetry is mostly pious and didactic. She glories in 'hallowed Reason's Fire within my Breast' inspiring the soul with 'Love and Gratitude'. 'There's nae Luck aboot the House' or 'Song of the Mariner's Wife' has been attributed to JA and was heard and admired by Robert Burns. It portrays a devoted wife, while a companion piece parodically describes the domestic reliance of a man on a woman. Although the poems may be by JA, neither resembles the usually pious tone of her ascribed works.

JA founded a girls' school at the quay head at Crawford's Bridge where she was known for her extraordinarily emotional renditions of Shakespeare. She was greatly impressed by Richardson's *Clarissa*, and she closed the school for six weeks to walk to London to visit the author. Failing to make a living either by poetry or school teaching she spent some years as a pedlar; she died in the Glasgow poorhouse. JANET JONES

Works: *Miscellany Poems, by Jane Adams in Crawfordsdyke* (1734); 'Song of the Mariner's Wife', in *Cromek's Select Scottish Songs* (1810).

References: *DNB*; Todd.

Adams, Sarah Flower

b. 22 February 1805, Great Harlow, Essex; d. 14 August 1848, London
Poet
(Also wrote under SY, SFA)

A lyric and dramatic poet best known for her hymns, SA was the daughter of radical political journalist Benjamin Flower and of Eliza Flower (*née* Gould) who shared her husband's commitment to free speech. SA and her sister were educated at home by their father and local schoolmasters. Orphaned by 1829, she lived then with the family of William Johnson Fox, liberal man of letters and Unitarian minister, until 1834, when she married William Bridges Adams, a civil engineer and political writer. She aspired to an acting career and actually made a few appearances on the stage.

Between 1832 and 1836 the *Monthly Repository* published more than twenty of SA's poems, essays and stories. Several of her contributions present the arts as a means of social improvement. She also wrote notices for the *Westminster Review*. Her review of Elizabeth Barrett's *Poems* (1844) compliments the poet's 'moral courage' in paying tribute to George Sand, comments on the chronic problem of domestic poverty, and notes that Barrett has addressed 'two of the leading topics of the day – War and Monopoly'.

Thirteen of SA's lyrics appear in *Hymns and Anthems* (1841), prepared for use in the Rev. Fox's Finsbury chapel. 'He sendeth sun, he sendeth shower' has been extensively used, and 'Nearer, My God, to Thee' remains universally popular. Uncomfortable with SA's Unitarianism, some editors of the latter poem have introduced references to Christ; many hymnals omit one or more of its five stanzas, thus obscuring its basis in Genesis 28:11–19, the story of Jacob's ladder.

Vivia Perpetua (1841), a blank verse drama based on the martyrdom of a Christian woman, Vivia, in AD 204, contrasts Christian and non-Christian values and explores the possibilities of female heroism. The protagonist's father Vivius despises the common citizens of Carthage but anticipates using them to overthrow the corrupt plebeian praefect. Advocate of 'the just supremacy of birth', he consigns slaves to 'their proper place', expects his widowed daughter to be cheerful as well as obedient, and encourages her infant son to be aggressive.

Vivia loves her father but can no longer respect the social and ecclesiastical hierarchies or dream of military glory for her son. Struggling with conflicting desires to proclaim her faith and to spare Vivius the shock of her conversion, she contemplates Antigone, who was loyal to blood ties, and the Dido of history, who sacrificed her life for 'her people's safety and her soul's dear honour' (not because Aeneas left her). She then takes Christ as exemplar and accepts slaves and labourers as her family. She vows to intercede in heaven for unconverted blood relatives and faces execution with a 'joy and wonder at [God's] mighty power' that the audience is invited to share. After the enemies of Vivius expose the Christians, their leading proselyte reaffirms Christ's example of a perfect life – and exhorts his 'brothers' to emulate Vivia's courageous death. The play expresses SA's religious faith, commitment to social justice, and belief that art, like heroism, has a greater 'power for good'.

MARY G. DE JONG

Works: Thirteen lyrics in *Hymns and Anthems* (1841); *Vivia Perpetua: A Dramatic Poem in Five Acts* (1841); review of Elizabeth Barrett's *Poems* (1844) in *Westminster Review* 42 (December 1844); *The Flock at the Fountain* (1845).

References: Allibone; *DNB*; Drabble; Julian, J. (ed.) *A Dictionary of Hymnology* (1907); Mineka, F. E., *The Dissidence of Dissent: The Monthly Repository (1806–1838)* (1944); Showalter, E., *A Literature of Their Own* (1977); Stephenson, H. W., *The Author of Nearer, My God, to Thee* (1922).

Adcock, Fleur
b. 10 February 1934, Papakura, New Zealand
Poet

FA writes with the nervous energy of a poet who never feels herself quite at home. Her childhood was divided between New Zealand and England, where her family spent the war years. In 1947, they returned to New Zealand and FA resumed an education begun in England. She attended Wellington Girls' College, and later received a master's degree in classics from Victoria University at Ellington. In 1952, she married Alistair Campbell, and in 1957 the couple were divorced. She has two sons. FA left New Zealand a second and final time in 1963, and emigrated to England. She worked in London as a librarian in the Foreign and Commonwealth Office for sixteen years, and has since held arts fellowships at several universities. Despite an absence of over twenty years, she is considered among New Zealand's foremost poets, receiving the New Zealand Book Award in 1984.

FA had already left New Zealand by the time her first collection of poems, *Eye of the Hurricane* (1964), was published. The poems, completed in New Zealand, are written in a style of determined detachment. In 'Invocation for Gregory' this operates to poignant effect, as the poet asks the elements to be gentle to the son she has left behind, while 'Voices' speaks with edgy quickness of 'a chronic convalescence from hope deferred'. Memories of an interrupted childhood in New Zealand are evoked with greater calm in *Tigers* (1967), a collection which otherwise overlaps with the first. In 'The Water Below' she recalls an early fantasy of a 'house floored with water' while the memory of 'a static, sunny, twenty-year old moment' in 'Remarks on Sernyl' unfolds in a brilliant image of a multi-coloured caterpillar. Adult memories, however, affirm her sense of personal exile. In *High Tide in the Garden* (1971) she makes several such return trips. In 'Stewart Island' she visits a place by the sea where 'it was too cold to swim', and where sandflies and 'a mad seagull' menace her sons. In contrast to this scene of inhospitable 'beauty', Wellington is 'a barren place'. FA's rejection of these native landscapes, however, inspires her most distilled verse.

Poems which confront the problem of dual identity directly seem verbose by comparison, somewhat given to fanciful wordplay. In 'Gas' she refers to her 'amoeba's trick' of self-division and replication; this trick soon becomes familiar to FA's reader. Travel affirms her continual sense of dislocation and alienation. She views the landscape subjectively, using it as a projection screen for aspects of her own condition. 'Playing tourist' in *The Scenic Route* (1974), FA visits Northern Ireland, the home of her ancestors. In 'Richey' the 'green hills' of her great-grandfather's birthplace are replaced by an image of the plum tree outside his New Zealand home; a childhood memory, this image returns FA to her unique place of origin. In her next collection, *The Inner Harbour* (1979), the poet is still in transit. 'Instead of an Interview' sends her back to England with 'a suitcase full of stones -/ of shells and pebbles, pottery and pieces of bark'. She turns over these fragments in poems like 'In Focus', 'Settlers', and 'Going Back', which blend images from family history with childish impressions. These 'receding pictures' appear with sudden clarity: 'a wall with blackboards; a gate where I swung, the wind bleak/ in the telegraph wires'.

Later poems move into dissociated regions of fantasy. In 'Lantern Slides' a wedding group is pictured in an 'underground station', while in 'Blue Glass' a little girl imagines herself lifted by blue flowers as she strokes the beads of a stolen necklace. FA's most recent work, *The Virgin and the Nightingale: Medieval Latin Poems* (1983), moves even further away from the confines of personal perception. These often erotic poems are treated with a lightness of style and humour which predict a new development in her own poetry.

AMY GAMERMAN

Works: *The Eye of the Hurricane* (1964); *Tigers* (1967); *High Tide in the Garden* (1971); *The Scenic Route* (1974); (ed.), *New Poetry 4* (with Anthony Thwaite) (1978); *The Inner Harbour* (1979); *Below Loughrigg* (1979); (ed.), *The Oxford Book of Contemporary New Zealand Poetry* (1982); *Selected Poems* (1983); *The Virgin and the Nightingale: Medieval Latin Poems* (1983).
References: CA.

Aguilar, Grace

b. 2 June 1816, Hackney; d. 16 September, 1847, Frankfurt, Germany
Novelist, historian
GA's parents were Jews of Spanish descent: her father was a merchant, whilst her mother ran a small private school for boys in which GA later assisted. She had a sheltered upbringing and was educated at home by both her parents, learning classics and history and also showing considerable musical talent. Her mother and father were both ailing and to improve their health the family moved in 1828 to Devon. GA began writing at an early age: before she was 12 years old she had finished a drama about Gustavus Vasa, and during her teens she worked on a series of poems published in 1835 as *The Magic Wreath*. But in the same year she suffered a serious attack of measles which left her health permanently impaired. Soon afterwards the death of her father obliged her to

write for a living. Her health continued to worsen until her death at the age of
31 in Germany where her mother had taken her to obtain medical help.

GA's first paid work was on Jewish subjects. *The Spirit of Judaism* was
published in America in 1842 after being printed for private circulation in
England. It was widely praised in the US despite the fact that it was printed
with a critical comment on it by an American rabbi. GA attacked what she
saw as the excessive interest in ritual and tradition of modern Jewish communities, and argued that Judaism's spiritualism and moral code as presented in the
Old Testament were of greater importance.

The Women of Israel (1845) is an especially interesting work because her
Judaism allows her to understand and criticize the part which Christianity has
played in the establishment of ideals of womanhood. She welcomes the 'many
valuable works relative to women's capabilities, influence and missions' which
have appeared, but remarks that their writers have unjustly identified feminine
virtue with Christian virtue: 'Education and nationality compel them to believe
that "Christianity is the sole source of female excellence" . . . that the value
and dignity of woman's character would never have been recognized but for
the religion of Jesus.' At the same time GA wishes to rebut charges that Mosaic
law is oppressive of women, and insists that, within Judaism, women 'have a
station to uphold, and a "mission" to perform, not alone as daughters, wives,
and mothers, but as witnesses of that faith which first raised, cherished and
defended them'. Nevertheless, GA's attitude towards the centrally important
question of Eve's transgression is ambivalent: although she daringly asks 'If He
permitted, ordained, why did He punish?', she accepts that 'The very first
consequence of woman's sin was to render her, in physical and mental strength,
inferior to man.'

GA's unusual perspective on Christian femininity and, especially, domesticity, provided her with difficulties as well as insights. In the introduction to
her novel *Home Influence* (1847) she is clearly anxious that her Judaism may be
thought to invalidate her as a purveyor of domestic piety, and insists that her
work is 'a simple domestic story, the characters in which are all Christians' and
that 'all *doctrinal* points have been most carefully avoided'.

GA's novels generally set out to illustrate a particular moral theme, sometimes
indicated in the title. She describes *Home Influence* as 'a story illustrative of a
mother's solemn responsibilities, intense anxiety to fulfil them, and deep sense
of the Influence of Home'. *Woman's Friendship* (1853) demonstrates the potential
strength of women's friendships and their ability occasionally to transcend class
barriers. Florence's 'mother' (later discovered not to be her real mother) warns
her that her friendship with Lady Ida Villiers can never come to anything
'because friendship, even more than love, demands equality of station'; but
despite a long estrangement and the discovery of Florence's true parentage the
two remain devoted friends at the close of the novel. GA comments in a final
chapter ('A Providence in All') on 'how much female friendship – in general
so scorned and scoffed at – may be the invisible means of strengthening in
virtue'.

Seven books were published posthumously. She was commemorated by the
Aguilar Free Library Service in New York which, during the time of the
great migrations, gave books to aid immigrants in assimilating themselves into
American culture.   JAMES SMITH

Works: *The Spirit of Judaism* (1842); *Records of Israel* (1844); *Women of Israel*
(1845); *The Jewish Faith* (1846); *History of the Jews in England* (1847); *Home
Influence* (1847); *The Vale of Cedars* (1850); *The Mother's Recompense* (1851); *The*

Days of Bruce (1852); *Woman's Friendship* (1853); *Home Scenes and Heart Studies* (1853); *Sabbath Thoughts and Sacred Communings* (1853).
References: Abrahams, B. Z., 'Pilgrimages to English shrines', *Art Union Journal* (1852); *BA* (19); *DNB*; Zeitlin, L. G., *The Nineteenth-Century Anglo-Jewish Novel* (1981).

Aiken, Joan
b. 4 September, 1924, Rye, Sussex
Novelist, writer of short stories and books for children and adolescents
JA is an extremely prolific writer, particularly in the genre of children's fiction. Her career began at the age of 17, when one of her stories was broadcast on the BBC's Children's Hour, and to date she has published over eighty books. Her background was a literary one (her father was the poet Conrad Aiken) and she admits that she always intended to be a writer; yet before becoming a full-time author in 1961 she worked for the BBC, the United Nations and in advertising. In 1945 JA married Ronald George Brown, whose death in 1954 left her with two young children to bring up alone.

JA's most successful works have been those written for adolescents. *The Whispering Mountain* won the 1969 Guardian Award and was runner-up for the Carnegie Award, while in 1972 *Night Fall* won the Mystery Writers of America Award. Her 'teenage' fiction is well written, attracting an overlapping readership of both adults and adolescents. JA finds little distinction between the process of writing for adults and for children. Her practical approach to writing forms the basis of a book published in 1982, *The Way to Write for Children*. Above all the book emphasizes that children must not be preached at or talked down to – one of the factors which makes her juvenile fiction equally readable for adults: 'I believe that an overt moral message is to be avoided like the plague, whether you are addressing toddlers, twelve-year olds or adolescents.' However she does draw important distinctions between the reading requirements of the varying age groups. Speaking about teenagers she comments, 'During this period of their developement they are in the process of breaking away from all the rules that have hitherto constrained them. They are not interested in plots; what they are interested in is emotion. The teenage novel has a duty to portray the successive tidal waves of feeling that wash over adolescents . . . the teenage novel is a novel of character.'

JA also holds strong views on the content of children's fiction. She believes that tragedy can be coped with, and that grief and fear need not be avoided, because children are resilient enough to cope with what are upsetting but basically straightforward emotions. Depression, on the other hand, should be avoided at all costs because of its extreme complexity and its often insoluble nature. Finally, she believes that children's books should never contain overt violence on the grounds that it is 'too easy to imitate'. She concludes that, 'Really good writing for children should come out with the force of Niagara. It ought to be concentrated; it needs to have everything that is in adult writing, but squeezed into smaller compass, in a form adapted to children's capacities and at shorter length.'

Midnight Is a Place (1974) answers this description. Critically well received and the subject of an Independent Television series, it is one of JA's most successful pieces of adolescent fiction. The action is unrelenting. The hero, Luke, undergoes a terrifying series of trials and tribulations, all of which are firmly grounded in a well-researched historical setting. It is also concerned with character: Luke is forced to abandon the self-centred outlook of a child and reassess his views of himself and those around him. By the end of the book he has emerged triumphant into a new maturity, which is a part of the general optimism of the ending. However, the harshness of reality is not avoided, and the happy ending is directly preceded by the tragic death of a 'good' character in a senseless duel. *Midnight Is a Place*, then, aims at and achieves a sense of positive reality. *Go Saddle the Sea* (1977) takes a different approach which is closer to fantasy. It chronicles the adventures of Felix as he journeys across early nineteenth-century Spain seeking passage to England where he hopes to find his family. The first-person narrative is written with much humour. Felix's conscious attempt to achieve an adult voice and his frequent asides addressed to God focus the reader's attention on the indisputable charms of the hero rather than the improbability of his adventures. Here Felix, finding himself in a particularly tight spot, has one of his quick conversations with God: 'Please listen to me, Father in heaven, for this is important! . . . if you think this danger I am in is a just punishment for these faults, bueno! . . . though I, for my part, consider it decidedly harsh of You, and it is more than *I* would do to someone who had behaved in such a way.'

When discussing the importance of characterization in *The Way to Write for Children*, JA suggests that in adult fiction it is possible to take certain short cuts in creating a character, providing that one is creating something which conforms to stock stereotypes easily recognizable to appropriate sectors of the reading public. That is to say, the thriller reader wants and expects to receive the standard portrait of a detective. The theory is probably a sound one, but it is possible to suggest that in her adult fiction JA takes this concept rather too far. Indeed her historical romances such as *The Smile of the Stranger* (1978) revel so much in their clichéd nature that it is impossible to read them without suspecting a pastiche, and on this tongue-in-cheek level JA's novels provide well-written and enjoyable entertainment.

Short stories are one of the most effective areas of JA's writing. The collections *A Touch of Chill* (1979) and *A Whisper in the Night* (1982) include what are described as stories of 'horror, suspense and fantasy', but their nature is far more ambivalent than this would suggest. They contain no overt violence and have been categorized as children's books by both the *New York Times* and the *Washington Post*. The horror tends to be in the past or in the imagination of the characters and the suspense of the stories is often based on the difficulty of telling where reality ends and the fantastic or horrific begins. Stories such as 'Power-cut' and 'The Helper' are successfully unpleasant; JA creates an oppressive and threatening atmosphere with considerable skill. 'The Story about Caruso' is particularly impressive: the shock of its ending comes from the intensely understated and matter-of-fact style of narration:

' "Can you send police and ambulance?" she said calmly. "I have just murdered my uncle."

Then she replaced the receiver, lifted up the divan mattress, pulled out a bar of raisin milk chocolate, and began eating it with controlled absent-minded haste.'   GILL PLAIN

Selected works: *All You've Ever Wanted* (1953); *More Than You Bargained For* (1955); *The Kingdom and the Cave* (1960); *The Wolves of Willoughby Chase* (1962); *The Silence of Herondale* (1964); *Nightbirds on Nantucket* (1966); *Dark Interval* (1967); *A Necklace of Raindrops and Other Stories* (1969); *Night Fall* (1969); *Armitage, Armitage, Fly Away Home* (1970); *Deadly Nightshade* (1971); *The Kingdom Under the Sea* (1971); *Winterthing: A Child's Play* (1972); *A Harp of Fishbones*

(1972); *Midnight is a Place* (1974); *Arabel's Raven* (1974); *Not What You Expected* (1974); *Tale of a One-Way Street* (1976); *The Skin Spinner* (1976); *A Bundle of Nerves* (1976); *Go Saddle the Sea* (1977); *The Faithless Lollybird* (1977); *Mice and Mendelson* (1978); *A Touch of Chill* (1979); *Arabel and Mortimer* (1980); *The Shadow Guests* (1980); *The Stolen Lake* (1981); *A Whisper in the Night* (1982); *The Way to Write for Children* (1982); *Bridle the Wind* (1983); *The Kingdom Under the Sea and Other Stories* (1984); *Up the Chimney Down and Other Stories* (1984); *The Last Slice of Rainbow and Other Stories* (1985); *Fog Hounds, Wind Cat, Sea Mice* (1985); *A Goose on Your Grave* (1987); *Mansfield Revisited* (1987).
References: *CA.*

Aikin, Lucy

b. 6 November 1781, Warrington; d. 29 January 1864, Hampstead
Poet, critic, historian

Daughter of John Aikin, author and physician, and niece of Anna Laetitia Barbauld, LA grew up in a household that encouraged learning in its daughters as well as its sons. The Aikin family moved to Yarmouth in 1784; LA was taught mostly at home, for her brief experience at school showed that local institutions could offer her little. Dr Aikin moved his practice to London in 1792; in 1797, on account of ill-health, he retired with his family to Stoke Newington where LA lived with her parents until her father's death in 1822. Subsequently she and her mother moved to Hampstead, where Mrs Aikin died in 1830. LA, who never married, continued to live in Hampstead until 1844. She then joined the household of her nephew, C. A. Aikin, in London until 1846, and then that of her niece and her husband, Philip Hemery LeBreton, in Wimbledon until 1852, when they all returned to Hampstead.

Educated primarily by her father, LA was fluent in French, Italian, and Latin. She was also very well acquainted with the English classics, and with her father's interests, history and biography. She knew intimately the works of her aunt Mrs Barbauld, many of which were written for educating the young. *Evenings at Home*, a book of essays compiled by her aunt and father for family reading, probably reflects the reading and opinions of the Aikin family. LA was widely acquainted with scholarly and literary people. Mrs John Taylor of Norwich and her family were among her closest friends; Joanna Baillie and her sister were neighbours and intimates in Hampstead. Among her correspondents was the Rev. Dr William Ellery Channing, a Unitarian minister of Boston; their correspondence lasted from 1826 to 1842 and is perhaps the best source for LA's views on literature, politics, and religion. A staunch Unitarian, she was a liberal but not a radical in politics. She was also a feminist who repeatedly protested against the prevailing view of woman's place and valuation in contempory society.

Encouraged by her father's praise of an eloquent remark, LA determined to seek a literary career, as his sister, Anna Barbauld, had done. She recorded that an early reading of her aunt's prose hymns for children had instilled in her a sense of the sublime, although her own style seldom ventures beyond rational and lucid expression of opinion and emotion.

Her anthology *Poetry for Children* (1801), although frequently reprinted, was outstripped in popularity by the Taylors' *Original Poems for Infant Minds* (1804–5). LA's selection of short verse and extracts draws mainly on Autgustan poetry; only in later editions does Wordsworth appear. Description is preferred to narration, and the emphasis is placed upon moral sentiment and natural history. Although the poems are intended for memorization, few concessions are made to the young reader in terms of poetic diction. Some simpler pieces include Southey's poem 'You are old, father William . . .' and her own contributions. Among these are a lyrical ballad on the suffering of a beggarman ('Cold blows the blast across the moor'), and verses on Lapland, in which a traveller gives a rhythmically lively account of 'icy oceans where the whale/Tosses in foam his lashing tail'. The main interest of the book for modern readers lies in its Preface to Parents, which suggests changing attitudes to the education of the child. The author regrets that 'Since dragons and fairies, giants and witches, have vanished from our nurseries before the wand of reason, it has been a prevailing maxim that the young child should be fed on mere prose and simple fact.' She suggests that poetry is a better form of nourishment. What is memorized with pleasure in youth will in future years soothe grief, strengthen piety, and fire the soul with virtuous indignation.

Epistles on Women (1810) was described by LA's biographer in 1864 as a moral and didactic work in the manner of Pope: 'terse and compact in language and smooth in versification, but not aiming at the higher qualities of imagination or invention'. Her novel *Lorimer* (1814) belongs to an outmoded tradition of sensibility. The dialogue is stilted: ' "Eustace", said she meekly, "have I merited this?" ' There is more vitality in the patterns of children's speech which she records in her handbook on letter-writing for the young, *Juvenile Correspondence* (1811). The usual dull and formal models are replaced here by conversational accounts of daily activities. Her aim is to encourage the production of letters that will reflect more of the imdividual character of the writer.

Later, she turned her attention to studies in history and biography. *Memoirs of the Court of Queen Elizabeth* (1818) is the first of her three substantial and readable historical works, the others being similar accounts of the courts of James I (1822) and Charles I (1833). In the preface to the first book, she defines the scope of her project: the 'memoir' is illustrative of the domestic history of a period, with biographical and literary observations. Her analysis of political and religious issues is cautious, yet her liberal sympathies are evident. Conventional standards are applied in her more confident literary judgements: Jonson is praised for the classical qualities which Donne lacks. Her aim – to provide 'a correct sketch' – is modest, but her method is professional. With the help of her publisher and friends, she gained access to original papers. She assures the reader that reliance may be placed on her fidelity to quoted sources – apart from modernized spelling and punctuation. Her commentary is restricted by the narrowness of her experience, particularly in the case of James I, but she is aware of the difficulties facing the historian in such matters as the interpretation of conflicting evidence.

As a biographer, she recorded in 1823 the life of her father. She wrote a short memoir of her aunt in 1825. Her biography of Addison, whom she regarded as morally superior to Pope and Swift, appeared in 1843. These books are informative and carefully researched; she takes pains to produce an objective account.

LA's experimentation in several genres, balancing invention with scholarship, helped to extend the concept of the modes of writing suitable for women.

BARBARA BRANDON SCHNORRENBERG AND CLARE MACDONALD SHAW

Works: *Epistle on Women* (1810); *Lorimer: A Tale* (1814); *Memoirs of the Court of Queen Elizabeth* (1818); *Memoirs of the Court of James I* (1822); *Memoirs of the Court of Charles I* (1833); *Life of Addison* (1843); *Memoirs, Miscellanies and Letters of the late Lucy Aikin*, ed. P. H. LeBreton (1864).

References: DNB; OCCL; Smith, B. G., 'The contribution of women to modern historiography in Great Britain, France, and the United States, 1750–1940', *American Historical Review* 89, (June 1984).

Allingham, Margery

b. 20 May 1904, London; d. 30 June 1966
Writer of detective fiction
MA attended the Perse School for Girls in Cambridge, but her main literary education happened at home. Her father, Herbert Allingham, was best known as an editor of and contributor to various boys' papers specializing in adventure stories, including detective tales. From her father and many of his friends, MA must have seen writing as a natural profession. Her first efforts were in the genre of the boys' tale and date from the 1920s. Surrounded by talk of deadlines and journalism, MA did not come to consider that writing for money need preclude producing work of lasting interest. G.R.M. Hearne, her father's friend who also wrote adventure stories, told her, 'They never mind you putting all you've got into this stuff. They never pay you any more for it, but they don't stop you.' In 1927 she married Philip Youngman Carter, also a writer of stories for boys.

For most of MA's writing career in detective fiction, she uses as protagonist the aristocrat Albert Campion, who hides his background and turns himself thereby into a self-effacing invisible man, with the implication that he himself is as deceiving and unknowable as the criminals he pursues. There are changes through the novels so that, beginning as a kind of Wodehousian idiot – he carries a water pistol and is said to have an inane expression – Campion becomes an individually realized character with a rather disturbing presence, although, like the heroes of Dorothy L. Sayers and Agatha Christie, he certainly draws on the reader's nostalgia. He has the conventionally eccentric manservant who lugubriously answers the telephone, but he also has a very unconventional wife who designs aircraft and who is portrayed as being highly significant in the development of fighting planes in the Second World War. She is one of many strong central female characters who are independent and oriented towards a career. MA herself was engaged in war work during the war years.

MA had moved from the thriller to the detective novel with *Police at the Funeral* (1931). Plots of this and subsequent novels are sometimes episodic and sometimes tightly structured, with settings ranging from the international crime scene to the English country house. Her late works were accused by critics of pretentiousness, an accusation which may reflect MA's efforts to make her detective story into a serious genre. *The Fashion in Shrouds* (1938) is however a successful synthesis of the detective story with the psychological novel.

London, as an historical entity, is an important subject in her books, especially in *More Work For The Undertaker* (1948) about a family of eccentrics who act as a foil for the marked eccentricity of Campion, and in *The Tiger in the Smoke* (1952), a menacing story of pursuit. The detective of the later works, Luke, is described with psychological subtlety and developed through a series of novels. In these works there is an acknowledgement, rare among detective writers, of the political function of the policeman.   JANET JONES

Works: *Blackkerchief Dick* (1923); *The White Cottage Mystery* (1928); *Crime at Black Dudley* (1929; published in the US as *The Black Dudley Murder*, 1929); *Mystery Mile* (1930); *Police at the Funeral* (1931); *Look to the Lady* (1931; published in the US as *The Gyrth Chalice Mystery*, 1931); *Sweet Danger* (1933; published in the US as *Kingdom of Death,* 1933); *Death of a Ghost* (1934); *Flowers for the Judge* (1936); *The Case of the Late Pig* (1937); *Mr Campion Criminologist* (1937); *Dancers in Mourning* (1937; republished in 1943 as *Who Killed Chloe?*); *Black Plumes* (1940); *Traitor's Purse* (1941); *The Oaken Heart* (1941); *The Dance of the Years* (1943; published in the US as *The Galantrys,* 1943); *The Case Book of Mr Campion* (1947); *Take Two at Bedtime* (1950; published in the US as *Deadly Duo,* 1949); *More Work for the Undertaker* (1949); *The Tiger in the Smoke* (1952); *No Love Lost: Two Stories of Suspense* (1954); *The Beckoning Lady* (1955; published in the US as *The Estate of the Beckoning Lady,* 1955); *Hide My Eyes* (1958); *Three Cases For Mr Campion* (1961); *The China Governess* (1962); *The Mind Readers* (1965); *Mr Campion's Lady* (1965); *Cargo of Eagles* (1967); *Mr Campion and Others* (1967); *The Allingham Case-Book* (1969); *The Allingham Minibus* (1973); *The Fear Sign* (1976).

References: *CA*; Craig, P. and Cadogan, M., *The Lady Investigates* (1981); Mann, J., *Deadlier Than the Male* (1981); Panek, L., *Watteau's Shepherds: The Detective Novel in Britain, (1914–40)* (1979); Steinbrunner, C. and Penzler, O., *Encyclopedia of Mystery and Detection* (1976).

Anger, Jane

fl. 1589

Polemical writer

Jane Anger, her Protection for Women was a pamphlet published in London in 1589 by Richard Jones and Thomas Orwin. According to the title page, it was written by Ja. A., Gent. This, in conjunction with the knowledge of Latin shown in the pamphlet, might suggest male authorship, although some Jane or Joan Angers have been discovered living at the time the pamphlet was written. Much is made of the femaleness of the author in the text, but this reference to feminine experience is common to other pamphlets that may or may not have been written by women. If Jane Anger is the author, then she is the first Englishwoman to enter into the gender controversies of the Renaissance. JA wrote her book in answer to *Boke, his Surfeyt in love,* entered in the Stationer's Company register for November 1588. This too was printed by Orwin and is now lost.

JA roundly asserts that women are morally purer than men; they were created last and from woman has come the salvation of the world. Their sorry state derives from their credulity and good natures, of which men have taken cruel advantage: 'a goose standing before a ravenous fox is in as good a case as a woman who trusteth to a man's fidelity.' Men are mocked as little game cocks, lecherous, voluptuous, vain and deceitful, and their masculinity becomes a sham, an absurd construction. Men need women as mirrors of themselves, and their conception of women derives entirely from their own base impulses: 'if then lust pricketh them, they will swear that love stingeth us; which imagination only is sufficient to make them essay the scaling of half a dozen of us in one night.'

The style of the pamphlet is eclectic, proverbial at times, learned at others. The robust sexual language echoes the traditional language of the misogynist writings which emphasize the physical horror of woman as painted decay. Possibly there is an influence from John Lyly's *Euphues,* not mentioned in the text but paralleled in the allusive, metaphorical style. Argument is through examples, fables, allusions to classical stories, and Biblical episodes.

There is no known response to JA and the pamphlet was not reprinted until 1985.   JANET JONES

Works: *Jane Anger her Protection for Women. To defend them against Scandalous Reportes of a Late Surfeiting Lover, and all other like Venerians that complaine so to bee overcloyed with womens kindnesse* (1589).

References: Kahin, H., 'Jane Anger and John Lyly', *Modern Language Quarterly* 8 (1947); Shepherd, S., *Amazons and Warrior Women* (1981); Shepherd, S. (ed.), *The Women's Sharp Revenge: Five Women's Pamphlets from the Renaissance* (1985); Travitsky, B., *The Paradise of Women* (1981); Warnicke, R., *Women of the English Renaissance and Reformation* (1983).

Arnim, Elizabeth von

b. 31 August 1866, Sydney, Australia; d. 9 February 1941, Charleston, South Carolina

Novelist

(Also wrote under Elizabeth, the author of 'Elizabeth and her German Garden', Alice Cholmondeley, Mary Annette Beauchamp Russell)

Born in Sydney the daughter of Henry and Lovey Lassiter Beauchamp, but reared in London, EvA, a first cousin of Katherine Mansfield, attended Miss Summerhayes's school in Ealing. In 1891 she married Count Henning August von Arnim, and in 1895 the family moved to his estate in Pomerania, the scene of her early novels. After von Arnim died in 1910, EvA wrote, entertained, and made a home for her five children at her château in Switzerland until the outbreak of the war. Returning to England, after an affair with H. G. Wells she embarked in 1916 on a disastrous marriage to Francis, second Earl Russell, brother of Bertrand Russell, which ended in 1919 when they separated. In 1939 EvA moved to America, where she died two years later.

The wit and irony of EvA's early work is softened by sentiment and optimism. Her best-known novel, *Elizabeth and her German Garden* (1898), published anonymously in England, achieved instant popularity and went into numerous editions. Based on her life in Pomerania, on its surface the novel is a pastoral idyll filled with the delights of nature and EvA's enjoyment of the Romantic poets. But its individuality and interest lie in the contrast of the rebellious 'Elizabeth's' freedom out of doors with her enslavement to the conventional demands made upon her by motherhood, German neighbours, and marriage to 'the Man of Wrath', a humorous caricature of her husband.

The other novels of EvA's early period pursue this vein of witty rebellion. Like all her books except *Christine* (1913) (published under the pseudonym 'Alice Cholmondeley'), *The Solitary Summer* (1899), *The April Baby's Book of Tunes* (1901), and *The Adventures of Elizabeth in Rugen* (1904) were attributed to 'Elizabeth, author of "Elizabeth and her German Garden" '. Although these three novels reveal her delight in nature, her children, and her husband, they express more strongly her ambivalence towards marriage and German conventionality, as well as her resentment of the necessity for women to excercise constant self-control and conceal their true feelings and opinions.

The unexplained imprisonment of EvA's husband in 1899 inspired *The Benefactress* (1901), the story of an Englishwoman who takes distressed German gentlewomen into her house. *The Caravaners* (1909) ridicules self-important German husbands; *Fräulein Schmidt and Mr Anstruther* (1907) makes fun of German gluttony and social ambition.

In her widowhood, EvA's writing becomes darker in tone and even at times malicious. *The Pastor's Wife* (1914) is a grimly realistic story of the marriage of an English clergyman's daughter to a German pastor more interested in East Prussia's soil than in his wife. The heroine's disappointment at not escaping in marriage the 'rush of barren duties' heaped upon her as a bishop's daughter, her horror at the toll exacted on family life and women's health by an uncontrolled birthrate, and her husband's coolness once they are married lead to her elopement with an artist, but she returns to her husband.

EvA's masterpiece, *Vera* (1912), inspired by her relationship with Russell, is a terrifying picture of the tyranny of men and the weakness of women in marriage. The immature Lucy Entwhistle, alone except for an ineffectual aunt, hastily marries Everard Wemyss without even considering the possible reasons for his wife's (Vera's) recent suicide and attributes his apparent lack of grief to courage rather than callousness. With his childlike sense of fun, Wemyss is at first too comical to be threatening, and his domestic tyrannies are merely amusing. But his callousness, cruelty, and self-pity manifest themselves as soon as Lucy behaves otherwise than as his 'duddely-umpty little girl', and her remorse at angering him becomes progressively less effective in restoring his love. It becomes clear that he drove Vera to suicide. The aunt, barred from the house, realizes that Lucy, unlike Vera, will not survive fifteen years of marriage to Wemyss. *Vera* uses shifting interior monologue with an effect both comic and macabre in its juxtaposition of Wemyss's point of view with everyone else's.

With *The Enchanted April* (1923), a best-seller that was later dramatized, EvA returns to a sunnier mood. The protagonist, unhappy because she has been 'good for years and years', escapes domestic duties on holiday alone in Italy; when her husband joins her, he too relaxes his hold on convention. They experience a rebirth of love, and the novel ends hopefully.

EvA's autobiography, *All the Dogs of My Life* (1936), contrasts her fourteen dogs' unfluctuating love for her with the ups and downs of human love. Despite her happy first marriage and numerous love affairs, EvA claims to have little use for husbands or lovers – 'A widow is the only complete example of her sex.' She finds joy chiefly in her children and her work. In her last novel, *Mr Skeffington* (1940), her ambivalence toward men and marriage is again evident, as Fanny, haunted by the ghost of the husband she divorced long ago, takes him back after she learns he is blind and cannot see the ruin of her looks.

EvA's work was much admired in her time. Barbara Pym has praised her novels' unsentimental portrayal of marriage and Alice Meynell described her as 'one of the three finest wits of her day'.   KATE BROWDER HEBERLEIN

Selected works: Elizabeth and her German Garden (1898); *The Solitary Summer* (1899); *The April Baby's Book of Tunes* (1900); *The Ordeal of Elizabeth* (1901); *The Pious Pilgrimage* (1901); *The Benefactress* (1902); *The Adventures of Elizabeth in Rügen* (1904); *The Princess Priscilla's Fortnight* (1906); *Fräulein Schmidt and Mr Anstruther* (1907); *The Caravaners* (1909); *Christine* (1913); *The Pastor's Wife* (1914); *Christopher and Columbus* (1919); *In the Mountains* (1920); *Vera* (1921); *Love* (1925); *Introduction to Sally* (1926); *Expiation* (1929); *Father* (1931); *The Jasmine Farm* (1934); *All the Dogs of My life* (1936); *Mr Skeffington* (1940).

References: Cooper, A. R., *Authors and Others* (1970); Charmes, L. de, *Elizabeth of the German Garden* (1958); Kunitz; Nichols, B., *Twenty-Five* (1926); Oppenheim, E. P., *The Pool of Memory* (1941); Richardson, K. (ed.), *Twentieth Century Writing* (1969); Swinnerton, F., *Swinnerton: An Autobiography* (1936); Usborne, K., *'Elizabeth': The Author of Elizabeth and her German Garden* (1986).

Ashford, Daisy

b. 7 April 1881, Petersham, Surrey; d. 15 January 1972, near Norwich

Novelist

DA's mother was Emma Walker, the daughter of a wealthy Nottinghamshire landowner. She married a soldier, moved to Ireland, and became a Roman Catholic. On her husband's death, she returned to England with her five children and met and married the middle-aged William Ashford, with whom she had three daughters, DA (Margaret) being the eldest. DA had a typical upper-middle-class childhood, full of other children, visitors, governesses, and servants. Her later education occured in Haywards Heath. Both DA's parents were staunch Catholics and both wrote in a small way, the father in a serious mode contributing articles to the Catholic Truth Society and the mother, more frivolously, composing limericks and other light pieces. In 1889 the family moved from Petersham to Lewes, considered healthier for raising children. DA took a secretarial course and went to live for a time with her artist sister in London. She married in 1920 and spent much of the rest of her long life in Norfolk.

Between the ages of 4, when DA is said to have dictated her first story, and 14, when she finished *The Hangman's Daughter*, she wrote fiction and plays, her most famous story, *The Young Visiters*, coming to the attention of J. M. Barrie many years after she had written it. He contributed a preface in which he suggested its appeal in the way it captured a child's excitement at the luxury of adult life, tea in bed for example, and in its free and easy treatment of grand personages like princes and popes; he insisted that, despite some remarkably felicitous misspellings and incongruities, the publication was authentic: 'The pencilled MS. has been accurately reproduced, not a word added or cut out.' DA's characters were often based on friends and relatives and her stories reflect her experience of extended families and Catholicism. Her style is a mixture of cliché and the unexpected, liberally sprinkled with semi-malapropisms, and her plots surprise by taking ordinary self-asserting girls into conventional melodramatic situations.

The earliest piece, 'A Life of Father McSwiney', reflects DA's Catholic environment and tells in haphazard prose the story of a boy who becomes a Jesuit priest because as a baby he has 'a saintly smile on his Jesuit-like face and is 'much more good than other people'. He is confirmed 'by the precise Bishop' and has a night out with the Pope in London where he visits the theatre to see 'a pious love affair'. *The Young Visiters* was written when DA was 9 and it tells of the unsuccessful efforts of Mr Salteena, 'an elderly man of 42' who is not quite a real gentleman, to marry the young Ethel, who is very pale because of the drains in the house. Despite Mr Salteena's attractions, which include 'black and twisty' whiskers and a becoming topper, Ethel prefers the 'presumshious' Bernard with his 'somber tastes' and Mr Salteena is reduced to crying loudly into his handkerchief at their wedding.

In her later work, *Where Love Lies Deepest*, written at the age of 12, and *The Hangman's Daughter*, written at 13, DA makes resolute attempts to be literary, and the works read like parodies of romantic fiction. Yet there are still appealing moments when clichés are unexpectedly juxtaposed and there is a robustness and naturalness about the resilient heroines who, when they encounter threatening men, mainly notice their clothes. True to DA's experience of late Victorian affluence, poor girls still have cook maids and £10 to spend on clothes, while faithful servants are always available. Helen, the heroine of *The Hangman's*

Daughter, nearly marries a villain with whom she lives in remarkable intimacy before the unmasking. In these stories DA tries to catch the moralizing tone of an omniscient narrator of conventional melodramatic fiction – 'Ah Helen!, happily for you that you can see the bright light appearing, but there are dark clouds gathering . . .' – but the work is more remarkable for such opinions as 'it is not always the bad that are rich'.

After *The Hangman's Daughter*, into which DA put considerable work, she published no more, although she began an autobiography which she destroyed. Although she declared, 'I adored writing and used to pray for bad weather, so that I need not go out but could stay in and write' and insisted that at 13 she had wanted to be an author, she also stated that her 'ambition . . . entirely left' her after her school days. Perhaps the silence had something to do with the diffidence which marked her character – she had not been a favourite child and her siblings had laughed at part of *The Hangman's Daughter* which she regarded as a serious piece of writing. In his preface to *The Young Visiters* Barrie described the reticent adult DA had become 'evidently a little scared' by the child she used to be.   JANET TODD

Works: *The Young Visiters* (1919); *Daisy Ashford: Her Book* (including *Where Love Lies Deepest* and *The Hangman's Daughter*) (1920).

References: Barrie, J. M., 'Introduction' to *The Young Visiters* (1919); Carpenter, H., 'Introduction' to *Love and Marriage* (1982); Drabble; Steel, M., 'Introduction' to *The Hangman's Daughter and Other Stories* (1983); OCCL.

Askew, Anne

b. 1521, Lincolnshire; d. 16 July 1546, London
Autobiographer and poet

AA was the second daughter of Dame Elizabeth and Sir William Askew (or Ayscough), knight, of South Kelsey, Lincolnshire. When her elder sister Martha died before her projected marriage to Thomas Kyme, the two families arranged that AA should marry him instead. According to John Bale, the marriage arrangements were made only 'for lucre . . . (as an vngodlye maner it is in Englande moch vsed amonge noble men)', and AA was 'compelled agaynst her wyll or fre consent' into the marriage. Bale goes on to say that they bore two children before religious differences (Kyme was an adamant Roman Catholic, AA an equally determined Reformer) led to his 'vyolentlye [driving] her oute of hys howse'. It may be that in 1544 AA made an unsuccessful plea to the bishop's court in Lincoln for a divorce; soon after, by this time once again using the name 'Askew' rather than 'Kyme', she travelled to London - perhaps to appeal to the Court of Chancery for a divorce.

Soon AA's radical Protestantism was well enough known to be perceived as dangerous to the state, and on 13 June 1545, with Thomas Lukine and Joan Sawtry, she was arraigned under the first of the Six Articles of 1539, which declared that persons denying the Anglican position on transubstantiation were to be burned at the stake. In the absence of adequate witnesses, the three were found not guilty of speaking against the sacrament, but in March of 1545 or 1546, AA was once again tried for heresy. (This trial is the one subsequently called her 'first examination'.) She was interrogated first at Sadler's Hall by Christopher Dare, then by a priest whom according to Bale she refused to answer 'because [she] perceyued him a papyst', by the lord mayor, and the bishop's chancellor. Most of the questions asked her had to do with her understanding of the sacrament (Dare began by enquiring 'yf I ded not beleue that the sacrament hangynge ouer the aultre was the very bodye of Christ realye', but the fact of AA's being a woman was also at issue (the bishop's chancellor 'sayd, that I was moche to blame for vtterynge the scriptures. For S. Paul [he sayd] forbode women to speake or to talk of the worde of God'. Having refused to satisfy her interrogators, AA was placed in prison, where she was again questioned by a priest. A person AA identifies as her 'cosyn Bryttayne' attempted to help her, but AA refused to cooperate when she was questioned further. Bishop Bonner wrote a confession which he claimed she signed but on which AA said she wrote, 'I Anne Askew do beleue all maner thynges contayned in the fayth of the Catholyck churche.'

AA was freed from imprisonment, but on 18 June 1546 she was again arraigned – this time at Greenwich (her 'second examination' recounts this final episode in her life). Once more AA was uncooperative, answering, for example, questions about the meaning of the sacrament by saying, 'I belieue, that so oft as I in a Christen congregacyon, do receyve the breade in remembraunce of Christes death, & with thankes geuing accordynge to hys holye instytueyon, I receyue therwith the frutes also of hys most gloryous passyon.' When the Bishop of Winchester then 'bad me make a dyrect answer', she responded, 'I wolde not syng a newe songe to the lord in a straunge lande.' Her countering questions with her own interpretations of scriptural passages must have been particularly galling to those who had approved of the 1543 Act for the Advancement of True Religion, which had forbidden the reading of the Bible by all women and by men under the rank of yeoman. Even when she was taken to the Tower of London and tortured by Sir Richard Rich and Lord Chancellor Thomas Wriothesley, AA refused to submit: finally the Lord Chancellor 'sent [her] worde if [she] wolde leaue my opynyon, I shuld want nothynge. If I wolde not, I shuld fourth to Newgate, and so be burned', and she responded, 'that I wolde rather dye, than to breake my faythe'. On 16 July AA was burned at Smithfield, on the same day as were John Lascelles, John Adams and Nicolas Belenian.

In 1546 the Protestant propagandist, John Bale, Bishop of Ossery, published *The first examinacyon of Anne Askewe, lately martyred in Smythfelde, by the Romyshe popes vpholders, with the Elucydacyon of Johan Bale*, and in 1547, *The lattre examinacyon of Anne Askewe, latelye martyred in Smythfelde, by the wycked Synagoge of Antichrist, with the Elucydacyon of Johan Bale*. On the title page of each volume is a woodcut representing AA as an emblem of Christian justice: holding the Bible in her right hand and a palm in her left, she stands triumphantly over a beast which wears the Pope's three-tiered crown. Throughout both volumes – in extensive prefaces, concluding essays, and the 'elucydacyons' with which he glosses AA's account of her examinations (most of the 'elucydacyons' are longer than the passages upon which they comment) – Bale presents AA as a saintly heroine whose brave words conquered representatives of the Antichrist. Describing AA as 'a gentylwoman verye yonge, dayntye, and tender', Bale asserts that her moral strength in the face of adversity was a gift from God: 'Whan she semed most feble, than was she most stronge. And gladlye she rejoyced in that weakenesse, that Christes power myght strongelye dwell in her.' The Preface to the first *Examination* includes an extensive comparison between AA and the early Christian martyr Blandina; the Preface to the second *Examination* places AA in a long line of Christian, especially English, saints. Noting Bale's polemical use – some would perhaps say his exploitation – of AA's story, one might well wonder about the extent to which he has edited, even written, words which he assures us were 'sent abroade by her owne handwriting'. The second *Examination*, Bale says, he prints, 'lyke as I receyued it in coppye, by serten duche merchauntes commynge from thens, whych had bene at their burnynge, and beholden the tyrannouse vyolence there shewed. First out of the preson she wrote vnto a secrete frynde of hers, after thys maner folowynge.' Two points suggest that AA did in fact write her own account of the examinations, and that what Bale published is at least close to her actual words. First, John Foxe, a careful, if polemical historian, reprints the examinations from Bale's volumes in *Actes and Monuments* (1653) with the assurance that they are 'as she wrote them with her own hande, at the instante desire of certaine faithfull men and women'. Second, the style of AA's concise and wittily enigmatic summary narration of her experience, representing herself as a stable and subtly intelligent woman, is very different from Bale's strident loquacity and religious fervour in the elucidations. That Foxe does not reprint the pieces with which Bale closes his two volumes – a paraphrase of Psalm 54 in the first instance and 'A Ballad which Anne Askewe made and sang when she was in Newgate' in the second – may indicate that he considered them apocryphal.

When Foxe reprinted AA's words from the *Examinations*, he replaced Bale's elucidations with more concise opening and closing comments, thus letting her story speak for itself: 'if thou marke diligently . . . thou maist easeliy perceiue', he writes sardonically, 'the tre by the frute and the man by his worke'. He inserts a copy of the confession Bishop Bonner wrote for AA to sign after the first examination and, at the end of the second examination, rewrites Bale's account of AA's death at Smithfield – including the detail that she was so broken by the torture that she had to be carried to her execution in a chair. Like Bale, Foxe emphasizes AA's constancy, beginning his account by noting that she was 'martred in Smithfield for the Constante and faithfull testimonye of the truthe' and ending by saying she is 'a singular example of Christen constancie for all men to folowe', and he comments on John Lascelles', John Adams', and Nicolas Belenian's good fortune in having been burned the same day as AA, for her steadfastness and brave words gave courage to even those 'strong and stout menne'.   ELIZABETH H. HAGEMAN

Works: *The first examinacyon of Anne Askewe, lately martyred in Smythfelde, by the Romysh popes vpholders, with the Elucydacyon of Johan Bale* (1546); *The lattre examinacyon of Anne Askew, lately martyred in Smythfelde, by the wycked Synagoge of Antichrist, with the Elucydacyon of Johan Bale* (1547).

References: Beilin, E. V., 'A challenge to authority: Anne Askew', in *Redeeming Eve: Women Writers of the English Renaissance* (1987); Fairfield, L. P., *John Bale: Mythmaker for the English Reformation* (1976); King, J. N., *English Reformation Literature: The Tudor Origins of the Protestant Tradition* (1982); King, J. N., 'The godly woman in Elizabethan iconography', *Renaissance Quarterly* 38 (1985); Travitsky, B., *The Paradise of Women: Writings by Englishwomen of the Renaissance* (1981); Wilson, D., *A Tudor Tapestry: Men, Women, and Society in Reformation England* (1972).

Astell, Mary

b. 6 November 1666, Newcastle-on-Tyne; d. 14 May 1731, Chelsea, London
Philosopher, polemicist

MA was born into a Newcastle coal merchant's family. Her father, Peter Astell, was a leading member of the coal Hostmen; her mother, Mary Errington, was also from a prosperous Newcastle coal-mining family. She is thought to have been educated when very young in philosophy, logic, and mathematics by her uncle Ralph Astell, her father's bachelor brother, a graduate of Cambridge University and a curate in St Nicholas Cathedral. At the age of 22, at the time of the Glorious Revolution, MA went to London, where she had great difficulty finding a means of providing for herself. Archbishop Sancroft came to her aid 'when even my Kinsfolk had failed, and my familiar Friends had forgotten me'. By 1692, thanks to his and/or others' charity, she had settled in Chelsea – where she was to stay until her death – and had begun to correspond with the Rev. John Norris of Bemerton, the last of the so-called Cambridge Platonists. For ten months they discussed in their letters how one owed one's love to God rather than to His creatures, how to respond to the misfortune and pain dispensed by Divine Providence, and other claims of the spirit as they might contradict the claims of the flesh. Norris wanted to publish their correspondence; while he was negotiating this, MA published anonymously her first book, *A Serious Proposal To the Ladies* (1694), which, together with the correspondence with Norris published the following year under the title of *Letters Concerning the Love of God* (1695), established her reputation as an intellectual and a writer.

In *A Serious Proposal To the Ladies*, MA suggested that wealthy women who did not intend to marry could use their dowries to finance residential women's colleges – Protestant nunneries – to provide the recommended education for upper- and middle-class women and to serve as living quarters for 'hunted heiresses' or decayed gentlewomen. The book was followed by *A Serious Proposal To the Ladies Part II* (1697), whose purpose was to provide the rules for rational thought, a distillation of the Port Royal logic and Descartes' method, for women who were still unprovided with an institution of higher learning. These books were subsequently published together. Her next book may be the most clearly feminist in emphasis. *Some Reflections on Marriage* (1700) discusses the obedience that a wife owes her husband and concludes that, since it is the most potentially tyrannical of relationships, no woman ought to undertake this slavery lightly, and that the morally responsible nature of one's husband-to-be is his most important qualification to consider. The preface added to the 1706 edition is an excellent early example of seventeenth-century liberal, political rhetoric applied to the issue of women's rights. MA writes wittily, sometimes sarcastically, exhorting women to rise above the petty concerns of dress and flirtation, and to be worthy of their natures as creatures of a divine being. 'You may be as ambitious as you please, so you can aspire to the best things . . . Remember, I pray you, the famous Women of former Ages . . . and blush to think how much is now and will hereafter be said of them, when you your selves . . . must be buried in silence and forgetfulness! . . . Let us learn to pride our selves in something more excellent than the invention of a Fashion, and not entertain such a degrading thought of our own *worth* as to imagine that our Souls were given us only for the service of our Bodies, and that the best improvement we can make of these is to attract the Eyes of Men.'

In 1704, the Whigs and Tories of Parliament continued to polarize on the issue of the Occasional Conformity Bill, a bill designed to bar Dissenters from holding public office by making it illegal for them to qualify by occasionally conforming, or taking the Anglican communion. Politically a conservative Tory, MA was concerned about the Church of England's struggles to maintain political power in England. She published three political works that year: two of them, *Moderation Truly Stated* and *A Fair Way With Dissenters and Their Patrons*, argued in favour of the Occasional Conformity Bill and were much appreciated by religious conservatives. The third, *An Impartial Enquiry Into The Causes of Rebellion and Civil War*, a royalist manifesto, argued that the subversive, individualistic element in Whig and Dissenting ideology had led to the war. MA's conservative religious convictions were as well developed and central to her intellectual system as her political or feminist views. Throughout her life she campaigned for conservative Anglicanism as the necessary basis for personal morality and national politics as well as spiritual understanding. She followed the Tory Atterbury's debates with Dr Hoadley over the doctrine of Divine Right and passive obedience (the degree to which subjects ought to submit passively to their rulers), and offered Atterbury advice on his rebuttal of Hoadley's *The Measures of Submission to the Civil Magistrate Considered* (1705). She worked with John Walker on his polemical *The Sufferings of the Clergy* (1714) and collected and transcribed for him the information on the persecutions of the Anglican clergyman Dr Squire. In 1705 MA published her religious manifesto, *The Christian Religion As Profess'd By a Daughter of the Church*, in which she seeks to establish the philosophical principles of her religion – her own version of the Cartesian sequence from the existence of reason to a belief in God – and to refute the materialistic thinking of her own day – like Locke's – which led to scepticism. Her last book was an attempt to bolster up seventeenth-century religious piety before the onslaughts of a tolerant, latitudinarian individualism: *Bart'lemy Fair, or, An Inquiry After Wit* (1709) was written as an answer to Lord Shaftesbury's *Letter Concerning Enthusiasm*, the first treatise of his *Characteristics*. In it, MA scorns 'this Blessed Age of Liberty! which has made us so much Wiser than our Fathers', and notes that never before was it 'thought a Service to the Public to expose the Establish'd Religion, no not when it was ever so false and ridiculous in it self, to the Contempt of the People'. She wrote a new preface to *Bart'lemy Fair* in 1722, and issued new editions of *Letters Concerning the Love of God* and *Some Reflections Upon Marriage* in 1730 just before she died. Her style in her religious works is less vivacious than in her feminist ones and tends toward the rhapsodic or lugubrious.

MA's importance as the first widely read, expressly feminist polemicist is incalculable. She was perhaps the first respectable woman prose writer in England, the prototype for the Bluestockings of the next generation. She inspired many of the women intellectuals of her own time: Elizabeth Thomas, Lady Chudleigh, Elizabeth Elstob, and Lady Mary Wortley Montagu. She was satirized in the *Tatler* for her otherworldly Platonism, but her ideas – and often her language – were picked up and imitated by the leading male authors of the day. Defoe, Steele, and Richardson all make reference to *A Serious Proposal To the Ladies*: Defoe in *Essay on Projects* (1697), Richardson in vol. II of *Sir Charles Grandison* (1753–4), and Steele, who actually uses more than 100 pages of it verbatim, without attribution, in his *The Ladies Library* (1714). The fact that MA's active role in the public realm did not damage her reputation is probably due to the extreme conservatism of her political and religious views, her unimpeachably pious and ascetic habits, and the wealth and social standing of her particular friends, the pious and philanthropic Lady Elizabeth Hastings, the Countess of Coventry, and Lady Catherine Jones. Through these women MA came to know the famous scholars, antiquarians, and clergymen who sought their patronage and, with their backing, she opened a school for the poor daughters of out-pensioners at the Royal Hospital in 1709. MA died after an operation for a breast tumour and was buried in the churchyard at Chelsea.

RUTH PERRY

Selected works: *A Serious Proposal To the Ladies* (1694); *Letters Concerning the*

Love of God (1695); *A Serious Proposal To the Ladies Part II* (1697); *Some Reflections Upon Marriage* (1700); *Moderation Truly Stated, or, A Review of a Late Pamphlet Entitul'd Moderation a Vertue* (1704); *A Fair Way with the Dissenters and Their Patrons* (1704); *An Impartial Enquiry into the Causes of Rebellion and Civil War in this Kingdom* (1704); *The Christian Religion, As Profess'd by a Daughter of the Church of England* (1705); *Reflections Upon Marriage. The Third Edition. To Which is Added a Preface, in Answer to Some Objections* (1706); *Bart'lemy Fair, or, An Enquiry after Wit* (1709).

References: *DNB*; Ferguson, M. (ed.), *First Feminists* (1985); Halsband, R., 'Note 163. Two facts about Mary Astell', *Book Collector* 10 (Autumn 1961); Harris, J., *Samuel Richardson* (1986); Hill, B. (ed.), *The First English Feminist* (1986); Janes, R., 'Mary, Mary, quite contrary, or, Mary Astell and Mary Wollstonecraft compared', in R. C. Rosbottom (ed.), *Studies in Eighteenth-Century Culture* (1976); Kinnaird, J. K., 'Mary Astell and the Conservative contribution to English feminism', *Journal of British Studies* 19 (1979); McIlquham Mrs, 'Mary Astell: a seventeenth-century advocate for women', *Westminster Review* 149 (April 1898); Norton, J. E., 'Some uncollected authors 27: Mary Astell, 1666–1731', *Book Collector* 10 (Spring 1961); Perry, R., *The Celebrated Mary Astell* (1986); Perry, R. 'The veil of chastity: Mary Astell's feminism', in R. Runte (ed.), *Studies in Eighteenth-Century Culture*, vol. 9 (1980); Reynolds, M., *The Learned Lady in England, 1650–1760* (1920); Rogers, K., *Feminism in Eighteenth-Century England* (1982); Smith, F., *Mary Astell* (1916); Smith, H. L., *Reason's Disciples* (1982); Upham, A. H., 'English femmes savantes at the end of the seventeenth century', *Journal of English and Germanic Philology* 12 (1913); Wallas, A., *Before the Blue Stockings* (1929).

Aubin, Penelope
b. 1679, London; d. 1731, London
Novelist, translator, playwright
PA seems to have had a Catholic upbringing. Her novels often refer to locations in south-west England and Wales, indicating that she may have lived in these regions during the earlier part of her life. The circumstances of her marriage are not known, but it may have taken place in the thirteen-year period between the first publication of her poetry in 1708 and the beginning of her career as a novelist in 1721, when financial difficulties forced her to turn to writing as a means of support. PA lived in London for most of her life, writing three poems, seven novels, one play, and four translations from the French, and editing two collections of French works. By 1729 she had preached to great public acclaim, from her own oratory in the York Buildings near Charing Cross. She died shortly after an unsuccessful staging of her play, *The Humours of the Masqueraders*.

PA's intention as a writer was clearly to instruct as well as entertain; her preface to *The Life of Madam de Beaumont* states that 'in this story I have aim'd at pleasing, and at the same time encouraging virtue in my readers'. Unlike her predecessors such as Aphra Behn, or her contemporary Eliza Haywood, she combined the elements of travelogue and romance with morality, thereby incorporating her career as preacher into that of the romance writer. The traditional theme of lovers' separation and reunion are fused with instruction 'to encourage virtue and excite us to heroic actions'. Many of her central characters are married, and moral considerations determine their behaviour in their various extreme adventures. The popular prose style of the day is discarded in favour of a pious polemical style of extreme moral and emotional simplicity, illustrating the battle between Good and Evil, or the struggle between fidelity to duty and self-immolation in illicit passion. Her novels clearly indicate a stage in the progress of popular literature from the ponderous seventeenth-century French romance to the moralistic sentimental novels of the eighteenth century.

GABRIELLE OSRIN

Selected works: 'The Extasy' (1708); 'The Wellcome: a poem to his Grace the Duke of Marlborough' (1708); (trans.), *The Illustrious French Lovers*, by Robert Challes (1720); *The Strange Adventures of the Count de Vinevil and His Family* (1721); *The Life of Madam de Beaumont* (1721); *The Noble Slaves, or, The Lives and Adventures of Two Lords and Two Ladies upon a Desolate Island* (1722); *The Life and Amorous Adventures of Lucinda* (1722); (trans.), *The Life of the Countess de Gondez*, by Mme de Beaucour (1722); (trans.), *The Adventures of the Prince of Clermont and Madam de Ravezan*, by Mme de Beaucour (1722); *The Life of Charlotte du Pont* (1723); *The Life and Adventures of Lady Lucy* (1726); *The Life and Adventures of the Young Count Albertus, the son of Count Lewis Augustus, by the Lady Lucy* (1728); *The Humours of the Masqueraders* (1733).

References: Dooley, B., *Penelope Aubin: Forgotten Catholic Novelist* (1959); McBurney, W. H., *Mrs Penelope Aubin and the Early Eighteenth Century English Novel* (1957); Shugrue, M. F., *The Sincerest Form of Flattery: Imitation in the Early Eighteenth-Century Novel* (1971); Spencer, J., *The Rise of the Woman Novelist* (1986); Todd.

Austen, Jane

b. 16 December 1775, Steventon; d. 18 July 1817, Winchester

Novelist

JA was the seventh of eight children of the Rev. George Austen and his wife Cassandra and grew up in a cultured, affectionate, and moderately prosperous family. Her father, who educated her, encouraged her writing and her reading of the established eighteenth-century writers. She also had a wide acquaintance with contemporary fiction and poetry. A major disturbance of her otherwise outwardly uneventful life occurred on her father's sudden retirement and the subsequent removal of the family to Bath in 1801. On his death in 1805, she moved with her mother and sister to Southampton and then in 1809 to Chawton where her brother Edward settled them in a house on his estate. This was her home until very shortly before her death when she went to Winchester to seek medical treatment for Addison's disease which overshadowed her last years. She never married, though she once accepted a proposal which she refused on the following day after a night of anguished reflection. Her opportunities for vicarious experience of a larger world were however considerable: an aunt was wrongfully imprisoned for shoplifting; a cousin, the widow of a French count guillotined in the Terror, fled from revolutionary France and married JA's brother Henry (whose own colourful career embraced both bankruptcy and ordination). Two brothers were in the navy: one was a friend of Nelson and both rose to the rank of admiral. The second Austen son was mentally defective and never mentioned, while the third, Edward, was adopted by a childless relative and inherited a fortune. Her limitation of subject matter to '3 or 4 families in a Country Village' was evidently the result of choice rather than deficiency of information.

JA's juvenilia, written in her teens for her own and her family's entertainment, reveal a detached and precocious enjoyment of absurdity, particularly in her parodies of the novel of sensibility. *Love and Freindship* ridicules the egotism of emotional self-indulgence and *A Collection of Letters* and *Lesley Castle* are sprightly burlesques of the epistolary form. *A History of England* (by a self-confessed 'partial, ignorant and prejudiced historian') contains 'very few dates' and its purpose is chiefly to vindicate Mary Queen of Scots and vilify Elizabeth I, an interesting and somewhat uncharacteristic early preference for the victim of passion over the cool rationalist. *Lady Susan* marks an advance both in complexity of story telling and in characterisation. The concerns of JA's mature work are to some extent prefigured in the relationship between the monstrous adulteress Lady Susan, whose dynamic energy is wholly destructive, and her feeble but virtuous daughter.

JA's early novels went through a number of major revisions before publication, the most significant modification being her liberation from the epistolary convention and adoption of an ironic and sceptical narrative persona. The order of composition does not correspond to the order of publication of her work. *Elinor and Marianne*, written in 1795–6, was redrafted twice as *Sense and Sensibility* before publication in 1811. *First Impressions*, refused by a publisher in 1797, was rewritten as *Pride and Prejudice* in 1809 and published in 1813. *Northanger Abbey*, written in 1788–9, sold to Crosby & Sons in 1803 and mysteriously withheld from publication, came out posthumously in 1818. *The Watsons*, begun in 1804, was abandoned, perhaps at the death of JA's father. After an apparently inactive period of seven years, she wrote *Mansfield Park, Emma*, and *Persuasion*, and was working on the unfinished *Sanditon* at the time of her death.

JA's fictional territory is the domestic life of the class into which she was born – the provincial gentry, socially confident in the hereditary possession of land, allied by marriage to the lower reaches of the aristocracy and to the upper levels of trade and providing for its younger sons a respectable independence in the church or the armed services. She represents this class at the historical point where its sphere of influence is beginning to be penetrated by the capitalist bourgeoisie and where its assumptions are therefore coming under pressure. The world of her novels is materialistic and secular: the precise amount that people own or expect to inherit is public information, and while respect is paid to the forms of religion, none of her characters (with the possible exception of Anne in *Persuasion*) shows much awareness of spirituality. Edmund in *Mansfield Park* takes his ordination seriously, but the majority of her clergy are career persons, the value of whose livings is easier to ascertain than the nature of their ministry.

JA's novels all address the question of how, in the absence or failure of proper authority, a scheme of values may be articulated which will be independent both of the market place and of irrelevant class distinctions. Conduct is sanctioned or condemned by reference to the convention that the possession of property entails responsibilities of which the public expression is good manners. While her values are thus essentially conservative, her treatment of her society is always ironic and often profoundly critical. Those responsible for the preservation and transmission of values are neglectful or decadent, while vulgarity and materialism in all classes signify a moral coarseness that corrupts feeling and jeopardizes relationships. The failure of aristocratic responsibility is comically represented in the grotesque arrogance of Lady Catherine de Burgh in *Pride and*

Prejudice, but the vanity of Sir Walter Elliot in *Persuasion* actually threatens the loss of his estate and thus the traditional social order itself. Parental authority is treated with an equivalent scepticism: in *Mansfield Park* Sir Thomas Bertram's chilly aloofness leaves his children vulnerable to the corrupting indulgence of Mrs Norris, and in *Pride and Prejudice* the abdication of responsibility by Mr Bennet, who is characteristically shown in the act of withdrawing from the family circle, leaves his younger daughters without guidance in the control of their impulsive and pleasure-seeking natures. None of JA's heroines can look to a parent or parental surrogate either for useful precept or example – they are all absent, careless, inadequate, or, like Lady Russell in *Persuasion*, themselves flawed in judgement. If hierarchical authority is compromised, equally danger-ous is vulgarity like that of warm-hearted Aunt Philips in *Pride and Prejudice*, whose chaotic, indecorous supper parties blunt Elizabeth's capacity to assess Wickham's duplicitous personality and also help to create the conditions for Lydia's moral and social disaster. The ridiculous Mr Collins's linking of Mrs Philips with Lady Catherine de Burgh in his comparison of her parlour to 'the small summer breakfast-room at Rosings' is a pointer to the fact that they do fail equally in social responsibility though in opposite ways: Lady Catherine by excluding, Mrs Philips by including all without discrimination. The operation of proper discrimination is demonstrated by Mr Knightley in *Pride and Prejudice* and by Fanny Price in *Mansfield Park*, both of whom assess correctly the moral worth of others independent of their wealth, rank and physical attractiveness and in opposition to the judgement of those whom they love.

Without engaging overtly in the contemporary debate on feminism, JA focuses on women's experience of a society which conspicuously fails to meet their needs, while assigning to each of them a precise cash value. (In *Mansfield Park*, Lady Bertram's looks have gained her a husband to whom she was 'at least three thousand pounds short of any equitable claim'.) Marriage is not only, as Charlotte Lucas bluntly recognizes in *Pride and Prejudice*, a woman's 'pleasantest preservative from want', it is also her only guarantee of social consequence. The marginalized social position of Miss Bates and Jane Fairfax's shrinking from the 'offices for the sale – not exactly of human flesh – but of human intellect' in *Emma* illustrate the alternatives. Though Emma herself fantasizes about a life of independence, liberated by birth and fortune from the subordination of marriage, her continued pre-eminence is in fact dependent upon her becoming the wife of Mr Knightley. JA's novels attempt to elucidate the terms upon which marriage can become an institution providing for the fulfilment of women's aspirations, sanctified by love but validated by prudence. Each of them describes a courtship, marking out the stages by which a man and a woman negotiate the terms of a relationship which will satisfy the needs of both. Sexual passion is invariably disastrous: it clouds the judgement and concludes in disgrace at worst and mutual indifference at best. Unions based on purely material considerations, like that of Mr Rushworth and Maria Bertram in *Mansfield Park*, are a degradation. Though motherhood may provide some occupation, it can reduce a woman's intellectual life to the imbecile doting of Lady Middleton in *Sense and Sensibility* or the hypochondriac obsessions of Isabella Knightley in *Emma*. Mrs Bennet's nerves in *Pride and Prejudice*, Mrs Norris's miserliness in *Mansfield Park*, and Emma's mischievous meddling are all symptoms of a morally corrosive ennui.

The tension between JA's recognition of the frustration of women's aspir-ations and her innate conservatism is apparent in her ambivalent attitude to women's energy. In *Northanger Abbey* Catherine's physical robustness is a marker of her moral health, but also of a fertile imagination which, untutored, leads her to mistake the conventions of Gothic fiction for clues to the meaning of adult life. The resultant perceptual confusion is corrected by the sensible Henry Tilney, whose instruction in aesthetics and pedantic attention to her grammar signify his function in teaching her to see correctly and to articulate, and thus control, her feelings. In *Sense and Sensibility* Elinor reacts to the absence of parental guidance by a scrupulous observation of the rules of good behaviour, Marianne by a passionate assertion of her individuality. Like Catherine, she confuses literature with life, taking the reprehensible Willoughby for the hero of her own romance and the cult of sensibility for a series of moral precepts. While Elinor's self-control negates the possibility of intimacy, Marianne's uninhibited expression of feeling causes pain to others and undermines her health. Both sisters reach equilibrium in marriage to rational men, but where Elinor's is the vindication of all the choices she has made, Marianne's is achieved at the cost of her vitality. In *Pride and Prejudice* Jane and Elizabeth exhibit a similar polarity, but in this novel Jane's tranquillity temporarily puts at risk Bingley's confidence in her, while Elizabeth's energy, which is both the cause and effect of her superiority to her environment, is also a potential pitfall: her imaginative self-confidence, unsupported by experience, leads her to mistake Wickham's physical attractions for indicators of sensitivity, and Darcy's shyness for caste arrogance. Her experience of visiting Pemberley, Darcy's family home, initiates her into the values of a life of tradition, order, and repose. Her love for Darcy develops both out of gratitude for his altruistic redemption of her family's honour, and from the recognition that her sprightliness requires a compromise with his solidity if it is to become a genuninely useful tool of discrimination. In *Mansfield Park* the arguments are all on the side of passivity. Fanny's physical feebleness is the outward sign of grace, while the restlessness of her cousins and the Crawfords is a symptom of the moral vacuum they inhabit. The amateur theatricals, which are an affront to the good order of Mansfield, provide this energy with a dangerous outlet in the enactment of illegitimate desires. Fanny's visit to her parents' chaotic home reinforces her conviction that quietness and propriety are an expression of consideration for others. On the other hand, Lady Bertram's torpor represents repose without moral awareness - a total abdication of responsibility. *Emma* is a detailed study of the collapse of female self-confidence (which is equated with arrogance) and a reinforcement of the patriarchal norm. Like Catherine and Marianne, Emma is an 'imaginist' who seeks to construct the world and other people in accordance with her own desires. Like Elizabeth Bennet's, her energy is an expression of a superior but undisciplined intelligence. The painful realization that each of her independent judgements has been wrong causes her gratefully to accept the authority in marriage of clear-sighted Mr Knightley, whose attempts at guidance and control she has resisted since childhood. *Persuasion* also records a woman's recognition that she has been mistaken, but in terms which radically depart from the assumptions of the previous novels. Anne's respect for propriety has led her, seven years previously, to value the advice of her godmother above her own feelings and to break her engagement. She has since come to understand that in relationships intuition may be a surer guide than authority, though she retains a confused conviction that, while the advice she acted upon was wrong, her respect for its giver was right. Where JA's previous heroines have found fulfilment in the surrender of their energy to the rational direction of their husbands, Anne's fading vitality is revived by renewed contact with Captain Wentworth. The moral worth of previous heroes has been verified by their connection with inherited land: Wentworth stands for order rooted in naval discipline, where both respect and fortune have to be earned. Anne's marriage will remove her from the decadent society of her ancient family to the bracing companionship of the sailors, just as Kellynch Hall has passed from the unworthy proprietorship of Sir Walter Elliot to Admiral Croft's careful tenancy. While the novel's tone is elegaic and autumnal, its subject is renewal and the enduring power of love. It contains JA's most encouraging portrayal of a marriage in that of Admiral and Mrs Croft, whose comic, touching, and unself-conscious interdependence is symbolized when she saves the gig he is driving from overturning by seizing the reins herself. The difficult equipoise thus achieved is a perfect metaphor for the condition to which all JA's couples aspire – a mutually supportive balance of opposite but equal powers.   ELIZABETH JOYCE

Works: *Sense and Sensibility* (1811); *Pride and Prejudice* (1813); *Mansfield Park* (1814); *Emma* (1816); *Persuasion* (1818); *Northanger Abbey* (1818); *The Watsons and Lady Susan* (1871); *Love and Freindship* (1922); *Collected Letters* (1932; revised edn 1952); *Volume the First* (1933); *Volume the Third* (1951).

References: Austen Leigh, J. E., *A Memoir of Jane Austen* (1870); Butler, M., *Jane Austen and the War of Ideas* (1975); Cecil, D., *A Portrait of Jane Austen* (1978); Drabble; *DNB*; Lascelles, M., *Jane Austen: Her Mind and Art* (1939); Litz, A. W., *Jane Austen: A Study of Her Artistic Development* (1965); Monaghan, D., *Jane Austen: Structure and Social Vision* (1980); Mudrick, M., *Jane Austen: Irony as Defense and Discovery* (1968); Southam, B. C., (ed.), *Jane Austen: The Critical Heritage* (1968); Tanner, T., *Jane Austen* (1986); Williams, M., *Jane Austen: Six Novels and Their Methods* (1986); Wright, A. H., *Jane Austen's Novels: A Study in Structure* (1954).

Ayres, Ruby

b. January 1883, Watford; d. 14 November 1955, Weybridge
Romantic novelist

RA was the daughter of a Hertfordshire architect. At the age of 26 she married Reginald William Pocock, a London insurance broker, and settled in Harrow. Following Pocock's death in a train accident in the 1940s, RA spent her final years at her sister's home in Weybridge. She had no children.

RA was a prolific writer of romance fiction who managed to publish almost 150 novels during her life, as well as serials for the *Daily Chronicle*, the *Daily Mirror*, and countless other newspapers and magazines. Her fiction was an innocuous blend of humour and romance which proved to be immortal and, in fact, many of her novels were being reissued well into the 1970s with new covers and slight alterations to the text (for example, a hero recently returned from India in an original edition resurfaced years later as a man just returned from an oil-related job in the Middle East).

Once, when asked whether she herself really believed in romance, RA responded, 'More marriages have been ruined by a nagging wife than there can ever be by an atomic bomb. I firmly believe that romance can be lively even when the strawberry season is over and there is only bread and cheese in the larder and no matter whether you agree with me or not, I'll go on writing love stories with happy endings.'   JEAN HANFF KORELITZ

Selected works: *Richard Chatterton, VC* (1915); *The Making of a Man* (1915); *The Littl'st Lover* (1917); *The Winds of the World* (1918); *The Remembered Kiss* (1918); *The Second Honeymoon* (1918); *The Phantom Lover* (1919); *The Scar* (1920); *A Bachelor Husband* (1920); *The Woman Hater* (1920); *The Marriage of Barry*

Wicklow (1920); *His Word of Honour* (1921); *A Loveless Marriage* (1921); *The Street Below* (1922); *The Matherson Marriage* (1922); *The Romance of a Rogue* (1923); *The Man Without a Heart* (1923); *Candle Light* (1924); *The Man the Women Loved* (1925); *Overheard* (1925); *Charity's Chosen* (1926); *Spoilt Music* (1926); *The Planter and the Tree* (1926); *The Luckiest Lady (1927); Life Steps In* (1928); *Broken* (1928); *Lovers* (1929); *One Month at Sea, Together with George Who Believed in Allah* (1929); *In the Day's March* (1930); *One Summer* (1930); *Men Made the Town* (1931); *By the World Forgot* (1932); *So Many Miles* (1932); *Changing Pilots* (1932); *Look to the Spring* (1932); *Always Tomorrow*(1933); *Come to My Wedding* (1933); *Love Is So Blind* (1933); *From This Day Forward* (1934); *Much-Loved* (1934); *Feather* (1935); *The Man in Her Life* (1935); *Some Day* (1935); *The Sun and the Sea* (1935); *Compromise* (1936); *After-Glow* (1936); *High Noon* (1936); *Somebody Else* (1936); *Too Much Together* (1936); *Living Apart* (1937); *Owner Gone Abroad* (1937); *Unofficial Wife* (1937); *The Tree Drops a Leaf* (1938); *And Still They Dream* (1938); *One to Live With* (1938); *The Thousandth Man* (1939); *Week-End Woman* (1939); *Little and Good* (1940); *The Little Sinner* (1940); *Still Waters* (1941); *Where Are You Going?* (1946); *The Day Comes Round* (1949); *The Man from Ceylon* (1950); *Love Without Wings* (1953); *Old-Fashioned Heart* (1953).
References: Beauman, N., *A Very Great Profession* (1983); RGW.

Bacon, Anne, Lady
b. 1528, Gidea Hall, Essex; d. 1610, Gorhambury, Hertfordshire
Translator, letter writer
(Also wrote under Anne Cooke)
AB was the second daughter of Ann Cawnton and Sir Anthony Cooke. Reports that she spoke Latin, Greek, French, and Italian, 'as her native tongue', and that she was associated with Edward VI as governess, suggest that she received a thorough education. In 1556 she married Sir Nicholas Bacon, with whom she had two sons, Antony in 1558 and Francis in 1560. The last decade of her life is remarkable for the lack of information surrounding it, a silence broken only by Bishop Goodman's comment: 'But for Bacon's Mother, she was but little better than frantic in her age.'

AB's extant letters are characterized by a continual concern for her sons and testify to the consistent financial support she gave them: 'I have been too ready for you both till nothing is left.' Around 1550 AB published her first work, a translation of sermons by the Italian Franciscan Bernadino Ochino (1487-c. 1504). These were then reprinted in an enlarged edition in 1564. As the printer John Day remarks, the translation is fluent and concise and is notable for being by someone 'that neuer gaddid farder then hir Fathers house to learne the language'. In her dedication to her mother which prefixes the later edition, AB testifies to the difficulties she had encountered and introduces the work with a characteristic, though perhaps deceptive, posture of humility: 'I descend, therefore, to the understanding of mine own debilitie.'

AB's outstanding achievement is her translation of Bishop John Jewel's *Apologia pro Ecclesia Anglicana* (1562). The first methodical statement in the vernacular of the position of the Church of England in relation to that of Rome – 'we have declared unto you the very whole maner of our religion' – the *Apologie or Aunswer in defence of the Church of England* was and remains an important work. The huge impact of the book sparked off the long-standing controversy between Jewel and Thomas Harding and led to its reissue in 1600 and again after her death. It was AB who introduced the work to the English reader; as

Mathew Parker, the Archbishop of Canterbury, remarked in his preface, it is she who 'delivers him by your cleane translation from the perrils of ambiguous and doubtful constructions: and in makinge his good worke more publikely beneficiall'.   CATHERINE S. WEARING

Works: *Certayne sermons of the ryghte famous and excellente clerk master Bernadine Ochine, borne within the famous university of Sienna in Italy, now also an example in this lyfe, for the faithful testimony of Jesus Christ, 25 sermons, translated into English from the Italian by a gentleman, and the last 25 translated by a young lady* (c.1550); *Sermons of Bernadine Ochine (to the number of 25) concerning the predestination and election of God* (1564); *An Apologie or Aunswer in defence of the Church of England* (1564); correspondence in Spedding, J.(ed.), *The Works of Francis Bacon* (1862).

References: Allibone; Ballard; Barnes, S., 'Cookes of Gidea Hall', *Essex Review* 21 (1912); *DNB*; Hogrefe,P., *Women of Action in Tudor England* (1977); Hughey, R., 'Lady Anne Bacon's translations', in *Review of English Studies* 10 (1934); Lewis, C. S., *English Literature in the Sixteenth Century, Excluding Drama* (1954).

Bagnold, Enid

b. 27 October 1889, Rochester; d. 31 March 1981, London
Novelist, dramatist

EB was the daughter of Ethel and Arthur Bagnold, a professional soldier. Her early years were spent in Jamaica, returning to the UK in 1902 to go to boarding school. This was a quite exceptional school run by a grand-daughter of Dr Arnold of Rugby, who was also the mother of Aldous Huxley. There, EB first displayed her literary talents by winning first prize in an essay and poetry competition. EB's education was completed abroad, in Marburg and in Paris. In 1907 her poem appeared in *New Age*. She was allowed a surprising degree of freedom from the early 1900s and at the age of 19 she was permitted to share a flat in Chelsea and also given an allowance of £75 a year by her parents. She did not waste her time by indulging in the typical social activities of a girl in her position. EB embraced the Bohemian scene enthusiastically and quickly befriended writers and artists including Gaudier-Brzeska, Ralph Hodgson, H. G. Wells, Vita Sackville-West, and Rudyard Kipling. She also studied with Walter Sickert at his drawing school in Camden.

In 1912, EB met the notorious Frank Harris and began a two-year affair with him. At the same time she worked with him as a journalist on *Hearth and Home* and *Modern Society*. Her letters to him were later published. EB was emancipated in all senses of the word. There were no neurotic dabblings in the emotional side of life. She entered relationships as an equal and emerged an equal, learning from her lovers. Prince Antoine Bibesco taught her to record events as they happened. This she did and the process resulted in *A Diary Without Dates* (1917), a record of her time as a VAD nurse at the Royal Herbert Hospital, Woolwich, during the First World War. It made national headlines and resulted in her instant dismissal!

She later went to France as a driver with the First Aid Nursing Yeomanry and this was to provide the material for her first novel, *The Happy Foreigner* (1920). The conditions in France directly after the war were appalling; food was scarce and disgusting when secured. EB doubted she could survive such a regime of deprivation and the work which lasted literally from dawn to dusk. There was no time for the ritual diary and all EB could manage was to send numbered letters home to her mother who carefully preserved and typed them. From these she later reconstructed her novel.

The Happy Foreigner is a love story rising out of the devastion in France in the aftermath of war. The heroine, an English VAD, falls in love with a French captain, and her meetings with him make her feel a woman, in the midst of a routine as gruelling as any man's. She is representative of a new type of young woman and reflects the views and attitudes of her creator, EB: if she is expected to carry out man's work, then she is entitled to be equal on all levels, including an emotional one. EB was at this time in the aftermath of her affair with Prince Bibesco and she was almost certainly taking a defiant line in her writing. A character in *The Happy Foreigner* remarks that 'love is based on illusion' and when the heroine meets the hero out of uniform, a little plumper and full of plans for their future, she understands what is meant by this remark.

In 1920 EB met Roderick Jones, chairman of Reuters, and subsequently married him. As Lady Jones, with four children to bring up, EB had to be disciplined in her approach to her writing, reserving a certain space of time each day for it. In 1938 *The Squire* appeared. It was a novel of birth and of death. The 'squire' of the title is awaiting the birth of her fifth child. In charge of a large household of children and servants, she rules a world of women: cooks, midwife, maids. Her husband is abroad and will not be back until long after the birth is expected. The squire bears his absence well, as she does most things, calmly and stoically. There is no fear at the approaching birth, of pain or of death, but as she watches her sleeping children, she thinks of the transience of life, of approaching middle age, and of the knowledge that she will not always be there to look after her children. In *The Squire*, EB dealt with childbirth in a very direct and open way and she extolled the virtues of breastfeeding. This was not met with general approval, but EB was so involved with child-bearing and rearing, personally and in the wider context, that she wanted to communicate her pleasure and satisfaction to her readers – even if it meant shocking H. G. Wells!

National Velvet appeared in 1935 and has since become a classic of children's literature. Velvet was a young girl who won a pony in a raffle, on which she eventually won the Grand National. It was an improbable plot, but it began the genre of the 'pony story' and achieved even more fame when it was filmed in 1944, with Elizabeth Taylor in the starring role. ALISON RIMMER

Selected works: A Diary Without Dates (1918); The Sailing Ships and Other Poems (1918); The Happy Foreigner (1920); Serena Blandish, or, The Difficulty of Getting Married (1924); Alice and Thomas and Jane (1930); National Velvet (1935; as a film in 1944, as a play in 1946); The Door of Life (1938); The Squire (1938); Lottie Dundas (1942); The Loved and Envied (1951); The Chalk Garden (1953); Call Me Jack (1968); Enid Bagnold's Autobiography (1969); A Matter of Gravity (1976).

References: OCCL; Sebra, A., *Enid Bagnold: The Authorized Biography* (1986).

Baillie, Lady Grisell

b. 25 December 1665; d. 6 December 1746

Poet, day-book keeper

GB, the daughter of Sir Patrick Hume of Polwarth and Grisell Ker, is perhaps as well known for her legendary heroism as she is for her writings. According to the story made famous by Joanna Baillie's *Metrical Legend*, she saved the life of her father (then under suspicion for participating in the Rye House Plot) by braving 'witch-fires, dancing in the dark/ owlets shriek, watch dogs bark' to hide him in the family vault near Redbraes Castle. In 1685, after her father's friend Robert Baillie had been hanged, drawn, and quartered on the same charge, the Hume family fled to Utrecht, finding solace if not material ease in the company of other exiled Scottish Presbyterians. The eldest daughter of eighteen children, GB managed the household and once made a secret voyage back to Scotland to rescue a sister and obtain the money that would sustain the family during their exile. At the Revolution of 1688, she and her mother returned to Britain in the company of the Princess of Orange who invited her to become a maid of honour at the English court. Instead, in 1692 she married George Baillie, Robert's son and, like her brother, a soldier in King William's army. During their long and happy marriage she took over many of the responsibilities of her husband's and her father's restored estates, and often travelled with her two daughters to 'southern climes' which included the Belgian city where she had spent the most exciting years of her life.

The *Day Books* she began to keep after her marriage are meticulous and prosaic, filled with necessary domestic accounts, recipes, menus, and travel itineraries, useful for understanding the daily life of a woman of her time and position but of limited literary interest. GB's daughter, however, writing in 1749, states that while in Utrecht her mother composed a book of songs which had unfortunately disappeared by the time Lady Murray's *Memoir* was published in 1822. One delightful poem, 'Were Ne My Hearts Light I Wad Dye', first published anonymously in *Orpheus Caledonius* (1726), and a fragment, 'The Ewe-butchin's Bonnie', sometimes printed with additional verses by Lady John Scott, are believed to have come from this lost book, and have often served as examples of the Scottish ballad tradition at its best.   SUSAN HASTINGS

Works: 'Were Ne My Hearts Light I Wad Dye', *Orpheus Caledonius or a Collection of the best Scotch Songs set to Music by W. Thomson* (1726); 'The Ewe-butchin's Bonnie' ('Absence'), broadsheet, with music by Charles Sharpe (1839); *The Household Book of Lady Griselle Baillie 1692–1733*, ed. R. Scott-Montcrieff (1911).

References: Baillie, J., *Metrical Legends of Exalted Characters* (1821); Chambers, R. (ed.), *The Songs of Scotland Prior to Burns* (1862); Eyre-Todd, G. (ed.), *Abbotsford Series of Scottish Poets* (1891–6); Murray, G., *Memoirs of the Lives and Characters of the Right Honourable George Baillie of Jerviswood, and of Lady Grisell Baillie* (1822); Ramsay, A., *The Tea-Table Miscellany: A Collection of Choice Songs, Scots and English, in Two Volumes* (1788); Warrender, M., *Marchmont and the Humes of Polwarth* (1894).

Baillie, Joanna
b. 11 September 1762, Bothwell, Lanarkshire; d. 23 February 1851, Hampstead
Dramatist, poet, religious writer
JB's father James, dour, intellectual and undemonstrative (it was said that he never kissed or caressed his children), was a minister of religion in Bothwell, and later Professor of Divinity at Glasgow; her mother Dorothea came from a family distinguished by its medical men. JB's uncles, William and John Hunter, were both famous physicians and anatomists. JB's twin sister died shortly after birth but she enjoyed close and lasting companionship with Matthew and Agnes, her elder brother and sister. At her boarding school in Glasgow JB was a bright and vivacious pupil, showing a keen interest in drama, writing plays, stage managing and designing costumes. Her imagination was already active: there were, she wrote, 'ghosts and witches in my busy brain'. Her father died in 1778 and a few years later the family moved to London, where Matthew,

now a medical student, had inherited property from his Uncle William. JB published her first book, *Fugitive Verses*, in 1790, an anonymous production that had one review and no sales. Undaunted, JB then wrote a tragedy, *Arnold*, which she later destroyed.

Her prospects improved when she moved with her mother and sister to 'Hampstead's healthy height'. Here she found not only health but literary inspiration. Her Aunt Anne (Mrs John Hunter) had become a lyric poet of distinction, and her graceful verses (set to music by Haydn) were as pleasant and popular as her London *conversazioni*. JB, an eager guest, enjoyed the company of Henry Mackenzie, Samuel Rogers, and a variety of authors and Bluestockings.

This encouraged her to continue with her writing, and in 1798 she anonymously published the first volume of a planned series of plays attempting to 'delineate the stronger passions of the mind', each passion to be the subject of both a tragedy and a comedy. This volume contained a sprightly little comedy on love, *The Trial*, together with two of her most powerful blank verse tragedies, *Basil* (love) and *De Monfort* (hate), prefaced by a lengthy introduction, in which JB's emphasis on the importance of genuine feeling, simplicity, and realism to replace false and artificial representations of nature linked her to the authors of *Lyrical Ballads*, published in the same year. Reviews were highly favourable, everyone (except that perceptive Bluestocking Hester Piozzi) assuming that the plays were written by a man. *De Monfort* was performed at Drury Lane with lavish Gothic trappings, and with Kemble and Siddons giving fine performances as brother and sister. De Monfort's hatred drove him to murder, and this dark, brooding, self-tormented hero–villain, forerunner of the Byronic figure, was to become a feature of her plays, giving ample scope to the talents of Kemble and Kean.

JB brought out a second volume of plays in 1802, dedicated to her brother Matthew (her identity had already been revealed to the world in the third edition of her first volume in 1800). This contained the 'companion' comedy to *De Monfort*, an amusing play called *The Election*, which eventually appeared in London as a musical, with a huge cast and an indifferent reception. Nor did *Ethwald*, a long, diffuse Gothic tragedy on ambition, heavily influenced by *Macbeth*, find favour with the public. Complaints were made about the grisly battlefield scenes. (JB tended to overpopulate her tragedies with corpses; an interest in dead bodies was of course a family trait, her brother and both her medical uncles being keen dissectors and enthusiastic embalmers.)

Still haunted by the gruesome and the Gothic, she produced a volume of 'miscellaneous' plays in 1804, the two most interesting being *Rayner* and *Constantine Paleologus*. *Rayner* boasted another brooding hero, moping and meditating with excessive sensibility, and *Constantine Paleologus* was a more showy and horrific tragedy, written especially for Siddons and Kemble, who refused it. It was also rejected by all the London managers to whom it was submitted.

By this time JB had begun to realize that, in spite of her brilliant reputation, most of her tragedies, like those of so many later Romantics, were regarded as 'literary' rather than 'acting' plays. This was a disappointment to her, and for some years she published no more drama, devoting herself to lyric poetry and to household duties. She resembled Elizabeth Carter in her combination of learning and domesticity, and visitors were impressed by the fact that she darned her own stockings and made her own puddings. Helped by Agnes, she also nursed her elderly mother, blind and paralysed after a stroke.

She remained single, but with an increasingly large social circle. One of her greatest friends and admirers was William Sotheby, author of that splendid

Gothic drama *Julian and Agnes*. In 1806 Sotheby introduced her to Scott, who had himself ventured into Gothic territory with his tragedy *The House of Aspen*. Sotheby and Scott vied in their praise of JB; they dedicated works to her, consulted her on a variety of subjects, and sent her presents. Scott was particularly generous, and JB was delighted with his pebble brooch from Iona, his giant Scottish thistle for her Hampstead garden, and his glowing tribute in *Marmion* to her 'inspired strain'. She visited him after her mother's death in 1808, travelling with Agnes to Edinburgh and fitting in a trip to the Lake District to see Southey.

With heart 'on flame' with Romantic inspiration, JB now set to work to compose a Scottish Gothic drama, *The Family Legend*. This time Siddons accepted the leading part, and the play was acted in Edinburgh in 1810, complete with a prologue by Scott and an epilogue by Henry Mackenzie. It introduced some spectacular stage effects, the heroine at one point being perched precariously on a craggy rock in the sea (a triumph for the master-carpenter and scene painters), prayerfully exercising the virtue of hope in the best Gothic tradition (a triumph for Siddons as the audience sobbed uncontrollably).

JB considered hope as a 'passion' in her next volume of plays in 1812, with a 'serious musical drama', *The Beacon*, which proved to be one of her most popular plays. Even the critic Jeffrey, who thought the volume a failure and viewed the whole idea of writing plays on individual passions as perverse and fantastic, was entirely captivated by *The Beacon* and its lyrics. This volume also contained the richly Gothic but unfortunately named tragedy of fear *Orra*, whose eponymous heroine, avid, like Austen's Catherine Morland, for stories of ghosts and horrors, was driven mad by supposedly supernatural happenings. It was never performed on the London stage – a further disappointment for JB.

In 1815 Byron tried unsuccessfully to revive *De Monfort* at Drury Lane. Both he and his wife knew and admired the talented Baillies: Byron consulted Matthew about his club foot and was given a brace – which he never bothered to wear – and Annabella consulted him about her husband's sanity. Byron considered JB unique, and, after seeing Mrs Wilmot's dull play *Ina* (one of the numerous feeble attempts at Gothic drama by JB's many female imitators), he declared, 'women, saving Joanna Baillie, cannot write tragedy; they have not seen enough nor felt enough of life for it' – an odd comment, in view of JB's extremely sheltered life.

JB announced that the 1812 volume would be her last, in spite of Scott's efforts to persuade her otherwise. She visited Scott again in 1817, and saw the ruins of Melrose Abbey by moonlight (she remarked what a beautiful embroidery pattern it would make). Other patterns occupied her attention from time to time and she acknowledged her debt to Scott in matters of rhyme and versification in her *Metrical Legends of Exalted Characters* in 1821. In the legend of Lady Griselda Baillie she promulgated her views on the ideal woman – brave, tender, cheerful, generous, modest, wise – and hit out against the aggressive feminism and anti-domestic stance typical of many a learned lady of the time, whose ink-stained finger scorned 'with vulgar thimble to be clipt'.

The following year JB brought out a *Collection of Poems* for the benefit of a friend whose business had failed. Scott provided a drama *Mac Duff's Cross*, and from the Lake District came Southey's *The Cataract of Lodore* and Wordsworth's sonnet *Not Love Nor War*. JB herself contributed two ballads, *The Robber Polydore* being one of her most rousing.

By this time JB was vastly popular as a writer of songs and ballads, and her work was eagerly sought after by that enthusiastic musician George Thomson, friend of Burns and indefatigable collector of national songs, who employed Beethoven, Haydn, Pleyel, and Kozeluch to 'decorate' his airs. JB was one of his most valued correspondents and contributors. She sent him *The Maid of Llanwellyn* for his Welsh collection and over the years she supplied him with batches of Scottish lyrics, including such favourites as *Poverty Parts Gude Companie*, *Hooly and Fairly*, *Fy*, *Let us A' to the Wedding*, *The Wee Pickle Tow*, *The Weary Pun o' Tow* and *Saw Ye Johnnie Comin'?* Some were new versions of 'coarse' old Scottish songs, but in JB's hands they lost none of their native vigour and verve. Thomson paid her, as he paid her Aunt Anne, with Indian-style shawls and scarves, since they both refused to accept money. Haydn provided the music for JB's song *The Gowan Glitters on the Sward* and for her Welsh airs *O Welcome Bat and Owlet Gray* and *Goodmorrow to Thy Sable Beak*, and also for the famous *Woo'd, and Married, and A'*. Beethoven 'improved' the traditional Scottish air that accompanied JB's song *O Swiftly Glides the Bonny Boat*. JB's reputation as a 'songstress' now equalled her reputation as a dramatist. She was less successful when she essayed hymns and religious plays, her drama *The Martyr* (1826) being tame and undistinguished except for the cheerful song of the martyrs on their way to execution.

In old age JB grew more interested in religion and theological matters. She inclined towards Arianism and wrote a pamphlet on the nature of Christ. Philanthropical activity occupied her too: in her seventies she would visit the poor and sick in all weathers and most of her earnings went to charity. Wordsworth considered her 'the model of an English gentlewoman' and Harriet Martineau looked upon her as an ideal example of 'intellectual superiority in women', devoid of 'pedantry, vanity, coquetry and manners ruined by celebrity'.

In 1836 she staged a comeback with three volumes of drama, completing her plays on the passions and adding several others. (Her total output was over twenty-six plays.) None, however, attained the popularity of her 1798 volume. In the 1840s her reputation dwindled and her health declined. Longmans brought out a complete edition of her works in 1851, but by this time it was too late for her to take much pleasure in it. At 88, her mind was beginning to fail and she died shortly after the book appeared. Her death, occurring less than a month after that of Mary Shelley, occasioned a last outburst of extravagant praise, one critic vowing that he 'would rather have written one "Beacon" than one hundred "Frankensteins".' Few would echo such sentiments today or award her a place second to Shakespeare. Her exclusive concentration on one passion tends to weaken rather than strengthen the presentation of character in her tragedies, but her combination of horrid happenings, spectacular scenery, and a moral message proved a popular package, and, at best, her Gothic drama easily surpasses that of Lewis, Whalley, and Southey; her bright comedies outsparkle those of Hannah Cowley and Elizabeth Inchbald and her delightful lyrics deserve a far better fate than a rare nod from a discerning anthologist.

MARGARET MAISON

Works: *Fugitive Verses* (1790) (all original copies now lost, but verses included in *Works*, 1851, see below); *A Series of Plays: in which it is attempted to delineate the stronger passions of the mind, Each passion being the subject of a tragedy and a comedy* (usually called *Plays on the Passions*), vol. 1 (1798); *Plays on the Passions*, vol. 2 (1802); *Miscellaneous Plays* (1804); *The Family Legend: A Tragedy* (1810); *Plays on the Passions*, vol. 3 (1812); *Metrical Legends of Exalted Characters* (1821); *A Collection of Poems, Chiefly Manuscript, and from Living Authors* (1823); *The*

Martyr (1826); *A View of the General Tenour of the New Testament regarding the Nature and Dignity of Jesus Christ* (1831); *Dramas*, 2 vols (1836); *Ahalya Baee: A Poem* (1849); *The Dramatic and Poetical Works of Joanna Baillie* (1851).
References: Badstuber, A., *Joanne Baillie's Plays on the Passions* (1911); Carhart, M., *The Life and Work of Joanna Baillie* (1923); Carswell, D., *Sir Walter* (1930); Dix, J., *Lions: Living and Dead* (1852); Evans, B., *Gothic Drama from Walpole to Shelley* (1947); Grierson, H. (ed.), *The Letters of Sir Walter Scott*, 12 vols (1932–7); Insch, A., 'Joanna Baillie's *De Monfort* in relation to her theory of tragedy', *Durham University Journal* 54, 3 (June 1962); Manvell, R., *Sarah Siddons* (1970); Meynell, A., *The Second Person Singular and Other Essays* (1921); Nicoll, A., *British Drama* (1925); Norton, M., 'The plays of Joanna Baillie', *Review of English Studies* 23, 90 (April 1947); Pieszczek, R., *Joanna Baillie* (1910); Plarr, V., 'Sir Walter Scott and Joanna Baillie', *Edinburgh Review* 216, 442 (October 1912) and 217, 443 (January 1913); Rogers, C., *The Modern Scottish Minstrel*, 6 vols (1855); Thomson, G., *The Select Melodies of Scotland, Interspersed with those of Ireland and Wales*, 5 vols (1822); Tytler, S. and Watson, J., *The Songstresses of Scotland*, 2 vols (1871); Ziegenrücker, E., *Joanna Baillie's Plays on the Passions* (1909).

Bainbridge, Beryl

b. 21 November 1934, Liverpool
Novelist, television playwright
Educated at Merchant Taylor's School, Liverpool, and at a ballet school in Hertfordshire, BB worked from 1949–60 as an actress with provincial repertory companies and from 1961–73 as a clerk with the publishers Gerald Duckworth. She also had a brief period of employment in a London bottle factory in 1970. In 1954 she married Austin Davies, whom she divorced in 1959. She has a son and two daughters. She was awarded the Guardian Fiction Prize in 1974 for *The Bottle Factory Outing*, and the Whitbread Award in 1977 for *Injury Time*. *The Dressmaker* (1973) and *The Bottle Factory Outing* were both runners-up for the Booker Prize.

In various interviews with the press and on television, BB has claimed an autobiographical basis for her fiction, including its more bizarre episodes and characters ('It is always me and the experiences I have had'), while justifying her recurrent motif of violence and death as providing the 'strong narrative line' essential to fiction. It is the juxtaposition of banality and menace that gives her writing its characteristic tone, in which desperation, emotional dereliction, and horror are represented in a style of jaunty detachment, and the mundane strategies of everyday living are punctuated by startling intrusions of absurdity. From the black farce of *Harriet Said* (1972) to the muted tragedy of *Watson's Apology* (1983), her work to date shows developing subtlety in the handling of an essentially consistent theme: the lonely quest for acceptance in a world whose ground rules are largely unintelligible.

The discursive form of *A Weekend With Claude* (1967) and *Another Part of the Wood* (1968) represented a false start. Both novels were revised in the 1980s to conform to the pared-down economy established in *Harriet Said* (1972) and refined in succeeding novels. In *Harriet Said*, *The Dressmaker* and *A Quiet Life* (1976), the claustrophobic respectability of family life in lower-middle-class Liverpool during and after the Second World War is subverted by adolescent sexuality and murder. *The Bottle Factory Outing* (1974), *Sweet William* (1975) and *Injury Time* (1977) are all set in London, where characters in flight from the suffocating tyrannies of 'home' pursue affection with varying degrees of persistence and energy but little real optimism and less success. The enigmatic William's complex liaisons are his insurance against loneliness but impose it upon his victims. The violence latent in the comic misunderstandings and cross purposes of *The Bottle Factory Outing* explodes in the grotesque farce of Freda's murder. In *Injury Time*, violence located in the outside world intrudes upon domestic privacy to embarrassing as well as alarming effect, when guests at a dinner party given by a married man and his mistress are taken hostage by armed criminals.

Young Adolf (1979) draws upon historical speculation, *Winter Garden* (1981) upon international relations, to represent the disorientation and panic experienced by a character isolated in an alien environment by his inability to interpret either its language or its customs. In *Young Adolf*, the reader's historical awareness provides a chilling and ironic commentary on the ludicrous humiliations which bedevil the youthful Hitler's inept pursuit of acceptance on a visit to relatives in Liverpool in 1912. The consequences will be a revenge sufficiently terrible to restore his shattered self-esteem. In *Winter Garden*, Ashburner joins his mistress on a cultural visit to the Soviet Union and after her unexplained disappearance finds himself totally isolated by his inability either to interpret the meaning of what he sees, or to communicate his needs and fears. Detached from all contact with the familiar, his perceptions become increasingly hallucinatory and the novel concludes with his bewildered recognition that he is about to be arrested for spying in a country where he cannot be sure of the reality of anything he has seen.

Watson's Apology (1985), written with the same spare elegance as the previous novels, marks a deepening psychological penetration and a more ambitious scope in its treatment of a story whose grotesque aspect is closer to the tragic than the comic mode. Characteristically intrigued by the *Dictionary of National Biography*'s description of Watson as 'author and murderer', BB set out to explore the meaning of an historical event – the brutal murder of his wife by an inoffensive clergyman. The emotional wasteland of a Victorian marriage of convenience is dissected with compassion and the corrosive bitterness engendered by mutual disappointment is discovered to be more horrible than the act of violence which is its ultimate expression.

The world of BB's novels is reminiscent of the early plays of Pinter. The lurking menace inherent in the drab ordinariness of the settings, the dogged eccentricities of behaviour, the comic inanities of the dialogue, and the deft precision of style create a characteristic blend of Gothic horror and comedy of manners. Her characters are victims, whose partial, confused, and inaccurate perceptions of their situation doom them to the isolation from which they strive to liberate themselves. Grotesque and incongruous details puncture the narrative with startling reminders of the intrusion of the unexpected into the mundane. Except for *Watson's Apology*, all BB's novels are comic: they are all disturbing.   ELIZABETH JOYCE

Works: *A Weekend with Claude* (1967, 1981); *Another Part of the Wood* (1968, 1979); *Harriet Said* (1972); *The Dressmaker* (1973); *The Bottle Factory Outing* (1974); *Sweet William* (1975); *A Quiet Life* (1976); 'Tiptoe Through the Tulips' (television play) (1976); *Injury Time* (1977); 'Blue Skies From Now On' (television play) (1977); 'The Warrior's Return' (television play, Velvet Glove series) (1977); *Young Adolf* (1978); 'Words Fail Me' (television play) (1979); *Winter Garden* (1980); *Sweet William* (screenplay) (1980); 'The Journal of Bridget Hitler', with Philip Saville (television play) (1981); 'Somewhere More Central' (televi-

sion play) (1981); *English Journey, or, The Road to Milton Keynes* (1984); *Watson's Apology* (1984).
References: Cobb, R., 'Portrait of the dictator as a young artist', *New Society* (16 November 1978); Johnson, D., 'The sufferings of Young Hitler', *Times Literary Supplement* (1 December 1978); Phelps, G., 'The Post War Novel' in B. Ford (ed.), *The New Pelican Guide to English Literature* (1983); Rumens, C., 'Cutting down to size', *Times Literary Supplement* (11 September 1981).

Banks, Isabella
(Mrs George Linnaeus Banks)
b. 25 March 1821, Manchester; d. 5 May 1887, Dalston
Novelist, journalist, poet
As the daughter of James Varley, a successful tradesman and amateur painter, IB enjoyed a childhood suffused with cultural contacts. Artists, local poets, and literary figures were frequent visitors to the household; IB's relatives included Harrison Rinsworth, and Walker of *The Original*. Home tuition complemented IB's education, sharpening not only her interest in topography and history but her critical awareness of her social milieu.

At 17 IB took charge of a school outside the squalour of industrial Manchester, and in 1846 she married the writer and poet George Linnaeus Banks (1821–81). A year later they left Manchester; IB was rarely to return. Despite ill-health she led a full life, her interests extending well beyond fine needlework and contributions to her husband's periodicals. IB joined the Harrogate Mechanics' Institute and took active advantage of its library and lecture facilities. One of her own lectures was entitled, in somewhat utopian manner, 'Woman . . . as She was, as She is, and As She may Be'.

IB was only 16 when the poem 'A Dying Girl to her Mother' appeared in the *Manchester Guardian*. George Faulkner's inclusion of some of her writing in *Bradshaw's Three* in 1841 and 1842 must have kindled her literary aspirations; and in 1876 she published her most famous novel, *The Manchester Man*. Here IB's precocious interest in local affairs is something of a salvation. The book survives as a document of life in Manchester during the nineteenth century, treating the 1816 riots with especial vigour. IB's focus on the Manchester area persisted, leading to her being labelled the 'Lancashire novelist'. *Wooers and Winners* (1880), subtitled *A Yorkshire Story*, was found 'rather old-fashioned' even in 1880; more generous readers might attribute this to an intentional unity between homely subject and style.

Caleb Booth's Clerk (1878) is perhaps the fastest-moving and best-plotted novel amongst IB's prolific output. Her oeuvre in its entirety, however, stands as a solid monument to a departed generation and its environment. A wealth of specific detail conspires to inform the author's, and thus the reader's, perspective; and so, at best, the reader is persuaded to give up the criticial reins to identify with what plot there is.   E. LEVY

Works: *Ivy Leaves: A Collection of Poems* (1844); *Daisies in the Grass: Songs and Poems* (1865); *God's Providence House* (1865); *Stung to the Quick* (1867); *The Manchester Man* (1876); *Glory: A Wiltshire Story* (1877); *Ripples and Breakers (Illustrated Poems)* (1878); *Caleb Booth's Clerk* (1878); *Wooers and Winners: A Yorkshire Story* (1880); *More Than Coronets* (1881); *Through the Night: Tales of Shades and Shadows* (1882); *The Watchmaker's Daughter and Other Tales* (1882); *Forbidden to Marry* (1883); *Sybilla and Other Stories* (1884); *In His Own Hand*

(1885); *Geoffrey Oliphant's Folly* (1886); *A Rough Road* (1892); *Bond-Slaves* (1893); *Slowly Grinding Mills* (1893); *The Bridge of Beauty* (1894).
References: Allibone; Burney, Edward L., *Mrs G. Linnaeus Banks* (1969); *DNB;* *Manchester Faces and Places* 4, 40 (December 1982); Plarr, V. G. (ed.), *Men and Women of the Time*, 14th edn (1895).

Bannerman, Helen
b. 25 February 1862, Edinburgh; d. 13 October 1946, Edinburgh
Writer for children
One of seven children of Robert Boog Watson, a scientist and minister in the Free Church of Scotland, and of Helen (*née* Cowan) Watson, HB went at the age of 2 with her family to Madeira, where she was taught by her father and became a voracious reader. Returning in 1874, HB went to school in Edinburgh and began writing stories which already showed her later penchant for the macabre and for tigers. In 1875 a bank collapse ruined the fortune of her mother, and her father, then on a scientific expedition, had to return to the Church for a living. The family moved to Glasgow and in 1879 HB became engaged to Will Bannerman who was working in public health and medical research for the Indian Medical Service. While he was in India she took an external degree in language and literature at the University of St Andrews, since women were still prevented from being full members. In 1889 they were married and set off for India, where they lived in various places, especially Bombay, Bangalore and Madras. They remained in India until 1918, with periodic leaves in England, producing four children who at the appropriate ages returned to Edinburgh for education, much to HB's regret; during an early separation from her eldest daughter she wrote a sentimental poem, 'Far Away, Far Away, Over the Sea'. In India HB lived the life of an English memsahib but her establishment was modest by the standards of others and she avoided much socializing. She was devoted to raising her children and spent much time in writing and drawing. In 1896 there was an outbreak of plague in India and Bannerman was engaged with Haffkine in experimenting with vaccines; the drama of this work greatly influenced HB's life, as the couple moved frequently for Bannerman to pursue his controversial research. While the children were in India they were sent into the hills during the most unhealthy months; HB disliked the separation and on one of the journeys from the hill town of Kodaikand to Madras she wrote *The Story of Little Black Sambo* for her daughters of 2 and 5. She was later offered £5 for the copyright of this work which her friend in England accepted although HB wished very much to retain control of her books. The work had a phenomenal success, going through four editions in the first year and achieving similar success in the US; it was translated into most European languages, as well as Hebrew and Arabic. The work was set in an imaginary jungle land and the wily protagonist Sambo, drawn in HB's caricatured style, had mixed racial features; the most Indian aspect was the use of some Hindustani words. Later works on the same pattern went to other publishers so that HB could retain her copyright, but none had the same success as *Little Black Sambo*. *The Story of Little Black Mingo* (1901) makes the protagonist a black girl and the villain a crocodile rather than a tiger, while *The Story of Little Black Quibba* (1902) drew on HB's recent illness and tells of a sick mother whose child cures her by finding mangoes. Beside works for publication, HB wrote weekly letters to her daughters in Edinburgh with coloured illustrations, later bound in more than seventeen volumes. When her children were grown up she started writing

stories for adults and she edited a magazine for the Young Woman's Christian Association, but she did not have the success in this genre that she had had with her children's books. Her last years in India, unpunctuated by leave in England because of the First World War, were marred by ill-health.

HB's books exemplified the new type of children's literature, using direct visual pictures and lacking an overt moral, which she mocked in *The Story of Little Degchie-Head* (1903). When first published, they were criticized by some for their violence, and certainly her animals are far less idealized than those of her contemporary Beatrix Potter, having a very animal obsession with eating their prey. In recent years the books, especially *Little Black Sambo*, have come in for considerable criticism first in the US and then, with West Indian immigration, in England for alleged racism and they have been banned from many establishments. In part this reaction was due to corruptions of HB's original conception, particularly in America, since, without owning the copyright, she could not control later editions of her work which often had more grotesque illustrations than she had originally provided. In part it was due to the name Sambo which she had used as a specific name, but which some later readers felt was a racial epithet and a reference to slavery. In 1965 Nancy Larrick's *The All White World of Children's Books* found *Little Black Sambo* objectionable and there was protest that Sambo's eating of 169 pancakes made blacks appear greedy. Certainly the reaction would have surprised HB who caricatured whites and blacks alike – in *Pat and the Spider* (1904) she used her own young son Pat for the illustrations – and who set her stories in an entirely imaginary world where blackberries and bamboo grow together. A more recent approach has drawn on psychoanalytical theories and found in the stories castration anxieties and the guilt of the forbidden.   JANET TODD

Works: *The Story of Little Black Sambo* (1899); *The Story of Little Black Mingo* (1901); *The Story of Little Black Quibba* (1902); *The Story of Little Degchie-Head* (1903; published in the US as *The Story of Little Kettlehead*, 1904); *Pat and the Spider* (1904); *The Story of the Teasing Monkey* (1906); *The Story of Little Black Quasha* (1908); *The Story of Little Black Bobtail* (1909); *The Story of Sambo and the Twins* (1937); *The Story of Little White Squibba* (1966).

References: Arbuthnot, M. H., *Children and Books* (1964); Hay, E., *Sambo Sahib* (1981); Kujoth, E. H., *Best Selling Children's Books* (1973); Larrick, N., *The All White World of Children's Books* (1964); McDonald, M., 'Little Black Sambo', *Psycho-Analytic Study of the Child* 29 (1973); OCCL; Schiller, J. G., 'The story of Little Black Sambo', *Book Collector* 23 (1974); Stokes, F. A., foreword to *The Jumbo Sambo* (1942); Yuill, P., *Little Black Sambo: A Closer Look* (1976).

Barbauld, Anna Laetitia

b. 1743, Kibworth, Leicestershire; d. 1825, Stoke Newington

Poet, essayist, educational writer, editor

The only daughter of the noted classicist and Nonconformist minister John Aikin, ALB was educated mainly by her father. In 1785 Aikin became one of the teachers at the new Dissenting academy in Warrington. There ALB's close friends and teachers included many of the leading intellectuals in Britain, among them Joseph Priestley. In 1774 she married Rochemont Barbauld, a student at Warrington and a Nonconformist cleric. He was called to minister to a congregation in Palsgrave, Suffolk, where ALB took charge of a school for young boys. She was apparently a superb teacher, and the school was very successful until the Barbaulds left Suffolk in 1785. They travelled on the continent for about a year and then settled in Hampstead where Barbauld ministered to a congregation. ALB took a few pupils, mostly older girls, in Hampstead and also in Stoke Newington where they moved in 1802 to be near her brother John. Barbauld briefly ministered to another congregation there but, never a very stable person, he soon collapsed; he died insane in 1808. They had no children but adopted one of ALB's nephews, Charles Rochemont Aikin, later a well-known scientist.

ALB's early education under her father included the English classics, French, Italian, Latin, and Greek, although in her later writing she played down the need for such education for women. She was very close to her brother John who encouraged her first publication, a book of verse, in 1773, and with whom she collaborated on a volume of essays published the same year. She also contributed several pieces to his later work, *Evenings at Home* (1792). Her friends included many of the Bluestocking circle, Joseph Johnson the publisher, Joanna Baillie, Mrs John Taylor of Norwich, Gilbert Wakefield, and many other leading dissenters and liberals. She wrote feelingly on behalf of the abolition of the slave trade, the removal of civil disabilities for Dissenters, and freedom of speech and public worship. Her later reputation rested primarily on a few poems and her work as editor. In 1804 she published the *Correspondence of Samuel Richardson* in six volumes with a long biographical and critical introduction. In 1810 she edited *The British Novelists* in fifty volumes. *The Female Speaker* (1811) was a volume of selections of the best British prose and poetry, long used in the education of girls.

ALB's experience of teaching her husband's pupils gave her the insight into the minds of young children which is reflected in the direct and simple prose of *Lessons for Children of Three Years Old* (1788), written for her adopted son. She had noted that no suitable books were available for the very young. Instead of moralizing, she relies on observation of the external world to develop the child's sentiments: 'Here is a bird dropped down just at your feet. It is all bloody. Poor thing! how it flutters. . . . It is going to die.'

However, in the more influential *Evenings at Home* (1782–6, 6 vols), written in conjunction with her brother, Dr Aikin, she addresses older children in more rigorous terms. 'A Lesson in the Art of Distinguishing' is attributed to her by her niece. In this catechism on the nature of the horse, the child, who wishes to describe the animal as 'a fine large prancing creature', is corrected by a Gradgrindian father who urges him to define the quadruped with greater precision.

Her ideas on the education of girls are disappointingly conventional, in view of her own career. In the essay 'On Female Studies' she argues that, since young ladies can be called to no profession beyond that of wife, mother, and mistress of a household, they should confine themselves to the acquisition of a 'general tincture' of knowledge. Literature is particularly useful for 'adorning and improving the mind . . . refining the sentiments and supplying proper stores of conversation'.

Breaking this traditional mould, she combined the profession of writing with that of teaching. As a critic, she wrote prefaces to editions of Collins and Akenside in addition to those for the series of *British Novelists*, published in fifty volumes (1810) with an introductory essay on fiction. These are designed to inform and entertain the general reader. The critical assessment is often shrewd and objective, in spite of her usual bias towards elegance and moral purpose in literature.

Her early poetry in the quarto of 1773 owes much to her reading of the classics and the major Augustan writers. She draws on the pastoral tradition in imitative verses; her meditations and descriptions are more expressive. Her elevated style, technically accomplished, but conventional in its use of epithets and personification, is sometimes exchanged for a lighter and more distinctive manner of writing, as in 'The Mouse's Petition' – for release from the trap where, according to her niece, she had found it confined by Priestley for an experiment on air.

Blandness vanishes, to good effect, when her political passions are aroused, especially in her later verse. She is vehement in her defence of liberty, writing a verse epistle to Wilberforce (1791) on the rejection of the Bill for the abolition of the slave trade, and supporting with enthusiasm the ideals of the French Revolution. In the poem 'To the Poor' (1795), she expresses indignation at the way in which sermons are made to serve a political purpose. She mocks the rich, who bear the afflictions of the poor with Christian resignation, and urges the poor not to fear 'the God whom priests and kings have made'. Her long prophetic poem, *Eighteen Hundred and Eleven* (1812), published as a pamphlet, attacks British social and political corruption; she predicts the fall of London, with pilgrims meditating in the ruins. She was disappointed by the public's hostile response; the poem was regarded as unpatriotic. Her most popular lyric, 'Life', was admired by Wordsworth and Tennyson. The lines of the last stanza ('Life, we've been long together') have survived the obscurity into which much of her verse has fallen.

She is best known today for a hybrid form, the *Hymns in Prose for Children* (1781). In this book she adopts 'measured prose' as her medium because she doubted 'whether poetry ought to be lowered to the capacities of children'. This work was intended 'to impress devotional feelings as early as possible in the infant's mind by connecting religion with the wonder and delight of the child's response to the natural world'. Her rhythms, parallel constructions, and cumulative effects are influenced by the Psalms; the vision of nature here is much fresher than that of her formal verse: 'I have seen the insects sporting in the sunshine and darting along the streams; their wings glittered with gold and purple; their bodies shone like green emerald. . . . I returned. . . . They were brushed in the pool . . . the swallow had devoured them, the pike had seized them.'

AB may have met Blake at the house of her publisher, Joseph Johnson. There are several interesting verbal correspondences between her *Hymns* and his *Songs*, but her vision rests in the natural world as an expression of God's system; her writing is addressed to the 'Child of Reason', and her intention is to develop the heart and mind rather than the imagination.

BARBARA BRANDON SCHNORRENBERG AND CLARE MACDONALD SHAW

Works: *Poems* (1773); *Miscellaneous Pieces in Prose* (with John Aikin) (1773); *Devotional Pieces* (1775); *Early Lessons for Children* (c. 1776–8); *Hymns in Prose for Children* (c. 1776–8); *Address to the Opposers of the Repeal of the Corporation and Test Acts* (1790); *Epistle to William Wilberforce* (1791); *Letter to John Bull* (1792); *Evenings at Home* (with John Aikin) (1792); *Remarks on Mr Gilbert Wakefield's Enquiry* (1793); *Correspondence of Samuel Richardson* (1804); *The British Novelists* (1808); *The Female Speaker* (1811); *Eighteen Hundred and Eleven, a Poem* (1812); *Works, with a Memoir by Lucy Aikin* (1825).

References: BA (19); Messenger, A., 'Heroics and mock heroics: John Milton, Alexander Pope, and Anna Laetitia Barbauld', in *His and Hers: Essays in Restoration and Eighteenth-Century Literature* (1986); Moore, C. E., ' "Ladies . . . taking the pen in hand": Mrs Barbauld's criticism of eighteenth-century women novelists', in M. A. Schofield and C. Macheski (eds), *Fetter'd or Free? British Women Novelists 1670–1815* (1986); Oliver, G. A., *The Story of the Life of Anna Laetitia Barbauld* (1886); *OCCL;* Rodgers, B., *Georgian Chronicle: Mrs Barbauld and her Family* (1958); Todd; Whiting, M. B., 'A century-old friendship: unpublished letters from Mrs Barbauld', *London Mercury* 26 (September 1932); Williamson, M. L., 'Who's afraid of Mrs Barbauld? The Blue Stockings and feminism', *International Journal of Women's Studies* 3 (January-February 1980).

Barker, A. L.
b. 13 April 1918, St Paul's Cray, Kent
Short story writer, novelist

ALB is the daughter of Harry and Elsie Barker and attended a county secondary school which she left at the age of 16. She found secretarial work in London offices and later became a junior sub-editor for the Amalgamated Press. In the Second World War she served for six months with the Land Army and then for over three years with the National Fire Service. After the war she did some freelance work and wrote for the BBC. She has adapted some of her stories for the screen.

There was a fifteen-year gap between ALB's first two novels, *Apology for a Hero* (1950) and *A Case Examined* (1965). The central character of *A Case Examined*, Rose, chairs a charity committee which has to choose whether to support the church hassock fund or to give to the needy. ALB contrasts Rose's petty concerns with the real ones of her impoverished friend, Solange, who is living in Paris having suffered under the Nazi regime. At first Rose dismisses her friend's difficulties, saying that they are self-inflicted; following a visit to Paris, however, she is obliged to change her mind. Rose's new knowledge brings the two women to a deeper understanding of each other.

A Heavy Feather (1978) begins with a father and young daughter drawn close together by the mother's absence. The child has no alternative but to accompany her father as he goes around on his not very successful work of odd-jobbing. ALB captures the child's worst moments – chilblains on the hands without gloves (someone eventually gives her some, too big but delightful to her) and portrays her joy at the simplest relief in an unrelentingly hard childhood. On one occasion her father's plumbing repair goes wrong: 'I lowered myself from the table. When my feet touched the water I knew that this did not come into any of the categories of refusal I was familiar with, i.e. that it couldn't be afforded, that it would make me sick, that it wasn't mine. This pretty tide pearling round the legs of the furniture, the blue-and-rose-mottled shawl of water not completely covering the kitchen floor, was in fact mine.' Characters are minutely observed and described in detail. She says of Miss Velva, the music teacher in *A Heavy Feather*, 'She wore her weird grubby clothes with an air, even a flair. Her features were fine and regular, the skin without a pucker or crease, smooth as ivory, and much the same yellow as her piano keys.' There is the violence of death, separation, and alienation in the abrupt ending of *A Heavy Feather*, contrasting the lives of two girls, one normal, free, and the other retarded and captive.

ALB's most highly regarded writings are her collections of short stories. These are unusual for the often complex links among the individual stories in each collection. Her first book, *Innocents: Variations on a Theme* (1947), which won the Somerset Maugham Award in the first year of its existence, is a collection of eight stories, each of which deals centrally with a single innocent confronting experience or evil for the first time. Although most of these figures are children (and ALB has been widely praised for her skill in adopting a child's viewpoint), two of them are adults who are victimized by children. *Femina Real* (1971) is another of ALB's collections in which the stories are united by a common theme: the central figures in all of these stories are women of varying ages and social positions. Critics have sometimes regarded ALB's view of women as an unsympathetic one, but the passion for revenge of her heroines is shown to be closely related to their subjugated status.

In other collections, ALB sometimes links her stories not simply at this general thematic level, but also at the level of plot. *The Joy-Ride and After* (1963) consists of three stories, 'The Joy-Ride', almost of novel length, 'The Narrow Boat', and 'A Likely Story'. In the title story, a garage worker who borrows his employer's car to take his cousin Esther for a drive is involved in an accident in which a woman is injured. The injured woman's consequent loss of memory is explored in the second story, whilst the third concerns Esther's dramatically exaggerated account of the joy-ride to the man whom she has now married.

Perhaps ALB's most startling use of an interrelated group of stories is in the sequence *Life Stories* (1981). The book begins with the declaration that 'I wanted to write something about myself and my writing': but the distinction between self and writing remains a difficult one to draw throughout the volume. It consists of a series of autobiographical accounts of particular episodes within ALB's life punctuated by a series of stories. The autobiographical episodes are further interrupted by substantial quotations from ALB's earlier stories relevant to those episodes. The autobiographical significance both of the complete and of the quoted stories is implied but rarely clarified. Moreover, the autobiographical episodes are scarcely less literary or more naturalistic in style than the stories themselves. The result is that the narrative detachment which in many of the other collections offers the reader a secure refuge here becomes somewhat disquieting: such detachment is now itself made the principal subject of the work, which consequently appears empty at what should be its centre. ALB's constellation of related but separate stories can examine the isolation and fragmentation of the self in a way which is more difficult in the integrated form of the novel.   ALISON RIMMER

Works: *Innocents* (1947); *Apology for a Hero* (1950); *Novelette and Other Stories* (1951); *The Joy-Ride and After* (1963); *A Case Examined* (1965); *John Brown's Body* (1969); *Penguin Modern Stories 8* (1971); *Femina Real* (1971); *A Source of Embarrassment* (1974); *A Heavy Feather* (1978); *Life Stories* (1981); *No Word of Love* (1985).

References: CA; DLB; Kunitz, J. and Colby, V. (eds), *Twentieth Century Authors, First Supplement: A Biographical Dictionary of Modern Literature* (1955).

Barker, Jane
b. 1652, Blatherwicke, Northamptonshire; d. c. 1727, France?
Poet, novelist
(Also wrote under 'Galesia', 'Fidelia')
JB was a royalist spinster, baptized into the Church of England in 1652 but later converted to Roman Catholicism. She was the daughter of a farming tenant of the Earl of Essex, Thomas Barker, and his wife Anne Connock. Early in her life the family moved to Wilsthorpe near Stamford. JB received considerable education in Latin, philosophy, and medicine from her elder brother who attended Oxford and Leyden universities. Later when her father

and her beloved brother died, she would take over the management of the house and farm.

In 1688 her *Poetical Recreations* appeared, prefaced by a series of complimentary verses by young men from the universities comparing her with Sidney, Jonson, Shakespeare, and Katherine Philips. Shortly after its publication she went into exile with James II, remaining in France for about a decade. While there she suffered from cataracts which she treated herself, being proud of her medical competence. She returned to England during the reign of Queen Anne and began writing prose fiction. She was suspected of Jacobitism and may have been in correspondence with the Jacobite leaders. She seems to have returned to France in 1727.

JB was a committed royalist, for whom Charles II had a mythical quality as the 'compleat Mirror of Christianitie' whose death 'put a Stop to the Wheel of all Joy and Happiness in England'. In her autobiographical fiction she describes how her male relatives died fighting for James II, first against the usurping Duke of Monmouth and then against William of Orange, while her mother died of grief 'for the Death of this her Royal Lord' (Charles II).

Having a small income from a royal grant made to her father, she had the option of spinsterhood, which she seems to have embraced with much self-consciousness, investigating both in her poetry and in her fiction the awkward role of the autonomous and intellectual woman in a society which did not much appreciate the type. In her poem 'A Virgin Life' she begs 'Suffer me not to fall into the Pow'rs of Men's almost Omnipotent Amours' and she hopes to be 'Fearless of Twenty five and all its train,/ Of slights or scorns, or being call'd Old Maid' which she sees as a threat that pushes many girls into inappropriate marriages. In place of matrimony she describes communities of women whose friendship is called 'a Gem, whose Lustre do's out-shine/ All that's below the heav'nly Crystaline':

> Friendship is that mysterious thing alone,
> Which can unite, and make two Hearts but one;
> It purifies our Love, and makes it flow
> I'th'clearest stream that's found in Love below.

JB's first prose work to be written was *Exilius*, which was not however published until 1715, a lengthy romance in the French heroic style. Next came *Love Intrigues: or the History of the Amours of Bosvil and Galesia* (1713), and the continuations: *A Patch-Work Screen for the Ladies* (1723) and *Lining of the Patch-Work Screen* (1726). The centre of interest in the prose works is the autobiographical heroine Galesia whose abortive romance with Bosvil is anatomized. Occasionally failure is blamed on the villainy and mysterious inconsistency of men and Galesia responds in heroic fashion, setting out to kill the faithless man in the name of her sex: 'The false Bosvil shou'd now disquiet me no more, nor any other of our Sex; in him I will end his Race, no more of them shall come to disturb, or affront Womankind; this only Son, shall dye by the hands of me an only Daughter.' Mostly, however, Galesia accepts that there is a reluctance to marry within herself, and the later works are much concerned with the role of the single woman, and especially of the single woman writer. Sometimes she complains of this lonely destiny, 'how useless, or rather pernicious, Books and Learning are to our Sex'; at other times she accepts literature as a fate that she cannot escape:

> All this, my Fayte, all this thou didst fore show,
> Ev'n when I was a Child,
> When in my Picture's Hand,
> My Mother did command,
> There should be drawn a Laurel Bough.
> Lo! then my Muse sat by, and smil'd. . . .

Later her mother is described as less approving of this undomestic role, although she does in the end accept it, saying, 'if there be a fatal Necessity that it must be so, e'en go on, and make thyself easy with thy fantastick Companions the Muses . . . as thou sayest in this Poem, thou hast try'd divers means to chase away this unlucky Genius that attends thee; and I am sensible, out of a true design'd Obedience to me; But since it will not do, I shall no more oppose thy Fancy, but comply and indulge so innocent a Diversion.'

A Patch-Work Screen and *Lining* are fragmentary biographies interspersed with recipes, poems, religious meditations, satirical sketches, and bits of news, the form expressing the fragmentary nature of the female life. Galesia helps some female friends make a patch-work screen of bits of her writing, so forming a work of art from her life. Tales and anecdotes are presented baldly without sentiment, often suggesting psychological patterns never investigated, as for example in the odd tale of a man, his wife, and his mistress. In this story a homely lady marries and her husband takes a mistress who moves in to form a *ménage à trois*. Soon the wife 'becomes a perfect Slave to her, and, as if she was the Servant, instead of the Mistress, did all the Household-Work, made the Bed, clean'd the House, wash'd the Dishes; nay, farther than so, got up in the Morning, scour'd the Irons, made the Fire, &c. leaving this vile Strumpet in Bed with her Husband; for they lay all Three together every Night.' The man tires of the mistress but the wife won't part with her and when Galesia's mother visits she finds 'the Servant sitting in a handsome Velvet Chair, dress'd up in very good lac'd Linnen, having clean Gloves on her Hands, and the Wife washing the Dishes'. When the husband ejects the mistress the wife goes too and is soon reduced to begging but she will not leave the other woman even though offered money by friends and even the Queen. 'Sure,' comments the listener to this tale, 'This poor Creature was under some spell or Inchantment, or she could never have persisted, in so strange a manner. . . .'   JANET TODD

Works: *Poetical Recreations* (1688); *Love Intrigues, or the History of the Amours of Bosvil and Galesia* (1713); *Exilius, or the Banish'd Roman* (1715); *The Christian Pilgrimage* (1718); *The Entertaining Novels of Mrs Jane Barker* (1719); *A Patch-Work Screen for the Ladies* (1723); *Lining of the Patch-Work Screen* (1726).

References: Backscheider, P., 'Woman's influence', *Studies in the Novel* 11 (1979); DLB; Greer, G. *et al., Kissing the Rod: An Anthology of Seventeenth-Century Women's Verse* (1988); Horner, J., *The English Women Novelists and Their Connection with the Feminist Movement 1688–1797* (1929–30); McBurney, W. H., 'Edmund Curll, Mrs Jane Barker, and the English novel', *PQ* 37 (1958); MacCarthy, B., *Women Writers: Their Contribution to the English Novel 1621–1744* (1944); Richetti, J. J., *Popular Fiction Before Richardson: Narrative Patterns 1700–1739* (1969); Spencer, J., *The Rise of the Woman Novelist* (1986); Spacks, P. M., *Imagining a Self* (1976); Todd; Todd, J., *Women's Friendship in Literature* (1980).

Barnard, Lady Anne

b. 8 December 1750, Balcarres, East Fife, Scotland; d. 6 May 1825, London
Poet, memoirist

AB was born, the eldest of eleven children, at Balcarres Castle overlooking the Firth of Forth, twenty miles from Edinburgh. Her father, James Lindsay, 5th Earl of Balcarres, was a retired soldier who had fought in the Stuart cause in the uprising of 1715, but who supported George II at Dettingen in 1743 and at Fontenoy in 1745. When he was 60, he married Anne Dalrymple, a young woman of 22, who at first rejected her ageing suitor, but relented when she learned that he had fallen seriously ill and that he had already settled half of his estate on her. Not surprisingly, in view of his advanced years, the old soldier left the rearing of the children to the young mother, who proved to be a stern disciplinarian. Her punishments of whippings and bitter potions caused him to remark on one occasion, 'Odsfish! Madam! I will not have it so; you will break the spirit of my young troop.' Yet AB felt the strongest affection for her mother, as she reveals in her Memoirs.

AB acquired her formal education from her tutor and from her governess, Lady Henrietta Cumming, and her remarkable devotion to honour, duty, and practical wisdom from her parents. Her nephew wrote of the relationship between AB and her aged father, 'she was for several years his constant companion, and imbibed much of his chivalrous character, which became the foundation of her own.' Her visits to her grandmother in Edinburgh allowed her to meet, among others, Hume, Mackenzie, Adam Smith, Monboddo, and Dr Johnson. When she joined her widowed sister Margaret in Berkeley Square, London, their house became a gathering place for the famous people of the day including Pitt, Burke, Walpole, and Sheridan. A contemporary describes AB as 'graceful, witty, and elegant, full of life and animation. . . . She had in society a power of placing herself in sympathy with those whom she addressed, of drawing forth their feelings, their talents, their acquirements.' She aroused the romantic feelings of two of her visitors, William Windham and Henry Dundas. Although she married neither, her friendship with Dundas influenced her life.

Finally, in 1793 at the age of 42, she married Andrew Barnard, an impecunious ex-military officer and son of the Bishop of Limerick. He was twelve years her junior. It was a happy marriage, despite the difference in age and a lack of money. To solve the financial problem, AB sought help from her friend Henry Dundas, now Lord Melville and Secretary of State for War and the Colonies. After two years she was successful, and in 1796 Andrew was appointed Colonial Secretary to Lord Macartney, first governor of the newly acquired Cape Colony in South Africa.

Lord Melville had reason to be pleased with the appointment, for Barnard was a gifted administrator, and AB a remarkable first lady of the colony, a role forced on her because the governor's wife remained in England. She soon endeared herself to the various factions among both the English and the Dutch. As she wrote in her journal, 'What I wished chiefly to effect was, if possible, to bring the nations together on terms of good will, and, by having public days pretty often at the Castle, to reconcile the Dutch to the sight of their masters by the attraction of fiddles and French horns.' In 1802, England returned the colony to the Dutch and, after five years of doing her duty with tact and wisdom, AB left Cape Town, never to return. However, her husband returned in 1807 after England had retaken the colony. He expected his wife to join him, but he died soon after his arrival. She sought comfort from her sister Margaret at the house in Berkeley Square, where she remained until her death in 1825.

After her husband's death AB led a full social life. She developed a friendship with Mrs Fitzherbert, mistress to the Prince Regent, with whom she travelled to Paris during the French Revolution. She also maintained a close friendship with the Prince himself, who called her 'Sister Anne' and who showed his affection with a gift and the words, 'I love you and beg you to accept this gold chain for my sake.' She continued to be a talented hostess. As her mother neared death, she visited 'the dear old nest' at Balcarres. Her own last years were spent in her 'drawing room forty feet long, surrounded with papers and drawings'. She writes during these last years, 'I have got into the habit of living on other days with those I loved, reflecting on the past. . . . I compile and arrange my memorandums of past observations and events; I retouch some sketches and form new ones from souvenirs taken on the spot.'

Although AB wrote throughout her adult years, her reputation as a writer came in the last two years of her life when the public learned that she was author of 'Auld Robin Gray', the most popular Scottish ballad of the nineteenth century. Today her reputation depends on her family chronicles, her journal, and her letters, a small canon with intrinsic literary merit and historical value, especially concerning South African colonial development. Tantalizing to scholars are eighteen volumes of manuscripts concerning her life in London, Edinburgh, and the continent which remain unpublished because she left strict orders forbidding publication, an injunction carefully observed by her descendants.

Her refusal to acknowledge authorship of 'the queen of all Scottish ballads', 'Auld Robin Gray', arose from shyness. Although she wrote the ballad when she was 21, she did not admit the fact until Sir Walter Scott named her the author in his novel *The Pirate* and ended fifty years of speculation. In a letter to Scott AB describes her substitution of her poem for the crude words that she heard sung to a lovely tune. In the poem, Jeanie, a village girl, falls in love with Jamie, who is reported lost at sea. Under parental pressure, Jeanie marries old Robin Gray, the local shepherd, a character from AB's childhood. Jamie returns, and Jeanie sends him away: 'I darena think o' Jamie, for that would be a sin,/ But I'll do my best a good wife to be,/ For, O, Robin Gray, he is kind to me.' Originally Scott published the poem with other songs by AB, and with songs by other members of the Lindsay family, in a volume entitled *Lays of the Lindsays* (1824). However, AB withdrew her permission, and Scott limited publication to 'Auld Robin Gray', two continuations, and AB's letter. She left Scott £50 in her will, perhaps to offset the losses he suffered on the venture.

AB's chronicles were printed in *Lives of the Lindsays* (1840) by her grandnephew, Alexander W. C. L. Crawford, Lord Lindsay. He quotes her extensively. She believed that recording her family's and her own life was her duty: 'It was a maxim of my father's that the person who neglects to leave some trace of his mind behind him, acording to his capacity, fails not only in his duty to society, but in gratitude to the author of his being, and may be said to have existed in vain.' She wrote sensitively of her family, including her mother, as in this description of her at 93: 'Her lamp burns cheerily; her Bible is read with delight, and a remark often made which proves that a clear flame sparkles in the socket still. So happy is she with the excellent Robert and his wife, that she believes the patriarchal house of Balcarres is her own, and Robert and his wife are her guests.' Of her own old age she wrote, 'OCCUPATION is the best nostrum in the great laboratory of human life, for pains, cares, mortifications, and ennui; it amuses in sickness, it lightens the distress of circumstance, it acts as a general opiate to ill-requited love, it is solace to the heart.'

AB described her South African experiences in a journal intended for her sisters and in many letters. Some of this material is published in three collections, 'Extracts from the Journals of a Residence at the Cape of Good Hope', (1840), *South Africa a Century Ago: Letters Written From the Cape of Good Hope* (1901), which includes letters to Lord Melville, and *Lady Anne Barnard at the Cape of Good Hope* (1924) which contains letters to the Earl of Macartney, plus sketches by AB. The selections provide a vivid acount of life in Cape Town during the five years of England's first administration of the colony. Her efforts to know the people moved her to travel to the farm areas and into the interior. So successful were these efforts at uniting Dutch and English that a century later, during the Boer War, a commentator asserted that war would have been avoided had her policy been England's policy; 'She would deserve the epithet queenly, could queens be found who equalled her.'   PHILIP BORDINAT

Works: Poem in *Lays of the Lindsays* (1824); *Auld Robin Gray: A Ballad* (1825); *Auld Robin Gray:* Continuation; Second Continuation (1840?); 'Anne Countess of Balcarres' and 'Lady Anne Barnard [Portions of her Memoirs]', in Crawford, A. W. C. L., Lord Lindsay, *Lives of the Lindsays*, vol. 2 (1840); 'Extracts from the journal of a residence at the Cape of Good Hope, and of a short tour into the interior', in Crawford, A. W. C. L., Lord Lindsay, *Lives of the Lindsays*, vol. 3 (1840); *South Africa a Century Ago: Letters Written From the Cape of Good Hope, 1797–1801*, ed. W. H. Wilkins (1901); *The Cape of Good Hope 1797–1802*, ed. D. Fairbridge (1924); *Letters, 1778–1824*, ed. A. Powell (1928); *The Letters of Lady Anne Barnard to Henry Dundas, together with Her Tour into the Interior, and Certain other Letters* (1973).

References: Anderson, W., *The Scottish Nation . . . and Biographical History of the People of Scotland* (1863); *BA* (18); *DNB*; Dorlund, W. A. N., *The Sum of Feminine Achievement* (1917); Fairbridge, D., *Lady Anne Barnard at the Cape of Good Hope* (1924); Fullove, A. A., 'Lady Anne Barnard: her poetry', *Quarterly Bulletin of South African Libraries* 30 (1976); Graham, H., 'Lady Anne Barnard', in *A Group of Scottish Women* (1908); Graham, W. H., 'Lady Anne Barnard', *Contemporary Review* (August 1950); Kannenmeyer, M. J. and Lewin Robinson, A. M., 'The Lady Anne Barnard letters in the South African Public Library, Cape Town', *Quarterly Bulletin of the South African Libraries* (September 1949); Masson, M., *Lady Anne Barnard: The Court and Colonial Service under George III and the Regency* (1948); Mills, G., *First Ladies of the Cape* (1948); Murray, J. C., *The Ballads and Songs of Scotland* (1874); Taylor, M. S., *Auld Robin Gray: An Emotional Drama in Five Acts* (1881); Todd; Tyler, S. and Watson, J. L., *Songstresses of Scotland*, vol. 2 (1871).

Bawden, Nina

b. 19 January 1925, London

Novelist, writer for children

Daughter of C. and E. U. M. Mabey, NB was educated at Ilford High School and in Wales as an evacuee before winning a scholarship to Somerville College, Oxford. Her first marriage, in 1946, was to Henry Walton Bawden, by whom she had two sons. In 1954 she married Austin Steven Kark, the future head of the BBC World Service. From 1946 to 1947 she worked as an Assistant at the Town and Country Planning Association. In 1968 she served as a JP in Surrey. She has contributed fiction reviews to *The Daily Telegraph*.

NB's novels for adults are accurate and sensitive studies of shifts of feeling and desire in close relationships. A *Woman of My Age* examines the resentments and conflicts of an eighteen-year marriage by focusing on tensions during a holiday in North Africa. *Familiar Passions* and *The Ice-House* also look at marriage through the eyes of women who have to face their husbands' infidelity after years of trust, and succeed in showing how such traumas affect a woman's sense of her individuality. The male protagonist of *George Beneath a Paper Moon* works as a travel operator and this enables NB to use a variety of foreign locations and to reveal a sense of the injustice of dictatorial regimes. Her many other works include *Afternoon of A Good Woman* which was the *Yorkshire Post* Novel of the Year in 1976. Some of her novels for children such as *Rebel on a Rock* (set in the Greece of the military junta) and *Runaway Summer* create exciting plots around children's perception of and accidental involvement in adult intrigue, political and criminal. Her best-known works concentrate on domestic conflict; *The Peppermint Pig* (winner of the Guardian Children's Fiction Award in 1975) and *Carrie's War* (commended for the Carnegie Medal) explore children's awareness of adult vulnerability and their growing familiarity with the moral and emotional confusion of their society. The latter also draws on NB's own experience of wartime evacuation. Faithful to the feelings of her audience, NB skilfully portrays frustration, loneliness, and boredom and the mingled fear and excitement with which children face the prospect of growing up. *Kept in the Dark* combines the suspense of suspected evil-doing with a perceptive study of relationships; it shows the reactions of a family of three children to a young man's manic instability.   MARINA TZAMOURANIS

Selected works: *Who Calls the Tune* (1953); *The Odd Flamingo* (1954); *Change Here for Babylon* (1955); *The Solitary Child* (1956); *Devil by the Sea* (1958) (abridged for children, 1976); *In Honour Bound* (1961); *Tortoise by Candlelight* (1963); *The Secret Passage* (1963); *A Little Love, A Little Learning* (1965); *The Witch's Daughter* (1966); *A Woman of My Age* (1967); *The Grain of Truth* (1969); *The Runaway Summer* (1969); *Carrie's War* (1973); *George Beneath a Paper Moon* (1974); *The Peppermint Pig* (1975); *Afternoon of a Good Woman* (1976); *Rebel on the Rock* (1978); *Familiar Passions* (1979); *Kept in the Dark* (1982); *The Ice-House* (1983); *Princess Alice* (1985); *Circle of Deceit* (1987).

References: Gordon, C., 'The end of innocence', *Times Literary Supplement* (1 October 1976); Kemp, P., 'Maud and Mrs Mudd', *Listener* (1 March 1979); Kemp, P., 'Hard to bare', *Times Literary Supplement* (17 April 1981); *OCCL*; Wade, R. 'Quarterly fiction review', *Contemporary Review* (October 1983).

Bedford, Sybille

b. 16 March 1911, Charlottenburg, Germany

Historical novelist, biographer, travel writer

SB was privately educated in Italy, England, and France. She married in 1935 and has lived in France, England, the United States, and Italy. Her writings include literary journalism, travel books, fiction and biography. She also worked as a law reporter, covering the Auschwitz trial at Frankfurt, the trial of Jack Ruby at Dallas, and the *Lady Chatterley* and Stephen Ward trials at the Old Bailey, London. Further writings on law include *The Faces of Justice* (1961), a comparison of legal procedures in European countries. Her first novel, *A Legacy*, was published in 1956; her most important recent publication is a two-volume biography of Aldous Huxley (1973–4). She was vice-president of PEN in 1979, became a Fellow of the Royal Society of Literature in 1964, and was awarded the OBE in 1981.

Her three published novels are historical fictions, set against the backgrounds of the Kaiser's Germany and the First and Second World Wars respectively. Generational and family history are interwoven with political events and intrigues, and her aristocratic characters play an active role in European power struggles. In *A Legacy*, SB's strongest novel, she portrays marriages between two wealthy German families in the context of the fraught unification of Germany, moving to a close with the country's *fin-de-siècle* corruption. *A Favourite of the Gods* (1963) and its sequel, *A Compass Error* (1968), tell the stories of three generations of women: the imperious Anna, an American heiress who marries an Italian prince, her beautiful and ebullient daughter Constanza, and her grand-daughter Flavia, heroine of *A Compass Error* and occasionally glimpsed as narrator of both works. *A Favourite of the Gods* is set in a Jamesian world of smart London residences and Italian villas, and spans some thirty years from the late nineteenth century to the 1920s, its subjects being affairs, betrayals, sexual jealousy, and sexual knowledge. Although SB is concerned to emphasize the fact of her characters' anti-fascist activities, the nature of these is not substantially explored. It is probably fair to say that she is most interested in politics when it offers scope for representing, or hinting at, intrigues and enigmas. In *A Compass Error* the political background of war and anti-fascism is subordinated to the story of the heroine's sentimental education as a 17-year-old in the South of France, and the plot turns to melodrama.

Critical opinion tends to divide over the question of the relevance and interest of SB's aristocratic and upper-class settings. The allusiveness and opacity of her prose has been highly praised, although her detractors might claim that the appearance of depth and substance beneath the surface is illusory. To date, she has not been significantly discussed within the context of feminism and women's writing, although there may be scope for such discussion in her use of female narration and her portrayal of relationships between women.

LAURA MARCUS

Works: *The Sudden View: A Mexican Journey* (1953); *A Legacy* (1956); *The Best We Can Do: An Account of the Trial of John Bodkin Adams* (1958); *The Trial of Dr Adams* (1959); *A Visit to Don Otavio: A Traveller's Tale from Mexico* (1960); *The Faces of Justice: A Traveller's Report* (1961); *A Favourite of the Gods* (1963); *A Compass Error* (1968); *Aldous Huxley: A Biography* (1973–4).

References: Furbank, P. N., *Encounter* (April 1964); Levin, B., article in *Daily Mail* (12 September 1966); Pritchett, V. S., *New Statesman* (11 January 1963); Vansittart, P., 'Introduction' to *A Favourite of The Gods* and *A Compass Error* (1984); Waugh, E., *Spectator* (13 April 1956).

Beer, Patricia
b. 4 November 1924, Exmouth, Devon
Poet

PB's poetry evokes the scenes of past experience. Much of her life has been spent in the West Country, and childhood memories blend with the Devon landscape in the poems that they inspire. Her father, Andrew Beer, was a railway clerk. The family received free rail passes, and the 'thousands' of train rides taken in her youth provided PB with an enduring subject for her poetry. Her mother Harriet (nicknamed 'Queen') was a teacher before she married, and strongly encouraged both her daughters to become teachers as well. She died while PB was still a child, and Andrew Beer later remarried. Educated at

Exmouth Grammar School and Exeter University, PB went on to complete a B.Litt. degree at St Hugh's College, Oxford. In 1946 she went to Italy, where she spent seven years lecturing in English at various institutions. Back in England, she lectured at Goldsmiths College, London (1962–8) before making poetry her full-time occupation. She is married to Damien Parsons.

Her first collection of poems, *Loss of the Magyar*, takes its title from an incident in her family history, the sinking of a ship (the *Magyar*) owned by her great-grandfather, Andrew Beer. This was followed by a second collection, *Survivors*, in 1963. Later verse draws more directly on her Devon childhood. An autobiography, *Mrs Beer's House*, continued in prose form the process of recounting begun in the 1967 collection of verse, *Just like the Resurrection*. Her next collection, *The Estuary*, is as concerned with the activity of remembrance as with the past itself. In the title poem the adult poet reinterprets her own experience as she studies the landscape of her home. The walls of a familiar estuary suddenly appear as 'two/Distinct pieces of countryside'. Suspended between memory and perception, the image marks a moment of discovery. The poem's simplicity of style and layered imagery are typical of her developing style. Particular objects have a rich imaginative value; a bronze statue and a kitchen calendar become points of departure. Trains are used to travel in memory. A train on its final run in 'The Branch Line' (*The Estuary*) is described as the 'Bright dragon of childhood', while in 'Southern Railway' (*Lie of the Land*), the poet takes a backward ride to a moment when, as children, 'we half-hopped, half-stood/Looking towards London'.

In *Lie of the Land*, PB evokes the Devon landscape with vivid, often funny images. 'Watercolour' describes trees as 'parsley magnified', while in 'Icicles' pieces of ice are variously described as elephants' trunks and crossed legs. Time and the passage of time remain dominant concerns; in 'A Street in Padua' she returns to a scene from her Italian adulthood, but the sunny square is shadowed by her memories. Her history of a country cottage begins in the reign of Elizabeth I and winds down to the ticking of 'the clock on the night storage heating'. *Moon's Ottery*, her one novel, is set backward in history, in Elizabethan Devon. In all her work death is a familiar presence, referred to with intimacy and humour. This may have particular roots in her family history; PB's paternal grandfather made coffins, and her maternal grandfather carved tombstones. In 'The Conjuror', the death of a magician is unblinkingly described: 'the quick deceiving hand was changing/to flyaway dust under a ton of soil'. The magician's trick, like the poet's, becomes the prelude to a larger disappearing act.

In PB's poetry, even the inanimate is given quirky life. Short, straightforward, and highly descriptive, her poems invest the ordinary world with a quality of surprise.   AMY GAMERMAN

Selected works: *Loss of the Magyar* (1959); *The Survivors* (1963); *Just like the Resurrection* (1967); *Mrs Beer's House* (1968); *The Estuary* (1971); *Reader: I Married Him* (1974); *Driving West* (1975); *Moon's Ottery* (1978); *Selected Poems* (1979); *Lie of the Land* (1983); *Patricia Beer's Devon* (1984).

References: CP; Drabble.

Beeton, Isabella

b. 1836, London; d. 1865, Greenhythe

Editor, journalist, cookery writer

IB was the daughter of Elizabeth Jerram and Benjamin Mayson, a linen draper who died leaving IB, aged 4, and three younger siblings. In 1843 her mother married Henry Dorling, a printer and clerk of the Epsom race course; he was a widower with four small children and together they had thirteen more.

For most of the year, except when the Derby was held, the children lived apart from their parents in a 'nursery' in the Grand-Stand which overlooked the Epsom Downs race course; IB and her sister Bessie, along with their maternal grandmother, looked after the younger children. Their parents lived in the Epsom High Street nearby and paid them frequent visits. When the race meetings were held, the 'living cargo of children', as IB put it, were distributed among relatives and friends in Epsom or, in summer, frequently sent to Brighton. IB was educated briefly at an Islington school and later in Heidelberg at a school run by two sisters.

In 1856 she married a young publisher, Samuel Orchart Beeton. His health was frail, and IB was determined to excel at home management. During the lengthy preparation for the wedding, she is reported by her sister to have exclaimed, 'Why has no one written a book – a good book for brides? To help them learn these things?' The gap was to be filled by one of the most successful cookery books ever published, Mrs Beeton's *Book of Household Management*.

This was begun in 1857, after the death of the Beetons' first child, Samuel Orchart, at the age of three months. The volume is an all-purpose reference manual for the mistress of a household of some substance and contains, as promised on the title page, 'a history of the origin, properties, and uses of all things connected with home life and comfort'. There are instructions for paying calls, handling servants, feeding invalids, and making wills. The book covers kitchen equipment, culinary history, and a seasonal guide for foods (an innovation in cookery books). Her encyclopedic knowledge and engaging style were widely appreciated, and the book became a staple of the nineteenth-century home. A character in *A Duet with an Occasional Chorus* by Conan Doyle remarked that it contained 'more wisdom to the square inch than any work of man'.

Doyle may have been charmed, as many readers had been, by her descriptions of the various types of edible animals. In her description of pigs, for instance, she warns of the young pig 'who is the dwarf of the family circle, a poor, little, shrivelled, half-starved anatomy, with a small melancholy voice, a staggering gait, a woe-begone countenance, and a thread of a tail, whose existence the complacent mother ignores'. The Chinese sow, when properly fattened, 'looks like an elongated carcase, a mass of fat, withut shape or form, like a feather pillow'. This pig, however, when 'judiciously fed', has an 'extremely delicate and delicious' flesh.

The book is replete with recipes for special occasions: a common cake suitable for sending to children at school, a christening cake, a bill of fare for a ball supper, picnic, or summer wedding, along with dozens of menus for plain family dinners. The duties of the butler, footman, coachman, valet, lady's maid, upper and under housemaid, dairy-maid, and sick-nurse are described in detail. There are instructions for removing paint spots from silk cloth, packing trunks for lengthy visits, dressing and nursing children, and insuring access to drains when purchasing land.

The book contains a brief history of dining, from ancient Greece to contemporary London. Many of the recipes themselves, however, are simple and economical, reflecting her conviction that 'frugality and economy are home virtues, without which no household can prosper'. Her ultimate aim was, as she put it, to avert 'family discontent' and lessen the temptation of men to dine at their clubs and taverns by enabling the mistress of a house to be 'thoroughly acquainted with the theory and practice of cookery, as well as be perfectly conversant with all the other arts of making and keeping a comfortable home'.

The *Book of Household Management* began to appear in monthly parts in September 1859; it was published in book form in October. Over 60,000 copies were sold the first year. The recipes and those portions of the book related to the kitchen were published separately in 1863 as *The Englishwoman's Cookery Book*. The book went through many editions and was a standard wedding gift for many decades, finding a wide and appreciative audience.

In addition to *Household Management*, IB had other journalistic and editorial pursuits. Samuel Beeton had founded *The Englishwoman's Domestic Magazine* in 1852, and it was here that she published her first article in April 1857. She became the magazine's fashion correspondent and editor in 1860. She also edited women's features for *The Queen*, launched by the Beetons in 1861, and assisted with *The Young Englishwoman*.

The Beetons lost a second child, also named Samuel Orchart, at the age of 3 at the end of 1862. A third son, Orchart, was born in 1863 and a fourth, Mayson, in 1865, both of whom survived to adulthood. Unfortunately, IB contracted puerperal fever after the birth of Mayson, and died at the age of 28.

SARAH BIRD WRIGHT

Works: Book of Household Management (1861); The Englishwoman's Cookery Book (1863); Mrs Beeton's Dictionary of Every-day Cookery (1865).

References: Freeman, S., Isabella and Sam: The Story of Mrs Beeton (1977); Hyde, H. M., Mr and Mrs Beeton (1951); Spain, N., The Beeton Story (1956).

Behn, Aphra

b. 1640, Harbledown, Kent (?); d. 16 April 1689, London

Playwright, poet

AB's origins are uncertain, but recent evidence suggests that she was the Aphra Johnson christened in 1640 in Harbledown, Kent, although the yeoman status of her supposed father, Bartholomew Johnson, does not accord with her education, which is that of a gentlewoman. According to her novel *Oronooko*, she travelled to Surinam in 1663–4 when she was a young woman. Upon her return to London she probably married a merchant named Behn, of Dutch extraction, who perhaps died of the plague in 1665; however, she never once refers to such a person. The earliest indisputable external evidence about her life is a series of letters documenting her employment in 1666 as a secret agent for the English government, when she was sent to Antwerp to obtain information about exiled Cromwellians and to relay Dutch military plans. She used 'Astrea' as her code name and later as her literary name. In the Netherlands she ran into debt, and in 1667, when she returned home, was briefly committed to a debtors' prison. She was noted among a wide circle of friends and fellow writers for her wit and generosity; Sir Peter Lely and Mary Beale painted portraits of her. Her strong Tory sentiments and personal loyalty to the royal family led to a political outspokenness that earned her enemies among some powerful Whigs. She satirized the Earl of Shaftesbury, the Whig leader, in *The City Heiress* (1682) but offended the King in the same year when she attacked his illegitimate son Duke of Monmouth in an epilogue, for which she was arrested. During her life she was forced to fend off not only political and personal attacks but also attacks on her as a woman who wrote with the same freedoms as a man. In her last years she suffered from poverty and severe illness, and her political hopes were crushed by the Revolution of 1688.

AB first achieved literary celebrity as a playwright, entering the theatre in 1670 and producing seventeen extant plays; two more plays have been lost – *Like Father, Like Son* (1682) and *The Wavering Nymph* (1684). Four anonymous plays have been attributed to her – *The Woman Turned Bully* (1675), *The Debauchee* (1677), *The Counterfeit Bridegroom* (1677), and *The Revenge* (1680); these, however, may have been written by Thomas Betterton. AB's dramatic speciality was the 'Spanish' comedy of intrigue written in brisk, colloquial prose. Typically she combines material from several sources into a complex, fast moving plot. A number of couples – eluding the unwanted marriages arranged for them – meet, bed, and/or wed after innumerable intrigues, mistaken identities, duels, disguises, and practical jokes. Her plays abound in bedroom farce and scenes of comic lowlife with delightful portrayals of landladies, bawds, buffoons, and prostitutes. She provides spectacle in masquing, costuming, and dance and uses stage machinery and other technical resources to create special effects.

The best of AB's intrigue comedies is *The Rover, or, The Banished Cavaliers* (1677), set at carnival time in Naples, where impoverished English cavaliers-in-exile become entangled with Spanish ladies and win their persons and fortunes. AB's rover, Willmore, is her distinctive version of a favourite Restoration character, the wild gallant. *The Rover* stayed in the repertory until the middle of the eighteenth century, the role of the witty heroine being taken by such famous actresses as Elizabeth Barry, Anne Bracegirdle, Anne Oldfield, and Peg Woffington. Also among AB's best plays is *Sir Patient Fancy* (1678), an amusing tangle of the amours of two neighbouring London families. Her *Emperor of the Moon* was an instant success in 1687. A gay and extravagant combination of *commedia dell'arte*, operatic spectacle, sumptuous costuming, dance, song, satire, intrigue, and some manners comedy, the play was performed for nearly a hundred years.

A number of her plays deal centrally with her most distinctive theme, forced marriage. She entitled her first play *The Forced Marriage* (1670) and went on to write *The Town Fop* (1676) and *The Lucky Chance* (1686), respectively a sentimental and a harsher treatment of the same subject. While New Comedy in general depicts the witty stratagems of young lovers who outwit their elders in order to marry according to their own choice, AB goes beyond this to attack the arranged marriage as an institution. In doing so, she uses in distinctive ways two stock characters, the courtesan and the amazon. In *The Rover*, Parts 1 and 2 (1677, 1681) and *The Feigned Courtesans* (1679) AB uses the courtesan to suggest that marriage for money is a form of prostitution. In *The Young King* (1679) and *The Widow Ranter* (1689) the woman warrior in both romantic and comic versions provides a visual metaphor for the battle of the sexes and suggests the compatibility of lovers who are equals in wit and war.

AB was a versatile and sometimes distinguished poet. She wrote topical and witty prologues and epilogues for the theatre. Her elegies and panegyrics in baroque pindarics for members of the royal family and the nobility were usually published in folio or quarto to celebrate a state occasion. Her elegies for the Earl of Rochester and the Duke of Buckingham display her personal affection and admiration for these two fellow wits. AB had a fine lyric gift; her elegant and sophisticated songs appeared both in her plays and in contemporary collections. Her best known song, 'Love in Fantastic Triumph Sat', appeared in her one tragedy, *Abdelazer* (1676), and has often been reprinted.

AB made a number of miscellaneous translations from Latin and French in the latter part of her career, apparently for financial reasons. She had no Latin and worked from an English prose paraphrase; her French, however, was fluent, and she produced able, sometimes improved, versions of Tallement, La Rochefoucauld, Bonnecorse, Aesop, and de Fontenelle.

In the last years of her life she also wrote fiction, producing more than a dozen novels, some of which were published posthumously. Her novels achieved great popularity: two were dramatized, and collections of them appeared throughout the eighteenth century. In her fictions AB pioneered the transition from romance to novel by providing extensive circumstantial detail. Her two best tales *The Fair Jilt* and *Oronooko*, are based on events she herself witnessed. Oronooko, the story of an African prince enslaved in Surinam, displays great originality in theme and structure and is perhaps her best-known work.

Another of her novels, *Love Letters Between a Nobleman and His Sister*, is significant as a full-length pre-Richardsonian epistolary novel of unusual technical competence and dramatic interest. AB varies the style, length, and time sequence of letters to display nuances of emotion and thought in the characters. The novel has an additional historical interest as a *roman à clef* based on the scandalous 1682 elopement of Lord Grey of Werk with his wife's sister, Lady Henrietta Berkeley. The next year Grey was involved in the Rye House Plot to murder King Charles. The novel was a best-seller, reprinted numerous times until 1759.

AB wrote ably in a number of genres. She is significant not only as an artist but also as the first professional woman writer and the first woman whose writing won her burial in Westminster Abbey, On her tombstone are these verses: 'Here lies a proof that wit can never be/Defence enough against mortality.'   NANCY COTTON

Selected works: *The Forced Marriage* (1670); *The Amorous Prince* (1671); *The Dutch Lover* (1673); *Abdelazer* (1676); *The Town Fop* (1676); *The Rover* (1677); *Sir Patient Fancy* (1678); *The Feigned Courtesans* (1679); *The Young King* (1679); *The Second Part of The Rover* (1681); *The False Count* (1681); *The Roundheads* (1681); *Like Father, Like Son* (1682); *The City Heiress* (1682); *Poems upon Several Occasions* (1684); *Love Letters Between a Nobleman and His Sister* (1684); *The Wavering Nymph* (1684); *A Pindaric on the Death of Our Late Sovereign* (1685); *A Poem to Catherine Queen Dowager* (1685); *A Pindaric Poem on the Happy Coronation* (1685); *The Lucky Chance* (1686); *The Emperor of the Moon* (1687); *To Christopher, Duke of Albermarle* (1687); *To the Memory of George, Duke of Buckingham* (1687); *The Amours of Philander and Sylvia* (1687); *A Congratulatory Poem to Her Most Sacred Majesty* (1688); *The Fair Jilt* (1688); *A Congratulatory Poem on the Happy Birth of the Prince of Wales* (1688); *Oronooko* (1688); *Agnes de Castro* (1688); *A Poem to Sir Roger L'Estrange* (1688); *To Poet Bavius* (1688); *A Congratulatory Poem to Queen Mary* (1689); *The History of the Nun* (1689); *The Lucky Mistake* (1689); *A Pindaric Poem to the Reverend Dr Burnet* (1689); *The Widow Ranter* (1689); *The Younger Brother* (1696); *The Adventure of the Black Lady* (1698); *The Court of the King of Bantam* (1698); *The Nun* (1698); *The Unfortunate Happy Lady* (1698); *The Wandering Beauty* (1698); *The Dumb Virgin* (1700); *The Unhappy Mistake* (1700); *Works*, 6 vols. ed. Montague Summers (1915).

References: Cameron, W. J., *New Light on Aphra Behn* (1961); Cotton, N., *Women Playwrights in England c. 1363–1750* (1980); Duffy, M., *The Passionate Shepherdess* (1977); Goreau, A., *Reconstructing Aphra* (1980); Guffey, G., *Two English Novelists* (1975); Link, F., *Aphra Behn* (1968); Loftis, J., *The Spanish Plays of Neoclassical England* (1973); Sackville-West, V., *Aphra Behn* (1928); Todd; Todd, J., *The Sign of Angellica* (1989); Woodcock, G., *The Incomparable Aphra* (1948).

Bell, Gertrude

b. 14 July 1868, Washington, County Durham; d. 12 July 1926, Baghdad

Archaeologist, poet

Born into an affluent gentry family with a fortune in iron, GB was the daughter of Hugh and Maria (*née* Shield) Bell. Her mother died in 1871 after the birth of her brother, and her father, a Liberal MP, married Florence Olliffe in 1876. GB had a good relationship with her stepmother, who encouraged her in her interest in history and travel, and she remained close to her father throughout her adult life, even asking his approval before she made her daring trips. After a period at school in London, she went to Lady Margaret Hall, Oxford, where she obtained a first-class degree in history in 1888; she then began a series of travels in eastern Europe and the Middle East using the highly placed contacts of her relatives and friends. In 1892 she met the diplomat Henry Cadogan in Iran and became engaged to him despite her family's disapproval of his financial status; he died of pneumonia before the marriage could take place. In 1893 she travelled with her father in Europe and Algeria and in 1897 took the first of her round-the-world trips, then fashionable for the rich.

Her travelling was without overriding purpose until 1899 when she went to Jerusalem and became fired with enthusiasm for both archaeology and the desert. Although she was in Europe between 1901 and 1904, gaining fame from her climbing in the Alps, she spent most of the rest of her life committed to the exploration and study of the desert regions of the Middle East. She travelled extensively, and in some style, with a few servants, fine linen, cutlery, and platters. Her interest was mainly in ruins, especially the palace of Ukhaidir, 120 miles south-west of Baghdad, and the forts and monasteries near the Euphrates.

In 1894 she had published a book of travel sketches called *Safar Nameh: Persian Pictures*, followed in 1897 by translations from Persian poetry, *Poems from the Divan of Hafiz*. More enthusiastically received than these early works was her lively account of Syria, *The Desert and the Sown* (1907). Her other publications of the period were more restrained and less popular, concerned to give details of places and their ruins, such as the record of her trip in 1901, *Amurath to Amurath*, and her accounts of excavations in Ukhaidir.

Although she mentions friendships with women, GB's most famous attachment was to the married Lieutenant-Colonel Charles Doughty-Wylie, whom she met before the First World War. Her letters to him have not survived, but it is clear that she was much involved. When he left England, she set off for Damascus but was delayed in Hail because of the increasingly difficult political stituation. With her attachment to Doughty-Wylie in her mind, she wrote, 'I have known loneliness in solitude now, for the first time, and in the long days of camel riding and the long evenings of winter camping, my thoughts have gone wandering far from the camp fire into places which I wish were not so full of acute sensation.' Back in war-torn Europe, she worked for the Red Cross in France, but was soon shattered to learn of Doughty-Wylie's heroic death at Gallipoli.

Famous for her knowledge of the middle east, GB was asked by the British war government to join the Arab intelligence bureau in Cairo and to obtain information about northern Arabia with the aim of fomenting rebellion by the Arabs against the Turks. She worked in Baghdad and in Basra and liaised between the British and the desert tribes. With the flamboyant T. E. Lawrence, she supported the Arab wish for independence against some of the imperialist aims of Britain and by 1920 she was advising both the British and the new ruler in Iraq, the Hashemite Emir Feisal. Her influential account of the British role in the Persian Gulf and Arabia in the period from 1914 to 1920, *Review of the Civil Administration in Mesopotamia*, provides a good warning to all declining colonial powers: 'I had no idea before coming to Baghdad of the extent to which Turkey is a country of red tape and blind and dumb officialdom, or of the degree in which the Turkish position in Iraq is unsupported by physical force. One cannot but admire, however, the dogged and uncomplaining resolution with which the Turkish civil bureaucracy and skeleton army persist in their impossible tasks.' Between 1923 and 1926 GB was Director of Antiquities in Baghdad where she founded the museum. She died suddenly from an overdose of drugs, probably accidental, and was buried in the British cemetery.

GB showed many contradictions. She combined the intrepidity and conventionality so marked in Victorian women of achievement. She travelled further into Arabia alone than any other European woman and yet thought it improper to go out unchaperoned in London. She shocked some by smoking and yet her hands were always busy with needlework. She was impatient with what she saw as the ineptness of most women and was not a feminist, disliking any assertion of equality; yet, when her views clashed with theirs, she felt it appropriate to quarrel with her male superiors, who disliked what they regarded as her 'status snobbery'. She was deeply patriotic and often imperialist in her outlook, but she saw the absurdity of the territorial claims of Europe in Arabia where the people had little sense of nationhood.   JANET TODD

Works: *Safar Nameh Persian Pictures* (anon.) (1894); *Poems from the Divan of Hafiz* (1897); *The Desert and the Sown* (1907); 'The vaulting system at Ukhaidir', *Journal of Hellenic Studies* 30 (1910); *Amurath to Amurath* (1911); *Palace and Mosque at Ukhaidir* (1914); *The Arabs of Mesopotamia* (anon.) (1918); *Review of the Civil Administration in Mesopotamia* (1920); *The Arab War* (dispatches from the *Arab Bulletin*) (1940); *Letters of Gertrude Bell* (1927).

References: Burgoyne, E., *Gertrude Bell: From Her Personal Papers* (1958, 1961); Cowlin, D., *A Woman in the Desert* (1967); Curtis, M. (ed.), *People and Politics in the Middle East* (1971); Davidson, Sir J. H., *Political Strategy, Mesopotamia* (1922); Glubb, Sir J., *Britain and the Arabs* (1959); Hill, S., articles in *Antiquity* (1976), and *Observer* (9 May 1976); Kamm, J., *Gertrude Bell, Daughter of the Desert* (1956); Ridley, M.R., *Gertrude Bell* (1941); Van Ess, D., *Pioneers in the Arab World* (1974); Winstone, H. V. F., *Gertrude Bell* (1978).

Belloc-Lowndes, Marie

b. 5 August 1868, London; d. 14 November 1947, Eversley Cross, Hampshire
Novelist, memoirist
(Also wrote under Marie Belloc, Philip Curtin, Elizabeth Rayner)
MB-L was the only daughter of Louis Belloc and the Victorian feminist Elizabeth (Bessie) Rayner Parkes, and sister of the writer Hilaire Belloc. Her early childhood, much of it spent at La Celle St Cloud, near Paris, was idyllically happy and inspired her with a lifelong devotion to France. Her formal education was sketchy, but she quickly became a voracious reader and a keen observer of the world around her. In the 1890s she took up journalism, working for the *Pall Mall Gazette* and other magazines, with assignments in England and France. Liberated and unchaperoned, she travelled and interviewed extensively.

In January 1896 she married Frederick Lowndes, a *Times* journalist; they settled in Westminster and had three children. Since Lowndes's work took him out of the house from 3 p.m. to 3 a.m. MB-L felt free to pursue her two favourite occupations: writing and socializing. Her quill pen was busy at 5 a.m. and later in the day the luncheon, cocktail, and dinner parties took over.

This routine, during the course of nearly half a century, resulted in over forty-five novels, and an acquaintance with most of the celebrities of the time. MB-L's charm and vivacity won her many distinguished friends: she lunched frequently with Henry James, attended the Sunday 'At Homes' of Oscar and Constance Wilde, captivated the ageing George Meredith, and encouraged the young Graham Greene to write. She also enjoyed the political scene, and was a welcome guest at 10 Downing Street, especially when Herbert Asquith was Prime Minister. Age could not wither her *joie de vivre* and she survived the Second World War and her husband's death (1940) with undiminished vitality and literary activity.

Addicted to gossip, she found the topics of love and crime particularly enthralling, and her fiction reflects these interests. Her romances, although tending towards the novelettish (with an abundance of sweet trembling lips yielding to ardent masterful love), reveal a sharp eye for detail and an impressive knowledge of the human heart. Her crime stories display narrative skill and a considerable talent for mystery and suspense, shown to their best advantage in *The Lodger* (1913), based on the Jack the Ripper murders and later made into a play, an opera, and several films. Good runners-up are *The Chink in the Armour* (1912), greatly admired by Ernest Hemingway ('the people credible and the action and the terror never false'), *The Story of Ivy* (1927), and *The Chianti Flask* (1934).

Her biographies (chiefly of royalty) are chatty and informative, but it is her memoirs, full of anecdotal reminiscences and fascinating sidelights on life and literature through two World Wars, that have proved almost as popular and enduring as her most famous thriller.   MARGARET MAISON

Selected works: HRH *The Prince of Wales* (1898); *Barbara Rebell* (1905); *When No Man Pursueth* (1910); *The Chink in the Armour* (1912); *The Lodger* (1913); *The Red Cross Barge* (1916); *Love and Hatred* (1917); *From the Vasty Deep* (1920); *What Really Happened* (1926); *The Story of Ivy* (1927); *Cressida: No Mystery* (1928); *The Net is Cast* (1933); *The Chianti Flask* (1934); *And Call it Accident* (1936); *Lizzie Borden* (1939); *I, Too, Have Lived in Arcadia* (1941); *Where Love and Friendship Dwelt* (1943); *The Merry Wives of Westminster* (1946); *A Passing World* (1948); *The Young Hilaire Belloc* (1956).

References: Iddesleigh, E. and Lowndes-Marques, S., 'Foreword' to *Diaries and Letters of Marie Belloc-Lowndes 1911–1947* (1971).

Bennett, Anna Maria

b. date unknown, Merthyr Tydfil; d. 13 February 1808, Brighton
Novelist

AMB achieved some literary status in her lifetime: she is listed in Mary Robinson's roll of literary honour; Scott valued her work; and Coleridge called *The Beggar Girl* (1797) 'the best novel . . . since Fielding', and praised her and Jane Austen equally. Her obituary notice in *The Athenaeum* rates her the equal of Fielding and Richardson. All 2,000 copies of *Vicissitudes Abroad* (1806), were sold on the day of publication, although the price was thirty-six shillings, several times the usual cost. She was the most commercially successful of the authors associated with the Minerva Press. Evidently her readers enjoyed the length of her works but the reviewers, no doubt forced to read them within an editor's deadline, complained of this feature. AMB did not receive a sound education: the reviewers of her early work criticize her faulty grammar and she corrected later editions.

AMB was the daughter of David Evans, who brought her from Merthyr Tydfil to Bristol, where he kept a grocery shop on the Back. She married a tanner called Bennett in Brecknock, and became a seller of ready-made naval clothing in London. Admiral Sir Thomas Pye sheltered from the rain in the shop, and she became his housekeeper in Surrey. They separated in 1785 because Pye sent a letter intended for another woman to AMB. However, when he died three weeks later, he left her a comfortable legacy and a house. She superintended a workhouse for some years before employing a deputy. Her children were Thomas Pye Bennett, RN, and Harriet Pye Bennett. The latter, who became the actress Mrs Esten, obtained a legal separation from her husband, AMB paying off his debts, and entered a supposed bigamous marriage to the Duke of Hamilton, by whom she had a child. AMB managed her daughter's career, and helped diffuse the scandal. In 1793 AMB managed the Theatre Royal in Edinburgh, then in the gift of the Duke, but his relations with Mrs Esten cooled, and, after a ruinous dispute, AMB and her daughter returned to London. The preface to *Ellen* (1794) tells of the consequent 'mental derangement' from which writing fiction was an escape. Her first two novels were published anonymously. In the dedication which prefaces *The Beggar Girl* (1797), she writes that she had lived for 'some time' near to the Duchess of York's residence. This was at Oatlands Park, Weybridge, Surrey. The dedications which preface her novels show devotion to the royal family and to an elevated ideal of feminine propriety and piety which she did not consistently emulate in her own life. Her books reveal a knowledge both of elevated society and of poverty.

AMB's works were entitled novels and were intended not as romance but as realistic portrayals of modern life. Yet she used romantic elements: for example, *Anna* (1785) is a reworking of the Cinderella story, and *Ellen* echoes the story of patient Grizelda. However, she also mocks the conventions of the romance: *The Beggar Girl* contains chapters headed 'The long story', 'The long story continued', and 'No end to the long story' and satirized the Gothic romanticist in Mrs Wouldbe who, too old to intrigue, attempts to write *The Grim Abbess* and *The Dumb Nun of St Bog-and-moat*. *Ellen* ends with the statement that although her heroine must have human faults, they are concealed 'by the impenetrable veil of immense riches'. Coleridge thought that the characters of Colonel Bahanun and Betty Brown in *The Beggar Girl* had not been bettered by any of Scott's colourful creations. Rosa, the ugly duckling heroine of *The Beggar Girl*, is also an original creation which may have contributed to the liveliness of Jane Austen's Catherine Morland. AMB well depicts the blending of high society and the demi-monde in *The Beggar Girl*, and society gatherings by the side of a shabby boarding school in *Juvenile Indiscretions* (1786). She developed the number of plot lines woven into a single narrative to picture a changing society. *Vicissitudes Abroad* successfully interweaves an account of the progress of the French Revolution with the stories of individuals attendant on Marie-Antoinette. AMB controls her potentially unwieldy material and, although partisan, creates a convincing and moving portrait of the beleaguered court.

A part of her readers' enjoyment lay in discovering the real personages portrayed in the novels. AMB herself states that some of the characters in *Juvenile Indiscretions* are founded on real people, and *The Gentleman's Magazine* carried a report that characters in *The Beggar Girl* were founded on a family living in Tooting and requested further information.   WILLIAM R. EDE

Works: *Anna or, Memoirs of a Welch Heiress, Interspersed with Anecdotes of a Nabob* (1785); *Juvenile Indiscretions: A Novel* (1786); *Agnes De Courci, A Domestic Tale,* (1789); *Ellen, Countess of Castle Howel, A Novel,* (1794, 1805); *The Beggar Girl and her Benefactors* (1797); *De Valcourt, A Novel* (1800); *Vicissitudes Abroad, or, The Ghost of My Father: A Novel* (1806).

References: Blakey, D., *The Minerva Press 1790–1820* (1935); Coleridge, H. N., *Table Talk and Omniana of Samuel Taylor Coleridge,* ed. T. Ashe (1884); Coleridge, S. T., *Collected Letters of Samuel Taylor Coleridge,* ed. Earl Leslie Griggs (1956–71); Fuller, J. F., *A Curious Genealogical Medley* (1913); Lee Lewes, C., *Memoirs* (1805); Price, M. B., and Price, L. M., *The Publication of English Literature in Germany in the Eighteenth Century* (1934); Randall, A. F., *Letter to the Women of England* (1799); Rogers, K. M., *Feminism in Eighteenth-Century England* (1982); Summers, M., *A Gothic Bibliography* (1938); Todd; Tompkins, J. M. S., *The Popular Novel in England 1770–1800* (1932).

Benson, Stella
b. 1892, Shropshire; d. 1933, Hongay, Tongking, China
Novelist, poet, short story writer
In 1913, after a sheltered childhood which was plagued by illness, SB rejected the overprotective concern of her parents and left for London with the intention of becoming a financially independent writer. Working life proved beneficial to her health and in the two years before the publication of her first novel, *I Pose* (1915), she worked in such diverse enterprises as charity organizations, paper bag production, and gardening.

SB was first exposed to feminism in her late teens and her adoption of the feminist position is reflected both in her activities and her writing. While living in London she campaigned to improve conditions of life for prostitutes, and later, during her years in China, she fought to control the selling of young girls into government brothels.

Personal experience was fundamental to SB's writing, forming ideas and prejudices which would recur throughout her novels and short stories. Perhaps the most deep-rooted and recurrent of her themes is alienation: her central characters are usually extremely isolated individuals whose detachment causes them to lose contact with reality. Loneliness receives frequent and contrasting treatment in SB's short stories. In 'Hope against Hope' (1931), a sad and simple story, the loneliness of a plain woman is depicted with a detached and deceptively unsympathetic perspective through its narration by a misogynist patient. The humour is grotesque and the portrayal of Nurse Hope is cruel: ultimately the story reveals above all the inability of men to understand women who fail to conform to their allotted stereotypes.

The Man Who Missed the 'Bus (1928) is also about loneliness, but here the sensation of alienation is achieved through a more surreal approach. As the story progresses it becomes increasingly difficult to tell whether Mr Robinson is dead or alive. His inability to perceive faces is dreamlike, and when he can no longer see his own face in the mirror, this inability becomes ghostly. The story presents a frightening and uncanny portrayal of loneliness.

Finally the idea of isolation receives comic and absurd treatment in 'An Out Islander Comes In' (1913). Rose, the 'Out-Islander', finds herself alone in a world populated entirely by replicas of her new husband Willie, a man whose sensitivity is encapsulated in his remark, 'Foller the crowd, that's what I always say – it's only crazy folks that try to be different.' Gradually Rose finds she cannot distinguish her Willie from all the other 'Willies' surrounding her: 'Opposite to her was Willie, and there two women down on her left, was another unmistakeable Willie. In the whirl and the dusk she could, uneasily, see other Willies grouped in the stern. As the boat twitched itself skilfully parallel with the ribs of the tender, Rose realized that the larger vessel was lined with Willies. She felt altogether alone in the midst of this superfluity, and began to cry unobtrusively.'

The isolation of these characters is to a degree autobiographical. In 1918 SB sailed to America and was soon caught up in the heady and hectic social circle of California. The initial enjoyment she experienced was short-lived. She found it impossible to identify with the Californian experience and her antipathy found expression in her 1922 satire of American life, *The Poor Man.*

In 1921 SB married James O'Gorman Anderson, an official in the Chinese customs service, and in 1922 they moved to China. It was here that SB's isolation became extreme. The role of women in China was one to which she could not conform and in consequence her self-confidence waned and she came to feel painfully inadequate: 'In China . . . what I have of my own is not despised so much as entirely unsuspected. None of these neighbours here know me as anything but a plain woman, a poor housekeeper, a woman who has not even had a child . . .' The pain caused by the social stigma of childlessness was exacerbated by SB's personal desire for children. Her potential maternal affection was transferred to her dogs – a situation on which she commented in an article of 1931, where she suggested that pets were a substitute for children, who are a substitute for immortality.

Tobit Transplanted (1930) was SB's most successful novel, winning the Vie Heureuse Prize and the ACC Benson silver medal for services to literature. It is an allegorical story of White Russian exiles in China based on the apocryphal story of Tobit, and the work is characterized by a humorous detachment which relieves the intensity of the often quite disturbing central themes.

The structure of *Tobit Transplanted* is complex. Contrasting narrative techniques are juxtaposed and SB moves skilfully from the intimacy of the 'dear reader' approach to an abstract and detached style of narration through the voice of a non-comprehending observer. This unusual perspective is often achieved through the eyes of a dog, but the technique is best displayed in the central scene of the novel, where the signing of a marriage contract between two Russian families is narrated by a drunken Chinese observer who speaks not one word of Russian.

The central characters of the book, Seryozah and Tanya, are both seeking a point of contact with a world in which they do not feel they properly belong. Tanya is struggling to avoid the social obligation of marriage because she feels her individuality will be destroyed by the relationship. The prospect of two 'mes' becoming an 'us' is anathema to her, and her fears are exacerbated by the attitudes of those around her. Katya, the servant, defines marriage thus: 'I'll tell you what marriage is Tatiana Pavlovna – it's just getting out of bed, cooking three meals, and getting back into bed again.' Escape only becomes possible for Tanya because in Seryozah she finds someone with whom marriage can be the alliance of two individuals, not the creation of an all-consuming 'us'.

The characters of *Tobit Transplanted* are personally involved in a struggle between illusion and reality. They seek to preserve the illusions of their 'vanity', while reality seeks to impose itself. The parent-child relationship and man's urge for immortality are inextricably linked to this struggle. Even for the most isolated individual, such as Tanya, the failure of parents to live up to externally and internally imposed expectations is of vital importance, because the imperfection of one's creator is ultimately a reflection on oneself. Tanya and Seryozah's marriage is a compromise, and this is what makes it so important, for, in forming a relationship and rejecting the perfection of the isolated individual, they have gained a foothold in reality, which alone can provide happiness.

GILL PLAIN

Works: *I Pose* (1915); *This is the End* (1917); *Twenty* (1918); *Living Alone* (1919); *Kwan-yin* (1922); *The Poor Man* (1922); *Pipers and a Dancer* (1924); *The Awakening, a fantasy* (1925); *The Little World* (1925); *Goodbye, Stranger* (1926); *The Man Who Missed the 'Bus* (1928); *Worlds Within Worlds* (1928); *The Far Away Bride* (1930; published in England in 1931 as *Tobit Transplanted*); *Hope against Hope and Other Stories* (1931); *Christmas Formula and Other Stories* (1932); *Pull Devil, Pull Baker* (1933); *Poems* (1935); *Mundos* (unfinished) (1935); *Collected Short Stories* (1936).

References: Bedell, R. M., *Stella Benson* (1983); Clarabut, C. (ed.), *Some Letters of Stella Benson* (1938); Roberts, R. E., *Portrait of Stella Benson* (1939).

Bentley, Phyllis
b. Halifax, Yorkshire, 1894; d. Yorkshire, 1977

Novelist, biographer

It is a somewhat sad testimony to PB that despite her interest in, and devotion to, the form of the regional novel – she published a book on the subject in 1941 – very few of her many titles now survive. *Inheritance* (1932) alone survives with acclaim due in part to its televisation. It is her secondary work, on the Brontës, which ensured that she remained in print up to her death in 1977 and *The Brontës and Their World* (1957) is still a classic.

PB was born in Halifax, in the West Riding of Yorkshire, and, apart from short spells spent in London, and travelling in the USA, remained attached to the county of her birth. She was the youngest child, and only daughter, of a textile manufacturer, whose status within the Yorkshire community was assured. Despite the recessions of the trade, he remained comparatively affluent, so being able to indulge PB. When the family moved to Huddersfield, she was boarded at a school in Halifax and remained there until her mother, for reasons unknown, took her away from this school, and both went to the south of England, the mother travelling and PB attending an Ursuline Convent school near Hythe. On returning to Halifax PB went briefly to Halifax High School for Girls but eventually finished her education at Cheltenham Ladies' College where she took, and passed, a University of London external examination which allowed her a BA degree.

She then worked as a teacher in north London and began her largely autobiographical novel, *Environment*, which was eventually published in 1922. Four allegorical stories, *The World's Bane*, were published in 1918 and were influenced – a debt acknowledged by the author – by Olive Schreiner's *Dreams*. By this time PB was working as a librarian and subsequently as a writer on *John O'London's Weekly*. During this period her novels *Cat-in-the-Manger* (1923), *The Partnership* (1928), and *The Spinner of the Years* (1929) were published along with *Carr* (1929), the biography of a textile manufacturer.

PB was beginning to feel the pull of her native Yorkshire, especially of the West Riding, strengthened by her friendship with Winifred Holtby, another prominent Yorkshire writer, whom she met in 1929. Through Holtby, PB met Vera Brittain who was instrumental in furthering her career. Her blunt nature led to squalls in relationships but her strong spirit did not lose her friends. 1932 saw the publication of *Inheritance*, PB's best-known novel. It chronicles the lives of the Yorkshire families involved in the textile industry and was a forerunner of the contemporary family saga novels but written with complete integrity without regard to mass-market appeal. Much of the material was drawn from her mother's recollections of her family and the central character, 'Joth', is based on her great-uncle, James Hanson.

PB's home in Halifax was just ten miles from Haworth, home of the Brontës, and she knew the countryside intimately. *The Brontës and Their World*, published in the Thames & Hudson Literary Lives series, is much more than the standard illustrated biography. It relates the history of the family from the late eighteenth century and begins in Ireland with the birth of Patrick Brontë, in 1777. Her description of Haworth and the surrounding countryside equal her narrative on the family itself, expressing her deep feeling for the place and her attachment to it. That the Brontës drew inspiration from it was no mystery to PB for she herself drew from it and it influenced her writing profoundly: 'these are Pennine miles: the roads have steep gradients, and are wild and windy, exposed to every kind of weather. In the Brontës' days there was no railway from Haworth and no bus service; if one wanted to leave the village one walked or rode if one could afford a horse, or hired a gig or a covered carrier's cart. Readers from the south of England and more distant places have said that they never understood the Brontës' writings until they had seen Haworth.'   ALISON RIMMER

Selected works: The World's Bane and Other Stories (1918); *Environment* (1922); *Cat-in-the-Manger* (1923); *The Partnership* (1928); *The Spinner of the Years* (1928); *Carr* (1929); *Inheritance* (1932); *A Modern Tragedy* (1934); *Freedom, Farewell* (1936); *The English Regional Novel* (1941); *The Rise of Henry Morcar* (1946); *The Brontës* (1947); *Life Story* (1948); *Quorum* (1950); *Love and Money: Seven Tales of the West Riding* (1957); *Kith and Kin: Nine Tales of Family Life* (1960); *Tales of the West Riding* (1965); *The New Venturers* (1973); *More Tales of the West Riding* (1974).

References: Baker and Packman, *Guide to the Best Fiction* (1932); *CA; DNB.*

Berridge, Elizabeth
b. 3 December 1921, London
Novelist, short story writer
EB is the daughter of Albert Berridge, an estate manager, and his wife Phyllis (*née* Drew) Berridge. She studied French and German at a private school in Geneva and attended the Regent Street Polytechnic in London. In 1940 she married the author and publisher Ronald Moore, and the couple have two children. She took jobs as a secretary and as a journalist, and later as a publisher's editor, from 1956 until 1960. She has worked as a critic for *The Daily Telegraph, Books and Bookmen,* and *Country Life*. From 1964 until 1971 she appeared on Radio 4's *Woman's Hour*. In 1964 she won an award for the best novel of the year from the *Yorkshire Post* for *Across the Common*.

EB is sometimes described as a characteristically English writer, and most of the stories in her first collection, published in 1947, deal with major or minor crises in the lives of predominantly middle class English characters. EB shows a particular interest in the way in which such crises can produce apparently unlikely psychological reactions. In 'Tell It to a Stranger' Mrs Hatfield returns to her house to find that she has been burgled, but remains entirely calm, consoled by the prospect of telling her friends about her loss. When she arrives at her friends' house, only to find that it has been destroyed in a bombing raid and her friends killed, her immediate reaction is an intense frustration at having no one to tell about the burglary. EB's stories are also often preoccupied with the internal jealousies and hatreds of families: in 'The Shrine' with a struggle between two daughters learning musical instruments to win the affection of their mother, a pianist; in 'The Bare Tree' with the tensions caused within a family by the failure of the father, a sculptor, to sellhis work.

When EB ventures beyond such territory her work can be disappointing, as in the unconvincing 'The Greatest Good', which envisages a totalitarian society of women run by a bureaucratic 'Organisation'. The 'supervisor' explains to the narrator that women have risen to power through the increasing delegation of unwelcome tasks by men, culminating in women being made to fight wars in place of men and thereby assuming control of the military. However, EB's subsequent work shows an increasing sureness of tone and breadth of subject matter. *People at Play* (1982) takes for its central figure Stanislaus Spolianski, a Pole living in London, and the tenants to whom he lets the remaining floors of his house. The novel's syntax is typically looser than in EB's earlier work, allowing her a greater flexibility in following the moods and reflections of her characters. JAMES SMITH

Works: *House of Defence* (1945); *The Story of Stanley Brent* (1945); *Selected Short Stories* (1947); *Be Clean, Be Tidy* (1949); *Rose under Glass* (1961); *Across the Common* (1964); *Sing Me Who You Are* (1967); *Family Matters* (1980); *Run For Home* (1981); *People at Play* (1982).
References: *CA.*

Betham-Edwards, Matilda
b. 1836, Westerfield, Suffolk; d. 1919
Novelist, essayist, travel writer
Brought up on the family's Suffolk farm, MB-E was 12 when her mother Barbara Betham died, 'a beautiful, refined and, for her day, highly educated woman. From that time, partly owing to domestic affairs, partly owing to the fondness of an adoring father, the direction of my life was left in my own hands.' Most influentially, at 10 years old, MB-E attended a day-school directed by a devotee of French Grammar, to whom she attributed 'the passionate interest afterwards taken by me in France and French affairs'. Later in life she made annual journeys, writing magazine articles and editing *Murray's Handbook for Central France*. She also edited Arthur Young's *Autobiography* (1898) and wrote a biographical sketch and notes for his *Travels in France during the years 1787, '88, '89* (1890). In 1891 she was made an Officier de l'Instruction Publique de France, the only Englishwoman to be so honoured, and went on to write many books on France and French life.

After her mother's death MB-E educated herself, reading books brought for her in a frail of market groceries from the Mechanics' Institute in Ipswich. She went briefly as a pupil-governess to a school in Peckham, which she loathed, and began her novel *The White House by the Sea* (1857) in her teens, completing it soon after she returned home. It was reprinted continuously for the next forty years but she received nothing from it because she had initially accepted twenty-five new novels as a payment. MB-E wrote fiction prodigiously for over sixty years. *Dr Jacob* (1864), a popular early novel, was based on 'an elderly

English clergyman of noble presence and most winning manners' about whom she heard in Frankfurt during her travels on the continent. He successfully raised money for a crusade against Judaism in Jerusalem; he then squandered it and absconded in debt. In her own estimation, *Forestalled* (1880) and *Love and Marriage* (1884) were her best novels.

When her father Edward died, the management of the farm fell to MB-E and her only unmarried sister for the next two or three years. On the breaking up of her Suffolk home she travelled in France, Spain, and Algeria with Barbara Bodichon, recording this in *A Winter with the Swallows* (1866) and *Through Spain to the Sahara* (1867). Her French, German, Spanish, and Italian were fluent. She moved to Kensington, where she met Charles Bradlaugh, whom she very much admired, and George Eliot, whose power as a writer she fully admitted, while finding her 'sombre realism' repellent. For MB-E George Sand was the greatest novelist of the age.

MB-E was an anti-vivisectionist and Nonconformist, fervently anti-Catholic and very critical of the hypocrisies of the Church of England, but when Moody and Sankey, the American revivalists asked her to write them a story on the lines of *Kitty* (1869) with a distinctly evangelical bias, she 'regretfully refused'. Politically she had wide liberal sympathies. She assumed women's equality and felt that recognition of this would inevitably occur, although she was not prepared to agitate for it. When *Sylvesters* (1871) first ran in *Good Words* as a serial, the socialist views in the novel caused many subscribers to give up the family journal. She wrote articles on the International Working Men's Association for *Fraser's Magazine* (July–September 1875) and attended a meeting in High Holborn at which Karl Marx presided.

MB-E and her cousin, Amelia Blandford Edwards, were often mistaken for each other because of their initials. Amelia kept her middle name for the sake of euphony, MB-E kept hers because it was her mother's maiden name and had literary associations. She wrote about her aunt and godmother Matilda Betham, author of *A Biographical Dictionary of Celebrated Women* (1804), in *Six Life Studies of Famous Women* (1884). In 1898 she brought out *Reminiscences* and in the year of her death *Mid-Victorian Memories*.   CHRISTINE DEVONSHIRE

Selected works: The White House By The Sea (1857); Now or Never (1859); Charles and Ernest or, Play and Work: A Story of Hazelhurst School (1859); Ally and her Schoolfellow: A Tale for the Young (1861); John and I (1862); Snow-Flakes and the Stories they told the Children (1862); Scenes and Stories of the Rhine (1862); Doctor Jacob (1864); Lisabee's Love Story (1865); The Wild Flower of Ravensworth (1866); A Winter with the Swallows (1866); Through Spain to the Sahara (1867); Campany's Courtship (1868); Kitty (1869); The Sylvesters (1871); Mademoiselle Josephine's Fridays and Other Stories (1874); Bridget (1877); Forestalled, or the Life-Quest (1880); Six Life Studies of Famous Women (1880); The Starry Blossom, and Other Stories for the Young (1881); Poems (1884); Love and Marriage or, The Waiting on an Island, and Other Tales (1884); Half-Way: An Anglo-French Romance (1886); The Parting of the Ways (1888); For One and the World (1889); 'Introduction', biographical sketch and notes to Travels in France, by A. Young (1890); selected and introduced, Poems of Owen Meredith (1890); A Dream of Millions and Other Tales (1891); A North-Country Comedy (1891); Two Aunts and a Nephew (1891); The Romance of a French Parsonage (1892); France of Today (1892–4); A Romance of Dijon (1894); (trans), Passages in the Life of a Galley Slave, by J. Marteilhe (1895); (ed.), The Autobiography of Arthur Young (1898); A Storm-Rent Sky: Scenes of Love and Revolution (1898); Reminiscences (1898); The Lord of the Harvest (1899); Mock Beggars' Hall: A Story (1902); Barham Brocklebank, MD (1903);

Home Life in France (1905); *From an Islington Widow: Pages of Reminiscent Romance* (1914); *Under the German Ban in Alsace and Lorraine* (1914); *Hearts of Alsace: A Story of Our Time* (1916); *War Poems* (1917); *Mid-Victorian Memories* (1919); (trans.), *French Fireside Poetry* ed. B. Miall, with metrical translations and an introduction (1919).
References: NWAD.

Bishop, Isabella Bird
b. 15 October 1831, Boroughbridge; d. 7 October 1904, London
Travel writer
IBB was the daughter of a curate, Edward Bird, and a Sunday school teacher, Dora Lawson. She had one sister, Henrietta Bird, and a half-brother from her father's first marriage, who died as a boy. Educated at home, IBB's first foray into public life was in 1848, when she taught Sunday School classes at her father's church in Birmingham to girls of her own age. Her first publication was a privately printed pamphlet endorsing protectionism written when she was 16. In the autumn of 1848, Edward Bird received a permanent place at Wyton, Huntingdonshire, where IBB retired in later years.

In 1854 IBB began her travels abroad. Her notes and letters from her first trip to America were published by John Murray in 1856 as *The Englishwoman in America*. It was an immediate best-seller and IBB began her distinguished career as a travel writer. Part of the profits from the sale of the first book were used for the relief of the poor fishermen in the Scottish Highlands whom she had seen each summer since 1850 when her family holidayed there.

During her second American journey, her father died. She had been researching the religious beliefs of Americans for him and published her findings first as a series of nine articles for the *Patriot* newspaper and then as her second book, *Aspects of Religion in America* (1859). In 1859, Mrs Bird moved her daughters to Edinburgh. Increasingly bothered by a spinal condition that plagued her all her life, IBB wrote articles for inspirational magazines such as *Leisure Hour, Family Treasury, Good Words,* and *Sunday at Home*. From 1862 to 1866, she was involved in helping clothmakers from the Hebrides to emigrate to Canada where they would find work. She travelled to Canada in 1866 to see how they were faring.

In August 1866, IBB's mother died. To distract herself from grief, she began revising her journal of a voyage to the Hebrides made in 1860 for publication in *Leisure Hours*. This was followed by a political pamphlet, *Notes on Old Edinburgh*, which graphically described the plight of the poor in the slums of Edinburgh and called for social reform. Later that year, IBB published a series of papers in *Leisure Hours* on eighteenth-century hymn writers which was a companion to an earlier series in the same magazine on the Emblematist poets, Donne, Quarles, and Herbert.

In 1871, IBB went to Australia and the Sandwich Islands in a vain attempt to cure her spinal ailment. The notes from her voyage were published as *Six Months in the Sandwich Islands* in 1874. In 1878, she embarked on her first trip to Japan. The details of her journey were published in 1880 as *Unbeaten Tracks in Japan* and in 1883 as *The Golden Chersonese*, which described her travels through Hong Kong, Saigon, Singapore, and Malaysia. In 1879, upon her return, she published an account of her second American trip as *A Lady's Life in the Rocky Mountains*.

IBB never fully recovered from the death of her sister, Henrietta, in June

1880. In December of that year she became engaged to Dr John Bishop, who had been her sister's physician and with whose character as a noble, religious man she was well acquainted. The two were married in the Birds' home in Warwickshire on 8 March 1881. Shortly after their marriage, Dr Bishop contracted a fatal blood disease and, despite IBB's many efforts to find a cure for it, he died in 1886.

IBB then became involved with the Young Women's Christian Association (YWCA) and studied nursing. Feeling the call of the missionary life, as a result of her hospital work and recent widowhood, IBB joined the Church Missionary Society (CMS), a Baptist organization dedicated to bringing Christianity to the peoples of the Middle East and Asia. During this period, she decided to build a hospital in her husband's honour in Nazareth in recognition of his lifelong interest in missionary medicine. She set out in 1889 for the Middle East, travelling through the Suez to India and Islamabad where a site was chosen for the 'John Bird Memorial Hospital'. Palestine, at this time, was involved in territorial wars which made her initial goal impossible. Once the limestone building, with its operating room and thirty-two patient beds, was under construction, IBB travelled on to Tibet, Central Asia, and Persia. Returning to India, she set up a smaller women's hospital in Srinagar in memory of her sister. From Srinagar, IBB returned to Edinburgh in December 1890 via America, Syria, and Trebizond.

In 1891, IBB began compiling *Journeys in Persia* based on her surviving letters and diaries. Bad weather ruined some of her notebooks, some of her letters miscarried, and several times her possessions were stolen during this trip. Her articles on the persecution of the Christians by the Turks published in the *Contemporary Review* led to her addressing the House of Commons on the Armenian and Syrian immigration problem. She was made a fellow of the Royal Scottish Geographical Society in November 1891, following a successful series of lectures on the Middle East to learned societies in England and Scotland.

In 1894, IBB departed for another missionary trip to Yokohama and China, despite her recent diagnosis of heart disease and her continual suffering from rheumatic gout. This was her last successful trip abroad for the CMS. With no immediate family and no children, IBB was at her leisure in the Orient, going about Japan, Manchuria, and Korea in the company of fellow British subjects. In 1896, she sailed up the Yangtze River and went 300 miles alone on mule back into the Szechuan provinces. During this trip, she built three hospitals and an orphanage in memory of her husband, parents, and sister, and financed the projects by selling the silver plate she had brought along with her for this purpose. She returned to London in March 1897 where she resumed a successful speaking career and prepared *Korea and her Neighbours*, published in January 1898. Her adventures sailing up the Yangtze were published in November 1899 as *The Yangtze Valley and Beyond*.

Her final missionary trip was to Morocco from December 1900 to June 1901. Seriously plagued by poor health, IBB could do little and published just one article describing the people and country in the *Monthly Review*. In 1903, she began to feel herself dying from a tumour. Although unable to write extensively, she kept up her correspondence until her death. She was buried in Dean Cemetery beside her husband, whose body was returned from Cannes to rest with hers.

IBB's writings are characterized by natural curiosity, detail, and unprejudiced reporting. No aspect of colour, sound, or movement is too trivial to record.

She employed the language of the people she visited in her accounts of them as well as the horticultural names of the plants and flowers she saw. Although she travelled in places where the British presence was known, IBB's journey up the Yangtze and into the lands of the Chi-Po tribe of Tibet were pioneering. Her writings reflect a woman of unusual courage and energy.

B. E. SCHNELLER

Works: *The Englishwoman in America* (1856); *Aspects of Religion in America* (1859); *The Hawaiian Archipelago: Six Months among the Palm Groves, Coral Reefs, and Volcanoes of the Sandwich Islands* (1874); *A Lady's Life in the Rocky Mountains* (1879); *Unbeaten Tracks in Japan* (1880); *The Golden Chersonese and the Way Thither* (1883); *Journeys in Persia and Kurdistan: With a Summer in the Upper Karum Region and a Visit to the Nestorian Rayahs* (1891); *Among the Tibetans* (1894); *Korea and Her Neighbours* (1898); *The Yangtze Valley and Beyond* (1899); *Chinese Pictures* (1900).

References: *BA* (19); *DNB*; Stoddart, A., *The Life of Isabella Bird (Mrs Bishop)* (1908).

Blessington, Marguerite, Countess of

b. 1 September 1789, Clonmel, County Tipperary; d. 1849, Paris

Novelist, gossip writer, salon hostess

MB had a life as colourful, dramatic, and full of reversals of fortune as characters in any of her writings. From humble beginnings in Ireland she became 'the most gorgeous Lady Blessington' whose home was the resort of many famous writers, and with whom many, including Byron, Dickens, and Disraeli, corresponded. She was the fourth child of Edmund Power. Noticeable as the only plain child in a good-looking family, she was also intelligent and imaginative: from an early age she entertained her six brothers and sisters by improvising stories for them. She received some education from a friend of her mother. Her father, the dissolute only son of a small Irish landowner of ancient Roman Catholic stock, constantly lived above his income. When MB was 8 years old, he became a magistrate in Waterford and Tipperary and hunted down insurgents with the help of dragoons, consequently becoming hated in the neighbourhood. He attempted several business enterprises, including starting a newspaper, but sank deeper into debt and became a tyrant to his family. His extravagant taste in buckskins, top boots, lace ruffles, and cravats earned him locally the nicknames 'Shiver the frills' and 'Beau Power'. His strong will, energy, and extravagance seem to have been inherited by MB, who in later years experimented in many different kinds of writing to pay off her debts while unable to economize on the grand scale of her lifestyle.

When MB was 14 years old, her father found a way of solving his financial difficulties by virtually selling her to a sadistic captain, Maurice St Leger Farmer, from County Kildare. In spite of her entreaties and his relatives' warnings to her father that he had bouts of insanity, she was forced to marry him. After three months of enduring his 'ungovernable outbursts of passion', MB refused to go with him to join his regiment, returning, unwelcomed, to her home. Perhaps because of this experience, many of her heroines are victims of sadistic or tyrannical men. Fortunately for MB, her husband's fiery temper led him to draw his sword on his colonel; he was forced to sell his commission and join the East India Company. In 1817 he was involved in a drunken orgy and was killed by falling from a window in the King's Bench prison. At the age of 28, MB was at least officially a free woman.

By the time she was 20, MB had become conspicuously beautiful, and in Dublin drew many admirers. Her portrait was painted by Sir Thomas Lawrence. Four months after her husband's death, she married again, this time a widower, Charles Gardiner, the second Viscount Mountjoy and the first Earl of Blessington. Seven years her senior, he had estates in Ireland yielding an income of £30,000 and a town mansion in St James's Square. He lavished gifts on his beautiful wife and they lived extravagantly in London, where their house was a centre of social attraction and provided MB with plenty of material for her writing.

In 1822 she published anonymously her first book, *The Magic Lantern, or Sketches of Scenes from the Metropolis*. Later that year the Blessingtons embarked on a continental tour, during which MB met Byron and became his confidante. She wrote in her diary, 'Am I indeed in the same town with Byron? . . . I hope he may not be fat . . . for a fat poet is an anomaly, in my opinion.' After her meeting with him she remarked, 'I have seldom seen finer teeth than Lord Byron's.' Both these comments seem to justify Byron's opinion, 'Were I to point out the prominent defect of Lady Blessington, I should say it was flippancy.' Apart from enjoying his company, it was later a financial advantage to her, as her *Journal of Conversations with Lord Byron* (1832) was immediately popular. These vivacious conversations are valuable for the light they shed on Byron. His attitude to Leigh Hunt, his partner with Shelley in the periodical *The Liberal*, is made clear in his remark to MB, 'Our tastes are so opposite that we are totally unsuited to each other. . . . We are more formed to be friends at a distance than near,' and his rashness is illustrated by MB's comment, 'It appears to me that Byron is a person who, without reflection would form engagements, which when condemned by his friends and advisers, he would gladly get out of . . . without reflecting on the humiliation such desertion must inflict.' During the next year the Blessingtons and Byron met daily, and when they eventually parted, Byron cried. He sold his yacht, *Bolivar*, to the Earl, and wrote a poem to MB.

Four years later, the Earl's daughter (by his previous marriage) was married to the Count D'Orsay in Naples at the age of 15. Two years afterwards (1829) the Earl died from apoplexy in Paris, his fortune almost exhausted. By now MB had a relationship with the Count D'Orsay which lasted the rest of her life. In 1831 they moved to Mayfair, becoming again a social focus. In 1833 her first novel *Grace Kennedy, or The Repealers* appeared in three volumes; MB then started writing for periodicals, and in 1834 began editing *The Book of Beauty*. She moved to Gore House in Kensington, soon followed by D'Orsay, and for fourteen years her home was the resort of famous contemporary writers. Her splendid lifestyle necessitated her writing for publication every year. Her travels on the continent were put to good use in *The Idler in Italy* (1839) and *The Idler in France* (1841), which were both very popular. MB also experimented in verse and published a verse story, *The Belle of a Season* (1840). The Irish potato disease of 1845 greatly reduced her income; in the following year she became a highly paid gossip writer for the new *Daily News*, and displayed a gift for discovering exciting snatches of up-to-date gossip. In spite of this success, however, her debts were mounting at a rate that her earnings could not match. In April 1849 D'Orsay fled to Paris with his valet and one portmanteau, and a few days later MB followed him. Gore House was auctioned to satisfy the creditors. Shortly afterwards MB died in D'Orsay's Paris house, and was buried in Chambourcy.

In the year of her death, MB's edition of *The Book of Beauty, or, Regal Gallery* was published. It begins with a portrait of the young Queen Victoria and a sonnet in her honour. The lives of eleven other English queens follow, three of which are written by MB, and show the qualities which throughout her writings make her style so attractive to her readers. Her tone is stately and resonant: 'But as the brightest mornings are often followed by the darkest days, so was the early and brilliant youth of the Infanta succeeded by the gloom which surrounded her life soon after she exchanged the sunshine of her natal clime of Granada for the cloudy and chilly one of England.' Her comments are forthright: 'Rarely does it occur that mothers-in-law feel any warm affection for the wives of their sons'; and her style is dramatic and eloquently descriptive: 'Her fair hair in rich profusion floated down her back, confined to her head by a network of gold and a circlet of precious stones, the dazzling lustre of which seemed to give a glory to the seraphic character of her face.'

SHIRLEY EACHUS

Selected works: The Magic Lantern, or, Sketches of Scenes from the Metropolis (1822); *Sketches and Fragments* (1822); *Journal of Conversations with Lord Byron* (1832); *Grace Cassidy and the Repealers* (1833); *The Book of Beauty* (1834–49); *The Two Friends* (1835) *The Victims of Society* (1837); *Gems of Beauty* (1838); *The Governess* (1839); *The Idler in Italy* (1840); *The Belle of a Season* (1840); *The Idler in France* (1841); *The Lottery of Life and Other Tales* (1842); *Memoirs of a Femme du Chambre* (1846); *The Book of Beauty, or, Regal Gallery for 1849* (1849); *Country Quarters* (1850).

References: BA (19); *DNB*; Fitzgerald Molley, J., *The Most Gorgeous Lady Blessington* (1896); Madden, R. R., *The Literary Life and Correspondence of the Countess Blessington* (1855); Marshall, W. J., *Byron, Shelley, Hunt and The Liberal* (1960); Uglow.

Blind, Mathilde

b. 1841, Mannheim; d. 1896, London

Poet, biographer, translator, editor

(Also wrote under Claude Lake)

MB was the daughter of an elderly retired banker, but adopted the surname of her mother's second husband Karl Blind, a political writer and revolutionary. After leading the Baden revolt in 1848–9 he was forced to seek refuge in Belgium, where MB's schooling began, and then, three years later, in London. She attended two or three unsatisfactory schools, but her most reliable training came from her mother. In 1859 she went on a walking tour by herself through Switzerland and met a group of 'brilliant revolutionists' who taught her Latin, Old German, and Middle German. On her return she began a rigorous programme of self-education and became acquainted with foreign exiles like Louis Blanc and Garibaldi who frequented her parents' house. The *Fortnightly Review* (May 1891) later published her 'Personal Recollections of Mazzini'. Her brother Ferdinand attempted to assassinate Bismarck and then committed suicide in 1866, leaving his property to her. Shortly afterwards her first volume of *Poems* (1867) was published under the pseudonym Claude Lake.

She had hopes of succeeding as a lecturer, advocating female franchise, the raising of the status of women, and their entry into all professions except the military and naval. She focused on the inferiority of women's education and probably the idea of bequeathing her estate to an institution which conformed to her educational ideal was formed at this time. A lecture on Shelley was printed and prompted an article in the *Westminster Review* (July 1870) which embodied textual corrections; the work made her known as a sympathetic and skilful editor and critic. She later wrote an abridged biography for Tauchnitz and edited the *Letters and Journals of Lord Byron* and *Poems of Lord Byron* (1886).

While still on good terms with her family, in 1871 she set up a home of her own. In 1873 she translated Strauss's *The Old Faith and the New*, wrote a life of the author, and made a tour of the Scottish Highlands which inspired *The Prophecy of St Oran* (1881). She had discovered the legend, telling of the love of one of St Columba's monks for a Pictish woman, on a lonely farm on the Isle of Skye. It was believed that Heaven's anger prevented the church on Iona from being built until Oran was punished by being buried alive. This was done but he rose again to deny his faith. The poem was not finished until some years later when MB had moved to Manchester to be near Ford Madox Brown and his wife. In the meantime she was occupied with her romance *Tarantella* (1884). *The Heather on Fire* (1886) was written after a second visit to Scotland in 1883. It tells of the violent clearance of whole communities of crofters from Highland estates 'to make way for sporting grounds rented by merchant princes and American millionaires', which MB regarded as a national crime. At the same time she worked on biographies of *George Eliot* (1883) and *Madame Roland* (1886), the result of her passion to celebrate illustrious women. Her health was failing but she attempted an ambitious epic poem, *The Ascent of Man* (1888), on Darwin's theory of evolution. On a visit to Nice she met Marie Bashkirtseff whom she respected for her intellectual energy; she translated Bashkirtseff's *Journal* (1890) and provided a sympathetic introduction.

When she became sole heir to the fortune of her stepbrother, she was enabled to travel widely, and she spent considerable time in Rome and twice visited Egypt. The collections *Dramas in Miniature* (1891), *Songs and Sonnets* (1893), and *Birds of Passage* (1895) reflect her travels. On her return she visited rural England, staying with her friend Mona Caird and spending time in Stratford, an experience from which her last collection, *Shakespeare Sonnets* (1902), dates. She died in an invalids' home in south London and left the greater part of her estate to Newnham College, Cambridge. CHRISTINE DEVONSHIRE

Selected works: (under Claude Lake), *Poems* (1867); *Shelley: A lecture* (1870); (ed. and memoir), *A Selection from the Poems of P. B. Shelley* (1872); (trans.), *The Old Faith and the New*, by D. F. Strauss (1873); *The Prophecy of St Oran* (1881); *George Eliot* (1883); *Tarantella* (1884); *The Heather on Fire: A Tale of the Highland Clearances* (1886); *Madame Roland* (1886); (ed.), *The Poetical Works of Lord Byron*, (1886); *The Ascent of Man* (1889); (trans. and intro.), *The Journal of Marie Bashkirtseff* (1890); *Dramas in Miniature* (1891); *Songs and Sonnets* (1893); *Birds of Passage* (1895); *Shakespeare Sonnets* (1902).

References: *DNB*; Robertson, E. S., *English Poetesses* (1883); Symons, A. (ed.), *The Poetical Works of Mathilde Blind*, with memoir by R. Garnett (1900).

Blyton, Enid

b. 11 August 1897, East Dulwich, London; d. 28 November 1968, Hampstead, London

Writer for children

(Also wrote under Mary Pollock)

One of England's best-known writers for children, EB experienced childhood as troubled and lonely. The only child of unhappily married parents (her father left home when she was 13), EB spent her formative years at boarding school, like most of her characters. Educated at St Christopher's School for Girls

(1907–15), she became both head girl and captain of games. Parents are absent figures in her books, appearing at the margins to deposit their children at school or on holiday. Teachers and headmistresses remain her most visible and highly defined adult characters. EB trained as a kindergarten teacher at the Froebel Insitute, Ipswich High School (1916–18), and subsequently became governess to a family of small boys. During this time she began writing stories for children, the first of which were published in magazines. In 1924, EB married Hugh Pollock, her editor at Newnes. The couple had two daughters. Marital tensions, intensified by Pollock's alcoholism, resulted in divorce in 1942. EB remarried a year later, to a London surgeon, Kenneth Darrel Waters.

During a career spanning roughly thirty-five years, EB produced a wide range of books for children. In addition to original stories and novels, she wrote adaptations of fables by Aesop and Uncle Remus, books on nature and animals, verse, plays, and prayer books. Successful early in her career, she published a collection of her first stories, *The Enid Blyton Book of Fairies* (1924) two years after they began to appear in magazines. Her early stories featured fairies and circus people, subjects with strong appeal for young children. Her fantasy books *Adventures of the Wishing Chair* (1937) and *The Enchanted Wood* (1939) were especially popular. Today's child readers are usually more familiar with her later creations. During the 1940s, EB began writing short novels for older children, placed in middle-class English settings. The first of her school stories, *The Naughtiest Girl in the School* (1940) was continued as a series, as were later *The Twins at St Clare's* (1941) and *First Term at Malory Towers* (1946). Other series took children out of the school and into more fantastic locales. The Famous Five made their first appearance in *Five on a Treasure Island* (1942) and went on to enjoy dozens of new adventures. Equally popular were the Secret Seven, who were introduced in a book of that name in 1949. At her peak during the 1940s, EB produced over thirty books a year. At the end of this decade she began writing the picture books for younger children that featured the infamous Noddy. During the 1950s she added substantially to this series, although she continued to write new adventures for her earlier creations. Libraries in England and abroad began to ban her books at this time. Undaunted, EB continued to write more Noddy books during the 1960s, slowed only by her diminishing mental clarity.

EB's novels depict an enclosed children's world. Breezy, unemotional, the children are happiest in their own company, whether in the institutional environment of the school or in more exotic settings. Children serve as one another's companions, guides rescuers, tutors, and occasional tormentors. Adults exist to control or limit their activities, administering more severe forms of discipline and punishment. Often ambiguous figures, their presence in the children's world is invariably intrusive. Uncle Quentin of the Famous Five series is a stern and forbidding guardian, emerging from his study only to glower at the children for making noise. Teachers are fair-minded disciplinarians, alternately respected and ridiculed by their charges. In the adventure stories the figure of the adult is reinvented as the criminal; the flip side of the protective guardian, the criminal wields an inverted power of law or punishment. Children are made powerful against such adults through the group. In school and adventure stories alike, co-operation is the highest good. In school stories especially, good sportsmanship and school spirit are valued above individual achievement. Telling tales, or tattling, is the worst offence, and children who betray other children to adults are regarded with contempt.

Although distinct from the adult-world, the children's community shares its attitudes and duplicates its social and economic structures. EB's world is unabashedly middle-class; children are uniformly well-provided for, with French lessons, games of tennis, and plenty of cake for tea. *Five on a Treasure Island* introduces 'Alf, the fisherboy'. Paid to look after one of the children's dog, this character represents the child as servant. While the dog joins the Five on their adventure, Alf remains behind. Beneath an egalitarian gloss, the children's world is rigidly exclusive. Well-travelled stereotypes are used to evoke the outsider; Carlotta in *Summer Term at St Clare's* impresses the other girls with her 'fantastic acrobatics', the legacy of a circus background, while the rich American Zerelda in *Third Year at Malory Towers* uses too much make-up and resorts constantly to the adjective 'wunnerful'. Exclusion operates on the basis of gender as well. The girls of the Famous Five and Secret Seven are left out of the more exciting and potentially dangerous adventures. In *The Secret Seven* the boys are adamant that 'boys only are in the performance tonight', although their dog, Scamper, is admitted as a useful companion. The tomboy is a recurring figure (George of the Famous Five, Bobby of St Clare's, Bill of Malory Towers) whose negated femininity permits a certain freedom of action. Characters are roughly distinguished from one another, and in the adventure stories enjoy the same minimal development given to their canine companions. In part, this is due to the EB ethos, which favours conformity. In the school stories, plot arises from the new pupils, who must each be brought into line with their peers. Whether they are too rebellious (Elizabeth in *The Naughtiest Girl in The School*), or too studious (Pam in *Summer Term at St Clare's*), an extreme of any kind must be corrected. Children, largely through peer pressure, 'knock the corners off' these initiates.

Noddy, the elf-like inhabitant of EB's Toyland, is her most controversial creation. With his little car, 'his taxi in Toyland', Noddy gets into innumerable scrapes and mishaps. Invariably distressed and confused, he is bullied by the other inhabitants of Toyland, with the exception of his friend Big Ears. Despite EB's assurance to her readers that 'he really can be very clever sometimes', Noddy presents children with a model of relentless stupidity. Accused of racism, the Noddy books always feature a black-faced Dr Golly.

Contemporary critics of EB's work become caught up in the controversy surrounding her. Racist, sexist, and determinedly middle-class, her books can also be dismissed on the basis of their fundamental mediocrity: their limited vocabulary, stunted plots, and minimal character development. But her ongoing popularity among child readers is cited in her defence, and critics are hard-put to reconcile this phenomenon with her defects.   AMY GAMERMAN

Selected works: *Enid Blyton Book of Fairies* (1924); *Adventures of the Wishing Chair* (1937); *Mr Galliano's Circus* (1938); *The Enchanted Wood* (1939); *Naughty Amelia Jane!* (1939); *The Naughtiest Girl in the School* (1940); *The Adventurous Four* (1941); *The Twins at St Clare's* (1941); *Five on a Treasure Island* (1942); *The Caravan Family* (1945); *First Term at Malory Towers* (1946); *The Secret Seven* (1949); *Hurrah for Little Noddy* (1950); *Noddy and his Car* (1951); *Noddy in Toyland* (1955).

References: OCCL; Ray, S. G., *The Blyton Phenomenon: The Controversy Surrounding the World's Most Successful Children's Writer* (1982); Stoney, B., *Enid Blyton: A Biography* (1974).

Bodichon, Barbara

b. 18 April 1827, London; d. 11 June 1891, Robertsbridge, Sussex

Polemical writer

BB was the illegitimate daugher of Benjamin Leigh Smith, a Unitarian and the Radical MP for Norwich at the period of the repeal of the Corn Laws, and Anne Longden, a milliner's apprentice. She was educated at home by the unorthodox James Buchanan, who believed that lengthy readings from *The Arabian Nights* and other works of fiction provided a better education than more organized study. BB's illegitimacy led to few social disadvantages, for when she came of age her father took the unusual step of settling an income of £300 annually on her. In the following year she enrolled (together with her Aunt Julia) in the new Ladies' College in Bedford Square, one of the few British institutions of higher education open to women.

BB chose to follow the course given by the Professor of Drawing, Francis S. Cary. She had begun painting and drawing at an early age, but for her this was to become more than a gracious accomplishment. Cary's course was the only opportunity for women artists to receive expert instruction in drawing: the Academy School refused to admit women and consequently women artists found difficulty in exhibiting their work. BB continued to draw and paint throughout her life: her work was admired by, amongst others, Corot, in whose Paris studios she worked for a time. Later in her life her work was widely exhibited and earned her substantial sums of money.

But painting was by no means a full-time occupation for BB. She started a school with the help of Elizabeth Whitehead and other friends. Although founding a school was a widely recognized form of amusement for wealthy Victorian women, BB's school was in many respects unusual: it was co-educational, there was no uniform, and it had no system of punishments. Moreover BB and her friends did much of the teaching themselves. Perhaps more remarkably, the school was attended by children from a wide variety of social backgrounds: the charge for each pupil per week was sixpence, and most of the school's expenses were met by BB and her sisters and friends. Education remained a lifelong preoccupation of BB and she was closely involved in helping Emily Davies set up Girton College, Cambridge, in 1869.

In 1854 BB published a *Brief Summary in Plain Language of the Most Important Laws Concerning Women*. The pamphlet acted as a powerful stimulus to early movements for legal reform, revealing as it did that most married (and divorced) women had virtually no legal rights whatever, and in particular had no right to any property separate from their husband's. The pamphlet also addressed a matter of evident personal concern to BB: it pointed out that illegitimate children had no legal existence of any kind. The Society for the Amendment of the Law agreed to refer the question of the legal status of married women to their Committee on Personal Laws. Meanwhile, a public meeting was arranged which was attended by many leading women writers, including Mary Howitt and Anna Jameson. In some cases, women who had been abandoned by their husbands and subsequently supported themselves by writing or acting had been legally obliged to make over their entire earnings to their husbands. BB's subsequent campaign for a Married Women's Property Bill led her to collect substantial amounts of such empirical information.

In the autumn of 1854 BB's health broke down and she made a long trip to Italy in the hope of improving it. Regular winter trips to the Mediterranean subsequently became a necessity. In 1856 she travelled to Algiers and met a

French doctor, Eugene Bodichon, who despite his descent from an aristocratic Breton family was a convinced republican and revolutionary. They married, and initially BB hoped that Eugene would establish a practice in England. But Bodichon (who was eighteen years older than BB) would not uproot himself, and the couple consequently agreed to live apart for several months of the year. However, they also travelled widely together: in 1857–8 they visited the slave states of America. BB's reflections on Southern culture are recorded in her *American Diary* (1872).

Another figure of central importance in BB's life was George Eliot (Marian Evans). When *Adam Bede* was published anonymously and sold out its first printing of 14,000 copies, BB guessed that Eliot was its author from quotations which she read in book reviews. She was even sufficiently sure of this to write a letter of congratulation to her friend. One strong bond between Eliot and BB was the fact that they had both suffered the attentions of John Chapman, the editor of the *Westminster Review*, who attempted in a series of letters to persuade BB that the only sure remedy for her ill-health was 'the reinvigorating effect on your system of a fulfilment of love's physical desires' and suggested that they should live together as lovers, offering Eliot's relationship with G. H. Lewes as proof of how successfully this could be done. There is no evidence, however, that BB was ever, as has been claimed, Chapman's mistress. Chapman was probably the model for the seducer Tito in Eliot's *Romola*, whilst many of the heroine's physical and mental characteristics are reminiscent of BB.

BB's pamphlet *Women and Work* (1857), arguing that all professions should be open to women, was soon followed by the first number of the *Englishwoman's Journal*, which appeared in 1858. The journal published biographical accounts of women who had demonstrated that contemporary restrictions of the scope of women's tasks and opportunities were arbitrary, such as Florence Nightingale and BB's friend Elizabeth Blackwell, the first woman to qualify as a medical practitioner. French and German literature were closely followed by the journal, which also included reviews of new books in English: an early number contained a witty review of Coventry Patmore's *The Angel In The House*. More surprisingly, the journal acted as a focus for practical projects. Large numbers of unemployed women visited its offices looking for work: a register was taken of their names which formed the basis of the new Society for Promoting the Employment of Women. A successful print shop was set up: the *Journal* was able visibly to demonstrate its assertions that women could do almost any kind of work.

BB was actively involved in the suffrage campaign of the 1860s. The campaign faced severe internal difficulties, for while Emily Davies wished explicitly to restrict the campaign to asking for votes for propertied women, John Stuart Mill (who was to present the petition to Parliament and who was campaigning at the same time for an extension of the franchise in general) threatened to refuse to present the petition if it contained any such restriction. BB played an important role in devising a compromise formulation which implied, though it did not state, that the petition was not immediately concerned with enfranchising unpropertied women. BB's wish to see the universities opened to women came nearer to realization with the establishment in 1869 of Girton College (which moved to its present site in 1873.) In 1877 BB suffered a stroke which left her health permanently impaired. For the last decade of her life after her husband's death she lived all the year round in England. She died in the cottage which she herself had built in Sussex, leaving £10,000 to Girton.

BB's two pamphlets on suffrage, *Reasons for the Enfranchisement of Women*

(1866) and *Objections to the Enfranchisement of Women Considered* (1866) both of which originated as papers given to the National Association for the Promotion of Social Science, are models of careful reasoning. The latter pamphlet is the more interesting, for it calls forth BB's most powerful arguments. The idea that women do not want votes is wittily confuted: 'It is impossible to say positively which side has the majority, unless we could poll all the women in question . . .' And BB equally points out that no suggestion of compulsory voting is being made: women who do not wish to vote simply need not register. But in BB's paper, more explicitly than in the petition, it is made clear that the proposal for enfranchisement 'practically concerns only single women and widows who have 40s. freeholds, or other county qualifications, and for boroughs, all those who occupy, as owners or tenants, houses of the value of £10 a year'.

Reasons for the Enfranchisement of Women indicates the usefulness of the empirical information which BB had gathered during the course of her career about the difficulties faced by women. She was able to show that in certain instances women had been caused considerable hardship through no other reason than their disenfranchisement: in agricultural districts where landlords considered representation in Parliament as a valuable commodity, women were often turned out of their tenancies once their husbands had died. She gives as an example 'one estate on which seven widows have been ejected, who, if they had had votes, would have been continued as tenants'.

Equally interesting with her polemical writings is BB's record of her visit to all but one of the fifteen American slave states, the *American Diary*. BB spent time both with slave-owners and with slaves; her anger at the injustice of slavery continually reminded her of the condition of women in her own country. Moreover, she felt that both cases were not accidental instances of injustice which simply called for particular reforming legislation, but were entirely morally disabling to each country: 'I cannot come amongst these people without the perception that every standard of right and wrong is lost – that they are perverted and degraded by this one falsehood. . . . I feel in England how incapable men and women are of judging rightly on any point when they hold false opinions concerning the rights of one half of the human race.' BB's *American Diary* suggests, where her polemical writings do not, that a movement for the emancipation of woman needs to go beyond legislative reform.

JAMES SMITH

Selected works: *A Brief Summary in Plain Language of the Most Important Laws Concerning Women* (1854); *Women and Work* (1857); *Objections to the Enfranchisement of Women Considered* (1866); *Reasons for the Enfranchisement of Women* (1866); *American Diary* (1872).

References: Burton, H., *Barbara Bodichon 1827–1891* (1949); Haight, G. (ed.), *The George Eliot Letters* (1954–5); Herstein, S. R., *A Mid-Victorian Feminist, Barbara Leigh Smith Bodichon* (1986); Reed, J. (ed.), *Barbara Leigh Smith Bodichon: An American Diary 1857–8* (1972); Spender, D., *Women of Ideas and What Men Have Done to Them* (1983); Stephen, B., *Emily Davies and Girton College* (1927).

Bonhote, Elizabeth
b. 1744, Bungay, Suffolk; d. July 1818, Bungay
Novelist, educational writer
EB appears to have lived an uneventful life in Suffolk, at Bungay and Bury. She married a solicitor, Daniel Bonhote, with whom she had several children. Her husband died in 1808.

Her first work, *The Rambles of Mr Friendly*, was published anonymously in 1772. It purports to describe various characters to be met in Hyde Park, but is in fact a series of essays on the differing morality of the town and country. It was translated into German in 1773. EB published several novels between 1773 and 1796: *The Fashionable Friend, Olivia, Darnley Vale, Ellen Woodley*, and *Bungay Castle*. All are conventional Gothic and romantic works with extremely elaborate plots and little delineation of character, time or place. *Bungay Castle* (1796) is probably the best as it draws on EB's memory of the castle from her childhood.

In 1788 EB wrote a series of essays on education, *The Parental Monitor*. This work was published by subscription and was reprinted in 1796. She claims to have written the essays when in ill-health, fearing she would not live to bring up her children. The work, in two volumes, one for girls and one for boys, was to guide those who would be responsible for her family. Like her novels, this work is typical of its time and the contents differ little from any standard conduct books of the day. EB's final publication was *Feeling* (1810), a book of verse.
         BARBARA BRANDON SCHNORRENBERG

Works: *The Rambles of Mr Friendly* (1772); *The Fashionable Friend* (1773); *Olivia* (1786); *The Parental Monitor* (1788); *Darnley Vale* (1789); *Ellen Woodley* (1790); *Bungay Castle* (1796); *Feeling* (1810).
References: *DNB*; Todd.

Bonner, Hypatia Bradlaugh
b. 31 March 1858, London; d. 25 August 1935, London
Esayist, pamphleteer, writer for children
HBB was the daughter of Charles Bradlaugh, the champion of free thought who became famous as the first Member of Parliament to refuse to swear the oath of allegiance on the grounds of his atheism. The influence of her father and his friends and political allies is everywhere apparent in the work of HBB which is largely comprised of political and propagandist literature.

She was educated at a small school in London run by two sisters, Miss Maria and Miss Annie Burnell, and at a school in Midhurst, Kent, although at her father's request she was withdrawn from all religious instruction. Later a friend of her father's paid for a period of schooling in Paris, but this was cut short by illness. In 1877 she attended the classes of J. H. Levy in political economy at the City of London College, but after only one term the college decided to exclude women students. In this same year, at the age of only 19, she made her first public speech; she spoke in defence of her father and Mrs Besant who were at that time being prosecuted for having published Charles Knowlton's *Fruits of Philosophy* in which the author advocated birth control.

Two years later HBB resumed her studies and enrolled in a course in inorganic chemistry taught by Dr Edward Aveling, the common-law husband of Karl Marx's daughter, Eleanor. She was awarded a first-class certificate in the examination set by the Science and Art Department of the Council for Education. She went on to take examinations in mathematics, mechanics, and biology and eventually matriculated at London University. By 1880 she was herself teaching elementary chemistry at the Hall of Science in London, and her first publication, *Chemistry of the Home*, was a collection of four of her lectures.

In 1881 she met Arthur Bonner, whom she married at Marylebone Registry Office in June 1885. Arthur was the son of a clergyman, but met HBB when he joined the National Secular Society and rejected his father's faith. The couple had two children, Kenneth, born in April 1886, who died when he was only six months old, and Charles, born in April 1890. Throughout her married life HBB campaigned for the causes in which she fervently believed. She continued her father's agitation for a secularized society and wrote many pamphlets on this topic, as well as editing *The National Reformer* and *The Reformer*, both organs of the National Secular Society. All of HBB's work is meticulously researched and vigorously argued.

The only fiction she wrote was a volume of children's stories, although even these were designed to carry a free thought message to young readers. There is very little original in the stories; 'Princess Vera', the main one in the collection, is a tale about a young boy's adventures as he tries to leave a world of exploitation and persecution to quest after an ideal world which can only return when the Princess Vera is released from her prison. The best course for achieving this turns out to be through earnest study of science and nature. In another tale, 'How the World Was Made', an old man explains to his grandchildren that what they have been told about the world being created in six days is merely 'a Jewish fable, believed in by a great many people at one time, but no sensible people believe it today'. Science is again recommended to the children. These stories are of considerable period interest, but probably had little appeal to the audience for whom they were intended.   JUDITH VINCENT

Works: *Chemistry of the Home* (1882); *Princess Vera and Other Stories* (1886); *Charles Bradlaugh: A Record of His Life and Work*, 2 vols (1894); *The Labour System in Assam* (1904); *The Death Penalty* (1908); *Penalties Upon Opinion* (1912); *The Christian Hell* (1913); *Christianity and Conduct* (1919); *Belief, Make-belief and Unbelief* (1920); *Christianizing the Heathen* (1922).

Reference: Bonner, A. and Bonner, C.B., *Hypatia Bradlaugh Bonner* (1942).

Boston, Lucy
b. 1892, Southport, Lancashire
Novelist, poet, writer for children
LB was born into a devout Wesleyan Methodist family, the fifth of the six children of James Wood, an engineer, and Mary Garrett. In her account of her childhood and youth, *Perverse and Foolish* (1979), LB explains how her mother's oppressive puritanism set her on a course of 'outrageous and defiant unconventionality whenever opportunity offered'. She was educated at Downs School, Seaford, Sussex, a Quaker school in Surrey, and a Paris finishing school, before going up to Somerville College, Oxford, to read Classics in 1914. With the outbreak of the First World War, however, she left Oxford to train as a nurse. In 1916, having been dismissed from Addenbrooke's Hospital, Cambridge, on account of 'unfitting conduct for a decent girl', she went to serve in a French military hospital. In 1917 she married her cousin, Harold Boston, an officer in the Royal Flying Corps. Her one son, Peter, was to illustrate most of books.

When her marriage was dissolved in 1935, LB left England for an itinerant life in Italy and Austria, spent chiefly painting. Driven back to England by political circumstances in 1939, she purchased the 700-year-old Manor House in Hemingford Grey, Huntingdonshire, which was to become the 'Green Knowe' of the series of children's novels for which she is best known.

LB did not start writing novels until the age of 60. Her first novel, *Yew Hall* (1954), was written for adults and inspired by the Manor House; in it the narrator accepts her destiny to be 'the temporary vessel of the consciousness of the long, unremembered life of the house'. This theme of continuity was to run through the whole of the *Green Knowe* series, from *The Children of Green Knowe* (1954) in which Tolly, the central character, refers to Green Knowe as 'the Ark' and arrives there through flooded fens, establishing the house as a symbol of renewal, to *The Stones of Green Knowe* (1976), in which each of Roger d'Aulneaux's travels into the future is motivated by his desire to know whether or not the house has survived. Green Knowe transcends the fragmentation of time in several ways; not only is history made palpable by the alterations that have been made to the house across 700 years, but children who have lived in the house in bygone ages reappear. In its inclusiveness and ability to assimilate the past, Green Knowe is the antidote to a world in which human effort has culminated in the madness of war and 'the lunacy of hydrogen bombs', radically undermining our faith in development.

The simultaneity experienced at Green Knowe is in part dependent upon the synthesizing powers of the child's perception. LB claims that reality, in her work, 'has no outside edge' in that the child's imagination can expand it. This is true not only of the *Green Knowe* stories but also of *The Sea Egg* (1967), *Nothing Said* (1971), and *The Fossil Snake* (1975): each of these stories presents an 'impossible' ocurrence (a sea egg, a dryad, a regenerated reptile) which is none the less 'true' in imaginative terms.

LB claims that all her child heroes and heroines are 'dispossessed and looking for what they have lost'. Tolly's parents have gone to live in Burma; blind Susan in *The Chimneys of Green Knowe* (1958) is, on account of her handicap, treated with contempt by most of her family, and her friend-and-servant Jacob has been uprooted from his native Barbados; *The River at Green Knowe* (1959) centres around the refugees Oskar from Poland and Ping from China. In *A Stranger at Green Knowe* (1961), for which LB won the Library Association Carnegie medal in 1962, Ping befriends another displaced 'child', Hanno the gorilla, wrenched from the jungle home which, like Green Knowe itself, is the antithesis of the artificial urban civilization represented by Hanno's soulless concrete cage at London Zoo. Through Hanno's affinities with Ping, LB asserts a strong link between the human and animal worlds, and questions the self-conferred status of humanity; a man-centred conception of the universe is, she insists, 'false and crippling'. Like *The Chimneys*, in which Susan struggles to achieve her independence against all odds, *A Stranger* is an investigation of freedom and the violation of freedom.

LB also wrote poetry throughout her life. The anthology *Time is Undone* (1977) collects twenty-five poems written during the previous fifty years, and includes the sonnet sequence 'Poems in Old Age', much praised by I. A. Richards.   ANNE FERNIHOUGH

Works: *Yew Hall* (1954); *The Children of Green Knowe* (1954); *The Chimneys of Green Knowe* (1958; published in the United States as *The Treasure of Green Knowe*); *The River at Green Knowe* (1959); *A Stranger at Green Knowe* (1961); *An Enemy at Green Knowe* (1964); *The Castle of Yew* (1965); *The Sea Egg* (1967); *The House that Grew* (1967); *Persephone* (1969; published in the United States as *Strongholds*); *The Horned Man, or, Whom Will You Send to Fetch Her Away?* (1970); *Nothing Said* (1971); *Memory in a House* (1973); *The Guardians of the*

House (1974); *The Fossil Snake* (1975); *The Stones of Green Knowe* (1976); *Time is Undone* (1977); *Perverse and Foolish* (1979).
References: Cameron, S., *The Green and Burning Tree* (1977); Chambers, A., 'The reader in the book', *Signal* (23 May 1977); Crouch, M., 'A visit to Green Knowe', *Junior Bookshelf* 26 (December 1962); Crouch, M., 'Lucy Boston at 80', *Junior Bookshelf* 36 (December 1972); Crouch, M. and Ellis, A., *Chosen for Children* (1977); Hollindale, P., 'The novels of L. M. Boston', in *Good Writers for Young Readers* (1977); Robbins, S., 'A nip of otherness, like life: the novels of Lucy Boston', *Children's Literature in Education* 6 (November 1971); Rose, J. A., *Lucy Boston* (1965); Rosenthal, L., 'The development of consciousness in Lucy Boston's *The Children of Green Knowe*', *Children's Literature* 8 (1979); Stott, J. C., 'From here to eternity: aspects of pastoral in the *Green Knowe* series', *Children's Literature* 11 (1982); Townsend, J., *A Sense of Story* (1971); Wintle, J. and Fisher, E., *Pied Pipers: Interviews with Influential Creators of Children's Literature* (1974).

Bottome, Phyllis
b. 31 May 1882, Rochester, Kent; d. 22 August 1963, Hampstead
Novelist, miscellaneous writer
PB was the daughter of an American clergyman, William MacDonald Bottome, and of Margaret Leatham of Yorkshire. She was the third of the couple's four children and the youngest daughter. Educated primarily at home, PB received her formal training in a Catholic girls' boarding school in New York City while her father was pastor at Grace Church from 1890 to 1895. She records in her memoirs, *Search for a Soul* (1948), that she was always interested in novel writing: 'I may truthfully say I became a novelist at age four or five', and goes on to describe herself as 'an imaginative young girl with observant eyes'. In 1896, the family returned to England, settling in Bournemouth. PB began acting lessons in London, but her theatrical debut was cancelled because she contracted pneumonia. She never resumed her studies. As a child, PB noted that she was influenced by Charlotte Brontë's *Jane Eyre*, Olive Schreiner's *Story of an African Farm*, and the poetry of Shelley and Tennyson. Her first novel, *Life the Interpreter*, was published in 1899 when PB was 17.

Both the world wars had a profound effect on PB who abhorred repression of individuality and liberty to an extreme degree. She was especially sensitive to the ravages of war on Austria, where she vacationed and lived for many years, primarily in Vienna. At the same time, her interest in the psychological theories of Alfred Adler, which began around 1930, had a great influence on her prose.

In 1916, PB married Captain Alban Ernan Forbes-Dennis to whom she had been engaged before the war. During the First World War the couple lived first in Marseilles and afterwards in Vienna. It was not until the publication of *Old Wine* (1926), a novel that describes the Austrian aristocracy, that PB received any critical attention, although it was her eighth novel.

Throughout the Second World War, PB apparently lived in Europe and by 1947 had published twenty-four novels after *Old Wine*. Of these, *Mortal Storm* (1937), a novel that shows her sensitivity to persons with psychiatric problems, and *Within the Cup* (1943) (published in America as *Survival*) are representative of her work. *Within the Cup*, a highly successful book, is set in 1939 during the Nazi invasion of Austria. It is the story of Rudi, a Jewish Adlerian psychiatrist, who must flee to England to escape persecution and learn how to survive in his adopted country. *Within the Cup* is virulently anti-Nazi and full of Adler-inspired commentary on individual behaviour and definitions of cultural identity. Although well thought out, the characters are more types than individuals and PB is unable to create sympathy for Rudi's plight or his English hosts because they psychoanalyze each other far too much.

After the war, PB and her husband continued to travel in Austria and Italy and maintained a residence in Kitzbühl in the Alps. Between 1950 and 1961, when PB ceased publishing, she wrote five more novels, two collections of short fiction, a collection of essays, and two more memoirs. In 1963, Daphne du Maurier edited a group of PB's stories entitled *The Best Stories of Phyllis Bottome*.

The strengths of PB's novels are their conscientious craftsmanship, clear style, and absorption of the theories of Adler in a natural way. Unfortunately, she relied excessively on the Adlerian alienated hero as the central character of much of her fiction after 1940 and she limited herself, as a result, to plots that dealt only with psychological problems within the fictive society. In addition to her forty-seven novels, PB also wrote a clear and informative biography of Adler (1939), a life of the author Stella Benson (1943), and, during the wars, pamphlets for the British Ministry of Munitions. Her works have been translated into many languages.   B. E. SCHNELLER

Selected works: Life the Interpreter (1899); The Master Hope (1904); Raw Material (1905); The Imperfect Gift (1907); Broken Music (1907); The Dark Tower (1909); The Crystal Heart (1911); Crooked Answers (with H. de L. Brock) (1911); Secretly Armed (1916); A Certain Star (1917); Second Fiddle (1917); The Derelict and Other Stories (1917); Helen of Troy and Rose (1918); The Kingfisher (1922); The Victim and the Worm (1923); The Perfect Wife (1924); The Depths of Prosperity (with Dorothy Thompson) (1925); The Belated Reckoning (1925); Old Wine (1926); The Rat (1927); The Messenger of the Gods (1927); Wild Grapes (1928); Plain Case (1928); Strange Fruit (1928); Tatter'd Loving (1929); Windlestraws (1929); Devil's Due (1931); Wind in his Fists (1931); The Advance of Harriet (1933); Private Worlds (1934); Stella Benson (1934); Innocence and Experience (1935); Level Crossing (1936); Mortal Storm (1937); Danger Signal (1939; published in the US as Murder in the Bud); Alfred Adler: Apostle of Freedom (1939); The Heart of a Child (1940); Masks and Faces (1940); Formidable Tyrants (1941); London Pride (1941); The Mansion House of Liberty (1941); Within the Cup (1943; published in the US as Survival); From the Life (1944); Individual Countries (1944); The Life-Line (1946); Austria's Contribution towards our New World Order (1946); Search for a Soul (1948); Under the Skin (1950); Fortune's Finger (1950); The Challenge (1953); Man and Beast (1954); Against Whom? (1954; published in the US as The Secret Stair); Not in Our Stars (1955); Eldorado Jane (1956); Walls of Glass (1958); The Goal (1961); Best Stories of Phyllis Bottome, ed. Daphne du Maurier (1963).
References: BA (20); CA; DLB; Dictionary of Literature in the English Language, Living Authors (1931); Kunitz.

Bowen, Elizabeth

b. 1899, Dublin; d. 1973, Hythe, Kent
Novelist
EB, the daughter of Anglo-Irish parents, spent much of her childhood and adolescence in England. In 1923 she married Alan Cameron, later Secretary for Education at the University of Oxford and subsequently Secretary to the Central Council of School Broadcasting at the BBC. In the same year her first

collection of stories was published, under the title *Encounters*. Her first novel, *The Hotel*, appeared in 1927. It was well received, and her subsequent literary career was smooth and successful, although her post-war novels did not invariably win a favourable reception. In 1935 she moved to London, making her home in Clarence Terrace overlooking Regent's Park, an area featured in a number of her novels and tales; henceforward she became a prominent figure in the literary life of the metropolis. During the Second World War she worked at the Ministry of Information. Throughout her life she maintained her links with Ireland, and kept up the family home, Bowen's Court in County Cork, only selling it towards the end of her life when no longer able to afford it. In her final years she lived at Hythe in Kent, the Seale on Sea of *The Death of the Heart*. A history, *Bowen's Court* (1942), and two pieces of autobiographical writing, *Seven Winters* (1942) and *Pictures and Conversations* (1975), describe aspects of her life and background.

EB was a careful and dedicated writer, and everything she wrote is of some degree of interest. Although the ten novels form her principal achievement, she was also an excellent short story writer, publishing seven collections in all (a collected edition in one volume appeared in 1980). She also wrote a history of the Shelbourne Hotel in Dublin and a highly individual travel book, *A Time in Rome* (1960). Two collections of her articles and reviews were published in her lifetime, and two more since her death. A woman of great personal charm and distinguished appearance, she was an accomplished hostess, a witty public speaker, and a popular member of the literary world. Among her friends were Virginia Woolf, Cyril Connolly, Iris Murdoch, and Lord David Cecil.

The Hotel showed not only her gift for comedy but also a brooding sense of the emptiness waiting to engulf the lives of the leisured and well-to-do, about whom, following in the tradition of Henry James and Edith Wharton, most of her fiction was to be concerned. The heroine is the first in a line of clear-sighted innocents who act as catalysts in social dramas which that very innocence has been instrumental in promoting. *The Last September* (1929) depicts an Irish country house at the time of the Troubles of 1920. It draws on memories of Bowen's Court, and makes telling use of landscape, generating a sense of unease that seems to relate to more than the period in which the novel is set. *Friends and Relations* (1931) returns to the world of purely domestic life; even so, the comedy of manners and misunderstandings has troubling overtones. The power of withheld emotion vibrates through all EB's pre-war novels.

The next four mark the middle phase of her achievement. They are concerned with the destructive force of innocence and single-mindedness in a world of necessity ruled by compromise. In *To the North* (1932), the most narrowly focused of them, infatuation and betrayal result in violent death; at the same time much of the book is couched in terms of delicate comedy. *The House in Paris* (1935) works partly through flashback in a moving and intense account of the reverberations upon two small children of a bygone love affair. *The Death of the Heart* (1938) is probably the author's most well-known novel, certainly her most assured if most conventional one. It gives a poignant yet sharply humorous portrayal of the devastation of three lives at the hands of a teenage girl: the outcome, at an intellectual level, is tragic, but there is much deft comedy and acute social observation on the surface. *The Heat of the Day* (1949), like many of the stories in *The Demon Lover* (1946), provides a haunting portrait of life in wartime London. It is EB's most ambitious novel, and represents a widening of her fictional concerns, with a tale of espionage as the fulcrum of the plot. It also contains two prominent working-class characters.

The book's overall success has been a matter of critical controversy, and it contains some of its author's most passionate and brilliant writing. To this extent it is EB's equivalent of Henry James's *The Princess Casamassima*.

Her last three novels deal in variety of styles and methodologies with the impact upon the present of the past. *A World of Love* (1955), the briefest and most lyrical of them, is the tale of a momentary haunting in a dilapidated Irish country house; it is the most mannered and enigmatic of its author's works. *The Little Girls* (1964), more brisk and satirical, constitutes an unnerving investigation into the dangers of trying to bring the past back to life; the final novel, *Eva Trout* (1967), is to some extent a study in heredity and the nature of violence. Both books are notably free from the introspective and meditative quality that characterized their immediate predecessors, and represent an attempt by the author to free herself, if not from her preoccupations, then from the expectations of her readers as to how she would handle them. A posthumously published fragment called 'The Move-In' suggests that she was prepared to develop still further along these lines.

EB has a number of enviable gifts as a writer. From its inception, a persistent vein of mordant humour informed her work, and she belongs to the tradition of those novelists, usually women, who specialize in the satirical portrayal of social snobberies and self-awareness, and their effect upon the nuances of human relationships. Her female characters are more memorable than her male ones; she has a particular understanding (often put to comic effect) of the wayward awkwardness of adolescent girls. Purely on the surface level, her work can be extremely entertaining.

Balancing this interest in human behaviour and motivation one finds a strong sense of physical environment. Whether rural or urban, the setting of EB's tales is always graphically presented (she is especially precise in her descriptions of interiors); but her particular distinction lies in her ability to convey not only the physical but also the psychic impact of any given place. It is this gift which generates much of the emotional intensity in her novels and stories; and it finds its fullest expression in *A Time in Rome*, a highly personal book which was among its author's favourites.

This ability to suggest suprarational, if not supernatural experience not only enriches the presentation of the novels, but also results in a number of successful short stories dealing with the mysterious and uncanny, as well as others of a more visionary nature – 'Mysterious Kor' and 'The Happy Autumn Fields' are examples of the latter. But even here, potential solemnity is often laced with ironic observation. In EB's finest work this sense of the macabre and disturbing is elevated into the perception of underlying mystery.

The imaginative intensity extends to moral concern. A feature of the novels of the middle period is the proliferation of authorial comment, a brooding and at times almost declamatory exposition of the issues raised by the events which the narrator, through these indirect means, describes. At times the novel can be saturated in this authorial voice, one whose impact is furthered by what is occasionally overmannered and quirky prose. The eccentric syntax and phrasing is usually justified in terms of emphasis and exactness of meaning; but in *The Heat of the Day* and *A World of Love*, her two most visionary novels, the mannered can at times degenerate into mannerism.

EB's novels are the product of an aristocratic world. But, although most of her characters are well-to-do and possessed of servants, this aristocracy is less a matter of social rank than of fineness of outlook and emotional fastidiousness. EB is a writer who assumes her readers into her world, thus establishing a fictitious intimacy: she makes great play with the personal pronoun 'one'. Coupled with this, her manner is allusive, at times even cryptic. Much has to be inferred and, in the later novels, much deduced. There is no verbal slack: she works with maximum deliberation even when not at maximum intensity. At their finest, the novels and tales achieve a remarkable fusion of physical with psychic impressions: she is akin to Virginia Woolf in her stress on the act of perception, in her concern to render the quality of livingness. But, unlike Woolf, she is interested in plot and narrative as well: the nature of time is a constant preoccupation in her work. Her novels are never merely impressionistic or absorbed in the present moment only.

The persistent theme throughout her fiction is the power and the unsettling nature of love. For all her sense of literary form, her concern with restraint ('life with the lid on', as she called it) and her eye for detail, she is a romantic novelist. She does not merely record appearances, she explores possibilities. The power of feeling and the shaping capacities of observation are always prominent in her world, making it, for all its physicality, a mental and imaginative one. If she writes very much from within the traditions and manners of her own class, the idiosyncratic and personal character of her work transcends the limitations of mere contemporaneity. It is a great deal more than the distinguished and distinctive product of a particular time.   GLEN CAVALIERO

Selected works: Encounters (1923); Ann Lee's (1926); *The Hotel* (1927); *The Last September* (1929); Friends and Relations (1931); *To the North* (1932); *The Cat Jumps* (1934); *The House in Paris* (1935); *The Death of the Heart* (1938); *Look at Those Roses* (1941); *Bowen's Court* (1942); *Seven Winters* (1943); *The Heat of the Day* (1949); *A World of Love* (1955); *A Time in Rome* (1960); *The Little Girls* (1964); *A Day in the Dark* (1965); *The Good Tiger* (1965); *Eva Trout* (1969); *Pictures and Conversations* (1975); *The Mulberry Tree*, ed. H. Lee (1986).

References: Blodgett, H., *Patterns of Reality: Elizabeth Bowen's Novels* (1975); Kenney, E. J., *Elizabeth Bowen* (1974).

Braddon, Mary

b. 4 October 1835, London; d. 4 February 1915, Richmond

Novelist, poet, playwright

A prolific, controversial, and best-selling novelist, MB also wrote poetry, plays, and short fiction. She edited several magazines owned by her husband, the publisher John Maxwell, including *Belgravia* and *The Mistletoe Bough*, and contributed to *Punch, The World*, and *Figaro*. Her life was in some ways as sensational as the fiction which became her trade mark. Her father, Henry Braddon, deserted the family while MB was still a child. To help support the family, she went on the stage at the age of 19 under the name Mary Seyton. The financial support of an admiring Yorkshire squire named Gilby allowed her to leave the stage and finish *Garibaldi and Other Poems* (1861), 'The Loves of Arcadia' (a comedietta produced at the Strand Theatre in 1860), and her first novel, *Three Times Dead* (1860), revised and released by Maxwell as *The Trail of the Serpent* (1861). By mid-1861 MB was living with Maxwell, whose actual wife, Mary Anne, remained in a Dublin insane asylum until her death in 1874. Only then did MB and Maxwell marry legally, after she had already borne him five children and helped raise the five from his first marriage. Maxwell's attempts to present MB as his lawful wife before 1874 were publicly refuted by his in-laws, leaving his and MB's standing in society painfully ambiguous.

MB's sufferings at the hands of Victorian respectability are reflected in the subtle undermining of social conventions that marks her most interesting novels. MB became adept at manipulating the intricately plotted suspense in the everyday settings that had been popularized by Wilkie Collins's *Woman in White*. In *Lady Audley's Secret* (1862), the spectacular best-seller which defined the 'sensation novel' of the 1860s, the blue-eyed, flaxen-haired 'angel in the house' turns bigamist in order to marry well and murders in order to protect her position; the insanity which constitutes her deepest secret metaphorically underlines her subversion of feminine stereotypes. The heroines of *Aurora Floyd* (1863) and *John Marchmont's Legacy* (1863) similarly confound convention by combining all the traits of the model woman with heinous villainy. In *The Lady's Mile* (1866) MB uses the circular bridal path in Hyde Park to represent the constriction of respectable female lives and the moral and social wilderness beyond it. Despite the fact that *Lady Audley* had made her rich, MB never slackened her pace. Several of her novels during this period began as blood-thirsty serials turned out for magazines like *The Halfpenny Journal* and *Belgravia*, some under the pen name 'Babington White'. MB herself maintained a wry distance from such work, joking in her frequent letters to Edward Bulwer-Lytton about 'the amount of crime, treachery, murder, slow poisoning, and general infamy required by the halfpenny reader'. Some of her experience as a journalist colours the portrait of Sigismund Smith in *The Doctor's Wife* (1864), MB's English version of *Madame Bovary*. *Birds of Prey* (1867) and its sequel, *Charlotte's Inheritance* (1868), offer the best examples of what MB referred to as writing of 'the Balzac-morbid-anatomy-school'.

MB's early novels came under attack for their 'immorality' and 'sensuality' – criticism that often carried innuendoes about her private life with Maxwell. Later MB learned to be more skilful in appearing to satisfy middle-class ideals while subtly satirizing them. In *Strangers and Pilgrims* (1873) and *Lost for Love* (1874) evangelical cant is her target. *Joshua Haggard's Daughter* (1876) was the first of many novels criticizing the irresponsibility and conspicuous consumption of the idle rich, among them *Vixen* (1879), *Just As I Am* (1880), *One Thing Needful* (1886), *Gerard* (1891), and *Rough Justice* (1898). MB's interest in Zola is reflected in the settings and detail of works like 'Under the Red Flag' (1883), *Ishmael* (1884), and *Like and Unlike* (1887). She returned to the sensation novel with spectacular success in *The Fatal Three* (1888). MB's contemporaries often appeared in fictional guise in her works: Gladstone in *The One Thing Needful*, Gerard de Nerval in *Ishmael*, Wilde in *The Rose of Life* (1905). During the 1880s and 1890s MB also produced condensations of Scott's novels for the penny press, children's stories, short sentimental fiction, and several plays. *Dead Love Has Chains* (1907), like several novels in her final years, offers penetrating psychological studies of the sexual ambivalence of the 1890s and 1900s.

Although she may, out of deference to the advice of Bulwer-Lytton and Charles Reade, have tried to make her work more 'serious' and artistic', MB remained an unabashed popularizer. As she herself admitted, she was too often struck by the ridiculous side of things to be swayed much by the sentimental; she always maintained an ironic distance from the very stereotypes she was exploiting. Notwithstanding the unevenness of her work, she stands out as a shrewd and skilful manipulator of plot, convention, and detail who earned the admiration of Thackeray, Bulwer-Lytton, Reade, Stevenson, George Moore, Henry James, and others. Her tremendous success sprang from her ability to satisfy popular tastes, but her lasting interest derives from the skill with which she questioned and unsettled popular values.   ROSEMARY JANN

Selected works: Three Times Dead (1860); *The Black Band* (1861); *Garibaldi*

(1861); *The Lady Lisle* (1862); *Lady Audley's Secret* (1862); *Captain of the Vulture* (1863); *Aurora Floyd* (1863); *Eleanor's Victory* (1863); *John Marchmont's Legacy* (1863); *Henry Dunbar* (1864); *Only a Clod* (1865); *Sir Jasper's Tenant* (1865); *Ralph the Bailiff and Other Tales* (1867); *Rupert Godwin* (1867); *Charlotte's Inheritance* (1868); *Run to Earth* (1868); *Fenton's Quest* (1871); *Robert Ainsleigh* (1872); *To the Bitter End* (1872); *Milly Darrell* (1873); *Lucius Davoren* (1873); *Taken at the Flood* (1874); *A Strange World* (1875); *Dead Men's Shoes* (1876); *Joshua Haggard's Daughter* (1876); *An Open Verdict* (1878); *Vixen* (1879); *Aladdin and Other Stories* (1880); *The Missing Witness* (1880); *Just as I Am* (1880); *Asphodel* (1881); *Mount Royal* (1882); *Flower and Weed* (1883); *The Golden Calf* (1883); *Ishmael* (1884); *Wyllard's Weird* (1885); *One Thing Needful* (1886); *Under the Red Flag and Other Stories* (1886); *Mohawks* (1886); *Like and Unlike* (1887); *The Fatal Three* (1888); *The Day Will Come* (1889); *Gerard* (1891); *The Venetians* (1892); *The Christmas Hirelings* (1894); *Sons of Fire* (1895); *London Pride* (1896); *In High Places* (1898); *Rough Justice* (1898); *The Infidel* (1900); *A Lost Eden* (1904); *The Rose of Life* (1905); *The White House* (1906); *Dead Love Has Chains* (1907); *During Her Majesty's Pleasure* (1908); *Beyond These Voices* (1910); *The Green Curtain* (1911); *Miranda* (1913); *Mary* (1916).

References: Allibone; *DNB*; Drabble; Garrison, D., 'Immoral fiction in the late Victorian library', *American Quarterly* 28 (Spring 1976); Hoys, F., *Women of the day* (1885); Hughes, W., *The Maniac in the Cellar* (1980); James, H., *Notes and Reviews* (1921); Sadleir, M., *Things Past* (1944); Showalter, E., *A Literature of Their Own* (1977); Wolff, R. L., *Sensational Victorian* (1879).

Bray, Anna Eliza
b. 25 December 1790, Newington, Surrey; d. 21 January 1883, London
Novelist, miscellaneous writer
AB was the daughter of John Kempe, a bullion carrier in the Mint, and of Ann Arrow of Westminster. She had one brother, Alfred Kempe, an artist. AB studied for the stage but illness prevented her theatrical debut in 1815. In 1818, she married the artist Charles Alfred Stothard, who specialized in the illustration of sculptured monuments in Britain. Her first published work, *Letters Written During a Tour Through Normandy, Brittany and Other Parts of France in 1818* (1820) contains thirty-two letters written during her travels with her husband from July to November of 1818. Illustrated by her husband, the volume contains architectural and historical descriptions of French towns as well as anecdotal descriptions of the people the couple encountered. The largest section of this 300-page book is devoted to the Bayeux tapestry, a part of which AB was falsely accused of stealing by the curators in the 1860s. AB's marriage to Charles Stothard ended prematurely with his accidental death in May 1821. In 1832 AB completed and published the book on which Stothard was working, *Monumental Effigies of Great Britain*. Also that year she published *Memoirs of Charles Stothard* and in 1851, the life of her father-in-law, Thomas Stothard, a distinguished artist.

In 1822, AB married the Rev. Edward Atkyns Bray of Tavistock. From 1826 to 1874, she published fourteen novels, three historical biographies, two descriptive sketches, one topical history and her collected novels in ten volumes covering publications from 1826 through 1844. *The White Hoods* (1828) and *Warleigh, or, The Fatal Oak: A Legend of Devon* (1834) are characteristic of her fiction. Both are historical romances, set in the wilds of the English countryside and incorporating legends and folklore. Well in excess of 300 pages long, the novels have flat characters, trite dialogue and obvious plots, but were, nevertheless, all extremely popular.

AB was best known for her series of letters to the poet Robert Southey on the superstitions and traditions of Tavistock, published as *A Description of that Part of Devonshire Bordering on the Tamar and the Tavy in a Series of Letters to Robert Southey* (1836). These sixty-odd letters were written between February 1832 and October 1835 and contain vignettes of British history, personal news, descriptions of important persons of Devonshire, such as the poet, William Browne, and anecdotes of local history. She also included specimens of her husband's poetry which she was to publish separately after his death in 1857 as *Poetical Remains* (1859). Following the success of *A Description*, AB published *A Peep at the Pixies, or, Legends of the West* (1854) for children, written in the same clear, reporting style as her previous non-fictional writings, and again it contained romantic legends of the West Country. In 1857 she moved to London and published a life of Handel. From 1859 to 1870, she published nothing. Then in 1870 she brought out two non-fictional works based on episodes in French history and a life of Joan of Arc in 1874. Her last three novels were published in 1871, 1874, and 1880. In 1884, her *Autobiography* appeared with an introduction by her nephew, John A. Kempe. This work, which covers her life up until 1843, is clearly and more energetically written than her other non-fictional writing.

In commenting on why AB was obscure even in her own day, John Kempe states, 'The truth is, that save for Southey, she had made but few acquaintants among the leading spirits of her day. . . . Her understanding of current events . . . was guided more by feeling than reflection. A great speech would rouse her by its eloquence but she would have little real perception of [the events] bearing upon the present. If she spoke of them, they did but lead her back to the past. . . . It was this failure of mental grasp which prevented her from ranking as a letter-writer and therefore, a receiver of letters.' Kempe also faults her novels for excessive detail, saying she did not know how to 'condense' and suggests that, although popular, they were out of date in their own day.

B. E. SCHNELLER

Selected works: Letters Written During a Tour Through Normandy, Brittany, and Other Parts of France in 1818 (1820); *Memoirs . . . of the late C. Stothard and Some Account of a Journey in the Netherlands* (1823); *DeFoix, or, Sketches of the Manners and Customs of the Fourteenth Century* (1826); *The White Hoods* (1828); *Warleigh, or, The Fatal Oak: A Legend of Devon* (1834); *A Description of that Part of Devonshire Bordering on the Tamar and the Tavy in a Series of Letters to Robert Southey* (1836); *Trelawny of Trelawne, or, The Prophecy: A Legend of Cornwall* (1837); *Courtney of Warbeddon: A Romance of the West* (1844); *The Life of Thomas Stothard with Personal Reminiscences* (1851); *A Peep at the Pixies, or, Legends of the West* (1854); *Handel: His Life, Personal and Professional* (1857); *Silver Lining, or, Light and Shade* (1874); *Joan of Arc and the Times of Charles VIIth King of France* (1874); *Autobiography*, ed. J. A. Kempe (1884).

References: BA (19); *DNB*; Hale, Mrs, *Woman's Record* (1870).

Brazil, Angela

b. 30 November 1869, Preston, Lancashire; d. 11 March, 1947, Coventry
Writer for girls
AB was the fourth child and second daughter of Clarence Brazil, a cotton mill manager of Irish descent and Angelica McKinnal, part Scottish, part Spanish

from Rio de Janeiro. She was educated at Ellerslie College, Manchester, where she was both a day and boarding pupil, experiencing the kind of fervent friendships that would be so prominent a feature of her schoolgirl novels and learning the joys of bossing and mothering younger children. During this time her family took a cottage in Llanbedr overlooking the Conway Valley; AB's love of the wild countryside of Wales and the rustic living in the cottage finds expression in many of her later stories. On leaving school she studied at Heatherley's art school in London and after her father's death in 1899, travelled with her mother, settling around 1911 in Coventry with her doctor brother, Walter. Her elder sister Amy joined them after their mother's death in 1915 to form what one acquaintance called 'a kind of holy trinity' (the other brother Clarence was the only one to marry). In Coventry she played an active part in cultural life, being a tireless committee woman, and was famous for her children's (and probably less enjoyable adult) parties of jellies and games. She was also an active conservationist, very much concerned to arrest the exploitation of the land. As a person she was found rather intimidating by many, with her bossy manner and cultured demeanour, and she no doubt displayed something of the snobbishness which is expressed in her books. She was famous for wearing mauve and was easily associated with the Lavender Lady, a character in *For the School Colours* (1918), who was a 'poetess' and 'wore a soft lavender dress and an old lace fichu' and was deeply loved by a young girl (the fictional friendship bears some resemblance to that between AB and Dolly Milward, with whom AB travelled in later years).

AB started her writing career with *The Mischievous Brownie* (1899), four plays for children, but she found her characteristic subject only in her mid-30s with *A Terrible Tomboy* (1904), published with illustrations by herself and her sister Amy, in which she gave to the eager energetic Peggy at the age of five many of her own perceived traits. The book was well-received and was followed by *The Fortunes of Philippa* (1906), the first of her school tales which drew movingly on her mother's experience of being a child from South America coming to boarding school in England. More characteristic of AB's later style was, however, *The Third Class at Miss Kaye's* (1908) which describes in detail the school round of sports and friendships; it was followed by *The Nicest Girl in the School* (1909), probably her most popular book, and over forty similar schoolgirl titles. Since she published her books often at the rate of several a year, they were inevitably written to a formula and many of the heroines with names such as Aveline, Rosemunde, Arduine and Merle are interchangeable. Yet, since she resisted the temptation to write series, she could respond to changes in style and public concern. During the First World War her books became virulently anti-German; in *A Popular Schoolgirl* (1920) the girls help in 'their small way, not to let the Great War be forgotten.' AB also wrote copiously for periodicals such as *Little Folks* and *Our School Magazine*. As an adult she kept in touch with schoolgirl life by constant visits to schools and by schoolgirl penfriends.

The schoolbooks with their foundlings and castaways draw on AB's own childhood experiences as well as on fantasies fed by fairy tales. They heartily approve the robust, plucky, cheery girl who likes fair play, has 'jolly hols' and finds things 'absolutely ripping', while they despise the goody-goody type. Mothers are usually sympathetic and fathers noble but distant. The books are famous for their jolly-hockey-sticks ethos – AB thought hockey, which had played no part in her own schooldays, broke down barriers between people and constructively used up adolescent energy – and for their use of schoolgirl slang which some readers find fanciful, believing that schoolgirls could never have used such whimsical expressions, while others claimed that they served as informants for AB's works. The books are also famous or notorious for their lack of modern sex consciousness, for AB describes both in her novels and in her autobiography *My Own Schooldays* (1925) 'white-hot' friendships between girls which draw on her fascination with mystical experiences and reveal souls reaching to souls. These intense friendships are conveyed in the language usually reserved for adult passion, with the participants being jealous and love-lorn, falling in love, kissing, adoring, and swearing eternal fidelity. 'There are in this world those who love and those who are loved,' she wrote in one novel, 'and Isobel was ready with spendthrift generosity to offer her utmost in way of friendship, finding Belle's pretty thanks and kisses a sufficient reward for any trouble she might take on her account.' Over the years as society became more sexually conscious, her descriptions tended to lessen in intensity and by the 1930s there is little mention of the warm physical contact so stressed in the early books.

AB saw herself in adulthood as 'an absolute schoolgirl' and her apparently arrested development is mirrored in her fictive Peter Pan world of secret benevolent societies – *The Little Green School* (1931) and *The School in the South* (1922) – where sweets are always a comfort and solace, and life a clear contest between duty and the baser self; nice boys can be friends but need not become romantic options. Yet, despite the naive quality of AB's books and the falling off in the later ones, she remains important as the originator of a genre, developing the children's novel of the 1880s and 1890s, associated with L. T. Meade and concerned with the years in boarding school, into an investigation of the nature of schooling and the schoolgirl as a type. Her books, whether true or not to childhood slang, do chart the changes in education over the forty years of her writing. Her early ones tend to describe small schools as well as large public boarding institutions, while her later ones reflect the more professional establishments of the 1920s and 1930s, with their emphasis on examinations, which AB always disapproved as a 'relic of the barbarous age' (*Loyal to the School*, 1921), and their stress on a graded hierarchy of teachers, monitors and prefects, which she much approved. In *The Leader of the Lower School* (1913), she described a school as 'a state in miniature'. AB's books also well reflect the changing ideal of girlhood; the emphasis on being a lady disappears to be replaced by concern for being a good type and a good sport.

JANET TODD

Selected works: *The Mischievous Brownie* (1899); *The Fairy Gifts* (1901); *The Enchanted Fiddle* (1903); *A Terrible Tomboy* (1904); *The Fortunes of Philippa* (1906); *The Third Class at Miss Kaye's* (1908); *The Nicest Girl in the School* (1909); *The Manor House School* (1910); *The New Girl at St. Chad's* (1911); *A Fourth Form Friendship* (1911); *A Pair of Schoolgirls* (1912); *The Leader of the Lower School* (1913); *For the Sake of the School* (1915); *The Madcap of the School* (1917); *For the School Colours* (1918); *Loyal to the School* (1920); *The School in the South* (1922); *My Own Schooldays* (1925); *The Little Green School* (1931); *The School at the Turrets* (1936); *Jill's Jolliest School* (1937); *Five Jolly Schoolgirls* (1941); *Three Terms at Uplands* (1945); *The School on the Loch* (1946).

References: Avery, G., *Childhood Patterns* (1975); Cadogan, M. and Craig, P., *You're a Brick, Angela!* (1976); Freeman, G., *The Schoolgirl Ethic: The Life and Work of Angela Brazil* (1976); OCCL.

Bridge, Ann

b. 1889, Bridgend, Surrey; d. 1974

Novelist, travel writer

The wife of a British Foreign Official, AB was aware throughout her career of the possibility of censorship and the need for decorum and strict pseudonymity. This did little to restrict her huge output of popular fiction, however. Although AB's mother was American and her father English, AB passed much of her childhood in northern Italy. *Enchanter's Nightshade* (1937), a detailed and sporadically lively cameo of Italian provincial society in the early 1900s, benefits from her observations at this time.

AB's education continued back in Surrey and at the London School of Economics. Subsequently she married Sir Owen O'Malley, with whom she had one son and one daughter. Active in war relief work during the Second World War, she travelled widely with her husband and encountered a variety of dignitaries. AB spent over a year in the States, settling finally in Ireland, by which time she was fluent in French, German, Italian, and Chinese. Indeed China, where AB spent some time, provided the inspiration for her first novel, *Peking Picnic* (1932). Doing for China what *A Passage to India* had done for the subcontinent, the novel immediately won the *Atlantic Monthly* Prize and remains interesting for its combination of a deftly managed plot with some insight into the obscure workings of human relationships. Still set in the Far East, *Four Part Setting* (1939), in which a party journeys from Peking into the mountains, sees AB shed some of her authorial aloofness, almost making real protagonists of her characters.

AB contrived a blend of travel writing, history, and romance; exotic locations remain a staple of her work. In *Illyrian Spring* (1935), Yugoslavia is the backdrop to an examination of the relationship between a painter, Lady Kilmichael, and a younger man. Ostensibly the heroine is thus forced to recognize her own past mistakes; but the author's judgmental voice – 'Lady Kilmichael had no dramatic sense about herself; it never occurred to her to take herself romantically' – works against the notion of such new-found self-discovery. *Singing Waters* (1945), set in Albania, similarly depicts a woman tackling life with fresh resolve after initial disorientation in a foreign country.

AB's most successful novel is *The Dark Moment* (1952), based in revolutionary Turkey under Mustafa Kemal Ataturk. The fabric of the text is cross-stitched with detail researched by AB in Turkey in 1940. Once more AB demystifies an alien culture for a western readership. Evidently fascinated by Kemal, AB makes a real attempt to sound out his enigmatic personality through the eyes of her heroine, Fanny. At the same time the novel communicates the difficulty faced by Feride, a pasha's daughter, in adopting western standards and mores.

AB's work is uneven. Often she provides a superabundance of lucid dialogue and travelogue, as in *The Numbered Account* (1960). She is adept at evoking peaceful landscapes in which characters gently meditate upon their own or others's situations and emotions and her authorial comments on human behaviour are perceptive, sometimes profound; incidents are well-structured, and she does not push plots to inappropriately happy endings. However, she has an inconsistent narrative stance, especially in some of the later novels fluctuating between authorial omniscience of a character's innermost thoughts and a remote detachment; this weakens the credibility of her characters, making them insubstantial rather than vital, complex individuals. There is a degree of stereotyping in the characterization too, which includes an element of unattractive snobbery. At her best, though, AB's interest in the comedy of manners is rescued from two-dimensionality by her awareness of the potential tragedy of personal responsibility for happiness.   E. LEVY AND JUDITH ALDRIDGE

Selected works: *Peking Picnic* (1932); *Ginger Griffin* (1934); *Illyrian Spring* (1935); *The Song in the House: Short Stories* (1936); *Enchanter's Nightshade* (1937); *Four-Part Setting* (1939); *Frontier Passage* (1942); *The Singing Waters* (1945); *And Then You Came* (1948); *The House at Kilmartin* (1951); *The Dark Moment* (1952); *A Place to Stand* (1953); *The Light-hearted Quest* (1956); *The Portuguese Escape* (1958); *The Numbered Account* (1960); *The Tightening String* (1962); *Emergency in the Pyrenees* (1965); *Episode at Toledo* (1967); *The Malady at Madeira* (1970); *Permission to Resign: Goings On in the Corridors of Power* (1971).

References: Cadogan, M. and Craig, P., *Women and Children First*; Hoehn, M. (ed.), *Catholic Authors* (1974); Reilly, J. M. (ed.), *Twentieth Century Crime and Mystery Writers* (1980).

Brittain, Vera

b. 29 December 1893, Newcastle-under-Lyme; d. 29 March 1970, London
Novelist, biographer, lecturer, journalist, poet

VB achieved lasting fame for her poignant autobiographical account of the First World War, *Testament of Youth* (1933). In the second part of her autobiography, *Testament of Experience* (1957), she described the writing of the book as a cathartic experience through which the ghosts of the war years were finally laid to rest: 'the actual decanting into words of past grief for lost loves is a form of exorcism, leaving the way clear for new patterns of tenderness.' Yet *Testament of Youth* did not end VB's preoccupation with war, and the shadow of her experience remains over practically her entire life and works.

VB was brought up in Buxton, Derbyshire to what she termed 'provincial young ladyhood'. She found the intellectual restrictions of this lifestyle deeply frustrating, and saw university as her only hope of escape. She campaigned vigorously against parental opposition to her plans, and succeeded in gaining an exhibition to Somerville College, Oxford in 1914. She received vital support from her younger brother Edward, to whom she was very close. It was through Edward that VB met and fell in love with Roland Leighton, who was also to have gone to Oxford in 1914. These plans were shattered by the outbreak of war, and VB found herself alone at college while Edward and Roland went to fight in the 'Great War'.

The war was to alter fundamentally the course of VB's life. By 1915 she was unable to bear the inactivity of Oxford, and in her desire for positive action she had joined a Voluntary Aid Detachment (VAD) as a nurse. The work was demanding, but when the news came at Christmas 1915 of Roland Leighton's death, VB volunteered for service abroad. Throughout her life VB maintained the belief that work was the only way to assuage the pain of grief and bereavement. In 1916 she was sent to Malta and afterwards served at Etaples in France. By 1918 she had lost not only her fiancé, but also her brother and almost every male acquaintance of her generation.

VB found temporary relief in poetry. Her *Verses of a VAD* were published in 1918 and reissued with some new work in 1934 as *Poems of the War and After*. The poetry has been described as 'extremely banal', but seen within context it represents a remarkable attempt to express emotions and experiences which defied the literary vocabulary of the day. One of the most impressive of these poems, 'Sic Transit', achieves considerable effect through its extremely economical style. Elevated diction and a complex sentence structure are juxtaposed to simple monosyllabic statements, achieving a rhythm in which the hope and happiness the poet desires is destroyed with exhausting regularity.

> I am so tired
> The dying sun incarnadines the west,
> And every window with its gold is fired;
> And all I loved the best
> Is gone, and every good that I desired
> Passes away, an idle hopeless quest,
> Even the highest whereto I aspired
> Has vanished with the rest.
> I am so tired.

In *Testament of Youth* VB describes the pain and confusion into which she was thrown by the death of Roland. 'Numerous other correspondents counselled patience and endurance; time, they told me with maddening unanimity, would heal. I resented the suggestion bitterly, I could not believe it, and did not even want it to be true. If time did heal I should not have kept faith with Roland, I thought, clinging assiduously to my pain, for I did not then know that if the living are to be of any use in this world, they must always break faith with the dead.' *Testament of Youth* is very long, at times overwritten, but always sincere, poignant, and moving. It was the first set of war memoirs to chronicle the impact of the war on non-combatants.

The book does not end with the war. The passionate memorial to the dead concludes with the second part of the book; part 3 continues with a chronicle of the healing process of the post-war years, including VB's return to Oxford in 1919. It was there that she met Winifred Holtby whose friendship would help her adjust to post-war life. Although Holtby was several years younger than VB, she too had experienced the war, albeit briefly, as a volunteer in Queen Mary's Army Auxiliary Service. This bond of common experience underpinned a friendship which would survive VB's subsequent marriage. In 1922 the two left Oxford with second-class degrees in history, and set up house together in London with the intention of pursuing careers as freelance journalists and writers. Initially it was Holtby who achieved the greater success. Her first novel, *Anderby Wold* (1923), was well received, while VB's *Dark Tide* (1923) struggled to find a publisher. Yet while Holtby found professional success, VB found personal happiness in her relationship with George Catlin. Catlin first saw her at Oxford, but their romance was largely conducted by post. Their meeting forms the climax of *Testament of Youth*, being symbolic of the end of VB's period of mourning for the war dead and representing the beginning of a new life.

The couple married in 1925 and moved initially to the US where Catlin was a professor at Cornell University. The move was not a successful one for VB, who could get nothing published there; she was bored and depressed by the restricted social life of the isolated academic community. The outcome was a 'semi-detached marriage'; she returned to England for the sake of her career, while Catlin remained in the US for the sake of his. The arrangement succeeded and continued through the birth of VB's two children, John and Shirley, although VB's life without her husband was greatly dependent upon the assistance of Winifred Holtby.

When in 1936 Holtby died, VB lost a truly devoted friend. VB became

Holtby's literary executor, and was responsible for the posthumous publication of her most famous book, *South Riding*. She was immediately asked to produce a biography of Holtby, and in 1940 *Testament of Friendship* appeared after some delay. It is a comprehensive, if rather flowery, tribute to her friend, helped by the success of *South Riding*, which ensured the biography a far wider audience than it would have received in 1936.

None of VB's five novels achieved the success of Holtby's, although she did acquire a small but loyal corpus of regular readers. Her fourth and fifth novels, *Account Rendered* (1945) and *Born 1925* (1948), have been recently reissued, and while they shed interesting light on VB's concerns and preoccupations, they also clearly reveal why she will be remembered as a chronicler rather than as a novelist. The novels are readable, if sometimes long-winded and digressive, and areas which relate to her personal experience are usually well-written and effective. The problems arise with her attempts to describe events and emotions outside her experience. VB was an extremely reserved and controlled woman who seldom exhibited emotion. In *Account Rendered* her imagination failed her when she attempted to depict the devoted love of the young and ill-educated Enid for her much older employer Francis. The characterization of Enid is uncomfortably melodramatic; unable to overcome the difficulties of creating emotional moments, VB resorts to clichés: 'murder! Oh, then let me hang instead of him! cried her sorrowful heart.' Another problem is VB's tendency to lecture, in this case on the profound and persistent consequences of war and the unseen damage it causes to humanity. Throughout the book there are largely digressive sections discussing the themes of war and pacifism.

Born 1925 suffers less than *Account Rendered* from VB's tendency to overdramatize and to stereotype lesser characters. She seems much more secure in this family saga contrasting the response of two generations to the Second World War. Robert and Sylvia both experienced the First World War, and it had affected them in a way that their children, Adrian and Josephine, cannot understand. Robert's pacifism and his decision to enter the ministry are well drawn, but by far the most impressive piece of characterisation is VB's portrayal of the actress Sylvia who has been left emotionally numb by the wartime loss of her first husband. When Sylvia is approached by another man after her marriage to Robert her response is thus: 'She feared she might surrender to Damon out of the same profound indifference that had been responsible for her consent to marry Robert.' It is a considerable achievement that VB is able to put herself outside her beliefs and provide a credible description of Adrian's cynical reaction against his father's pacifist beliefs.

While VB struggled at fiction, she found herself naturally gifted at public speaking. From her early days in London supporting the Labour Party, the United Nations, and the Six Point Group, she progressed to several successful lecture tours of the US. The initial invitation to tour the US resulted from the success of *Testament of Youth*, but subsequent invitations stemmed from her ability as a speaker and the intense American interest in Europe.

By the 1930s the central theme of VB's public speaking and journalistic work was pacifism. In 1936 she joined the Peace Pledge Union of Canon Dick Sheppard, and maintained her pacifist stance throughout the Second World War, in spite of the personal consequences. In *Testament of Experience* she described the dilemma which faced her. 'For three years now I had enjoyed outstanding success in different parts of the world, and had savoured that rare experience the more fully owing to the long period of frustration before it. Everything in me recoiled from the prospect of exchanging this welcome stimulus for public disapproval.' Whatever her political feelings about the war, though, VB worked tirelessly throughout its duration. She refused to assist the Ministry of Information with government propaganda, but she produced a regular newsletter addressed to peace lovers everywhere. She also assisted with the evacuation of children and wrote a documentary book, *England's House* (1941), based on her visits to some of the worst hit areas of London. The conclusion of the war, however, brought an unexpected vindication of both VB and her husband, who was also a committed pacifist. In spite of spending the war distrusted by the British authorities, both their names appeared on the Gestapo death list of conspicuous enemies of the Third Reich. The following excerpt from an article published in the *Christian Century* reveals the deep pain caused her by man's inhumanity to man: 'Not, probably, until next winter will the full price of massacre bombing come home to half-starved, half-frozen Europeans. It made no undeniable contribution to military victory, and it relegated men, for whose salvation Christ died, to the level of hunted and outraged beasts. It has postponed to a degree not yet calculable the true dawn of peace and reconstruction, which arises, and can only arise, from international security, confidence and hope.'

In the 1950s VB became a staunch supporter of the Campaign for Nuclear Disarmament.   GILL PLAIN

Works: *Verses of a VAD* (1918); *The Dark Tide* (1923); *Not Without Honour* (1924); *Women's Work in Modern England* (1928); *Halcyon, or, The Future of Monogamy* (1929); *Testament of Youth* (1933); *Poems of the War and After* (1934); *Honourable Estate* (1936); *Thrice a Stranger. New Chapters of Autobiography* (1938); *Testament of Friendship* (1940); *England's Hour* (1941); *Humiliation with Honour* (1942); *One of These Little Ones. A Plea to Parents and Others for Europe's Children* (1943); *Seed of Chaos: What Mass Bombing Really Means* (1944); *Above All Nations* (1945); *Account Rendered* (1945); *On Becoming a Writer* (1947); *Born 1925* (1948); *In the Steps of John Bunyan* (1950); *Search After Sunrise* (1951); *The Story of St Martin's* (1951); *Lady into Woman: A History of Women from Victoria to Elizabeth II* (1953); *Testament of Experience* (1957); *Selected Letters of Winifred Holtby and Vera Brittain* (1960); *The Women at Oxford: A Fragment of History* (1960); *Pethick-Lawrence: A Portrait* (1963); *The Rebel Passion: A Short History of Some Pioneer Peace-Makers* (1964); *Envoy Extraordinary. A Study of Vijaya Lakshmi Pandit* (1965); *Radclyffe Hall: A Case of Obscenity?* (1968).

References: Bailey, H., *Vera Brittain* (1987); Berry, P., 'Introduction' to *Testament of a Generation: The Journalism of Vera Brittain and Winifred Holtby* (1985); Bishop, A. (ed.), *Chronicle of Youth: Vera Brittain's War Diary 1913–17* (1981); *CA; DLB; DNB;* Drabble.

Brontë, Anne
b. 17 January 1820, Thornton, Yorkshire; d. 28 May 1849, Scarborough
Novelist
As the youngest member of the Brontë family, AB has always suffered by comparison with her sisters. It is still a moot point whether we would read her at all if she had not been the sister of Emily and Charlotte, forming a sad part of their tragic story, and offering comparisons between her novels and the far more famous *Jane Eyre* and *Wuthering Heights*.

AB was the sixth child and fifth daughter of the Reverend Patrick Brontë and Maria Branwell. When she was very young her family moved to Haworth, and in the next year her mother died. The children's aunt, Elizabeth Branwell, came to live with the family and appears to have educated AB largely at home. Around 1836 AB went with Charlotte to Miss Wooler's school, but was not happy there. Spells as a governess with the Inghams of Blake Hall and the Robinsons of Thorp Green were not happy either, although in the latter post she stayed for about five years, and apparently won the respect of her pupils. Returning home in June 1845, probably because of her brother Branwell's disgraceful conduct while tutor with the Robinsons, she joined her sisters in publishing some of the poems she had been writing. A love affair with William Weightman, curate at Haworth, who died in 1842, has been postulated, but there is no certain evidence for this, although some sad love poetry might suggest it. *Agnes Grey* was published in 1847 together with *Wuthering Heights*, and *The Tenant of Wildfell Hall* in 1848. The first novel received little critical attention, the second was regarded as shocking. AB fell ill at the end of 1848, and, although she lingered through the winter, she died in May 1849, having made a final journey to Scarborough, where she is buried.

Charlotte Bronte was very fond of her sister but, in preparing a second edition of *Agnes Grey* in 1850, she made disparaging remarks about AB's work, saying of *The Tenant of Wildfell Hall* that the choice of subject was an entire mistake. Modern critics have tended to see both novels as aids to biography. *Agnes Grey* tells the story of a governess who is badly treated by two families until eventually she is rescued by a kindly clergyman who marries her. William Weightman and Anne's two employers are supposed to be models for this tale, although there are many differences between fact and fiction. Instead, *Agnes Grey* should be seen as a novel about education, with lessons to be learnt from the poor upbringings in both families and, more subtly, from the exploitation of innocence in Agnes. *The Tenant of Wildfell Hall* is about the unhappy marriage of Helen Huntingdon to the dissolute and adulterous Arthur. There are links with Branwell here, although Arthur's conviviality seems unlike the sordid drinking habits of Branwell. Although the novel is heavily moral, with Helen's virtue rewarded by the death of Arthur and marriage to Gilbert Markham, who is the narrator of the first and third sections, Helen's diary in the centre contains disturbing hints that she may be partly responsible for the breakdown of the marriage through her innocent piety. TOM WINNIFRITH

Works: *Agnes Grey* (1847); *The Tenant of Wildfell Hall* (1848).

References: Bronte, C., 'Biographical notice of Ellis and Acton Bell', in 2nd edn of *Wuthering Heights and Agnes Grey* (1850); Chitham, E. (ed.), *The Poems of Anne Bronte: A New Text and Commentary* (1929); Craik, W. A., *The Bronte Novels* (1968); *DNB;* Drabble; Eagleton, T., *Myths of Power: A Marxist Study of the Brontës* (1975); Ewbank, I. S., *Their Proper Sphere – A Study of the Bronte Sisters as Early Victorian Novelists* (1966); Gérin, W., *Anne Bronte* (1959); Hale, W. T., *Anne Bronte: Her Life and Writings* (1929); Harrison, A. and Stanford, D., *Anne Bronte: Her Life and Work* (1950).

Bronte, Charlotte

b. 21 April 1816, Thornton; d. 31 March 1855, Haworth

Novelist

In her lifetime CB was easily the most famous of the Bronte sisters, and Mrs Gaskell's biography made her more so. This biography, great work of art though it is, has meant that we have tended to see CB through Victorian spectacles, especially since Mrs Gaskell relied heavily on correspondence to

CB's rather conventional friend, Ellen Nussey. Recent scholarship and criticism have shown CB in a more original light.

After her mother's death in 1821 she remained at home in Haworth until 1824. In that year her father, the Rev. Patrick Brontë, sent her to school with her elder sisters, Maria and Elizabeth, at the Clergy Daughters' School at Cowan Bridge, Lancashire. Both Elizabeth and Maria fell ill at this school and returned home to die. CB's experiences at Cowan Bridge have certain affinities with those of Jane Eyre at Lowood. After returning home in 1825 she stayed in Haworth for six years. During these years she began a precocious career as a writer of poems and romantic fiction. The juvenilia of both CB and her brother Branwell have received much attention recently, although the affinities between the mature novels and the juvenilia, and the literary merits of the latter have been exaggerated. In 1831 she went to school at Roe Head, where she stayed for a year, meeting her two closest friends, Mary Taylor and Ellen Nussey. In 1835 she returned to the school at Roe Head, this time as a teacher. She did not find teaching easy either at this school, where she stayed until 1838, or in two posts as governess with the Sidgwick family of Stonegappe in 1839 and with the White family of Rawdon in 1841. There were not many other careers open, although CB did in these years turn down two offers of marriage. Ambitious to found her own school, she went in 1842 with Emily to Belgium to improve her foreign languages.

Belgium produced more unhappiness. In her first year she suffered a little from loneliness, but made good academic progress. When her aunt died she and Emily returned home, but CB went back to Belgium at the beginning of 1843. This was a result of the pleas of both Madame Heger, the proprietress of the school, and her husband, who taught at the school. Monsieur Heger was a brilliant teacher, and some of the excesses of CB's juvenile prose were curbed under his influence. Respect for his teaching gradually turned into embarrassing affection, and both love and loneliness made CB's second year in Belgium an unhappy one. She left Brussels on 1 January 1844. Attempts to found a school in Haworth failed, and she wrote unhappy letters to Monsieur Heger. The disgrace of Branwell in June 1845 may have exacerbated feelings of guilt. Solace came from an unexpected quarter. In the autumn of 1845 Charlotte came across a volume of her sister's poems. After initial objections on the part of Emily, the three sisters decided to publish a selection of their poems. Very few volumes were sold but, now embarked upon a literary career, the Brontës wrote three prose stories. These were *Agnes Grey, Wuthering Heights*, and *The Professor*. Smith & Elder rejected *The Professor* in July 1847, a year after it had been completed, but said they would welcome a three-volume novel by the same author. CB hastened to finish *Jane Eyre* and sent off the manuscript on 24 August. It was published on 19 October and was an immediate success.

1848 opened promisingly for the Brontës, although there were some hostile reviews, and confusion as to which Brontë had written which book, since they had published under the pseudonyms Acton, Currer, and Ellis Bell. In July Anne and CB travelled to London and met George Smith. The year ended in tragedy with the deaths of Branwell in September and of Emily in December. Anne lingered on until May 1849, but not surprisingly CB's novel *Shirley*, begun in such promising circumstances and completed heroically in August 1849, shows a certain lack of unity. After finishing *Shirley*, CB took some time to embark upon her next novel. Attempts were made to revive *The Professor*, which was eventually published posthumously, and in 1850 she worked on a second edition of her sisters' works. *Villette* was finally started in 1851 and reflects not only her memories of loneliness in Belgium, but also her increasing isolation at Haworth as she struggled to complete her task in spite of depression and ill-health. James Taylor, who worked at Smith & Elder, had proposed to her in April 1851, and there are hints of a possible romance with Smith himself; both men, as well as Monsieur Heger, appear in some form in *Villette*. Eventually, after completing *Villette* at the end of 1852, CB received another proposal from her father's curate, Arthur Bell Nicholls. Initially both she and her father were opposed to the match, but Mr Nicholls won his way, marrying CB on 29 June 1854. She died, possibly pregnant, on 31 March 1855.

The publication of CB's biography by Mrs Gaskell in March 1857 confirmed CB's high reputation and her pathetic story attracted much sympathy. Earlier accusations of unfeminine coarseness were rendered vain. Throughout the nineteenth century her standing remained high, but the publication of the Haworth edition, with introductions by Mrs Humphry Ward, at the turn of the century marked the point where Emily was considered a greater novelist than CB. Mrs Ward drew attention to the faulty plot construction of CBs novels, with their melodramatic touches and numerous coincidences. Biographical speculation was always ready to link events in the lives of the Brontës with events in their books, and this speculation was increased by the discovery in 1913 of some letters by CB to Monsieur Heger. The discovery that she had been in love with a married Belgian schoolmaster drew attention to the fact that her heroes tended to be married or Belgians or schoolmasters or a combination. Thus critics began to dismiss her works as narrowly autobiographical romances.

In the past forty years there has been more interest in CB. The realistic eccentricities and incoherence of her novels have been excused because of their allegorical significance. Jane Eyre's extraordinary adventures can be seen as a vehicle of a struggle between Duty and Passion. *Shirley* is not just an everyday story of Yorkshire folk, but contains several penetrating insights into the oppression of women by men, and of workers by masters, although the two themes are not very well integrated in the third-person narrative. *Villette* has been seen for too long as a fictional account of CB's experiences in Belgium, as has *The Professor*, although in the latter case CB rather clumsily made the narrator a man. *Villette* can also be seen as an allegory of the conflicting claims of Duty and Imagination. All of CB's novels and her life are interesting for the feminist critic, although extreme claims for the novels as exemplary are sometimes misplaced, since, as contemporary critics rather sternly noted, CB's heroines do seem to need the affection of a man to fulfil them.

Opinions about the merits of the novels will probably continue to vary. Some contemporary critics were shocked by *Jane Eyre*, admired *Shirley* and were baffled by *Villette*. *Jane Eyre* is always likely to be the most popular work, but discriminating critics may find *Villette* the more interesting and exciting novel. *Shirley* and *The Professor*, with their obvious faults of construction, would not seem to have much merit were it not for the fact that CB wrote them.   TOM WINNIFRITH

Works: *Jane Eyre* (1847); *Shirley* (1849); *Villette* (1853); *The Professor* (1857).

References: Alexander, C., *The Early Writings of Charlotte Brontë* (1983); Allot, M. (ed.), *The Brontës: The Critical Heritage* (1974); Bjork, H., *The Language of Truth* (1974); *DNB;* Drabble; Duthie, E., *The Foreign Vision of Charlotte Brontë* (1975); Gaskell, E., *The Life of Charlotte Brontë* (1857); Gérin, W., *Charlotte Brontë: The Evolution of Genius* (1967); Martin, R., *The Accents of Persuasion* (1966); Tillotson, K., *Novels of the Eighteen Forties* (1954); Winnifrith, T., *The Brontës* (1977); Winnifrith, T., *A New Life of Charlotte Brontë* (1987).

Brontë, Emily

b. 30 July 1818, Thornton; d. 19 December 1848, Haworth

Novelist, poet

EB's reputation rests upon one novel and a handful of poems. Her juvenile prose stories have not survived, while much of her poetry, largely unpublished in her lifetime, is commonplace. Her surviving letters and diary papers are pathetically few, although some French essays written in Belgium are powerful. It is as the author of *Wuthering Heights* that EB is known.

Her life is badly documented, but seems singularly unlike the life depicted in her novel. She was the fifth child of the Rev. Patrick Brontë and Maria Branwell; her mother died before she was 3. Her father's stories of Yorkshire life and his Irish forbears may have provided some inspiration for her, although she seems to have adopted an unorthodox position on religious matters. She was briefly at school at Cowan Bridge in 1824 and 1825 and at Roe Head in 1835, but was otherwise educated at home. In the winter of 1838 and 1839 she was a teacher at Law Hill near Halifax, possibly gaining some ideas for *Wuthering Heights* from that locality. Like her two sisters and brother, she wrote copiously in both prose and verse from a very early age. A diary fragment of 1834 reveals that already by this time EB and Anne had broken away from Charlotte and Branwell to write about an imaginary realm called Gondal. They continued to write about this until the end of their lives, although none of the prose about Gondal survives. EB's earliest surviving poetry dates to 1836. Not all of it is about Gondal, nor is it possible to establish the history of Gondal with any certainty, although it seems to have been peopled by characters of a passionate nature similar to that of Heathcliff and Catherine in *Wuthering Heights*. Some of EB's later poetry has the same metaphysical depth as her novel.

After returning from Law Hill EB stayed at home while her sisters went out as governesses. In 1842 she accompanied Charlotte to Belgium. Monsieur Heger appreciated her originality, although she would not seem to have been successful as a teacher. Her aunt's death summoned her and Charlotte back to Haworth, and she remained there for the rest of her life. Various hints in Charlotte's letters and Anne's and EB's diary notes suggest that she was always the most domesticated of the sisters. She was certainly the least able to survive away from home.

In February 1844 EB copied her poems into two notebooks, one of which she called Gondal Poems. During the next two years she continued to write poetry: her best poems, 'Remembrance', 'The Prisoner', 'The Philosopher', 'Stars', and 'No Coward Soul is Mine' date from this period. All but the last-named were published in May 1846 after Charlotte's discovery of the poems in the autumn of the previous year; Gondal references were largely eliminated. EB did not seem pleased with the discovery of her poems, and appears to have shunned any publicity for her literary ventures. *Wuthering Heights* was completed by July 1846, and thereafter nothing of EB's survives apart from one poem. We do not know when *Wuthering Heights* was begun. It is possible that some of 1846 and 1847 was spent extending *Wuthering Heights* from one volume to two.

When eventually published in December 1847, *Wuthering Heights* baffled the critics. The publication of *The Tenant of Wildfell Hall* in June 1848 appeared to confirm the impression that the Bells were a bad lot, although it seems more likely that Anne wrote this novel as a counterblast to EB's unorthodox views.

EB's meagre output in the last two years has led some to believe that publication killed the inspiration in her, even that it led to her premature death at the end of 1848. She died of tuberculosis, resolutely refusing medical aid. Charlotte was very fond of her sister, but somewhat in awe of her. It took some time for critics to appreciate EB's greatness, although Matthew Arnold in 'Haworth Churchyard' perceptively linked her with Shakespeare.

Throughout the twentieth century, critics have been agreed on the greatness of *Wuthering Heights*, although they have taken widely different views about its meaning. Heathcliff has been seen alternately as a romantic hero and an unscrupulous ruffian, Nelly Dean, the main narrator, as a representative of Yorkshire common sense and the villain of the novel. It is possible to make similar judgements about almost every character and indeed about the two houses around which the action revolves, Wuthering Heights, bracing though rough, and Thrushcross Grange, more luxurious but less homely. EB's device of introducing two narrators has the effect of making us view the action through the distorted vision of the uncomprehending and silly Lockwood, and through the vision of Nelly Dean with her pious half-truths. It is difficult to see the point of the second generation, on which Heathcliff wreaks a cruel revenge by creating in Hareton, Linton Heathcliff, and the younger Catherine a grotesque parody of the relations between himself, Edgar Linton, and the elder Catherine. The happy ending of the novel with Hareton's and Catherine's impending marriage and removal to Thrushcross Grange does not seem as important as the suggestion that Heathcliff is reunited with Catherine after death. The elegiac ending in which Lockwood looks at the graves of the elder generation and says he cannot think of unquiet slumbers for those quiet sleepers is both appropriate and mysterious. In the love of Heathcliff and Catherine EB portrays a passion that rises above ordinary sexual love which seems trivial in comparison with it, just as the ordinary world of Lockwood and indeed of most readers seems trivial in comparison with the savage but strangely beautiful world through which the lovers roam.   TOM WINNIFRITH

Work: *Wuthering Heights* (1847).

References: Blondel, J., *Emily Brontë: Expérience spirituelle et création poétique* (1956); Cecil, D., *Early Victorian Novelists* (1934); Gérin, W., *Emily Brontë* (1971); Hewish, J., *Emily Brontë* (1969); Ratchford, F. E., *Gondal's Queen: A Novel in Verse* (1955); Petit, J. F. (ed.), *Emily Brontë* (1973); Robinson, A. M., *Emily Brontë* (1883); Spark, M. and Stanford, D., *Emily Brontë* (1953); Visick, M., *The Genesis of 'Wuthering Heights'* (1958); Winnifrith, T., *The Brontës and Their Background* (1973).

Brooke, Frances

b. 1724, Claypole, Lincolnshire; d. 1789, Sleaford, Lincolnshire
Novelist, playwright
(Also wrote under Mary Singleton)

FB was the eldest daughter of the Rev. Thomas Moore and Mary Knowles. After her father died in 1727 she, her mother, and her younger sister Sarah lived with her grandmother in Peterborough. After the deaths of their grandmother and mother, FB and Sarah lived with an aunt.

Her first publication, a weekly periodical, *The Old Maid*, by 'Mary Singleton, Spinster', ran for twenty-two numbers from 15 November 1755 until 10 April 1756, and was reprinted in one volume in 1764. In 1756 she published *Virginia: A Tragedy, with Odes, Pastorals, and Translations*. The play was never acted;

written some years earlier, it had been rejected by David Garrick. In the same year FB married the Rev. Dr John Brooke, a Norfolk man with several benefices in Norwich and surrounding places. Their son, John Moore Brooke, was born in 1756 or 1757. In 1760 her translation of Marie-Jeanne Riccoboni's *Lettres de Milady Juliette Gatesby* (1759) appeared: Riccoboni's fiction became an influence on FB's own. *The History of Lady Julia Mandeville* was published in 1763 and translated into French the following year. In July 1763 FB, with her son and her sister, sailed to Canada to join her husband, now Chaplain to the British garrison in Quebec. Samuel Johnson is described as taking leave of her on this occasion with a kiss, an anecdote which also indicates that she was friendly by this time with Boswell, Hannah More, and Anna Seward. FB revisited England in 1764 and had returned permanently by 1769, when her Canadian novel *Emily Montague* was published. *Memoirs of the Marquis of St Forlaix*, translated from Framéry, followed in 1770, and *Elements of the History of England*, from Abbé Milot, in 1771. She now tried the theatre again. From 1773 to 1778 she was joint manager of the Haymarket Opera House with her close friend, the actress Mary Ann Yates. FB's second tragedy, *The Siege of Sinope*, was rejected by Garrick, but later produced at Covent Garden with Mrs Yates in the principal role, and published in 1781. Meanwhile FB had continued to write fiction. *All's Right at Last, or, The History of Miss West* (1774), another novel with Canadian scenes, has been attributed to her, but the sympathetic account of Methodism found in it is most untypical of FB, who elsewhere expresses herself strongly in favour of the established Church. *The Excursion* (1777) is definitely hers. Unlike her first two novels, both epistolary, it has an omniscient narrator. Its heroine, like the young FB, goes to London with literary ambitions and has her work rejected by Garrick, who is lampooned in the novel.

FB's greatest commercial success was a comic opera, *Rosina*, with music by William Shield. First produced at Covent Garden on New Year's Eve 1782, it was acted over 200 times before 1800, making it the second most popular afterpiece on the London stage in that period, outdone only by *Comus*. It went through fourteen editions by 1800. A second, less successful opera, *Marian*, was performed at Covent Garden in 1788. By this time FB was living with her son (now a vicar) at Sleaford, Lincolnshire. She died there in January 1789 of a 'spasmodic complaint'. *The History of Charles Mandeville: A Sequel to Lady Julia*, probably by her but conceivably by someone else exploiting the continued popularity of her first novel, appeared in 1790.

A versatile writer, FB achieved most in her refreshingly witty variants on the sentimental novel, but some of her other work is of interest. *Virginia* is a limp attempt at blank-verse tragedy, *The Siege of Sinope* not much better. The light pastoral *Rosina* is slight, as is *Marian*. The poems published with *Virginia* are interesting for their insight into FB's early ambitions: she praises Elizabeth Carter and hopes to achieve fame in her turn. *The Old Maid* is a much stronger work. In conversational prose, FB follows the example of Addison and Steele. She creates the persona of an old maid nearing the age of 50, whose love of gossip is the stated motive for the periodical. Self-mockery, dry wit, and tender concern for her fictional niece make the old maid an interesting character, who offers us Tory reflections on current affairs, and theatrical criticism which defends Shakespeare's original *Lear* against Nahum Tate's then popular version with its happy ending.

Lady Julia Mandeville, which made FB's name, is a tale of sentimental mis-understanding enlivened by mockery from Lady Anne Wilmot, a foil to the over-delicate hero and heroine. The novel's most noted feature was its tragic ending. With hero and heroine dead, Lady Anne changes her tone to lamentation: 'Bellville! Where are now all our gay schemes? Where the circle of happy friends? How vain are the designs of man!' The many objections to this denouement actually suggest its power for contemporary readers: the reviewer in the *Monthly Review* claimed he could not read it 'without giving way to the tender emotions which the ingenious unknown writer so well knows how to inspire'.

Emily Montague resolved sentimental difficulties in happy marriages, and is most interesting for its Canadian background, which inspires Arabella Fermor to reflections on women's role in different societies: 'I will marry a savage, and turn squaw . . . they talk of French husbands, but commend me to an Indian one, who lets his wife ramble five hundred miles, without asking where she is going. . . . I will not be a squaw . . . they are slaves: the mothers marry their children without consulting their inclinations. . . . They may talk of the privilege of chusing a chief; but what is that to the dear English privilege of chusing a husband?' The epistolary form allows FB to air ideas on various other topics, including the benefits of British as opposed to French rule of Canada.

In *The Excursion* FB mingled the uncommon topic of a woman's writing ambitions with the common ones of the dangers to chastity and reputation facing an indiscreet girl. With gentle irony FB steers her heroine away from writing for the stage, 'a pursuit', a friend advises her, 'in which her sex, her delicacy of mind, her rectitude of heart, her honest pride, and perhaps her genius, were all against her success'.

FB was well-known and highly esteemed. Fanny Burney, meeting her in 1774, commented, 'Mrs Brooke is very short and fat, and squints; but has the art of showing agreeable ugliness. She is very well bred, and expresses herself with much modesty upon all subjects; which in an *authoress*, a woman of *known* understanding, is extremely pleasing.' A blander judgement was printed in the *European Magazine* shortly after FB's death, praising her work and calling her 'as remarkable for her gentleness and suavity of manners as for her literary talents'.   JANE SPENCER

Works: *The Old Maid* (1755–6); *Virginia: A Tragedy* (1756); (trans.), *Letters of Lady Juliet Catesby*, ed. M.-J. Riccoboni (1759); *The History of Lady Julia Mandeville* (1763); *Emily Montague* (1769); (trans.), *Memoirs of the Marquis of St Forlaix*, ed. Framéry (1770); (trans.), *Elements of the History of England*, by A. Milot (1771); *All's Right at Last, or, The History of Miss West* (attrib.) (1774); *The Excursion* (1777); *The Siege of Sinope* (1781); *Rosina* (1782); *The History of Charles Mandeville* (attrib.) (1790).

References: Burpee, L. J., 'Introduction' to *The History of Emily Montague* (1931); Ellis, A. R. (ed.), *Early Diary of Fanny Burney, 1768–1778* (1889); *The London Stage, 1660–1800: Part 5, 1776–1800*, vols 1–3; Poole, P. E., 'Introduction' to *The History of Lady Julia Mandeville* (1930); Spencer, J., *The Rise of the Woman Novelist* (1986); Todd; Todd, J., *The Sign of Angellica* (1989).

Brookner, Anita
b. 16 July 1938, London
Novelist, art historian

The daugher of Newson and Maude Brookner, AB was educated at James Allen's Girls' School, King's College, London, the Courtauld Institute, and in Paris. A visiting lecturer at the University of Reading from 1959 to 1964, she was Slade Professor of Fine Arts at Cambridge, the first woman to hold the position. She is a Fellow of New Hall, Cambridge, and currently teaches at the Courtauld Institute. An authority on eighteenth- and nineteenth-century French art, she is the author of four specialized studies in the field. In addition she is known for her reviews such as those in the *Times Literary Supplement* which applaud controlled, conventional scholarship and often denigrate feminist criticism regarded as political.

AB has written six novels, the first of which, *A Start In Life* (1981) (published as *The Debut* in the US), tells the story of Dr Ruth Weiss, a quiet scholar devoted to the study of Balzac. At the age of 40 she decides that literature has ruined her life and that the virtuous are passive victims doomed to unsatisfying lives. The novel has rather a tentative plot, perhaps more suited to a short story, and an uncertain voice. In *Providence* (1982) AB better paces events; and sure wit and irony enrich a repertory of voices. The novel is the story of a woman lecturer who specializes in the Romantic tradition, delivering a series of presentations on Constant's *Adolphe*. She lives in two worlds, one of her doting but demanding French grandparents and the other of British academe. Her perceptions clouded by fantasies, she misreads the meaning of an affair with a colleague and retreats into a life of disappointment.

AB's third novel, *Look at Me* (1983), is a work of metafiction about a lonely and sensitive library cataloguer who catalogues and observes rather than experiences the people she meets. In the end she retreats to the bed in which her mother died in order to write the novel we read. Initially described as a 'beggar at the feast', she takes revenge, consuming her enemies while making literature a substitute for living. In *Hotel du Lac* (1984), which won the Booker Prize, the protagonist is again a writer but of romantic fiction, sent to Switzerland after an 'unfortunate lapse'; there in an elegant hotel she joins in the rituals of hotel residence, writing undelivered letters to her lover and working on sections of a new novel. She achieves some insight into her own predicament but chooses to reject a life of pragmatic arrangements to return to London and a life of romantic fictions.

Family and Friends (1985) is a striking departure from AB's previous works and an answer to critics who have claimed that her fiction is essentially autobiographical. It chronicles the affairs of a wealthy Jewish family during the late 1930s and the 1940s. The novel embraces not only a larger cast of characters but also a wider geography than the previous four. Transplanted to London before the Second World War, the family continues to prosper without their recently deceased patriarch. Inevitably disappointed in her search for romance, the heroine, who has taken over the role of patriarch, returns to London and ends up caring for her invalid widowed father, consumed anew by her study of virtue and vice in the fiction of Balzac.

AB's most recent novel, *The Misalliance* (1986), again concerns a woman alone. The newly divorced Blanche, seeming eccentric to others, blames her isolation on her genteel and caring personality. Her efforts to find a relationship with a mother and a mute 3-year-old child result in her understanding that love can be another trap and a misappropriation.

AB's slightly precious style is full of allusions to Dickens, Balzac, Colette, and Henry James. She usually presents lonely women of early middle age, exiled or orphaned, bound to, if not oppressed by, traditions, whether intellectual or social. Lonely and inhibited, they yet venture timidly into love affairs which follow a preordained course to disappointment; the experience is transmuted to artistic creation of one sort or another, while the loneliness is intensified.

ROBERT E. HOSMER, JR AND JANET JONES

Works: *Watteau* (1968); *The Genius of the Future* (1971); *Greuze* (1972); *Jacques-Louis David* (1980); *A Start in Life* (1981; published in the US as *The Debut*); *Providence* (1982); *Look At Me* (1983); *Hotel du Lac* (1984); *Family And Friends* (1985); *The Misalliance* (1986).
References: *CA; DLB.*

Brophy, Brigid
b. 12 June 1929, London
Novelist, critic and essayist, short story writer
BB is the daughter of novelist John Brophy and of Charis Grundy. She was educated at St Paul's Girls' School, from where she won a Jubilee Scholarship to read Classics at St Hugh's College, Oxford in 1947. Subsequently she began to work at her literary career, supporting herself for a time through the distribution of pornographic books. In 1954 she married Michael Levey (deputy keeper of the National Gallery) and that same year won first prize at the Cheltenham Literary Festival for her first novel, *Hackenfeller's Ape*. Throughout the 1950s and 1960s she continued to write prolifically, both fiction and non-fiction, winning in 1962 the *London Magazine* prize for prose but provoking mixed reactions in readers and critics as she developed her own very particular interests in her work and life. She is a vegetarian, an active member of the Writers' Guild of Great Britain, and a campaigner for public lending rights. She contributed essays to the *New Statesman*, *The Sunday Times*, the *London Magazine*, the *New York Herald Tribune*, the *Texas Quarterly*, and *Queen*, and to psychoanalytic journals, and she continues to contribute to a number of journals; she is an astringent reviewer, with little sympathy for academic feminism. Of later years she has been a sufferer from multiple sclerosis. BB lives in London. She has one daughter.

Although BB's name is widely known among the reading public, relatively few seem to have close acquaintance with her books, which are rarely mentioned by the authors of critical works. Her dislike of censorship and espousal of the cause of sexual freedom, and her denunciation of the possible hypocrisies of marriage, could have won her a place in the vanguard of the women's movement, but the imaginative leap which causes her to write as though she already had the freedom, as a woman and an intellectual, to write as she chooses, and her apparent refusal to use her time to demand that freedom, seem to have caused bewilderment.

Her first novel, the attention-winning *Hackenfeller's Ape*, already displays something of the breadth of the writer's erudition and her ability to view humanity from an unexpected point of view. The opening itself reveals this freshness of vision; from the title, from the description of a park 'alive with the murmuring vibration of the species which made it its preserve', the reader thinks herself in a zoo park; correctly, as it happens, but the species observed here is *homo sapiens*. The viewpoint shifts throughout, the writer's psychological knowledge allowing her to adopt a position of detachment sharply contrasted to that of the omnipresent author or the author-as-camera stance. The remarkable closing sequence, detailing the physical and psychological development of an embryonic monkey acquiring before birth an apparatus of anxiety and guilt, suggests acquaintance with the work of Melanie Klein.

This applied psychology caused disturbance among BB's critics, especially on the publication of her non-fiction works. *Black Ship to Hell* (1962) was described by a contemporary as 'an avalanche of erudite self-indulgence in mythology, classical literature, history of music, philosophy and psychoanalysis'. So it is, but its 'feminine' refusal to acknowledge conventional boundaries is precisely the freedom which embodies BB's perception of the dark side of human nature. The book has been viewed as a study of man as a self-destructive animal; BB brings to it the lack of sentimentality observed in *Hackenfeller's Ape*.

In 1964 she published a novel, *The Snow Ball*, and a massive, complex study, *Mozart the Dramatist*. The novel takes its cue from the study, its setting a party in eighteenth-century fancy dress, in which the protagonists, dressed as Don Giovanni and Dona Anna, investigate the question of whether, in the opera, Dona Anna was in fact seduced. Here, she is and there is a memorable description of female orgasm which made the book notorious. The setting is baroque, a style that fascinated BB; the characters are observed about the business of satisfying sexual requirements at different stages of life (adolescence, mid-life, later middle age). The story occupies an evening, beginning with a bird's eye viewpoint which, with the mask motif, 'makes strange' and ending with the reverberations of an unexpected death.

BB's acknowledgement of the expression of the shadow side through eroticism occurs in her essay contributions to various journals. A collection, *Don't Never Forget*, was published in 1966. 'Monogamy', from *Queen* (April 1965), aired views that would soon be espoused by the women's movement; perhaps BB's light-handed approach was too sophisticated to be adopted as a war cry. Similarly, the essay on Sade's *Justine*, greatly predating Angela Carter's treatment in *The Sadeian Woman*, deftly exposes Sade's masturbation fantasies as being bereft of the decadent and imaginative power which fuels other work (Genet's, perhaps) and points up de Beauvoir's book on Sade as possessing 'much uneconomical existentializing about the interchangeability of subject and object' (satirizing de Beauvoir's own Sartrian style). Her interest in decadence and masturbation fantasy, 'the unmentionable portion of the literary iceberg' ('Sade', *New Statesman*, 1964) led her into extensive work on Aubrey Beardsley. *Black and White* was published in 1968; with its analysis of the pictures (illustrated), the book is of immense value in its study of the erotic elements of Beardsley's art. Two further studies of Beardsley followed, as well as one of Ronald Firbank, *Prancing Novelist*. In it BB displays the qualities panned by the critics of *Black Ship to Hell*, and elucidates, interprets, and palpably enjoys Firbank, taking particular delight in bringing into focus history's varied applications of the symbols he uses.

The collection of stories published the same year, *The Adventures of God in his Search for the Black Girl*, contains some works structured in the conventional mode of the fairy story. BB abandons the Gothic atmosphere and writes in a thoroughly modern idiom; the universal application of 'The Singularly Ugly Princess' or 'The Woodcutter's Upright Son' is clear. The gem of the collection is the title story; an intellectual game played with Voltaire, Gibbon, and representatives of other schools of thought, it gives BB ample scope for stating views on censorship, public lending rights, and other favourite topics, but also reveals her remarkable ability to lay bare the inconsistencies and shibboleths encountered in intellectual argument.

Her prolific early output has slowed somewhat over the last years, but the later fiction is more substantial and developed; *The Snow Ball* is a mere observation compared to *Palace Without Chairs* (1978). This is written with all the wit, depth, and playfulness apparent in her non-fiction from the beginning, and fulfils the observational function of earlier fiction without distancing the reader. It can be read on many levels; its progression is the psychological balance between innocence and experience and the inevitability of movement from one to the other. Her protagonists are a royal family. When she makes use of kings and nobles in fiction they perform the same function as in the tragic genre, that is, as expression or symbols of the parts of ourselves that we take seriously. She also recognizes in the nature of art 'the one justifiably aristocratic system'.

JENNIFER PLASTOW

Selected works: The Crown Princess and Other Stories (1953); *Hackenfeller's Ape* (1953); *The King of a Rainy Country* (1956); *Flesh* (1962); *The Finishing Touch* (1963); *The Snow Ball* (1964); *Mozart the Dramatist* (1964); *Don't Never Forget* (1966); *Religion in State Schools* (1967); *Black and White* (1968); *In Transit* (1970); *Prancing Novelist* (1973); *The Adventures of God in his Search for the Black Girl* (1973); *Palace without Chairs* (1978); *The Prince and the Wild Geese* (1983); *Baroque n' Roll* (1986).
References: Drabble.

Broster, D.K.

b. 1878, near Liverpool; d. 7 February 1950, Bexhill, Sussex
Historical novelist
DKB was the eldest daughter of Thomas Mawdsley Broster and Emilie Kathleen Gething. She was educated at Cheltenham Ladies' College and at St Hilda's College, Oxford, where she read history. Her first novel, *Chantemerle* (1911), was written jointly with G.W. Taylor, as was *The Vision Splendid* (1913).

During the First World War, DKB served with a voluntary Franco-American hospital in France, after which she returned to Oxford and became secretary to the Regius Professor of History for a number of years, before making her home at Catsfield, near Battle, Sussex. She produced the main body of her writing in the 1920s and 1930s, but her last book *The Captain's Lady* (1947), was one of her most popular novels.

A novelist noted for historical veracity and the gift of evoking the atmosphere of place and time, DKB achieved her greatest success with her Scottish trilogy of the 1745 Rebellion and its aftermath. *The Flight of the Heron* (1925), *The Gleam in the North* (1927), and *The Dark Mile* (1929) are vividly and sympathetically written from the perspective of the Scottish people who became caught up in tragic events. Of her other works, *Almond, Wild Almond* (1933), and *Child Royal* (1937) were particularly successful.   MARGARET ASHBY

Works: Chantemerle (with Miss G.W. Taylor) (1911); *The Vision Splendid* (with Miss G.W. Taylor) (1913); *Sir Isumbras at the Ford* (1918); *The Yellow Poppy* (1920); *The Wounded Name* (1922); 'Mr Rowl' (1924); *The Flight of the Heron* (1925); *The Gleam in the North* (1927); *The Dark Mile* (1929); *Ships in the Bay* (1931); *A Fire of Driftwood* (1932); *Almond, Wild Almond* (1933); *World Under Snow* (with G. Forester) (1935); *Child Royal* (1937); *The Sea Without a Haven* (1941); *Couching at the Door* (1942); *The Captain's Lady* (1947).
References: OCCL; Richardson, K. (ed.), *Twentieth-Century Writing* (1969).

Broughton, Rhoda

b. 29 November 1840, Denbighshire, North Wales; d. 5 June 1920,
Headington Hill, Oxford
Novelist
RB was the daughter of Delves Broughton, a clergyman, and of Jane Bennet of Dublin. The youngest of five children, RB was brought up in Staffordshire.

She began to write novels at the age of 22, inspired by Anne Thackeray's 'Story of Elizabeth'. With the death of her father in 1863, RB went to live with one of her sisters, Mrs William Charles Newcombe, until 1892. She then moved to live with a cousin in Headington, Oxford, where she was well-known for her literary dinner parties and academic gatherings. Few details of her private life are known, but it is probable that many of her sketches of rural life and domestic scenes were based on her own experiences.

RB's first novel, *Not Wisely but Too Well*, was first published in the *Dublin University Magazine* prior to its publication in book form in 1867. Between 1867 and 1914, she published twenty-six novels. Letters written to her London publisher Bentley reveal that she was extremely self-conscious as a novelist and always strove to present her best work to the public. Her success is evident in the prices she was paid by Bentley for her copyrights: *Cometh up as a Flower* £300, *Nancy and Belinda* £1,000, and *Alas!* £1,300. Her principal theme was love and it was always her intention to present it vigorously and passionately. Her plots frequently centred on marriages which destroyed the woman involved. She often used as a heroine a headstrong young woman subdued into marriage who would have a scandalous affair with a robust lover.

RB's deliberately suggestive titles and romance plots won her a wide audience and a reputation for audacity. In the 1930s she was considered among the best-selling novelists of the Victorian period and ranked alongside Anthony Trollope, Wilkie Collins, and Lewis Carroll in popularity. Yet her writing was often ungrammatical and her descriptive passages absurd and cumbersome: 'In the way of virility he had already broken a kitchen poker with his biceps; and as proof of his devotion he had travelled back from a vague Asia region, where he had been working off some of his superfluous agony upon the biggest game in pestilential jungles, merely to catch a glimpse of his lady's chignon, as in the company of her husband . . . she stepped into her brougham at a London terminus' (*A Fool in her Folly*). Her humorous descriptions of country parish life, especially the behaviour of children in the presence of their elders, show, however, that she could on occasion write lively, brisk, naturalistic dialogue.

B.E. SCHNELLER

Selected works: Not Wisely, but Too Well (1867); Cometh up as a Flower (1867); Red as a Rose is She (1870); Goodbye Sweetheart: A Tale (1872); Tales for Christmas Eve (1872); Nancy: A Novel (1873); Joan: A Tale (1876); Second Thoughts (1880); Belinda (1883); Betty's Visions and Mrs Smith of Longman's (1886); Alas! (1890); Mrs Bligh: A Novel (1892); A Beginner (1894); Scylla or Charybdis? A Novel (1895); Dear Faustina (1897); The Game and the Candle (1899); Foes in Law (1900); Lavinia (1902); The Waif's Progress (1905); Mamma (1908); The Devil and the Deep Sea (1910); Between Two Stools (1912); A Thorn in the Flesh (1917); A Fool in her Folly (1920).

References: BA (19); DLB; Dictionary of English Authors; Dictionary of Literature in the English Language; Drabble; Heywood, J.C., How They Strike Me, These Authors (1877).

Browning, Elizabeth Barrett

b. 6 March 1806, Coxhoe Hall, near Durham; d. 29 June 1861, Casa Guidi, Florence

Poet

EBB was born in 1806. She was the eldest of eleven children of Edward Moulton Barrett and Mary Graham Clarke. In 1809 the family moved to Hope

End, a large country house in Herefordshire which Mr Barrett had built with proceeds from his sugar plantations in Jamaica. EBB spent a happy and precocious childhood at Hope End. She was encouraged in her prolific reading and writing by both her parents, but especially by her father. It was he who gave her the free use of his library (with the exception of some few censored works), who allowed her to share her brothers' classical tuition and who had her first volume of poems privately published when she was 14.

The idyll of her childhood was disrupted by a number of events, however. At about the time when her favourite brother Bro left for school, EBB began to suffer from some vague pulmonary and nervous disorder, which was to afflict her for the rest of her life and render her, for long periods, an invalid. In 1828 her mother died, leaving the children to the care of their increasingly anxious and demanding father. In her early twenties, EBB continued her education under the tutelage of a local classical scholar, Hugh Stuart Boyd, who, being almost totally blind, relied on her good offices as a reader of the Greek texts he was studying. It seems, however, that he was unaware of the extent to which her intellectual need for him had become a stormy and miserable infatuation. Finally, in 1832, as a direct result of the movement for Abolition, Mr Barrett was forced to sell Hope End and move to London.

By 1838, when the family settled in Wimpole Street, EBB was effectively an invalid. She was too weak to leave her bedroom, and too nervous to receive any except the most familiar of visitors. In this seclusion, however, she composed much of her first successful volume of poems: the *Poems* of 1844. She also, at this time, became a close friend and regular correspondent with Miss Mitford. The two confined women encouraged each other in their writing, and formed a strong intellectual and emotional bond which survived years of separation.

In 1838, EBB was sent to Torquay to recuperate from a lung haemorrhage. It was there that the great tragedy of her life occurred. Against her father's will, she insisted that Bro should remain with her as a companion. One summer's day, in June 1840, Bro had a mysterious sailing accident and drowned. For the rest of her life, EBB was unable to speak or write of the event for which she felt guiltily responsible.

The publication of her 1844 collection of poems brought her widespread acclaim, as well as inspiring the younger Robert Browning to write his first warmly admiring letter to the unseen poet of Wimpole Street. The correspondence led to a friendship and courtship which, as a result of Mr Barrett's increasingly fanatical edicts against marriage, was conducted clandestinely. On 12 September 1846, the two poets were married in secret and, a week later, EBB escaped from her father's house to Italy.

The couple settled in Florence, in Casa Guidi. In 1849, at the age of 43, EBB gave birth to a son, Robert Wiedeman Barrett Browning, known affectionately as Pen. Throughout the 1850s she followed with eager interest the revolutionary turmoil of Europe, and her poetry became ever more sharply focused on the contemporary political world. *Casa Guidi Windows* was the product of her observations and meditations on the Italian Risorgimento. During these years she also found renewed health and strength for several long journeys, to Rome, Siena, Venice, Paris, and back to London. However, in spite of her long cherished hopes, Mr Barrett refused any reconciliation with his once best-loved daughter. He returned her many letters unopened, and continued to deny her entry to his house.

In December 1856, EBB published the poem she had been writing over the past ten years: *Aurora Leigh*. It was something of a *succès de scandale*, and firmly established her reputation as a poet. In April of the following year, Mr Barrett died.

The remaining four years of EBB's life were spent mainly in Florence and Rome. At this time, she caught the widespread craze for spiritualism, and attended meetings in the hope of communicating with the spirits. Her hopes were never realized. Meanwhile, the direct and propagandist message of the *Poems Before Congress* bears witness to her continuing political passions. Although, in her last years, she had become very weak and tired, she wrote poetry to the end, and *Last Poems*, published posthumously, contains some of her most powerful lyrics. She died, unexpectedly and quietly, on 29 June 1861.

Sonnets from the Portuguese, *Casa Guidi Windows*, *Aurora Leigh*, and *Last Poems* represent the best of EBB's work. The maudlin poeticisms of her early style have given way, in these, to a sinewy and idiosyncratic colloquialism, and the too easy sing-song of her immature verses to a new, distinctive, tussling register of speech.

In the *Sonnets from the Portuguese*, EBB expresses her love for Robert with a fulsome and yet witty energy, which flirts and skirmishes with the inherited conventions of the love sonnet. The sometimes embarrassingly elevated language of desire is, in the best of these sonnets, counterbalanced by a levelling sense of humour. *Casa Guidi Windows* is a discursive poem about the ideals and disappointments of the Italian Risorgimento. It shows EBB at her most passionately cosmopolitan, and, as a poet, surprisingly capable of turning the intractable issues of papal power, British imperialism, and nationalistic mythologizing into a strong and musical poetry.

Aurora Leigh, EBB's novel in verse, is both a love story and a forceful, polemical statement about the roles of women in the contemporary world. Its two heroines, the poet Aurora and the fallen woman Marian Erle, are subtly allied in a joint defiance of the conventions and laws of their society. On one level, the poem presents a strong protest against the wrongs of women. On another level, it confronts the emotional and psychological inhibitions of the woman who would be a poet and earn her living independently by the pen. Both a briskly readable story and a quieter, semi-autobiographical exploration of the growth and development of the woman poet's mind, *Aurora Leigh* in many ways marks the height of EBB's achievement as a poet.

Last Poems contains some of the most stringent and beautiful lyrics EBB ever wrote. Poems such as 'A Musical Instrument', 'Bianca among the Nightingales', 'Lord Walter's Wife', 'My Heart and I', 'Mother and Poet', and 'De Profundis' capture, in their exquisite repetitions and refrains, a dramatic sense of melancholy, neurosis, or dancing gaiety, which should finally confirm the reputation of this major nineteenth-century woman poet. ANGELA LEIGHTON

Works: *The Battle of Marathon* (1820); *An Essay on Mind, with Other Poems* (1826); *Prometheus Bound . . . and Miscellaneous Poems* (1833); *The Seraphim and Other Poems* (1838); *Poems*, 2 vols (1844); *Poems*, 2 vols, revision and enlargement of 1844 edition, including *Sonnets from the Portuguese* (1850); *Casa Guidi Windows* (1851); *Aurora Leigh* (1856); *Poems Before Congress* (1860); *Last Poems* (1862).

References: Diehl, J. F., ' "Come slowly – Eden": An exploration of women poets and their muse', *Signs* 3 (1978); Forster, M., *'My Heart and I': The Life and Work of Elizabeth Barrett Browning* (1988); Gelpi, B. C., '*Aurora Leigh*: The vocation of the woman poet', *Victorian Poetry* 19 (1981); Gilbert, S., 'From *Patria* to *Matria*: Elizabeth Barrett Browning's Risorgimento', *PMLA* 99 (1984); Hewlett, D., *Elizabeth Barrett Browning: A Life* (1952); Kaplan, C., 'Wicked fathers: A family romance', in *Sea Changes: Essays on Culture and Feminism* (1986); Leighton, A., *Elizabeth Barrett Browning* (1986); Mermin, D., 'The female poet and the embarrassed reader: Elizabeth Barrett Browning's *Sonnets from the Portuguese*', *English Literary History* 48 (1981); Mermin, D., 'Elizabeth Barrett Browning through 1844: becoming a woman poet', *Studies in English Literature: 1500–1900* 26 (1986); Rosenblum, D., 'Face to face: Elizabeth Barrett Browning's *Aurora Leigh* and nineteenth-century poetry', *Victorian Studies* 26 (1983); Steinmetz, V., 'Beyond the sun: patriarchal images in *Aurora Leigh*', *Studies in Browning and His Circle* 9 (1981); Steinmetz, V., 'Images of "mother-want" in EBB's *Aurora Leigh*', *Victorian Poetry* 21 (1983); Taplin, G.B., *The Life of Elizabeth Barrett Browning* (1957); Woolf, V., ' "Aurora Leigh" ', in *The Common Reader*, 2nd series (1932).

Brunton, Mary

b. 1 November 1778, Barra, Orkney; d. 19 December 1818, Edinburgh

Novelist

Little is known of the early life of MB except through the memoir written by her husband and published with the fragment of her last novel *Emmeline* in 1819. She was the daughter of Col. Thomas Balfour of Elwick and Frances Ligonier, sister of the Earl of Ligonier. She appears to have received little formal education and there is mention of 'early unkindness'; by the age of 16 she was running the household and a few years later, although offered the chance to live in London with Viscountess Wentworth, she chose instead in 1798 to marry a scholarly Calvinist minister, Alexander Brunton, with a church in Bolton, East Lothian. It was apparently a happy union; the couple studied together, read history and theology, and learned German. In 1803 they moved to Edinburgh where Brunton had a new parish and in about 1809 MB began writing a novel for publication. The novel was *Self-Control* (1811), published anonymously but soon known to be MB's. Inculcating duty, feminine propriety, and self-reliance all together, it tells of Laura, who manages to fend off the passionate advances of Captain Hargrave, a would-be seducer whom she initially loves, and of de Courcy who has been helping her by buying her paintings. Despite the shame and the opposition of her impoverished father to this work, it has in fact supported them both. After her father's death, she becomes a companion to an intolerable mistress and then is kidnapped by Hargrave and taken to America where Hargrave, realizing that he will never gain her love, kills himself. Laura returns from America to marry de Courcy. In the novel much is made of the difficulty of a woman's earning her own living and of the horror of total financial dependence on another.

Discipline (1814) repeats many of the motifs of *Self-Control* but has a very different heroine, the assertive Ellen, fashionably educated by a rich father who yet intends her for the serious reforming Maitland. She, however, becomes interested in a man who tries to elope with her and Maitland himself cools as he contemplates her triviality. When her father loses his money and commits suicide, Ellen is rescued by a poor invalid spinster who begins her real education; after her friend's death, Ellen becomes a governess and undergoes many ordeals – one of her jealous employers even manages for a while to have her committed to an asylum. In the end, the reformed Ellen marries Maitland who turns out to be a Highland chief. Part of the novel is set in the Highlands in which MB had a particular interest, and it seems that she would have made more of this setting had it not been for the overwhelming example of Walter Scott who was using this material at the same time.

Although always accepting that money was an object in any art, MB insisted that her prime motive in writing was to inculcate religion; consequently her books avoid the 'easy flexible sort of virtue' popular with the public. Both her novels criticize the romantic expectations of young girls which she believed were encouraged by other writers of fiction. But, despite their moral and religious purpose and despite their exotic and fantastic plots, her novels have considerable psychological realism in their pictures of the heroines struggling to control inappropriate infatuation and to earn a living.

Emmeline was intended as the first of several moral tales; it is a schematic story which tells of the unusual pedicament of a feminine and passive woman married to a man of her choice but who, to marry that man, has been divorced from her earlier husband; despite the couple's wealth and initial position in society, they are ostracized by all. The work was unfinished when MB died of puerperal fever after giving birth to a stillborn child.   JANET TODD

Works: *Self-Control* (1811); *Discipline* (1814); *Emmeline. With Some Other Pieces* (1819).

References: Brunton, A., 'Memoir', in *Emmeline* (1819); Smith, S. W. R., 'Men, women, and money: the case of Mary Brunton', in *Fetter'd or Free?*, ed. M. A. Schofield and C. Macheski (1986); Taylor, I. and Luria, G., 'Gender and genre', in *What Manner of Woman?*, ed. M. Springer (1977); Todd.

Bryher

b. 2 September 1894, Margate, Kent; d. 28 January 1983, Vevey, Switzerland
Novelist
(Also wrote under Winifred Bryher)

B was the daughter of Sir John Reeves, an industrialist and financier, and Hannah Ellerman. She travelled so much with her family that she had to be privately educated, which she felt to be fortunate ('Fate was kind and I did few formal lessons in my childhood, with the result that my mind developed freely and was ravenous for knowledge'). Their travels through Europe, Egypt, and the Middle East gave her a background for the archaeology and history that were always to fascinate her. She legally changed her name to Bryher (the name of one of the Scilly Isles) when she began to write, so as not to be identified with her father's massively influential name. She was a friend of the poet HD, and met, on a trip with her to the United States, Robert McAlmon whom she married in 1921, the day after their first meeting. (They divorced in 1927, and she married Kenneth Macpherson, with whom she founded the film journal *Close-Up*; they divorced in 1947.)

Man Ray's haunting portrait of Bryher depicts her with two clenched fists and an elegantly tense face slightly turned to the side, sad, wistful, serious, and strangely determined, in a fur collar white against the black of her dress. There seems nothing frivolous about her – Marianne Moore, celebrating her and her 'undeceived eye for beauty', celebrates, in the same breath, her 'passion for moral beauty'.

There is, to be sure, something of the moral, even moralizing, about the tone of her historical novels. They are static and stylized, written in a mode we may currently find difficult to digest. (*The Coin of Carthage* (1963), found by many to be her most important work, ends forgettably: 'What pity, what pity is there ever for the vanquished!') This even in a book that tries, in recounting the tale of the Roman Republic during the Second Punic War, to give a sort of common reader's view through the description of the lives of two Greek traders, quite simply. The *New York Times Book Review* said with some justice that her novel served 'Rome and Carthage as Edith Hamilton's essays serve Greece'. Of her own attachment to history Bryher says, in her autobiography, that it largely depended on the inspiration of G. A. Henty, the author of *The Young Carthaginians*. Her heroes can be imposing, like Hannibal of Carthage, who somehow managed to pay the tribute the Romans imposed and who fought at a young age ('I was just the same age as Hannibal when he had sworn his famous oath to fight Rome'; 'I wanted to be a cabin boy and found that I could reply to tiresome arguments'; 'If Hannibal was old enough to go on a campaign when he was nine, I am old enough to go to sea!').

But there is, in spite of the high moral spirit of the whole adventure, none the less a tone of distress over what is irrecoverable from the past; lost libraries, destroyed by the Romans symbolize a whole civilization losing its soul: 'They kept only a few agricultural books and these subsequently disappeared.' Carthage was courageous, losing out because her empire had been founded upon her control of the sea, when the Romans developed new methods of warfare; England was brave and depressed in the 1940s – over and over, the comparisons are suggested: 'It is as if England had been defeated in 1940 and we were trying to describe the last hours of London only from many accounts', or, in *Gate to the Sea* (1959), the port of Paestum besieged by tyrants. In *Beowulf* (1956), the bombing of London in the Second World War ends with a wonderful exclamation by one of the female characters: 'Oh dear,' she said, 'I do think it is very embarrassing to be bombed.' All B's novels are historical and, in some extended sense, actual. Horace Gregory writes of her renewal of the writing of the past that her 'short, highly charged analogies to situations and problems that bedevil our days and nights' is equal to the perception of a poet. The project of recreating the historical times she chooses, together with her preoccupation for the present, makes her will-to-the-past seem strangely contemporaneous.   MARY ANN CAWS

Selected works: *Amy Lowell: A Critical Appreciation* (1918); *Development: A Novel* (1920); *West* (1925); *Film Problems of Soviet Russia* (1929); *Film in Education* (1937); *The Fourteenth of October* (1952); *The Player's Boy* (1953); *Beowulf* (1956); *Gate to the Sea* (1959); *The Heart to Artemis: A Writer's Memoirs* (1962); *The Coin of Carthage* (1963); *The Days of Mars: A Memoir* (1972).

References: Beach, S., *Shakespeare and Company* (1959); *CA*; Hanscombe, G. and Smyers, V. L., *Writing for their Lives* (1987).

Bulwer-Lytton, Rosina

b. 3 November 1802, Ballywire, Co. Limerick; d. 12 March 1882, 'Glenômera', Upper Sydenham

Novelist

RBL was born in Ireland, the daughter of Francis Mass Wheeler and Anna Mass Wheeler (daughter of Archdeacon Doyle). Her parents had married at an early age and family life was unsettled. In 1816, when Anna Wheeler left her husband to live in France, RBL went to live in London under the guardianship of her uncle, Sir John Doyle, the retired Governor of Guernsey. She became a member of the Bohemian literary circle which centred around Byron's ex-lover, Lady Caroline Lamb. RBL was introduced to Edward Bulwer in April 1826; at the age of 22, he was on the threshold of a literary career. They became lovers, but their marriage was opposed by Edward's mother, Lady Bulwer; their engagement was broken and renewed several times prior to their marriage in August 1827. Lady Bulwer stopped Edward's allowance, and he turned to writing for profit. RBL and Edward began a tempestuous marriage in Woodcot House, Oxfordshire, and then moved to 36 Hertford Street. Edward claimed that the marriage took place only because he had 'dishonoured' her, and displayed violence towards RBL between 1828 and 1834; his apologetic letters to her at this time seem to support this view of their relationship. A daughter, Emily, was born in 1828, and a son, Edward Robert (subsequently the first Earl of Lytton), was born in 1831. In 1835, the family moved to Berrymead Priory, Acton. RBL wrote in her diary on 13 December 1835 'What a life mine has been! A sunless childhood; a flowerless youth; and certainly a fruitless womanhood.' Edward was openly unfaithful for many years during their marriage, and a final separation was signed in April 1836. RBL spent the next two years in Ireland with her children, but in 1838 her children were removed from her charge. She was forbidden any form of communication with her son, and saw her daughter Emily only once, when she died in 1848 at the age of 20.

In 1838, RBL travelled from Bath to Paris, Florence, and Geneva. She wrote various articles depicting Edward and his circle in an uncomplimentary light, and began writing novels. She believed herself to be continually persecuted by agents of her husband, a belief that may have had some basis in fact. She returned to England in 1847 to petition for an increased allowance, a request that was not granted. At this time she began a correspondence with A.E. Chalon which continued until Chalon's death in 1860; it clearly charts her legal battle with her husband, who is referred to as 'Sir Liar'. By 1857, a public appeal had been launched for financial assistance to cover her debts. RBL's public attempts to sabotage Edward's political career resulted in his attempt to incarcerate her in an asylum in 1858. She was forcibly detained and removed to a private establishment for the mentally deficient at Inverness Lodge, Brentford. This was followed by a public scandal which prompted her release after three weeks of 'treatment'. She then travelled to France with her son, but they parted after severe quarrels. RBL became a peeress in 1866, yet remained in debt. Edward died in 1873 after a successful literary and political career. RBL moved to 'Glenômera' in Upper Sydenham in 1875, and lived as a recluse until her death in 1882. She was buried in St John the Evangelist churchyard, Shirley, Surrey.

RBL's literary work consisted primarily of several-volumed novels. Several of these novels were written in the style of 'true histories' of which it is implied that she is only the editor. *Memoirs of a Muscovite* (1844) is a fantasy romance which ends in a happy marriage. Her fictional portrait of Molière in *School for Husbands* (1852) makes the 'tragedy' of his life heroic; it is notable for the preface in which RBL details her literary persecution by various publishers. Although her novels seem to paint a whimsical portrait of the aristocracy, it is difficult to avoid relating her art with her life. Novels such as *The World and his Wife* (1858) convey a bitterness towards the misuse of power: 'Not only do men, but as it would appear the most eminently profligate and immoral men, make and administer the laws . . . but they are . . . grossly immoral and unjust.' These themes of injustice are often incongruously combined with sentimental motifs. RBL wrote *A Blighted Life* (1880) in response to an advertisement requesting information to expose the practice of illegal incarcerations in madhouses. It was published without her knowledge in 1880, and stands as an eloquent defence for women committed to confinement against their will.

GABRIELLE OSRIN

Works: *Cheveley, or, The Man of Honour* (1839); *The Budget of the Bubble Family* (1840); *The Prince-duke and the Page* (1841); *Bianca Cappello: An Historical Romance* (1843); *Memoirs of a Muscovite* (1844); *The Peers' Daughters* (1849); *Miriam Sedley, or, The Tares and the Wheat: A Tale of Real Life* (1851); *The School for Husbands, or, Molière's Life and Times* (1852); *Very Successful!* (1856); *The World and his Wife* (1858); *Shells from the Sands of Time* (1876); *A Blighted Life* (1880); *Unpublished Letters of Lady Bulwer Lytton to A.E. Chalton RA* (1914).

References: Devey, L., *Life of Rosina, Lady Lytton* (1887); Sadleir, M., *Bulwer: A Panorama; Edward and Rosina 1803–36* (1931).

Burnett, Frances Hodgson

b. 24 November 1849, Manchester, England; d. 29 October 1924, Long Island, USA

Novelist, playwright, writer for children

FHB's reputation now rests almost entirely on her three major children's books: *Little Lord Fauntleroy* (1886), *A Little Princess* (1905), and *The Secret Garden* (1911). All three are continuously in print and have been seen regularly on cinema and television screens. But FHB's first success was as a novelist for adults. Her early novels, including the first one, *That Lass o' Lowries* (1877), remain remarkable. At the time, the critical acclaim was tremendous. The *Boston Transcript* said of *That Lass,* 'We know of no more powerful work from a woman's hand in the English language, not even excepting the best of George Eliot.' By the time she published *Through One Administration* (1883), her most serious and impressive novel, she had a high reputation on both sides of the Atlantic. An article in the 1883 issue of the *Century* listed FHB as one of those (with Henry James) 'who hold the front rank today in general estimation'. *Through One Administration* is both a political novel and a study of a failed marriage, the consequences of marrying the wrong person.

FHB was born in Manchester in comfortable circumstances. Her father's death and the resultant poverty caused her mother to take her children to a brother in Tennessee in 1865. Throughout her life, FHB moved back and forth between England and America, crossing the Atlantic thirty-three times. She started writing to help her family financially, and sold her first story when she was only 18. She married Swan Burnett in 1873 and supported him with her writing while he completed his medical studies in Paris. There were two sons of the marriage, one of whom died as a boy. FHB was divorced in 1898, rationalizing a situation that had existed for many years. A newspaper report at the time commented, 'Mrs Burnett entertained very advanced ideas as to the rights of women and the duties of a wife.' She married Stephen Townsend, who had been her partner for many years, in 1900, but left him soon afterwards. In spite of her success as a writer, for the stage and in books, and the considerable wealth and fame this success brought her, FHB's life was not a happy one.

Little Lord Fauntleroy, a book that has been much derided, turned FHB into a famous writer for children. Like many of her adult stories, it has a Cinderella, rags-to-riches theme. It has been criticized for its sentimentality and the unnatural goodness of its small hero. But the boy was very closely modelled on FHB's younger son, a fact which caused him lifelong embarrassment. The book changed FHB from being a serious writer, striving to master an art, into a craftswoman who had discovered she had the Midas touch. The more money she earned, the more she seemed to need. Earlier adult novels had left her 'completely exhausted' as 'she had entered into the joys and griefs of the men and women she pictured; she had shared their anxieties, suffered and endured all the trials they had passed through', as a contemporary interviewer put it. *Fauntleroy*, on the other hand, she had written quickly and easily.

After its success, FHB regularly published children's books. The quality was variable, and her most impressive work continued to be for adults until the publication in 1905 of *A Little Princess*, an enlarged version of a story that had originally appeared as *Sara Crewe* (1887) and which she had then dramatized. The best of the later adult works not only have humour and a strong narrative drive (she was always a fine storyteller) but also show an attractive social conscience. Memorable later characters include Rosalie Vanderpoel in *The Shuttle* (1907), a powerful story of an international marriage, and Emily Fox-Seton, the unselfish heroine of *The Making of a Marchioness* (1901), a harshly realistic portrait of Edwardian society.

The Secret Garden did not have the same initial impact as *Fauntleroy*, but its reputation has continued to grow since its publication in 1911. The most original thing about the book is that its heroine and one of its heroes are both thoroughly unattractive children. The story is the entirely convincing transformation of these children through their contact with the natural world. FHB was far too good a writer to spoil her story with overt propaganda, though there is one lapse at the beginning of chapter 27 with an explicit explanation of her symbolism and a bald definition of what the rest of the book conveys so subtly. Far from encouraging the Victorian attitudes instilled in her as a child, FHB suggested that children should be self-reliant and listen to their own hearts and consciences.

FHB's achievements were not purely personal and literary. Gladstone, when prime minister, suggested that *Fauntleroy* would help Britain and America to understand each other, and a lawsuit she brought over an unauthorized dramatization of that book helped to change the copyright laws of England.

ANN THWAITE

Selected works: *That Lass o' Lowries* (1877); *Surly Tim and other Stories* (1877); *Theo* (1877); *Dolly* (1877); *Earlier Stories*, 1st series (1878); *Kathleen* (1878); *Miss Crespigny* (1878); *A Quiet Life* and *The Tide on the Moaning Bar* (1878); *Our Neighbour Opposite* (1878); *Jarl's Daughter* (1879); *Natalie and Other Stories* (1879); *Haworth's* (1879); *A Fair Barbarian* (1881); *Through One Administration* (1883); *Little Lord Fauntleroy* (1886); *A Woman's Will, or, Miss Defarge* (1887); *Sara Crewe* (1888); *The Fortunes of Philippa Fairfax* (1888); *The Pretty Sister of José* (1889); *Children I Have Known* (1892); *The One I Knew the Best of All* (1893); *The Captain's Youngest* (1894); *The Two Little Pilgrims' Progress* (1895); *A Lady of Quality* (1896); *The Making of a Marchioness* (1901); *The Methods of Lady Walderhurst* (1901); *In the Closed Room* (1904); *A Little Princess* (1905); *The Dawn of a Tomorrow* (1906); *Racketty Packetty House* (1906); *The Spring Cleaning* (1908); *The Shuttle* (1907); *The Good Wolf* (1908); *Barty Crusoe and His Man Saturday* (1909); *The Land of the Blue Flower* (1909); *The Secret Garden* (1911); *My Robin* (1912); *The Lost Prince* (1915); *The White People* (1917); *Robin* (1922); *In the Garden* (1922).

References: Burnett, V., *The Romantick Lady* (1927); Laski, M., *Mrs Ewing, Mrs Molesworth, Mrs Hodgson Burnett* (1950); *OCCL*; Thwaite, A., *Waiting for the Party: The Life of Frances Hodgson Burnett* (1974); Townsend, J. R., *Written for Children* (1974).

Burney, Fanny

b. 13 June 1752, King's Lynn, Norfolk; d. 6 January 1840, London

Novelist

(Also wrote under Frances d'Arblay)

The novelist FB was one of the several children of Dr Charles Burney, noted music teacher and music historian. Her mother Esther Sleepe died when FB was 10, and her father allowed her to grow up in great freedom. She read both serious literature – sermons, histories, courtesy or conduct books – and eighteenth-century fiction, and she eagerly and frequently attended the theatre. Despite her general high spirits and talent for mimicry (honed, no doubt, by frequent association with her father's friend, the actor-manager David Garrick), she was shy and thoughtful around strangers, earning the sobriquet of 'The Old Lady' when only 11 years old.

She began a diary when she was 15, which served as excellent practice for her future writing. Read by her family and close friends, the journals included character sketches, anecdotes, and conversations as well as chronicles of her activities and opinions. FB continued her journals into old age, leaving for future years lively sketches of literary, court, and social life in England as well as chilling descriptions of such terrors as France just after Waterloo and a masectomy without anaesthesia.

The journals gave FB a way of making sense of her life. From seemingly random happenings, she could shape a coherent narrative and gain control of her experiences. The journals also provided her with an escape from the image she revealed to the world. In writing her journal entries, she freed herself from the decorous façade she presented to her social and literary critics, thereby fortifying and nourishing her inner life. The tension between the stifling social and the liberating private life that the journals show also informs each of RB's novels.

Her first novel, *Evelina*, originally written in spare moments to amuse her family, was published anonymously in 1778 and succeeded triumphantly, earning even Dr Johnson's praise. In this epistolary account of a young lady's somewhat rocky entrance into the social world, FB combined small doses of sound morality in the courtesy book tradition with several highly theatrical and farcical sketches of human foibles and social pretensions. Her strength lay particularly in inventing realistic dialogue that deftly revealed the character and class of the speaker. She particularly excelled in mimicking the middle classes.

Once the secret of her authorship came out, FB found herself, to her discomfort, courted by high literary and social circles. Her friends urged her to indulge her gift for satire and apt dialogue by writing a comedy and she created 'The Witlings' (1779), a sentimental comedy containing a sub-plot that satirized the Bluestockings. Her father advised her to suppress the scandalous work in order to preserve her social character; consequently, 'The Witlings' saw neither the stage nor print.

FB wrote her next novel, *Cecilia* (1782), under uncomfortable circumstances. Her family and publisher pressured her to write quickly, so she could not revise or condense as much as she wished to do. The work, nevertheless, was popular and influenced Austen's *Pride and Prejudice*. *Cecilia* contains several memorable comic characters, but the novel is more serious and less satiric than its predecessor, discussing in more harrowing terms the perils a rich young woman faces in society.

FB's second novel also treats the real economic problems of genteel eighteenth-century men and women who do not know how to handle money, an issue that reappears more pessimistically in her last two novels. The ending, too, is less romantic than *Evelina*'s and more melodramatic: the heroine goes mad (in, however, as believable a manner as possible) from financial and amatory worries. Once again, FB's interest in theatricality surfaces, because the final section of the novel draws from the tragedy *Venice Preserved*. Perhaps FB's novel was responsible for the renewed popularity of Otway's play at Drury Lane the season after the novel appeared.

In 1786, FB accepted the post of Second Keeper to the Robes of Queen Charlotte, a position she did not want or like, but could not refuse for economic and family reasons. During her five years of service, she wrote some ponderous historical tragedies, no doubt inspired by her residence in a royal castle and her depressed frame of mind. Of the tragedies, only *Edwy and Elgiva* (1790) was performed (at Drury Lane in 1795); it was an immediate failure.

In 1793, FB married the French emigré, Alexandre d'Arblay. The couple suffered from money troubles, which FB was able to remedy with another novel planned during her period at court. *Camilla* (1796) is close in plot to *Cecilia*: the heroine again suffers financial difficulties, endures seemingly unrequited love, and loses her self-control in a gripping sequence at the end of the book. FB develops this novel differently, however. It follows several siblings and cousins from childhood to adulthood, thereby showing the effects of nature versus nurture and the value of practical social experience over merely theoretical education. The novel contains more melodramatic material and less of the social satire at which FB excelled. Despite lacking the popularity of *Evelina*, the novel realized huge profits for the author.

Financially secure, FB turned her pen to drama gain, this time to comedies. None was ever performed. One of the plays interested Harris of Covent Garden, but Dr Burney urged FB to avoid another potential public fiasco. A comedy of manners, *A Busy Day*, returns to the idiom and light style of *Evelina*, with its satire on social pretension and class conflict. It is the play of hers most worth reviving.

After a lengthy residence in France, FB published her final novel, *The Wanderer* (1814), a novel of suspense, but it did not prove as profitable as she had hoped. The public expected a witty novel exposing French foibles; instead they received another heroine suffering from even greater economic distress, with romantic embellishments. Juliet, unlike other of FB's heroines, finds herself required to fend for herself equipped only with a gentlewoman's training and a disguised identity, and discovers the dangers of being a woman unprotected by family or friends. Evelina Anville had to worry about social *faux pas*; Juliet must cope with sexual harassment, attempted rape, and loss of social status as she tries to earn her keep. Genuine terrors, we learn, stem from real life, and attack the powerless.

Of course, Juliet does find herself rescued from social isolation, anonymity, and penury by the end of the book, but her survival until then has really depended on her maintaining the role of the conventional woman rather than adopting the more militant feminist ideals of her foil, Elinor. *The Wanderer*, written in a heavy-handed and melodramatic style, offers the same solution to feminine difficulties as the other novels: good sense combined with a careful adherence to social custom will ensure a woman's survival in a hostile world.

In general, FB's fiction realistically depicts the social and economic insecurity that plagued many middle-class women (and men). Within the romance structure of each of her novels, she tries to teach her readers how to conquer that

insecurity by learning prudence in all aspects of conduct, even if that prudence
requires suppressing some individuality.   LINDA V. TROOST

Works: *Evelina, or, A Young Lady's Entrance into the World* (1775); 'The Witlings'
(1779); *Cecilia, or, Memoirs of an Heiress* (1782); *Edwy and Elgiva* (1790); 'Hubert
De Vere' (1790–1); 'The Siege of Pevensey' (1790–1); *Brief Reflections Relative
to the Emigrant French Clergy* (1793); *Camilla, or, A Picture of Youth* (1796); 'Love
and Fashion' (1798–9); *A Busy Day* (1800–1); 'The Woman Hater' (1800–1); *The
Wanderer, or, Female Difficulties* (1814); 'Narrative of the Illness and Death of
General d'Arblay' (1823); *Memoirs of Dr Burney* (1832); *The Journals and Letters
of Fanny Burney*, ed. J. Hemlow *et al*. (1972–84); *Selected Letters and Journals*, ed.
J. Hemlow (1986).

References: Adelstein, M., *Fanny Burney* (1968); Bloom, L. and Bloom, E.,
'Fanny Burney's novels: the retreat from wonder', *Novel* 12 (1979); Copeland,
E. W., 'Money in the novels of Fanny Burney', *Studies in the Novel* 8 (Spring
1976); Cutting, R., 'Defiant women: the growth of feminism in Fanny Burney's
novels', *SEL* 17 (1977); Drabble; Grau, J., *Fanny Burney: An Annotated Bibli-
ography* (1981); Hemlow, J., 'Fanny Burney and the courtesy books', *PMLA*
65 (1950); Hemlow, J., 'Fanny Burney: playwright', *University of Toronto Quar-
terly* 19 (1950); Hemlow, J., *The History of Fanny Burney* (1958); Simons, J.,
Fanny Burney (1987); Spacks, P., *Imagining a Self* (1976); Spacks, P., ' "Ev'ry
Woman is at Heart a Rake" ', *Eighteenth-Century Studies* 8 (1974); Staves, S.,
'Evelina, or, Female Difficulties', *Modern Philology* 73 (1976); Straub, K., 'Fanny
Burney's *Evelina* and the "gulphs, pits, and precipices" of 18th-century female
life', *Eighteenth Century: Theory and Interpretation* 27 (1986); Todd; Todd, J.,
The Sign of Angellica: Women, Writing and Fiction 1660–1800 (1989).

Bury, Lady Charlotte

b. 18 February 1775, London; d. 31 March 1861, London

Novelist, diarist, poet

CB, the younger daughter of John Campbell, 5th Duke of Argyll, and his wife
Elizabeth Gunning, Duchess of Hamilton, was famous for her beauty, her
'silver-fork' fiction, and her royal *chroniques scandaleuses*.

Educated privately, and presented at court, she was married on 21 June 1796
to a penniless cousin, Colonel John Campbell, by whom she had nine children.
In 1797 she produced a mediocre volume of verse. Widowed in 1809, she
accepted the post of Lady-in-Waiting to the Princess of Wales, later Queen
Caroline. She left the royal service in 1815, after publishing her first novel and
keeping a detailed private diary of her experiences at court. On 17 March 1818,
in Florence, she married, against the wishes of her family, the Rev. Edward
John Bury, an Anglican clergyman of artistic leanings, extravagant tastes, and
limited means. Two more children were born, and she continued writing fiction
to support the family. As a clergyman's wife she wrote an insipid book of
prayers, much ridiculed by Thackeray.

Bury died in 1832 and a pressing need for money led CB to publish something
more *piquant*. Colburn paid her £2,000 for her diary, which appeared anonymously in 1838 – a breach of confidentiality, revealing the indiscretions of the
Princesss of Wales, her sufferings at the hands of her husband and mother-in-
law, and the political intrigue with which she was surrounded. This, as
expected, had an enormous sale, but CB was severely criticized for her 'betrayal'
and ostracized by many of her aristocratic acquaintances. She continued with
her writing in the 1840s, much of it hackwork, including a cookery book. Her

output dwindled in the 1850s, and, saddened by the deaths of eight of her children, and almost forgotten by the literary world, she died in poverty at the age of 86.

Her work suffers from triviality, sentimentality, and a slipshod style, but there are some vivid pictures of high society and court life (drawn from genuine experience rather than imagination or servants' gossip), and some spirited castigation of fashionable vices, particularly self-indulgence, illicit passion, flirtation ('the demon of coquetry'), and the ambitious matchmaking of manoeuvring mothers. One of her best novels, *The Divorced (1837),* anticipates *East Lynne* in depicting the horrors, humiliations, and maternal torments that await the guilty *divorcée.*   MARGARET MAISON

Selected works: *Poems on Several Occasions* (1797); *Self Indulgence* (1812); *Conduct is Fate* (1822); *Alla Giornata* (1826); *Suspirium Sanctorum* (1826); *A Marriage in High Life* (1828); *Flirtation* (1828); *The Exclusives* (1830); *Journal of the Heart* (1830, 2nd series 1835); *The Separation* (a revision of *Self Indulgence*) (1830); *The Three Great Sanctuaries of Tuscany* (1833); *The Disinherited, and the Ensnared* (1836); *The Divorced* (1837); *Diary Illustrative of the Times of George IV* (later renamed *The Diary of a Lady-in-Waiting*) (1838); *The History of a Flirt* (1840); *The Manoeuvring Mother* (1842); *The Lady's Own Cookery Book* (1844); *The Wilfulness of Woman* (1844); *The Lady of Fashion* (1856); *The Two Baronets* (1864).
References: Dixon, W., *Queens of Beauty and Their Romances* (1907); Prucher, A., *Figure Europee del Primo '800* (1961); Rosa, M. W., *The Silver-Fork School* (1936); Steuart, A. F., 'Introduction' to *The Diary of a Lady-in-Waiting* (1908); White, E. M., 'Thackeray, "Dolly Duster" and Lady Charlotte Campbell Bury', *Review of English Studies* 26, 61 (February, 1965).

Byatt, A. S.
b. 24 August 1936, Sheffield
Literary critic, scholar, novelist
ASB is the daughter of Kathleen Marie Bloor and John Frederick Drabble, QC. Her sister is Margaret Drabble, the novelist. ASB's first marriage (1959) to Charles Raynor Byatt was dissolved in 1969; she has one daughter from this marriage, a son died. She also has two daughters from her second marriage to Peter John Duffy (1969). ASB was educated at Sheffield High School, and the Mount School, York. She went to Newnham College, Cambridge, where she gained an honours degree in English in 1957. She then went to Bryn Mawr College, Pennsylvania, on an English Speaking Union Fellowship, and in 1958–9 was at Somerville College, Oxford. She taught at Westminster Tutors from 1962 to 1965, was an extra-mural lecturer at the University of London from 1962 to 1971, lectured part-time in literature at the Central School of Art and Design from 1965 to 1969, and from 1972 to 1983 was a lecturer in English at University College, London. She has been an Associate of Newnham College since 1977, and was a member of the Social Effects of Television Advisory Group, BBC, from 1974 to 1977. ASB was also a member of the Board of Communications and Cultural Studies, CNAA, from 1978 to 1984, and is a member of the Board of Creative and Performing Arts. She is a Fellow of the Royal Society of Literature. She regularly reviews for *The Times* and *New Statesman.* She lives in London.

ASB has gained a reputation as both a scholar and a novelist. Her study of Iris Murdoch, *Degrees of Freedom: The Novels of Iris Murdoch* (1965), was the first book on that writer and remains one of the most sensitive analyses of

Murdoch's work. This may be due to the fact that both writers, although almost a generation apart, underwent similar experiences, being students, scholars, and novelists as well as women in post-war Oxbridge and London. Both have academic and novelistic interests in an intellectual world dominated by men, and both have a very intellectual, ideas-based approach to their fiction. ASB wrote a second book on Murdoch, *Iris Murdoch*, in 1976. She also wrote a study of *Wordsworth and Coleridge in Their Time* (1970), and edited George Eliot's *Mill on the Floss* (1979).

Her first novel, *Shadow of a Sun*, was published in 1964. Taking its title from a Ralegh poem, it deals with the attempt of Anna, the teenage daughter of an important English novelist, Henry Severell, to free herself from the overpowering personality of her father. The oppressive atmosphere experienced by Anna is highlighted for the reader by the small number of characters in the novel. ASB's *The Game* (1968) has the same intensity as her first novel; it centres on the relationship of two sisters, one, Cassandra, an Oxford don, the other, Julia, a popular novelist. The sisters shared a childhood game based on the creation, in Brontë-like fashion, of an imaginary world. As adults they have prolonged this game through their respective professional interests. The re-entry into their lives of a childhood friend, Simon, reactivates childhood conflicts between the sisters, and their uneasy relationship with reality and the imaginary culminates tragically in Cassandra's suicide.

In 1979 ASB published the first volume of what is to be a quartet, followed by the second volume in 1985. Both *The Virgin in the Garden* and *Still Life* deal with life in the second Elizabethan age. The first novel is set in 1952–3, and presents the early history of Bill Potter's three children Stephanie, Frederica, and Marcus. The second novel covers the years 1954–9. Both texts are full of literary allusions, and constitute an attempt to fuse symbolism and realism through the exploration of English history and cultural tradition and that of individual lives.   GABRIELE GRIFFIN

Works: *Shadow of a Sun* (1964); *Degrees of Freedom: The Novels of Iris Murdoch* (1965); *The Game* (1968); *Wordsworth and Coleridge in Their Time* (1970); *Iris Murdoch* (1976); 'Daniel', *Encounter* (April 1976); *The Virgin in the Garden* (1979); *Still Life* (1985); *Sugar and Other Stories* (1987).

References: Dusinberre, J., 'Forms of reality in A. S. Byatt's *The Virgin in the Garden*', *Critique* 24, 1, (Fall 1982); Kenyon, O., *Women Novelists Today* (1988).

Cable, Mildred

b. 1878, Guildford; d. 1952, Dorset

Travel and religious writer

MC is primarily known as a writer of travel journals, although she also wrote other books of a more straightforwardly religious nature and biographical studies of missionaries. Most of her books were written in collaboration with Francesca French.

Having decided at a very early age that she wanted to join the Protestant China Inland Mission, she studied medicine at London University to equip her for this purpose, rather than studying music as her parents wished. At the age of 23, she joined the Mission. In China she met Francesca French who by then was a well-known mission worker in the Shansi province. They were later joined by Francesca's sister, Evangeline, and together they set up a school for girls in Hwochow. Several years later, she was ordered to go to the Gobi Desert by the Commander-in-Chief of the Mission in an attempt to convert the inhabitants. One of her earlier books, *Through the Jade Gate and Central Asia* (1927), describes the journey the three women made across the Gobi Desert, through the Sian region of China and finally to Russia, and depicts their missionary activities: MC describes the setting up of a 'pioneer band' of Chinese converts in Kanchow to go into areas where Christianity had not previously penetrated. The women taught many people to read the Chinese government's phonetic script so that they could read the Bible and Christian tracts in their own language; they travelled to fairs and other gatherings to sell bibles and to sing songs accompanied by a portable organ. One other effective method of conversion which they discovered was to interest the women and thereby gain an entrance into the home to visit the men. Although the contemporary reader may be impressed by the sincerity and depth of MC's Christian belief, the descriptions of Buddhists ('a blinded people') and Moslems ('self-righteous Pharisees') clearly create difficulties.

The book for which she is most famous is *The Gobi Desert* (1942), which gained the Royal Central Asian Society's award, and which has been reprinted by Virago (1984). In this book, she describes her travels through the Gobi Desert with Francesca and Evangeline French (they were the first Englishwomen to cross the desert, and the first missionaries to go there since the sixth century). The conditions in which they travelled were extremely difficult, transport being exceptionally limited, and water and food scarce; they also travelled in constant fear of attack by bandits and robbers. Unlike *Through the Jade Gate*, there is little evidence of proselytizing in the book; much of it is taken up with descriptions of the vastness and the surprising productiveness of the desert, and the ways in which the various ethnic groups, (Chinese, Turki, Qazaq, and Russian) survive there, where westerners with western technology could not. In neither of these books is MC aware of the problems created by the missionaries' presence in China, especially the rifts within families caused by conversion to Christianity. Nor does she seem to be aware of the political implications of the missionaries' presence.

MC and the French sisters left China in 1936, and continued to work for the British and Foreign Bible Society, writing over twenty books. MC did not marry, but with Francesca French, her lifelong companion, she adopted a girl from the Gobi whom they called Topsy. Marina Warner, in her introduction to the Virago edition of *The Gobi Desert*, discusses the question of whether MC and Francesca were lesbian; it would seem inappropriate to attribute lesbianism to everyone who refused to act in a 'feminine' way, especially where evidence is so lacking. However, their lives were clearly woman-centred as other women travellers' lives were not. SARA MILLS

Selected works: Despatches from North West Kansu (1925); *Through the Jade Gate and Central Asia* (1927); *Something Happened* (1933); *Ambassadors for Christ* (1935); *The Making of a Pioneer: Percy Mather* (1935); *The Journey with a Purpose* (1935); *The Story of Topsy, Little Lonely of Central Asia* (1937); *Grace, Child of the Gobi* (1938); *The Gobi Desert* (1942); *China, Her Life and Her People* (1946); *The Book Which Demands a Verdict* (1946); *Dhina, Her Life and People* (1946); *George Hunter, Apostle of Turkestan* (1948); *Wall of Spears: The Gobi Desert* (1951); *Why Not For the World: The Story of God Through the Bible Society* (1952).

References: Allen, A., *Travelling Ladies – Victorian Adventuresses* (1980); Warner, M., 'Introduction' to *The Gobi Desert* (1984).

Caird, Mona

b. 1858, Isle of Wight; d. 4 February 1932, Hampstead, London

Novelist, miscellaneous writer

MC was the daughter of John Alison, an English inventor. Her date of birth and other facts about her life are uncertain, but it seems that as a child she wrote stories and plays that reveal she was proficient in French and German as well as knowledgeable in English literature, philosophy, and science. In 1877 she married James A. Henryson-Caird and lived in Hampstead from then until her death. In addition to her career as a romance novelist, MC was active in propaganda, writing for the temperance movement and the anti-vivisection campaigns. Her views on marriage caused her to be labelled a feminist in her day. Both her fiction and non-fiction argue for a more liberated and honest look at marriage than Victorian society permitted. For example, in *The Morality of Marriage and Other Essays* (1897), MC defines marriage as a continuation of the ancient practice of wife-purchasing and focuses on means of reforming attitudes towards it by changing male habits, increasing opportunities for female education, and correcting the laws to equalize child custody and divorce settlements. In her indignation, she is frequently sarcastic and derisive of societies that cling to patriarchal systems. The characters in her novels frequently give long set speeches on marriage reform that reflect these views. In *A Romance of the Moors* (1891), the young lovers Dick and Bessie encounter the liberated Margaret who counsels the pair to know themselves first so as to shake off traditional expectations of married life, and to approach their love as mature, independent individuals who are as sufficient with each other as without. At one crucial point, Margaret tells Bessie, 'You shall come away with me and see if you can't form other interests that will bring you closer to Dick, not take you farther away from him.' A frequent theme of MC's novels, then, was the damage wrong marriages could do to women. In *The Wings of Azreal* (1889), Viola Sedley's marriage to the evil, selfish Phillip ends with her murdering him in self-defence, then fleeing her lover's attempts to help her by rushing on to the moors and into oblivion.

A direct result of MC's outspokenness on marriage was a public controversy carried on in the pages of the *Review* in August 1888, that culminated in her book-length study, *The Morality of Marriage and Other Essays*. In an effort to dispute her own belief that for 'the woman of the nineteenth century there is nothing but discouragement, opposition, eternal admonitions and reminders as to duty', MC creates heroines in her novels who are able to rise above society's expectations and determine not only their own fate but that of those around them. Bessie chooses not to marry Dick, and practically rejects him, until his period of wanderlust has passed and he is at peace with himself, just as Viola rejects Henry Lancaster to save him from the certain destruction she faces for murdering her husband.

In an effort to focus on the psychological dilemma of the female character, MC sacrifices characterization and dialogue; her characters are frequently shallow and verbose and they utter many banalities. Her plots tend to be simple and obvious; yet she can use suspense skilfully, as in *The Wings of Azreal*.

B. E. SCHNELLER

Works: *Whom Nature Leadeth* (1883); *One that Wins* (1887); *The Wings of Azreal* (1889); *A Romance of the Moors* (1891); *The Daughters of Danaus* (1894); *Beyond the Pale* (1896); *The Morality of Marriage and Other Essays* (1897); *Romantic Cities of Provence* (1906); *Stones of Sacrifice* (1915).

References: Allibone; *BA* (19); Cunningham, A. R., 'The "New Woman Fiction" of the 1890s', *Victorian Studies* 17 (December 1973); Stetz, M. D., 'Turning points: Mona Caird', *Turn-of-the-Century Women* 2, 2 (Winter 1985).

Carey, Rosa Nouchette

b. 24 September 1840, Stratford-le-Bow, London; d. 19 July 1909, London
Novelist, short story writer

RNC was the eighth child and fourth daughter of a shipowner, William Henry Carey, and his wife, Maria Jane. Considered delicate, she was educated at home during her early years in Hackney and then at the Ladies' Institute, St John's Wood. She wrote plays and poems for her brothers and sisters, and told stories to one sister in particular as she worked at her needlework. Her first novel, *Nellie's Memories* (1868), was composed entirely in this manner and only written down seven years later. The novel proved a success, going through multiple editions; thirty-eight more novels were to follow. RNC also became a prolific writer of short stories, published in *Girls' Own Paper* which was started by the Religious Tract Society as a counterweight to the violent and sensational reading matter aimed at young people; for some years she was on the staff of this periodical, which had a wide readership, stretching from servants to royalty, and which addressed social issues of the day, such as the changing concept of the lady at a time when women often earned their living outside the home. RNC also published stories with the Religious Tract Society and compiled a volume of brief biographies, *Twelve Notable Good Women of the Nineteenth Century* (1899). She led an outwardly uneventful life, first in Hampstead and then in Putney, and was a close friend of both Mrs Henry Wood and Mathilde Blind, although the friendship with the latter, started in school years, foundered on religious differences. For more than eighteen years, RNC lived with her widowed sister, Helen Burnside, a fellow contributor to *Girls' Own Paper.*

RNC believed steadfastly in the domestic role of women, at one stage even trying to avoid writing in case it interfered with her duties in the home. When her brother died, she cared for his children, and she gave classes to girls and servants through the Fulham Sunday School. Her sister said of her that she '*lived* her religion' so that 'family duty and devotion to its many members have always come first'. RNC herself stated that her ambition was 'to try to do good and not harm by my works, and to write books which any mother can give a girl to read'. *The Lady* described her novels as 'immaculately pure, and very high in tone'. Although a conservative writer, she managed to some extent to adapt to the changing social situation and so she largely retained her initial popularity.

Wee Wifie (1869) is about a child bride married to an older man who rapidly tires of her. The book is her trial by ordeal; in the end female suffering triumphs but at the expense of the heroine. The unacknowledged masochism of the work can be illustrated by the lengthy scene depicting the heroine's painful labour with her first child. *Not Like Other Girls* (1884) depicts a family of girls whose fortune disappears and who are left unprovided for and without education. The novel shows the effect of this loss on their status in the community and on their attitude to themselves as ladies. *Our Bessie* (1888) appeared first as a serial in *Girls' Own Paper*; it presents a simple, sensible heroine and a rich young lady, Edna, who must learn wisdom and humility. Pathos is provided in the story of Bessie's sister who is sickly and fretful but who is addressed firmly by Bessie: 'Why don't you look on your unhappy nature as your appointed cross,

and just bear with yourself as much as you expect others to bear with you? . . .
why don't you say to yourself . . . "my one effort shall be to prevent other
people suffering through me"?'   JANET JONES
Selected works: Nellie's Memories (1868); Wee Wifie (1869); Wooed and Married
(1875); Not Like other Girls (1884); Uncle Max (1887); Only the Governess (1888);
Our Bessie (1888); The Rosa Nouchette Carey Birthday Book (1901); The Sunny
Side of the Hill (1908); Barbara Heathcote's Trial (1909).
References: DNB; NWAD; Plarr, V., People of the Period (1897).

Carlyle, Jane Welsh

b. 14 July 1801, Haddington, East Lothian; d. 21 April 1866, London
Letter writer
At first sight it is surprising that JC remains famous. She alone among celebrated
Victorian women owes her fame not to what she did, like Florence Nightingale,
or to what she wrote, like Emily Brontë, but to her personality and to the
strange, impossible genius of the man she married. She traced descent from
two families called Welsh, and reckoned John Knox among her family connections. The family had long been settled at the manor house of Craigenputtock.
She was taught Latin by Edward Irving, friend of Carlyle, and later rival with
him for JC's hand. She was described as 'bright and self-willed', and her
precocity is shown by her passionate response to the story of Dido in *Aeneid
VI* – she burnt her doll on her tenth birthday. She had strong family affections,
and in 1819 was passionately grieved by the death of her father, John Welsh,
as she was later by that of her mother, Grace Welsh. Irving, who for a time
wavered about his own forthcoming marriage, in the hope of marrying JC,
introduced her to his friend Carlyle in 1821. A rough, uncouth peasant with
wide reading and (when roused) a brilliant flow of passionate talk, he soon
impressed her more than more eligible and wealthier suitors. But she managed
to retain for a time a tone of imperious superiority. Such tactics could not be
permanent in dealing with a man of fierce pride and independence, an explosive
temper, and a firm belief in the necessity of male dominance. When she married
him in 1826, her motives were perhaps not completely known to herself. Partly,
perhaps, she was reacting against her own thwarted affection for Irving; partly
she was motivated by intellectual ambition – she was among the first to sense
the presence of a budding genius - partly she was flattered by the devotion of
a man whose rough masculinity could border on the brutal, and whose
unswerving honesty (coupled with contempt for most of the world's inhabitants) forbade him to pay insincere compliments. She admired him more than
she loved him. But in all the frustrations and vicissitudes of a marriage lasting
nearly forty years, she never ceased to desire his affection and good opinion as
the greatest earthly good.
     For a time they lived a lonely life in Scotland, but in 1831 moved to London,
which remained their home for the rest of their married life, as it was Carlyle's
in his widowerhood of nearly fifteen years. Visitors to the house in Cheyne
Row will be surprised that is is described in the *DNB* as 'small', that an
impecunious, childless couple could possibly fill so much space. If it were not
now a museum, it would probably be occupied by a millionaire. Nevertheless,
their financial anxieties were genuine. Carlyle's fame came slowly, and it was
not until 1837, when Carlyle was 42 and JC 36, that *The French Revolution*,
rewritten after the first manuscript had been accidentally destroyed, definitely
established Carlyle's fame. Meanwhile JC had emerged from the loneliness of

her early married life, acquired her own female friends, notably the novelist Geraldine Jewsbury, and become the hostess of a salon, to which both literary lions and political exiles, like Mazzini and Cavaignac, resorted.

The marriage fascinated contemporaries. The wag who said it was a good marriage because it meant two unhappy people instead of four, though unkind, was pointing to a truth, that the two were in some ways extraordinarily alike. They were both clever, egoistical, brittle, short-tempered, and endlessly fond of complaining. But the difference in their complaints was this: Carlyle would quarrel, complain, and rail at her over the most trivial matters, but was always loyal in speaking of her to others, and most notably in his self-reproachful comments on her letters after her death. She was outwardly more submissive, but complained endlessly to others. Geraldine Jewsbury, her friend rather than his, thought his the nobler nature. Both, though entirely free from the placidity and sloth of Jane Austen's Lady Bertram, were like her in their shared delusion that nothing could ever be troublesome or fatiguing to anyone but themselves. Reading their tirades of complaint against each other and the world, it is sometimes hard to remember the comfort, success, and, after 1837, comparative security of their lives. When no greater disasters were to be had, headaches, insomnia, and constipation could be described in language most people would reserve for shipwrecks, earthquakes, and bankruptcies.

Two of JC's troubles, however, were more substantial. The evidence that Carlyle was impotent, though not absolutely conclusive, has been found convincing by most of those who have studied the question. Froude, Carlyle's disciple and biographer, omitted direct mention of the issue in his book, but wrote a personal memoir (posthumously published in 1903) which leaves no doubt of his opinion. From this point of view, JC's tiresomely sentimental attitude to dogs acquires a poignancy that it would otherwise lack; and her death, clutching a lap dog in a London street, becomes ironically emblematic. Her other trouble was jealousy of Lady Harriet Baring (Lady Ashburton), who dazzled Carlyle, and painfully patronized JC. Perhaps (since for several different reasons it was impossible that Lady Harriet should become Carlyle's mistress) envy was as strong an emotion as jealousy in JC's heart. Deeply concerned as she was in her husband's burgeoning public reputation, she did not wish him to have social ambitions or achievements separately from herself; and it was difficult for her, being clearly better-born than he, to accept that he might, more easily than she, soar into high social circles. Perhaps, too, she blamed her self for naivety in not having discerned earlier Carlyle's powerful vanity, concealed but not obliterated under a crust of Scots independence and deliberate bad manners.

After 1850, Carlyle, though wearily recognized as a 'great man', became a back number in English intellectual life. His temper deteriorated yet further, and JC's self-pity did not grow less. They staggered on together as they always had, retaining amid all their troubles a strong mutual respect. The end was sudden. Carlyle had been elected Rector of Edinburgh University, and went there to deliver the address at his installation, as he characteristically said, 'in a mood of defiant despair, and under the pressure of nightmare'. He was at Dumfries when he heard the news of her death, which inspired a remorse never afterwards forgotten. Her epitaph speaks of her 'soft invincibility' and 'noble loyalty of heart' and as the light of her husband's life.

JC's only literary monument is to be found in her letters – on average over a hundred a year to friends and family. They are vivid, sharp, and witty, but they hardly convince us that a notable author was lost by her failing to publish on her own account. She could be as savage and ruthless as her husband, and it is a question how far we should attribute this to his influence, and how far to the similarity of their natures. For instance, she wrote to him (10 April 1866) about the case of Governor Eyre, who had executed a large number of West Indians; 'He [Hayward] told me *women* might patronize Eyre. . . . But no *man* living could stand up for Eyre now! "I hope Mr Carlyle does," I said. . . . "I should be surprised and grieved if I found him sentimentalizing over a pack of black brutes." '

Domestic trivia abound, especially complaints about servants (in this she rather resembled Lady Bertram's sister, Mrs Price), criticisms of her husband, mostly justified, and catty remarks about Lady Ashburton, together with more substantial matter, her abiding affection for him and tender reminiscences of the past, especially of her Scottish childhood. The dominant mood is self-pity. Her own sharp wit might have been stirred if she had heard of another woman writing (April 1864), 'Oh, what I have suffered, my aunts! what I may still have to suffer! Pray for me that I may be enabled to endure. Don't write to myself; reading letters excites me too much . . . Ah, my aunts, I shall die; that is my belief!'

But she was the ultimate victor in the long contest of wills with her husband. Death, as he felt for the rest of his life, is the unanswerable repartee.

A. O. J. COCKSHUT

Works: *Letters and Memorials of Jane Welsh Carlyle*, prepared by T. Carlyle, ed. J. A. Froude (1883); *New Letters and Memorials of Jane Welsh Carlyle*, ed. A. Carlyle (1903); *Jane Welsh Carlyle: Letters to her Family 1839–63*, ed. L. Huxley (1924); *Letters of Jane Welsh Carlyle to Joseph Neuberg 1848–62*, ed. T. Scudder (1931); *Jane Welsh Carlyle: A New Selection of Her Letters*, ed. T. Bliss (1950); *I Too Am Here: Selected Letters of Jane Welsh Carlyle*, ed. A. and M. M. Simpson (1977).

References: Campbell, I., *Thomas Carlyle* (1974); Carlyle, T., *Reminiscences* (1881); Clubbe, J. (ed.), *Carlyle and His Contemporaries* (1976); Hardwick, E., 'Jane Carlyle', in *Seduction and Betrayal* (1970); Kaplan, F., *Thomas Carlyle* (1983); Mormson, N. B., *True Minds: The Marriage of Thomas and Jane Carlyle* (1974); Smiles, S., *A Publisher and His Friends* (1911); Woolf, V., 'Geraldine and Jane', in *Second Common Reader* (1932).

Carrington

b. 29 March, 1893, Hereford; d. 11 March 1932, Ham Spray, Hampshire
Letter writer, diarist, painter
C was born into the middle-class family of Samuel Carrington, a retired railway builder for the East India Company, and his much younger wife Charlotte Houghton, the former governess to the children of one of his nieces. C (who from her Slade student days to the end of her life never used her first name) detested her mother's fussiness and conformity but idealized her father: 'I loved my father for his rough big character, his rather rustic simplicity and the great way he lived inside himself,' she wrote in one of her letters to her fellow student Mark Gertler, with whom she carried on an intermittent love affair for many years. Her other close friends at the Slade, C. R. W. Nevinson, Paul Nach, and Stanley Spencer, encouraged her in her art, as Roger Fry, whose criticism she greatly admired, never did. She rarely exhibited, and felt herself a failure, constantly comparing herself not just with Piero della Francesca, Tintoretto, and her other favourite artists, but – probably more tragically –

with the brilliant talkers and creators of her acquaintance, closely or loosely attached to Bloomsbury: 'It's rather maddening to have the ambition of Tintoretto and to paint like a mouse,' she wrote.

C's ambition for herself never included the standard marriage and children; having met Lytton Strachey through Virginia and Leonard Woolf, and having fallen quite absolutely in love with him, she devoted her life to nursing and nourishing him. Lytton Strachey, being homosexual, feared her devotion in its possibly dependent form, and encouraged her marriage to Ralph Partridge. Together they set up a *ménage à trois* in 1921 at Tidmarsh Mill, near Pangbourne, intended as a calm retreat for Strachey, who asked C to be his housekeeper. Later they removed to Ham Spray, near the Hampshire downs. By this time Strachey's royalties from *Queen Victoria* were sufficient to purchase the house. C decorated it as she had done the other homes, as well as painting inn signs, and doing tinsel and glass paintings, but leaving less and less time for serious painting: 'I am not strong enough to live in this world of people *and* paint,' she wrote in her diary. For the time taken up by constant entertaining and the mode of life she had chosen was forever inimical to her dedication: of this she was fully aware and, to some extent, she consented to it, and became involved over and over again in various love affairs – with Gerald Brenan and with 'Beakus' Penrose, ten years her junior, who reminded her of her brother Teddy, killed in the War, and who in the end tired of her. As Strachey was dying of cancer, C tried to take her own life with carbon monoxide fumes, was rescued, and, six weeks after his death, shot herself with a gun she claimed she had borrowed to kill rabbits. Not making a very clean job of it, for the gun had not gone off at once, and she had had to reset it, she felt she had 'bungled' her death, as she had her life.

Tormented for much of her life by feelings of insufficiency, C nevertheless succeeded in a quite extraordinary fashion in showing and sharing a unique style of living, thinking, and writing, which is, at its best, delightful, and, at its most depressing, profoundly troubling for what it indicates of a woman's often problematic stance towards her own work and towards the intertwinings of relations with the others around her. C's low evaluation of herself and her work, coupled with the intensity of her observations, written and painted, of nature and other people, makes a case study for psychology enthusiasts. She has other attractions for enthusiasts of superb 'epistolary style'. C's unpublished ventures into short fiction and drama and her poetry pale beside the variety of tone and temper in her letters, profusely and drolly illustrated, and always quite exactly vectored towards the recipient. They are alternately cajoling, flirtatious, tender, gossipy, encouraging, affectionate, digressive, and focused. Her acknowledged bisexuality finds a parallel ambivalence in all her attitudes, so that she advances and retreats, discloses and then hides, offers and then withdraws. In the art of letter writing, she ranks among the very first of practitioners.

And in the art of diary writing, that most ambivalent art of the secret and the manifest, she ranks no less high. Her life with all its peculiarities of the personal and the professional (can an art not displayed except in its craft aspect be said to fulfil the self? what is, precisely speaking, the professional?) finds its truest fulfilment in its self-writing through the letters to others and to herself. 'I feel there is nothing to prevent my now fervent image of the nymph who turned into a stag so perfectly that it could be no disgrace,' she observed in a letter of 1924 to Gerald Brenan. But in 1931, in a letter to Rosamond Lehmann, after quoting from what she calls Lytton Strachey's creed, that 'it's *no* good being anything but what you are and the great thing is never to do anything one doesn't feel genuinely inside onself', she continues in a self-accusatory mode: 'For really I used every excuse not to do any proper painting. It's partly I have such high standards that I can't bear going on with pictures when I can see they are amateurish and dull.'

C alternated between a secretive delight at solitude, declaring that 'the pleasure of being alone in my bedroom is very great', and a playful passion for gossip: 'all the very intimate and indiscreet things I meant to tell you in France,' she says to Sebastian Sprott, one of her favourite correspondents, have to her regret been forgotten in English discretion, back at Tidmarsh. 'I confess I rather enjoyed for once the company of anyone as stupid as myself,' she teased him before enjoining him about Lytton Strachey's comfort, 'as one mistress to another'. The funny informal brightness of her letter-writing art is matched, at other moments, by her extremes of 'melancholly', as she always spelled it, and by her nightmares and dreads, coupled with sharp feelings of guilt towards anyone with whom she was involved. Even her all-encompassing love for Lytton Strachey was to her 'the most self-debasing' sort anyone could have, predicting years of 'misery' for herself, and yet it alone seemed to her worth creating for and dwelling upon. Her peculiar genius for friendship and its written art outshone her other writing, if not her painting. The presentation of her extraordinary diary, called by her, in a strange distancing act, 'D. C. Partride: Her Book' is characteristic: her married name was Partridge, and by dropping a letter from it, it is indeed as if she is refusing to take that other name quite as she had promised: 'To you,' she wrote to Mark Gertler, 'I shall ever be Carrington, and to myself.'   MARY ANN CAWS

Works: *Carrington: Letters and Extracts from her Diaries*, ed. D. Garnett (1970).
References: Carrington, N., *Carrington: Paintings, Drawings and Decorations* (1978); Brenan, G., *Gerald Brenan: Personal Record 1920–1972* (1972).

Carswell, Catherine
b. March 1879, Glasgow; d. March 1946, Oxford
Novelist, biographer, critic

CC was the second of the four children of George and Mary Anne MacFarlane. She was brought up in a militantly Presbyterian environment: her father, who negotiated the shipping of textiles to the West Indies, was president and one of the founders of the YMCA, and both her grandfathers were church ministers who had helped to form the United Free Church of Scotland. Her mother was zealously pro-Jewish, and at the age of 12 CC helped her to give informal English lessons to impoverished Polish refugees. She attended schools in Glasgow, and in 1897 went to Frankfurt for two years, studying music at the Schumann Conservatorium. Returning to Glasgow, she gave up music and turned instead to lecturing in art history. In 1904 she married the artist Herbert Jackson after a very brief courtship. When, the following year, she told him of her pregnancy, he attempted to kill her and was later certified insane. Returning to Glasgow with her daughter Diana, born in October 1905, she began to attend classes in English literature at the university, but could not as a woman be admitted for a degree. In May 1908 she made legal history by winning the case for the annulment of her marriage.

In 1907, CC became reviewer and dramatic critic for the *Glasgow Herald*, working first in Glasgow and then, in 1912, in London. A meeting with D. H.

Lawrence in 1914 marked the beginning of a close and enduring friendship, and in 1915 she was sacked as a result of a favourable review of Lawrence's *The Rainbow*, which she sent directly to the printer without the editor's intervention. In the same year she married the journalist Donald Carswell, with whom she had one son. (Her daughter had died of pneumonia in 1913.) Her next job was as assistant dramatic critic for *The Observer*, but by now she was engaged on her first novel, *Open the Door* (1920). In 1916 she and Lawrence exchanged manuscripts of *Open the Door* and *Women in Love*, and, with Lawrence's encouragement, CC's novel was finally completed in 1918; though initially rejected by Duckworth, it was published by Melrose in 1920, winning the Melrose prize. Another novel, *The Camomile*, followed in 1922.

CC then turned to biography, making her name with *The Life of Robert Burns*, which shocked orthodox Burnsites in its attempt to uncover the 'real' Burns from the adulation with which tradition had smothered him. Her biography of Lawrence, *The Savage Pilgrimage*, for which she is best known, appeared two years afer Lawrence's death, in 1932. It was written partly as an attack on John Middleton Murry's 'destructive hagiography' of Lawrence in *Son of Woman* (1931); initially published by Chatto & Windus, it was withdrawn from circulation as a result of a writ for libel served by Murry. It was reissued by Secker, with certain changes, in 1933. Finally, a life of Boccaccio, *The Tranquil Heart*, appeared in 1937; CC claimed to have chosen Boccaccio because 'No writer before him dreamed of writing avowedly for women readers . . . yet none but men have written about him.'

After the death of her husband in an accident during a black-out in 1940, CC lived alone in London, working on various anthologies and her autobiography, *Lying Awake*, which was published posthumously and incomplete in 1952. She counted among her close friends Vita Sackville-West, Storm Jameson, Edwin Muir, Rose Macaulay, Hugh McDiarmid, and John Buchan.

Both CC's novels draw heavily on her own experiences as a young woman and her early training in music and art. As its title suggests, *Open the Door* is a *Bildungsroman*, following Joanna Bannerman's struggle to break free from the oppressively puritanical environment in which she has grown up. As an art student in Edinburgh she falls passionately in love with and quickly marries Mario Rasponi, but shortly after the marriage he is killed, and Joanna returns to the stifling atmosphere of her family home. A letter from her Bohemian Aunt Perdy in Italy opens 'an unsuspected door of escape' and Joanna becomes acquainted with her aunt's eccentric personal philosophy, with the 'Father-Motherhood of God' and the 'Central Sphere of the Senses'. Returning to Edinburgh, she adopts a less conventional life, becoming an artist and the mistress of the painter Louis Pender (modelled on Maurice Greiffenhagen, with whom CC had an unsuccessful love affair after the break-up of her first marriage). She plans to bind Pender to her by bearing his child, but does not conceive and is eventually rejected by him. The break with her Calvinistic upbringing is finally made when she discovers, in a passage suggestive of Lawrence's influence on the novel, that 'evil' quite as much as 'good' had made her 'alive . . . an individual . . . a divine creation herself capable of creative life'.

The Camomile is centred on the letters and journal of a young music teacher recently returned from Frankfurt to Glasgow who is disillusioned with music and overcome by a 'tormenting desire to express herself in writing'. In order to fulfil it, she rejects the predictable married life expected of her. Both CC's novels, like her biographies, are concerned with the breaking out of conventional moulds and the development of individual genius.

Her autobiography includes a number of poems, and a selection of letters which show Lawrence's influence in their antipathy towards the intellect: 'One can and should *think* with all one's being – *thought* to be real must be linked up with the stream of the blood.'   ANNE FERNIHOUGH

Works: *Open the Door* (1920); *The Camomile: An Invention* (1922); *The Life of Robert Burns* (1930); *The Savage Pilgrimage: A Narrative of D. H. Lawrence* (1932); (ed.), *A National Gallery: Being a Collection of English Characters* (with Daniel George) (1933); (ed.), *The English in Love: A Museum of Illustrative Verse and Prose Pieces from the 14th Century to the 20th* (with Daniel George) (1935); (ed.), *The Fays of the Abbey Theatre: An Autobiographical Record* (with W. G. Fay) (1935); (ed.), *The Scots Weekend and the Caledonian Vade-Mecum for Hosts* (with John Carswell) (1936); *The Tranquil Heart: Portrait of Giovanni Boccaccio* (1937); *Lying Awake: An Unfinished Autobiography and Other Posthumous Papers* (1950). **References:** *The Letters of D. H. Lawrence*, vols 2–7 (1981–).

Carter, Angela

b. 7 May 1940, Eastbourne, Sussex

Novelist, short story writer, journalist, critic

AC was born in Eastbourne because her mother, Olive Stalker, had gone there to escape the wartime bombing of London. Her father, Hugh, a journalist, stayed behind to work, but visited them often. The family moved again, for safety, to a South Yorkshire mining village, the birthplace of Olive's mother. There AC spent her early childhood, with her older brother, part of an 'obsessive family . . . sustained by a subjectively rich if objectively commonplace folklore'. At the war's end, the family returned to south London. AC spent school holidays with her grandmother in Yorkshire or at her father's family home in Scotland.

AC read English at Bristol University. Her first novel, *Shadow Dance* (1965), introduced the images of catabolism and the questioning of received notions of sexuality characteristic of her later work. In 1967, *The Magic Toyshop* won the John Llewellyn Rhys Memorial Prize. The story of Melanie's journey from secure childhood into dangerous and bewildering adolescence has the resonance of dream or fairy-tale; the narrative moves from apparent realism to nightmare dislocation with disturbing ease.

This ability to create compelling narrative, then distort it, to juxtapose the rational and improbable, and to use and subvert myth, has led to AC's inclusion among the Magic Realists. *The Company of Wolves*, adapted for cinema by AC and Neil Jordan, re-interprets the story of Little Red Riding Hood. Its mixture of black humour, eroticism, and horror frightens, seduces, and entertains: the audience's expectations are confounded. The title story of the collection of short stories *The Bloody Chamber* (1979) seems firmly placed in the Gothic tradition: an innocent bride, a depraved husband, an island castle, a locked door . . . yet the avenging angel is a strong, worldly-wise woman with a keen sense of the ridiculous. No passive fate seems possible for her daughter.

AC's work is informed by a strongly feminist perspective. She suggests, in *The Sadeian Woman* (1979), that a 'terrorist of the imagination, a sexual guerrilla' might explode accepted definitions of masculine and feminine, and of relations between the sexes. She agrees that gender differences exist, but seeks to separate that knowledge from culturally defined modes of behaviour which, through unquestioning acceptance, become 'translated in the language of common usage to the status of universals'.

It is precisely those 'universals' which AC challenges in her work. In 1969, a Somerset Maugham Travel Award enabled her to visit and work in another country. She chose Japan, as a culture with no Judeo-Christian tradition. She stayed for two years; the experience formed the basis for a series of articles for *New Society*. A collection of these and other essays was published in 1982 as *Nothing Sacred*. In it, acute observations of Japanese and Western culture show an awareness of the constraints imposed on human behaviour by social or ideological repression, and the attempts people make to free themselves through fantasy, festival, and myth.

For AC's characters, the products of historical forces and the offspring of the human imagination occupy the same arena. There are no simplistic solutions to hand, no comforting balm for the human condition. They observe their present age with a wide open eye which fails to blink at violence or cruelty: they react to the bizarre and grotesque as children do, with glee or with the analytical interest of the anthropologist. Sometimes, as in *Heroes and Villains* (1969) or *The Passion of New Eve* (1977), they inhabit a landscape of the future where civilization's thin skin is torn and inchoate impulses break through, raw and bloody.

In an introduction to *Come Unto These Yellow Sands* (1985), a collection of radio plays, including *The Company of Wolves*, there is a discussion of the appeal of the radio play as voices in the dark. AC's vision is undeniably dark, but the voices that speak through it weave spells, ask questions, and prophesy.

In *Nights at the Circus* (1984), Fevvers is seen as New Woman: 'the pure child of the century that just now is waiting in the wings, the New Age in which no women will be bound down to the ground'. Fevvers has her own wings; she incorporates both Leda and the swan. She is no longer at the mercy of myth or history. The contract of compliance is ended through the exercise of flight, through the power of the written and spoken word, of creative imagination and eroticism. When Fevvers and her New Man meet again, they have escaped being 'mutilated by history'. The last voices in the dark are laughing with gusto.   ELFRIDA LAUGHARNE

Works: *Shadow Dance* (1966; republished as *Honeybuzzard*); *The Magic Toyshop* (1967); *Several Perceptions* (1968); *Heroes and Villains* (1969); *Love* (1971); *The Infernal Desire Machines of Doctor Hoffman* (1972; republished as *The War of Dreams*); *Fireworks* (1974); *The Passion of New Eve* (1977); *The Fairy Tales of Charles Perrault* (1979); *The Sadeian Woman: An Exercise in Cultural History* (1979); *The Bloody Chamber* (1979); *Nothing Sacred* (1982); *Nights at the Circus* (1984); *Black Venus* (1985); *Come Unto These Yellow Sands* (1985); (ed.), *Bad Girls and Wicked Women* (1986).

References: DLB; Harrenden, J., *Novelists in Interview* (1985); Punter, D., 'Angela Carter: supersessions of the masculine', *Critique* 24 (1984); Punter, D., *The Literature of Terror* (1980); Rose, E. C., 'Through the looking glass: when women tell fairy tales', in *The Voyage In*, ed. E. Abel, M. Hirsch and E. Langland (1983); Sage, L., 'The savage sideshow: a profile of Angela Carter', *New Review* 39/40 (1977).

Carter, Elizabeth

b. 16 December 1717, Deal; d. 19 February 1806, London

Poet, translator, essayist, scholar, letter writer

(Also wrote under Camilla, Chariessa, Eliza, A Lady)

EC was certainly the most erudite and possibly the most influential of all the eighteenth-century Bluestockings. She was the eldest daughter of the Rev. Nicholas Carter, Perpetual Curate at Deal, and his first wife Margaret Swayne, who died when EC was 10.

Although a slow learner, she was highly gifted linguistically and acquired French from a Huguenot refugee, and Latin, Greek, and Hebrew from her father; she then taught herself Italian, Spanish, German, Portuguese, and Arabic. In her youth she wrote plays, novels, sermons, and poems, and corresponded in French and Latin with a fellow prodigy, John Philip Baratier, who had mastered five languages by the age of 9. Not surprisingly, she suffered for most of her life from severe nervous headaches, partially alleviated by snuff, flute playing, gardening, and long country walks (she once walked the seventeen miles from Canterbury to Deal).

Her talents were soon noticed by Edward Cave, that enterprising journalist and founder-editor of the *Gentleman's Magazine*. EC wrote for this periodical and Cave helped her to publish a small collection of her poems in 1738. Cave also introduced her to Samuel Johnson, and they formed a friendship lasting nearly half a century. Johnson took a great interest in her work, and revised her translation from the French of the critique by Professor Creusaz of Pope's *Essay on Man*. Cave published this in 1739. EC, an admirer of Pope, toned down the professor's allegations that the essay was fatalistic and hostile to revealed religion.

In the same year Cave published EC's translation from the Italian of Count Algarotti's dialogues on Newton's philosophy 'for the use of ladies'. The count was convinced that Italian women needed 'a new Mode of Cultivating the Mind' that did not involve head-dresses and curls, and he proceeded to give it to them. By making available to British women this high-powered excursion into the realms of science and philosophy EC won considerable applause from the Bluestockings.

Another long and fruitful friendship began in 1741 with Catherine Talbot, the adopted daughter of Dr Secker, Bishop of Oxford (later Archbishop of Canterbury). Like EC, Talbot was *virgo supra fidem erudita*, who read Epictetus before breakfast. These two studious young women visited each other frequently and corresponded regularly. Elizabeth Montagu, 'Queen of the Blues', also sought out EC's acquaintance and introduced her to some of the most brilliant and stimulating minds of the age. EC continued to write poetry and her *Ode to Wisdom* captivated Richardson, who used it in his novel *Clarissa* and had it set to music.

In the 1750s EC was extremely active. Often getting up at four or five o'clock in the morning, she worked hard for nearly a decade on her translation of Epictetus, wrote essays for Johnson's *Rambler* and coached her half-brother Henry for Cambridge, to the amazement of the dons. She also made his shirts. (Not many undergraduates at that time could boast a sister who was both their tutor and tailor.)

She was busy too with her cookery, her specialities being brandy puddings and christening cakes, meriting Johnson's famous compliment that she could 'make a pudding as well as translate Epictetus from the Greek, and work a handkerchief as well as compose a poem'. Her achievements inspired John Duncombe to extravagant eulogy in his *Feminiad* (1745), where Plato was shown rejoicing in the discovery of his genius 'glowing in a female Mind'.

The long-awaited translation of Epictetus appeared in 1758. It brought her fame and fortune, neither of which changed the serenity of her outlook or the simplicity of her lifestyle. When urged to follow up her success with a biography of the Stoic philosopher, she gave a characteristic response: 'I have a dozen shirts to make.' However, when pressed by Mrs Montagu and Lords Lyttelton and Bath, she did manage to lay down her needle and produce a second volume of verse in 1762, which ran into several editions and was translated into French and Latin.

Excessive study and sewing affected her nerves, and in 1763, accompanied by Lord Bath and the Montagus, she travelled to Spa, in Flanders, to take the waters, but bad weather and worsening health soon brought her home.

The last forty years of her life were uneventful. She remained single, having declined many offers. In addition to her mental, spiritual, and domestic accomplishments, she possessed a 'handsome' countenance, a cheerful and attractive personality and a remarkably sweet voice; it was rumoured that the Archbishop of Canterbury, the Bishop of London, and Lord Bath all wished to marry her. The historian and antiquary Dr Thomas Birch once courted her with passionate love letters in Latin, but to no avail. EC chose to live quietly by the sea with her father, in her little 'vinegar bottle' house, where they both had separate libraries, and met at meals, often conversing in Latin. She wrote long letters to her friends but nothing for publication.

Every winter she spent a few weeks in London, taking rooms in Clarges Street with her maid and dining out almost every night. Her circle of female admirers included Fanny Burney, Hannah More, and Mesdames Montagu, Vesey ('our dear Sylph'), Chapone, Hunter, and Boscawen.

Her father's death in 1774 was a great blow, which she bore with Christian rather than Stoic fortitude. 'I should never think of finding consolation from the Stoics under any important troubles, though I think them admirable against little teasing vexations,' she wrote to Mrs Montagu on this occasion: a sensible reply to critics who accused her of promoting non-Christian morality and attempting to convert the human heart 'into a flint'.

The educationist Hester Chapone had been one such critic but the two women remained friends and EC was pleased to receive an affectionate dedication when Chapone's *Miscellanies* appeared in 1775. She was less happy when her 'zealous Admirer' William Hayley published his *Philosophical, Historical and Moral Essay on Old Maids* in 1785, dedicated to EC 'as a Poet, as a Philosopher and as an Old Maid', and as 'President' of the 'chaste Community' that Hayley purported to honour but frequently ridiculed in his three-volume work.

As she grew older EC's circle of admirers grew even wider and more illustrious. The Empress Catherine III enthused over *Epictetus*, and EC was praised in Russia for her piety, modesty, and outstanding talents. In 1791 Queen Charlotte expressed a wish to meet her and an introduction was arranged at Lord Cremorne's house in Chelsea; they discussed German literature and afterwards the Queen sent her German books and 'flattering messages'. Later the Duke of Cumberland called on her at Deal, and the Princess of Wales went to tea with her.

EC wore her laurels with outward composure but an aching head. The pain worsened with the years, and she had frequent fainting fits. She could no longer walk very far, and she put on considerable weight. But her intellect and judgment remained unimpaired.

At 88 she insisted on taking her usual winter trips to London, where she attended several dinner parties, but became very weak, took to her bed, died peacefully, and was interred in the burial ground of Grosvenor Chapel.

Epictetus continued to flourish well into the nineteenth century and even acquired two new editions in the twentieth, its sound and conscientious scholarship standing the test of time better than the inaccurate translation of the *Enchiridion* (from the Latin) hastily dashed off by Lady Mary Wortley Montagu in 1710.

Her poetry has not fared so well. The once popular 'Ode to Wisdom' has an air of elevated banality; she is at her most original and vigorous in 'A Dialogue' (between Body and Mind) and at her most polished in her appeal 'To Dr Walwyn' to spare his trees. Her charming poem to her father expresses deep filial gratitude for his enlightened guidance of her studies, and her many poems to women, although supportive, emphasize the ephemeral and illusory nature of earthly satisfactions. EC's ideals for feminine achievement were set firmly in a domestic and Christian context (she disliked Wollstonecraft).

Her letters show her good humour, good sense, and good judgment: it is regrettable that her pious nephew, in his anxiety to minimize 'trifling chit-chat' and 'confidential communications', exercised such a heavy-handed censorship in editing her correspondence.   MARGARET MAISON

Works: (Confusion exists over EC's poetical contributions to the *Gentleman's Magazine*, some being unsigned, others signed 'Eliza', a name also used by another contributor. Several of these poems appear in her collections of verse and also in her nephew's 'new edition' of 1807.) *A Riddle* (unsigned), *Gentleman's Magazine* 4 (November 1734); translation of the 30th Ode of Anacreon (signed 'Camilla'), *Gentleman's Magazine* 5 (September 1735); *A Riddle* (signed 'Eliza'), *Gentleman's Magazine* 8 (February 1738); *Poems upon Particular Occasions* (1738); 'On the Death of Mrs Rowe' (signed 'Elizabeth Carter') *Gentleman's Magazine* 9 (March 1739); *An Examination of Mr Pope's Essay on Man. Translated from the French of M. Crousaz* (1739); *Sir Isaac Newton's Philosophy Explain'd for the Use of Ladies. In Six Dialogues, on Light and Colours. From the Italian of Sig. Algarotti*, 2 vols (1739); 'To Melancholy' (unsigned), *Gentleman's Magazine* 9 (November 1739); 'To the Rambler' (unsigned), *Rambler* (18 August 1750); 'To the Rambler' (signed 'Chariessa'), *Rambler* 100 (2 March 1751); trans. *All the Works of Epictetus, which are now extant, consisting of his Discourses, preserved by Arrian, in four Books, the Enchiridion, and Fragments. Translated from the Greek* (1758); *Poems on Several Occassions* (1762); *Memoirs of the Life of Mrs Elizabeth Carter, with a new edition of her Poems, some of which have never appeared before; to which are added, some miscellaneous essays in prose, together with Notes on the Bible and Answers to Objections Concerning the Christian Religion*, ed. M. Pennington (1807); *A Series of Letters between Mrs Elizabeth Carter and Miss Catherine Talbot from the year 1741 to 1770. To which are added, Letters from Mrs Elizabeth Carter to Mrs Vesey between the years 1763 and 1787*, ed. M. Pennington, 4 vols (1809); *Letters from Mrs Elizabeth Carter and Mrs Montagu between the years 1755 and 1800. Chiefly upon Literary and Moral Subjects*, ed. M. Pennington, 3 vols (1817).

References: Anon., Obituary, *Gentleman's Magazine* 76, 1 (February 1806); Balderston, K. (ed.), *Thraliana* (1942); Blunt, R. (ed.), *Mrs Montagu 'Queen of the Blues': Her Letters and Friendship from 1762 to 1800* (1923); Climenson, E. (ed.), *Elizabeth Montagu, The Queen of the Bluestockings: Her correspondence from*

1720 to 1761, 2 vols (1906); Elwood, A., *Memoirs of the Literary Ladies of England*, 2 vols (1843); Gaussen, A., *A Woman of Wit and Wisdom* (1906); Hayley, W., *A Philosophical, Historical, and Moral Essay on Old Maids*, 3 vols (1785); Hill, G. (ed.), *Boswell's Life of Johnson* (1934–50); Huchon, R., *Mrs Montagu and her Friends* (1907); Johnson, R., *Bluestocking Letters* (1926); Montagu, M. (ed.), *The Letters of Mrs Elizabeth Montagu, with some of the Letters of her Correspondents*, part 2, 2 vols (1813); Pennington, M. (ed.), *Memoirs of the Life of Mrs Elizabeth Carter* (1807); Rogers, K., *Feminism in Eighteenth-Century England* (1982); Ruhe, E., 'Birch, Johnson and Elizabeth Carter: an episode of 1738–9', *PMLA* 73, 5, part 1 (December 1958); Tinker, C., *The Salon and English Letters* (1915); Todd; Wheeler, E., *Famous Bluestockings* (1910).

Cartland, Barbara

b. 9 July 1901, Vectis Lodge, Edgbaston

Romantic novelist

(Also writes under Barbara McCorquodale)

BC, the daughter of Mary (née Scobell) and Bertram Cartland, was educated at Malvern Girls' College and Abbey House in Hampshire. Her mother came from an upper-class family which could trace its history back to before the Norman Conquest, and her father from a very wealthy middle-class background. In 1903 however, her father's family lost most of its money, which led to a change in lifestyle for the Cartlands; they moved to a small house in Pershore. BC recalls in one of her autobiographies growing up surrounded by politics. Her father was involved in the work of the Primrose League, and was appointed Private Secretary to an MP. According to BC, he had ambitions of becoming an MP himself, but he was killed in the First World War. His death left the family in even more straitened circumstances: BC's two brothers were still at school, and BC was about to be launched into society. Her mother contrived to manage on a low budget, building up a knitwear business. BC managed to dress well by a friendly agreement with Norman Hartnell, then a little-known designer, whereby she bought his clothes at cost price, and in return gave him publicity and persuaded her friends to buy from him. BC must have been something of a social success, for apparently she received forty-nine proposals of marriage (a number of which she accepted then changed her mind) before deciding on Alexander McCorquodale, whose father was chairman of the company owning the largest printing group in the world. They had one child, but divorced a few years later. In 1936 BC married again, this time to Alexander's cousin, Hugh, with whom she had two children.

BC's writing career began in 1923, when she began to contribute to the *Daily Express* gossip column for 5 shillings a paragraph. She soon started writing articles for the paper, and received advice and encouragement from Lord Beaverbrook. She began writing her first novel, *Jig-Saw* (1925), to overcome her boredom on a family holiday in Bredon where she missed the social whirl of London. The central character, Mona, has been to a convent school in Paris, and is about to return to England for the first time in years. She feels considerable trepidation at the thought of seeing her family who have neglected her, but also excitement at the sensation of being on the brink of adulthood. BC describes appealingly her conflicting and changing feelings, and tells an entertaining story about Mona's romance, marriage, separation from her husband, and their eventual reunion. The critics were not especially impressed with the novel, but the reading public was: *Jig-Saw* was published in six editions and translated into five languages.

BC has since written in a variety of genres, including drama, biography, sociology, and verse, but she is best known for her romantic novels, of which she has written over 300, and has a reputed readership of over 400 million. She appears in the *Guinness Book of Records* as the most prolific living author and in 1977 wrote twenty-four books, breaking her own world record for yearly output. She produces her books methodically: apparently she dictates to a secretary for two hours each day while relaxing on a sofa. Her novels now lack the freshness and fun of her early works and have become rigidly formulaic and much shorter. The heroine is always virginal and vulnerable (often a cruelly treated orphan), who meets an older, wealthier, more experienced (often sexually), desperately attractive man who, weary of his numerous *affaires de coeur* with society women, cannot resist her 'unusual' beauty and her 'spirituality'; he generally rescues her from a predicament, then their mutual love is revealed, much to the heroine's amazement, for she never considers herself worthy of him. It would be unjust, however, to say that her heroines are utterly indistinguishable: although they are not (and have no desire to be) as clever as their men, some are unusually talented, for example, the heroine of *Magic or Mirage?* (1978): 'The *Mauretania*'s sirens began to blow the farewell, and Devina, who was musical, realised that it was pitched two octaves below middle-A.' In contrast to this extraordinary display of talent, Viola, the heroine of *Vote for Love* (1977), is 'gentle, ineffectual and only too willing to have everything decided for her by someone she thought wiser and more intelligent'. Viola is lucky enough to meet a man willing to fill this role when she tries to plant a bomb in his drawing room. He is a prominent member of the government, and Viola, at the insistence of her wicked suffragette stepmother who beats her, frequently within an inch of her life, has to assassinate him. The attempt fails, thanks to Viola's softness and Rayburn's quick-wittedness. BC paints an unflattering (and unusual) picture of the suffragettes; on one occasion Viola spends a night in prison with a group of them: 'When they were not shouting they were giggling and gossiping amongst themselves, criticising their leaders and the way in which the campaigns and meetings were being conducted.' Viola likens them to 'naughty children who had raided an orchard or were enjoying a midnight feast that was not permitted by their teacher'. Needless to say, Rayburn and Viola are absolutely in accord about the pointlessness of female emancipation, as one telling exchange indicates:

> His voice deepened and he went on:
> 'No vote, no act of Parliament, no alteration of a woman's status could make you more important to me, than you already are just by being a woman.'
> 'I want to be . . . your woman,' Viola whispered.
> Then because she was shy she hid her face against his neck.

The heroine of *A Shaft of Sunlight* (1982), Giona, has more initiative than Viola. She too is an orphan who is beaten by a wicked relative, and befriended by a dazzlingly attractive man. She tries to write a poem to her beloved, but encounters difficulties, as she explains to him: 'It is so inadequate. There are no words even in poetry to describe you, and when I have written a page I tear it up . . . ashamed that I am . . . unable to convey adequately what I am . . . feeling in . . . words.' The beloved helpfully suggests she might write it in Greek. This punctuated style of speech is typical of BC's heroines (quavering Viola's monosyllables are even punctuated with pauses: 'Y.yes'). This feature, together with the very short paragraphs BC prefers (they are rarely more than one sentence long) makes a BC text easily recognizable from its layout alone. This paragraphing is clearly a conscious choice (presumably designed to make the novels easy to read) because in her *Library of Love* (a series of abridged versions of novels by other romantic writers, for example Elinor Glyn and Ethel Dell), BC alters the texts to conform to this style.

BC is proud of the escapism her novels provide for her millions of readers, saying the stories take them away, for a while, from unromantic modern life. Although the reality of BC's life in many ways is at odds with the fantasy she produces (notably her divorce, and the pattern of marriages in her own family where it is the *men* who have married someone of higher social standing), in others there seems to be an element of fairy-tale: after experiencing financial difficulties as a young woman, she now lives in a stately home, Camfield Place, and in 1981, on the marriage of Lady Diana Spencer to the Prince of Wales, became step-grandmother to the future Queen of England.   LUCY SLOAN

Selected works: *Jig-Saw* (1925); *Blood Money* (1925); *If the Tree is Saved* (1929); *A Virgin in Mayfair* (1932); *A Beggar Wished* (1934); *Touch the Stars* (1935); *But Never Free* (1937); *Stolen Halo* (1940); *Ronald Cartland* (1942); *The Isthmus Years 1919–35* (1943); *Love is an Eagle* (1951); *Elizabethan Lover* (1953); *Bewitching Women* (1955); *Polly - My Wonderful Mother* (1956); *The Scandalous Life of King Carol* (1957); *Love, Life and Sex*(1957); *The Private Life of Elizabeth, Empress of Austria* (1959); *Love Under Fire* (1960); *Diane de Poitiers* (1962); *The Many Facets of Love* (1963); *Metternich, the Passionate Diplomat* (1964); *Woman the Enigma* (1965); *The Private Life of Charles II* (1968); *Health Food Cookery Book* (1971); *Men Are Wonderful* (1973); *Food for Love* (1975); *Vote for Love* (1977); *Magic or Mirage?* (1978); *The Drums of Love* (1979); *A Song of Love* (1980); *Romantic Royal Marriages* (1981); *Love Wins* (1982); *A Shaft of Sunlight* (1982); *Tempted to Love* (1983); *Dangerous Experiment* (1983); *Moonlight on the Sphinx* (1984); *Love is a Gamble* (1985); *Paradise Found* (1986); *A Runaway Star* (1987).

References: *CA*; Cloud, H., *Barbara Cartland, Crusader in Pink* (1979); Robyns, G., *Barbara Cartland* (1985); *RGW*.

Centlivre, Susanna

b. ? ; d. 1 December 1723, London
Playwright
(Also wrote under Susanna Carroll)

Accounts of SC's life before 1700 are conjectural, but her frequent visits to Holbeach, Lincolnshire,, support the tradition that she was born there. She first appeared in print in 1700, under the name Susanna Carroll; at this time she was living in London and contributing fashionable correspondence to *Familiar and Courtly Letters* and similar collections. In 1707 she married Joseph Centlivre, a royal cook, and in 1713 the couple moved to Buckingham Court, where they lived for the rest of their lives. SC was an ardent Whig, attracting a wide circle of friends among Whig writers; her politics and her anti-Catholicism were the main reasons for Pope's including her in the 1728 *Dunciad*. SC was buried at St Paul's in Covent Garden. An edition of her plays was advertised for 1732, but the first collected editions did not appear until 1760; her letters and incidental poems remain scattered in eighteenth-century periodicals and anthologies.

The most famous female comic playwright in the early decades of the eighteenth century, SC wrote sixteen full-length plays and three short pieces. Her plays are typically farcical comedies of intrigue leading to the marriage of an honest hero (often a soldier) and a sensible heroine. Using a wide variety of sources in French, Spanish, and earlier English drama, her plays depend more on fast-paced plots than on witty dialogue: her tone is on the whole genial and light-hearted rather than biting. She is an adroit stage technician who writes for an audience rather than for readers. Her four most accomplished comedies became stock repertory pieces.

The first of these, *The Gamester* (1705), initiated a series of plays about gambling. The hero, Valere, faces ruin because of his addiction to gaming, but the rich and resourceful Angelica reclaims him by disguising herself as a man and winning his money, watch, ring, and finally her own portrait set with diamonds, a love token with which he had solemnly sworn never to part. When Valere is penitent, Angelica forgives and marries him. Ostensibly writing sentimental reform comedy, SC actually exploits the audience's interest in gaming. Valere's obsession is more convincingly portrayed than his reformation, and the liveliest scene in the play depicts the sharpers and suckers hot over the gaming table, absorbed in their own colourful jargon.

SC's next success was *The Busy Body* (1709), an intrigue comedy in which two young couples outwit two comic old men. The unusual ingredient is the character of Marplot, the busybody. In his impertinent but good-natured eagerness to discover his friends' secrets, Marplot repeatedly brings the young lovers near to disaster. The plot set up an interesting tension: the audience sympathizes with the lovers and at the same time with Marplot.

The action of *The Wonder* (1714) turns on Violante's promise to protect the secret of Isabella's romance. Although every event conspires to make Violante appear false, she keeps her friend's secret to the point of passionate quarrels with her beloved Don Felix. Around the central pair of lovers revolve delightful minor comic characters. Plot and dialogue are compressed so that a surprising turn occurs every few minutes. The role of Don Felix was one of David Garrick's triumphs, and he chose it for his farewell performance in 1776. SC's last success, *A Bold Stroke for a Wife* (1718), is similarly ingenious. The plot turns on a single premise. Colonel Fainwell, in order to marry Anne Lovely, must gain the consent of four amusingly different guardians – a beau, a virtuoso, a businessman, and a Quaker. He wins the lady by assuming five successive disguises, the last being an impersonation of the real Simon Pure, adding that expression to the language.

Of these four comedies, the most popular in the eighteenth century was *The Busy Body*. *The Wonder* and *A Bold Stroke for a Wife* continued to grow in popularity, and while *The Gamester* was replaced in the repertory by other plays about gambling, SC's three later successes were performed regularly throughout the nineteenth century, not only in England but also in the United States and Australia.   NANCY COTTON

Works: *The Perjured Husband* (1700); *The Beau's Duel* (1702); *The Stolen Heiress* (1702); *Love's Contrivance* (1703); *The Gamester* (1705); *The Basset-Table* (1705); *Love at a Venture* (1706); *The Platonic Lady* (1706); *The Busy Body* (1709; reprinted with introduction by Jess Byrd, 1949); *The Man's Bewitched* (1709); *A Bickerstaff's Burying* (1710); *Marplot* (1710); *The Perplexed Lovers* (1712); *The Masquerade* (1713); *The Wonder* (1714); *A Poem Humbly Presented to His Most Sacred Majesty* (1714); *An Epistle to Mrs Wallup* (1714); *The Gotham Election* (1715); *A Wife Well Managed* (1715); *The Cruel Gift* (1716); *An Epistle to the King of Sweden from a Lady of Great Britain* (1717); *A Bold Stroke for a Wife* (1718; ed. Thalia Stathas,

1968); *A Woman's Case* (1720); *The Artifice* (1722); *Works* (1760); *The Plays of Susanna Centlivre*, 3 vols, ed. R. Frushell (1982).
References: Allibone; Bateson, F. W., *English Comic Drama 1700–1750* (1929); Boas, F. S., *An Introduction to Eighteenth-Century Drama 1700–1780* (1953); Bowyer, J. W., *The Celebrated Mrs Centlivre* (1952); Cotton, N., *Women Playwrights in England c. 1363–1750* (1980); *DNB*; Drabble; Hume, R. D., 'Marital discord in English comedy', *Modern Philology* 74 (February 1977); Lock, F. P., *Susanna Centlivre* (1979); Todd.

Chandler, Mary
b. 1687, Malmsbury, Wiltshire; d. 11 September 1745, Bath
Poet
MC was the eldest daughter of a Dissenting minister and, for financial reasons, was not formally educated like her brothers. Instead, she was taught how to manage a business and in 1705 she opened her own millinery shop in Bath, which she managed for thirty-five years despite a severely damaged spine, the result of a childhood accident. To remedy her deficient education, she studied modern authors and classical writers in translation during her spare time. She wrote verses for the amusement of her friends, who requested so many copies that she decided to have her work printed.

Her most popular poem was the 322-line *A Description of Bath* (1734), which gives a lightly satirical history and description of the town and the hot baths, a picture of the social scene there, and a moral commentary on Bath. The third edition of the satire in 1736 included several others poems by her, which address such topics as the manifestation of God's benevolence through Nature, the delights of solitude, and the importance of true friendship. Much of her verse was occasioned by personal experience. When she was 54, for example, a wealthy sexagenarian, impressed by the good sense expressed in her poem, 'The Wish', travelled eighty miles in order to propose marriage to her. She decided that she could not endure 'loss of liberty' and refused him. This episode became the poem 'A True Tale', a blend of satire and serious reflection. She also wrote poems on subjects inspired by conversations or visits with particular friends. Her later work became more reflective, and, at her death, she left a lengthy but unfinished poem on 'the being and attributes of God'.

MC's verse displays her admiration for Horace's satires, with their accessible and realistic subjects, gracious style, and clear messages. Pope's work also influenced her strongly. He once visited her, probably in the autumn of 1734, when he 'approved' her newly published satire. She alludes to him, refers to his works, and borrows the form of the heroic-couplet epistle in *A Description of Bath*; in addition, part of his 'Epistle to Burlington' (1731) provided the structure for the final section, a eulogy of Ralph Allen, Bath's leading citizen and the reformer of the national postal service. Although contruction work on Allen's residence, Prior Park, had barely started, MC presented it in verse as the best in art and nature, an inversion of Timon's villa which represents the worst.

MC was a popular poet in Bath. Her volume of poetry ran to eight editions, the last published as late as 1767. She was one of the first to see the potential of Bath and its society as a subject of literary interest. Works such as Anstey's epistolary verse satire, *The New Bath Guide* (1766), are indebted to MC. Her own descriptions of Bath were frequently in other works, such as the 1742 revision of Defoe's *Tour Through the Whole Island of Great Britain*, probably the

work of Samuel Richardson, whose brother-in-law in Bath published MC's
poetry.   LINDA V. TROOST
Works: *A Description of Bath: A Poem. In a Letter to a Friend* (1734; with several
poems added, 1736, 1738, 1741; with 'A True Tale' added, 1744).
References: Boyce, B., *The Benevolent Man* (1967); Cibber, T. (ed.), *Lives of
the Poets* (1753); *DNB*; Todd.

Chapone, Hester

b. 27 October 1727, Twywell, Northants; d. 25 December 1801, Hadley,
Middlesex
Conduct book writer, poet
(Also wrote under Hester Mulso)
HC, the daughter of Thomas Mulso, became one of the Bluestockings. She
displayed a talent for writing at an early age, but her mother discouraged
her literary ambitions. After her mother's early death, HC embarked upon a
programme of self-education, studying French, Italian, and Latin. Through
Samuel Richardson, she met John Chapone, an attorney, whom she married in
1760 after a lengthy engagement; he died within nine months. In the remaining
forty years of her life, she occasionally published essays and poems and visited
her relatives. Her most notable associates were Richardson, Samuel Johnson,
Elizabeth Carter, Fanny Burney, and Elizabeth Montagu. She died after several
years of physical and mental decline, having outlived every member of her
immediate family and many of their descendants.

Her first published work appeared in the *Rambler* (1750) and in the *Adventurer*
(1753). During these years, she also published poems and carried on an epistolary debate about filial obedience with Samuel Richardson. In the letters (published posthumously), HC argues that, although a daughter should not marry
without the consent of the parents, she may refuse anyone the parents might
propose. Richardson, on the other hand, conservatively argues that a daughter
has no right of refusal and must obey her parents in all things. HC and
Richardson eventually quarrelled, apparently over his objection to her permitting her verses to be read too publicly.

HC's elegant poetry addresses a range of topics in several forms. She wrote
or translated from the Italian many stanzaic poems on conventional themes
such as the virtues of solitude, peace, and nature, but she also composed a
highly polished Pindaric ode addressed to Elizabeth Carter that denounces the
philosophy of Epictetus (this originally appeared as a preface to Carter's 1758
translation of his work). Her verses generally display a sharp wit. In one poem,
she remarks that her own verses cure her of insomnia, and, in an early poem,
she manipulates the Miltonic and classical conventions of love as she discusses
the superiority of platonic feminine friendship over heterosexual love. Johnson
quoted from the poem (still at that time unpublished) to provide an example
of a quatrain for his dictionary in 1755.

HC's essays won her a considerable reputation, especially her *Letters on the
Improvement of the Mind* (1773). She originally wrote these letters to a favourite
niece, but Mrs Montagu advised her to publish them. The letters outline a
practical course of self-education for young women, complete with a list of
recommended primary and secondary sources. In addition to the usual instruction in French, dancing, and manners, HC recommends extensive reading,
particularly in the Bible, British and European history, the natural sciences,
moral philosophy, selected literary works, and geography. The programme

which HC outlines is ambitious and reveals her concern that women should receive a solid education. When it was first published, *Letters* sold quickly, and by its final appearance in 1851, it had been through about sixty editions in Great Britain, France, and the United States.

In 1775, HC published *Miscellanies in Prose and Verse*, which included her early poems and 'The Story of Fidelia', reprinted from *The Adventurer*. Two years later, she published *A Letter to a New-Married Lady* (1777), a practical treatise which she subsequently included in *Miscellanies*. After her death, her relatives brought out a four-volume edition of her works, including her letters to Carter and Richardson.   LINDA V. TROOST

Works: *Letters on the Improvement of the Mind* (1773); *Miscellanies in Prose and Verse* (1775); *A Letter to a New-Married Lady* (1777); *The Works of Mrs Chapone* (1807); *The Tenbury Letters*, ed. E. Fellowes and E. Pine (1943); *Bluestocking Letters*, ed. R. Johnson (1926).

References: Allibone; Cole, J., *Memoirs of Mrs Chapone* (1839); *DNB*; Drabble; Elwood, A., *Memoirs of the Literary Ladies of England* (1843); Gaussen, A., *A Later Pepys* (1904); Moers, E., *Literary Women* (1976); *OCCL*; Todd; Wheeler, E., *Famous Blue-Stockings* (1910); Wilson, M., *These Were Muses* (1924).

Charke, Charlotte
b. 1713; d. c. 1760
Autobiographer, playwright

CC tried many roles in life, including actress, valet, barmaid, and seller of groceries and sausages. She gained notoriety from her autobiography (*A Narrative of the Life of Mrs Charlotte Charke*), published during 1755.

CC was the last of twelve children of Colley Cibber, actor, playwright, and manager of the Theatre Royal in Drury Lane, and of a former actress, Katherine Shore. She had a minimal education, and, when she was 17, Cibber arranged for her marriage to Richard Charke, an actor and violinist at Drury Lane, with whom she soon had a child. She was a dancer at Drury Lane until she was sacked in 1733 and made her debut as an actress in *The Provoked Wife* in 1730. She subsequently played in *The Tender Husband, Othello, Oronooko,* and *The London Merchant*. Separated from Charke, she worked with Henry Fielding's company until its collapse after the Licensing Act of 1737 and in 1735 wrote a dramatic attack on Charles Fleetwood, the manager of Drury Lane who had sacked her: a bombastic and rather coarse play entitled *The Art of Management*.

In financial difficulties, CC toured with a puppet theatre around London and took many non-theatrical jobs such as grocer, drawer, soup seller, and servant. She occasionally adopted men's clothes, a habit she had often followed in the theatre. As a man she almost married an heiress but confessed the truth immediately before the wedding and gave proof of her sex to the incredulous girl. She took a lover, and, later, when her husband had died, she probably married John Sacheverelle, whom she seems to have abandoned after a few months. For many years she and a woman friend set up as Mr and Mrs Brown and were itinerant players. When they returned to London in poverty, CC threatened her father with the publication of her autobiography in order to persuade him to support her. The attempt was unsuccessful, and so the work was published nevertheless. It is a rollicking account which veers between presenting the author as a humorous and resourceful character and appealing to the reader's pity. *The Gentleman's Magazine* ran it as a serial during 1755.

In her last years CC lived in a 'wretched hovel', writing to fend off poverty and using incidents and experiences from her varied life in her writings. *The Mercer, or, Fatal Extravagance* appeared in 1755 and describes a bankrupt who kills himself, while *The Lover's Treat, or, Unnatural Hatred* (1758) concerns an innocent girl who is confined to a brothel. The short tale *The History of Charles and Patty* is undated and also attributed to CC.   JANET JONES

Works: *The Art of Management* (1735); *A Narrative of the Life of Mrs Charlotte Charke* (1755); *The Mercer, or, Fatal Friendship* (1755); *The History of Henry Dumont, Esq. and Miss Charlotte Evelyn* (1756); *The Lover's Treat, or, Unnatural Hatred* (1758); *The History of Charles and Patty* (n.d.).

References: Browne, A., *The Eighteenth-Century Feminist Mind* (1987); Cotton, N., *Women Playwrights in England c. 1363–1750* (1980); Todd.

Charlesworth, Maria

b. 1 October 1819, Little Blakenham, Ipswich; d. 16 October 1880, Nutfield, Surrey

Writer for children

MC's father, the Rev. John Charlesworth, was an Evangelical clergyman who moved during MC's childhood to a living in Ipswich, where she was educated. In her teens her father took a London living near St Paul's; there her health failed and she became something of an invalid. She began to write in her early twenties and continued writing didactic stories throughout her life. On the death of her parents she lived at Nutfield, Surrey, but she was a frequent visitor to her brother's parish in Limehouse and to Bermondsey where she set up a mission and a 'ragged school'. MC is a striking example of nineteenth-century Evangelical piety, greatly influenced by her parent's concern for the poor in both their rural and city parishes. Her first book, *The Female Visitor to the Poor*, was published as 'By a Clergyman's Daughter' and drew on her own experiences in helping her parents give food, clothing, bibles and pious exhortations to their more unfortunate parishioners. It was well received but it was its fictionalized version aimed at the juvenile market which became a best-seller. *Ministering Children* (1854) sold 170,000 copies in the author's lifetime and was translated into French, German, and Swedish. Extracts were published as separate stories and a sequel came out in 1867. It was rapidly established as a suitable Sunday School prize and one of the best known of the 'Reward Books'. MC wrote other works with, frankly, more attractive titles: *England's Yeomen* (1861), *The Old Looking-Glass, or, Mrs Dorothy Cope's Recollections of Service* (1877), and *Oliver of the Mill* (1876), but it is on *Ministering Children* that her reputation rests.

It is difficult today to realize how widely the book was read (though not always with unmitigated pleasure as those 'Would-be-Goods', E. Nesbit's Bastable family, testify). As a book for the young it has a simple vocabulary and style, a resoundingly clear message, and, despite its descriptions of poverty and illness, a comfortable view of life in which any kind of 'ministering' is met by a grateful response and an amelioration of both physical and spiritual states. It is this and the vision of an England full of helping squires and old ladies going to church in scarlet cloaks, which seems meretricious to the modern reader. There is no awareness of the horrors of urban life or the real squalor of rural life nor of the political and social reforms of the period. Everyone in the end is converted to Bible-reading contentment by the children who minister in tenement, workhouse, farm, and hall. The story is slow to start and MC does not know how to vary our interest in the children, though she can display a little humour in the rich boy who finds charity 'capital fun', and some shrewdness of observation in Mrs Smith's attitude to her daughter, Rose, but it is really a series of loosely linked episodes with hardly any tension generated. Its interest today is historical, as evidence of Evangelical, individualistic piety.

MARY SHAKESHAFT

Works: *The Female Visitor to the Poor, or, Records of Female Parochial Visiting, by a Clergyman's Daughter* (1846); *The Light of Life, dedicated to the young* (1850); *Ministering Children* (1854); *The Cottage and its Visitor* (1856); *Oliver of the Mill: A Tale* (1876); *The Old Looking-Glass, or, Mrs Dorothy Cope's Recollections of Service* (1877); *The Broken Looking-Glass* (1879).

References: Avery, G., *Nineteenth-Century Children* (1965); Avery, G., *Childhood's Pattern* (1975). Cutt, M. C., *Ministering Angels* (1978); *DNB*; Darton, F. H., *Children's Books in England* (1932; 3rd edn revised by Brian Alderson, 1982); Muir, P., *English Children's Books* (1954);

Cholmondeley, Mary

b. 3 June 1859, Hodnet, Shropshire; d. 15 July 1925, London

Novelist

MC was the third child and the eldest daughter of the Rev. Hugh Cholmondeley, eventually made Rector of Hodnet, and Emily Beaumont Cholmondeley. Her grandmother was Mary Heber, sister of Bishop Heber, the hymn writer. MC suffered all her life from ill health, a condition identified in her later life as asthma. Her invalid sister Hester, author of miscellaneous verse, died at the age of twenty-two. Although in *Under One Roof: A Family Record* (1918), MC gives a vivid picture of the happy family of her childhood, social and secure, in her journals she writes with quite a different emotional tone: 'I was nothing, a plain silent country girl, an invalid whom no one cared a straw about. I don't see why they should. But in all those early years, those enormously long years, a sort of dull, smouldering fire of passion seemed to be gradually kindling in me, a determination which I can liken to nothing but a slow fire to overcome all these dreadful obstacles of illness and ugliness and incompetence. . . . It is not my talent which has placed me where I am, but the repression of my youth, my unhappy love-affair, the having to confront a hard dull life, devoid of anything I cared for intellectually, and being hampered at every turn I feebly made by constant illness.'

MC never married and lived with her family until she died. The family moved to London in 1896 after MC had some success with her first three novels. At the age of forty-one she achieved overnight fame (or notoriety), with her novel *Red Pottage* (1899), which was both denounced from the pulpit and hailed by the *Spectator* as 'brilliant and exhilarating'. MC remarked of this period in her life, 'I will not pretend that the turmoil gave me unmixed pain'. Later, she suffered greater pain from the novel's and her own fall from fame; her later novels were scarcely noted. After her father's death, she lived quietly in an apartment with her sisters. The gatherings she held there are recounted in Percy Lubbock's sketch.

The contemporary reading public took *Red Pottage* to be a brilliant satirical portrait of the clergy and country life. At the heart of it lies the friendship of two strong, idealistic women, Hester Gresley and Rachel West. In its comments about the importance but misunderstood nature of women's friendships, the novel's narrative voice achieves its best moments and avoids the pontifical and moralistic tone into which it lapses at other times. Hester is a talented writer in poor health who lives with her clergyman brother and his wife. Her brother is portrayed as dogmatic, intellectually limited, petty, and egocentric; his wife, jealous and narrow. In spite of the limitations such companions impose upon Hester, she self-sacrificially makes the best of her spinster situation, at the cost of her health, accommodating her writing schedule to the inflexible pettiness of the household and saving the life of one of her brother's children by cradling him through the nights. The work's climax occurs when Hester's clergyman brother burns the only copy of the novel which has cost Hester so dearly, because he believes it immoral. The reader, however, knows that the work is brilliant and important. Parallel to the plot of Hester's artistic and moral struggles (the theme recurs in a late story, 'The Goldfish' in *The Romance of His Life* (1921)), is the more conventional, if implausible and melodramatic romantic plot involving Rachel West. Rachel has had several reversals of fortune. As the novel begins, she is an heiress of a great fortune but she has been very poor and remains the outspoken champion of the poor. Hugh Scarlett, the object of her new romantic interest, has had an affair with a married woman, Lady Newhaven. Her husband makes a dramatic proposal to preserve his honour suggesting that, in lieu of a duel, the two men draw straws to determine which one will commit suicide within three months. Hugh breaks the terms of the agreement and so Rachel finds him dishonourable; conveniently he dies so that her relationship with him does not have to be resolved. Her romantic fate is revealed in an afterword. Although there is much that is unattractive to the modern reader in this novel, its moralizing, melodrama, and inflated prose, it is redeemed by its comic scenes and realistic portrayal of women who care about their work, ideas and each other.   MARTHA SATZ

Works: *The Danvers Jewels* (1887); *Charles Danvers* (1889); *Diana Tempest* (1893); *Devotee* (1897); *Red Pottage* (1899); *Moth and Rust* (1902); *Prisoners* (1906); *The Lowest Rung* (1908); *Notwithstanding* (1913); *Under One Roof* (1918); *The Romance of His Life* (1921).

References: Colby, V., ' "Devoted Amateur": Mary Cholmoneley and *Red Pottage*', *Essays in Criticism* 20, April 1970; *Times*, 17 July, 1925; Lubbock, P., *Mary Cholmondeley: A Sketch from Memory* (1928); Showalter, E., *A Literature of Their Own* (1977).

Christie, Agatha

b. 15 September 1890, Torquay, Devon; d. 12 January 1976, Wallingford, Oxfordshire

Detective novelist

(Also wrote under Mary Westmacott)

AC was the child of Frederick and Clarissa Miller, rich parents who brought her up with little formal education in the years before the First World War. Nostalgia for the settled life of these years is a conspicuous feature of her work. She made an unhappy marriage in 1914 to Colonel Archibald Christie, and her first ventures into writing may be seen as escapes from the strains of this marriage. Her first novel, *The Mysterious Affair at Styles* (1920), is one of her best. *The Murder of Roger Ackroyd* (1926) is famous in the annals of detective fiction for its surprising murderer. The political stance of some of the early stories, like *The Seven Dials Mystery* (1929), strongly condemning socialists and anarchists, makes them appear dated. After a divorce in 1928 AC married the archaeologist Max Mallowan in 1930 and thereafter kept up a steady stream of books at the rate of more than one a year. Archaeology and the Middle East form the background of several of her stories in the 1930s; in the Second World War, apart from the stilted *N or M* (1941), she was principally popular because she provided an escape from harsh reality. After the war, books about people inhabiting large country houses remained a source of enjoyment for people living in more straitened circumstances. Attempts to enter the modern world, as in *Third Girl* (1966), were less successful. Her play *The Mousetrap* has run without interruption since 1952, probably because of its period charm. Her two principal detectives, Hercule Poirot and Miss Marple, are almost entirely sexless, although passion as a motive for crime plays a considerable part in her novels.

The question whether crime is ever excusable is rarely treated by AC although she does raise it in the contrived *Murder on the Orient Express* (1934). The unjustly neglected *Curtain* (1975) and the earlier *Ten Little Niggers* (1935) do offer some thoughts about crime and punishment, but readers of AC cannot expect to find philosophical depth in the intellectual puzzle of discovering the identity of a murderer from a series of ingenious clues. As a crime writer she does succeed in pleasing and teasing her audience, although her characters are hackneyed and plots mechanical. She knew her limitations and within these limitations was a supreme performer.

Under the pseudonym Mary Westmacott, AC also wrote six romantic novels.

TOM WINNIFRITH

Selected works: The Mysterious Affair at Styles: A Detective Story (1920); The Murder on the Links (1923); The Murder of Roger Ackroyd (1926); The Seven Dials Mystery (1929); The Murder at the Vicarage (1930); Peril at End House (1932); Lord Edgware Dies (1933); Murder on the Orient Express (1934); The A.B.C. Murders: A New Poirot Mystery (1936); Murder in Mesopotamia (1936); Death on the Nile (1937); Appointment with Death: A Poirot Mystery (1938); Murder is Easy (1939); Ten Little Niggers (1939); Death Comes as the End (1942); Sparkling Cyanide (1945); Crooked House (1949); The Mousetrap and Other Stories (1949); A Murder is Announced (1950); They Came to Baghdad (1951); A Pocket Full of Rye (1953); Dead Man's Folly (1956); 4:50 from Paddington (1957); Ordeal by Innocence (1958); Cat among the Pigeons (1959); At Bertram's Hotel (1965); Endless Night (1967); Curtain: Hercule Poirot's Last Case (1974); An Autobiography (1977).

References: Keating, H. (ed), Christie: First Lady of Crime (1977); Morgan, J., Agatha Christie: A Biography (1984); Ramsey, G., Christie: Mistress of Mystery (1967); Robyns, G., The Mystery of Christie (1978); Sanders, D. and Lovallo, L. (eds), The Agatha Christie Companion (1985).

Chudleigh, Mary, Lady

b. August 1656, Winslade, Devon; d. 15 December 1710, Ashton, Devon
Poet, essayist

MC enjoyed a wide popularity in her own day. Having established her reputation with *The Ladies' Defence* (1701), the first appearance of her *Poems* two years later was followed by three subsequent editions, and her *Essays* (1710) was printed for no fewer than ten different booksellers in London.

Born to Richard Lee and his wife, to whom MC refers in a poem as 'Philinda', little is known about her except what can be gleaned from her work. She married late, in 1685, and her union with Sir George Chudleigh of Ashton appears to have been far from happy. She bore two sons and a daughter, Eliza Maria, whose early death occasioned MC's most heart-rending poem, a dialogue between herself ('Marissa') and a bosom friend she calls 'Lucinda'. MC found pleasure primarily in solitary reading, and her own work reveals a wide acquaintance with poetry, history, philosophy, and theology. Verse provided her with the opportunity to ' Inspect each Action, ev'ry Word dissect,/ And on the Failures of my Life reflect' ('To Clorissa'), while the essays 'were the Products of my Retirement, some of the pleasing opiates I made use of to lull my mind to a delightful Rest, the ravishing amusements . . . of my lonely Moments'. She died at the age of 55, having long been confined to her room by rheumatism, and was buried without a memorial.

Despite her protestations of solitude, MC was part of a circle of like-minded literary women. Many of her poems were addressed to female friends to whom MC gave classically allusive pseudonyms in the contemporary style. Her first (anonymous) publication, *The Ladies' Defence*, was in response to a misogynist sermon by John Sprint published two years earlier as *The Bride-Woman's Counsellor*. Two other anonymous women had already attacked this diatribe in print. Their pamphlets, *The Female Preacher* (1699) and *The Female Advocate* (1700), have both been ascribed to MC by the *Dictionary of Anonymous and Pseudonymous English Literature*. The latter is probably not hers; the former was written by one 'Eugenia', whom MC may well have known since in her poem 'To Eugenia' she praises that lady's 'ingenious Pen'.

Although MC later, after an unauthorized reprinting of *Ladies' Defence*, denied that the work was an invective on marriage, 'insisting' it was but merely a satire on vice, her views on marriage are made perfectly clear elsewhere: 'Marriage is but a fatal Lott'ry made:/ Where some are Gainers, but the most betrayed' ('A Dialogue between Alexis and Astrea'). On romance she wrote

> Oh wondrous Woman! Prodigy of Wit!
> Why didst thou Man to thy fond Heart admit? . . .
> What Pity 'twas thou shouldst to Love give way.
> To Love, to vicious Love, become a Prey.
>   ('The Resolution')

MC greatly admired her younger contemporary, Mary Astell, whom she addressed in verse as 'Almystrea', and she distilled Astell's *Reflections upon Marriage* into the acerbic 'To the Ladies':

> Then shun, oh! shun that wretched State,
> And all your fawning Flatterers hate:
> Value your selves, and Men despise,
> You must be Proud if you'll be wise.

MC wrote chiefly for 'the Ladies' entertainment' and her subjects are particularly female. All of the individuals in her poems are women, with the exception of one Dr Musgrave, to whom she wrote a paean in thanks for alleviating her daughter's lingering illness. The essays discuss such topics as Knowledge, Pride, Humility, Friendship, and finally Solitude in suitably pious and undistinguished phrases. But before lapsing into sentimentality MC urges her readers not to let men monopolize learning and to prefer 'rational instructive Thoughts' as the only satisfying alternative to 'treacherous Man . . . who's composed of nothing but Deceit'.

According to Ballard's *Memoirs*, MC left unpublished two tragedies, two operas, a masque, and verse translations of Lucian. Several of her letters appear in collections, such as *The Duke of Wharton's Poetical Works*, vol. 2, and *Curll's Collection*, vol. 3.   AMY ERICKSON

Selected works: *The Female Advocate, or, A Plea for the Just Liberty of the Tender Sex, and Particularly of Married Women* (Attrib.) (1700); *The Ladies' Defence, or, The Bride-Woman's Counsellor Answer'd: A Poem in Dialogue Between Sir John Brute, Sir Wm Loveall, Melissa, and a Parson* (1701); *Poems on Several Occasions* (1703); *Essays upon Several Subjects in Prose and Verse* (1710); some poems and *Ladies' Defence* reprinted in *Poems of Eminent Ladies* (1775).

References: Allibone; Ballard; *DNB*; Smith, H.L., *Reason's Disciples: Seventeenth-Century English Feminists* (1982); Stenton, D.M., *The English Woman in History* (1957); Todd.

Churchill, Caryl

b. 3 September 1938, London

Playwright

CC addresses social and political questions with audacity and wit. Her father, Robert Churchill, a political cartoonist, and her mother, a model, actress, and secretary, moved to Canada in 1948 where CC attended the Trafalgar School, Montreal. Returning to England in 1956, she began to write plays at Lady Margaret Hall, Oxford. *Downstairs* (1958) and *Having a Wonderful Time* (1960) were produced there before she received her BA in English in 1960 and the Richard Hilary Memorial Prize in 1961. CC married the barrister David Harter in 1961 and stayed at home throughout the decade, having three sons, and writing more than a dozen plays for radio and television. Her plays connect personal and political oppression by depicting conflicts about sexuality, mothering, and violence. They are often Brechtian in form, and use popular devices like song and documentary or historical material to emphasize social rather than psychological conflicts.

In 1972, Michael Codron commissioned CC to write a play for the Royal Court, the theatre that established John Osborne, David Storey, and David Hare. The play was *Owners*, about property values in rowhouses, butcher's meat, infants, and senile mums. The style recalls Joe Orton's savage mockery of cosy family life; the plot concerns a patriarchal butcher who plans to murder his ambitious wife. As resident dramatist at the Royal Court (1974–5), CC wrote a science fiction play, now called *Moving Clocks Go Slow* (1975), and *Objections to Sex and Violence* (1975). *Objections*, staged in 1975, puts a middle-class divorcée into a caretaker's job and involves her with terrorists and flashers. In *Traps*, written immediately afterwards but not staged until 1977, CC began to experiment with dramatic time. Four men, two women and an infant explore the possibilities of change in a commune which is like an impossible Escher drawing: their changing relationships form flexible traps. Similar traps prevent the audience from knowing whether the commune is in the country or the city, and whether Syl has a child she doesn't want or wants a child she doesn't have. The play ends with a hope for Utopia as the characters bathe serially in an old washtub, the most violent one bathing last and smiling, in the dirtiest water.

Until this time CC had worked alone on plays about contemporary life. When she began to work with fringe theatre workshops, she found the experience exhilarating, exhausting, and fruitful. With Monstrous Regiment, a feminist touring company, she wrote *Vinegar Tom* (1976), a play which shows how the witch-hunts of the seventeenth century used non-conforming women (old, poor, single, or skilled as healers) as scapegoats in a time of social unrest. Working with the Joint Stock Theatre Group and its director, Max Stafford-Clark, on *Light Shining in Buckinghamshire* (1976), CC used ideas derived from improvisations to dramatize the attempts of Diggers, Levellers, and Ranters to build a New Jerusalem in the England of the 1640s. Both workshop plays use a historical perspective to show that social change can occur, both set groups of people in a political context, both are ensemble pieces without star roles, and both use short, self-contained scenes, interrupted by songs, to raise political questions.

Working again with Monstrous Regiment and with her co-authors David Radford, Bryony Lavery, and Michelene Wandor, CC developed *Floorshow* (1977) as a group of sketches and lyrics for a cabaret about women and work. Then, in a workshop on sexual politics with Joint Stock, she developed her best-known play, *Cloud Nine* (1979), a satirical farce set in an African colony in 1880 and in a London park in about 1980. Through music-hall devices and cross-sex casting, she connects colonial, sexual, and class oppression. In the first act, Clive, the Victorian patriarch, insists that both his family and his Africans must live out his ideas, while the exuberant and farcical action ridicules his pretences. A male actor plays his wife, Betty, who is an exaggerated stereotype of feminine compliance. Because the butler has assumed white values, a white actor plays African Joshua, for whom the walls of Empire finally come tumbling down. In the second act the members of Clive's family, only twenty-five years older, are no longer his property. With new working-class characters encountered in the public space of a London park, they try out new social arrangements in a tenderer questioning of class, gender, and homophobic oppression. *Cloud Nine* opened at the Royal Court in 1979, and the 1981 New York production, which ran for two years, won three Obie awards.

Three More Sleepless Nights (1980), about two couples trying to change by changing partners, followed *Cloud Nine* but did not win the same critical acclaim. There followed *Top Girls* (1982), which led Benedict Nightingale to rank CC as one of the half-dozen best contemporary dramatists.Its brilliant opening brings famous and successful women from the past millennium to a dinner celebrating Marlene's latest promotion. Of the top girls, only Dull Gret, a peasant from a Brueghel painting, has challenged the patriarchal hierarchy. Pope Joan, Lady Nijo, and the others, like Marlene herself, have sacrificed sexuality, maternity, or self-assertion to succeed in a man's world. In a final naturalistic scene in Marlene's working-class sister's home, we see that nothing has changed at the bottom, although there is some room for women at the top.

Remembering *Top Girls*, several critics referred to CC's next play as 'Bottom Girls'. *Fen* (1983) peoples the potato farms in a bleak East Anglian landscape with figures, five women and one man, playing twenty-two roles. In the fog which steams from the fen, distinctions between past and present, illusion and reality, are obscured. Val, a central figure, torn between her lover and her children, dies because she can't get used to how things are. CC won the Susan Smith Blackburn Prize for *Fen* in 1984. Most critics found her next play, *Softcops* (1984), which deals with crime and punishment in nineteenth-century France, too dependent on its intellectual source, *Discipline and Punish* by the French philosopher Michel Foucault. *Midday Sun* (1984), a script for a dance group at the Institute of Contemporary Arts, presents four British tourists who fantasize about, experience, and then remember a holiday on a Moroccan beach and an encounter with an Arab beggar.

In 1986, working with co-author David Lan and the Joint Stock Theatre Group, CC wrote *A Mouthful of Birds* for an autumn tour. Using Euripides' *The Bacchae* as a ground, the play sets seven people free from their usual fears through temporary ecstasy or possession. Dionysus is called forth by a West Indian medium who works, appropriately, as a switchboard operator. *Serious Money* (1987), a City comedy about greed, an easier target than her earlier complex ones is the most recent result of CC's long collaboration with Joint Stock and Max Stafford-Clark. Cleverly staged, it opens with a brief look at seventeenth-century speculators in Thomas Shadwell's *The Volunteers, or, The Stockjobbers.* As in *Cloud Nine*, doubling presents shifting identities, this time between City traders and their investigators, County riders and their mounts, and Third World opportunists and their victims, all set forth in unheroic couplets. The play ends with a song, 'Five More Glorious Years', an ironic celebration of Margaret Thatcher's 1987 election victory. After a successful run in London, the production transferred to New York's Public Theatre and then to Broadway.   MARY R. DAVIDSON

Works: (dates are of first performance) *Downstairs* (1958); *Having a Wonderful Time* (1960); *Easy Death* (1961); *Owners* (1972); *Schreber's Nervous Illness* (1972); *Moving Clocks Go Slow* (1975); *Objections to Sex and Violence* (1975); *Light Shining in Buckinghamshire* (1976); *Vinegar Tom* (1976); *Floorshow* (1977); *Traps* (1977); *The Legion Hall Bombing* (1978); *Cloud Nine* (1979); *Three More Sleepless Nights* (1980); *Top Girls* (1982); *Fen* (1983); *Softcops* (1983); *Midday Sun* (1984); *A Mouthful of Birds* (with David Lan) (1986); *Serious Money* (1987).

References: *CA; CD*; Diamond, E., 'Refusing the romanticism of identity: narrative interventions in Churchill, Benmussa, Duras', *Theatre Journal* 37 (October 1985); *DLB*; Drabble; Itzin, C., *Stages in the Revolution: Political Theatre in Britain since 1968* (1981); Keyssar, H., 'The dramas of Caryl Churchill: the politics of possibility', *Feminist Theatre* (1984); Klein, J., 'Seeing double: theatrical conceits in *Cloud Nine*', *Journal of Dramatic Theory and Criticism* 1 (Spring 1987); Wandor, M., *Understudies* (1981); Wandor, M., *Carry On, Understudies* (1986).

Clarke, Mary Cowden

b. 22 June 1809, London; d. 12 January 1898, Genoa
Critic, novelist, poet

MCC was the eldest daughter of the composer and arranger Vincent Novello and of his wife Mary Sabilla Hehl. Novello was friendly with many of the most celebrated *littérateurs* and artists of his day, and MCC became acquainted in her early years with, amongst others, Keats, Leigh Hunt, and Charles and Mary Lamb. She later turned these acquaintances to professional use in the *Recollections of Writers* which she wrote with her husband. MCC was taught initially at home (at one time Mary Lamb taught her English verse and Latin) and then completed her education at a school in Boulogne. Afterwards she worked for a short time as a governess in England before abandoning the profession because of her poor health.

In the summer of 1828 she married Charles Cowden Clarke, one of her father's circle of literary acquaintances. Her own prolific literary career had already begun in the previous year with her publication of a piece entitled 'My Arm Chair' in *Hone's Table Book* for 1827. Much of her subsequent career was devoted, in one form or another, to Shakespeare: in 1829 she began compiling a concordance to his works which took her sixteen years to complete and see through the press, and which remained the standard concordance for half a century. She also produced a collection of tales dealing with *The Girlhood of Shakespeare's Heroines* (1852) and later edited and annotated his works in collaboration with her husband. In addition she was from 1853 until 1856 the editor of the *Musical Times* and translated several musicological treatises from French and Italian. Moreover, she found time to produce novels, several volumes of verse and metrical prose stories, and an autobiography. For the last thirty-five years of her life she pursued her career from the continent, first in Nice and later, after her father's death, from his villa in Genoa.

Much of MCC's creative work has an implicitly pedagogical cast. *The Girlhood of Shakespeare's Heroines* offers a collection of *Bildungsromanen* which seek 'to imagine the possible circumstances and influences of scene, event, and associate, surrounding the infant life of his heroines, which might have conduced to originate and foster those germs of character recognized in their maturity. . . .' Many of the stories thus become educational parables whose events become important only in so far as they influence permanent features of adult character. 'Katharina and Bianca: the Shrew, and the Demure' offers countless opportunities for a favourite instructive antithesis of MCC's: Bianca's unwillingness to offend the self-love of her elders is treated no less ironically than Katharina's wilfulness. But, although MCC occasionally criticizes the educational practices which produce such submissive creatures as Bianca and recognizes that, in the words of Katharina's wise aunt, 'high spirits . . . form an admirable basis for character, if only directed properly', she emphasizes that such instruction, as in Shakespeare's play, is best received at the hands of a man. At one point Giulio, a youth whom Katharina has been teasing, ties her to a tree, with exemplary results: she feels 'A perplexed feeling of shame and surprise take possession of her, at finding herself completely overcome - *mastered.*'

A similar antithesis to that between Katharina and Bianca is developed in more detail in MCC's novel *The Iron Cousin* (1854), in which the 'high-spirited' Kate Ireton is contrasted with the demure and well-bred Alicia White. Here, however, the fatherly art of taming is considered in more detail: Kate's 'iron cousin', Fermor Worthington, improves Kate by means of carefully administered doses of approval and disapproval: 'She found herself giving way at his change of voice, as it dropped into his earnest depth of tone . . .' But *The Iron Cousin* also indicates an awareness of wider social influences on character absent from 'Katharina and Bianca': the poverty which Kate undergoes after her uncle dies without leaving a will is as educational as Fermor's stern precepts.

SIMON JARVIS

Works: *The Complete Concordance to Shakespeare* (1845); *Shakespeare Proverbs* (1848); *A Book of Stories for Young People* (1848); *Kit Bam's Adventures* (1849); *The Girlhood of Shakespeare's Heroines* (1852); *The Iron Cousin* (1854); *The Song of a Drop o' Wather* (1856); *World-Noted Women* (1858); *The Life and Labours of Vincent Novello* (1864); *The Trust and the Remittance* (1873); *Short Stories in Metrical Prose* (1873); *A Rambling Story* (1874); *Verse Waifs* (1883); *A Score of Sonnets to One Subject* (1884); *Uncle Peep and I: A Child's Novel* (1886); *Memorial Sonnets* (1888); *Centennial Biographic Sketch of Charles Cowden Clarke* (1887); *My Long Life* (1896).

References: Altick, R. D., *The Cowden Clarkes* (1948); Gittings, R., 'Introduction' to *Recollections of Writers* (1969); Novello, S. (ed. and condenser), *The Girlhood of Shakespeare's Heroines*, new edn. (1955).

Clifford, Lady Anne

b. 30 January 1590, Skipton Castle, Yorkshire; d. 22 March 1676, Brougham
Castle, Westmorland

Diarist, biographer, letter writer

AC was the daughter of Lady Margaret Russell and George Clifford, Earl of
Cumberland. She was educated by a governess, Mrs Anne Taylor, and the poet
Samuel Daniel. The account of her life survives in two forms; the first is a
diary and the other, in the third person, is named 'A summary of the records
and a true memorial of the life of me, the Lady Anne Clifford'. The latter
manuscript forms part of an extensive three-volume work, *Great Books of the
Records of Skipton Castle*, which AC compiled to cover the history of her family
from King John to 1652. AC's childhood memories highlight the tension
between her parents: when her father returned home from his long voyages
abroad they 'did show the dislike they had of one another'. AC's father died
in 1605, leaving his estate to his brother. By ignoring the deed dating from the
reign of Edward II which stated that land must be entailed upon children
irrespective of sex, her father left behind a legal wrangle that was to dominate
her life and to remain unsolved until 1643. As AC did not begin writing until
after this date it seems that the manuscripts are as much a historical validation
of her actions as an autobiography.

In 1609 AC married Richard Sackville, Earl of Dorset. With him she had
five children, two of whom survived infancy, Margaret (b. 1614) and Isabella
(b. 1622). Dorset was eager to stop the lawsuit and thereby please the king. His
attempts to persuade AC verged at times on the ruthless; emotional blackmail,
enforced separation from her child, and abuse coloured the marriage: 'Your
land transports you beyond yourself and makes you devoid of all reason'
(Dorset, in *Diary*, p. 14).

Dorset died in 1624 and, in 1630 AC remarried. Philip Herbert, Earl of
Pembroke, was, like his predecessor, unsupportive in his wife's legal battles. AC
felt 'condemned by most folks because I would not consent to the agreement, so
as I may truly say, I am like an owl in the desert' (*Diary*, p. 28). After
Pembroke's death in 1650 AC began a new and varied career. She began
writing, founded an almshouse in Appleby for thirteen homeless women and
a school in Mallerstang 'to teach the children of the dale to write and read
English', and held the position of 'Sherriffwich' in the county of Westmorland.
In addition AC inaugurated an extensive programme of renovation on her now
numerous estates – five castles and seven churches being rebuilt by the time of
her death. In his sermon at AC's funeral Bishop Rainbow called her 'a most
critical searcher into her own life'.   CATHERINE S. WEARING

Works: *Lives of Lady Anne Clifford and her Parents*, ed. J. P. Gilson (1916); *The
Diary of Lady Jane Clifford*, ed. V. Sackville-West (1923); *Clifford Letters of the
Sixteenth Century*, ed. A. G. Dickens (1962).

References: Allibone; Ballard; Costello, L. S., *Memoirs of Eminent Englishwomen*
(1844); *DNB*; Notestein, W., *Four Worthies* (1956); Palmer, A. and Palmer, V.,
Who's Who in Shakespeare's England (1981); Rainbow, E., *A Sermon Preached at
the Funeral of the Right Honorable Anne, Countess of Pembroke, Dorset and Montgomery* (1677); Sackville-West, V., *Knole and the Sackvilles* (1923); Walpole, H.,
'Letters of ladies', *World* (5 April 1753); Williamson, G., *Lady Anne Clifford*
(1922); Wilson, V., *Society Women of Shakespeare's Time* (1924).

Clifford, Lucy
b. 1853, Barbados; d. 21 April 1929
Novelist, playwright, writer for children
(Also wrote under Mrs W. K. Clifford)
LC was the daughter of John Lane, a West Indian planter. As an art student in
London she met and in 1875 married W. K. Clifford, professor of mathematics
and 'delicious *enfant terrible*', as William James called him, on the literary and
scientific scene. Through her husband, she became part of a circle which
included Leslie Stephen, James Russell Lowell, and Henry and William James.
She was one of the few women invited to George Eliot's Sunday afternoon
parties at the Priory. When in 1879 she was left a widow with two small
daughters (one of whom, Ethel, later Lady Dilke, became a poet), Eliot helped
her to get a small Civil List pension and gave her the introductions that enabled
her to augment it by writing articles for the *Standard*.
    W. K. Clifford, who before his death at 34 had made several contributions
to mathematics, had also developed two philosophical concepts to which he
gave the terms 'mind-stuff' and the 'tribal self'. The first asserts that the mind
is the only reality, but defines mind as the elements – much like the atomic
particles of physical matter – which form the mind, rather than the complex,
conscious mind of common definition. The second, 'the tribal self', posits a
morality developed by the individual regulating his conduct to assure the
'welfare of the tribe'. These theories were explored fictionally in LC's novels
and tales, as, for example, her first book, *Anyhow Stories* (1882); this literary
fairy tale directed to an audience of all ages was so successful that an enlarged
edition appeared in 1899.
    Mrs Keith's Crime (1885) explores the 'tribal self' of a woman with an incur-
able, suffering child; she finds a solution in euthanasia. The book caused a
sensation amongst critics and the public and was much admired by Robert
Browning and Thomas Hardy. *Aunt Anne* (1893), considered by some to be
LC's best novel, recounted the effort of the title character to establish herself
as the dominant power in a family – the tribe. Henry James, LC's friend from
1880 to his death in 1916, teasingly called LC 'Aunt Lucy', echoing this work,
because of her assertive if warm personality. Of her work he wrote critically,
'you don't *squeeze* your material hard and tight enough . . . this is the fault of
all fictive writing now.'   ELEANOR LANGSTAFF
Selected works: Anyhow Stories (1882; enlarged edn, 1899); *The Dingy House at
Kensington* (1882); *Mrs Keith's Crime* (1885; new revised edn, 1925); *Love Letters
of a Worldly Woman* (1891); *A Woman Alone* (1891; produced as a play 1914);
The Last Touches and Other Stories (1892); *Aunt Anne* (1893); *A Wild Proxy*
(1894); *A Flash of Summer: The Story of a Simple Woman's Life* (1895); *The
Dominant Note and Other Stories* (1897); *A Long Duel: A Serious Comedy in Four
Acts* (1901); *Woodside Farm* (1902); *A Honeymoon Tragedy: A Comedy in One Act*
(1904); *The Getting Well of Dorothy* (1904); *The Modern Way* (1906); *Mrs Hamil-
ton's Second Marriage* (1909); *Thomas and the Princess* (1909); *Sir George's Objection*
(1910); *The Searchlight: A Play* (1913); *Two's Company: A Play* (1915); *The
House in Marylebone* (1917); *Miss Fingal* (1919); *Eve's Lover* (1927).
References: Ekstein, R. 'Childhood autism, its process, as seen in a Victorian
fairy tale', *American Imago: A Psychoanalytic Journal for Culture, Science, and the
Arts* 35 (1978); Lurie, A., 'A tail of terror', *New York Review of Books* (11
December 1975); Randell, L., 'Mrs W. K. Clifford', *Bookman* 57 (1920).

Cobbe, Frances Power

b. 4 December 1822, Newbridge, Dublin; d. 5 April 1904, Wales

Essayist

FPC's detailed autobiography records her eventful life, from her childhood in Newbridge where she lived with her brothers and parents, Charles and Frances Cobbe, to her work as a suffragist, feminist, philanthropist, and anti-vivisectionist.

As the only daughter of 'well-born' parents, FPC had a comfortable though lonely childhood and was educated by governesses until 1836 when she attended school in Brighton. The formal education she underwent appeared to her to be 'shallow', 'senseless', and 'pretentious', and FPC soon began to develop her own interests, for example in architecture and history. Later she was moved to argue for an adequate and fulfilling education for women.

An income inherited from her father in 1837 allowed FPC to travel extensively throughout Europe. She was to draw upon these experiences in her sophisticated travel writings, for example *Italics*. FPC came to know such respected writers as Arnold, Browning, Mill, and Tennyson. She wrote copiously on religion and morality. Her first publication in 1855 (*Essay on the Theory of Intuitive Morals*) was well-received, and the fact that it was published anonymously led to some interesting reviews: 'the work of a lofty and masculine mind' wrote the *Caledonian Mercury*. In her autobiography FPC speaks of Theism as her 'staff of life', and, although her religious writings are sometimes not particularly profound or explorative, she writes with sincerity and assurance. These attributes are prominent in *Darwinism In Morals and Other Essays*, a lively and controlled response to a provocative issue.

An important aspect of FPC's life was her continued work for social reform. She was involved in the welfare of those in reform schools and workhouses in Bristol, and was exposed to social injustice and poverty. Her experience caused her to become an advocate of women's rights, wanting influence so that she could help her 'less fortunate sisters': she stated in a speech made before the Recorder of London on 13 May 1876 that she advocated women's suffrage as the 'natural and needful' constitutional means of gaining 'protection for the rights of the weaker half of the nation'. FPC spoke often at women's conferences and her writings upon the duties and rights of women are forceful and emotive, firmly linking social, political and Christian duty. Her main concern was that women's talents and powers were wasted, and her account of her own life seeks to demonstrate 'how pleasant and interesting, and . . . not altogether useless a life is open to woman'.

LORNA DAMMS

Works: *Essay on the Theory of Intuitive Morals* (1855); *Essays on the Pursuits of Women* (1863); *Thanksgiving* (1863); *Religious Duty* (1864); *Broken Lights: An Inquiry into the Present and Future Prospects of Religious Faith* (1864); *The Cities of the Past* (1864); *Italics* (1864); *Studies New and Old on Ethical and Social Subjects* (1864); *Hours of Work and Play* (1867); *Dawning Lights, Secular Results of the New Reformation* (1868); *Darwinism in Morals and Other Essays* (1872); *Doomed to be Saved* (1874); *Essays on Life and Death and the Evolution of Moral Sentiment* (1874); *The Hopes of the Human Race* (1874); *The Moral Aspects of Vivisection* (1875); *False Beasts and True* (1876); *Re-echoes* (1876); *The Duties of Women* (1881); *The Peak in Darien* (1882); *The Scientific Spirit of the Age* (1888); *The Friend of Man, and His Friends, the Poets* (1889); *Health and Holiness* (1891); *Life, by Herself* (1894); *Life of Frances Power Cobbe* (1904).

References: Allibone; *Letters of Matthew Arnold 1843–84* (1903); *BA*; Chappell, J.,

Women of Worth (1908); *DNB*; Hickok, K., *Representations of Women: Nineteenth-Century British Women's Poetry* (1984); Plarr, V. G., *Men and Women of the Time*, 15th edn (1899).

Colegate, Isabel
b. 10 September 1931, London
Novelist

IC is the youngest daughter of an MP, Sir Arthur Colegate, and of Lady Colegate Worsley. As both historical novelist and novelist of manners, she records relationships amongst the powerful and not so powerful in the first half of this century. She left school at the age of 16 to concentrate on her writing and produced a finished novel within a year. In 1950 she began work for Anthony Blond, a literary agent turned publisher who brought out her first novel, *The Blackmailer*, in 1958. Its central characters are Judith Lane, the widow of a Korean war 'hero', Anthony Lane, who keeps alive the myth of his valour in battle, and Baldwin Rees, who had served under Lane and confronts Judith with the 'real' story of Lane's cowardice. Rees extorts money from her by threatening to sell the story to a newspaper. Although afflicted with overwriting, syntactical awkwardness, and somewhat abrupt, implausible character changes, *The Blackmailer* introduced what later became dominant concerns for IC: money, class, and power.

The same concerns are apparent in IC's next novel, *A Man of Power* (1960). Here the young woman who undergoes an education is Vanessa, the daughter of Lady Essex Cooper, who narrates the story of her mother's involvement with Lewis Ogden, 'the man of power'. IC's use of Vanessa as the first-person narrator makes *A Man of Power* at once more assured and more engaging than *The Blackmailer*. IC regards her third novel, *The Great Occasion* (1962), as her most technically successful. This ambitious (and partly autobiographical) work follows the five daughters of Gabriel Dodson, a wealthy financier, as they mature in the England of the 1950s. Only one of the women achieves any real independence. The book is remarkable for its psychological insight, but the task of trying to trace the careers of one man and his five daughters through two decades of turbulent history is a burden to the reader.

Statues in a Garden (1964), while related thematically to IC's first three novels, is a departure in stylistic terms. It deals with the family of Sir Aylmer Weston, a prominent Liberal politician, during the summer of 1914. When Aylmer's nephew and adopted son, Philip, seduces Lady Weston, the family's gracious Edwardian world collapses. The novel is more than a social chronicle: it ambitiously questions the view that the Great War was alone responsible for the social transformations which occurred immediately after it. Philip's very attempts to join the society of the Westons are part of what bring that society to an end.

The three novels of the 'Orlando trilogy' combine perceptive characterization with an identifiable historical context. In *Orlando King* (1968) the 21-year-old protagonist, after a sheltered upbringing on an island off the coast of Brittany, establishes a brilliant business career for himself in the London of the 1930s. Unwittingly, he marries his father's widow, Judith, whose failed attempt at suicide causes her complete mental breakdown. Orlando discovers his father's identity; partially blinded in the bombing of London, he forsakes his business and political careers and goes into exile. *Orlando At the Brazen Threshold* (1971) details the last few moments of Orlando's life. He returns to the island of his childhood and clarifies some of the mysterious circumstances of his early life. He is reunited with his daughter, Agatha, and returns to London for a brief visit before retiring to Tuscany where he dies. *Agatha* (1973), the final novel in the trilogy, makes significant use of historical events, and especially of the Guy Burgess case. The trilogy is marked by ambiguity: the novels must be read together in order to appreciate IC's carefully engineered construction of character and her references to the Oedipus story.

IC's next novel, *News From the City of the Sun* (1979), explores patterns of historical activity within the specific context of England from 1931 until the early 1970s. Three brothers have established a utopian community in the grounds of an unused abbey, gathering members who are distinctly representative of the times. The novel's young female narrator, although she participates in some of the action, remains essentially detached in her presentation of the class conflicts and power games played out in the community. IC's most recent novel, *The Shooting Party* (1980), received the W. H. Smith Literary Award and was subsequently filmed. It is her most technically assured work to date. She skilfully interweaves documentary history and fiction to chronicle one weekend in the autumn of 1913 on the Oxfordshire estate of Sir Randolph Nettelby. The guests have assembled for shooting, sherry, and sexual intrigue. IC's technical finesse renders this somewhat familiar material entirely plausible.

IC's attempts at short fiction have been less successful than her novels and *A Glimpse of Sion's Glory* (1985), a collection of three stories, consists of one mediocre retelling of the 'bright promise never fulfilled' theme, a failed attempt at science fiction, and a single successful story, 'The Girl Who Lived Among Artists', which has a dark, fairy-tale quality.   ROBERT E. HOSMER, JR

Works: *The Blackmailer* (1958); *A Man of Power* (1960); *The Great Occasion* (1962); *Statues in a Garden* (1964); *Orlando King* (1968); *Orlando at the Brazen Threshold* (1971); *Agatha* (1973); *News from the City of the Sun* (1979); *The Shooting Party* (1980); *A Glimpse of Sion's Glory* (1985).

References: *CA*; *DLB*.

Coleridge, Mary

b. 23 September 1861, London; d. August 1907, Harrogate

Poet, novelist, critic

(Also wrote under Anodos)

MC was the daughter of Arthur Duke Coleridge, who was Clerk of the Assize to the Midland Circuit, and his wife Mary Anne Coleridge. She was the great-great-niece of the poet Samuel Taylor Coleridge. Her parents had a varied circle of artistic and literary friends: Tennyson, Browning, and Ruskin were often guests at the house, as also were the painter Millais and the actress Fanny Kemble. MC was taught by her father's friend William John Cory, a retired schoolmaster who had been obliged to leave Eton after being involved in a scandal. Cory described MC, the favourite of his pupils, as 'the industrious wise clever modest & supremely unselfish Mary Coleridge'. She learned six languages, including Greek and Hebrew, and her early literary efforts showed considerable promise.

Although MC never left the family home where she grew up, she travelled on the continent with four similarly well-educated and well-off friends; the group called themselves the 'Quintette'. Her first appearance in print was as an essayist for the *Monthly Packet*, at the age of 20, and contributions to *Merry*

England and other periodicals followed. Her first novel, *The Seven Sleepers of Ephesus*, appeared in 1893; the novel which established her reputation was *The King With Two Faces* (1897). From 1902 onwards, MC wrote for the *Times Literary Supplement*. She died of appendicitis in Harrogate at the age of 45.

MC is now primarily remembered for the poems which she was reluctant to print when alive. Although many of her literary friends admired her work MC herself found it difficult to take the prospect of publication seriously until, unknown to her, the poems were put before Robert Bridges anonymously and won his enthusiastic approval. Bridges even offered to help her correct her poems for publication, writing somewhat self-importantly that 'I am willing to take some trouble . . . if she is inclined to work.' It is clear that MC did indeed act on many of Bridges' suggestions for improvements; in one instance two poems which he had considered would be more effective if combined were amalgamated. But she also disregarded many of his promptings. Beside the poem 'Larghetto' he had written 'I can't stand the title' but it remains the same in her first published collection, *Fancy's Following* (1896).

MC's poetry displays a wider range than the whimsical titles of her collections would suggest. Many of the poems are love lyrics or ballads recalling the work of the Pre-Raphaelites, but there are also poems of urban life handled in a manner more reminiscent of the French poets of the *fin-de-siècle*. MC's attempts at technical impressionism can sometimes become obtrusive, as in this couplet from 'Street Lanterns', with its excessive alliteration: 'Lit, throughout the lengthy night / By the little lantern's light.' But her work also hints at the changed aesthetic priorities of the new century. It often shows a precise and epigrammatic wit, even when dealing with the most deeply felt topics, as in 'Broken Friendship':

> Give me no gift! Less than thyself were nought.
> It was thyself, alas! not thine I sought.
> Once reigned I as a monarch in this heart,
> Now from the doors a stranger I depart.

The concentration of some of her poems upon individual striking images also anticipates the development of lyric poetry in the early years of the twentieth century. 'Street Lanterns' is organized as a series of couplets each of which offers a discrete visual image and which are laid alongside each other rather than combined into a developing whole.

Although MC could occasionally become passionate about social reform, it rarely features in her literary work as more than an aesthetic moment. In an essay on the novels of Mrs Gaskell she celebrates the ethical zeal of the mid-century novelists: 'As the sonnet, which had been as a lute for lovers, became in Milton's hand a trumpet, so the novel, which had been once (and was to be again) a toy, became in theirs a sword with which to fight in the cause of the oppressed.' But the essay soon settles down to the business of choosing a 'favourite character from this long gallery' and MC's choice is the Lady Ludlow of exquisite aesthetic sensibilities who can relish 'the scent of decaying strawberry leaves in the autumn . . . cherished by her because only a nose of gentle birth can detect it'. And the layers of irony in 'An Insincere Wish Addressed to a Beggar' ('You can't forget that I am rich, / Nor I that you are telling lies') emphasize further MC's belief that the refined pleasures so important to her poetry are only available to those of wealth and breeding.

Apart from her novels and poems, MC also wrote a collection of essays, *Non*

Sequitur (1900), and a biography, *Holman Hunt*, written at the artist's request
and published in 1908, after her death. JAMES SMITH
Works: *The Seven Sleepers of Ephesus* (1893); *Fancy's Following* (under Anodos)
(1896); *The King with Two Faces* (1897); *Fancy's Guerdon* (under Anodos) (1897);
Non Sequitur (1900); *The Fiery Dawn* (1901); *The Shadow on the Wall* (1904);
The Lady on the Drawing-Room Floor (1906); *Holman Hunt* (1908); *Poems*, ed. H.
Newbolt (1908); *Gathered Leaves from the Prose of Mary E. Coleridge*, with
memoir by E. Sichel, includes six unpublished poems (1910); *The Collected
Poems of Mary Coleridge*, ed. T. Whistler (1954).
References: Evans, B. I., *English Poetry in the Later Nineteenth Century* (1933);
Reilly, J. J., 'In praise of Mary Coleridge', in *Of Books and Men* (1942); Whistler,
T., 'Introduction' to *The Collected Poems of Mary Coleridge* (1954).

Coleridge, Sara

b. 23 December 1802, Greta Hall, Keswick; d. 3 May 1852, London
Editor, writer for children, poet
'When there is not mere carelessness but a positive coldness in regard to what
I have done, I do sometimes feel as if I had been wasting myself a good deal
– at least so far as worldly advantage is concerned,' wrote SC in her diary.
Most of her writing life was spent editing the work of her father, Samuel
Taylor Coleridge. Though it is always as well to be wary of defining people
in terms of their famous parents, SC linked her own life so forcibly to her
father's that, in her case, it is unavoidable. From an early age she identified
closely with her father and his later estrangement from her mother helped to
enhance the attraction. As her brother wrote, 'Sara is the inheritrix of his mind
and of his genius.' But with multiple pregnancies, an invalid mother, and a
dependent brother to cope with, her own creative output was limited to what
she could produce in her spare moments.
SC grew up in the shadow of the monolithic figures of William Wordsworth
and Robert Southey, spending the first twenty-seven years of her life under
Uncle Southey's roof (Mrs Coleridge and Mrs Southey were sisters). SC was
a serious child prone to morbid ill-health, which she later attributed to falling
in the River Greta at the age of 2, though it probably had more to do with her
father's habit of taking her into his bed and telling her horror stories late into
the night.
Although Coleridge was appreciative of SC's overdeveloped imagination, he
turned away from her when it became obvious that she preferred the company
of her mother. This terrible alienation is reported in her unfinished memoir
and gives some idea of how haunting her prose could be: 'truly nothing does
so freeze affection as the breath of jealousy. The sense that you have done very
wrong, or at least given great offence, you know not how or why – that you
are dunned for some payment of love or feeling which you know not how to
produce or to demonstrate on a sudden, chills the heart, and fills it with
perplexity and bitterness. My father reproached me, and contrasted my coldness
with the childish caresses of the little Wordsworths. I shrunk away and hid
myself in the wood behind the house.'
By the age of 20 her translation of Martin Dobrizhoffer's *Account of the
Abipones* (1822) was giving her a small income with which she eased the financial
straits imposed on her and her mother by her father's excesses. Her reading,
although it included Jane Austen and Cervantes, was mainly theological. 'The
thing that would suit me best of anything in the whole world,' she confided

to Derwent, 'would be the life of a country clergyman.' She was an Anglican of the staunchest kind and heartily disapproved of the Oxford Movement, which she felt to be 'contrary to the principles of the Reformation'.

In 1829 she married her cousin Henry Coleridge after a lengthy courtship. The two cousins were brought together by a common obsession with her father, and together they began rescuing his reputation by editing his unpublished work (under Henry's name). Despite attacks of hysteria SC educated her two children, Edith and Herbert, at home, developing elaborate games to make learning more fun. These were later published as *Pretty Lessons in Verse for Good Children* (1834). Even during one of her worst bouts of illness she wrote her fairy-tale in verse, *Phantasmion* (1837).

After Henry's death in 1843, SC began to receive full credit for her editorial work and in seven years she brought four major works of her father's to publication. These included *Biographia Litteraria* (1847) and *Notes on Shakespeare* (1849), the books on which his reputation as a literary critic rests.

It was also during this period that she began to write her memoir, which ends so unsatisfactorily halfway through a sentence, 'On reviewing my earlier childhood, I find the predominant reflection'; this statement is tantalizingly followed by a triple row of dots, as inconclusive as her own life. By 1850 her health was failing; she developed cancer of the breast and abandoned the idea of a memoir.   MARTIN BRIGHT

Works: *An Account of the Abipones, an Equestrian People of Paraguay, from the Latin of Martin Dobrizhoffer* (1822); *The Right Joyous and Pleasant History of the Facts, Tests, and Prowesses of the Chevalier Bayard, the Good Knight without Fear and without Reproach: by the Loyall Servant* (1825); *Pretty Lessons in Verse for Good Children* (1834); *Phantasmion* (1837); (ed.), *Biographia Litteraria*, by S. T. Coleridge* (1847); (ed.), *Notes and Lectures upon Shakespeare . . . of S. T. Coleridge* (1849); (ed.), *Essays on His Own Times*, by S. T. Coleridge (1850); (ed.), *The Poems of Samuel Taylor Coleridge* (with Derwent Coleridge) (1852); *The Memoir and Letters of Sara Coleridge*, ed. Edith Coleridge (1873); *Minnow among Tritons: Mrs S. T. Coleridge's Letters to T. Poole 1799–1834*, ed. S. Potter (1934); *Sara Coleridge and Henry Reed: Reed's Memoir of Sara Coleridge; Her letters to Reed including her comment on his memoir of Gray; Her marginalia in H. Crabb Robinson's copy of Wordsworth's memoirs*, ed. L. N. Broughton (1937).

References: Griggs, E. L., *Coleridge Fille* (1940); Mudge, B. K., 'Burning down the house: Sara Coleridge, Virginia Woolf, and the politics of literary revision', *Tulsa Studies in Women's Literature* 5 (Fall 1986); *OCCL*; Towle, E. A., *A Poet's Children* (1912); Woolf, V., 'Sara Coleridge', in *Death of the Moth and Other Essays* (1942).

Collier, Mary

b. 1689/90 near Midhurst, Sussex; d. after 1762, Alton, Hampshire
Poet

MC appears to have been the first published working-class woman poet in England. Her most important poem, *The Woman's Labour: An Epistle To Mr Stephen Duck* (1739), subverts the genre of the georgic even more radically than does Duck's *The Thresher's Labour* (1736), for she introduces a feminist critique of male prejudices about women workers alongside the new poetical subject matter of agricultural and domestic work as experienced, not observed. The publication of such a text as early as 1739 suggests that English working-class feminism has a history that predates its usual association with the nineteenth century. And MC's skilful appropriation of 'high literary' neo-classical tropes for her own purposes demonstrates that a plebeian female poet can take aesthetic advantage of her distance from the dominant literary culture in this period.

In 'Some Remarks of the Author's Life drawn by herself', her autobiographical preface to her collected poems of 1762, MC tells us that she was the child of 'poor, but honest Parents' who taught her to read when she was very young. Her mother's death prevented her from ever going to school; as she grew up, she was 'set to such labour as the Country afforded'. She nursed her ailing father, and after his death moved to Petersfield where she worked as a laundress, brewer, domestic servant, and occasional field hand. At 63 MC retired from her work as a washerwoman to take up the post of housekeeper at a farm near Alton; at 70 she retired to 'a Garret (The Poor Poets Fate)' in that town, where she lived until her death, as she claimed, 'in Piety, Purity, Peace, and an Old Maid'. Throughout her life reading was her chief recreation, and at some point she learned to write to 'assist' her memory. Her various employers seem to have regarded her as a curiosity, an example of that popular eighteenth-century phenomenon, a 'natural genius'. According to the 'Advertisement' to a collected edition of her poems, with proper education she 'would have ranked with the greatest poets of [the] kingdom'.

In 1739 she published, at her own expense, *The Woman's Labour*, in which she vindicated the women of her own class in reply to Duck's accusations of their frivolity, laziness, and garrulity. She had got his poems by heart, admiring his 'unlettered' genius and his descriptions of the rigours of agrarian labour, but she thought he had been 'too Severe' on the female sex. *The Woman's Labour* mounts a proto-feminist critique of men's refusing to see women's work as productive, and, in so doing, gives us vivid descriptions of what amounts to a triple shift of wage labour, housework, and caring for children. Laundering fine linen for the gentry becomes an epic contest:

> Until with Heat and Work, 'tis often known,
> Not only Sweat, but Blood runs trickling down
> Our Wrists and Fingers; still our Work demands
> The constant Action of our lab'ring Hands. (11. 184–7)

Unlike Duck or James Thomson in *The Seasons*, Collier gives us a powerful evocation of a winter of labour, for women's work is seasonless as well as ceaseless. And the empirical testimony that Collier offers – of wages of 'Sixpence or Eight-pence' a day at best, so that women's projections of the future could only linger on the prospect of 'Old Age and Poverty' (11. 199–201) – has been subsequently confirmed by social historians. *The Woman's Labour* appeared together with MC's *The Three Wise Sentences, from the First Book of Esdras, Ch. III and IV*, in which competing arguments as to what constitutes the greatest power on earth are offered. One of the contestants proposes 'Woman', only to claim that divine truth, as the creator of all things including Woman, is indisputably the greatest power. These poems went through three editions, the third of which includes a statement by nine respectable Petersfield residents testifying to MC's authenticity.

In 1762 MC published by subscription her collected *Poems, on Several Occasions*. In addition to the two poems mentioned above, the volume includes two elegies, a dialogue on marriage, versifications of 1 *Samuel* 1–2 and the *Spectator*, no. 375, a celebration of the marriage of George III, and a reply to an exciseman 'Who doubted her being the Author of the Washerwoman's Labour', in which she advocates female education as a means to sexual equality. Another edition of the same poems was also published, entitled *The Poems of Mary Collier, the Washerwoman of Petersfield . . . A New Edition*, with a new 'Advertisement' venerating her talents and indicating that she maintained a strong local following until her death.   DONNA LANDRY

Works: *The Woman's Labour: An Epistle to Mr Stephen Duck; In Answer to his late Poem, called The Thresher's Labour. To which are added, The Three Wise Sentences, Taken From The First Book of Esdras, Ch. III. and IV* (1739); *Poems, on Several Occasions* (1762); *The Poems of Mary Collier, the Washerwoman of Petersfield* (n.d.).

References: Ferguson, M., *First Feminists: British Women Writers 1578–1799* (1985); Landry, D., 'The resignation of Mary Collier: some problems in feminist literary history', in *The New Eighteenth Century*, ed. L. Brown and F. Nussbaum (1987); Todd.

Collyer, Mary

b. 1716?; d. December 1762 or January 1763, Islington, London

Translator, novelist

MC married John Collyer the elder, an editor, compiler, and translator who often printed her books. Her first known publication was a translation of Marivaux's *La Vie de Marianne*, possibly dated as 1742, though a claim has been made for 1735. The interpretative nature of the translation is suggested in the new title, *The Virtuous Orphan, or, the Life of Marianne*. A later pirated edition appeared with changes in 1746 as *The Life and Adventures of Indiana*, and many other editions occurred throughout the eighteenth century, during which MC's partial translation was the standard presentation of Marivaux. MC admitted that the French novel was put into 'English dress' and directed to female readers in particular; both MC's translation and *Pamela* have girls of lower social status improving the morality of their higher-placed lovers. In addition, the style adopted is closer to Samuel Richardson than to Marivaux. MC's second published work, *Memoirs of the Countess of Bressol*, a group of moral tales, appeared in 1743, and in 1744 the first volume of *Felicia to Charlotte: Being Letters from a Young Lady in the Country to a Friend in the Town*, telling of the romantic entanglements of Felicia. Written in a style both mocking and sentimental it describes the overpowering sensations of love and the physical manifestations of melting softness, greedy looks, and swelling breasts. Yet there is simultaneously a more realistic voice that mocks this style: 'You are now ready to imagine I shall describe him throwing himself at my feet, while with a flow of rapture, he admires my superlative goodness . . . if these were your thoughts, you were extremely mistaken'. The two styles and stances are oddly mixed and the 'engaging youth' who is the hero, said to attract her through his enthusiastic talk of virtue and nature, and to be too good a Christian to 'deify his mistress', is yet as overwhelmed by her effect as any sentimental hero, and he has the typical 'feminine' characteristics as well as the 'natural curis' so common in women's romantic fiction of the time. The style of the second volume (1749) is more restrained than both the sentimental and more realistic styles of Part I, since Felicia's 'romantick adventures' have ended in marriage:

'I have nothing more to do with the affecting scenes of fond distress, the pangs of jealousy, or the fears of incurring a father's displeasure'; the aim becomes the one clearly stated in the preface: to prove 'that the Seeds of Virtue are implanted in the Mind of Every Reasonable Being'. Conjugal felicity is interrupted only by the death of a child and some inset stories of distress. The volume presents the married lady and mother who unfashionably insists on suckling her baby, perhaps an echo of MC's own practice since she had borne her only known child not long before the publication. In its concern for a woman's life *after* marriage, it forms part of a group of novels directed at women which include Part II of Richardson's *Pamela* and Sarah Fielding's *Countess of Dellwyn*. The tenor of Part II, as well as the slight mockery of sentimental postures in Part I, explains the approval of MC by the Blue-stocking ladies including Elizabeth Carter, not usually impressed by sentimental fiction.

In *Felicia to Charlotte* MC mentions a work for children, *The Christmas Box* of 1748–9, but apart from this work MC seems to have been silent until in 1761 her translation of Salomon Gessner's *Der Tod Abels* appeared as *The Death of Abel* dedicated to the Queen. Despite her apologetic preface in which she described the work of a female pen as but a 'faint representation of the glowing beauties of the original', it was extremely popular, going through 27 editions in the next 25 years and remaining in print in the next century. The dedication suggests that MC was in some financial difficulties since she was writing, she claimed, to support her family. The translation is a sentimental version of the Cain and Abel story in which Abel becomes a man of feeling and Cain in due course a romantic outsider who dramatizes his outcast situation. The popularity of *The Death of Abel* encouraged MC to undertake another translation, of Gottlieb Klopstock's *Messiah*; completed and published by Joseph Collyer, volumes 1 and 2 appeared in 1763 after her death and volume 3 in 1772.

JANET TODD

Works: (trans.), *The Virtuous Orphan*, by Marivaux (1735); (ed.), *Memoirs of the Countess of Bressol* (1743); *Felicia to Charlotte* (1744); *Letters from Felicia to Charlotte*, vol. 2 (1749); *The Christmas Box* (1748–9); (trans.), *The Death of Abel*, by S. Gessner (1761); (trans.), *The Messiah*, by G. Klopstock (1763).

References: DLB; Hughes, H. S., 'Translations of the *Vie de Marianne* and their relation to contemporary English fiction', *Modern Philology* 15, 7 (1917); Rogers, K., *Feminism in Eighteenth-Century England* (1982); Spencer, J., *The Rise of the Woman Novelist: From Aphra Behn to Jane Austen* (1986); Todd.

Compton-Burnett, Ivy

b. 5 June 1884, Pinner, Middlesex; d. 27 August 1969, London
Novelist

The first child of James Compton Burnett and Katharine Rees, IC-B was followed by two brothers and four sisters. James had been previously married to Agnes Thomas (who died after bearing five children), so IC-B grew up in a large household including servants appropriate to a gentleman's family. IC-B's mother was the first to hyphenate her husband's family names, thinking that doing so increased the family's distinction.

IC-B's early childhood was fairly happy, although there was friction between the two sets of children. She studied the literary classics with her brothers' tutor while her sisters preferred music. She was a very clever, rather solitary girl, even while attending the Addiscombe College for the Daughters of Gentlemen. Now settled in Hove, the family was held together by the love and generous spirit of James Compton Burnett, whose death in 1901 deeply affected all remaining family members.

The following year IC-B went to the Royal Holloway College for Women to read classics, where she took a second-class honours degree in 1906. She then moved back home to Hove to teach her younger sisters, and started writing her first novel, published five years later and reviewed as a work of great promise. Katharine Compton-Burnett increasingly became the family tyrant, dying in late 1911 of breast cancer. IC-B became head of the household, wielding her power also with a heavy hand, and her four younger sisters moved out after four years under her rule.

The early deaths of her two younger brothers (one by illness, the other in the Second World War) and the double suicide of her two youngest sisters in 1916 caused IC-B severe emotional upheaval. Fortunately, she had made the acquaintance of the sisters Dorothy and Tertia Beresford, whose support helped her through these crises, and who later became models for her characters' witty dialogue. In 1918 a severe case of Spanish influenza incapacitated IC-B and she suffered the after-effects for years, but her tyrannical tendencies largely dissolved during the illness and in her convalescence she took up the hobby of intricate embroidery for chair seats.

Dorothy Beresford's 1919 marriage separated her from IC-B, but her place was soon taken by Margaret Jourdain, the poet and furniture historian. The two friends lived together for the next thirty-two years. The happiness IC-B felt through their companionship gradually gave her the impetus to start writing again. Her casual approach to work, sitting in an armchair with an exercise book propped open on her knee, belied her profound and carefully thought-out prose. *Pastors and Masters* appeared in 1925, followed every two years (except during the Second World War) by another novel. After eleven well-received novels, the now-famous IC-B was made a Fellow of the Royal Society of Literature. She and Margaret led quiet, busy, non-eventful lives. Speculation arose regarding their sexuality, but Margaret considered herself 'asexual'; IC-B termed them both 'neuters', and passion never seemed to be a part of their relationship. IC-B was very dependent on her companion until Margaret grew sick, when IC-B's dominance took on the unpleasant, tyrannical aspect of her 1911–15 period. In early 1951 Margaret died after a brief illness and her loss was a severe shock to IC-B.

The first book she wrote after Margaret's death revealed a technique even sharper, cleaner, and deeper than before. The following volume, *Mother and Son,* won the James Tait Black Memorial Prize, to IC-B's great satisfaction. Several of her novels were adapted to very successful radio scripts in the 1950s; to many of her audience, the radio versions are more accessible than the printed novels themselves. In 1960 the University of Leeds awarded her an honorary Doctor of Letters degree.

The 1960s were not particularly happy for IC-B: many of her close friends were dying or already dead; she was concerned about her income, although she had comfortable amounts of capital in reserve; and she fell and broke each hip on separate occasions. Living alone with her housekeeper and omnipresent exercise book, she had a steady flow of visitors. From her girlhood, IC-B was always a 'watcher', listening and observing the events around her. She grew up into a peculiar individual, delicate and ironic. New acquaintances often expected her to speak like one of her characters, and were disappointed by her flat speech and long silences. In 1967 she became Dame Commander of the British Empire, and the following year received the Companion of Literature title from the Royal Society of Literature. The last four years of her life were often solitary, as she preferred to see visitors singly, and she grew increasingly eccentric. She died after an attack of bronchitis.

Late in life, IC-B described her first thirty-five years as miserable. Many of her novels, reflecting that unhappiness, contain themes of family tension owing to emotional tyranny, violence, crime, homosexuality, and incest. She wrote twenty novels, but in later years often ignored the first, *Dolores*, as 'sentimental juvenilia'. Her novels are all set in country houses or school environments, around 1890–1910, inhabited by variously sized casts of characters who tend to say exactly what is on their minds in a highly mannered style. This stylized speech is the key to the novels, because IC-B relies on the power of words rather than action to carry the interest. Plot exists, and plenty of it, but it is revealed by the dialogue instead of the typical, more accessible narrative description, of which there is a minimum. The language used is non-metaphorical in the extreme; its intense clarity and directness take many first-time readers aback. Their words, indeed the characters themselves, are concentrated, distilled, reduced to their essentials. IC-B felt that people are not strongly defined enough to show up on paper, so she had to concentrate their characters in order to do them prose justice.

Her characters possess unusual names – Cassius, Flavia, Hereward, Ninian – but the author claimed to have no hidden intent. Her character motivation is the most basic possible: the self. From her use of dialogue and astute perception of the dynamics of family life, IC-B has often been compared to Jane Austen.

Owing to the difficulties of IC-B's writing, she is not a universally loved writer. It is objected that the novels contain insufficient characterization, artificial and stilted dialogue, unlikely plots, and a static environment. But an acceptance of the characters' manner of verbal communication opens the reader to the full import of their complex personalities, fascinating insights, painfully sharp observations, and dramatically revealing actions, *given* the world in which they live. The bare, highly formalistic literary structure has been compared to the Cubist movement in painting, owing to the similar technique of revealing aspects – and eliminating non-essential details – in a superbly precise, brilliant exposure of the subject. AMALIA E. ERICKSON

Works: *Dolores* (1911); *Pastors and Masters* (1925); *Brothers and Sisters* (1929); *Men and Wives* (1931); *More Women than Men* (1933); *A House and Its Head* (1935); *Daughters and Sons* (1937); *A Family and A Fortune* (1939); *Parents and Children* (1941); *Elders and Betters* (1944); *Manservant and Maidservant* (1947; published in the US as *Bullivant and the Lambs*); *Two Worlds and Their Ways* (1949); *Darkness and Day* (1950); *The Present and the Past* (1953); *Mother and Son* (1955); *A Father and His Fate* (1957); *A Heritage and its History* (1959); *The Mighty and Their Fall* (1961); *A God and his Gifts* (1963); *The Last and the First* (1971).

References: Baldanza, F., *Ivy Compton-Burnett* (1964); Burkhardt, C. (ed.), *Twentieth Century Literature* 25, 2, 'Ivy Compton-Burnett Issue' (1979); *Crawford Liddell, R., A Treatise on the Novel* (1947); Sprigge, E., *The Life of Ivy Compton-Burnett* (1973); Spurling, H., *Ivy* (1974).

Comyns, Barbara

b. 1909, Bidford-on-Avon, Warwickshire

Novelist

BC was one of six children. Her father, managing director of a chemical firm, was 'a violent, impatient man'; her mother was an invalid, deaf since the age of 25. Thus BC's early life was characterized by seclusion, punctuated by a series of poorly qualified governesses. She spent much time in boats – and the theme of water runs through such works as *Sisters by a River* and the flood novel *Who Was Changed and Who Was Dead*. BC started her authorial career at the age of 10. She illustrated many of her own works, moving on to art schools in Stratford-on-Avon and London. Subsequently, she scraped a meagre living in a small advertising agency, while she made use of the wealth of literature available in London libraries.

In 1931 BC married a young artist with whom she had a son and a daughter. Later they were to separate amicably, but in the meantime BC worked as an artist's model, also dealing in old cars and converting and letting flats. With the onset of war, BC and her children moved to the country, where she felt unfulfilled until she started writing once more; the fruit was the autobiographical *Sisters by a River* (1947).

BC returned to London in 1942 where she traded in antique furniture and bred poodles. *Our Spoons Came From Woolworths* was published at the same time as the earlier novel. In 1945 BC married her present husband; the couple spent their honeymoon in Snowdonia, where BC was inspired with the idea for *The Vet's Daughter* (1959). This novel, located in the consciousness of Alice Rowlands, the daughter of a bullying vet in Edwardian London, is haunted by lifelessness. Alice is lonely, trapped, and oppressed, we are told. Apparently she longs for love interest in the plot of her own life – and she gets it, diluted and drawn out in the form of dull suitor Blinkers, and concentrated but evanescent in the striking figure of sailor Nicholas. With the manifestation of Alice's occult powers things could, for a moment, come to life; but the somehow false naivety of Alice's deadpan reportage (perhaps BC's attempt to portray a lost innocence) is like double glazing separating reader from heroine, insulating her within unsatisfying inscrutability amidst professed candour. *The Vet's Daughter* is sometimes used to exemplify BC's 'off-beat' talent; but there is much to be said for beating in time with the rest of humanity at least occasionally.

At the same time as she was writing *The Vet's Daughter* BC began researching a book on Leigh Hunt. She became an expert on the subject, but the book was never published. Her next novel was based on newspaper reports of an epidemic of ergot poisoning in a French village. *Who Was Changed And Who Was Dead* is often macabrely comic; but again too studied an authorial aloofness may leave the reader with little with which to identify. BC's prose, though, is brilliantly paced. Her novels would make excellent short stories; and that is not to detract from them, for perhaps the novel is sometimes arbitrarily seized upon as the best form for writing fiction. BC herself has successfully made the transition not only into another genre but into another medium, her novels being performed on BBC Radio as serials, plays – even a musical. Maybe these forms are better vehicles for BC's inclination towards the bizarre, abstracting out to some extent the reader's struggle to identify. With whom? That is the question which BC's novels, for all their undoubted vigour and appeal, leave unanswered.   E. LEVY

Works: *Sisters by a River* (1947); *Our Spoons Came From Woolworths* (1950); *Who*

Was Changed And Who Was Dead (1955); *The Vet's Daughter* (1959); *Out of the Red into the Blue* (1960); *The Skin Chairs* (1962); *Birds in Tiny Cages* (1964); *A Touch of Mistletoe* (1967); *Mr Fox* (1987).
References: Holden, U., 'Introduction' to *Sisters by a River* (1984).

Cook, Eliza
b. 24 December 1818, London; d. 23 September 1889, Wimbledon
Poet, essayist
EC was a middle-class Victorian writer of feminist essays on women and work and of verses that ranged from angry and powerful political ballads which found a working-class readership to sentimental treatments of domestic themes appealing largely to the middle class.

EC was the youngest of eleven children and was entirely self-educated. She grew up in the country, living from 1827 onwards in Horsham, Sussex. She defiantly dressed in a manner considered masculine, and unself-consciously displayed a passionate attachment to the actress Charlotte Cushman.

She began writing at the age of 15 and published her first verses, *Lays of a Wild Harp*, at 17; the favourable reception of the book led her to submit poems to the *Weekly Dispatch*, the *Metropolitan Magazine*, and the *New Monthly Magazine*. Her most famous poem, 'The Old Arm Chair', a sentimental tribute to her deceased mother, appeared in the *Dispatch* in 1837. This and many of her other poems on the subject of her mother's death expressed a genuine grief that contemporary readers were likely to share. *Melaia and Other Poems*, published in 1838, was a great success in both England and the United States. This volume has some lively satire (including the title poem), along with the simple and sentimental poems for which EC was best known to a domestic middle-class readership.

Despite the popularity of EC's poetry, her real talent was for journalism. *Eliza Cook's Journal*, which she wrote and edited virtually single-handedly from May 1849 to May 1854, was a miscellany of sketches, reviews, social essays, and verses intended to improve the lives of uncultured middle-class women – by entertaining and informing them and by contributing a feminist voice to contemporary debates about women's proper role in society. In the pages of this journal, EC particularly addressed the difficulties and despair of English working women, be they governesses, seamstresses, factory workers, or servants. She attacked the interpretation of English law that allowed husbands to 'discipline' their wives physically, she defended 'old maids', and she criticized the superficiality of English girls' education. The journal ceased publication after five years because of her failing health and consequent poor business management, not for lack of an audience. A large portion of the contents of the journal was reissued in 1860 as *Jottings from My Journal*.

In 1863 EC was awarded a civil list pension of £100 per year. *New Echoes and Other Poems* (1864) was her last book of poems, and a collection of aphorisms, *Diamond Dust* (1865), her last book of prose. For the last twenty-five years of her life she was an invalid. She died at the age of 71, having outlived her popularity as a poet but not her reputation as a feminist.

KATHLEEN HICKOK

Works: *Lays of a Wild Harp* (1835); *Melaia and Other Poems* (1838); *Poems, Second Series* (1845); *Eliza Cook's Journal* (1849–54); *I'm Afloat: Songs* (1850); *Jottings from My Journal* (1860); *New Echoes, and Other Poems* (1864); *Diamond Dust* (1865); *The Old Armchair* (1886).

References: Allibone; *DNB*; Drabble; Faderman, L., *Surpassing the Love of Men* (1981); Hickok, K., *Representations of Women: Nineteenth-Century British Women's Poetry* (1984); Mitchell, S., *The Fallen Angel: Chastity, Class, and Women's Reading 1835–1880* (1981); Woodring, C., *Victorian Samplers: William and Mary Howitt* (1952).

Cookson, Catherine

b. 20 June 1906, Tyne Dock, Durham
Novelist
(Also writes under Catherine Marchant)
CC grew up in East Jarrow, the illegitimate daughter of a woman she believed to be her sister for most of her childhood. She began work in service before moving south to Hastings, where she met and married a local school teacher, Thomas Cookson, in 1940. It was not, however, until after she was 40 that she started to write. She now lives in Northumberland.

CC is a remarkably prolific and popular author of women's romantic fiction. Many of her books are set in the area in which she grew up, and she has a reputation as a regional writer. Her books generally enact a female fantasy of sorts: a spirited heroine meets an attractive man, whose attitude to her is often patronizing; he eventually falls in love with her, she overcomes her initial dislike for him and they live happily every after. Yet there is much variety in the novels, which range from the historical tale of the landed gentry of the 'Mallen' series, to the stories of a farmer's daughter in the 1970s in the 'Mary Ann' books. This set of stories has been particularly popular, translated with great success into German, Dutch, and Italian. Two of her novels have been made into films.   VIRGINIA CROMPTON

Selected works: Our Kate: An Autobiography (1969); Fanny McBride (1977); The Gambling Man (1977); Feathers in the Fire (1978); The Unbaited Trap (1978); Pure as the Lily (1978); Mrs Flannagan's Trumpet (1978); The Glass Virgin (1978); Joe and the Gladiator (1978); The Tide of Life (1978); The Man Who Cried (1979); Go tell it to Mrs Golightly (1979); The Mallen Novels (The Mallen Girl; The Mallen Letter; The Mallen Streak) (1979); Maggie Rowan (1979); The Nice Bloke (1979); Slinky Jane (1979); The Blind Miller (1980); Tilly Trotter (1980); Lanky Jones (1980); Fenwick Houses (1980); Nancy Nutall and the Mongrel (1982); The Whip (1983); Tilly Trotter Widowed (1983); Marriage and Mary Ann (1984); A Dinner of Herbs (1985); The Moth (1986); Bill Bailey (1987); Bill Bailey's Lot (1987).

Cooper, Lettice

b. 1897 Eccles, Lancashire
Novelist, biographer, writer for children
LC was educated at secondary school in Southbourne and at Lady Margaret Hall, Oxford, from 1916 to 1918. She worked briefly on *Time and Tide* as editorial assistant and drama critic at the start of the Second World War, was Public Relations Officer in the Ministry of Food from 1940 to 1945, and President of English PEN from 1979 to 1981. LC is best known as the author of delightful stories for children, *Blackberry's Kitten* (1961) and *Parkin* (1977), and of more robust tales for juveniles, *Robert the Sky Hunter* (1973) and *Contadino* (1964). Her popularity as children's writer has obscured her deserved reputation as a novelist for adults.

Her writing career began in the 1920s and spans half a century. *We Have*

Come to a Country (1935) is set in a centre for the unemployed in the 1930s and describes the conflicting personalities and the battle between condescension and self-determination (epitomized by the attitudes to the unemployed held by the Ladies' Committee and the Men's Committee). Generally, however, her themes are more domestic. *The New House* (1936) takes place during one day in which a widow and her daughter move from the old family home to a smaller house. The upheaval brings to the surface hidden conflicts as the daughter steps over the threshold of childhood into maturity. LC returns to the dramas within institutions, this time an Adult Education Centre, in *Three Lives* (1957); unlike the earlier work it is without political overtones. *Late in the Afternoon* (1971) has a topical setting, the unrest of 1968. The perspective is that of an old lady and the suggestion is that the young are sometimes lacking in humanity. LC's particular strengths are her ability to span and understand the generations, and her grasp of the nuances of middle-class English domestic life.

MARY JOANNOU

Selected works: *The Lighted Room* (1925); *Likewise the Lyon* (1929); *The Old Fox* (1927); *Good Venture* (1928); *The Ship of Truth* (1930); *Private Enterprise* (1931); *We Have Come to a Country* (1935); *The New House* (1936); *National Provincial* (1936); *Black Bethlehem* (1947); *Robert Louis Stevenson* (1948); *Yorkshire West Riding* (1950); *George Eliot* (1951); *Fenny* (1953); *Great Men of Yorkshire* (1955); *Three Lives* (1957); *A Certain Compass* (1960); *Blackberry's Kitten* (1961); *The Double Heart* (1962); *The Young Victoria* (1962); *The Bear Who Was Too Big* (1963); *James Watt* (1963); *Garibaldi* (1964); *The Young Edgar Allan Poe* (1964); *Contadino* (1964); *The Fugitive King* (1965); *The Twig of Cypress* (1966); *We Shall Have Snow* (1966); *A Hand Upon the Time* (1968); *Robert Louis Stevenson* (1969); *Gunpowder, Treason and Plot* (1970); *Late in the Afternoon* (1971); *Robert the Sky Hunter* (1973); *Tea on Sunday* (1973); *Snow and Roses* (1976); *Parkin* (1970); *Desirable Residence* (1980).

References: Beauman, N., *A Very Great Profession* (1983); Duffy, M., 'Introduction' to *The New House* (1987); King, F., 'Introduction' to *Fenny* (1987).

Corelli, Marie

b. 1 May 1855, Bayswater, London; d. 21 April 1924, Stratford-upon-Avon
Novelist

MC was the illegitimate child of Charles Mackay, poet and journalist, and Mary Mills, a servant. After the death of his first wife in 1861, Mackay married MC's mother. MC was educated at home by governesses, and when her mother died in 1876 Bertha Vyver joined the household as companion to MC. From 1883 until 1889 MC ran the Mackay household. During this period she had pretensions to a musical career, and devised the name 'Marie Corelli' for her recitals. She also began to publish poems. In 1886 when she was 31 George Bentley published her first novel *A Romance of Two Worlds*. This made little impact, but several later publications, *Ardath* (1889), *Barabbas* (1893), and *The Sorrows of Satan* (1895), established her as a best-seller. By the turn of the century she was said to be earning £10,000 for each of her novels. Her readers included Edward VII, Gladstone, Asquith, and Oscar Wilde. In 1901, following a severe breakdown, and the death of her brother, MC and Vyver moved to Stratford-upon-Avon, where MC claimed affinity with Shakespeare. Here in 1902 she bought two Shetland ponies and a miniature chase-cart in which she and Vyver took their afternoon rides. In 1905 she ordered a specially crafted gondola, 'The Dream', from Venice and had it delivered with a uniformed gondolier (soon to be replaced by the gardener). Over a period of several years, she pursued a one-sided love affair with her neighbour, the artist Arthur Severn, who withstood her assaults with amused contempt. MC was more successful with the crowds who waited outside the halls where she lectured. Tourists gathered each afternoon to glimpse her as she emerged from her house at Stratford-upon-Avon. Surprisingly, however, MC combined her efforts to seek fame with desperate attempts to maintain personal privacy. She refused to be photographed, and lied about her parentage, upbringing, and date of birth. Her attempts to maintain an image of herself as elfin, coy, and 17 became the object of public ridicule. She lived with Bertha Vyver in Stratford-upon-Avon until her death.

MC's Edwardian romances displayed the same bizarre combination of sensational love, spiritualism, science, and religious bigotry and prejudice as her previous works. She waxed hysterical on subjects like women who smoked or rode bicycles, Parisians who drank and read cheap novels, socialists, suffragists, and Carnegie libraries. Her novels were overwritten, full of clichés, archaisms, adjectives, adverbs, and repetitions. They were also longer than those of her contemporaries, and loaded with descriptive passages. But many of her readers regarded her as a kind of sage and truth-teller. In 1902 *Temporal Power*, her novel attacking socialism, in its first week sold the entire first edition of 120,000 copies, and 50,000 of a second edition. The story of a socialist attempt to overthrow the monarchy, *Temporal Power* is also a *roman à clef*. The main characters are easily identifiable with prominent public figures: the ineffectual king with Edward VII, his austere queen with Queen Alexandra, and the feckless secretary of state with Joseph Chamberlain. None of the portraits, except that of the rags-to-riches heroine, clearly MC herself, is flattering.

Another of MC's hobby horses was suffrage. *Woman or Suffragette? A Question of National Choice* (1907) reflected one of the recurrent preoccupations of her Edwardian romances. Like Angel in *Angel's Wickedness* (1903) and Innocent in *Innocent: Her Fancy and His Fact* (1914), MC's heroines are all childlike, innocent, and passive. She attacks the current 'cycling mania, rough games, and general throwing to the winds of all dainty feminine reserve - delicacy and modesty'. The intensity of her love scenes is due to the woman's agonizing repression. But if her heroines are dumb, the author's voice is quick to interrupt or frame her sexual scenes with moralistic generalizations, and to sustain interest in the scene of passion by placing it in strange or bizarre settings – temples, pyramids, mausoleums – or in exotic lands or other periods of history. Despite occasional rumours that MC and Vyver were lovers, there is nothing in the novels to suggest this. The two women remained together throughout MC's life, and Vyver died in poverty in 1941.

A number of MC's early novels had focused on sensational aspects of spiritual experience, and on religion. She claimed that she had changed her plans to be a concert pianist after a mystical experience in which she was directed to make a career of writing. She had a penchant for portraying angels, devils, and even Christ appearing visibly to her characters. Satan becomes a prominent figure in several of her books, most notably *The Sorrows of Satan*. He appears again in *The Devil's Motor* (1910), a story in which the devil in smoked glasses drives a huge touring car around the world and is so shocked at human sin that he drives off the cliff with all humankind following to destruction. *The Treasure of Heaven* (1906), *Holy Orders* (1908), and *The Life Everlasting* (1911) are full of religious bigotry and prejudice, with particularly hysterical attacks on Judaism and Catholicism. In each case the plots, composed with a reformer's zeal, are designed to show how much nobler are sentimental motives than either doctrinal or pecuniary ones. *The Treasure of Heaven* reputedly reduced George Meredith to tears. *Holy Orders* was the first of MC's novels to reflect an appreciable decline in sales, its mélange of romantic heroines and attacks on the clergy being out of place in the new climate for realism. SANDRA KEMP

Selected works: *A Romance of Two Worlds* (1886); *Thelma: A Society Novel* (1887); *Ardath: The Story of a Dead Self* (1889); *My Wonderful Wife: A Study in Smoke* (1889); *Wormwood: A Drama of Paris* (1890); *The Soul of Lilith* (1892); *Barabbas: A Dream of the World's Tragedy* (1893); *The Sorrows of Satan* (1895); *The Murder of Delicia* (1896); *Cameos* (1896); *Zisha: The Problem of a Wicked Soul* (1897); *Boy: A Sketch* (1900); *The Master Christian* (1900); *A Christmas Greeting of Various Thoughts, Verses and Fancies* (1901); *'Temporal Power': A Study of Supremacy* (1902); *God's Good Man: A Simple Love Story* (1904); *The Strange Visitation of Josiah McNason: A Christmas Ghost Story* (1904); *Free Opinions Freely Expressed on Certain Phases of Modern Social Life and Conduct* (1905); *The Treasure of Heaven: A Romance of Riches* (1906); *Woman or Suffragette? A Question of National Choice* (1907); *Holy Orders* (1908); *The Devil's Motor* (1910); *The Life Everlasting: A Reality of Romance* (1911); *The Young Diana: An Experience of the Future* (1918); *My Little Bit* (1919); *The Secret Power* (1921); *Love and the Philosopher* (1923); *Open Confession to a Man from a Woman* (1925); *Poems*, ed. B. Vyver (1925).

References: Bigland, E., *Marie Corelli: The Woman and the Legend* (1953); Carr, K., *Miss Marie Corelli* (1901); Masters, B., *Now Barabbas Was a Rotter: The Extraordinary Life of Marie Corelli* (1978); Scott, W. S., *Marie Corelli: The Story of a Friendship* (1953); Showalter, E., *A Literature of their Own* (1977); Vyver, B., *Memoirs of Marie Corelli* (1930).

Cornford, Frances

b. 30 March 1886, Cambridge; d. 19 August 1960, Cambridge
Poet

The grand-daughter of Charles Darwin and daughter of Sir Francis Darwin and his second wife, FC was educated at home and spent most of her life in Cambridge. She married Francis Macdonald Cornford, a Fellow of Trinity College, in 1909 and in the years before the First World War was an important figure in the group of friends who became known as the Neo-Pagans, acting as confidante and advisor in the complicated emotional dramas surrounding Rupert Brooke. From her marriage there were five children, the eldest of whom, John, the poet and communist, was killed in the Spanish Civil War in 1936.

FC began publishing poetry in 1910, with volumes appearing at regular intervals until she produced her *Collected Poems* in 1954. During the Second World War she collaborated with Esther Polianowsky Salaman in *Poems from the Russian*, and other translations include Paul Eluard's *Le Dur désir de durer*, written with Stephen Spender in 1950. She was awarded the Queen's Medal for Poetry in 1959 and one further volume, *On a Calm Shore*, appeared in the year of her death, 1960.

As a poet, FC owes much to the Georgian poetry movement with which she was associated by many ties of friendship. Even as late as 1960 her poems retain their allegiance to Georgian themes, only developing in her treatment of such themes an increased sharpness and starkness of expression and perception, until she comes to appear the elegist of that movement and the values it espoused. Repeatedly invoking an English pastoral muse particularly associated with her native Cambridge, and a way of life that continues 'in a rhythm reachless by modernity', FC's poetry explores the dysfunction between such images of permanence and security and a poetic consciousness which, while able to deploy them and to find a limited shelter within their traditions, knows too that it cannot be adequately defined and identified by them. She writes with nostalgia of a lost simplicity of outlook still possessed by country folk and is impressed by their calm and strength in the face of mortality. Set against this, she invokes a modernity shot through with anxieties: the peacefulness of time is shattered by the ringing of a telephone and, after 'the human chaos of the night' in war-blitzed England, the cycles of the natural world continue with a vivid and estranging persistence.

Especially in the volumes that follow *Travelling Home* (1948), FC reiterates a deepening sense of pessimism about the nature of human vitality and of what will stand as epitaph to 'our angry lives'. This growing horror of life's tyrannical impositions finds its most terse and epigrammatic expression in the somewhat deceptively titled final volume, *On a Calm Shore*. Here FC attempts to reach a still and peace-giving meditative centre from which to confront the terrifying multiplicity of experience. The mysterious specificity of things that she had celebrated in her earlier work is now rendered as the merely accidental, with death as the democratic leveller uniting a Theban priest and a modern lorry driver ('In the Egyptian Room'). As part of that process of paring things down to their bare, enigmatic, and often shocking essentials, which is responsible for much of FC's characteristic wit, the themes of this volume are precisely listed: Time, Children, Night and Morning, Love, Places and Seasons, Transience – as if in an effort of tidiness. Her revisions for the *Collected Poems* show her to be disturbed even by the vitality of her own images and the startling conceits of the original volumes are frequently replaced by words less obviously seeking to draw attention to themselves. The elegiac strain always present in her work increasingly defines itself in formal terms, and such 'hieratic' power as poetry retains for FC is inevitably attracted towards the epitaphic:

> The wrong you did is gentle, like the trust
> You put in us, and like your voice and air,
> The wrong you have done is very quiet, just
> Not being there. (from *Different Days*, 1928)

                                                                   DIANA BASHAM

Works: *Poems* (1910); *Death and the Princess: A morality* (1912); *Spring Morning* (1915); *Autumn Midnight* (1923); *Different Days* (1928); *Mountains and Molehills* (1934); *Poems from the Russian* (with Esther Polianowsky Salaman) (1943); *Travelling Home* (1948); (trans.) *The Dour Desire to Endure* (with Stephen Spender), by P. Eluard (1950); *Collected Poems* (1954); *On a Calm Shore* (1960); (trans.), *Fifteen Poems from the French* (1976); some letters of FC included in John Cornford, *Understand the Weapon, Understand the Wound* (1976).

References: Anderson, A., *A Bibliography of the Writings of Frances Cornford* (1975); Delaney, P., *The Neo-Pagans* (1987); McFadden, G., *Discovering the Comic* (1982).

Cowley, Hannah

b. 1743, Tiverton, Devon; d. 11 March 1809, Tiverton, Devon

Dramatist

(Also wrote under Anna Matilda)

Although HC was reared in a remote part of Devon, she was educated and encouraged in her taste for literature – 'You gave my youthful Fancy wings to soar' (Dedication to *The Maid of Arragon*) – by her father Philip Parkhouse, a bookseller and excellent classical scholar whose mother was a cousin to John Gay. Few details of her early life survive: there is dispute even about the date of her marriage, which took place around 1768 according to the introduction to her *Works* (1813), about 1772 in the account of the *Biographica Dramatica* (1812), as well as about whether she was the mother of three or four children. In 1783 her husband, a captain in the East India Company, went abroad to serve in the Bengal colony and died there in 1897. HC herself remained attached to her remote village, where she retired after gaining a paradoxical reputation as a chronicler of fashionable London society: 'In her plays,' remarks the editor of her collected *Works*, 'Posterity may perhaps find as complete specimens as will reach them, of english Colloquy towards the close of the eighteenth Century, and of Manners as characteristic of the day, as the style of the elder Dramatists is of their's.'

HC appears rather to have stumbled on to the stage. After attending a dismal play she is said to have commented to her husband that she could have done better herself and then to have decided to prove it, writing *The Runaway* (1776) in less than a fortnight. Whatever the impetus, HC's career began on an auspicious note. She submitted her comedy to Drury Lane, where David Garrick read it with enthusiasm and undertook it early in 1776 as his last production, casting the unknown Sarah Siddons for the ingenue in her stage debut. The play enjoyed great success, the first of a succession of comedies by which over the next decade HC established herself as a major force in the London theatre. Although the notice in the *Biographica Dramatica* claims, 'In her writings nothing was laboured; all was spontaneous effusion: she had nothing of the drudge of literature; and fame was not half so much her object as the pleasure of composition,' and although, too, she was said never to have attended an opening night nor cared much about her reception, quite another picture comes from observing the pattern with which she moulded her considerable popularity. Following the romantic comedy that established her name, she seems systematically to have expanded her range, producing in succession a tragedy, an interlude, and a farce, then switching literary roles wholly by publishing her lengthy metrical tale, *The Maid of Arragon*, in 1780. Moreover, the tragedy *Albina, Countess Raimond* (1779) occasioned a newspaper battle with Richard Sheridan and Hannah More, the first of whom HC accused of conspiring to delay production and the second of plagiarizing from her plot. In the spirited preface to *Albina* she complained, 'I have been deprived of a reasonable prospect of several hundred pounds, and have spent *years* of fruitless anxiety and worry.' Such sentiments indicate that her pride was as well developed as her sense of professionalism. When she left the theatre in 1797 with *The Town Before You*, she prefaced the printed version of the play with an attack against the bad taste of current audiences, vowing never again to write for the stage. She kept her pledge in a novel manner, returning to the public in 1801 with an epic poem, *The Siege of Acre*, which celebrated Sir Sidney Smith's successful defence of the beleaguered Syrian outpost against Napoleon's assault. It is the solitary epic of the many written during England's Romantic period that attempts to render the contemporary wars into heroic verse. Characteristically, in her poem HC holds a mirror up to her achievement and exhorts her fellow poets to emulate her in confronting historical truth. The quality of her verse notwithstanding, in range, ambition, and sheer pluck HC was a hard act to follow.

In truth, little of HC's poetry merits comparison with her comedies. Her poetic style is generally overwrought and stilted, making her epics seem quaintly bombastic and her shorter poems merely mannered. To modern eyes her mistake as a poet was to have trained in the wrong school, among the Della Cruscans. While achieving her greatest successes on the stage, HC was simultaneously maintaining a second persona, as perhaps the best known of the pseudonymous women poets of the Della Cruscan school, Anna Matilda, under which name she published a volume of verse in 1788. To read these poems, as well as the collective effort to which Anna Matilda contributed, *The Poetry of the World*, against the comedies is to discern a tongue-in-cheek attitude toward Della Cruscan excesses. Whether or not she intended it, HC found herself receiving the impassioned advances of Robert Merry, Della Crusca himself, which she parried over a long poetic correspondence, countering his celebrations of unrestrained sensibility with paeans to indifference, asserting that it would be far preferable to be a Newton or Locke than any man's mistress. In context, then, the contributions of Anna Matilda to *The World* (recast as *The British Album*) strike a remarkably feminist pose. The charade came to an end in a denouement that could have come from one of HC's comedies – indeed, as almost an exact parody of how Letitia Hardy wins the haughty Doricourt through an elaborate masquerade in *The Belle's Stratagem* (1780) – with HC at last agreeing to an assignation with Della Crusca, where Robert Merry discovered that he had been wooing a portly mother of 45. True to his shameless nature, Merry wrote it all up in 'The Interview', one of the funniest pieces of high seriousness to come from English Romanticism. Since only a couple of Anna Matilda's numerous effusions were incorporated into HC's *Works*, one can assume that she enjoyed the joke without herself overcrediting the verse that so sparked Merry's ardour.

Comedy was HC's natural bent, and she attracted a broad following that continued for many years after her death. Certain of her roles – for instance, that of Letitia Hardy, which secured the reputations of Mrs Younge and Mrs Jordan in HC's day and later prompted Ellen Terry's revival of *The Belle's Stratagem* - were coveted theatrical vehicles. Her writing is very much in the spirit of Sheridan, as indeed is most comedy of the later eighteenth century; and as manager of Drury Lane he had a major influence on her professional success. But the difference between them is signal. In almost all her dramatic works HC's strongest characters are women who are determined to succeed in circumstances that constrain their futures. The note HC appended to *The Belle's Stratagem* indicates her express intention to alter the terms of the eighteenth-century comedy of manners and, with necessary adjustments, could preface all her plays: 'In the Following Comedy my purpose was to draw A FEMALE CHARACTER that, with the most lively Sensibility, fine Understanding, and elegant Accomplishments, should in her natural character unite that graceful Reserve and Delicacy, which, veiling those charms, render them still more interesting.' Even with such a citation of virtues, however, HC is conscious of the necessity of feminine veiling. The imperative for a woman on HC's stage, as expressed by Lady Bell Bloomer in *Which is the Man?* (1782), is to conduct herself in such a manner that she 'is mistress of her whole situation, and cannot be surprised', and the result is a constant role playing that doubles the theatrical fiction. In *A Bold Stroke for a Husband* (1783) Olivia pretends to be a shrew in order to ward off the suitors her father brings her; her cousin Victoria, married to the dissolute scoundrel Carlo, dresses *en travesté* and successfully woos his mistress away from him. In *School for Greybeards* (1786) Seraphina encourages Don Octavio's mistaken suit so that her stepdaughter can circumvent her father's arrangements and marry the youth. In her last play, *The Town Before You* (1795), HC expands the role playing across gender and class lines to provide a fascinating glimpse of London lowlife attempting to swindle and seduce the rich. As even these few examples suggest, veils are endemic and continually shifting, at one point a means of liberation, at another a trap. The young are generally at the mercy of their elders; women are at the mercy of men. The resource of the swindlers of *The Town Before You*, who remark that 'Our wits are our means of preying on Vanity and Folly', is not far different from that of HC's heriones in their efforts not to be preyed on by the same forces. As with all distinguished comedy, HC's, under its own veils of elegant wit and intricately twining strands of plot, is deeply serious and even subversive.

STUART CURRAN

Works: *The Runaway* (1776); *Who's the Dupe?* (1779); *Albina, Countess Raimond* (1779); *The Maid of Arragon* (1780); *The Belle's Stratagem* (1780); *The School for Eloquence* (1780); *The World as it Goes* (recast as *Second Thoughts are Best*) (1781); *Which is the Man?* (1782); *A Bold Stroke for a Husband* (1783); *More Ways than One* (1783); *School for Graybeards, or, The Mourning Bride* (1786); *The Scottish Village, or, Pitcairne Green* (1786); *The Fate of Sparta* (1788); *The Poetry of Anna Matilda* (1788); *The British Album: Containing the Poems of Della Crusca, Anna Matilda, etc.*, 3rd edn (1790); *A Day in Turkey* (1792); *The Town Before You* (1795); *The Siege of Acre* (in six books, 1801; in four books, 1810); *The Works of Mrs Cowley*, 3 vols (1813).

References: *BA* (18); Cumberland, J., 'Preface' to *A Bold Stroke for a Husband* (1837); *DNB*; Todd.

Crompton, Richmal

b. 15 November 1890, Bury, Lancashire; d. 11 January 1969, Farnborough, Kent

Novelist, writer for children

RC's continuing literary importance is as the creator of the anarchic 11-year-old, William Brown, forever at odds with his quiet middle-class Home Counties background. He first appeared in a story for adults in the *Home Magazine* in February 1919, and has since appealed to generations of children as well as to their parents. By the 1980s the stories had been translated into at least sixteen languages and been used as the basis of a radio series, two television series and four films. Nearly 10 million William books have been sold worldwide.

RC was the second daughter of a curate and schoolmaster, the Rev. Edward John Sewell Lamburn and his wife Clara (*née* Crompton). Her elder sister Gwen and younger brother Jack remained close to her throughout her life and it is possible that Jack's exploits and non-bookish character helped inspire the creation of William. The family were brought up with a strong Anglican faith which RC retained throughout her life, and in her eleventh year she followed her sister to board at St Elphin's Clergy Daughters' School, at first in Warrington, Lancashire and later in Darley Dale, Derbyshire. In 1911 she won an open entrance scholarship to the Royal Holloway College, London. She was awarded a university scholarship in 1912 and a Driver scholarship in classics from the college in 1914. That year she left with a second-class honours degree to become classics mistress at her old school. In 1917 she followed her sister and widowed mother south, becoming classics mistress at Bromley High School for Girls in Kent. In 1923 an attack of poliomyelitis left her with a permanently crippled leg, and she was forced to give up teaching for writing. She had already begun to write short stories and the William stories, after being transferred from the *Home Magazine* to the *Happy Mag*, had been published in a rather random selection in 1922 by George Newnes Ltd in two books called *Just William* and *More William*. RC's ambition was to write adult novels and, from the early 1920s until 1960 when her last adult novel appeared, she was always busy with two books at a time, one for adults, the other for children. She never married, but remained very close to her family, her nephew Tommy and later her great-nephew Edward providing later inspiration to her studies of boyhood. She supported many Church and Christian charities, as well as the Muscular Dystrophy Group and the British Polio Fellowship. In later years she grew increasingly interested in psychic research and in reincarnation while remaining a devout member of the Church of England. She was a lifelong adherent of the Conservative Party. She died suddenly at the age of 79, with a William story still unfinished. This was eventually completed by her niece as the thirty-eighth and last of the William books, *William the Lawless* (1970).

While RC's forty-one novels are rather gentle studies of middle-class family life, the William stories turn the same material into farcical comedy. Their strength lies in their extravagant situations and verbal exuberance. The plots are in the mainline of English farce, event piled on event with Dickensian gusto: when William runs away from home and accidentally finds himself working as a bootboy in a large house, it is inevitable that his father should be the honoured guest whose meal he ruins: ' "Good Lord!" said the guest, "it's William!" "Oh crumbs!" said the Boots, "It's father!" ' The verbal wit is reminiscent of P. G. Wodehouse, based often on William's wilful misunderstanding of adult speech. ' "Did you say I could have a party, father?" he said casually. "No I did *not*," said Mr Brown firmly.' William, who has learnt at school that two negatives make an affirmative, takes this as permission to go ahead and, while his parents are away, their house is wrecked by an invasion of boys. At the centre of the books' appeal is the original character of William himself, an imp of misrule let lose amid the gentilities of English suburbia. He is of course spontaneous, adventurous, and full of initiative, like so many earlier boy heroes, but he achieves mythic dimensions by being much more than the 'lovable scamp' of sentimental reviewers: he can be coarse, violent, ruthless, and blissfully selfish. His primary function, is to be an iconoclast, a centre for saturnalian and anarchic impulses. It is tempting to see him as a manifestation of the well-concealed 'id' of his author's highly civilized personality.

By the end of the 1950s, RC's adult novels had fallen out of favour. As she herself observed, 'There's not much call nowadays for quiet stories about families and village life – that's rather a vanished world.' The William books, however, their content modernized over the decades (*William's Television Show* and *William and the Pop Singers* both appeared in the 1960s) continued to appeal. At one level they are a humorous record of changes in middle-class mores over the decades, although there are some dubious touches of anti-semitism and even of cruelty to animals in two of the original 1930s stories. But their enduring appeal is not simply as a period piece, for William has taken his place in literary folklore, alongside Tom Sawyer and Huckleberry Finn, as a symbol of boyhood, at once destructive and regenerative, struggling to achieve authentic life in a stifling society. VALERIE PURTON

Selected works: *Just William* (1922); *More William* (1922); *The Innermost Room* (1923); *William the Conqueror* (1926); *William the Outlaw* (1927); *Sugar and Spice and Other Stories* (1929); *William's Crowded Hours* (1931); *Portrait of a Family* (1932); *William the Detective* (1935); *Caroline* (1936); *William the Dictator* (1938); *William and the ARP* (1939; reprinted as *William's Bad Resolutions* 1956); *William and the Evacuees* (1940; reprinted as *William and the Film Star* 1956); *Jimmy* (1949); *William the Bold* (1950); *William and the Moon Rocket* (1954); *William's Television Show* (1958); *The Inheritor* (1960); *William and the Pop Singers* (1965); *William the Lawless* (1970).

References: Cadogan, M. *Richmal Crompton* (1986); Craig, P. and Cadogan, M., 'That boy again', *Sunday Times Magazine* (6 February 1977); Lofts, W. O. G. and Adley, D., *William: A Bibliography* (1980), OCCL.

Crowe, Catherine

b. 1800?, Borough Green, Kent; d. 14 June 1872, Folkestone
Novelist and short story writer
CC was the daughter of John Stevens, of Clarges Street, Piccadilly, London. In October 1822 she married Lt. Col. John Crowe, and moved to Edinburgh with him; they had one son, John William. During her time in Edinburgh, she was a widely read, successful writer, and she knew many prominent people. She counted herself one of the followers of George Combe, the phrenologist, and was interested in the scientific study of supernatural phenomena. On the death of her husband in 1860, she moved to Folkestone.

CC was a prolific writer of novels and short stories; she also wrote plays and articles, and she translated from German. Her first work, *Aristomedus*, a tragedy written on classical lines, was published anonymously in 1838. She then published two novels which established her as a successful writer, *Manorial Rights* (1839) and *Susan Hopley* (1841). Her other five novels were also well-received. Her characters in these novels are ordinary working people, who are the victims of violent intrigues, caught in melodramatic situations. Her female characters, for example in *Linny Dawson* (1847) and *Susan Hopley*, have a remarkable strength in adversity; they are the victims of circumstance and lack of education, yet they are often portrayed overcoming social obstacles through the force of their will. *Susan Hopley* was adapted for the stage and played in London for three hundred performances. In 1853, her own play, *The Cruel Kindness* was performed at the Haymarket Theatre, London. In 1844 she was believed to be the author of the anonymously published controversial work *Vestiges of the Natural History of Creation*, actually by Robert Chambers; she seems to have been reluctant to undeceive the public.

However, CC is principally known for her writing on the supernatural; in 1848 *Night Side of Nature or Ghosts and Ghost Seers*, a collection of supernatural stories, appeared and ran to several editions. In these stories and vignettes, she described the existence of the spirit world with great conviction. Her interest in phrenology, physiology and spiritualism led her to attempt to give supposedly objective accounts of the paranormal. Following the publication in 1859 of an article, 'Spiritualism and the Age we Live in', she became subject to attacks of madness, and her writing output declined. She continued to write stories for children and in 1861 she published *Adventures of a Monkey*; she also abridged *Uncle Tom's Cabin* for a younger audience.

Her work is a fascinating mixture of the prosaic and the romantic, often with intricate plots contrasting with rather mundane dialogue. CC is skilful at holding her reader's attention with a curious mingling of factual and imaginary material.   SARA MILLS

Selected works: Aristodemus (1838); *Manorial Rights* (1839); *Susan Hopley* (1841); *Men and Women* (1843); (trans.), *Seeress of Provost*, by Kerner (1845); *Lilly Dawson* (1847); *Pippie's Warning* (1848); *Night Side of Nature* (1848); *Light and Darkness* (1850); *Adventures of a Beauty* (1852); *The Cruel Kindness* (1853); *Linny Lockwood* (1854); 'Spiritualism and the Age we Live in' (1859); *Adventures of a Monkey* (1861).

References: Boase, F. (ed.), *Modern English Biography* (1965); Clapton, G. T., 'Baudelaire and Catherine Crowe', *Modern Language Review* 25 (1930); Dalziel, M., *Popular Fiction 100 Years Ago* (1957); *DNB*; Keegan, P. Q., 'Mrs Crowe's and Mrs Gaskell's Novels', *Victoria Magazine* 33 (1879); Mitchell, S., *The Fallen Angel: Chastity, Class and Women's Reading 1835–1880* (1981); Sergeant, A., 'Mrs Crowe' in *Women Novelists of Queen Victoria's Reign* (1897).

Custance, Olive

b. 7 February 1874, Weston, Norfolk; d. 12 February 1944, Hove, Sussex
Poet

OC was the elder child of Eleanor Constance Jolliffe and Colonel Frederic Hambledon Custance of the Grenadier Guards. More than any other woman poet of her time she captured the shifting moods of brilliance and despair which characterized the aesthetic ideals of the 1890s, and what she wrote was quintessentially an expression of late Victorian decadence. Her initiation into that strange coterie of writers later referred to by W. B. Yeats as 'the tragic generation' came in a timely way in 1890. At the age of 16 she met the poet John Gray, and while her 'Prince of Poets' seemingly failed to return her affections (he later became a Roman Catholic priest in Edinburgh) they continued to exchange letters and OC dedicated several poems to Gray.

In 1897 John Lane published *Opals*, the first collection of poems from OC, at the famous Sign of the Bodley Head, and in the same year Aubrey Beardsley designed a bookplate for the aspiring decadent poet. By the turn of the century she had established a friendship with the American writer Natalie Clifford Barney, who invited her to join the Sapphic group of poets gathered around Renée Vivien in Paris. OC arrived in Paris in the spring of 1901, in the company of her mother and George Montagu, later the Earl of Sandwich. In January 1902 she became engaged to Montagu, a social liaison welcomed by both families, but for some time OC had been meeting in secret with Lord Alfred Douglas, still in public disgrace after his role in the trial and imprisonment of Oscar Wilde. After his return from a short period of exile in America, Douglas persuaded OC to break off her engagement and they were married by special licence at St George's, Hanover Square on 4 March 1902.

The inspiration which Douglas provided is clear in the poem 'Antinous' in OC's second volume of poems, *Rainbows* (1902), but it was short-lived and only two further collections of work appeared in her lifetime: *The Blue Bird* (1905) and *The Inn of Dreams* (1911). After a stay in the south of France, Corsica, and Ostend in the early part of the century, the couple settled at Lake Farm in Amesbury, Wiltshire. By 1913, however, OC had returned to her father in Norfolk and 'Bosie' was involved in long and serious litigation with Colonel Custance over the future of his and OC's son Raymond, eventually being charged with criminal libel. In 1920 OC settled in Bembridge, Isle of Wight; in 1930 she went to London, and in 1932 she moved to Hove, close to her husband. Although she met Lord Alfred Douglas frequently, their separation was final.

No single volume by OC remains in print, but a small number of poems, including her contributions to the *Yellow Book* – 'The White Statue' and 'Pierrot' – have appeared in anthologies of late Victorian poetry. Her writing displays a characteristic yearning for strange and unnatural forms of beauty, for exquisite sensations and secret pleasures - the gorgeous colours of peacocks' feathers, the tremulous warmth of candlelight, the brilliant hardness of jewels, the intoxicating perfume of flowers - but desire sickens and 'the laughing mouth of song' is struck dumb with despair. Her intense preoccupation with artifice is wholly typical of the decadent generation and best seen, perhaps, in those poems which draw upon the Pygmalion myth and worship lifeless clay with passionate abandonment. There is, as Mario Praz has pointed out in *The Romantic Agony*, something deeply erotic and perverse about such overtures, but these lines of forbidden love are far from being indulgent exercises in depravity. The poems of OC are the cry of a woman against the moral constraints of an oppressively philistine society. She was, in her own words, 'a freeborn singing child, in this dull sordid age of ours'.   STEPHEN REGAN

Works: *Opals* (1897); *Rainbows* (1902); *The Blue Bird* (1905); *The Inn of Dreams* (1911).

References: Beckson, K., *Aesthetes and Decadents of the 1890's* (1966); Douglas, A., *The Autobiography of Lord Alfred Douglas* (1929); Sewell, B., *Olive Custance: Her Life and Work* (1975); Thornton, R. K. R., *The Poetry of the 'Nineties* (1970).

Dane, Clemence

b. 1887, Blackheath; d. 28 March 1965, London

Playwright, novelist

CD, whose real name was Winifred Ashton, is one of those writers who, despite a prolific output, has so far received little critical attention. She was educated in England, Germany, and Switzerland. After studying art in Dresden and at the Slade School she tried acting, making her debut in February 1913 under the stage name of Diana Portis at the Criterion in H. V. Esmond's *Eliza Comes To Stay*. When CD's health broke down during the First World War she stopped acting, taught for a time in a girls' school, and then settled down to become a writer, taking her *nom de plume* from a church in London. She lived in London's Covent Garden for over thirty years, paying tribute to it in 1964 in her *London has a Garden*. She loved the theatre, wrote many plays (among them several such as *Mr Fox* and *Shivering Shocks, or, The Hiding Place* specifically 'for boys'), and counted among her friends actors such as Sir Lewis Casson and Dame Sybil Thorndike. Upon CD's death the London publisher Heinemann republished many of her works, but they are at present out of print.

CD wrote plays, novels, short stories, and essays. Her first novel, dedicated to her woman friend 'EA', *Regiment of Women* (1917), describes life at a girls' school, and the effect which one mistress, Claire Hartill, has on another, Alwynne Durand, as well as on those girls whom she selects for her 'special class'. Portrayed as an essentially heartless woman who is interested in power for its own sake, incapable of maintaining a long-term relationship, unable to respond to the sensitive affection of those emotionally dependent upon her,

Claire Hartill drives one pupil to suicide and Alwynne into the arms of a man who promises her a marriage of the most conventional type, devoid of any independence for the woman. As an indictment of both lesbianism and segregational schooling the novel makes an interesting comparison to Muriel Spark's *The Prime of Miss Jean Brodie* and Rosemary Manning's *The Chinese Garden*. Following her next novel, *First the Blade* (1918), CD wrote *Legend* (1919), in which the character of a dead woman writer is reconstructed from people's retrospective responses to her. A number of CD's works deal with theatrical themes: *Enter Sir John* (1930) and *Re-Enter Sir John* (1932), both detective stories, have as their central character an actor-manager. *Broom Stages* (1931) and *The Flower Girls* (1954) portray theatrical families. Other novels include *Wandering Star* (1924), *The Babyons* (1928), *The Moon is Feminine* (1938), *The Arrogant History of White Ben* (1939), and *He Brings Great News* (1939). CD's short stories were published under the title *Fate Cries Out* (1935). She produced three anthologies: *The Nelson Touch* (1942), *The Shelter Book* (1940), and *A Hundred Enchanted Tales* (1937).

Of her plays, many achieved long runs, especially *A Bill of Divorcement* (1921), a study of the complex and interwoven love lives of a mother and daughter. CD's next play, *Will Shakespeare* (1921), was an ingenious reconstruction of the poet's life. *Mariners* (1927) details the tragic effects of a clergyman's marriage to an insensitive woman. Of special interest for the study of woman writers is *Wild Decembers*, a play about the Brontës. Other plays include *Granite, The Way Things Happen, Naboth's Vineyard, Adam's Opera, Moonlight is Silver, Come of Age, Cousin Muriel, The Saviours, The Lion and the Unicorn,* and *Call Home the Heart*. Some of these were written for radio and BBC television.

CD's essays were published under the titles *The Women's Side* and *Tradition and Hugh Walpole*. She adapted Rostand's *D'Aiglon* and Hebbel's *Herod and Mariamne*. In 1953 she was awarded a CBE. Her work still awaits critical recognition.   GABRIELE GRIFFIN

Selected works: *Regiment of Women* (1917); *First The Blade* (1918); *Legend* (1919); *A Bill of Divorcement* (1921); *Will Shakespeare* (1921); *Shivering Shocks, or, The Hiding Place* (1923); *The Way Things Happen* (1924); *Wandering Star* (1924); *Naboth's Vineyard* (1925); *Granite* (1926); *The Women's Side* (1926); *The Dearly Beloved of Benjamin Cobb* (1927); *Mr Fox* (1927); *The Babyons* (1928); *Adam's Opera* (1928); *Tradition and Hugh Walpole* (1929); *Enter Sir John* (1930); *Printer's Devil* (1930); *Broome Stages* (1931); *Re-Enter Sir John* (1932); *L'Aiglon* (1934); *Moonlight is Silver* (1934); *Fate Cries Out* (1935); *A Hundred Enchanted Tales* (1937); *Herod and Mariamne* (1938); *The Moon Is Feminine* (1938); *The Arrogant History of White Ben* (1939); *He Brings Great News* (1939); *England's Darling* (1940); *The Shelter Book* (1940); *The Nelson Touch* (1942); *The Saviours* (1942); *Call Home the Heart* (1947); *Bonnie Prince Charlie . . .* (1948); *The Flower Girls* (1954).

References: Drabble; Faderman, L., *Surpassing the Love of Men* (1985).

D'Arcy, Ella

b. 1851, London; d. 1939, Kent

Short story writer, novelist, translator

ED is known chiefly for her connection with the *Yellow Book;* she contributed stories to ten of the thirteen issues of that periodical and also acted as assistant editor. She was born of Irish parents in London, but spent a considerable amount of time in her early years in the Channel Islands and received part of her education in Germany and France. She studied art at the Slade School in London, but deterioration of her eyesight forced her to relinquish her ambition to become a painter. She has been described as one of the most elusive writers of the 1890s, and very little is known about her life. From the end of the nineteenth century she wrote nothing, although she did translate into English André Maurois's fictionalized biography of Shelley, *Ariel*. She spent the latter part of her life chiefly in Paris.

ED published stories in *All Year Round*, *Blackwood's Magazine*, and *Temple Bar* as well as in the *Yellow Book*. These stories were gathered together into two volumes, *Monochromes* (1895) and *Modern Instances* (1898). ED's stories matched perfectly the tone the editor, Henry Harland, desired for the *Yellow Book* when he described its aim as being 'to preserve a delicate, decorous, and reticent mien and conduct . . . [and] at the same time have the courage of its modernness'. Many of her stories and her only novel, *The Bishop's Dilemma* (1898), explore the loneliness and isolation of modern life, and her characters are frequently portrayed as the victims of the institutions of society or of the greed or selfishness of others. Her themes are those found often in the writing of the 1890s: in seven of her stories marriage is depicted as inflicting misery on both husbands and wives; in stories such as 'The Death Mask' and 'The Villa Lucienne' she is concerned with subjectivity and shifting perception; and in other stories influences of contemporary feminism and psychology are apparent. Her writing skills are considerable; her style is economical and understated and she experiments with a variety of narrative techniques. Her friend Netta Syrett attributed the very small amount of ED's published work to inveterate laziness.

JUDITH VINCENT

Works: *Monochromes* (1895); *Modern Instances* (1898); *The Bishop's Dilemma* (1898); (trans.), *Ariel*, by A. Maurois (1924).
References: Beckson, K., *Henry Harland: His Life and Work* (1978); Mix, K., *A Study in Yellow* (1960).

Daryush, Elizabeth

b. 5 December 1887, London; d. 7 April 1977, Oxford
Poet
(Also wrote under Elizabeth Bridges)
ED was the daughter of the Poet Laureate Robert Bridges and his wife Monica (*née* Waterhouse) Bridges, herself the daughter of the architect Alfred Waterhouse. She spent most of her childhood in the Bridges' home at Yattendon in Berkshire. The family moved to Boar's Hill, overlooking Oxford, when she was 20; amongst her acquaintances in Oxford were the poets John Masefield and Robert Graves. She also met Thomas Hardy and knew the art critic and painter Roger Fry, who painted her portrait. Fry's sister Margaret introduced ED to Ali Akbar Daryush, a Persian government official, in 1923, and they were married at the end of that year. They travelled to Persia together and lived there until 1927, when her husband's poor health obliged him to return to England. The couple moved into another house on Boar's Hill, where ED lived until the end of her life.

Her first book of poetry, *Charitessi* (1911), was published when she was 23, and impressed W. B. Yeats, who was a correspondent of her father's. Her subsequent volume, the modestly entitled *Verses* (1916), began a series of similar collections, most of them published in the 1930s, up to *Verses: Seventh Book* (1971). ED also published her work in periodicals, notably the *Southern Review*;

her poetry was for most of her life somewhat better known in the US than in her own country, and was occasionally anthologized there. For many years the American poet and critic Yvor Winters was the most enthusiastic champion of her work. Towards the end of her life, however, her poetry began to attract the attention of a group of poets and critics associated with the Carcanet Press, who published her *Collected Poems* (1976) shortly before her death.

ED described modernist formal experiments as 'the weedy garden of instant verse', and her own poetry is staunchly traditional. Although she wrote a substantial number of poems in syllabic meters, these are very seldom unrhymed, and the majority of her work is in familiar forms and meters. Her poems frequently fall into rhetorical patterns of a symmetry which few other poets of the century have found congenial: 'How long, said spirit . . .' for example, is a poem of four stanzas each of which is introduced by a rhetorical question asked in turn by 'spirit', 'mind', 'life', and 'heart'. Her sonnets, similarly, often seek to accentuate rather than elide the break between octave and sestet.

There is, however, a notable development in the subject matter of ED's poetry during the course of her career: whereas the poems in *Charitessi* and *Verses* employ an almost entirely traditional vocabulary of topics drawn from the natural world, ED began in the 1930s to address a broader range of subjects. Her new resentment of social injustice, and her related sense of the decline of the English gentry to which she belonged, are evident in the apocalyptic warnings which close 'Children of wealth in your warm nursery . . .' and in the ironic yet sympathetic portrayal of an heiress in 'Still-Life'. But ED is as often anxious about as she is eager for social levelling: 'The Warden's Daughter' contrasts 'A squalid July street, a sweaty crowd, / Shop-staring, jostling . . .' with the girl who is the poem's subject, 'a girl whose bearing showed, / Like a cool background, all from whence she came, / Her spacious, quiet home . . .' The lines suggest the intimate dependence of the girl's graceful bearing on her comfortable circumstances; but whereas 'Still-Life' subtly explores just such a dependence, this poem goes on to consider the girl's bearing as reflecting a 'beauty . . . that's of the mind', an inner beauty which the 'sweaty crowd', by implication, congenitally lack.

Critical interest in ED's work was initially concentrated upon her use of syllabic meters. Bridges had himself frequently employed such meters, and this is likely to have been the starting point for ED's interest in them, since she was almost entirely unacquainted with the contemporaneous experiments of Marianne Moore. ED's 'Note on syllabic meters,' prefixed to her *Collected Poems* indicates that the poet herself believed such apparently technical questions to have a wide thematic significance. She takes a work of art, and its every detail, to exist as 'a contrived relation between the known and the uncomprehended': thus, for example, the syllable count in the syllabic line is regarded as a known constant against which its accentual pattern represents the unfixed and unpredictable.

It is difficult to demonstrate the operations of such large forces in a single line, but the metrical freedom of ED's syllabic verse certainly allows it to achieve mimetic contrasts in tone and lexicon which her accentual verse can rarely (and rarely aims to) provide. The opening stanza of the poem 'Invalid Dawn' is heavily freighted with alliteration and stressed syllables which, together with the slightly unusual diction, apparently announce a somewhat ornate treatment of the subject:

> Above the grey dawn
>   gather, wan, the glows:
> relieved by leaden
>   gleams a star-gang goes;

but the abruptly unstressed third stanza introduces the 'watchers'

> that were there all night –
>   factory, station
> and hospital light . . . ,

where the second and third lines of the stanza fall into a mundanely trochaic pattern which accompanies the dullness of the city beneath the dawn. Because in syllabic verse the verse is not explicitly organized around stress patterns, variations in these patterns can be used to thematic effect without drawing undue attention to themselves. Where such technical labour is expended upon genuinely complex subject matter, ED's poetry discovers a distinctive and original style.   SIMON JARVIS

Works: *Charitessi* (1911); *Verses* (1916); *Sonnets from Hafez and Other Verses* (1921); *Second Book Verses* (1932); *Third Book Verses* (1933); *Fourth Book Verses* (1934); *The Last Man and Other Verses* (1936); *Sixth Book Verses* (1938); *Verses: Seventh Book* (1971); *Collected Poems* (1976).

References: Davie, D., 'Introduction' to *Collected Poems* (1976); *DLB*; Fuller, R., 'Preface' to *Verses: Seventh Book* (1971); Stanford, D. E., 'Elizabeth Daryush (1887–1977) and Ezra Pound (1885–1972)', *Southern Review* 13 (1973); Winters, Y., *Uncollected Essays and Reviews* (1973).

Davie, Elspeth
b. Kilmarnock
Novelist, short story writer

Although ED spent her early years in the South of England, she returned to Scotland to complete her schooling. After training at Edinburgh University and the local College of Art, ED began to teach painting. She married and, with the arrival of one daughter, lived for some years in Ireland before returning once more to Scotland. It quickly became evident that writing was to be the focus of ED's creative life, to the fruitful extent that in 1978 she was awarded the Katharine Mansfield Prize for her story 'The High Tide Talker'.

A hallmark of ED's storytelling is the intent precision of the author's control over utterance. The location of her subject matter skates dizzyingly from one consciousness or country or confrontation to another. Yet ED is consistently compelling – and often drily humorous – describing a bus crossing the lonely wastes of Australia: 'You asked for a wilderness - you've got it!' growls the driver in *The Night of the Funny Hats*. So too she depicts an awkward encounter in a suburban shoe shop, in *The Foothold*: ' "Can I help?" said Thomas loudly from between the curtains. It was a phrase which never failed to irritate independent customers. Thomas himself had a disliking for it. He seldom uttered it. Yet it had its uses. . . . "Can you – *can* you help?" said the young man suddenly.' Thus an epiphany is made of an everyday experience, a trite phrase investigated and invested with significance. Whether the ostensible material is a train journey, a hospital visit, or a sign-painter's labours, ED achieves a viewpoint which, if often unfamiliar and disorientating, is equally 'worth the carriage' – and to which, vitally, the reader feels invited to share, in the possibility of a laugh or a sigh.

ED's rapid shifts of register from the comic to the macabre and back again lead the reader to examine his or her own attitude to quotidian happenings. The bevelled edge of ED's prose cuts deeply and directly into the hearts of her characters, frequently lonely or disillusioned people whose aspirations and disappointments are exposed with intellectual rigour, yet with honest sympathy. A writer with a painter's eye for observation, ED is sensitive to the landscapes of her stories not as mere backdrops but as constituents of the action themselves: 'Each bush, tree, stone and flower lived in the naked light with its own black shadow sharply defined.' This responsibility – sometimes almost hostageship – to exactitude extends to ED's involvement with her characters, where, crucially for an age in which many excellent woman novelists discriminate in favour of their female protagonists, ED balances a sharp interest in the strength of women with a wider perspective permitting access into the minds of men.   E. LEVY

Works: *Providings* (1965); *The Spark and Other Stories* (1969); *Creating a Scene* (1971); *The High Tide Talker* (1976); *Climbers on a Stair* (1978); *The Night of the Funny Hats* (1980); *A Traveller's Room* (1985).
References: *CA.*

Davys, Mary

b. 1674, Dublin; d. 1732
Novelist, playwright
When the Rev. Peter Davys, master of the Free School of St Patrick's in Dublin, died young in 1698, he left his widow MD without means of support. Both he and his wife had been part of the circle of Jonathan Swift who occasionally gave her a little financial assistance, but mostly she had to fend for herself. She soon left for England, where she lived first in York for fifteen years and then in Cambridge; in the latter she established a coffee house probably with the proceeds from her play *The Northern Heiress* (1716).

MD started her literary career with *The Lady's Tale* (1700), *The Amours of Alcippus and Lucippe* (1704), and *The Fugitive* (1705), romantic tales with firm morals that were not especially successful. In 1716 her play *The Northern Heiress, or, The Humours of York* by a 'Female Muse, from Northern Clime' was produced at Lincoln's Inn Fields. In many ways it was a conventional play with two sets of lovers, a fop, and a country squire, and it made the usual attack on marriage for money. But it was unusual in being set in a country boarding house in York (possibly MD had earned her living during the previous years in this way) and in revealing characters and speech patterns of various types from that city. Despite the opposition of some 'York Gentlemen', the play was a success.

In 1724 MD published *The Reform'd Coquet*, the subscription list of which included the names of Pope and Gay; the work proved popular and went through several editions. It tells of an unwise girl who is reformed by her lover disguised as a wise old guardian who teaches her through controlled but harsh experience that to leave a family is always wrong and that men are not always chivalrous. After the course of instruction, the heroine stops being 'self-will'd' and 'head-strong' and following her 'own Inventions', and she learns to accept the patriarchal world without becoming its victim. In the history of fiction it has some importance in helping to establish the moral love tale in opposition to the erotic fiction of such writers as Delarivier Manley and Eliza Haywood.

In 1725 MD published her *Works* which included her earlier tales, *The Lady's*

Tale, The Cousins, The Modern Poet, a satiric look at the professional poet, *The Self-Rival*, a lively comedy which includes portrayals of good-natured and sour old maids, *The Merry Wanderer*, a series of anecdotes based on visits to various great houses, and *Familiar Letters Betwixt a Gentleman and a Lady*. The last of these is probably her most interesting work for what it reveals of her social and political attitudes.

In it a lady with Whig leanings and a Tory gentleman discuss political and social matters. The Tory, exiled in the 'dull Country' presumably for his Jacobite activity, considers that 'Kings are such sacred Things, that no Hand, but that of Providence shou'd touch' and that belief in their sacred position is necessary for belief in any public justice. The Whigs he sees as heirs of the disgraced Puritans, implicated in the crime of regicide. The lady, in turn, sees the Tories as a romantic anachronism in Hanoverian England, associated with a naive nostalgia for the Stuart kings. The theory of divine right makes a mockery of the modern conception of the rights of citizens, she asserts. In her words a new vision of England is conjured up, a country not embodied in royalty although it serves it when appropriate, but one that is distinct in its libertarian tradition that will not allow its laws and religion to be 'sacrific'd to the Caprice of a whimsical King'. Her work breathes compromise and the *Familiar Letters* ends with party faction obliterated in the assumed marriage of the Tory gentleman and the Whig lady. The series also tells of friendship between a man and a woman which the reader is intended to see as a strong basis for marriage, while sexual passion is mocked; none the less there remains some grumbling at the inequalities of marriage, as well as complete acceptance of the male prerogative within it: 'The Notion I have always had of Happiness in Marriage, is, where Love causes Obedience on one side, and Compliance on the other, with a View to the Duty incumbent on both: If any thing can sweeten the bitter Cup, 'tis that.'

As a woman writer MD was aware of her need to separate herself from the lewd image of Manley and Haywood, and she insisted that she was aiming to 'restore the Purity and Empire of Love'. She was concerned, also, to indicate her own unblemished reputation as 'the relict of a Clergy-man'. She was, she declared in the preface to her works, writing out of necessity, for financial reasons: 'If [critics] find any thing there offensive either to God or Man, any thing either to shock their Morals or their Modesty, 'tis then time enough to blame. And let them further consider, that a Woman left to her own Endeavours for Twenty-seven Years together, may well be allow'd to catch at any Opportunity for that Bread, which they that condemn her would very probably deny to give her.'

MD's assessment of her writings was moderate: 'I never was so vain, as to think they deserv'd a Place in the first Rank, or so humble, as to resign them to the last.' But her work is interesting for its relative freedom of expression, its mention of such subjects as would later be taboo for a respectable woman, such as fornication and venereal disease. Rigidly moral in her messages, she was none the less harsher than later moral sentimental writers. In her last novel, *The Accomplish'd Rake* (1727), for example, she describes a seducer who is tricked for revenge into sleeping with a woman with venereal disease, while in *Familiar Letters* a selfish beauty who 'thinks all Mankind born to do her Homage, and despises the tasteless Fool that can resist her Charms' ridicules a lover who goes so absurdly far as to offer her a private income as wife and widow; when his love turns to contempt, he takes his revenge by bringing the lady to the

altar only to jilt her there, both correspondents in the letters agreeing that the
lady is well served.   JANET TODD

Works: *The Amours of Alcippus and Lucippe* (1704); *The Fugitive* (1705); *The
Northern Heiress, or, The Humours of York* (1716); *The Reform'd Coquet* (1724);
Works of Mrs Davys (incl. *Familiar Letters Betwixt a Gentleman and a Lady* and
The Merry Wanderer) (1725); *The Accomplish'd Rake* (1727); *The False Friend*
(expansion of a piece in *Works*) (1732).

References: Cotton, N., *Women Playwrights in England* (1980); Day, R. A.,
'Introduction' to *Familiar Letters* (1955); Day, R. A., *Told in Letters* (1966);
McBurney, W. H., 'Mrs Mary Davys: forerunner of Fielding', *PMLA* 74
(1959); Spencer, J., *The Rise of the Woman Novelist* (1986); Swift, J., *Journal to
Stella*, ed. H. Williams (1948); Todd.

Delafield, E. M.

b. 9 June 1890, Sussex; d. 2 December 1943, Devon
Novelist, playwright, author of articles

EMD (as she was known to her friends) wrote lightly satirical novels which
were very popular in the inter-war years. Her greatest success was with *The
Diary of a Provincial Lady* (1930). Her pseudonym Delafield was a loose translation of her French maiden name, de la Pasture.

The daughter of Count Henry de la Pasture (d. 1908), whose family had
come to England after the French Revolution, EMD had a sheltered Edwardian
girlhood and endured several (usually French) governesses. She was close to
her sister and based *The Pelicans* (1918) on the theme of close, almost suffocating
love between two sisters. Her dominating, sociable mother, who wrote novels
and plays under the name of Mrs Henry de la Pasture, expected her daughters
to be married by the time they were 20; she herself remarried promptly when
she was widowed and became Lady Hugh Clifford. She retained her former
name for professional purposes partly in order to avoid confusion with the
novelist Mrs Lucy Clifford.

When EMD was 21 she entered a French convent for nine months; she spent
two years with relations in Devon recuperating from this experience and then,
from 1914 to 1917, served as a VAD in Exeter. From 1917 to 1918 she worked
in the Ministry of National Service; her second novel, *The War-Workers* (1918),
drew on this experience. In 1919 she married Major Arthur Dashwood; they
lived in Devon with their son and daughter and EMD played the part she often
described and satirized in her novels, the wife/mother/housekeeper, cheerful
but harassed, who takes an active role in the local community, in her case as a
Justice of the Peace and a member of the Women's Institute. Her marriage was
only superficially a happy one and she had close friendships with other writers,
for example Kate O'Brien. Although much in her work was autobiographical,
she was wittier and more elegant than some of her rather downtrodden heroines,
but she shared with others of them a gentle, generous, and commonsensical
spirit. Five of her novels have a strong Catholic element: *The Pelicans* and
Consequences (1919) (and its dramatized version *The Glass Wall*, 1933) are about
girls becoming nuns; *Zella Sees Herself* (1917), her first novel, and *Turn Back
the Leaves* (1930) are about the effect of Catholicism on family life. Yet EMD
never alluded to her time in a convent and her public reputation was based on
her lightly witty novels about domestic life and ordinariness, the seriousness
of which can be overlooked; the *Times* obituary referred to her 'almost uncanny
gift for converting the small and familiar dullnesses of everyday life into laugh-

ter'. Of her forty or so published works the most characteristic are *Thank Heaven Fasting* (1932), which is about the tyranny of the marriage market, and *The Way Things Are* (1927), which is about a 'happily married' woman who was a precursor of the nameless heroine of *The Diary of a Provincial Lady* (1930). These exceedingly funny diary extracts first appeared in instalments in *Time and Tide*, the feminist magazine of which EMD was a director and to which she contributed numerous articles. (The third *Provincial Lady* volume was based on articles for *Punch*.) EMD was also interested in criminology and wrote *Messalina of the Suburbs* (1924), based on the Thompson-Bywaters case (cf. also F. Tennyson Jesse's *A Pin to See the Peepshow*, 1934). 'All that I have tried to do,' she once wrote in the typically self-deprecating tone of someone whose work was not only popular and financially necessary but also vital to her self-esteem and happiness, 'is to observe faithfully, and record accurately, the things that have come within my limited range. The fault that I have most tried to avoid is sentimentality.'   NICOLA BEAUMAN

Works: *Zella Sees Herself* (1917); *The War Workers* (1918); *The Pelicans* (1918); *Consequences* (1919); *Tension* (1920); *The Heel of Achilles* (1921); *Humbug* (1921); *The Optimist* (1922); *A Reversion to Type* (1923); *Messalina of the Suburbs* (1924); *Mrs Harter* (1924); *The Chip and the Block* (1925); *Jill* (1927); *The Entertainment* (1927); *The Way Things Are* (1927); *What is Love?* (1928); *The Suburban Young Man* (1928); *Women Are Like That* (1929); *Turn Back the Leaves* (1930); *To See Ourselves* (1930); *The Diary of a Provincial Lady* (1930); *Challenge to Clarissa* (1931); *Thank Heaven Fasting* (1932); *The Provincial Lady Goes Further* (1932); *General Impressions* (1933); *Gay Life* (1933); *The Glass Wall* (1933); *The Provincial Lady in America* (1934); *The Bazalgettes* (1935); *The Mulberry Bush* (1935); *Faster! Faster!* (1936); *Nothing is Safe* (1937); *Straw Without Bricks: I Visit Soviet Russia* (1937); *Ladies and Gentlemen in Victorian Fiction* (1937); *As Others Hear Us: A Miscellany* (1937); *The Brontës* (1938); *Three Marriages* (1939); *Love Has No Resurrection* (1939); *We Meant to be Happy* (1939); *The Provincial Lady in War-Time* (1940); *No One Now Will Know* (1941); *Late and Soon* (1943).

References: Beauman, N., 'Introduction' to *Diary of a Provincial Lady* (1984); Cooper, T., 'Introduction' to *Diary of a Provincial Lady* (1979); Gawsworth, J., *Ten Contemporaries: Notes Towards Their Definitive Bibliography* (1937); Johnson, R. B., *Some Contemporary Novelists: Women* (1920).

Delany, Mary

b. 14 May 1700, Coulston, Wiltshire; d. 15 April 1788, Windsor
Letter writer
Daughter of a well-connected though poor gentleman, Bernard Granville, MD expected to be introduced into Queen Anne's court by her uncle Lord Lansdowne and her aunt Lady Stanley. However, the death of the Queen in 1714 removed her father and other Tory relatives from any influence or power. The family retired to Gloucestershire where MD apparently attracted a suitor regarded by her family as unacceptable. She was sent to stay with Lord Lansdowne at Longleat. He arranged a marriage between MD and Alexander Pendarves, a Cornish landowner of nearly 60; the marriage took place in February 1718, despite MD's objections. The couple retired to Cornwall where Pendarves proved to be a jealous, peevish, and often drunken husband. He died suddenly in March 1725, leaving his widow no income but her marriage settlement. In the following years MD lived mostly in London where she was courted by several men, most notably Lord Baltimore. She made a long visit

to Ireland in the early 1730s. As a member of court and aristocratic circles, MD became friendly with the leading social and intellectual figures of her day. Her closest friend was Margaret, Duchess of Portland; her friends also included members of the Bluestocking circle and both Whig and Tory hostesses. She knew Swift, Handel, and Burke. In June 1743 she married Patrick Delany, a learned Irish Anglican cleric. They made their home in Ireland, where he was appointed Dean of Down, and made frequent trips to England. After Delany's death in 1768, MD lived in London and often spent months in the country with the Duchess of Portland. After the Duchess's death in 1785, George III gave MD a house at Windsor where she was a great favourite with the whole royal family.

MD's education was not particulary extensive in a formal sense. She did not read Latin or Greek, but she did know French and some Italian. She read very widely in the classics and contemporary literature in both English and French. Reading aloud was a regular feature of the Delany household; MD's letters show an intelligent and eclectic appreciation for what she read. She was not musical herself but was devoted to Handel's works especially and attended performances at every opportunity. She was extremely skilled with her needle and made various furnishings for her own houses and those of friends and relations. Her knowledge of and appreciation of art was extensive; she was a skilful copyist and sketcher. Like her friend the Duchess, MD collected shells, china, and plants and was an enthusiastic gardener and decorator. In her later years her artistic talents were devoted largely to her paper mosaics, as she called them. She cut from various coloured papers and pasted together botanic specimens of exceptional accuracy. Volumes of these are now in the British Museum.

During her long life, MD was an energetic and superb letter writer. Her main correspondents were her sister Ann Dewes (1707–61), Ann's daughter Mary Port, and her daughter Georgina Mary Ann. MD had no children herself, but she regarded her niece and great-niece much as her own children. In addition to her family, MD wrote to a wide variety of friends. There is no system or plan to her letters. She tells what has happened to her, what she has seen, what she has read and heard, the latest gossip, a menu, or a cure for some ailment. Her observations are usually kind but always frank. She seldom wrote of political events, but for an account of the daily life of the upper-middle-class gentry and some nobility in the eighteenth century there is no better source.

                                    BARBARA BRANDON SCHNORRENBERG

Works: *The Autobiography and Correspondence of Mary Granville, Mrs Delany*, ed. Lady Llanover (1861); *Letters from Mrs Delany to Mrs Frances Hamilton* (1820).
References: Brimley Johnson, R. (ed.), *Mrs Delany at Court and among the Wits* (1925); Hayden, R., *Mrs Delany: Her Life and Her Flowers* (1980); Vulliamy, C. E., *Aspasia: The Life and Letters of Mary Granville, Mrs Delany* (1935).

Delaney, Shelagh
b. 1939, Salford, Lancashire
Dramatist, screenwriter, short story writer
SD's first literary acclaim came in 1958 with the production of her stage play, *A Taste of Honey*. She was 18 when she wrote it and, although she rejects this fact as unimportant, or less important than the work itself, it still remains remarkable that it was written by a young woman who had rejected formal education at 16. After failing her 11-plus SD had gone to a secondary school,

but her late development was recognized and she was moved to a grammar school. She always wanted to be a writer; she initially began with prose and *A Taste of Honey* derived from her first attempts at a novel.

After leaving school she had a variety of jobs – salesgirl, cinema usherette, and assistant in a photographic laboratory. Her observation of what was going on around her was to provide material for her work. Post-war Britain was moving towards an affluence which the majority of the population had never before experienced; the welfare state was born and the working class had a new security. Employment was high and for the first time young people had disposable incomes; the 'teenager' had arrived. The theatre which, from the turn of the century up to the war, had offered mainly middle-class drama in drawing-room situations, was hit by the 'New Wave' dramatists, Osborne, Wesker, Arden, and Pinter. SD is usually grouped with them. She was concerned with real life as opposed to the images of life presented by advertising and the new media.

A Taste of Honey centres around five characters: Helen, Jo, her daughter, Peter, Helen's boyfriend, The Boy (Jo's unnamed boyfriend), and Geoff, who befriends Jo. The main tensions arise between Helen and Jo, the daughter resentful of the life her mother has imposed upon her. But Jo, although talented, like SD, turns her back on education and despite her dislike of her mother's life seems set to follow in her footsteps. She becomes pregnant by a black sailor who soon disappears; even the arrival of the compassionate Geoff cannot fracture the cycle of frustration and futility. Jo is left, in the first stages of labour, repeating one of the childhood rhymes she finds comforting – she is, after all, still very much a child. 'As I was going to Pippin Hill/Pippin Hill was dirty/and there I met a pretty miss.' This ending combines reality with optimism: Jo is still young and the world may change. *A Taste of Honey* was first performed by members of the Theatre Workshop Company at the Theatre Royal, Stratford, East London, and produced by Joan Littlewood to whom SD had first sent the play. The experimental and improvisational nature of the Theatre Workshop suited *A Taste of Honey* and although the company's approach was frequently to change and add to authors' lines, this play reached the stage largely unchanged. Some critics were less than kind to SD, dismissing her play as a phenomenon not to be taken seriously because of the author's age. But they were proved wrong. The play was transferred to the West End of London in 1959 and ran for a long time; in 1960 it was put on in New York, in 1961 it won the New York Drama Critics Circle award and in 1962 it was filmed. SD wrote the screenplay along with Tony Richardson who also directed it and won the British Film Academy Award. Roundabout Theatre staged a revival of the play, off-Broadway, in 1981, directed by Tony Tanner and later transferred to the Century Theatre, Broadway.

In 1963 SD's collection of short stories, *Sweetly Sings the Donkey*, was published. Since then she has worked principally for television and the cinema. In 1966 she wrote the screenplay for the film *The White Bus*, which was directed by Lindsay Anderson, followed in 1968 by her screenplay for the film *Charley Bubbles*, directed by Albert Finney. Her television plays, *Did Your Nanny Come from Bergen?*, *The House That Jack Built*, and *Find me First* were broadcast in 1970, 1977, and 1979 respectively. In 1985 she wrote the screenplay for the film, *Dance With a Stranger*, which won the Prix Populaire at the Cannes Film Festival. SD was made a Fellow of the Royal Society of Literature in the same year.   ALISON RIMMER

Selected works: *A Taste of Honey* (1958); *The Lion in Love* (1960); *A Taste of*

Honey (with Tony Richardson) (1962); *Sweetly Sings the Donkey* (1963); *The White Bus* (1966); *Charley Bubbles* (1968); *Dance with a Stranger* (1982).
References: Allsop, K., *The Angry Decade* (1958); Goorney, H., *The Theatre Workshop Story* (1981); Kitchin, L., *Mid-Century Drama* (1962); Taylor, J. R., *Anger and After* (1969).

Dell, Ethel M.

b. 2 August 1881, Streatham, London; d. 17 September 1939, Hereford.
Romantic novelist
EMD was a highly successful novelist in the mainstream of popular fiction of the 1920s and 1930s whose works were reprinted until the mid–1950s. She perfectly captured the mood of the generation between the wars, which looked above all for security – happy endings were *de rigueur* – and for the reinforcement of its own social values. These centred on the paramountcy of the marriage bond and the submission of the female to the benevolent dictatorship of the male. A competent and lively writer, EMD often sets up potentially disturbing situations in which the heroine is caught between desire and duty, but invariably her writing backs away from introspection and it is the plot, rather than any inner development of the characters, which neatly resolves all conflict.

EMD was the younger daughter of John Vincent Dell, who worked for the Equitable Life Assurance Company, and of his wife Irene (*née* Parrott). She was educated in Streatham, at a private school, and subsequently lived first at Knockholt, near Sevenoaks, Kent, and then at Ashford, Middlesex. From childhood she wrote copiously. An early story, 'The Sea Urchin and the Prince', won second prize in a competition in *The Red Magazine* in 1909, and after more successes with magazine stories, EMD published her first novel, *The Way of the Eagle*, in 1912 at the age of 31. Its enormous success led to a nationwide following which remained loyal for four decades and obviously influenced what she wrote. *By Request* (1927), for example, is 'written at the request of some of my readers' and picks up the fortunes of two characters from an earlier novel. In 1922 when she was 41, following the deaths of her parents, EMD married Lieutenant-Colonel Gerald Tahourdin Savage of the Royal Army Service Corps, and thereafter lived a secluded country life, hiding from her fame and delighting in her dogs, gardening, and motoring. She was by all accounts a charming, generous, and retiring person, and these qualities are evident in the novels. She died in a Hereford nursing home at the age of 58 and was survived by her husband. Her books retained their huge popularity; some were even translated into Spanish. *The Keeper of the Door* was reprinted in 1952 and *The Knave of Diamonds* reached its 34th impression in 1954. Thereafter tastes changed dramatically and EMD, with so many others of her literary generation, was relegated to the role of period piece.

EMD's strengths and weaknesses remained unchanged during her long and uniformly successsful career. Her upper-middle-class characters are immediately identifiable as spirited heroine, faithful and morally impeccable hero, shallow and usually philandering villain, loveable younger brother, naughty but good-hearted child, etc. The only tension – and the source of titillation – comes from the many devices of the plot to keep the hero and heroine apart, or at least estranged, until the final consummation. Sexual attraction, which is the pivot of all the stories, is always presented in coded form: the heroine 'quivers', is 'scorched like a flaming fire' by the hero's passion, which erupts like 'the red fire of a volcano'. The value system consists of: a vague and undogmatic

Christianity; the sanctity of male friendship (one chapter on this theme is called 'Greater Love'); the nobility of the relation between servant (especially if foreign) and master; the healthy effect of strict discipline (physical chastisement of children and underlings by the hero is relished and approved); and, at the heart of the philosophy *and* of the plot, the supremacy of the marriage bond, often conceived in the most rigid legal terms. Any deviations from the mono-gamous norm in the shape of illegitimate children or supernumerary lovers are amended by the deaths of the unwanted characters, leaving the way clear for the happy ending. A summary of the plot of a single novel, *The Lamp in the Desert* (1919) may stand as a paradigm: spirited heroine, orphaned, joins soldier brother in India and rashly marries rakish officer whom she does not love; the hero (best friend of brother), who truly loves her, finds out that the rake has committed bigamy and chases him off; hero and heroine marry; sickly child is born; to his horror, hero discovers the original marriage *was* valid (the rake's first wife having died in England just before the wedding); he cannot reveal the full horror of the situation to the heroine and many misunderstandings soon separate them; eventually both the rake and the baby die and hero and heroine can be *properly* (i.e. legally) united, with the prospect of *legitimate* offspring to replace the doomed illegitimate child.

In the novels the action moves briskly and even the minor characters are well-drawn. Sentimentality is usually avoided; but EMD's work resolutely aims not to challenge but to comfort, and thus never develops beyond the well-defined confines of 'romance'.   VALERIE PURTON

Selected works: *The Way of the Eagle* (1912); *The Knave of Diamonds* (1913); *The Desire of his Life* (1914); *The Rocks of Valpre* (1914) *The Keeper of the Door* (1915); *The Bars of Iron* (1916); *Greatheart* (1918); *Her Compensation* (1918); *The Lamp in the Desert* (1919); *The Top of the World* (1920); *Rosa Mundi and Other Stories* (1921); *Tetherstones* (1923); *Verses* (1923); *The Unknown Quantity* (1924); *The Gate Marked Private* (1928); *The Prison Wall* (1932); *Dona Celestis* (1933); *Where Three Roads Meet* (1935); *The Serpent in the Garden* (1938); *Sown Among Thorns* (1939).

Bibliography: *DNB*; Obituary, *Times* (19 September, 1939).

Dick, Kay

b. 29 July 1915, London.

Novelist, critic, editor

(Also wrote under J. Scott)

KD was educated in English boarding schools in Geneva and at the Lycée Français in London. Initially she worked for publishing and bookselling firms in various capacities, from editing to publicity and production. During the Second World War she became assistant editor of *John O'London's Weekly*, and there met Stevie Smith. Under a pseudonym, she took up the editorship of *The Windmill*, a literary quarterly published by Heinemann. KD has also worked as a publisher's reader and a broadcaster, and has contributed freelance articles and reviews to both literary magazines and broader journals like *The Times Saturday Review* and *Harper's Bazaar*. She published the first of her seven novels, *By the Lake*, in 1949 and has also edited several anthologies, including one of selections from Edgar Allen Poe.

KD's best-known non-fictional work is *Ivy and Stevie* (1971), a record of two intimate, revealing conversations with Ivy Compton-Burnett and Stevie Smith, preceding personal reflections by KD on the work and characters of these close friends. *Pierrot* (1960) traces the Commedia dell'Arte figure of Pierrot from its medieval origins through several ages of European culture to its most recent appearances in opera, ballet, and literature.

In 1977, KD won the South-East Arts Literature Prize for *They: A Sequence of Unease* (1977). Its short chapters follow a lonely woman artist living in an uncertain, dangerous world of the future. She visits the houses of her friends, all musicians, authors, and painters devoted to their art, living in a society which persecutes anybody who deviates from the standardized life. Insisting on communality, 'they', an unspecified, omnipresent group of people, abhor any communication other than small talk. They erect towers where those who create, grieve or love are cured of 'unsocial, inadmissible, contagious' indications of originality and individualism. Prevailing in the novel is a veiled sense of threat, and an absolute need for self control as the 'artists' attempt to preserve love and friendship and to outwit the system by memorizing, copying, and practising art without attracting punishment. A heightened attention to nature and a repetitive, ritualistic style and structure characterize *They*, a powerful novella on the state of fear.

The Shelf (1984), KD's latest novel, could be the conventional heterosexual tragic love story. It features Anne, a mysterious beloved woman who eventually commits suicide. The situation is, however, transposed on to a lesbian relationship, the story told by a lonely, bisexual character, Cassie. When, after the suicide, Cassie recovers her love letters to Anne from a police shelf, she writes out her past distrust and passion for the mysterious, tragic woman in a long letter to a male friend.   SABINE VANACKER

Selected works: *At Close of Eve: An Anthology of Curious New Stories* (1947); *By the Lake* (1949); *Young Man* (1951); *An Affair of Love* (1953); *Solitaire* (1958); *Pierrot: An Investigation into Commedia Dell'Arte* (1960); *Sunday* (1962; *Bizarre and Arabesque: Selections from Edgar Allen Poe* (1970); *Ivy and Stevie: Ivy Compton-Burnett and Stevie Smith, Conversations and Reflections* (1971); *Writers and Their Work: The Paris Review Interviews* (1972); *Friends and Friendship* (1974); *They: A Sequence of Unease* (1977); *The Shelf* (1984).

References: review of *The Shelf*, *Times Literary Supplement* (24 February 1984); review of *They*, *Times Educational Supplement* (23 December 1977); review of *Ivy and Stevie*, *Times* (7 October 1971); review of *Friends and Friendship*, *Times* (18 April 1974).

Dickens, Monica
b. 10 May 1915, London
Novelist, writer for children, autobiographer

MD is the youngest child and second daughter of Henry Charles Dickens, a barrister, and Fanny Runge. Her paternal great-grandfather was Charles Dickens and her mother was of German descent. She was educated at St Paul's Girls' School and at a finishing school in Paris, after which her life followed the then traditional upper-middle-class pattern, culminating in a debutante season.

Untrained for a career, MD, on impulse, took up work as a cook-general and her experiences provided the raw material for her first book, the autobiographical *One Pair of Hands* (1939). The success of this led her to write a novel *Mariana*, based on her own childhood and youth. She then took up nursing and wrote about life in a London hospital in *One Pair of Feet* (1942). During the Second World War she was directed to work in a factory repairing Spitfires for the Battle of Britain, and her novel *The Fancy* (1943) grew out of this experience. Wishing to return to nursing, she found considerable difficulty in obtaining another post, because of hostility towards *One Pair of Feet* on the part of hospital authorities, but eventually she was successful, and nursed for most of the rest of the war.

After the war, she bought a cottage at Hinxworth, in north Hertfordshire, and lived there alone except for her dogs and horses. At this period she worked for a year as a local reporter at the *Hertfordshire Express* newspaper's Hitchin office, and wrote *My Turn to Make the Tea* (1951) as a result. She had also, since 1946, been a regular columnist for *Woman's Own* magazine. In 1951 she married Commander Roy Olin Stratton, of the US Navy, and shortly after-wards they adopted two daughters, and made their home at North Falmouth, Massachusetts.

MD continued writing her column for *Woman's Own* until 1965, and also made regular trips back to England. Her method of research for her books now became that of a journalist and she devoted considerable time to the communi-ties and organizations in which she was interested, watching, listening, and taking part in the lives of others. *Cobbler's Dream* (1963) resulted partly from her own extensive knowledge of horses and partly from working with the RSPCA. It was then suggested to her that she should turn her attention to the ill-treatment of children, and she wrote *Kate and Emma* (1964), after a great deal of research with the NSPCC and at juvenile courts. Similarly, *The Listeners* (1970) developed out of her work with the Samaritans.

MD's first children's book, *The House at World's End* (1970), drew on her own childhood memories of horses and the countryside. During the following years she went on to write a succession of books for children, including the immensely popular *Follyfoot* series, which was serialized for television.

The Samaritans had made a great impression on MD and, after initial discouragement, she was able to found a Samaritan movement in the USA, instituting the first branch at Boston, Massachusetts in 1974. MD's husband, Roy Stratton, died in 1985 and she came back to England, living for a time in Berkshire and then returning to north Hertfordshire.

MD's work tends to fall into distinct groups, although with overlapping subject matter and always with material drawn from first-hand experience. The early autobiographical books – *One Pair of Hands, One Pair of Feet* and *My Turn to Make the Tea* – achieved immediate popularity for their lightness of touch and precise, witty observation. The earlier novels, such as *Thursday Afternoons* and *Flowers on the Grass*, were similar in tone and content to the autobiographical books, but gradually MD developed a more serious, even sombre approach to both style and subject-matter. *The Heart of London*, concerned as it is with inner-city social problems, *The Winds of Heaven* and *The Room Upstairs*, both treating old age, and *Kate and Emma*, are typical of this stage of her work.

MARGARET ASHBY

Selected works: *Mariana* (1940; published in the US as *The Moon Was Law*); *The Fancy* (1943, published in the US as *Edward's Fancy*); *Thursday Afternoons* (1945); *Joy and Josephine* (1948); *Flowers on the Grass* (1949); *My Turn to Make the Tea* (1951); *No More Meadows* (1953; published in the US as *The Nightingales are Singing*); *The Winds of Heaven* (1955); *The Angel in the Corner* (1956); *Man Overboard* (1958); *Cobbler's Dream* (1963); *The Room Upstairs* (1966); *The Land-lord's Daughter* (1968); *The Great Fire* (1970); *The Listeners* (1970; published in the USA as *The End of the Line*); *Follyfoot* (1971); *The Great Escape* (1971); *World's End in Winter* (1972); *Dora at Follyfoot* (1972); *Spring Comes to World's End* (1973); *Follyfoot Farm* (1973); *Last Year When I was Young* (1974); *The Horses*

of Follyfoot (1975); *Stranger at Follyfoot* (1976); *An Open Book* (1978); *Ballad of Favour* (1985).
References: *CN*; Ward, A. C. (ed.), *Longman Companion to Twentieth-Century Literature* (1981).

Dixie, Lady Florence
b. 24 March 1857, London; d. 7 November 1905, London
Travel writer, novelist, pamphleteer
FD attracted attention initially as a 'lady travel writer' and subsequently as a vigorous campaigner on behalf of Zulu nationalism, women's rights, vegetarianism, and Irish Home Rule. Her aristocratic rank gave a piquancy to her activities in the eyes of her contemporaries. She and her twin brother were the youngest children of the 7th Marquess of Queensbury, who died when they were 3 years old, and her unconventional girlhood was spent largely in wandering about Europe with her mother and riding and hunting on equal terms with her brothers. In 1875 she married Alexander Beaumont Churchill Dixie and, after the birth of two sons in three years, marked her rejection of the domestic role by undertaking an expedition to South America in 1878 with her husband and others. In 1881 she toured South Africa to report on the Boer War peace negotiations for the *Morning Post*. An opponent of the Land League, she nevertheless visited the West of Ireland in 1882 in support of Home Rule. As her consciousness of the causes of oppression developed, she renounced big-game hunting, joined the Humanitarian League, and until her death from diptheria in 1905 engaged in writing fiction, articles, and pamphlets in support of humanitarian and feminist causes.

FD's juvenilia, published as *Songs of a Child* (1901) and *Abel Avenged: A Dramatic Tragedy* (1877), are strongly influenced by her adolescent admiration for the Byronic rebel-hero, and reveal growing religious scepticism and passionate identification with all victims of cruelty, particularly animals. *Across Patagonia* (1880) is chiefly of interest as a record of FD's assumption of an energetic 'masculine' persona. *In the Land of Misfortune* (1882), the account of her South African travels, is a personal odyssey, in which her patriotic contempt for the Boers and disgust at their cruelty are gradually complicated by her growing awareness that the British are betraying both the interests and the trust of the Africans. In Cetshwayo, the deposed Zulu king, she finds a focus for her sympathy with the oppressed. *A Defence of Zululand and Its King* (1882) helped to stimulate the public interest which led to his eventual restoration. FD's fiction transposes incidents and personalities from her life into exotic or imaginary settings to give expression to her views on women's experience. In *Redeemed in Blood* (1889) much of the action takes place in Patagonia. The assertive heroine, Maeva, finally resolves to work with her husband for the general good. *Gloriana, or, The Revolution of 1900* (1890) is a dream novel in which the heroine avoids the limitations of gender by disguising herself as a man, so successfully that she becomes prime minister and introduces legislation to correct the inequality of the sexes and thus bring about an ideal state. *The Story of Ijain, or, The Evolution of a Mind* (1903), a romanticized autobiographical account of FD's childhood, concludes with the heroine's dedication of herself to the overthrow of oppression. *Izra, or, The Child of Solitude* (1903–5), published in instalments and left unconcluded on the author's death, explores the restraints of gender roles and advocates a liberated and liberating attitude to sexuality. She also wrote two adventure stories for children, *the Two Castaways*

(1889) and *Aniwee, or, The Warrior Queen* (1890), both of which have energetic and competent heroines who reject the conventional feminine role, and didactic narrators who direct the young reader to question gender stereotypes.

ELIZABETH JOYCE

Works: *Abel Avenged: A Dramatic Tragedy* (1877); *Across Patagonia* (1880); 'Afflums, a true story', *Vanity Fair* (7 December 1881); *An Address to the Tenant Farmers and People of Ireland with Advice and Warning* (1882); *A Defence of Zululand and Its King: Echoes from the Blue Books* (1882); *In the Land of Misfortune* (1882); *Ireland and Her Shadow* (1882); *Waifs and Strays, or, The Pilgrimage of a Bohemian Abroad* (1884); 'Woman's Mission', *Vanity Fair* (6 August 1884); *Redeemed in Blood* (1889); *The Young Castaways, or, The Child Hunters of Patagonia* (1889); *Aniwee, or, The Warrior Queen: A Tale of the Araucanian Indians* (1890); *Gloriana, or, The Revolution of 1900* (1890); *Woman's Position and the Objects of the Women's Franchise League* (1891); 'Memories of a Great Lone Land', *Westminster Review* (March 1893); 'The True Science of Living', *Westminster Review* (October 1893); 'The Horrors of Sport', *Humanitarian League: Cruelties of Civilisation* 2 (1895); *Songs of a Child and Other Poems by 'Darling'* (1901–2); *Isola, or, The Disinherited: A Revolt for Women and All the Disinherited* (1902); *The Story of Ijain, or, The Evolution of a Mind* (1903); 'Izra, or, The Child of Solitude', *Agnostic Journal* (January 1903, November 1905); 'President Roosevelt's Gospel of Doom', *Weekly Times and Echoes* (18 April 1903); *Towards Freedom: An Appeal to Thoughtful Men and Women* (1904).

References: Roberts, B., *Ladies in the Veld* (1965); Stevenson, C. B., *Women Travel Writers in Africa* (1982).

Douglas, O.

b. 1878 (?), Pathhead Manse, Fife; d. 24 November 1948, Bank House, Peebles

Novelist

The pseudonym 'O. Douglas' was one of the few devices that separated Anna Buchan's life from her fiction. The eldest daughter in a large family, her father (the Rev. John) was a minister in the Free Church of Scotland, and her mother Helen (*née* Masterton) occupied herself with their six children and 'good works'. OD's early childhood – spent with her adored brothers in the Scottish 'borders' – was especially happy. During her adolescence she moved with her family to Glasgow, where her father was minister of the John Knox Church. She attended private schools there and in Edinburgh. She later returned to the 'bright attractive county town' of Peebles, on which the fictional 'Priorsford' is based. At the age of 28 she took over the maintenance of the family home, and there looked after her mother and kept house for various brothers, as well as participating in community affairs. In 1907 OD made a rare trip out of Scotland to visit her younger brother, a civil servant in Calcutta. This experience prompted her to write her first novel, *Olivia in India* (1912), which was well received.

Olivia in India differs in content from later novels but it sets the predominant tone. A 'happy book', it narrates in letters a young girl's adventures abroad. Olivia's travelogue is interspersed with childhood reminiscences, and Scotland intrudes on more immediate impressions of India. Her descriptions of a visit to a Calcutta bazaar, her brother's club, and tea at the Mission House, form an amusing portrait of colonial insularity. *The Setons* (1917), OD's next novel, stays closer to home. Set in Glasgow, it features a large 'Church' family, in which the eldest daughter fills the role of her absent mother. Golden-haired Elizabeth is just impudent enough to make her virtues tolerable to the reader;

a 'sunny soul', she, like other OD heroines, seems a wishful projection of the author herself. Elizabeth's charismatic brothers appear, under different names, in later novels ('adorable' Buff becomes 'Bat' in *The Day of Small Things* (1930)), which are often closely similar in plot. *Ann and Her Mother* (1922) takes the form of a protracted reminiscence, as Ann's mother (again, divisions between fiction and autobiography become quite indistinct) recalls various episodes in her life as the maternal head of a large 'church' family in Scotland. Her unmarried daughter is self-reliant and optimistic, a mature realization of the sunny Elizabeth. Cheerful spinsters are perhaps OD's most enduring protagonists. Although Jean Jardine of *Penny Plain* (1920) marries a lord (she returns, complete with her own small children in *Priorsford* (1932)), most of OD's heroines, like Kirsty in *Pink Sugar* (1924) or Nicole in *The Day of Small Things*, occupy themselves with good works, ageing mothers, or second-hand children. Small children and their antics are a subject dear to OD and extraordinary plot developments are required to bring them under the care of these committed spinsters.

OD's novels demonstrate, in a friend's words, 'faith in the ultimate decency of things'. These 'things' could be loosely described as family, community life, and material well-being. The cottages and houses in the novels are described with great detail; the gleaming old wood furniture, the bowls of flowers, and the lavish teas with scones and seedcake are invested with a sense of worthiness, a near-moral value. The married protagonist of *Jane's Parlour* (1937), delights in her special room (off-limits to the children), and Nicole and her mother find solace for life's disappointments in their well-appointed home with its view of the sea. The First World War is the only discordant element in this sunny environment. Although confined to the margins of her novels, its presence is felt, often in the death of a beloved brother or son (OD's youngest brother was killed in the war). OD's novels attracted a wide readership throughout her lifetime. Her autobiography, *Unforgettable, Unforgotten* (1945), is a fond account of family life and a successful literary career.   AMY GAMERMAN

Works: *Olivia in India* (1912); *The Setons* (1917); *Penny Plain* (1920); *Ann and Her Mother* (1922); *Pink Sugar* (1924); *The Proper Place* (1926); *Eliza for Common* (1928); *The Day of Small Things* (1930); *Priorsford* (1932); *Taken by the Hand* (1935); *Jane's Parlour* (1937); *People like Ourselves* (1938); *The House that is Our Own* (1940); *Unforgettable, Unforgotten* (1945); *Farewell to Priorsford* (1950).

References: Reekie, A. G., 'Introduction' to *Farewell to Priorsford* (1950).

Douglas, Lady Eleanor

b. c. 1598, Ireland; d. 1652, England
Pamphleteer
(Also wrote under Lady Audley, Lady Davies)

ED was infamous in her own time as a mad prophetess. She predicted, accurately, the deaths of her two husbands and Archbishop Laud, as well as the birth and sex of Charles I's first son. Notorious throughout England, from the court to the lowliest, she appears to have been a victim of religious mania, declaring, in one of her innumerable and incoherent tracts, that she was possessed by the spirit of the prophet Daniel. She concluded with a play on her name: REVEAL O DANIEL ELEANOR AUDELEY. ED's mental instability may have been hereditary; her father's letters seem the product of an unbalanced mind, her elder brother was hanged for sexual crimes against minors, and her only son by John Davies was said to be deaf, mute, and mentally handicapped, dying in his childhood. One of her contemporaries writes of her reputation as a 'Cunning Woman amongst the ignorant people', although Queen Henrietta Maria, too, consulted her for predictions. A scholar of the time found reason to praise her: 'She was learned above her sex, humble below her fortune, having a mind so great and noble that prosperity could not make it remiss, nor the deepest adversity cause her to shrink, or discover the least pusillanimity or dejection of spirit, being full of the love of God.'

She was the fifth daughter of George Tuchet, Lord Audley and Earl of Castlehaven, and Lucy Mervin, daughter of Sir James Mervin of Wiltshire. Her father was probably well acquainted with Sir John Davies, attorney-general in Ireland, now best known for his poem *Orchestra*. Some time before 1612 ED married Sir John and bore a son and daughter in Dublin. Their marriage must have been an unhappy one: Sir John burned ED's literary productions, whereupon she predicted his death in three years' time. Three days before his actual death in 1626, before witnesses, she 'gave him pass to take his long sleep.' A few months later, ED married Sir Archibald Douglas, who also burned her books, and who also died, in 1644, after his wife's prophecy of his death.

During her marriage to Sir Archibald ED was imprisoned and fined £3,000 for publishing false prophecy without a licence. Although her sentence was harsh, allowing her no books, pen, paper, or bible, and little attendance from servants, once released she continued to write and publish at least twenty-eight tracts throughout the 1640s and 1650s. Her daughter, Lucy Hastings, Countess of Huntingdon, appears to have been her only friend, petitioning the courts for clemency for her mother and welcoming her to her home, despite ED's published accusations against the countess's in-laws. JESLYN MEDOFF

Selected works: From the Lady Eleanor, Her Blessing to her Beloved Daughter (1644); *The Day of Judgements Modell* (1646); *The Lady Eleanor: Her Remonstrance to Great Britain* (1648); *The New Jerusalem at Hand* (1649); *The Dragons Blasphemous Charge Against Her* (1651).

References: Ballard; *DNB*; Fraser, A., *The Weaker Vessel* (1984); Hays, M., *Female Biography* (1807); Spencer, T., 'The history of an unfortunate Lady', *Harvard Studies and Notes in Philology and Literature* xx (1938).

Drabble, Margaret
b. 5 June 1939, Sheffield
Novelist, critic, essayist

MD is the second child of John Frederick and Marie Bloor Drabble. The family of four children includes an elder sister, A. S. Byatt, a novelist, critic, and essayist; a younger sister, Helen, an art historian; and a much younger brother who is a barrister. Growing up in Sheffield, Yorkshire, the family was, MD points out, of the same size and constitution as the Brontës, and like them, composed childhood stories together. Their father was a barrister, then a circuit judge, and later, in retirement, a novelist. Their mother was an English teacher at The Mount in York, a Quaker boarding school. MD followed her elder sister to The Mount and later, on a scholarship, to Newnham College, Cambridge, where she received a starred first in English. After university, in 1960, MD married Clive Swift, a Cambridge graduate in English who became an actor. After a brief acting career MD turned to novel writing and childrearing. The couple had three children before separating and divorcing in 1972. MD has lived in a comfortable house in Hampstead for many years; in 1982 she married the biographer and man of letters Michael Holroyd.

Widely read and well received by both critics and the general audience, MD plays a lively role in British culture. In addition to nine novels, she has written several stories and screenplays and a biography of Arnold Bennett, and has re-edited *The Oxford Companion to English Literature* (1985). She has written or edited several books on literary subjects and scores of reviews and other pieces for journals, newspapers, and magazines. She writes for both school children and adults, for both scholars and laymen. Frequently interviewed and photographed, the subject of much critical commentary, she also appears on televised literary programmes, participates on government councils and Arts Council tours, and for many years taught adult education one day a week at Morley College. While her fiction is located within, enriched by, and played off against the literary language, traditions, and characters she knows so well, MD chooses not to be a high-culture artist, disengaged from everyday realities. Eminently accessible and readable, she is attuned to herself and to ordinary experience, vividly rendering the ordinary with intelligence and learning, insight and humour. Her informal, intimate, personal voice seems to speak directly for a whole generation of readers, particularly women, in Great Britain, the United States, and other countries.

The protagonists of MD's novels have followed the course and concerns of her own life: young women leaving university, getting married and separated, bearing children, having affairs, raising progressively older children, reaching mid-life, and wondering what next. The tension between surface and meaning gives to MD's work an unresolved, exploratory quality quite different from the popular women's fiction it deceptively resembles. She examines with subtlety and moral acuity the very tissue and structure of women's lives. From her first, comparatively slight novel, *A Summer Bird-Cage* (1963), her first-person characterizations grow in depth and subtlety, reaching their culmination in her most technically experimental narrative, *The Waterfall* (1969), which records Jane Gray's orgasmic breaking out of the constrictions of female identity and her equivocal examination of this experience.

The third-person novels of MD's middle period move further out of the solipsistic spaces of the early novels. They record a more graphic exodus from the constricting world of childhood: its geography, class-bound values, and moral outlook. Northern landscapes are rejected in each novel for the cosmopolitan environment of London, duplicating the journey MD herself made from Sheffield to London. While born into a liberal, professional, middle-class family, MD draws from her family's rural, working-class roots in her fiction, dramatizing particularly the 'need to escape' from oppressive provincial limitations. 'By will and by strain', her characters create new selves and new worlds out of preconceived 'golden' fantasies: a golden Jerusalem, a Bunyanesque holy city, realms of gold.

While these novels link up to the socio-moral tradition of the English novel – which MD outspokenly values over modernist experiment – like her earlier work, they continue to be in many ways double-voiced and equivocal, mediating between traditional realistic humanism and modern perspectives. 'Omniscience has its limits,' the narrator of *The Realms of Gold* (1975) candidly admits, calling attention to the fictionality of this carefully constructed world. Similarly, character is not at all stable, and perhaps not knowable. Because the characters' lives are such a composite of psychological determinism and wilful self-creation, the boundaries between the real and the imagined are unclear for characters and readers alike. MD's use of houses and landscapes as objective correlatives of mental states lends considerable subtlety and depth to these works, dramatizing her intense preoccupation with the 'effect of landscape upon the soul'. The search for a suitable moral and human habitation is the compelling genesis of her art. The tension within these middle novels resides in the apparent freedom of the individual to create a new self coupled with his or her necessary circumscription within geographical, communal, and historical contexts.

In her later two novels, *The Ice Age* (1977) and *The Middle Ground* (1980), MD focuses on the commonly shared contexts and experiences of urban middle-class life, detailing the texture, the trends, and the trappings of mass culture. The most vividly memorable passages of both books depict the dehumanized, noisy, dirty, ugly, and graffiti-ridden world that is modern urban Britain. The environment in which characters live is largely shaped from without. The individual may be, like Anthony Keating in *The Ice Age*, no more than a 'weed upon the tide of history' doomed to enact a drama which differs only in particulars from those of other members of his or her generation.

Like their author, the characters, successful in their professional lives, are now experiencing a midlife reappraisal of self. What is happening to individuals reflects, in turn, what is happening to the British nation as a whole, which is getting older, tired, staid, facing crises, and going through some strange and disorienting metamorphosis. *The Ice Age* is highly controlled, a visibly plotted work, and so too are the lives of the characters it chronicles, whereas *The Middle Ground* is plotless and shapeless, the novel's structure open to contingency just as the lives of its characters are.

MD's fiction is constantly nourished by her own personal development. Her mediating position between 'male' and 'female' concerns and traditions, literary and popular issues and perspectives, the literary and the real, the traditional and the modern gives resonance and strength to her fiction. Her attempt to 'only connect' these diverse strains is the generating energy of her work.

JOANNE V. CREIGHTON

Works: *A Summer Bird-Cage* (1963); *The Garrick Year* (1964); *The Millstone* (1965); *Wordsworth* (1966); *Jerusalem the Golden* (1967); *The Waterfall* (1969); *The Needle's Eye* (1972); *Virginia Woolf: A Personal Debt* (1973); *Arnold Bennett: A Biography* (1974); *The Realms of Gold* (1975); *The Ice Age* (1977); *For Queen and Country: Britain in the Victorian Age* (1978); *A Writer's Britain: Landscape in Literature* (1979); *The Middle Ground* (1980); *The Tradition of Women's Fiction: Lectures in Japan* (1982); (ed.), *Oxford Companion to English Literature* (1985); *The Radiant Way* (1987).

References: Creighton, J. V., *Margaret Drabble* (1985); Hannay, J., *The Intertextuality of Fate: A Study of Margaret Drabble* (1986); Korenman, J. S., 'A Margaret Drabble bibliography', in *Critical Essays on Margaret Drabble* (1984); Moran, M. H., *Margaret Drabble: Existing Within Structures* (1983); Myer, V. G., *Margaret Drabble: Puritanism and Permissiveness* (1974); Rose, E. C. (ed.), *Critical Essays on Margaret Drabble* (1984); Rose, E. C., *The Novels of Margaret Drabble: Equivocal Figures* (1980); Schmidt, D. (ed.), *Margaret Drabble: Golden Realms* (1982).

Duff Gordon, Lady

b. 24 June 1821, London; d. 14 July 1869, Cairo

Travel writer, translator

LDG (Lucie), the daughter of John Austin and Mary Taylor, moved in exalted intellectual circles throughout her life. When only 5 she travelled with her family to Bonn where she became fluent in German. As a young girl she met Heinrich Heine who remembered her when he saw her again at the end of his life. In 1840 she married Sir Alexander Duff Gordon. The couple lived first in London then in Esher; their home became one of England's most celebrated salons. LDG was a personal friend of Thackeray and, after she moved to Paris in 1857, of August Comte and Alfred de Vigny.

Her literary career commenced with a translation of Barthold Georg Niebuhr's *Studies of Ancient Grecian Mythology* (1839). While still a child she had heard the German classical scholar tell these mythological tales to his son. In 1844 she translated Meinhold's *Mary Schweidler, The Amber Witch*, a narrative purporting to derive from a seventeenth-century chronicle, and then the *Narrative of Remarkable Criminal Trials* by Anselm Ritter von Feuerbach. Her translation of Leon de Wailly's *Stella and Vanessa* from the French appeared in 1850. She collaborated with her husband on a translation of *Memoirs of the House of Brandenburg* by Leopold von Ranke, a German historian who visited her in London.

LDG suffered from consumption for most of her life. She survived a critical attack of the disease in 1849 after the birth of her son, Maurice, but in 1860 she was obliged to leave England for the milder climate of the Cape of Good Hope, where she made many friends among the Malay population and wrote her 'Letters from the Cape'. In 1862 she moved to Egypt, where her eager interest in the life and manners of its inhabitants resulted in her famous *Letters from Egypt* (1865). She died of consumption in 1869 and is buried in the English cemetery in Cairo.

LDG's literary reputation rests on her *Letters from Egypt* and *Last Letters from Egypt* (1875). She made no secret of her dislike for English cultural condescension, and asked pointedly, 'Why do the English talk of the beautiful sentiment of the Bible and pretend to feel it so much and when they come and see the same life before them, they ridicule it?' Her account is marked not only by the vigour of her commentary but also by a rare breadth of interests: her letters include remarks on the pictorial complexity and splendour of Arab architecture and on the calligraphic beauty of Arab art, as well as ethnological speculations concerning the differences between Arab, Turkish, and Coptic life. She countered a widely held belief that Middle Eastern government was especially despotic with arguments that 'social equality' existed to a greater degree in the Levant than elsewhere. She had an unusual sense of Egypt's cultural complexity, writing that 'This country is a palimpsest in which the Bible is written over Herodotus, and the Koran over that. In the town the Koran is most visible, in the country Herodotus.' The *Letters* are especially moving in their concern for the indigence of the *fellahin* (peasants) who came to esteem LDG as 'Sitt-el-Kebeer', 'the great lady'.   JANET JONES

Works: (all trans.): *Studies of Ancient Grecian Mythology*, by B. G. Niebuhr (1839); *Mary Schweidler, the Amber Witch* by W. Meinhold (1844); *Narrative of Remarkable Criminal Trials*, by P. J. A. von Feuerbach (1844); *The French in Algiers*, by de France and Lamping (1845); *Stella and Vanessa*, by A. F. L. de Wailly (1850); *The Village Doctor*, by S. D'Arbouville (1853); *Ferdinand I and Maximilian II of Austria: The State of Germany after the Reformation*, by L. von Ranke (1853); *The Russians in Bulgaria and Rumelia . . .* , by H. C. B. von Moltke (1854); *The History and Literature of the Crusades*, by H. C. L. von Sybel (1861); other works: *Letters from the Cape* (1863); *Letters from Egypt* (1865); *Last Letters from Egypt* (1875).

References: Norton, C., 'Lady Duff Gordon and her works', *Macmillan's Magazine* 20 (1869); Searight, S., 'Introduction' to *Letters from Egypt* (1983); Waterfield, O. H. G., *Lucie Duff Gordon in England, South Africa, and Egypt* (1937).

Duffy, Maureen

b. 1933, Worthing, Sussex

Novelist, dramatist, poet

MD was educated at Trowbridge High School for Girls, Wiltshire and Sarah Bonnell High School for Girls. She read English at King's College, London, and after graduating she worked as a school teacher for five years.

Her first novel, *That's How it Was*, appeared in 1962. It was a powerful work about the relationship between a mother and her daughter. The mother is fiercely and clearly portrayed. 'She stood there, thin as brown paper, her bird's bones and lean flesh held together by a steel-wire will. It would have been like trying to fight a small fierce flame.' It is a novel of survival; the mother surviving on her own with a small child, the child surviving during a temporary separation from her mother. MD writes with simplicity about the love between mother and child, a love which survives deprivation and insecurity.

Her next novel, *The Single Eye* (1964), was a bold experiment. MD attempted to put herself into the character of Mike, a young photographer married to Toni, an Italian girl. *The Microcosm* (1966) was seen at the time as a controversial novel, tackling as it did the question of lesbian relationships in contemporary society. It begins – and ends – in a 'gay' club where the women come to dance, assume their night-time disguises and put away, for a few hours, their conventional 'normal' roles. MD's talent is for the non-direct approach; her description of the action is clothed in a rich language: 'Gone under grass yet not stirring this spring morning as bulb and tuber poke through the top soil with blunt leaf fingers, resurrecting; the dancing legs rigid in bone, muscles liquid, taut tendons dissolving, only the hair still bright-tipped, grown long and thick, darker at the roots.' *The Microcosm* is a blend of fantasy and reality which questioned the nature of 'minorities' within society.

The Paradox Players (1967) contains some of MD's best writing. A novelist retreats from the world to live on a houseboat, moored on the Thames, near Hampton Court. The people he meets on the river during one bitter winter make up the kaleidoscope of action, the tensions and triumphs of a small world.

MD is a prolific author and her work extends beyond the novelist's territory to literary criticism and poetry. *The Erotic World of Faery* was published in 1972 and *The Passionate Shepherdess: Aphra Behn 1640–1689* in 1977. This second work did much to revive interest in the dramatist Aphra Behn, who had long been neglected.

MD has published six collections of verse in which her writing is tight and controlled and frequently draws inspiration from the visual arts and classical and religious themes. She revisits areas often examined by other poets:

> Yesterday, Lucy's forever now,
> Shortest though old style your calendar
> Gave a different figure
> Primed with ill-luck black enough,
> You might well have thought,
> For perpetual mourning, I forgot,
> I confess your obsequies. Unsought
> By my usual pilgrim and limping feet,
> Grave divine, I offer you this chaplet.
> ('Nocturnal for the Winter Solstice', from *The Venus Touch*, 1971).

If MD's public thought that she would continue in the same vein as her earlier novels, they were wrong. She has explored many new territories in her later novels from *Capital* (1975) to *Gor Saga* (1981). The latter deals with one of MD's main concerns, animal rights. Gor, a young gorilla created by AID, in a laboratory, is brought up as a human child. The issues which this raises are examined in detail. Her most recent novel, *Change* (1987), is set in wartime Britain and deals with young people growing to maturity in extreme and dangerous conditions.

MD co-founded the Writers Action Group in 1972 and since 1985 she has been President of the Writers Guild of Great Britain. She was also one of the prime movers in the campaign for Public Lending Right.   ALISON RIMMER

Works: *That's How it Was* (1962); *The Single Eye* (1964); *The Microcosm* (1966); *The Paradox Players* (1967); *Lyrics for the Dog Hour* (1968); *Wounds* (1969); *Love Child* (1971); *The Venus Touch* (1971); *The Erotic World of Faery* (1972); *I Want To Go To Moscow: A Lay* (1973); *Actaeon* (1973); *Capital* (1975); *The Passionate Shepherdess: Aphra Behn 1640–1689* (1977); *Housespy* (1978); *Memorials of the Quick and the Dead* (1979); *Inherit the Earth: A Social History* (1980); *Gor Saga* (1981); (as D. M. Cayer) *Scarborough Fear* (1982); *Londoners: An Elegy* (1983); *Man and Beast: An Animal Rights Handbook* (1984); *Collected Poems* (1985); *Change* (1987).

References: CA.

Du Maurier, Daphne
b. 13 May 1907, London
Novelist, short story writer, playwright, biographer

D du M succeeded to a popular and lively literary heritage; she is the second daughter of the late Sir Gerald du Maurier, the renowned actor-manager and creator of the role of 'Bulldog Drummond'. Her mother, Muriel Beaumont, was an actress and her grandfather, George du Maurier, an artist for *Punch* and author of *Trilby* and *Peter Ibbetson*. D du M was educated at home in London with her sisters and then in France at Meudon and Paris. In 1932 she married Sir Frederick Arthur Montague Browning, then a Major in the Grenadier Guards, later wartime Commander of Airborne Forces, Chief-of-Staff to Mountbatten and, until 1958, treasurer to the Duke of Edinburgh. He died in 1965 leaving her with three children, all of whom are married. Since the war D du M has made Cornwall her home; first at Menabilly and now at Kilmarth, Par. She describes her politics as 'centre' and is a member of the Brontë Society, a fellow of the Royal Society of Literature, and in 1969 was made Dame Commander, Order of the British Empire.

D du M's childhood was characterized by a tension between a desperate need for solitude and familial/financial security. She confessed to feeling 'inadequate' through this period and only discovered peace with books and play-acting. Resisting growing up until her late teenage years, she rejected the conventional entry into the debutante scene and nepotistic opportunities of an acting career.

D du M began her long and prolific literary career in 1928 by writing short stories and articles. Her first novel *The Loving Spirit* (1931) was completed during a ten-week stay at her parents' country home on the Cornish coast. This romantic family chronicle was an immediate best-seller and it made her a fashionable reputation, enhanced by a further Cornish romance set in the nineteenth century, *Jamaica Inn* (1936), and her frank biography of her father, *Gerald: A Portrait* (1934). *Rebecca* (1938), however, has proved her most enduringly popular novel; within twenty years of publication it had run to thirty-nine impressions and been translated into over twenty languages. The work revived interest in the Gothic novel, a form that had apparently died out over a century before, by resurrecting a narrative formula which oscillates mysteriously between the familiar and the supernatural. The novel is an expression of women's fears about husbands; the Girl marries a man whom she subsequently suspects of still harbouring a transcendent love for his dead, first wife, but who has actually murdered Rebecca, scandalized by her promiscuity. The new couple occupy a private, claustrophobic existence and yet are paradoxically distanced by introversion and their own self-critical attitudes. The ghostly Manderley, the architecture of which is quintessential Gothic, is the haunting context for the ghoulish intrusions in each protagonist's sense of identity; the Girl is never named and seems defined by an enigmatic anonymity when she inhabits the place of Rebecca, the first Mrs de Winter, whose strong sexuality has been an insurance against the threat of impersonality. But this invitation of Rebecca is suppressed by the middle-class prudence of the Girl, Maxim's second wife.

Of the contemporary critics, V. S. Pritchett located the plain reason for the novel's immense success: 'Many a better novelist would give his eyes to be able to tell a story as Miss du Maurier does, to make it move at such a pace and to go with such mastery from surprise to surprise . . . from the first sinister rumours to the final conflagration the melodrama is excellent.' This emphasis on her gift for story telling is the right one; even though the prose of *Rebecca* now seems opaque and dated, it had in its time an intensity and rhythm which matched the unsettled and tentative mood of the story.

My Cousin Rachel (1951) was hailed as another *Rebecca* and the similarity of the plots is striking; here it is the woman who is haunted by a previous marriage and whose affection for her late husband, Ambrose, is ambivalent. This is coloured and confused by the narrator, Philip Ashley, who bears a strong likeness to his dead cousin and who is himself 'vanquished' by Rachel's elusive, Italianate beauty. Again, D du M is broadly concerned with the spectacle of irrational happenings in a supposedly rational and ordered universe. The narrative's momentum is sustained by the base-line integrity of D du M's approach: 'The point is, life has to be endured, and lived. But how to live it is the problem.'

This concern makes the author immensely practical in terms of plot and character; she admits that she is 'not so much interested in people as in types – types who represent great forces of good and evil. I don't care very much whether John Smith likes Mary Robinson, goes to bed with Jane Brown and then refuses to pay the hotel bill. But I am passionately interested in human cruelty, human lust and human avarice – and, of course, their counterparts on the scale of virtue.' This is her vindication of the charge that her figures are two-dimensional and the plots turgid.

In *My Cousin Rachel* and the earlier *Frenchman's Creek* (1941) she appears to invite and refute criticism; Rainaldi, the suspicious and machinating executor, makes easy sense of male/female behaviour: 'Women, especially Rachel, act always from emotion. We men, more usually but not always so, with reason.' D du M often avoids these simple gender divisions by juxtaposing seemingly antithetical forces within the individual; Dona St Columb, the heroine of *Frenchman's Creek*, has to choose between two impulses, 'a longing to throw modesty and reserve to the winds and confess everything, and an equal determination to conceal the love forever . . . to die rather than admit a thing so personal, so intimate'. This sense of isolation and anonymity between recognized character and societal expectation confronts many of her protagonists; they appear as fugitives from roles forced upon them and their knowledge of self, like the vulnerable, terrorized Girl in *Rebecca* and Dona St Columb who, in her prescribed place, feels an 'outlaw at heart'. Some critics, however, have been unsympathetic about the consistency of design; familiarity with the broad outlines of *Rebecca* and *My Cousin Rachel* has aroused charges of complacency in the facile reworking of stock material in the later novels such as *Frenchman's Creek*.

D du M is passionately devoted to Cornwall. The four Cornish novels, *Jamaica Inn, Rebecca, Frenchman's Creek* and *My Cousin Rachel*, are cast as romantic historical fiction. In each there is a strong nostalgia and sense of heritage, not just a sentimental evocation of the past but a demonstration and experiment in how our experience relates to that past. In the contemporary opening chapter in the eighteenth-century *Frenchman's Creek* the lone yachtsman is suspended as the 'past becomes the present'. There is a fascination in these works with the history of the world we inhabit. *The King's General* (1946) tells the story of her Cornish home, Menabilly, during the Civil War. These themes are most directly addressed in *The House on the Strand* (1969), a late novel which examines the deep influence of past on present and recognizes complementary worlds across six centuries.

The result is only partially successful and the power of the Cornish landscape is often disfigured by romantic clichés of dark waters and absolving sunsets. Kate O'Brien in the *Spectator* said of *Rebecca*, 'it is a Charlotte Brontë story minus Charlotte Brontë' and laments a lack of real engagement between the natural and human world. But it is not appropriate to approach D du M's work as great literature. The assumption she has consistently worked upon is her reader's simple desire to know what is going to happen next and to be transported by an ingenious, exciting and engagingly romantic tale.

DOMINIC FYFE

Selected works: *The Loving Spirit* (1931); *I'll Never Be Young Again* (1932); *The Progress of Julius* (1933); *Gerald: A Portrait* (1934); *Jamaica Inn* (1936); *Rebecca* (1938); *Happy Christmas* (1940); *Frenchman's Creek* (1941); *Consider the Lilies* (1943); *Hungry Hill* (1943); *Nothing Hurts For Long; and Escort: Two Tales* (1943); *Leading Lady; The King's General* (1946); *My Cousin Rachel* (1951); *Mary Anne* (1954); *The Scapegoat* (1957); *The Glass Blowers* (1963); *The Birds and Other Stories* (1963); *The House on the Strand* (1969); *The Blue Lenses and Other Stories* (1970); *Don't Look Now* (1971); *Growing Pains: The Shaping of a Writer* (1977); *The Rendezvous and Other Stories* (1980); *The Rebecca Notebook and Other Memories* (1980).

References: Drake, R. Y., 'Manderley revisited', *Mississippi Quarterly* 12 (1959); Light, A., 'Rebecca', *Feminist Review* (1984); Radcliffe, E. J., *Gothic Novels of the 20th Century: An Annotated Bibliography* (1979); Rowntree, I. J., ' "Frenchman's Creek" as a variation of "The Gypsy Laddie" ', *Tennessee Folklore Society Bulletin* 25 (1959); Stockwell, L. T., 'Best sellers and the critics: a case history', *College English* 16 (1956).

Dunn, Nell

b. 1936, London

Essayist, novelist, playwright

ND's work emerged in the 1960s as part of an investigative, naturalistic movement in British culture. It was a movement that focused upon working-class life as both economically deprived and spiritually alienated, and often took as its subject the most marginalized victims of a society that prided itself on never having had it so good. These concerns were central to the work of film and television directors Ken Loach and Roland Joffee and playwrights like Jeremy Sandford and David Mercer, as well as to ND.

In 1959 ND moved from Chelsea across the Thames and went to live with her husband Jeremy Sandford in the working-class area of Battersea. They both began to gather material about the people of the area, augmenting observation and interviews with research and collation of material sifted from newspaper clippings, and sought to shape and condense it into forms that would be of interest to a mass audience. In the process ND developed a style of investigative journalism and docudrama that both caught public attention and transformed her into an early 1960s media personality, perhaps more looked at (the girl on the motorcycle in Battersea) than listened to.

Her first book, *Up the Junction* (1963), was a collection of short sketches about life in the Clapham Junction commercial centre of Battersea. The vignettes are concise and candid pictures of life in Clapham; girls getting dressed and putting on their make-up for a Friday night out; sexual flirtations at the pub; life at home for young unwed mothers; women talking to each other as they work in a local candy factory. The author's precise and observant narrative documents the character of their existence, finding interest and dignity in the little struggles that colour their life without shrinking from the vulgarity of the milieu. Although many critics accused her of slumming and censured her for being coarse and sensational, D. A. N. Jones in the *New Statesman* noted her strong comment on 'English class relations', and Edgar Z. Friedenberg praised her successful 'use of ethnology' in her accounts of 'lower-depths poverty'. Friedenberg's comment is perceptive, for it places ND in a line of writers from Gorky and late nineteenth-century naturalists to the 1960s' school of 'culture of poverty' writers in the US, of documentary writers who present rather than analyse, but nevertheless succeed in validating common experience to a large audience and thus stretch the accepted boundaries of writing. *Up the Junction* won the John Llewellyn Rhys Memorial Prize for short story collections in 1964 and was subsequently made into a feature film. *Talking to Women* (1965), a collection of shaped and edited interviews, and *Poor Cow* (1967), a novel, were also developed from ND's Battersea research, being in a sense both social documents and imaginative creations. In these works ND focuses upon the struggles and passions of a stratum of working-class women, giving expression not only to their dialect and language but to their perceptions of the world.

In 1969 ND collaborated with director Ken Loach on a film adaptation of *Poor Cow*, a work that was, unfortunately, far more sentimental and less hard-edged than its source, and less successful than Loach's notable productions of Sandford's and Mercer's docudramas. Thus by the end of the 1960s the reputation of ND's work tended to be eclipsed in critical circles by other documentary realists of the period. During the decade of the 1970s she tended to fade from public view although she wrote a number of novels about a range of concerns.

ND's feminism resurfaced in 1981 in *Steaming*, a play with documentary roots, which was an instant popular success both in England and North America. It follows the pattern of her early work as the audience, in a sense, listens in on a group of women talking. The setting is the Turkish Lounge of a dilapidated public bath in the East End of London. There the play's five principal characters meet to relax and share their troubles. As the characters undress they shed their social inhibitions and begin to share confidences about men and sex and what qualities and achievements they value as most important in their lives. Although their accents range from genteel to working-class, their concerns, it turns out, are all not so different. And ND unites the characters politically as well, when the baths are threatened with closure. The play was awarded the Susan Smith Blackburn Prize in 1981, and its popularity attests to ND's ability to give voice to feminist feelings of solidarity and aspiration. It also sparked debate in feminist circles, being replied to, perhaps, by Caryl Churchill's *Top Girls* in the following year (1982), a Brechtian play that questions whether working-class and middle-class experiences of women's oppression are identical and takes a hard look at the price of success for women in competitive societies. It is a measure of the times and of ND's pioneering achievement that, while debates about her work in the 1960s centred about the validity of her subject, they now tend to focus on how she problematizes and evaluates her chosen material. MICHAEL KLEIN

Works: Up the Junction (1963); *Talking to Women* (1965); *Poor Cow* (1967); *Poor Cow* (screenplay, with Kenneth Loach) (1968); *The Incurable* (1971); *I Want* (with Adrian Henri) (1972); *Tear His Head Off His Shoulders* (1974); *Living Like I Do* (1976); *The Only Child* (1978); *Steaming* (1981).

References: Drabble; *New Statesman* (22 November 1966); *New York Times Book Review* (6 November 1966); *New York Review of Books* (18 May 1967); *Yale Review* (Spring 1968); *New York Times* (12–13 December 1982).

Eastlake, Elizabeth, Lady
b. 1809, Norwich; d. 1893, London
Journalist, art critic, letter writer, translator
(Also wrote under Elizabeth Rigby)

EE was born to Dr Edward Rigby and Anne Palgrave, their fifth child and fourth daughter. Her father died when EE was 11, and she received little subsequent formal education. After a serious bout of typhoid fever, she was taken by her mother to convalesce in Heidelberg from 1827 to 1829. Upon her return in 1830 EE began translating a German book on British art collections (not published until 1854) and wrote a short fictional story about Salzburg. From then on she wrote extensively, keeping voluminous notebooks and journals, in addition to regular correspondence.

EE studied literature, art, and music in London, lived on and off with her mother, returned to Germany in 1835, and in 1838 made an extended visit to a married sister in Russia. The descriptive letters she sent to her mother during that trip were published in a popular volume entitled *A Residence on the Shores of the Baltic.*

In 1842 Mrs Rigby and her daughters moved to Edinburgh, where EE especially was welcomed into the upper-middle-class intellectual circles. She travelled on the continent, visited the Baltic a second time, and continued her critical and creative writing, publishing frequent articles in the *Quarterly Review* and the *Edinburgh Review.*

Her marriage in 1849 to Charles Lock Eastlake, RA (knighted the following year), a highly esteemed art critic, admitted her to that exalted circle of London society which included Thomas Macaulay, John Ruskin, Sir Robert Peel, the Duke of Wellington, Benjamin Jowett, Charles Kingsley, Charles Dickens, and Mrs Grote, to name just a few. Charming, witty, and self-confident, EE observed and recorded countless scenes of social history, both significant and commonplace. She translated volumes from both French and German, as well as publishing her own critical essays and prose collections.

Starting in 1854, EE and her husband took numerous trips to the continent, and she memorialized their experiences at great length in her journals and letters. Following Sir Charles's death in 1865, she wrote an anonymous volume, *Fellowship: Letters Addressed to my Sister Mourners*, which made her many friends. In 1870 she edited her husband's *Contributions to the Literature of the Fine Arts*, and reworked some of his other previously published writing. In 1880 she published her father's letters from his 1789 tour of France and southern Europe. The discussion of politics in these letters interested EE, who went on to read de Tocqueville extensively, her interest leading to a study of Mme de Staël and the Jacobin movement.

An impressively active woman, EE loved beauty, honesty, and refinement. Her outspoken, decisive speech and writing were characteristic of her manner. Strongly conservative, she was not a feminist, considering women weaker and less able than men in all ways. Indeed, she felt that to 'keep down the redundancy of mere word, and keep up the succession of real thought is a task beyond the usual strength of women. It always appears an unfair strain on my mind.'

EE's extensive writings possess little literary significance. The pages and pages she covered with her pen are excellent social history records – the clever and often arbitrary notes of an English *grande dame* – written with good taste, care, and compositional accuracy. Her art critiques are highly subjective, yet impressive in their scope. The letters and journals are filled with lengthy descriptions, social and political commentary, amusing chatter, and smatterings of French, German and Italian.   AMALIA ERICKSON

Selected works: *A Residence on the Shores of the Baltic* (1841; republished in 1844 as *Letters from the Shores . . .*); *The Jewess: A Tale from the Shores of the Baltic* (1843); *Livonian Tales* (1844); *The History of Our Lord as Exemplified in Works of Art* (with Anna Brownell Jameson) (1860); *Fellowship: Letters Addressed to my Sister Mourners* (1868); (ed.), *Life of John Gibson, RA, Sculptor* (1870); *Mrs Grote: a Sketch* (1880).

References: Allibone; *DNB*; Lockhead, M. C., *Elizabeth Rigby, Lady Eastlake* (1961); Smith, C. E. (ed.), *Letters and Journals of Lady Eastlake* (1895).

Eden, Emily

b. 3 March 1797, Westminster; d. 5 August 1869, Richmond

Novelist, letter writer

EE was the seventh daughter of William Eden, first Baron Auckland, and of Eleanor Elliot, a sister of the first Earl of Minto. EE had a privileged and comfortable childhood, in the company of her mother, tutors, and her younger sister, Fanny. When Lady Auckland died in 1818, the two sisters established a household with their brother George in London. EE's quick wit, lively intellect, staunch Whig beliefs, and skill at debate made her an excellent hostess. In May 1827, George was appointed First Lord of the Admiralty. Fanny and EE subsequently moved to Ham Common near Richmond where EE wrote her first novel, *The Semi-Attached Couple*, although it was not published until 1860.

When Lord Melbourne was elected prime minister he appointed George Governor-General of India, a post he held from 1835 until 1842. Fanny, EE and he moved to India; EE's years there were decidedly unhappy. She missed her family, hated the intense Calcutta heat, and was bored by the rigid formality of social calls, dinners, drives, and balls. Worse still, George had practically no time to spend with her, so, to occupy herself, she wrote letters to her sisters and friends. These were later collected and published as *Up the Country* (1866) (the title referred to the state visits George and his sisters made from Calcutta through the northern provinces to Simla in the Punjab). Her letters reveal sensitivity, thoughtfulness, humour, and a keen descriptive quality. She was concerned about the plight of the poor, women, and animals, and was fascinated by the opulent lives of the nobility in the midst of the general poverty. All of the letters, numbering nearly 200, express disdain for the eccentricity of Indian life, and the unhealthy living conditions of her party who were trying to maintain a 'proper' camp, replete with dinners and entertainments. From Simla in 1838, she wrote 'We had a great dinner on Monday, and another fainting lady. Somebody always faints here. I myself believe, that though they do not like to say so, it is the *fleas* that make them ill. You cannot imagine the provocation of those animals during the rains. . . . The worst of it is, the more the house is cleaned and tormented, the worse the fleas get. . . . They say the plague is to cease next month, which is a comfort.'

EE's accounts of the habits and manners of the Sikh rajahs and the Afghani shahs add another, more candidly personal, dimension to the historical accounts of the first Afghan War (1838–42). George's diplomatic blunderings were one of the causes of the war, and led to his replacement in 1842 by Lord Ellenborough. The Edens returned to England soon after, and immediately on their return the sisters set about visiting relatives while George remained at home enduring criticism from both the press and the government.

In 1849 both George and Fanny died. Remarkably, EE rallied against her sorrow by turning again to writing. Her niece moved in with her at Eden Lodge, and her lifelong friend, Theresa Lewis, became her literary 'agent' and principal source of literary encouragement. EE's first project was editing her father, William Eden's journals for publication; then in 1858 her first published novel, *The Semi-Detached House* appeared. She was paid £300 for it by the publisher, Bentley, and was enormously pleased by the letters she received from friends praising her for its humorous portrayal of city and country manners. The central character is Blanche, a young, upper-class woman, who goes to the country while her husband is away on a diplomatic mission. Blanche has many preconceptions about country people, which she is obliged to alter by the end of the novel. Through her acquaintance with a local family, Blanche learns that social position, wealth, and beauty have little to do with filial devotion and married love.

Following the success of *The Semi-Detached House*, in 1860 EE published *The Semi-Attached Couple*, her novel written thirty years before. It focuses on the unfulfilling marriage of Lord and Lady Teviot. They both misunderstand each other's character – he thinks she is too attached to her family and she thinks he is cold – until on a diplomatic mission to Lisbon, Teviot contracts a deadly fever and is rushed home, near death. This provides the supercilious, Helen with the chance to discover that her husband really loves her, and allows Teviot to appreciate what Helen's closeness to her family means, and to come to love the family himself. The novel is populated by characters from different social backgrounds, the most amusing of which is Fisherwick, secretary to the cabinet minister known only as 'G'. In Fisherwick, EE successfully combines her knowledge of political types with humour; when G becomes prime minister, Fisherwick is said to 'have reached the summit of his Mont Blanc'.

B. E. SCHNELLER

Works: *Portraits of the Princes and People of India* (1844); *Up the Country: Letters from India* (1866); *The Semi-Detached House* (1858); *The Semi-Attached Couple* (1860); *Miss Eden's Letters*, ed. V. Dickinson, (1919).
References: Allibone; *Biographica Dramatica*; Drabble; Dunbar, J., *Golden Interlude: The Edens in India 1836–1842* (1956).

Edgeworth, Maria
b. January 1768, Black Bourton, Oxfordshire; d. May 1849, Edgeworthstown, Co. Longford, Ireland
Novelist, educational writer

ME was the daughter of the former Anna Maria Elers (1743–73) and Richard Lovell Edgeworth (1744–1817). When Anna Maria Edgeworth died in childbirth, her widower speedily married the efficient Honora Sneyd who exacted reverence rather love from her stepchildren. R. L. Edgeworth took his family to settle on his estate in Ireland, but his two elder children, a son and ME, proved uncooperative and had to be sent away to school in England. Honora Edgeworth died of tuberculosis in 1780, and after some reluctance from himself and the Church of England, Edgeworth married her sister Elizabeth to provide a mother for his children. In 1782 the family went once more to Ireland, ME accompanying them. For the remainder of her life, apart from tours of a few months to England, Scotland, France, and Switzerland, her home was the family house at Edgeworthstown, County Longford, in the Irish Midlands.

Richard Lovell was the emotional and intellectual focus of ME's life. During his second marriage, when she was aged between 5 and 7, her behaviour was disturbed, partly because her father and stepmother were too mutually absorbed to attend to her needs. On her return to Ireland at 15, she trained herself to become her father's amanuensis and assistant in running the estate, with its rental income during her lifetime of between £1,600 and £3,500 a year; in these roles, she rivalled her new stepmother for his time and attention. Edgeworth was a man with the wide-ranging interests and liberal political sympathies characteristic of the Enlightenment. During his years in England, especially 1764–73, he developed his interest in experimental science, mechanics, and became one of the original members of the Lunar Society of Birmingham, along with the industrialists James Watt, Matthew Boulton, and Josiah Wedgewood, the doctor and poet Erasmus Darwin, and the chemist and Unitarian polemicist Joseph Priestley. An even closer friend was the eccentric Thomas Day, with whom Edgeworth shared an interest in education, particularly in the theories of Rousseau. ME became acquainted with her father's friends in childhood, and stayed for some school holidays with Day, who attempted to instruct her in the Rousseauistic ideal of womanhood, which was feminine, passive, and unintellectual.

Once in Ireland, Edgeworth and ME took up this educational work together. Although he had early rejected much of Rousseau's *Emile* as impractical, Edgeworth retained his interest in current French educational writing, and ME's first literary attempt was a translation of Madame de Genlis's *Adèle et Théodore*, which was completed but recalled before publication in 1783. As child after child was born to his Sneyd wives in the 1770s, 1780s, and 1790s, Edgeworth experimented with various teaching methods and kept notes of the children's comments and reactions. By the late 1780s, ME had begun to compose stories for the domestic circle of children, which from the 1790s were gradually published in series such as *The Parent's Assistant* (1796) and *Early Lessons* (1801).

The theories on which the stories are based, together with the notes, are explained in R. L. Edgeworth and ME's *Practical Education* (1798), a work immediately accepted as important in Napoleonic Europe as well as in Britain.

Meanwhile ME's fiction for adults, which is more independent of her father, began to establish her separate reputation. *Letters for Literary Ladies* (1795) contains three stories with feminist themes, the first a dialogue between two progressive gentlemen (resembling Day and Edgeworth) who differ over whether women should become authors. This was followed in 1800 by the most celebrated of her books, *Castle Rackrent*, supposedly the memoirs of the Irish servant of a family of feckless Anglo-Irish gentry. This brilliant and apparently wholly original book draws richly on ME's domestic experience and family background. The Rackrent dynasty resembles her own forbears, while the tones of the narrator are patterned on the Edgeworths' steward. R. L. Edgeworth's liberal and tolerant attitudes in Irish politics are reflected in *Castle Rackrent*'s well-disposed (if arguably external) treatment of the native Irish. A concern for the dignity of the common man tends increasingly to coincide with an interest in the manners and in the distinctive language of the different classes and regions in the era of the American and French Revolutions. This egalitarian approach to language is illustrated in the work of the Edgeworths' favourite grammarian, John Horne Tooke (*Diversions of Purley*, 1787–1805), in Wordsworth's Preface to the *Lyrical Ballads* (1800), and in their own further defence of the Irish dialect, *Irish Bulls* (1802), where they represent Irish speech patterns as warm, witty, and eloquent, and of equal dignity with standard English.

During the 1790s, the Edgeworths' liberalism and supposed pro-French sympathies cut them off from their Protestant Anglo-Irish neighbours, somewhat isolating them on their Co. Longford estate. After the French invasion of Ireland was repelled in 1798 and Ireland's political union with England was engineered in 1800, animosities among the local gentry subsided, and the Edgeworths' social circle widened. Gradually ME's fiction reflects these changed circumstances, becoming richer in observed character and incident, and more conventional in attitude. For fifteen years she published continually: two full-length novels, *Belinda* (1801) and *Patronage* (1804), and, more characteristically, novellas and tales, *Popular Tales* (1804), *The Modern Griselda* (1805), *Leonora* (1806), and the six-volume *Tales of Fashionable Life* (1809 and 1812), which contains some of her finest writing, with 'Ennui' and 'Manoeuvring' included in the first issue, and 'Vivian', 'Emile de Coulanges' and 'The Absentee' in the second.

In 1802, during the brief lull in the Napoleonic Wars, Edgeworth took his fourth wife, Frances Beaufort, and his two elder unmarried daughters, ME and Charlotte, to Paris. They stayed there from October 1802 until March 1803, and moved in scientific and intellectual circles which already knew their work through the translations which were published in the Swiss periodical *Bibliothèque Brittanique*. While in Paris, ME met and considered marrying a Swedish courtier of scientific pursuits, Abraham Niclas Clewburg-Edelcrantz, an experience she recalled with emotion for many years. She gave as her reason for refusing him her reluctance to leave her father and her home.

ME had no equivalent experience of London society until her first lengthy visit there in 1813. Before that, however, her name attracted fashionable visitors to Edgeworthstown in increasing numbers, and during the first decade of the century, she corresponded with fellow writers and intellectuals such as Anna Laetitia Barbauld, Elizabeth Inchbald, Walter Scott, and Etienne Dumont (a friend of Mirabeau and Bentham). Her commanding position as a serious novelist ended when Scott took over her regional subject matter with *Waverley* in 1814. She wrote one more fine Irish novel, *Ormond*, in 1817, the year her father died. After this she declared that her motive for writing sustained fiction was gone; nevertheless, her last novel of domestic and fashionable life, *Helen* (1834), is probably her best on this theme. In her last thirty years she travelled in Ireland, England, and on the continent, recording her social encounters in pleasing, amusing letters, while at home she showed toughness and resourcefulness in helping her surviving stepmother to run the Edgeworthstown estate.

ME was undoubtedly the most commercially successful and prestigious novelist of her heyday, 1800–14. The £2,100 she earned from *Patronage* (1814) is three times Scott's £700 for *Waverley* (1814), which Lockhart thought unprecedented, and seven times Jane Austen's £300 for *Emma* (1816). ME calculated that in all she earned £11,062 8s. 10d. from her writing, and this for books which, unlike most other novels, were singled out for full-length and largely favourable reviews by the *Edinburgh Review* and the *Quarterly Review*. No Englishwoman had a comparable literary career before George Eliot's. For contemporary women, the most significant fact about ME may well have been her successful competition with men. Although she used a woman's form, she wrote for both sexes and (notably in *Patronage*) ignored the convention that politics and professional life could be discussed, as they could be experienced, only by men. But while not a doctrinaire feminist like Mary Wollstonecraft, ME was always consciously a woman writer who identified herself with a women's literary tradition. She acknowledged debts to Fanny Burney, Elizabeth Inchbald, Anna Laetitia Barbauld, Mme de Genlis, and Mme de Staël. Together with her father, she proposed to Barbauld in 1799 that they might combine to inaugurate a politically liberal women's journal, *The Feminead*, an idea scotched by Barbauld because women were ideologically too divided: 'Mrs Hannah More would not write along with you or me, & we should probably hesitate at joining Miss Hayes, or if she were living, Mrs Godwin.' Like other moderate feminists, ME was clearly embarrassed by Wollstonecraft's unconventional career; ME's novel *Belinda*, which urges that women should think and act independently, contains a hostile caricature of a mannish woman, Mrs Harriott Freke. (Writing even more pointedly in favour of women's self-sufficiency in *The Wanderer* (1814), Fanny Burney also includes an unflattering portrait of a feminist, Elinor Jodrell.) Having prudently disavowed at the outset that she wanted sexual emancipation for women, ME consistently claims equality of treatment for them. Her novels of English fashionable and domestic life portray women rather than men, and counter the contemporary tendency to polarize the sexes by denying that any personal characteristics, except the most foolish ones, are feminine. ME's women sound like women, for she is the first novelist to apply an insight articulated by Wollstonecraft, that women have their own language. But her women vary as much as her men, from the simplistic (Virginia in *Belinda*) to the intellectually pretentious (Olivia in *Leonora*), the manipulative (Mrs Beaumont in *Manoeuvring*), and the masterful (Lady Delacour in *Belinda*, Lady Davenant in *Helen*). The range of women character-types, which is unprecedented, amounts to a denial of typing. Almost as notable, ME deploys the stereotyped romance-and-marriage plot, but insists that marriage for women is an economic partnership with a man, and leads to a socially responsible task, the education of children. Her handling of plot reassesses the assumptions behind the conventions of the 'women's novel', even if she falls well short of Wollstonecraft's wholesale challenge.

Until recently ME's interesting position as a woman writer has been overlooked in favour of her more obviously innovatory treatment of Irish common life, in four short novels – *Castle Rackrent* (1800), *Ennui* (1809), *The Absentee* (1812), and *Ormond* (1817). In these works, Edgeworth documents Irish society, from the Anglo-Irish in their great houses to the peasants in their hovels, and she analyses the relations between classes with a subtlety belied by her didactic tone. The fundamentally liberal concern with the language of different orders and regions has already been defined as characteristic of the late Enlightenment. These were the features of ME's Irish fiction that helped to stimulate Scott's *Waverley*, as he acknowledges in his postscript, and thus to become key formal elements in the nineteenth-century European realistic novel.

ME's aesthetic assumptions, outside or prior to Romanticism, and her debts to an eighteenth-century genre, the moral tale, have cast long shadows over her work for the modern reader. Criticism has been overwhelmingly biographical, and crudely inclined to blame R. L. Edgeworth for his supposed appropriation of his daughter's work: Virginia Woolf does this, in a superficial essay in *The Common Reader*. Certainly ME resembles many women writers of her period, including Burney, Hester Thrale, Barbauld, de Staël and Jane Austen, in seeking a special intimacy with her father, and in viewing her writing as in some sense his. There is virtually no substance in the often-repeated charge that he interfered in the detail of her stories. During her most productive decades, 1795–1814, he probably steered her, consciously and unconsciously, toward more writing on public, masculine, 'serious' subjects, less in the accepted feminine mode of what he called 'pretty stories and novellettes'. In this he acted unlike other patriarchal mentors, and arguably to her advantage. On the other hand, the scale of values he thus communicated may have inhibited her from identifying with her female protagonists, as other women writers were wont to do. The great exception is the novel she wrote without him, *Helen*, a sympathetic study of the conflicting loyalties of two young women caught between patriarchal authority, with its moral absolutes, and their affection for one another. This intelligent and characteristically individual book was admired and imitated (in *Wives and Daughters*) by Elizabeth Gaskell, the Victorian novelist who most resembles ME.   MARILYN BUTLER

Selected works: Letters for Literary Ladies (1795); *The Parent's Assistant* (1796); *Practical Education* (1798); *Castle Rackrent* (1800); *Moral Tales for Young People* (1801); *Belinda* (1801); *Popular Tales* (1804); *The Modern Griselda* (1805); *Leonora* (1806); *Tales of Fashionable Life* (1809, 1812); *Patronage* (1814); *Harrington: A Tale; and Ormond: A Tale* (1817); (ed.), *Memoirs of Richard Lovell Edgeworth*, vol. 2 (1820); *Thoughts on Bores, Janus* (1826); *Little Plays for Children* (1827); *Helen* (1834).

References: Butler, M., *Maria Edgeworth* (1972); Colvin, C., *Maria Edgeworth: Letters from England* (1971); Hare, A. J. C., *The Life and Letters of Maria Edgeworth* (1894); Lawless, E., *Maria Edgeworth* (1904); Newby, P. H., *Maria Edgeworth* (1950); Simon, B., *Studies in the History of Education, 1780–1870* (1960); Tompkins, J. M. S., *The Popular Novel in England 1770–1800* (1932); Zimmern, H., *Maria Edgeworth* (1883).

Edwards, Amelia

b. 7 June 1831, London; d. 15 April 1892, Weston-super-Mare, Somerset
Novelist, travel writer
AE was the daughter of a banker and educated at home by her mother. She began her literary career as a journalist writing lead articles and fine arts criticism

for periodicals such as the *Morning Post* and the *Saturday Review*. In 1855 her first novel, *My Brother's Wife*, was published. This first success was followed by seven more of the same type of romantic story. Of her novels, *Barbara's History* (1864) and *Lord Brackenbury* (1880) are most representative of AE's fiction. Both are set outside England and tell the story of unhappy and unsuccessful love. *Barbara's History* is the story of a young, immature girl who goes to college in Germany and is married only to be estranged from her husband for mysterious reasons. In addition to these early fictional works, AE also wrote *The History of France* (1856) and *A Summary of English History* (1858), translated Fanny Lavoit's *A Lady's Captivity among Chinese Pirates in the China Seas* (1858) and edited and appeared in *Home Thoughts and Home Themes: Poems* (1865). AE has three poems in this eighty-page volume and her fellow contributors included Jennett Humphreys, Dora Greenwell and Mrs Norton. The volume is tastefully illustrated with pictures by A. B. Houghton based on engravings of domestic scenes by the Dalziel brothers. AE's poetry is amateur and sentimental. Only one piece, 'The Scramble for Sugarplums', is written in a standard poetic form (octosyllabic couplets). This poem also shows the influence of Thomas Gray and Charlotte Smith in lines such as, 'Laugh and scramble, shout and play/ Happy children, while you may/ Life soon loses its completeness.' Another poem, 'Mock Burial', takes as its subject some children the author has seen on the beach who are burying their pet dog in mock ceremony, which allows AE to speculate on the seriousness of death and the children's cavalier attitude towards it. Finally, 'The Pleasures and Pains of Childhood' is an interesting poem. Addressed to a sibling, the piece describes how children are easily frightened by the fairy stories and tall tales intended to amuse them and this idea is re-evaluated by the mature adult.

1873 was the turning point in AE's career. After publication of *Untrodden Peaks and Unfrequented Valleys*, which described her travels in Switzerland, she journeyed into Egypt with a companion indentified only as 'L'. In 1877, AE published an account of her trip illustrated with her own excellent and accurate drawings. *A Thousand Miles up the Nile*, which went into three editions in her lifetime, describes AE's trip from Cairo to Abu Simbel and into the Nubian Desert. As the narrative shows, AE was deeply inspired by what she saw and was especially encouraged when she and her companions found a previously undiscovered temple dedicated to Ramses and his followers. To commemorate the discovery the group's initials were carved on an empty stone near the entrance and a letter was sent to *The Times* dated 16 February 1874 announcing the find. The discovery of this monument to ancient civilization with its painted atrium, chambers, and stairways, moved AE to work towards conservation of such treasures. Upon her return to England in 1874, she laid the foundation for the Egypt Exploration Fund, whose primary purpose was to excavate artefacts and locate temples and monuments for preservation. In 1882, AE was made an honorary secretary of the organization.

After 1880, AE devoted herself exclusively to lecturing and writing on Egyptian treasures and civilization. During a lecture tour in America in 1889, she broke her arm and her health began to decline. She published her second book-length study of Egyptian culture in 1892, the year of her death. *Pharoahs, Fellahs and Explorers* is an encyclopedia of Egyptian culture. Her translation of Sir Gaston Maspero's *Manual of Egyptian Archaeology: For the Use of Students and Travellers* was published posthumously. In the late winter of 1892, AE contracted influenza and died in the spring. Her collection of artefacts was bequeathed to University College in London along with her library and £2,415 for the first chair in Egyptology in the United Kingdom. AE contributed the article on 'Egyptology' to the *Encyclopedia Britannica*; she received an honorary doctorate from Columbia University; and she was a member of the Biblical Archaeological Society and the Society for the Promotion of Hellenic Studies.

B. E. SCHNELLER

Works: *My Brother's Wife* (1855); *A Summary of English History* (1856); *The Ladder of Life* (1857); *A History of France* (1858); (trans.), *A Lady's Captivity Among Chinese Pirates in the China Sea*, by Fanny Lavoit; *Hand and Glove* (1859); *The Story of Cervantes* (1863); *Barbara's History* (1864); *Sights and Sounds* (1865); *Home Thoughts and Home Themes: Poems* (1865); *Debenham's Vow* (1869); *In the Days of My Youth, Monsieur Maurice* (1873); *Untrodden Peaks and Unfrequented Valleys: A Mid-summer Ramble in the Dolomites* (1873); *A Thousand Miles up the Nile* (1877); (ed.), *A Poetry Book of Modern Poets* (1879); (ed.), *A Poetry Book of Elder Poets* (1879); *Lord Brackenbury* (1880); *Pharoahs, Fellahs, and Explorers* (1892); (trans.), *A Manual of Egyptian Archeology: For the Use of Students and Travellers* by Sir Gaston Maspero (1902).

References: Allibone; BA (19).

Egerton, George

b. 1859, Melbourne, Australia; d. 1945, Ifield Park, Crawley, Sussex
Short story writer, novelist

GE (Mary Chavelita Dunne) was born in Melbourne, Australia, and grew up travelling around the world. She worked in London and New York as a nurse and at various other occupations, before she began travelling again with her father's friend, Henry Higginson, and his lady companion. Higginson was a bigamist, and he and GE eloped to Norway in 1887.

Two years later, Higginson died; GE stayed in Norway, studying the works of Strindberg, Ibsen, Bjornsen, and other Scandinavian writers. She met Knut Hamsen (a meeting recorded in her story 'A Cross Line') and on her return to London in 1890 she translated his novel *Hunger*. In 1891 she married George Egerton Clairmonte and moved to Ireland, where she began to write seriously. In the same year, a publisher, John Lane, accepted the series of six short stories published as *Keynotes*, which became a literary sensation, bringing their author both fame and notoriety, which were confirmed by the second series, *Discords*, the following year. A son was born to GE in 1895; after this her marriage ended. In 1901 she married drama critic Reginald Golding Bright, and began to try her hand at plays and adaptations, but her later writing was unsuccessful; her earlier fame waned fast. She died at her Sussex home in 1945.

GE's notorious literary success in the 1890s was largely forgotten until the republication by Virago of her first and best-known works in 1983, and even at the time her fame, though considerable, was short-lived. Her early works are worth reading now, however, for their vision and for the celebration of the potential in women's lives, in which their author passionately believed.

The publication of *Keynotes* in 1893 placed GE in the vanguard of the 'New Woman' movement, which explored the possibilities which might open up for women once patriarchal attitudes in society began to change. Unlike her contemporary Sarah Grand, who confined her attention to the improvement of women's lot within marriage, GE chose to emphasize the importance of honouring women's sexuality and regarded respectability as a male construct. She is an idealist, involved in the creation of literary symbols and the celebration of potential, rather than one dealing with the minutiae of how to live in society without irredeemably compromising one's aims, which links her more closely to the literary movement of the times than the social one in which many women were involved. Despite this she owes less, stylistically, to the fashion for decadence than she does to the spiritual symbolism of the Scandinavian writers. Her critics failed to notice this; *Punch* satirized her as 'Borgia Smudgiton', and *Blackwood's Magazine* contributor Hugh Stutfield classed her (along with most other female writers, especially Sarah Grand who was really not eligible) as an 'erotomaniac'. Her writing in fact cannot be said to be erotic compared with other contributors to *The Yellow Book*, such as Beardsley, but it does regard the physical and emotional realities of life in the way that is now regarded as typical of women's writing. 'Now Spring Has Come' is a wry acceptance of the perishable quality of romantic illusion; in 'A Cross Line', a woman rejects the possible development of deep friendship with a man, not out of fidelity to her husband so much as from recognition that she will require all her spiritual energy to give birth to her newly conceived child. The stories of *Discords* are darker and chilling, to this day, in their acknowledgement of the lasting damage caused to young girls by ignorance ('Virgin Soil') and of the ungovernable, destructive nature of human passions when diverted from their natural courses ('Wedlock'). The opening of this story shows GE's writing at its best; the break-up of a stately garden into lots for the building of mean houses is an eloquent symbol of the ruin of a woman's life by the imposition of restrictions by society and unimaginative men. Unfortunately GE did not build on this strength; her style has a tendency to gallop through events without proper attention to the atmosphere necessary for successful symbolism, and she veers uneasily between past and present tenses; despite her talents – and her exposure to society had given her insight into the lives and preoccupations of many classes which she used creatively – her subsequent work represents a falling-off.   JENNIFER PLASTOW

Works: *Keynotes* (1893); *Discords* (1894); *Young Ofeg's Ditties* (1895); *Symphonies* (1897); *Fantasias* (1898); *The Wheel of God* (1898); *Rosa Amorosa* (1901); *Flies in Amber* (1905).

References: Cunningham, G., *The New Woman and the Victorian Novel* (1978); De Vere White, T., *A Leaf from the Yellow Book: The Correspondence of George Egerton* (1958); Harris, W. V., 'Egerton: forgotten realist', *Victorian Newsletter* (Spring 1968); Stubbs, P., *Women and Fiction: Feminism and the Novel 1880–1920* (1979); Vicinus, M., 'Introduction' to *Keynotes* and *Discords* (1983).

Egerton, Sarah

b. 1670(?), London; d. 13 February 1723, Winslow, Buckinghamshire

Poet

(Also wrote under S.F.; S.F.E.; Clarinda; Mrs Field)

SE was the daughter of Thomas Fyge, physician and city councilman of London, and Mary Beacham of Seaton, Rutland. In 1686, at the age of 16, SE published *The Female Advocate*, a response in verse to Robert Gould's scathing satire on women, *Love Given O'er, or, A Satyr against the Pride, Lust, and Inconstancy, of Woman* (1682). According to her autobiographical poems in *Poems on Several Occasions* (1703), her father, angered by SE's act of publishing and the ensuing notoriety, banished her from their London home to the country.

Within the next few years SE married, apparently against her will, an attorney, Edward Field. SE appears to have been an avid student, ostentatiously displaying in her poems some knowledge of Latin, Greek mythology, history, and philosophy. Edward Field encouraged SE in her scholarly pursuits, but because she married unwillingly, she showed little appreciation for his support until after his death, which occurred around 1695. She then fell in love with her husband's clerk, Henry Pierce, a married man whom she calls 'Alexis'. SE wrote over 120 love letters to him, and made him gifts of money. When she was nearly 30, she was made to marry a distant cousin, Thomas Egerton, of Adstock, Buckinghamshire, an elderly clergyman with grown-up children. SE's former friend, the writer Delarivier Manley, describes violent physical battles between SE and her second husband, and claims that SE tried to choke Egerton's daughter with her bare hands. In 1703 SE sued Egerton for divorce on the grounds of cruelty, claiming that he neglected to send for medical help when she was having fits; Egerton in turn claimed that she had run off to London for a time with Pierce, taking Egerton's money with her. In the same year, SE, her father, and Pierce were subpoenaed to appear in Chancery, where Egerton sued for money and property left to SE by her first husband. Apparently, the divorce suit was unsuccessful. Egerton died in 1720, and SE three years after him. She was buried in Winslow, the home of her landowning gentry ancestors.

Her literary reputation was primarily based on her earliest work, *The Female Advocate*, in which she defends women's position in society.

> Surely then she a Noble Creature is,
> Whom Heav'n thus made to consummate all Bliss.
> Tho' Man had Being first, yet methinks She
> In Nature should have the Supremacy.

Similar viewpoints are expressed in 'The Liberty' (*Poems on Several Occasions*) in which SE complains,

> My Sex forbids, I should my Silence break,
> I lose my Jest, cause Women must not Speak.
> Mysteries must not be, with my Search Prophan'd,
> My Closet not with Books, but Sweat-meats cram'd

and in 'The Emulation':

> And shall we Women now sit tamely by,
> Make no excursions in Philosophy,
> Or grace our Thoughts in tuneful Poetry?
> We will our Rights in Learning's World maintain,
> Wits Empire, now, shall know a Female Reign.

SE knew a number of literary and theatrical figures of her day. She was a friend of John Froud, whose *The Grove, or, The Rival Muses* (1701) praises 'Clarinda['s] . . . immortal Fire'. SE addressed poems to Joshua Barnes, a noted antiquarian, the poet laureate, Nahum Tate, and Elizabeth Bracegirdle, the actress. Her pastoral 'The Fond Shepherdess' is dedicated to Congreve. SE and Elizabeth Thomas (the 'Corinna' of Pope's *Dunciad*) were the only women to publish poems on Dryden's death in the collection *Luctus Brittanici, or, The Tears of the British Muses* (1700). Along with Manley, Catharine Trotter, Lady Sarah Piers, Mary Pix, and Susannah Centlivre, she published three more elegies in *The Nine Muses, or, Poems upon the Death of the Late Famous John Dryden Esq.* (1700). SE's last known work is unpublished, 'The Essay Address'd to the Illustrious prince and Duke of Marlboro after the long Campaigne 1708' (Huntington Library MS EL 8796).

Although SE's work, as a whole, will never establish her as anything more than a minor literary figure, it is a testament to the concerns of women of her time, their need for self-expression, their longing for education, and their suffering under the constraints of 'Tyrant Custom'. The poems are alternately forceful in their claims for women's rights, and plaintive in their depiction of SE as a tragic victim of fate, a misunderstood, intellectual woman of artistic sensibilities.   JESLYN MEDOFF

Works: *The Female Advocate, or, An Answer To A Late Satyr Against the Pride, Lust, and Inconstancy Of Woman: Written by a Lady in Vindication of her Sex* (1686); 'An Ode, on the Death of John Dryden, Esq. By a Young Lady', in *Luctus Brittanici* (1700); 'Erato: the amorous muse', 'Euterpe: the lyric muse', and 'Terpsichore: a lyrick muse', in *The Nine Muses* (1700); *Poems on Several Occasions, Together with a Pastoral* (1703).

References: Anderson, P. B., 'Mistress Delarivière Manley's biography', *Modern Philology* 33 (1936); Ferguson, M., *First Feminists: British Women Writers 1578–1799* (1985); *The Gentleman's Magazine* (December 1780, March 1781, October 1781); Greer, G. et al. (eds), *Kissing the Rod* (1988); Hobby, E., *Virtue of Necessity: British Women Writers 1640–1688* (1988); Köster, P. (ed.), *The Novels of Mary Delarivière Manley* (1971); Medoff, J., 'New light on Sarah Fyge (Field, Egerton)', *Tulsa Studies in Women's Literature* 1 (1982); Nussbaum, F., *The Brink of All We Hate: English Satires on Women 1660–1750* (1983); Nussbaum, F., 'Introduction' to *Satires on Women* 180 (1976); Smith, H. L., *Reason's Disciples: Seventeenth Century English Feminists* (1982).

Eliot, George

b. 22 November 1819, South Farm, Arbury, Warwickshire; d. 22 December 1880, Cheyne Walk, Chelsea, London
Novelist, essayist, poet

GE (Mary Ann Evans) was the third child of Robert Evans and his second wife, Christiana Pearson. Evans, a carpenter by trade, had been agent for Francis Parker, who in 1806 became heir to the Newdigate-Newdegate family estates, when Sir Roger Newdigate, who had redesigned Arbury Hall in the Gothic revival style, died childless. Evans accompanied Francis Parker Newdigate to Warwickshire, taking up residence at South Farm. In spring 1820, a few months after the birth of his third daughter, Evans moved his family to Griff House, on the Coventry Road; the young Mary Ann, along with her brother Isaac, three years her senior, attended a dame school across the road from Griff House until 1824, when she joined her sister Chrissey at Miss Lathom's School in Attleborough. In 1828, she was sent to Mrs Wallington's School in Nuneaton, where the principal governess was Maria Lewis, whose Evangelical fervour influenced GE throughout her adolescence, even after GE transferred to the Miss Franklins' school in Coventry in 1832. After her mother's death in 1836, GE managed her father's household, first at Griff and then at Foleshill, where she and her father moved in 1841 to make room at Griff House for Isaac and his new bride. She continued her studies at home, and her extensive reading and her growing friendship with Charles and Caroline Hennell Bray, beginning in November 1841, led her to question the Evangelical doctrines she had so enthusiastically espoused in the 1830s; an estrangement from her father resulted from her refusal to attend church, a situation remedied after many months when she again went to church and Robert Evans asked no questions about her beliefs. Her first publications indicate the transformation in her views; in January 1840 a fervently Evangelical poem signed 'M.A.E.' appeared in the *Christian Observer*; in 1846, her translation of David Friedrich Strauss's *Das*

Jesu was published, without her name, under the title *The Life of Jesus, Critically Examined.*

GE continued to read and study and to take charge of Robert Evans's house until he died in 1849, leaving her £2,000 in trust and £100 cash. Shortly afterwards, she began a continental tour with the Brays and remained behind in Geneva, where she spent eight months. Her father's legacy being insufficient to support her, on her return from Switzerland GE rented a room in the house of London publisher John Chapman at 142 Strand and became the actual though not nominal editor of the *Westminster Review* from 1852 to 1854. In the essays she wrote for the *Westminster*, the *Leader*, and other periodicals during the 1850s, she continued the attention to fiction that she had begun in her reading at the Miss Franklins' school and in her reviews for the *Coventry Herald* in the late 1840s. Two principles these reviews and articles establish are essential for understanding her own fiction: the importance of portraying the ordinary lives of ordinary people in a realistic rather than an idealized fashion, and the necessity of showing the demoralizing effects of poverty and oppression for both oppressors and oppressed. Among the most important essays addressing the first idea are 'The Morality of Wilhelm Meister' (*Leader*, 21 July 1855), in which she stresses the immorality of a fictional ending in which events are arranged 'according to those notions of justice on which the novel-writer would have recommended that the world should be governed if he had been consulted at the creation', and 'The Natural History of German Life' (*Westminster Review*, July 1856), in which she urges that the role of the artist is to make his audience 'feel, not for the heroic artisan or the sentimental peasant, but for the peasant in all his coarse apathy, and the artisan in all his suspicious unselfishness'. In this essay, she stresses too the 'miserable fallacy that high morality and refined sentiment can grow out of harsh social relations, ignorance, and want', a point that she makes later the same year in a review of Harriet Beecher Stowe's *Dred (Westminster Review*, October 1856), when she condemns Stowe's too-optimistic picture of blacks under slavery: 'If the negroes are really so very good, slavery has answered as moral discipline. But apart from the argumentative suicide involved in this one-sidedness, Mrs Stowe loses by it the most terribly tragic element in the relation of the two races – the Nemesis lurking in the vices of the oppressed.'

In 1854 she published a translation of Ludwig Feuerbach's *Das Wesen des Christenthums* and assisted George Henry Lewes with his columns in the *Leader* when he became ill that spring. Lewes, a successful writer in many fields, and a contributor to the *Westminster Review*, had, partly out of principle and perhaps out of a sense of guilt at being responsible for his wife's infidelity, acknowledged as his own a son born to Agnes Lewes on 16 April 1850, whose father was in fact Thornton Hunt. Agnes, who had three more children by Hunt in the 1850s, continued to be supported by Lewes, with the children taking his name; because he had in effect condoned the adultery, Lewes was unable to obtain a divorce. Hence, to form their own union which both regarded as a marriage though the law did not, he and GE were forced to defy Victorian mores, an act which caused both considerable soul searching and resulted in GE's estrangement from her beloved brother Isaac and from many of the women of her society, who could not risk visiting her without danger to their own reputations. The couple first made their union public when they went together to Weimar, leaving London on 20 July 1854 and remaining in Germany for eight months. Though many of GE's friends feared the consequences for her of an unsanctioned union with a man they regarded as unreliable, the 'marriage' lasted twenty-four years, until Lewes's death on 30 November 1878.

GE's diffidence about publishing as well as the problems posed by her relationship with Lewes made it imperative that her first work of fiction, *Scenes of Clerical Life*, be published anonymously. Lewes handled the transactions with John Blackwood, setting the pattern of managing her dealings with publishers throughout her career. She had begun the first story of the three included in this series in September 1856, soon after sending off to John Chapman an essay called 'Silly Novels by Lady Novelists' (published in the *Westminster*, October 1856), in which she condemned the unreality of many women's novels, singling out the 'white-neck cloth species', the Evangelical version of the High Church 'oracular' type – both equally silly. In *Scenes*, despite her personal unbelief, she presents sympathetically but realistically the human beings within the Evangelical branch of the Established Church. The settings are so distinctly those of her childhood that one can, for instance, use the middle story, 'Mr Gilfil's Love Story', as a guide to Sir Roger Newdigate's Gothic renovations of Arbury Hall. Published in *Blackwood's* from January to November 1857, *Scenes* appeared in two volumes in January 1858. Though at times during the serialization John Blackwood had thought the stories almost too realistic, the reviews were favourable and encouraged GE in the early parts of *Adam Bede*, which were already underway.

Though she had originally conceived of *Adam Bede* as another scene from clerical life, GE was disheartened by Blackwood's hesitations and decided to stop the series with 'Janet's Repentance' and expand her new story. This story began with two characters out of her childhood: Adam Bede is clearly based on her father, Robert Evans, and Dinah Morris, in her role as a Methodist preacher and ministrant to a young girl condemned for child murder, is based loosely on her aunt, Mrs Samuel Evans. With the possible exception of the 'The Harvest Supper', chapter 53, there is none of the 'coarse' peasantry that Eliot advocated in her earlier essays as showing a true picture of rural life; still, the book, as its famous chapter 17 states, was intended to give a picture of life among people 'more or less commonplace and vulgar'. Published on 1 February 1859, *Adam Bede* received enthusiastic reviews. Its popularity made it the benchmark by which her subsequent fiction was judged; reviews of even her last two novels tended to refer to GE as 'the author of *Adam Bede*'. Popularity also increased speculation about the author's identity, and GE's anonymity could no longer be preserved, particularly in the face of claims made by a Warwickshire clergyman, Joseph Liggins, to have written both *Scenes* and *Adam Bede*.

The composition of her next book, *The Mill on the Floss*, was interrupted by what she called an 'outré' story, 'The Lifted Veil', which appeared in *Blackwood's* in July 1859. It is a melancholy tale of clairvoyance, in the mode Dickens and Gaskell were popularizing. With *The Mill on the Floss*, however, GE returned to her more typical realistic mode. Though it is dangerous to identify any fictional character too closely with its creator, Maggie Tulliver is in many ways a young GE; the Tulliver farm is Griff House, with its Round Pool; the Dodson sisters are her Aunts Pearson, her mother's sisters with a penchant for respectability; and Tom Tulliver is her brother Isaac, whose disapproval of her 'marriage' to Lewes, which she announced to him in May 1857, nearly three years after it began, ended any intercourse between them until after Lewes's death and GE's marriage to John Walter Cross. The pain of that separation and the disapproval that occasioned it are evident throughout the novel in Maggie's need to please her conventional brother. From its opening chapters in which Maggie is, in her father's judgement, too acute for a girl, and in her mother's too unruly, the novel protests against the sexual stereotyping of children, as well as the failures of love and sympathy that GE saw as flaws in human relationships. In this as in her first two works of fiction, she attempted to extend the knowledge of others' lives, knowledge she saw as essential to developing human understanding and human sympathy. Although Lewes originally considered serialization, in imitation of Dickens's popular method of publishing, *The Mill on the Floss* was published in three volumes by Blackwood, in April 1860.

Eliot and Lewes had already left for Rome, where John Blackwood kept them informed of outstanding sales and enthusiastic reviews. In mid-May they went on to Florence, where GE began to contemplate an ambitious new project, a historical novel dealing with the life of Savonarola. Back in England, in summer 1860, however, GE turned to the story that became 'Brother Jacob' (it appeared in the *Cornhill Magazine* in July 1864) and in September began work on *Silas Marner*, published by Blackwood in one volume in April 1861. GE said the story came to her first as a 'legendary tale', but that she soon turned to a 'more realistic treatment' (*Letters* III, 382). The bare outlines recall the powerful simplicity of the legend of St Ogg in *The Mill on the Floss*, but it was the realism and humour of Mrs Winthrop, the Lammeters, and the scene at the Rainbow that appealed to John Blackwood and attracted readers and reviewers. The *Saturday Review* notice (13 April 1861) could have been written by GE herself in the mid–1850s, so closely does it connect her achievement with the goals she outlined for fiction: 'it is in the portraiture of the poor . . . that this writer is without a rival. [The work gives] a new revelation of what society in quiet English parishes really is.' Comparing Dolly Winthrop with the 'model cottager's wife' of the usual 'lady-novelist', the notice concludes, 'The one is a living woman, the other is an improveable puppet.'

The predominance of the legendary and ideal is more noticeable in her next novel, *Romola*, despite the realistic texture provided by details on Savonarola and his times, carefully researched through extensive reading and a second trip to Florence in May and June 1861. Though generally 'diffident' about her writing (a word Lewes used frequently to refer to her uncertainty about the artistic value of her work), she was particularly anxious about publishing a historical novel which, despite the genre's popularity since Sir Walter Scott, did not offer the setting which readers had come to expect from her – rural England one or two generations in the past. The method of publication also posed difficulties. Though she had considered instalments in *Blackwood's*, George Smith made a lucrative offer of £10,000 for sixteen monthly parts in the *Cornhill*, which GE altered to £7,000 for twelve instalments. With illustrations by Frederic Leighton, *Romola* began in July 1862, and having been extended to fourteen instalments, ended in August 1863. The three-volume edition was issued in July 1863 by Smith, Elder. Despite its intellectual appeal to many readers, *Romola* was not the popular success that her earlier, English novels had been, nor was it the financial success George Smith had anticipated. Yet, though the setting is different, the novel is unmistakably GE's in its moral thrust. The story of Tito Melema illustrates the irrevocable and widespread consequences that result from a single choice of good or evil and the dangers of a life that is not 'rooted in memories' (chapter 9). The decisions of conscience that Tito faces anticipate the struggles of Gwendolen Harleth in GE's last novel, *Daniel Deronda*.

Her next two novels return to the Midlands of her early work, the scenes of her childhood. Despite the familiar setting, GE did extensive research for *Felix Holt, the Radical*, which was published by Blackwood in three volumes in June 1866. Her correspondence with Frederic Harrison regarding the legal complexities on which the plot turns reveals her attention to the details of her novels. *Felix Holt* continues GE's probing of the consequences of human actions and her emphasis on sympathy through knowledge of other human lives. At the same time, the novel incorporates several features popular from the sensation fiction of the 1860s: the child of unknown or unrevealed parentage, the complex inheritance problem, adultery, and illegitimacy. Though sometimes referred to as GE's 'political novel', because of its focus on the first Reform Bill and its appearance one year before the second, *Felix Holt* manifests GE's concern with broad human issues rather than with narrowly topical ones.

Throughout much of 1867 and early 1868, GE was occupied with *The Spanish Gypsy*, a long poem published by Blackwood in June 1868. Reviews generally were favourable and sales were good, despite the melodramatic, rather far-fetched subject and treatment. Working on other poems and her new idea for 'A Novel called Middlemarch' (GE Journal, 1 January 1869) in 1869, she and Lewes were also preoccupied with the illness of his son Thornton, who died in October 1869 at the Priory, where he had been with them since returning in May from six years in Natal. The design for *Middlemarch* was not complete until May 1871, when GE realized that it would run to four volumes. Lewes began to consider a new method of publication – serialization in eight parts, each forming a half-volume. Blackwood approved, and the first part appeared in December 1871, followed by bimonthly parts until October 1872; the November and December instalments completed the work, which was widely acclaimed, even though many reviewers found the serialization, especially with the two-month intervals, confusing and annoying.

Like *Felix Holt*, *Middlemarch* is set at the time of the first Reform Bill, but its concerns are with failed human aspirations in its central characters, Dorothea Brooke and Tertius Lydgate. In particular it delineates the disastrous effects of the narrow scope permitted to women in the nineteenth century. The nemesis in the vices of the oppressed that GE had discussed in her essay on Stowe's *Dred* is demonstrated in Rosamond Vincy, where the superficiality and self-centredness encouraged by her education and upbringing as a 'model' young woman lead to misery not only for herself but for others as well. In Dorothea too is illustrated the waste of human potential that comes when women are measured only as adjuncts to someone else, not as beings who are themselves capable of taking up some great work. The novel's four linked plots provide a comprehensive view of English provincial society. Humorous characters like Mr Brooke and Mrs Cadwallader, whose sharp tongue reminded readers of *Adam Bede's* Mrs Poyser, also connected *Middlemarch* with her early work.

The idea for the opening scene of her last novel, *Daniel Deronda*, came in September 1872, when GE noted a scene at a roulette table in Homburg, but work proceeded slowly, being interrupted in 1874 for the completion of poems that made up *The Legend of Jubal, and Other Poems*, published in May that year. Though *Middlemarch* had been hailed by many reviewers as the greatest work of England's 'greatest living novelist', initial reviews of *Deronda* were equally enthusiastic. With the commercial as well as artistic success of *Middlemarch*, Lewes and GE had decided to repeat part publication, though without the confusing shift from bimonthly to monthly numbers. Appearing from February to September 1876, *Deronda* was a break with practice in several respects: it is set contemporaneously, frequently in London or on the continent; it deals with the upper classes of English society; and it offers a detailed exploration of Anglo-Jewish life. Many reviewers felt, and some later critics have agreed, that the 'Gwendolen' portion of the plot was GE at her finest, but that the so-called

'Jewish' portion had little appeal. In fact, the two parts are closely linked. Gwendolen is a fully developed type of which Rosamond Vincy (*Middlemarch*) and Esther Lyon (*Felix Holt*) are, comparatively, sketches: the young woman with no view beyond her own wishes. Deronda, an outsider in English society, is a foil to this narrow self-centredness – not only Gwendolen's, but also that of the whole of English society of the 1860s. The social criticism results in no definite plan for Gwendolen or for England, but Deronda, the ideal character, finds his mission in establishing a Jewish homeland in the East. Hailed by the Anglo-Jewish press as an unusually sympathetic treatment, *Daniel Deronda* was still being celebrated in Israel on its centenary in 1976.

Particularly in the 1870s, in the face of her growing fame, GE began to be 'visited' and invited to dinner even by women of high social standing. Lewes died in November 1878, and after his death, she turned for solace to completing his *Problems of Life and Mind* and her own *Impressions of Theophrastus Such*, a collection of essays, including one, 'The Modern Hep! Hep! Hep!', which took up again the Zionist theme of *Daniel Deronda*. They were published by Blackwood in May 1879, along with *The Study of Psychology*, volume 1 of Lewes's work. She began to depend more and more on their common friend and business adviser, John Walter Cross, whose third proposal of marriage GE accepted. They were married in May 1880. After a wedding trip to Venice, they returned to the house they had purchased in Chelsea, where GE died a few months later.   CAROL A. MARTIN

Works: (trans.), *Das Leben Jesu*, by D. F. Strauss (1846); (trans.), *Das Wesen des Christentums*, by L. Feuerbach (1854); *Scenes of Clerical Life* (1858); *Adam Bede* (1859); *The Mill on the Floss* (1860); *Silas Marner* (1861); *Romola* (1863); *Felix Holt* (1866); *The Spanish Gypsy* (1868); *Middlemarch* (1872); *Legend of Jubal and Other Poems* (1874); *Daniel Deronda* (1876); *Impressions of Theophrastus Such* (1879); *Letters*, ed. G. S. Haight (1954–5, 1978–9); *Essays of George Eliot*, ed. T. Pinney (1963); *Some George Eliot Notebooks: An Edition of the Carl H. Pforzheimer Library's George Eliot Holograph Notebooks*, ed. W. Baker vols 1–4, (1976–85).

References: Bonaparte, F., *Will and Destiny, Morality and Tragedy in George Eliot's Novels* (1975); Carroll, D. (ed.), *George Eliot: The Critical Heritage* (1971); Cross, J. W., *The Life of George Eliot* (1885); Ermarth, E. D., 'George Eliot's conception of sympathy', *Nineteenth-Century Fiction* 40 (1985); 'George Eliot 1880–1980', *Nineteenth-Century Fiction* 35, special issue (December 1980); Graver, Suzanne, *George Eliot and Community* (1984); Haight, G. S., *George Eliot: A Biography* (1968); Hardy, Barbara (ed.), *Critical Essays on George Eliot* (1970); Harvey, W. J., *The Art of George Eliot* (1963); Leavis, F. R., *The Great Tradition* (1948); Mann, K. B., *The Language That Makes George Eliot's Fiction* (1983); Mintz, A., *George Eliot and the Novel of Vocation* (1978); Redinger, R. V., *George Eliot: The Emergent Self* (1975); Welsh, A. *George Eliot and Blackmail* (1985); Woolf, V., 'George Eliot', *The Common Reader* (1925).

Elizabeth I, Queen

b. 7 September 1533, Greenwich; d. 24 March 1603, Richmond
Poet, devotional writer, orator

After a youth which included the execution of her mother, Anne Boleyn, her brother's accession to the throne after Henry VIII's death in 1547, and her own imprisonment during the reign of her Catholic sister Mary, E became Queen of England in 1558. Roger Ascham and his pupil William Grindal, who were amongst the finest scholars of the emerging Protestant humanism, had guided her education. Besides maintaining an interest in history and classical literature, she cultivated her knowledge of modern languages, which enabled her to treat directly with foreign emissaries. Much of her literary accomplishment depended on this linguistic facility. She knew not only some Spanish, Flemish, and German, but was expert enough in French, Italian, Latin, and Greek to write *A Book of Devotions* in these four languages as well as in English. These private prayers, compiled perhaps in the 1570s, are the most personal of E's writings, but they nevertheless reflect her sense of her political position.

Her translations demonstrate her linguistic competence rather than accomplished versifying. At the age of about 11, she rendered the 13th Psalm into tetrameters and Marguerite de Navarre's *Le Miroir de L'Ame Pecheresse* into prose (as *The Mirror of the Sinful Soul*). When 65 years old, she tackled Horace's 'Ars Poetica'. Her most polished piece is an early verse translation of ninety lines from Petrarch's 'Trionfo dell' Eternita'. Her longest is of Boethius's *De Consolatione Philosophiae* (1593). The frequent alliteration of this version may sound awkward to a modern ear, but some passages have considerable vigour. The numerous mistranslations and the Latinate word order may result from the rapidity with which E translated, according to contemporary accounts.

E also wrote original poems, although not all of those subsequently ascribed to her. Of the six definitely genuine pieces, three are only two- to four-line epigrams, and the others are under twenty lines long. This small body of work none the less has distinctive characteristics: the poems touch her particular situations, political and personal. They do not so much complain against fortune as assert her determination to overcome it. 'When I was fair and young' is a treatment of the familiar *carpe diem* topic: the poet regrets her rejection of all suitors in youth. Whilst its sentiments could evidently be applied to E's own refusal to marry, its treatment of them is indistinguishable from that of the many contemporary discussions of the same theme. The two other substantial pieces are less fashionable and are marked by the frequent alliteration and rougher meters characteristic of more traditional mid-century lyrics.

In her roles as princess and queen, E wrote many and varied letters. She could be remarkably direct, even with other monarchs, but, when her own feelings were ambivalent or when her purposes required that she should not commit herself, she could cloud her meaning in high diction, extended metaphors, and philosophical aphorisms.

Over a dozen of E's speeches survive and, although their occasions vary, they typically express trust in her people's goodwill and a desire for their security. Whilst some rhetorical features, such as a dependence on deductive reasoning and a penchant for comparisons and metaphors, remain fairly constant, her style changes: early speeches rely on an obfuscating adorned prose, while, as her political confidence increases, later performances grow more bold, if only in stating her evasiveness. In one case, she herself calls her response to a request an 'answer answerless'. The two most famous speeches, that at Tilbury to her troops as the Spanish Armada approached, and her final 'Golden' oration to Parliament, are unusually direct and dramatic.

SAYRE N. GREENFIELD AND JAMES SMITH

Works: *A Book of Devotions Composed by Her Majesty Elizabeth R*, trans. A. Fox and intro. J. Hodges (1970); *Mirror of the Sinful Soul*, ed. P. Ames (1897); *Marguerite de Navarre: Le Miroir de L'Ame Pecheresse: Edition critique et . . . la traduction faite par la princesse Elisabeth*, ed. R. Salminen (1979); *Queen Elizabeth's Englishings of Boethius . . . Plutarch . . . Horace*, ed. C. Pemberton (1899); *The Poems of Queen Elizabeth I*, ed. L. Bradner (1964); *The Letters of Queen*

Elizabeth I, ed. G. Harrison (1935); *The Public Speaking of Queen Elizabeth I: Selections*, ed. G. Rice (1951).
References: Allibone; Brooke, T., 'Queen Elizabeth's prayers', *Huntington Library Quarterly* 2 (1938); Erickson, C., *The First Elizabethan* (1983); Hageman, E., 'Recent studies in women writers of Tudor England', *English Literary Renaissance* 14 (1984); Haugaard, W., 'Elizabeth Tudor's *Book of Devotions*: a neglected clue to the queen's life and character', *Sixteenth-Century Journal* 12, 2 (1981); Heisch, A., 'Queen Elizabeth I: parliamentary rhetoric and the exercise of power', *Signs* 1 (1975); Hodges, J., *The Nature of the Lion* (1962); Johnson, P., *Elizabeth I: A Study in Power and Intellect* (1974); Levine, J., *Great Lives Observed: Elizabeth I* (1969); Neale, J., *Queen Elizabeth* (1934); Plowden, A., *The Young Elizabeth* (1971); Travitsky, B., *The Paradise of Women* (1981).

Elliott, Janice
b. 1931, Derbyshire
Novelist, writer for children
JE was educated at Nottingham High School for Girls and St Anne's College, Oxford. She married Robert Cooper in 1959, and has one son; they now live in Fowey, Cornwall.

Between 1954 and 1962 JE worked on the editorial staff of *House and Garden, House Beautiful, Harper's Bazaar* (as Beauty Editor), *The Sunday Times* Woman's Page, and *The Sunday Times Colour Magazine* at its launch; since then she has worked regularly as a reviewer, most recently, from 1969 until 1986, for *The Sunday Telegraph*. She also wrote a regular column in *Twentieth Century Magazine*, has published short stories, and has broadcast on radio and television, including scripting and presenting programmes on Saul Bellow and Patrick White for BBC television. Two of her novels have been filmed: *The Buttercup Chain* in 1970, and *Secret Places* in 1984.

JE's fiction is satirically inventive. The recent novels, especially, combine vivid and sympathetic portrayals of middle-class Britain in decline and fear with a world in which private dreams and nightmares manifest themselves terrifyingly in public life, and public events and images become the stuff of private hallucinations; the ironic narration also allows one to laugh at the plight of the characters. In *Secret Places* (1981), set in a girls' school and a Midlands city during the Second World War, a society wthout men is shown replicating the hatred and scapegoating of the public war; in *The Country of her Dreams* (1982) a Congress of European Arts squabbles hilariously over preserving its past in a future holocaust, while an English woman finds her individual identity dissolving among public violence and threats; in *Magic* (1983) pilgrims troop to a newly publicized shrine of the ancient British, to be acquired by the Ministry of Defence; the shrine hums noisily, its historian relives his other incarnations and is seen leaving this one on television, and his grandson eats Kentucky Fried Chicken during the dark night of the soul; in *The Italian Lesson* (1985) E. M. Forster's Italians, revisited, are now terrorists and their English admirers, in the 1980s, have become incompetent tourists, learned, kindly, full of liberal intentions, but overwhelmed by private griefs; in *Dr Gruber's Daughter* (1986) Hitler is manifested in an attic in a north Oxford house during the coronation spring of 1953, while a woman don downstairs succumbs suddenly to the lasciviousness of medieval literature, a housewife next door has regular chats with Lilibet while a policeman lusts for her flannel nightgown and spotted dick, and Anglican nuns across the road watch a hired television. S. F. P. REID

Works: *Cave with Echoes* (1962); *The Somnambulists* (1964); *The Godmother* (1966); *The Buttercup Chain* (1967); *The Singing Head* (1968); *Angels Falling* (1969); *The Kindling* (1970); *The Birthday Unicorn* (1970); *A State of Peace* (1971); *Private Life* (1972); *Alexander in the Land of Mog* (1973); *Heaven on Earth* (1975); *A Loving Eye* (1977); *The Honey Tree* (1978); *Summer People* (1980); *Secret Places* (1981); *The Country of her Dreams* (1982); *Magic* (1983); *The Italian Lesson* (1985); *Dr Gruber's Daughter* (1986); *The King Awakes* (1987); *The Sadness of Witches* (1987).

Ellis, Alice Thomas
b. Liverpool
Novelist, writer of non-fiction
(Also writes under Anna Haycraft)
ATE writes stylish novels of a range of themes including bereavement, love, class difference, and sexuality. She also writes non-fictional books under her real name, Anna Haycraft.

ATE was born in Liverpool before 1939; she was educated at Bangor Grammar School and Liverpool School of Art. Her parents belonged to the Church of Humanity, but she became a Catholic convert at the age of 19, and she is a practising Catholic, in favour of full ritual and formality: her religious beliefs pervade her novels. She describes herself as 'extremely feministic'. She is married to Colin Haycraft, chairman and managing director of Duckworth publishers, of which she is a director and the fiction editor. The have five children, and live in London.

ATE's books are extremely witty, carefully crafted analyses of the moral choices facing a range of female characters. Her female protagonists are invariably rather eccentric or scatty, and are frequently not completely aware of the effects of their actions. Her novels often deal with the absurd situations which develop when people fall in love. Each of the characters seems to be acting in the knowledge of a perfect good, and yet never manages to measure up to that ideal; as she says, 'only the good were *able* to believe in God' (*The 27th Kingdom*, 1982). Her wit involves a very dry, calculated, almost cruel detachment from her characters.

John Walsh suggests that ATE is the leading member of what he terms 'the Duckworth gang': a group of novelists consisting of ATE, Beryl Bainbridge, Patrice Chaplin and Caroline Blackwood. These writers have developed a form of writing which could be called the 'Duckworth style': short novels centring on women characters in domestic and marital traumas. In all of their work, there is little sustained character analysis, and instead, there is a concern with the bizarre and the obsessive.

ATE is the author of *The Sin Eater*, which, in 1977, won the Welsh Arts Council Award for 'a book of exceptional merit'. This tense, brooding tale of a Welsh family waiting for the patriarch to die presents, as Peter Ackroyd remarks, 'the relentlessness of domestic life, the knives only just sheathed in time, the tart little phrases bouncing around like Molotov cocktails'. The story centres around Rose and her interactions with members of her family, but these conflicts are set within a wider context of the conflicts between the family and the rest of the village.

The 27th Kingdom was nominated for the Booker Prize in 1982, and has gained ATE most notice as a writer. The story is about Valentine, an ex-nun with extraordinary thaumaturgical powers. *Unexplained Laughter* (1985) won the Yorkshire Post Fiction Award in 1985, and is concerned with Lydia's attempts to recover from a broken heart. The main focus is on her malice towards her companion Betty, and the lurking presence of Angharad, a deranged child who runs wild on the surrounding hills.   SARA MILLS

Works: *The Sin Eater* (1977); *The Birds of the Air* (1980); *Darling, You Shouldn't Have Gone to So Much Trouble* (with Caroline Blackwood) (1980); *The 27th Kingdom* (1982); *The Other Side of the Fire* (1983); *Unexplained Laughter* (1985); *Natural Baby Food* (1985); *Home Life* (1986); *Secrets of Strangers* (with Tom Pitt-Atkins) (1986).

References: Ackroyd, P., 'Out of sight', *Spectator* 239 (24 December 1977); *CA*; Gertler, T., 'Arms and the men', *New York Magazine* 17, 41 (15 October 1984); Treglown, J., 'A handful of dust', *New Statesman* 94 (16 December 1977).

Ellis, Sarah Stickney

b. 1799, Holderness, Yorkshire; d. 16 June 1872, Hoddesdon, Hertfordshire
Novelist, writer of conduct books

SSE published over thirty books, established a school based on the principles she expounded, and did much to promote the cause of temperance. Yet the *DNB* credits her only with the achievement of being married to one William Ellis, missionary. She fails to merit an individual entry and her writing career is condensed into the brief description, 'a lady who acquired quite considerable literary fame'. The importance of a woman's supportive role is central to SSE's conduct books, and it would seem that both in her life and after her death she fulfilled this role.

It is extremely difficult to decide how far SSE actually accepted the male superiority which she advocated in her books. In spite of the confidential first-person narrative, her own opinion remains curiously unclear. However, in the case of the conduct books, attempts to impose a twentieth-century feminist reading will not work. It is dangerous to read too much into the sometimes striking inconsistencies present in books such as *The Wives of England* (1843). A passage from the first chapter, entitled 'Thoughts before Marriage', begins, 'It is one of the greatest misfortunes to which women are liable, that they cannot, consistently with female delicacy, cultivate, before an engagement is made, an aquaintance sufficiently intimate to lead to the discovery of certain facts which would at once decide the point', but concludes, 'the less a woman allows her name to be associated with that of her husband before marriage, the better.' However, later in the same chapter all ambiguity is destroyed: 'One important truth sufficiently impressed upon your mind will materially assist in this desirable consummation – it is the superiority of your husband, simply as a man. It is quite possible you may have more talent, with higher attainments, and you may also have been generally more admired; but this has nothing whatsoever to do with your position as a woman, which is, and must be, inferior to his as a man.'

In *The Wives of England*, SSE is offering a handbook for survival. It provides sisterly advice telling women how to make the best of their lot within the bounds of a system which SSE makes no attempt to challenge. She advocates the community of sisterhood, but emphasizes its subservience both to the authority of men and to God. She concludes that a woman's only true hope of happiness lies in trusting that spiritual love which transcends all others.

SSE was born a Quaker, but she rejected the Society of Friends and joined the Congregationalists. In 1837 she became the second wife of William Ellis, a missionary whose involvement in the Madagascan crisis brought him considerable fame. SSE shared her husband's interest in missionary activity and the strength of her faith is evident in all her work. She takes a morally uncompromising stance, and is strongly anti-romantic in her stated disapproval of conventional 'light reading'. Yet she was not opposed to fiction as a genre, only to the kind of novel which she believed encouraged folly and caprice. Indeed she believed that fiction could serve a positive and beneficial purpose. In the preface to *Pictures of Private Life* (1833) she states, 'Fiction may be compared to a key, which opens many minds that would be closed against a sermon.' Such a remark suggests that her novels would be straightforward tracts on morality, but they cannot be so easily categorized. While they fulfil her avowed purpose of moral education, they also suggest that SSE felt uneasy about society's sexual double standard.

The poem *Janet – One of Many* (1862) supports this suggestion. Superficially the work appears to be a condemnation of women who let their hearts control their heads, and who, through sinning for the sake of 'love', become corrupted and depraved. Janet is uncompromisingly damned for her acts and the fallen woman is described thus:

> So walks the shadow on its darkening way –
> A thing of night, unfit to meet the day;
> Still scattering broadcast on its downward course
> The poison seeds of anguish and remorse.

Yet in spite of this, SSE seems to conclude that Janet was, above all, a victim; a woman deserted by men who paid no price for their sins. As Janet is spurned by her second lover, this point is made clear. 'Quick falling raindrops on his eyeballs glistened, / They were not tears – he left his grief behind.' SSE holds the man responsible for his act, and passes bitter comment on the injustice of women's lot; yet she remains unforgiving towards the woman who has sinned.

Some of the ambiguity present in SSE's work can be attributed to the difficult position of all nineteenth-century women writers, who in pursuing this profession laid themselves open to charges of unwomanly behaviour from the male establishment. The frequent condemnation of literary women resulted in many anonymous publications, which in turn led to considerable confusion and speculation over authorship. A novel by Francis Eliza Notley, *Agatha Beaufort, or, Family Pride* was for many years mistakenly attributed to SSE. Other women authors chose to avoid patriarchal criticism by meticulous conformity to the accepted stereotype of helpless femininity.

Authorship was seen as something which distracted women from their responsibility to the home, and SSE's conduct books emphasize again and again the importance of the woman's place in the home. A woman should work for others, not for her own gratification. Consequently SSE's novels contain considerable evidence of the pressure brought to bear by the female guilt of authorship. The fate of the characters in *Pique* (1850) illustrates this, and the novel also provides an example of SSE's justification of fiction for the purposes of morality.

Pique is full of lively and attractive female characters who come into contact with personified virtue, and are duly chastised for their deplorable lack of gravity. Their capacity for independence is replaced by the all-consuming duty of marriage. *Pique* also demonstrates SSE's belief that, in the wordly domain at least, men are essentially superior to women. Only men are capable of coping with the real 'adult' world. They treat the female characters as children and marriage seen in this light simply becomes the replacement of one father figure with another. Similarly, women are seen as something in which it is dangerous for a man to place too much trust. Throughout the novel the faith, love, and honesty of the women is constantly being tested.

SSE expressed considerable concern regarding the moral dangers of fiction. She did not fear overblown portrayals of larger-than-life characters, romantic figures painted black or white, with no grounding in reality. Her fear was rather of more natural characters whose charm disguised less obvious but more insidious evils. Her novels sought to show these evils, and to illustrate that they too would be punished, however superficially harmless they might appear. Mildred, the heroine of *Pique*, is one such character. Her spirit and independence are attractive, and her comments are often highly sympathetic: 'Lord Alyresford is a great deal too good for me, Helen. I detest these marvels of propriety. Give me instead poor human nature, with all its failings.'

Exactly how far SSE accepted the premises of her conduct books is impossible to tell. She was an unconventional woman and it is possible that she expected her audience to 'read between the lines'. Indeed, it is unlikely that her female readership would have responded to *The Women of England* in the same way as the reviewer in the *London Spectator*: 'At a time when women are becoming anxious to shine in other spheres than that humble but holiest of all – home, to inculcate the truth that the paramount and peculiar duties of woman consist in ministering to the wants, comforts, and happiness of her fellow creatures, is a salutary task.'   GILL PLAIN

Selected works: Pictures of Private Life (1833); The Poetry of Life (1835); Home, or, The Iron Rule (1836); The Women of England (1838); Summer and Winter in the Pyrenees (1841); The Dangers of Dining Out, or, Hints to Those Who Would Make Home Happy (1842); The Daughters of England (1842); Mrs Ellis' Housekeeping Made Easy (1843); The Mothers of England (1843); The Wives of England (1843); The Irish Girl and Other Poems (1844); Temper and Temperament (1844); The Young Ladies' Reader (1845); Prevention Better than Cure (1847); The Family Monitor (1848); Fireside Stories (1850); Social Distinction, or, Hearts and Homes (1850); Pique (1850); Home is Home (1851); The Brother, or, the Man of Many Friends (1855); Family Pride (1852); Friends at Their Own Fireside (1858); The Mothers of Great Men (1859); The Mother's Mistake (1856); Chapters on Wives (1860); Janet: One of Many (1862); The Widow Green and Her Three Nieces (1865); False Pride (1866); Rainy Days and How to Meet Them (1867); The Melville Family and Their Bible Readings (1871); Education of the Heart, Woman's Best Work (1872).
References: Allibone; Colby, V., Yesterday's Woman: Domestic Realism in the English Novel (1974); Showalter, E., A Literature of Their Own (1977); The Home Life and Letters of Mrs Ellis Compiled by her Nieces (1893).

Elstob, Elizabeth
b. 29 September 1683, Newcastle-upon-Tyne; d. 3 June 1756, Bulstrode, Berkshire
Scholar
In spite of the deplorable poverty of her middle years, EE prided herself on an 'antient lineage' of Wales. Her father was Ralph Elstob, a country clergyman (though sometimes listed as a Newcastle merchant); her mother Jane promoted female education, and trained EE at home in the rudiments of Latin and Grammar.

After the death of her father in 1688, and then of her mother in 1691, EE and her brother William Elstob, ten years her senior, came under the guardianship of their uncle, the Rev. Charles Elstob of Canterbury, and his wife Martha. The Rev. Elstob, observing his niece's interest in ancient languages, restrained EE's progress, quoting Milton, 'One tongue is enough for a woman!' Martha Elstob, more enlightened, persuaded him to permit EE to study French, one of eight languages she mastered during her youth. William went on to pursue theology and English antiquities at university.

From about 1702 to 1714, EE enjoyed a period of intellectual freedom and astonishing productivity. When William was appointed Rector of Stone, near London, EE was able to leave the confining environment of her uncle's home, and live with William. The twelve years with William were the happiest and most productive in her life. William was a linguist and antiquary, and he directed his young sister in Saxon studies. This branch of antiquarian learning was flourishing following the religious controversies of the Glorious Revolution; the Church of England wanted to trace the roots of the English Church to the original Saxon Fathers, so establishing an alternative theological tradition to Papism and Dissent. With her brother EE met many charter-members of the new Society of Antiquaries, and learnt methods of research. Her rapid progress soon enabled her to become a faithful Saxon translator and, by 1709, a valuable collaborator.

EE's first recorded publication was *An Essay on Glory* (1708), from Mme de Scudéry, 'done into English by a Person of the same Sex'. EE probably turned to Scudéry under the influence of her new London friend, the feminist Mary Astell. Her early exposure to Scudéry and Astell made a permanent impression; moreover, their writings prompted EE to compile a workbook of biographical sketches of learned Englishwomen, which later formed the foundation of Ballard's *Memoirs of Several Ladies of Great Britain* (1752). EE's first publication was suitably dedicated to her aunt, Martha Elstob, another feminist guardian of EE's early beginnings.

At the age of 26, EE launched her scholarly career with the publication by subscription of *An English-Saxon Homily on the Birthday of St Gregory* (1709), a parallel-column Saxon-English text, based on one of eighty extant Saxon homilies of Aelfric (c. 955–1006), an early Christian grammarian. A collaboration between brother and sister, the Elstob *Homily* was dedicated to Queen Anne and, like all EE's works, was printed by William Bowyer. Supported by a sound scholarly apparatus of notes and glosses, the *Homily* includes a letter in Latin to EE from her brother, wherein he promotes Saxon studies and warmly receives EE into the scholarly community. About half of her subscription list were women. The preface is as historically valuable as the scholarship, for it makes a significant contribution to developing English traditions of feminist polemic. In addition to championing Saxon studies as an investigation into England's own mother tongue, EE argues for enlightened attitudes towards female education. Both in content and organization, her preface manifests the influence of Anna Maria van Schurman's feminist *Dissertatio* (1641; English translation, 1659), and the essays of Bathsua Makin and Mary Astell. Like other early women writers, such as Aphra Behn, EE was sensitive to charges of plagiarism ('I have been askt the Question, more than once, whether this Performance was all my own').

After her auspicious debut, EE's astonishing industry continued unabated, with plans for a more ambitious project – a grand edition of all of the eighty extant Saxon homilies of Aelfric. In preparation for this edition, EE began to cultivate subscribers through correspondence and discussion with Saxon antiquaries. Most strategically, she published the fruits of her preliminary networking, *Some Testimonies of Learned Men in Favour of the Intended Edition of the Saxon Homilies* (1713). This small pamphlet was dedicated to EE's uncle.

Women readers were now beginning to take notice of the young 'Saxon Nymph', as EE was called, who had become the toast of scholarly circles. As EE wrote to George Hickes, she was approached by a female scholar, who asked her to prepare an English grammar of the Saxon language for women untrained in Latin and foreign tongues. 'I was gratified,' she wrote, 'with the new friendship . . . of a young Lady, whose Ingenuity and Love of Learning is well known and esteem'd.' EE published for female initiates *Rudiments of Grammar for the English-Saxon Tongue* (1715), dedicated to the Prince of Wales and, like the Elstob *Homily*, published by subscription. In her preface, addressed to Hickes, EE uses the occasion of the publication to take on several conservative English grammarians who had registered harsh criticism of Hickes's *Thesaurus* and the contemporary vogue in Saxon studies, among them Jonathan Swift.

EE's glorious progress was stopped by the death of her two most effective allies and promoters, her beloved brother and George Hickes. At the age of 32, EE found herself utterly alone in the world. With only a small family inheritance and no hope of material support from the universities, her immediate priority shifted from scholarship to survival. She suffered several blows. First was the failure (and subsequent financial embarrassment) of a boarding school for girls, founded at Chelsea, which folded after six months. More heartbreaking was the financial impossibility of launching her edition of Aelfric's sermons and only a small fragment of the thirty-six page MS text of the homilies was printed at Oxford in 1717. As extant copies of this ambitious project show, the press literally stopped in mid-sentence. Only five copies of EE's remarkable *Saxon Homilies* were printed, now preserved in the British Library.

The records of the Chelsea poor rates list EE as living in a large house in Paradise Row during the first half of 1718; by the end of that same year, records show she was no longer occupying this dwelling. Hickes's correspondence of 1718 states that EE was in desperate straits. Some commentators suggest she was imprisoned for debt shortly after 1715 and the failure of the Chelsea school. As her sole converse had always been with books, EE's only recourse was again to set up as a teacher. She found a small post in Evesham, Worcestershire, instructing lower-class children for a groat a week. As she wrote to George Ballard in 1735, her schedule was gruelling: 'I have no time to do anything till six at night, when I have the duty of the day done, and am then frequently so fatigu'd that I am oblig'd to lye down for an hour or two to rest myself and recover my spirits.' The next year she wrote, 'I assure you, these long winter evenings to me are very melancholy ones, for when my school is done, my little ones leave me incapable of either reading, writing, or thinking, for their noise is not out of my head till I fall asleep, which is often late.' During this dark period, EE withdrew from society and assumed the name 'Mrs Frances Smith', in an attempt, perhaps, to elude creditors and hide her personal shame. Commentators have suggested that to supplement her income, EE suffered additional humiliations as a hired domestic.

Only after several years of servitude and misery did EE's fortunes begin to change. Throughout the late 1730s, she was aided by three new allies: Mary Delany, Sarah Chapone, and George Ballard. A letter written by Chapone, soliciting money for EE, restored the celebrated Saxon Lady and saved her and her scholarship from obscurity. A strategic epistolary network, consisting of

Mrs Delany, Lady Hastings, and Mrs Pointz (tutoress to Prince William) effectively brought the 'historic Chapone epistle' (as Delany called it) to the attention of Queen Caroline in 1733, who was so moved by EE's circumstances that she granted her a royal pension of £100 every five years. The Chapone letter also raised for EE an annual annuity of twenty guineas, arranged by the Delany-Chapone-Ballard circle. Unfortunately, Caroline's royal bounty ceased with her death in 1737.

The final phase of EE's life consisted of seventeen years of relative peace and happiness as a resident governess at Bulstrode, Berkshire. After the queen's death, EE's new coterie made certain that the Chapone letter went to the Duchess of Portland, who received EE into her employ in 1739 as live-in governess of her three daughters, at an annual salary of £30. EE called Delany the 'authoress' of her happiness. In addition to her duties at Bulstrode, EE was developing close ties with the antiquarian Ballard. At her suggestion and under her direction, he launched his book of biographical profiles of England's learned ladies, from Juliana of Norwich (d. 1416) to Constantia Grierson (d. 1733), *Memoirs of Several Ladies of Great Britain* (1752). In this venture, Ballard relied on EE's workbook on learned Englishwomen, which she began in about 1708. Ballard's fifteen-page biography of Astell was taken directly from EE's notes on Astell, based on their friendship in London. Ballard was saddened by the reduced circumstances in which he found EE; he saw her life as a negative exemplum of the fate of learned ladies in an ignorant age. But he was nourished, none the less, by her early achievements and feminism, and together they enjoyed a love of English antiquities and feminist research. EE attempted to promote Ballard before her patroness the Duchess of Portland, but this proved fruitless. Ballard died in 1754. In her last years EE suffered from rheumatism. She was attended during her final days by two female relatives, and she died at the Portland estate at Bulstrode.   MAUREEN MULVIHILL

Works: (trans.), *An Essay on Glory*, by M. de Scudéry (1708); *An English-Saxon Homily on the Birthday of St Gregory: Antiently used in the English-Saxon Church, Giving an Account of the Conversion of the English from Paganism to Christianity* (1709); *Some Testimonies of Learn'd Men in Favour of the Intended Edition of the Saxon Homilies* (1713); *Rudiments of Grammar for the English-Saxon Tongue* (1715); *A Saxon Homilarium* (a fragment of the intended project; only five copies printed) (1717).

References: Adams, E. N., *Old English Scholarship in England from 1566 to 1800* (1917); Beauchamp, V. W., 'Pioneer linguist: Elizabeth Elstob', *University of Michigan Publications in Women's Studies* 1 (October 1974); *DNB*; Green, M. E., 'Elizabeth Elstob: the Saxon nymph', in *Female Scholars*, ed. J. R. Brink (1980); Hale, S., in *Woman's Record, or, Sketches of All Distinguished Women, from the Creation to AD 1854* (1855); Hughes, S. F. D., 'Mrs Elstob's defense of antiquarian learning in her *Rudiments*', *Harvard Library Bulletin* 27 (April 1979); Murphy, Michael, 'The Elstobs: scholars of Old English and Anglican apologists', *Durham University Journal* 58 (June 1966); Murphy, M. (ed.), *Elizabeth Elstob's Apology for the Study of Northern Antiquities* (1956); Perry, R. (ed.), *Memoirs of Several Ladies of Great Britain . . . By George Ballard* (1985); Reynolds, M., *The Learned Lady in England* (1920); Todd.

'Ephelia'

fl. c. 1678–82

Poet

One of the most intriguing of many 'lost' writers of the later Stuart period, E is the author of *Female Poems On Several Occasions: Written by Ephelia* (1679, 1682). Its epistle-dedicatory, to Mary Stuart *née* Villiers, is signed 'Ephelia', as is the last page of the first edition. E's is one of the rarest, most elegant books of the Restoration. It is also one of the earliest recorded poetic collections by an English woman. E also wrote a 'lost' play, which received an amateur production at a dancing school, evidently a satiric comedy or farce, directed at Charles II and his brother James, or possibly two of the many royal bastards. It may well have been a reworking of Beaumont and Fletcher's *Coxcombs*. Her play's prologue, epilogue, and two songs are printed in both editions of *Female Poems*. A staunch Royalist, E also produced two political broadsides: one to Charles II on the Popish Plot, unsigned but reprinted in *Female Poems*, the other a cautionary poem to Monmouth, signed 'Ephelia'.

Contemporary evidence confirms E as a *bona fide* Restoration personality: Aphra Behn playfully refers to 'a Poet Joan' (prologue, *Sir Pat. Fancy*); the satirist Gould links E to Behn, 'Sylvia', and 'Ariadne' as disreputable, hackney writers (*Satyrical Epistle*); Ken(d)rick complains of E's overt feminism and sexuality; and, in the nineteenth century, Ebsworth, in his edition of the Roxburghe Ballads, provides the highly important information that 'one of Mulgrave's mistresses was "humble Joan" ' (most certainly Joan Phillips). E was identified in the 1880s as 'Mrs Joan Phillips' by H. B. Wheatley, on evidence no longer extant. It seems that E was born about 1650 into a pedigreed Welsh, possibly English, family; she might have been connected with the Tilly family. Edmund Gosse's hypothesis that E was the only daughter of Katherine Philips ('Orinda') lacks credible support, to date. E acknowledges that the early death of both parents left her destitute. Evidently, she first set up in London as a playwright, modelling herself on Behn, to whom she pays homage in *Female Poems* and whose circle of writers she may have joined. Because of E's acknowledged poverty, she may have become involved with the London *demi-monde* (cf. Garfield's *Wandering Whore* and Neville's *Parliament of Ladies*). As we do not hear from E after 1681, she may have died in poverty or married and departed the literary scene. The second edition of *Female Poems* may have been occasioned by E's death. It exists in a completely different state from the first edition, as it reprints all of the 1679 text but adds several verses by Rochester, Etherege, Behn, 'Orinda', D'Urfey, Scroope, and others of E's coterie and (perhaps) family background.

E's contribution to Restoration verse is the poem of feminine regret, represented in her lament to Bajazet (John Sheffield, Lord Mulgrave), beginning, 'How far are they deceiv'd that hope in vain'. Since the nineteenth century, this fine lyric has been attributed to Etherege by several Restoration scholars on the authority of a single, ambiguously worded couplet in Buckingham's *Epistle to Mr Julian*. Other poetic forms in *Female Poems* include acrostic, broadside, epistle-dedicatory, encomium, elegy, panegyric, pastoral, satire, verse-epistle, amorous lyric, and song, several set to music. A dark book, *Female Poems* reconstructs with poignant emotional and psychological veracity the romantic crises in the life of a young woman writer. Its centre is a linked group of impassioned lyrics to 'Strephon' (E's 'J G'), who appears to be a gold trader, attached to the Crown's Tangier interest (cf. E's 'On Wealth'). E also reveals that J G is 'twice [her] Age, and more', and the elected 'Steward' of his social club, 'The Society', which may be the Society of Sea-Serjeants, a secret conclave of Welsh royalists of the Interregnum and Jacobite periods. E brilliantly reconstructs the full cycle of their affair, from romantic bliss to bitter betrayal, when J G abandons E (and her former rival 'Mopsa') to marry a wealthy beauty in Tangier. E gracefully punctuates the J G affair with a magnanimous tribute to J G's bride, 'To Madam G', which closes *Female Poems* on a note of emotional calm. MAUREEN MULVIHILL

Works: *A Poem To His Sacred Majesty, On The Plot: Written by a Gentlewoman* (1678; reprinted in *Female Poems . . . by Ephelia, 1679*); *Female Poems On Several Occasions: Written by Ephelia* (1679); *Advice To His Grace* (1681).

References: Greer, G. et al. eds. *Kissing the Rod* (1988); Gosse, Sir E., *Seventeenth-Century Studies* (1885); Hobby, E., *A Virtue of Necessity* (1988); John, G., 'Ephelia: an unknown poet of the Restoration', *Fortnightly* 108 (1920); Reynolds, M., *The Learned Lady in England* (1920); Todd; Vieth, D. M., *Attribution in Restoration Poetry* (1963).

Evans, Margiad

b. 1909, Uxbridge, Middlesex; d. 1958, Sussex

Novelist, poet

ME grew up near Ross-on-Wye in southern Herefordshire, a landscape frequently portrayed in her books. Between 1932 and 1936 she published four novels; then, following a seven-year interval, a collection of nature journals called *Autobiography*. In 1940 she married a schoolteacher, Michael Williams. While expecting her first child she discovered that she was epileptic, and her reaction to this experience is recorded in *A Ray of Darkness* (1952).

It is her novels and autobiographies that are of interest, rather than her poems. The earliest of the novels is *Country Dance* (1932), a triangular love story written in the form of a diary and set in the Welsh border country during the nineteenth century. It is a skilfully controlled performance, and was illustrated by the author under her true name, Peggy Whistler. In *The Wooden Doctor* (1933) the narrator is the victim of an obsessive and unrequited passion, as is the protagonist of *Turf or Stone* (1934). *Creed* (1936), the most substantial of the novels, is a powerful study of a religious fanatic, whom loss of faith converts into a visionary humanist; like its predecessors it has a provincial setting. In all these novels human relationships are tumultuous, painful and constricting. *Autobiography* (1943), on the other hand, portrays a life consciously seeking to lose itself in the contemplation of natural forces; much of the writing is singularly beautiful, and the book relates interestingly to Richard Jefferies's *The Story of my Heart*. The more directly autobiographical *A Ray of Darkness* (1952), in addition to its immediate occasion, provides a critique of attitudes and responses found in the earlier books, and qualifies the worship of the inanimate with the assertion of the need for human ties. It is a record of great honesty and courage. But all six books have a singular directness, occasionally violent and bitter in expression but always intensely personal. ME is a good example of those novelists of narrowly focused vision and stylistic idiosyncrasy in which English fiction has always been prolific. GLEN CAVALIERO

Selected Works: *Country Dance* (1932); *The Wooden Doctor* (1933); *Turf or Stone* (1934); *Creed* (1936); *Autobiography* (1943); *Poems from Obscurity* (1947); *A Ray of Darkness* (1952); *A Candle Ahead* (1956).

References: Kavanagh, P. J., introduction to *Autobiography* (2nd edition, 1974); Savage, D. S., *The Withered Branch* (1950).

Ewing, Juliana Horatia
b. 3 August 1841, Ecclesfield, Yorkshire; d. 13 May 1885, Bath
Writer for children
JHE was the second child of Margaret and the Rev. Alfred Gatty. Her mother, reporting on her recitation of the catechism in church at the age of 3, called her (and her elder sister) 'most refined little teapots indeed'. No doubt Mrs Gatty was describing her daughter's shape, but she could well have been referring to the way the teapot was filled with the stories of Andersen, Grimm, and Bechstein to be poured out later as Aunt Judy's (her nickname) stories for the benefit of her younger brothers and sisters. She was educated entirely by her mother and father.

Together with her mother, JHE organized the Black Bag Club to encourage other members of the family to write. They were to place their contributions in the bag to be read out at a later date. The younger ones, all known by number rather than name (eight survived), often had their stories written for them by JHE. She organized plays and games and kept her brothers and sisters happy for hours. She would save her money and spend it on presents and holidays for them, a personality trait she used for a character in one of her early novels, *Madame Liberality* (1877). Her book *The Brownies* (1870) inspired Baden-Powell to use the name for the younger section of the Girl Guides. She helped her mother in her scientific collection of seaweeds and amused the family by writing a parody of Charles Kingsley's 'The Sands of Dee', beginning,

> Oh, Gattys, go and call your Mother home
> Call your Mother home
> At least in time for tea
> The breakfast, lunch and dinner come and go
> Unheeded at the sea.

Her first published story was in Charlotte's Yonge's *Monthly Packet* in 1861 and this was followed by contributions to her mother's periodical for children, *Aunt Judy's Magazine*, notably *Mrs Overtheway's Remembrances* (1869). In 1869 she married Major Ewing and they lived for two years in Canada and then in various parts of England, JHE having to remain at home through ill-health when her husband was posted to Malta and then Ceylon. JHE capitalized on her own and her husband's experiences abroad and she succeeded in creating realistic setting and characters even when her novels were set in places which she had not visited herself. She could also make use of incidents from her mother's childhood as she did in basing Nurse Bundle, in *A Flat Iron for a Farthing* (1872), on the nurse who helped to educate the 2-year-old Margaret Scott (later to become Mrs Gatty) when her mother died. There is a distinct echo in both name and outlook of Nurse Bundle in Russell Hoban's Aunt Cosy-Joy Bundle-Sweet in his book, *How Tom beat Captain Najork and His Hired Sportsmen*. JHE was always on the side of the child.

JHE took over the editorship of *Aunt Judy's Magazine* when her mother died in 1873. Her hundreds of stories for children included fairy-tales and longer, realistic novels like *Jan of the Windmill* (1876). Her mother had recognized her skill as early as 1861: 'Julie will go far beyond me in pathos and power, there is no doubt.'

JHE herself, when writing about her mother, referred to a writer's need for 'strict fact and genuine feeling', and one young critic quoted by Mrs Molesworth, another children's writer, summed up JHE's ability to give 'us nice thinkings afterwards'. JHE knew the power of books when she wrote, 'A wicked book is all the wickeder because it can never repent.' Conversely, it would be nice to say a good book remains good but although JHE was immensely popular in her own period, her books do not appeal to modern children. Her moralizing and sentimental attitudes, such as the sacrifice of the young soldier to save his friend in *Jackanapes* (1883), are hard to accept nowadays, but some of her characters, her descriptions, and her sense of humour do still make her books worth reading. John Sannell the mill hand and Cheap John from *Jan of the Windmill* bear comparison with some of Dickens's less respectable characters; and she can make her readers laugh in *Jackanapes* when she describes the village as seen through the eyes of a goose, or when the two small boys visit the fair and take a ride on the giddy-go-round: Jackanapes 'held out the ingenious hope that the round-and-round feeling would very likely cure the up-and-down sensation.' This story also includes a plea for girls to learn 'some robuster virtues than maidenliness and not to move the antimacassars'.

JHE had read Ruskin and claimed that his laws of composition, Principality, Repetition, Continuity, Contrast, and Harmony, were equally applicable to writing. However, she was not always successful in applying them. *Jan of the Windmill*, for all its virtues, is not well constructed and the same could be said of *Jackanapes*. Her best constructed books are *A Flat Iron for a Farthing* and *Mrs Overtheway's Remembrances*, which contains stories within the story. Whatever criticisms are made of JHE's books, it is worth remembering that Mrs Molesworth called them 'powerful levers for good'.

Many of JHE's books were illustrated by famous artists including Randolph Caldecott and George Cruickshank.　　　　　　　　　　　　　　　　LIZ CASHDAN

Selected works: (the first date refers to publication in magazine form, the second to publication in book form): *Melchior's Dream and Other Stories* (1861, 1862); *The Brownies* (1865, 1870); *Mrs Overtheway's Remembrances* (1866–8, 1869); *Old-fashioned Fairy-Tales* (1869–75, 1882); *Christmas Crackers* (1869, 1870); *A Flat Iron for a Farthing* (1870–1, 1872); *The Peace Egg* (1871, 1873); *Six to Sixteen* (1872, 1875); *Jan of the Windmill* (1872, 1876); *Lob Lie by the Fire* (1873); *Madam Liberality* (1873, 1877); *Verse Books for Children* (1874–81, 1883–8); *Dandelion Clocks* (1876, 1895); *We and the World* (1877–9, 1880); *A Soldier's Children* (1879, 1883); *Jackanapes* (1879, 1883); *Daddy Darwin's Dovecot* (1881–2, 1884); *Laetus Sorte Mea: The Story of a Short Life* (1882, 1885); *Mary's Meadow* (1883, 1886); *Letters from a Little Garden* (1884, 1886).

References: Avery, G., *Mrs Ewing* (1961); *BA* (19); Doyle, B., *Who's Who in Children's Literature* (1968); Eden, Mrs H. F. K., *Juliana Horatia Ewing and Her Books* (1890); Green, R. L., *Tellers of Tales* (1969); *OCCL*; Laski, M., *Mrs Ewing, Mrs. Molesworth and Mrs Hodgson Burnett* (1950); Maxwell, C., *Mrs Gatty and Mrs Ewing* (1969); Molesworth, L., *Stories and Studies* (1893).

Fainlight, Ruth

b.1931, New York

Poet, dramatist

RF's background is cosmopolitan. Her mother was born in what was part of the Austro-Hungarian Empire and is now part of the Soviet Union. Her father was born in London and she herself in New York; she has lived in Britain for over thirty years. She was educated in both America and England and she studied art in Birmingham and Brighton. She married the novelist Alan Sillitoe in 1959 and they have a son and a daughter. She now lives in London.

Her poetry is generally 'unwordy' and sparse and conveys meaning in a direct form. RF is very much involved in personal experience and repeatedly returns to the theme of isolation, the poet's role in the 'normal' world, and being a woman in a world defined by men. This feeling of being 'apart' from society RF considers as the price she has to pay for the gift of being a poet. In 'Unseemly' (from *To See the Matter Clearly*, 1968) RF states that she has abandoned her 'race', her 'family', simply to learn about herself. Intrinsically she finds the act of doing this a betrayal. In 'To Break the Silence' (*Climates*, 1983) there is a tone of reconciliation, an indication that she has accepted her 'different' life and in part found it sweet.

RF considers that the distancing enables a poet to observe others' suffering and to be able to use the experience as the raw material for work. Suffering and death are continuing themes in her work, from a dream of killing her own child to the early death of her brother, an event which affected her profoundly. In 'In Memoriam HPF' (*Fifteen to Infinity*, 1983) RF approaches the subject. She realizes that she will never again meet her brother, except in her dreams or poems. When RF employs her brief telling form she is at her best; abandoning it, her language loses some of the tautness and discipline which are her strengths. In 'Sleep-Learning' (*To See the Matter Clearly*) the 'stern son' whose eyes move behind 'mauve eyelids' and, in dreams, 'roams through the night-forests, desolate', is less effective than the feeling created in 'A Child's Fear of Spiders', where RF transforms the child's basic fear of spiders, through the image of the parents copulating to the further image of limbs symbolizing two swastikas, to the concept of absolute power, then, finally, returns to the child's fear of spiders.

RF is constantly aware of the poet's 'other life', whether in a domestic situation or abroad in India or the Sinai desert. In 'Stubborn' (*Fifteen to Infinity*) she asserts that her fundamental self, her 'stone-age self', scorns the veneer of civilization that men and women have adopted: the attempt to prove that we are anything more than 'upright animals'. But, in contradiction, RF goes on to say that this stone-age self cannot understand what shapes, gives pain to, and haunts the poet, the woman caught in this contradiction. Doubt and struggle are always evident in RF's work but in the midst of poems marked by these themes are poems of bright imagery which appear like small jewels. In 'Silk Kimonos' (*Fifteen to Infinity*) we have an example of this striking use of language:

> Jade green and pale gold
> under dark autumn cloud, worn flimsy
> by rain and frost and wind, the plane's
> leaves shift across their boughs
> and the closed fronts of houses like silk
> kimonos over dancers' limbs.

Like many poets, RF draws inspiration from the visual arts. Her five poems based on Leonard Baskin's *Death Drawings* draw together her acute observation and her preoccupation with death.

> It is the death you saw –
> the hands of a Japanese wrestler
> reaching out for you, tendons tense

and stretched, the brutal forearms
of a weightlifter, a prizefighter
a porter from the meat market . . . .
It is the death that comes with no pity
to thrust you in the charnel-pit.
Death with no wings.
('Death with no wings', *Fifteen to Infinity*)

RF also has the ability to explore minute areas of personal experience with delicacy and accuracy. *The Function of Tears*, a long poem published separately in 1979, was used to analyse the effect of weeping, as opposed to the verbal communication of feeling. Weeping, she argues, serves as language, and, although the most anguished weeping is generally solitary it is also a first communication before words, expressing a full spectrum of emotional response.

As RF returns to the duality of the poet's life, the doubt and anguish which marks it, she also returns to poems which deal with motherhood, children, the feelings between women and those between mother and child. In 'That Smile' (*Sybils and Others*, 1980), RF tries to communicate to the mother of two unruly little boys on an underground train her shared experience, her memory of what it was like to be in her position, for the mother to enjoy the children:

I now
wanted to catch the mother's furious eye
and make her delight in them, acknowledge her own
two children as emanations of wisdom
and joy; and more than this, as empty
station platforms hurtled past,
I wished that she would smile at me.

RF was longing to be drawn into this experience, to share the mother's frustration, to moderate it and, in the light of common maternal past, to make the woman enjoy these two small children. ALISON RIMMER

Selected works: *A Forecast, a Fable* (1958); *Cages* (1966); *Eighteen Poems from 1966* (1967); *To see the Matter Clearly and Other Poems* (1968); *Poem with Alan Sillitoe and Ted Hughes* (1971); *The Region's Violence* (1976); *Twenty-One Poems* (1973); *Another Full Moon* (1976); *Two Fire Poems* (1977); *Sybils and Others* (1980); *Two Wind Poems* (1980); (trans.), *Navigaciones*, by S. de Mello Breyner Andressen (1983); *Climates* (1983); *Fifteen to Infinity* (1983).

References: *CA*; Plath, A. S. (ed), *Letters Home by Sylvia Plath* (1975); *The Times Literary Supplement* (8 April 1977 and 23 May 1980).

Fairless, Michael

b. 7 May 1869, Rastrich, Yorkshire; d. 24 August 1901
Novelist

MF (Margaret Fairless Barber) was the youngest of three daughters. Her parents, Fairless and Maria Barber, were well-educated, and MF read 'omnivorously' throughout her youth, completing all of Dickens and most of Sir Walter Scott by the age of 12. She trained in nursing and worked for a time as a parish nurse, but was increasingly ill herself from her early twenties. Following her parents' deaths, MF, now financially independent, lived for a time in Germany but ultimately returned to England in declining health. She began to write at this time and, although all three of her works were published posthumously, she lived to correct proofs of two of them.

She was cared for in her final illness by her friend M. E. Dowson who, as 'William Scott Palmer', published a memoir of her a decade later, recalling her perseverance and courage: 'When writing could not be done in a sitting position, she propped the paper on her chest and wrote lying down; by and by the right hand could no longer be used, so she wrote with her left, a beautiful legible script. When increased physical weakness made writing in every way impossible, she dictated.'

MF's first work became her most famous; *The Roadmender* (1902) had sold 250,000 copies by 1922. It is a strikingly simple book in which the roadmender himself, a 'delicate literary artifice' according to C. Lewis Hind, reflects on his happy life as a servant of his fellow men and of his God, and gives thanks for the many blessings around him: 'I have attained my ideal: I am a roadmender, some say stone breaker . . . . All day I sit by the roadside on a stretch of grass under a high hedge of saplings and a tangle of traveller's joy, woodbine, sweetbriar, and late roses. Opposite me is a white gate, seldom used, if one may judge from the trail of honeysuckle growing tranquilly along it: I know now that whenever and wherever I die my soul will pass out through this white gate; and then, thank God, I shall not have to undo that trail.' Some twenty years after *The Roadmender*'s publication, Hind wrote that 'this small volume stands as proof of the statement that everyone has one book in him or her, if they but have the gift of expression'.

MF's second book, *The Gathering of Brother Hilarius* (1901), relating the adventures of a travelling monk, was actually published several months before *The Roadmender*, but never achieved its popularity. *The Grey Bretheren* (1905) was posthumously edited from her stories, sketches and poems by M. E. Dowson.   JEAN HANFF KORELITZ

Selected works: The Gathering of Brother Hilarius (1901); The Roadmender (1902); The Grey Bretheren (1905).

References: Palmer, W. S. (M. E. Dowson) and Haggard, A. M., *Michael Fairless: Her Life and Writings* (1913); Hind, C., *More Authors and I* (1922).

Falkland, Elizabeth Cary, Lady

b. 1585 or 1586, Burford, Oxfordshire; d. October 1639, London

Poet, dramatist

The only child and heiress of a wealthy Oxford lawyer, Lawrence Tanfield, later Lord Chief Baron of the Exchequer, EF was a startlingly precocious child who taught herself several ancient and modern languages. In 1602 when she was about 16 she was married to Henry Cary, ten years her senior, who later became a member of the Privy Council, a viscount, and Lord Chief Deputy of Ireland. In about 1607, after Henry had returned from military service abroad, they began twenty years of life together during which EF bore eleven living children, most of whom she nursed herself; her eldest son, Lucius, was reared by her father. When EF mortgaged her jointure to advance her husband's career, her father disinherited her in favour of Lucius. In 1626 she converted to Roman Catholicism, damaging her husband's career as a courtier in a Protestant court. He responded by abandoning her, taking custody of her children, and stripping her house of the necessities of life. EF appealed to the court for help, and in 1627 the Privy Council ordered Lord Falkland to support his wife, but seven months later he had still not complied with the order. In her last years she kidnapped two of her sons and smuggled them to the continent to become

Catholics. Three of her daughters became nuns; one of them wrote a detailed biography of her mother emphasizing her sufferings for her faith.

EF began making translations at an early age. Between 13 and 15 she translated *Le Miroir de Monde* and dedicated it to her great-uncle, Sir Henry Lee. She later translated the works of Cardinal Du Perron. One of these, *The Reply to the King of Great Britain*, published in 1630, was ordered to be publicly burned. Towards the end of her life she was translating the writings of Blosius, a Flemish Benedictine monk.

She began writing poetry shortly after her marriage, while living with her mother-in-law. When Lady Cary, angry at her daughter-in-law for reading constantly, took away her books, EF 'set herself to make verses', completing a life of Tamburlaine in verse and a tragedy set in Sicily (both are lost). *Mariam, the Fair Queen of Jewry*, a Senecan tragedy based on Josephus's *Antiquities*, also dates from this period. The first of many English plays about Herod and Mariamne, *Mariam* is carefully constructed and attentive to historical details. EF's dramaturgy is competent but conventional: the action is discussed rather than dramatized, and details of the execution are left to the messenger. The play is written in quatrains with occasional couplets and sonnets inserted. When *Mariam* was published in 1613, some ten years after it was written, EF became the first Englishwoman to publish a full-length original play. EF began writing again after her separation from her husband. She wrote verse lives of several women saints and poetry about the Annunciation. The only surviving creative work from this period, however, is her life of Edward II.

EF was reputed to be both eccentric and generous. Literary works dedicated to her include *England's Helicon*, the *Works* of John Marston, and Michael Drayton's *England's Heroicall Epistles*. She was also the subject of verses by William Basse and John Davies of Hereford. She died of a lung disease and was buried in the chapel of the Catholic queen, Henrietta Maria.

NANCY COTTON

Works: (trans.), *The Mirror of the World*, by A. Ortellius (c. 1598–1602); *Mariam* (c. 1602–5), ed. A. C. Dunstan and W. W. Greg (1914); *The History of Edward II* (1627); (trans.), *The Reply to the King of Great Britain*, by Cardinal du Perron (1630).

References: Allibone; Ballard; Cotton, N., *Women Playwrights in England c. 1363–1750* (1980); *DNB*; Dunstan, A. C., *Examination of Two English Dramas* (1908); Fullerton, G., *Life of Elisabeth, Lady Falkland* (1883); Murdock, K., *The Sun at Noon* (1939); Simpson, R. (ed.), *The Lady Falkland: Her Life* (1861); Stauffer, D. A., 'A deep and sad passion', in *Parrott Presentation Volume* (1935).

Fanshawe, Ann, Lady

b. 25 March 1625, London; d. 30 January 1680, Ware?
Biographer

AF's life is described in her memoir of her husband, Sir Richard Fanshawe, a cavalier, poet, and diplomat. *The Memoirs of Ann, Lady Fanshawe, Wife of the Right Honble Sir Richard Fanshawe Bart., 1660–1672: Written in 1676 for Her Only Surviving Son, Sir Richard Fanshawe, 2nd Baronet* was first printed in 1829 and reissued in 1830 by Sir N. Harris Nicolas from a transcript made in the late eighteenth century by AF's great-granddaughter, C. Colman. A manuscript of the *Memoirs* in the British Library is signed by AF but is not in her handwriting although it may be corrected by her; this formed the basis of another edition in 1907. Sometimes the *Memoirs* suffers from a rather confused chronology since AF uses both old and new dating and is often writing long after the events she describes; none the less, in all its versions, the work is a vivid account of the Commonwealth and Restoration period of English history from the perspective of a royalist wife, charting both personal and political events and their constant intermingling.

The daughter of Sir John Harrison and Margaret Harrison of Hertfordshire, AF described herself as a 'hoyting girl' (a hoyden); she had an adequate education for the time, being instructed in music, needlework, dancing, and French. With the Civil War came poverty and she and her family moved to Oxford where they lived, surrounded by sickness and news of war, in 'a baker's house in an obscure street' and where she had to 'lie in a very bad bed in a garret' and receive only 'one dish of meat and that not the best ordered'. In 1642 her father was briefly imprisoned by order of Parliament. In 1644 she married her cousin, the 35-year-old Richard Fanshawe (made a baronet in 1650) who held a position under the young Prince Charles. According to AF the marriage, which produced fourteen children, only five of whom survived their father, was utterly happy: 'I thought myself a queen, and my husband so glorious a crown that I more valued myself to be called by his name than born a princess.' Partings and reunitings are described with emotion and the relationship is presented as extraordinarily intimate and supportive. 'We so studied one the other that we knew each other's mind by our looks; what ever was real happiness, God gave it me in him.'

Combined with her emphasis on marital harmony was a stress on the political difficulties of her life described as 'nearly thirty years suffering by land and sea, and the hazard of our lives over and over'. She told, for example, of how, when her husband was captured after the Battle of Worcester in 1651 and briefly imprisoned at Whitehall, she came to his cell window very early each morning and worked tirelessly to release him through obtaining a certificate of ill-health. Even more impressive adventures occurred during their flight from England. In Ireland, the couple was caught in the plague-ridden town of Galway and later AF was almost taken as a slave by Turks; she effected her escape by donning men's clothes. Sometimes they were near starvation and sometimes almost shipwrecked. The account is often matter-of-fact, and the recounting of adventures is punctuated with ordinary observations on clothes, customs, scenery, and food.

After the Restoration Richard Fanshawe enjoyed royal favour; he was made a Privy Councillor and ambassador first to Portugal and then Spain. AF describes the revelry at the court of Charles II and her impressions of royal events. Richard died in 1667 while still in Spain; after his death the queen mother offered AF residence in Spain providing she became a Roman Catholic, but AF refused and she returned with her children and her husband's body to England. A decade later she wrote the *Memoirs* as tribute to her husband, presenting his heroic image to her son and carefully depicting their close and loving marriage. Friction was rare; as a young bride, she once tried to overcome her husband's proper discretion in political matters, but then admits that his 'reason' overcame her 'folly'.   JANET TODD

Works: *The Memoirs of Ann, Lady Fanshawe. . . .* , ed. Sir N. Harris Nicolas (1829).

References: *DNB*; Fraser, A., *The Weaker Vessel* (1984); Kunitz, S. and Haycroft, H., *British Authors before 1800* (1952); Loftis, J. (ed.), *The Memoirs of Anne, Lady Halkett and Ann, Lady Fanshawe* (1979); Spender, D., *Mothers of the*

Novel (1986); Todd; Ward, A. W. and Walter, A. R., (eds.), *Cambridge History of English Literature*, vol. 8 (1952).

Farjeon, Eleanor
b. 13 February 1881, London; d. 5 June 1965, Hampstead, London
Poet, novelist, playwright, writer for children
EF was born into a lively bohemian family. Her father, Ben Farjeon, after an adventurous youth, became a successful playwright and novelist and married Margaret Jefferson of a famous American theatrical family. They encouraged their four children to be artists: Harry became a musician and EF, Joe, and Herbert writers. Their unconventional, happy childhood is recalled in EF's *A Nursery in the Nineties* which begins, 'I pine for my childhood, and the childhood of my brothers.' At their increasingly splendid Hampstead homes EF saw many of the writers, actors, and musicians of the day and she was to retain an active interest in the theatre all her life. She had governesses, but her real education came from her wide reading, encouraged by a father who owned 8,000 books and who gave each child a new book weekly after Sunday lunch. They were also encouraged to write, their father copying their best efforts into a notebook of his own. There was an unusually close bond between the children fostered by Harry, whom his niece likens to Svengali. In his hypnotic game of TAR EF readily became characters in made-up situations. She was involved in this make-believe until she was almost 30 and, while it encouraged her facility with words, it also hampered her emotional growth. She says of her shyness in her twenties, 'I was ignorant of my human longings.' Ben Farjeon died in 1903, leaving his family quite poor and, after her first visit to America in 1904, EF began to write in earnest, publishing her first volume of poetry, *Pan-Worship*, in 1908. Today probably her best-known poem is the hymn 'Morning has Broken', written in the twenties. She wrote over eighty books and composed some songs. She lived all her life in Hampstead, apart from a short time in Sussex at the end of the First World War, and in 1960 gave a collection of her works to Hampstead Public Libraries. She never married but at 40 went to live with George Earle with whom she stayed until his death in 1949. She miscarried their only child. In 1951 she became a Roman Catholic. It is clear from accounts of those who knew her that she had a strong need for love and expressed love vigorously to the crowds of friends who poured out their troubles to her. Her friends compose a roll-call of distinguished twentieth-century writers: Robert Frost, David Garnett, D. H. Lawrence (whose manuscript of *The Rainbow* she helped to type), Walter de la Mare, Christopher Fry, and Edward Thomas, of whom she has left a moving account in *Edward Thomas: The Last Four Years*. A centenary radio portrait by Anne Harvey, *A Life Kept Always Young*, stresses her kindness and her noisiness. She once described herself as 'a cheerful suet pudding' and her enthusiasm for life showed itself in all her writings, in her friendships, her love of children and cats and her unfailing propensity, even in old age, to fall in love. Her friends found her poem 'Mrs Malone' (1950) almost a self-portrait of a generous-hearted woman. Her writings brought her awards such as the Library Association Carnegie Medal and the Hans Andersen Medal in 1956 for *The Little Bookroom* (1955), and the first award of the American Regina Medal in 1959. An EF Award was established in 1965 and is given annually for distinguished services to children's books during the preceding year. *The Times* obituary described her as 'best known as a writer of children's verses and stories, in which capacity she must indeed be counted among the

happiest and most charming writers of her kind'. She excelled as a writer of whimsical fairy-tales, often derived from English folk-tales, and light verse, some of which was printed daily in the *Daily Herald* under the name of 'Tom Fool'. 'Facile' is the most critical word which can be used of her work but the dangerous word 'charming' is rightly applied to the Martin Pippin books and her poetry for children, such as *Then There Were Three* (1958) and *Kings and Queens* (1936) in which she collaborated with her brother Herbert.

MARY SHAKESHAFT

Works: *Pan-Worship* (1908); *Nursery Rhymes of London Town* (1916); *Martin Pippin in the Apple Orchard* (1921); *Kings and Queens* (with Herbert Farjeon) (1936); *Martin Pippin in the Daisy-Field* (1937); *The New Book of Days* (1941); *Silver Sand and Snow* (1951); *The Little Bookroom* (1955); *Then There Were Three* (collection of three previous books of poetry) (1958).

References: Blakelock, D., *Eleanor: Portrait of a Farjeon* (1966); Colwell, E., *Eleanor Farjeon: A Biography* (1961); Farjeon, A., *Morning Has Broken* (1985); *OCCL*.

Feinstein, Elaine

b. 24 October 1930, Bootle, Lancashire

Poet, novelist, translator

The daughter of Fay and Isidore Cooklin, EF was educated at Wyggeston Grammar School, Leicester. A happy childhood was interrupted when as a teenager she realized the horrors of the Second World War and, in her own words, 'became Jewish for the first time'. She won a scholarship to study English at Newnham College, Cambridge, and read for the Bar. In 1956, she married an immunologist, Dr Arnold Feinstein, and they have three sons. From 1960, she was on the editorial staff of Cambridge University Press, but in 1963 she moved to a three-year lectureship in English at Bishop Stortford Training College, Hertfordshire, and from there to an Assistant Lectureship in Literature at the University of Essex. At 36, she published her first collection of poems, *In a Green Eye* (1966), and has since proved a prolific author, her work comprising eight novels, two short story collections, translations, biography, and editorial work. EF has won several awards and grants, among others an Arts Council Grant in 1970, 1979, and 1981, the Daisy Miller Award for fiction in 1971, and the Kelus Prize in 1978, and she became a Fellow of the Royal Society of Literature in 1980. She now lives and works in Cambridge.

In a recent introduction to her poems, EF described the function of poetry as 'trying to make sense of experience'. Indeed, her second volume, *The Magic Apple Tree* (1971), at first seems purely confessional, a woman poet's musing on everyday happenings, fears, and feelings. However, everyday reality in several poems undergoes a process of 'transformation'. The poet is an alchemist, merging divergent images from reality in the 'alembic' of the poem, until the presence of the one image poignantly, unavoidably, evokes the potentiality of the other. In the title poem, the sight of drab winter streets is affected by the memory of the trees in a bright Samuel Palmer painting:

> I remembered Samuel Palmer's garden
> Waterhouse in Shoreham, and at once
> I knew: that the chill of wet
> brown streets was no more literal
> than the yellow he laid there against
> his unnatural blue   because

> together they worked upon me like
> an icon   infantine.

Feinstein tries, moreover, to remain true to her experience, her relationship
with contemporary reality. 'Mother Love', translated into a modern vocabulary
and stripped of sentimentality, focuses on the exhaustion of motherhood. As
the child physically and mentally drains the mother, an altogether truer picture
of mother love emerges, harder and more tender at the same time. Other poems
in this second volume portraying reality with a modern voice and urgency are
'Sundance in Sawston' or the unsatisfactory morning of 'I Have Seen Worse
Days Turn'.

> Outside, the rain
> and humus taste of old potatoes, which
> in unfastidious hands could
> blow up the whole alembic.
> How do you change the weather in the blood?

Our own constant re-creation in everyday life is paralleled formally in EF's
choice of a new poetic form for every poem. Sentence and stanza length, and
punctuation are adapted, in the same way as the poem's images are merged
with others.

EF repeated the struggle with reality on a larger scene with a gloomier
urgency. *The Celebrants and Other Poems* (1973) is a sequence tracing through
the ages the human obsession with knowledge and death. Sections are devoted
to Melusine, 'bewitched into a myth' and turned into a serpent, to women
possessed by 'hostile' spirits, to the sorcery of Paracelsus, and the art of Michel-
angelo Buonarotti, who shows 'the pressure of death' in every torso he creates.
The Celebrants deals with this human search for knowledge about reality just
beyond the accepted boundaries, by magicians, by suffering artists. Connected
with two sections about a Jewish past ('nomads, wilderness people . . . or
magicians'), this poem also presents a wary I-figure, heir to both this Jewish
history and to the search for dangerous knowledge through science and art.

For her early poetry, EF claimed such varied influences as Emily Dickinson
and modern Americans, like Wallace Stevens and William Carlos Williams.
Certainly her formal experiments with punctuation and her expressive use of
pauses and silence remind one of the Black Mountain Group. EF's discovery of
a near-forgotten twentieth-century Russian poet, Marina Tsvetayeva, however,
influenced her profoundly, resulting in a longer, more daring verse line, a
toning-down of formal expertise in favour of vision, and the strong, more
biting image. In admiration for Tsvetayeva's 'raw' self-exposure in her poetry,
EF's poems poignantly deal with the topics of pain, suffering, and fear in, for
example, 'For Malcolm Lowry' or the physical pain and courage of 'Calliope
in the Labour Ward'.

EF has since translated a selection of Tsvetayeva's poetry, and written a
sensitive, balanced biography, *A Captive Lion* (1987), making this important
poet better known in Britain. Her most recent collection, *Badlands* (1986), was
well-received and registers the continuing influences of Tsvetayeva and a return
of the questions about reality, myth, and magic. Eternal mythical figures like
Eurydice or Penelope, in 'Songs for Eurydice: A Sequence', now function in a
reinterpreted myth, leading to a discussion of the suffering of artists in repressive
societies. Another poem ultimately focusing on artists is 'The Water Magician

of San Diego', linking the artist with magicians and others who work outside the rules of society.

To a certain extent, EF carries over the themes and interests from her poetry into the novels: contemporary couples, families, scientists, and artists are combined with a vision of reality reminiscent of her poetry. In this respect, the title of the third novel is significant: *The Glass Alembic* (1973). Here, too, everyday reality and relationships suddenly become warped with other images, are mixed up and then seemingly restored to the previous situation, re-thought by a mystical experience of reality. The arrival of his estranged wife and children, mysteriously invited, unbalances the main character and sets off rapid switches in all the relationships at his laboratory, until the situation slowly returns to a restored balance.

The activity of unreality, imagination, and myth on reality increased in the next novels. Dr Miriam Garner sinks into a coma artificially induced by her scientist-husband and in visions relives a Jewish past in Spain in *The Ecstasy of Dr Miriam Garner* (1976). The scope in *The Shadow Master* (1978) was even bolder, as a Jewish myth becomes reality. A new Messiah wins an international, modern-day following. The novel moves to an apocalyptic ending as fanatic followers and anti-semitic groups call up chaos over Britian and Europe. When the Messiah disappears from sight, life again returns to an altered normality, but this strong novel has briefly called up the returning horrors of the Second World War.

EF's prose is raw and often nightmarish: violence and especially a dark sexuality pervert the reality of the contemporary, civilized characters. The topics of fear, pain, and the question of humanity return as most characters are haunted by their knowledge of the recent horrors in their Jewish history. *The Border*, (1984) is a softer, closely knitted novel tracing the flight of a Jewish scientist-artist couple out of Nazi Austria to a border town between France and Spain, a flight from horror to freedom. With this novel, EF seems to have reached a more formalized investigation into present and past reality.

SABINE VANACKER

Selected works: *In a Green Eye* (1966); *The Circle* (1970); (trans.), *The Selected Poems of Marina Tsvetayeva* (1971); *The Magic Apple Tree* (1971); *The Amberstone Exit* (1972); *At the Edge* (1972); *The Celebrants and Other Poems* (1973); *The Glass Alembic* (1973); *The Ecstasy of Dr Miriam Garner* (1976); *Some Unease and Angels: Selected Poems* (1977); *The Shadow Master* (1978); *The Silent Areas* (1980); *The Feast of Euridice* (1980); *The Border* (1984); *Bessie Smith* (1985); *Badlands* (1986); *A Captive Lion* (1987).

References: Byers, M., 'Cautious vision: recent British poetry by women', in Schmidt, M. and Lindop, G. (eds), *British Poetry since 1960: a Critical Survey* (1972); CD; Halio, J. L. (ed.), *British Novelists Since 1960* (1983); Mitchell, D., 'Modes of realism: Roy Fisher and Elaine Feinstein', in Jones, P. and Schmidt, M. (eds), *British Poetry since 1970: A Critical Survey* (1980); Zeman, A., *Presumptuous Girls: Women and Their World in the Serious Woman's Novel* (1977).

Fell, Margaret

b. 1614, Marsh Grange, near Dalton, Lancashire; d. 1702, Swarthmoor Hall, near Ulverston, Lancashire

Quaker pamphleteer

Little is known of MF's life before 1652, when she first met the Quaker George Fox, except what she tells us in her own 'Relation' (in *A Brief Collection*, 1710).

Her parents, John Askew and Margaret Pyper(?), were 'good and honest, and of honourable repute'. In 1632 she married Thomas Fell (1599–1658), a barrister who subsequently held many positions of prominence, including being MP for Lancaster in the Long Parliament (he was expelled and fined in 1647 for non-attendence), and from 1651 Judge of Assize for the Chester and North Wales Circuit. They had nine children, including George who for some years before his death was a source of misery to his mother as he pursued her through the courts for property he claimed as his.

In 1652, whilst Thomas Fell was away in London, George Fox visited Ulverston on a preaching tour, and MF, her children and servants were all converted to Quakerism. Thomas Fell (who was never converted) was quickly reconciled to the change, and under MF's supervision Swarthmoor Hall became a nerve-centre of Quaker organization. She constantly exchanged letters with Friends travelling at home and abroad, distributing funds for their support and overseeing the circulation of news. In 1653 she also wrote to Oliver Cromwell, the first of a series of letters appealing for religious toleration that she sent or delivered by hand to the nation's rulers, including Charles II, James II, and William III.

She first began to write for publication in 1655, when with others she produced *False Prophets, Anticrists* [sic], *Deceivers*, a pamphlet advising its readers to test the validity of Church ministers' assertions against their own understanding of the Scriptures. The measured authoritative style of this pamphlet, which is illustrated with detailed reference to the Bible, differentiates MF's work from that of her female contemporaries, whose tone was generally less confident and more ecstatic. All her writings are indeed characterized by their confidence in her right to instruct others. She consistently claimed the authority to reprove Friends like James Nayler and Martha Simmonds who challenged George Fox's version of Quakerism, and *A Testimonie of the Touch-stone* includes a polemic against people devoted to 'the Ranters principles'. Several of her most substantial independent publications were addressed to the Jews (readmitted to England in 1655, ending the banishment imposed by Elizabeth I). *For Manasseth-Ben-Israel* and *A Loving Salutation*, like her later *A Call to the Universal Seed, A Call unto the Seed of Israel* and *The Daughter of Sion Awakened*, use Old Testament references in an attempt to convert Jews to Quakerism. *A Loving Salutation* was also translated into Hebrew by Spinoza.

MF took part in the flurry of Quaker pamphleteering concerning the Restoration of the monarchy, in 1660 making the first of her many visits to London to see the king and other members of the royal family (including Henrietta Maria and Elizabeth of Bohemia) to protest against the persecution of Friends. (Her last such trip was made in 1684, when she was 70 years old.) A great traveller, in 1663 she also made a 1,000 mile trip through England visiting Friends.

In 1664 she was arrested, had a sentence of praemunire passed against her (effectively, a sentence of outlawry), and was imprisoned until 1668 in Lancaster Castle. These four years were her second most productive period as a pamphleteer. Among other works she wrote *The Standard of the Lord Revealed*, a commentary on the entire Bible, and her *Womens Speaking Justified*, a carefully argued case for some women's right to participate in religious matters. (Though often described as the first Quaker pamphlet of its type, and revolutionary, this is in fact a more conservative and cautious document, though longer and more authoritative, then those written by various Quaker women in the 1650s. In 1669, some eleven years after the death of her first husband and after much public speculation, MF married George Fox. He signed an undertaking never to interfere with her estate, and the couple did not live together for any extended period for several years. All her daughters, especially Isabel (later Yeamans, then Morrice), Sarah (later Meade) and Rachel (later Abraham), became prominent Quakers in their own right.

The oft-repeated assertion that MF was the much-loved 'nursing mother' of Quakerism needs to be treated with some caution. Most of the manuscript sources cited are not originals, but are copies of correspondence made by William Caton, a servant of the Fell family who was clearly devoted to MF and might have been selective in what he recorded. The previously unpublished letters that appeared in 1710 as part of *A Brief Collection* have also been edited by another hand. It is clear that, from the early 1650s, errant Friends, especially women, were referred to MF for disciplining or re-education. Quakers were a more divided body than some of their chroniclers suggest, and many Quaker women were more radical than MF, if finally less influential in the development of its organization.   ELAINE HOBBY

Selected works: *For Manasseth-Ben-Israel* (1656); *A Loving Salutation* (1656); *A Testimonie of the Touch-stone* (1656); *A Paper Concerning Such as Are Made Ministers* (1659); *To the General Councel, and Officers of the Army* (1659); *The Citie of London Reprov'd* (1660); *A Declaration and Information from Us* (1660); *An Evident Demonstration to Gods Elect* (1660); *This Is to the Clergy* (1660); *This Was Given to Major Generall Harrison* (1660); *A True Testimony from the People of God* (1660); *To the Magistrates and People of England* (1664); *A Call to the Universall Seed* (1665); *A Letter Sent to the King* (1666); *Womens Speaking Justified* (1666); *The Daughter of Sion Awakened* (1677);*The Standard of the Lord Revealed* (1667); *A Touch-stone, or, A Perfect Tryal by the Scriptures* (1667); *A Call Unto the Seed of Israel* (1668?); *A Brief Collection* (1710).

References: Brailsford, M., *Quaker Women 1650–1690* (1915); Braithwaite, W., *The Beginnings of Quakerism* (1912); Crosfield, H., *Margaret Fell* (1913); Foulds, E., *A Lily Among Thorns* (1950); Latt, D. (ed.), Margaret Fell *Women's Speaking Justified* (1979); Ross, I., *Margaret Fell, Mother of Quakerism* (1949).

Fenwick, Eliza
b. ?; d. 1840, Rhode Island
Novelist

EF was part of the liberal and radical circle in London in the 1790s, associated with the publisher Joseph Johnson and with William Godwin, Mary Wollstonecraft, and Mary Hays. She married an editor and translator, John Fenwick, on whom Charles Lamb's portrait of a likeable but impecunious and constantly borrowing man, Ralph Bigod, was based. In 1795 she published anonymously *Secresy; or, The Ruin on the Rock*, her only novel. This was a sentimental epistolary work which both warned against excessive sensibility and showed its seductive charms for women. The book investigated some of the current questions about women's nature and education through the upbringing and future development of two girls. The heroine has been secluded from the world and confined to a castle, necessarily growing enthusiastic and intense, as her friend notes. She falls imprudently in love and the attachment which she cannot forego leads in the end to her death. And yet the moral is by no means simply on the side of common sense and social knowledge, for, although the sentimental character proves ineffective, it is still preferable to the debased qualities of most of the other worldly and selfish people in the novel.

The only comfort in *Secresy* is female friendship and over the following years EF herself had to find much solace and support in such friendly ties. In 1797 she was with Mary Wollstonecraft when the latter died following childbirth; later she helped Godwin notify friends of her death and took some part in caring for the baby Mary over the next few weeks. In 1799 her husband had to flee from London to escape creditors and he left EF permanently in 1800; he emigrated to the US. With her son and daughter, EF stayed part of a summer with the former actress turned poet and novelist, Mary Robinson, and she corresponded with Mary Hays into old age. These letters, together with those to Crabb Robinson from 1798 to 1828, give a view of her difficult and impoverished life, trying to earn a living for herself and her children, writing against constant interruptions and struggling to avoid the temptation (to which she frequently succumbed) of self-pity and bitterness.

In 1806 EF worked for a short time for Godwin helping him with his recently founded Juvenile Library; she wrote several educational works for children, including *The Life of Carlo, the Famous Dog of Drury Lane Theatre* (1804) and *Lessons for Children*, intended as a sequel to a children's work by Anna Laetitia Barbauld. EF's daughter became an actress with the help of Thomas Holcroft and went on the stage in the West Indies, while EF worked as a governess in Ireland. When her daughter's husband abandoned her and her four children in 1818, EF and her son went to Barbados to help set up a school. In 1816 her son died, causing immense distress to EF. The school languished and later EF and her daughter went to America where EF obtained work as a teacher. After her daughter died in 1828 EF and her four grandchildren moved several times. The two older boys drowned and a third married; EF spent her last days with the remaining granddaughter in Rhode Island.   JANET TODD

Works: *Secresy; or, The Ruin on the Rock* (1795); *The Life of Carlo, the Famous Dog of Drury Lane Theatre* (1804); *The Class Book; or, Three Hundred and Sixty-five Reading Lessons Adapted to the Use of Schools* (1806); *Infantine Stories, Composed Progressively, in Words of One, Two and Three Syllables . . .* (1810); *Lessons for Children . . . A New Edition* (1811); *Rays from the Rainbow* (1812); *Lessons for Children: A Sequel to Mrs Barbauld's Lessons* (1828).

References: Cameron, K. N. (ed), *Shelley and His Circle 1773–1822* (1961); Todd; Wedd, A. F. (ed), *The Fate of the Fenwicks* (1927).

Ferrier, Susan

b. 17 September 1782, Edinburgh; d. 5 November 1854

Novelist

SF was the youngest of the ten children of James Ferrier, a manager of the Fifth Duke of Argyll's estates and later a principal clerk of the sessions, and of Helen Coutts, the daughter of a farmer and a local beauty in her native Kincardineshire. SF had six brothers and three sisters. Her only formal education was at Mr Stalker's Academy in Edinburgh where she excelled at French. Her father was an acquaintance of Sir Walter Scott, whose friendship with the Ferrier family eased SF's reception into Edinburgh's literary society and assisted her in the publication of her first novel, *Marriage* (1818). Chief among SF's childhood friends were the daughter of the Duke of Argyll, Lady Charlotte Campbell (later Lady Bury) and his niece, Charlotte Clavering. In 1810, Clavering proposed to SF that they write a novel about the many unusual visitors they saw coming to conduct business with the Duke. Shortly after the project began, Clavering dropped out, but her 'History of Mrs Douglas' was retained by SF for the published text. The theme of *Marriage* is virtue rewarded, pride abased. The story describes the happy and unhappy consequences of marrying for love in the lives of Lady Juliana Courtland and her daughters, Adelaide and Mary. Sub-themes of the novel include the conflict between poverty and wealth and the corrupting influence of the city on country morality. SF was paid £810 for her first novel. *Marriage*, published anonymously, was attributed to Scott by the London presses. It is the first Scottish novel of manners and country life. Its satire is friendly and its scope is broad as the story moves through London to Edinburgh and into the Scottish countryside.

SF's second novel, *The Inheritance* (1824), was also published anonymously. Because of the success of *Marriage*, she was paid £1,000 by her publisher, Blackwood. Influenced by Jane Austen's *Emma* and *Pride and Prejudice* and the novels of Maria Edgeworth, *The Inheritance* has a more tightly controlled plot and more concrete descriptions of people and places than *Marriage*. Gertrude St Clair, a young heiress, is cheated of her inheritance by her spiteful father who thinks she is not really his daughter; but she is still able to marry the man she loves because her kindly uncle, Adam Ramsey, takes her into his care when her father abandons her. Ramsey's character was based on SF's father and reveals his strengths and weaknesses. He expresses the opinion that no good writing could be done by a woman, and yet in one comic scene is described going furtively to his study to read the latest romantic novel. The narrator comments, 'Novel writers he always conceived to be born idiots, and novel readers he considered as something lower on the scale of intellect. It was, therefore, with feelings of the deepest humiliation he found himself irresistibly carried along [by his reading].'

Destiny, set in the Scottish Highlands, was SF's third and final novel, published anonymously and dedicated to Walter Scott. For this work, she received £1,700 from Blackwood. An artistic failure, the theme of the novel is encapsulated in its title. The characters are exaggerated and the merits of the story and its humour are overshadowed by this defect. *Destiny* is the story of an arrogant Scottish chieftain and his silly wife who entertain a variety of 'fashionable' London guests assisted by a faithful retainer and an uncouth clergyman. Although popular, *Destiny* disappointed SF who ceased writing after its publication in part because of failing eyesight and in part, perhaps, because she was aware of the inferior quality of this work.

From the time of her mother's death in 1797 until her father's in 1829, SF managed James Ferrier's household, since she was the only unmarried daughter. On three occasions, 1811, 1829, and 1831, she visited Walter Scott, who described her in his diary as 'simple, full of humour, and exceedingly ready at repartee'. In February 1874, SF's descriptions of her visits were posthumously published in the *Temple Bar Magazine*. After 1831, SF was approaching total blindness and spent most of her time in a darkened room entertaining only a few guests. Described in her own time as equal to Jane Austen and better than Fanny Burney, SF has not received much attention in modern times. A deeply nationalistic writer, she yet satirized pretension and eccentricity in Scottish society with lively good humour. She was also moralistic, believing that 'the only good purpose of a book is to inculcate morality and convey some lessons of instruction as well as delight'.

SF's *Works* was published anonymously in 1841 and reissued under her name in 1851. Most of her letters were destroyed at her death, in accordance with her instructions.   B. E. SCHNELLER

Works: *Marriage* (1818); *The Inheritance* (1824); *Destiny* (1831); *Works* (1841).

References: *BA* (19); *DNB*; Hale, Mrs, *Woman's Record, or, Sketches of All Distinguished Women* (1870); Parker, W., *Susan Ferrier and John Galt* (1965); Paxton, N. L., 'Subversive feminism: a reassessment of Susan Ferrier's *Marriage*', *Women & Literature* 4 (Spring 1976); Sackville, M., 'Introduction' to *Works* (1970).

'Field, Michael'

Bradley, Katherine Harris, b. 27 October 1846, Birmingham; d. 26 September 1914, Hawksyard Priory?
(Also wrote under Arran Leigh)
Cooper, Edith Emma, b. 12 January 1862, Kenilworth, Warwickshire; d. 13 December 1913, Richmond, Surrey?
(Also wrote under Isla Leigh)
Poets, playwrights
Katherine Bradley and Edith Cooper were constant companions from 1865, when Bradley joined the household of her invalid older sister, Cooper's mother, and assumed the care and tutelage of her niece. KB corresponded with John Ruskin between 1875 and 1880; she and EC came to dislike the 'speckled silliness in Ruskin's dealings with women'. In 1878 the family moved to Bristol, where Bradley and Cooper attended University College together, participating in debating societies, women's suffrage organizations, and anti-vivisectionist activities. By the time Cooper was 20, the two women had sworn 'Against the world, to be/ Poets and lovers evermore'. For the remainder of their lives, they collaborated on more than twenty-five tragic dramas and eight volumes of lyrics; after their deaths, their journal *Works and Days* revealed the great joy they had found in the life they led.

The first volume issued under the pseudonym 'Michael Field' was a pair of tragic dramas, *Callirrhoë and Fair Rosamund* (1884). Like most of their plays, these were never performed, but the book was hailed by the popular press as the work of a promising new writer. When it was revealed that the author was not a man ('some avatar of Waring'), but a spinster aunt and her spinster niece, public acclaim quickly subsided. Nevertheless, praise from Robert Browning, George Meredith, and other late nineteenth-century poets encouraged Bradley and Cooper to continue. Their many plays, mostly on classical or historical subjects, are slow and stiff, though well-researched and often at least mildly feminist in theme. The only one that was performed in their day was a commercial failure.

Their poetry, on the other hand, can be compared with the work of Oscar Wilde and George Moore (both of whom they knew) in its turn-of-the century aestheticism. *Long Ago* (1889), for example, is a collection of intense and sensuous verses based on poems by Sappho; this volume also contains 'Tiresias', a passionate appreciation of femine 'receptivity of soul' and 'the mystic raptures of the bride'. *Underneath the Bough* (1893) includes 'A Girl', Bradley's rhapsodic description of Cooper; this poem concludes with an explanation of the deeply collaborative method of 'Michael Field's' poems:

> Our souls so knit,
> I leave a page half-writ –
> The work begun
> Will be to heaven's conception done,
> If she come to it.

In 'Stream and Pool', KB elaborated on this theme: 'Mine is the eddying foam and the broken current, /Thine the serene-flowing tide, the unshattered rhythm.' Although KB wrote many of the poems in *Underneath the Bough* and *Mystic Trees* (1913) and EC wrote *Poems of Adoration* (1912), the majority of their work, including the journal *Works and Days*, was a joint effort.

Near the end of their lives, fearing the separation of death, the two women converted to Roman Catholicism.

When EC subsequently developed cancer, KB nursed her until her death then she herself died of the same illness within six months. *Works and Days*, originally written for a personal rather than a public audience, was entrusted to T. Sturge Moore, who asked to open it at the end of 1929 and publish whatever seemed fitting; he did so. The journal offers many insights into the self-definition of two talented and mutually devoted women artists.   KATHLEEN HICKOK

Selected works: The New Minnesinger and Other Poems, by Arran Leigh (1875); *Bellerophon and Other Poems*, by Arran and Isla Leigh (1881); *Callirrhoë (1884); Fair Rosamund* (1884); *The Father's Tragedy (1885); William Rufus, Loyalty or Love* (1885); *Brutus Ultor: A Play in Verse* (1886); *Canute the Great (1887); The Cup of Water* (1887); *Long Ago* (1889); *The Tragic Mary* (1890); *Stephania: A Trialogue* (1892); *Underneath the Bough: A Book of Verses* (1893); *A Question of Memory: A Play in Four Acts* (1893); *Attila, My Attila: A Play in Verse* (1896); *The World at Auction: A Drama in Verse* (1898); *Noontime Branches* (1899); *The Race of Leaves* (1901); *Julia Domna: A Drama in Verse* (1903); *Brogia: A Period Play* (1905); *Wild Honey from Various Thyme: Poems* (1908); *The Tragedy of Diane* (1911); *Poems of Adoration* (1912); *Mystic Trees* (1913); *Dedicated: An Early Work of Michael Field* (1914); *Whym Chow, Flame of Love* (1914); *Deirdre (1918); A Question of Memory (1918); Ras Byzance* (1918); *The Wattlefold: Unpublished Poems* (1930); *Works and Days: Extracts from the Journals of Michael Field* (1934).

References: BA(19); Bax, C. and Stewart, M. (eds), *The Distaff Muse* (1949); Faderman, L., *Surpassing the Love of Men* (1981); Hickok, K., *Representations of Women* (1984); Moore, T.S., 'Introduction' to *A Selection from the Poems of Michael Field* (1923); Ricketts, C., *Michael Field*, ed. P. Delaney (1976); Sturgeon, M., *Michael Field* (1922).

Fielding, Sarah

b. 8 November 1710, East Stour, Dorset; d. 9 April 1768, near Bath
Novelist, writer for children, translator

SF was the third daughter of Sarah and Colonel Edmund Fielding, and third sister of the novelist, Henry Fielding. Her father was an impoverished scion of the Earl of Denbigh, who had made his career in the army, and distinguished himself in service under Marlborough. Her mother was the daughter of Sir Henry Gould, a Judge of the Queen's Bench, and it was he who bought the small estate at East Stour on which SF was born. In 1718 SF's mother died, and her six surviving children (Henry, Catherine, Ursula, Sarah, Beatrice, and Edmund) were put under the care of their great-aunt, Mrs Catherine Cottington. Colonel Fielding left his family and moved to London, and the following year he remarried. His new wife was a Catholic, the English widow of an Italian, and shortly after their marriage the couple came to join the children at East Stour. The result was chaos. The Fielding children, encouraged by their grandmother and great-aunt, rebelled against their stepmother and continually misbehaved. They became very 'headstrong and undutiful' and so in 1719 the family was dispersed. Henry was sent to Eton, Catherine, Ursula, and Sarah to a boarding school in Salisbury, and Beatrice and Edmund to the house of their maternal grandmother, Lady Gould.

In February 1721 Lady Gould filed a bill of complaint against Edmund Fielding, in order to get not only custody of the children, but also control of the East Stour estate, for the income from this was supposed, according to her husband's will, to be used entirely for the benefit of the children. This case was won by Lady Gould in May 1722, and from that time SF was resident either at her boarding school or with her grandmother. After Lady Gould's death in 1733 the Fielding sisters continued to live in her house in Salisbury, chaperoned by an aunt, and it is not known when they left Dorset, or where they went.

During the 1740s SF lived in London, sometimes with her brother and his family, sometimes with her sisters, and it was at this time that she started her writing career. In 1742 Henry Fielding's *Joseph Andrews* was published, to which SF had contributed the letter from Leonora to Horatio. This was followed in 1744 by her first novel, *The Adventures of David Simple*, which gained its author considerable literary prestige. Over the next twenty years SF wrote two sequels to *David Simple*, a translation of Xenophon that was still a standard text at the beginning of this century, at least four more novels (including one co-written with her childhood friend, Jane Collier), and the first known full-length English novel for children. She is also thought to have been the author of a rather slavish appraisal of Richardson's *Clarissa*, and of two issues of her brother's periodical *The Covent Garden Journal* (nos. 63 and 64) on the need to give accurate references for domestic servants. The Bluestockings Elizabeth Carter and Elizabeth Montagu attributed to her the anonymous novel *The Histories of Some of the Penitents in the Magdalene House: As Supposed to Be Related by Themselves* (1760), and she had been suggested as the writer of *The History of Charlotte Summers* (1749) and *The History of Betty Barnes* (1753), although there is no evidence, either textual or circumstantial, for the last two attributions.

SF's motive for writing seems to have been largely financial. In 1738 the East Stour estate had been sold, and the proceeds divided between the Fielding siblings, but SF's share was insufficient to render her economically independent. For most of her life she was forced to rely on the generosity of her friends and relatives, and her writing provided a valuable supplementary source of income. Her wealthy cousin, Lady Mary Wortley Montagu, considered SF's literary activities as an unfortunate necessity. 'I . . . heartily pity her,' she wrote, 'constrained by her circumstances to seek her bread by a method I do not doubt she despises,' and SF suggested in the 'Advertisement' to *David Simple* that she was driven into print by 'distress of circumstances'.

While resident in London SF became a member of the circle of admiring females around Samuel Richardson. She often attended the gatherings at Richardson's house at North End, during which the great man would read aloud from his own works. Richardson thought highly of SF's novels, three of which he printed, and it was he who retailed Samuel Johnson's famous comment on her work. 'What a knowledge of the human heart!' he exclaimed in a letter to SF. 'Well might a critical judge of writing say, as he did to me, that your late brother's knowledge of it was not (fine writer as he was) comparable to yours. His was but as the knowledge of the outside of a clockwork machine, while your's was that of all the finer springs and movements of the inside.'

Following the deaths of her three sisters between 1750 and 1751, and of her brother Henry in 1754, SF retired from London society, and in 1758 she took up permanent residence in Bath, possibly at Widcombe Lodge. From here she was a frequent visitor to Claverton, the house of the philanthropic Ralph Allen, and on Allen's death in 1764 he bequeathed her £100. SF died in April 1768, and was buried in the parish church of Charlcombe on the outskirts of Bath. The Rev. John Hoadley erected a tablet to her memory in the Abbey church in Bath.

Nowadays SF tends to be remembered as the sister of Henry Fielding, rather than as a novelist in her own right, but in the eighteenth century the situation was different. It was not only Richardson who believed that the two writers were of comparable status. Clara Reeve wrote in *The Progress of Romance* that SF's works 'are not unworthy next to be mentioned after her brother's. If they do not equal them in wit and learning, they excell in some other material merits, that are more beneficial to their readers', and the anonymous author of the *Critical Remarks on Sir Charles Grandison* preferred SF's novels to Richardson's final work. On its publication many critics believed that *David Simple* (which, like all SF's works except her translation of Xenophon, was published anonymously) was the work of her brother. The second edition of the novel therefore contained a preface by Henry, disclaiming responsibility for the book, declaring it to be the work of 'a young woman . . . nearly and dearly allied to me'.

Much of this preface is given over to Fielding's refutation of the suggestion that he was the author of *The Causidicade*, a rather scurrilous piece of doggerel attacking members of the legal profession. But he also provides what now reads as a rather patronising recommendation of his sister's work. He claims that apart from making a few suggestions about the novel's structure and the direction of the plot, his role in the production amounted 'to little more than the Correction of some small Errors, which Want of Habit in Writing chiefly occasioned, and which no Man of Learning would think worth his Censure in a Romance; nor any Gentleman, in the writings of a Young Woman'. Many of these corrections involved the removal of that characteristic feature of female writing – the dash. Fielding regularized his sister's punctuation, and corrected some of her colloquial expressions, in order to make the work conform to his model of the correct, masculine style.

Despite these interventions, *David Simple* is very different from the work of Henry Fielding. Many modern readers have been dissatisfied with the flatness of the characterization and the absence of psychological development, but to read the novel in these terms is to fail to realize what SF was trying to achieve. She saw the novel as a fundamentally moral rather than a realistic form, and used her characters to embody certain moral positions within an allegorical structure. The novel portrays the experiences of a naive but virtuous character, as he travels through society in search of a friend. In the process he encounters numerous people, who recount their experiences of the villainy of the world, so that the hero and the reader are gradually brought to recognize that corruption and hypocrisy are endemic in society. This recognition leads, at the end of the novel, to his retreat from the complex modern world, to a simple-life community in the countryside with the select group of friends that he gathered in the course of his travels.

The pessimism inherent in this narrative was brought out in 1753, with the publication of a sequel entitled *David Simple, Volume the Last*. This traces the adventures of David Simple and his wife and friends after their retreat into the countryside, and represents a succession of bleak disasters. It is not only deeply depressing, but carefully structured and tightly written, bringing out the full potential of the allegorical narrative form. Lady Mary Wortley Montagu commented after its publication, 'Sally has mended her style.'

SF's experiments with allegorical form were developed even further in 1754 with the publication of *The Cry: A New Dramatic Fable*, which she co-wrote with Jane Collier. *The Cry* is an allegorical assembly of censorious individuals, to whom the central character, Portia, must present her narrative. Portia is supported by Una, the allegorical figure of truth, and in the discussions between these figures SF dramatized the major issues of eighteenth-century literary theory. Questions of the nature of truth and fiction, and of the role of narrative and experience, are implicit in the interrogation and defence of Portia, and in the progressive clarification and expansion of her story.

The Cry was not, however, a popular work. Lady Mary Wortley Montagu condemned it as 'the most absurd [fable] I ever saw', while asserting that its sentiments were 'just'. Greater success greeted the publication in 1759 of the more structurally orthodox novel *The Countess of Dellwyn*. This story of female infidelity was written to 'display the natural tendency of virtue towards the attainment of happiness' and to show 'that misery is the unavoidable consequence of vicious life'. In its prioritization of moral and didactic structure above realistic characterization and psychological depth, this novel in many ways exemplified the limitations but also the power and potential of the narrative form developed by SF, for her bold and experimental use of narrative was primarily used to inculcate a scheme of conventional moral precepts. It was this combination of innovation and pedagogy that generated *The Governess*, her lively and morally improving novel for children, and encouraged her to analyse the moral characters of two of the most striking women of the ancient world, in *The Lives of Cleopatra and Octavia*.   LIZ BELLAMY

Works: *The Adventures of David Simple: Containing an Account of his Travels thro' the Cities of London and Westminster, in the Search of a Real Friend* (1744); *Familiar Letters between the Principal Characters in David Simple, and Some Others . . . To which is added, A Vision* (1747); *The Governess, or, Little Female Academy* (1749); *Remarks on Clarissa, Addressed to the Author* (1749); *The Adventures of David Simple, Volume the Last in Which His History is Concluded* (1753); *The Cry: A New Dramatic Fable* (with Jane Collier) (1754); *The Lives of Cleopatra and Octavia* (1757); *The History of The Countess of Dellwyn* (1759); *The History of Ophelia* (1760); *Xenophon's Memoirs of Socrates: With the Defence of Socrates Before His Judges: translated from the original Greek* (1762). In addition SF may have been the author of *The Histories of Some of the Penitents in the Magdalene House: As Supposed to be Related by Themselves* (1760).

References: Kelsall, M., 'Introduction' to *David Simple* (1969); Richardson, S., *The Correspondence of Samuel Richardson*, ed. A. L. Barbauld (1804); OCCL; Spencer, J., *The Rise of the Woman Novelist* (1986); Todd; Todd, J., *Sensibility: An Introduction* (1986); *The Sign of Angellica* (1989).

Fiennes, Celia

b. 1662, Newton Toney, near Salisbury; d. 1741, Hackney

Travel writer

The travels of CF between about 1684 and 1712 are the only ones that we know of undertaken and recorded by a woman at a time when travel memoirs were particularly popular. Hers was the first comprehensive survey of England since those of Harrison and Camden in the sixteenth century, predating the better-known tour of Defoe and contemporary with that of Henri Misson. CF's work remained unpublished until the nineteenth century.

CF was the daughter of Colonel Nathaniel and Frances (née Whitehead) Fiennes, and came of a prominent Puritan family distinguished for its opposition to Charles I. CF's Nonconformist upbringing is reflected in her comments on the size and quality of preaching at Dissenting meetings in the towns she visited. At the age of about 22 she began her journeys in south-western England and in the ensuing eighteen years visited every county in England and the border areas of Scotland and Wales. Nothing is known of CF except what she herself recorded, so the last thirty years of her life after she wrote the journals remain a blank.

In 1697 CF made her first large tour of the north, probably in the company of two kinswomen. If modest and at times prim, she was undoubtedly intrepid, travelling on horseback over roads in poor repair with two servants (on one occasion these are identified as male), staying at inns and occasionally with relatives. On one occasion her horse throws her (this she dismisses with a cursory 'indeed mercy and truth allwayes have attended me') and on another she is dogged by highwaymen, but her narrative is always matter-of-fact, recording her surroundings for posterity rather than expressing her personal reactions to it. CF's taste is for the modern, the technical, and for curiosities – from skeletons used for teaching anatomy to the fantastic waterworks and architectural minutiae of aristocratic country houses, which she describes in detail. Haddon Hall in Derbyshire is dismissed as 'a good old house . . . and good Gardens but nothing very curious as the mode now is'.

The other main subject of CF's commentary was manufacturing, particularly textile production (she observes that in East Anglia people commonly spin outdoors in the lanes) and mineral industries (tin mining, salt making, the use of coal and peat). Her vocabulary is limited: the most descriptive praise she can muster is 'a pretty neat market town with streets well-pitched'. She rarely notices people, especially not those of a lower social level than herself, with the exception of the Scottish borderers, whose poverty she attributes to sloth, and an occasional landlady, of whom she enquires about the local ways. In one rare intellectual observation she describes a Dissenting meeting of several hundred people and observes, 'I was glad to see soe many tho' they were but of the meaner sort, for indeed its the poor receive the Gospell.' Her style has been called naive, but is, rather, the product of an active, unromantic and technical mind, curious to see the world more than to reproduce it with any kind of literary finesse.

The ostensible motive for CF's travels was her health. She describes each of the newly fashionable spas throughout England, down to the music played for entertainment and the quality of the patrons. But from her activities her health appears to be more than adequate, and her motive for travelling and for writing can better be found in her own preface, where she recommends, especially to the ladies, 'the studdy of those things which tends to improve the mind and make our Lives pleasant and comfortable as well as proffitable . . . and render Suffering and Age supportable and Death less formidable and a future State more happy'.

CF compiled most of her notes in 1702 but her work was not printed until 1812 when Southey included two extracts from the manuscript anonymously in a miscellany. The work first appeared in its entirety in 1888, edited by a kinswoman of CF to whom the manuscript had descended.   AMY ERICKSON

Works: *Through England on a Side Saddle in the Time of William and Mary*, ed. E. Griffiths (1888), re-ed. by C. Morris as *The Journeys of Celia Fiennes*, (1947). **References:** *DNB*; Hillaby, J., 'Introduction' to *The Journeys of Celia Fiennes* (1983); Morris, C., 'Introduction' to *The Journeys of Celia Fiennes* (1947); Parkes, J., *Travel in England in the 17th Century* (1925); Todd; Willy, M. E., *Three Women Diarists* (1964).

Figes, Eva

b. 15 April 1932, Berlin

Novelist, critic, translator

EF was born in Berlin of German Jewish parents, Emil Eduard and Irma Unger, but has now taken British nationality. Her European background – she lived seven years of her early life in Germany – remains a powerful influence, with the shadow of the holocaust recurring in her work.

She was educated at Kingsbury Grammar School and Queen Mary College, London, graduating in 1953. After university she worked as an editor at Longman, Weidenfeld & Nicolson, and Blackie. Her first novel, *Equinox*, was published in 1966. She acknowledges Kafka and Beckett as being influential to her writing and to these two writers must be added a third, Virgina Woolf. She is concerned with developing new forms in her fiction in an attempt to break away from what she sees as the conservative tradition in the British novel. By doing this she aligns herself with the Modernist school. Without abandoning a formal structure she also explores the inner self.

EF treats the man or woman set apart from society; Janus in a *Winter Journey* (1967), Lily in *Light* (1983), and Konek in *Konek Landing* (1969), who suffers the ultimate in loneliness, the refugee displaced by war, stateless, surviving by the harshest means possible in order to survive. In some sections of her novels EF has a strong lyric sense, and they read like verse, rich in descriptive and sensuous quality. This quality serves to bind together themes which may be dislocated or interrupted. In *Light* the continuity realized in EF's lyric style is personified. Claude (Monet), the artist who seeks perfection in light and landscape, is at the same time troubled by the realities of death and the passing of the things he values.

In one of her recent books, *The Seven Ages* (1986), EF evokes 1,000 years of women's history. Through the mind of a retired midwife we hear the voices of women from the dawn of history to the modern age. The cycle of women's lives, adolescence, maturity, pregnancy and death, remains the same from that time to this. Again there is a strong poetic impulse in the work and a lyric beauty.

Her latest novel, *Ghosts* (1988), is written in short paragraphs. The woman's voice, running through these paragraphs, talks about 'ghosts'; the ghosts of her children now grown up and gone, the ghost of her husband, the ghost of her mother and father, the ghost of another country and the ghost of her younger self. Again this novel has the concentration and intensity of verse. The repetition of certain words for emphasis adds to the rhythmic sense of the whole and gives it a unified and moving quality.

As a critic EF has gained a substantial reputation. In particular, *Patriarchal Attitudes* (1970) has achieved the status of a classic text. It appeared before either Germaine Greer's *The Female Eunuch* or Kate Millett's *Sexual Politics* and is an examination of the ideas which have contributed to the placing of women in subservient roles in most societies. It discusses the influence of Christianity, the rise of capitalism, and Freudian psychoanalysis in relation to the subject.

EF has translated books by Martin Walser, Elisabeth Borchers, Bernhard Grizmek, and George Sand.   ALISON RIMMER

Works: *Equinox* (1966); *Winter Journey* (1967); *The Musicians of Bremen* (1967); *The Banger* (1968); *Konek Landing* (1969); *Patriarchal Attitudes* (1970); *Scibble Sam* (1971); *B* (1972); *Days* (1974); *Tragedy and Social Evolution* (1976); *Nelly's Version* (1977); *Little Eden* (1978); *Waking* (1981); *Light* (1983); *The Seven Ages* (1986); *Ghosts* (1988).

References: *CA*; *DLB*; Drabble.

Findlater, Mary

b. 28 March 1865, Lochearnhead, Perthshire; d. 22 Novenber 1963, Comrie, Perthshire
Novelist

Findlater, Jane

b. 4 November 1866, Lochearnhead, Perthshire; d. 20 May 1946, Comrie, Perthshire

Novelist

JF and MF were the daughters of Eric Findlater and Sarah Borthwick. They had an elder sister, Sarah. They were brought up in the Free Church manse at Lochearnhead where their father was the minister. Story telling was a favourite winter occupation and the sisters' relations and friends made it into a fine art. The stringencies of their economic position were not made any better by their mother's old-fashioned taste – the girls were acutely conscious that their clothes made them look ridiculous. The girls were educated by governesses and started to write when they were children. When Eric Findlater died in 1886, the family moved to Prestonpans. JF's first novel was accepted by Methuen in 1895 and after this the sisters supported themselves and their mother and older sister by their writing. JF's novel was admired by many famous people: Sir Edward and Lady Grey, Lady Frances Balfour, Ellen Terry, and William Gladstone. It was in this sort of society that the gregarious sisters continued to move.

In 1900 they went to Devon for the sake of their mother's health; there they were happy to meet Miss Vulliamy, the sister-in-law of George Meredith whose novels they greatly admired. They also met an American writer, Kate Douglas Wiggin, who, one dismal weekend, persuaded MF and JF and another friend, Charlotte Stewart (pseudonym Allan McAulay), to collaborate on a novel which was published as *The Affair at the Inn* (1909). Kate Wiggin suggested they should tour America and their publishers in America agreed; they left in 1905. They found New York overpowering but felt happier in New England where they met and became friendly with William and Alice James. They continued writing steadily and to great critical acclaim until the outbreak of the First World War which disrupted the world they had known. They did voluntary work in a local hospital during the war. In 1923 they proposed to build a new house in Rye. MF was operated on for cancer but recovered successfully to enjoy happy years there. By this time the sisters' popularity was fading and, when their work was set beside that of D. H. Lawrence or Virginia Woolf, it was labelled 'Victorian'. They moved back to Perth in 1940 to escape threats of a German invasion. JF died of a heart attack some years later but MF lived on quietly, preparing materials for a biography.

Crossriggs (1908), the Findlater sisters' finest collaboration, examines the life of an intelligent, capable woman in the late nineteenth century. Alexandra Hope has to provide financially for her eccentric father, widowed sister, and five children, at a time when it was not thought fitting for middle-class women, even if impoverished, to work for a living. She also thinks of her own personal fulfilment. The physical strain of work, nursing her family through a series of illnesses and managing a house, make Alex irritable and tired, a fact the family notices but finds hard to accept. In love with a married man and courted by an eligible young bachelor, Alex's emotions and sexual desires, described with a mixture of discretion and frankness, admit no easy resolution. In the end the writers avoid the position of marriage to a second-best choice or of second best status for Alex as a mistress by releasing her for a world tour; she begins it as a forward-looking, self-reliant, emotionally stable individual.

In their work JF and MF affirm and develop the insights of earlier women authors; they work self-consciously in a tradition of women's fiction. Thus, while they describe reactionary or confused attitudes to women, their heroines themselves do not find it surprising that they are able to be educated as well as men, to earn their own living, and to exist quite happily without being married. In the haunting *The Green Graves of Balgowrie*, JF discusses the place of education in a woman's development; in this novel she also describes the effects of mental cruelty on two young sisters who live alone with their increasingly insane mother. *The Ladder to the Stars* (1906) contains the story of a woman who discovers her own creativity as a novelist despite the drawbacks of a narrow-minded family and the necessity of caring for a sick mother. MF's singly authored work is arguably less subtle than JF's or the collaborations. However, her sense of humour and intelligence makes a novel like *The Rose of Joy* (1903), a study of the merits of marriage, a pleasant and informed piece of writing. The work of both sisters possesses an arresting sense of place, which, especially in the Scottish novels, produces a background of gentle melancholy.

BETH DICKSON

Works: MF: *Songs and Sonnets* (1895); *Over the Hills* (1897); *Betty Musgrave* (1899); *A Narrow Way* (1901); *The Rose of Joy* (1903); *A Blind Bird's Nest* (1907); *Tents of a Night* (1914); JF: *The Green Graves of Balgowrie* (1895); *A Daughter of Strife* (1897); *Rachel* (1899); *The Story of a Mother* (1902); *Stones from a Glass House* (1904); *All That Happened in a Week* (1905); *The Ladder to the Stars* (1906); *Seven Scots Stories* (1912); *A Green Grass Widow and Other Stories* (1921); MF and JF: *Tales that are Told* (1901); *Crossriggs* (1908); *Penny Monypenny* (1911); *Content with Flies* (1916); *Seen and Heard Before and After 1914* (1916); *Beneath the Visiting Moon* (1923); MF and JF with Kate Douglas Wiggin and Allan McAulay: *The Affair at the Inn* (1904); *Robinetta* (1911).

References: Mackenzie, E., *The Findlater Sisters: Literature and Friendship* (1964).

Fitzgerald, Penelope

b. 17 December 1916

Novelist

PF was born into a family distinguished by achievement in letters and religion; her father, Edmund Valpy, was the editor of *Punch* and her mother the niece of Monsignor Ronald Knox, the celebrated Biblical scholar. At Somerville College, Oxford, she read English and graduated with first-class honours in 1939. In 1941 she married Desmond Fitzgerald. She has worked as a journalist and as a programmer for the BBC. Before her first work of fiction in 1977, she published two biographies, one of Edward Burne-Jones, the other of her uncles, the four Knox brothers. She has also written *Charlotte Mew and her Friends* and edited *The Novel on Blue Paper*, an incomplete work by William Morris.

PF is the author of six novels which have enjoyed both critical and popular success. She published no fiction until the age of 61, and has employed throughout a remarkably fluent and economical prose style. Her work is characterized by her careful illumination of limited social contexts and an unsentimental, although not unsympathetic, treatment of character.

The Golden Child, a thriller set 'in the great hive of the unnamed museum with the Golden Treasure at its heart', presents the stifling world of that museum and its competing personalities, obsessed with the ritual of their institution, as a metaphor for society. Sir William Livingstone Simpkin, with his sympathy for the crowds of cold children queueing for admission around the building, is the humane and moral centre of gravity in the novel. Knowing that the golden treasure is a forgery, he shuns any role in the commercial spectacle and dies when crushed between two shelves in the museum's library. In an explosive climax, the glass case containing the golden child breaks and 'reveals the ancient royal child as an undernourished, recently deceased African child'.

PF's subsequent novel, *The Bookshop* (1978), also concentrates on an individual of courage and conviction living within a world of competing forces. The town of Hardborough is a depressed area where Florence Green decides to open a bookshop in a damp and haunted building. From the outset, the physical setting, economic conditions, and social context of the town collaborate against her. PF creates a carefully localized drama of individual courage and determination assaulted by inhospitable natural forces and knowing political powers. *The Bookshop* is a novel about the oppression imposed both by class divisions and by the divisions within an individual consciousness.

In her third novel, *Offshore* (1979), for which she won the Booker Prize, PF's powers of specific and richly atmospheric description enable her to present a whole community with extreme brevity. Set in 1961 in a community of houseboat dwellers, a classless cast of characters living on the tidal Thames at Battersea Reach, the novel presents men and women living in a divided world, half of the time stranded in the mud, the other half drifting. As in her depiction of Florence Green, PF is interested in the ways in which human beings live within particular contexts; some succeed, some do not, and once again PF is particularly successful at creating children who are knowing survivors in an adult world. *Offshore* ends neither at sea nor on dry land but in flux: the houseboat dwellers remain subject to the threat of cruel tides on the one hand and gelatinous mud on the other.

Human Voices (1980), written mainly in dialogue, is perhaps PF's least engaging novel. This time the fictional microcosm is the BBC's Recorded Programmes Department in the summer and autumn of 1940, a hive of power games and territorial intrigue. Here, too, the figure of a child is of considerable significance, for it is 16-year-old Annie Asra who is the novel's most fluent speaker of truth. More than in any other PF novel, style functions as content; in her use of both speech and silence, in her attempts to capture the nuances and peculiarities of human communication, PF has in *Human Voices* extended the range of her own voice. With the delightful *At Freddie's* (1982), PF returns to a world of aged eccentrics and knowing children, in this case the Temple Stage School, founded and run by Miss Freddie Wentworth. For nearly forty years she has trained child actors for the London theatre, but a crisis occurs when the government decides to establish a National Stage School. Realizing that she may go out of business, Freddie orchestrates a letter-writing campaign to *The Times*. In the end, although the government's plans are shelved, Freddie decides that she will in future train her charges for television commercials. Like Florence Green of *The Bookshop*, Freddie is a survivor; unlike her, she is a successful one.

The readers of PF's fiction should resist the temptation to dismiss it as mere light entertainment. While not overburdened with metaphysical concerns, it is distinguished by undeniable excellences of style, by sharply focused insights into character, and by a consistently humane concern for the moral dimension of existence. ROBERT E. HOSMER, JR

Works: *Edward Burne-Jones* (1975); *The Knox Brothers* (1977); *The Golden Child* (1977); *The Bookshop* (1978); *Charlotte Mew and Her Friends* (1979); *Offshore* (1979); *Human Voices* (1980); (ed.), *The Novel on Blue Paper* by W. Morris (1981); *At Freddie's* (1982); *Innocence* (1986).
References: *CA*; *DLB*.

Forbes, Rosita

b. 16 January 1890, Swinderley, Lincolnshire; d. 30 June 1967, Bermuda
Travel writer, novelist
RF was the daughter of Herbert Torr, a Lincolnshire landowner, and his wife Rosita (*née* Graham). She was the eldest of the couple's six children. Little is known of her childhood other than that she was an avid reader of books. In 1911 she married Colonel Ronald Forbes but, after travelling with him to Australia and India, they were divorced in 1917. Meanwhile, RF served the war effort by driving ambulances on the Western Front, a service for which she received two decorations. Subsequently she travelled around the world with a woman friend and recorded her experiences in her first book, *Unconducted Wanderers* (1919).

The highly placed figures whom RF met in the Middle Eastern capitals gave her a long-lasting concern for the life and politics of the region, and also facilitated the planning of her first genuinely exploratory journey, that over the Libyan desert to Kufara, an oasis which had only once before been visited by Europeans. She was accompanied by the Egyptian explorer Ahmed Hassanein Bey, whose understanding of regional politics and of desert conditions was of vital importance to her expedition. Hassanein Bey felt that RF greatly underestimated his part in their joint exploits in her *The Secret of the Sahara: Kufara* (1921), despite that book's acknowledgement that his 'knowledge of the Senussi . . . was invaluable to me'. Because the Italian authorities in Libya were reluctant to allow RF to travel through the Arab kingdoms she was obliged to escape the Italian zone disguised as an Islamic woman, 'Khadija'.

In 1921 she remarried, again to a military man, Colonel Arthur McGrath. The early years of the decade were marked by a series of awards recognizing her explorations: the Gold Medals of the Royal Antwerp and French Geographical Societies in 1921 and 1923 respectively were followed by the Silver Medal of the Royal Society of Arts in 1924. She continued to travel widely in Africa and the Middle East, visiting a brigand chief in the Atlas Mountains whose biography she had been commissioned to write, and journeying through Ethiopia with a film maker. During the 1930s RF expanded her repertoire with journeys to South America and through Afghanistan to Samarkand; in the Second World

War she lectured in the US and Canada in support of the war effort. In their later years RF and her husband retired to the Bahamas, where McGrath died in 1962. RF herself died five years later in Bermuda.

The bulk of RF's travel books is made up of chapters of anecdote recounting the discomforts of travel with grim amusement. The indigenous populations of RF's chosen countries can often appear in such chapters simply as the objects of humour or curiosity. In *From Red Sea to Blue Nile* (1925) her expedition arrives in a village stricken by disease to be greeted by pleas for help from the villagers: 'There was one funny case of a small imp with a pain in his middle, when his older brother explained that he had caught a young bird and eaten it alive . . . . We agreed that this was most unfortunate.' But such chapters are punctuated by anthropological sections in which African society and ethics are given serious and respectful attention. RF shows a particular interest in the fortunes of women in the countries through which she travelled, which often contrasted strongly with the independence which her own bravery, as well as her wealth and social connections, afforded her. In a chapter 'Concerning Women' in *From Red Sea to Blue Nile* RF notes that 'Money is the alpha and omega of Abyssinia, and, through the traditional law of inheritance in its only definite, enduring form – land – it is in the hands of the men'.

RF's novels often share the African settings of many of her travel books. Their heroes, however, are not generally Africans, but typically military men serving one or other of the colonial powers in Africa: in *If the Gods Laugh* (1925) Colonel Navarro, 'the conqueror of Tripolitania, uncrowned king amongst the Arabs', in *A Fool's Hell* (1923) Michael Treherne of the 59th Lancers. Their heroines, correspondingly, are well-to-do but bored young women in search of travels and adventure such as Victoria Torini of *If the Gods Laugh* ('I want to race through life, with the wind in my face . . .').   JAMES SMITH

Works: *Unconducted Wanderers* (1919); *The Secret of the Sahara: Kufara* (1921); *The Jewel in the Lotus* (1922); *Quest* (1922); *A Fool's Hell* (1923); *El Raisuni* (1924); *If the Gods Laugh* (1925); *Sirocco* (1927); *Adventure* (1928); *From Red Sea to Blue Nile* (1926); *One Flesh* (1930); *Conflict* (1931); *Ordinary People* (1931); *Eight Republics in Search of a Future* (1933); *The Extraordinary House* (1934); *Women Called Wild* (1935); *The Golden Vagabond* (1936); *Forbidden Road* (1937); *These Are Real People* (1937); *A Unicorn in the Bahamas* (1939); (ed.) *Women of All Lands* (1939); *India of the Princes* (1939); *The Prodigious Caribbean* (1940); *These Men I Knew* (1940); *Gypsy in the Sun* (1944); *Appointment with Destiny* (1946); *Sir Henry Morgan* (1948); *Appointment in the Sun* (1949); *Islands in the Sun* (1949). **References:** CA: DNB; Hassanein Bey, A. M., *The Lost Oases* (1925); Philby, H. St J., *Forty Years in the Wilderness* (1957); Wilson, H. W., *Twentieth Century Authors* (1942).

Forest, Antonia
b.?, London
Writer for children

An only child, AF was born in London, where she later received her education at a Girls' Public Day School Trust school. Her father was of Russian descent, her mother was Irish. She has written thirteen books, ten of which are about the Marlow family in the present century. Without originally intending to add to the genre of historical novels, she was inspired by the Shakespeare Quatercentenary celebrations in 1964, to write two books, *The Player's Boy* (1970), and *The Players and the Rebels* (1971), extensions of the 'Marlow' series into the sixteenth century. These deal mainly with the Elizabethan theatre. *The Thursday Kidnapping* (1963), is unconnected with the 'Marlow' books: it was commended by the Library Association.

AF is distinctive as a children's writer, as her books do not fall easily into the category marked 'Books for children'. This is partly because of her method, which can be elliptical, as in *The Ready-made Family* (1967), where Karen Marlow's marriage to a middle-aged widower with three children is understood more through the silences that surround the event, than through any straightforward explanations. There is a complex psychology in all her work that indicates an author as worthy of adult as of juvenile attention. The literary vehicle of the 'series', which builds up slowly, demands not only a consistency in the quality of writing but also a coherent and developing vision of the characters.

AF's themes and interests are not always accessible to the child reader. One such theme is the concept of 'being', which is dealt with in *Peter's Room* (1961), where the younger Marlows act out their own version of the Brontë's Gondal saga, attempting under cover of their roles to probe their own potentialities. Her other books show a similar concern with literature, history and esoterica, such as falconry. The subjects are treated with sensitivity and offer the reader many new perceptions (see, for example, her treatment of *The Tempest*, in *The Cricket Term*) as well as contributing to the life and consciousness of the Marlows.   SUSAN ANG

Works: *Autumn Term* (1948); *The Marlows and the Traitor* (1953); *Falconer's Lure* (1957); *End of Term* (1959); *Peter's Room* (1961); *The Thursday Kidnapping* (1963); *The Thuggery Affair* (1965); *The Ready-Made Family* (1967); *The Players' Boy* (1970); *The Players and the Rebels* (1971); *The Cricket Term* (1974); *The Attic Term* (1976); *Run Away Home* (1982).
References: *CA*; *OCCL*.

Forster, Margaret
b. 25 May 1938, Carlisle, Cumberland
Novelist, biographer, reviewer
MF is unusual in that she had a working-class background which was also culturally 'deprived': her father was a fitter, her mother a housewife, 'better educated, but though intelligent and artistic, no more a reader than he was'. School introduced her to books and she read avidly, an activity not endorsed at home; lack of rapport with an elder brother and younger sister resulted in time spent on her own. A teacher identified her writing ability very early, and increasingly MF felt compelled to try to emulate the books she admired, among them *Wuthering Heights*; writing, for her, 'arose directly out of being a voracious reader.' In 1949 MF gained an eleven-plus scholarship place at Carlisle and County High School for Girls, and in 1957, an Open Scholarship to Somerville College, Oxford, to read history, partly a tactical choice of subject, and partly because the English syllabus 'ended mid-C19th which was where I wanted to start'. On completing her degree, she married, in June 1960, the writer and journalist Hunter Davies, whom she had known since her schooldays; he had just been appointed to *The Sunday Times*, and they settled permanently in London. Her first novel, in the manner of Balzac, was written between June and September, but rejected (later reworked as *The Bogeyman*). In 1961, as a reaction, she wrote *Dames' Delight* while teaching English at Barnsbury Girls' School (1961–3). Its publication in 1964 successfully launched her, but also, in her view, 'in the wrong direction', only to be reversed in 1974 with *The*

Seduction of Mrs Pendlebury. In the intervening years, further novels steadily appeared, and writing was fitted in with family commitments (a daughter was born in 1964, a son in 1966). Increasing dissatisfaction with the novels led her to turn, instead, to the different demands and discipline of biography, a dialectic in her writing that she has maintained. The birth of her third child, a daughter, in 1972 saw a return to the novel through constraints on time, but with the determination to write differently. Although a disappointment, *Mrs Pendlebury* remains, for her, a significant work, together with *Mother Can You Hear Me?* and *Private Papers*. From 1977 to 1980 she was chief non-fiction reviewer for the London *Evening Standard*, she has been a judge for the Booker Prize, and in 1975 she was elected Fellow of the Royal Society of Literature. She has recently completed a biography of Elizabeth Barrett Browning, together with an edited selection of the poems, and has plans for a further novel.

MF's novels have received little critical attention beyond reviews. Consistently intelligent, perceptive, and forcefully unsentimental, they are preoccupied with relationships and their inherent difficulties. MF has come, increasingly, to see her work as feminist, especially in its focus on the family and mother-daughter relationships. A distinctive feature is the exploration of gender and class.

Dames' Delight (1964) is loosely based on MF's Oxford experience. Morag, clever *and* beautiful, recounts her negotiation of sexuality, achievement, and class. Disillusion comes from the outset ('Oxford, the Home of Pressed Steel' announces the station hoarding); worse is to follow in the all-women college and the university, over both of which Morag triumphs. She is the prototype of MF's central female characters: usually extraordinary, their perspective functions to question superficial conformity and the 'hypocrisy underlying all relationships' (*Mrs Pendlebury*), which are seen as invasive, oppressive in their obligations, yet possibly essential to social existence. The heroine of *Georgy Girl* is unbeautiful, obstinately, often hilariously, refusing to conform to femininity; however, she needs heterosexual relations for her self-realization. *Fenella Phizackerley* is handicapped by excessive, merely physical beauty, and society's evaluation of her in these terms; she does, however, achieve self-knowledge. The protagonist of *Miss Owen-Owen is at Home* does not: dominating, achievement-orientated, as appointed headmistress she takes the Girls' Grammar School (and local community) in hand; denying sexuality herself, she arrogantly dictates the lives of others. In these earlier novels, MF presents the 'community of women' (school, college, relationships) as negative and divisive; in *The Park*, six women remain divided, rather than united, by their experiences, albeit different, as wives and mothers. *The Seduction of Mrs Pendlebury* expresses more openly the ambivalence in MF's work about the desirability of relationships, and Rose Pendlebury swings excessively and disastrously from one pole to the other. MF's use of multiple perspectives, however, mostly refuses any authorial resolution. In *The Bride of Lowther Fell*, Alexandra distances herself physically in remote Cumberland: 'I had escaped the chains of motherhood and the servitude of marriage. I was my own person.' Events, however, lead her to begin to overcome her fear of involvement and here a clearer emphasis emerges.

The family, and mother-daughter relationships as its embodiment, is a recurrent theme. Morag's family do not communicate. The Roberts (*The Bogeyman*) articulate, but destructively, family tensions: the father appears central, but the catalyst is the uncompromising teenage daughter – a recurring figure in MF's work – overshadowing her passive mother. Morag, too, rejects everything her mother's life stands for (as does Fenella Phizackerley), particularly its class-bound impoverishment of potential. The mother-daughter continuum is central to *Mother Can You Hear Me?* and *Private Papers*, MF's best novels to date. Both are studies in middle/later life; both use memory as a means of resolving crises of identity and relationships. *In Mother Can You Hear Me?*, Angela, working-class daughter become middle-class wife/mother travels, literally and emotionally, between the two roles. Unable to identify with her ailing mother ('Mother had been nowhere at all') or to understand her daughter's 'rejection' of her ('she had attempted to mould her relationship with Sadie differently'), she experiences failure and guilt in both directions. Working through her mother's death, she finally achieves acceptance and balance, and hope for relations with her daughter. *Private Papers* is a wider, impressive study. Penelope, in her old age, records in her 'diary' her life as wife (widowed by the Second World War) and as mother to her daughters. Struggling to come to terms with her attempts to be a 'good' mother (instilling her conviction of 'the family' as necessarily 'happy'), and the reality of her daughters' personalities and chosen ways of life, she rehearses the past as a form of explanation and self-justification. Discovering the diary, the eldest daughter vehemently challenges the account, recording her own version in secret. The daughter has the last word, but attributes the diary's abrupt cessation to positive causes: 'We stand alone . . . we are three strong, assertive people to whom the Family is not sacrosanct. But what Mother came to appreciate was that perhaps this does not amount to failure on her or our part'.   JUDITH SKEELS

Works: *Dames' Delight* (1964); *Georgy Girl* (1966); *Georgy Girl* (screenplay) (with Peter Nichols) (1969); *The Bogeyman* (1966); *The Travels of Maudie Tipstaff* (1967); *The Park* (1968); *Miss Owen-Owen is at Home* (1969); *Fenella Phizackerley* (1971); *Mr Bone's Retreat* (1971); *The Rash Adventurer: The Rise and Fall of Charles Edward Stuart* (1973); *The Seduction of Mrs Pendlebury* (1974); *William Makepeace Thackeray: Memoirs of a Victorian Gentleman* (1978); *Mother Can You Hear Me?* (1979); *The Bride of Lowther Fell* (1981); *Marital Rites* (1982); *Significant Sisters: The Grassroots of Active Feminism 1839–1939* (1984); *Private Papers* (1986).
References: CN.

Fothergill, Jessie

b. June 1851, Cheetham Hill, Manchester; d. 28 July 1891, Berne, Switzerland
Novelist

JF was the first child born to Thomas Fothergill, who was a manager in the cotton business, and his wife Anne. While she was still young they moved from Manchester to a house in Bowdon, Cheshire, ten miles from the city. Her father died when she was 15, and soon afterwards the family moved to Littleborough, near Rochdale; JF was sent to a Harrogate boarding school. After her first visit to Germany in 1874, she began her literary career by publishing her first novel, *Healey* (1875), in three volumes, drawing on her experience of the relationship between genteel and working life in Littleborough. Her first popular success came with her third novel, *The First Violin* (1877), which was later dramatized. She continued to live in Littleborough but spent her last years on the continent, where she died at the age of only 40.

The themes considered in *Made or Marred* (1881) are typical of those treated in much of JF's fiction. Principal amongst these is a romantic liaison between characters of differing social backgrounds. Philip Massey, an office clerk in the large north-western city of Irkford, falls in love with Angela Fairfax, a young gentlewoman recently impoverished who has been reduced to giving music lessons in order to support herself. Angela's aim, however, is simply to secure through marriage the standard of living to which she has previously been accustomed, and when Philip returns from company business in China, she has already married a rich but ageing cotton broker. The novel raises the theme announced by its title in an early chapter called 'What is Success?', and the denouement answers this question in somewhat schematic fashion: Angela, apparently made, is inwardly marred by a loveless marriage, whilst her younger sister Mabelle eventually marries Philip and is thereby rewarded for her earlier virtue in reproaching Angela for her conduct towards him. Despite the triteness of its concluding paragraphs, however, the novel's portrayal of Angela's remorseless exploitation of her younger sister is a subtle one.

Similar themes are considered in greater depth and at greater length in *Healey*. Once more JF is interested in a romantic affair across barriers of class, but this interest is far less simply the novel's chief concern than its subtitle ('A Romance') might suggest. The novel shows how complex and enduring are the obstacles to any relationship between Katharine Healey, the sister of a colliery owner, and Ughtred Earnshaw, his 'overlooker': it is not until the end of the novel that the two can admit to any affection for each other, having made a painful transition through an uncomfortably agreed-upon 'friendship'. In marked contrast to the unmitigatedly positive conclusion of *Made or Marred*, Earnshaw's marriage to Katharine is accompanied by a sense of the ineradicable suffering caused to Katharine by the discovery that the brother whom she idolizes is a cynical seducer who is perfectly prepared to banish his sister from their house when she confronts him with the fact.

The optimism about the possibility of overcoming social differences suggested by the provisionally successful marriage between Katharine and Earnshaw is thus counterbalanced by the secret marriage which Wilfrid Healey arranges with Sara, the working-class woman whom he has seduced. JF's sense of Katharine's isolation after she discovers her brother's marriage is cast in almost theological terms: it is regarded as a vicarious fall from which any recovery can only be partial.   JAMES SMITH

Works: *Healey* (1875); *Aldyth* (1876); *The First Violin* (1877); *The Wellfields* (1880); *Kith and Kin* (1881); *Made or Marred* (1881); *One of Three* (1881); *Peril* (1884); *Borderland* (1886); *The Lasses of Leverhouse* (1888); *From Moor Isles* (1888); *A March in the Ranks* (1890); *Oriole's Daughter* (1893).
References: *NWAD*; Crisp, J., *Jessie Fothergill: A Bibliography* (1951); *DNB*; *NWAD*; Speight, *Romantic Richmondshire* (1897).

Frankau, Pamela
b. 3 January 1908, London; d. 8 June 1967, London
Novelist
PF was one of the most popular writers in Britain and America in her lifetime. A novelist who wrote over thirty books, she also worked as a journalist and non-fiction writer, as a critic for BBC radio, and produced three collections of short stories. Her family background abounded with literary achievement: her grandmother and her sister, Mary Wilson, were novelists; her great-aunt was the 'amusing' journalist Mrs Aria, and her father was the well-known novelist Gilbert Frankau. PF was educated at the P.N.E.U. School, Burgess Hill, Sussex, and after her parents' marriage broke up, lived with her mother and sister in Windsor. She declined a place at Cambridge, and worked at the Amalgamated Press and as sub-editor on *Woman's Journal*.

Her circle of friends included Noel Coward, G. B. Stern and Rebecca West. In the Second World War she served with the A.T.S. Her lover for nine years, Humbert Woolfe, died in 1940, and in 1942 she was received into the Roman Catholic Church. She married Marshall Dill Jnr, of San Francisco in 1945; their one child died in infancy, and the marriage later dissolved. PF died of cancer, having shared a house with Margaret Webster, a theatrical producer, for the last ten years of her life. Her will ended: 'I give praise and thanks to Almighty God for the gift of life. I thank my loves, my friends, my acquaintances and my benefactors for helping to make it such a good adventure.'

She published her first novel at the age of nineteen, and had three novels and a book of short stories in print by the time she was twenty-one. Her most acclaimed work, *The Willow Cabin*, was a Book Society choice on its publication in 1949. Its heroine, Caroline, abandons her brilliant stage career to become the mistress of a distinguished surgeon, a man much older than herself. The novel revolves around her love for him, her jealousy towards his wife, and the reconciliation of the two women after his death. The character of Caroline was described in *The Times Literary Supplement* (3 June 1949), as 'an illustration of the type most favoured by contemporary women novelists. She is the epitome of that legendary figure, the modern girl'. PF's final three novels form a trilogy which has been regarded as Galsworthian, and at her death she left a further novel, a detective story, unfinished.

PF's novels are in the main mystery thrillers with strong overtones of morality. Well-constructed, totally professional, they are polished rather than innovative, and uncontroversial in style and content. Her realistic character construction won the praise of critics of the time, who acclaimed the apparent autonomy of her characters. With great regard for detail, she conveys era, place and social strata; her backgrounds have great credibility at one level, although without political depth. A dichotomy between good and evil, light and dark, runs through her work, and in her trilogy on the life of Thomas Weston (*Clothes for a King* – comprising *Sing for your Supper* (1963), *Slave of the Lamp* (1965), and *Over the Mountains* (1967)) this is manifested in the central struggle between the young Thomas and an ageing sorcerer. Elements of fantasy and magic colour her works – the gifts of second sight and healing (*Sing for your Supper*), a soul in limbo contemplating its past (David Nelson in *The Bridge* (1957)). In many novels some vagueness in the symbolism, and a fanciful sentimentality are compensated for by a neat, clear style and close detailed surveys of social behaviour, as well as by witty and sharply satirical asides.   SHÂN WAREING

Selected works: *Marriage of Harlequin* (1927); *I Find Four People* (1935); *Shaken in the Wind* (1948); *The Willow Cabin* (1949); *The Offshore Light* (1952); *A Wreath for The Enemy* (1954); *The Bridge* (1957); *Ask Me No More* (1958); *Road Through The Woods* (1960); *Pen To Paper* (1961); *Sing For Your Supper* (1963); *Slave of The Lamp* (1965); *Over The Mountains* (1967).

References: Barker, R., introduction to *A Wreath for the Enemy* (1988); *Chamber's Biographical Dictionary*; *CA*; *The New York Times*, 9 June 1967; York, S., introduction to *The Willow Cabin* (1988).

Fraser, Antonia
b. 27 August 1932, London
Novelist, historian, translator
AF is a versatile and popular author, known primarily for her historical biographies and mysteries. The daughter of Frank and Elizabeth Pakenham (*née*

Harman), the 7th Earl and Countess of Longford, she graduated in history from Lady Margaret Hall, Oxford in 1953. Three years later she married the Rt Hon. Sir Hugh Fraser, MP (d. 1984). After the birth of six children, their marriage was dissolved in 1977. AF married the playwright Harold Pinter in 1980, and currently lives in London. She was a member of the Arts Council in 1970–2, chairwoman of the Society of Authors in 1974–5, and became a Fellow of the Royal Society of Literature in 1983.

Her mother, Elizabeth Longford, is a historian of Victorian England and was a close friend of C.V. Wedgwood at Lady Margaret Hall. It is the latter's subject matter and historical period which AF's work most closely resembles: both write biographies of famous people in sixteenth- and seventeenth-century England, although AF's treatment is more romantic than Wedgwood's. AF's first historical biography, *Mary, Queen of Scots* (1969), resulted from three years of original research, especially in letters and memoirs. It received immediate acclaim, winning the James Tait Black Memorial Prize. The portrayal of Mary is uncommonly sympathetic, going into great detail on her health, and gives to history the first human, multidimensional characterization of the Scottish queen.

AF's subsequent biographies were less successful. Her prose is hackneyed, and would be florid if it were not so bland. For instance, in *Mary*, we are told that Henry VIII wanted to rear the girl queen in the English court 'in order to check any possible fluttering for liberty in the Scottish dove-cots'; and later, when the queen conceived a passion for the English Lord Darnley, 'the honeyed trap . . . was sprung.' AF's sentence structure is not infrequently cumbersome, as in, 'Huntly told Somerset that she had smallpox, but as Mary was to suffer a much better attested attack of smallpox later in her childhood, it seems to have been measles, the explanation given to La Chapelle in Edinburgh, which was responsible for her collapse on this occasion.' Despite AF's popular audience, she fails to translate foreign language passages, appealing perhaps to a perverse snobbery in the non-French-speaking reader who nevertheless believes that history is made up of kings and queens, lords and ladies, all of whom speak French.

In *The Weaker Vessel* (1984) AF broadens her usual aristocratic focus to include a few merchants' wives, prostitutes, and actresses. However, the work remains an essentially ahistorical catalogue of anecdotes about various aristocratic ladies 'between the death of one Queen Regnant and the accession of another'. While the stories are interesting (*The Weaker Vessel* has been on many best-seller lists since its publication), AF's use of sources is highly selective and she offers no explanatory context besides the romantic belief that although affection played women false, love *would* find a way.

In addition to the works listed below, AF has written mystery stories in anthologies and various plays for television, including the series, *Jemimah Shore Investigates* (based on *A Splash of Red*), and *Quiet as a Nun*.   AMY ERICKSON

Works: *King Arthur and the Knights of the Round Table* (1954); (trans.) *Monsters in China*, by J. Monsterleet (1956); *Robin Hood* (1955); (trans.) *Dior*, by C. Dior (1957); *Dolls* (1963); *A History of Toys* (1966); *Mary, Queen of Scots* (1969); *Cromwell, Our Chief of Men* (1973; published in the US as *Cromwell, The Lord Protector*); *King James, VI of Scotland, I of England* (1974); *Quiet as a Nun* (1977); *The Wild Island: A Mystery* (1978); *King Charles II* (1979); *A Splash of Red* (1981); *Cool Repentance* (1982); *The Weaker Vessel: Woman's Lot in 17th Century England* (1984).
References: CA.

Fullerton, Lady Georgiana

b. 23 September 1812, Tixall, Staffordshire; d. 19 January 1885, Bournemouth
Novelist, biographer, translator, poet, religious writer

GF was the younger daughter of Lord Granville Leveson-Gower and his wife Lady Harriet Cavendish. Educated privately, GF grew up with a keen relish for parties, balls, operas, and worldly pleasures in which religion 'had no part'. She lived with her parents in Paris for some years and in 1833 married Alexander Fullerton, an embassy attaché and former Guards officer. Nominally an Anglican, she became interested in the Oxford Movement in the 1840s, and her husband's sudden conversion to Roman Catholicism in 1843 influenced her profoundly.

Back in England she finished her first novel, *Ellen Middleton* (1844), showing the need for confession, which caused a *furore*. In 1846 she followed her husband into the Catholic Church and from then on led a life of devotion, self-denial, and good works. The loss of her only child just before his twenty-first birthday deepened her faith; her personal sanctity became as famous as her writings. She was admired by Gladstone, revered by Newman, and even associated with miracles by certain nuns after her death.

As an author she made a valuable contribution to Oxford Movement fiction by combining the sensation novel with the religious novel and making conversion exciting and theology thrilling. *Ellen Middleton* worked wonders for the sacrament of penance; *Grantley Manor* (1847), portrayed a fierce passion and faith conflict, and in *Mrs Gerald's Niece* (1869) GF, with considerable dramatic and psychological skill, described marital discord arising from Oxford Movement controversies. Such powerful tales for the times caused many conversions. Her poems, some in French, are less successful, her historical fiction is often overloaded with research, but her last novel, *A Will and a Way* (1881), a passion and faith conflict set in France during the Reign of Terror, is one of the most vivid and gripping of all her stories.   MARGARET MAISON

Selected works: Ellen Middleton (1844); Grantley Manor (1847); Lady-Bird (1852); *The Life of St Frances of Rome* (1855); *The Countess of Bonneval* (1858) (previously published in French, 1857); *Laurentia* (1861); *Rose Leblanc* (1862); *Too Strange Not to Be True* (1864); *A Stormy Life* (1867); *Mrs Gerald's Niece* (1869); *The Gold-digger and Other Poems* (1871); *The Life of Luisa de Carvajal* (1873); *The Miraculous Medal* (1880); *A Will and a Way* (1881); *The Life of Elisabeth, Lady Falkland* (1883).

References: Anon., *The Inner Life of Lady Georgiana Fullerton* (1900); Anon., *Lady Georgiana Fullerton* (1905); Craven, P., *Life of Lady Georgiana Fullerton,* trans. H. J. Coleridge (1888); Maison, M., 'The Anglican Agony', *The Month* 201, 1066 (June 1956); Maison, M., *Search Your Soul, Eustace* (1961); Pollen, J. H. (ed.), 'Letters of Cardinal Newman to Lady Georgiana Fullerton', *The Month* 129, 634 (April 1917); Wolff, R., *Gains and Losses* (1977); Yonge, C. M., 'Lady Georgiana Fullerton' in *Women Novelists of Queen Victoria's Reign* (1897).

Gardam, Jane

b. 11 July 1928, Coatham, Yorkshire
Novelist, short story writer, writer for children

JG is an exciting and accomplished writer whose major achievement is in shifting the boundaries between children's fiction and adult fiction in a series of novels which move unflinchingly through the no-man's-land of adolescence into the adult world. She has also probed new possibilities for the short story in several books of 'incidents' in which the same characters reappear in different settings. Although her short stories can be set in Jamaica, the Far East, or Italy, she is most truly herself when writing of the north of England; her ability to create a 'sense of place' may yet be seen as her most enduring gift.

JG is the daughter of William Pearson of Coatham School, Redcar, and his wife Kathleen Mary Pearson (*née* Helm). She was educated at Saltburn High School for Girls and at Bedford College, University of London, from where she graduated with an honours degree in English in 1949. After three more years at Bedford doing research, she became a sub-editor of *Weldon's Ladies Journal* in 1952 and from 1953 to 1955 was Assistant Literary Editor of *Time and Tide*, working for C. V. Wedgwood. In 1952 she married the barrister David Hill Gardam, now a QC with an international practice. With him she has travelled widely, especially in the Far East, though she still spends as much time as she can in the north of England. They have two sons and a daughter.

Black Faces, White Faces shared the 1975 David Higham Award for a promising first work of fiction and won the Winifred Holtby Memorial Prize in 1976; *God on the Rocks* was a runner-up for the Booker Prize in 1978; *The Hollow Land* won the Whitbread Literary Award in 1981; and *The Pangs of Love* received the Katherine Mansfield Award in 1984. In 1976 JG became a Fellow of the Royal Society of Literature.

JG's work is characterized by freshness, honesty, and an eagerness to experiment, whether she is writing about modern Jamaica (*Black Faces, White Faces*) or about the north-east coast of England at the beginning of the century (*Crusoe's Daughter*, 1985). In her short stories the urge to experiment with styles and with a wide range of subject matter inevitably makes for unevenness of achievement, and her most complete and successful works are those in which she can explore the inner landscape of female adolescence against an external landscape which is equally familiar to her. *Crusoe's Daughter* (1985) satisfies these criteria, charting the life of Polly Flint from the age of 6 until extreme old age in a large house on the marshes at Saltburn, where JG herself went to school. The tension between a strict and joyless religious upbringing and developing sexuality is central to this novel, as it is to another of JG's best works, *God on the Rocks*. The tone of these books – unsentimental, witty, yet compassionate – is JG's truest voice, and it can be heard again in *The Hollow Land*, another story of a northern childhood, although this time set further west and with a small boy as protagonist. The humour of novels of adolescence like *Bilgewater* (1977) holds in check a tendency towards a slightly self-indulgent literariness. JG's young heroines are fictional creations who continually hark back to literary sources: Athene Price in *The Summer after the Funeral* (1973) identifies with Emily Brontë: Marigold ('Bilgewater') Green dreams of Joyce and Hardy; Polly Flint draws throughout her life on her experience of *Robinson Crusoe* – the hero more real to her ultimately than a human lover.

Set against this is a vivid particularity of detail which can evoke a middle-class child's impression of an outrageous Geordie housemaid or a 13-year-old's first experience of menstruation with uncomfortable clarity. The historical settings are occasionally rather forced, but the emotional and geographical locations are impeccably observed and truthful. There is an unfussy directness of approach in the opening sentences which epitomizes JG's characteristic strength: 'I'm Bell Teesdale. I'm a lad. I'm eight.' 'I am Polly Flint. I came to live at the yellow house when I was six years old.'

JG experiments continually with shifts in genre. Her short stories may be ghost stories, wistful comedies of manners in the Katherine Mansfield mode, wittily adapted fairy-tales, or superior romantic fiction. Within a novel she may juxtapose the epistolary form, third-person narrative, and even excursions into drama. The effect is to create an excitement and a sense of freedom which always holds out the promise of further development. VALERIE PURTON

Selected works: A Few Fair Days (1971); *A Long Way from Verona* (1971); *The Summer after the Funeral* (1973); *Black Faces, White Faces* (1975); *Bilgewater* (1977); *God on the Rocks* (1978); *The Hollow Land* (1981); *Bridget and William* (1981); *Horse* (1982); *The Pangs of Love and Other Stories* (1983); *Kit* (1983); *Crusoe's Daughter* (1985).

References: OCCL; *The Writers Directory 1986–88*; *World Dictionary of Children's Writers* (1978).

Gardner, Helen

b. 13 February 1908, London; d. 4 June 1986, Oxford

Critic

HG was a distinguished literary critic and scholar who had a marked influence on the reception of English poetry, especially that of the late sixteenth and early seventeenth centuries, the period that includes the 'metaphysical poets'. She was especially noted for her careful interpretative and textual studies of John Donne's poetry and prose, for her appreciation of T. S. Eliot and for her criticism of Milton and Shakespeare in whose tragedies she controversially found Christian elements.

The daughter of Charles and Helen Mary Gardner, HG began her literary education at the North London Collegiate School. She received her BA in 1929 from St Hilda's College, Oxford. Although she had begun a thesis on the medieval mystic Walter Hilton, she took a job as assistant lecturer in the University of Birmingham in 1930 and remained there until 1941, when she returned to St Hilda's as a tutor in English literature. She became University Reader in Renaissance English Literature in 1954 and Merton Professor of English Literature in 1966. She also held various lectureships in the United States.

HG sets out her general views on literature and criticism in two main works, *Criticism* (1959) and *In Defence of the Imagination* (1982). In *The Business of Criticism* she wrote, 'The primary critical act is a judgement, the decision that a certain piece of writing has significance and value.' Yet HG avoided prescriptively evaluative judgement and tended not to rank literary works. She did believe, however, that certain critical readings were preferable to others, the best ones aiming as far as possible to approximate the reading intended by the author. In other words, she assumed a stable meaning within a text which it was the critic's business to try to uncover. It was not the business of the critic to create new and idiosyncratic interpretations but simply to help other readers to see themselves what the works held. She had a firm belief in a neutral criticism purged of subjectivity and ideology. Feeling should be cast aside 'so that the poem which my mind recreates in the reading becomes more and more a poem which my mind would never have created'. Given her literary principles, HG inevitably supported an historical approach to literature, although she warned against a simple reading of a work in the light of the history of ideas. The modern critic must understand that he or she is historically bound like the text. The only way forward is minute and painstaking attention to the linguistic nuances of the text.

In her last work, *In Defence of the Imagination*, HG assesses her literary life and considers modern literary theory. She dislikes the new approaches of recent years, through deconstruction, structuralism, and psychoanalysis. The methods arising from such theory she finds detrimental to literary pleasure and she accuses its proponents of doubting the purpose of literary study in general. She also objects to the overemphasis of universities in recent years on publication rather than teaching, which she felt was responsible for the proliferation of literary theories.   JANET JONES

Works: *The Art of T. S. Eliot* (1949); (ed.), *The Divine Poems of John Donne* (1952); *The Limits of Literary Criticism: Reflections on the Interpretation of Poetry and Scripture* (1956); (ed.), *The Metaphysical Poets* (1957); *The Business of Criticism* (1959); (ed.), *Elizabethan and Jacobean Studies presented to F. P. Wilson* (with Herbert Davis) (1959); (ed.), *The Sonnets of William Alabaster* (with G. M. Storey) (1959); *Edwin Muir* (1961); (ed.), *John Donne: A Collection of Critical Essays* (1962); (ed.), *The Elegies and the Songs and Sonnets of John Donne* (1965); *A Reading of Paradise Lost* (1965); *T. S. Eliot and the English Poetic Tradition* (1966); (ed.), *King Lear* (1967); *Literary Studies* (1967); (ed.), *Selected Prose of John Donne* (with Timothy Healy) (1967); (ed.), *F. P. Wilson: Shakespearian and Other Studies* (1969); (ed.), *F. P. Wilson: Shakespeare and the New Bibliography* (1970); *Religion and Literature* (1971); (ed.), *The Faber Book of Religious Verse* (1972); *Poems in the Making* (1972); *The Waste Land* (1972); *The Composition of 'Four Quartets'* (1977); *In Defence of the Imagination* (1982).

References: Carey, J. (ed.), *English Renaissance Studies presented to Dame Helen Gardner* (1980); *CA*; Drabble.

Garnett, Constance

b. 1861, Brighton; d. 1946, Edenbridge

Translator

(Also wrote under C. C. Black)

CG was the daughter of David Black and Clara Patten Black. Considered delicate, she was educated for some years at home, then attended Brighton High School which she detested. At the age of 17 she won a scholarship to Newnham College Cambridge, where she gained first-class honours in the Classical Tripos, although no degrees were awarded to women until 1947. In 1889 she married the scholar and critic Edward Garnett; in 1892 when she was pregnant with their only child (the novelist and autobiographer David Garnett) she began to learn Russian to occupy herself.

CG visited Russia on a number of occasions, and she had two particular connections with the country: first through her father, who grew up there, while his father was employed by Tsar Nicholas I as naval architect; and second, through Russian revolutionary exiles living in England with whom she and her husband were friends. One of these, Felix Volkhovsky, taught CG Russian. CG soon put her linguistic skills to use, and in 1893 her first translation, Goncharov's *A Common Story*, was published.

Over the following years CG translated seventy volumes from Russian, including all the works of Turgenev, Dostoevsky, and Gogol, most of Chekhov's plays and short stories, and Tolstoy's *Anna Karenina* (1901) and *War and Peace* (1904). Her translations received considerable critical acclaim for their authority and sensitive use of language: 'Mrs Garnett's translations from the Russian are always distinguished by most careful accuracy and a fine literary flavour', wrote a contemporary reviewer. She always tried to use a style appropriate to the period in which the author had written, which may account for what *The Times Literary Supplement* critic called her 'wilful quaintness of language'. Her translations, still current in many cases, brought Russian literature to a wide readership in Britain, and helped create a climate of sympathetic interest in Russian affairs. CG's literary involvement with Russia was linked with a concern with the country's politics. Although never a communist, CG was, as a Fabian, initally sympathetic to the revolutionary cause, and in 1894 secretly carried letters to revolutionaries in Russia from their exiled friends in England. However, later she grew disenchanted with the revolutionary movement, and refused an invitation to act as interpreter for Lenin at the Russian Social Democratic convention in England in 1907. LUCY SLOAN

Selected works: *Catalogue of the Books in the Library of the People's Palace for East London* (1889); (trans.), *Tales*, by A. Chekhov (13 vols) (1916–22); (trans.), *Letters to his Family and Friends*, by A. Chekhov (1920); (trans.), *Three Sisters and Other Plays*, by A. Chekhov (1923); (trans.), *The Cherry Orchard and Other Plays*, by A. Chekhov (1935); (trans.), *The Brothers Karamazov*, by F. Dostoevsky (1912); (trans.), *The Idiot*, by F. Dostoevsky (1913); (trans.), *Letters from the Underground*, by F. Dostoevsky (1913); (trans.), *Crime and Punishment*, by F. Dostoevsky (1914); (trans.), *The House of the Dead*, by F. Dostoevsky (1915); (trans.), *The Insulted and the Injured*, by F. Dostoevsky (1915); (trans.), *The Revolt of the 'Potemkin'*, by K. Feldman (1908); (trans.), *Works*, by N. Gogol, 6 vols (1922–8); (trans.), *A Common Story*, by I. Goncharov (1893); (trans.), *My Past and Thoughts*, by A. J. Herzen (1924); (trans.), *The Storm*, by A. N. Ostrovsky (1899); (trans.), *The Kingdom of God is Within You*, by L. Tolstoy (1894); (trans.), *Anna Karenina*, by L. Tolstoy (1901); (trans.), *War and Peace*, by L. Tolstoy (1904); (trans.), *Christianity and Patriotism*, by L. Tolstoy (1922); (trans.), *Novels*, by I. Turgenev, 15 vols (1894–9); (trans.), *Knock, Knock, Knock and Other Stories*, by I. Turgenev (1922); (trans.), *Three Famous Plays: A Month in the Country, A Provincial Lady, A Poor Gentleman*, by I. Turgenev (1951). *References:* Crawford; *DNB*; Drabble; Garnett, D., *The Golden Echo* (1954); Heilbrun, C., *The Garnett Family* (1961).

Gaskell, Elizabeth

b. 29 September 1810, Chelsea, London; d. 12 November 1865, Alton, Hampshire
Novelist, biographer, short story writer
(Also wrote under Cotton Mather Mills)
Eighth child of William Stevenson, former Unitarian minister and, from 1806 to 1829, a civil servant, and Elizabeth (*née* Holland) Stevenson, EG, along with her brother John, twelve years her senior, were the only Stevenson children to survive infancy. Thirteen months after EG was born, her mother died and she went to live with her mother's elder sister, Mrs Hannah Lumb, and her daughter Mary Anne, an invalid, in Knutsford, Cheshire. There she acquired her lifelong love of the country, which was enhanced by regular visits to the Holland family farm three miles away at Sandlebridge. Though her father remarried four years after his first wife's death, EG remained with her aunt in Knutsford until she was 12, when she went to the Miss Byerlys' school in Warwickshire, first at Barford and then at Straford-upon-Avon, where she remained until June 1827. To the disappearance of her brother John on a voyage to India in 1828 is attributed the recurrence in EG's fiction of the motif of the lost sailor's return (e.g. Frederick Hale in *North and South*, Charley Kinraid, in *Sylvia's Lovers*, and

Peter Jenkyns in *Cranford*). EG assisted with the nursing of her father during his last illness, and after his death in 1829 remained in London with Holland relatives, going after a few months to Newcastle-upon-Tyne for an extended visit to the family of the Rev. William Turner, a distant connection by marriage. Turner became the model for the minister Thurstan Benson in *Ruth*. With the Turners' daughter Anne, EG paid a visit in late 1831 to Anne's sister Mary, the wife of a Unitarian minister, John G. Robberds, in Manchester. There, at the Cross Street Unitarian Chapel, EG met Robberds's assistant, William Gaskell, son of a manufacturing family from Lancashire. They were married on 30 August 1832 in the Knutsford Parish Church (Unitarian marriages, to be legal, had to be solemnized by a clergyman from the Established Church), and after a brief honeymoon in Wales went to live in Manchester, where she remained (in a succession of houses) until her sudden death at the country home in Hampshire which she was buying from her earnings as a novelist and had planned as a surprise for her husband, a retreat and eventual retirement residence for them and a home for any of her daughters who did not marry.

EG had six children: a stillborn girl, on 4 July 1833; Marianne, born 12 September 1834; Margaret Emily (Meta), 5 February 1837; Florence Elizabeth (Flossy), 7 October 1842; William, 23 October 1844; and Julia, 3 September 1846. All lived to adulthood except William, who died of scarlet fever in 1845; the death of her only son may have occasioned EG's writing of *Mary Barton*, said to have stemmed from her husband's suggestion to distract her from her grief.

EG had however been writing stories since her teens. In *Blackwood's* of January 1837 she and her husband jointly published a poem intended as part of a series of sketches of ordinary life, in the Wordsworthian mode; the series was never completed. Ten years later, under the name Cotton Mather Mills, she published three short stories in *Howitts' Journal*, run by William and Mary Howitt, translators, writers of nature books, children's literature, novels, and other genres; they gave EG encouragement in her publishing career. Before this she had published 'indirectly', by furnishing William Howitt with two items for his own books, *Visits to Remarkable Places* (1840) and the second edition (1840) of *The Rural Life of England*. In 1847 Howitt initiated the contact with Chapman and Hall that led to the publication of *Mary Barton*, which appeared anonymously in two volumes in October 1848. Although some reviewers, including W. R. Greg (*Edinburgh Review*, April 1849), criticized the book for presenting factory owners in an unfavourable light, it brought EG rapid acclaim from established authors such as Thomas Carlyle and Charles Dickens; the latter invited her to dinner during her first trip to London and invited her to contribute to his new weekly publication, *Household Words*. Although their collaboration was sometimes an uneasy one, especially during the serialization of *North and South*, EG was to publish both novels and short stories in *Household Words* and its successor *All the Year Round*.

One of the marks of EG's fiction is the skill with which she handles many different subjects. Like other Victorian writers she viewed the novel as a way of drawing public attention to problems outside the reader's ordinary knowledge. Her preface to *Mary Barton*, subtitled 'A Tale of Manchester Life', attests to her need to write the truth about the 'unhappy state of things' between owner and worker, with the implication that this might contribute to a 'public effort' to ameliorate the situation. The strength of the novel lies in its engaging plot and in its detailed depiction of the life of the poor, but, together with the realistic descriptions, there are elements of melodrama (for instance, Mary

Barton's collapse at the end of the court proceedings) and sentimentality (such as John Barton's deathbed reconciliation with the man whose son he killed).

After this industrial novel, EG returned to the Knutsford of her childhood for *Cranford*, whose quiet picture of a community of women, spinsters, and widows, for the most part, makes it unique in mid-century fiction, where readers often desired both sensational incident and at least one love-plot with a concluding marriage. At the same time, EG's interest in social problems caused her to interrupt her tales of Cranford to work on *Ruth*, a novel in which she attempted to awaken sympathy for a 'fallen woman'. Her interest in this subject came from her acquaintance with a girl of 16, a seamstress like Ruth, who had been seduced by the doctor who attended her; the girl, a Miss Pasley, turned to prostitution and theft. With the advice and assistance of Charles Dickens, EG helped the girl, upon her release from prison, to get passage to the Cape to begin a new life. This incident led her to record in *Ruth*, published in January 1853, the 'plain and earnest truth' about such young women. Though there are hints in her letters that she was apprehensive about publishing the work, the letters also record her surprise and dismay at the hostile reception given this work on a tabooed subject, the first volume of which was burned by two members of William Gaskell's congregation. Anticipating Thomas Hardy's Tess, EG's heroine is presented as a pure girl, an orphan seamstress, seduced at 15, who redeems herself by the love with which she raises her illegitimate son and the self-sacrifice with which, after nursing her seducer back to health during a cholera epidemic, she dies of the disease. The plot is direct and engaging, but the sentimentality and emphatic didacticism have made it less highly regarded than her other works. Both the seducer and the hypocritical evangelical, Mr Bradshaw, are stereotypical figures, but the Benson family, who pass Ruth off as a widow for many years, enabling her to establish her character for goodness, are rounded and sympathetic, and their servant Sally is one of the finest comic characters of Victorian fiction. Despite the initial shock caused by the sympathetic treatment of the unwed mother, the book had many admirers, including Charlotte Brontë and George Henry Lewes, although the former found fault with the conventional ending in which the repentant sinner must die, and the latter found Ruth *too* pure for EG's social purpose.

As the last instalments of *Cranford* appeared in the spring of 1853, EG was at work on a new idea for a novel. Remembering the criticism that *Mary Barton* did not present a fair picture of employers, she attempted to right the balance in *North and South*, where the factory owner John Thornton gradually engages the sympathy of the reader and the love of the heroine, Margaret Hale. Here EG contrasts the agricultural south, with its lovely scenery and its ignorance and supersitition, with the new industrial town of Milton Northern (a thinly disguised Manchester), a forward-looking, vital place despite its problems. The novel is more intricately plotted than her earlier ones and shows EG's increasing ability to present scenes of suffering and death without lapsing into sentimentality.

EG's settings generally come directly from her own experience, and perhaps because fame had brought her into London drawing rooms, she includes not only the familiar country people and Manchester's urban poor, but also London gentility. Her heroine represents an advance over the more stereotypical figures of *Mary Barton* and *Ruth*. Assuming the responsibilities of her weak parents and others around her, Margaret Hale is a fully realized individual as well as a symbol of the adjustment to change necessary in the new industralized England. Responding to Dickens's pleas for a novel for *Household Words*, EG published

North and South serially from 2 September 1854 to 27 January 1855. The letters of both reveal their mutual frustration. Dickens atrributed the declining sales of *Household Words* to the lack of interest in the story, and EG found it impossible to adjust her work to the demand for short weekly instalments, each ending in a climactic incident.

North and South was to be EG's last novel for several years. In 1850 she had met Charlotte Brontë and formed a friendship that lasted until Brontë's death in 1855 at the age of 39. Patrick Brontë asked EG to prepare a biography of his daughter, a task that EG herself had already considered, although on a lesser scale than he had envisaged. Published in March 1857, the *Life* received positive notices and sold so well that within six weeks a second edition was underway. It is clear from EG's letters that she thought she was speaking truth, yet her partisanship of her friend is also evident in the *Life;* there is little doubt, for instance, that EG knew of Brontë's feelings for M. Heger, her teacher in Brussels, and deliberately suppressed the information. Though the work reflects what Charlotte Brontë told EG of her early life, as well as the contents of Brontë's letters, the *Life* can be seen also as a novel in which Charlotte Brontë is the heroine whose creator has chosen the details that most clearly project the desired image.

EG's intention to portray Charlotte Brontë, 'the woman', in a way that would enable the public to understand the suffering of her life had led to criticism of those she thought had contributed to Brontë's ill-health, especially Wiliam Carus Wilson, the proprietor of Cowan Bridge School, and Mrs Robinson (in 1857, Lady Shaw), the alleged temptress of Branwell Brontë. Both were still alive in 1857 and threatened legal action. When EG returned in late May from an extended visit to friends in Rome, she immediately began to work on revisions for the third edition, which was published in August 1857. It tempered the criticism of Wilson and Mrs Robinson and also corrected the portrait of Patrick Brontë.

In 1856–8, EG overstrained her energies in writing the *Life*, in dealing with subsequent criticisms, and in preparing the revised third edition, at the m time as she was coping with family problems. Her daughter Meta had become engaged to a Captain Hill, shortly to be assigned to India. Meta made preliminary preparations to go out with him immediately, then decided to marry him later, in Egypt, and go from there to India. After his departure, however, she broke off the engagement upon hearing unfavourable reports of his character. All of this caused EG grave concern and her health suffered, as it frequently did when she was overworked or under stress. Needing funds, in part for travel for Meta, she hastened to write the tales collected in *My Lady Ludlow*, which was serialized in *Household Words* from 19 June to 25 September 1858. 'The Manchester Marriage', published later that year in *Household Words*, reverts to her theme of the return of the long-lost sailor and anticipates its fuller development in her next novel, her only historical one, *Sylvia's Lovers* (1863). For this EG travelled to Whitby (Monkshaven in the novel) which is described vividly with its whaling ships and the press-gang riots of the 1790s. The fine description, characterization, and plotting of the first two volumes give way in the last to the overuse of the return-of-the-missing-person motif, and to maudlin sentimentality, in a battlefield encounter and a father's fatal rescue of his daughter from the sea. This unevenness may be attributed in part to the interruptions in the book's composition. Though in a letter tentatively dated 9 December 1861 EG records that she has completed the first two volumes and is ready to finish the third, she was unable to do so for another year. The year

1862 brought distractions, in addition to normal family responsibilities, in Marianne's worrying proclivity towards Roman Catholicism and in EG's work in relieving the needs of distressed cotton workers during the Lancashire Cotton Famine caused by the American Civil War.

Although EG published a number of short pieces in Dickens's weeklies, including the melodramatic novella *A Dark Night's Work* in *All the Year Round* (24 January to 21 March 1863), she disliked his editorial strictness and the demands of weekly serialization. Preferring to work with George Smith, she published her last two major works in the *Cornhill*, where monthly serialization permitted longer instalments: *Cousin Phillis* (November 1863 to February 1864) and *Wives and Daughters* (uncompleted), which began in August 1864 and ended in January 1866, the last two numbers appearing posthumously. Both *Cousin Phillis* and *Wives and Daughters* return to the Knutsford of EG's youth, perhaps in consonance with her growing wish for a more health-giving country house away from the smoke and fog of Manchester, the wish that led her to purchase 'The Lawn'. In both novels she treats young girls growing up, experiencing first love in a supportive and comforting rural setting. Both works avoid the melodramatic in favour of quiet family relationships in which ordinary events are delineated with the humour found earlier in *Cranford*. Set in the pre-Reform Bill era, *Wives and Daughters* is a nostalgic look at the small town; no mere wish to return to the past, however, the novel, through the character of naturalist Roger Hamley, acknowledges the inevitability and largely positive nature of change.

Assessments of EG's work have changed according to changes in literary tastes since her death. Revived interest in the social problem novel in the past two decades has given new prominence to *Mary Barton, Ruth*, and *North and South*. At the same time, *Cranford, Cousin Phillis*, and *Wives and Daughters*, earlier admired for their feminine charm, are seen anew as pictures of parts of women's experience often ignored in nineteenth-century fiction – especially the lives of middle-aged spinsters and widows in *Cranford*, and of young girls in the female *Bildungsromane* represented by *Cousin Phillis* and *Wives and Daughters*. *The Life of Charlotte Brontë* continues to draw praise as one of the finest examples of nineteenth-century biography, and EG's short tales, especially the ghost stories, are being re-examined.   CAROL A. MARTIN

Selected works: (dates for works originally published serially are given for the volume edition): *Mary Barton* (1848); *Ruth* (1853); *Cranford* (1853); *North and South* (1855); *Lizzie Leigh and Other Tales* (1855); *The Life of Charlotte Brontë* (1857); *Round the Sofa* (including 'My Lady Ludlow' and other stories) (1859); *Right at Last and Other Tales* (1860); *Sylvia's Lovers* (1863); *Cousin Phillis and Other Tales* (1865); *The Grey Woman and Other Tales* (1865); *Wives and Daughters* (1866); *My Diary*, ed. C. Shorter (privately printed) (1923); *Letters of Mrs Gaskell*, ed. J. A. V. Chapple and A. Pollard (1966).

References: Craik, W. A., *Elizabeth Gaskell and the English Provincial Novel* (1975); Easson, A., *Elizabeth Gaskell* (1979); Fowler, R., 'Cranford: cow in grey flannel or lion couchant?', *Studies in English Literature* 24 (1984); Ganz, M., *Elizabeth Gaskell: The Artist in Conflict* (1969); Gérin, W., *Elizabeth Gaskell: A Biography* (1976); Hopkins, A. B., *Elizabeth Gaskell: Her Life and Works* (1952); Lansbury, C., *Elizabeth Gaskell: The Novel of Social Crisis* (1975); Lansbury, C., *Elizabeth Gaskell* (1984); Lucas, J., 'Engels, Mrs Gaskell and Manchester', in *The Literature of Change* (1977); Martin, Carol A., 'Gaskell, Darwin, and North and South', *Studies in the Novel* 15 (1983); Pollard, A., *Mrs Gaskell: Novelist and Biographer* (1965); Rubenius, A., *The Woman Question in Mrs Gaskell's Life* *and Works* (1950); Sharps, J. G., *Mrs Gaskell's Observation and Invention* (1970); Tillotson, K., *Novels of the Eighteen-Forties* (1961); Weiss, B., 'Elizabeth Gaskell: the telling of feminine tales', *Studies in the Novel* 16 (1984); Wright, E., *Mrs Gaskell: The Basis for Reassessment* (1965).

Gatty, Margaret

b. 3 June 1809, Burnham Vicarage, Essex; d. 4 October 1873, Ecclesfield Vicarage, South Yorkshire

Writer for children, botanist

MG was the daughter of Dr Alexander Scott, one time chaplain to Lord Nelson, and Mary Frances Ryder who died when MG was 2 years old. She was brought up together with an older sister, Horatia, partly in the house of her grandfather Ryder and partly by her father with the help of a nurse, Maria Booth, who became the model for the character of the nurse in MG's daughter, Juliana Horatia Ewing's book, *A Flat Iron for a Farthing* (1872).

Lacking formal education which in those days was reserved for sons, she nevertheless managed to learn enough German and Italian to translate poetry by Klopstock and Dante. She wrote poems herself and knew the works of Scott, Southey, and Coleridge. She was a competent pianist and sufficiently confident in her own expertise as an etcher on copper to send examples of her work to the British Museum where they are still preserved. As they grew up she and her sister spent an increasing amount of time in a whirl of social engagements, but in spite of this she was the sort of woman who in a later period might well have gone to university to study botany or possibly literature. Along with her interest in books, religion, and seaweeds (in 1863 she published a two-volume account of British seaweeds with her own illustrations which became one of the main sources for the scientific study of seaweeds over the next eighty years; she also had a seaweed and a sea serpent named after her), she developed a love of writing and a sense of humour that made her famous as a children's writer in the middle of the nineteenth century.

In 1839 she married Alfred Gatty and settled with him in Ecclesfield Vicarage where he had inherited the living. She had ten children, eight of whom survived into adulthood. Her time was spent running the household, bringing up the children, and looking after women and children from local factories, encouraging them to accept the use of chloroform and homoeopathy. Her children became both readers and co-writers; her second daughter, Juliana Horatia (later Mrs Ewing), being the one who worked most closely with her mother in telling stories to the younger members of the family, and in contributing to her mother's books, particularly *Aunt Judy's Tales* (1859) and *Aunt Judy's Magazine*. 'Aunt Judy' was in fact a pseudonym for Juliana. As a young woman MG and her sister had set up a Black Bag Club for writers where contributors put their piece of writing into the bag for reading or publication at a later date. MG and Juliana organized a similar club for the family so that story telling and listening became an important part of family life. Each child was known by a number rather than his or her name.

Apart from the Aunt Judy books and the book on seaweeds, she published several volumes called *Parables from Nature* (1855–71), which contained stories based on the facts of natural history with strong moral teaching, legendary tales which had the same moral purpose, and a book about sundials.

Most of the moralizing is likely to stick in the throats of modern children, but there is no doubt about the strength of appeal in her sense of humour. MG was always firmly on the side of the child both in her own stories and in those she chose to publish or review in her Aunt Judy books. Reviewing *Alice in Wonderland*, she called it an 'exquisitely wild, fantastic, impossible yet most natural history' and praised the Tenniel illustrations for entering 'equally into the fun and graceful sentiment of his author'. She managed to get Tenniel and other famous artists such as Millais, Holman Hunt, and Burne Jones to illustrate her own books.

MG suffered from a disease which increasingly affected her physical movement, including her ability to write. She bravely fought off its effects so that she could continue to visit friends and writers, one of whom was Tennyson, but eventually she was forced to accept a sedentary life with presents of seaweeds, instead of going off in search of them herself. After her death her daughter Juliana took over the editorship of *Aunt Judy's Magazine*.

MG was a woman with an individual outlook which was nevertheless trammelled by the conventions of Victorian family life. Her advice to women seaweed hunters was, 'It is both wasteful, uncomfortable and dangerous to attempt seaweed hunting in delicate boots. . . . Next to boots comes the question of petticoats and if anything could excuse a woman from imitating the costume of a man, it would be what she suffers as a seaweed collector from those necessary draperies.' In the end she saw men's control of women as 'necesary draperies', on one occasion comparing the sound of women speaking in public to 'bells rung backward'. Perhaps it is our loss that her writings are out of print, and that all we have is her name preserved in the seaweed *gattya pinella* and the sea serpent *gattya spectabilis*.   LIZ CASHDAN

Selected works: The Fairy Godmothers (1851); Parables from Nature, 1st series (1855); Worlds Not Realized (1856); Parables from Nature, 2nd series (1857); Proverbs Illustrated (1857); The Poor Incumbent (1858); Legendary Tales (1858); Aunt Judy's Tales (1859); Parables from Nature, 3rd series (1861); Aunt Judy's Letters (1862); History of British Seaweeds(1863); Parables from Nature, 4th series (1864); Domestic Pictures and Tales (1865); Christmas Crackers (1870); Waifs and Strays of Natural History (1870); Parables from Nature, 5th series (1871); The Book of Sundials (1872).

References: Doyle, B., *Who's Who in Children's Literature* (1968); Green, R. L., *Tellers of Tales* (1969); Maxwell, C., *Mrs Gatty and Mrs Ewing* (1969); *OCCL*.

Gems, Pam

b. 1 August 1925, Bransgore, Hampshire

Playwright

PG is best known for four plays, *Dusa, Fish, Stas and Vi* (1976), *Queen Christina* (1977), *Piaf* (1978), and *Camille* (1986), each of which shows that conventional gender roles force difficult choices for even the most talented women. She usually writes about women, finding them 'very funny, coarse, subversive', but her *Aunt Mary* concerns creative male transvestites and her 1986 play, *The Danton Affair*, has a very large cast, nearly all of whom are male Reign of Terrorists.

PG, the first child of working-class parents, Jim and Elsie Mabel Annetts Price, was brought up, along with two brothers, by her mother after her father's death in 1929. She won a scholarship to Brockenhurst County Grammar School, left school to join the WRENS in the Second World War, took a degree in psychology at Manchester University in 1949, and, in the same year, married Keith Gems, a model manufacturer. The family lived at first in Paris, the setting for several later plays, then on the Isle of Wight, and then in London after 1965. There are four children.

PG worked briefly for the BBC in the 1960s, writing three plays for television, of which only *A Builder by Trade* (1961) was produced. After the move to London, she began to work with lunchtime theatres and with the feminist movement. For Al Berman's Almost Free Theatre, she wrote *My Warren* (about ageing and sexuality) and *After Birthday* (about childbirth) in 1973, followed by *The Amiable Courtship of Miz Venus and Wild Bill* for Almost Free's Women's Season. Her first play to reach the West End, *Dusa, Fish, Stas and Vi* (1976), was originally called *Dead Fish*. Rich and radical Fish shares her flat with Dusa, searching for the children her divorced husband has kidnapped, Stas, working as a physiotherapist by day and a party girl by night, and Vi, revelling in anorexia. The women support each other in a coarse and funny community, but they cannot overcome Fish's depression when her lover, and fellow radical organizer, leaves her to marry a more submissive woman. Stas mocks romantic love and treats Fish's claim to property rights in her lover as upper-class regression in the otherwise radical Fish. Stas makes enough money to become a postgraduate student; Vi consents to eat and gets a job. But, pessimistic about change in the relations between men and women, Fish ends her masochistic obsession by poisoning herself, an act discovered, ironically, just as the women's joint efforts have recovered Dusa's children.

The question of children and achievement for women is also central to PG's next play, *Queen Christina* (1977). Christina of Sweden (1626–89), having watched her mother destroyed by repeated, but vain, efforts to produce a living male heir, is brought up to rule as a man. She learns that only power is respected, and abdicates rather than accept her duty, in turn, to provide an heir. Travelling south to Rome she is converted to Catholicism by an attractive cardinal but he refuses to become her lover and offers her only a new kingdom, an arena for her military skills. Christina feels cheated of her woman's life, of the warmth and the babies she finds among her kitchen staff, and, refusing further violence, she retreats to her library where she hopes to find out what women are. The play, rejected by the Royal Court Theatre as too sprawling, expensive, and slanted towards women, was produced at The Other Place in Stratford and revived in London.

PG's *Franz into April*, about a psychiatrist and a repressed Englishwoman, was produced in 1977. The next year, the Royal Shakespeare Company produced *Piaf*, which she had written earlier, and which became her second play to reach the West End, and her first to cross the Atlantic to Broadway, in 1981. As Piaf, the Parisian streetwalker who became a cabaret star, Jane Lapotaire was funny and desperate, vulgar and elegant, maintaining a community of two with her woman-friend, Toine, from the same background. Piaf's series of lovers make the play episodic in structure, joined by her songs. New York critics were less enthusiastic about the play than the British had been.

In *The Treat*, set in a French brothel, PG satirized the enactment of cruel fantasies, and in *Aunt Mary* she celebrated a group of literary male transvestites in a provincial English town. The campy, quarrelsome, generous community defeats a television producer who would exploit them on her show. These plays of 1982 were followed by *Camille* in 1984. When her Camille leaves Paris to share a cottage with her lover, she regretfully abandons a circle of dependants, and when she gives up her lover, it is not to save his reputation, but because his father has promised to educate her son for a place in the class she depends on. This more pragamatic, less romantic, *Camille* again pleased British audiences more than American.

PG, who has written adaptations of plays by Duras, Ibsen, and Chekhov, most recently adapted a stage chronicle by Stanislawa Przybyszewska, *The Danton Affair* (1986), produced at the Barbican by the Royal Shakespeare Company. The cast of forty acts out bread riots and political faction fights until the populist Danton challenges the incorruptible, visionary Robespierre. This Danton, who forces himself on his peasant-born child-bride, is a sensual opportunist, unlike the heroic Danton in Georg Büchner's better-known play, *Danton's Death*. Few critics liked the chronicle play; some blamed its original Polish author, and others suggested that PG should return to working on a smaller scale. Whether she does that, or learns to please on the heroic scale, PG continues to connect history with contemporary experience, and the private with the public life, in provocative plays about difficult choices.   MARY R. DAVIDSON

Selected works: *Betty's Wonderful Christmas* (1972); *My Warren* (1973); *After Birthday* (1973); *The Amiable Courtship of Miz Venus and Wild Bill* (1974); *Go West, Young Woman* (1974); *Up in Sweden* (1975); *Dead Fish*, later called *Dusa, Fish, Stas and Vi* (1976); *Guinevere* (1976); (trans.), *My Name is Rosa Luxemburg*, by Marianne Awicoste (1976); (trans.), *Rivers and Forests*, by Marguerite Duras (1976); *Queen Christina* (1977); *Franz into April* (1977); *Piaf* (1978); *Sandra* (1979); *Ladybird, Ladybird* (1979); (adapt.), *Uncle Vanya*, by Anton Chekhov (1979); (adapt.), *A Doll's House*, by Henrik Ibsen (1980); *Pasionaria* (1982); *The Treat* (1982); *Aunt Mary* (1982); *Camille* (1984).

References: Chambers, C., *Other Spaces* (1980); *DLB;* Itzin, C., *Stages in the Revolution* (1980); Keyssar, H., *Feminist Theatre* (1985); Wandor, M., *Understudies* (1981); Wandor, M., *Carry On, Understudies* (1986).

Gibbons, Stella

b. 5 January 1902, London

Novelist, journalist, poet

SG was born in London, the daughter of a doctor, and was educated first at home by a series of governesses and then at North London Collegiate School. She then studied journalism at University College, London, and was a working journalist for ten years before turning to the writing of poetry and fiction. In 1933 she married Allan Bourne Webb, an actor and singer, who died in 1959, and with whom she had one daughter. She is a Fellow of the Royal Society of Literature.

SG's first novel, *Cold Comfort Farm* (1932), probably inspired by Mary Webb's *Precious Bane*, was an accomplished and hilarious satire on the primitivism of D. H. Lawrence, Thomas Hardy, and the popular regional novels of the 1920s. Its heroine Flora Poste, on a visit to her rural relatives, reforms their gloomy, secretive household along contemporary lines. She subjects their brooding misery and emotional intensity to a no-nonsense rationalism, and introduces them to the pleasures of modern commerce and high fashion. 'Purple' prose passages were marked in the text with asterisks, adding to the deliberate, mocking stylization of the work. The book became a best-seller, won the Femina Vie Heureuse Prize for 1933, and has since achieved classic status. Sequels to *Cold Comfort Farm* (the short stories *Conference at Cold Comfort Farm*, 1949, and *Christmas at Cold Comfort Farm*, 1940) did not have the same topicality or literary astringency as the original. SG continued to produce well-observed, witty novels of manners, largely set in the north London literary community she knew well, but none had the outstanding success of her first book.

Many of SG's novels deal with the effects of the larger group on the individual. *The Charmers* (1965) focuses on the idea of sacrifice; Christine Smith, a spinster, has looked after her parents for most of her life before she is engaged as a housekeeper for 'the charmers', a group of artists or would-be artists. She sacrifices much for the group who disastrously let her down. *The Snow Woman* (1969) looks again at the life of an older woman. A perceptive first-person account of disappointment and boredom, the 'Snow Woman' finds her attitudes challenged by old acquaintances and a puzzling young couple.

A polished technician, with a talent for caricature and ironic commentary, SG was also a highly professional short story writer. Despite her prolific prose output, she always thought of herself as a poet. SG retired from writing fiction in 1970.   JUDY SIMONS AND LISA BUCKBY

Selected works: The Mountain Beast and Other Poems (1930); Cold Comfort Farm (1932); Bassett (1934); The Priestess and Other Poems (1934); The Untidy Gnome (1935); Enbury Heath (1935); Miss Linsey and Pa (1936); Roaring Tower and Other Short Stories (1937); Nightingalewood (1938); The Lowland Venus and Other Poems(1938); My American: A Romance (1939); Christmas at Cold Comfort Farm and Other Stories (1940); The Rich House (1941); Ticky (1943); The Bachelor (1944); Westwood (1946); The Matchmaker (1949); Conference at Cold Comfort Farm (1949); Collected Poems (1951); Fort of the Bear (1953); Beside the Pearly Water (1954); The Shadow of a Sorcerer (1955); Here Be Dragons (1956); White Sand and Grey Sand (1958); A Pink Front Door (1959); The Weather at Tregulla (1962); The Wolves Were in the Sledge (1964); The Charmers (1965); Starlight (1967); The Snow Woman (1969); The Woods in Winter (1970).

References: BA (20); CN; Jacqueline, A., 'Cold comfort from Stella Gibbons', *A Review of International English Literature* 19, 3 (1978).

Gilliatt, Penelope

b. 25 March 1932, London

Novelist, short story writer, playwright

PG has established a considerable reputation as a woman of letters. She grew up in Northumberland, the daughter of a prominent barrister and his Scots wife, Cyril and Mary (née Douglas) Conner. She was educated at Queens's College, London (1942–7) and Bennington College (1948–9), and has worked for the British *Vogue*, *The Observer*, and, as a film critic, for *The New Yorker*. Since leaving the last position she has continued to write stories and profiles for the magazine.

PG's first major publication, a novel, *One by One*, appeared in 1965. She has since written three other novels: *A State of Change* (1967), *The Cutting Edge* (1978), and *Mortal Matters* (1983). Each of them concerns the ways in which human beings can cope with integrating the past and ordering the present. PG's telling psychological accuracy is manifested in all four novels. Nevertheless, her layered use of elements from allegory and parable produces somewhat tentative and diffuse narratives. The erudition of her novels, their elaborate puns and well-turned phrases, cannot compensate for their minimal plot and occasional repetition of character types. Her fiction is somewhat cerebral entertainment.

The confines of the short story perhaps suit PG's talents better. All five of her collections demonstrate the virtues which have earned her a reputation as the quintessential *New Yorker* writer. The nine stories in *Come Back If It Doesn't Get Better* (1969), published in England as *What's It Like Out?*, are character studies which show PG's interest in the workings of the human psyche. The eight stories and one play in *Nobody's Business* (1972) are comparable, both in their concentration on character and in their mood: each story's static focus on a particular situation is only slightly relieved by their verbal sophistication and humour. *Splendid Lives* (1978) contains nine stories, almost all about the last years of aged characters. *Quotations from Other Lives* (1981), with its eleven stories and one play, continues PG's examination of lives in contemporary England and America in rather disappointing fashion: she repeats not only names and remarks but even jokes, a tactic suggested by the title of the collection. Nor does *They Sleep Without Dreaming* (1985) break any new ground.

In each of PG's last four collections the finest piece is a play, and, given her talent for dialogue, this is perhaps not surprising. The screenplay for *Sunday, Bloody Sunday* (1971) is one of her most impressive works. It treats the lives of a trio of characters: Daniel Hirsh, a homosexual Jewish doctor; Alex, a divorced businesswoman; and Bob, a young artist who is lover to both. While little happens in *Sunday, Bloody Sunday*, for it is simply the story of Bob leaving Daniel and Alex behind to go to America, the juxtaposition of carefully rendered personalities and the shifting dynamics of their interaction make for riveting drama. The screenplay, with its emphasis on dialogue rather than action, its abrupt cuts from one scene to another with a minimum of transition, and its need for immediacy, is a genre well adapted to PG's strengths.

PG's critical writing about film and theatre spans her entire professional career. She has published two collections of reviews: the first, *Unholy Fools: Wits, Comics, Disturbers of the Peace: Film and Theatre* (1973), presents profiles of great comics like Keaton and Chaplin as well as short critical essays. Two of the profiles in this volume became full-length critical studies: *Jean Renoir* (1975) and *Jacques Tati* (1976). The second collection, *Three-Quarter Face: Reports and Reflections* (1980) extends PG's biographical interests to a study of over two dozen directors and entertainers.   ROBERT E. HOSMER, JR

Works: *One by One* (1965); *A State of Change* (1967); *What's It Like Out?* (1969; published in the US as *Come Back If It Doesn't Get Better*); *Sunday, Bloody Sunday* (1971); *Nobody's Business* (1972); *Unholy Fools* (1973); *The Western* (1975); *The Method* (1975); *Living on the Box* (1975); *The Flight Fund* (1975); *Jean Renoir* (1975); *Jacques Tati* (1976); *Splendid Lives* (1977); *The Cutting Edge* (1978); *In the Unlikely Event of an Emergency* (1979); *Three-Quarter Face* (1980); *Property* (1980); *Nobody's Business* (stage version, 1980); *In Trust* (1980); *Beach of Aurora* (1981); *Quotations from Other Lives* (1981); *Mortal Matters* (1983); *They Sleep Without Dreaming* (1985); *22 Stories* (1986).

References: *CA; DLB;* Moers, E., *Literary Women* (1976).

Glasse, Hannah

b. 1708, Holborn, London; d. 1770, Newcastle

Cookery writer

HG's father Isaac was the son of the Rev. Major Allgood, rector of Simonsburn; her mother was the daughter of Isaac Clark, a London vintner. HG and her husband John Glasse had three sons and six daughters, many of whom died in infancy. In 1751 she was 'Habit Maker to Her Royal Highness the Princess of Wales, in Tavistock Street, Covent Garden'. Possibly she was the 'Hannah

Glass of St Paul's Co. Garden' on the May 1754 bankruptcy list in the *Gentleman's Magazine*.

HG was the author of *The Compleat Confectioner*, printed in Dublin in 1742. Many editions followed. She is best known, however, for *The Art of Cookery, Made Plain and Easy*, first published in 1747 as 'by a lady'; it attracted nearly 200 subscribers and went through numerous editions. The cookery book first bore HG's name in 1788. While some, including Dr Johnson, disputed her authorship and others noted the unscientific nature of her recipes, the book was widely appreciated for its clear directions and its orderly presentation. By 1812 *The Art of Cookery* had appeared in twenty-six editions, including two in America. HG may later in life have been the author of several books for children.

HG claims that she is not so presumptuous as to 'direct a Lady how to set out her Table', but her advice in *The Art of Cookery* obviously reached mistresses as well as servants. She combined basic instructions about cooking ingredients with suggestions about presentation and domestic economy. It was important not to be wasteful but also to be genteel. She was unimpressed by extravagant French cooks who 'used six Pounds of Butter to fry twelve Eggs' when 'Every Body knows, that understands Cooking, that Half a Pound is full enough'. Some of her recipes demand phenomenal amounts of ingredients such as eggs, and extraordinary devotion to cookery such as two hours of beating. The instruction is often clear, if disconcerting. Pigs should be roasted until 'the Eyes drop out'. HG considers the medicinal qualities of food. A few eels stewed in broth may remedy 'weakly and consumptive constitutions', 'plague water' was a complicated concoction while 'hysterical water' demanded a quarter of a pound of dried millipedes.   JANET JONES

Works: *The Compleat Confectioner* (1742); *The Art of Cookery, Made Plain and Easy; Which Far Exceeds Anything of the Kind Ever Yet Published, etc. [by a Lady]* (1747); *The Servant's Directory or Housekeeper's Companion* (1760).

References: Todd.

Glyn, Elinor

b. 17 October 1864, Jersey; d. 23 September 1943, London

Novelist, film script writer

EG was the second child of Douglas and Elinor Sutherland, both impoverished aristocrats. Her father died of typhoid fever, leaving his wife with little money, two children, Lucy (aged 2) and Elinor (three months), and an injunction to bring them up to revere their noble ancestors and never demean their gentle birth. Too poor to stay in England, she took the children to her parents' home in Canada, where EG spent her first six years learning the rigid etiquette of the French aristocracy (her grandfather was French and had escaped the Revolution when most of his family were guillotined). Though often escaping from her rigorous upbringing into an imaginary world, EG never forgot the lessons in aristocratic self-control: 'Tears, like terror are servants' behaviour.'

In 1871 her mother remarried and finally settled in Jersey. Hating her domineering stepfather, EG again escaped from outward unhappiness by reading indiscriminately everything she could reach in his library. She wrote stories and, at 15, began *The Diary of Miss Nellie Sutherland* which she continued intermittently for the rest of her life. She had believed her red hair and green eyes were ugly but discovered they were not, after a brief romance with an Eton schoolboy and a visit to her French relatives in Paris, where she experienced 'a sudden awakening to the possibilities of life'.

When she was launched into society, the complexities of her upbringing and situation were apparent: 'an elegant girl with a haughty poise, no money, a courtly manner and home-made clothes'. Before she was 21 she had received and refused three marriage proposals, longing for a great romance. At a house-party, four men, competing for her, threw each other into a lake and then had baths in their host's champagne. This story reached Clayton Glyn, a country gentleman, who determined to meet her. EG thought him the 'most pefect grand seigneur' that she had ever met, and in 1892 they were married, settling in Durrington, Essex, where their first daughter, Margot, was born.

As Glyn's wife, EG enjoyed an assured social position, house-parties, and travel. Her first journalistic commission was a series of articles for *Scottish Life* with descriptions of the latest fashions and beauty advice. The first instalment appeared in May 1898 as *Les Coulisses de l'Elegance*. In December, her second daughter, Juliet, was born. Shortly afterwards, convalescing from rheumatic fever, EG began her first novel, *The Visits of Elizabeth*, based upon her experiences of society and her visits to France. It was first published anonymously, and as a comic satire on society was very well received.

In 1902, again convalescing, she began a second novel, *The Reflections of Ambrosine*. Ambrosine, like EG, had an ancestor who was guillotined, and was brought up in proud poverty by her grandmother. She marries an 'unspeakably common man', who fortunately dies of measles, leaving her free to marry the more socially desirable Sir Anthony Thornhirst. In her third novel, *The Vicissitudes of Evangeline* (1905), the red-haired, green-eyed heroine enters the world of society much as her author had done, innocent, adventurous, and observant. She is surprised by the reaction of her puritanical hostess to her night-dress: – ' "Becoming!" almost screamed Mary Macintosh. "But no nice woman wants things to look becoming in bed!" '

Her next novel, *Three Weeks*, shocked society. A young Englishman, Paul, is seduced by a passionate, anonymous foreign lady ('The lady was a Slav and must not be judged by English standards') so that she could present her royal husband with a worthy heir. The setting is exotic: she lies on a tiger-skin rug, 'quivering with the movements of a snake' and later lay 'in his arms on the couch of roses crushed deep and half-buried in their velvet leaves'. Millions of copies were sold, with translations into nearly every European language.

In the following year, EG visited America where she became influenced by 'New Thought', seeking an elixir of eternal youth and a belief in reincarnation. She wrote *Elizabeth Visits America*, a sequel to her first novel, Elizabeth travelling roughly the same route as EG. Three other travel books followed later: *His Hour, Love's Hour* (about Hungary), and *Letters from Spain*.

Discovering her husband was badly in debt, she had from then on to write for money. She had an eventful visit to Russia, once being caught in a snowstorm in a troika, and nearly kidnapped on another occasion. Her resulting book, *His Hour*, gives a vivid picture of the Russian court of 1910. The *Daily Express* commented, 'As one reads one thinks all the time of Versailles before the Revolution with its elegant . . . aristocrats dancing while their doom is being prepared.' Times were changing: in 1912 she published her first book in which the hero had a career, *Halcyone*. The next year, returning to her successful theme of English country house society, she wrote *The Sequence*. The hero, Sir Hugh Dremont, was described as 'one of EG's most attractive heroes' by Barbara Cartland (who has condensed this and several other of EG's books in

Library of Love). Typically, there is passion ('My foolish heart was still beating tempestuously'), fashion (Letitia 'in a ravishing confection of lace and chiffon, blooming like a peach') and class-consciousness ('These tragic looks are bourgeois'). After many setbacks, the two lovers are finally free to marry, Guinevere's unpleasant husband and son and Sir Hugh's disastrous wife luckily having all died.

In 1915, Clayton Glyn died. EG worked in a London canteen and later, in France, as a war correspondent for America. She recalled sheltering in a dugout: 'Only the memory of my grandmama's teaching kept me from screaming aloud.' She still managed to find time to write novels; *The Career of Katherine Bush* was published in 1917. At the signing of the peace treaty in Versailles, she was one of only two women present. After the war she continued her busy life of writing and travel and at the age of 56 embarked on a new career, writing for silent films in Hollywood. She criticized bad sets and anachronisms, and coached the actors, including Rudolph Valentino, to be better stage lovers. Mr Goldwyn commented, 'EG's name is synonymous with the discovery of sex appeal for the cinema.' Several of her novels were filmed, including the highly successful *It*. Returning to England in 1929, she founded a small film company and directed two talking pictures.

In 1933, she was the second most popular author in the 2d. libraries. Her reputation is indicated by Beverley Nichols: 'The average young man in the street . . . would tell you that she spent most of her time on a tiger-skin, smoking scented cigarettes, writing passionate passages with a purple pen and occasionally sipping a liqueur.' During the Second World War she wrote articles about wartime England for America, until her death, aged 78.

SHIRLEY EACHUS

Works: *The Visits of Elizabeth* (1900); *The Reflections of Ambrosine* (1902); *The Damsel and the Sage* (1903); *The Vicissitudes of Evangeline* (1905); *Beyond the Rocks* (1906); *Three Weeks* (1907); *Sayings of Grandmama* (1908); *Elizabeth Visits America* (1909); *His Hour* (1910); *The Reason Why* (1911); *Halcyone* (1912); *The Contrast and Other Stories* (1913); *The Sequence* (1913); *Letters to Caroline* (1914); *The Man and the Moment* (1915); *Three Things* (1915); *The Career of Katherine Bush* (1917); *Destruction* (1918); *The Price of Things* (1919); *Points of View* (1920); *The Philosophy of Love* (1920); *Man and Maid* (1922); *The Great Moment* (1923); *Six Days* (1924); *Letters from Spain* (1924); *This Passion Called Love* (1925); *Love's Blindness* (1926); *The Wrinkle Book* (1927); *It and Other Stories* (1927); *Love – What I Think of It* (1928); *The Flirt and the Flapper* (1930); *Love's Hour* (1932); *Glorious Flames* (1932); *Saint or Satyre?* (1933); *Sooner or Later* (1933); *Did She?* (1934); *Romantic Adventure (an Autobiography)* (1936); *The Third Eye* (1940).

References: *DNB;* Drabble; Etherington-Smith, M., and Pilcher, J., *The It Girls: Lucy, Lady Duff Gordon, the Couturière Lucile and Elinor Glyn, Romantic Novelist* (1986); Glyn, A., *Elinor Glyn* (1955).

Godden, Rumer

b. 10 December 1907, Sussex
Novelist, writer for children, poet
RG was the second of the four daughters of Arthur Leigh Godden, who worked for a large steamer company, and Katherine Norah Hingley. She was brought up in India, chiefly in Narayangunj, East Bengal (now Bangladesh), a period she has described in *Two Under the Indian Sun* (1966), written with her sister Jon. She was educated by governesses at home in India, then at 12 was sent to

England to an Anglo-Catholic convent, where she found the adjustment difficult. She attended five schools during the next six years, settling eventually at Moira House, Eastbourne, Sussex, where she concentrated on French literature and music. In her early teens she had some poems published at her own expense, but was unable to sell them.

At the age of 20 she trained as a dancing teacher, then in 1929 went to Calcutta to set up her own dance school. In 1934 she married Lawrence Sinclair Foster, a stockbroker, and shortly afterwards gave birth to a son, David, who died within four days of his birth. Her first novel, *Chinese Puzzle* (1936), was accepted by Peter Davies the day her first daughter was born. (Two earlier novels had been rejected.) It is the whimsical life story of a Chinaman of the tenth century who has been reincarnated a thousand years later in the form of a Pekingese dog. Another novel, *The Lady and the Unicorn*, about a Eurasian family and the difficulties of living between two cultures, appeared in 1937. RG's first real success was *Black Narcissus*, finished in 1938 a month before her second daughter was born. Centred around a small party of nuns who attempt to settle in the Himalayan foothills, it became an immediate best-seller.

In 1941 RG's husband left her after going bankrupt through unsuccessful gambling on the Stock Exchange, and she went with her children to stay on the Rungli-Rungliot Tea Estate in Darjeeling. The diary she kept there was published as *Rungli-Rungliot: Thus Far and No Further* in 1943. She then settled with her children in Kashmir, living in harsh conditions and surviving, amongst other things, her servant's attempt to poison her.

In 1949 she married James Lesley Haynes Dixon, settling in Britain. She lived for some years in Lamb House at Rye, the long-time home of Henry James, and now lives in Dumfriesshire, Scotland. She has continued to write prolifically, producing over twenty novels and as many children's books. Among her best known novels are *The Greengage Summer*, a mystery involving a family of English children in a French hotel, and *An Episode of Sparrows*, a tender story of street urchins in London. She has also written poetry and various non-fictional works, including *Bengal Journey* (1945), an account of women's war work in Bengal, and critiques of Hans Christian Andersen and Beatrix Potter. Various of her works, including *Black Narcissus, The River* (directed by Jean Renoir), *The Greengage Summer*, and *An Episode of Sparrows*, have been made into films.

A first volume of her autobiography, *A Time to Dance, No Time to Weep* (1987), has recently appeared. It deals with her unconventional childhood in India, her disastrous first marriage and her struggle, in the face of considerable domestic hardship, to become a writer. She is currently working on a second volume of autobiography.

Roman Catholicism is central to much of RG's fiction (including several children's stories). Both *In This House of Brede* (1969) and *Five for Sorrow, Ten for Joy* (1979) are set in nunneries; in the latter, the convent life follows life in a Paris brothel, a murder, and years of penitence in a women's prison. In *Black Narcissus*, for which RG is best known, five nuns settle in a disused palace in the Himalayan foothills only to find that all their projects fail. The mountain visible from the palace garden begins to fill their imaginations (like the caves in Forster's *A Passage to India*), making their Christian ritual seem 'small and petty' in comparison. Their faith is also rigorously challenged by the continual presence of a general turned holy man whose unworldliness makes theirs look worldly, as well as by the blunt pragmatism of the worldly Mr Dean. As the nuns prepare to leave India, the rains come to wipe away all remaining traces of them: the convent has proved to be 'no more than a cobweb that would be brushed away'. Sister Phillippa voices a view of India held by Kipling and Forster when she argues that 'there are only two ways to live in this place. . . . You must either live like Mr Dean or like the Sunnyasi; either ignore it completely or give yourself up to it'. It is a view also expressed in *Kingfishers Catch Fire* (1953), where the heroine's attempts to live like a Kashmiri lead to disaster. What she imagines to be her own frugality is seen by the Kashmiris as excess, and her 'assistance' is construed as interference. The differences between the two cultures are perceived, as in Forster, as 'a muddle'.

Another preoccupation in RG's work is adolescence and the coming to awareness that it entails. Frequently children prove to be more resourceful than the adults around them. In *The Greengage Summer* a group of children abandoned by their sick mother in a French hotel, deceived and manipulated by the charming, enigmatic Eliot and his besotted mistress, are ultimately able to provide the police with the vital information for which they have been searching for years. The experiences at *Les Oeillets*, filtered through the consciousness of the 13-year-old girl Cecil, necessitate a loss of innocence, an irreversible widening of the horizons of these protected middle-class children brought up in a drab English seaside resort. We witness their being forced, stage by stage, to abandon their naive idolization of the glamorous Eliot, and to accept, contrary to all their preconceptions, that he is a callous murderer and jewel thief. In *An Episode of Sparows*, Lovejoy Mason, left by her promiscuous actress mother to be brought up by the inept proprietors of a restaurant in a London slum, overcomes the elements and the opposition of the slum's inhabitants to create a beautiful garden in a bombed-out churchyard. Here as elsewhere RG displays a fascination with walls, limits, and their effects, both enervating and invigorating.

The majority of RG's novels display a strong emphasis on plot and little formal experimentation, though some works, including *A Fugue in Time* (1945) and *China Court* (1961), show the influence of Bergson in their preoccupation with time and memory and their fusion of past and present. *The River* (1946) attempts through its structure (it opens and closes with the same lines) to reproduce the sense of timelessness RG associates with Hinduism.

RG's first children's story, *The Doll's House* (1947), provides the subject for a string of children's books in which the protagonists are dolls, e.g. *Impunity Jane* (1954) and *The Story of Holly and Ivy* (1958). The doll's world is the adult world in microcosm (RG describes *The Doll's House* as 'a murder story'). Whilst retaining their doll-like characteristics, the dolls reflect, in their personalities and relationships, the complexities of family life. Other children's books include *The Mousewife* (1951), the story of a friendship between a caged dove and a mouse, based on an entry in Dorothy Wordsworth's journal, and *The Kitchen Madonna* (1967), about two children who make an icon of the virgin and child for their Ukrainian nanny. *The Diddakoi* (1972) was winner of the Whitbread Award.   ANNE FERNIHOUGH

Selected works: *Chinese Puzzle* (1936); *The Lady and the Unicorn* (1937); *Black Narcissus* (1939); *Breakfast with the Nikolides* (1942); *Rungli-Rungliot: Thus Far and No Further* (1943); *Bengal Journey* (1945); *The River* (1946); *The Doll's House* (1947); *A Candle for St Jude* (1948); *The Mousewife* (1951); *Kingfishers Catch Fire* (1953); *Impunity Jane* (1954); *Hans Christian Andersen: A Great Life in Brief* (1954); *The Fairy Doll* (1956); *Mouse House* (1957); *Mooltiki: Stories and Poems from India* (1957); *The Greengage Summer* (1958); *The Story of Holly and Ivy* (1958); *St Jerome and the Lion* (1961); *Miss Happiness and Miss Flower* (1961); *China Court:*

The Hours of a Country House (1961); *Home is the Sailor* (1964); *The Kitchen Madonna* (1967); *In This House of Brede* (1969); *Operation Sippacik* (1969); *The Tale of the Tales: The Beatrix Potter Ballet* (1971); *The Diddakoi* (1972); *The Old Woman Who Lived in a Vinegar Bottle* (1972); *The Peacock Spring* (1975); *The Rocking Horse Secret* (1978); *The Butterfly Lions: The Story of the Pekingese in History, Legend and Art* (1978); *Five for Sorrow, Ten for Joy* (1979); *Thursday's Children* (1984); *A Time to Dance, No Time to Weep* (1987).
References: Greenberger, A. J., *The British Image of India* (1969); Simpson, H. A., *Rumer Godden* (1973); Tindall, W. Y., 'Rumer Godden, public symbolist', *College English* 13 (March 1952); Wintle, J. and Fisher, E., *The Pied Pipers: Interviews with the Influential Creators of Children's Literature* (1974).

Gore, Catherine
b. 1799, East Retford, Nottinghamshire; d. 1861, Linwood, Hampshire
Novelist, playwright
(Also wrote under CD, CFG, Mrs Charles Gore, Albany Poyntz)
Although she made her reputation as a novelist with her stories of high society, and came to move in fashionable circles, CG was not born into the upper classes; she was the daughter of a wine merchant, C. Moody. Educated at home in London, she showed promise as a writer at an early age (Joanna Baillie praised her work), although she published nothing until after her marriage to Captain Charles Gore in 1823. From then on she wrote fairly consistently until she became blind in her old age, producing around seventy volumes; the only real gap in her writing came when the family inherited some money. She nursed her husband who was an invalid for many years, and with him had ten children, only two of whom survived her.

Her first publication, *The Two Broken Hearts*, a verse story, appeared in 1823, and was followed in 1824 by a novel, *Theresa Marchmont, or, The Maid of Honour*. The central character is Helen, the epitome of passive female virtue: neglected by her husband Greville, she 'nourished an intensity of wife-like devotion and endurance which no unkindness could tire.' When she sees what she believes to be the ghost of Gréville's first wife, Theresa, a dreadful secret is uncovered: Theresa is alive, but insane. Helen is deeply shocked, but to protect Greville's name, sacrifices the rest of her life to caring for Theresa. Though the novel is at times mawkishly sentimental, CG's ability as a story teller is apparent in the swift, exciting narrative, as is her relish of complicated human relationships and the devastating results of hypocrisy and deceit, which in her subsequent novels fuel much of the comedy.

In 1830 appeared *Women as They Are, or, The Manners of the Day*, the novel that first brought CG recognition as one of the 'silver fork' school of writers. Numerous others of the same style followed, bringing CG to the forefront of the school. Without being merely formulaic, these novels contain recognizable, recurrent features: they tend to be set in contemporary high society, described in close material detail, which creates a sense of actuality as the characters go to familiar places like Almacks or Vauxhall, order ice-creams from the most fashionable caterers, Gunters, and even the shops they visit and the clerks they employ were well-known at the time. Written for and about members of fashionable society, fashion itself is an important theme of the novels: the latest styles are closely described, and the novels came to act as handbooks for aspirants to fashion. The action usually centres on marriage, which is treated both romantically, as a wish-fulfilment, and satirically, when characters use it as a means of social or financial advancement. An example of the latter is *Mothers and Daughters, A Tale of the Year 1830* (1831), in which two generations of women scheme and matchmake: first Lady Maria ('Charles Willingham very properly fell in love, and Lady Maria very naturally fell into a fit of musing'), then her daughters, Claudia, who is determined to marry an aristocrat, and Eleanor, who would be satisfied with vast wealth. But however well these women seem to be manipulating their unfortunate victims, CG never allows them complete success; for example Eleanor is convinced of her power over one stupendously dull but wealthy man, and spends hours trying to give him the confidence to propose, only to discover that all he wants is advice on courting her cousin.

CG and her family lived in a number of different places, including a stay of some years in Paris. Her varied lifestyle informed many of her novels, notably *Cecil, or, The Adventures of a Coxcomb* (1841) in which the narrator, Cecil, who is a friend of Byron, describes his riotous life in Britain and on the continent. Through the character of Cecil, CG satirizes dandyism, with its vanity, pretension, and selfishness. The only way of controlling Cecil's tantrums as a baby was to place him in front of the mirror, where the sight of his own beauty calmed him. His father intended him for the Church, 'But the wig!' Cecil protests. His ambition is to be 'dictator to the world of fashion', and to make as many women as possible fall in love with him: 'I was never more cruel to them than could be helped. Why, why has Providence created them with such feeble temperaments, or the coarser sex with such powerful attractions!' Cecil becomes the victim of his own vanity, however, when he believes one beauty to be in love with him, and gets more involved than usual, only to discover that she is engaged to his arch-enemy.

CG was renowned as a witty conversationalist, and the dialogue in her novels has similar energy. For a while she exploited this skill writing for the stage, and met with some success. Her first play, *The School for Coquettes*, ran for thirty nights at the Haymarket in 1832. Six more plays of varying popularity followed, then in 1843 CG won a £500 prize for an 'English comedy', with *Quid Pro Quo, or, The Day of Dupes*. Against a sub-plot of county political wrangling, the main plot concerns class difference and social climbing, and involves the hero in disguise, everyone in amateur theatricals, and the four young people in love. Though the judges liked it the play was a box-office failure, and was attacked by audiences and critics alike. CG wrote no more drama.

CG was good at business and knew how to exploit her market. Once she published two novels anonymously in one week to stimulate sales through competition. She published *Cecil* anonymously, suggesting in the preface that it was a first novel, to capture the public's interest in a new writer. In 1855 she lost £20,000 in a banking scandal, but made the most of the publicity, recouping some of the loss by a reissue of her 1843 novel, *The Banker's Wife*, about a corrupt banker. When the Duchesse de Praslin was murdered while reading *Mrs Armytage, or, Female Domination* (1836), CG ordered a double reprint of the novel, while stressing that her intentions were entirely moral, for the novel pointed out 'the injurious effects produced upon the female character by an extension of the rights and privileges of the sex'.   LUCY SLOAN

Selected works: *The Two Broken Hearts* (1823); *Theresa Marchmont, or, The Maid of Honour* (1824); *Lettre de Cachet: A Tale, and The Reign of Terror: A Tale* (1827); *Hungarian Tales* (1829); *Romances of Real Life* (1829); *Women As They Are, or, The Manners of the Day* (1830); *Mothers and Daughters: A Tale of the Year*

1830 (1831); *The School for Coquettes* (1832); *The Sketchbook of Fashion* (1833); *The Maid of Croissey, King O'Neil,* and *The Queen's Champion,* in *Webster's Acting National Drama* (1835); *The Diary of a Désennuyée* (1836); *Mrs Armytage, or, Female Domination* (1836); *The Woman of the World: A Novel* (1838); *The Cabinet Minister* (1839); *Dacre of the South, or, The Olden Time: A Drama* (1840); *Preferment, or, My Uncle the Earl* (1840); *The Abbey and Other Tales* (1840); *Cecil, or, The Adventures of a Coxcomb: A Novel* (1841); *Cecil, a Peer* (1841); *Paris in 1841* (1842); *The Ambassador's Wife* (1842); *The Money-Lender* (1843); *The Banker's Wife, or, Court and City: A Novel* (1843); *Agathonia: A Romance* (1844); *Quid Pro Quo, or, The Day of the Dupes* (1844); *The Story of a Royal Favourite* (1845); *The Debutante, or, The London Season* (1846); *Temptation and Atonement and Other Tales* (1847); *The Diamond and the Pearl: A Novel* (1849); *The Dean's Daughter, or, The Days We Live In* (1853); *Mammon, or, The Hardships of an Heiress* (1855); *The Two Aristocracies: A Novel* (1857); *Heckington: A Novel* (1858).

References: Adburgham, A., *Silver Fork Society: Fashionable Life and Literature 1814–1840* (1983); Allibone; Anderson, B., 'The writing of Catherine Gore', *Journal of Popular Culture* 10 (1976); *BA* (19); Cook, D., *The Theatre* (August 1882); *DNB;* Drabble; Hale, S. J., *Woman's Record* (1855); Horne, R. H. (ed.), *A New Spirit of the Age* (1844); Moers, E., *Literary Women* (1976); Rosa, M. W., *The Silver-Fork School: Novels of Fashion Preceding* Vanity Fair (1936).

Goudge, Elizabeth

b. 24 April 1900, Wells, Somerset; d. 1 April 1984, near Henley-on-Thames
Novelist, biographer, writer for children

EG, the only child of Ida de Beauchamp Collenette and Henry Leighton Goudge, a clergyman, lived in cathedral towns until her father's death. In 1911 the family moved to Ely. From 1914 to 1918 she attended Southbourne, a boarding school. After studying at the Art School at Reading College for two years, EG taught design and applied art at home in Ely and Oxford (where her father had become Regius Professor of Divinity in 1923) from 1922 to 1932. EG's love of the theatre, which began in her school days, inspired her to write plays, but although her first was produced in London in 1932, her interest in the theatre was better adapted to depicting actors in novels than to playwriting. She began writing fiction in Devon, where after the move to Oxford her invalid mother lived. EG's first novel was published in 1934, but while building a reputation with her books, she made her living writing stories for magazines, particularly *The Strand.* She suffered a nervous breakdown in the mid–1930s, and, after her father's death in 1939 and her mother's in 1944, she left Devon to live with Jessie Monroe near Henley-on-Thames. *Green Dolphin Country* (published in America as *Green Dolphin Street*) (1944) won an M-G-M film prize of $125,000 and became a best-seller and made her a success. *The Little White Horse* (1947), a children's book, won the Carnegie Medal. She died in 1984.

EG wrote a great many books, but except for an increased proportion of non-fiction in her later life, her writing shows little development. Rather, her work falls into several categories with examples from each appearing at widely spaced intervals. Throughout her career, she wrote short stories, historical novels, novels of place, children's books, and non-fiction on religious subjects. The categories overlap – all of her work exhibits her deeply held Christian faith, her understanding of the world of children, her love of the English countryside and her sense of place, and her interest in English history and legend.

Her best-known historical novels are *Green Dolphin Country* (1944), *Gentian Hill* (1949), and *The Child from the Sea* (1970). The first is about a Guernsey great-uncle of hers, who, having emigrated, writes home for a bride but confuses her name with that of her sister and gets the wrong one. He never tells her and the marriage is successful. The second, a retelling of the West Country legend of the Chapel of St Michael, is set in the Napoleonic period. The third is the story of Lucy Waters, the secret wife of Charles II; its theme is forgiveness.

Some of EG's novels of place also have historical settings. Of her three novels of cathedral towns, two are set in the past: *Towers in the Mist* (1938) in sixteenth-century Oxford and *The Dean's Watch* (1960) in nineteenth-century Ely. *A City of Bells* (1936), set in modern Wells, concerns a young bookseller's efforts to win the love of an actress and to rescue a writer from obscurity and reunite him with his young daughter. *Island Magic* (1934), EG's first novel, is about her maternal grandparents' lives on the island of Guernsey in the last century.

Devon is the setting for EG's series of novels about the Eliots of Damerosehay – the saintly but outspoken matriarch Lucilla, her middle-aged children, and their families, particularly her grandson David, a famous actor. These books stress the values of family, spiritual testing and growth, and proper action as the catalyst of proper feeling, and show a beautiful house with an instructive past in a spectacular natural setting to be a major force in fostering these values. In *The Bird in the Tree* (1940), EG's own favourite of her books, Lucilla prevails on David and Nadine, the ex-wife of his uncle, to renounce their love so that Nadine may be reconciled with her husband and children. In *The Herb of Grace* (1948), Nadine, under the influence of her new home, The Herb of Grace, formerly a pilgrims' inn, finally completes her renunciation of David, freeing him to marry and take his place as Lucilla's heir at Damerosehay. In *The Heart of the Family* (1953), a concentration camp victim who has lost his family in the bombing of Hamburg teaches David, a pilot on that mission, the meaning of forgiveness, enabling David to rededicate himself to his own family.

EG's books for children are characteristically mysteries set in the English countryside, mixing fantasy and reality, often having an historical setting as well. The award-winning *The Little White Horse* (1947), a mystery set in the 1840s, is sometimes over-sweet but very appealing to an imaginative child. *Smokey House* (1940), a story of smuggling in the post-Napoleonic era, is notable for its exquisite style and its portrayal of friendships between the young and the old. *The Valley of Song* (1951), an eighteenth-century fable about shipbuilders who are helped by an imaginative child, appeals less to children than to adults with a taste for EG's luscious scenic description and sentimental yet modern spirituality. *Linnets and Valerians* (1964) involves the four Linnet children in a mystery concerning the Valerian family.

Not surprisingly, considering her novels' emphasis on the spiritual life, EG also wrote non-fiction on religious subjects. *God So Loved the World* (1951) is a biography of Jesus; *My God and My All* (1959) is a biography of St Francis of Assisi. Her autobiography, *The Joy of the Snow* (1974), is a highly impressionistic account of her life with her parents, her family history, her spiritual growth, her writing career, and the places she lived. It is almost devoid of dates and gives few details of her life after her mother's death.

Although all of EG's writing suffers from sentimentality, excessive description, and didacticism, her novels of place and her children's books show great insight into human character – especially the very young and the very old –

and lyrically evoke the English countryside and English legend. Her novels about the Eliot family are her most adult in theme and treatment, her least characteristic but certainly her most interesting to readers who desire neither escape nor inspiration. KATE BROWDER HEBERLEIN

Selected works: *Island Magic* (1934); *The Middle Window* (1935); *A City of Bells* (1936); *A Pedlar's Pack* (1937); *Towers in the Mist* (1938); *The Sister of the Angels* (1939); *Three Plays* (1939); *Smokey House* (1940); *The Bird in the Tree* (1940); *The Golden Skylark* (1941); *The Well of the Star* (1941); *The Blue Hills* (1942); *The Castle on the Hill* (1942); *The Ikon on the Wall* (1943); *Green Dolphin Country* (1944; published in the US as *Green Dolphin Street*); *The Elizabeth Goudge Reader* (1946); *The Little White Horse* (1947); *Songs and Verses* (1947); *At the Sign of the Dolphin* (1947); *Henrietta's House* (1947); *The Herb of Grace* (1948; published in the US as *Pilgrim's Inn*); *Christmas at the Herb of Grace* (1949); *Gentian Hill* (1949); *Make Believe* (1949); *The Reward of Faith* (1950); *The Valley of Song* (1951); *God So Loved the World* (1951); *White Wings* (1952); *The Heart of the Family* (1953); *David, the Shepherd Boy* (1954); *The Rosemary Tree* (1956); *The Eliots of Damerosehay* (1957); *The White Witch* (1958); *My God and My All: The Life of St Francis of Assisi* (1959); *The Dean's Watch* (1960); *The Scent of Water* (1963); *Linnets and Valerians* (1964); *A Book of Comfort* (1964); *Three Cities of Bells* (1965); *A Diary of Prayer* (1966); *A Book of Peace* (1967); *A Christmas Book* (1967); *I Saw Three Ships* (1969); *The Ten Gifts* (1969); *The Child from the Sea* (1970); *The Lost Angel* (1971); *The Joy of the Snow* (1974); *A Book of Faith* (1976); *Pattern of People* (1976).

References: *CA*; Leasor, J., *Author by Profession* (1952); *OCCL*.

Grand, Sarah

b. 10 June 1854, Donaghadee, County Down, Northern Ireland; d. 12 May 1943, Calne, Wiltshire

Novelist

One of five children, SG was born in Ireland of English parents, Edward John Bellenden Clark and Margaret Bell Sherwood, but when her father, a naval officer, died in 1861, her mother moved the family back to England. SG was educated at home until she was 14 when she was sent to boarding school. She escaped from school at 16 by marrying a naval surgeon twenty-three years her senior, apparently an unhappy match. After *Ideala* (1888) was published she moved away from her husband and son to live in London where her career flourished, and when her husband died in 1898, SG joined the Women Writers' Suffrage League and became active in the women's suffrage movement in Tunbridge Wells. In 1922, two years after moving to Bath, she became the city's mayoress for six years. One of the 'New Women' writers of the 1890s, SG used her controversial novels to criticize the oppression of women. She also wrote many socially conscious short stories and articles for women's magazines, such as 'Is It Ever Justifiable to Break Off an Engagement?' and 'Should Irascible Old Men Be Taught to Knit?'. Severly criticized in some quarters both for her subject matter and for her style, she was admired by others such as Mark Twain and George Bernard Shaw.

Her first successful novel, *Ideala*, forms a trilogy with *The Heavenly Twins* (1893) and *The Beth Book* (1897). A first-person narrative about Ideala by a male friend, it examines a number of social problems as well as the question of the proper goal for women. *The Heavenly Twins*, a best-seller, experiments with narrative voice, producing some disconcerting breaks, and it has many themes and sub-plots. Above all it concerns the disastrous effects of inadequate female education on women, although it shows some characters surmounting their conditioning. The title refers to the twins Angelica and Diavolo, female and male, and their upbringing, but the novel actually focuses on Evadane, a highly intelligent and self-educated woman who, through being kept in ignorance by her parents, inadvertently marries a brutish man with a sordid past.

The Beth Book, based loosely on her own life, successfully conveys the strong, fascinating character of Beth and well describes the Victorian upbringing of a young girl. Instead of being a pathetic, sentimental account of the oppression of the female children, the novel presents Beth unexpectedly refusing to submit. There are short ironic character descriptions, such as that of the Vicar of Rainharbour: 'Self denial and morality were his favourite subjects. He had had three wives himself, and was getting through a fourth as fast as one baby a year would do it.' Unfortunately there are structural problems in the novel resulting from SG's desire to stay with the central character's point of view; in one scene, for example, Beth trails her corrupt Uncle James around his estate for an unbelievably long time, unseen yet close enough to hear his conversation. Sometimes characterization can be inconsistent; there is an abrupt change in Mr Caldwell, Beth's father, from a harsh, domineering and critical husband ('not to disturb him was the object of everybody's life') to a patient, appreciative and understanding father to Beth shortly before his death. The advice he gives Beth is necessary for the continuation of the novel, but the change in his personality is explained only perfunctorily in a few hasty scenes in the garden.

Unlike her trilogy, *Singularly Deluded* (1893) caused no controversy and has little interest beyond plot except in its vivid description of a fire at sea. Her next two novels, *Adnam's Orchard* (1912) and *Winged Victory* (1916), deal with the problem of land reform, and in them SG focuses on lower-class characters, considering at length what makes a person 'noble'. In *Adnam's Orchard* we see a land laid waste by its unambitious noble landowners, the workers and their families either unemployed or impoverished in substandard housing. The absurdity of the landowners' raising rent as soon as tenants make any improvements in the property is apparent. *Winged Victory* follows the life of Ella Banks, a character in *Adnam's Orchard*, and her attempts to improve the lives of women workers in the sweatshops.   CAROL PULHAM

Works: *Two Dear Little Feet* (1880); *Ideala: A Study From Life* (1888); *A Domestic Experiment* (1891); *Singularly Deluded* (1893); *The Heavenly Twins* (1893); *Our Manifold Nature* (1894); *The Beth Book* (1897); *The Modern Man and Maid* (1898); *Babs the Impossible* (1900); *Emotional Moments* (1908); *Adnam's Orchard* (1912); *The Winged Victory* (1916); *Variety* (1922).

References: Cunningham, G., *The 'New Woman' and the Fiction of the 1890s* (1978); Huddleston, J., *Sarah Grand: A Bibliography* (1979); Kersley, G., *Darling Madame: Sarah Grand and Devoted Friend* (1983); Showalter, E., *A Literature of Their Own* (1977).

Greenwell, Dora

b. 1821, Lanchester, County Durham; d. 1882, Clifton, Bristol
Theological writer, poet, essayist
DG was the only daughter of the five children of Dorothy Smales and William Thomas Greenwell, a country squire and magistrate who for a while was Deputy Lieutenant of the county. The family were initially well-off and she was educated at home by a governess. She spoke French and Italian fluently

and could read German and Spanish. By 1848 the family's fortune had diminished and their home, Greenwell Ford, had to be sold. Shortly afterwards she published her first book of verse, *Poems* (1848), reprinted in 1850 as *Stories That Might Be True with Other Poems*. She stayed at her brother's home at Ovingham Rectory, Northumberland, for two years where she met and began a long friendship with Josephine Butler to whom she dedicated her early prose work, *The Patience of Hope* (1860). In 1850 the family moved to Golbourne in Lancashire and in 1854, when her brother resigned his living because of ill-health, Dora and her mother moved back to Durham, where they lived for the next eighteen years and where most of her writing was done.

Her first prose work was *A Present Heaven* (1855); in subsequent editions she changed the title to *The Covenant of Life and Peace*. *Two Friends* (1863), which she described as 'a conversation with myself', was dedicated to her publisher Thomas Constable with whose family in Edinburgh she became close friends. She uses an imaginary interlocutor, Philip (who also appears in the sequel *Colloquia Crucis*, 1871), to represent 'the practical working side' (as opposed to the imaginative) of her own mind and creates a dialogue full of sensitive insight and characteristic broad sympathy. She reflects on states of perception, on what she felt as a painful contradiction 'between the brokenness of Christ and the clear perfection of Art', on political crimes – among which she counted war and slavery – and on the reality of evil. She was personally sympathetic to Evangelicals and the book contains detailed and appreciative references to the 'eminently social' sect of Methodism, as well as discussion of the best and worst aspects of Catholicism. She cuts across traditional Christian ideas about the value of suffering: 'Sorrow is essentially separative. What is its extremest form – insanity – but isolation? The French, with as much truth as tenderness, call the insane "les aliénés".'

Having worked among the paupers in Durham workhouse and prison, she wrote an article 'On the education of the imbecile' (*North British Review*, September 1868) after the founding of the Lancaster asylum and argued that 'this ought not to be left to philanthropy'. It attracted the attention of the medical faculty and there was much discussion about which eminent doctor could have written it. *Essays* (1866) contains five articles mostly reprinted from the *North British Review*, including 'Hardened in good', which tells of her own experiences with the poor in Durham and 'Our single women', in which she argued for greater recognition (including financial), utilization, and organization of women's capacities. She also wrote a biography of *Lacordaire* (1867), a Dominican friar with whom she felt close sympathy, and a memoir of the Quaker *John Woolman* (1871).

When her mother died in 1871 she moved to London, and also lived for some time in Torquay and at her brother's home in Clifton. She wrote on 'The East African slave trade' for the *Contemporary Review* (June 1873) and published two more collections of essays, *Liber Humanitatis* (1875) and *A Basket of Summer Fruit* (1876), dedicated 'To the American Evangelists' (probably Moody and Sankey) 'who lately visited England'. She was a friend of Jean Ingelow and continued to write poetry on aspects of spiritual and social life throughout her later years, producing collections in 1861 and 1867 (both simply called *Poems*). The second is more humorous and secular and contains a dialogue between two Durham pitmen about the Lancashire cotton famine in 1863 and verses on the American Civil War. These were followed by *Carmina Crucis* (1869), containing the powerful poem 'Sita' about the maligned wife of the god Rama,

Songs of Salvation (1873) – some of the poems in this volume are better-known as hymns – *The Soul's Legend* (1873), and *Camera Obscura* (1876).

CHRISTINE DEVONSHIRE

Selected works: *Poems* (1848); *Stories That Might Be True, with Other Poems* 1850); *A Present Heaven* (1855); *The Patience of Hope* (1860); *Poems* (1861); *Two Friends* (1863); *Essays* (1866); *Poems* (1867); *Carmina Crucis* (1869); *On the Education of the Imbecile* (1869); *Colloquia Crucis* (1871); *Songs of Salvation* (1873); *The Soul's Legend* (1873); *Liber Humanitatis* (1875); *Camera Obscura* (1876); *A Basket of Summer Fruits* (1877).

References: Bett, H., *Dora Greenwell* (1950); Dorling, W., *Memoirs of Dora Greenwell* (1885); Maynard, C. L., *Dora Greenwell* (1925).

Greer, Germaine

b. 29 January 1939, Melbourne, Australia

Journalist, feminist theorist, art historian, literary critic

GG is the daughter of Margaret Lanfrancan and Eric Reginald Greer, a newspaper advertising manager. She earned an honours degree from the University of Melbourne in 1959, an MA with first-class honours from the University of Sydney in 1963, and a PhD (on Shakespeare) from Newnham College, Cambridge in 1968. The same year she married newspaperman Paul de Feu (whom she divorced five years later) and began lecturing in English at Warwick University, where she worked until 1973. She founded the Tulsa (Oklahoma) Center for the Study of Women's Literature, serving as its director from 1979 to 1982. She contributes articles to many journals, appears frequently on television, and has recently collaborated in compiling a book of seventeenth-century women poets, *Kissing the Rod* (1988). She is at present editing the writings of Aphra Behn.

The Female Eunuch created an instant sensation in 1971, and has become a classic text of the later twentieth-century feminist movement. It is an outrageous and supremely readable critique of the role of women in western society, which vigorously reveals the havoc wreaked on women's sexuality by the patriarchal stereotype of the 'eternal feminine'. The book sounds a ringing call to women to take joy in the overwhelming of their psychic prison walls and to create a 'festival of the oppressed'.

In *The Obstacle Race* (1979), GG argues that the internal, psychological obstacles to western women's 'greatness' in painting were much more powerful in keeping them out of art history books than overt, societal coercion. (She introduces an abundance of women painters from the past; the work sometimes degenerates to a mere listing of names, since sadly so little is known about their lives or art. She is careful to state that these women are only a selection – many more about whom even less is known might have been included.) Unlike other more timid art historians, GG has a refreshing perspective on the subject that allows her to draw comparisons between artists across centuries, and the audacity to advocate activism in an academic book. In this, as in all her work, she combines thorough intellectual rigour with a striking ability to inspire her readers in a practical way. Here, she urges that, for the recovery and preservation of women painters, 'women by the thousand must begin to sift the archives of their own districts, turn out their own attics, haunt their own salerooms and the auctions in old houses'.

Sex and Destiny (1984), in GG's usual erudite and entertaining style, attacks the idea of a population explosion and the western world's enforcement on the underdeveloped world of what it euphemistically calls 'family planning'. She discusses the importance of children and attitudes to sexuality and contraception to peoples other than those of north-western European origin, drawing on sources from government statistics to her own conversations, ranging regionally from Tuscany to Syria, India, and Java.

Her emphasis on the importance of children, particularly to women, has been raucously denounced by feminist and non-feminist critics alike as a menopausal recantation of her stance in *The Female Eunuch*. But while *Sex and Destiny* sometimes takes an unduly idealistic view of family life in underdeveloped countries, its analysis of the global problem challenges every reader to examine her own views, and rightly points out the hypocrisy of western contraceptive policies. The charge that GG has deserted the feminist ship is merely an unfortunate symptom of the media-created 'decline of feminism in the 1980s'. The integrity of her work is reflected in GG's own words in *The Female Eunuch*: 'All literature, however vituperative, is an act of love.'   AMY ERICKSON

Selected works: *The Female Eunuch* (1970); *The Obstacle Race: The Fortunes of Women Painters and Their Work* (1979); *Sex and Destiny: The Politics of Human Fertility* (1984); 'Women and Power in Cuba', in *Women: A World Apart* (1985); *Shakespeare* (1986); (ed.), *Kissing the Rod* (1988).

References: *CA*; Callil, C., 'Twenty who changed our lives', *Sunday Times Magazine* (22 February 1987); Plante, D., *Three Difficult Women* (1983).

Gregory, Augusta, Lady

b. 15 March 1852, Roxborough, County Galway; d. 22 May 1932, Coole, County Galway

Dramatist, folklorist

Though, like other key figures in the Irish literary renaissance, AG was by birth and upbringing a member of the Protestant ascendancy, her sympathies were those of a 'nationalist rebel'. Her achievement was to provide for the Abbey Theatre in Dublin between 1902 and 1927, the period when it was the focus of Irish cultural nationalism, much of what was genuinely popular and innovative in its repertoire, and to become, as Yeats acknowledged, 'the founder of modern Irish dialect literature'. She was the twelfth child and youngest daughter of Dudley Persse, a Protestant landowner whose family and connections were hard riding, proselytizing gentry with few intellectual or cultural interests. From her Catholic, Irish-speaking nurse AG absorbed Galway legends and folk history and an early sympathy with the Fenians. She was educated by a series of governesses and spent her early adult life in humanitarian work among the local cottagers, the squalor and deprivation of whose lives made a lasting impression. Her marriage in 1880 to Sir William Gregory, a neighbouring landowner thirty-five years her senior, who had recently retired as Governor of Ceylon, liberated her into a world which was larger both literally and in its intellectual outlook. She travelled with him in Europe and to Egypt, India, and Ceylon, and became acquainted with cosmopolitan artistic and literary circles. Sir William died in 1892, and their only son, William Robert, born in 1882, predeceased his mother when as a member of the Royal Flying Corps he was shot down in Italy in 1918. During her long widowhood AG found in practical and creative work for the Abbey Theatre both an expression of her patriotic sentiments and a satisfying outlet for her energy, organizational capacity, and imaginative powers.

AG's earliest writings illustrate the formation and development of her political views. In 1882 she published a defence of the revolt against Turkish rule of the Egyptian Arabi Bey, a protest against unjust 'over government' which was reiterated in an Irish context in her editions of her husband's autobiography (1894) and of the letters of her grandfather-in-law, a former Secretary of State for Ireland (*Mr Gregory's Letter Box 1813–1830*, 1898). Her first contribution to the literary movement was an edition of essays by Ireland's 'image makers' including Standish O'Grady, Douglas Hyde, and W. B. Yeats (*Ideals in Ireland*, 1901). The particular role she was to play in Irish cultural history, however, began to emerge in 1893, when Yeats's collection of Sligo folk tales, *The Celtic Twilight*, and Hyde's *Love Songs of Connacht* prompted her to begin her lifelong task of collecting, collating, and publishing Galway tales and legends. This material, with its matter-of-fact acceptance of the supernatural, its relish for quirks and eccentricities of character, and its delight in the poetic and the marvellous, was to provide her with a fertile source of inspiration for her dramatic writings. It also gave her a style of dramatic discourse. In listening to and transcribing local speech, she developed a cadenced, rhythmic, and lyrical representation of 'Kiltartan' dialect which formed the basis of peasant dialogue in her own plays and those of Yeats and Synge. Having learnt the Irish language she further extended her familiarity with Irish culture back into the heroic past with her lively translations of the ancient epics, published as *Cuchulain of Muirthemne* (1902) and *Gods and Fighting Men* (1904). These became accessible for the first time to a wide audience and also provided Yeats with much of his dramatic material.

In the plan for a 'national theatre' proposed at the famous meeting of AG, Yeats, and Edward Martyn in 1897, LG's role was identified as that of fund-raiser. However, from acting as Yeats's amanuensis she progressed to collabor-ation with him (*Cathleen ni Houlihan*, 1902) and eventually to independent authorship, her first play, *Twenty-Five* (1902), being produced in her fiftieth year. For the next twenty-five years she achieved a regular output of plays composed with the specific requirements of the Abbey and its company in mind and written for an essentially didactic purpose, 'the theatre . . . being intended for art and a thinking Democracy'. She was equally versatile in her practical contributions to the life of the theatre and in the range of her dramatic writings, the desire for experimentation being, she wrote, 'like a fire in the blood'.

Her most consistently popular and successful plays were her comic one-act fantasies of peasant life (*The Jackdaw*, 1902, *Spreading the News*, 1904, *Hyacinth Halvey*, 1906). These are constructed on the principles of farce but distinguished from it in her own assessment by their dependence for humour upon character rather than incident. In each, an initial misunderstanding initiates a series of increasingly absurd amplifications through the obsessive commitment of each character to an individual and erroneous view of what has occurred, an illus-tration of the 'incorrigible genius' of the Irish for 'myth making'. Thus in *Spreading the News* the villagers persist in maintaining that a murder has been committed in the presence of its alleged, but palpably living, victim. The preference of the Irish for myth over reality and the dissipation of their energy in talk rather than action were recurrent motifs in AG's work. Her treatment of peasant characters is not reductive however: in *Cathleen ni Houlihan* and *The Rising of the Moon* (1907) her comic representation is successfully blended with fervent patriotism to produce potent images of 'the dignity of Ireland'. In the one-act tragedy *The Gaol Gate* (1906) the simplicity and powerlessness of three bewildered women rise to nobility in Mary Cahel's keen, which proclaims the absolute value of her son's decision to face execution rather than inform on another man.

In her 'tragic comedies' (*The Canavans*, 1906, *The White Cockade*, 1905, *The Deliverer*, 1911) AG draws upon folk history to find analogies for modern dilemmas. *The Deliverer* uses the story of Moses as a vehicle to explore the meaning of Parnell as Ireland's 'lost king'. In each play a 'myth maker' or visionary offers to the people an ideal: the urgency of his dream, the inevitability of its refusal, and his heroic apotheosis through acceptance of his isolation form the tragic pattern. The 'tragedies' (*Kincora*, 1905 revised 1909, *Devorgilla*, 1907, *Grania*, 1911) draw freely upon the ancient epics for their portrayals of powerful, strong-minded women frustrated by fate and circumstance from the attainment of their desires. The theme of conflicting loyalties, highly relevant to contemporary Ireland and recurrent throughout AG's work, is explored in these plays in passages of acute psychological insight and in a heroic idiom which makes the legendary characters both impressive and accessible.

AG's experiments with dramatic form include translations of Molière and Goldoni, with whose comic methods she had a strong affinity, poetic 'fairy plays' for children (*The Jester*, 1918, *The Dragon*, 1919), a number of miracle plays with a religious theme (*The Travelling Man*, 1909, *Dave*, 1927), a ghost play (*Shanwalla*, 1915) and a passion play in an Irish idiom (*The Story Brought by Brigit*, 1924). All her dramatic writings were intended to serve her personal ambition for the Abbey: that it should reach as wide a range of audiences as possible, touring all parts of Ireland with plays designed to enhance a sense of national identity and awareness of Irish culture. In *Our Irish Theatre* (1913) she gives an informative, lively, and personal account of the early years of the Abbey Theatre. To this institution she herself contributed unflagging energy, aristocratic habits of leadership, generous encouragment, and support for other writers (including J. M. Synge and Sean O'Casey), numerous well-received plays, and an unshakeable conviction of the importance of the theatre's role in the preparation of Ireland for independent nationhood.   ELIZABETH JOYCE

Selected works: *Arabi and his Household* (1882); *Over the River* (1888); *A Phantom's Pilgrimage, or, Home Ruin* (1893); (ed.), *The Autobiography of Sir William Gregory* (1894); 'Ireland, real and ideal', *Nineteenth Century* (November 1898); (ed.), *Mr Gregory's Letter Box 1813–1830* (1898); *Ideals in Ireland* (1901); *Cuchulain of Muirthemne* (1902); *Gods and Fighting Men* (1904); *A Book of Saints and Wonders* (1906); *Seven Short Plays* (1909); *The Kiltartan Molière* (1910); *The Kiltartan Wonder Book* (1910); *Irish Folk History Plays*, 1st series (1912); *Irish Folk History Plays*, 2nd series (1912); *New Comedies* (1913); *Our Irish Theatre* (1913); *The Golden Apple* (1916); *The Kiltartan Poetry Book* (1919); *Visions and Beliefs in the West of Ireland*, 2 vols (1920); *Hugh Lane's Life and Achievement* (1921); *The Image and Other Plays* (1922); *Three Wonder Plays* (1923); *Mirandolina* (1924); *The Story Brought by Brigit* (1924); *A Case for the Return of Sir Hugh Lane's Pictures to Dublin* (1926); *On the Race Course* (1926); *Three Last Plays* (1928); *My First Play: Colman and Guaire* (1930); *Coole* (1931); *Lady Gregory's Journals 1916–1930*, (1946); *The Coole Edition of Lady Gregory's Writings* (1970); *Seventy Years* (1974).

References: Adams, H., *Lady Gregory* (1973); Cothead E., *Lady Gregory: A Literary Portrait* (1961, revised 1966); *DNB*; Drabble; Gregory, A., *Me and Nu: Childhood at Coole* (1966); Kohfeldt, M. L., *Lady Gregory* (1985); Saddlemyer, A., *In Defence of Lady Gregory, Playwright* (1966); Saddlemyer, A., 'Augusta Gregory, Irish Nationalist', in *Myth and Reality in Irish Literature*, ed. J. Ronsley (1977).

Greville, Frances

b. (probably) December 1726, Ireland or London; d. 30 July 1789, Petersham, Surrey

Poet

FG was born the seventh of the nine children of James and Catherine Coote Macartney, her father originally of Longford, Ireland, with a house in Dublin, but, by the time of FG's birth, living almost entirely in London, where she grew up in houses in St James's and Hanover Squares. Macartney had inherited an Irish estate of about £2,000 a year, was a member of the Irish Parliament (1713–60), and in London frequented White's and the circle of the 2nd Duke of Richmond. Her mother died in 1731, probably of the family weakness, consumption, leaving her surviving three younger daughters, Catherine, Frances, and Mary, to the supervision of the eldest, Alicia, known subsequently in Irish, London, and Bath society as Bad, Wicked, or Evil Mac. Horace Walpole, who included FG among *The Beauties*, a 1746 tribute to the women of the Fox circle, and who mentioned her in his letters, thought her at the time somewhat racy. Until she married she lived an apparently unrepressed and gay life in the fashionable circles frequented by Walpole. Her particular friend, Lady Caroline Lennox, daughter of the 2nd Duke of Richmond, had eloped with Henry Fox in 1744, and Fox, later Lord Holland, was to be the prop of FG, her husband, and her children until his death in 1774. Several of FG's manuscript poems date from this early period when she was already celebrated among her friends for beauty, wit, and talent.

FG's goddaughter Fanny Burney described her fine 'feminine' features, 'masculine' understanding, croaking voice, manner of lounging at her ease 'in such curves as she found most commodious, with her head alone upright', her eyes fixed 'with an expression rather alarming than flattering' on her objects, and noted that to strangers she was often forbidding but to intimates was the kindest and most solicitous of mortals.

In 1747 FG made the unlucky conquest of Fulke Greville (1717–1808) of Wilbury House, Wiltshire, a dashing, charming man but, as a Burney acquaintance put it, 'constitutionally inconstant'. Greville lived well beyond his means with the splendour of a Renaissance prince and dedicated himself to connoisseurship of the arts and all the sports, but particularly to the turf and gambling, which was to ruin him. On 26 January 1748 the couple 'eloped' round the corner to St George's, Hanover Square. 'Mr Greville has taken a wife out of the window when he might just as well have taken her out of the door,' said James Macartney. Happy at first, the Grevilles purchased for their amusement from Dr Arne the apprenticeship indentures of Charles Burney and installed him at Wilbury as confidant, protégé, and concert master. At Wilbury on 28 November 1748 was born their first child, Frances Ann, later the celebrated Whig hostess Lady Crewe.

Though elected to Parliament in 1747, Greville went abroad to live in mid-1749. The family stayed in Paris (where, probably, a son, Algernon, was born in summer 1750) for over a year, and then went for nearly three years to Lunéville to the small court of King Stanislas of Lorraine, where two more sons, William and James, were born in 1751 and 1753.

The family returned to Wilbury in 1753 and over the subsequent twenty years Greville slowly ruined them all through his compulsive extravagance and his gambling, meanwhile supporting his vanity through the acquisition of art, expensive alterations to Wilbury, feats on the racetrack, and authorship. In 1756 he published his *Maxims, Characters, and Reflections*, a well-received work which Walpole and others believed to be at least half written by FG. Her husband's serious resentment of FG's talents stems from this attribution and was increased when in 1758 her celebrated 'Ode to Indifference' first circulated among their friends and then found its way into print. The ode was apparently a *cri de coeur* supposed to derive from her grief over her son Algernon's death in 1756 and her husband's derelictions.

The Grevilles travelled in Italy in 1756–58, and on their return added to the family three more sons, Robert (1758), Henry (1760), and Charles (1762). In 1763 Henry Fox staved off the Grevilles' ruin by providing Greville with a temporary post worth £700 a year. In 1766 FG contrived to marry off her beautiful daughter Frances Ann to the rich and eligible John Crewe of Crewe Hall, Cheshire, before she departed for exile in Bavaria where Fox, now Lord Holland, had obtained for her husband a post as Envoy Extraordinary to the Court. Made ill by the Bavarian climate, FG returned home in 1767, leaving her sons in her husband's charge. Robert died suddenly in 1768, after which Greville returned home broken both mentally and physically. He resigned his post in 1770.

In that year FG's father died, leaving his fortune for life between her and her sister Catherine, and thereafter to his grandsons. FG now had an income of about £800 which for the next fifteen years she struggled to retain for the use of herself and her children, while her husband extorted at least half of it even after she had separated from him by measures which included threats of, if not attempts at, abduction and incarceration.

FG spent a large part of these years in Ireland or in France, often on extended visits to protectors like Lady Longford and Lady Louisa Conolly or with her daughter Frances Ann Crewe, and at the same time used all her skill and her connections to establish her now resourceless sons. James took orders and obtained preferment through relations. Harry and Charles had army commissions; Harry was adopted by Evil Mac and Charles eventually married a daughter of the Duke of Portland. William Fulke, FG's eldest surviving son, attained the rank of admiral in the navy and after her death inherited her portion of his grandfather's estate. In the mid-1780s a final separation agreement with her husband was reached, but FG's health was already ruined. She died in her lodgings at Petersham, surrounded by four of her five children.

A born writer, FG was celebrated for her innumerable letters and never ceased to scribble verse, but she was constrained by both class and her husband to confine her talents to a social use, the writing of graceful letters or of occasional verses sent as thank-you notes or compliments or written as charades or riddles to enliven a social occasion. An important exception are her occasional social satires meant to entertain a few close friends. These are of a type which show why her wit was feared:

> Close to a Title still is Peggys place
> An Index to a fashionable Face
> Who there Crys Peggy? only Miss N – oh!
> I'm sorry Madam I'm oblig'd to go. . . .

Peggy proceeds through the room trading upward till finally she is deserted by all.

The celebrated ode in favour of indifference, and opposing the growing cult of sensibility, begs for an anodyne against too much feeling:

> Nor ease nor peace that Heart can know,
> Which like the Needle true,
> Turns at the touch of Joy or woe,
> But turning trembles too. . . .
> Then take this treach'rous sense of mine,
> Which dooms me still to Smart,
> Which pleasure can to pain refine,
> To pain new pangs impart.

For a hundred years the verses were copied and recopied, reprinted and anthologized, and they elicited many answers in defence of sensibility.

Her sense that women of her station did not publish was for some years no doubt a restraining force, but her husband's sanctions against her writing made her truly fearful. He was a rigorous censor; in a letter to Lady Susan O'Brien after her elopement with the actor William O'Brien, FG apologizes for not having written to offer her support sooner, but says she has seized the first opportunity when she was alone to send her kind comments (with which her husband did not concur). Her friends were instructed never to reveal those rare bits of verse which she sent when pressed to do so, and she instructed them to burn her letters without showing them, for all too often they were passed about. She quarrelled with Madame du Deffand, who had apparently put her letters into an album with others, including Voltaire's.

The *Maxims* undoubtedly reveal her good sense, for her husband's other writings are frequently incoherent, but for the most part it is impossible to say which part of them is hers. Perhaps after her daughter's friend Georgiana, Duchess of Devonshire, published a novel, *The Sylph* (1780), FG began her own novel, which survives unfinished in manuscript. The novel is finely satiric and has interesting characters but FG demonstrates no great ability at plotting a long work of fiction. The manuscript and a manuscript notebook of FG's poems are in the possession of a descendant. Many manuscript poems by FG also survive in various collections and archives.   BETTY RIZZO

Selected works: 'Ode to Indifference' (1758).
References: Burney, C., *Memoirs* (1832); Leinster, Duchess of, *Correspondence* (1949), Todd; Todd, J., *Sensibility* (1986).

Grierson, Constantia

b. 1706, Graiguenamanagh, County Kilkenny, Ireland; d. 1733, Dublin
Poet, classicist

CG was a member of the circle of women poets befriended by Swift which included Mary Barber and Laetitia Pilkington. She was born to a poor and uneducated Irish country family, possibly named Phillips or Crawley. She mastered the classical languages, mathematics, and history largely through her own application, aided by some books provided by her father, and by some instruction from the minister of the parish. At the age of 18, she went to Dublin, where she was apprenticed to Dr Van Lewen, a Dutch immigrant who had become Ireland's first male midwife and who had a distinguished reputation as a physician. In his household she became acquainted with his daughter, later Laetitia Pilkington.

CG abandoned midwifery when she married George Grierson, a Scottish printer who had come to practise his trade in Dublin. She seems to have assisted in her husband's business, for she is referred to in the patent by which her husband was made the King's Printer in 1729, which claims that 'Mr George Grierson of the city of Dublin, printer, and Constantia his wife, have brought the art of printing to a greater perfection than was ever heretofore done in this kingdom . . .'. CG edited the works of Virgil, Terence, and Tacitus: her editions were published by Grierson's press. She was apparently working on an edition of Sallust immediately before her death. These editions, with their elegant Latin introductions, have been much admired by subsequent scholars. One of CG's two sons died in childhood and is commemorated in consolatory verses by her friend Mary Barber. Her other son, George Abraham Grierson, succeeded his father as King's Printer, but died at the age of 27.

Only nine of CG's poems are known to be extant, and these owe their preservation to Mary Barber and Laetitia Pilkington, who included them in their own volumes. CG's first poetic publication may have been in the year before her death, when 'The Art of Printing' was distributed as a broadside. Her other poems appeared posthumously, first in Barber's *Poems on Several Occasions* (1734) and later in *Poems by Eminent Ladies* (1755). They are mostly occasional works, addressed to her women friends – two to Pilkington, one to Barber, and one to Barber's son, Con, in praise of his mother. In passing she notes the evils of British rule in Ireland, and attacks absentee landowners who 'squander vast estates at balls and play,/ While public debts increase, and funds decay'.   SIOBHAN KILFEATHER

Selected works: (ed.), P. *Virgilii Maronis Opera* (1724); (ed.), *C. Cornelii Taciti Opera* (1730); poems in Barber, M.(ed.), *Poems on Several Occasions* (1734); poems in *Poems by Eminent Ladies* (1755); *The Art of Printing* (n.d.).

References: Allibone; Ballard; *DNB*; *Memoirs of Mrs Laetitia Pilkington* (1748); Todd; Wilson, C. H., *Brookiana* (1804).

Griffith, Elizabeth

b. 1727(?), Dublin (?); d. 5 January 1793, Naas, County Kildare
Playwright, novelist
Elizabeth Griffith was the daughter of Thomas Griffith (1680?–1744), a well-known comic actor in Dublin and London and manager of the Theatre Royal in Aungier Street, Dublin, and of Jane Foxcroft Griffith (1694–1773), daughter of Richard Foxcroft, rector of Portarlington. Thomas Griffith's immediate forebears were Welsh and Jane Foxcroft's from Yorkshire, but EG grew up a thorough Irishwoman on the verges of the theatre, as a girl lively, gay, and voluble. Her education, much under the direction of a loving and indulgent father, seems to have been designed to make her an actress. Her reading included all the polite new publications in English and French; she could both write and recite verse, and she studied both novels and plays, probably conning parts. She learned no Latin. Her deportment later, in England, was so studied as to cause some acquaintances to call her affected.

Thomas Griffith's death left his family with slender resources and EG may have tried the theatre in the Irish provinces not long after. Her known debut was in 1749 in the company of her father's old friend Thomas Sheridan at Smock-Alley in Dublin, where for two seasons she played such roles as Juliet to the ageing Sheridan's Romeo, Jane Shore, and – a breeches part – Nottingham in *The Earl of Essex*. Her speciality was tragedy roles.

In 1746 EG had met a charming and well-connected but penniless Kilkenny farmer, Richard Griffith (1716?–1788), self-styled an 'honourable libertine', and they had fallen in love, indulging in a sentimental correspondence and relationship which eventually wounded EG's reputation. Griffith's father, a selfish aristocrat, had married a fortune and dissipated it; his provision for his children was the advice to do likewise. Griffith, trying to support himself as a farmer, did not consider marrying EG and for years tried to seduce her, but found her both provocative and adamant. 'I have often wondered that a person, who has as much wit, spirit, and wildness in her imagination, as any one I know, should have, in reality, more delicacy in her sentiments, and more decency in her expressions, than I ever met with in any other woman,' he lamented. Though without formal education, a lack he deeply felt, Griffith was attracted to letters and found deep gratification in his correspondence with EG in which they both spiritedly and sententiously discussed their readings, their acquaintance, and their ideas, copiously demonstrated their sensibility, and bestowed on one another vast quantities of approval. Perhaps Griffith justified this exchange with a woman by elevating her to equal status and thus instituting a model for their relationship which made them both famous and which inspired her in her first plays to attempt to reform the rest of mankind in regard to women.

By 1751 the relationship was generally thought to have progressed too far and, EG having threatened to remove herself to London, Griffith married her privately. The exact dates of marriage and of the birth of their son Richard (c. 1752) remain mysterious. With both events still secret, EG departed in early 1753 for the Covent Garden Theatre in London, where for three seasons she played without progressing past minor roles. The acting of her brother Richard was regarded by Garrick as affected, and probably EG's acting style, formed under the stilted Sheridan, was similarly condemned. In the meantime, at Maidenhall in Kilkenny, Griffith essayed an ambitious linen manufactory which failed at about the time she relinquished her acting career. A daughter, Catherine, was born to the couple in 1756.

Various friends had applauded the Griffiths' correspondence and in 1757, desperate for funds, they published the first two volumes, by subscription, of *A Series of Genuine Letters between Henry and Frances*. Publication made them both famous and a sentimental success, and at last in 1760 the Duke of Bedford provided Griffith with Irish employment. Thereafter his apparent lack of ambition and occasional employment as political manager for friends like Lord Charlemont and Henry Flood, impelled EG in 1764 – by which time she had completed two plays and a novel – to move to London, where she could better further her literary projects. Probably with the profits from her second play, *The Double Mistake*, she settled in 1766 into her house in Hyde Street, Bloomsbury. Griffith thereafter spent much of his time in Ireland, thus ensuring the continuation of the polite correspondence which resulted in two more volumes of the letters, in 1767 and again in 1770.

EG was always subject to depression, caused in part by her husband's fickle nature and in part by her belief that the failure of the family finances was her own fault for having made Griffith marry her, and she wrote unceasingly in an effort to make reparation. Considering the fragile state of her health, and the poor condition of her eyesight, her total output is impressive. The publication of their letters ceased in 1770 and perhaps the fabled polite marriage had too; Anna Seward repeated a story that in the 1780s Griffith had eloped with a young heiress, but if so his defection was brief. In 1770 the pair had equipped their son to depart for India as a clerk of the East India Company and in the 1780s he returned a nabob to buy an estate, Millicent, at Naas, Co. Kildare, to sit in the Irish Parliament, to marry, and to establish an eminent family. After her son's return from India, EG virtually retired from her literary labours. Griffith died at Naas in 1788, EG in 1793.

EG was most ambitious as a playwright. Between 1765 and 1779 she had five plays produced at major London theatres and worked on seven or eight others of which she published two or three. *Amana* (1764), a verse tragedy without proper dramatic structure, was published by subscription. EG was never a poet, and her focus on the viewpoint of Amana, who prefers death to the sultan's embraces, rather than on her honest merchant-lover, must have baffled her readers. *The Platonic Wife*, produced at Covent Garden in January 1765, had a heroine modelled on EG's own persona in the *Genuine Letters* with the added initiative and plotting skills of a Restoration female wit. She insists that her English husband treat her (like Griffith) after marriage with tenderness, courtliness, and flattery. When he refuses she leaves him, and while separated entertains (but refuses) the propositions of three lovers. When she repents and returns, her husband relents and capitulates, promising all the sentimental admiration she can desire. A cabal was got up to destroy the play before the first night, the reviews were harsh, and through the condemnation of this play EG learned she must choose between being a successful playwright and advancing the status of English wives. With two children to establish in life, her debate must have been brief. She took up the role of female moralist.

For *The Double Mistake*, produced at Covent Garden in January 1766, EG borrowed the structure of an old play (George Digby's *Elvira*), and made both her sensible and her silly heroines lacking entirely in initiative, plotting skills, and effectiveness; they are saved from disaster only through the twists of the plot. Moreover, the silly heroine studies languages while the sensible one prefers 'working' (needlework), and a comic lady pedant has been added so the public could be quite sure where EG stood on the delicate subject of female learning. The play was a great success, and one performance was by royal command. EG, now sure of her ground, next began her celebrated manipulation of David Garrick, which was to result in his assigning her the task of and assisting her in the translation of Beaumarchais's play *Eugenie*, which, as *The School for Rakes*, opened at Drury Lane in February 1769. With her structure provided and her characters doctored by Garrick, EG was further assisted by a basically misogynistic plot, in which the heroine is restored to the arms of her beloved only through plot developments. The play was a great hit and provided the funds to outfit EG's son for India. EG renewed her attack on Garrick who was determined never to produce a play for her again. But in March 1772 at Covent Garden Colman produced *A Wife in the Right*. In this play the errant husband nearly destroys not only his wife's but his wife's friend's marriage, and in the end is reclaimed without either of his victims having displayed much resourcefulness; on the contrary, the woman of contrivances and initiative is the husband's villainous mistress, who is, of course, unmasked and punished. The play, promising success, failed the first night because of the drunkenness of the popular comic actor Ned Shuter, who first delayed the debut and then spoiled the play through his inability to learn his lines. Colman not only withdrew the play after one performance, but also refused EG any share of the profits. EG, now resolved never to deal with him again, returned to the adamant Garrick, and her final play, *The Times*, was produced at Drury Lane in 1779 only after Garrick's retirement. In this play, a translation of Goldoni's *Bourru Bienfaisant*, a long-suffering wife spends all her efforts to reform her extravagant gambler of a husband, and at last succeeds. The play ran the standard nine performances. In addition to *Amana* and her five performed plays, EG was probably the translator of Beaumarchais's *The Barber of Seville* (1776) and possibly of Diderot's *Dorval* (1777), and worked on other translations and original plays including both a comedy and a tragedy.

Following EG's identification of her literary forte, the detailed description of feminine sufferings and anatomy of feminine psychological distress, she wrote three highly popular epistolary novels. An important theme in all three is that one cannot be blamed for one's passions but must be held accountable for what one does about them. Both wives and husbands may perhaps in spite of themselves love others, but are duty-bound not to hurt their spouses. *The Delicate Distress*, by 'Frances' (1769), was published with 'Henry's' *The Gordian Knot* as *Two Novels, in Letters*. EG's novel details the various trials in love of several men and women and contains many romantic sub-plots. Another theme that emerges in EG's work is that beauty and charm are formidable in woman, but her most effectual weapon is moral superiority which in the end – her only revenge – man is forced to recognize. Here Lucy, jilted by her unworthy lover who then marries his appropriate punishment and becomes impoverished, secretly bestows an annuity on him and is fully avenged when he learns the identity of her benefactor. In EG's work, the wife who perseveres in her long-suffering and uncomplaining virtue often wins her husband back in the end.

The History of Lady Barton (1771) is the story of a thoroughly admirable heroine of this type, married to an unworthy husband and presented with a lover worthy in every way, who finally dies from a complication of cruel machination and inner conflict. *The Story of Lady Juliana Harley* (1776) presents the mystery of the heroine who at the end of the book confides the secret of her lost love and enters a convent. Other characters play variations on the marriage plot, including the gambler and roué who returns to the arms of his wife and the young woman almost ruined by the adventurer whom she has foolishly married. All of EG's novels are skillfully compounded of interwoven plots; her tone is refined, and her psychological skills (particularly in recounting long-enduring subtle torments) acute.

EG's bibliography includes almost a dozen full-length translations from the French besides the plays she translated. She was a competent translator who, however, indulged in the addition of moral comments perhaps to justify her choice of sometimes racy French texts. She was undoubtedly the author of translations that appeared anonymously, and almost certainly translated four volumes of Voltaire, *The Spirit of Nations*, for Kenrick's edition of Voltaire in 1779–81. She was the author of short stories that appeared in the *Westminster Magazine* (to which she contributed heavily) and then in her collected *Novellettes* (1780). She undoubtedly did some editing work. Finally, two of her most important late works were *The Morality of Shakespeare's Drama Illustrated* (1775) in which she excerpted passages from Shakespeare and commented on them in order to vindicate his moral purposes, and *Essays, Addressed to Young Married Women* (1782) in which she brought her literary career to a close by apprising wives of their position and advising them that their best course was to suffer passively all their errant husbands' behaviour, lest their complaints and recriminations only drive them further away. Only the most self-contained art could keep a husband at home, for 'a love of power and authority is natural to men and wherever this inclination is most indulged, will be the situation of their choice.' EG had come a distance from her dreams of equal consideration in the first volumes of letters. Her peculiar triumph was that she contrived, despite her position as a woman, to establish her children and to wrest a respectable livelihood as a professional author. BETTY RIZZO

Selected works: *A Series of Genuine Letters between Henry and Frances* vols 1 and 2 (1757); (trans.), *The Memoirs of Ninon de L'Enclos, with her Letters to Mon*^r. *de St Evremont and to the Marquis de Sévigné. Collected and translated from the French. By a Lady* (1761); *Amana: A Dramatic Poem* (1764); *The Platonic Wife: A Comedy* (1765); *The Double Mistake: A Comedy* (1766); *Dorval, or, The Test of Virtue* (probable) (1767); *A Series of Genuine Letters between Henry and Frances,* vols. 3 and 4 (1767); *The School for Rakes: A Comedy* (1769), *The Delicate Distress* (1769); *A Series of Genuine Letters between Henry and Frances,* vols 5 and 6. (1770); *The History of Lady Barton; A Novel, in Letters* (1771); *A Wife in the Right: A Comedy* (1772); (trans.), *The Fatal Effects of Inconstancy, or, Letters from the Marchioness de Syrce. Translated from the French* (1774); *The Morality of Shakespeare's Drama Illustrated* (1775); (trans.), *The Barber of Seville, or, The Useless Precaution: A Comedy in Four Acts. By the Author of Eugenie,* by Pierre Beaumarchais (1776); *The Story of Lady Juliana Harley: A Novel, In Letters* (1776); (trans.), *The Princess of Cleves,* (probable) (1777); *The Times: A Comedy* (1779); (trans.), *The Spirit of Nations,* by Voltaire, 4 vols, part of William Kenrick's translation of Voltaire (1779–81); (trans.), *Zayde: A Spanish History* (1780); *Essays, Addressed to Young Married Women* (1782).

References: Eshleman, D., *Elizabeth Griffith: A Biographical and Critical Study* (1949); Garrick, D., *Private Correspondence of David Garrick with the Most Celebrated Persons of His Time,* ed. J. Boaden (1831–2); Tompkins, J. M. S., *The Polite Marriage* (1938).

Grymeston, Elizabeth

b. before 1563; d. before 1604

Writer of Advice Book

Fifth child of Margaret Flint and Martin Bernye (or Berney) of Gunton, Norfolk, by 1584 EG had married Christopher Grymeston (or Grimeston), eighth and youngest son of Dorothy Thwaytes and Thomas Grymeston of Smeeton, Yorkshire. They lived in Cambridge until 31 January 1592 or 1593, when Christopher Grymeston left Caius College, where he had been a student and where he was then bursar, and entered Gray's Inn, London. In 1599 he was admitted to the bar. Although his eldest brother Marmaduke inherited his father's property, Christopher and EG were named heirs of Martin Bernye's estate. EG bore nine children, only one of whom survived her. No record of her death is extant, but the introductory verses by Simon Grahame in her *Miscelanea* indicate that she was no longer living when it was published in 1604.

Both the Bernye and Grymeston families had Roman Catholic connections: Caius, Christopher Grymeston's college, for example, was known for its 'popish' leanings, and the recusancy rolls of 1592/1593 list an Elizabeth Grymeston of Yorkshire as having been fined for refusing to attend Anglican church services. By the time Simon Grahame, whose Spenserian sonnet opens EG's *Miscelanea*, died in 1614, he was a Roman Catholic, and the two poets whose work EG uses most extensively in the *Miscelanea* – her kinsman, Robert Southwell, and Richard Rowlands (or Verstegen) – were also Catholic writers.

In the dedicatory epistle 'To her living sonne Bernye Grymeston', EG contrasts her concern for her son with her mother's ill treatment of her when she was a child and indicates that she has written this book to be for him 'the true portrature of thy mothers minde'. EG clearly indicates that her volume is a miscellany of others' work 'gathered' as is a bee's honey, 'out of many flowers'. Twentieth-century ideas of original composition are altogether irrelevant to an author who says, 'neither could I ever brooke to set downe that haltingly in my broken stile, which I found better expressed by a graver authour' and who then urges her son to be equally reliant on traditional wisdom: 'God send thee too, to be a wits Camelion,/ That any authours colour can put on'. EG's style is, however, anything but halting as she recasts and combines prose paraphrased from various Church fathers, excerpts from the Vulgate version of the Bible, and poetic passages from classical, continental, and English writers – the latter by way of Richard Allott's *England's Parnassus* (1600).

The 1604 edition of the *Miscelanea* includes fourteen short chapters; three later editions include six additional chapters. Chapter XII consists of a madrigal EG says was 'made' by her son Bernye 'vpon the conceit of his mothers play to the former ditties'; and Chapter XIII (XIX in the three later editions) prints Rowland's seven penitental psalms (first printed in Antwerp in 1601) in reverse order. Elsewhere, EG does more to transform her sources – altering poems to fit their prose contexts, for example, correcting erroneous translations, even transforming passages so they will make two different points in two different parts of her book. The sombre tone of the whole work may be indicated by its first and last strictures: 'When thou risest, let thy thoughts ascend, that grace may descend: and if thou canst not weepe for thy sinnes, then weepe, because thou canst not weepe', and 'What harme the heart doth thinke, and hand effect, that will the worme of conscience betray'.   ELIZABETH H. HAGEMAN

Selected works: Miscelanea, Meditations, Memoratives (1604).

References: Beilin, E. V., *Redeeming Eve: Women Writers of The English Renaissance* (1987); *DNB*; Fletcher, B. Y. and Sizemore, C. W., 'Elizabeth Grymeston's *Miscelanea, Meditations, Memoratives*: Introduction and Selected Texts', *The Library Chronicle* 47 (1981); Mahl, M. R. and Koon, H., ed., *The Female Spectator: English Women Writers before 1800* (1977); Travitsky, B. S., 'The New Mother of the English Renaissance: Her Writings on Motherhood', in *The Lost Tradition: Mothers and Daughters in Literature*, ed. C. N. Davidson and E. M. Broner (1980).

Gunning, Susannah

b. 1740(?), London; d. 1800, London
Novelist
(Also wrote under Miss Minifie)
SG was the daughter of James Minifie, DD, and at the publication of her first novel in 1763 lived in Fairwater, Somerset. Five years later, she married Captain (soon to be Lieutenant-General) John Gunning, the articulate and spoiled brother of the famous beauties, whose mother was the daughter of a viscount. Gunning's parents had so successfully advanced his sisters through marriage that SG may have attempted a parallel coup for her daughter, born in 1769. Her plans went awry, however, resulting in the hullabaloo of forgeries and adulteries which Horace Walpole called the 'Gunninghiad'. In the midst of this fracas, SG published in the guise of mother-writ-large an open letter (over 100 pages long) defending her daughter against allegations that she had written a forged letter. SG blamed her husband, among others, complaining, 'I have been so long in a scene of mysteries, of which he is the artificer, that I never expect to get out of them as long as I live,' adding that she regretted twenty-

two of her twenty-three years of marriage. Not long after, General Gunning, who had maintained a high moral tone during the family crisis, was himself fined £5,000 for 'criminal conversation' with his tailor's wife. Gunning and his mistress hastened to Naples, where he wrote an *Apology* (1792), in which he boasted of myriad, detailed, and exaggerated conquests, especially of aristocratic women. In 1797, in response to a letter from his daughter, he altered his will the day before he died, leaving £8,000 to her and to his wife, and his Irish estate to the latter. During this final period SG wrote steadily. At her death she left an unfinished novel, *The Heir Apparent*, which her daughter revised and published two years later.

In all, SG wrote thirteen novels (six of them epistolary), one long poem, and the defence of her daughter's conduct. She and her sister Margaret Minifie initiated their own careers when SG was in her early twenties, publishing by subscription their collaborative *Histories of Lady Frances S— and Lady Caroline S—* (1763). Commercial publishers printed the next five novels, which followed in quick succession. One of these, *Family Pictures* (1764), claims to be 'literally true' and is addressed to the 'female part of this metropolis'. In fact, however, the plots of these early novels are conventional (distressed virgins achieve aristocratic marriages), and the language formal. When after fifteen years of marriage SG published her next novel, *Coombe Wood* (1783), the satiric element had increased, and marriage itself was the occasional object. Whether life or literature had taught her the satiric mode, we cannot be sure. Marriage is certainly one of the chief butts. Lady Lucy in *Coombe Wood* considers marriage an 'incumbrance', so she sweetens her choice by settling on a £200,000 man, even though he resembles 'a frightful bird I once saw in a menagerie'. This charmlessness is compounded by 'a detestable dapperness wriggled into his whole person', but Lady Lucy takes much comfort in the fact that his clawlike hands glitter with diamonds. The heroine loves her cousin but does not intend to marry him, a posture which even at this early date appears to reflect the situation which engendered the 'Gunninghiad'. Nine years later, in an advertisement prefacing the *Anecdotes of the Delborough Family* (1792), SG denied the allegation that she had included family details. Regarding the *Anecdotes*, the denial may stand, but the theme of her poem *Virginius and Virginia* (1792) is that a father and child should never 'be debar'd', and in *Memoirs of Mary* (1793), where the heroine suffers because of a forged letter and the writing is notably more idiomatic, SG certainly plundered her daughter's life, if not her own. She tried a new direction in 1796 in *Delves*, 'A Welch Tale', which is a young boy's picaresque 'Quixotting expedition', though her other publication that year was merely a four-volume alteration of a French novel. Her last two books were novels of manners, with the interesting twist that in *Love at First Sight* (1797) the heroine's husband pours all his affection on his first-born son, refusing even to see his other offspring, a pointed exaggeration of patriarchy. However, since the title page says that this novel is 'from the French with alterations and additions', SG may not be responsible for this invention. In *Fashionable Involvements* (1800), the stylized characters include a rapacious money-lending Jew named Isaac (he asks £60 for a debt of £7), and a widow who is 'one of the few women who come under the description of *rational*'. SG's writing was most pungent when she was fictionalizing her personal experiences, but her rather innocent novels do not truly reflect the lurid complications attendant on marriage to John Gunning.

In her most dramatic scenes, SG tends towards hyperbole, a habit for which Lady Harcourt coined the word 'minific'. In *Memoirs of Mary* Lord Auberry says of his daughter (the heroine's mother), 'I would a thousand times rather see her dead, than the wife of your favourite Montague.' Yet metaphoric keenness, compressed vigour, and occasional understatement also characterize SG's satirical descriptions and dialogue. In *Fashionable Involvements*, we are told that 'Lady Isleworth, at fourteen, was a romp – at fifteen, a wife, and at sixteen, a mother.' Since the married Isleworths are children themselves, they bicker so aggressively that the best they were ever able to achieve was that occasionally their 'domestic harmony was . . . restored to its usual standard'. In *Memoirs of Mary* Sir Ashton Montague writes to Mrs Oxburn, 'Was you ever hippish? Do you know anything about the vapours? I have an odd sort of feeling, and can't make out what it is; no wonder, for I am confined to a bed, where none but a dwarf can lie straight, in a room not ten feet square, half my body swathed with poultices, half-covered with plasters, and fed on milk-sops like a baby.' Although SG here ascribes a feminine complaint to a male character, the sexual attitudes she reflects are almost unrelievedly conventional. Her women, in particular, consistently jibe at their erring sisters and rivals. This persistent denigration of women serves to emphasize how difficult it was to query the literary and cultural stereotypes of the period.   JANICE FARRAR THADDEUS

Selected works: *Histories of Lady Frances S— and Lady Caroline S—* (1763); *Family Pictures* (1764); *The Picture* (1766); *Barford Abbey* (1768); *The Cottage* (1769); *The Hermit* (1770); *Coombe Wood* (1783); *A Letter from Mrs Gunning, Addressed to His Grace the Duke of Argyll* (1791); *Anecdotes of the Delborough Family* (1792); *Virginius and Virginia: A Poem, in Six Parts* (1792); *Memoirs of Mary* (1793); *Delves: a Welch Tale* (1796); *Love at First Sight* (1797); *Fashionable Involvements* (1800); *The Heir Apparent* (1802).

References: Burney, F., *The Early Diary of Frances Burney, 1768–1778*, ed. Annie Raine Ellis, (1913); *A Friendly Letter to the Marquis of Lorn, on the Subject of Mrs Gunning's Pamphlet, With Some Explanations of the Gunning Mystery Never Before Published. By a Knight of Chivalry* (1791); Gantz, I., *The Pastel Portrait: The Gunnings of Castlecoote and Howards of Hampstead* (1963); Gunning, J., *An Apology for the Life of Major General G—, Written by Himself. Containing a Full Explanation of the G-nn-g mystery, and of the author's connection with Mr D-ber-y's family of Soho Square* (1792); Kunitz, S. and Haycroft, H. (eds), *British Authors before 1800* (1952); *Notes and Queries*, 6th series, 7 (1883); 8 (1883); Todd; Todd, J., 'Marketing the self: Mary Carleton, Miss F and Susannah Gunning', *Studies on Voltaire and the Eighteenth Century* 217 (1983); *The Sign of Angellica: women, writing and fiction 1660–1800* (1989); Walpole, H., *Correspondence* 11, ed. W. S. Lewis *et al.* (1944).

Halkett, Anne, Lady

b. 4 January 1622, London; d. 22 April 1699, Edinburgh
Devotional writer, autobiographer

AH was the daughter of Thomas Murray, the Provost of Eton and former tutor to Charles I, and Jane (*née* Drummond) Murray, who was previously governess to Princess Elizabeth. AH was tutored in music, French, needlework, and dancing, but in her 'Autobiography' (1677–8), she records that she is most indebted to her mother's care of her religious education: 'even from our infancy we were instructed never to neglect to begin and end the day with prayer, and orderly every morning to read the Bible, and ever to keepe the church as often as there was occasion to meet there, either for prayers or preaching.' This enabled her to regard all misfortune, both personal and national, as part of

God's purpose. AH was an active Royalist sympathizer, and in 1648 helped the Duke of York to escape from London by dressing him as a woman. From 1650 she lived with Royalists in Scotland and during the Civil War she aided wounded soldiers. In 1658 she married Sir James Halkett, with whom she had four children, three of whom died in infancy. After the Restoration she received little compensation for the loss of her estate and tutored the children of the Scottish nobility for two years before James II granted her a pension in 1685. On her death AH left over twenty manuscript volumes, most of which were sober religious meditations full of biblical diction. A selection from these papers was published in Edinburgh in 1701 prefaced by a 'Life' which was derived from the autobiography.

AH's lively autobiographical writing reveals a strong-willed woman who often had to struggle to make herself submit to what she saw as restrictions imposed by God on her personal desires. The writing mainly concerns her trials and misfortunes, and how she learned to live with them. The flow of the narrative is frequently stopped by AH so that she can reflect on the spiritual significance of these various episodes. God is seen behind both personal concerns and those that affect the Royalist cause; for instance the meditation on the execution of Charles I concludes that his death was personally and politically necessary, for in being given an opportunity to reveal his true nobility, Charles won the support of many people. Disappointments are suffered for God in the hope that He will eventually bring good out of suffering. AH saw in retrospect that God had intended her to marry Halkett, for she would have married the Royalist agent Colonel Bampfield had not conflicting reports of his wife's death dissuaded her.

When Sir James Halkett began courting her, AH refused him, but soon afterwards learned that Bampfield's wife was in fact alive. She fell ill: 'what ye trialls were that I mett with under that sicknesse are knowne to some yett living, and the submission under them was, I hope, acceptable to him that gave it.' Soon afterwards she married Halkett out of gratitude for his kindness, and in obedience to God's clear command.

AH concludes that the lesson of the death of her second child is 'to teach me not to love this world or anything that is in it'. CAROLINE COLEMAN

Works: 'Meditations upon the Seventieth and Fifth Psalm' (1701); 'Meditations and Prayers upon the First Week; with Observation on Each Day's Creation and Consideration on the Seven Capital Vices to be Opposed: and Their Opposite Virtues to be Studied and Practised' (1701); *Instructions for Youth* (1701); *Autobiography* (1875).

References: Ballard; *DNB*; Fraser, A., *The Weaker Vessel* (1984); Loftis, A. (ed.), *The Memoirs of Anne, Lady Halkett and Ann, Lady Fanshawe* (1979); Todd.

Hall, Radclyffe

b. 1880 in West Cliff, near Bournemouth; d. August 1943, London

Poet, novelist

(Also wrote under Marguerite Radclyffe-Hall)

RH was born Marguerite to Radclyffe Radclyffe-Hall and Mary Jane Sanger (of Philadelphia). Her father's father, a tuberculosis specialist, made his fortune in a sanatorium in Torquay in the mid-Victorian era. His son, known as Rat, was a dilettante who occupied himself by travelling around Europe on his yacht. Rat left his wife weeks after RH was born, approximately at the same time as RH's only sibling, 2-year-old Florence, died from unspecified convulsions.

Her parents' divorce settled a small maintenance on her mother (now called Marie), with the bulk of the money held in trust for RH. In search of money, Marie married Alberto Visetti, a singing master at the Royal College of Music, and in 1889 settled in Kensington. RH was taught by a series of governesses; in her teens she attended various day schools. The lack of structure in education or family life caused her to rely upon her own creativity; she invented verses and rhymes, matching her words with her own piano music. Alienated, rejected, and often ignored by her now warring mother and stepfather, she idealized her absent father, but realized that men as a whole held little attraction for her.

When RH was 18 her father died of tuberculosis. At 21 she inherited her grandfather's fortune and moved from home, taking her maternal grandmother with her as companion. For the next six years she lived in London, then Malvern Wells, and took a lengthy trip to the US, visiting her mother's family and travelling with two of her cousins. Her time in England was spent hunting and amusing herself. She took the name John in private life, and in 1906 paid for publication of her first poetry volume, a well-received book of unremarkable poems.

In 1907 RH met and fell instantly in love with Mabel Veronica Batten, known as 'Ladye', fascinated by her social graces, delicacy, and childlike helplessness. Her friendship with Ladye, a talented *lieder* singer and beautiful socialite, developed slowly, but in the summer of 1908 they quietly became lovers. That autumn RH's second volume of poetry demonstrated greater happiness, increased confidence, and heightened maturity. Two poems have subtle references to lesbianism: 'Ode to Sappho' and 'The Scar'.

Late in 1910 RH's maternal grandmother and Ladye's husband, George Batten, died, allowing RH and Ladye to buy a London flat. They lived happily for seven years, socializing with Ladye's many friends and travelling frequently to the continent. During this time RH converted to Catholicism.

In 1915 RH met Una Vincent Troubridge at a tea party. The effect was immediate. RH, then 35, cut a striking figure dressed in 'very simple tailor-made clothes', with a face like that 'of a very handsome young man'. Una, wife of the respected navy admiral Jack Troubridge, had a very unhappy marriage and suffered countless psychological and physical illnesses. The two women began a surreptitious affair which Ladye soon suspected. RH and Ladye's relationship deteriorated into frequent rages and anguished weeping on both sides. RH knew how much she loved and owed Ladye who, then 58, was rapidly becoming an invalid. In 1916, after a hysterical accusation of RH's unfaithfulness, Ladye died from a cerebral haemorrhage.

RH and Una soon moved in together, but their mutual reverence for and guilt about Ladye was revealed during their twenty-eight years together by the memorabilia of Ladye kept throughout their home. They also spent many years trying to contact her spirit through psychic mediums. RH and Una bought a home north of London – their first in a series of country houses and city flats – and spent many months over the coming years travelling in Europe. Residing in Paris, they met Colette, the artist Romaine Brooks, and the American Natalie Barney, among others, in the expatriate lesbian set which made Paris its home from the early 1900s to the 1930s.

RH began her first published prose in 1919, the work which was to become *The Unlit Lamp*. Inspired by the sight of a fussy elderly woman attended hand-

and-foot by her late-middle-aged daughter at an English seaside resort, RH resolved to publicize the plight of this long-suffering class of spinster daughters who devoted their otherwise-wasted lives to the care of crotchety parents. Owing to publishing difficulties, *The Forge* appeared first, in 1924, although it was written second. Both books received good reviews and popular acclaim. By this time RH had decided to publish under the name Radclyffe Hall, dropping the hyphen she had always considered pretentious.

Throughout their years together, Una served as household manager, secretary, accountant, and social go-between (RH was often startlingly gruff and blunt). Both women adored animals and bred show-dogs. *Adam's Breed* was published in 1926 to an outstanding reception. The novel was awarded both the prestigious Prix Femina and the James Tait Black Memorial Prize, an achievement matched only by E. M. Forster's *A Passage to India*. Only four years after publication of her first novel, RH was amazed to find herself at the top of her profession.

In 1928 the largely autobiographical *The Well of Loneliness* was daringly published, tracing the life of the wealthy young woman Stephen Gordon from birth to her full realization that she is a 'congenital invert' (as she terms it), a lesbian by nature. The cry of immorality was immediately raised; the subsequent trial of RH and Jonathan Cape, the novel's publisher, found the book to be an obscene libel which could not be printed in England. The trial was a turning point in RH's life, her first public stand on her sexual orientation. Becoming, in her mind, a spokeswoman for female homosexuality, she took it upon herself to research and theorize on its existence.

After the trial, the public watched RH and Una more closely, but their mutual devotion and complete lack of shame remained strong. Then, in France in 1943, Una fell ill and was nursed by Eugenia Souline, a half-Russian woman who spoke little English. RH fell passionately in love with her. After nineteen years of virtual marriage, RH forced Una to suffer the anguish caused by Souline's presence on and off over the next nine years. There is no indication that Souline ever returned the affection, although hundreds of RH's letters remain as proof of her infatuation.

Between 1932 and 1936 RH published three more novels, none of which carried the weight or impact of *The Well*. Her risk taking had declined; much of her writing contained clearly Catholic imagery and themes. In late 1939 RH's health began to fail; she never completely recovered. A severe relapse occurred in 1943, and after five stoic months, she died from cancer of the rectum. She was buried in Ladye's tomb in Highgate cemetery. Una chose the inscription: 'And If God Choose I Shall But Love Thee Better After Death.' RH's mother died two years later at the age of 89. Una Troubridge was faithful to RH's memory, publishing her *Life and Death of Radclyffe Hall*, and carefully guarding copyrights and interests. She died of liver cancer in 1963 and was buried in Rome, although she also had requested burial in Ladye's tomb.

The Well, the work for which RH is best known, is a largely autobiographical, though romanticized version of RH's life. It is the first full, rich portrait of a lesbian in literature. At the time the publication was an act of outstanding bravery. But, because the women's movement of the 1970s declared lesbianism guilt-free, the guilt evident within *The Well* has caused the novel to be despised by some modern lesbians. Indeed, those passages which are autobiographical accounts stand out through their guilty, often wrenching realism. Much of the writing is overblown and contrived, in the popular style. Many sophisticated and/or experimental writers, such as Virginia Woolf, expressed private regret that a better-written novel was not the one challenging the censorship law. But a less bluff, tough, and financially independent author may not have possessed the character, honesty, and remarkable belief in herself which RH had.

AMALIA ERICKSON

Works: *'Twixt Earth and Stars* (1906); *A Sheaf of Verses* (1908); *Poems of the Past and Present* (1910); *Songs of Three Counties and Other Poems* (1913); *The Forgotten Island* (1915); *The Forge* (1924); *The Unlit Lamp* (1924); *A Saturday Life* (1925); *Adam's Breed* (1926); *The Well of Loneliness* (1928); *The Master of the House* (1932); *Miss Ogilvy Finds Herself* (1934); *The Sixth Beatitude* (1936).

References: Baker, M., *Our Three Selves* (1985); Dickson, L., *Radclyffe Hall at the Well of Loneliness* (1975); Fairbairns, Z., 'Introduction' to *The Unlit Lamp* (1981); Franks, C. S., *Beyond 'The Well of Loneliness': The Fiction of Radclyffe Hall* (1982); Hennegan, A., 'Introduction' to *Adam's Breed* (1985); Hennegan, A., 'Introduction' to *The Well of Loneliness* (1982); Ormrod, R., *Una Troubridge, The Friend of Radclyffe Hall* (1985); Troubridge, U. B., *The Life and Death of Radclyffe Hall* (1961).

Hall, Mrs S. C.

b. 6 January 1800, Dublin; d. 30 January 1881, East Molesey
Novelist, short story writer
(Also wrote under Anna Maria Hall)

SCH's mother, Sarah Elizabeth Fielding was left a widow around the time of her daughter's birth and shortly afterwards went to live with a relative, George Carr, of Craigie in Wexford. SCH lived in Ireland until 1815 when she moved to England with her mother. In 1824 she married Samuel Carter Hall, a journalist and proprietor of journals, and from 1826 onwards her mother lived with them in London. Her mother died there in 1856 at the age of 83. SCH's first published work was an Irish sketch entitled 'Master Ben' which she wrote for the periodical *The Spirit and Manners of the Age.* The sketch was well received and SCH began a series of Irish vignettes which she collected as *Sketches of Irish Character* (1829).

The success of these stories prompted SCH to take up writing as a career, and over the next fifty years her output was both varied and prolific, including nine novels, several plays, and many collections of stories. Many of her Irish stories, including 'The Groves of Blarney', appeared in her husband's *New Monthly Magazine.* In December 1868 she was granted a civil list pension of £100 annually. Towards the end of her life she became increasingly interested in philanthropic projects: she founded several hospitals and nursing homes, including the Home for Decayed Gentlewomen and the Hospital for Consumption at Brompton. She was active in the temperance movement and in 1875 produced a collection of temperance tales under the title of *Boons and Blessings.* She also campaigned for women's rights but nevertheless opposed female suffrage.

Perhaps because of her Irish subject matter, SCH's writings, particularly *Marian* (1840), were often compared with those of Maria Edgeworth. But, as SCH herself pointed out, a more immediate model, especially for the stories, was Mary Russell Mitford's *Our Village.* Although SCH's pastoral tales are almost all set in Ireland her work was never popular there. The 'Introduction' to the fifth edition of *Sketches of Irish Character* (1855) suggests that they were in any case intended purely for an English audience. SCH is careful to point out that her subjects are to be distinguished from the vulgar mass of the Irish peasantry by their English ancestry: 'The inhabitants are, chiefly, descendants of the Anglo-Norman settlers . . . and retain most of their English character. This is apparent . . . in the skilfully farmed fields, the comparatively comfortable cottages . . .'.

This emphasis on a peasantry poor but (because English) decent is pursued in the sketches themselves. In 'Mary Ryan's Daughter', Daddy Denny, a Wordsworthian beggar, spends less time asking for food and money than he does forgoing offered gifts in the pursuit of noble ends. Similarly, when Mary Ryan, an outcast whose virtue is considered suspect by the other villagers, takes refuge in the poorest dwelling in the village, a one-room hovel, it is decently kept: 'the floor was even and well-swept, the chimney did not smoke, and the bed of dried heather was raised from the floor by some long boards, and covered by a patch quilt.' The entire community's essential decency is implicitly confirmed when Mary is discovered to be the legitimate wife of a landowner who has dishonestly disowned her, and Mary's daughter to be heir to his estate.

Despite the collection's promise of 'sketches', as many of the tales are organized around moral or proverbial tags as around single characters. 'Larry Moore' begins, ' "THINK of to-morrow!" – that is what few Irish peasants ever do', and develops as a series of variations on this theme, in which a well-born female narrator chastises Larry for his indolence, never losing an opportunity to reiterate, ' "Oh, Larry, I'm afraid you never think of to-morrow!" ' The narrator conclusively enforces her moral by pointing out that ' "the English think of *to-morrow*." ' 'Take It Easy' is similarly constructed: an old widow who has been married three times tells a dissatisfied newly-wed that 'All ye can do with him, Aileen, when he gets into those humours, is – to take it asy'. Once more the stoical injunction to 'take it asy' recurs with monotonous regularity.

Such methods of organizing stories hint at the influence of folk stories and fairy tales on SCH's work. There are occasional appearances of the supernatural in her stories, but the culmination of this vein in her writing is the lavishly illustrated and extremely popular *Midsummer Eve* (1848), a 'Fairy Tale of Love' set in Ireland and employing Irish legends. Even here, however, SCH was delighted to discover that entertainment could be immediately improving: 'How fertile of Thought are the Fairy Legends of Ireland,' she writes in her introduction, 'full of natural poetry and seldom without a moral!'   JAMES SMITH

Works: *Sketches of Irish Character* (1829); *The Juvenile Forget-me-Not* (1829); *Chronicles of a School-Room* (1830); *Tales of a Woman's Trials* (1835); *Uncle Horace* (1837); *St Pierre, the Refugee* (1837); *Lights and Shadows of Irish Life*, 3 vols (1838); *The Book of Royalty: Characteristics of British Palaces* (1839); *Tales of the Irish Peasantry* (1840); *Marian, or, A Young Maid's Fortunes*, 3 vols (1840); *The Hartopp Jubilee* (1840); *Sharpe's London Magazine, Conducted by Mrs S. C. Hall* (1845); *The White Boy: A Novel*, 2 vols (1845); *Midsummer Eve: A Fairy Tale of Love* (1848); *The Swan's Egg: A Tale* (1850); *Pilgrimages to English Shrines* (1850); *Stories of The Governess* (1852); *The Worn Thimble: A Story* (1853); *The Drunkard's Bible* (1854); *The Two Friends* (1856); *A Woman's Story*, 3 vols (1857); *The Lucky Penny and Other Tales* (1857); *Finden's Gallery of Modern Art, with Tales by Mrs S. C. Hall* (1859); *The Boy's Birthday Book* (1859); *Daddy Dacre's School* (1859); *Can Wrong Be Right? A Tale*, 2 vols (1862); *Nelly Nowlan and Other Stories* (1865); *The Playfellow and Other Stories* (1866); *The Way of the World and Other Stories* (1866); *The Prince of the Fairy Family* (1867); *Alice Stanley and Other Stories* (1868); *Animal Sagacity* (1868); *The Fight of Faith: A Story*, 2 vols (1869); *Digging a Grave with a Wineglass* (1871); *Chronicles of a Cosy Nook*

(1875); *Boons and Blessings: Stories of Temperance* (1875); *Grandmother's Pockets* (1880).
References: Hall, S. C., *Retrospect of a Long Life* (1883); *BA* (19); Hogan, R. (ed.), *Macmillan Dictionary of Irish Literature* (1980); Mayo, I. F., 'A recollection of two old friends: Mr and Mrs S. C. Hall', *Leisure Hour* 38 (1889).

Hamilton, Cicely

b. 15 June 1872, London; d. 5 December 1952, London
Playwright, novelist, journalist, social commentator
CH was a professional writer, totally dependent for her income on what she wrote; as a result she produced twenty-two books, ten full-length plays, nine one-act plays and a very large body of journalism. CH remains an important writer because she participated in, and recorded her responses to, most of the social and political events of the first half of the twentieth century which have been significant for women.

CH was born in Kensington, the daughter of Captain Denzil and Maude Hammill (*née* Piers). She was educated at private schools in Malvern and in Bad Homburg, Germany, and then worked for a short time as a pupil-teacher before earning her living by a combination of hack-journalism, writing of pulp-fiction, and acting in touring companies. In 1908 her play *Diana of Dobsons* established her reputation as a playwright and from then on she made her living by writing plays and novels and by serious journalism. She was active in the suffrage campaign, a member of the Women's Freedom League and a founder of the Women Writers' Suffrage League. In 1914 she became administrator for the Scottish Women's Hospital at Royaumont and from 1917 to 1919 ran a repertory company entertaining troops in France and Germany. In 1920 she ran the Press Office at the International Suffrage Congress in Geneva and on her return to England continued to be involved in feminist activities. She was on the editorial committee of *The Englishwoman*, a director of *Time and Tide*, and a member of the Six Point Group and of the Open Door Council. In 1938 she was awarded a civil list pension for her services to literature. She was editor of the Press Bulletin of the British League for European Freedom from 1945 until her death. CH remained unmarried and celebrated her spinsterhood and the opportunity it gave for close friendships with like-minded women.

Despite the diversity of her output there are three main themes which recur throughout CH's work: an insistence that the true emancipation of women depends on financial independence and that until this comes about the relations between the sexes will remain tainted by the cash nexus; a conviction that man is naturally war-like and that science will always be used to make ever more terrible weapons; and a deep distrust of what she calls the 'herd instinct' and its adverse effect upon both public and private morality.

CH's most successful plays were *Diana of Dobsons* (1908) and *The Old Adam* (1924). The first is a comedy about the gulf between working people, especially working women, and the leisured classes; before the hero is allowed to marry Diana he has to prove himself capable of honest toil. In this play CH combined serious social points about the power and freedom conveyed by money with a romantic plot which appealed to the public. As a result the play toured continuously for twenty years. *The Old Adam* is an original and imaginative work about the inevitability of war. When an inventor discovers rays which will paralyse all machinery within a selected area, Paphlagonia declares war on its old enemy Ruritania; Ruritania has made a similar discovery and the weapons of both sides are useless. But, instead of this bringing an end to the conflict, the combatants continue fighting with clubs and stones. Some of the play's humour draws too much on obvious jokes about politicians but it makes the point forcefully that men have 'the love of strife, for itself, for its own dear sake'.

Grimmer images of war are presented in the novels *William, an Englishman* (1919) and *Theodore Savage* (1922). In *William*, written in the aftermath of the first World War and for which CH won the Femina Vie Heureuse Prize in 1919, the eponymous hero and his wife Griselda are passionate but unquestioning supporters of women's suffrage and pacificism. Griselda dies after being raped by a German soldier in Belgium at the beginning of the war and William becomes pro-war. CH attacks their narrowness and lack of independent judgement and at times her contempt for her characters is a barrier for the reader, especially when one remembers CH's own involvement with the suffrage campaign. William's behaviour, however, is credible as that of a man who followed the herd until tragedy made him face the reality of war. In *Theodore Savage* civilization has been destroyed by total scientifiic warfare; mankind becomes concerned only with survival and all moral restraints disappear. Later, as communities form, people try to understand their lives and a dread of science and learning develops, since these are seen as the source of all destruction. In this powerful and apocalyptic book CH expresses a cyclical view of history in which mankind endlessly refines the tools of its own destruction and emerges from the ruins to repeat the process, mythologizing its past as it does so.

During the suffrage campaign CH wrote plays for the Actresses' Franchise League: *How the Vote was Won* (1909) still works well in performance and *A Pageant of Great Women* (1910), hugely popular with suffrage audiences, is a stirring, if slightly bombastic celebration of women's achievements. Her major contribution to the suffrage debate was *Marriage as a Trade* (1909), a witty, hard-hitting demonstration of the argument that women only marry because they have no other means of earning a living. The book debunks romantic love and celebrates spinsterhood with an exuberance and confidence which CH never recaptured in her writing after the First World War. The plays *Phyl* (1913), *Just to Get Married* (1910), and *A Matter of Money* (1911), which CH later turned into novels, explore the reality of the theories of *Marriage as a Trade* – women's choices in marriage and in love are limited by financial restraints. *Just to Get Married* has a weak and conventional final act but is otherwise perceptive and convincing.

In her journalism CH concentrated on feminist and social issues; she was especially concerned with true equality of opportunity for women and with the need to assert the supremacy of the individual conscience over the 'herd-instinct' in both public and private life. Of her travel books those about Italy and Germany and the effects of fascism and about Russia and the effect of socialism are particularly illuminating. Her autobiography, *Life Errant*, is disappointingly reticent and minimizes the variety of her experiences, the richness of her friendships, and the intensity of her commitment.

CH was a writer who appealed to contemporary taste and who was, in much of her work, characteristic of her period. Her great skill, however, lay in introducing elements of more experimental dramatic forms and quite radical feminist and social ideas into her work without alienating mainstream audiences.

ELISABETH J. WHITELAW

Selected works: *The Sixth Commandment* (1906); *The Sergeant of Hussars* (1907); *Mrs Vance* (1907); *Diana of Dobsons* (1908); *How the Vote was Won* (with

Christopher St John) (1909); *The Pot and the Kettle* (1909); *Marriage as a Trade* (1909); *The Homecoming* (1910); *A Pageant of Great Women* (1910); *Just To Get Married* (1910); *A Matter of Money* (1911); *Just To Get Married* (1911); *Jack and Jill and a Friend* (1911); *The Constant Husband* (1912); *Lady Noggs* (1913); *Phyl* (1913); *A Matter of Money* (1916); *William, an Englishman* (1919); *The Brave and the Fair* (1920); *Mrs Armstrong's Admirer* (1920); *Theodore Savage* (1922); *The Old Adam* (first performed as *The Human Factor*) (1924); *The Beggar Prince* (1929); *Full Stop* (1931); *Modern Germanies* (1931); *Modern Italy* (1932); *Life Errant* (1935); *Lament for Democracy* (1940).

Bibliography: Lewis, J., 'Introduction' to *Marriage as a Trade* (1981); Spender, D., *Women of Ideas (and What Men have Done to Them)* (1982).

Hamilton, Elizabeth

b. 1758, Belfast; d. 1816, Harrogate

Essayist, poet, satirist, novelist

Since EH's life was in many ways uneventful, it is important to note her own assessment of her personality: 'I have always found myself in more danger of being forsaken by my prudence than my spirits.' Her mother, Katherine MacKay, was Irish, but her father, Charles Hamilton, came from a distinguished though poor Scottish family and worked as a merchant. EH was their third and last child. Her father died within the year, her mother when she was 9. From the age of 6 she lived in Stirlingshire, with her paternal aunt Mrs Marshall, who had defied family pride by marrying a worthy and dignified farmer. EH became a tomboy, climbing over the countryside in summer and sliding over it in winter. Although she did not receive a classical education, she studied until the age of 13 under a master in a mixed school. Her aunt appreciated literature, but warned her niece to avoid pedantry, with the result that EH once hid Lord Kames's *Elements of Criticism* under a chair cushion, 'well knowing the ridicule to which I should have been exposed, had I been detected in the act of looking into such a book'. She was happy with the Marshalls, but she chafed somewhat under the realization that she was intellectually superior to her surroundings, and she idolized her brother and sister. As she was finishing her formal schooling, her brother left for a fourteen-year tour of military duty in India. Their voluminous correspondence constituted what her friend and biographer Elizabeth O. Benger called 'a *second* education'. In 1788 Charles Hamilton returned from India to translate the *Hedaya*, one of the two chief commentaries on Moslem law. When EH visited her brother in London, she realized she had at last met a group of people who were her intellectual equals. Her aunt had died in 1782, and, after her uncle's death in 1790, she moved to London to live with her brother. Although two years later he also died, he was undoubtedly the chief intellectual and emotional influence on her life, so much so that as late as 1803 she wrote, 'With him, my every hope of happiness expired.' EH was resilient, however, and she had made other friends, including the writer and clergyman Dr George Gregory, who encouraged EH in her literary ventures. After her brother's death, she lived in England with her married sister Katherine Black, and she settled ultimately in Edinburgh in 1804, a move which inspired her vernacular poems, including the famous 'My Ain Fireside' and a spirited welcome to old age. She held weekly literary gatherings, won a government pension, and was generally recognized as a powerful intellectual force. Although inhibited by weak eyes and at times nearly incapacitated by gout, she helped to found a house of industry for women and continued publishing works on education. Her infirmities at last forced her to move to London. She died in Harrogate.

From the start EH had always been ambitious; she wanted to be known beyond her own circle. While in Stirling she wrote a journal of a tour through the Highlands, which to her surprise her aunt caused to be published in a 'provincial magazine'. She also began an historical novel about Arabella Stuart, which is most remarkable for a series of letters between two sisters who have been separated and yearn to meet. In 1785, she published essays and poetry in the *Lounger*. One of these essays warned women that they could expect 'an inexhaustible source of delight' in learning, but that they would not thereby attract men (17 December 1785, signed Almeria). EH's three novels differed widely in form and content. The first, *Letters of a Hindoo Rajah* (1796), uses the device of satirical Oriental letters, following Montesquieu and Goldsmith. This book, which she called 'my black baby' (her books were her metaphorical children: she called *Letters on Education* 'my bantling'), contains a long and learned preface, but its chief theme is that women need not faint at the sight of blood nor engage in other fashionable timidities – they can be strong and competent. The book attracted excellent reviews. Her second novel, which raced through a number of editions, was *Memoirs of Modern Philosophers* (1800), a spoof of the Godwin circle. The anti-heroine Bridgetina Botherim, who soon became 'a proverbial point in conversation' (*Gentleman's Magazine*, 1816), represents Mary Hays. Botherim is stupid, headstrong, deformed, and – perhaps for these reasons – metaphysically inclined. She recklessly attempts to force men to love her. By following similar principles, her unfortunate counterpart, the sweet and lovely Julie Delmond, allows herself to be seduced and abandoned, and finally commits suicide. One of EH's most effective satirical techniques is to put Godwin's literal words into the mouth of Julie's seducer, Vallaton. Interestingly, in spite of EH's usually loyal support of her own sex, the most evil character in this book is her *femme fatale* Emmeline, who elicits from the authorial voice this wholesale attack: 'The wickedness of even the worst of men seldom equals the wickedness of woman.' When Emmeline tires of Vallaton, she conveniently betrays him to the guillotine. The objects of EH's satire seem chiefly to have been the extremists of the modern philosophers, among whom she did not include Mary Wollstonecraft. In her third novel, *The Cottagers of Glenburnie* (1808), the commonsensical Mrs Mason comes to stay with her well-meaning but lazy and disorderly cousin Mrs MacClarty, who never seems to get around to washing her children, cleaning her butter churn, planting flowers, or even keeping her husband alive. Although Mrs MacClarty proves resistant, Mrs Mason eventually organizes and reforms the whole neighbourhood, introducing ideals of cleanliness, economy, and education. The characters speak in the vernacular and are eminently believable. The MacClarty family's refrain, '*I cou'd no be fashed*' (I couldn't be bothered), became a saying of the day, and F. Jeffrey in the *Edinburgh Review* suggested that the book be circulated among Scottish cottagers themselves, providing them with a more vivid and subtle encouragement to change their ways than Hannah More's *Cheap Repository Tracts*, which were too condescending.

Interspersed among her novels, EH published a number of other influential works. Her *Letters on Education* (1801) had gone through eight editions by 1837. Here, her concern was chiefly that women, as mothers, should raise their children intelligently, treating boys and girls equally, nurturing their moral and intellectual life primarily by monitoring their early associations of ideas. Her biography of *Agrippina, the Wife of Germanicus* (1804) was an important attempt to deal seriously with the life of an admirable Roman woman, although EH's lack of a classical education hindered her researches. After living for six months as the invited tutor in an aristocratic household, she published *Letters Addressed to the Daughter of a Nobleman on the Formation of the Religious and the Moral Principle* (1806). It is worth noting that her religious beliefs were non-sectarian, which is not surprising considering her varied upbringing.

Although initially EH's chief intellectual mentors were male, she had many women friends, including Joanna Baillie and Maria Edgeworth. She directed all of her books primarily to her own sex, whose qualities of mind she admired and defended. Women's minds were truly her subject, not women's bodies or their desires. Mrs Mason imposes her woman's virtues on the town of Glenburnie, and she immeasurably improves the place. Bridgetina Botherim and Julie Delmond are corrupted and victimized alike by an improbable romanticism which men – the modern philosophers – have fostered as a social good. EH's books were popular, and Jane Austen was pleased that such a 'respectable writer' had read *Sense and Sensibility*. After EH's death Maria Edgeworth praised her 'as an original, agreeable, and successful writer of fiction', but argued that her works on education were of a 'higher sort', chiefly because they opened a new field of investigation to women, metaphysical study, which was 'not only practicable, but pleasant; and not only pleasant, but what is of far more consequence to women, safe' (*Gentleman's Magazine*, 1816).

JANICE FARRAR THADDEUS

Selected works: *Translation of the Letters of a Hindoo Rajah, with a Preliminary Dissertation on the History of the Hindoos* (1796); *Memoirs of Modern Philosophers: A Novel* (1800); *Letters on The Elementary Principles of Education* (1801); *Letters Addressed to the Daughter of a Nobleman on the Formation of Religious and Moral Principle* (1806); *The Cottagers of Glenburnie* (1808); *Exercises in Religious Knowledge* (1809); *A Series of Popular Essays, Illustrative of Principles Essentially Connected with the Improvement of the Understanding, the Imagination, and the Heart* (1812).

References: BA (19); Benger, E. O., *Memoirs of Mrs Elizabeth Hamilton* (1818); Edgeworth, M., 'Character and writings of Mrs Elizabeth Hamilton', *Gentleman's Magazine* Supplement 86, 2 (1816); Jeffrey, F., 'Mrs Hamilton's *Cottagers*', *Edinburgh Review* (July 1808); Luria, G., 'Introduction' to *The Cottagers of Glenburnie* and *Letters Addressed to the Daughter of a Nobleman* (1974); Luria, G., 'Introduction' to *Memoirs of Modern Philosophers* (1974); Moler, K. L., *Jane Austen's Art of Allusion* (1968).

Harraden, Beatrice

b. 24 January 1864, Hampstead; d. 5 May 1936
Novelist

BH was the daughter of Samuel and Rosalie Harraden and, later, the ward of Mrs Lynn Linton. She was educated at Cheltenham College and Bedford College, London. She travelled much in the United States and in Europe, and was active in the suffragette movement, despite some doubting of the extent of her own personal commitment to the cause. Of one contemporary suffragette leader, she said 'I always feel I've failed her by not giving up absolutely everything for the cause.' BH's seventeen novels, written between 1891 and 1928, often reflected her suffragette leanings. She described *Interplay* (1908), for example, as being about the 'conception of woman as an independent being'. In *The Guiding Thread* (1916), a woman leaves a restrictive marriage, and the heroine of *Katherine Frensham* (1903) is a happily unmarried 40-year-old woman with 'the calm independence of a man'.

The First World War made its mark on BH's fiction. In *Where Your Treasure Is* (1918), a sequel to the earlier *Out of the Wreck I Rise* (1912), the heroine Tamar Scott works as a gem dealer in wartime London, seemingly oblivious of the fighting across the channel. An appraisal leads her to Holland where she meets Belgian refugees and confronts the full reality of war.

JEAN HANFF KORELITZ

Selected works: *Things Will Take a Turn* (1891); *Ships that Pass in the Night* (1893); *In Varying Moods* (1894); *Hilda Strafford: A California Story* (1897); *Hilda Strafford and the Remittance Man: Two California Stories* (1897); *Untold Tales of the Past* (1897); *The Fowler* (1899); *The Scholar's Daughter* (1906); *Interplay* (1908); *Out of the Wreck I Rise* (1912); *Where Your Treasure Is* (1918; published in the US as *Where Your Heart Is*); *Spring Shall Plant* (1920); *Thirteen All Told* (1921); *Patuffa* (1923); *Youth Calling* (1924); *Rachel* (1926); *Search Will Find Out* (1928).

Harrison, Jane
b. 9 September 1850, Cottingham, near Hull; d. 15 April 1928, London
Classicist, anthropologist

JH was one of three daughters of a timber merchant, Charles Harrison, and of Elizabeth (*née* Nelson) Harrison, who died young. JH was educated first at home and then at Cheltenham Ladies' College; later she went to Newnham College, Cambridge, where she was one of the first students and in time became a fellow in classics, very popular with students for her enthusiastic lecturing on ancient Greece. When she left Cambridge, JH studied Greek art and antiquities in the British Museum and was excited by the ideas of J. G. Frazer and the archaeological discoveries of Schliemann and Arthur Evans, which supported her interest in comparative religion.

An outstanding classical scholar, JH was one of a group labelled the 'Cambridge ritualists' who used social anthropology and psychology to illuminate classical studies, especially Greek religion. The views were controversial at a time when such studies were primarily text-based, as she describes in her last work, *Reminiscences of a Student's Life* (1925). Despite immense erudition, JH was often criticized as unscholarly and impulsive because of her passionate adherence to her ideas on religion, and she was especially opposed by her former teacher William Ridgeway; at one time she was even denounced by the Provost of King's College for her contention that primitive myth lay behind the story of John the Baptist's head. JH insisted that Greek religion should not be seen through literature. Homer was for her the end not the beginning of a tradition and her analysis began with actual rites rather than with the artificial figures of the Olympian gods. Her aim was to uncover the primitive, savage stratum in Greek religion, overlaid in later sophisticated festivals. The intellectual excitement of JH's work on Greek religion and the religious impulse in general, studied through ethnology and psychology, is conveyed in the many letters she wrote to Gilbert Murray, the translator of Greek poetry and a great admirer of her work, and in her major books such as *Prologomena* (1903), a prelude to the study of Greek religion, and *Themis* (1912), a study of its social origins.

During the First World War, since she held pacifist sentiments and saw the conflict as the result of a savage craving for sensation, JH went abroad. She was accompanied by her friend and companion Hope Mirlees, with whom she had a close personal and professional relationship and whom she described as 'a ghostly daughter'. The two women studied Russian together and later published translations. JH returned to England and lived in Bloomsbury until her death.

JH received numerous awards for her work. Apart from classical scholars, she met many famous people of her day, such as George Eliot (briefly), whose mixture of conventional demeanour and intellectual daring she much admired, Tennyson, Browning, Burne-Jones, and Ann Thackeray Ritchie. She travelled widely, visiting Greece, Crete, Italy, Algeria, France and Sweden.

JANET TODD

Selected works: *Myths of the Odyssey in Art and Literature* (1882); *Introductory Studies in Greek Art* (1885); *Manual of Mythology* (1890); *Prolegomena to the Study of Greek Religion* (1903); *The Religion of Ancient Greece* (1905); *Themis* (1912); *Ancient Art and Ritual* (1913); *Epilogomena to the Study of Greek Religion* (1921); *Mythology* (1925); *Reminiscences of a Student's Life* (with Hope Mirlees) (1925); (trans.), *The Book of the Bear* (1926); *Life of the Arch-Priest Avvakum* (with H. Mirlees) (1926); *Myths of Greece and Rome* (1927).

References: Holroyd, M., *Lytton Strachey* (1967–8); Murray, G., *Inaugural Lecture*, Newnham College (1928); Macmillan, S. J. G., *Jane Ellen Harrison* (1959); Peacock, S. J., *Jane Ellen Harrison* (1988); Woolf, V., *The Diary of Virginia Woolf, 1925–1930*, vol. 3 (1980); West, F., *Gilbert Murray: A Life* (1984).

Havergal, Frances Ridley

b. 14 December 1836, Astley, Worcestershire; d. 3 June 1879, The Mumbles, Swansea

Hymn writer

FRH was the youngest of the six children of the Reverend Henry Havergal, a writer of sacred music. Her sister, Maria, in her *Memorials of FRH* (1880), gives an attractive picture of a closely knit, evangelically pious Victorian family. FRH, nicknamed 'Little Quicksilver', was a lively, precocious child, reading her Bible at 4 and showing early linguistic skill. Later she read French, German, Welsh, Hebrew, and New Testament Greek, despite her only formal education being a few months at schools in Worcester and Germany. She was an agile tree climber who read poetry and left books lying around in the stables and gardens but she early on showed the piety which marked her life and writing, and it is interesting to note that her godmother, Lucy Emma, wrote religious verse. Her mother died when FRH was 11, and her bitter grief found expression later in her story *The Four Happy Days*. Her father remarried, and after his death in 1870 she devoted herself to her stepmother who died in 1878. She then set up house with her sister Maria in The Mumbles, Swansea, where she died the next year.

FRH had a wide circle of friends, and according to her biographer, T. H. Darlow, she refused several offers of marriage, though Maria is discreet about these. She was accomplished, singing in oratorios and embroidering beautifully, and despite ill-health she played croquet and skated and went on walking tours in Wales and Switzerland. She paid visits to her clergyman brothers and married sisters, helping to educate their daughters, and kept up a huge correspondence. Outwardly uneventful, her life was inwardly ardent and self-critical. She regarded significant dates in her life as her confirmation on 17 July 1854, an anniversary she always observed, an undefined spiritual crisis on 2 December 1873, and her father's death. In a letter to a friend in March 1864 she defined his churchmanship and her own: '1. Evangelical Doctrine i.e. Christ and his

Atonement are above and before all things: Conversion . . . ; that good works follow out of and are not any means of justification which is only by faith in Christ; that outward forms and ceremonies have no merit or virtue in themselves whatever. 2. Loyal Church Practice'. Her letters give a lively and often humorous account of parish events, Sunday School teaching, day school visits, Bible studies and addresses to girls' groups and parties ('a grand hymn-spree (!)'), and of work for the YWCA, the Bible Society, various missions and the Keswick Convention, still an important annual event for Evangelicals.

She published over thirty collections of hymns which brought her an enormous correspondence. In a letter of 1872 she outlines a typical day, and Maria shows how in her last months she still aimed at devoting every minute to the service of her 'King'. She rose and studied early in what she called her 'workshop', turning out hymns, letters of counsel, and tracts, on her American typewriter. Maria says sternly, 'she refrained from late hours and frittering talks at night.'

She was a versifier of great capacity but it would be vain to look for literary influences other than that of the Bible where, to her, every verse had equal authority. She loved what she called 'a bit of Bible mosaic', and that is largely what her hymns are. Her favourite poets were Milton, Herbert, and E. B. Browning. She read no contemporary novels, never went to the theatre and found Shakespeare 'earthy' when she read him as an adult. In her hymns, with their commonplace rhymes and rhythms, she encapsulates the earnestness and drama of self-dedication which sees life's events, however trivial, as part of an eternal struggle. Her own favourite, found in her pocket bible, was:

> I am trusting Thee, Lord Jesus,
>   Trusting only Thee;
> Trusting Thee for full salvation,
>   Great and free.

Her theology, if simple and narrow, gives the individual in a congregational setting the emotional satisfaction of an ardent personal response. On her tomb is inscribed, 'By her writings in prose and verse, she "being dead yet speaketh".' It is doubtful if her prose is now widely known, but many still sing with fervour her best known hymn, 'Take my life, and let it be' with its ending, 'Ever, only, all for Thee', so characteristic of its writer's thought.

MARY SHAKESHAFT

Works: *Poetical Works*, ed. M. G. Havergal (1884); *Letters*, ed. M. G. Havergal (1885).

References: Bullock, C., *The Crown of the Road* (1884); *DNB*; Darlow, T. H., *Frances Ridley Havergal, a Saint of God* (1927); Enoch, E. E., *Frances Ridley Havergal* (1929); Havergal, M. V. G., *Memorials of Frances Ridley Havergal* (1880).

Hawkes, Jacquetta

b. 1910, Cambridge

Archaeologist, fiction writer

JH is the younger daughter of the Nobel Prize Winner Sir Frederick Hopkins and of Jessie Stephens Hopkins. She was educated at the Perse School, Cambridge, and went on to read archaeology and anthropology at Newnham College, Cambridge, where she obtained a first-class honours degree. From 1931 to 1940 she was involved in research in Britain, Ireland, France, and Palestine.

In 1933 she married Christopher Hawkes by whom she had one son. In 1940 she was made a fellow of the Society of Antiquaries. The next four years were spent in the wartime civil service. She became assistant principal in the Post-War Reconstruction Secretariat and then moved on, through the Ministry of Education, to become principal and secretary of the UK National Commission for UNESCO. She stayed there until 1948 when she returned to archaeology and writing. From 1949 to 1955 she acted as vice-president for the Council of British Archaeology, as archaeological advisor for the Festival of Britain, and as a governor of the British Film Institute. She received an OBE in 1952.

In 1953 she was divorced from Christopher Hawkes; in the same year she married J. B. Priestley with whom she collaborated on *The Dragon's Mouth* (1952) and *Journey down a Rainbow* (1955). She became joint author with Sir Leonard Woolley of the first volume of the UNESCO *History of Mankind* (1963), entitled *Prehistory and the Beginnings of Civilization*. As archaeological correspondent first of *The Observer* and then of *The Sunday Times*, she visited many distant excavation sites. She contributed articles to the *Spectator* and other national periodicals, as well as to learned journals.

JH was a popularizer of archaeology, and many of her works have a mingled scientific and literary flavour. *A Land* (1951), which won the Kemsley Award, is an imaginative study of the geological evolution of Britain, containing clear black-and-white photographs by Walter Bird which help to capture the feeling of the gradual process of evolution. In her preface JH tells the reader, 'In this book I have used the findings of the two sciences of geology and archaeology for purposes altogether unscientific. I have tried to use them evocatively and the image I have sought to evoke is of an entity, the land of Britain, in which past and present, nature, man and art appear all in one piece.' To create her impression she uses not only geology and archaeology but the poetry of writers such as Wordsworth, Hardy, and Clare, as well as references to artists such as Constable: 'Hardy's poems grew from the Wessex Downlands, Clare's from the tiny stretch of the Midlands in which alone he felt at home'; and 'It is a countryside [East Anglia] owing something of its present character to Constable who saw it with such a briliant eye.' She also adds her own imaginative descriptions: 'The land that had always been silent and undisturbed began not only to be minutely stirred by small burrowings and by the growth of plants, but was marked by the impress of feet, even though between the footsteps went the groove of a scaly tail.'

Guide to Prehistoric and Roman Monuments in England and Wales (1951) is arranged in the manner of a guided tour. The reader is introduced to many different antiquities, including tombs, caves, and sanctuaries, the White Horse of Uffington and the Rollright stones, through JH's easy, clear style and through the inclusion of some excellent photographs and maps. Sometimes she mentions her own experience: 'I am now entering the countryside where I myself grew up and every part of it is alive with sharp, indestructible memories of childhood.' Information is detailed and invites readers to participate: 'If we take the road back towards Morvah, it leads us close to Chun Castle, a fine round fort on a hill which commands all the country behind Lands End.' The loose insert map of 'The Principal Prehistoric and Roman Monuments in England and Wales' suggests that readers must do some investigation for themselves.

Fables (1953) moves from archaeology to fiction. The work consists of eighteen fables of varying length, the characters being mainly gods and animals. As in her archaeological works, JH is able to call on her knowledge of nature: the habits of animals, birds, and fish and the changing landscapes. Many of the fables are short and sardonic, with clear morals. An example is the 'Elopdatery', the name of a fictitious offence which ceases to exist when the name ceases to exist. At the end 'frogs dived joyfully into the water and lived to beget a whole new race among whom the word Elopdatery was unknown.' Other fables are more opaque and suggestive, such as 'A Woman as Great as the World', told in a resonant poetic style that demands close reading and avoids any obvious moral.

LISA BUCKBY

Selected works: *Archaeology of Jersey* (1939); *Prehistoric Britain* (with Christopher Hawkes) (1944); *Early Britain* (1945); *Symbols and Speculations* (1948); *A Land* (1951); *Guide to Prehistoric and Roman Monuments in England and Wales* (1951); *Fables* (1953); *Man on Earth* (1954); *Journey Down a Rainbow* (with J. B. Priestley) (1955); *Providence Island* (1959); *Man and the Sun* (1962); *UNESCO History of Mankind*, vol. 1, part 1 (1963); (ed.), *The Worlds of the Past* (1963); *King of the Two Lands* (1966); *Dawn of the Gods* (1968); *The First Great Civilizations* (1973); *The Atlas of Early Man* (1976); *A Quest of Love* (1980); *Mortimer Wheeler: Adventurer in Archaeology* (1982); *The Shell Guide to British Archaeology* (1986).
References: Drabble.

Hawkins, Laetitia Matilda

b. 1759, London; d. 1835, Twickenham
Novelist, memoirist

The daughter of Sidney (*née* Storer) and Sir John Hawkins, the musicologist, biographer, and unclubbable friend of Dr Johnson, LMH was the author of memoirs, devotional works, and an unknown quantity of minor fiction. In 1759, shortly after LMH's birth, her mother inherited a substantial fortune, and so the family was able to move from London to Twickenham, where in 1761 Sir John became magistrate for Middlesex. With neighbours such as David Garrick and Horace Walpole, the Hawkinses' house soon became a resort of the cultural lions of the eighteenth century, visited by the intellectuals and literati who made up the coterie of Samuel Johnson. Sir John Hawkins was the author of a *Life of Samuel Johnson* (1787) and *A General History of the Science and Practice of Music* (1776), as well as an editor of Johnson's works and Izaak Walton's *The Compleat Angler*. The rather sickly LMH was therefore brought up in a highly literary environment, and, like her brothers John and Henry, she seems to have taken to writing from her youth. Little is known, however, about her early output, for it was not until fairly late in her career that she began to publish her works under her own name, and scholars have so far been unable to identify many of her anonymous writings. For much of her life her writing was shrouded in secrecy, and, although she had written her first (unidentified) novel before her father's death in 1789, Sir John, who strongly disapproved of novel reading and writing, never found out about his daughter's literary activities. The first of LMH's works which has been securely identified was the *Letters on the Female Mind* published in 1793, the year of her mother's death. This was devoted to an analysis of women's capacity, and attempted to counter Helen Maria Williams's *Letters from France*. As well as indicating LMH's ideas of the rather limited role of women in society, the *Letters* reveal the two themes that were at the heart of her fiction – her ideas on education and child rearing and her conservative politics. In 1811 LMH published her first novel under her own name, *The Countess and Gertrude, or, Modes of Discipline*, and this was followed by three more novels and two collections of memoirs about Dr Johnson and the literary circles amongst which she was brought up. She is also thought to be the author of two devotional works, and has been tentatively identified as the writer of *Siegwart: A Tale from the German* (1806). LMH never married, and after the death of her parents she went to live in the Twickenham house of her younger brother Henry, where she died.

LMH's work received the praise of Isaac D'Israeli in the *Gentleman's Magazine* (July 1814). In an article attacking her father and brother he wrote that 'the redeeming genius of that family – the genius which, like the figure of the antients, bears wings on its shoulders and flames on its head – must be a female'. To modern readers, however, LMH's works tend to be rather too moralistic and overtly didactic for comfort. They are informed with all the proselytizing Christian zeal of Hannah More, without More's wit, pace, and vivacity. As an anonymous reviewer wrote in the *New Monthly Magazine* of August 1821 (3,404), 'Miss Hawkin's characteristics in writing are verbosity tedious as Richardson's, without his power of giving interest to trifles; [and] quaintness sometimes bordering on vulgarity.' Moreover, 'there is a tone of self-conceit, of imaginary superiority . . . that prevents her from either affecting . . . or instructing in the degree which . . . she wishes and intends.'

In common with the works of Mary Wollstonecraft, Elizabeth Inchbald, and Maria Edgeworth, LMH's novels emphasize the importance of education in the formation of female character, but, unlike Wollstonecraft and Inchbald, LMH explicitly and emphatically rejected the new ideas of education propounded by the supporters of the French Revolution. In *Rosanne, or, A Father's Labours Lost* (1814), for example, the heroine is given an atheistical, free-thinking education, so that by the age of 15 she has never heard of, let alone seen, a bible. Despite, therefore, good natural parts and inclinations Rosanne is headstrong, wilful, and selfish. All turns out well in the end, however, for, having stumbled across a bible in the course of the story, the heroine is not only converted herself, and thus rendered a paragon of virtue, but also manages to convert her misdirected philosophical father. The overt didacticism of the story is emphasized by LMH's extensive use of lengthy footnotes. These give the works a scholarly appearance, and serve to underline their message, recommending certain educational methods, attacking the French, and celebrating the work of the anti-Jacobin which 'contributed to save us as a nation from revolution'.   LIZ BELLAMY

Selected works: Letters on the Female Mind (attrib.) (1793); Siegwart: A Tale from the German, 3 vols (attrib.) (1806); *The Countess and Gertrude, or, Modes of Discipline*, 4 vols (1811); *Sermonets Addressed to Those Who Have Not Yet Acquired the Inclination to Apply the Power of Attention to Compositions of a Higher Kind* (1814); *Rosanne, or, A Father's Labour Lost*, 3 vols (1814); *Heracline, or, Opposite Proceedings*, 4 vols (1821); *Devotional Exercises, Extracted from Bishop Patrick's Christian Sacrifice; Adapted to the Present Time* (1823); *Anecdotes, Biographical Sketches and Memoirs* (1824); *Memoirs, Anecdotes, Facts and Opinions Collected and Preserved by L.M.H.*, 2 vols (1824); *Annaline, or, Motive-Hunting*, 3 vols (1824).

References: De Castro, J. P., 'Laetitia Hawkins and Boswell', *Notes & Queries* 185 (1943); Skrine, F. H., *Gossip about Dr Johnson and Others, Being Chapters from the Memoirs of Miss Laetitia Matilda Hawkins* (1926); Todd.

Hays, Mary

b. 1760; d. 1843, London

Novelist, essayist, letter writer

(Also wrote under 'Eusebia')

MH spent her early life in Southwark with her widowed mother and two sisters. She attended lectures at the Dissenting Academy in Hackney, and also studied French, mathematics, and religious literature. Intellectual work helped her to overcome her grief at the death of her fiancé John Eccles; they had met in 1777 and had remained attached despite parental opposition, meeting clandestinely and writing hundreds of letters.

MH's first publication, a pamphlet defending the Dissenters' public worship against Gilbert Wakefield's *Enquiry into the Expediency and Propriety of Public Worship*, appeared in 1792 under the pseudonym 'Eusebia'. It received considerable attention and brought MH into contact with radical thinkers among the Dissenters. Her friends included Robert Robinson, John Disney (for whom she composed sermons which he preached at Essex Street Chapel), Joseph Priestley, and George Dyer, who brought her a copy of Mary Wollstonecraft's *Vindication of the Rights of Woman* in 1792. MH soon got to know Wollstonecraft, who gave her advice about the publication of her *Letters and Essays, Moral and Miscellaneous* (1793), and was mentioned in its preface as 'the sensible vindicator of female rights.'

In 1794 MH's friendship with Godwin began when she asked him to lend her a copy of *Political Justice*. She wrote to him frequently in 1795 and 1796, confiding to him her unrequited passion for William Frend. The experience bore fruit in her first novel, *Memoirs of Emma Courtney* (1796), in which the heroine declares her love for Augustus Harley while Mr Francis, a character based on Godwin, tries to argue her out of a hopeless passion. Her conversations with him insist that his belief in the power of reason must take account of women's circumstances and feelings. Emma's pursuit of Harley and her offer to live with him outside marriage 'for the individuality of an affection constitutes its chastity' made MH notorious, despite her claim that the heroine's story was 'calculated to operate as a *warning*, not an example.' MH was caricatured as the man-chasing Bridgetina Botherim in Elizabeth Hamilton's *Memoirs of Modern Philosophers* (1800), and she was also ridiculed in Charles Lloyd's *Edmund Oliver* (1798).

During 1796 and 1797 MH wrote for the *Monthly Magazine*: she argued for the equality of male and female intellects against another contributor's denial, and also defended novel writing and her own practice of creating faulty characters. Her interest in the difficult fate of noble minds inspired her second novel, *The Victim of Prejudice* (1799), in which the orphaned heroine, Mary, learns that she is illegitimate and that her mother, after having been seduced and driven into prostitution, was hanged for involvement in a tavern killing. Mary reads her mother's autobiographical account, which accuses society of allowing a seduced woman no hope of reform. The daughter equally becomes a victim of prejudice when her lover's family opposes their marriage because of her illegitimacy, and she is pursued and finally raped by a baronet. After this she, like her mother before her, can find no harbour in respectable society and she wastes away from the effects of poverty, disease, and time spent in debtors' prison. Like *Emma Courtney*, *The Victim of Prejudice* is written in the sentimental and declamatory style then current. It shows an interesting use of symbolic incident when Mary's childhood threat of stealing 'a large and tempting cluster of grapes, of uncommon ripeness, bloom and beauty' from the lord of the manor, carried out to prove her courage and her love for the playmate William, leads to her receiving sexual attention for the first time in her life. The novel is similar in its concerns to Wollstonecraft's *The Wrongs of Woman*, published posthumously a year earlier. MH had remained a close friend of Wollstone-craft's, and she and another writer, Eliza Fenwick, helped nurse Wollstonecraft before her death in 1797. After this MH wrote a memoir of her friend in the *Monthly Magazine*, praising her 'active and incessant' efforts on behalf of women. MH's feminist ideas were also expressed in the *Appeal to the Men of Great Britain in Behalf of Women*, published anonymously in 1798. A second memoir of Wollstonecraft in the *Annual Necrology for 1797-8*, published in 1800, is rather more reserved about its subject, seeming to consider her as one of MH's own noble but erring heroines: 'Persons of the most exquisite genius have probably the greatest sensibility, consequently the strongest passions, by the fervour of which they are too often betrayed into error.' By the turn of the century, with strong reaction in England against all kinds of radical ideas, MH was obliged to modify her feminism. However, her six-volume *Female Biography* (1803) still shows her commitment to 'the happiness of my sex, and their advancement in the grand scale of rational and social existence,' and includes nearly 300 entries for distinguished women of the past. By this time MH was acquainted with Crabb Robinson, who remained a lifelong friend, Southey, who gave her advice about publication, and Coleridge, who did not like her and objected to hearing intellectual talk from 'a thing, ugly and petticoated'. She also knew Charles and Mary Lamb. She published little in the following years, which she spent partly with her brother and family in Wandsworth and partly in a school at Oundle, Northamptonshire. She was in Hot Wells, Clifton, in 1814. In 1824 she settled in London, where she died at the age of 83. Her last books were moral tales for the poor: *The Brothers, or, Consequences* (1815) and *Family Annals, or, The Sisters* (1817). *Memoirs of Queens* (1821) was based on *Female Biography*.

MH's fame was short lived. During the 1790s reactions to her were polarized on political grounds. To the liberal *Monthly Magazine* she was 'a favourite author,' with 'strong natural powers, and an unrestricted freedom of thinking'. The *Critical Review*, though it praised her second novel for some passages 'scarcely inferior to the effusions of Rousseau,' criticized her 'splendid irrita-bility', and attacks on social institutions. The *British Critic*, reviewing *Emma Courtney*, advised her that if she would stop mingling exclusively with the radicals who had formed her ideas, she would not only write more entertain-ingly but be better able 'to discharge the duties of her sex'.   JANE SPENCER

Works: Cursory Remarks on An Enquiry into the Expediency and Propriety of Public or Social Worship (1792); Letters and Essays, Moral and Miscellaneous (1793); Memoirs of Emma Courtney (1796); Appeal to the Men of Great Britain in Behalf of Women (attrib.) (1798); The Victim of Prejudice (1799); Female Biography (1803); Historical Dialogues for Young Persons (1806-8); Memoirs of Queens Illustrious and Celebrated (1821); The Love Letters of Mary Hays, ed. A. F. Wedd (1925); The Fate of the Fenwicks, ed. A. F. Wedd (1927).

References: Adams, M. R., 'Mary Hays, disciple of William Godwin', *PMLA* 60 (1940); Allibone; Luria, G., 'Introduction' to *Appeal . . .* (1974); Moers, E., *Literary Women* (1976); Pollin, B. K., 'Mary Hays on women's rights in the *Monthly Magazine*', *Etudes Anglaises* 24 (1971); Todd; Todd, J., *The Sign of Angellica: women, writing and fiction 1660-1800* (1989).

Haywood, Eliza

b. 1693, London; d. 1756, London

Novelist, playwright, translator, periodical writer, poet

Little is know about EH's life, although she alludes in her later work to a past 'engrossed by a hurry of promiscuous diversions'. Probably the most prolific and versatile writer of her age, she never turned her hand to autobiography, nor sought to vindicate herself from the scandalous accusations her contemporaries levelled at her.

The daughter of a London shopkeeper named Fowler, she evidently learnt French and Spanish since her works include seven 'translations' from these languages. Yet she displays little or no knowledge of the classics, and complained in the dedication to *The Fatal Secret* (1724) that she was, like most women, 'depriv'd of those Advantages of Education which the other Sex enjoy'. She married Valentine Haywood, a clergyman with a living in Norfolk, and their son was baptized in London in 1711. There are no records of other children by her husband or any other man.

Her first interest was in the theatre, where there was a strong, if recent, tradition of women playwrights and actresses by the 1700s. In 1715 she may have appeared as Chloë in *Timon of Athens, or, The Man Hater* at Smock-Alley, Dublin. Her first novel, *Love in Excess* (1719), published in three parts, was an instant success and went into four editions before 1724 when it was published in her *Works*. Along with Swift's *Gulliver's Travels* and Defoe's *Robinson Crusoe* it was one of the best selling works of fiction before the publication of Richardson's *Pamela* in 1740. *Love in Excess*, the story of a young rake, Delmont, his amours, unhappy marriage, and eventual conversion to true love at the hands of his young ward, Melliora, has all the hallmarks of EH's writing. It combines conventions from the idealized world of the French romance with the earthiness of the Italian novella. The elevated language and semi-religious language of love common to the aristocratic romances of late seventeenth-century France, such as Madeleine de Scudéry's *Clelia*, is now employed for the purposes of voyeuristic eroticism. Amena's seduction at the hands of Delmont is a typical example of EH's rhetoric of desire in which female sexuality is presented as an irresistible unconscious force: 'he found her panting Heart beat Measures of Consent, her heaving Breast swell to be press'd by his, and every Pulse confess a Wish to yield; her Spirits all dissolv'd, sunk in a Lethargy of Love.'

Letters, their exchange, loss, and interception, are an important plot device in *Love In Excess*. In 1720, EH capitalized on the popularity of the letter form for the novel and the pathos of the Portuguese style by producing a loose translation of Edmé Boursault's *Lettres Nouvelles* (1699) entitled *Letters from a Lady of Quality to a Chevalier*. The second part was published by subscription and the list gives an interesting indication of her readership in that 123 out of the 309 subscribers were female. Few of the names are distinguished, which suggests that EH was catering to a middle-class readership. This was EH's only venture into subscription publication and, at a cost of one to three shillings for an octavo novel, her works were obviously out of the financial reach of labouring women or men. The *Letters* are accompanied by a long 'Discourse concerning Writings of this Nature' by EH, warning her female readers about the dangers of corresponding with men.

In January 1721 the *Post-Boy* carried an advertisement in which her husband announced that EH had left him in November 1720 without his consent and disclaimed any responsibility for her debts. From this point onwards, EH published novel after novel at great speed. Her biographer,George Whicher, lists sixty-seven single works by her over a period of thirty-seven years. Clearly, writing was her sole source of subsistence. She could command only one to ten guineas per book from her publisher, so rapid output was a necessity. Dedications to wealthy patrons might have won her an extra guinea per book.

The stage was slightly more lucrative, if a less secure livelihood. In March 1721 EH's tragedy *The Fair Captive* was first performed at Lincoln's Inn Fields. EH appeared as Mrs Graspall in her own comedy *A Wife to Be Lett* in August 1723 at Drury Lane when the actress fell sick. The prologue boldly admonished her 'Criticks! be dumb to-night – no Skill display;/ A dangerous Woman-Poet wrote the Play.' EH maintained her interest in the stage throughout her career, although it was never her main means of subsistence. In 1729 a tragedy by EH, *Frederic, Duke of Brunswick-Lunenburgh* was performed at Lincoln's Inn Fields. In 1730 EH played the part of Achilles' ex-mistress, Briscis, in William Hatchett's play *Rival Father*, and in 1736 she appeared as Mrs Arden in *Arden of Faversham*, a play she may have adapted herself. In 1733, EH and Hatchett collaborated on a highly successful adaptation of Fielding's *Tragedy of Tragedies*.

However, it was her novels for which she became (in)famous. In 1724 alone she published ten 'romances' and a translation. Her publisher, William Rufus Chetwood, further increased his profits by rapid re-editions and collections of her works. In the early 1740s, EH herself tried a short-lived publishing venture. She set up at the Sign of Fame in Covent Garden, and published a miscellaneous collection of attacks on Richardson's *Pamela* entitled *Anti-Pamela* in 1741 along with a French translation, *The Busy-Body*.

EH's works divide into two periods. An unaccountable publishing 'silence' (she may have published anonymously or pseudonymously) between the years 1728 and 1744 has generated a series of myths about her literary and personal career. When she reappeared on the literary stage with her periodical *The Female Spectator* and a novel, *The Fortunate Foundlings*, her style had undergone a distinctive shift in moral perspective. Her salacious and exotic stories of seduction and betrayal were replaced by moral speculation upon London society and domestic love. In *The Female Spectator* she attacks the authors of 'Romances, Novels, and Plays' who 'dress their Cupid up in Roses' and make 'every woe that Love occasions, appear a Charm'. Clara Reeve in *The Progress of Romance* (1785) saw this change as a moral conversion, stating that 'she employed the latter part of her life in expiating the offences of the former'. It might equally well have been a response to the changes in the reading market that Richardson's *Pamela* occasioned. Romances were now out of fashion and moral realism had become the order of the day.

EH's disappearance from the publishing scene coincided with Alexander Pope's aggressive attack upon her in his 1728 *Dunciad*. EH is the prize for which the two publishers Chetwood and Curll compete in the goddess Dulness's 'Olympic' games. Pope's description of her with 'Two babes of love close clinging to her waste' has led critics to assume that EH had two illegitimate children. It seems more likely, however, that the two 'babes of love' are EH's two scandal novels, *Memoirs of a Certain Island* (1724) and *The Court of Carimania* (1726), to which Pope refers in his footnote, attacking the 'profligate licentiousness of those shameless Scribblers' of scandal fiction. Pope was offended by EH's portrayal of George II's mistress, Mrs Henrietta Howard, as Ismonda in *The Court of Carimania*. EH's scandal novels are deeply indebted to those of Mary Delarivier Manley. Like Manley, she attacked Sarah, Duchess of Marlborough in her *Memoirs of a Certain Island*, the very title of which echoed her predecessor's *New Atalantis*. However, her later scandal novel, *Adventures of Eovaai*, was dedicated to the duchess. In this work EH joined Henry Fielding's campaign against the prime minister, Walpole, by presenting him as the evil magician and minister Ochihatou in pursuit of her heroine's sexual favours by fair means or foul. More generally, EH's debt to Manley lay in her use of the seduction and betrayal formula of amatory fiction and its concomitant moral symbol of the embattled virgin to dramatize political conflict and propagandize on behalf of Tory ideology. She seems to have been more at home with Manley's 'gossip-mongering' vein than in full-blown satire of major political events, as the considerable success of her *Bath-Intrigues* (1726), a series of letters from the popular watering place concerning minor dignitaries and celebrities, indicates.

Also like Manley, EH seems to have had a number of troubled literary friendships. In particular, Richard Savage, who had praised her amatory fiction in verses prefixed to *Love in Excess* and *The Rash Resolve* (1724), joined Pope's *Dunciad* lobby in 1732 criticizing EH for 'writing Novels of Intrigue, to teach young Heiresses the art of running away with Fortune-hunters, and scandalizing Persons of the highest Worth and Distinction'. In her preface to the *Memoirs of Baron de Brosse* (1725), EH laid out the critical double bind the successful woman writer faced: 'If her Writings are considerable enough to make any Figure in the World, Envy pursues her with weary'd Diligence; and, if on the contrary, she only writes what is forgot as soon as read, Contempt is all the Reward.'

She defended her writing practice by claiming that love was a topic suitable to women which 'requires no Aids of Learning, no general Conversation, no Application' (*The Fatal Secret*, 1724) and indeed her greatest success lay in her short romances of passion. Crammed with event, these stories frequently act out a conflict between evil seductress and innocent maiden, offering a variety of strategies for survival in the dangerous world of love to her women readers. EH allows her readers to indulge the pleasures of sexual fantasy but always ensures that female sexuality is suitably punished. In *Idalia* (1723) she warns that 'guilty Pleasures are never of any long Continuance; the inconsiderate Heart, which quitting Virtue places its whole Felicity in *Love*, sooner or *later* must confess the Error and curse in unavailing Penitence the luscious Crime which lured them on to ruin.' EH's early heroines are surrounded by a conspiracy to love, pursued by ardent admirers, unprotected by parents and society. Nature itself is an accomplice to seduction. In *Love in Excess*, the young Amena is unable to resist Delmont's advances since 'all Nature seem'd to favour his Design, the Pleasantness of the Place, the Silence of the Night, the Sweetness of the Air'. In *Fantomina* (1724) and *The Masqueraders* (1724), her heroines manage to escape, at least temporarily, the position of victim commonly offered in her novels by learning to adopt the disguises and manipulative strategies of the male rake.

EH maintained a thoroughly cynical view of male desire throughout her fiction. She argues in her treatise on love, *Reflections on the Various Effects of Love* (1726), which consists of a loose series of exemplary narratives tempered with some amateur philosophy, that the 'Winter of Indifference and Neglect . . . rarely, if ever, fails to succeed the sultry Summer of too fierce Desire in Man's unconstant Heart'. In her later work, the eroticized seduction scenes are considerably weakened and her concerns become more social and domestic. She produced a number of conduct books for instance, *A Present for a Serving-Maid* (1743), *The Wife* (1756) and *The Husband* (1756). Her fiction shows the influence of Richardson and Fielding in particular, and looks forward to the concerns of women novelists such as Fanny Burney in its discussion of female propriety. Her heroines no longer face death or decline as a result of indulging their sexual passions. Rather their discretion is tested and social disgrace is the major threat to their futures. Exotic and romantic names are replaced by names that indicate character such as Mr Trueworth, Miss Forward, Mrs Marlove, etc. *The Fortunate Foundlings* (1744) and *Life's Progress through the Passions* (1748) both indicate EH's new direction in her writings. In the former, Louisa's romantic development is contrasted with the martial achievements of her foundling brother, Horatio. In the latter, the hero Natura is followed from childhood to a peaceful death in order to show the growth and management of the different passions in a representative man. The fruition of her mature powers is shown in EH's *The History of Miss Betsy Thoughtless* (1751), the story of a young girl's romantic disasters and final happiness in the arms of her first lover, Mr Trueworth, following a disastrous marriage to the mean-spirited Mr Munden. The *Monthly Review* clearly found it tame after EH's earlier work, asking 'how can we greatly interest ourselves in the fortune of one whose character and conduct are neither amiable nor infamous, and which we can neither admire, nor love, nor pity, nor be diverted with?' However, it was to be EH's best-remembered work and it does demonstrate a mature realism without the moral insipidity of much domestic fiction of the period. *The History of Jemmy and Jenny Jessamy* (1752) commences with the engagement of EH's hero and heroine and then proceeds to follow their lives as a dishonest friend, mishaps, and misunderstandings threaten the prospect of their marriage. Finally the pair are married and EH's new moral perspective is shown in her conclusion that leaves them 'to enjoy, in calm retirement, the more pure and lasting sweets of a well govern'd and perfect tenderness'.

Despite the seeming gulf between these novels and her earlier work, there is a remarkable consistency in EH's concern 'to inculcate into young girls all imaginable precaution, in regard to their behaviour towards those of another sex' (*Betsy Thoughtless*). If her aim is to prepare her young female readers for the perils of romantic love in both cases, her method is different since in *Betsy Thoughtless* she adds, 'yet I know not if it is not an error to dwell too much upon that topic.' Her most successful venture into periodical writing, *The Female Spectator*, pursues a similar vein, presenting itself as the mature deliberations of a reformed woman, offering her worldly knowledge to innocent and unsuspecting women readers. *The Female Spectator*, like its illustrious male counterpart, had a fictional editorial board which was representative of the new hegemonic class, a married lady of good family, a widow of quality, and the beautiful daughter of a wealthy merchant. Published monthly from April 1744 to May 1746, EH's periodical addressed a variety of issues of interest to women, from masquerades to natural philosophy. It printed 'letters' from male and female correspondents asking advice from the 'Female Sage' or laying out their own educational and moral plans for the female sex. A letter from 'Cleora' is a particularly powerful and considered attack upon women's oppression, insisting, 'There is, undoubtedly, no sex in souls, and we are as able to receive and practise the impressions, not only of virtue and religion, but also of those sciences which the men engross to themselves, as they can be.' EH's other ventures into the periodical market for women were *The Parrot*, published weekly from August to October 1746, and *The Young Lady* (three numbers in January 1756).

EH continued to write up to her death in February 1756. *Clementina* (1768), *A new Present for a Servant-Maid* (1772) and *The History of Leonora Meadowson*

(1778) were all published posthumously. However, despite her ventures into domestic and sentimental fiction in the 1740s she was best remembered and finally damned for her early romances of passion. The *Monthly Review* dismissed a reprint of *The Agreeable Caledonian* in 1768 with the comment that it was 'written in a tawdry style, now utterly exploded'. ROSALIND BALLASTER

Selected works: *Love in Excess,* (1719–20); (trans.), *Letters From a Lady of Quality to a Chevalier* (1720); *The Fair Captive* (1721); *The British Recluse, or, The Secret History of Cleomira* (1722); *The Injur'd Husband, or, The Mistaken Resentment* (1722); *Idalia, or, The Unfortunate Mistress* (1723); *Lasselia, or, The Self-Abandoned* (1723); *The Rash Resolve, or, The Untimely Discovery* (1724); *The Surprise, or Constancy Rewarded* (1724); *The Fatal Secret, or, Constancy in Distress* (1724); *The Masqueraders, or, Fatal Curiosity* (part 1 1724, part 2 1725); *The Force of Nature, or, The Lucky Disappointment* (1724); *Fantomina, or, Love in a Maze* (1724); *Bath-Intrigues in Four Letters to a Friend in London* (1725); *The Tea-Table, or, A Conversation between Some Polite Persons of both Sexes at a Lady's Visiting Day* (part 1 1725, part 2 1726); *The Dumb Projector: Being a Surprising Account of a Trip to Holland Made by Mr Duncan Campbell* (1725); *Memoirs of the Baron de Brosse* (1725); *Fatal Fondness, or, Love Its Own Opposer* (1725); (trans.), *Mary Stuart, Queen of Scots* (1725); *The Mercenary Lover, or, The Unfortunate Heiress* (1726); *The Distress'd Orphan, or, Love in a Mad-house* (1726); *Reflections on the Various Effects of Love* (1726); *The City Jilt, or, The Alderman Turned Beau* (1726); *The Double Marriage, or, The Fatal Release* (1726); *The Secret History of the Present Intrigues of the Court of Carimania* (1727); *Letters From the Palace of Fame* (1727); *The Fruitless Enquiry* (1727); (trans.), *The Life of Madam de Villesache* (1727); *The Perplex'd Duchess, or, Treachery Rewarded* (1727); (trans.), *Love in its Variety* (1727); *Philidore and Placentia, or, L'Amour Trop Delicat* (1727); *The Agreeable Caledonian, or, Memoirs of Signora di Morella, a Roman Lady,* (part 1 1728, part 2, 1729); *Irish Artifice* (1728); *Persecuted Virtue, or, The Cruel Lover* (1728); (trans.), *The Disguised Prince, or, The Beautiful Parisian* (part 1 1728, part 2 1729); *Frederick, Duke of Brunswick-Lunenburgh* (1729); *The Fair Hebrew, or, A True but Secret History of Two Jewish Ladies . . .* (1728); (trans.), *Mrs Haywood's Select Collection of Novels and Histories, Written by the Most Celebrated Authors, in Several Languages. All newly Translated from the Originals by Several Hands* (1729); *Love Letters on All Occasions Lately Passed between Persons of Distinction* (1730); *Secret Memoirs of the Late Mr Duncan Campbell* (1732); *The Opera of Operas, or, Tom Thumb the Great,* with songs by E. H. and W. Hatchett (1733); *Adventures of Eovaii, Princess of Ijaveo: A Pre-Adamitical History* (1736); (trans.), *The Virtuous Villager, or, The Virgin's Victory* (1742); *A Present for a Servant Maid* (1743); *The Fortunate Foundlings* (1744); *The Female Spectator,* in monthly numbers (1744–6), and then in 44 vols (1747); *The Parrot* (1746); *Life's Progress through the Passions, or, The Adventures of Natura* (1748); *Epistles for the Ladies* (1749); *Dalinda* (1749); *The History of Miss Betsy Thoughtless* (1751); *The History of Jemmy and Jenny Jessamy* (1753); *The Invisible Spy* (1755); *The Wife* (1756); *The Husband, in Answer to the Wife* (1756); *The History of Leonora Meadowson* (1778).

References: *DNB*; MacCarthy, B., *Women Writers: Their Contributions to the English Novel 1621–1744* (1944); Richetti, J. J., *Popular Fiction before Richardson: Narrative Patterns 1700–39* (1969); Schofield, M. A., *Quiet Rebellion: The Fictional Heroines of Eliza Fowler Haywood* (1982); Schofield, M. A., 'Descending angels, salubrious sluts and petty prostitutes in Haywood's fiction,' in M. A. Schofield and C. Macheski (eds), *Fetter'd or Free? British Women Novelists 1670–1815* (1985); Todd; Todd, *The Sign of Angellica: women, writing and fiction 1660–1800* (1989) Whicher, G. F., *The Life and Romances of Mrs Eliza Haywood* (1915).

Hemans, Felicia

b. 23 September 1795, Liverpool; d. 16 May 1835, Dublin

Poet, hymn writer, essayist

FH was the fifth of seven children, the daughter of George Browne, a merchant of Irish ancestry, and Felicity Wagner, of German and Italian descent. Owing to financial troubles, the Browne family moved before FH was 7 to Gwrych, near Abergele in North Wales. She was tutored by her mother and later by friends and neighbours. In her first book of poems, published in Liverpool when she was 15, she shows her love of family and nature, her spirituality and her facility in composing in French. The charm and tenderness of her youthful verse were qualities central to her mature poetry as well. In 1809, FH met her future husband, Captain Alfred Hemans, an Irishman, who served in the Royal Welch Fusiliers with her brothers. When FH married in 1812, she had published three books of verse, *Poems* (1808), *England and Spain, or, Valour and Patriotism: A Poem* (1808), a narrative poem inspired by her brothers' participation in the Peninsular Campaign, and *Domestic Affections and Other Poems* (1812), a collection which shows greater fluency with poetic forms but little depth of thought. The topical nature of her early writings illustrates FH's lifelong interest in current affairs.

Between 1812 and 1818 FH bore five sons and published three books, *The Restoration of Works of Art in Italy* (1816), *Modern Greece* (1817), and *Translations from Camoens and other Poets* (1818). *Modern Greece* is an ambitious narrative poem about the Greek Revolution which suffers from a lack of first-hand knowledge of the situation. Byron, upon receiving a copy of the poem from his bookseller, Murray, angrily wrote him to send no more verse by this 'Mrs He-Woman'. Shortly after the birth of her fifth son, Charles Isidore Hemans, who was to become a noted antiquarian, her marriage ended and the captain departed for Rome. Although he never saw FH again, the separation was amicable. The precise reason for the end of the marriage is unclear, but it has been suggested that the captain's pension from the army was too small to support his family and he left to ease the financial burden on his wife and her family, with whom they were forced to live. FH continued to write while raising the children. In 1819, she won a prize for her poem *Wallace's Invocation to Bruce* and in the same year she published *Tales and Historic Scenes*. In 1820 *The Sceptic*, regarded as her finest religious poem, was published, and in 1822 *Welsh Melodies*. In 1823, FH turned briefly to playwrighting. Her *Vespers of Palermo*, a five-act tragedy, was performed with some success first at Covent Garden and then in Edinburgh. Her other two plays, *The Siege of Valencia* (1823) and *De Chantillion* (n.d.), were never performed. In 1825, FH began studying German and she published two more books of verse, *Lays of Many Lands* and *The Forest Sanctuary*, the latter being her favourite among her works, concerning the mental and physical suffering of a Spaniard suffering religious persecution.

In 1827, after the death of her mother and in declining health herself, FH moved to Wavertree, near Liverpool, then in 1831 to Dublin. During this period, she published four books, *Hymns for Childhood* (1827 US, 1834 UK), *Casabianca* (1828), published as part of the second edition of *The Forest Sanctuary*, *Records of Woman* (1828), dedicated to Joanna Baillie and based on stories of noble women found in D'Israeli's *Curiosities of Literature*, and *Songs of the Affections* (1830). EH was also a contributor of poetry and essays on foreign literature to the *Edinburgh Monthly Magazine* and *Blackwood's*, among other periodicals. Prior to her death, she published *Hymns on the Works of Nature for the Use of Children* (1833), *National Lyrics and Songs for Music* (1834), and *Scenes and Hymns of Life with Other Religious Poems* (1834). She was buried in St Anne's churchyard in Dublin.

A contemporary of Wordsworth, Byron, and Shelley, FH owes more to the eighteenth century than to her own. Her poetry is distinguished by its clear syntax, good diction, and her competent use of established verse forms. Her choice of subjects, exotic settings, and celebration of religious and domestic themes, along with her clear style, made her one of the most popular poets of her day, although today much of her writing seems sentimental and superficial. Writing in 1853 Frederic Rowton described her works as 'a perfect embodiment of a woman's soul: – I would say that they are intensely feminine. The delicacy, the softness, the pureness, the quick observant vision, the ready sensibility, the devotedness, the faith of a woman's nature find in Mrs Hemans their ultra representative. . . .'

B. E. SCHNELLER

Selected works: Poems (1808); *England and Spain, or, Valour and Patriotism: A Poem* (1808); *Domestic Affections and Other Poems* (1812); *The Restoration of Works of Art in Italy* (1816); *Modern Greece* (1817); *Tales and Historic Scenes* (1819); *Wallace's Invocation to Bruce* (1819); *The Sceptic* (1820); *Dartmoor* (1820); *Welsh Melodies* (1822); *Lays of Many Lands* (1825); *The Forest Sanctuary* (1825); *Hymns for Childhood* (1827); *Casabianca* (1828); *Records of Woman* (1828); *Songs of the Affections* (1830); *Hymns on the Works of Nature for the Use of Children* (1833); *National Lyrics and Songs for Music* (1834); *Scenes and Hymns of Life and Other Religious Poems* (1834); collected works: *The Poetical Works of Hemans, Heber and Polock*, ed. Crissy and Goodman (1831); *Works*, ed. H. Brown Hughes (1839); *Poems*, ed. R. Griswold (1875).

References: BA (19); Chorley, H.F., *Memorials of Mrs Hemans* (1836); Courtney, J. E., *The Adventurous Thirties: A Chapter in the Women's Movement* (1933); *DNB*; Hale, Mrs, *Woman's Record, or, Sketches of All Distinguished Women* (1870); *OCCL*; Reiman, D. H., 'Introduction' to *Poems* (1978); Rowton, F., *The Female Poets of Great Britain* (1853).

Heyer, Georgette

b. 16 March 1902, London; d. 1974
Novelist

GH was educated at seminary schools and Westminster College, London. She married in 1925 and lived in East Africa from then until 1928, and in Yugoslavia from 1928 to 1929. She was the author of nearly sixty historical romances and detective novels, the first of which was written at the age of 17.

GH is best known for her historical romances, most of which are set in the Regency period. A careful historical researcher, she filled her novels with details of Regency fashion, manners, and slang and created a further sense of authenticity through the introduction of historical figures (Beau Brummell, the Prince Regent) among her fictional characters. Her romantic plots usually employ the stock figures of the aristocratic rake, the virtuous, though spirited, heroine, and a supporting cast of Regency fops and blades. GH claimed Jane Austen as her literary model, and sought to emulate her ironic tone, though there is little of Austen's social satire in her work.

GH's dozen detective novels are less well known, although they contribute interestingly to the development of the detective genre in the 1920s and 1930s. Set in the confined worlds of the country house or the London party, the family becomes the source and location of the drama, and inheritance is usually revealed as the motive for murder. Sub-plots are reminiscent of GH's Regency romances, with the hero-rake being ultimately cleared of suspicion and declaring his love for the heroine.

GH's writing has usually been criticized for its conventional plots and characterizations and 'escapist' qualities, or alternatively lauded for its wit and period 'feel'. Such discussions have overlooked other aspects of her novels which link her firmly to a tradition of women's popular romances, and in which the portrayal of relationships between the sexes suggests a different reason for her popularity. For example, in one of her best-known historical romances, *Regency Buck* (1935) the heroine is 'tamed' by her guardian, and love and marriage come with female submission to the stern but dashing hero. Sexual fantasy is arguably a more important element in GH's fiction than has been allowed for.

LAURA MARCUS

Selected works: *The Black Moth* (1921); *The Great Roxhythe* (1922); *Simon the Coldheart* (1925); *The Masqueraders* (1928); *The Barren Court* (1930); *Footsteps in the Dark* (1932); *The Convenient Marriage* (1934); *Regency Buck* (1935); *The Talisman Ring* (1936); *An Infamous Army* (1937); *Royal Escape* (1937); *The Spanish Bride* (1940); *The Corinthian* (1940); *Beau Wyndham* (1941); *The Reluctant Widow* (1946); *Arabella* (1949); *The Quiet Gentleman* (1951); *Cotillion* (1953); *Bath Tangle* (1955); *Sprig Muslin* (1956); *April Lady* (1957); *A Civil Contract* (1961); *Freedom* (1965); *Lady of Quality* (1972).

References: *CA*; *DNB*; Hodge, J. A., *The Private World of Georgette Heyer* (1984); *The Times Literary Supplement* (18 April 1935, 12 June 1937, 18 January 1957).

Hobbes, John Oliver

b. 3 November 1867, Chelsea, near Boston, Massachusetts; d. 13 August 1906, London

Novelist, dramatist, journalist

Witty, fragile, sensitive, and stylish, JOH was one of the most scintillating stars in the literary firmament of the 1890s. The eldest child of a wealthy American businessman, John Morgan Richards, and his wife, Laura Arnold, JOH came to England as a baby in 1868 when the family settled in London. She was educated locally and at a finishing school in Paris, and was presented at court in 1886.

In February 1887 she married Reginald Craigie, a handsome young banker possessed of considerable vanity, a roving eye, and a passion for drink. JOH was ill on her honeymoon and unhappy ever after. In 1891 she left him and, with her only child John, returned to her parents. She always remained close to her father, but she suffered continually from her mother's domineering and eccentric behaviour.

Study and writing were her refuge; she attended lectures at University College, London, reading Latin and Greek, and writing her highly successful first novel *Some Emotions and a Moral*, published by Fisher Unwin in his Pseudonym Library in 1891. In 1892 she became a Catholic, to the horror of her Nonconformist family (she always claimed she had read herself into the Church). She then turned to playwriting, which brought her a warm friendship with Ellen Terry and a tempestuous relationship with George Moore. Her first comedy, *Journeys End in Lovers Meeting*, was well received, and, after Gladstone's cataract operation, she was summoned to his sofa to read her play as a tonic for the invalid.

In 1895 she was divorced; parental pressure on her to remarry was strong, and she had no shortage of admirers, Lord Crewe, Lord Curzon, and Dr (later Bishop) Welldon being the most distinguished. But JOH opted for Catholic chastity and dedication to her profession. She was president of the Society of Women Journalists 1895–6, went on lecture tours and, invited to India by Lord Curzon, attended the great Delhi Durbar of 1903, reporting on it for several newspapers. Her health was poor, and after her travels she would return completely exhausted to her parents' London home or to their castle near Ventnor on the Isle of Wight, often taking to her bed for weeks on end and from there dictating her novels and plays to her secretary. Constant friction with her mother wore her out too, and both JOH and her sister made several suicide attempts.

An American tour in 1905–6 (undertaken to avoid a family Christmas) proved so fatiguing that she broke her contract, returned home and suffered a mild heart attack in March 1906. In July of that year Curzon's wife died, and maternal pressure on JOH to remarry was redoubled. A few weeks later, after a weekend of 'family gales' on the Isle of Wight, JOH was found dead in bed by the housekeeper at the Richardses' London home. The official verdict was heart failure, but George Moore was not slow to spread stories of an overdose. In 1908 Curzon unveiled a memorial plaque to her in University College, and recalled the charm of her personality, the brilliance of her conversation and the clever 'dissection of soul' in her writings.

Today her comedies, although sparkling with Wildean epigrams, seem too lightweight and superficial to merit revival – but her novels contain more than that peculiar blend of faith and frivolity so popular in the 1890s; they have, besides their flashes of wit and cynicism, a depth of philosophical thoughtfulness, a rather sad wisdom, and a consistently good style.

Her first novel broke new ground with its offbeat title and oblong-shaped volume, no larger than a cheque book. Its story of disappointed idealists and ill-assorted marriages set the theme for most of JOH's subsequent fiction. Her 'Catholic' novel, *The School for Saints* (1897), and its sequel, *Robert Orange* (1900), offer a sensitive portrayal of the conflict between passion and faith, and her last novel, *The Dream and the Business* (1906), shows a clash between the Nonconformist and Catholic mentalities, wittily described, crisply argued and tinged with that subtle bitter-sweet flavour characteristic of her work.

MARGARET MAISON

Selected works: *Some Emotions and a Moral* (1891); *The Sinner's Comedy* (1892); *A Study of Temptations* (1893); *Journeys End in Lovers Meeting* (1894); *The Gods, Some Mortals and Lord Wickenham* (1895); *The Herb-Moon: A Fantasia* (1896); *The School for Saints* (1897); *The Ambassador* (1898); 'Osbern and Ursyne', *Anglo-Saxon Review* 1 (June 1899); *The Wisdom of the Wise* (1900); *Talks about Temperaments* (1902); *Love and the Soul Hunters* (1902); *Imperial India* (1903); *Dowries* (1904); *Letters from a Silent Study* (1904); *The Science of Life* (1904); *The Vineyard* (1904); *The Flute of Pan* (1905); *The Art of Portraiture* (Dante Society Lectures), (1906); *The Dream and the Business* (1906).

References: Archer, W., *Real Conversations* (1904); Baring, M., *Have you Anything to Declare?* (1936); Brown, W. F., *Through Windows of Memory* (1946); Chesterton, G. K., *Heretics* (1905); Clark, B. H., *Intimate Portraits* (1951); Clarke, I., *Six Portraits* (1935); Colby, V., *The Singular Anomaly* (1970); Courtney, W. L., *The Feminine Note in Fiction* (1904); Gerber, H. E., *George Moore in Transition*

(1968); Hind, C. L., *Authors and I* (1921); Hind, C. L., *Naphtali* (1926); Howells, W. D., 'The Fiction of John Oliver Hobbes', *North American Review* 31 December 1966); Maison, M., *Search Your Soul, Eustace* (1961); Maison, M., *John Oliver Hobbes* (1976); Mitchell, S., *George Moore* (1916); Mix, K. L., *A Story in Yellow* (1960); Proctor, Z., *Life and Yesterday* (1960); Richards, J. M., *With John Bull and Jonathan*, (1905); Richards, J. M., *The Life of John Oliver Hobbes* (1911); Richards, J. M., *Almost Fairyland* (1914); Terry, E., *The Story of My Life* (1908).

Holden, Molly

b. 7 September 1927, London
Poet, writer of children's novels
MH was educated at Commonweal Grammar School, Swindon, Wiltshire, and at King's College, London. She graduated with a BA (Hons) in English in 1948 and obtained an MA in 1951. In 1949 she married Alan Holden; they have two children. Since 1964 she has suffered from multiple sclerosis. She received an Arts Council Award in 1970 and the Cholmondley Award in 1972.

MH has written three novels for young readers, successfully depicting family relationships and dealing unsentimentally with the difficulties of living in harsh surroundings or in turbulent communities. Their plots are weak, however, and the narration lacks pace, problems which, together with a dominantly bleak mood, have prevented the books appealing strongly to young readers. MH's main achievement is as a rural poet. She writes quietly but intensely, conveying an impression of strong involvement with the scenes and people described. Her poems are characterized by their accurate observation, careful selection of details appropriate to the theme or mood to be captured, and vivid, economical turns of phrase. Her choices and treatments of subject are free from nostalgia or romanticizing.

Her verse-forms are usually free, but disciplined to the demands of her themes. She uses emjambment and the occasional rhyming form effectively to enhance the movement of ideas or to highlight important details. Sometimes slight, but never trivial, the poems progress logically and suggest a sense of an underlying natural order to existence. MH writes in the tradition of Clare and Thomas, although as a woman writing nature poetry in the second half of the twentieth century she has received less critical attention and a narrower readership than her works merit.   JUDITH ALDRIDGE
Selected works: The Bright Cloud (1964); To Make Me Grieve (1968); The Unfinished Feud (1970); Air and Chill Earth (1971); White Rose and Wanderer (1972); Reivers' Weather (1973); A Speckled Bush (1974); The Country Over (1975); New and Selected Poems (1986).
References: Byers, M., 'Cautious vision: recent British poetry by women', in M. Schmidt and G. Lindop (eds), *British Poetry Since 1960* (1972); *CA*; *CP*; *DLB*; Alma, R., 'The poetry of M. Holden', *Poetry Nation* 2 (1974).

Holme, Constance

b. 1880, Milnthorpe, Westmorland; d. 1955, Arnside, Westmorland
Novelist
CH was a member of a family who for generations had acted as Land Agents in Westmorland (now part of Cumbria). In 1916 she married Frederick Punchard, the agent for Underley Hall, Kirkby Lonsdale; the estate was the property of Lord Henry Bentinck, a brother of Lady Ottoline Morrell, who was to

become an admirer of CH's work. The rest of her life was spent in Westmorland.

The first three novels, *Crump Folk Going Home* (1913), *The Lonely Plough* (1914), and *The Old Road from Spain* (1915), provide affectionate but not uncritical portrayals of the social life of the region, centring on the old county families, and on feudal loyalties and relationships as they existed at a time of radical change; they reveal a sympathetic and by no means acquiescent awareness of the limitations of a woman's role in such a world. *The Old Road from Spain* makes effective use of a supernatural theme, and all three novels exhibit a deeply felt response to local landscape and traditions.

Beautiful End (1918), *The Splendid Fairing* (1919), *The Trumpet in the Dust* (1921), and *The Things which Belong—* (1925) differ from their predecessors in concentrating on the lives and aspirations of elderly working people, small farmers, charwomen, and a gardener and his wife. Although conservative in sentiment and presentation, they are technically sophisticated, focusing on the events of a single day and making ingenious and extensive use of flashback in the manner of Virginia Woolf's *Mrs Dalloway*, a technique which CH anticipated by several years. Although her reputation has probably suffered through the excessive compliment that Oxford University Press paid to her when it included all her novels in its World's Classics series, her work is regional only in its setting, and is an example of provincial writing at its most authentic and assured.   GLEN CAVALIERO

Works: *Crump Folk Going Home* (1913); *The Lonely Plough* (1914); *The Old Road from Spain* (1915); *Beautiful End* (1918); *The Splendid Fairing* (1919); *The Trumpet in the Dust* (1921); *The Things which Belong—* (1925); *He-Who-Came?* (1930); *The Wisdom of the Simple* (1937).

References: Cavaliero, G., *The Rural Tradition in the English Novel 1900–1939* (1977).

Holtby, Winifred

b. 23 June 1898, Rudstone, Yorkshire; d. 25 September 1935, London

Novelist, journalist

WH was an intensely active and prolific woman, a journalist, a lecturer, a feminist, and a novelist. She suffered from the competing pulls of her diverse interests and activities, and was caught between the poles of politics and art, between the tug of her own generosity towards friends and the need for the solitude to work. In a letter to her friend, Jean McWilliam, she remarks that she 'was half-smothered by people who all want me to be and say what they want rather than what I want'. Lady Rhondda, editor of *Time and Tide*, recalls that in replying to a request to be literary editor, she said, 'Oh, no, Margaret, I'll do anything else in the world but *not* that, you *know* I can't say "NO" to people.' But in spite of this predilection for granting others' demands, WH had published six novels before she died at the age of 37, enough short stories to fill two volumes, a book of poems, the first English critical study of Virginia Woolf's writing, two works of satire, and a book on women. In addition, she had her play produced, wrote numerous newspaper articles, lectured, and conducted a vigorous lifelong campaign for the rights of blacks in South Africa.

WH's father, David Holtby, was a farmer. Her mother, Alice Holtby, the alderman of East Riding, is commonly regarded as the source of one of the most endearing characters of *South Riding*, Mrs Beddows; WH paid tribute to her mother in the preface. WH was a brilliant student at the Queen Margaret's

School, Scarborough. When she was only 13 she found at a bookseller's a volume of her own poetry, *My Garden and Other Poems*, that her mother had had published for her. She later described this experience: 'I have known since then countless moments of pleasure, several of rapture and a few of pride, but as I walked back to school with my first published work I knew so dazzling an ecstasy of achievement that nothing experienced since has ever approached it.' A sympathetic schoolmistress persuaded WH's parents to send her to Somerville College, Oxford, where her work was interrupted for a year of service during the First World War in the Women's Army Corps. She met Vera Brittain at Oxford, and later they shared a flat; their relationship was the most important of WH's life. When Vera Brittain married, WH shared the couple's home, loving and caring for the children as her own. WH herself loved one man for many years, but they never married, and only became engaged on her deathbed.

WH wrote for the *Manchester Guardian, News Chronicle*, and *Time and Tide*, of which she became director in 1926, and was described as 'the most brilliant journalist of London'. Her journalistic views are surprisingly contemporary. Her lectures on education, for example were directed to developing the individual talent in each person. Her study of Virginia Woolf focused on the political nature of Woolf's writing, the problems of women in wartime, and the antagonistic pulls on women between work and art. Her book on women, published in 1934, is an account of women's position throughout the ages, and especially of their developing status in the twentieth century. The book's imaginative, sparkling writing emphasises its thesis that the history of women is not the record of their relationship to men but the story of their place in the universe. In conclusion, WH emphasizes 'that the inequality of the sexes mainly arises from the deep subconscious belief that women have less right to be at work than men'.

South Riding, WH's masterpiece, is a complex tale which mixes politics and human fortunes. Set in WH's native Yorkshire, in the fictional South Riding, it tells of the regional council and the way its decisions influence a variety of lives. WH wrote in the preface, 'What fascinated me was the discovery that apparently academic and impersonal resolutions passed in a county council were daily revolutionising the lives of men and women whom they affected. The complex tangle of motives prompting public decision, the unforeseen consequences of their enactment in private lives, appeared to me as part of the unseen pattern of the English landscape.' A second theme is the struggle between the old and the new, embodied in the conflict between the conservative Robert Carne and the new school mistress, Sarah Burton, who indefatigably fights for reforms. But the drama is personal too. Carne is obsessed by the hopes that his insane wife will recover. Meanwhile, he worries about his schoolgirl daughter whom he fears has inherited his wife's insanity. He falls in love with Sarah Burton, a strong woman who is constantly overturning conventional views and who works for the unhappy and unfortunate. Mrs Beddows, an older woman and alderman, nurtures Carne and loves him. There are myriad poignant dramas and deftly described characters in this work: the poor, brilliant schoolgirl who must give up her education to care for her younger brothers and sisters; the innkeeper's wife dying of cancer who tries to keep her pain away from her husband; the respectable councilman blackmailed by his lover to whom he has turned because he has not received 'marital comforts'.

Of WH's other novels, *Poor Caroline* and *Mandoa! Mandoa!* are probably her best. *Poor Caroline* tells the ironical story of the Christian Cinema Company, its ridiculous yet indomitable founder Caroline Denton-Smyth, and the way in which both affected the fortunes of a miscellaneous group of people. The protagonist is self-deceiving and has an unbalanced devotion to hopeless projects; yet in some way she remains inspirational. *Mandoa! Mandoa!*, a biting and clever satire, tells of an enterprising travel agency's attempt to advertise an isolated principality in Central Africa. MARTHA SATZ

Selected works: *Anderby Wold* (1923); *The Land of Green Ginger* (1927); *Eutychus, or, The Future of the Pulpit* (1928); *Poor Caroline* (1931); *Virginia Woolf: A Critical Study* (1932); *The Astonishing Island* (1933); *Mandoa! Mandoa!* (1933); *Truth is Not Sober and Other Stories* (1934); *Women and a Changing Civilisation* (1934); *South Riding* (1936); *Pavements at Anderby* (1937); *Letters to a Friend* (1937).

References: Brittain, V., *Testament of Friendship* (1940); Gray, J., 'Hypatia at the helm', in *On Second Thought* (1946); Handley-Taylor, G., *Winifred Holtby: A Concise and Selected Bibliography together with Some Letters*, foreword by Vera Brittain (1955); Heilbrun, C. G., 'Introduction' to *Testament of Friendship* (1981); White, E., *Winifred Holtby as I Knew Her* (1938).

Howard, Elizabeth Jane

b. London, 1923

Novelist, short story writer

EJH was educated privately and trained as an actress. She played at Stratford-upon-Avon and in repertory in Devon. In 1942 she married for the first time. Her third husband, whom she married in 1965, was the novelist Kingsley Amis. Like her first two marriages this ended in divorce, in 1983. EJH has had various occupations; model, radio and television broadcasting, and as an editor first at Chatto & Windus and then at Weidenfeld & Nicolson.

Her first novel, *The Beautiful Visit*, was published in 1950. There is nothing experimental about EJH's writing and she belongs to the straightforward tradition of British novelists. She writes about people rather than social issues. If one considers the period in which she began to write and the social upheaval of the 50s it must have been quite a positive decision not to be influenced by this material. *The Long View* appeared in 1956. It deals with the break-up of a marriage and examines its history from 1950 back through the years to its beginning in 1926. There is a feeling in EJH's writing that one must be constantly aware of others, that hurt to others should be avoided and that a sense of responsibility should predominate.

After Julius appeared in 1965. In it EJH explores, in detail, the concept of guilt; the consequences of one person's actions on other people. The long-dead Julius still casts his shadow over the three women in his life, his wife and two daughters. EJH introduces the people who will enact the drama, analysing them individually and in conjunction with the others. Out of the events of one weekend new alliances are formed; the daughters begin to free themselves from the past and move towards a new life. Only the wife, bereft of husband, lover, daughters, and her carefully constructed life, at last begins to realize that it is she alone who misses Julius. EJH has a delicate touch in dealing with young girls adrift in the world. Equally sympathetic is her handling of the displaced elderly like Major Hawkes in *After Julius*. Her satire and humour are gentle but totally without sentimentality. In *Odd Girl Out* (1972), Arabella, rich and amoral, disrupts the peaceful ordered lives of the Cornhills. Arabella believes that love is everywhere and is hers by right of claiming it or giving it. The Cornhills have been married for ten years and believe that their relationship is inviolate and well-ordered, like many created by EJH. This sense of 'control' regularly recurs in EJH's prose and is frequently an illusion. The linen may be laundered and put neatly away, meals planned and cooked in advance, but the unpredictability of human nature works constantly, directly or indirectly, to undermine this order. Arabella, the catalyst, despite her honesty, her unwillingness to believe in illusion, and her desire to confront the Cornhills with reality, is defeated by their need to believe in what they have constructed, rather than what they could be.

Something in Disguise (1969) is a sinister novel. If EJH has been involved in examining the consequences of one person's actions on others, then here the theme is presented *par excellence*. Having brought up two children on her own May marries Colonel Brown-Lacey, ostensibly a bore but evil underneath. Brown-Lacey is a killer and step by step the truth is unravelled. In the process there are the extra tensions of May's children being alienated and Brown-Lacey's own daughter fleeing the home. This is the force of consequence at its most extreme, driving through conventional life-patterns and ordinary desires.

EJH's taste for the sinister and macabre reappears in the first short story in her collection *Mr Wrong* (1975). She also displays humour and wit in this collection but it is the story of the ordinary girl pursued by the far from ordinary Mr Wrong that sets the tone of the book. From the homely background with the loving parents EJH switches to lonely motorways and the girl turned victim.

ALISON RIMMER

Selected works: *The Beautiful Visit* (1950); *We Are For the Dark: Six Ghost Stories* (with Robert Aickman) (1951); *The Long View* (1956); *Bettina* (with A. R. Helps) (1957); *The Sea Change* (1959); *The Very Edge* (1963); *After Julius* (1965); *Something in Disguise* (1969); *Wife Swapping 7–10.30 PM* (1970); *Odd Girl Out* (1972); *Mr Wrong* (1975); *Howard and Maschler on Food* (with Fay Maschler) (1987).

References: *CA.*

Howitt, Mary

b. 12 March 1799, Coleford, Gloucestershire; d. 30 January 1888, Rome
Novelist, nature writer, writer for children, editor, translator
Second of four children born to strict Quaker parents, Samuel and Ann (*née* Wood) Botham, MH, along with her sister Anna, eighteen months her senior, was at first left with a nursemaid to educate herself. When a servant taught her by example how to write a love letter, at the age of 9, her disapproving father sent both girls to a school run by neighbour Mary Parker, on condition that his daughters should not sit with the other girls for fear of acquiring contaminating ideas and habits. In 1809 the two girls went to a Society of Friends' school in Croydon, then returned shortly to the family home in Uttoxeter because of their mother's serious illness. After her recovery, MH followed her sister to a Friends' school in Sheffield in 1811. In 1812 she returned home to receive instruction briefly from two male tutors and then was left to self-education. Because of the family's strict observance of the Quaker prohibition against art and literature, the Botham daughters had to indulge their growing interest in both surreptitiously. MH's introduction in 1818 to another Quaker, William Howitt, soon led to the revelation of a common interest in literature and the mutual desire to make their livelihoods through writing. They were married in a Quaker ceremony at Uttoxeter in April 1821. They had five surviving children.

After William worked briefly in his own chemist's shop, the couple began to rely on writing, translating, and editing for their income. Their first works, *The Forest Minstrel and Other Poems* (1823) and *The Desolation of Eyam and Other Poems* (1827), were joint productions, as was much of their enormous later literary output; sometimes they shared a title page, often they simply assisted each other. These poems and much of their subsequent work were strongly influenced by the Romantics, of whom they were among the first popularizers. MH's work contains clear echoes of Coleridge and Wordsworth, with whom the Howitts later became friends after Mrs Wordsworth had recovered from an illness in the Howitts' house in 1831. MH recognized Keats's work early on, and she and her husband admired Byron and defended him against calumniators after his death. Later she admired the Pre-Raphaelites.

MH as much as her husband contributed to the family income, which was never large, and to family literary ventures, most notably *Howitt's Journal*, which was devoted, according to 'William and Mary Howitt's Address to their Friends and Readers' in the first number of 2 January 1847, to 'the entertainment, the good, and the advancement of the public'. Because of several problems, including the careless record keeping, the venture lasted only a year and a half and resulted in William Howitt's bankruptcy, wherein even the couple's copyrights were lost. A wage-earning woman who none the less had no legal right to her income, MH was an early supporter of the efforts of her friends, especially Barbara Bodichon, to persuade Parliament in 1856 to enact a Married Women's Property Act; the signed petitions were pasted together by MH and Octavia Hill. Her interest in the rights of women was part of her lifelong concern for working conditions in the factories, the cause of peace, political reform, and comprehensive education. Among her other friends was Elizabeth Gaskell, who also signed the petition and whose earliest stories were published in *Howitt's Journal* and, although she was not named, in the pages of two of William Howitt's most famous works, *The Rural Life of England* (in the second and subsequent editions) and *Visits to Remarkable Places*. In her *Autobiography*, MH proudly notes the encouragement they gave to Gaskell on her first novel, *Mary Barton*. Other friends included the feminists Bessie Raynor Parkes and Fredrika Bremer, whose Swedish novels MH introduced into England with her translation of *Neighbours* in 1842; although Bremer at times complained of errors in MH's translations, she continued to favour her, providing MH with early copies of her work to circumvent other translators (in the days before international copyright agreements). MH was an early translator of Hans Christian Andersen's work and that of several German authors. She and her husband collaborated on a history of Scandinavian literature, *The Literature and Romance of Northern Europe* (1852). MH also wrote novels, short stories, and children's stories, including *The Children's Year* (1847) and its companion piece, *Our Cousins in Ohio* (1849), gleaned from information her sister Emma sent from her new home in the United States.

Most of MH's work has been out of print since its early success although some of her poems have been included in twentieth-century anthologies; her very readable *Autobiography* and her Bremer translations have been reprinted in this century. The *Cambridge Bibliography* credits her with 110 works, and her articles are practically uncountable. She wrote for most of the major and minor Victorian periodicals, including the *Athenaeum, Household Words*, and *All the Year Round*. She published both poetry and prose in the *People's Journal* and in *Howitt's Journal*. The quality of her work no doubt suffered from the pressure of earning an income, and she lamented in a letter to her sister Anna in 1848 that a new residence gave her 'no little working-room to myself', but that this

too had 'its bright side, because I can bear interruptions better than William or
Anna Mary [their daughter, also a writer and an artist]' (*Autobiography*). Her
life both reflected and influenced the religious and philosophical struggles of
many Victorians: from her family legacy of membership in the Society of
Friends, she later became interested in Unitarianism, then spiritualism, and
finally in her old age she became a Roman Catholic.   CAROL A. MARTIN

Selected works: The Forest Minstrel and Other Poems (with William Howitt)
(1823); The Desolation of Eyam and Other Poems (with William Howitt) (1827);
The Seven Temptations (1834); Wood Leighton, or, A Year in the Country (1836);
Birds and Flowers and Other Country Things (1838); Hymns and Fireside Verses
(1839); Little Coin, Much Care, or, How Poor Men Live: A Tale (1842); (trans.),
The Neighbours; A Story of Everyday Life, by Bremer (1842); The Home, or,
Family Cares and Family Joys, by Bremer (1843); Ballads and Other Poems (1847);
The Heir of Wast-Waylan (1847); (trans.), Brothers and Sisters: A Tale of Domestic
Life, by Bremer (1848); Our Cousins in Ohio (1849); The Literature and Romance
of Northern Europe (with William Howitt) (1852); (trans.), The Homes of the New
World: Impressions of America, by Bremer (1853); Birds and Flowers and Other
Country Things (1855); (trans.), Hertha, by Bremer (1856); (trans.), Travels in
the Holy Land, by Bremer (1862); Ruined Abbeys and Castles of Great Britain
(with William Howitt) (1862); (trans.) Greece and the Greeks, by Bremer (1863);
The Cost of Caergwyn (1864); Autobiography, ed. Margaret Howitt (1889).

References: Butler, J. A., 'Wordsworth's funeral: a contemporary report', ELN
13 (1975); de Groot, H. B., 'R. H. Horne, Mary Howitt and a mid-Victorian
version of 'The Echoing Green', Blake Studies 4 (1971); Lee, A., Laurels and
Rosemary: The Life of William and Mary Howitt (1955); OCCL; Paston, G., Little
Memoirs of the Nineteenth Century (1902); Woodring, C. R., Victorian Samplers,
William and Mary Howitt (1952); Woodring, C. R., 'William and Mary Howitt:
bibliographical notes', Harvard Library Bulletin 5 (Spring 1951).

Hughes, Molly

b. 1867, London; d. 1956, Johannesburg, South Africa
Autobiographer, family biographer

MH was the only daughter and youngest child of the five children of Thomas
Thomas, a former mining engineer turned member of the London Stock Exchange, and Mary Vivian, daughter of a well-to-do farming and mining family
from Camborne in Cornwall. Her childhood, girlhood, and early adulthood
are chronicled in A London Child of the 1870s, A London Girl of the 1880s, and
A London Home of the 1890s; her Cornish connections are described in Vivians;
and her widowhood and later teaching career are detailed in A London Family
between the Wars.

MH attended the North London Collegiate School under the famous Miss
Buss; A London Girl . . . vividly captures the school's strengths and attractions
but also its mistakes and less appealing features as these seemed to a pupil and,
later on, a well-known educationalist. In 1885 MH was one of the first small
group of women to attend the Cambridge Training College under Miss E. P.
Hughes (founded with the help and direction of Miss Buss), an interesting
account of which is contained in A London Girl. . . . MH's teaching career
began in 1886, a year in which she also registered for a part-time BA at the
University of London. As A London Home . . . describes, she gave up a better-
paid job in 1892 to become the first principal of teacher training at Bedford
College. Her teaching career was much aided by a prolonged ten-year engage-

ment to Arthur Hughes, a teacher who struggled against great financial odds to become a barrister; they finally married in 1897. MH gave birth to a daughter, Bronwen, who died in infancy (her brief life, then death, is movingly described in *A London Home . . .*) and three sons, Vivian, Barnholt, and Arthur.

MH's husband was killed in a road accident in 1918; as a result she returned to teaching, becoming an inspector for the University of London and for the Board of Education, and also, for a shorter period, for Surrey County Council. Tributes from contemporaries after her death remember MH as a kind, clever, modest, humorous woman, courageous in the face of her various personal tragedies, but also an outstanding HMI of schools. This latter tribute of course befits a woman who was the product of the teaching of some of the best-known pioneers of woman's education in England.

MH's now lesser-known published works include various books of gentle religious instruction and, in collaboration with Walter Rippmann, a Latin course, a Latin reader, and a 'key' to both. However, her best-known and best-loved books are the five autobiographies/family biographies she wrote to show her sons the shifts and changes of her life. It is difficult not to feel that a wider motivation, which she was typically too modest openly to express, was to share with many other people through publication the small, fascinating details of the fabric of a life and a social world gone by, and also (and perhaps more importantly to her) a view of 'Victorian parents' and 'Victorian family life' which is in complete contrast to modern stereotypes.

MH's patent honesty and sincerity and also her consummate art in telling a story (despite an apparent artlessness) characterize her best-known writings. These qualities allow readers to empathize with her even when she says things (for example, concerning the innate superiority of brothers and the innately greater importance of men as a group) that otherwise would jar on the politically aware. At her best, she has the rare ability to enable readers to see and feel through her eyes and experience, thus letting us into the vanished world of a Victorian child, girl and adult.   LIZ STANLEY

Works: *The King of Kings* (1903); *The Story of Christ's First Missioners* (with M. Penstone) (1911); *From Baptism to Holy Communion* (1913); *Good Will towards Men* (1915); *A Rapid Latin Course* (with W. Rippmann) (1923); *A Latin Reader* (with W. Rippmann) (1925); *Key to A Rapid Latin Course and A Latin Reader* (with W. Rippmann) (1926); *About England* (1927); *America's England* (1930); *London at Home* (1931); *The City Saints* (1932); *Hidden Interests in the Bible* (1932); *A London Child of the Seventies* (1934); *Vivians: A Family in Victorian Cornwall* (1935); *A London Girl of the Eighties* (1936); *A London Home in the Nineties* (1937); *Scripture Teaching Today* (1939); *A London Family between the Wars* (1940).

References: Kamm, J., *How Different From Us: A Biography of Miss Buss and Miss Beale* (1958); Murray, J. H., *Strong-Minded Woman* (1984); Vicinus, M., *Independent Woman* (1985).

Hungerford, Margaret

b. around 1854, Roscarberry, County Cork, Ireland; d. 24 January 1897, Bandon, County Cork, Ireland

Novelist

(Also wrote under Mrs Hungerford and 'The Duchess')

MH was born Margaret Wolfe Hamilton. Her father, the Rev. Canon Hamilton, was rector and vicar choral of St Faughnan's cathedral. She married Edward Argles, a Dublin solicitor, and had three daughters. After six years of marriage,

Argles died and she married Henry Hungerford of Cahermore, Bandon, with whom she had two sons and one daughter. She herself died of typhoid fever.

MH began to write at a very young age and eventually published well over thirty works of fiction, including love stories, ghost stories and humour. Her books were published under a variety of pseudonyms, (primarily 'The Duchess' and occasionally 'The Author of *"Phyllis"* ' or 'The Author of *"Molly Bawn"* ') and were enormously popular in England, America and Australia. It was said of her that she sold her novels as fast as she could write them. Helen C. Black, one of Mrs Hungerford's contemporary admirers, attributed her success to 'the delicacy of her love scenes, the lightness of touch that distinguishes her numerous flirtations [which] can only be equalled by the pathos she has thrown into her work every now and then, as if to temper her brightness with a little shade. Her descriptions of scenery are especially vivid and delightful, and very often full of poetry.' Other critics were slightly more grudging (reviews were, Mrs Hungerford said, 'my one great dread and anxiety'). According to the *Spectator*, 'There is no guile in the novels of the author of "Molly Bawn", nor any consistency, nor analysis of character; but they exhibit a faculty truly remarkable for reproducing the vapid small-talk, the shallow but harmless "chaff" of certain strata of modern fashionable society.'   JEAN HANFF KORELITZ

Selected works: Phyllis (1877); *Molly Bawn* (1878); *Airy Fairy Lillian* (1879); *Beauty's Daughters* (1880); *Faith and Unfaith* (1881); *Moonshine and Marguerites* (1883); *Rossmoyne* (1883); *Monica* (1883); *Portia, or, 'By Passions Mocked'* (1883); *A Week in Killarney* (1884); *The Witching Hour* (1884); *Doris* (1884); *Sweet is True Love* (1884); *Mildred Trevanion* (1885); *Green Pleasure and Grey Grief* (1886); *Lady Branksmere* (1886); *A Mental Struggle* (1886); *A Modern Circe* (1887); *Marvel* (1888); *The Hon. Mrs Vereker* (1888); *In Durance Vile and Other Stories* (1889); *A Born Coquette* (1890); *Life's Remorse* (1890); *A Little Irish Girl* (1891); *Nor Wife Nor Maid* (1892); *The Hoyden* (1894); *The O'Connors of Ballynahinch* (1894); *The Coming of Chloë* (1897); *Nora Creina* (1903).

References; Black, H. C., *Notable Women Authors of the Day* (1893); *BA* (19).

Hunt, Violet

b. 28 September 1862, Durham (?); d. 16 January 1942, London

Novelist, short story writer, biographer

VH was the daughter of Margaret Raine Hunt, novelist, and Alfred William Hunt, landscape painter and watercolourist. Her father intended that she should follow his profession: until VH was 28 it seemed likely that she would. She was educated at home and at Notting Hill High School, London, where she was a contemporary of Jenny and May Morris.

VH and her sisters, Silvia and Venice, spent their childhood in the company of their parents' friends, many of whom were distinguished artists and writers. In *The Flurried Years* (1926) VH recalls her invitations to 'Pre-Raphaelite parties at the Seddons and the Tebbs'. There she met Ford Madox Hueffer (later Ford Madox Ford), eleven years her junior; she often had to 'rap the fingers of the two high-spirited Hueffer boys for playing ball with the penny buns'. Although she recognized the attractions of this artistic, fashionable milieu, VH was later to treat her youthful experiences with biting satire. In *The Celebrity at Home* (1904) and *The Celebrity's Daughter* (1913), the self-indulgence of a successful author and the charmed circle he inhabits is seen through the eyes of a precocious child: it is a far from flattering picture.

The Hunt household was a meeting place for political ideas as well as literary lions. Margaret Hunt's commitment to women's suffrage influenced VH to work with the Pankhursts and to develop her own views on the changing role of women in society, notably her belief in freedom of artistic, political, and sexual expression. In later life she was to support her friend Marguerite Radclyffe-Hall against the suppression of *The Well of Loneliness*. VH's first novel, *The Maiden's progress* (1894), showed the emergence of her distinctive voice, also evident in journalism for *Black and White* and the *Pall Mall Gazette*. Later novels, particularly *White Rose of Weary Leaf* (1908) and the autobiographical *Sooner or Later* (1904), established her reputation. Her acerbic wit, shrewd eye for observation and willingness to tackle the difficult themes of adultery, promiscuity, and prostitution invited comparison with the French realists. Somerset Maugham, H. G. Wells, and Henry James admired her work.

In 1908, at the suggestion of H. G. Wells, VH took some short stories to Ford Madox Hueffer, who was editing the *English Review*. He chose, apparently at random, her macabre tale 'The Coach', in which dead souls reminisce over the manner of their deaths. Its tone, a mixture of Grand Guignol and high farce ('I was disgracefully cut up. I couldn't possibly have worn a low-cut dress again!') contributes to the atmosphere of menace which pervades VH's *Tales of the Uneasy* (1910). Hueffer's decision to publish VH's story, and their subsequent conversation, marked the beginning of a relationship which was to move from a shared passion for literature, through a period of emotional intensity and painful litigation, to an acrimonious end.

At first, there were 'high hopes, both personal and literary' for the *Review*. Its founders, who included Wells, Conrad, and Edward Garnett, intended, in Hueffer's words, to give 'imaginative literature a chance in England'. The quality of the *Review* was apparent from its first issue, with contributions from Henry James, Thomas Hardy, and John Galsworthy. During the time of Hueffer's editorial control, established writers rubbed shoulders with new 'discoveries', most notably D. H. Lawrence.

VH's involvement with Hueffer and the *Review* grew throughout 1909. She had boundless enthusiasm, contacts, money of her own and faith in Hueffer's ability as an editor and author. Together, they made a formidable team. South Lodge, the London house which VH had bought in 1908, and in which she cared for her mother after her father's death, became a centre for ebullient gatherings of writers and artists. When it became clear that the *Review* was in severe financial difficulties, VH persuaded a wealthy friend to buy it, only to find that a condition of the transaction was Hueffer's replacement as editor.

Further problems arose when Hueffer's wife refused to divorce him so that he and VH could marry. The ensuing scandal was exacerbated by a lawsuit which ended in damages being awarded to Mrs Hueffer against a weekly paper, the *Throne*, which had described VH in print as Mrs F. M. Hueffer. Friends and colleagues were divided in their loyalties: a complicating factor was VH's insistence that she and Hueffer had, in fact, married during a trip to Germany, although she was unable to supply proof. One consequence of the scandal was that VH's niece, Rosamond, was forbidden to visit South Lodge by her parents. VH's relationship with her sisters, already strained because of their belief that she was mismanaging their mother's affairs, deteriorated further. When Margaret Hunt died in 1912, Venice and Silvia contested her will.

VH embarked on a programme of protracted correspondence, in the wake of Mrs Hueffer's libel action, in an attempt to clear her name and re-establish her position as society hostess. Many of her letters went unanswered; invitations were refused, or not acknowledged. H. G. Wells remained a friend, as did Ezra

Pound, Rebecca West, and Wyndham Lewis. In the years before the war, South Lodge was the focus for much social and artistic activity. VH and Hueffer presided over gatherings where vorticism was argued over and where *Blast*, the hoped-for magazine of the modern movement, was read from: the first draft of Hueffer's novel *The Good Soldier* appeared in the inaugural issue. *The Desirable Alien*, a collaborative acount of their travels in Germany, was published in 1913. Despite its companionably argumentative tone, their relationship was under considerable strain. When Hueffer sought a commission in 1915, it was without VH's knowledge. By the war's end, they were estranged.

After the war, VH published *More Tales of the Uneasy* (1925) and *The Tiger Skin* (1924). Of all her work, the stories of horror and suspense are most clearly realized; Henry James preferred them to her novels. They show a narrative control and imaginative richness, and each has its own dreamlike logic. In *The Tiger Skin*, the central woman character, Adelaide Favarger, pursues her obsession with giving birth to a perfect child to monstrous lengths. When sitting at dinner with potential suitors she 'glowed in her dark setting, a meagre Circe who gathered the ready-made beasts about her, and shook no deterrent wand at them.' The tiger skin, a gift from the man she chooses to father her child, is a recurring image of barbarism. It is not, however, the animal's savagery that threatens, but the human's relentless pursuit of beauty for its own sake, the desire to capture and preserve youth. The effect of Adelaide's intense, distorted vision is profoundly disturbing.

The Flurried Years, VH's last attempt to clarify her part in the legal wrangling over Hueffer's name, and to give an account of their relationship, served only to rekindle the scandal which had lain dormant for a decade. Its publication made her rift with Hueffer (now Ford) wider still. There was more controversy to come. VH's biography of Lizzie Siddall, *The Wife of Rossetti* (1932), in its melodramatic depiction of her death and its suggestion that Dante Gabriel Rossetti might have caused it through neglect, brought a storm of protest. The Rossetti family and literary historians questioned VH's version of events. Once more, VH set out to defend her position, which grew more untenable as time went on. The letters printed in *Time and Tide* and *The Times Literary Supplement* reveal, at last, her resignation. Admitting that Lizzie died before she was born, VH writes, 'Hearsay seems to be the only way of getting at the facts.'

VH wrote nothing after *The Wife of Rossetti*. She still gave parties, no longer insisting that guests should dress for dinner. For years, Gaudier-Brzeska's massive head of Ezra Pound dominated her front garden. Ford Madox Ford died in 1939 and VH in 1942, in South Lodge. 'I have always been up against something – wanting to alter something – fighting something. I do not invite contest exactly; it comes to me.'   ELFRIDA LAUGHARNE

Works: *The Maiden's Progress* (1894); *A Hard Woman* (1895); *The Way of Marriage* (1896); *Unkist, Unkind!* (1897); *The Human Interest* (1899); *Affairs of the Heart* (1900); *The Celebrity at Home* (1904); *Sooner or Later* (1904); *The Cat* (1905); *The Workaday Woman* (1906); *White Rose of Weary Leaf* (1908); *The Wife of Altamont* (1910); *Tales of the Uneasy* (1910); *The Doll* (1911); *The Desirable Alien* (with Ford Madox Hueffer) (1913); *The Celebrity's Daughter* (1913); *The House of Many Mirrors* (1915); *Their Lives* (1916); *Zeppelin Nights: A London Entertainment* (with Ford Madox Hueffer) (1916); *The Last Ditch* (1918); *Their Hearts* (1921); *The Tiger Skin* (1924); *More Tales of the Uneasy* (1925); *The Flurried Years* (1926); *The Wife of Rossetti* (1932).

References: Adcock, A. St J., *The Glory That Was Grub Street* (1928); Drabble;

Goldring, D., *South Lodge* (1943); Mizener, A., *The Saddest Story: A Biography of Ford Madox Ford* (1971); Richards, G., *Memories of a Misspent Youth.*

Hutchinson, Lucy

b. 29 January 1620, Tower of London; d. late 1670s

Biographer, autobiographer

LC was the daughter of the Royalist Sir Allen Apsley, Lieutenant of the Tower, and Lucy St John, his third wife, who breastfed her alone of all her ten children. Her mother was eager that her delicate daughter become learned and she was taught French at an early age and 'carried to sermons' which she could remember and repeat exactly. Later her father tutored her in Latin and LH soon outshone her three brothers who were receiving formal education at school. She was a voracious reader, ranging over the classics, Hebrew texts and theology: 'every moment I could steal from my play I would employ in any book I could find.' By this time her mother was worried over her health (and her marriage prospects) and took to locking up her books to prevent her from reading too much and from neglecting the more feminine arts of dancing, music, and needlework, the last of which she 'absolutely hated'. With her learning and solemnity she was rather unprepossessing to other children, she admitted in her account of her life. Her mother had been attracted to Calvinism as a young girl and must have influenced LH in her later Puritan religious opinions.

Despite her mother's fears, it was her learning that attracted her future husband, who noted in a song of hers an intelligence 'beyond the customary reach of a she-witt'. When he feared that she was already married, in her description he turned 'pale as ashes, and felt a fainting seize his spiritts.' When they finally met, his heart was already 'prepossesst with his owne fancy' while she who had formerly shied away from men was 'surpriz'd with some unusuall liking in her soule, when she saw this gentleman'. On the day when they should have married, she fell ill with smallpox which disfigured her for a time, but none the less Hutchinson married her as soon as possible, in 1638. The marriage, in LH's account of it in her *Memoirs of the Life of Colonel Hutchinson* (not published until 1806), was a happy one: 'if he esteem'd her att a higher rate than she in herselfe could have deserv'd', she wrote, 'he was the author of that vertue he doted on, while she only reflected his own glories upon him: all that she was was *him*, while he was here.' He was so devoted to her that 'when she ceast to be young and lovely, he began to shew most fondnesse'. After their marriage the couple lived for some months in London and then went to Enfield, where they had twin sons in 1639. They then went to Owthorpe in Nottinghamshire, Hutchinson's family home. LH translated Lucretius into English verse in a room full of children learning their lessons.

In the Civil War Hutchinson became a parliamentarian. He was made governor of the castle in Nottingham where LH doctored the wounded – of both sides, much to the annoyance of a Roundhead captain, for she argued that what she did was 'her duty in humanity to them, as fellow creatures, not as enemies'. In 1646 Hutchinson became a member of the Long Parliament. Reluctantly he acted as one of Charles I's judges, but played little further part in politics after the execution because of ill-health and because of his dislike of Cromwell's increasing power. In 1659 he was summoned to Parliament and was there when Charles II was welcomed. After the Restoration LH claimed that she wrote a rather obsequious letter on her husband's behalf but not with his approval and initially, with the help of royalist relatives, he did not share the extreme fate of other regicides. But he was uncomfortable in this favouritism and refused to flee the country or sue for any further protection. In 1663 he was arrested on a trumped-up charge and confined to the Tower, then imprisoned in Sandown Castle in Kent where LH and two of their children followed him. LH trudged every day to visit him 'with horrible toyle and inconvenience' and she brought him shells to keep him amused. Despite her attendance Hutchinson soon died, leaving his wife his last message: 'let her, as she is above other women, show herself in this occasion a good christian, and above the pitch of ordinary women.' After his death she described herself as a shadow and a nothing.

Between 1664 and 1671 LH wrote her *Memoirs* 'to moderate my woe, and if it were possible to augment my love', prefaced by a fragment of autobiography, 'The Life of Mrs Lucy Hutchinson written by herself', and by a eulogy of Hutchinson, 'Mrs Hutchinson to her children, concerning their father "To my Children" '. The work was not intended for immediate publication, although she no doubt expected it to be preserved, and it was probably modelled on the published biography and autobiography of the Duchess of Newcastle of whom LH profoundly disapproved. The biography presents a portrait of an upright, punctilious, rather irascible Puritan despite all the praise from LH, while the picture of herself, although subordinated to her husband's, is more appealing in its energy and wittiness.

In her last years LH struggled in poverty, managing, however, to keep her interest in learning; she dedicated her translation of Lucretius to the Earl of Anglesey in 1675, although the dedication does speak of 'the sin of amusing myself with such vain philosophy'. Among her other works are two books on religious subjects for her daughter, one of which was published in 1817.

JANET TODD

Works: *Memoirs of the Life of Colonel Hutchinson* (1806); *The Life of Mrs Hutchinson Written By Herself* (1806); *On the Principles of the Christian Religion* (1817).
References: Braund, E., 'Mrs Hutchinson and her teaching', *Evangelical Quarterly* 31 (1959); *DNB*; Firth, C. M., 'Introduction' to *Memoirs* (1906); Fraser, A., *The Weaker Vessel* (1984); Handley, G. M., 'Notes on the *Memoirs*' (1906); Hobby, E., *Virtue of Necessity* (1988); Mayo, R., *Epicurus in England* (1934); Mendelson, S. H., *The Mental World of Stuart Women* (1987); Schucking, L. L., *The Puritan Family* (1969); Todd; Weiss, S. A., 'Dating Mrs Hutchinson's translation of Lucretius', *Notes & Queries* 100 (1955).

Huxley, Elspeth
b. 23 July 1907
Novelist, travel writer

Daughter of Major Josceline Grant of Njoro, Kenya, EH followed her parents to East Africa at the age of 5 to live on a coffee farm near Thika, thirty-five miles from Nairobi. She was educated at the European school at Nairobi. In 1925 she returned to England to attend Reading University, where she obtained a Diploma in Agriculture. She then studied at Cornell University in New York State. In 1929 she joined the Empire Marketing Board as a press officer, and in 1931 she married Gervas Huxley, cousin of Aldous and Julian. They had one son and travelled extensively. From 1952 to 1959 she was a member of the General Advisory Board of the BBC. She then joined the Monckton Advisory Commission Central Africa. She farmed in Wiltshire with her husband while continuing her work as a radio broadcaster and freelance journalist. She also worked as an editor on a biographical anthology of the Kingsleys, and on a travel memoir by M. H. Kingsley in 1973 and 1976 respectively. She was awarded the CBE in 1962 and was widowed in 1971.

EH's best-known work is *The Flame Trees of Thika* (1959), an evocative account of her childhood in Kenya before the First World War, in which the people, landscapes, and animals of that country are brought tenderly and lovingly to life. The book was filmed for a television serial in 1981. *The Mottled Lizard* (1962) is the sequel to *The Flame Trees of Thika*. *Death of an Aryan* (later called *The African Poison Murders*) (1986) also has its roots in EH's childhood experiences, portraying a farming community in colonial East Africa; Kenya is again described in *Out in the Midday Sun* (1985). EH has also used a colonial background for several crime novels, among them *Murder on Safari* (1938) and *Murder at Government House* (1937). The complex issues involved in colonialism are the matter of *The Walled City* (1948), which deal with two British administrators, and *White Man's Country* (1935), a two-volume history of Lord Delamere and his pioneering work in Kenya. Other non-fictional works on Africa include *The Challenge of Africa* (1971), a comprehensive and beautifully illustrated history of travel in the continent and serial accounts of EH's own travels. Among writings on England are the autobiographical *Love Among the Daughters* (1968), set in the 1920s, and *The Prince Buys the Manor* (1982), a skilfully comic romp through a sleepy market town in the Cotswolds where socialites, badger lovers and international terrorists are driven into a frenzy of plotting by the decision of a royal prince to buy the local manor. EH's experience of farming in Wiltshire lies behind *Gallipot Eyes* (1975), and *Back Street New Worlds* (1964) is a study of immigrants in Britain.   MARINA TZAMOURANIS

Works: *White Man's Country* (1935); *Murder at Government House* (1937); *Murder on Safari* (1938); *Red Strangers* (1938); *Atlantic Ordeal* (1941); *East Africa* (1941); *Race and Politics in Kenya* (with Margery Perham) (1944); *The Walled City* (1948); *The Sorcerer's Apprentice* (1948); *I Don't Mind if I Do* (1951); *Four Guineas* (1954); *A Thing to Love* (1954); *The Red Rock Wilderness* (1957); *The Flame Trees of Thika* (1959); *A New Earth* (1960); *The Mottled Lizard* (1962); *The Merry Hippo* (1963); *Forks and Hope* (1964); *A Man From Nowhere* (1964); *Back Street New Worlds* (1964); *Brave New Victuals* (1965); *Their Shining Eldorado* (1967); *Love Among the Daughters* (1968); *The Challenge of Africa* (1971); (ed.), *The Kingsleys* (1973); *Livingstone and His African Journeys* (1974); *Forence Nightingale* (1975); *Gallipot Eyes* (1975); (ed.), *Travels in Africa*, by M. H. Kingsley (1976); *Scott of the Antarctic* (1977); a memoir in *Nellie: Letters from Africa*, by Nellie Grant (1980); (ed.), *Pioneers' Scrapbook: Reminiscences of Kenya* (with Arnold Curtis) (1980); *Whipsnade: Captive Breeding for Survival* (1981); *The Prince Buys the Manor* (1982); *Last Days of Eden* (with Hugo van Lawick) (1984); *Out in the Midday Sun* (1985); *The African Poison Murders* (1986).

References: Courtauld, S., 'Only man is vile', *Spectator* (6 February 1982); Furness, M., 'Small-town times', *Times Literary Supplement* (29 October 1982); Shills, E., 'Further observations on Mrs Huxley', *Encounter* 97 (October 1976); Shills, E., 'Reluctant hero', *Economist* (12 November 1977).

Inchbald, Elizabeth
b. 15 October 1753, Stanningfield, Suffolk; d. 1 August 1821, Kensington
Novelist, playwright
EI was the eighth child of John and Mary Simpson, Catholic farmers at Stanningfield near Bury St Edmunds. She had no formal schooling but she read at

home and shared her family's love of the theatre, which they attended in Bury and Norwich. In 1772, having tried to join Richard Griffith's theatre in Norwich, she ran away from home to seek her fortune in the London theatre. She had considerable beauty but she suffered from a stammer which she managed to control on the stage only through prolonged rehearsal. Her youth, beauty, and lack of protection made her vulnerable in London and she was frightened by the attempt of the actor James Dodd to molest her when she turned to him for help. Her unprotected state encouraged her to accept a marriage proposal from a fellow Catholic, the actor and portrait painter, Joseph Inchbald, a man seventeen years her senior with two illegitimate children, whom she had earlier rejected.

EI made her debut in Bristol as Cordelia to Joseph Inchbald's Lear, roles which used their obvious difference in age; she was to repeat the role in Glasgow. For the first four years of their marriage she travelled impecuniously round the provincial theatres of England and Scotland, often quarrelling with her husband over possible infidelities. At the same time she tried to educate herself through reading and learning French. In July 1776 they moved to Paris where Joseph tried to earn money through painting, and EI tried writing comedies. By September 1776 they were once more in Brighton, almost destitute. No work was available in London and they moved to Liverpool when they began a friendship with Mrs Siddons and her brother, John Philip Kemble. EI fell in love (unrequited) with the latter. After playing in several towns in Yorkshire, Joseph Inchbald died of a heart attack leaving EI a widow at 26. Over the next few years she rejected several offers of marriage from, for example, William Godwin and Thomas Holcroft, perhaps hoping that Kemble would propose or perhaps dreading another difficult marriage. In 1780 she played Bellario in London but had only mediocre success, and she left the stage in 1789.

EI had written several plays before 1784 when her first one was performed. This was *The Mogul Tale, or, The Descent of the Balloon* which played for ten days at the Haymarket in 1784 and earned her 100 guineas. After this play, inspired by the French craze for ballooning, EI received consistently high fees for her plays, most of which were both produced and printed. She managed her affairs shrewdly, investing her earnings so well that she provided a substantial income for herself. Clearly she feared the poverty she had known with Inchbald, and she was extremely careful with her own expenditure while behaving generously to her family.

EI shows her humanitarian and social concerns in many of her successful plays. The comedy *I'll Tell You What* (1786) probed marriage and divorce, and in its contrasting of types, considered the qualities required for a literary heroine. Other plays showed independent women, but always crowned their independence with marriage, although her plots suggest support for the idea of divorce. *Such Things Are* (1788) makes its social purpose clear in its depiction of the prison reformer John Howard. Today her most famous play may be *Lovers' Vows* (1798), a free translation of a Kotzebue play, the acting of which upturns the household in *Mansfield Park*. EI translated several plays from German, naturalizing them into English through her skilful rendering of dialogue: she trimmed plots and characters and generally made them more theatrical. Through this work she was instrumental in introducing German sensational drama to late eighteenth-century English audiences.

Athough her first professional writing was for the theatre, EI is now better known for her novels. *A Simple Story* had been circulated among friends in

1777; a first version was ready in 1779, but she failed to obtain a publisher, and so began a second novel. In 1791 when, on the advice of Holcroft and Godwin, she combined the stories, EI succeeded in selling the book to a publisher. *A Simple Story* may have been inspired by her friendship with Kemble since there is a resemblance between him and the hero Dorriforth, a Catholic priest who grows to love his ward, Miss Milner, an attractive, high-spirited, faulty girl. Dorriforth agonizes over his vocation, Miss Milner's faults, and his love for her. He inherits an earldom, leaves the priesthood and marries his ward. The second part of the novel takes place sixteen years later; his wife proves unfaithful, and the sternly moral Dorriforth visits her sin on her daughter until he learns to forgive. This second part is far more didactic than the first, and the two parts are not satisfactorily welded in tone or fable. The concluding moral, that the novel demonstrates 'the pernicious effects of an improper education' seems inappropriate to the earlier vivid depiction of Miss Milner and to the later portrait of the arrogant Dorriforth. The novel has been much admired, both by Maria Edgeworth for its realistic presentation of character and, in the twentieth century, for its enactment of the restraints both on the spirited Miss Milner and on the woman writer.

Nature and Art (1796), her second novel, takes up the concluding moral of *A Simple Story* and shows the influence of the pedagogic theories of both Godwin and Rousseau (whose *Confessions* she translated). After their father's death, Henry, a fiddler, supports his brother, William, until he rises in the Church; the ingratitude Henry receives sends him to Africa. Later his naturally educated son returns to live with his uncle, and encounters his cousin William. The novel contrasts the two cousins; William seduces a virtuous girl, then punishes her for the prostitution which he has forced on her; Henry, meanwhile, marries his faithful and virtuous lady. Some of the most interesting parts of the novel concern the girl who falls into prostitution; EI's concern for this theme may have been quickened by her experience with her sister who died after being a prostitute.

In her later years EI took up reviewing and editing. She provided critical and biographical prefaces for *The British Theatre* (in twenty-five volumes, 1806–9), so becoming the first professional woman theatre critic. She is in tune with the views on drama of her time and is concerned for the morality of the stage. Defending herself from a critic, she admitted she was an 'unlettered woman', but her knowledge of drama on and off the stage made her a competent judge of what was theatrically workable and innovative. She also wrote articles and reviews and selected works for *A Collection of Farces* (1809) and *The Modern Theatre* (1811).

EI knew many of the liberal writers of her day such as Anna Laetitia Barbauld, Maria Edgeworth, Holcroft, and Godwin, although she reacted unpleasantly to news of the latter's marriage to Mary Wollstonecraft. After her husband's death she lived independently except when she joined a sort of convent for Catholic ladies in 1803. She ended her life in Kensington House, a Roman Catholic residence for ladies. Her confessor had urged her to destroy her memoirs on which she had been working.   JANET TODD

Selected works: The Mogul Tale (1784); *Appearance is Against Them* (1785); *I'll Tell you What* (1786); (trans.), *The Widow's Vow*, by Patrat (1796); (trans.), *The Midnight Hour*, by Damaniant (1787); (trans.), *The Child of Nature*, by Mme de Genlis (1788); *Such Things Are* (1788); *The Mogul's Tale* (1788); *Animal Magnetism* (1788 or 1789); (trans.), *The Married Man*, by Destouches (1789); *A Simple Story* (1791); (trans.), *Next-Door Neighbours*, by Mercier (1791); *The Massacre*

(1792); *Everyone Has His Fault* (1793); *The Wedding Day* (1794); *Nature and Art* (1796); *Wives as They Were and Maids as They Are* (1797); (trans.), *Lovers' Vows*, by Kotzebue (1798); (trans.), *The Wise Man of the East*, by Kotzebue (1799); *To Marry or Not to Marry* (1805); (ed.), *The British Theatre* (1806–9); (ed.), *A Collection of Farces* (1809); (ed.), *The Modern Theatre* (1811); *A Case of Conscience* (1833); *The Massacre* (1833); *Perfidy Punished* (1787) is sometimes ascribed to EI. **References:** Allibone; Backsheider, P., 'Introduction' to *The Plays of Elizabeth Inchbald* (1983); Boaden, J., *Memoirs of Mrs Inchbald* (1833); *DNB*; Drabble; Joughin, G., 'An Inchbald bibliography', *University of Texas Studies in English* 14 (1934); Kelly, G., *The English Jacobin Novel 1708–1805* (1976); Kunitz, S. and Haycroft, H. (eds.), *British Authors before 1800* (1952); Littlewood, S. R., *Elizabeth Inchbald and Her Circle . . . 1753–1821* (1921); KcKee, W., Moers, E., *Literary Women* (1976); McKee, W., *Elizabeth Inchbald, Novelist* (1935); Todd; Tompkins, J. M. S., 'Introduction' to *A Simple Story* (1967).

Ingelow, Jean
b. 17 March 1820, near Boston, Lincolnshire; d. 20 July 1897, London
Poet
(Also wrote under 'Orris')

JI has been called a 'lost Pre-Raphaelite', for her poetry and prose, published during the second half of the nineteenth century, exhibit the form, style, and subject matter of Pre-Raphaelite art. She and her numerous brothers and sisters were educated at home by their mother, Jean (*née* Kilgour) Ingelow, who encouraged their creativity; together they produced a family periodical, where JI first saw her poems 'in print'. However it was financial need that prompted her to begin publishing in earnest, in the 1850s; mostly children's tales, under a pen name 'Orris' (illustrated by John Millais), and an anonymous book of poems.

Her second volume of poetry (1863) went through thirty editions. In this many of her best poems appeared, including 'Songs of Seven' and 'Divided', a wistful tale about a couple walking on opposite sides of a streamlet that becomes ever wider and faster, until it divides them absolutely and forever. The natural descriptions and emotional appeal in this poem made it one of her best loved and most quoted pieces.

'Divided' led to speculation that in her youth JI must have lost a sweetheart herself. Certainly she never married; a spinster aunt Rebecca, who was anti-marriage, may have influenced her opinions on the subject. And although she was essentially conservative in attitudes, in many of her poems she expressed reservations about marriage, for example in 'Katherine of Aragon to Henry VIII' (1850), 'Brothers, and a Sermon' (1863), and 'Wedlock' (1867). Yet even more frequently she wrote of love, courtship, and marriage as a desirable progress and of the wife as an 'angel of the house'.

'The High Tide on the Coast of Lincolnshire, 1571' (1883), a ballad about a sixteenth-century disaster, was her most popular poem. Contemporary readers were also moved by her poems about childhood deaths; the best of these is probably 'Katie, Aged Five Years', written for her friend (and first editor), the Rev. Edward Harston, who had lost three children in rapid succession. In her later years JI wrote mostly fiction, including several novels – *Off the Skelligs* (1872) and *Sarah de Berenger* (1879) – and numerous children's tales. Her most successful children's story is *Mopsa the Fairy* (1869), presenting an imaginary world in a graceful, Pre-Raphaelite style.

JI was on friendly terms with Ruskin, Longfellow, and Tennyson, as well as Christina Rossetti and Jane and Ann Taylor of Ongar. When Tennyson died in 1892, JI was mentioned as a candidate for the poet laureateship, although she was actually better known in the United States than in England.

KATHLEEN HICKOK

Works: *A Rhyming Chronicle of Incidents and Feelings*, ed. Edward Harston (1850); *Allerton and Drieux, or, The War of Opinion* (1857); *Tales of Orris* (1860); *Poems* (1863); *Studies for Stories* (1864); *Stories Told to a Child* (1865); *Home Thoughts and Home Scenes* (1865): *Songs of Seven* (1866, 1881); *The Wild Duck Shooter and I Have a Right* (1867); *A Story of Doom and Other Poems* (1867); *A Sister's Bye-Hours* (1868); *Mopsa the Fairy* (1869); *The Little Wonder-Horn* (1872); *Fated to be Free* (1875); *One Hundred Holy Songs, Carols and Sacred Ballads* (1878); *Off the Skelligs* (1879); *Sarah de Berenger* (1879); *Poems* (1880); *Don John: A Story* (1881); 'The High Tide on the Coast of Lincolnshire, 1571' (1883); *Poems: Third Series* (1885, 1888); *Poems of the Old Days and the New* (1885); *John Jerome, His Thoughts and Ways: A Book without Beginning* (1886); *Very Young and Quite Another Story* (1890); *A Motto Changed* (1894); *The Old Man's Prayer* (1895).

References: Anon., *Some Recollections of Jean Ingelow and Her Early Friends* (1901); Black, H. C., *Notable Women Authors of the Day* (1893); *BA* (I9); Hickok, K., *Representations of Women: Nineteenth-Century British Women's Poetry* (1984); Lewis, N., 'A lost Pre-Raphaelite', *TLS* (8 December 1972); Peters, M., *Jean Ingelow, Victorian Poetess* (1972); Robertson, E. S. (ed.) *English Poetesses* (1883); Stedman, E. A., *An Appreciation* (1935); Symons, A., 'Jean Ingelow', *Saturday Review* 84 (1897).

Jacob, Naomi

b. 1 July 1884, Ripon, Yorkshire; d. 27 August 1964, Sirmione, Lake Garda, Italy

Novelist, memoirist

NJ was the daughter of Samuel Jacob, a German Jew, and Nina Ellington Collinson, daughter of an old Yorkshire family. She was educated privately and at Middlesbrough High School, but left at the age of 15 to earn her own living, her parents' marriage having run into difficulties. She began work as a pupil-teacher, earning £12 per year at a Church of England School in Middles-brough, and managed, by self-education, to qualify as a teacher.

Having become disillusioned with education, NJ left her teaching post to become manager and secretary to the variety artiste Marguerite Broadfoote, and met many famous stage performers. At this time she became an active supporter of both the Woman's Suffrage Movement and the Labour Party. She was received into the Roman Catholic Church in 1914.

When the First World War started, NJ enlisted as an officer in the Women's Legion and became the superintendent of a munitions factory. She contracted tuberculosis in 1917 and spent the following three years in a sanitorium. When she recovered, she found it difficult to obtain work, and eventually turned to the stage, making her debut in 1920 and achieving considerable success in West End productions and in films during the next ten years.

In 1926, NJ's first novel *Jacob Ussher* (based on a play by H. V. Esmond) was published and achieved immediate success. Thereafter she wrote prolifically, producing two books a year for most of the rest of her life.

NJ became ill again in 1930 and, having been advised to live in a milder climate, she settled in Sirmione, on the shores of Lake Garda, Italy. Her health improved rapidly and she continued her writing there, returning to England every summer to give lecture tours on the subjects of peace, literature, and the theatre. She also worked for the cause of animal welfare.

In 1939 NJ returned to England and on the outbreak of the Second World War she again enlisted as an officer in the Women's Legion and served in ENSA in North Africa, Sicily and Italy. She made a brief return to the London stage, appearing in 1942 in *The Nutmeg Tree* by Margery Sharp, and also wrote two one-act plays herself, *The Dawn* and *Mary of Delight*.

After the war NJ was able to go back to her Italian home, 'Casa Micki', but she revisited England every year. She had by now left the Labour Party and become a Conservative. As well as her continuing output of novels, she was now writing a series of autobiographical works, beginning with *Me: A Chronicle about Other People* in 1933. Her last two books, *Me – and the Stage* and the novel *The Long Shadows* were published on her eightieth birthday in 1964, six weeks before she died.

NJ's novels achieved a wide popularity which continues to the present day. Her style is sympathetic and easy to read and her plots are straightforward and traditional, with an emphasis on family stories and character studies. The influence of both her parents is obvious in her work. Her mother's family had farmed the same land in Yorkshire for over 300 years and she drew on this heritage for some of her most successful novels, such as *They Left the Land* (1940). NJ's father was Jewish and his background was the inspirational source for *Young Emmanuel* (1932) and *Four Generations* (1934) which achieved instant success and were later reissued as part of the two-volume *Gollancz Saga*. While all her novels are characterized by a warmth and a tolerant understanding of human nature, the *Gollancz Saga* books, written during the Nazi era, make a contribution to a concept of the brotherhood of man, and are probably her most lasting work.

NJ's non-fiction works include a popular biography of Marie Lloyd entitled *Our Marie* (1936) and the eleven lightly written and amusing autobiographical volumes variously titled *Me*, which were generally less successful than her novels.   MARGARET ASHBY

Selected works: *Jacob Ussher* (1926); *Power* (1927); *Rock and Sand* (1929); *The Beloved Physician* (1930); *Roots* (1931); *Props* (1932); *Young Emmanuel* (1932); *Me: A Chronicle about Other People* (1933); *The Plough* (1934); *Four Generations* (1934); *The Loaded Stick* (1934); *Me – in the Kitchen* (1935); *Timepiece* (1936); *Our Marie* (1936); *Me – Again* (1937); *Fade Out* (1937); *The Lenient God* (1938); *Straws in Amber* (1938); *Full Meridian* (1939); *They Left the Land* (1940); *Me – in Wartime* (1940); *Cap of Youth* (1941); *Private Gollancz* (1943); *Susan Crowther* (1945); *Me and the Mediterranean* (1945); *Honour's a Mistress* (1947); *Me – Over There* (1947); *Mary of Delight* (1949); *Me and Mine* (1949); *Every Other Gift* (1950); *Heart of the House* (1950); *Me – Looking Back* (1950); *Robert, Nana and – Me* (1952); *The Gollancz Saga* (2 vols 1952–3); *Morning Will Come* (1953); *Antonia* (1954); *Me – Likes and Dislikes* (1954); *Gollancz and Partners* (1958); *What's to Come* (1958); *Great Black Oxen* (1962); *The Long Shadows* (1964); *Me – and the Stage* (1964).

References: *CA*; Daiches, D. (ed.), *Penguin Companion to Literature* (1971); Richardson, K. (ed.), *Twentieth Century Writing* (1969); *Twentieth Century Authors: A Bibliographical Dictionary of Modern Literature* (1942); Ward, A. C. (ed.), *Longman Companion to Twentieth Century Literature* (1981).

James, P. D.

b. 3 August 1920

Crime novelist

Daughter of Sidney and Dorothy James, PDJ was educated at Cambridge High School but did not go to university as her father did not wish to pay for a girl's education. At the age of 16 she started work at a local tax office and a few years later she became assistant stage manager at the Festival Theatre in Cambridge. In 1941 she married a doctor, Ernest Connor White, with whom she had two daughters. She went back to work in 1949 to support her husband who had returned from the war seriously ill. From 1949 to 1968 she rose through the ranks of the NHS to become a hospital administrator. In 1968 she passed a competitive examination for senior placement in the Criminal Division of the British Home Office, becoming a specialist in juvenile delinquency in the Children's Division in 1971. She was awarded the OBE in 1983.

PDJ is best known for her novels featuring the detective Adam Dalgleish, of Scotland Yard. An intellectual and sensitive man, he ages and rises in rank with each book but remains as devoted to his work and as introspective as he was in the first novel *Cover her Face* (1962). PDJ uses the rather conventional setting of a grand old English house for this, but uses her own working environment in *A Mind to Murder* (1963), *Shroud For a Nightingale* (1971) and *The Black Tower* (1975) where murders take place in medical institutions (the last two won a Gold and a Silver Dagger from the Crime Writers' Association). Her extensive grounding in hospital procedure provides meticulous detail for her complex but well-controlled plots. A forensic science laboratory and its routines are used in *Death of an Expert Witness* (1976). This work contains some of PDJ's most convincing characters in a compassionate study of anguish and love in the motherless family of a pathologist, the affairs of a fickle widow, and the moving relationship of a writer and her young companion. In *Unnatural Causes* (1967) we follow Adam Dalgleish to the small coastal settlement where he goes to rest with his aunt and chances upon a murder among an isolated community of writers. With skilful characterization and evocative descriptions of the unwelcoming landscape, PDJ builds up an oppressive atmosphere of jealousy and resentment to match Dalgleish's personal frustration as he decides whether to marry and finds himself at odds with the policeman officially handling the case. He appears only as a secondary character in *An Unsuitable Job For a Woman* (1972) in which the protagonist is Cordelia Gray, a 22-year-old private detective. In *The Skull Beneath the Skin* (1982) she solves the murder of an actress in a mystery influenced by Jacobean tragedy. In *Innocent Blood* (1980) PDJ shows the effects of a past murder on the daughter of two murderers, and stresses, as in most of her novels, the shattering consequences of crime on innocent people. She uses the conventions of a murder mystery to build up suspense, but does not allow a fresh murder to take place as it would focus attention away from the sadness and deprivation she is pointing to. Adam Dalgleish returns in *A Taste For Death* (1986) where a senior woman detective, Kate Miskin, is introduced to solve the murder of an MP. Also set in London, this work, like *Innocent Blood*, reveals unsatisfactory relationships as it cleverly plays with the conventions of detective fiction, but the violent climax it builds up to is most seriously concerned with innocence and endurance. PDJ's one non-fictional work is *The Maul and the Pear Tree* (1971), written with Thomas A. Critchley, concerning a series of real crimes that took place in London's East End in 1811.

MARINA TZAMOURANIS

Works: *Cover Her Face* (1962); *A Mind to Murder* (1963); *Unnatural Causes* (1967); *Shroud For a Nightingale* (1971); *The Maul and the Pear Tree* (with Thomas A. Critchley) (1971); *An Unsuitable Job For a Woman* (1972); *The Black Tower* (1975); *Death of an Expert Witness* (1976); *Innocent Blood* (1980); *The Skull Beneath the Skin* (1982); *A Taste for Death* (1986).

References: Bailey, P., 'Between two worlds', *Times Literary Supplement* (20 March 1980); Bannon, B. (ed.) 'PW interviews; P. D. James', *Publishers Weekly* (5 January 1976); Cannon, M., 'Mistress of malice domestic', *Macleans* (30 June 1980); James, P. D., 'Ought Adam to marry Cordelia?', *Murder Ink*, ed. D. Wynn, (1977); Siebenheller, N., *P. D. James* (1981); de la Torre, L., 'Cordelia Gray: the thinking man's heroine', *Murder Ink*, ed. D. Wynn (1977); Winks, R. W., *Murder and Dying* (1976).

Jameson, Anna B.

b. 17 May 1794, Dublin; d. 17 March 1860, Ealing

Essayist, travel writer, art historian

AJ came to England at the age of 4, when her father, Dennis Brownell Murphy, a miniaturist painter, brought his English wife and young family to live in Whitehaven, eventually settling at Hanwell, near London. AJ, the eldest of five daughters, was a high-spirited and gifted child, who dominated over and led her sisters, and revolted against her governess, preferring to undertake her own course of reading and learning, including teaching herself Italian. Acquainted early on with her father's financial ineptitude, at one time she planned a runaway trip to Brussels where she and her sisters could learn lacemaking and help to alleviate family monetary difficulties. Despite a somewhat desultory education, she was considered well enough equipped to become a governess when she was 16, first to the sons of the Marquis of Winchester, then to the Rowles family of Bradbourne Park, Kent, and finally to the Littletons of Teddersley, Staffs, an occupation in which she remained until 1825.

Around the end of 1820 she met Robert Jameson, lawyer and friend of Hartley Coleridge, to whom she begame engaged in spring 1821, but the engagement was broken off shortly afterwards, and later that year AJ went with the Rowleses on a continental tour. The result of this trip was her first major publication, *The Diary of an Ennuyée* (1826, reissued in 1834 together with other travel pieces and commentary on German art and female writers as *Visits and Sketches*), a curious fictionalized travel biography in which her self-indulgently morbid persona, suffering from some unspecified and debilitating grief and clearly to some extent embodying her creator, recounts her impressions of Italy; despite its maudlin sentimentality, it contains some valuable observations and is not without humour. Jameson resumed his courtship when AJ returned to England the following year, and after some apparent reluctance she married him in 1825. The marriage was unsuccessful from the beginning, perhaps because of personality differences: in 1829 Jameson went to Dominica as puisne judge, while AJ stayed behind and accompanied her father and a friend on a tour of the Low Countries and Germany; in 1833 he returned, but departed in a few months to become Attorney General in Upper Canada, again leaving AJ who made several more trips to Germany, establishing there a passionate friendship with Ottilie von Goethe. In 1836 she went out to join him in Toronto, but the visit proved disastrous and she left in September 1837, never seeing her husband again. A separation was agreed between them, and he made her a small allowance, but on his death in 1854 his will made no provision for her.

The rest of her life was divided between travel and writing, the latter increasingly necessitated as her family relied on her financial support, especially after her father's death in 1842; an additional commitment was the welfare of her niece, Gerardine, for whom she made herself responsible after her brother-in-law's financial downfall. Her widening circle of friends included Elizabeth Barrett and Robert Browning – whom she accompanied from Paris to Pisa after their secret marriage and whom she several times visited in Florence – Lady Byron, Fanny Kemble, and Elizabeth Gaskell. She continued to travel frequently, particularly in Germany and Italy, ostensibly to collect material for her voluminous *Sacred and Legendary Art* (1848–52) but also to escape the constraint of home life and domestic duties and enjoy freedom of movement.

Her literary work, which gained her considerable popularity, is rarely iconoclastic, her art criticism aiming at elucidating painting from a moral and religious perspective for the general public rather than establishing revolutionary aesthetic principles, and her social commentaries being more descriptive than destructive, but it shows a growing concern for women and female-oriented topics, even where the subject is not overtly feminist. Her *Characteristics of Women* (1832), for example, while basically treating Shakespeare's heroines, encompasses discussion of female education and the difference between men and women, and the fruit of her Canadian trip, *Winter Studies and Summer Rambles* (1838), a travel book on the New World, contains many observations about the need for changed attitudes towards women's roles and education, material which provoked attacks from several reviewers. In 1842 she published pseudonymously an article in the *Athenaeum* on the recent Royal Commission Report on the employment of women and young people in mines, in which she demanded better support for working women, and in 1845 she produced a pamphlet entitled *On Mothers and Governesses* blaming the deficiencies of female education for the inferior status of governesses; both works were republished in 1846 in an essay collection. In 1855, she gave the first of two public lectures, on *Sisters of Charity*, printed later that year; one on women's employment followed, published as *The Communion of Labour* (1856). In both of these she pleaded strongly for wider opportunities for women and for the breaking-down of rigid sexual, social and economic divisions. At this time, too, she sponsored a group of educational and feminist reformers, including Barbara Bodichon, Adelaide Proctor, and Bessie Parkes, encouraging their work and suggesting the idea of the *Englishwoman's Journal*. While never militant in outlook (she did not argue for complete equality and regarded domestic happiness as the prime female goal), she learnt from her own experience the importance of independence and consistently called for fairer treatment of women. Widely respected as a philanthropist, social critic, and art historian, she died from bronchial pneumonia in 1860, while still working on the last of her *Sacred and Legendary Art* series, *History of Our Lord*.   SHIRLEY FORSTER

Selected works: *A First or Mother's Dictionary for Children* (1825); *The Diary of an Ennuyée* (first issued anonymously as *A Lady's Diary*) (1826); *Memoirs of the Loves of the Poets* (1829); *Memoirs of the Beauties of the Court of Charles II* (1831); *Characteristics of Women*, 2 vols (1832); *Visits and Sketches at Home and Abroad* (1834); *Winter Studies and Summer Rambles in Canada* (1838); *Handbook to the Public Galleries of Art in or Near London* (1840); *Companion to the Private Galleries of Art in London* (1844); *Memoirs of Early Italian Painters* (1845); *The Relative Position of Mothers and Governesses* (1846); *Memoirs and Essays on Art, Literature* *and Social Morals* (1846); *Sacred and Legendary Art* (1848); *Legends of the Monastic Orders* (1850); *Legends of the Madonna* (1852); *A Commonplace Book of Thoughts, Memories and Fancies, Original and Selected* (1854); *Sisters of Charity, Catholic and Protestant, at Home and Abroad* (1855); *The Communion of Labour* (1856); *The History of Our Lord, as Exemplified in Works of Art* (completed by Lady Eastlake) (1864); *Early Canadian Sketches* (1958).

References: BA (19); Banks, O., *The Biographical Dictionary of British Feminists, vol. I: 1800–1930* (1985); Erskine, Mrs S. (ed.), *Anna Jameson: Letters and Friendships, 1812–1860* (1915); Macpherson, G., *Memoirs of Anna Jameson* (1878); Thomas, C., *Love and Work Enough: The Life of Anna Jameson* (1967).

Jameson, Storm

b. 1891, Whitby; d. 30 September 1986, Cambridge

Novelist, critic, essayist, memoirist, translator

(Also wrote under William Lamb, James Hill)

SJ was born into a northern family with strong seafaring connections, her mother a shipowner's daughter, her father a master mariner. Educated at Scarborough Municipal School, she obtained English honours from Leeds University in 1912 followed by an MA from London University. SJ's early novels, *The Pot Boils* (1919), *The Happy Highways* (1920), *The Clash* (1922) and *The Pitiful Wife* (1924), deal with the gap between men who fought in the First World War and the women who stayed at home, detailing the destructive effects of the war on personal relations and sexual morality and the opportunities it provided for marital infidelity. In 1925 SJ married the historian Guy Chapman, and learned something of the fascination of war, which she expressed in *Three Kingdoms* (1926) and *Farewell to Youth* (1928).

The *Triumph of Time* trilogy, consisting of *The Lovely Ship* (1927), *The Voyage Home* (1930), and *A Richer Dust* (1931), chronicles the life of Mary Hervey and a middle-class northern family across generations. *A Day Off* (1933) is a sharply observed segment in the life of an ageing woman fearing desertion by her lover, a character study of petty deceptions and strong emotional need. Her second trilogy, *The Mirror of Darkness* sequence containing *Company Parade* (1934), *Love in Winter* (1935), and *None Turn Back* (1936), reveals SJ's interest in the interface of the personal and the political and focuses on a cross-section of characters to explore the nature of these connections. In *None Turn Back* she concentrates on Hervey Russell and on a social spectrum of rich and poor, fascist and communist, men and women, industrialists and intellectuals and their interactions and interrelationships in the week of the General Strike.

In the 1930s SJ was increasingly occupied with the threat of fascism and she became active in a number of left-wing, liberal, and humanitarian causes. The fear of fascism was the impetus behind *In the Second Year* (1936), a terse dystopian thriller set in the second year of an imaginary English dictatorship. In her autobiography, *Journey from the North* (1970), she describes the impulses which turned creative artists into pamphleteers and amateur politicians. 'There really was a stench. On one side Dachau, on the other "the distressed areas" with their ashamed workless men and despairing women.' SJ explains that not many English writers had the hardness of heart to remain detached from such suffering.

In 1939 she became President of the British section of International PEN and actively engaged in helping refugee writers. *Europe to Let* (1940), *Cousin Honoré* (1941), and *Cloudless May* (1944) focus on occupied Europe. *Cousin Honoré* provides a portrait of a French province as a microcosm of those forces representing and resisting the threat to French civilization. In *Cloudless May* she anatomizes a French township awaiting the arrival of the Germans; she examines the greed, courage, vanity, loyalty, honesty and cowardice of its different inhabitants. The novel is centred not on an individual but on the community as a whole. SJ was an admirer of France where she spent time happily, and she translated de Maupassant. She visited Poland and Czechoslovakia, witnessing the devastation of war at first-hand. *The Black Laurel* (1948) unfolds in Berlin and eastern Europe. In this novel SJ retains characters, David Renn and William Cory, from *The Mirror of Darkness*. Two of her later novels, *The Green Man* (1953) and *A Cup of Tea for Mr Thorgill* (1957) contain careful satires of the political and social intrigues of the establishment world.

SJ wrote prolifically, publishing forty-five novels, and was highly critical of her own work. In *Journey from the North* she mentions only *That was Yesterday* (1932), *A Day Off* (1933), *Cousin Honoré*, *Cloudless May*, *The Journal of Mary Hervey Russell* (1945), *Before the Crossing*, *The Black Laurel* and *The Green Man* as having been worth writing. However, her cameo *A Day Off* displays the ability to investigate a range of emotions and convey the essence of character that is prominent throughout all her writing.   MARY JOANNOU

Selected works: *The Pot Boils* (1919); *Modern Drama in Europe* (1920); *The Clash* (1922); *Lady Susan and Life* (1923); (trans.), *Mont-Oriel*, by Guy de Maupassant (1924); (trans.), *Horla and Other Stories* by Guy de Maupassant (1924); *The Lovely Ship* (1927); *Farewell to Youth* (1928); *The Decline of Merry England* (1930); *The Voyage Home* (1930); *A Richer Dust* (1931); *That was Yesterday* (1932); *A Day Off* (1933); *No Time Like the Present* (1933); *Challenge to Death* (1935); *Love in Winter* (1935); *The Soul of Man in the Age of Leisure* (1935); *None Turn Back* (1936); *In the Second Year* (1936); *The Moon is Making* (1937); *The World Ends* (under pseudonym William Lamb) (1937); *Loving Memory* (under pseudonym James Hill) (1937); *No Victory for the Soldier* (under pseudonym James Hill) (1938); *The Novel in Contemporary Life* (1938); *Here Comes a Candle* (1939); *The Captain's Wife* (1939); *Europe to Let* (1940); *Cousin Honoré* (1941); *The Fort* (1941); *London Calling* (1942); *Cloudless May* (1944); *The Journal of Mary Hervey Russell* (1945); *The Writer's Situation* (1950); *The Green Man* (1953); *A Cup of Tea for Mr Thorgill* (1957); *A Ulysses Too Many* (1958); *Morley Roberts: The Last Eminent Victorian* (1961); *A Month Soon Goes By* (1963); *The Early Life of Stephen Hind* (1966); *Journey From the North* (1970); *Parthian Words* (1971); *There Will Be a Short Interval* (1973); *Speaking of Stendhal* (1979).

References: Beauman, N., *A Very Great Profession* (1983); Drabble.

Jellicoe, Ann

b. 15 July 1927, Middlesbrough, Yorkshire

Dramatist, director

AJ is the daughter of John Andrea Jellicoe, described by her as a 'sophisticated . . . aristocratic . . . also rather intelligent' man from the south, and Frances Jackson Henderson, a 'practical, solid Methodist' from the north. Her parents separated when she was eighteen months old and AJ received her early education in the north at Polam Hall School in Darlington, County Durham, and Queen Margaret's School in Castle Howard, Yorkshire. AJ remembers wanting to be an actress as a child; however, when she studied at the Central School of Speech and Drama in London (1944–7), where she was awarded the Elsie Fogerty prize in 1947, she 'discovered herself' as a director.

After beginning her career in the theatre as an actress, stage manager, and director in repertory, she travelled abroad to learn languages and study theatre architecture. She married C. E. Knight-Clarke in 1950. The marriage ended in 1961 and the following year she married Roger Mayne, with whom she has a son and a daughter. In the early 1950s, AJ founded and ran for two years the Cockpit Theatre Club, an open-stage experimental theatre club in London. She directed several plays, including an early one of her own, described by John Russell Taylor as a 'one-act indiscretion' in the style of Christopher Frye, which she prefers to forget. AJ returned to the Central School of Speech and Drama in 1953 as a lecturer and director, where she directed and produced student plays for two years. In 1956, hoping to break into professional theatre as a director, AJ wrote *The Sport of My Mad Mother*, which won joint third prize in the *Observer* playwriting competition in 1957. During the years 1973–5 she served as Literary Manager of the Royal Court Theatre in London and continued her improvisational work on the stage by writing and directing plays for children. Since 1979 she has been the Founding Director of the Colway Theatre Trust, a group involved in large-scale community theatre productions. AJ was awarded the OBE in 1983 for her work in the theatre.

The Knack and *The Sport of My Mad Mother*, AJ's two best-known plays, explore the basic hostilities between people and use experimental theatrical techniques. *The Sport of My Mad Mother* (the title comes from the Hindu hymn 'all creation is the sport of my mad mother') presents a series of ritualistic episodes of arbitrary violence acted out instinctively by a group of teenagers. Greta, an earth-mother goddess figure, guides the destruction and gives birth to a child at the end of the play. AJ attempts to convey thought and emotion through group action, gesture, rhythm, music, and noise rather than through dialogue. Consequently, language in the play operates less on the level of rational meaning than as incantatory sounds used to release emotion. More recent criticism has been supportive of AJ's anti-intellectual approach to theatrical form and content. John Russell Taylor, for example, likens the written text of *Sport* to a 'short score from which a full orchestral sound can be conjured by a skilled musician'. Reviewers of the 1958 production, co-directed by AJ and George Devine, were less taken with AJ's 'verbal jazz' and the play was deemed a critical as well as a commercial failure.

The Knack was more successful, owing in large part to the film adaptation (*The Knack . . . and How to Get It*) which won the best picture award at the 1965 Cannes Film Festival. The 'knack' in the title refers to the ability to seduce women. Three young men, Tolen, Tom, and Colin, live together in a house in London. Two of the men are obsessed by sex. Tolen is successful sexually, with frequent conquests, Colin wishes he were, whilst Tom seems to be indifferent. When Nancy enters requesting directions to the YWCA, the comical plot begins as each of the four characters explores his or her feelings about sex. As in *Sport*, the action of the play often has little to do with what is said. When Colin and Tom persuade Nancy to participate in their fantasy that the bed in the room is actually a piano, the dialogue becomes a prolongued series of uninterrupted 'pings' and 'plongs'. AJ has argued that *The Knack* is not about sex, but about how people should treat other people. In her preface to *Shelley*, she describes Tolen's use of sex and sexual advice as a form of power. She prefers Tom's indirect approach. Tom does not provide Colin with ready-made answers to his problems; instead, he tries to place Colin in situations where he 'will be able to recognize the nature of his problems and perhaps find his own answers; . . . The man who understands seldom makes a direct statement.'

AJ's other plays exhibit the diversity of her approach to the theatre. Although *The Giveaway* (1969) uses techniques similar to those in *The Knack, Shelley, or, The Idealist* (1966) proved that she could write a more orthodox, intellectual play. In this almost documentary account of Shelley's life, AJ relies on language as the principal vehicle of communication. *The Rising Generation*, a parable of intolerance and totalitarian rule that was commissioned and later rejected by the Girl Guide organization, was written for a cast of 800 girls, 100 boys and a few adults.

AJ has translated and produced plays by Chekhov and Ibsen and she has written and directed three plays for children. More recently, she has become involved in large-scale community theatre. *The Reckoning*, a historical play about Lyme Regis produced in 1978, involved more than 200 people, including many of the people of Lyme Regis itself. These community theatre projects have seemed of less importance to the publishing industry, which still prefers more conventional individual literary achievement. This is unfortunate, because *The Reckoning* and *The Tide* (1980), by blurring the distinction between actor and spectator, exhibit AJ's most recent attempts to expand the possibilities of theatre.   CHARMAINE EDDY

Works: (trans.), *Rosmersholm*, by Henrik Ibsen (1960); 'The rising generation' *Ark* 25 (1960); (produced), *The Lady from the Sea*, by Henrik Ibsen (1961); *The Knack* (1962); (produced), *Der Freischutz*, libretto by Friedrich Kind (1963); *The Sport of My Mad Mother* (1964); *Shelley, or, The Idealist* (1966); *Some Unconscious Influences in the Theatre* (1967); *The Giveaway* (1970); (trans.), *The Seagull*, by Anton Chekhov (1975); *Three Jelliplays* (includes 'You'll Never Guess', 'Clever Elsie, Smiling Jack, Silent Peter', and 'A Good Thing and a Bad Thing') (1975); *Devon, A Shell Guide* (with Roger Mayne) (1975).

References: Clurman, H., *The Naked Image: Observations on the Modern Theatre* (1958); Findlater, R. (ed.), *At the Royal Court* (1981); Gottfried, M., *A Theatre Divided: The Postwar American Stage* (1967); Lumley, F., *New Trends in 20th Century Drama* (1967); McCrindle, J. F. (ed.), *Behind the Scenes: Theatre and Film Interviews from the Transatlantic Review* (1971); Taylor, J. R., *Anger and After* (1962).

Jenkins, Elizabeth

b. 31 October 1907, Hitchin, Hertfordshire

Novelist, biographer

EJ, daughter of James Heald (a headmaster) and Theodora (*née* Caldicott Ingram) Jenkins, was educated at St Christopher's School, Letchworth, and Newnham College, Cambridge (1924–7). In 1929 she published her first novel, *Virginia Water*. The same year she accepted a position as senior English mistress at King Alfred School, where she remained until 1939. During the war she worked for the British civil service. Since 1945 EJ has devoted herself full-time to research and writing. She was awarded an OBE in 1981.

Her most memorable fiction depicts with chilling matter-of-factness the victimization of her protagonists and the obdurate selfishness of their otherwise ordinary antagonists. EJ won the Femina Vie Heureuse Prize in 1934 for her second novel, *Harriet*, a psychological study of criminals' minds, based on a true story of a simple-minded woman and her infant son systematically starved to death by her husband and in-laws, who wanted her small inheritance. *The Tortoise and the Hare* (1954), the least sentimental or sensational of her novels, takes the point of view of the victim, tracing the psychological changes in a passive, weak, conventional woman whose husband is in the process of leaving her for an active, strong, capable, and passionate rival. Although the protagonist is treated with great gentleness and sympathy by EJ, the author does not gloss over the degree to which her heroine's shortcomings are directly responsible for her marital disaster. *Brightness* (1963) and *Honey* (1968), both novels about sensitive adolescent boys victimized by loveless adults around them, succeed better as exemplars of Christian charity than as realistic novels, but some of the background characters are finely drawn.

In contrast to the victimized protagonists of her fiction, the subjects of EJ's biographies are strong characters. Her short critical biography *Henry Fielding* approaches its subject with energetic appreciation of the man, his works, and his age. *Lady Caroline Lamb* (1932) is a lively, vivid and informally organized account openly partisan to its subject. Similarly lively, anecdotal, and personal are her *Elizabeth the Great* (1958) and *Elizabeth and Leicester* (1961), praised for their convincing psychological explanation of Elizabeth's refusal to marry. *Jane Austen: A Biography* (1949) is of EJ's biographies the most scholarly in tone and documentation, a meticulous, thorough, and readable presentation of the novelist's life and milieu. In addition to writing biographies valued primarily for their novelistic qualities, EJ wrote *The Phoenix Nest* (1936), an historical novel based on the life of Christopher Marlowe, and two collections of biographical essays, *Six Criminal Women* (1949) and *Ten Fascinating Women* (1955).

KATE BROWDER HEBERLEIN

Works: *Virginia Water* (1930); *The Winters* (1931); *Lady Carolyn Lamb: A Biography* (1932); *Portrait of an Actor* (1933); *Harriet* (1934); *Doubtful Joy* (1935); *The Phoenix Nest* (1936); *Jane Austen: A Biography* (1938); *Robert and Helen* (1944); *Henry Fielding* (1947); *Six Criminal Women* (1949); *The Tortoise and the Hare* (1954); *Ten Fascinating Women* (1955); *Elizabeth the Great* (1958); *Joseph Lister* (1960); *Elizabeth and Leicester* (1961); *Brightness* (1963); *Honey* (1968); *Dr Gully* (1972); *The Mystery of King Arthur* (1975); *The Princes in the Tower* (1978); *The Shadow and the Light: A Defence of Daniel Dunglas Home, the Medium* (1982).

References: *CA*; McNeil, H., 'Introduction' to *The Tortoise and the Hare* (1983).

Jennings, Elizabeth

b. 1926, Boston, Lincolnshire

Poet

EJ's early childhood was spent in the Lincolnshire town of Boston, an area which provided the stimulus for some of her most refreshing and evocative poetry. It is probable however that it was her years as an undergraduate at St Anne's College, Oxford, from 1945 to 1949 that began to influence how she translated her experiences into poetry. At Oxford EJ associated and worked with various of those writers who came to form the 'Movement' group. Though her inclusion amongst the Movement writers has been disputed, it is evident that characteristics of Movement thinking influenced her work: contemporary imagery and regulated rhyme and metre gradually replaced Romantic, inventive, sensuous imagery and archaisms. EJ's poems have recorded her progress, whilst consistently exhibiting a fluent lyricism and technical diversity. This is apparent not only in her original work, but in the translations she made, for example those from Rimbaud (*Lucidities*, 1970).

EJ's earlier work is technically accomplished and balanced. She shows evidence of an ability to feel sympathetically and to create animated and diverse poetry, memorable through its imaginative awareness, as in 'Fishermen', 'My

Grandmother', and 'Song at the Beginning of Autumn', from which the following extract is taken:

> But I am carried back against
> My will into a childhood where
> Autumn is bonfires, marbles, smoke;
> I lean against my window fenced
> From evocations in the air.
> When I said autumn, autumn broke.

Not all of EJ's poems exude such an air of confidence in the sanity of life as those written at the time when her involvement with the Movement was at its height: *Song for a Birth or a Death* (1961) contains violent and unsettling visions, while the experience of a nervous breakdown in the early 1960s markedly influenced her work. The poems maintain their control and cool reflection, but there is a painful awareness and sharp authenticity about the imagery which startles, as in *The Mind Has Mountains* (1966) and 'Sequence in Hospital' from *Recoveries* (1964) from which the following extract is taken:

> The huge philosophers depart,
> Large words slink off, like faith, like love,
> The thumping of the human heart
> Is reassurance here enough.
>
> Only one dreamer going back
> To how he felt when he was well,
> Weeps under pillows at his lack
> But cannot tell, but cannot tell.

EJ's poems of the 1970s and 1980s celebrate nature, love, and, particularly, her Catholic faith. Her sincerity and sensibility have been acclaimed in these meditations and evocations. The generous candour with which she writes allows us a view into thoughts and experiences which seem simultaneously private and eminently sharable as the following extract from 'Easter Duties', from *Growing Points* (1975), shows:

> And, yes, I want to bear
>
> Anticipated laughter, jokes which once
> Meant calibre and bite but did not make
> Anyone sad. Prayer yet could be a dance
> But still a cross. I offer small heartbreak,
> Catch grace almost by chance.

EJ acknowledged her belief in the importance of interplay between poet and reader, stating in *Christianity and Poetry* (1965) that a poet can only write interestingly and alertly if the reader is somehow allowed to feel involved: 'What I want is art for man's sake and for God's sake,' she wrote.

LORNA DAMMS

Works: *Poems* (1953); *A Way of Looking* (1955); *A Sense of the World* (1958); *Song for a Birth or a Death* (1961); *Recoveries* (1964); 'The Making of a Movement', *Spectator* (2 October 1964); *Christianity and Poetry* (1965); *The Secret Brother* (1966); *The Mind Has Mountains* (1966); *Collected Poems* (1967); *The Animals' Arrival* (1969); *Lucidities* (1970); *Relationships* (1972); *The Annunciation: Two Poems by R. Southwell and Elizabeth Jennings* (1972); *Growing Points* (1975); *Seven Men of Vision: An Appreciation* (1976); *Consequently I Rejoice* (1977); *After the*

Ark (1978); *Moments of Grace* (1980); *Celebrations and Elegies* (1982); *Extending the Territory* (1985); *Collected Poems* (1986).
References: Bedient, C., *Eight Contemporary Poets* (1974); Morrison, B., *The Movement* (1980).

Jesse, F. Tennyson

b. 1888, Chislehurst, Kent; d. 6 August 1958, St John's Wood, London
Novelist, dramatist, criminologist

FTJ was the second of three daughters of the Rev. Eustace Tennyson d'Eyncourt Jesse and his wife Edith Louisa James. At an early age she was sent to study art at the school of Mr and Mrs Stanhope Forbes at Newlyn. In 1911 she moved to London to work for *The Times* and the *Daily Mail* as a reporter. She also wrote book reviews for *The Times Literary Supplement* and the *English Review*.

In 1914 she spent a brief period in New York working on the *Metropolitan Magazine*. She then returned to Europe and throughout the First World War acted as correspondent for various newspapers as well as for the Ministry of Information, being one of the first woman journalists to report from the front. She was also involved in work for the National Relief Commission and the French Red Cross.

In 1918 she married the famous playwright H. M. Harwood. The couple had become friends when Harwood had written to her asking 'Mr Jesse' for permission to dramatize 'his' novel, *The Milky Way* (1913). After their marriage they moved often, setting up homes in both England and France. They collaborated on many plays, as well as jointly publishing their letters to friends in America under the titles of *London Front* (1940) and *While London Burns* (1942). Early on in her career she lost the fingers of her right hand and had patiently to teach herself to write again.

FTJ's most striking quality is her diversity. Beyond writing novels, plays and poems, she also made valuable contributions to the field of criminology. One of her main ideas was that, just as there are 'born murderers', there are also people who seem destined to be murdered and who may thus be termed 'born murderees'. In 1927 she was asked by the *Notable British Trials Series* to edit the trial of Madeleine Smith. FTJ was the first woman to be offered this job by the publishers and she went on to edit a number of famous cases. She became a member of the Royal Society of Literature in 1947.

In *Murder and its Motives* (1924) FTJ classifies murderers and their crimes according to six different motives, namely gain, revenge, elimination, jealousy, lust of killing, and conviction. Of other people she wrote, 'It has been observed with some truth, that everyone loves a good murder.' She describes murderers in great detail since for her this is where the fascination lies; the victim is usually of little interest, she believes. The book is especially attractive for the inclusion of a detailed description of late-nineteenth-century London.

Moonraker (1927) focuses on issues that are still current such as gender and race. The story, set in 1801, concerns a young boy called Jacky who runs away to sea and experiences a life of adventure, surprises, and new friendships. The political themes contrast with the swashbuckling setting, but the combination creates an intense atmosphere of cruelty and innocence. Jacky assists the famous black general, Toussaint L'Ouverture, in his fight against slavery and becomes a friend and companion of the strong woman, Captain Lovel, noting of both, 'they were the faces of the two most real people he had ever known.' Both stand for heroic but traditional virtues. Of Captain Lovel, it is implied, 'Virtue need not always go with a smooth face . . . women have lived strange and hard lives and been as chaste as snow,' while Toussaint L'Ouverture declares as he departs for France, 'I shall not be unhappy; if my people are treated well, it is all that matters, I will plough my fields and read my books.'

The Lacquer Lady (1929) is considered FTJ's best novel. The ideas behind it were inspired by a visit she made to Burma, where she grew fascinated by the fantastic story behind the Annexation of Upper Burma, related to her by Rod Swinhoe, one of the earliest dwellers in Mandalay after the Annexation. From his words she created the character of Fanny and many others, noting in the preface her indebtedness to Swinhoe: 'For it was he who told me the true causes which led to the Annexation of Upper Burma, how it was "Fanny" and her love affair.' She also spoke to other people who remembered the time. In the novel young, naïve Fanny travels from everyday life in Brighton to the terror and beauty of Mandalay; here in the name of what she believes to be love she reveals a secret that changes the future of Burma. FTJ feelingly evokes the exotic impression of Burma, but does not relinquish a sense of experienced reality.

A Pin to See the Peepshow (1934) is a story based on an English murder, the Thompson and Bywaters case, which took place in London in 1922. FTJ ironically studies the character of a woman, Julia, who almost dreams her way through life. It begins with her as a schoolgirl and ends with her last hours in prison. In between she is married to a dull husband mainly because she believed that he 'would mostly be away at the war, and she would have that lovely flat in St Clements Square'. She fantasizes about love and pleasure that exceed all reality, and the arrival of a lover only strengthens her belief in a world based on dreams, where comfort and passion are intermingled. Eventually it is Julia's fanciful nature that leads to her trial for murder because of the 'make-believe' letters she writes to her lover: 'but it was another thing to write about what life would be like if only Herbert was not there.' Julia's dreams lead her eventually to harsh reality; only then can she see her lover, the real murderer, in his true light: 'How could she love anyone who had done to her what he had done.' The most bitter irony is that Julia sacrificed for her dream world the only thing that could have saved her from death – the baby in her womb: 'This was the last irony. If she had not got rid of Herbert's child, she would have been safe now.' FTJ conveys sympathy for the silly but vital Julia, just as she felt sympathy for the original, Edith Thompson. Throughout the trial FTJ highlights the prejudice of the jury: 'The judge went on and on. He talked about their love, which he called adultery – had he never been to bed with anyone but his wife?' For Julia to admit to an abortion would have answered many of the prosecution's questions, but the reader is made to realize that the admission would simply make her death more certain. *A Pin to See the Peepshow* was dramatized and produced in New York in 1953. It was poorly received and closed after a very brief run. It was televized by the BBC in 1972.

LISA BUCKBY

Selected works: *The Mask* (1912); *The Milky Way* (1913); *Beggars On Horse-Back* (1915); *Secret Bread* (1917); *The Happy Bride* (1920); *The White Riband* (1921); *Murder and its Motives* (1924); *Anyhouse* (1925); *Tom Fool* (1926); *The Pelican* (with H. M. Harwood) (1926); *Moonraker* (1927); *Many Latitudes* (1928); *The Lacquer Lady* (1929); *Solange Stories* (1931); *A Pin to See the Peep Show* (1934); *Sabi Pas* (1935); *Act of God* (1936); *London Front* (with H. M. Harwood) (1940); *While London Burns* (with H. M. Harwood) (1942); *The Saga of San Demetrio* (1942); *The Story of Burma* (1946); *Comments on Cain* (1948); *The Alabaster Cup*

(1950); *The Compass* (1951); *A Pin to See the Peep Show* (with H. M. Harwood) (1953); *The Dragon in the Heart* (1956); editor in *Notable British Trials Series* for the following trials: *Madeleine Smith* (1927); *S. H. Dougal* (1928); *Sidney Fox* (1934); *Rattenbury & Stoner* (1935); *Ley & Smith* (1947); *Evans & Christie* (1957). *References:* Brander, J. C., 'Introduction' to *The Lacquer Lady* (1978); *A Portrait of Fryn* (1984); Jesse, J., '*The London Front* and *While London Burns*', *John O' London's Weekly* (6 January 1939); Leeson, B., 'Introduction' to *Moonraker* (1980); Morgan, E., 'Introduction' to *A Pin to See The Peep Show* (1978).

Jewsbury, Geraldine

b. 22 August 1812, Measham, Derbyshire; d. 23 September 1880, London

Novelist, journalist, writer for children

A popular and contoversial writer and promoter of women's causes. GJ was 6 when her mother died in 1818; together with her three brothers, she was brought up by her sister Maria Jane, twelve years her elder, who was also a successful writer. The stimulating literary environment, which included visits to and from British and American literary notables, continued until 1833 when Maria Jane married and sailed for India; GJ assumed responsibility for the household until the death of her father, Thomas, in 1840.

GJ's two principal philosophical mentors were George Sand and Thomas Carlyle. She discovered Carlyle's writings, notably *Past and Present*, at a time of spiritual crisis, and they affected her so deeply that she wrote to him, perhaps following the example of her sister who had received encouragement from Wordsworth. In 1841 she visited Thomas and Jane Carlyle in Cheyne Row and began a lifelong and sometimes tempestuous friendship with both of them. Although demanding the support of the Carlyles, GJ refused to be wholly guided by them, disgusting Thomas by her enthusiasm for George Sand. She returned to keep house for her favourite brother, Frank, in Lancashire, where she wrote her first novel, *Zoë* (1845). GJ remained there for ten years, housekeeping, writing, and entertaining visitors such as Ralph Waldo Emerson and George Henry Lewes. 'Faith and Scepticism' was sent to the *Westminster Review* by Lewes on her behalf in 1849 and was well received in certain literary circles. In 1854 she moved to Chelsea in order to be near the Carlyles; she continued to write for periodicals and to produce novels until 1859. In 1866, after the death of Jane Carlyle, she moved to Kent where she lived in retirement but continued to read for the publishing house of Bentley & Sons and to review for the *Athenaeum* until illness forced her back to London, where she died. GJ enjoyed a full career as a journalist, but her principal influence on English reading was through her work for Bentley & Sons from 1858 to 1880 and her reviews of more than 1,800 books for the *Athenaeum*.

While GJ is often remembered as a writer of popular fiction, she saw herself as a serious writer of social novels, although she spent only twelve years of a long career producing them. The hero's conflict between religion and love in *Zoë* is used to question the validity of organized religion and made the book an instant success. While the development of the hero was influenced by GJ's interest in the Oxford Movement, the treatment of the heroine was an exploration of passion in the manner of George Sand. *The Half-Sisters* (1848) showed a woman rising above her illegitimate birth and lack of social standing to a respected place in society. *Marian Withers* (1851), GJ's most impressive novel, discussed women's education and society's requirement that a woman establish herself by an appropriate marriage. George Henry Lewes described it, to GJ's annoyance, as a reply to Elizabeth Gaskell's *Mary Barton*; George Eliot criticized GJ in general for making all women heroines and all men villains. *Marian Withers* powerfully evokes its setting in Manchester and the surrounding countryside. GJ's unusually rapid narration enables her to provide Marian with a detailed social background; and Marian's emergence as an educated and active woman is considered in tandem with the difficulties which this education causes her.

GJ's later novels are generally of less interest. *The Sorrows of Gentility* (1851) explores the widespread social approbation of a husband's exploitation of his wife. *Constance Herbert* (1855) examines the fate of a woman who chooses power over other possible human relationships. In *Right or Wrong* (1856), her last novel, GJ returns to religion in a denunciation of the celibacy of a Catholic priest. In all her novels the pace is brisk, the characters well drawn, the description vivid, and the tone didactic. GJ wrote two books for children, *The History of an Adopted Child* (1852) and *Angelo, or, The Pine Forest in the Alps* (1856), as well as numerous children's stories for *Juvenile Budget* and *Household Words*.

ELEANOR LANGSTAFF

Works: *Zoë* (1845); *The Half-Sisters* (1848); *Marian Withers* (1851); *The History of an Adopted Child* (1852); *Constance Herbert* (1855); *Right or Wrong* (1856); *The Sorrows of Gentility* (1856); *Angelo, or, The Pine Forest in the Alps* (1856); *Selections from the Letters of Geraldine Endsor Jewsbury to Jane Welsh Carlyle* (1892).

References: Allibone; Cary, M., 'Geraldine Jewsbury and the woman question', *Research Studies* 42 (1974); *DLB*; *DNB*; Drabble; Fahnestock, J. R., 'Geraldine Jewsbury: the power of the publisher's reader', *Nineteenth Century Fiction* 28 (1973); Fryckstedt, M. C., 'Geraldine Jewsbury and *Douglas Jerrold's Shilling Magazine*', *English Studies* 4 (1985); Fryckstedt, M. C., 'New sources on Geraldine Jewsbury and the woman question', *Research Studies* 51 (1983); Griest, G. L., *Mudie's Circulating Library and the Victorian Novel* (1970); Howe, S., *Geraldine Jewsbury* (1935); Mercer, E., 'Geraldine Endsor Jewsbury', *Manchester Quarterly* 17 (1898); Showalter, E., *A Literature of Their Own* (1977); Thomson, P., *George Sand and the Victorians* (1977); Woolf, V., *Collected Essays* (1967).

Jewsbury, Maria Jane

b. 25 October 1800, Measham, Derbyshire; d. 4 October 1833, Poona, India
Poet, essayist

The daughter of Thomas Jewsbury, MJJ received some early formal education at Mrs Adams's School, Shenstone, but returned home for health reasons at the age of 14. At 18, upon the death of her mother and the family's removal to Manchester, she took charge of her younger sister Geraldine and her three brothers, one an infant. In spite of her intellectual isolation, she longed for a literary career, writing to Felicia Hemans, 'the ambition of writing a book, being praised publicly and associating with authors, seized me. . . .'

Alaric A. Watts, editor of the *Manchester Courier*, encouraged her in her ambition and sponsored her first book, *Phantasmagoria, or, Sketches of Life and Character*, published in Leeds in 1825 with a dedication to Wordsworth, whom she did not as yet know. The resulting correspondence began a lifelong friendship with the Wordsworth family, especially with Dora Wordsworth, the poet's daughter. Wordsworth appreciated MJJ as an accurate observer of simple people and he urged her to write of life and manners. The youthful, lively, satirical tone of *Phantasmagoria* was generally criticized by the reviewers even as it caught their attention. A poem written at the same time, 'Song of the Hindoo Women

While Accompanying a Widow to the Funeral', reflects MJJ's love of exoticism, so much a feature of the period. MJJ's collections of Lancashire carols and ballads were published in *The Rural Life*, edited by Mary Howitt.

After MJJ fell ill in the summer of 1826, the tone of her writing became more serious and religious. *Letters to the Young* (1828), a meditative work, discusses belief in God, intellectual snobbery, and 'the true end of education'. Its popularity required a second edition in 1829 and a third in 1832. *Lays of Leisure Hours* appeared in 1829 and *The Three Histories* in 1830; subtitled *The History of an Enthusiast, the History of a Nonchalant, the History of a Realist*, the last work owes much to Madame de Staël's *Corinne*.

MJJ was praised for her eloquent style by Letitia Landon and Christopher North, and her work appeared frequently in the *Athenaeum* from 1830 to 1832. But in keeping with her new seriousness and religious fervour, she married William Kew Fletcher, a chaplain for the East India Company, in August 1832. As a closing to her life in English letters – although she kept a diary of her trip to India, parts of which later published – she wrote to Hemans that she regretted her early reputation and desire for premature publication. She died of cholera in India, without seeing Wordsworth's 'Liberty' which he had dedicated to her and of which she was the subject.   ELEANOR LANGSTAFF

Works: *Phantasmagoria, or Sketches of Life and Character* (1825); *Letters to the Young* (1928); *Lays of Leisure Hours* (1829); *The Three Histories: The History of an Enthusiast, the History of a Nonchalant, the History of a Realist* (1830); extracts from MJJ's journal of her voyage and early days in India were published in Espinasse's *Lancashire Worthies*, 2nd series (1874–7).

References: *DNB*; Fryckstedt, M. C., 'The hidden rill: the life and career of Maria Jane Jewsbury', *Bulletin of the John Rylands University Library of Manchester* 66 (1984); Howe, S., *Geraldine Jewsbury: Her Life and Errors* (1930).

Jhabvala, Ruth Prawer

b. 7 May 1927, Cologne, Germany
Novelist, writer of short stories and of plays for cinema and television
RPJ is the younger child and only daughter of a Polish/Jewish lawyer, Marcus Prawer, and of his wife, Leonora Cohn Prawer. Her childhood encompassed both the comfortable security enjoyed until the early 1930s by assimilated German Jews in Cologne and the hostility shown to Jewish families there once Hitler came to power in the later years of that decade. RPJ's first stories were written in German, but when the family emigrated to England in 1939 she rapidly made the change to a new language. In the Nazi holocaust the Prawers lost every member of Marcus's family and part of Leonora Cohn's, most of their friends, and most of the children RPJ and her brother had known at school. The experience of living as part of a dispossessed expatriate Jewish community in Britain is captured by RPJ in an early story, 'A Birthday in London' (1962). In 1948 Marcus Prawer committed suicide, a family tragedy that RPJ recalls under fictional disguise in an early novel, *A Backward Place* (1965).

RPJ completed her education in England, first in Coventry, then at Hendon Grammar School, and later read English at Queen Mary College where she wrote her MA thesis for the University of London on 'The Short Story in England, 1700–1750'. In 1951 she married Cyrus S. H. Jhabvala, a Parsi architect, and returned with him to his home in Delhi, India. Between 1951 and 1960, nine years of Indian experience that RPJ invariably describes in terms of delight and the excitement of discovery, the Jhabvalas' three daughters were born and RPJ published four novels, all of which are set in Delhi.

The first of these, *To Whom She Will* (1955), republished in 1956 in the USA with the new title of *Amrita*, is a romantic comedy of Indian manners in which the family conflicts attending an oriental arranged marriage are shaped by the author to fit the balanced, patterned structures of English eighteenth-century drama and fiction that literary study had made familiar to her. *The Nature of Passion* (1956) is a satiric exposure of corruption in the worlds of business, officialdom, and the arts on the one hand, and a celebration of India's indestructible vitality of spirit on the other. By tracing, in *Esmond in India* (1958), the steady disillusionment with India suffered by an English resident in Delhi, RPJ plots the stages by which what she was later to term the 'experience of India' affects the western sensibility. *The Householder* (1960), a work delicately poised on the fine line between comedy and tragedy, tells a story of the growth of love and maturity within an arranged marriage. These novels earned RPJ a reputation as a satirist acutely aware of the comic incongruities of the Indian life around her.

In 1960 RPJ paid Britain a brief visit and found, on returning to Delhi, that her attitude towards India had altered. Her next novel, *Get Ready for Battle* (1962), focuses on the exploitation of India's poorest and most helpless classes by their corrupt, wealthy, and hypocritical fellow-countrymen and women. Here her earlier inclination to view dishonesty and corruption as materials for amusing character study (e.g. in *The Nature of Passion*) gives way to straightforward condemnation. RPJ's disillusionment with India found expression between 1960 and 1975 in three collections of short stories: *Like Birds, Like Fishes* (1963), *An Experience of India* (1966), and *A Stronger Climate* (1968). In an essay titled 'Myself in India' that prefaces the second of these volumes, RPJ describes a cycle of intense emotional variations to which she sees all sensitive westerners who spend an appreciable time in India (and this category includes herself) as being inevitably bound: 'There is a cycle that Europeans – by Europeans I mean all Westerners, including Americans – tend to pass through. It goes like this: first stage, tremendous enthusiasm – everything Indian is marvellous; second stage, everything Indian not so marvellous; third stage, everything Indian abominable. For some people it ends there, for others the cycle renews itself and goes on. . . . When I meet other Europeans, I can usually tell after a few moments conversation at what stage of the cycle they happen to be.' These perceptions provide the basis for RPJ's characterizations of westerners in India in her next three novels: *A Backward Place* (1965), which focuses on the social interaction of western expatriates and English-educated Indians in Delhi, *A New Dominion* (1972), and *Heat and Dust* (1975). The last two works bring to the subject of India's impact upon western sensibilities the deep perspective of colonial history as well as certain new fictional techniques developed by RPJ from her experience as script writer for a number of films set in India.

The first screenplay RPJ wrote was for a cinematic version directed by James Ivory of her own novel *The Householder*, released by Merchant-Ivory Productions in 1963. Since then she has divided her time between writing fiction and writing for the cinema, and no study of her recent work as a novelist would be complete that does not take into account the effect upon it of her cinematic experience.

Merchant-Ivory films, with which she has been associated since 1963, include the following: *Shakespearewallah* (1965), which is based on the experiences of the Kendalls, an English theatrical family that spent many years travelling India with productions of Shakespeare plays; *The Guru* (1969), which follows the adventures of two young people from the west who come to India in the 1960s, one to study the sitar and the other in search of the meaning of life; *Bombay Talkie* (1970), a visually beautiful, witty satire on India's popular film industry; *Autobiography of a Princess* (1975), a sixty-minute requiem for India's luxurious and brilliant, yet decadent royal past, and a film that has very close technical links with RPJ's novel *Heat and Dust*, published in the same year that *Autobiography* was released; *Roseland* (1977), a film about the live music dance hall and Broadway landmark that acts as a magnet for serious dancers and lonely people of all races and classes; *Hullabaloo Over Bonnie and Georgie's Pictures* (1978), which focuses on the efforts of two western art collectors to acquire, by fair means or foul, a Maharaja's famous follection of Indian miniature paintings; *The Europeans* (1979) and *The Bostonians* (1984), cinematic adaptations of two novels by Henry James; *Jane Austen in Manhattan* (1980), a film about an experimental theatre company in New York that decides to mount a presentation of a play (recently discovered) by the youthful Jane Austen; and *Quartet* (1981), a film based on a novel by Jean Rhys. While some of these ventures reflect RPJ's own interest in India, and in the themes of exile and isolation, others have given her an opportunity to rework for cinematic presentation the writings of authors she personally regards as being among the masters of the English novel: Jane Austen, Henry James, and – in the case of her most recent film for Merchant-Ivory, *A Room With A View* (1986) – E. M. Forster.

In 1975 RPJ took up residence in New York where she now spends nine months of every year, revisiting India in winter and Britain in early spring. *How I Became A Holy Mother* (1976) is a collection of short stories that focus on the experiences of lonely, ageing, exploited, and unhappy women. The title story indicates that RPJ has begun to turn on her new American milieu the ironic eye she formerly exercised on India. This impression is fully borne out by her ninth novel, *In Search of Love and Beauty* (1983). Set in New York, this book combines the author's three backgrounds of Europe, India, and America, and is of particular interest since in its picture of European Jewish refugees in America RPJ makes sustained contact for the first time in her published fiction with the obliterated world of her German childhood. Spirituality and opportunism are in conflict here as they were in earlier novels such as *Get Ready for Battle* and *A New Dominion*, embodied this time in the character of Leo Kellermann, a naturalized American version of Indian 'swamis', gurus, and charlatans. RPJ's most recent work, a novel titled *Three Continents*, was published in 1987.

In New York today (as formerly in Delhi) RPJ prefers to write in complete isolation. Her novels show that she splits up certain modern phenomena that interest her into various aspects that she embodies in the characters and settings of her fiction. By this means she contrives to study the whole, and explores with remarkable detachment her own identity in its relation to her milieu: especially, in her work up to 1975, to India. The major and minor concerns that interweave in her fiction arise from personal or observed experience. While some of her characters reflect her own disillusionment with India, others almost certainly reflect her personal affection for, and commitment to, that country. Her Indian novels depict contemporary Indian society, and a world that is subject to change and development. Her characters do not shape history but must accept events that, taking place at a political level, involve them and affect their lives and personalities.

As an artist, RPJ strives tirelessly for very fine and delicate effects. Her development from the broad satirical comedy of her earliest novels to the subtle ironies of her later work gives the reader a demonstration of an extraordinarily rapid artistic growth in a great living literary contemporary.

RPJ's work in fiction has been recognized by the award to her in 1975 of the Booker-McConnell prize for her novel *Heat and Dust*, and in 1979 of the Neil Gunn International Fellowship. In 1983 the University of London honoured its former student by conferring upon her the degree of Doctor of Letters. In February 1984 RPJ was awarded a MacArthur Foundation Fellowship, under the terms of which her writing is supported for five years with an annual tax-free grant of $52,000.

Although she lists 'writing film scripts' as merely a recreation in *Who's Who*, RPJ is (with James Ivory and Ismail Merchant) part of a trio of film makers whose productions are recognized as among the major achievements in post-war cinema. Her writing for film has been attracting increasing attention and praise. In 1983 the National Film Theatre saw the Film Section of the Critics Circle nominate *Heat and Dust* as the best screenplay of the year; and in 1984 the British Academy of Film and Television Arts nominated *Heat and Dust* in eight categories including that of the best adapted screenplay. RPJ excels, it would seem, in novel adaptations, her most distinguished recent work in that field having been done for *The Bostonians* and *A Room With A View*. She has described her simultaneous engagement with the genres of film and fiction as 'a two-way traffic' in which 'what I have learned in films I put back into my books, and what I have learned about characterization, relationships, happenings, and everything else that goes into writing fiction I've put to use in writing films. I can't think what it would have been like for me to have had one and not the other.'   YASMINE GOONERATNE

Selected works: *The Nature of Passion* (1956); *To Whom She Will* (1955; published in the US as *Amrita*, 1956); *Esmond in India* (1958); *Get Ready for Battle* (1962); *Like Birds, Like Fishes and Other Stories* (1963); *A Backward Place* (1965); *An Experience of India* (1966); *A Stronger Climate* (1968); *A New Dominion* (1972; published in the US as *Travelers*, 1973); *Shakespearewallah* (screenplay, 1973); *Autobiography of a Princess* (screenplay, 1975); *Heat and Dust* (1975); *How I Became A Holy Mother and Other Stories* (1976); *In Search of Love and Beauty* (1983); *Out of India* (1986); *Three Continents* (1987).

References: Blackwell, F., 'A European emigré in India', *Asiaweek Literary Review* (15 February 1985); Blackwell, F., 'Perception of the guru in the fiction of Ruth Prawer Jhabvala', *Journal of Indian Writing in English* 5, 2 (January 1977); *Contemporary Literary Criticism: Excerpts from the Criticism of Today's Novelists, Poets, Playwrights and Other Creative Writers* (1975); *CB*; De Souza, E., 'The blinds drawn and the airconditioner on: The novels of Ruth Prawer Jhabvala', *World Literature Written in English* 17, 1 (April 1978); Ezekiel, N., 'Cross-cultural encounter in literature', *Indian PEN* 43, 11 and 12 (1977); Gooneratne, Y., 'Apollo, Krishna, Superman: the image of India in Ruth Prawer Jhabvala's ninth novel (*In Search of Love and Beauty*)', in *Ariel* 15, 2 (April 1984); Gooneratne, Y., 'Contemporary India in the writing of Ruth Prawer Jhabvala', in *Westerly* 4 (December 1983); Gooneratne, Y., 'Film into fiction: the influence upon Ruth Prawer Jhabvala's fiction of her work for the cinema, 1960–1976', in *World Literature Written in English* 18, 2 (November 1979); Gooneratne, Y., 'Ruth Prawer Jhabvala', in H. Bock and A. Werttheim (eds.), *Essays on Contemporary Post-Colonial Fiction* (1986); Gooneratne, Y., *Silence, Exile and Cunning: The Fiction of Ruth Prawer Jhabvala* (1983); Ivory, J., *Autobiography of a Princess: Also Being the Adventures of an American Film Director in the Land of the Maharajas* (1975); Pym, J., *The Wandering Company: 21 Years of Merchant-Ivory Films* (1983);

Rutherford, A. and Petersen, K. H., 'Heat and Dust: Ruth Prawer Jhabvala's experience of India'; World Literature Written in English, 15, 2 (November 1976); Williams, H. M., 'R. K. Narayan and R. Prawer Jhabvala: two interpreters of modern India', Literature East and West 16, 4 (April 1975 for December 1972); Williams, H. M., The Fiction of Ruth Prawer Jhabvala (1973).

Jocelin, Elizabeth
b. 1595 or 1596; d. October 1622
Writer of Advice Book
EJ was the only child of Sir Richard Brooke of Norton in Chester and of Joan Chaderton (or Chatterton), daughter of William Chaderton, Bishop of Lincoln. In *A Briefe View of the State of the Church in England* (1608) John Harington writes that the Bishop of Lincoln had 'one onely daughter married to a Knight of good worship, though now they living asunder, he may be thought to have had no great comfort of that matrimony, yet to her daughter he means to leave a great patrimony' (p. 84); but in 'The Approbation' with which he introduced EJ's *The Mothers Legacie*, Thomas Goad says nothing about EJ's parents having been separated. Instead, he stresses continuity and loyalty within the family by noting 'the deepe impression, long since, when shee [EJ] was not aboue six yeeres old [i.e., in about 1602], made in her minde by the last words of her owne Mother, charging her vpon her blessing to shew all obedience and reuerence to her Father . . . and to her reuerend Grandfather' and then describes the excellent education EJ subsequently received from her maternal grandfather. Bishop Chaderton died when EJ was about 12 years old, in April 1608, and in 1616 EJ married Tourell Jocelin of Cambridgeshire.

Pregnant with her first child in 1622 and aware that she might die in childbirth, EJ wrote a book of advice to her future son or daughter. The child, Theodora, was born on 12 October, and nine days later EJ died. The manuscript of *The Mothers Legacie, To her vnborn Childe* is now in the British Library; it was printed seven times between 1625 and 1635 – and then again in 1684. Reprinted in the eighteenth, the nineteenth, and (in excerpts) the twentieth centuries, the book has struck many readers as, in the words of Randall T. Roffen in the Introduction to his edition of 1894, a 'rare combination . . . of earnest piety, quiet womanly counsel, and vigorous common sense'.

Like many other seventeenth-century women writers, EJ introduces her work with the humility *topos*: in her introductory letter to her 'Trvly louing, and most dearly loued Husband', she says that when she thought of writing the *Legacie*, 'mine owne weaknes appeared so manifestly, that I was ashamed, and durst not vndertake it. But when I could find no other means to expresse my motherly zeale, I encouraged my selfe. . . . Thus resolued, I writ this ensuing Letter to our little one, to whom I could not finde a fitter hand to convey it than thine owne, which maist with authority see the performance of this my little legacy, of which my Childe is Executor'. Tourell Jocelin's actual part in the publication of the *Legacie* is not clear, for it is prefaced, as noted above, by Thomas Goad's *Approbation*, an extended defence of the printing of a work by a woman. Building on the legal imagery with which EJ describes her treatise, Goad's argument begins by distinguishing between women's earthly rights and powers and their spiritual possibilities. He admits that civil law prohibits those 'that are vnder *Couert-baron* from disposing by Will and Testament any temporall estate' and then reminds his readers that 'vertue and grace haue power beyond al empeachment of sex or other debility, to enable and instruct the possessor to employ the same vnquestionably for the inward inriching of others', and justifies the value of EJ's words by recounting her own education in piety, her dutiful obedience to her father and grandfather and then to her husband, and her modest writing of the *Legacie* 'privatly in her Closet between God and her'. Were EJ an ordinary woman, or were the circumstances of her writing the book more mundane, it is clear, Goad would not think the *Legacie* worthy of print. But in his mind, it gains special validity from the details mentioned above – and from its having been composed while its author faced imminent death with 'more than womanly fortitude'.

If the child is a son, EJ hopes he will become a clergyman; if a daughter, she should be raised 'learning the Bible . . . good houswifery, writing, and good workes: other learning a woman needs not: though I admire it in those whom God hath blest with discretion'. Fearing pride in a daughter ('Pride being now rather accounted a vertue in our sex worthy praise, than a vice fit for reproofe'), EJ thus stresses the necessity of training in Christian humility – even while she notes that secular learning is a great complement to piety in extraordinary women. In the body of the work, EJ presents thirteen 'charges' which emphasize the value of a life void of pride and recommends that her child – male or female – devote its full energies to serving God's will.   ELIZABETH H. HAGEMAN

Work: *The Mothers Legacie, To her vnborne Childe* (1624).

References: Beilin, E. V., *Redeeming Eve: Women Writers of the English Renaissance* (1987); *DNB*; Sizemore, C. W., 'Early Seventeenth-Century Advice Books: The Female Viewpoint', *South Atlantic Bulletin*, 41 (1976); Travitsky, B., 'The New Mother of the English Renaissance: Her Writings on Motherhood', in *The Lost Tradition: Mothers and Daughters in Literature*, ed. Cathy N. Davidson and E. M. Broner (1980), and *The Paradise of Women: Writings by Englishwomen of the Renaissance* (1981).

Johnson, Pamela Hansford

b. 29 May 1912, London; d. 18 June 1981, London
Novelist, critic
(With Nick Stewart also wrote under 'Nap Lombard')

PHJ was a highly acclaimed popular novelist. Her novels still sell well, and she is widely read. The first child of a prosperous marriage between R. K. Johnson, a colonial administrator in the Gold Coast, and his ex-actress wife Amy (*née* Hanson), PHJ was 7 before her sister Beryl, her only sibling, was born. The baby lived only a few months, and when PHJ was 11, her father also died while home on leave from Africa; he left nothing but debts. Reared by her mother and an aunt, PHJ was educated at London schools and by her mother's theatrical background, but received no formal higher education. The Church of England in childhood, and the Congregational Church in her teens, influenced the development of her thought and shaped the way in which she expressed emotion. She began to publish poetry at 14, and her first novel, *This Bed Thy Centre*, was published in 1935, during the years she later described as seeing the peak of her political consciousness and activity. In 1936 she married Gordon Stewart, with whom she had two children, Andrew Morven and Lindsay Jean, and she published fiction throughout the 1930s and 1940s, adding critical and other writings to her output after the war. In 1950 she married novelist C. P. (later Lord) Snow; they had one son, Philip. She continued to write until her death.

PHJ said of her own work that she had written many novels, but few she respected. There is a curious sense of emotional and intellectual circumscription about much of her work, which is perhaps best described as 'quintessentially British'. In the beleaguered period of her earlier work, this ensured her popularity, but throughout her writing life her style changed rather little. She approached narrative with a straightforwardness which appealed to a large audience; her characters are carefully observed and drawn; she has been described as 'the literary equivalent of sterling', writing novels about love which avoid any suggestion of 'permissiveness' (an idea to which she was opposed) and which diffuse an atmosphere of calm and of trust in the sturdy British values of reliability and humour. There is, however, an apparent failure to engage at depth intellectually which causes the modern reader some dissatisfaction, for, while capable of penetrating insight at times, PHJ does not choose to pursue her thought with intellectual rigour, and, while she takes on changes of fashion in the attitudes of society, allowing her work to become nominally more explicit in the area of sexuality, for example, there is no corresponding emotional frankness, and no risks are taken. This is the more extraordinary since she was clearly interested in the causes of deviant behaviour; witness 'On Iniquity' (1967), an extended essay on the subject of the Moors Murders, and her introduction to *Corvo: The Fascination of the Paranoid Personality* (1961).

The 1950s, the 'Angry Decade', was a period of experimentation in form for PHJ, beginning with a play, 'Corinth House', in 1948, and moving on through the six 'Proust Reconstructions' for BBC Radio, continuing into the 1960s with a number of additions to her critical work including studies of Thomas Wolfe, Charles Dickens and Ivy Compton-Burnett. This innovation seems to have been undertaken as a matter of literary good form rather than in response to any pressing need for extension of the intellectual boundaries, and by the time of the writing of *Important to Me*, a series of autobiographical flashbacks, there is in some of the essays more than a suggestion of middle-aged priggishness, especially in her attitude to 'the young' and to the issue then known as women's liberation. This is the more distressing for the clear evidence of a mind capable of something better; in the essay 'Auschwitz' (which she visited in 1967) for example, she remarks, 'It seemed a very small gallows.' This quiet comment opens a floodgate of emotion, for both writers and reader; one regrets that, further on, the same woman can boast of reading a 'novel' 'in a couple of hours'. To what kind of novel can she be referring?

Her final fictional work, *A Bonfire*, is set in Clapham from 1924 to 1937, and the childhood of the heroine, Emma, has similarities with PHJ's own, with the loss of a father at the age of 11. It might be supposed, therefore, to give the writer the opportunity of reworking emotional realities and interpreting the attitudes of the society of the time with the benefit of hindsight and of the greater freedom of expression won for women's writing during the twentieth century. Though the latter is apparently attempted, PHJ's inability to create either an emotional or a social atmosphere makes the work disappointing. The defloration of the heroine, a virgin bride, is described flatly: 'Without a word he took her again and, still gently, broke the hymen.' The honeymoon was 'a week of sexual and romantic bliss'. Throughout her writing career PHJ's work was to observe the relationship between character and society, but while her gentle, amused detachment and good taste provided her public, in troubled times, with pleasant distraction, there is no major engagement with social issues, and little experiment with narrative or form in the quest for clarity or the definition of character.   JENNIFER PLASTOW

Selected works: *Symphony for Full Orchestra* (1934); *This Bed Thy Centre* (1935);

Blessed above Women (1936); *Here Today* (1937); *Girdle of Venus* (1939); *Too Dear for my Possessing* (1940); *Winter Quarters* (1943); *The Grinning Pig* (with Nick Stewart, as 'Nap Lombard') (1943); *The Trojan Brothers* (1944); *Avenue of Stone* (1947); *Thomas Wolfe: A Critical Study* (1947); *Summer to Decide* (1948); *Philistines* (1949); *Catherine Carter* (1952); *Ivy Compton-Burnett* (1953); *An Impossible Marriage* (1954); *Corinth House* (1954, performed 1948); *Last Resort* (1956); *The Unspeakable Skipton* (1959); 'Introduction' to *Corvo*, ed. C. Woolf and B. Sewell (1961); *An Error of Judgement* (1962); (trans.), *The Rehearsal*, by J. A. Anouilh (with Kitty Black) (1962); 'Introduction' to *Barchester Towers*, by A. Trollope (1962); *Night and Silence; Who is Here?* (1963); *Cork Street, Next to the Hatter's* (1965); *On Iniquity* (1967); *Important to Me* (1974); *The Good Listener* (1975); *The Good Husband* (1978); *A Bonfire* (1981).
References: Allen, W., *The Modern Novel* (1965); *CA*; Quigley, I., *Pamela Hansford Johnson* (1968).

Johnston, Jennifer
b. 12 January 1930, Dublin
Novelist

JJ is the daughter of Denis Johnston, Ireland's leading playwright since O'Casey, and of the actress and producer Shelagh Richards. She is the author of seven highly regarded, tightly written novels, three of which have been adapted as television plays. She received her formal education at the Park House School and at Trinity College, Dublin. In 1951 she married Ian Smyth; they have four children. She now lives in Derry, Northern Ireland.

JJ's works, all of which are set in Ireland or Northern Ireland, focus on the lives of individuals who, often through unlikely friendships, challenge the restrictions imposed by social class, political persuasion, and religious belief. While these relationships generally end unhappily, they nevertheless provide the major characters with a means to emotional growth and a taste of the joy that friendship affords. JJ's technical detachment prevents her treatment of such subject matter from becoming sentimental: each of her works employs many narrative voices, ranging from those of diary writers to those of traditional omniscient narrators. This allows JJ to experiment with narrative time in a way which establishes the powerful influence of the past on the present.

Her first published novel, *The Captains and the Kings* (1972), won the Robert Pitman Award and the Yorkshire Post Prize for the best first book of the year. It is the first among several of her works to deal with the disintegration of the Anglo-Irish 'big house' tradition. The owner of the house is haunted by apparitions from his unhappy past. His rapid spiritual and physical decline is brought to a halt, however, when he meets Diarmid, a young working-class Catholic whom he attempts to protect from his violent parents. In *The Gates*, published in 1973, but written before *The Captains and the Kings*, JJ employs a complex structure in which the account given by a third-person narrator is framed by diary entries and brief summaries of historical fact. The Anglo-Irish protagonist is the first of several JJ characters who are aspiring writers, but none of whom receives much encouragement. Upon her return from England she conspires with a new friend to sell the gates of her ancestral estate, intending to use the money from the sale to help revitalize the estate and her ailing uncle. Although her friend, a stablehand, absconds with the proceeds to England, the novel ends on a guardedly optimistic note. JJ leaves no doubt that the days of the big house are numbered.

The opening lines of *How Many Miles to Babylon?* (1974) underscore the novel's self-conscious artifice: 'Because I am an officer and a gentleman they have given me my notebooks, pen, ink, and paper.' Alexander Moore, a young Anglo-Irishman, is awaiting execution during the First World War: the novel presents Alexander's memories of his unhappy childhood and military career. Like most of JJ's protagonists, he has a secret friend; in his case it is Gerry, a working-class Catholic boy, with whom Alexander shares his few joyful moments of childhood. They find, however, that the class distinctions of Irish civilian life also exist on the front. Alexander is sentenced to death for the mercy killing of Gerry, who was to be executed by firing squad. *Shadows on Our Skin* (1977), which was shortlisted for the Booker Prize, is set in modern-day Derry and centres on yet another unlikely alliance, in this case between an adolescent Catholic boy and a young female Protestant school teacher. Their relationship lifts them, albeit temporarily, above the sectarian tensions of Ulster. The novel is punctuated by the boy's poems, which provide him with an escape both from the drudgery of school and from the difficulties epitomized by his drunken father, who lives on the memories of his Republican activities of years past.

The Old Jest (1979), the winner of the Whitbread Award, is set in the rural environs of Dublin in 1920. The narrative viewpoint alternates between the diary entries of Nancy Gulliver, another of JJ's would-be writers, and the account of a third-person narrator. The story opens on Nancy's eighteenth birthday, on which she declares, 'I want to start to become a person.' As Nancy matures, she frees herself from her Ascendancy past, experiences unrequited love, and befriends an Irish terrorist, who is eventually killed by the Black and Tans. Throughout this compelling narrative, Nancy paradoxically laments her inability to find a suitable subject for her writing. *The Christmas Tree* (1981) presents JJ's fiction at its understated best. Set in mid-twentieth-century Dublin, the novel, focusing on a single character, traces the final days of Constance Keating, a woman of 45 who is dying of leukaemia only nine months after she has given birth to an illegitimate child. Her reflections on her own life become the novel which she has always wanted to write. JJ's characteristic dry humour and authorial distance save the work from sentimentality. Constance's narration of her grim final days alternates with flashbacks to her childhood and to her affair in Rome with the father of her child; the narrative of her servant closes the novel after her death.

JJ's seventh novel, *The Railway Station Man* (1984), explores the relationship between a widowed artist, Helen Cuffe, her son, and the title character, a Second World War veteran who comes to Donegal to pursue his hobby, the restoration of abandoned railway stations. JJ returns in this work to an examination of the influence that historical circumstances have on individual lives; the political Troubles of Ireland cast a tragic shadow on the otherwise positive portrayal of human friendship. While the novel is distinguished by JJ's evocation of time and place and by her delineation of character, it is marred by a looseness of construction, an uncertainty of narrative voice, and unconvincing dialogue.

PETER DREWNIANY

Works: *The Captains and the Kings* (1972); *The Gates* (1973); *How Many Miles to Babylon?* (1974); *Shadows on our Skin* (1977); *The Old Jest* (1979); *The Christmas Tree* (1981); *The Railway Station Man* (1984).

References: Benstock, S., 'The masculine world of Jennifer Johnston', in Staley, Thomas F. (ed.), *Twentieth Century Women Novelists* (1982); Burleigh, D., 'Dead and gone: the fiction of Jennifer Johnston and Julia O'Faolain', in Sekine, M.

(ed.), *Irish Writers and Society at Large* (1985); Hogan, R. (ed.), *The Macmillan Dictionary of Irish Literature* (1979); Kennealy, M., 'Q and A with Jennifer Johnston', *Irish Literary Supplement* (Fall 1984).

Julian of Norwich
b. c.1343; d. after 1416
Mystical writer

J of N, the only British woman generally accepted as a great mystic of the medieval church, is thought to have been a contemplative nun, possibly at Carrow, and later an anchoress enclosed at St Julian's Church, Norwich. During a near-fatal illness in 1373 she experienced sixteen visions recorded initially in her short text which she was to revise and expand some twenty years later in the light of subsequent meditation. Both versions of her *Revelations of Divine Love* survive; her alterations from short to long version indicate her developing skills both as writer and theologian. She interprets her sickness and visions as the divine response to her earlier request for three gifts from God: a true understanding of Christ's Passion; a physical sickness to serve as spiritual purgation; and the three 'wounds' of contrition, compassion, and desire for God. The influence of the continental female mystical tradition on these petitions is acknowledged in the short version in a reference to St Cecilia, while the initial focus of the *Revelations* on the crucified Christ corresponds to the by then established conventions of women's piety. Identification with tradition, a necessary safeguard against charges of heresy, ends here. The *Revelations* are wholly distinctive in the theological complexity of their meditative passages and in J of N's original response to the mystic's problem of reconciling the Word (Christ) and words.

The lack of biographical detail is due as much to J of N's deliberate authorial strategy as to historical accident. She is known only by a devotional pseudonym drawn from the church at which she was enclosed, and presents herself in her text merely as a medium through which her readers may see God. While the visionary's claim to be irrelevant save as a channel to God is a leitmotif of female mysticism, J of N is unusual in making such humility the organizing principle of her work. Self-reference is, where possible, edited from the later version of the *Revelations* and J of N's personal experience of Christ is subsumed to the relationship of the general human soul and the Trinity: 'And though I speak of myself I am really speaking of all my fellow Christians . . . where Jesus is spoken of, the Blessed Trinity is always to be understood.' Just as J of N and Christ signify beyond themselves, each section of the visions is inextricably linked to preceding and succeeding passages. The justly famous meditation of the mothering role of Christ develops from the vision of his crucifixion and the Christian mystery of the eucharist; his 'labour pains' are his death pangs on the cross bearing souls to life, and while 'the human mother will suckle her child with her own milk, . . . our beloved Mother, Jesus, feeds us with himself.' In the *Revelations*, just as no referent may be defined in a single analogical term, no term is limited to a single referent. Complex verbal echoes convey the intricate interrelations of J of N's God and his creation. Christ's mothering qualities of pity, self-sacrifice, and understanding relate to an earlier description of Mary as the mother of all, the loving care of human mothers and the later presentation of the Church as 'our mother's breast'. Just as Christ is God and man, the material is imbued with the spiritual, a message conveyed doctrinally in J of N's discussion of mutual indwelling, and stylistically in skilfully mixed metaphor. The significance of the 'misty example' of a lord and servant is explicitly 'double': the servant is now Adam (as all humankind), now Christ; the servant's fall is both man's original sin and the redemptive 'fall' of Christ into Mary's womb. Adam's tattered garments signify his own corrupt human flesh yet echo Christ's flesh on the cross, 'torn to pieces and hanging loose as a cloth'; and Christ, 'hanging up in the air as men hang a cloth up to dry', is later metaphorically identified with his Church 'shaken in sorrow in this world as men shake a cloth in the wind'.

Many mystics reduce the mysterious quality of their God to simply analogy. Others refuse any attempt to describe the divine, acknowledging the reductive effects of a limited language. J of N's linguistic solutions to this problem would seem to place her in a unique position; the continuous development and modification of complex analogies convey a God whom human language can touch on but never pin down. As she says at the close of her text, 'This book is begun by God's gift and his grace, but it is not yet done/completed'; the signification of the text is infinite. Her God has no term (ending) and so no term (single definition), bar the infinitely re-interpretable 'I it am'.

A contemporary of Chaucer, J of N is, like him, a pioneer in developing the art of rhetoric in English. Her alterations from short to long version involve not only extensive meditative additions but careful balancing of sentence structure, again communicating the mysterious nature of her God. The *Revelations* are notable for countless examples of rhetorical figures, lost in modern translations. The contemplative soul is described as 'able to do no more but . . . attend to God's motion, and joy in his loving, and delight in his goodness'. J of N explores the Trinity, the three separate qualities of her triune God, as three separate ideas in a single rhetorical figure: 'For God is endless sovereign truth, endless sovereign wisdom, endless sovereign love unmade; and man's soul is a creature in God which hath the same properties made.' Her text conveys both in metaphorical and grammatical structuring J of N's grasp of the complexity of Christian theology and linguistic theory. In her summary she states that 'Love is our Lord's meaning'; the logic of the text then is relationships between words and images, and man and maker. J of N's teaching is essentially concerned with the union of creator and creation, and rejection of the divisive 'contrary', sin. The *Revelations* look towards the time when the union shall be fully realized, and, in words which T. S. Eliot was to borrow in his *Four Quartets* 'all shall be well, and all shall be well and all manner of things shall be well.'

J of N's claim to being an 'unlettered woman' accords with traditions of women's piety; her right to write at the time was based on her authorship being conceived as wholly dependent on God, and she herself merely an amanuensis. However, her claim to being poorly educated has misled critics into underestimating her extensive knowledge. Her text embraces much learning in an original, almost poetic form. This 'first woman of English letters' raises fascinating questions of women's education in the Middle Ages; the *Revelations* outrank, in thematic complexity and stylistic execution, many of the more readily respected works of male mystical teachers.   POLLY BRIGGS

Works: *A Book of Showings to the Anchoress Julian of Norwich*, parts 1 (short version) and 2 (long version), ed. E. Colledge and J. Walsh (1978); *Revelations of Divine Love* (modern translation), ed. C. Wolters (1966).

References: Allchin, A. M., 'Julian of Norwich and the continuity of tradition', in M. Glasscoe, ed., *The Medieval Mystical Tradition in England* (3 in series: 1980, 1982, 1983); Bradley, R., 'The motherhood theme in Julian of Norwich',

Fourteenth Century English Mystics Newsletter 2 (1976); Bradley, R., 'Patristic background of the motherhood similitude in Julian of Norwich', *Christian Scholars Review* 8 (1978); Hanshell, D., 'A crux in the interpretation of Julian of Norwich', *Downside Review* (1978); Maisonneuve, R., 'The visionary universe of Julian of Norwich', in Glasscoe, op. cit.; Molinari, P., *Julian of Norwich: The Teaching of a Fourteenth Century Mystic* (1958); Stone, C. R., *Middle English Prose Style: Margery Kempe and Julian of Norwich* (1970); Walsh, J., 'God's homely loving: St John and Julian of Norwich on the Divine Indwelling', *The Month* 205, new series 19 (1958); Watkin, E., *On Julian of Norwich and in Defence of Margery Kempe* (1979); Windeatt, B., 'Julian of Norwich and her audience', *Review of English Studies* n. s. 28 (1977); Windeatt, B., 'The art of mystical loving: Julian of Norwich', in Glasscoe, op. cit.

Katherine of Sutton

d. 1376

Religious playwright

K of S, the first known woman playwright in England, was abbess of Barking Abbey near London from 1363 to 1376. Her Latin plays were adaptations and innovative extensions of the Easter Liturgy which she wrote '*desiderans dictum torporem exstirpare et fidelium devocionem . . . excitare*', or to arouse the devotion of hitherto indifferent worshippers. Although, in common with contemporary liturgical drama, her plays remain close to their sources and preserve ritualistic elements, they also show an early move towards mimetic representation. The *Elevatio Hostiae* contains a *Harrowing of Hell* in which the members of the convent represent the patriarchs and are kept behind the doors of the chapel of St Mary Magdalen. When released by the priest *repraesentabit personam Christi*, they process to the altar bearing palms of victory and singing the traditional antiphons. The *Visitatio Sepulchrum*, both in form and staging, is similarly potentially mimetic. The three Marys are played by nuns instead of the usual clerics, and have been dressed, confessed, and absolved by the abbess in preparation for their roles. In an attempt to represent character, Mary Magdalen, unconvinced by the news of the Resurrection, speaks with two angels instead of one, and there is a dialogue between the Marys and the clergy *in figuram Discipulorum Christi*. The play still uses traditional responses, but, as well as the innovations in staging, it also contains a considerable number of speeches which cannot be found in any other *Visitatio*. K of S's works have the sophistication of the extended French liturgical drama, rather than the comparative simplicity of their English contemporaries.   CAROLINE COLEMAN

Works: *Depositio Crucis, Elevatio Hostiae, Visitatio Sepulchri*, in *The Ordinale and Customary of the Benedictine Nuns of Barking Abbey*, ed. J. B. L. Tolhurst (1977–8). **References:** Cotton, N., *Women Playwrights in England c. 1363–1750* (1980); Young, K., *The Drama of the Medieval Church*, vol. 1 (1933); Young, K., 'The harrowing of Hell in liturgical drama', *Transactions of the Wisconsin Academy of Sciences, Arts and Letters* 16 (1910).

Kavan, Anna

b. 10 April 1901, Cannes, France; d. 5 December 1967, London

Novelist

(Also wrote under Helen Ferguson)

AK had an unhappy childhood as her father committed suicide, leaving her at an early age in the sole care of her mother, who seemed to resent her birth.

Sometimes she was abandoned to relatives or strangers, then would unexpectedly be taken by her mother on lengthy trips through the continent and America. She was educated in a Church of England School, and later by private tutors. AK did not suffer any financial hardship as she was well provided for as a child, and then in her late teens married a wealthy Scottish diplomat, Donald Ferguson. The marriage was not a success – probably AK's decision to marry was influenced by her desire to escape from her family – and within a few years AK left Donald in Burma and returned to England with their son Brian, aged 2. She soon began an affair with Stuart Edmonds whom she married in 1930, and who encouraged AK in her ambition to find a professional career. She then studied at the Central Academy of Art in London, but was for years worried by a sense of failure. She was in fact an accomplished painter and later held a number of interesting jobs, for example as assistant editor for the literary magazine *Horizon* and as a recorder in a military psychiatric unit. AK's second marriage also began to break down. She suffered mental illness and was twice admitted to an asylum. After the second time she changed both her appearance, by losing weight and dying her hair blonde, and her name, to Anna Kavan; during this period she divorced Edmonds. She was registered as a drug addict. AK then travelled to New Zealand and America before returning to work in London.

AK's early novels were published under her first married name, Helen Ferguson. The first, *A Charmed Circle* (1929), presents two sisters who try to achieve some independence despite their family's lack of support. A later novel, *Goose Cross* (1936) focuses on the lives of two married couples, tracking the intense social and sexual interrelationships of the village in which they live. Deeply passionate and detailed in its patterning of events and feelings, the novel already displays a preoccupation with mental processes, insecurity, and loneliness, which were to become of paramount importance in AK's work after her mental illness. AK concentrates particularly on one character, Judith, who has become estranged from her husband. Judith seems locked in a stagnant mental state; as she explains, 'It isn't any good trying to come back to life. At any rate now I've achieved a sort of mental anæsthesia which is valuable in its way and which I don't want to lose.' However, she is compelled to abandon it, as her sexuality reawakens. AK describes her changing feelings as she begins to make love with her husband's friend: 'Her whole being was turned inwards, absorbed in her profound female sensuality which needed the stimulus of this particular kind of love-making to arouse its most ardent response.'

After AK's change of identity her novels took on a different style and content, and she began to deal with the inhabitants of mental institutions and to focus on psychological matters. She began to write far more concentrated prose, presenting different levels of consciousness together in the text. *Asylum Piece* (1940) and *I Am Lazarus* (1945), collections of short stories, concentrate on the psychological processes of the mentally disturbed. One story, 'Black Out' from *I Am Lazarus*, captures the fluctuating mental state of a shell-shocked soldier and contrasts it with the unmoving mind of his doctor. The soldier resists reality, and gets lost in a welter of memories. He recalls childhood fear: 'himself feeling shakey and sick and trying not to make a noise with his crying as he hid there crouched up in a ball of misery under the table'. The only way he can interpret the present is through what he can feel, and he concentrates on, and seems to reach the very essence of his regulation hospital tie: 'The tie had been washed so often that it had faded from red to deep pink and the cotton fabric had a curious dusty pile on it, almost like velvet, which communicated an agreeable sensation to the tips of his fingers.'

Perhaps her best work is *Ice* (1967). It takes place under the shadow of a fast-approaching, human-created ice age. The narrator and another man (who is a high-ranking army officer) pursue an elusive girl from the chaos-ridden town beneath the glacier wall, to the war-torn and rapidly cooling tropics. There is no escape from the glacier: as the world freezes, people in the few remaining free areas gaze hopelessly at the horizon awaiting the approaching ice.

LUCY SLOAN AND JULIAN TODD

Works: *A Charmed Circle* (1929); *Let Me Alone* (1930); *The Dark Sisters* (1930); *A Stranger Still* (1935); *Goose Cross* (1936); *Rich Get Rich* (1937); *Asylum Piece and Other Stories* (1940); *Change the Name* (1941); *I Am Lazarus* (1945); *Sleep Has His House* (1948); *The Horse's Tale* (with K. T. Bluth) (1949); *A Scarcity of Love* (1956); *Eagle's Nest* (1957); *A Bright Green Field* (1958); *Who Are You?* (1963); *Ice* (1967); *Julia and the Bazooka* (1970); *My Soul in China* (1975).

References: Aldiss, B., *Billion Year Spree: The True History of Science Fiction* (1973); Centing, R., *Under the Sign of Pisces* (1970); Crosland, M., *Beyond the Lighthouse* (1981); Davis, R., 'Preface' to *Let Me Alone* (1975); Davis, R., 'Introduction' to *Julia and the Bazooka* (1970); Nin, A., *The Novel of the Future* (1968); Owen, P., 'Prefatory note' to *Asylum Piece* (1972).

Kavanagh, Julia

b. 1824, Thurles, Ireland; d. 28 October 1877, Nice, France

Novelist, biographer

JK lived for much of her early life in France, the scene of many of her novels. Settling in London in 1844, she began her writing career partly in order to support her mother and partly to promote her interest in social progress. Her family life was difficult: her mother was a lifelong invalid requiring constant supervision, although she survived JK by a decade; her father, Peter Morgan Kavanagh, himself a writer, damaged her literary reputation in 1857 by ascribing a poor novel of his own, *The Hobbies*, to his daughter.

JK's first book for adults, *Madeleine* (1848), based on the life of a peasant girl of the Auvergne, brought her critical acclaim. She continued to draw on her detailed knowledge of France in many of her novels. Charlotte Brontë praised *Nathalie* (1850), the heroine of which – small, defenceless, and deprived of compatible intellectual companionship – foreshadows Brontë's Lucy Snowe in *Villette*. The heroine's sister, Rose, was thought by Brontë to be an autobiographical figure. Set in a girl's school in northern France, *Nathalie* addresses itself to the question of whether experience is self-fulfilment, or, as the convent teaches, expiation for sin.

JK later returned from France to England for subject matter. In *Rachel Grey* (1856), she showed, through the eyes of an orphaned working girl, how a relentless struggle for success affected both the working and managerial classes of northern England. Rachel has difficulty surviving in her shabby-genteel world, and is constantly under attack from both the workers and the managers; but she departs from the pattern of the stereotypical Victorian heroine by learning to work well with her male relations and with outsiders. Although George Eliot was critical of the novel's depiction of regional speech and manners, it is nevertheless considered to have influenced her own work. Whether dealing with the condition of England or set, more exotically, on the continent,

JK's work was popular, reaching a large audience through both serialization in periodicals and publication as multi-volume novels.

JK's collections of biographies of women form a substantial part of her literary output. She saw such biographical work as an essential corrective to the silence of male historians on the topic: in *Woman in France during the Eighteenth Century* (1850) she remarks of the power held by women at that time that 'Though the historians of the period have never fully or willingly acknowledged its existence, their silence cannot efface that which has been'. The account of women's power which JK develops is remarkable for its historical subtlety and leads her to develop wider reflections on, for example, the distribution of influence in the French court or the institution of the intellectual salon. *Women of Christianity* (1852) deliberately challenges the use of an idea of female piety to restrict women to the domestic sphere: her work 'does not profess to include those women whose virtues went not beyond the circle of home, and whose piety was limited to worship.' Instead, JK often presents Christianity as a means by which women denied access to political power could exercise public influence.   ELEANOR LANGSTAFF AND JAMES SMITH

Works: *The Montyon Prizes* (1846); *The Three Paths* (1848); *Madeleine* (1848); *Nathalie* (1850); *Woman in France during the Eighteenth Century* (1850); *Women of Christianity* (1852); *Daisy Burns* (1853); *Grace Lee* (1855); *Rachel Grey* (1856); *Adele* (1858); *A Summer and Winter in the Two Sicilies* (1858); *Seven Years and Other Tales* (1860); *French Women of Letters* (1862); *English Women of Letters* (1863); *Queen Mab* (1863); *Beatrice* (1865); *Sybil's Second Love* (1867); *Dora* (1868); *Silvia* (1870); *Bessie* (1872); *John Dorrien* (1875); *The Pearl Fountain and Other Fairy Tales* (1876); *Two Lilies* (1877); *Forget-me-nots* (1878).

References: Colby, R., *Fiction with a Purpose* (1967); *DNB*; Drabble; Foster, S., 'A suggestive book': a source for *Villette'*, *Etudes Anglaises: Grande-Bretagne, Etats-Unis* 35 (1982).

Kaye-Smith, Sheila

b. 1887, St Leonards-on-Sea, Sussex; d. 14 January 1956, Northiam, Sussex
Novelist

SKS was the daughter of Edward Kaye-Smith, MRCS, LRCP, physician and surgeon. She was educated privately and began writing fiction as a child, her first novel being published when she was only 20.

In 1924 she married T. Penrose Fry who later became a baronet. In 1929 they were both received into the Roman Catholic Church. On her husband's retirement, the couple moved to a house in Northiam, Sussex, which they had already bought. There SKS helped run their farm and estate as well as continuing her career as a prolific writer and lecturer. Her novels were published in America as well as England.

SKS's early novels were historical romances, but she quickly found her metier as a portrayer of Sussex, its farming communities and landscapes in contemporary or near-contemporary settings. Indeed, reviewers of the novels published in the first two decades of her writing career described her as 'doing for Sussex' what 'Hardy had done for Wessex'. But this is an exaggerated view of her achievements.

Certainly, however, her novels express great affection for the land and realistically depict people and places. The plots give equal importance to landowners and labourers, and SKS treats the latter without condescension, using dialect with tact and discrimination. Unlike some rural novelists of the period, she accepts the changes taking place in the countryside and considers unsentimentally the problems these can cause. In her best novels, *Sussex Gorse* (1916), *Little England* (1918), *Green Apple Harvest* (1920), and *Joanna Godden* (1921), SKS creates lively, positive characters and also conveys the sense of the working community to which they belong. She succeeds too in both describing an episode and conveying its significance for the character and the theme.

Unlike Hardy, SKS fails to imbue Sussex with any significance beyond its use as a setting; the universality of Wessex is never achieved. A more serious fault is that, in the course of her long writing career, she becomes repetitive. The plots, dealing with emotional or economic entanglements, vary little; the ways in which they are resolved become predictable, and no new vision is offered. In terms of construction, too, the later novels seems mechanical, following a carefully worked-out formula. SKS confessed in her autobiography *Three Ways Home* (1937) that her first novels were totally unplanned and that she learnt to organize her materials from the novelist W. L. George. The lesson, once learnt, was clearly applied rigidly and consistently. The result is a series of very readable but facile novels, which lack the intensity of imagination or range and depth of ideas which would have kept them alive beyond the period of their creation.

Her two collaborative critical books, *Talking of Jane Austen* (1943) and *More Talk of Jane Austen* (1950), have remained in print longer. The essays make pleasant reading: they are written with SKS's usual fluency and contain perceptive comments on features of Jane Austen's novels. Their tone is too reverential for modern taste, however, and they lack rigorous analysis.

JUDITH ALDRIDGE

Selected works: *The Tramping Methodist* (1908); *Starbrace* (1909); *Spell-land* (1910); *Isle of Thorns* (1913); *Three Against the World* (1914); *Willow's Forge and Other Poems* (1914); *Sussex Gorse* (1916); *Little England* (1918); *Tamarisk Town* (1919); *Green Apple Harvest* (1920); *Joanna Godden* (1921); *The End of the House of Alard* (1923); *Saints in Sussex* (1923); *The George and the Crown* (1925); *Joanna Godden Married and Other Stories* (1926); *The Village Doctor* (1929); *The History of Susan Spray: The Female Preacher* (1931); *Mirror of the Months* (1931); *Summer Holiday* (1932); *The Ploughman's Progress* (1932); *Superstition Corner* (1934); *Selina is Older* (1935); *Rose Deeprose* (1936); *Three Ways Home* (1937); *The Valiant Woman* (1938); *The Faithful Stranger and Other Stories* (1938); *The Hidden Son* (1942); *Tambourine, Trumpet and Drum* (1943); *Talking of Jane Austen* (with G. B. Stern) (1943); *The Lardners and the Laurelwoods* (1948); *The Treasures of the Snow* (1950); *More Talk of Jane Austen* (with G. B. Stern) (1950); *Mrs Gailey* (1951); *Weald of Kent and Sussex* (1953); *The View from the Parsonage* (1954); *All the Books of My Life* (1956).

References: Cavaliero, G., *The Rural Tradition in the English Novel 1900–1939* (1977); Hopkins, E. T., *Sheila Kaye-Smith and the Weald Country* (1925); Mackenzie, C., *Literature in My Time* (1933); Mansfield, K., *Novels and Novelists* (1930).

Keane, Molly

b. 1904, County Kildare, Ireland

Novelist, playwright

(Also writes under M. J. Farrell)

MK was born into the hunting, shooting, and fishing county set. Her father came originally from Somerset and her mother had some reputation as a poet. Her education depended on governesses and was rudimentary.

MK embraced the world she was born to enthusiastically, riding with skill and ability, and hunting with the best packs. In that social setting, to be seen reading a book, let alone to acknowledge writing one, was a social stigma. But, in the 1920s MK did begin to write books and to preserve the necessary anonymity she adopted the pseudonym of M. J. Farrell. From 1928 to 1952 she wrote ten novels dealing, mainly, with the small world that was hers; Anglo-Irish society, moneyed, elitist, living their lives against a backdrop of the real Ireland which was in a state of political turmoil. It has been said that MK wrote only to supplement her £30 a year dress allowance but there is little evidence that the work produced was 'written to order'. There is no sign of commercial necessity in the prose which is dry, witty, and written with great spirit. Her accomplished style has been compared to that of Jean Rhys.

As well as novels, MK wrote a number of plays during this period, including *Spring Meeting* (1938), *Ducks and Drakes* (1942), and *Treasure Hunt* (1949). They were always directed by John Gielgud and were recognized favourably by the critics including James Agate who claimed that she could 'hold her own against Noel Coward'. Hugh Walpole could also write of *Spring Meeting* (which introduced Margaret Rutherford to London audiences), 'she has a real sense of drama . . . she can create character. There is beauty here with understanding and an original mind.'

MK was one of five children, brought up in an atmosphere of neglect, mainly owing to her mother's total lack of interest in her children. Living conditions were primitive, the winters fiercely cold; there was no heating in the house and an atmosphere of deprivation dominated. This engendered in MK the desire to be independent and free of her mother. In riding she found this freedom. In *The Rising Tide* (1937) she vividly described this passion for horses akin to lust and obsession. In the field the women found all they otherwise lacked in their lives: the thrill of the hunt, the danger, achievement, exaltation. This study of horses, hunting, and the narrow world of one family was written when the issue of Home Rule was nudging Ireland towards revolution. MK could dismiss this from her mind and choose to concentrate on the smallest details of a threatened society.

Taking Chances (1929) is a bitter-sweet comedy. The setting is the traditional MK one; the characters, her familiar breed. The plot and structure are sound. But a more audacious author is emerging; one who does not steer clear of sexual politics, who can write about abortions and sexual misconduct. The device of introducing a stranger into an enclosed world is one she uses frequently. In *Taking Chances* the outsider is May Fuller, one of MK's brightest and best creations, to whom she lends some of the facets of her own unconventional personality – for behind the MK who rode to hounds and belonged to an anachronistic society there was a rebel who found her own freedoms in literature and the theatre.

After this period of novel and play writing MK was silenced. Her husband died at the age of 36 and MK stopped writing. This silence lasted over twenty-five years until she sent a new manuscript to Sir William Collins, the publisher of her earlier books. He rejected it, but Peggy Ashcroft, staying with MK at the time, took a different view. She enjoyed this new novel and urged MK to send it to another publisher, André Deutsch. *Good Behaviour* was published in 1981 and was shortlisted for the Booker Prize. MK had returned as MK, no longer needing to hide behind M. J. Farrell. She had not, however, abandoned her traditional setting. *Good Behaviour* is set again in the Anglo-Irish community. The St Charles family is decaying elegantly. Human emotions of sex, money, jealousy, and love are overruled by the principles of 'good behaviour'. But this code, like the family, is crumbling. As the father lies dying good behaviour predominates. When he dies his wife is 'rigorously set on perfect behaviour'. The mother in *Good Behaviour* is as remote and powerful as MK's. Owner of the house, the inheritance, she governs her daughter Aroon's life completely. She is pampered, spoiled, and demanding and only in dying and leaving Aroon the estate can her father redress the balance. *Good Behaviour* is witty, clever, macabre, and sinister. It proved beyond doubt that MK was no passé writer.

Time after Time appeared in 1983, to confirm the re-establishment of MK as a novelist of standing. It is the story of the Swift family, April, May, June, and Jasper, who have little in common but the memories of a, yet again, remote mother and a large but crumbling house in southern Ireland. Their world is disrupted by the arrival of the outsider, their cousin Leda from Vienna, blind, beautiful, and disruptive. MK's wicked humour flashes as she juxtaposes blind Leda with deaf April and conducts a pantomime of the family falling under Leda's spell, except for June who remains unconvinced by her charm. Leda's fall comes with a sharp twist at the end of the novel.   ALISON RIMMER

Works: (as M. J. Farrell) *Taking Chances* (1929); *Mad Puppetstown* (1931); *Conversation Piece* (1932); *Red Letter Day* (with J. Perry) (1933); *Devoted Ladies* (1934); *Full House* (1935); *The Rising Tide* (1937); *Spring Meeting: A comedy in Three Acts* (1938); *Two Days in Aragon* (1941); *Treasure Hunt: A Comedy* (1950); *Loving Without Tears* (1951); *Dazzling Prophet: A Farcical Comedy in Two Acts* (with J. Perry) (1961); (as Molly Keane): *Good Behaviour* (1981); *Time after Time* (1983).

References *CA*; Higginson, J. H., *British and American Sporting Authors* (1949); *New York Review of Books* (12 April 1984); *Times Literary Supplement* (9 October 1981).

Kelly, Isabella

Date and place of birth and death unknown

Novelist, poet, educationalist

(Also wrote under Mrs Hedgeland)

IK was a prolific and moderately popular writer. It may be that there were more editions of her work than are now known: the title page to a translation of *Joscelina* printed in Brunswick in 1799 states that it was taken from the third edition, whereas only one edition is listed in the bibliographies. She had a long and successful career, five of her nine novels and romances being published by the Minerva Press.

IK has left no autobiographical record. It is only from the dedications which preface her work, and from her poems, that we learn something of her life. *A Collection of Poems and Fables* (1794) reveals that she was the daughter of Eliza Fordyce, and first married Colonel Arthur Kelly, a relative of Lord Hawke, who at that time commanded 'the centre army in the Carnatic' in India. Several of her published poems were written before she was 14. The collection includes a lyric on the death of her child. The preface to *Joscelina* (1799) states that she published in order to extricate her husband from financial distress and to provide for her children. Her poems were republished in 1807 under a different title, and from the preface it is clear that she was by then a widow. From the evidence of the title pages it seems that she married a man named Hedgeland, between 1811 and 1813. She writes in the preface to *Instructive Anecdotes for Youth* (1819) that she is educating her daughters at her home in King's Road, Chelsea.

The novels are set in the present but, as in *The Ruins of Avondale Priory* (1796), use the distancing techniques associated with the historical romances of Ann Radcliffe. IK's narratives are of interest for the forthright reactionary political outlook given in a genre which was thought of as feminine and therefore apolitical. In *The Ruins of Avondale Priory*, the grateful vassalage benefit from the notice of St Clair and Ethelinde. Their example, in protecting their tenants from an avaricious steward by residing on their country estate, is recommended to the reader. Sir Eldred and Rodolpha, in *The Abbey of St Asaph* (1795), gladden the hearts of the vassalage by living on Sir Eldred's provincial estate. He enters Parliament to earn the gratitude of his king and of a united people for his solid judgement and correct principles. In these novels the rot of radical politics is banished from society by Christian marriage and by landowners caring for their tenants. *A Modern Incident in Domestic Life* (1803) employs the disguise of gender and is set in Barbados. *The Baron's Daughter: A Gothic Romance* (1802) is interesting as an example of an historical romance which uses the supernatural without providing a natural explanation. IK's novels emphasize the propriety of the heroine and the Christian virtue imparted in the narrative.   WILLIAM R. EDE

Works: *A Collection of Poems and Fables* (1794); *Madeline, or, The Castle of Montgomery: A Novel* (1794); *The Abbey of St Asaph* (1795); *The Ruins of Avondale Priory* (1796); *Joscelina, or, The Rewards of Benevolence: A Novel* (1797); *Eva: A Novel* (1797); *Ruthinglenne, or, The Critical Moment: A Novel* (1801); *The Baron's Daughter: A Gothic Romance* (1802); *A Modern Incident in Domestic Life* (1803); *The Secret: A Novel* (1805); *Poems and Fables on Several Occasions* (1805); *The Child's French Grammar, Intended as an Introduction to the Practical French Grammar of N. Wanostrocht* (1805); *Literary Information, Consisting of Anecdotes, Explanations, and Derivations* (1811); *Jane de Dunstanville, or, Characters as They Are: A Novel*(as Mrs Hedgeland) (1813); *Instructive Anecdotes for Youth* (1819).

References: Summers, M., *A Gothic Bibliography* (1938); Todd; Tompkins, J. M. S., *The Popular Novel in England 1770–1800* (1932).

Kemble, Adelaide

b. 1814(?), London; d. 4 August 1879, Hampshire

Novelist

The daughter of the actor Charles Kemble and of Marie-Thérèse Camp, and the sister of Fanny Kemble, AK was a much acclaimed vocalist before she left the stage in 1843 to marry Edward John Sartoris. After her return to England in 1842 following a triumphant Italian tour during which she received lessons from Guidetta Pasta, AK helped revive the flagging fortunes of Covent Garden by her performances in *La Somnambula* and *Semiramide*. She turned to writing after her marriage. She had three children, one of whom died in infancy.

AK's first work, *A Week in a French Country House*, first appeared in the *Cornhill Magazine* in 1867, and was published in book form in the same year.

Described by its author as 'more than a sketch and less than a story', it owed its popularity to its portraits of contemporary celebrities. Throughout her works, however, AK explores the ambiguous and unhappy position of women in society. Bessie, the narrator, while displaying a biting wit and accuracy in her appraisals of character and situation, accepts the belief that woman is intellectually inferior to man and needs to be guided by him. Her ambitions are modest and she has no wish to establish herself in society, for she has loved, for eleven years, an impoverished curate, and regards this love as the only way in which she can fulfil herself as a woman and achieve true happiness: 'each [man and woman] might be, in their very unlikeness, a comfort, a joy and a completion to the other.' Bessie's new friend, Ursula, refuses to accept Bessie's view and attempts to assert her independence. Society deplores her unfeminine behaviour. Ursula's background has already made her an outcast because her mother was an Italian opera singer who had to work for a living. Scorned by the Count de Saldes, the man she loves, Ursula is emotionally destroyed: 'everything like happiness was at an end, and she became at once and for ever the stern, melancholy woman that you see her now.' When the count does propose, it is too late for Ursula, who resigns herself to a loveless marriage with a grand duke which will gain her an acknowledged and secure status in society. The story, told from Bessie's viewpoint, naturally passes unfavourable judgement on Ursula, but there none the less remains some sympathy for her in the reader.

For AK, women in society are exploited by men. In the short story 'Medusa' (1868) the heroine has been reduced to a beautiful shell of a woman, whose mind has been destroyed by the chauvinistic count, her father, and her cruel husband. Yet she too finds a way to fulfil herself through love and motherhood; Wanda's sanity returns when she gives birth or is allowed to nurse the children of others. Even this natural fulfilment is destroyed when her father seizes her child, which then dies. Unlike Mrs Brandes who achieves happiness in marriage despite her unexciting and potentially frustrated life, Wanda remains socially and mentally drifting, for her natural potential as a woman is always thwarted. AK's works instruct women in their roles, but also expose those faults in society which prevent those roles from being achieved. The pattern of AK's own career on the stage and her subsequent marriage which ends it mirrors the ways in which her heroines have to resign themselves to domestic ambitions.

CAROLINE COLEMAN

Works: *A Week in a French Country House* (1867); *Medusa and Other Tales* (1868) (republished as *Past Hours*, 1880).

References: Butler, F. K., *Records of a Girlhood* (1830); Butler, F. K., *Records of a Later Life* (1846); Chorley, H. F., *Thirty Years of Musical Recollections* (1862); *DNB*; Ritchie, A. T., 'Preface' to *A Week in a French Country House* (1903); Gordon, Mrs, 'Preface' to *Past Hours* (1880).

Kemble, Fanny

b. 27 November 1809, London; d. 13 January 1893, London

Actress, poet, autobiographer

FK was born into a prominent theatrical family: her aunt was the well-known Sarah Siddons, and her uncle John and her father Charles played leading acting and managerial roles at Drury Lane and Covent Garden theatres. From her mother, a Swiss-French dancer and actress, Marie-Thérèse Camp, FK also inherited talent for the stage. She was a high-spirited and wilful child; a year at a school in Bath kept by one of her father's sisters having failed to tame her, at the age of 7 she was sent to France where she was educated for two years at Boulogne, followed a few years later by four in Paris. She returned home at 16 and continued a course of self-chosen reading as well as enjoying the rural pleasures of her parents' new residence near Weybridge. In 1825 she met Harriet St Leger, a friend of Uncle John and his wife, with whom she kept up a correspondence until the latter's death in 1877; Harriet's letters, returned to her friend, provided much of the material for FK's autobiographical writings.

Nourishing early ambitions of a literary career, FK started to compose romantic poetry and also wrote a historical play about Francis I which she hoped to have performed, but in 1827 her work was interrupted when she went to Edinburgh to stay for a year with her cousin, Mrs Henry Siddons, to whom she was sent for a change of intellectual and physical environment. In 1829, financial difficulties at Covent Garden had become so acute that, in order to help the theatre's fortunes, FK's father, opposed to her offer of becoming a governess, decided to launch her on the stage, a career which for all of her acting life she regarded as a necessity rather than as self-fulfilment. In her first role as Juliet, she was an instant success, and immediately gained access to London's cultural and aristocratic circles, as well as becoming well known in the provinces when the company went on tour. But by 1832, bankruptcy loomed again and FK and her father, with her aunt Adelaide ('Dall') as companion, left England for a two-year tour of the United States, her experience of which she recorded in her *Journal* (1835). Not uncritical of the Americans, she found much to admire and enjoy in the New World; in June 1834 she married Pierce Mease Butler, a Philadelphia plantation owner who had admired her from the first and who had accompanied her on some of her travels in the north-east.

The marriage was not a success, owing partly to incompatibility of temperament, but even more to the fact of FK's avowed initial ignorance of the source of her husband's family's wealth. Increasingly distressed by Butler's slave ownership (she was determined to express her anti-slavery views as an Appendix to her *Journal*, but was dissuaded from including it, though not from abandoning publication altogether, as Butler would have liked), her horror and hostility reached a climax when, in December 1838, she visited the plantations in south-east Georgia and saw the atrocities for herself. Though she did not originally intend to publish her impressions, merely circulating her notes among English and American friends, the outbreak of the Civil War and the British government's apparent readiness to support the Confederate South impelled her to public pronouncement, and her *Journal of a Residence on a Georgian Plantation* appeared in 1863. The work is an embittered, impassioned attack on slavery, which includes her guilt and self-hatred for being the unwitting perpetrator of such a system; its descriptions of the conditions of slave life make moving reading.

Matrimonial difficulties increased thereafter (she was not permitted to revisit Georgia) and though she and her husband continued to live and travel for periods together, she was increasingly alone, either in Philadelphia or in England, while still subject to his whims about her movements and to his financial imprudence. She officially separated from him in 1845, and in September she returned to England, with the additional heartache of having been forced to give her two small girls into his custody; she finally obtained a divorce in 1849, as the only means of securing her children's financial future. After briefly resuming her acting career she abandoned it for public readings, which she continued successfully for nearly twenty years; the proceeds from these enabled her to buy a house in Lennox, Massachusetts, near her great friends the Sedgwicks. Subsequently she moved between America and Europe, travelling and giving readings on both sides of the Atlantic; a second visit to Italy in 1853 reproduced her enjoyment of her first trip there, about which she writes so evocatively in *A Year of Consolation* (1847). During the late 1870s, she lived in retirement in Philadelphia, close to her children, now both married, and started work on her reminiscences which she was to publish in three parts over thirteen years. In 1877 she left America for good, and settled in England until her death at the home of her younger daughter, Fan, in 1893. Though she found the writing of her memoirs tiring and often tiresome, they vividly depict her energetic, varied, and full, albeit often distressing, life. As they make clear, despite her American affiliations she always regarded herself as English, and throughout her works her careful and usually fair-minded accounts of her New World experiences make a valuable contribution to the genre of American travel writing; her recall of her acting career and social acquaintances are also characterized by sharpness of observation and a delightful sense of humour, qualities which demand that she be recognized as a writer of some talent, as well as a notable figure on the Victorian stage.   SHIRLEY FOSTER

Works: *Journal of Frances Anne Butler* (1835); *Poems* (1844); *A Year of Consolation* (1847); *Journal of a Residence on a Georgian Plantation 1838–9* (1863); *Records of a Girlhood* (1878); *Records of Later Life* (1882); *The Adventures of Mr John Timothy Homespun in Switzerland* (1889); *Far Away and Long Ago* (1889); *Further Records 1848–1883* (1891).

References: Driver, L. S., *Fanny Kemble* (1933); Furnas, J. C., *Fanny Kemble: Leading Lady of the Nineteenth-Century Stage* (1982); Marshall, D., *Fanny Kemble* (1977); Wright, C., *Fanny Kemble in the Lovely Land* (1972).

Kempe, Margery

b. c.1373, Bishop's Lynn (now King's Lynn), Norfolk; d. c.1439
Mystical writer

The Book of Margery Kempe is the only example in English of a genre of female mystical autobiography common on the continent, in which the depiction of the miraculous and of a familiar, intimate relationship with the lover, Christ, and other biblical figures are privileged over theological speculation and insight. The written 'lives' of those continental women who were honoured by the Church through beatification or canonization were composed or edited later to serve as orthodox religious exemplars; MK's ultimate rejection by the ecclesiastical authorities means her book survives, undoctored, as a uniquely frank, idiosyncratic record of an extreme form of affective piety and the extraordinary life of a fifteenth-century woman.

Daughter of John Brunham, mayor of Lynn, MK married John Kempe, a holder of civic office, in about 1493. Her first vision occurred after the difficult birth of the first of her fourteen children; Christ came to her bedside 'in likeness of a man, most seemly, most beauteous', and drove away the devils that were tormenting her, inspiring in her a religious fervour which would eventually lead her to reject her own business ventures (brewing and milling) and her family life. In 1413 she and her husband swore mutual vows of chastity, effectively freeing MK for her heavenly bridegroom. Her life was marked by frequent conversations, 'dalliances', with Christ, who, she believed, inspired her travels as far as the Holy Land and Rome, and directed her, an uneducated woman, to dictate her book to an amanuensis. She presents her dogged determination in pursuing a path of piety beset with difficulties.

Her flamboyant manner and heavenly inspired tears brought, at the time, social rejection, while modern critics label her an hysteric. She is of a religious type peculiar to the Middle Ages, the self-humbling 'fools of God', willingly embracing persecution as the pattern of Christ's own life, literally enacting allegorically inspired Christian teachings, marrying deed to word. She was frequently accused of involving herself in Lollardy, a sect which threatened social revolution by literal interpretation of scripture, and of refusing enclosure as an anchorite or nun.

For the enclosed contemplative pronounced dead to the world, mystical marriage and 'imitatio Christi' were intended as purely spiritual goals; MK, in contrast, enacts them literally in her daily life. The figurative is realized and Christian metaphor becomes MK's code for life, not as a sign of grace for the traditionally female disembodied soul, but as justification for her life as woman, the bride/daughter/sister to Christ. She creates of herself a living symbol, scandalizing onlookers in her virgin-bride's white clothing. Drawing little if any distinction, linguistic or otherwise, between the actual and the visionary, MK employs, for example, 'ravished' to signify both earthly rape and spiritual ecstasy. The theological content of her conversations and debates are not recorded: the central interest of the text is the interplay of the mundane with the allegorical, MK's proofs of divine favour being the peculiar intimacy of her intercourse with the divine. In the eighty-first chapter she recounts her making of a hot drink for the Virgin Mary when she and St John take Mary home after Christ's burial; in the eighty-sixth, Christ likens His relationship with MK to a married couple who 'may . . . go to bed together without any shame or dread of the people'. That her religious outlook was unusual even in the Middle Ages is attested to by the fact that the few extracts of her book printed in 1501 by Wynkyn de Worde avoid any mention of MK's worldly life, and the mystical experiences are represented only by her rare, quietly contemplative passages.

The book is a startlingly honest account of MK's psychological and physical experiences. She refers to herself throughout in the third person, as 'this creature', in apposition to God, her creator. However, although ostensibly a work written for the glory of God, her book reveals MK's presence as far stronger than that of her maker. It has been called the first autobiography in English.

POLLY BRIGGS

Works: *The Book of Margery Kempe*, ed. S. B. Meech and H. E. Allen (1940); modern translation, *The Book of Margery Kempe*, ed. W. Butler-Bowden (1944).
References: Atkinson, C., *Mystic and Pilgrim: The Book and the World of Margery Kempe* (1983); Beckwith, S., 'A very material mysticism: the medieval mysticism of Margery Kempe', in *Medieval Literature*, ed. D. Aers (1986); Cholmeley, K., *Margery Kempe: Genius and Mystic* (1947); Dickman, S., 'Margery Kempe and the English devotional tradition', in *The Medieval Mystical Tradition in England* (1980); Dickman, S., 'Margery Kemp and the continental tradition of the pious woman', in *The Medieval Mystical Tradition in England*, ed. M. Glasscoe (1984); Goodman. A., 'The piety of John Brunham's daughter, of Lynne', in *Medieval Women* ed. D. Baker (1978); Hirsch, J. C., 'Author and scribe in *The Book of Margery Kempe*', in *Medium Aevum* 44 (1975); Stone, C. R., *Middle English Prose Style: Margery Kempe and Julian of Norwich* (1970); Thornton, M., *Margery Kempe: An Example in the English Pastoral Tradition* (1960); Watkin, E., *On Julian of Norwich and in Defence of Margery Kempe* (1979).

Kennedy, Margaret

b. 23 April 1896, Hyde Park Gate, London; d. 31 July 1967, Adderbury, Oxfordshire

Novelist, playwright, biographer, critic

MK was the eldest of the four children of Elinor Marwood and Charles Moore Kennedy. Her father was a qualified barrister, but chose, on the death of his father, to become a country gentleman. MK was brought up in High House, near Bromley, and educated by governesses and at Cheltenham Ladies' College. In 1914 she won a poetry prize at the Eisteddfod, where the judge was W. B. Yeats. In 1915 she went up to Somerville College, Oxford, to read History, graduating in 1919. Her first published work was a volume of French history, *A Century of Revolution* (1922), which, at the recommendation of A. L. Smith, Master of Balliol, she was commissioned to write for Methuen. In 1925 she married David Davies, a barrister and later a County Court judge, knighted in 1953. They settled in Kensington and had a son and two daughters.

Her first novel was *The Ladies of Lyndon* (1923), in which the heroine, Agatha Cocks, rebels against the social role assigned to her, that of the desirable wife for a man of 'assured, unearned income'. Her second novel, *The Constant Nymph* (1924), brought her instant recognition, and was reprinted in several editions in Britain and America. It was also adapted by MK and Basil Dean for the stage, and successfully produced in both London and New York, with Noel Coward and subsequently John Gielgud playing the part of Lewis Dodd. Four film versions of the novel appeared.

MK went on to write a further thirteen novels, in spite of Bell's Palsy, which afflicted her from 1939, and a long interruption for war work. Three of these novels received special recognition: *The Feast* (1950), an allegorical novel of the seven deadly sins, and *Lucy Carmichael* (1951) were Literary Guild and Book Society choices, while *Troy Chimneys* (1952) was the recipient of the James Tait Black Memorial Prize for 1953. *The Midas Touch* (1938), in which the main character is a clairvoyante, had been inspired by MK's own telepathic experiences. In addition, she wrote five plays for the London stage including *Escape Me Never* (1933), starring Elisabeth Bergner. Other works include a short biography of Jane Austen (1950). Her last novel appeared in 1964, the year of her husband's death. She then moved to Woodstock, Oxford, and died in nearby Adderbury.

MK's novels, which lay a strong emphasis on plot and are not devoid of sensation and melodrama, led some critics to dismiss her as a popular writer. In her history of the craft of fiction, *The Outlaws on Parnassus* (1958), she launched an attack on these critics, defending pleasure and entertainment as sources of value for the novel.

A recurrent theme in her work is the breaking away from convention in pursuit of personal fulfilment through art or through love, and the suffering as well as the rich compensation which social ostracism can bring. *The Ladies of Lyndon* focuses on Agatha, who rebels against the image which has been cut out for her, abandoning her baronet husband and escaping to the continent, and on Agatha's brother James, a budding painter of genius treated by his family as a half-wit. Both are part of a clash between bohemianism and bourgeois philistinism which informs many of MK's works, for example *The Game and the Candle* (1926) and *The Oracles* (1955).

Another theme common to most of the novels is that of the shifting and often grimly tangled pattern of family relationships, and in particular the disorientation and anguish suffered by children in the making and breaking of adult relationships. *Together and Apart* (1936) is a study of divorce in all its phases of domestic conflict, and pays particular attention to the child affected by the divorce, who is bundled off to boarding school to suffer at the hands of a sadistic prefect.

All these elements feature in *The Constant Nymph*, for which MK is best known. Its heroine, Tessa, is the daughter of a brilliant composer, Albert Sanger, who with his 'circus' of precocious children, slovenly mistress and assorted hangers-on, lives in a rambling chalet high in the Austrian Alps. Through his excesses and infidelities, Sanger has been largely responsible for the death of two wives. Tessa herself is described as 'unbalanced, untaught and fatally warm-hearted'; at 14 she falls tragically in love with Lewis Dodd, another gifted composer. She is made to endure her father's sudden death and Lewis's marriage to her beautiful but ambitious and calculating cousin Florence. Florence's jealousy and victimization of Tessa eventually erode her own marriage away, and Tessa elopes with Dodd, but emotional and physical neglect have taken their toll and Tessa eventually dies in a squalid Brussels boarding house. For MK's characters, the ideals of art and love are attainable only at a terrible cost to themselves and to others. MK wrote a sequel to *The Constant Nymph*, *The Fool of the Family* (1930).   ANNE FERNIHOUGH

Works: *A Century of Revolution* (1922); *The Ladies of Lyndon* (1923); *The Constant Nymph* (1924); *The Game and the Candle* (1926); *Red Sky at Morning* (1927); *Come With Me* (with Basil Dean) (1928); *The Fool of the Family* (1930); *Return I Dare Not* (1931); *A Long Time Ago* (1932); *Escape Me Never* (1933); *Together and Apart* (1936); *Autumn* (with Gregory Ratoff) (1937); *The Midas Touch* (1938); *The Feast* (1950); *Jane Austen* (1950); *Lucy Carmichael* (1951); *Troy Chimneys* (1952); *The Oracles* (1955; published in the US as *Act of God*); *The Heroes of Clone* (1957; published in the US as *The Wild Swan*); *The Outlaws on Parnassus* (1958); *A Night in Cold Harbour* (1960); *The Forgotten Smile* (1961); *Not in the Calendar* (1964).

References: Beauman, N., 'Introduction' to *The Ladies of Lyndon* (1981); Birley, J., 'Introduction' to *Together and Apart* (1981); Powell, V., *The Constant Novelist* (1983).

Kesson, Jessie

b. 1916, Inverness
Novelist

JK was born in the Inverness workhouse, the illegitimate daughter of Liza MacDonald. She was brought up in a deprived area of Elgin and, when she was 9, she was taken away from her mother who was too ill to look after her, being in an advanced state of chronic syphilis. JK was put into an orphanage, where she stayed until she was 16. Well educated at the local school, she developed an interest in writing and from that period was determined to become a writer. She left the orphanage to become a housemaid, but was sacked within a year. She developed neurasthenia and was put into a mental hospital. In 1935 JK met the Scots poet Nan Shepherd who encouraged her to enter a short story competition, which she won. JK convalesced on a farm where she met Johnnie Kesson, a farm labourer, who became her husband in 1936. JK wrote steadily from this time on but was saddled by the local press with the reputation of a literary curiosity – a farm labourer's wife who wrote. In 1954, in order to be taken seriously as a writer, she left Scotland for London, keeping herself afloat by writing plays for BBC Radio and working in Woolworths. Her first novel was published in 1959. She has worked with delinquent children, spastic children, and in homes for the elderly. She and her husband now live in north London. Two of her novels, *The White Bird Passes* (1959) and *Another Time, Another Place* (1983), have been filmed.

JK is a highly accomplished stylist. Her literary apprenticeship for *The White Bird Passes* was served in a series of plays for BBC Radio. (These plays have not been catalogued.) The style which emerges is elegant, confident, and unemcumbered, the perfect vehicle for expressing the naivety and complexity of the developing consciousness of a young girl. It is a style which sees clearly, records accurately, and overstates nothing: it is not difficult to see why JK admires Virginia Woolf. JK balances a shrewdly realistic appraisal of the problems of women's lives with a lyrical description of their real but unrealized ambitions and aspirations; her novels are often based upon snatches of song. *The White Bird Passes* is a semi-autobiographical novel which describes the warmth of Lady's Lane, home of prostitutes and others who do not conform to the mores of society at large. Janie McVean grows up there, delighted by the tales of the inhabitants, afraid of the violence which erupts, heartbroken on being separated from her mother and saddened by her mother's loss of beauty because of syphilis. The orphanage tries to make Janie conform but does not succeed in repressing either her creativity or her emergent sexuality. In *Glitter of Mica* (1963) and *Another Time, Another Place*, JK discusses the effect of conservative rural Aberdeenshire society on women. The only ones who cope are those like the courageous Sue Tatt who are prepared to risk ostracism because of their gregarious behaviour. The destiny of others, like the intelligent Helen Riddel and the sensitive heroine of *Another Time, Another Place*, is darker – madness, suicide or simply an imprisonment in the confining society. In short, women, who are not taken seriously by a patriarchal society, either conform to society's expectations and find their humanity dulled or else rebel against social strictures and become social misfits, comforted only by their dreams.   BETH DICKSON
Works: *The White Bird Passes* (1959); *The Glitter of Mica* (1963); *Another Time, Another Place* (1983); *Where the Apple Ripens* (1985).

Killigrew, Anne
b. 1660, London; d. 16 June 1685, London
Poet, painter
AK was the daughter of the theologian Dr Henry Killigrew and the niece of the popular Royalist dramatists Thomas and Sir William Killigrew. Her father secured her a position as maid of honour to Mary of Modena, and one of her companions was Anne Finch, Countess of Winchilsea. AK was a painter in the popular Restoration style, and was acclaimed by Dryden for her portraits of the king and queen. The year after her death from smallpox, AK's father published an edition of her poetry, for which Dryden wrote the memorial ode 'To the Pious Memory of the Accomplisht Young Lady Mistress Anne Killigrew'.

AK's earliest works are conventional poems of praise. She was accused of plagiarism as a result of her use of stock phrases and epithets, a charge she vigorously denied. Yet she insisted that the grandeur of her subject created the grandeur of her style, which was inspired rather than commonplace. In 'Alexandreis' although she acknowledges her use of the conventional 'frozen style', she prays that this will be transformed by the inspiration given by her subject: 'His lofty Deeds will raise each feeble line/ And God-like Acts will make my Verse Divine.' In fact she rarely succeeds in transcending stylistic convention, although she claims that her praise carries the weight of moral truth. In 'To the Queen', addressed to the unpopular Mary of Modena, the familiar elevation of the queen into a paragon of virtue makes the circle of her friends into an ark; it would be spiritual damnation to refuse to enter this ark. The moral severity behind the conventional epithets in AK's poetry, present also in her pastoral works, reflects the religious fervour of the court of James II, and it is this, rather than notable 'poetique fire', that distinguishes AK's work. Some works, however, suggest a movement away from Restoration convention towards a freer poetic form that AK might have achieved had she lived, for example 'The Discontent' in which she writes 'take here no Care, my Muse . . . / The ruggeder my Measures run when read, / They'l livelier paint th' unequal Paths fond Mortals tread', and 'On the Birthday of Queen Katherine' which present a fine metaphysical paradox. Dryden wrote that 'Such noble vigour did her verse adorn, / That it seem'd borrow'd when 'twas only born'.   CAROLINE COLEMAN

Works: *Poems* (1636).
References: Ballard; Cibber, T., *Lives of the Poets* (1753); Clayton, E., *English Female Artists* (1876); Keast, W., *Seventeenth Century English Poetry* (1962); Miner, E., *John Dryden* (1972); Tillyard, E. M. W., *Five Poems 1470–1870* (1948); Todd; Vieth, D. M., 'Irony in Dryden's Ode to Anne Killigrew', *Studies in Philology* 62 (1965).

King, Sophia
b. 1781(?); d. ?
Novelist, poet

SK was a prolific author of cheap Gothic novels. Nothing is known of her parentage, education, or life after the age of 25, when she stopped publishing. Her presumed birthdate is calculated from her own statement of her age in the preface to her first work, a volume of poems written with her sister Charlotte. In fact Charlotte, about whom nothing at all is known, wrote most of these poems.

SK's work was reviewed by the literary periodicals *Monthly Review* and *Critical Review*, the latter noting her 'luxuriant imagination'. This assessment accurately describes the plots of her Gothic romances: one hero is a ladykiller atheist, another wears a 'plume of ebon die'; the shedding of innocent and not-so-innocent blood and the sacrifice of maidenhood abound. SK summarized her own style best in the preface to her second volume of poems, where she salaciously suggests that the 'fantastic imagination roves unshackled' amid the 'horrible' and 'extraordinary'.   AMY ERICKSON

Works: *Trifles of Helicon* (with Charlotte King) (1798); *Waldorf, or, the Dangers of Philosophy* (1798); *Cordelia, or, A Romance of Real Life* (1799); *The Fatal Secret, or, Unknown Warrior* (1801); *The Victim of Friendship: A German Romance* (1801); *Poems, Legendary, Pathetic and Descriptive* (1804); *The Adventures of Victor Allen* (1805).
References: Todd; Tompkins, J. M. S., *The Popular Novel in England 1770–1800* (1932).

Kingsley, Mary

b. 13 October 1862, Islington; d. 3 June 1900, Simon's Town, Cape Town, South Africa

Ethnologist, travel writer

MK, a pioneer in the exploration of West Africa, was the only daughter of Mary Bailey and George Henry Kingsley, the brother of the novelists Charles and Henry. MK passed her childhood in Islington with her mother and younger brother, Charles, while her father, a doctor, sailed the South Seas and toured Spain with the Earl of Pembroke and the American west with Lord Dunraven. In 1879, upon her return, the family moved to Kent where MK, who did not attend school, studied chemistry, electricity, anthropology, and ethnology, supervised by her father and using his excellent library. In 1886, when Charles entered Christ's College, Cambridge, the family moved there and MK, now 24, greatly benefited from the conversation of the scholarly men and women who were her family's guests. In 1888, she travelled to Paris, but was forced by the failing health of her parents to return to Cambridge in 1891. When her father and mother died in 1892, MK moved to her brother's home in London, and after a brief trip to the Canary Islands, began to plan her first trip to West Africa. Although she had intended to follow her father into medicine, she decided in 1893 to devote herself to one of his other interests, primitive cultures and their laws.

Financed by Cambridge University, MK departed for West Africa in August 1893 to travel the Congo River to collect beetles and freshwater fish in previously uncharted regions. On her second voyage, between December 1894 and November 1895, MK explored the Ogowé River Valley in Gabon and the Bay of Biafra, and climbed the highest mountain in Cameroon, Mungo Mah Lobeh. She collected over sixty-five previously unseen specimens of fish from the waters surrounding the island of Corisco, many species of plants, soil specimens, and a variety of shells. MK financed her trip by trading ivory and rubber and textiles with the natives of Gabon, the Congo Française, and Cameroon. In her diaries, first, and later as *Travels in West Africa* (1897), MK records information never before collected about tribal life among the primitive Ajumba, Adooma, and Fan who lived on islands in the Ogowé or along its banks, taking special note of their religious beliefs, systems of justice and trade, and special customs relating to food preparation and marriage. With a keen eye for colour and detail, she also describes the landscape and wildlife she encountered: 'there were a quantity of ants and flocks of very small birds, little finch-like people, with a soft, dull grey plumage, relieved by the shading of dark green on the back, and the little crimson bills; they have a pretty, twittering note, and a little bigger than butterflies.'

Upon her return to England, MK was inundated with requests for lectures on African traditional medicine, animals, and the condition of English life in the colonies. In 1896, she gave the Hibbert Lecture at Oxford on 'African Religion and Law' and in 1898 she was made a member of the Anthropological Society. During this period (1896–1900), she was also writing her three books on Africa: *Travels in West Africa* (1897); *The Story of West Africa* (begun in 1897, published in 1899); and *West African Studies* (1899). Although all three are clearly written in capable expository prose, MK lamented her inability to write well in the preface of each and urged the reader to concentrate on her ideas rather than her style. In the 'Preface' to *West African Studies*, for example, she referred to the *Travels* as a 'word-swamp' which would never have attracted any attention were it not for the puffing skills of George Macmillan. Whereas *Travels* is clearly descriptive of the people and places she encountered, *The Story of West Africa* is more historical and *West African Studies* both anthropological and polemical. In the latter, MK deals with the negative effects of the Crown Colony system on the Africans and the English as well as matters concerning the unchecked commercial development of the area. The photographs which she includes of tribal gatherings and important villagers are as valuable as the text of the adventures. Prior to her third departure for Africa in March 1900, MK completed her father's *Notes on Sport and Travel* and added a sympathetic personal memoir.

MK reached Cape Town in 1900 and began nursing wounded Boer soldiers in Simon's Town Palace Hospital. Overworked and in frail health herself, she contracted enteric fever and was dead in three months. At her request she was buried at sea with a military funeral. The Mary Kingsley West African Society was founded in her honour in England to continue studies of primitive cultures, and a hospital was dedicated to her in Cape Town.   B. E. SCHNELLER

Works: *Travels in West Africa, Congo Française, Corisco, and Cameroon* (1897); 'The fetish view of the human soul', *Folk Lore* 8 (June 1897); 'The forms of apparitions in West Africa', *Journal of the Psychiatric Research Society* 14 (July 1899); 'Administration of our West African colonies', *Manchester Monthly Record* (March 1899); *West African Studies* (1899); *The Story of West Africa* (1899); memoir in *Notes on Sport and Travel*, by George Henry Kingsley (1900); 'West Africa from an ethnological point of view', *Imperial Institute Journal* (April 1900); 'The development of dodos', *National Review* (March 1896); 'Liquor traffic with West Africa', *Fortnightly* (April 1898); 'West African property', a series of four articles appearing in the *Morning Post* (July 1898).

References: *BA* (19); Blyden, E. W., *The African Society and Miss Kingsley* (1901); Campbell, O., *Mary Kingsley: A Victorian in the Jungle* (1957); Clair, C., *Mary Kingsley: African Explorer* (1963); *DNB;* Frank, K., *A Voyager Out: The Life of Mary Kingsley* (1986); Gwynn, S., *The Life of Mary Kingsley* (1933); Howard, C., *Mary Kingsley* (1957); Kipling, R., *Mary Kingsley* (1932); Stevenson, C., 'Female anger and African politics: the case of two Victorian "lady travellers" ', *Turn-of-the Century Women* 2, 1 (Summer 1985); Wallace, K., *This is Your Home: A Portrait of Mary Kingsley* (1956).

Lamb, Lady Caroline

b. 13 November 1785, London; d. 24 January 1828, London

Novelist, poet

CL was born Lady Caroline Ponsonby, the fourth child and only daughter of the third Earl of Bessborough. Her mother and aunt, daughters of the first Earl Spencer, were both celebrated for their beauty and their scandalous manner of life. CL's claim that she spent part of her childhood in Italy in the care of servants is unsupported by other evidence. She was brought up in the household of her aunt, the Duchess of Devonshire, and experienced only a very brief period of formal schooling. Her temperament as a child was so highly strung that on medical advice she was taught nothing and was subject to no restraint. In 1802 she visited Paris with her mother. In 1805 she married William Lamb, later Lord Melbourne, prime minister to Queen Victoria. The wedding was followed by a period of intense nervous agitation but the first few years of her marriage were comparatively stable and happy. Her only son, Augustus, born in 1807, was mentally retarded. In 1812 she met Byron, recorded in her journal that he was 'mad, bad and dangerous to know', and began a romantic obsession with him which dominated the rest of her life. They were lovers for a few months: when Byron terminated the relationship, CL's behaviour became increasingly eccentric, exhibitionist, and even violent. In 1816 her in-laws attempted to have her certified as insane and to separate her from her husband, but she continued to live with him until 1824, when she accidentally encountered Byron's cortège. The frantic agony and despair into which this incident plunged her provoked William Lamb's decision that they must separate. CL lived briefly in Paris, but returned to Brocket, the Melbournes' Hertfordshire estate. A series of romantic entanglements with younger men (including Bulwer Lytton and an illegitimate son of the Duke of Bedford) amplified the notoriety of her reputation. On becoming ill, she returned to London where she died of dropsy at the age of 42.

CL's novels provided for their author a therapeutic outlet for powerful feelings and for her readers the pleasures of the *roman à clef*. *Glenarvon* (1816) is a Gothic imbroglio set in Ireland and London, whose main characters are readily recognizable portraits of members of contemporary London society. The heroine, Calantha, is a self-portrait of the author, and her enigmatic, melodramatic lover and betrayer is modelled upon Byron, one of whose letters to CL is produced in the text. There are passages of description which have some power and a real feeling for natural beauty, but the novel is formless and the central intrigue is obscured in a maze of sensational details. *Glenarvon* enjoyed a considerable, but brief success with contemporary readers. In *Graham Hamilton* (1820) CL pared away the Gothic extravagances and with them most of the life in her literary manner. *Ada Reis* (1823), her own favourite among her novels, is also the most bizarre. The action involves the struggle of the incarnate spirits of light and darkness for the soul of the beautiful, passionate, and wilful Fiormonda. It ranges from Georgia to Peru, and in the third volume breaks through the boundaries of the material world to describe the heroine's sojourn in Hades as the consort of the infernal emperor. The Byronic role is played by Candulmar, who is irresistible but faithless, and her spiritual struggle to overcome the temptation he represents restores Fiormonda to mortality, to end her days as a saintly hermit.

CL's verses are mostly conventional in form and diction. One elegy was written to be recited by a page while girls danced round the bonfire on which CL immolated Byron's gifts and copies of his letters to her. This incident, absurd in its form but pathetic in its personal significance, might serve as a symbol for all her literary compositions, and indeed for her life.

ELIZABETH JOYCE

Works: *Glenarvon* (1816); *Graham Hamilton* (1820); *Ada Reis* (1823); *A New Canto* (1819).

References: BA (19); Drabble; Jenkins, E., *Lady Caroline Lamb* (1932).

Lamb, Mary

b. 3 December 1764, London; d. 20 May 1847, London
Writer for children, poet

ML was the third-born child and only surviving daughter of John and Elizabeth Lamb, five of whose eight children died in infancy. Her childhood home was the Inner Temple, where her father was employed as a waiter and as servant to Samuel Salt, a Member of Parliament and director of the East India Company, whose benevolent patronage was of great assistance to the Lambs. The children had access to Salt's library, where ML read widely. After her brief formal education at an academy in Fetter Lane, she was apprenticed to a dressmaker. She was responsible for the earliest education of her young brother Charles, the essayist (born in 1775), and with him made two happy childhood visits to their mother's family in Hertfordshire. There was a history of mental instability in the family and it was ML's tragedy that this took a violent and recurrent form in her. In 1796, in a fit of madness, she stabbed her mother to death. Unselfishly determined to keep her out of the public hospital, Charles became her legal guardian and cared for her at various addresses in and near London for the rest of his life. During the remissions in her illness ML enjoyed visits with her brother to the Lake District, Cambridge, a number of seaside resorts and, in 1822, to France where sadly the excitement of travel abroad brought on a relapse into confusion and violent behaviour. Frequent changes of residence contributed to her instability, as did her sensitivity to the tragedies of others, such as the death at sea in 1805 of William Wordsworth's brother John. In 1821 Charles and ML adopted an orphaned girl, Emma Isola, and made themselves responsible for her care and education until her marriage in 1833. When Charles died in 1835 ML was too ill to understand what had happened. She outlived him, sinking further into the isolation of her madness, for twelve years. Her brother's vivid, affectionate tribute to her is his portrayal of the strong-minded and warm-hearted Bridget Elia in his essay on 'Mackery End in Hertfordshire'.

During her lucid intervals, which were often of many months' duration, ML's warm and gentle personality endeared her to Charles's literary acquaint-ances, who also responded to the originality, acuteness, and humour with which she expressed her views. Hazlitt distinguished her from all other women as 'thoroughly reasonable' and remarked on the chaotic brilliance of her utter-ances in madness. Her shrewd and ironic perception of the condition of contem-porary women is demonstrated in her sprightly essay 'On Needlework' in which she concludes that women 'may be more properly ranked among the contributors to, than the partakers of, the undisturbed relaxations of mankind' and in which, as in the preface to the *Tales from Shakespeare*, she deplores the inadequacies of the education reserved for girls. Perhaps partly to compensate for the deficiencies of her own schooling she learnt Latin in 1814 'in order to acquire a correct style' and later coached a number of pupils in the language, including Emma Isola whose struggles are recorded in the sonnet 'To Emma, learning Latin'.

Though ML always found writing 'a most painful occupation', the strain of which tended to make her ill, in order to assist with the family's finances she collaborated with Charles in several publications. In 1806 they were commis-sioned by Godwin's Juvenile Library to produce a number of works for young readers. *Tales from Shakespeare* appeared the following year. The six tragedies were adapted by Charles, but the bulk of the work, fourteen comedies and pastoral romances, were, as he acknowledges, 'done capitally' by ML. Never-theless, either through her own diffidence or the commercial instinct of the publisher, her name did not appear on the title page until the seventh edition of this immediately popular work. ML had considerable success in transforming the plays from dramatic to narrative form, retaining as far as possible the original words and where additions and explanations were required, supplying them with tact. She concentrated upon the intrigues and relationships among the lovers and noble characters, largely omitting the clowns, jesters, low-life characters, the figures of exuberant comedy such as Sir Toby Belch in *Twelfth*

Night and, rather unexpectedly, Portia's caskets in *The Merchant of Venice*. She thus achieved a clear and interesting story line but at the expense of much of the humour. The emphasis of her adaptations was undoubtedly influenced by the difficulties of making intelligible much of Shakespeare's word-play, of finding a narrative equivalent for physical clowning, and of disentangling the complexities of the comic sub-plots. Furthermore, the preface (almost entirely ML's work) makes clear that she envisages a readership primarily of girls who might be supposed to find masculine and earthy humour less interesting than the adventures of Shakespeare's heroines and the working out of their destinies.

In 1809 Charles and ML published *Mrs Leicester's School*, a collection of ten stories of which ML wrote seven. The book was immediately popular and went through numerous editions. ML's stories are sensitive and unsentimental accounts of the child's world, never heavy-handed in their moralizing and sometimes refreshingly down to earth, as when in *A Visit to the Cousins* the prescribed remedy for an attack of selfishness is a visit to the theatre, a pleasure which depends upon sharing for its enjoyment. *The Farm House* is an evocative recollection of the Lambs' childhood visits to Hertfordshire which presents a pastoral idyll through a child's fresh and vivid sensory experience of the countryside. Though many of the stories deal with a child bereft of one or both parents, they all end reassuringly with loving acceptance of a surrogate or reabsorption into the family group. In *The Sailor Uncle*, morbid fascination with the grave of 'dear mamma' is corrected by the robust affection of the living uncle. All the stories explore a child's relationships with others and her developing social as well as moral self-awareness.

It is impossible to identify with certainty the authorship of most of the individual poems in the Lambs' next collaborative venture, *Poetry for Children* (1809). Charles claimed to have written 'the best' but admitted that his contribution was 'but one third of the whole'. Intended by the Godwins to compete with the poems of Isaac Watts and the Watson sisters, this miscellany of verse fables, anecdotes, moral precepts and Bible stories in rhyme sold quickly but was not reprinted (though the majority of the verses soon appeared in other compilations published by Godwin). As in the prose stories, the didacticism is relatively unobtrusive – religious duties are scarcely glanced at, and the emphasis is on encouraging sensitivity to siblings, social inferiors, animals, and the disadvantaged. The verses based on Bible stories, which are almost certainly ML's, describe lively events, such as that in 'David and Goliath' and the finding of the baby Moses, for their narrative interest rather than for the sake of a moral lesson. Some of the poems are trite, and the rhythms are occasionally clumsy, but the majority show an affectionate, sympathetic awareness of the child's world that, as Charles himself observed, is 'remarkable in an old bachelor and an old maid'. ML also wrote a number of occasional verses, several inspired by engravings, which were intended for circulation among close friends, and which are scarcely more than competent at their best. The prose story for children was the vehicle which best expressed her sharp observation of human behaviour and her delight in the natural world.   ELIZABETH JOYCE

Works: *Tales from Shakespeare, Designed for the Use of Young Persons* (with Charles Lamb) (1807); *Mrs Leicester's School, or, The History of Several Young Ladies, related by Themselves* (with Charles Lamb) (1809); *Poetry for Children* (with Charles Lamb) (1809); *The Works of Charles and Mary Lamb* (with Charles Lamb), 7 vols, ed. E. V. Lucas (1903–5); *The Works in Prose and Verse of Charles and Mary Lamb* (with Charles Lamb), ed. T. Hutchinson (1908); 'On

Needlework', *British Lady's Magazine* (April 1815); 'To Emma learning Latin', *Blackwood's Magazine* (June 1829).
References: Anthony, K. S., *The Lambs: A Study of Pre-Victorian England* (1948); Ashton, H. R., *I Had a Sister* (1937); Cornwall, B., *Charles Lamb: A Memoir* (1866); Gilchrist, Mrs, *Mary Lamb: A Biography* (1883); Hazlitt, W. C., *The Lambs: Their Lives, Their Friends and Their Correspondence* (1897); Kirlew, M., *Famous Sisters of Great Men* (1905); Lucas, E. V. (ed.), *The Letters of Charles Lamb to Which Are Added Those of His Sister Mary* (1935); Lucas, E. V., *The Life of Charles Lamb* (1905); Marrs, E. W. (ed.), *The Letters of Charles and Mary Anne Lamb* (1975–8); Ross, E. C., *The Ordeal of Bridget Elia* (1940); Talfourd, T. N. (ed.), *The Letters of Charles Lamb with a Sketch of His Life* (1837).

Landon, Letitia Elizabeth

b. 14 August 1802, Chelsea; d. 15 October 1838, Cape Coast, Ghana
Poet
(Also wrote under L, L.E.L.)

LEL's output of verse was marked by a constant tone of melancholy, although in person, by all accounts, she was a cheerful and pragmatic young woman. In a preface to her poetical works LEL explained her emphasis on sentiment: 'Aware that to elevate I must first soften, and that if I wish to purify I must first touch, I have ever endeavoured to bring forward grief, disappointment, the fallen leaf, the faded flower, the broken heart, and the early grave. . . . [As to] my frequent choice of Love for my source of song, I can only say that, for a woman, whose influence and whose sphere must be in the affections, what subject can be more fitting than one which it is her particular province to refine, spiritualize, and exalt?'

Educated at the same school as Mary Mitford and Lady Caroline Lamb, LEL was considered a child prodigy. When William Jerdan ran across some of her early poems, he was so impressed that in 1820, when she was 18 years old, he launched her career in his *Literary Gazette*. Her verses were so well received that she went on to publish five full volumes of poetry between 1821 and 1828: *The Fate of Adelaide* (1821), *The Improvisatrice* (1824), *The Troubadour* (1825), *The Golden Violet* (1827), and *The Venetian Bracelet, The Lost Pleiad, A History of the Lyre, and Other Poems* (1828). Her work was acclaimed by contemporary critics and awaited eagerly by readers who imagined the life of the mysterious poetess to be as romantic as the recurrent subjects of her poems. She was hailed as a female Byron. Her unguarded professional relationships with the editors William Jerdan and William Maginn damaged her personal reputation and may have caused the biographer, John Forster, to break off his engagement to marry her. To the astonishment of her friends, she responded by marrying George Maclean, the governor of Cape Coast Castle, and setting sail with him for a three-year term in Africa, despite rumours that Maclean already had an African wife. A few months later, she was found dead in her room with a bottle of prussic acid in her hand. Whether she died by accident, suicide, or murder was never determined.

The immense popularity of LEL's poetry has sometimes been attributed to her ability to capture superficial aspects of Romantic poetry and combine them with moral themes. Furthermore, her continual characterizations of self-sacrificing femininity gratified the new social ideal of womanhood. *Blackwood's* 'Tickler' asked of LEL in 1825, 'Does not she throw over her most impassioned strains of love and rapture a delicate and gentle spirit from the recess of her own pure and holy woman's heart?' Yet LEL thought of herself as a professional writer, motivated by the financial need of her family. Thus in addition to half a dozen volumes of poetry, five novels and a book of moral tales, she also published numerous fugitive pieces in various annuals and periodicals, including the *Drawing-Room Scrapbook*, the *Keepsake*, and *Friendship's Offering*. A few of these she edited or co-edited with the Countess of Blessington and others.

The extensive recognition accorded to LEL in her teens encouraged her to think of writing as a spontaneous, improvisatory act rather than as a discipline. Consequently, she wrote effusively and seldom revised; often the sublime effect for which she aimed collapsed into triteness and sentimentality. In 'Erinna' (1826), however, abandoning her usual rhymed couplets for blank verse, she wrote a genuinely autobiographical poem. In this dramatic monologue on the subject of the ancient poetess, LEL revealed her own frustrations as a woman writer. Finally, in a poetical fragment found among her papers after her death, she lamented, 'Alas! that ever/ Praise should have been what praise has been to me –/ The opiate of the mind.' LEL's untimely death forestalled whatever maturation of her talents might have followed from this revelation.

KATHLEEN HICKOK

Works: *The Fate of Adelaide and Other Poems* (1821); *The Improvisatrice and Other Poems* (1824); *The Troubadour* (1825); *The Golden Violet* (1827); *The Venetian Bracelet, The Lost Pleiad, A History of the Lyre, and Other Poems* (1828); *Romance and Reality* (1831); *Frances Carrara* (1834); *The Vow of the Peacock and Other Poems* (1828); *Traits and Trials of Early Life* (1836); *Ethel Churchill, or, The Two Brides* (1837); *A Birthday Tribute, Addressed to the Princess Alexandrina Victoria* (1837); *Duty and Inclination: A Novel, edited by Miss Landon* (1838); *Flowers of Loveliness* (with Lady Blessington and T. H. Bayley) (1838); *The Easter Gift: A Religious Offering* (1838); *The Zenana, and Minor Poems of L.E.L.* (1839); *Life and Literary Remains of L.E.L.* ed. S. L. Blanchard (1841); *Lady Anne Granard, or, Keeping Up Appearances* (1842).

References: Allibone; Ashton, H. R., *Letty Landon* (1951); Bethune, G., *The British Female Poets* (1848); Courtenay, J., *The Adventurous Thirties* (1933); Drabble; Elwin, M., *Victorian Wallflowers* (1934); Elwood, A. K., *Memoirs of the Literary Ladies of England* (1842); Enfield, D. L., *A Mystery of the Thirties* (1928); Hall, S. C. and Hall, A. M., 'Memories of authors: Miss Landon', *Atlantic Monthly* (1865); Hickok, K., *Representations of Women: Nineteenth Century English Women's Poetry* (1984); Jerdan, W., *Autobiography of William Jerdan* (1852–3); Miles, A. H. (ed.), *The Poets and Poetry of the Century* (1892); Robertson, E. S. (ed.), *English Poetesses* (1883); Sheppard, S., *Characteristics of the Genius and Writings of L.E.L.* (1841); Showalter, E., *A Literature of Their Own* (1977); Stevenson, L., 'Miss Landon: the "Milk-and-Watery Moon of Our Darkness," 1824–1830', *Modern Language Quarterly* 8 (1947).

Lanier, Emilia

b. before 27 January 1569, London; d. April 1645, London

Poet

EL was the daughter of one of Queen Elizabeth's Italian musicians, Baptista Bassano, and his mistress, Margaret Johnson. Her father died in 1576 when she was 7 years old, and her mother died eleven years later, leaving EL with a dowry of £100 (which, however, she may never have received). After a period during which she was in the service of the Countess of Kent, EL became the mistress of Lord Hunsdon, the Lord Chamberlain. When in 1592 she was discovered to be pregnant with his child, she was married off to another of the queen's musicians, Alphonso Lanier, with an annuity of £40. Lanier enlisted as a volunteer in a naval expedition in 1597, and EL consulted an astrologer, Simon Forman, as to his likely prospects on the voyage. (Forman's notes are our principal source of information about EL's early life.) But she also told Forman that her husband had spent all her money and left her in debt. He wrote, 'She is now very needy, in debt and it seems for lucre's sake will be a good fellow, for necessity doth compel.' He later paid her for sexual favours himself.

EL published her only book, *Salve Deus Rex Judaeorum*, in 1611 to little public response. Together with the title poem it included poetic addresses to a variety of noblewomen and a topographical poem, 'The Description of Cooke-ham', which may be the first example of the 'country house poem' in the literature. EL's subsequent life is known to us only through a series of lawsuits in which she became involved. We learn from a Chancery case which she brought in 1619 that her husband had died by this date and that she kept a school in St Giles-in-the-Fields. In 1635 EL petitioned for money due to her from her husband's monopoly over straw and hay weighing in London and Westminster, in which she asserted herself to be 'in great misery and having two grandchildren to provide for'. Beyond the information provided by these two suits we know little of EL's later life, and A. L. Rowse's contention that she was the 'dark lady' of Shakespeare's sonnets relies almost entirely upon ambiguous internal evidence from the sonnets and upon judgements about EL's 'passionate' and 'intemperate' character supposedly to be deduced from *Salve Deus . . .* and from Forman's notebooks.

EL's book is a strongly feminist one, not only in the contents of its principal poem, but also in its dedicatory apparatus. All of the dedicatory pieces are addressed to women: the first to the queen and others to a series of noblewomen. These are diverse in form: that to the queen consists chiefly of a series of compliments, but that to the Countess of Pembroke (herself a poet) is a narrative of 'The Authors Dreame', whilst another to the Countess of Pembroke is a prose piece. Most significantly, EL last addresses 'the Vertuous Reader' and explicitly indicates that her work is intended for an audience of 'all vertuous Ladies and Gentlewomen of this Kingdome', and that it has been written 'to make known to the world, that all women deserve not to be blamed . . .'. EL goes on to cite a catalogue of virtuous biblical women so as to 'inforce all good Christians and honourable minded men to speak reverently of our sexe'.

The title poem takes every available opportunity to reinterpret Scripture so as to prevent its use as a justification for misogyny. It is principally concerned with the Passion, and at many points emphasizes the part played by men in Christ's crucifixion whilst, conversely, exonerating women. A section entitled 'The teares of the daughters of Jerusalem' sets up a general antithesis to this effect:

> When spightfull men with torments did oppresse
> Th'afflicted body of this innocent Dove,
> Poor women seeing how much they did transgresse . . .
> They labour still these tyrants' hearts to move.

The poem includes numerous polemical digressions, among the most interesting of which is 'Eves Apologie in Defence of Women'. EL begins this by reversing the traditional hierarchy of responsibility for the Fall (and that later endorsed by Milton): 'Her fault though great, yet hee was most to blame.' Moreover,

EL proceeds to attack the use of this myth as a justification for contemporary sexual inequality: addresssing men in general, she asks, 'Your fault being greater, why should you disdaine/ Our beeing your equals, free from tyranny?'

EL's feminism is often accompanied by a more defensive insistence on the importance of female chastity. Mary Magdalene is conspicuous by her absence from EL's version of the Passion. But this insistence rarely goes without qualification, whether implicit or explicit. One digression, unpromisingly entitled 'An Invective against outward beauty unaccompanied with virtue', soon becomes an invective against men who 'seeke, attempte, plot and devise,/ How they may overthrow the chastest Dame . . .', and EL then goes on to give fewer examples of beautiful but unchaste women than of virtuous women who have none the less been victimized by men.   SIMON JARVIS

Works: *Salve Deus Rex Judaeorum* (1611).

References: Lewalski, B. K., 'Of God and good women: the poems of Aemilia Lanyer', in *Silent but for the Word*, ed., M. P. Hannay (1985); Rowse, A. L., *The Poems of Shakespeare's Dark Lady* (1978).

Lavin, Mary

b. 1912, Walpole, Massachusetts

Short story writer, novelist

One of Ireland's major living fiction writers, ML lives on her farm in Bective, near Dublin. Her mother, Norah Mahon, who came from a large middle-class family in County Galway, had married Thomas Lavin and gone back with him to America but, miserable there, she finally returned to Athenry with ML, then 9 years old. The months spent in this provincial Irish town in 1921 made a lasting impression on ML's imagination. When ML's father rejoined them they moved first to Dublin, and then, when he became manager of a local estate, to Bective.

As his only child, ML was encouraged by her father to acquire a good education. After attending the Loreto Convent School, she gained a First in English at University College, Dublin, and went on to write an MA thesis on Jane Austen. A dissertation on Virginia Woolf was put aside when ML began teaching and writing fiction. In 1942, aged 30, ML published her first collection of stories, and married William Walsh, a Dublin lawyer.

They settled in Bective, on the Abbey Farm. Over the next ten years ML published five volumes of short stories and received the James Tait Black Memorial Prize. Then in 1954 her husband died, and ML was left with three young children to support and a farm to run. Years of real difficulty were to follow. A Guggenheim Fellowship in 1959 prevented her from abandoning her writing, and she gradually began to receive wider recognition in Ireland and America, being awarded the Katherine Mansfield Prize in 1961; she was appointed writer-in-residence at the University of Connecticut for several semesters, and was granted an honorary doctorate from UCD. In 1969 she married Michael Scott, an old friend from her college days, and now divides her time between Dublin and the Abbey Farm.

ML has said that she turned to the short story as a form because the demands on her time allowed her to write only in interrupted snatches. Like other women who have survived as writers, she has made a virtue of necessity, using the story's limited space to show lives narrowly hemmed in by circumstances, to cast a brief light on what may be their one odd moment of meaning. Habituated to limitation, her characters generally fail to recognize their moment. In the unusually emblematic story 'The Giant Wave', the boy can hardly miss his moment, which lifts him high on the wave that drowns his village, and his life is transformed accordingly, although we are left wondering at the cost. The more typical revelation is far meaner in scope, passing by unnoticed or recognized only when it is too late, as a final turn of the screw: in 'At Sallygap' the man realizes that his one chance for freedom had passed years before, as his fiddle smashed in the wake of the ship he had just failed to take.

At times the irony of lost opportunity turns to dark comedy. In 'Bridal Sheets' the newly widowed woman from an inland town laments the waste of the smart clothes she had brought with her but left unworn during the short months of her marriage to an island fisherman, as too good for his impoverished village. When the island women lay out his drowned body in her similarly unused bridal sheets, to assuage what they take to be her grief at the waste of the past, she furiously strips them off and locks them back away with the rest of the hoard in her trunk. The waste to which she in her sharpness is oblivious is apparent only to the island women, with their shared experience of loss.

Here and elsewhere in ML's work, women who are separated from the common fund of female experience (being unmarried or childless or genteel or educated) ironically – since they are apparently a cut above the rest – have less insight than those around them ('The Long Ago', 'The Nun's Mother', 'The Mouse', 'A Single Lady', 'A Visit to the Cemetery'). In 'A Cup of Tea' the daughter home from college sides with her father and rejects her mother and her bitter experience of married misery, prevented by her education from assuming the woman's perspective, but not, as it turns out, from assuming her role. The daughter is on the brink of marrying in her turn a 'stern and stiff' man like her father, about to repeat her mother's mistake; a momentary insight, brought about by seeing the likeness of herself and her future husband in old photographs of her parents in their youth, slips uselessly away.

As the recurrence of likeness in family photos suggests, time in ML's world is circular, repetitive. Drawing from her own experience conflated with that of her mother and her family before her, ML renders her time setting hazy. Apart from some notable exceptions, the stories are set somewhere in the last hundred years in a world where life goes on largely unchanged. Successive generations, particularly of women, retread the old paths, even while they imagine themselves to be breaking new ground. Thus in 'A Visit to the Cemetery' two as yet unwed sisters close the gates firmly behind them on the old graveyard where their mother, together with a lifetime's awful marriage and a child dead in infancy, lies buried. The girls are confident that they will never have to lie there, in such a shocking place – that is, in what amounts to the old female space – since their future husbands will provide lots for them in the smart new cemetery up the road.

Writing as she often does about death, ML shifts in and out of black comedy as she shows life to be only a temporary violation of the prevailing order. In 'The Cemetery in the Demesne' only the superstitious hope of a woman for her sick scrap of a baby keeps it from the choked graveyard that dominates their gatehouse. But the absurdity of that hope is soon exposed and squashed by a chance passer-by, a man eager to put the woman right and in need of a chat. 'The Living' swings effectively between tragedy and farce as the narrator recalls how as a boy he gatecrashed a funeral for a dare, only to run away howling from the body and his own first insight into death. He dashed back to the living, to what he then thought was the unbreachable security of his mother's warm kitchen. He now knows better: 'And in the excitement I forgot all about the living and the dead. For a long time.'   GILLIAN PARKER

Works: Tales from Bective Bridge (1942); The Long Ago and Other Stories (1944); The House in Clewe Street (1945); The Becker Wives (1946); At Sallygap (1947); Mary O'Grady (1950); A Single Lady and Other Stories (1951); The Patriot Son and Other Stories (1956); A Likely Story (1957); Selected Stories (1959); The Great Wave and Other Stories (1961); The Stories of Mary Lavin, vol. 1 (1964); In the Middle of the Fields and Other Stories (1967); Happiness and Other Stories (1969); Collected Stories (1971); The Second Best Children in the World (1972); A Memory and Other Stories (1972); The Stories of Mary Lavin, vol. 2 (1973); The Shrine and Other Stories (1977); A Family Likeness and Other Stories (1985).

References: Bowen, Z., Mary Lavin (1975); Eire-Ireland 3 (1968) and 7 (1972); Irish University Review 9 (1979); Kelly, A., Mary Lavin: Quiet Rebel (1980); O'Connor, F., The Lonely Voice: A Study of the Short Story (1963); Peterson, R., Mary Lavin (1978); Pritchett, V. S., 'Introduction' to Collected Stories (1971).

Lead, Jane

b. March 1623; d. 19 August 1704

Mystical writer

JL was the daughter of Schildknap Ward of Norfolk, a member of a respectable Anglican family, and had at least a rudimentary education. When she was 15, she had her first mystical experience; she heard a voice whispering to her during the Christmas festival. She suffered periods of melancholy which ended when she was 18 after she saw a vision of 'a pardon with a seal on it' which absolved her from a lie she had once told. At the age of 21 she married a distant relative, William Lead, with whom she apparently lived contentedly for twenty-seven years, although she wrote in her spiritual journal, A Fountain of Gardens (1697), that he had been an obstacle to her love of Christ. They had at least one daughter, Barbara. After William Lead's death in February 1670, JL devoted her life to religion, regarding herself as a 'widow of God'.

In 1663 she had become acquainted with Dr John Pordage, a follower of Jacob Boehme, who may have encouraged her belief in the value of mystical experience. This experience became more frequent until by 1670 she received almost nightly visions; these she recorded in her journal and later published as A Fountain of Gardens. In 1681 JL's first publication, The Heavenly Cloud Now Breaking, appeared and caused some controversy in Holland and Germany; consequently her second book, The Revelation of Revelations (1683), was translated into both Dutch and German and published in 1694 and 1695. It was in Holland that the Oxonian, Dr Francis Lee, heard of JL and the visit he made to her on his return to England began a lifelong association. JL thought of Lee as her son, and he became her son-in-law following divine prompting. In 1694 JL with Lee began the Philadelphian Society, absolutely not a Dissenting sect according to its members since they stressed their support of ecclesiastical and political authorities. The society was partially financed by Baron Knyphausen of Germany; Richard Roach, also from Oxford, helped Lee publish the society's monthly periodical, Theosophical Transactions by the Philadelphian Society. JL remained leader of the society, claiming to receive instructions about its development directly from God. Although she initially recorded her visions purely for her own use, she began to publish them when instructed by God to do so. She lost her sight in her later years, and her remaining works were dictated to Lee, until her death at the age of 81. The Philadelphian movement subsequently suffered owing to its disunity, although Roach propagated JL's teaching until his death in 1730.

JL's work is an important part of the extensive literature produced by the flourishing European theosophical movement of the late seventeenth and early eighteenth centuries. It attacks the prevalent contemporary idolatry of scientific reason as an obstacle to the attainment of genuine wisdom, or Sophia, whose visitations to JL are described in her mystical journal. Her work is remarkable for its emphasis (recalling the similar interests of Julian of Norwich) on the female aspects of God. God, she claims, is both male and female: accordingly, the unfallen Adam was androgynous and the division of humanity into male and female occurred at the Fall. JL's millenarianism anticipated a Third Coming which would abolish this postlapsarian sexual division.   JANET JONES

Selected works: *The Heavenly Cloud Now Breaking: The Lord Christ's Ascension-Ladder Sent Down* (1681); *The Revelation of Revelations, &c.* (1683); *The Enochian Walks with God, Found Out by a Spirituall Traveller, Whose Face towards Mount Sion above Was Set. With an Experimental Account of What Was Known, Seen, and Met Withal There* (1694); *The Wonders of God's Creation Manifested in the Variety of Eight Worlds, as They Were Made Known Experimentally unto the Author* (1695); *A Message to the Philadelphian Society Whithersoever Dispersed over the Whole Earth* (1696); *The Tree of Faith, or, The Tree of Life Springing up in the Paradise of God, from Which All the Wonders of the New Creation Must Proceed* (1696); *A Fountain of Gardens Watered by the Rivers of Divine Pleasure, and Springing up in All the Variety of Spiritual Plants, Blown up by the Pure Breath into a Paradise, Sending Forth their Sweet Savours and Strong Odours for Soul Refreshing* (1696–1701); *A Revelation of the Everlasting Gospel Message* (1697); *The Wars of David and the Peaceable Reign of Solomon* (1700); *A Living Funeral Testimony, or, Death Overcome and Drowned in the Life of Christ* (1702); *The First Resurrection in Christ* (1704).

References: Allibone; *DNB*; Reynolds, M., *The Learned Lady in England* (1920); Thune, N., *The Behmenists and the Philadelphians* (1948); Todd.

Leapor, Mary (Molly)

b. 26 February 1722, Marston St Lawrence, Northamptonshire; d. 12 November 1746, Brackley, Northamptonshire
Poet

The daughter of Philip and Ann Leapor, ML was born on the estate of Sir John Blencowe ('Judge Blencowe'), to whom her father was gardener. If her parents had other children, she was the only child to reach maturity. After the death of Judge Blencowe and when ML was about 5, her father moved the family back to his native town of Brackley and commenced work as a nurseryman and independent gardener. He worked hard, but barely eked out a living. ML was taught to read and write, but when, to the distress of her parents, she devoted herself to scribbling at about 10, they attempted to discourage her. Feeling obliged to empower her to earn her living, they sent her, probably in her mid-teens, to be cook-maid to an unidentified gentleman, the duties being to tend the dairy and roast the meat. In the days of her fame this gentleman, unpersuaded of her talents, described her as having been 'extremely swarthy, and quite emaciated, with a long crane-neck, and a short body, much resembling, in shape, a bass-viol', with the unfortunate habit of 'sometimes taking up her pen while the jack was standing still, and the meat scorching'.

ML was not of a strong constitution, and in 1722, when Ann Leapor died, her father determined to bring her home to tend house for him and help in the nursery; he also insisted she work as a sempstress to prepare herself for independence when he was gone. With all of her burdens and despite his remonstrances, ML spent the following years studying and writing whenever possible. At her death she had acquired a library of seventeen volumes including part of Pope, Dryden's fables, and several volumes of plays. She believed that to write she must be educated, that to acquire learning was as important as to write poetry:

> Whilst in laborious Toils I spent my Hours,
> Employ'd to cultivate the springing Flow'rs.
> Happy, I cry'd, are those who Leisure find,
> With Care, like this, to cultivate their Mind.

She filled a notebook with poems which circulated in Brackley, attracting both attention and some ridicule of her pretensions. Despite the propinquity of the Blencowes and other gentry, and professional people including the Brackley bookseller James Payne, no one seems to have offered her significant or concrete encouragement, and she had no one to thank in this period for either favours or books. Before mid-1745 she had completed her favourite work, a tragedy which, circulating in Brackley (ladies, she said, sent for it to amuse themselves on dull afternoons), was seen by Bridget Freemantle, the 46-year-old daughter of a former rector. Probably in August of 1745 Freemantle met ML in the street and asked to see more of her work. A close relationship ensued which resulted in ML's subsequent fame.

Freemantle, a practical and efficient woman of intelligence who believed in ML, determined to make her independent and able to devote herself to her chosen work, sent her tragedy up to Covent Garden Theatre to Rich (who rejected it), and set about collecting subscriptions for a volume of poems. Under this encouragement ML's talent flowered and she poured out a body of work that after her death rounded out two 300-page volumes. Her new hope and happiness ended in November 1746 when she contracted measles and died.

On her deathbed ML asked Freemantle to continue plans for the subscription volume for her father's sake. Proposals dated 1 January 1747 circulated and a splendid list of almost 600 resulted that included nobles, gentry, clergymen, Members of Parliament, and Bluestockings. When the book appeared in 1748, Philip Leapor realized about £75, and in 1749 he was a Brackley freeholder. The Samuel Richardson circle was involved in publishing, in March 1751, a second volume comprising poems, the tragedy, an unfinished play, and some letters, which was edited by Isaac Hawkins Browne and printed by Richardson. ML was subsequently much praised by another Richardson friend, John Duncombe, in the *Feminead* (1754), who named her nature's favourite in succession to Shakespeare. Thornton and Colman included her in their *Poems by Eminent Ladies* (1755). She remained established throughout the rest of the century as one of the most interesting of the natural poets.

While the critics of the period looked to these natural poets (those untainted by art) for fine original poetry like Homer's, Pindar's, or Shakespeare's, poets like ML really believed their disadvantages to derive from inadequate acculturation and studied Dryden and Pope to acquire the perfect neoclassical finish. Pope was ML's model and idol and she was never so delighted as when Parthenissa, an eleventh-hour patron, called her 'the Successor to Pope'. Her poetry, however, was of several kinds. She acquired an original manner, especially in her last year, of writing about herself as author, her dreams, hopes, setbacks, and encounters, in heroic couplets never so pointed, succinct, or deadly as Pope's but with a good-humoured, wry, sometimes trenchant satire both of herself and of her critics that is all her own.

> Once *Delpho* read – Sage *Delpho*, learn'd and wise,
> O'er the scrawl'd Paper cast his judging Eyes,
> Whose lifted Brows confess'd a Critic's Pride,
> While his broad Thumb mov'd nimbly down the Side.
> His Form was like some Oracle profound;
> The list'ning Audience form'd a Circle round:
> But *Mira*, fixing her presuming Eyes
> On the stern Image, thus impatient cries:
> Sir, will they prosper? – Speak your Judgment, pray.
> Replies the Statue – Why, perhaps they may.
> For further answer we in vain implore:
> The Charm was over, and it spoke no more.
> ('An Epistle to Artemisia. On Fame')

ML wrote a series of short moral essays designed principally – for perhaps she did not presume to instruct others – to sooth her own discontent. She was apparently a sincere Christian and also wrote poetic versions of the psalms, versifications of other parts of the Bible, and verses on Pope's 'Universal Prayer'. Some of these were stanzaic, as 'A Request to the Divine Being' in the hymn tune stanza which ends,

> And when thy Wisdom thinks it fit,
> To shake my troubled Mind;
> Preserve my Reason with my Griefs,
> And let me not repine.

Her blank verse tragedy, 'The Unhappy Father', demonstrates careful attention to the plays of Rowe and Otway, and is competently plotted, developed, and versified. Several of the poems not printed till the second volume show a strain of feminism, a suggestion that the single state is the only dignified condition for a woman, as perhaps Freemantle and ML agreed, and the tragedy includes a strong statement of this kind from the heroine Emilia:

> Thro' check'd Desires, Threatenings and Restraint,
> The Virgin runs, but ne'er outgrows her Shackles;
> They still will fit her, even to hoary Age:
> With lordly Rulers Women still are curs'd;
> But the last Tyrant always proves the worst.

Freemantle wrote that no one who knew ML's noble soul could regard her as mean, and the attributes reflected in her verse are real literary talent, excellent good sense, and high ideals. Freemantle's summation, 'Her friends are now left to lament her loss, and that so great a part of a short and valuable life was spent in obscurity,' is well-judged. If ML had lived longer into days of recognition and leisure for writing, she probably would have left a name far better known.

BETTY RIZZO

Works: *Poems upon Several Occasions, by Mrs Leapor of Brackley in Northampton-shire*, vol. 1 (1748), vol. 2 (1751).

References: Duncombe, J., *The Feminead: A Poem* (1754); Richardson, S., *Correspondence* (1804); Rizzo, B., 'Christopher Smart, the 'CS' poems, and Molly Leapor's epitaph', *The Library*, 6th series 5, 1 (March 1983); B. Thornton and G. Colman (eds), *Poems by Eminent Ladies* (1755); Todd.

Leavis, Q. D.

b. 7 December 1906, London; d. 17 March 1981, Cambridge

Literary critic

QDL was the daughter of a Jewish draper and hosier in Edmonton and his wife Jane Davis. She attended the Latymer School and was made Carlisle Scholar at Girton College, Cambridge, in 1925. Two significant influences on her thought as an undergraduate were I. A. Richards, the pioneer of 'Practical Criticism', and H. M. Chadwick, her Anglo-Saxon teacher, who insisted on studying Anglo-Saxon literature in conjunction with the arts, history, and social structure of early England. QDL later noted that 'his students acquired an anthropological attitude'. She graduated in 1928 and was awarded first-class honours with special distinction in the English Tripos. In the following year she was elected to a research fellowship, also at Girton. Her marriage to F. R. Leavis, then a supervisor at Emmanuel College, Cambridge, took place in the same year. Her parents strongly disapproved of the match because Leavis was not Jewish, and cut off all relations with her shortly afterwards.

QDL's doctoral dissertation concerned the unusually broad field of relations between novels and their readers from the early seventeenth century until the twentieth, and was published in revised form in 1932 under the title *Fiction and the Reading Public*. When the critical journal *Scrutiny* was founded soon afterwards, many of its interests and methods had already been anticipated by her own work. Although she played a crucial part in editing the volume (and carried out much of the secretarial work for it), she was never given an official place on its editorial board. She also contributed many reviews of contemporary writing, particularly fiction, until 1949. At the same time, she brought up a family and supervised undergraduates from a number of colleges. Moreover, she collaborated in writing several books with her husband (as well, once more, as doing much of his typing for him). The precise extent of her collaboration, however, is still a matter of dispute: whilst *Dickens the Novelist* (1970) was explicitly published as a joint work, it is difficult to assess claims that her contribution to F. R. Leavis's own books has never been fully acknowledged. Her wider achievements, however, were certainly never recognized by the award of a teaching fellowship or a university post.

After her husband's retirement, QDL went with him to Harvard: their joint *Lectures from America* appeared in 1969. She also travelled with him to York where he was visiting professor from 1965. He died after a severe illness in 1978: QDL herself died three years later. Both the Leavises considered themselves to have been unjustly excluded from the Cambridge English Faculty, and indeed from the literary establishment in general, despite the fact that *Scrutiny* was widely acknowledged to be the most prestigious critical journal of its time, and that neither of them at any time faced difficulties in having their work published. Within Cambridge itself, although university recognition was slow to come to F. R. Leavis and was never given to QDL, they were both extremely influential teachers.

QDL's critical work has been given surprisingly little attention independently of her husband's, although (as F. R. Leavis pointed out) their approaches were in some respects sharply divergent. Her best-known work is *Fiction and the Reading Public*, in which an unprecedented wealth of historical and sociological research is brought to bear in an analysis of the changing composition and habits of the English reading public. QDL well described her method as an 'anthropological' one, however, for its approach to empirical data is never merely statistical: the twenty-five replies to a questionnaire which QDL sent out to sixty writers are subjected to detailed practical criticism for the insights they yield into the structure of the book market. QDL's attempt to understand the entire process of production leads her to devote similarly careful criticism to advertising copy, to popular magazines and newspapers, and even to the implications of changes in typography. The impossibility of conducting an equally direct empirical investigation into the reading publics of previous centuries is compensated for by an innovative extrapolation of the composition and reading practices of the audience implied by the style and syntax of a piece of prose: chunks of Nashe, Aphra Behn, Defoe, and Sterne (amongst others) are read for what they tell us about those for whom they were successfully marketed.

QDL's insistence on the importance of reading and research outside the canon of 'literature' reveals a markedly different emphasis from her husband's effort to expel some writers from the canon and establish others in their place. But, if her method is more thoroughly historical than his, many of her conclusions rest on an idea of the decline of taste which they both held. It is clear that for QDL the dramatic rise in the numbers of those able to read in no way compensates for the falling quality of what is read. 'The sudden opening of the fiction market to the general public was a blow to serious reading', she writes, and adds that the pre-literate pursuits of that public (' "creative" interests – country arts, traditional crafts and games and singing') were preferable to the mass consumption of best-sellers. She diagnoses the increasing demand for prose that asks for little effort from the reader as a result of the advancing division and mechanization of labour. But her hopes for the re-establishment of literary standards rested not with any organized labour movement but with the energetic proselytizing of an informed minority. The Minority Press and *Scrutiny* were soon to meet her demand for 'an all-round critical organ and a non-commercial press'.

The essays which QDL published in periodicals throughout the rest of her career, many of them republished in the posthumous *Collected Essays* (1983), indicate her continuing desire to broaden the canon of English literature. Her essay on the then virtually unknown Richard Jefferies in 1938 did a great deal to awaken interest in his writing. In 1969 she persuaded Chatto & Windus to reissue the neglected *Miss Marjoribanks*, by Mrs Oliphant. Moreover, QDL was impatient of the provincialism of much of the English literary establishment: she complained of a general ignorance of Hawthorne's work in England and herself wrote many essays on American fiction. But she could also set herself against what she saw as the undeserved rehabilitation of a neglected writer: when Charlotte Yonge's novels were widely praised in the 1930s QDL wrote an essay arguing that they had become fashionable because they suited current Anglo-Catholic preferences rather than for their literary merit. Her promotion of little-known writing, however, extended beyond her published material to her vigorous discussion of such work with her students.   JAMES SMITH

Works: *Fiction and the Reading Public* (1932); *Lectures in America* (with F. R. Leavis) (1969); *Dickens the Novelist* (with F. R. Leavis) (1970); *Collected Essays* (1983).

References: Bradbrook, M. C., *Collected Papers* (1982); Kinch, M. B., *Q. D. Leavis 1906–1981* (1982); Robertson, P. J. M., *The Leavises on Fiction* (1981); Thompson, D. (ed.), *The Leavises* (1984); Walsh, W., *F. R. Leavis* (1980).

Lee, Sophia
b. 1750, London; d. 13 March 1824, Clifton, Bristol

Lee, Harriet
b. 1757, London; d. 1851
Novelists, playwrights
SL was one of five daughters of the actor-manager John Lee; her mother died young and SL had to help raise the younger children, including HL. In 1780 she wrote a play *The Chapter of Accidents*, based on Diderot's *Le Père de Famille*; it was produced at the Haymarket Theatre and then at Drury Lane and Covent Garden. With the profits, SL started a school for young ladies at Belvidere House, Bath, with which HL helped; it flourished until 1803. SL's first effort in prose fiction was the long epistolary *The Life of a Lover*, not published until 1804. Subsequently she wrote one of the earliest historical and Gothic romances, *The Recess, or, A Tale of Other Times*, (the first volume of which appeared in 1783, with the second and third following in 1785. The complicated story takes place in the reign of Elizabeth I, who is a character in the novel, together with Drake, Sidney, and the Countess of Pembroke, and it concerns the persecution by Elizabeth of two daughters supposedly born to Mary, Queen of Scots by a clandestine marriage. Although these girls are raised secretly, one manages to marry the Earl of Leicester while the other falls in love with the Earl of Essex. Like earlier Gothic writers, such as Clara Reeve and Horace Walpole, SL pretends that she is merely editing the work which deals very freely with historical events, the explanation of which appears to be personal and emotional rather than political. *The Recess* was well received and went into many editions; there was even a translation into Portuguese. It inspired the play *Maria Stuart und Norfolk* by Christian Heinrich Speiss. In 1786 SL published *Warbeck: A Pathetic Tale*, a translation of Baculard D'Arnaud's *Varbeck* which, like *The Recess*, blended historical fact with sentimental fiction. A ballad in 156 stanzas entitled *A Hermit's Tale, Recorded by His Own Hand and Found in His Cell*, followed in 1787. Another play, a tragedy in blank verse called *Almeyda: Queen of Granada*, was produced at Drury Lane in 1796, with Sarah Siddons as the leading lady, but it did not reproduce the success of SL's first attempt, while the comedy, 'The Assignation', SL's final work, was unfavourably received when it was produced at Drury Lane in 1807 and was not printed.

During these same years HL was publishing novels and plays. *The Errors of Innocence*, a sentimental epistolary novel, appeared in 1786, and *The New Peerage*, a social comedy, in 1787. A decade later, HL began her major work, *The Canterbury Tales* (1797–1805), to which SL contributed the introduction and two stories. 'The Clergyman's Tale, Pembroke', and 'The Young Lady's Tale, The Two Emily's', the latter an extremely pathetic story of a morally forceful but inactive heroine; together these stories comprised one and a half volumes of the total five. HL's contributions, far more arresting than her sister's, are striking for their satirical quality and their realistic social and psychological pictures. 'The Landlady's Tale', for example, sympathetically depicts an unwed mother, while 'The Scotsman's Tale' well captures the interaction of romantic feelings with a sense of nationality, family, status, and class as a couple of lovers move from an idyllic isolated environment back into their own societies of commerce and nobility. The best-known story is 'The German's Tale: Kruitzner', much admired by Byron, who dramatized it as *Werner* (1822). This subtly depicts the progress of a man who, while not being essentially evil, is utterly self-centred and lacking in self-control. HL's tragedy, *The Mysterious Marriage*, printed in 1798, proved a failure and was never acted.

Both SL and HL were notable for their conversation and sociability and they are referred to in many letters and memoirs of the period.   JANET JONES

Works: Sophia Lee: *The Chapter of Accidents* (1780); *The Recess, or, A Tale of Other Times* (1783–5); (trans.), *Warbeck: A Pathetic Tale* by B. D'Arnaud, (1786); *A Hermit's Tale* (1787); *Almeyda: Queen of Granada* (1796); 'Introduction' to 'The Young Lady's Tale' and 'The Clergyman's Tale', *The Canterbury Tales* (1797–1805); *The Life of a Lover* (1804); Harriet Lee: *The Errors of Innocence* (1786); *The New Peerage* (1787); *The Canterbury Tales* (1797–1805); *Clara Lennox* (1797); *The Mysterious Marriage* (1798).

References: Punter, D., *The Literature of Terror: A History of Gothic Fictions from 1765 to the Present Day* (1980); Rogers, K., *Feminism in Eighteenth Century England* (1982); Summers, M., *The Gothic Quest: A History of the Gothic Novel* (1938); Todd; Tompkins, J. M. S., *The Popular Novel in England 1770–1800* (1932); Varma, D., 'Introduction' to *The Recess* (1972).

Lee, Vernon

b. 14 October 1856, Chateau St Leonard, near Boulogne, France; d. 13 February 1935, Il Palmerino, San Gervasio, Florence, Italy
Essayist, novelist, short story writer

VL (Violet Paget) was the exceptional product of exceptional circumstances. The only child of her mother's second marriage, her childhood was a solitary one, spent largely in the company of adults. VL's half-brother Eugene Lee-Hamilton, born in 1845, was the apple of his mother's eye, and, while doting on the son, Mrs Paget proved largely incapable of providing any maternal affection for her daughter. Considerable attention was devoted however, to the process of VL's education. In the course of a peripatetic childhood spent moving around Europe, VL received the attentions of numerous governesses. Each one taught the child according to her individual preference, and to this disorganized flow of information Mrs Paget added her own contribution – everything from poetry to geometry, all imparted while walking at speed with VL at her heels. VL was trained from an early age to pursue the career which her mother envisaged for her, that of a writer. This educational process succeeded in creating an intensely intellectual child, but, combined with the solitude and lack of affection she experienced, it also laid the foundations for a lonely adulthood. In middle age VL experienced a series of nervous breakdowns, and throughout her life she displayed a total absorption in her own thought and work which made her unconsciously tactless and lost her many friends.

For all the controversies that would later surround her, her literary career made a promising start. Her first major work, *Studies of the Eighteenth Century in Italy* (1880), was critically well received and achieved some popularity, especially in Italy. When the age and sex of the author became known, VL became something of a celebrity in literary circles. In 1881 she visited London for the first time, and was introduced to many of the leading artistic figures of the day. These circumstances prompted VL to apply considerable thought to the philosophy of art, and gradually she arrived at a position diametrically opposed to the theories of Ruskin which were popular at the time. She rejected the belief that the basis of all art is moral, believing instead that its primary function is the creation of pleasure. Only literature could be involved with moral issues, the visual arts were there to be enjoyed: 'Beauty has no moral value in the great battle between good and evil beauty remains neutral, passive, serenely egotistic.'

VL's universal popularity was short-lived. In 1884 she published her first attempt at a novel. *Miss Brown* was intended to be a satire of the aesthetic society she had witnessed in London, but it emerged instead as an over-long and heavy-handed disaster which offended many of her friends and acquaintances. VL had dedicated the novel to Henry James, whose opinion she valued greatly. James's high respect for her is revealed by a letter to T. S. Perry in September 1884 concerning another work. 'I don't think VL *great*, but I think her a most astounding young female, and *Euphorion* most fascinating and suggestive, as well as monstrous clever. She has a monstrous cerebration . . .'. James, however, was embarrassed by *Miss Brown* and, while remaining friends with VL, thanks to a much-delayed and tactfully phrased letter about the book, he voiced his true opinion in another letter to Perry in December of the same year: 'as it is her first attempt at a novel, so it is to be hoped that it may be her last. It is very bad, strangely inferior to her other writing, and (to me at least) painfully disagreeable in tone . . . the satire is strangely without delicacy or finesse, and the whole thing without form as art. It is in short a rather deplorable mistake – to be repented of.'

In contrast to the whole-hearted condemnation of James, VL's obituary in *The Times* suggested *Miss Brown* was 'not unworthy to be remembered with *Patience*.' But this is a generous comment. *Miss Brown* has moments of singular aptness, as for example in the scathing portrayal of the aesthetic snobbery of Mrs Melton Perry: 'I always make it a rule to engage only handsome servants, because it spiritualizes the minds of our children to be brought up constantly surrounded by beautiful forms,' and in the poet Hamlin's attempts to turn Anne Brown into a literary allusion, providing a clever illustration of the essential superficiality of his interest in her. But in general VL lacked the subtlety, the consistency, and above all the economy to rival the satire of W. S. Gilbert.

The reception of her first novel warned VL against further attempts and she turned instead to a much more successful formula of short stories and essays. Her *Genius Loci*, essays on the spirit of places, were particularly successful. She combined an intimate, almost fictional style of narrative with a singular talent for the evocation of place. Unfortunately the experience of *Miss Brown* had failed to penetrate VL's artistic self-absorption. With regard to the feelings of others she remained as innocently tactless as before, and in 1892, with the publication of the short story 'Lady Tal' in *Vanitas*, she committed her second major social error. It was in her nature to write quickly, not stopping to analyse the source of her inspiration, and consequently when her story demanded the creation of an American psychological novelist, she unconsciously produced a portrait of Henry James. Superficially the damage was repaired in an exchange of contrite letters, but VL and Henry James did not meet again until 1912. 'Lady Tal' is however a far superior work to *Miss Brown*, and the portrait of James is not unpleasant. Marion, the author, becomes the victim of his own artistic detachment, when the real world in the vital form of Lady Tal manipulates him seemingly to the point of marriage. Once he becomes interested in Lady Tal the comfortable distance between him and society is destroyed by the advent of emotions with which he is unable to cope. The motivation of Lady Tal remains obscure throughout the story. The only perspective the reader receives is that of Marion and this enables VL to create a surprising and enigmatic ending in the form of an unexpected proposal from Lady Tal. The short story format makes 'Lady Tal' more succinct and economical than is usual for VL and the characters, particularly Marion, are carefully and effectively drawn. The following description of Marion is also interesting because of its proximity to the life and character of VL herself. 'To be brought into contact with people more closely than was necessary or advantageous for their intellectual comprehension; to think about them, feel about them, mistress, wife, son, or daughter, the bare thought of such a thing jarred on Marion's nerves. So the better to study, the better to be solitary . . . he had condemned himself to live in a world of acquaintances, of indifference.'

VL consciously cultivated an indifference to most people's opinion of her, and she had few close relationships. One of the most important friendships in her life was with Kit Anstruther-Thomson, with whom she published several articles and books on aesthetic issues. This work however became another source of controversy when in 1897 VL and Kit were accused of plagiarism by the art scholar Bernard Berenson. In this case friendly relations were not restored until 1922.

The final major controversy of VL's life was provoked by the First World War. When combined with her cosmopolitan upbringing, her Victorian reformist tendencies made the idea of nationalistic war anathema to her. She adopted a strong pacifist stance and alienated many friends through her refusal to see any distinction between the motivation of Germany and of England. In 1920 she published *Satan the Waster*, a war trilogy which incorporated her polemical play written during the war, *The Ballet of the Nations*. On its first publication *Satan the Waster* was almost universally condemned; only George Bernard Shaw spoke in favour of it and he proclaimed it a masterpiece. However, when it was reissued in 1930, the changed political climate enabled it to be recognized as a powerful and effective anti-war satire: '*The voice of HEROISM, a youthful and very pure tenor, is heard above the din of the orchestra singing the Marseillaise to the accompaniment of his drum.* SATAN: Do you hear him, Clio? He shall be made to sing the other splendid murderous songs by turns . . . for, as you are aware, Heroism is of no country but of all equally, a real cosmopolitan, although his chief business is international extermination.'

VL continued writing almost up to her death in 1935, undeterred by deafness and failing health. In 1934 several friends staged a performance in Florence of her play *Ariadne in Mantua*. However, much as she appreciated this tribute to her contribution to the world of letters, a letter to Maurice Baring written in 1906 shows that the twentieth century had brought her an increasing awareness of having failed as a writer: 'It is certain that I can never imagine what I write being read, still less by anyone in particular. . . . It gives, perhaps, a certain freedom and decency, but sometimes, not often, it makes one feel a bit lonely, as if one were the vox clamans – not in the desert, but inside a cupboard.'

GILL PLAIN

Selected Works: *Studies of the Eighteenth Century in Italy* (1880); *Tuscan Fairy Tales* (1880); *The Prince of the Hundred Soups* (1883); *Ottilie* (1883); *Euphorion* (1884); *The Countess of Albany* (1884); *Miss Brown* (1884); *A Phantom Lover* (1886); *Juvenilia* (1887); *Hauntings* (1892); *Vanitas* (1892); *Renaissance Fancies and Studies* (1895); *Limbo* (1897); *Genius Loci: Notes on Places* (1899); *Ariadne in Mantua* (1903); *Pope Jacynth* (1904); *Hortus Vitae* (1904); *The Enchanted Woods* (1905); *Sister Benvenuta and the Christ Child* (1906); *The Sentimental Traveller* (1908); *Gospels of Anarchy* (1908); *Laurus Nobilis* (1909); *Vital Lies* (1912); *The Beautiful* (1913); *Louis Norbert* (1914); *The Tower of Mirrors* (1914); *The Ballet of*

the Nations (1915); *Satan the Waster* (1920); *The Handling of Words* (1923); *The Golden Keys* (1925); *Proteus* (1925); *The Poet's Eye* (1926); *For Maurice* (1927); *Music and its Lovers* (1932); *The Snake Lady* (1954); *Supernatural Tales* (1955); *Pope Jacynth and More Supernatural Tales* (1956).
References: Colby, V., 'The Puritan Aesthete', in *The Singular Anomaly* (1972); Gunn, P., *Vernon Lee, Violet Paget 1856–1935* (1969).

Lehmann, Rosamond
b. 3 February 1901, Bourne End, Buckinghamshire
Novelist

RL was the second daughter of R. C. Lehmann, Liberal MP, writer and editor of *Punch*, and his American-born wife, Alice. She was educated privately in a household where artistic expression of all kinds was encouraged. Her brother, John, became a writer and critic, her sister, Beatrix, a well-known actress. In 1919 RL won a scholarship to Cambridge, where she read modern languages. She married twice, first in 1923, after which she moved to Newcastle where she wrote her first novel, and second in 1928; she had two children. Both marriages ended in divorce. In 1929 her father died after a long illness; later her second husband left to fight in the Spanish Civil War, and in 1940 RL returned to live with her mother for a time, taking the children with her.

She became a reader for *New Writing*, her brother John's literary magazine, and was persuaded by him to write short stories, published as a collection in 1946 under the title *The Gypsy Baby*, which, written from her Berkshire cottage, reflect the realities of wartime existence. Earlier, in 1939, she had written her only play, *No More Music*, with a Carribean island setting to which she was later to return for *The Sea-Grape Tree* (1976). In 1941 she began a long friendship with the poet C. Day Lewis, important to both according to Lewis's son Sean. In 1958 her daughter Sally, married to Patrick Kavanagh, died suddenly of poliomyelitis in Jakarta, and after this shattering event RL was driven to confront openly the spiritual questions which had always consumed her.

In her first novel, *Dusty Answer* (1927), RL began the exploration of the subject which was to dominate her work, the nature of feminine passion. It dealt with a young girl's facination for a wealthy and charismatic neighbouring family, a subject that RL was to re-use in the more assured *Invitation to the Waltz* (1932) and *The Ballad and the Source* (1944). Clearly based on RL's undergraduate experience, *Dusty Answer* drew a bitter portrait of Cambridge in the 1920s and conveyed with conviction the agonies of first love. It was an immediate success, but its latent eroticism and the implications of lesbianism it contained shocked many readers.

The process of growing up also formed the central subject of *Invitation to the Waltz*. In following the 17-year-old Olivia Curtis to her first dance at the house of aristocratic neighbours, RL used a delicate impressionistic technique to expose the pangs, uncertainties, and aspirations of youth, capturing both evanescent magic and the comic awkwardness of adolescence. In this work, and in *Dusty Answer, The Ballad and the Source*, and *The Sea-Grape Tree*, the world of childhood, with its imperfect understanding of adult affairs, was seen to create its own security through its innocence. The inevitable disillusionment of romantic idealism, implicit in this book, was given full expression in its sequel, *The Weather in the Streets* (1936). Here, RL portrayed the harsh realities of the socialite and Bohemian world of the 1930s, simultaneously glamorous and sordid. In describing an adulterous affair from the perspective of the 'other woman', she depicted the suffering of romantic betrayal with an explicitness unusual for one of her period and class.

In *The Ballad and the Source* and *The Echoing Grove* (1953), RL developed her major theme of the destructive effects of sexual power. Both works are substantial and compelling analyses of the magnetism, complications, and profundity of personal relationships. Both rely on recollection for their central narrative method; both recreate vividly the quality of individual isolation; both deal fundamentally with the processes of ageing.

The Ballad and the Source is the largest in scope of all her novels. The young Rebecca, who gathers the threads of the story, owes a great deal of the structure of her childhood to that of RL's own early life. Rebecca is dominated by Sybil Jardin, an elderly woman who briefly takes a house near her. The power Mrs Jardin exerts is mystic, a compound of energy and mystery, and the exertion of it has wrecked both her own life and those of others associated with her. Rebecca, completely under her poetic spell, draws together the fragments of Mrs Jardin's story and builds a collection of narratives into the – almost – complete tale of her life. The device by which this old story is unfolded, is a masterpiece of narrative technique. RL's interest in 'mystery' – the essence of reality which lies beyond expression – apparent from her interest in Cocteau's work (she translated *Les Enfants Terribles* for publication in 1955), is revealed here, not only in the structure of the book, but in the surreal power of the images: Mrs Jardin, the silent watcher in the blue cloak; the frozen face of the infant Ianthe, object of war between her parents; the indefinable essence of Cherry, Ianthe's youngest child, beyond reach forever after her death from meningitis. Images of stone recur, immutable as experience, culminating in the breakdown of Ianthe in the studio of the sculptor, Gil, to whom her mother is romantically attached. Ianthe believes that there are living people inside the stone's heads, a horrifying parallel to her emotional experience.

In earlier novels, RL had concentrated on the familiar realities of the family and love relationships, and she returns to them, as if for final culmination, in the superbly patterned *The Echoing Grove* which deals with the three-part relationship between the two sisters and the man who is husband to one, lover to the other. After *The Echoing Grove*, numbed by the shock of her daughter's death, RL wrote nothing until in *The Swan in the Evening* (1967) she tried to express her attempts to cope with bereavement. This memoir preserves the features that distinguished RL's fiction: the fragmentary style, the telling use of apparently inconsequential detail, the importance of memory, the emotional intensity that creates life's significance. It received sympathetic but uncomprehending critical notice. *A Sea-Grape Tree* (1976), her latest work, occupies uneasy ground, not so much because it attempts to deal with experience beyond the normal as because the heroine – the older Rebecca, once again in communication with the spirit of Mrs Jardin – is not a character of sufficient richness and complexity to carry the weight of experience available to her. She is too far removed from the pure essence of life of her childhood; she seems like one in search of easy solutions, and that of sexual union, although undoubtedly powerful, seems too facile here.

RL's work is both unashamedly romantic and deeply serious. At one time dismissed, but now acclaimed, for their frank concentration on women's emotional lives, her novels depict the exploitation and the suffering that accompany love. Although her heroines are frequently intellectuals and career women, their world is essentially defined by their responsiveness to personal situations. In *Dusty Answer*, a character senses 'Oh, the torment of loving!' It is this torment which is at the heart of RL's work.

JUDY SIMONS AND JENNIFER PLASTOW

Works: *Dusty Answer* (1927); *A Note in Music* (1930); *Letter to a Sister* (1931); *Invitation to the Waltz* (1932); *The Weather in the Streets* (1936); *No More Music* (1939); *The Ballad and the Source* (1944); *The Gypsy's Baby and Other Stories* (1946); *The Echoing Grove* (1953); *A Man Seen Afar* (with W. Tudor Pole) (1965); *The Swan in the Evening: Fragments of an Inner Life* (1967); *Letters from Our Daughters* (with Cynthia Hill Sandys) (1972); *A Sea-Grape Tree* (1976).

References: Atkins, J., *Six Novelists Look at Society: An Enquiry into the Social Views of Elizabeth Bowen, L. P. Hartley, Rosamond Lehmann, Christopher Isherwood, Nancy Mitford, C. P. Snow* (1977); Dorosz, W., 'Subjective vision and human relationships in the novels of Rosamond Lehmann', *Studia Anglistica Uppsaliensa* 23 (1975); Gindin, J., 'Rosamond Lehmann; a revaluation', *Contemporary Literature* 5, 15 (1974); Kaplan, S. J., *Feminine Consciousness in the Modern British Novel* (1975); Kaplan, S. J., 'Rosamond Lehmann's *The Ballad and the Source*, a confrontation with the Great Mother', *Twentieth Century Literature* (June 1982); LeSturgeon, D. E., *Rosamond Lehmann* (1965); Tindall, G., *Rosamond Lehmann: An Appreciation* (1965).

Lennox, Charlotte

b. 1729(?), possibly in Gibraltar; d. 4 January 1804, London
Novelist

CL, the daughter of an army officer, James Ramsay, was possibly born in Gibraltar. In 1739 her father obtained an appointment in New York province and moved the family there. After his death, in about 1743, CL returned to England and was patronized by two noble ladies (one of whom she was later to satirize in *Harriot Stuart*). In 1747 she married Alexander Lennox, perhaps an employee of the printer William Strahan, and published her undistinguished *Poems on Several Occasions* (1747). Alexander Lennox had difficulty in supporting the family; so CL tried acting – unsuccessfully – and then became a professional author, publishing *The Life of Harriot Stuart* in 1750. Samuel Johnson arranged a celebration in honour of this event and continued to be her friend: he wrote seven prefaces and dedications for her, as well as proposals for a collected edition of her works; he quoted her in his *Dictionary*; and he helped her with her scholarly translations and with her finest novel, *The Female Quixote* (1752). She 'has many fopperies,' he wrote, 'but she is a great genius.' Samuel Richardson also advised her on *The Female Quixote* and helped her to get it published.

CL's literary career was both prolific and diverse. She conducted a monthly periodical, *The Lady's Museum*, for a year, with considerable help from her friends. She learned Italian in order to compile *Shakespear Illustrated* (1753–4), a translation of nine of Shakespeare's sources, printed together with reprints of English ones and observations on his use of them. CL also tried to break into the more lucrative field of stage writing: her first play, *Philander* (1757), was rejected; her second, *The Sister* (1769), failed; her third, *Old City Manners* (1775), adapted from *Eastward Hoe*, was quite successful. But, despite her constant and generally successful writing, she remained in chronic financial distress and died penniless. Her marriage was unhappy – according to Johnson, Alexander Lennox treated her 'very harshly' – and they probably separated permanently in 1792. She had a daughter who died young, and a son, who got into some serious trouble and had to be sent off to America.

CL's first novel, *Harriot Stuart*, is apparently partly autobiographical: its heroine travels from New York to England, and is disappointed by false encouragement from 'Lady Cecilia', upon whom she has relied to help her. Harriot's mother, like most of the mothers in CL's fiction, is selfish, conventional, and anti-intellectual, and prefers an undeserving elder sister to the heroine.

CL's most original work is unquestionably *The Female Quixote*. The novel was published anonymously, but the identity of its author was widely known. It was extremely successful, soon running into a second edition and enthusiastically reviewed by, amongst others, Henry Fielding. Its heroine, Arabella, is a beautiful and intelligent young woman who, brought up in seclusion, accepts French romances as guides to life. In these romances by Scudéry and La Calprenède the central characters devote their lives to exquisitely refined love affairs and peerless virgins are courted for years on end by humbly devoted suitors. Arabella, accordingly, believes 'that Love [is] the ruling Principle of the World', compared with which any other motive or obligation is negligible. She thinks every man who sees her is in love with her, and rejects her eminently suitable suitor, Mr Glanville, because he has been selected by her father and because he simply proposes marriage instead of devoting years to silently worshipping her.

Arabella is, of course, absurd in her ignorance of normal behaviour, her excessive demands for excitement and attention, her self-centredness, and her conceit. But CL complicates the relationship between imaginary romance and 'real' life. For Arabella is also shown to be clearly superior to Miss Glanville, the conventional fashionable young woman who constantly laughs at her. Arabella has an idealism, a magnanimity, and an intellectual breadth inconceivable to the other. When she and Mr Glanville discuss Greek history, Miss Glanville can only play the harpsichord. After Miss Glanville has spent four hours dressing, in the hope of eclipsing Arabella, and Arabella ingenuously compliments her on her appearance, Miss Glanville immediately glances in the mirror to see what is wrong, for she cannot believe that one woman could praise another sincerely. In the end, after Arabella has been brought down to earth, she appropriately joins Mr Glanville in a marriage of true minds, while Miss Glanville takes an unprincipled young man in marriage 'in the common Acceptation of that word', meaning that they unite 'Fortunes, Equipages, Titles, and Expence'.

CL draws much humour from the misunderstandings and cross-purposes which develop when Arabella imposes exalted romance ideals upon normally self-interested young gentlemen or mistakes their conventional politeness for despairing love or attempts at abduction. But there is an intrinsic problem in CL's plan, namely, that a virtuous eighteenth-century young lady could not actively seek adventures (like Don Quixote), nor even make a serious mistake without imperilling her chastity or gentility. Hence CL is constrained in the range of events available to her plot and in her manner of curing Arabella of her illusions.

CL's two immediately subsequent novels, *Henrietta* (1758) and *The History of Harriot and Sophia* (1760–1), are straighforwardly didactic, although they are unconventional in the emphasis which they place on the intelligence of their heroines. *Euphemia*, her last novel, is also didactic but draws, like *Harriot Stuart*, on CL's own life. CL makes effective use of an American background and apparently models her heroine's marital trials upon her own. Having married to please her mother, the saintly Euphemia is dragged to America by her husband, an army officer, who does not even trouble to ask his wife how she feels about the move. Since he is both foolish and too proud to listen to a woman's advice, his wife is continually obliged to repair his mistakes. He is incapable of making or retaining money, and he leads their son into dissipation. Euphemia is throughout a model of conventional wifely obedience, but is at the same time acutely aware of her superior reasonableness. In a wish-fulfilling ending strikingly dissimilar to the end of CL's own life, Euphemia is left with an adoring son and control of the family money, whilst her husband is reduced to insignificance in the eyes of all.   KATHARINE M. ROGERS

Works: *Poems on Several Occasions* (1747); *The Life of Harriot Stuart* (1750); (trans.), *The Memoirs of the Duke of Sully* (1751–5); *The Female Quixote* (1752); (trans.), *The Age of Lewis XIV* (1752); *Shakespear Illustrated* (1753–4); (trans.), *The Memoirs of the Countess of Berci* (1756); (trans.), *Memoirs from the History of Madame de Maintenon* (1757); *Philander* (1757); *Henrietta* (1758); (trans.), *The Greek Theatre of Father Brumoy* (1759); *The History of Harriot and Sophia* (1760–1); *The Lady's Museum* (1760–1); *The Sister* (1769); *Meditations and Penitential Prayers . . . by the Duchess de la Vallière* (1774); *Old City Manners* (1775); *Euphemia* (1790).

References: Allibone; Drabble; Maynadier, G. H., *The First American Novelist?* (1940); Rogers, K. M., *Feminism in Eighteenth-Century England* (1982); Séjourné, P., *The Mystery of Charlotte Lennox, First Novelist of Colonial America* (1967); Small, M. R., *Charlotte Ramsay Lennox* (1935); Spacks, P. M., *Imagining a Self: Autobiography and Novel in Eighteenth Century England* (1976); Todd; Todd, J., *Women's Friendship in Literature* (1980); *The Sign of Angellica* (1989); Warren, L. A., 'Of the conversation of women: *The Female Quixote* and the dream of perfection', *Studies in Eighteenth-Century Culture* 11 (1982).

Lessing, Doris

b. 1919, Persia (now Iran)
Novelist, short story writer, playwright, essayist
(Also writes under Jane Somers)

DL (*née* Tayler) was raised on an impoverished homestead in the white-settler land of Southern Rhodesia, now Zimbabwe. Her father had given up his job as a bank clerk to farm the new frontier in response to an empire exhibition in London, but, badly wounded in the First World War, he lacked the drive to carve a new life or profits out of the territory. Her mother, who had met her future husband as his nurse, kept herself going on their isolated mud-built, grass-thatched farm with the endlessly deferred hope of returning to 'real life' back in London.

In the middle of these tensions DL spent most of her youth reading, a way of stepping out of the situation and of gaining an objective perspective on experience, a recurrent strategy in her life and work. Sent to school in Salisbury, she left at 14 in rebellion against her mother's academic aspirations for her, but continued her reading at home.

She found work as a secretary in Salisbury, and in 1939, at the age of 20, married Frank Wisdom, a civil servant, with whom she had two children, who stayed with their father when the marriage ended in 1943. Working again as a secretary, DL joined the local Labour Party, and a small Marxist group, composed mainly of wartime immigrants and British service men. In 1945 she married Gottfried Lessing, a Jewish-German exile and Communist, with whom she had a son, Peter. When they were divorced in 1949, Gottfried went to live in East Germany, and DL came to London, with her son and the manuscript of her first novel.

The Grass Is Singing was an immediate success. Although she was now living in London, until the early 1960s her works were still set mainly in southern Africa, although she was banned as a 'prohibited immigrant' by the Central African Federation in 1956. In the same year she left the British Communist Party, which she had joined on arriving in London, after the Twentieth World Congress, but she continued to be politically active, speaking at the first Aldermaston march and at CND rallies, and being involved in the founding of *The New Left Review* and, with Arnold Wesker, in the radical theatre movement.

By now the location of her fiction had shifted to London, and in 1962 she published *The Golden Notebook*, exploring the lives of women living independently in the city. Her most famous novel, celebrated as a herald of the new wave of feminism, it thrust the author reluctantly into the vanguard of the women's movement. In the late 1960s she became interested in eastern thought, finding the Sufi belief in the gradual evolution of human faculties through history a congruent extension of her own views. She continues to write prolifically, experimenting with a variety of forms including science fiction, as ways of gaining perspective on the present moment in history.

DL writes as a prophet for her times who, from her earliest work, has shown women to be not on the margins but at the central point of the interlocking contradictions of the age. In *The Grass Is Singing* (1950) Mary Turner, the white settler's wife trapped on the isolated farm on the veld, slowly goes mad under the weight of an untenable system which has her locked in the conflicting roles of perpetrator and victim. Her death is covered by a local conspiracy of silence, the meaning of her experience marginalized out of existence.

The following novel, *Martha Quest* (1952), shows the struggle of a daughter, raised on a similar farm on the veld, not just to escape from repeating the mother's life, but actively to take on the weight of history, instead of cracking under the strain. Martha, a figure for Lessing throughout the five books of *The Children of Violence* sequence, walks out of the woman's place, the farmstead, and on to the veld, freeing herself from the old role and taking on a new task, a new form of conception and birth: 'It was as if something new was demanding conception, with her flesh as host; as if there were a necessity, which she must bring herself to accept, that she should allow herself to dissolve and be formed by that necessity.' Her task is to be the bearer of the future, the prophet. But in this female *Bildungsroman* the novel ends with Martha marrying and about to get pregnant, turning the prophetic task of regeneration into the literal one of generation.

The dialectic of Martha's growth goes on, however, in subsequent volumes in the series, as she moves forward out of the marriage and becomes politically committed. The goal of the work seems originally to have been Martha's discovery, in the struggle for a new world after the war, of a partial realization of her task, a way of building the harmonious City that she envisioned as a girl. But even while Lessing was writing, the whole structure fell apart around her in uncontrollable, non-literary crisis. Far from rising to a new dawn the world fell back into what DL calls the 'bad times', and the pattern of her life and work stopped short.

At this point comes *The Golden Notebook* (1962) which, as the first lines tell us, is about cracking up. The novel has been seen as celebrating the end of ideology, embracing the insights of psychiatry as opposed to Marxism, and as culminating in a sexual version of achieved destiny. But it is explicitly the work of a writer (with Lessing's background, living unmarried in London with her child) who can no longer write because she has lost her vision. She can only give us fragments, in the form of four disconnected notebooks, the Golden being the fifth: the last volume of *Children of Violence* as it were, its non-culmination. When a friend's son reads the notebooks he tries to kill himself, ending up blind instead: the prophet's function has become a dark parody. One after another alternative ways of life fail Ann/Ella/Molly, aspects of the divided self.

In an attenuated resolution Anna rethinks her past again, this time with the focus on the bit-part players, the defeated. She will now write about 'a small painful sort of courage which is at the root of every life because injustice and cruelty is at the root of life'. This is what DL went on to do, particularly in the short stories, which accounts perhaps for their notably dry, slightly ironic tone (in 'To Room 19' for example, one of her best stories) – as if finally all the fuss is slightly absurd, because to no purpose. At the same time DL struggled to recover her prophetic function and voice.

In 1969 DL was able to return to the story of Martha Quest, covering the preceding twenty years in England and reaching forward into the future. The fifth novel in *The Children of Violence*, the work picks up from where Martha undertakes the significant journey to England and commitment in 1949. But the title, *The Four-Gated City* (1969) – DL's original name for the City of her vision – is an ironic reference to the oppressive reality of London, where Martha holes up during the cold war: the dark days before the Apocalypse, not the time for building the New Jerusalem.

The novel covers the same period as *The Golden Notebook* but from the perspective of a time of crippling political reaction, the direct cause of the breakdown of family life and personality that is the book's subject. Early on Martha sees in a vision a couple and their child walking across the plain of history, and then weeps at seeing herself twenty years on, an anxious middle-aged woman presiding over an unhappy household. The novel ends in future apocalypse, which casts its shadow before, its signals being picked up by the young – a sign of eventual social reconnection. At the end of her life, Martha sends a black child through the devastation to a tenuous new city being built in Africa: in a muted way, and with the structure of the novel 'shot to hell' as DL has said, the purpose of her life that Martha envisaged as a girl on the veld has been carried out.

As her generation's era passed, DL turned her attention to the heritage they were leaving to the next. In three novels ageing women confront younger ones in danger of living out the old female roles, now acutely untenable in a new stage of history. The prophet, seeing the cycles of generation mindlessly turn-ing, wants – as she did when she was young – a new leap forward in consciousness.

Mindless is the word for Alice, the younger (but no longer that young) woman in *The Good Terrorist* (1985) who numbs her mind with radical rhetoric while acting out, all unwittingly, her mother's old role. As den-mother of a commune she compulsively creates a parodic replica of her parents' expansive 1960s household (an option now gone, the house sold, but the only space she knows how to inhabit) in the group's squat. History returns the second time as tragic farce as Alice, acting out the self-sacrificing mother, gets sucked into a 'family' of manipulative terrorists. Her own mother, goaded beyond endur-ance by her daughter's depradations, rejects the maternal role herself, takes a stiff drink and cuts Alice off.

Here as elsewhere DL is setting about the Blakean task of naming and casting out error, sorting out the progressive legacy and its inheritors – and poor knee-jerk Alice, shoring up her old house, is disowned. In *The Summer before the Dark* (1973) Kate Brown, another mother escaping from her role, struggles to destroy her old identity lest it become a heritage. She casts out the error that in women is defined as goodness: 'Patience. Self-discipline. Self-control. Self-abnegation. Chastity. Adaptability to others – this above all. . . . It seemed to her that she had acquired not virtues but a form of dementia.' That way too went Alice, the good, mad terrorist.

In *The Memoirs of a Survivor* (1974) both mother and daughter figures work to form a new female identity, the older woman sorting out the rooms of the past, preserving some, destroying others, while the girl goes out into the world to be recast by experience. At the end a cumulative image of error, a girl writhing in a tight red evening dress like a latter-day whore of Babylon, shrivels away, allowing the young woman to emerge as the new Eve, striding into the future with her millennial beast and her mate hastening to catch up.

The combination of outrageously literal prophetic metaphors with realism is a form DL went on to adapt for her *Canopus in Argos* cycle. These modern cultural parables include *The Marriage between Zones . . .* (1980) which attempts to make a viable dialect out of sexual antithesis by marrying the queen of an exclusively feminine land to the king of a male warrior-caste, and *Representative for Planet 8*, where the inhabitants, caught in the grip of a new ice-age, die off while awaiting some external form of deliverance. These are all works of our times. The series starts with *Shikasta* (1979), a rewriting of *Paradise Lost* in which Lessing returns to the roots of the prophetic tradition from which she has always drawn her vision. The narrator's task, like that of the author, is to turn the fallen earth back on to its intended path, to achieve the ordered city which is the goal of history.

A major writer of our era, DL speaks out of her experience of a time of defeat. Her territory is a world where the signposts have all been turned around and we read her because she points out dead ends and false exits in the maze, while trying to hold on to the hope of a thread leading out. She is a writer of crisis, her characters typically those on whom converging contradictions have for the moment come to bear with most intensity: Martha Quest or Anna Wulf have become representative figures for our times, and the *Bildungsroman* of DL's life is now part of our collective imagination.

GILLIAN PARKER

Selected works: *The Grass Is Singing* (1950); *Children of Violence (Martha Quest,* 1952; *A Proper Marriage,* 1954; *A Ripple from the Storm,* 1958; *Landlocked,* 1965; *The Four-Gated City,* 1969); *Retreat to Innocence* (1956); *The Golden Notebook* (1962); *Particularly Cats* (1967); *Briefing for a Descent into Hell* (1971); *The Summer before the Dark* (1973); *This Was the Old Chief's Country: Collected African Stories* vol. 1 (1973); *The Sun between Their Feet: Collected African Stories,* vol.2. (1973); *A Small Personal Voice,* ed. P. Schlueter (1974); *The Memoirs of a Survivor* (1974); *To Room Nineteen: Collected Stories* vol. 1 (1978); *The Temptation of Jack Orkney: Collected Stories* vol. 2 (1978); *Canopus in Argos: Archives (Shikasta,* 1979; *The Marriage between Zones Three, Four and Five,* 1980; *The Sirian Experiments,* 1981; *The Making of the Representative for Planet 8,* 1982; *The Sentimental Agents in the Volyan Empire,* 1983); *The Diary of Jane Somers* (1984); *The Good Terrorist* (1985).

References: Brewster, D., *Doris Lessing* (1965); Budhos, E., *The Theme of Enclosure in Selected Works of Doris Lessing* (1987); *Doris Lessing Newsletter* (since 1976); 'Doris Lessing Number', *Modern Fiction Studies* 26, 1 (1980); Drabble, M., 'Doris Lessing: Cassandra in a world under siege', *Ramparts* 10 (1972); Gardiner, J., 'Evil, apocalypse and feminist fiction', *Frontiers* 7 (1983); Kaplan,

S., 'Passionate portrayal of things to come: Doris Lessing's recent fiction', in T. Staley (ed.), *Twentieth Century Women Novelists* (1982); Pratt, A. and Dembo, L. (eds), *Doris Lessing: Critical Studies* (1974); Sage, L., *Doris Lessing* (1983); Seligman, D., *Doris Lessing: an Annotated Bibliography of Criticism* (1980); Singleton, M., *The City and the Veld: The Fiction of Doris Lessing* (1977); Taylor, J. (ed.), *Reading and Re-reading Doris Lessing* (1982).

Leverson, Ada

b. 10 October 1862, London; d. 30 August 1933, London
Novelist, parodist

AL, the eldest daughter of Zillah Simon Beddington, an amateur pianist, and Samuel Beddington, a property investor, was brought up in a luxurious, artistic environment and educated privately at home. At the age of 19, against her parents' wishes, she married Ernest Leverson, a gambler and speculator. This loveless marriage to a humourless man produced two children, a son who died in childhood and a daughter, Violet Wyndham. Despite AL's many (probably platonic) relationships with other men and her husband's being cited as co-respondent in a highly publicized divorce case, AL's fear of scandal and devotion to her daughter kept the marriage intact until 1900, when Ernest, nearly bankrupt, emigrated to Canada alone.

AL's first publications were anonymous articles, parodies, and sketches in *Punch, Black and White* and *The Yellow Book*; in 1892, 'An Afternoon Party', her parody of *The Picture of Dorian Gray*, resulted in a friendship with Oscar Wilde, of whose exotic circle the Leversons soon became members. AL is still more famous as an Edwardian hostess and as Wilde's 'Sphinx' (a nickname he gave her in 1894 when the publication of his 'The Sphinx' was parodied by her 'The Minx') than as a novelist. Between his trials in 1895, Wilde stayed in AL's son's nursery, and when he was released from prison it was she who visited him first.

AL began writing novels in 1905, after the death of Wilde and others of her famous and fashionable friends (Beardsley, Kitty Martineau, Prince Henri d'Orleans) and her separation from her husband. Her six novels were all written in bed, dictated to a stenographer, and published between 1907 and 1916 by Grant Richards, who had urged her to write novels in the mid–1890s. AL dedicated two of her novels to Richards, a married man with whom she was in love. In the seventeen years after she stopped writing novels, she spent much of her time with a group of younger friends dominated by the Sitwells. In 1933, on one of her frequent trips to Italy, she became ill, and she died of pneumonia shortly after returning to London.

AL's novels are stylistically precise, understated, epigrammatic comedies of manners exploring the subject of marriage among the upper middle classes of Edwardian England. Conceptually as well as stylistically reminiscent of Jane Austen's work, AL's fiction focuses on the tension between the desire for personal fulfilment and the demands of marriage as a social, legal, and moral contract. The characters are satirically exposed primarily through dialogue, supplemented by the unsentimental observations of a third-person narrator.

Love's Shadow, *Tenterhooks*, and *Love at Second Sight*, written at four-year intervals and twice reprinted together as *The Little Ottleys*, chronicle the marriage of Edith and Bruce Ottley. For Edith, as for AL, a sense of humour functions as a moral corrective; Bruce, whose character is based on Ernest Leverson, is entirely lacking in humour. He descends in the course of the three novels from merely one of the greatest bores and hypochondriacs in English fiction, to a domestic tyrant, to a monster of immorality. In *Love's Shadow*, the oppression of the wife by a morally and intellectually inferior husband is openly dramatized in the main plot; the same conflict is suggested in the Ottley sub-plot. In *Tenterhooks*, Edith falls in love with Aylmer Ross, a man who is her moral equal, but she renounces him (despite Bruce's infidelities) for the sake of her children, to avoid scandal, and to 'save' Bruce from his own worst instincts. Re-encountering Aylmer in *Love at Second Sight*, she gradually decides that her earlier renunciation was too high a price to pay for a life with Bruce, that he has no interest in custody of the children, that she can face a scandal, and, most importantly, that she can entrust him to the care of the stupid but benign Madame Frabelle.

After finishing her novels, AL produced only one more work, a vivid depiction of the opening night of *The Importance of Being Ernest* ('The Last First Night') published by T. S. Eliot in *The Criterion* in 1926 and reprinted in *Letters to the Sphinx from Oscar Wilde, with Reminiscences of the Author* in 1930). The volume included some thirty letters and telegrams from Wilde, 'The Importance of Being Oscar' (characterizing the period of the early 1890s and describing Wilde's central role), and 'Afterwards' (an account of her relationship with Wilde from the time of his first trial in 1895 until his death).

KATE BROWDER HEBERLEIN

Selected works: 'The Minx – a poem in prose', *Punch* (1894); 'Suggestion', *Yellow Book* (1895); *The Twelfth Hour* (1907); *Love's Shadow* (1908); *The Limit* (1911); *Tenterhooks* (1912); *Bird of Paradise* (1914); *Love at Second Sight* (1916); 'The last first night', *Criterion* (1926); *Letters to the Sphinx from Oscar Wilde, with Reminiscences by the Author* (1930).

References: Brown, J., 'Edwardian sphinx', in *As They Appear* (1952); Burkhart, C., *Ada Leverson* (1973); Holden, I., 'The art of Ada Leverson', *Cornhill Magazine* 164 (1950); MacInnes, C., 'The heart of a legend', *Encounter* 16 (May 1961); Sitwell, O., *Noble Essences* (1950); Wilde, O., *The Letters of Oscar Wilde* (1962); Wyndham, V., *The Sphinx and Her Circle: A Biographical Sketch of Ada Leverson, 1862–1933* (1963).

Levy, Amy

b. 10 November 1861, Clapham, London; d. 10 September 1889
Novelist, poet

AL had rich Jewish parents, Lewis Levy and Isabelle Levin. She attended Brighton School and then became the first Jewish woman to enter Newnham College, Cambridge. Early on she showed a bent for literature and a ballad by her was published in 1875 in the *Pelican* magazine. As a student at Newnham she published her first book of poetry, *Xantippe and Other Verse* (1881), as well as short stories, including 'Euphemia, a Sketch' in the *Victoria Magazine* (August 1880). 'Xantippe' was a portrait of the traditional figure of Socrates' nagging wife but given from her own viewpoint. AL also contributed to Oscar Wilde's magazine *Woman's World*; she became a friend of Wilde, as well as of Olive Schreiner.

After Cambridge AL travelled on the continent writing about the Jewish experience in various countries, especially noting the degree of isolation of the different communities, ranging from the ghetto of Venice to awkward assimilation in other places. In her novel *Reuben Sachs* (1888) she takes up the problem of cultural assimilation and the tension between the present comfort of affluent and compromised Jewish society and more austere Jewish history. The book gives a detailed and not especially flattering picture of the insular, snobbish, and self-contained community in London in which AL was raised. It focuses on the relationship of Reuben, a wealthy young man who has come down from Cambridge and seems bound for a brilliant political career, and Judith, one of the Jewish *vieille noblesse*, who has better birth and more beauty than Reuben's family but very little money. The dismissal by Reuben's family of their relationship ('Reuben will do nothing rash' is his mother's favourite phrase) makes Judith feel that 'in loving Reuben she had committed a crime too shameful for decent people even to speak of'. Added to this intense family pressure is the misunderstanding between the couple arising from Reuben's jealousy. The result is that Judith marries an aristocrat who, after experimenting with a number of religions, horrifies his family by converting to Judaism. In the novel AL writes with close attention to material and emotional detail, building up an atmosphere of repression and constriction around both Reuben and Judith as they slowly lose control over their own lives.

The psychological problem that a Jewish identity causes is further elaborated in a short story, 'Cohen of Trinity' (1889), in which a character from *Reuben Sachs* is accepted into English society, while another Jew from a less assimilated background gains esteem from a book he writes; the latter subsequently finds assimilation impossible and kills himself. The plot of this story anticipated life when AL herself committed suicide. She had been stung by criticism from the Jewish community of *Reuben Sachs* which had received acclaim from other quarters, but a more important factor, according to a friend, Richard Garnett, was probably her melancholic temperament perhaps exacerbated by the tensions of feminist activity – she was active in feminist and radical organizations – and literary creativity.   JANET JONES

Works: *Xantippe and Other Verse* (1881); *A Minor Poet and Other Verse* (1884); *The Romance of a Shop* (1888); *Reuben Sachs* (1888); *Miss Meredith* (1889); *A London Plane Tree and Other Verse* (1889).

References: Abrahams, B. Z., 'Amy Levy, poet and writer', *American Jewish Archives Quarterly* 1 (1960); Allibone; *DNB*; Modder, M. F., *The Jew in the Literature of England* (1939); Showalter, E., *A Literature of Their Own* (1977); Zatlin, L. G., *The Nineteenth Century Anglo-Jewish Novel* (1981).

Lincoln, Elizabeth Clinton, Countess of

b. 1574; d. after 1623

Writer of Advice Book

One of three daughters and co-heirs of Elizabeth Stumpe and Sir Henry Knevett (or Knyvett) of Charlton, Wiltshire, C of L some time after 21 September, 1584, married Thomas Clinton (or Fiennes), who became third Earl of Lincoln in 1616, and whose estate then included Tattershall Castle, Sempringham Manor (the principal home, it seems, of the family), and houses in Boston and London. Their eighteen children included three – Charles, Arbella (b. 1600), and Susan – who were to emigrate to New England. In the summer of 1629, Charles Fiennes and Lady Arbella and her husband Isaac Johnson sailed (as did Anne Bradstreet, the future American poet, and her family) with John Winthrop, whose flagship the *Eagle* had been renamed the *Lady Arbella* in honour of C of L's eldest daughter. Lady Susan and her husband John Humphrey arrived in New England in May, 1635. We have no record of C of L's death, but we do know that it was she who represented Lady Arbella's family in consenting to her marriage in 1623.

When Thomas Clinton, Earl of Lincoln, died in January 1618 or 1619, the eldest surviving son, Theophilus (b. 1601), succeeded him as Earl. Theophilus's estate manager, Thomas Dudley (father to Anne Bradstreet, above), arranged his marriage to Briget Fiennes, daughter of William Fiennes, Viscount Say and Sele of Broughton, and it was Theophilus's wife Briget to whom Dudley later addressed his *Letter to the Countess of Lincoln* which describes the first ten months of the Massachusetts Bay Colony in America and to whom C of L dedicated *The Countess of Lincolnes Nurserie* when it was published in Oxford by John Litchfield and James Short in 1622.

In the dedication, C of L establishes her daughter-in-law as an exemplary woman who has '[given] the sweete milke of your owne breasts, to your owne childe; wherein you haue gone before the greatest number of honourable Ladies of your place, in these latter times'. The 'kinde perswasion' of her treatise, C of L goes on, will urge other women to follow that 'duty, which all mothers are bound to performe'. After an introductory letter in which Thomas Lodge (by 1603 a Roman Catholic and a medical doctor) commends the treatise as a corrective to the contemporary 'vnnatural practice' of sending one's children out to wet nurses, C of L argues '*the duty of nursing due by mothers to their owne children*'. She contrasts the unworthy women of her own degenerate age with four biblical women – Eve, Sara, Hannah, and the Virgin Mary – each of whom, she says, gladly nursed her children 'in those lesse corrupted times', and she takes pains to argue that refusing to breastfeed one's children is a denial of God's law. Toward the end of the treatise, C of L notes that she herself failed to nurse her own children – but 'it was not for want of will in my selfe, but *partly I was ouerruled by anothers authority*, and *partly deceiued by sommes ill counsell, & partly I had not so well considered of my duty in this motherly office*, as since I did, when it was too late for me to put it into execution'. C of L acknowledges 'the paine and trouble' of nursing, but she offers other women advice better than the 'ill counsell' she had received, and she contrasts mere earthly authority with God's law. Her Protestantism is especially noticeable in her reminding her reader that her child is 'perhaps one of Gods very elect'. The book ends with an apocalyptic image of a nursing mother with a baby 'sucking hartily the milke out of [her breast], and growing by it, [which] is the *Lords owne instruction*, euery houre, and euery day, that you are suckling it, instructing you to shew that you are his *new Borne Babes*, by your earnest desire after his word, & the syncere doctrine thereof, and by your daily growing in grace and goodnesse thereby, so shall you reape pleasure, and profit'.

ELIZABETH H. HAGEMAN

Work: The Countess of Lincolnes Nurserie (1622)
References: Beilin, E. V., *Redeeming Eve: Women Writers of the English Renaissance* (1987); *Complete Peerage*, VII; Mahl, M. R. and Koon, H. (eds), *The Female Spectator: English Women Writers before 1800* (1977); Nichols, J. Gould, (ed.), *Collectanea Topographica et Genealogica* (1834–43), VII; Travitsky, B. S., 'The New Mother of the English Renaissance: Her Writings on Motherhood', in *The Lost Tradition: Mothers and Daughters in Literature*, ed. C. N. Davidson and E. M. Broner (1980); White, E. Wade, *Anne Bradstreet: The Tenth Muse* (1971).

Linton, Eliza Lynn

b. 10 February 1822, Keswick, Cumberland; d. 14 July 1898, London

Novelist, polemicist

ELL's father, the Rev. James Lynn, was a scholarly man who was overwhelmed by the death of his wife, Charlotte Goodenough, five months after the birth of Elizabeth, as ELL was christened. Her mother's death, at the age of 39, was a significant factor in ELL's development. She later maintained that she had one of the most unhappy and painful childhoods that it was possible to endure; she felt guilty and rejected, and because of her father's failure to take an interest in his offspring, she was roughly treated by her eleven older siblings. Her father's contribution was to employ a nurse – whom ELL remembered as cruel and drunken – to commit his children to 'the care of Providence' and to instil the right faith and values in them with harsh whippings followed by close confinement in the dark closet under the stairs. Suffering from extreme short-sightedness which was interpreted as stupidity, the miserable ELL became deeply resentful of 'weak' men like her father, and resentful too of those who enjoyed the affection and warmth of family circles.

ELL also became extraordinarily self-reliant and determinedly ambitious; receiving no formal education, she read voraciously and taught herself French, Italian, German, and Spanish, as well as some Latin and Greek. Lonely, wilful, and attention-seeking, she flaunted her radical religious and political beliefs – and became convinced that most of her problems could have been overcome, had she been male. At 20, she made a passionate commitment to another young woman (Mrs Dalrymple, a newcomer to the area); the end of this relationship left her deeply depressed but her spirits were restored by the publication of two of her poems in *Ainsworth's Magazine* (May and June 1844). Her burning desire to be a writer was revived. On the basis that freedom and fame would provide her with the sense of acceptance and security that she needed, she persuaded her father to support her literary aspirations in London, for one year. She was 23 when in 1845 she embarked on her remarkable independent venture and moved to a boarding house in Russell Square.

In London, she gained entry to literary circles, making many friends, among them Walter Savage Landor whom she called her 'adopted father'. She also researched her first novel in the Reading Room of the British Museum; published at her own expense, the erudite *Azeth the Egyptian* (1846) received some positive reviews and justified her continued London existence. She began work on her second historical novel, *Amymone* (1848). The central character is the philosopher Aspasia, who tries to advance the position of women; with its call for female freedom, this novel is one of the first nineteenth-century novels which advocated women's rights. Again reviews were complimentary and ELL was reassured by her ready success. In characteristically confident style she applied for a position at the *Morning Chronicle* and became one of the first salaried women journalists in Britain. She wrote articles and reviews and earned the impressive sum of £250 a year.

Because of objections to some of the 'indecencies' in her next novel, *Realities*, she had difficulties with acceptance; but it appeared in 1851, though published at the author's expense. Geraldine Jewsbury thought the work clever but in very bad taste and it received derisive reviews. So critical was the reception and so demoralized was the author that it was to be fourteen years before she published a novel again. At much the same time the editor of the *Morning Chronicle* decided to dispense with her services and so the second and much more difficult stage of her professional life began. Depressed, distrustful, and desperate, she was grateful for a correspondent's job in Paris in 1853; she became a prolific writer for periodicals as she supported herself by freelance work. A consistent contributor to *Household Words*, she was given credit for her competence and reliability by Charles Dickens.

By the 1850s, the issue of women's rights was on the social/political agenda in advanced circles, and as a contributor to the radical *English Review* (edited by William Linton) ELL wrote a highly appreciative article on Mary Wollstone-craft's *Vindication of the Rights of Woman* in 1854. But, acutely and astutely aware of her audience, she wrote another article, at much the same time, on much the same topic for *Household Words* (1 April 1854) in which she was extremely critical of the emancipation of women.

During this period she became friendly with William Linton and his second wife, Emily, who was overburdened by childbirth and childcare; ELL helped to nurse her through a protracted illness and, on her death, felt that it was intended that she should take on the ready-made family and marry William Linton, which she did in March 1858. But the marriage was not a success and within two months she was expressing her doubts in her writing. She found her husband weak and contemptible and marriage disastrous for her work habits and her finances. The couple were permanently separated when he went to the United States in search of work.

Her sentiments during this phase were reflected in her numerous articles which were her major means of support. In the *National Magazine*, for example, she publicly justified her actions. 'The Crooked Stick' (June 1858) tells of a maid who proves to be too choosy and is left with 'the crooked stick'; this was followed in July with 'Tantalus and I' in which the author adopts a male persona, and declares that one of the greatest mistakes she ever made was to wed one who was widowed, who was jealous and resentful, and who turned out to be the greatest obstacle to literary success. On her own ELL unhappily watched her fame and finances decline. In 1862 she finished a novel, 'Isola', but it was twice rejected. In 1865 she published *Grasp Your Nettle* but was deeply distressed when it received unfavourable reviews and was damned as a poor imitation of the work of Mary Elizabeth Braddon. In 1865 *Lizzie Norton* was published and in 1867 the previously rejected 'Isola' appeared as *Sowing the Wind*; in it there are two contrasting characters, the beautiful and womanly Isola, and the independent and manly newspaper woman, Jane. If Isola is the woman ELL knew that she would never be, Jane is the one for whom she shows little empathy, and much of the author's ambivalence about herself, and women's rights, is given substance in the differing features and fates of these two fictional females.

In 1866, she joined the staff of the *Saturday Review*, initially as a (provocative) book critic, but later writing more general pieces. On 14 March 1868 her sensational essay, 'The Girl of the Period', appeared – anonymously. ELL was a talented, often brilliant writer, and when she uncompromisingly condemned women's emancipation, when she deplored the demise of pure women and suggested that the new bold women were no better than prostitutes, her forceful piece struck a chord and the reading community took note. The essay caused enormous controversy and when she stepped forward to claim authorship, she was once more at the centre of literary attention. 'The Girl of the Period' (GOP) became a generic term (there was even a GOP magazine produced) and ELL continued to write in this vein – in increasingly exaggerated tones – over the next decade; she became one of the most outrageous but one of the best-known writers of the day. The fact that she was an emancipated woman who vehemently opposed emancipation for other women in her writing was a contradiction that she could accommodate; some of her women critics contended that she opposed women because it paid better than defending them.

Certainly this success marked the end of her financial problems. She was free to choose the work she wanted to do – and she embarked on some serious novel writing. Hostile to hypocrisy in the church – and to indulgent clergymen – she turned her attention to a religious theme and employed her satirical talents in her most popular novel, *The True History of Joshua Davidson, Christian and Communist* (1872). A defiant and irreverent book, it envisaged the rebirth of Jesus Christ in Victorian England and insisted that in all good faith the man would have to be a communist. It was an immense success though much attacked.

Despite the fame and financial rewards not all was well. ELL had problems with her writing – although her output was still prodigious as she averaged more than 200 essays and one extended work of fiction each year. Her next novel, however, was much less taxing and much more decorous; *Patricia Kemball* (1874) drew on the author's unhappy childhood and was found much more acceptable by the critics. Three novellas which explored the woman question from different perspectives were published in 1875 as *The Mad Willoughbys and Other Tales*, followed by *The Atonement of Leam Dundas* in the *Cornhill Magazine* in 1875–6.

For the next eight years ELL spent most of her time outside England, much of it in Italy. She had as companion the young woman she labelled as her 'adopted daughter', Beatrice Sichel. She declared this to be the happiest time of her life and, apart from the many travel articles she wrote during these years, there was a steady stream of novels: *The World Well Lost* (1877), *Under Which Lord?* (1879) – another work in which clerics and the church were the target – and the highly autobiographical and extremely interesting *The Rebel of the Family* (1880), in which the author explicitly condemns lesbianism. In 1881, *My Love* appeared to positive though not effusive responses. Then in 1883 appeared the famous/infamous *The Girl of the Period and Other Social Essays*. In 1884, ELL returned to England, was reunited with Beatrice and re-established herself as a literary celebrity.

Her most extraordinary work was published in 1885: her autobiography, in which she attained her desire to be a man. Entitled *The Autobiography of Christopher Kirkland*, it is a frank and forthright coverage of the author's life – from the perspective of a male. While this makes some of ELL's encounters with women socially acceptable in the narrative, this was clearly not her only motivation. Though not a literary success in its own day, the novel affords many insights into the nature of the writer and the quality of her work.

Prior to the publication of *Paston Carew, Millionaire and Miser* (1886) to which the critics were primarily indifferent, ELL met the young woman graduate of the University of London, Beatrice Harraden, an aspiring writer and a firm supporter of women's rights. Though Beatrice Harraden seems often to have been infuriated by ELL's blind and inexplicable opposition to women's emancipation she was yet much supported by her. After all, ELL had lamented her lack of education, refused to live with her husband, supported Divorce Law Reform, had retained control of her own finances on her marriage, and had lived an independent and professional life. How could she then argue against these activities, particularly when opposition was no longer popular.

But by the late 1880s, ELL was not an anti-feminist force to be reckoned with. Far from mocking others, she was being mocked herself, by such figures as Milicent Fawcett and the writer Mona Caird. Sarah Grand even went so far as to write a counterpiece, 'The Man of the Moment', which satirized ELL as well as men. Clearly ELL was not a member of that group of women writers at the end of the nineteenth century who were using fiction to explore new possibilities of existence for women. She may have been the scourge of those who supported women's rights, but the climate changed and no matter how outrageous her denunciations, she no longer shocked – or was celebrated. When she decried everything from women's education to women's bicycle riding, her hostility and hypocrisy were seen as more a matter for bemusement than bemoaning.

But 1894 saw the publication of yet another belligerent novel; *The One Too Many* contained an astonishing attack on women's education. *In Haste and at Leisure* followed in 1895 and went further in its condemnation of 'The New Woman' (the title of the work in the United States). It is a testimony to her craft as a writer that she continued to have her work published.

Apart from *The Second Youth of Theodora Desages* (published posthumously), one of ELL's last literary efforts was a contribution to *Women Novelists of Queen Victoria's Reign: A Book of Appreciations*. Ever aware of 'audience' she wrote a flattering appraisal of George Eliot, a writer whom she had never liked.

DALE SPENDER

Selected works: *Azeth the Egyptian* (1846); *Amymone* (1848); *Realities* (1851); *Witch Stories* (1861); *The Lake Country* (1864); *Grasp Your Nettle* (1865); *Lizzie Norton* (1865); *Sowing the Wind* (1867); *Ourselves: Essay on Women* (1869); *The True History of Joshua Davidson, Christian and Communist* (1872); *Patricia Kemball* (1874); *The Mad Willoughbys and Other Tales* (1875); *The Attonement of Leam Dundas* (1877); *The World Well Lost* (1877); *At Night in a Hospital* (1879); *Under Which Lord?* (1879); *The Rebel of the Family* (1880); *My Love* (1881); *The Girl of the Period and Other Social Essays* (1883); *The Autobiography of Christopher Kirkland* (1885); *Paston Carew, Millionaire and Miser* (1886); *Through the Long Night* (1888); *The One Too Many* (1894); *In Haste and at Leisure* (1895); *My Literary Life* (1899); *The Second Youth of Theodora Desages* (1900).

References: Anderson, N. F., *Woman Against Women in Victorian England: A Life of Eliza Lynn Linton* (1987); Colby, V., *The Singular Anomaly: Women Novelists in the Nineteenth Century* (1970); DNB; van Thal, H., *Eliza Lynn Linton* (1979).

Lively, Penelope
b. 17 March 1933, Cairo, Egypt
Novelist, writer for children

PL was born in Egypt and spent much of her childhood there before going up to St Anne's College, Oxford, where she took a BA in modern history in 1956. She married Jack Lively in 1957, and they have one daughter and one son.

PL's books are characterized by two related preoccupations: the relation between the present and the past, and a threatening sense of 'the darkness out there' (the title of one of her short stories). 'The darkness out there' is often a sense of the dangers and horror of the past: in her books it tends to erupt disastrously into the present. Her first four children's books all deal with local folklore and the bizarre and frightening persistence of legend. *Astercote* (1970), her first book, describes the disruption of a village community by the removal of a chalice from the nearby ruins of a village wiped out by the Black Death of 1349. PL's children often hear voices and sense the presence of ghosts – experiences which, while heightening the suspense of her stories, also encourage author and reader to explore the complexities of memory and the survival of the past. Mair, in *Astercote*, frequently hears the bells of the lost village: 'the sensation of being no longer Mair now, but Mair then, a watcher Mair in some other time'. In *The Whispering Knights* (1971), a group of children become entangled with Morgan le Fay in a modern reincarnation, and in *The Wild Hunt of Hagworthy* (1971), a village pageant, based on an old legend, revives the sleeping ghosts of a village community and comes to a heady climax as Lucy is hunted by a pack of spectral hounds.

The Ghost of Thomas Kempe (1973), which won a Carnegie Medal, and *The Revenge of Samuel Stokes* (1981) are both concerned with the ghostly persistence of historical personality. Thomas Kempe is a sixteenth-century sorcerer who makes a twentieth-century boy his apprentice, and Samuel Stokes, an eighteenth-century landscape gardener, plays havoc with the houses on an estate built on the site of one of his gardens. *The Ghost of Thomas Kempe* integrates a sharply comic sense of anachronism (the sorcerer is particularly incensed by the usurpation of his functions by the doctor and the priest) with a serious investigation of a child's developing historical imagination. *The House in Norham Gardens* (1974) deals with a similar issue in a more melancholy, wistful mode, when Clare Mayfield finds an African shield in her anthropologist grandfather's attic. Other children's books on a similar theme are *The Driftway* (1972), *Going Back* (1975), and *A Stitch in Time* (1976). The Fanny stories (*Fanny's Sister*, 1976; *Fanny and the Monsters*, 1979; and *Fanny and the Battle of Potter's Piece*, 1980) all deal with the adventures of a Victorian child, and in *The Voyage of QV 66* (1978), set after the Second Flood, a group of animals set off for London Zoo in a boat.

PL's adult fiction also tends to explore the themes of memory and history. Many of her protagonists are researchers (see *Treasures of Time*, 1979; *Judgement Day*, 1980; and *According to Mark*, 1984), whose encounters with the past have unforeseen effects on their own emotional and sexual lives. In *Treasures of Time*, which won the National Book Award, and *According to Mark*, a growing sense of the untrustworthiness of historical record, coupled with unexpected sexual involvements, serves to undermine previous certainties, although in *According to Mark* by the end life is restored to its usual frustratingly predictable comfort. *Next to Nature, Art* (1982) describes a summer course at Framleigh Creative Centre, and *The Road to Lichfield* (1977) and *Perfect Happiness* (1983) explore two women's experiences of bereavement and sexual reawakening. Her novel *Moon Tiger* won the Booker Prize in 1987. SUZANNE RAITT

Works: *Astercote* (1970); *The Whispering Knights* (1971); *The Wild Hunt of Hagworthy* (1971); *The Driftway* (1972); *The Ghost of Thomas Kempe* (1973); *The House in Norham Gardens* (1974); *Going Back* (1975); *Boy Without a Name* (1975); *A Stitch in Time* (1976); *The Stained Glass Window* (1976); *Fanny's Sister* (1976); *The Presence of the Past: An Introduction to Landscape History* (1976); *The Road to Lichfield* (1977); *The Voyage of QV 66* (1978); *Nothing Missing But the Samovar and Other Stories* (1978); *Treasure of Time* (1979); *Fanny and the Monsters* (1979); *Fanny and the Battle of Potter's Piece* (1980); *Judgement Day* (1980); *The Revenge of Samuel Stokes* (1981); *Next to Nature, Art* (1982); *Perfect Happiness* (1983); *Corruption* (1984); *According to Mark* (1984); *Uninvited Ghosts* (1984); *Moon Tiger* (1987).

Lumley, Joanna, Lady

b. 1537(?), Sussex(?); d. 9 March 1576 or 1577, London(?)

Translator

Credited with making the earliest translation of a Greek tragedy into English, JL was the the elder daugher of Henry Fitzalan, twelfth Earl of Arundel, and his wife, Katherine Grey Fitzalan. At the age of about 12 she was married to John, first Baron Lumley, who knew her brother at Cambridge. Lumley was a member of the Elizabethan Society of Antiquaries and collected a famous library which, combined with that of his father-in-law, was purchased by James I after Lumley's death in 1609. Lumley was a scholar; in 1550 he translated the *Institution of a Christian Prince or Ruler* by Erasmus, and encouraged his wife in translation work too. She and Lumley had two sons and one daughter, all of whom died in infancy.

JL's *The Tragedie of Euripides Called Iphigeneia Translated out of the Greake into Englisshe* is preserved in a rough copy book in the British Library which also contains some translations of Isocrates into Latin. It was probably written in the early years of JL's marriage. In 1524 at Basle, Froben published Erasmus's translation of *Iphigeneia* alongside the Greek original, and it is certain that JL used this Latin translation, possibly working from an earlier edition which did not contain the Greek at all. The lengthy 'Argument' of the play does not appear in Euripides but is an addition from Erasmus. In a translation which is relatively free, JL follows many of Erasmus's mistranslations, and credits Clytemnestra with giving birth to three sons and one daughter, a mistranslation which is impossible from the Greek, but which could have arisen from the Latin. Yet the English version is not a straight translation of Erasmus, for JL omits all the choral odes and only uses the chorus to provide cue lines which introduce protagonists. She also cuts long speeches of the major characters, particularly those which concern the gods or which analyse character. The action of the play is consequently almost chaotically rapid, as there is no opportunity to reflect on its cause or possible effects. As with all Renaissance translations of the play, JL preserves the ending in which Iphigeneia is carried to Tauris by Artemis.

Whether she translated the *Iphigeneia* directly from the Greek or not, JL certainly studied the language, although possibly at a later date, for she wrote in *Epistola ad Dominum Patrem*, which is also contained in the British Library manuscript, that she was studying Greek literature. By the time of her death, JL's exceptional education and scholarship had gained her considerable contemporary acclaim.   CAROLINE COLEMAN

Works: *The Tragedie of Euripides Called Iphigeneia Translated out of Greake into Englisshe*, ed. H. M. Child (1909).

References: Allibone; Ballard; Cotton, N., *Women Playwrights in England, c. 1363–1750* (1980); Crane, F. D., 'Euripides, Erasmus, and Lady Lumley', *Classical Journal* 36 (1941); Hays, M., *Female Biography* (1802); Hogrefe, P., *Tudor Women* (1975); Reynolds, M., *The Learned Lady in England, 1650–1760* (1920); Warnicke, R. M., *Women of the English Renaissance and Reformation* (1983); Williams, J., *Literary Women of England* (1861).

Lyall, Edna

b. 1857, Brighton; d. 1903

Novelist

EL (Ada Ellen Bayly) was the youngest of the four children of Mary (*née* Winter) and Robert Bayly, a barrister of the Inner Temple. Both EL's parents died when she was young (her father when she was 11, and her mother three years later), so she and her sisters and brother were taken into their uncle's home in Caterham. As EL was delicate, she was educated at home at first, then later at private schools in Brighton. Some memories of her early life are recorded in *The Burges Letters* (1902). As an adult, EL lived at the homes of her two sisters, both of whom had married clergymen. Her brother, too, entered the Church, and EL's novels show that she shared the family's commitment to Christianity. Aside from writing, EL spent her time working for charitable, religious, and political causes. She believed firmly in political and social liberalism, and was secretary of the Eastbourne Women's Liberal Association. She was also a supporter of women's suffrage. EL wrote under a pseudonym which was an anagram of nine of the letters of her real name. The true identity of 'EL' was the cause of some speculation, and in 1886 a stranger claimed to be her. Other reports followed, including one that EL was in a lunatic asylum; at this point she declared herself, and in 1887 published *Autobiography of a Slander* which addressed the dangers of inaccurate gossip.

EL's first novel, *Won by Waiting* (1879), focuses on the life of a young girl growing up in France and England. It was not particularly well received until after the success of EL's later works. *Donovan* (1882), her second novel, in which EL's religious and spiritual beliefs play an important part, was given far more attention, including an admiring letter from Mr Gladstone. As a result of this novel EL began a long correspondence with the free-thinking MP Charles Bradlaugh, who was the father of the novelist Mrs Bradlaugh Bonner. Though EL could not share his views on religion, she supported him during the crisis which followed his refusal to take an oath on the Bible in the House of Commons, and three times gave money towards his electoral expenses. It was he who provided much of the material which informs EL's third novel *We Two* (1884), which fully established EL's reputation as a writer. The central character of *We Two* is Erica, daughter of an important atheist leader Luke Raeburn, whose character apparently bears a resemblance to Bradlaugh's. The story spans nearly a decade, from when Brian Osmond, a young, Christian doctor, first meets and falls in love with Erica when she is 16, through the years during which she works for her father's cause, until Luke's death, when, at last, she has time to be in love with Brian. The main interest of the novel, however, is not their romance, but the gradual conversion of Erica from atheism, 'so barren a creed', to Christianity. The narration is clearly weighted towards religion, but the tone is not moralistic and the novel is in fact deeply critical of the narrow-mindedness and intolerance of many professed Christians; it stresses, too, the sincerity and goodness of the atheists who are so appallingly treated by the press and by unthinking mobs (Luke's death is the result of a riot begun by his opponents). Brian's father, a clergyman, publicly defends Luke from spurious attacks, for he believes that 'peace and justice and freedom of speech must stand before all party questions'.

EL's work became very popular: her novels ran into numerous editions and were translated into many languages. *Hope the Hermit* (1898), a story set in Cumberland during the reign of William and Mary, which had been serialized in *Christian World*, sold 9,000 copies on its first day of publication in novel form. Throughout her writing career EL continued to be inspired by the issues of the day: in *Doreen* (1894), she backed the movement for Irish Home Rule; *Autobiography of a Truth* (1896) criticized Turkish attacks on the Armenians (all the profits of the book were donated to the Armenian Relief Fund); and her final novel, *The Hinderers* (1902), argued against the Boer War.   LUCY SLOAN

Selected works: Won by Waiting (1879); *Donovan* (1882); *We Two* (1884); *In the Golden Days* (1885); *The Autobiography of a Slander* (1887); *Derrick Vaughan, Novelist* (1887); *Knight Errant* (1887); 'Preface' to *The All-Father*, by P. H. Newnham (1889); *A Hardy Norseman* (1889); *Their Happiest Christmas* (1890); *Max Hereford's Dream* (1891); 'Preface' to *The Story of an African Chief*, by L. K. Bruce (1893); *Doreen* (1894); *To Right the Wrong* (1894); *Autobiography of a Truth* (1896); *How the Children Raised the Wind* (1896); *Wayfaring Men* (1897); *Hope the Hermit* (1898); 'Introduction' to *Mrs Gaskell and Knutsford*, by G. A. Payne (1900); 'Introduction' to *Was, Is It or Is It Not Consistent with Christianity?*, by J. J. Green (1901); *In Spite of All* (1901); *Burges Letters* (1902); *Hinderers* (1902).

References: Crawford; *DNB*; Escreet, J. M., *Life of Edna Lyall* (1904); *NWAD*; Payne, G. A., *Edna Lyall: An Appreciation* (1903).

Macaulay, Catherine
b. 2 April 1731, Olantigh, Wye, Kent; d. 22 June 1791, Binfield, Berkshire
Historian, political controversialist, philosopher

CM was the first Englishwoman to write a major work of history and one of the few female pamphleteers active in the political controversies of the 1760s and 1770s.

The daughter of John and Elizabeth (*née* Wanley) Sawbridge, CM was descended on both sides from wealthy mercantile familes. Her mother died young and CM was educated privately with her brother at their father's wish. Both children read extensively in Roman history and developed a deep commitment to liberty and republican values. CM's brother, John, was later active in the Wilkesite movement.

In June 1760, CM married Dr George Macaulay, aged 44, a graduate in medicine from Padua and a member of the Scottish circle in London. The first volume of CM's *History of England* appeared three years later, based on her own research in the British Museum collection of parliamentary and legal documents, as well as private letters. The work took London by storm at a time when political controversy was rife, and volume 2 was published in 1765. The following year George Macaulay died, leaving CM with a 6-year-old daughter in comfortable circumstances. In the ensuing eight years she held a radical salon in her London home and worked intensively on the next three volumes of her *History*, as well as writing pamphlets criticizing Hobbes and her contemporary Burke, and advising Corsica on the establishment of a democratic republic.

In 1774 CM removed to Bath, where she resided with an elderly admirer, the Rev. Dr Thomas Wilson. She was now active primarily in practical politics, contributing to the literary property debate and endorsing the American colonies' right to rebel against tyrannical government.. On two visits to Paris she was received with great honour as a champion of the republican cause, inspiring Madame Roland to be 'la Macaulay de son pays'.

At the age of 47, CM remarried in December 1778 William Graham, aged

21, the younger brother of a well-known quack doctor. Friends and critics alike reacted with derision. Dr Wilson forbade her his house in Bath and removed from his London church a six-foot marble statue of CM as the muse of history and the burial vault prepared for her, both of which he had installed the previous year. No stranger to criticism, she continued to write, completing the final three volumes of her *History* and *Moral Truth* (1783) in five years.

CM spent the year 1784 in America with her husband, staying at the homes of prominent Americans with whom she maintained political correspondence, including George Washington and John and Abigail Adams. She became a close friend of Mercy Otis Warren (who wrote one of the few extant defences of CM's remarriage) and undoubtedly inspired Warren's three-volume *History of the American Revolution*. CM's reputation in both America and in France was much less affected by her second marriage than in England. Her death at her home in Binfield followed a lengthy illness and there is a memorial in the parish church, set there by her husband.

CM's monumental history of the seventeenth century was widely acclaimed in her own time as the Whig answer to Hume's Tory interpretation (1754, 3 vols) of the Stuarts and Interregnum. Unlike Hume, CM meticulously footnoted her work with reference to the original sources. Her style, which has been called 'lively, vigorous and practical', was meant to equal Hume's and is certainly entertaining. Like all contemporary historians, CM did not shrink from making overt judgements on the personal character of historical figures: Cromwell, for example, was 'the most corrupt and selfish being that ever disgraced human form', and single-handedly killed the Commonwealth. CM's *History* fell into oblivion in the nineteeth century, despite praise from Lecky and the Americans, Elizabeth Cady Stanton, Susan B. Anthony and Matilda Joslyn Gage.

CM's attempt to follow her seventeenth-century history with a series approaching her own time was unsuccessful largely because it appeared in the same year as her scandalous remarriage, and sharply criticized Robert Walpole and other Whig notables. The format of this volume, in a series of letters to Dr Wilson, does not recommend itself to historical narrative. In *Moral Truth and Letters on Education* (1790), CM criticizes the pessimistic view of human nature taken by Hobbes, Mandeville, and her contemporary Lord Bolingbroke. She quotes widely from classical and more recent philosophers but is forced to rely on reason to make her feminist arguments that boys and girls should be educated alike, that a 'might makes right' argument is simply an excuse for the oppression of women, and that women's freedom to choose a husband is vital if only as 'the right of choice in their domestic tyranny'.

CM inspired women writers not only in France and America, but also in England. Mary Wollstonecraft considered her 'the woman of the greatest abilities that this country has ever produced'. In her own lifetime there were at least two statues and five portraits made of her, and uncounted engravings were available cheaply. CM's critics, notably Dr Johnson and John Wilkes, not only attacked her political stance but also accused her of personal vanity and of painting her face. Yet in *Moral Truth* and *Letters on Education* CM decries the preoccupation with physical appearance encouraged by girls' upbringing. CM's popularity probably never recovered from the shock of her remarriage. The injustice of this popular dismissal is compounded because in her later, more philosophical works, her style reaches a peak of energetic eloquence and persuasiveness.   AMY ERICKSON

Works: *A History of England from the Accession of James I to That of the Brunswick*

Line (1763–83); *Loose Remarks on Certain Positions to Be Found in Mr Hobbes's Philosophical Rudiments of Government and Society, with a Short Sketch in a Letter to Signior Paoli* (1767); *Observations on a Pamphlet, Entitled Thoughts on the Cause of the Present Discontents* (1770); *A Modest Plea for the Property of Copy Right* (1774); *An Address to the People of England, Scotland, and Ireland, on the Present Important Crisis of Affairs* (1775); *A History of England from the Revolution to the Present Time* (1778); *A Treatise on the Immutability of Moral Truth* (1783); *Letters on Education, with Observations on Religious and Metaphysical Subjects* (1790); *Catalogue of Historical Tracts* (British Museum; n. p. 1790).

References: Allibone; Anon., *The Female Patriot: An Epistle from C-t-e M-c-y to the Rev. Dr W-l-n on Her Late marriage* (1779); Anon., *Six Odes Presented to That Justly-celebrated Historian Mrs Catherine Macaulay on Her Birthday* (1777(?)); Boos, F., 'Catherine Macaulay's *Letters on Education* (1790); An Early Feminist Polemic', *University of Michigan Papers in Women's Studies* 2 (1976); Donnelly, L. M., 'The celebrated Mrs Macaulay', *William and Mary Quarterly* 6 (1949); Hays, M., *Female Biography* (1803); Hill, B. and Hill, C., 'Catherine Macaulay and the seventeenth century', *Welsh History Review* 3 (1966–7); Lofft, C., *Observations on Mrs Macaulay's History of England, from the Revolution to the Resignation of Sir Robert Walpole* (1778); Spender, D., *Women of Ideas* (1982); 'Stella' (author), *Modest Exceptions . . . To Mrs Macaulay's Modest Plea* (1774); Stenton, D. M., *The English Woman in History* (1957); Todd; Withey, L., 'Catherine Macaulay and the uses of history: ancient rights, perfectionism and propaganda', *Journal of British Studies* 16, IX (1976).

Macaulay, Rose

b. 1 August 1881, Rugby; d. 30 October 1958, London
Novelist, literary critic, essayist, travel writer, poet

RM's parents, George Macaulay, a university lecturer, and Grace Conybeare, were both descended from families of Anglo-Catholic clergymen and intellectuals. In 1887, they moved to the Italian village of Varazze, to cure Grace's tubercular infection, returning to Oxford in 1894. There, RM attended the Oxford High School for Girls, a sudden change to institutionalized discipline after the informal education provided by her parents and the freedom of Italy. She read history at Somerville College, Oxford, between 1900 and 1903, but failed to sit the final examinations. In 1906, the boredom of home life produced a well-received first novel, *Abbots Verney*, after which novels followed with, at most, two-year intervals. During the pre-war years, her friendship with Rupert Brooke and the literary hostess Naomi Royde-Smith resulted in a greater independence and an acquisition of literary friends. In 1918 she started a long, secret relationship with the married writer Gerald O'Donovan and because of this severed all official bonds with the church.

By 1925, RM had lost interest in the topical satires which were her speciality: the quality of her novels declined, as did the sales. She began an equally impressive output of lively and informal journalism. An ambulance driver during the Second World War, she was devastated by the destruction of her flat and its valuable notes and library in 1941, and in 1942 by Gerald's death from cancer. When after ten years she returned to the novel, the quality of her writing had deepened. In 1951, she received an Honorary Doctorate of Letters from Cambridge, and in 1958 became a DBE. Her return to the Anglo-Catholic faith in her seventies was recorded in letters to her one-time confessor, Father

Johnson, published posthumously as *Letters to a Friend* (1961) and *Last Letters to a Friend* (1962).

RM's long literary career covered many areas. Early poetry was followed by twenty-three novels, popular journalism, and criticism such as *Milton* (1934) and *The Writings of E. M. Forster* (1938). Extensive travelling through Europe, America, and the Levant led to travelogues such as *Fabled Shore: From the Pyrenees to Portugal* (1949) and a highly original book on the centuries of English travel to Portugal, *They Went to Portugal* (1946)

But undoubtedly her major impact stems from her fiction written over a period of fifty years. Her early novels, such as *Abbots Verney* (1906), *The Furnace* (1907), and *The Secret River* (1909) were gloomy moralistic stories of personal failure and family drama which she was later to try to suppress. With *Potterism* (1920), however, RM wrote her first full-blown satire, one of the earliest to tackle the vulgarity and hypocrisy of the popular press. Jane and Johnny Potter, initially much embarrassed by their father's popular newspaper and their mother's sentimental novels, eventually capitulate to the Potter world, while Arthur Gideon, its leading attacker, is murdered, thus falling prey to the very sensationalism he was fighting.

Among these early topical comedies, *Dangerous Ages* (1921) was the most popular, describing, in four generations, how women suffer the pitfalls of their age: only the great-grandmother is contented; the others know the problems of growing old or middle-aged, or being young and inexperienced. The novel also contains a powerful satire on contemporary psychoanalysis. *Orphan Island* (1924), again in a lighter vein, shows how Miss Smith, shipwrecked with fifty orphans, moulds a Victorian Utopia, establishing her descendants as landed gentry and herself as the new Victoria.

Orphan Island points to a concern increasingly central to RM's various writing: the nature of civilization. *Crewe Train* (1926) opposed the 'civilization' of London to the 'barbarian' Denham, an unworldly primitive effectively normalized by her family, that is, married off with a baby. This opposition of civilization and barbarism constantly reappeared in her work, as did ruins, the signs of decayed societies. *Pleasure of Ruins* (1953), for instance, was an extensively researched book on eastern and European ruins and our fascination with past civilizations. *They Were Defeated* (1932), RM's only historical novel, testified again to her attraction to the past. An evocation of the life of the seventeenth-century poet John Herrick in an enchanted Cambridge, it was one of her best novels and a linguistic *tour de force*, the dialogue being entirely written in contemporary English.

After ten years of journalism, *The World My Wilderness* (1950) again centred on ruins and ruined lives, tracing the effects of the Second World War on Barbary, whose life near the French maquis has spoilt her for normal society. Sly and suspicious, she lies and steals without qualms, relating only to her mother. Barbary hides among the post-war London ruins where she expects to find the 'London Resistance Movement'. It is significant that most 'barbarians' in RM's work are these unadapted, sullen young girls like Barbary, Denham or shy, unsociable Rosamond Thinkwell, only happy among the lush nature of *Orphan Island*.

RM's last completed novel, *The Towers of Trebizond* (1956), interwove many strands of the author's own varied interests. The ruined Turkish city of Trebizond symbolized the spiritual search of the main character Laurie, while her adulterous love affair, her banishment from the Church, and her grief over the lover killed in a car crash have autobiographical resonance. These tragic elements are countered by a topical and humorous world, a Turkey infested with spies, Oxonian defectors, travel writers and religious missionaries. Laurie's Aunt Dot, who leads the Anglician mission, is a feminist researching the position of women in Turkey. Impressive in its combination of an idiosyncratic, witty style with the subject, the grief and guilt of the heroine, *The Towers of Trebizond* won the James Tait Black Memorial Prize in 1957. When she died, RM was preparing another novel, *Venice Besieged*, partly published in *Letters to a Sister* (1964).   SABINE VANACKER

Selected works: *Abbots Verney* (1906); *The Furnace* (1907); *The Secret River* (1909); *The Valley Captives* (1911); *Views and Vagabonds* (1912); *The Lee Shore* (1912); *The Two Blind Countries* (1914); *Non-Combatants and Others* (1916); *What Not: A Prophetic Comedy* (1918); *Potterism: A Tragi-farcical Tract* (1920); *Mystery at Geneva* (1922); *Told by an Idiot* (1923); *Crewe Train* (1926); *Keeping up Appearances* (1928); *Staying with Relations* (1930); *Some Religious Elements in English Literature* (1931); *They Were Defeated* (1932); *Milton* (1934); *I Would Be Private* (1937); *The Writings of E. M. Forster* (1938); *And No Man's Wit* (1940); *Life among the English* (1942); *The World My Wilderness* (1950); *Pleasure of Ruins* (1953); *The Towers of Trebizond* (1956); *Letters to a Friend: 1950–1952* (1961); *Last Letters to a Friend: 1952–1958* (1962); *Letters to a Sister* (1964).

References: Babington Smith, C., *Rose Macaulay: A Biography* (1972); Babington Smith, C., 'Letters to a friend', *American Scholar* 31 (Spring 1962): Benson, A. R., 'The ironic aesthete and the sponsoring of causes: a rhetorical quandary in novelistic technique', *English Literature in Transition* 9 (1966); Crosland, M., *Beyond the Lighthouse: English Women Novelists in the Twentieth Century* (1981); Gerger, H. E. and Lauterback, E. S., 'Bibliography news and notes', *English Literature in Transition* 5 (1962); Lockwood, W. J., 'Rose Macaulay', in *Minor British Novelists*, ed. C. A. Hoyt (1967); Stewart, D., 'Rose Macaulay – Anglicanism', in *The Ark of God: Studies in Five Modern Novelists* (1961).

Makin, Bathsua

b. 1612(?), Southwick, Sussex; d. 1674(?), London
Polemical writer

BM, the scholar, school mistress and active campaigner for the liberal education of women, was the daughter of the Sussex rector John Pell and his wife Elizabeth Holland. Her brother was the mathematician John Pell, a graduate of Cambridge and a member of the Royal Society. Although there is no record of BM's schooling she was famed as the most learned Englishwoman of her time. Her knowledge of mathematics, Italian, Latin, Hebrew, Greek, Spanish and French gained her the post of tutor to Charles I's daughter Princess Elizabeth in about 1641. At about this time she began a correspondence with the Dutch scholar Anna Maria Van Schurman, the linguist from Utrecht whose tract *De Ingenii Muliebris* influenced both the ideas and the structure of BM's own educational work, *An Essay to Revive the Antient Education of Gentlewomen* (1673). BM's debt is acknowledged in the *Essay* where Van Schurman's skill as a theologian, linguist, philosopher, and logician is noted as an example of female potential. Both women attempted to counter the contemporary lack of interest in the academic education of women and condemned those schools that only taught 'accomplishments' proper to a place at court, but which 'bring forth and breed up a generation of Baboons, that have little more wit than Apes or Hobby-Horses'. BM attempted to practise her ideas as mistress of a school at Tottenham High Cross, where women could learn up to six languages but 'those that think one Language enough for a woman, may forbear the languages and learn only Experimental Philosophy.' As a concession to contemporary fashion, half the time was spent on 'all things ordinarily taught in other schools, works of all sorts, dancing, music, singing, writing, keeping accounts'.

BM was concerned for single women and she urged them to gain their financial indepencence. In *The Malady and Remedy of Vexations and Unjust Arrests and Actions* (1646), BM pleaded to Parliament to abolish debtors' prisons, a cause possibly made dear to her by the imprisonment of her brother John Pell; in this work she complained of the undoing of many thousands of females by the 'vexations and unjust actions and arrests for pretended debts'. In 1664 BM wrote on her friend, 'Upon the lamented death of the Right Honourable, the Lady Elizabeth Langham'; Lady Elizabeth's virtues as a mother and a wife are significiantly mentioned before her acomplishments in learning, but her ability in Latin, French, and Italian is also stressed. A letter of 1668 with BM's signature mentions her husband, Makin, and indicates that she had a son.

BM's intention in the *Essay* is 'not to equalize Women to Men, much less to make them superior. They are the weaker Sex, yet capable of impressions of great things, something like to the best of Men.' The *Essay* is a dialogue in letter form between a male champion of women's education and a male objector, who considers women to be so naturally inferior to men that there is no point in educating them, even though he claims to have 'no prejudice against the sex'. BM's answers to these objections show the influence of both humanist and Puritan educational doctrines, although both are modified. She refuses to follow earlier humanists such as Richard Mulcaster as far as advocating that education should prepare women for public careers, and consequently, as with all female educational reformers of her time, BM demands a different education for boys and girls. She adheres to the ideas of Erasmus in *De Institutione Christianae Feminae* (1523); her reasons for educating women include the fundamental Puritan one of instruction in the knowledge of good and evil as an aid to salvation. BM follows contemporary conduct books in urging that women be instructed how to teach in the nursery and how to manage the household. Although the latter was only to take place in the absence of the husband, the need for this had become pressing during the Civil War: 'In these late Times there are several instances of Women, when Husbands were serving their King and Countrey, defended their Houses, and did all things, as Souldiers, with Pride and Valour, like Men.' Yet BM did not think women could have careers in public life like men. Motherhood remained the prime occupation and, although education was important, it was intended to make the wife a more useful support to her husband, and an adequate teacher to their young male children. More than this ought not to be demanded, for 'to ask too much is to be denied all'. The end of a humanist education was 'to polish your Souls, that you may glorify God, and answer the end of your Creation, to be meet helps to your husbands'. The *Essay* looks back to what women have achieved both in the far and recent past and seeks to accommodate these achievements to the needs of society. In her practice and theory BM was a considerable influence on women's education, and her ideas were developed by later theorists such as Hannah Wolley and Mary Astell.   CAROLINE COLEMAN

Works: *The Malady and Remedy of Vexations and Unjust Arrests and Actions* (1646); 'Elegy on the Death of Henry, Lord Hastings' (1649); 'Upon the much lamented death of the Right Honourable, the Lady Elizabeth Langham' (1664); *An Essay*

To Revive the Antient Education of Gentlewomen, In Religion, Manners, Arts and Tongues, With An Answer to the Objections against this Way of Education (1673).
References: Allibone; Brink, J. R., 'Bathsua Makin: educator and linguist', in *Female Scholars: A Tradition of Learned Women before 1800* (1980); *DNB*; Fraser, A., *The Weaker Vessel* (1984); Gardiner D., *English Girlhood at School* (1929); Greer, G. *et al* (eds), *Kissing the Rod* (1988); Humphreys, A. R., 'The "Rights of Woman" in the Age of Reason', *Modern Language Review* 41 (1946); Mahl, M. and Koon, H. (eds), *The Female Spectator* (1977); Perry, R., *The Celebrated Mary Astell* (1986); Reynolds, M., *The Learned Lady in England 1650–1760* (1920); Smith, H., *Reason's Disciples* (1982); Stenton, D. M., *The Englishwoman in History* (1957); Todd; Upham, A. H., 'English femmes savantes at the end of the seventeenth century', *Journal of English and German Philology* 12 (1913); Wallas, A., *Before the Bluestockings* (1929).

Malet, Lucas
b. 4 June 1852, Eversley, Hampshire; d. 27 October 1931, Tenby, Wales
Novelist
LM (Mary Kingsley) was the youngest daugher of Charles Kingsley and Frances Grenfell. She chose the pseudonym 'Lucas Malet' from the surnames of a Kingsley relative and a Grenfell grandmother to avoid exploiting her family's literary fame. While she enjoyed a measure of contemporary success for her novels and travelled in renowned literary company, she now seems to be a victim of changing tastes in the literary marketplace.

LM was raised, along with her siblings Maurice, Rose, and Grenville, in a nurturing environment, according to her mother's memoirs. While the boys were sent to school and the girls educated at home, LM eventually attended University College and the Slade School of Fine Art. However, she abandoned any notion of a career when her father died in 1875. She married the Rev. William Harrison, her father's former curate, in 1876; but the match was ill-fated and they soon separated, childless. After Harrison died in 1897, LM became a Roman Catholic. She then travelled widely with her cousin Gabrielle Vallings, whom she adopted and with whom she lived until her death. Gabrielle inherited all LM's literary papers, as well as those of Charles Kingsley.

LM's literary career spans some fifty years. Her first novel, *Mrs Lorimer: A Sketch in Black and White* (1882), was largely ignored, although the *Saturday Review* and the *Spectator* both reviewed it, apparently unaware of LM's true identity. Her second novel, *Colonel Enderby's Wife* (1885), established her position as a popular but outspoken writer of 'character' novels in London literary circles. Her subsequent novels, often published at wide intervals, bear testimony to the slowness of her writing. All received notice in the book review columns. Contemporary critics of her early works lauded her style and characterization but criticized her outspokenness on subjects such as seduction, illegitimate children, and deformity, especially in *The Wages of Sin* (1891) and *The History of Sir Richard Calmady* (1901). She was best known for these, along with *The Gateless Barrier* (1900), an extraordinary study about the unseen world.

LM was not a forerunner of twentieth-century literary style. Her reputation for depth of characterization and excellence of description continued during her long publishing lifetime, as reviews show, but she was soon criticized as an 'anachronism', an old-fashioned writer of sentimental and pathetic, verbose prose containing only occasional flashes of humour. Yet she was awarded a civil list pension the year before her death in recognition of her literary achievement. A friend and contemporary of Henry James, LM seems to have been incapable of bridging that literary generational gap marking the transition from verbosity to sparseness of language, the dominant taste in early twentieth-century fiction. As a result, her novels now elicit only archival interest.

PATRICIA LORIMER LUNDBERG

Selected works: *Mrs Lorimer: A Sketch in Black and White* (1882); *Colonel Enderby's Wife* (1885); *A Counsel of Perfection* (1888); *Little Peter: A Christmas Morality* (1888); *The Wages of Sin* (1891); *The Carissima* (1896); 'Forget-Me-Not' (1899); 'Joan of Arc's Missing Mother' (1899); *The Gateless Barrier* (1900); *The History of Sir Richard Calmady* (1901); *The Far Horizon* (1906); *Golden Galleon* (1910); *Adrian Savage* (1911); *Damaris* (1916); *Deadham Hard* (1919); *The Tall Villa* (1920); *DaSilva's Widow and Other Stories* (1922); *The Survivors* (1923); *The Dogs of Want: A Modern Comedy of Errors* (1924); *The Private Life of Mr Justice Syme* (finished and published by Gabrielle Vallings in 1932).

References: *DNB*; Kingsley, F., *Charles Kingsley: His Letters and Memories of His Life, Ed. by His Wife* (1877); Pope-Hennessy, U., *Canon Charles Kingsley* (1948); Thorp, M., *Charles Kingsley 1819–1875* (1937).

Manley, Delarivier [Mary]

b. 1663, Jersey; d. July 1724, London

Novelist, journalist, playwright

DM was the daughter of the royalist army officer and historian Sir Roger Manley, best known for his *Commentariorum de Rebellione Anglicana* (1686). Her mother, Margaret (née Dorislaus), was the daughter of a Dutch diplomat, Isaac Dorislaus, assassinated in 1649 by exiled royalists. DM was an inveterate autobiographer, inserting passages from her own history into the series of scandalous narratives of court and public life for which she became so famous. Her autobiography and self-defence, *The Adventures of Rivella* (1714) and the story of Delia in her *New Atalantis*, Volume 2 (1709), are the major sources for DM's biography. Roger Manley became Lieutenant-Governor of Jersey in October 1667 and it was here that DM, her two sisters and two brothers grew up. She was educated at home, apart from a short stay with one of her brothers at the home of a Huguenot minister, where she learnt French. In July 1685 a young actor and playwright turned soldier, James Carlisle, came to Roger Manley's garrison at Landguard Fort for a month, and DM claims to have fallen passionately in love. Throughout her writing, love figures as a fatal 'Poyson' for which her own fiction ostensibly acted as a preventative, if not an antidote, in warning young women of its ruinous effects.

On her father's death in 1687, DM inherited £200 and the residue of her father's estate. Both the executors her father had appointed for his will were dead by 1688 and DM and her sister were left to the care of their cousin, John Manley, a Tory lawyer and later MP. In *New Atalantis*, Volume 2 DM claims to have stayed with 'an old out-of-fashion aunt' in the country who infected her with romantic notions from the 'Books of Chivalry and Romances' she read to them. On her aunt's death, DM married John Manley and a son, John, was born to the couple in 1691. In her autobiographies DM claims to have been persuaded that his first wife, Anne Grosse, was dead, although she admits living with him for a further three years after he confessed his bigamy to her. In January 1694, under protection of Barbara Villiers, Duchess of Cleveland, and long-term mistress to Charles II, she left her bigamous marriage. The duchess, however, threw her out of Arlington Street six months later, having accused DM of a flirtation with her son. As a result she became one of DM's many satirical targets, most famously as the Duchesse de l'Inconstant in *New Atalantis*, Volume 1, where the traditional eroticized seduction scene of amatory fiction is comically inverted to present the woman as predatory rake.

From 1694 to 1696 DM appears to have travelled around the south-west of England, living hand to mouth, and soliciting money from friends. These travels resulted in her first publication, *Letters by Mrs Manley* (1696), modelled on the popular epistolary travelogue of Marie Catherine de la Motte, Baroness d'Aulnoy, *Travels into Spain* (1691), from which DM quotes. Madame d'Aulnoy was probably the most important single influence upon DM's literary style as a whole, her scandalous memoirs of the courts of France, Spain and England in the late seventeenth century acting as the literary models for DM's satirical fiction. DM's *Letters*, addressed to JH (probably James Hargreaves), were published without her permission and she quickly had them withdrawn. The letters are a lively account of a stagecoach journey, filled with dialogue and humorous character description, especially with regard to the persistent attention of a baronet's son whom DM titles her 'Beau'. Towards their conclusion, however, DM rejects her earlier 'romantic ideas of retirements' and complains that there is 'no real satisfaction without conversation', expressing her intention to return to the scandal-filled streets of London.

DM's first play, *The Lost Lover, or, The Jealous Husband*, a comedy, was also performed at Drury Lane in Spring 1696. The cast included the young Colley Cibber, but the play was not a success. DM claimed to have written it in seven days, and in her preface to the publication bitterly complained, 'I am satisfied the bare name of being a woman's play damned it beyond its own want of merit.' Yet even as she wrote, the Lincoln's Inn Field rival breakaway company were preparing to perform her new tragedy, *The Royal Mischief*. In contrast, *The Royal Mischief* was met by critical acclaim and popular enthusiasm when it was produced in April 1696, not least because of its erotic content. DM met criticisms about the 'warmth' of the play, centred upon the self-seeking sexuality of her female lead, Homais, by arguing that 'I did not believe it possible to pursue . . . [gentle love] too far'. In December 1696, Catherine Trotter asked DM to help her secure the freedom of one John Tilly, a lawyer and Governor of the Prison at the Fleet accused of corruption and taking bribes. This was the start of a six-year affair between DM and Tilly, who appears as Cleander in *Rivella*. Tilly and DM became involved in the notorious Albermarle case during this period, attempting to make money by helping to resolve the long litigation on behalf of Lord Bath against Ralph Montagu's claim to the Albermarle estate. Much of *Rivella* is taken up with the intricacies and double-dealing in which they became entangled, and which ultimately left them out of pocket. On December 1702, Tilly's first wife died and DM claims that she nobly gave him up so that he could solve his financial problems through marriage with a rich heiress. DM was left impecunious once more, reliant on friends and her pen.

In the year of the parliamentary election which the Whigs eventually won, DM entered the paper war with the publication of *The Secret History of Queen Zarah and the Zarazians* (1705), which became so popular that 'Zarazians' became an everyday pseudonym for Whig supporters. This is one of the earliest *romans à clef* to be published in Britain, and takes as its target the 'unnatural' behaviour of Sarah, Duchess of Marlborough, favourite of Queen Anne. Zarah/Sarah, 'the Mirror of her Sex, and the Phoenix of a Qu—n', is portrayed as a monster of depravity, in that she exploits her sexuality to win political influence, thus inverting gender hierarchies and fostering political anarchy.

Queen Zarah proved so popular that a second part was brought out in the same year. There are some doubts as to DM's authorship, since the text so rarely uses her favourite piece of punctuation, the exclamation mark, and uncharacteristically retains some sympathy for individual Whigs. It does, however, set the scene for most of DM's writing, a spicy combination of scurrilous tales about important political figures which sets about destroying Whig supremacy by character assassination and moral disquisition. In the twentieth century, *Queen Zarah* is probably best known for its preface which makes an important contribution to the early theory of the novel, by rejecting the idealized world of the French romance for the psychological 'realism' of the 'little history'. DM reveals an astute awareness of reader response and attacks the impossible chastity of romance heroines as 'in no wise probable', whilst insisting that the historian's first duty is to the entertainment of the reader rather than to 'Moralizing or Describing'.

In December 1706, a second tragedy by DM, *Almyna*, was performed at the Haymarket by the Queen's Theatre Company. The year of 1707 saw the publication of a collection of letters to and from DM entitled *The Lady's Pacquet Broke Open*. They include DM's correspondence with Richard Steele between 1697 and 1699, concerned mainly with questions of alchemy and seduction. When Steele refused DM financial assistance after her separation from Tilly, their friendship was severed to be followed by a long and bitter series of mutual slanders. The letters are a diverse collection of scandal and seduction narratives, written in DM's customary racy style. In July 1709, DM may have started *The Female Tatler*, a thrice-weekly scandal sheet written by one Phoebe Crackenthorpe, 'a lady that knows everything'. Her authorship of this paper is uncertain. Although it bears many of the marks of DM's scandalous and gossipy style, its lack of political alignment make its attribution to her unlikely.

In May 1709 Volume 1 of *Secret Memoirs and Manners of Several Persons of Quality, of both Sexes, From the New Atalantis* was published. Purportedly a translation from a French manuscript, it consisted of 246 pages of narratives concerning the private lives of prominent Whigs and Tories. A second volume appeared in October 1709 and took the same format. The goddess of Justice, Astrea (whom we might also identify with 'Astrea'/Aphra Behn), returns to earth in order to gather information about public and private models of conduct for the young prince she has taken under her wing (probably George I or George II of Hanover). She and her mother, Virtue, are conducted around the scenes of vice in the island of Atalantis by Intelligence, who serves the Princess Fame. Intelligence's command of the narrative is occasionally interrupted by other narrators, including the midwife, Mrs Nightwatch, or by Astrea's judgements on the stories. In defence of her own practice of describing seduction scenes in minute and erotic detail, DM has Astrea determine that we cannot be 'polluted but by our *own*, not the Crimes of *others*.' The *New Atalantis* had immediate popular success especially amongst women, as Lady Mary Wortley Montagu's impatience when, in October, the second volume was suppressed bears witness. DM, her publisher, and her printer were arrested on 29 October and on 5 November, four days after her fellows, DM was admitted to bail. The trial was heard in February 1710 and DM was discharged, defending herself with the claim that she received her information by 'inspiration' and rebuking her judges for bringing 'a Woman to her Trial for writing a few amorous Trifles' (*Rivella*). The *New Atalantis* went into seven editions and was translated into French (1713–16). DM supposedly determined after her court case that 'henceforward her Business should be to write of Pleasure and Entertainment only, wherein Party should no longer mingle', on the grounds that 'Politicks is not the Business of a Woman' (*Rivella*).

However, in 1710 DM published the first volume of *Memoirs of Europe*, ostensibly the story of Europe in the time of Charlemagne, but once again a series of scandalous political narratives. Whereas the first volume is narrated by two men, the ambassador Merovius and his friend the Count de St Gironne, to the book's hero, Horatius (Lord Peterborough), the second volume, published in November of the same year, is a series of stories narrated to the princess Ethelinda (Maria Königsmarck). The dedication comments that 'the Entertainment being to a Lady, there's not so much of the Politick as in the first Part, more of the Gay'. Here, DM returns from political history to the surer ground of sexual scandal in order to hit her political arrows home. Jonathan Swift, a friend and co-author with DM on a number of projects, described the verbose style of the *Memoirs* as 'two thousand Epithets, and fine Words putt up in a bag, and . . . puled . . . out by the handfull'. Steele was more vicious in his attacks, referring to DM in the *Tatler* of 3 September 1709 as a creator of 'artificial poisons conveyed by smell'.

From 1711 to early 1713, encouraged by Jonathan Swift, DM gave herself over to political journalism, addressing immediate political events from a Tory perspective. She took over the editorship of the *Examiner* from Swift in June 1711, writing nos. 46–52, which consist of a series of direct attacks on Whig propaganda, and accusations of Whig hypocrisy and corruption. In entering the 'masculine' sphere of political debate, DM displayed remarkable courage and confidence. However, whereas her scandal novels present the female eye as having a particularly penetrating observer's understanding of the political world in which women are allowed no 'interest', her journalistic writing is written in a far more conventional 'masculine' voice of political commentary. Amongst the pamphlets, *The Duke of M——h's Vindication* in particular demonstrates her considerable control of the art of irony. Ostensibly written from a Whig perspective, it highlights Marlborough's most questionable actions.

In early 1712 DM fell ill with 'dropsy and a sore leg', as Jonathan Swift reported to Stella, adding a short description of her as having 'very generous principles for one of her sort; and a great deal of good sense and invention; she is about forty, very homely and very fat'. By this time, DM and her sister Cornelia were living in Queen's Head Alley with DM's printer, John Barber, with whom she was reputed to be having an affair.

On Anne's death in 1714 and the restoration of Whig supremacy with the accession of George I, DM seems to have abandoned the cause of Tory propaganda and turned to the stage and amatory fiction once more. In early 1714, in order to prevent the publication of a scandalous biography written by Charles Gildon, DM agreed to produce her own autobiography for the publisher Curll under Gildon's title, *The Adventures of Rivella*. *Rivella* is a far more honest account of her marriage and affairs than the whitewash DM attempted in the history of Delia in *New Atalantis*, Volume 2. The story of her life is told by Sir Charles Lovemore to the amorous young Count d'Aumont and constructs the romance authoress herself as the erotic centrepiece to the narrative. DM is cleared of immorality on the grounds that her life history enables her to write better fiction. Her 'noble Discoveries' in the passion of love mean that 'it would have been a *Fault in her, not to have been Faulty*'. The double standard of gender is attacked when we are informed that 'if she had been a Man, she had been without Fault'.

In 1717 DM received 600 guineas from Steele for the play *Lucius*, performed by his Drury Lane company, and the two were finally, if only publicly, reconciled. Three years later, DM's reworking of some tales from the sixteenth-century *Palace of Pleasure* by Painter, *The Power of Love in Seven Novels*, was published. They carry the distinctive mark of DM's work, racy plotting, eroticism, and voyeurism, a fondness for exoticism, and an unerring sense of the reader's desire both to indulge sexual fantasy and to see sexuality (in particular, female desire) ultimately punished. As such, they mark the high point of DM's story-telling art, if they lack the subtle blend of politics and sexuality she used to such effect in the *New Atalantis*.

The Power of Love was DM's last still extant work. She died in July 1724, John Barber having eloped with her nurse, Sarah Dovekin, only months beforehand. Her only payment for her services to the Tory party appears to have been £50 from Robert Harley, Earl of Oxford, in 1714. Despite the lack of recognition and respect afforded her by the politicians she supported, DM's success as a popularizer of political debates, and especially her weaving together of the fabric of early eighteenth-century ideologies of femininity and their seeming opposite, the masculine world of high politics, cannot be underestimated. She managed to deploy sexual myth to curry popular support. The vicissitudes of her life and writing, interwoven as they were, act as a challenge to the notion that still prevails today that eighteenth-century satire and wit were the exclusive preserve of the masculine imagination.

ROSALIND BALLASTER

Selected works: Letters Written By Mrs Manley (1696; reissued as *A Stagecoach Journey to Exeter*, 1725); *The Lost Lover, or, The Jealous Husband* (1696); *The Royal Mischief* (1696); *The Secret History of Queen Zara and the Zarazians* (1705); *Almyna, or, The Arabian Vow* (1707); *The Lady's Paquet Broke Open* (1707); *Secret Memoirs and Manners of Several Persons of Quality, of Both Sexes, From the New Atalantis, an Island in the Mediterranean . . .* (1709); *Memoirs of Europe Towards the Close of the Eighth Century* (1710); *The Examiner*, nos. 46–52 (1711); *The Duke of M—h's Vindication* (1711); *A Learned Comment on Dr Hare's Sermon* (1711); *A True Relation of the Several Facts and Circumstances of the Intended Riot and Tumult on Queen Elizabeth's Birthday* (1711); *The Honour and Prerogative of the Queen's Majesty Vindicated* (1713); *The Adventures of Rivella* (1714; reissued as *Memoirs of the Life of Mrs Manley*, 1725); *The Power of Love in Seven Novels* (1720).

References: Anderson, P. B., 'Mistress . . . Manley's Biography', *Modern Philology* 33 (1936); Anderson, P. B., 'Delarivière Manley's prose fiction', *Philological Quarterly* 13 (1934). Clark, C., *Three Augustan Women Playwrights* (1986); Köster, P. (ed.), *The Novels of Mary Delarivière Manley, 1705–1714* (1971); Morgan, F., *A Woman of No Character: An Autobiography of Mrs Manley* (1986); Needham, G. B., 'Mrs Manley, an Eighteenth Century Wife of Bath', *Huntingdon Library Quarterly* 3 (1938); Needham, G. B., 'Mary De la Rivière Manley, Tory Defender', *HLQ* 12 (1948–9); Todd; Todd, J., *The Sign of Angellica: women, writing and fiction 1660–1800* (1989).

Mannin, Ethel
b. October 1900, London
Novelist, travel writer, autobiographer
The eldest daughter of Robert Mannin, a postal sorter and Edith Gray Mannin, EM has an Irish ancestry. She attended boarding school from 1906 to 1914, and later described herself during these years as a sensitive, quiet child who

thought herself too ugly to make friends. She wrote in *Confessions and Impressions* (1930) that she began writing stories at the age of 7. Her first publications were on the children's pages of the *Lady's Companion* in 1910 and *Reynolds Newspaper* in 1913. As a student, EM excelled at essay writing and was pleased to note that twenty years after she had left school her prose was being used as a model for teaching composition. EM counted among her literary influences the poetry of Coleridge (especially 'Kubla Khan'), Tennyson (especially 'Ulysses'), the verse of Keats and Shelley, and the novel *The Story of an African Farm* by Olive Schreiner.

In 1915 EM won a scholarship to a commercial school in London and upon graduatiion became a typist at Charles Higham's advertising firm. Here she says she received her 'real education'. By 1916 she was writing advertisement copy and editing two in-house publications. In 1917, Higham purchased the *Pelican*, a theatrical paper, which EM edited and of which she served as literary critic until it folded in 1919. EM earned extra money freelancing articles on business for trade publications, and also during this period she learned about socialism from a co-worker in the firm.

In 1919 EM married John Alexander Porteus but soon after the birth of her only child, Jean, the marriage ended. EM believed that a woman could not be a professional writer and a housewife at the same time. During her pregnancy she wrote serial novels for a guinea per thousand words. By 1927 she had published four novels: *Martha* (1923), *Hunger of the Sea* (1924), *Sounding Brass* (1925), and *Pilgrims* (1927). *Sounding Brass*, her first critical success, was based on her experiences and observations in the advertising agency and *Pilgrims*, also a success, was inspired by the art of Vincent Van Gogh.

From the age of 16 EM had defined herself as a socialist and both her fiction and non-fiction throughout the 1940s reflect her interest in this political and social philosophy. She was also influenced by the writing of Bertrand Russell and the educational theories of A. S. Neill, who wrote the introduction to *Common Sense and the Child* (1931) which argued for better methods of childrearing. *Linda Shawn* (1932) is a novel based on the life of a child and incorporates Neill's theories. *Love's Winnowing* (1932) is an early novel set against the socialist-defined working-class background and *The Red Rose* (1941) is based on the life of Emma Goldman.

In 1936, EM travelled to the Soviet Union, and records her journey in *South to Samarkand*. It is evident from the work's preface that she was hoping to have a favourable view of the Soviet Union reinforced, which was not the case, and she was honest enough to view her experiences with detachment. Her personality is clearly evident in *South to Samarkand*. She wryly records her exasperation at constantly being asked about 'the conditions of the working class in England' and her growing impatience with the infinite bureaucracy that impeded her and her companion's attempts to see the 'real' USSR. Because of her candid examination of the Soviet socialist system and works such as *Women and the Revolution*, EM was called the most unpopular writer in England in 1942.

In 1938, EM married Reginald Reynolds, a fellow writer. From 1932 to 1974, she travelled throughout America, Russia, Italy, India, Burma, Jordan, and the Middle East. All these trips resulted in travel books which reflect her early training as a journalist in the detachment of her observations. Many are accurately illustrated as well. For example, *Jungle Journey* (1950) contains photographs taken by Jean Porteus as she accompanied her mother through India.

In addition to her novels and travel writings, EM also wrote two biographies, three children's books, and seven memoirs. The last, *Sunset over Dartmoor*, was published in 1977. At the height of her career, EM wrote that she intended to publish two books a year, one fiction and one non-fiction, and judging from her list of works she achieved that goal. She stated that she wrote from five to six hours per day.   B. E. SCHNELLER

Selected works: Martha (1923); *Hunger of the Sea* (1924); *Sounding Brass* (1925); *Pilgrims* (1927); *Confessions and Impressions* (1930); *Green Figs* (1931); *Common Sense and the Child: A Plea for Freedom* (1931); *Linda Shawn* (1932); *South to Samarkand* (1936); *Women and the Revolution* (1938); *Common Sense and the Adolescent* (1938); *The Story of the Dance Hostess* (1940); *Red Rose: A Novel based on the Life of Emma Goldman* (1941); *Common Sense and Morality* (1942); *Comrade, O Comrade* (1947); *Jungle Journey* (1950); *The Wild Swans and Other Tales of the Ancient Irish* (1952); *This was a Man: Some Memories of Robert Mannin by his Daughter* (1952); *Land of the Crested Lion: A Journey through Burma* (1955); *The Country of the Sea: Some Wanderings in Brittany* (1957); *Ann and Peter in Sweden* (1958) *Ann and Peter in Japan* (1960); *Ann and Peter in Austria* (1961); *The Road to Beersheba* (1963); *A Lance for the Arabs: Some Travels through the United Arab Republic* (1963); *The Burning Bush* (1965); *An American Journey* (1967); *The Saga of Sammy-Cat* (1969); *Free Pass to Nowhere* (1970); *England at Large* (1970); *My Cat Sammy* (1971); *Young in the Twenties* (1971); *Mission to Beirut* (1973); *Stories from My Life* (1973); *Kildoon* (1974); *An Italian Journey* (1974); *The Late Miss Guthrie* (1975); *Sunset over Dartmoor* (1977).

References: CA; DLB.

Manning, Anne

b. 17 February 1807, London; d. 14 September 1879, Tunbridge Wells

Historical novelist

AM was the daughter of an insurance broker whose own father had been a Unitarian minister. She received a reasonably wide education at home from her mother, who taught her languages, history, and science. She was also a gifted painter, and was awarded a gold medal by the Royal Academy for a copy which she made of a work by Murillo. Her writing career began when, given the task of teaching her younger brothers and sisters, AM wrote for them her first work, *A Sister's Gift*. She never married, and led a very quiet life in Surrey, first in Mickleham and later, after the death of her parents, at Reigate Hill. She died in her sister's house in Tunbridge Wells.

AM's most celebrated work was *The Maiden and Married Life of Mary Powell* (1850). Most of her subsequent novels and popular histories were advertised as being 'by the author of *Mary Powell*'. The book presents itself as Mary Powell's journal from her seventeenth birthday in 1643 until October 1646, after her marriage to the poet John Milton. The 'journal' aims not only at stylistic, but also at orthographic and typographic authenticity: all nouns are capitalized, and the letter 's' is printed according to seventeenth-century convention, whilst the spelling is similarly antiquated. It was for her attention to such matters of nice historical detail that AM was principally noted by her contemporaries.

AM portrays Milton as given to making lengthy and portentous speeches to which Mary's response often falls short of the expected mute admiration: 'Alle this, and much more, as tedious to heare as to write, did I listen to, firste with flagging Attention, next with concealed Wearinesse . . . it soe chanced, by ill-luck, that Mr *Milton*, suddainlie turning his Eyes from Heaven upon poore me, caughte, I can scarcelie expresse how slighte, an Indication of Discomfort in my

Face; and instantlie a Cloud crossed his owne. . . '. The couple are nevertheless married, but shortly afterwards separated, partly because of their divergent political loyalties at a time of civil war. Mary extends a short holiday at her parents' home beyond the period allowed by her husband: the poet's angry letters lead Mary to remark, 'methinks Mr *Milton* presumeth somewhat too much on his marital Authoritie, writing in this Strayn.' But the book ends with the couple at least temporarily reconciled, whilst Mary provides for her journal a list of her husband's admirable qualities.

The imaginative reworking of material in AM's many historical novels is scarcely a less prominent feature of her popular histories. Her *The Chronicles of Merry England* (1854), in which the age of 'Merry England' is taken as roughly coextensive with what are now referred to as the Dark Ages, is punctuated by lengthy fictional speeches distributed amongst the chief actors. Sweeping moral judgements are made on the major historical personages: William the Conqueror is crafty, dishonest, and, above all, foreign, whilst Harold is the representative of Merry England itself, 'Brave, bold, and popular'.   JAMES SMITH

Selected works: Stories from the History of Italy (1831); The Hill Side (1850); The Maiden and Married Life of Mary Powell (1850); The Household of Sir Thomas More (1851); The Colloquies of Edward Osborne (1852); The Drawing Room Table (1852); Cherry and Violet (1853); The Provocations of Madame Palissy (1853); The Chronicles of Merry England (1854); Claude the Colporteur (1854); The Adventures of the Caliph Haroun Alraschid (1855); The Old Chelsea Bun-House (1855); Tasso and Leonora (1856); The Week of Darkness (1856); The Good Old Times (1857); Helen and Olga (1857); The Ladies of Bever Hollow (1858); The Year Nine (1858); Poplar House Academy (1859); The Story of Italy (1859); Village Belles (1859); The Day of Small Things (1860); Deborah's Diary (1860); Town and Forest (1860); The Chronicle of Ethelfled (1861); The Cottage History of England (1861); Family Pictures (1861); Noble Purpose Nobly Won (1862); The Duchess of Trajetto (1863); Meadowleigh (1863); An Interrupted Wedding (1864); Belforest (1865); The Lincolnshire Tragedy (1866); Diana's Crescent (1868); The Spanish Barber (1869); Compton Friars (1872); The Lady of Limited Income (1872); Lord Harry Bellair (1874).

References: Allibone; *BA* (19); Showalter, E., *A Literature of Their Own* (1977).

Manning, Olivia

b. 1908, Portsmouth; d. 1980, London
Novelist, literary journalist

OM was the daughter of the second marriage of Commander Oliver Manning, RN. He had served in the navy in the days of sail; his accounts of distant times and places undoubtedly fostered OM's own astute sense of history and locality. Her mother came from Ulster; this mixed background intensified OM's sense of belonging nowhere. Mother-daughter relations were problematic, especially after the open favouritism accorded her younger brother clouded her position as a bright, only child. But she was a devoted sister, and shared her parents' grief when the young Oliver Manning was killed on active service. Memories of their Isle of Wight childhood are at the basis of *The Play Room* (1969). She later saw her formation as a novelist as being rooted in the need to justify her existence after this displacement: 'From my very earliest days, I've felt the need to explain myself, because I've felt myself so acutely in the wrong.' She also identified with the writing pattern of Katherine Mansfield, who had also published a promising early novel followed by a ten-year gap, been devastated by the loss of a brother, and felt perpetually *dépaysée*.

OM had written and painted since childhood and supplemented her pocket money with serial fiction under a pseudonym. Initially she wished to paint rather than write but, after attending a local school, the genteel poverty of a naval pension cut short OM's training at Portsmouth Technical College, and she went to London to eke out a living doing various jobs, including painting reproduction furniture. Her artist's eye was to serve her well as a novelist. Her first novel, written in the evenings, was *The Wind Changes* (1938). Her experiences at this time of being poor and single were incorporated into the later novel *The Doves of Venus* (1955).

All of OM's fiction has a basis in autobiography; 'My subject is simply life as I have experienced it, and I am happiest when writing of things I know,' she said. But her fictional personae should not be identified completely with her own personality, especially in the case of her main character, Harriet Pringle, protagonist of the Balkan and Levant trilogies. The sketches she published in *Punch, My Husband Cartwright* (1956) and her memoir on her Siamese cats, *Extraordinary Cats* (1967), counterbalance the picture of the strained, barely compatible marriage portrayed in the trilogies. These trilogies dramatize the adjustments between the introverted but acutely observant, hypersensitive Harriet and the frustratingly gregarious, left-inclined, impractical Guy, whereas the sketches indicate a woman's resilient, protective, humorous affection for, and adroit handling of, a frequently impractical and often exasperating man, who was also her best friend and critic.

It was her marriage in August 1939 to the British Council lecturer R. D. Smith which gave OM the essential material and especially the locale for her six great novels. Their first posting was to Bucharest; thence they were evacuated to Athens, then Cairo, where OM was press officer to the US embassy, and then from 1941 to 1945 to Jerusalem where she was press assistant to the Public Information Office. Her husband later worked in broadcasting and on returning to Britain was made a BBC Radio drama producer.

For OM the post-war years were largely devoted to assimilating and refining her observation of war and dislocation. She is one of the most acute and sensitive of war novelists. She was discouraged by tardy recognition from the wider reading public though she always enjoyed the respect of other writers. She was consequently pleased with paperback publication in the 1970s. In 1976 she was awarded the CBE. Her death in 1980 saw her at the peak of critical esteem, though little formal evaluation has been written to date. She included William Gerhardie and Stevie Smith among her friends, and she herself admired Patrick White and Malcolm Lowry, both, significantly, writers of books where the landscape is a powerful factor in the human drama. In addition to her fiction she also contributed to magazines and newspapers such as *The Spectator, The Sunday Times, Horizon, The Observer,* and *The New Statesman.*

Her writing is spare, exact, and pellucid. She is a mistress of tragi-comedy. Her intelligence seems truly androgynous, as for example when she depicts the masculine experience of battle in the Desert War, or portrays a shaky marriage from the standpoint of Geoffrey Lynd, focal character of *Artist Among the Missing* (1950). Her sympathies lie always with the awkward, lonely, displaced, and less robust; this could be characterized as an essentially feminine perception of art, but her achievement is so complete it renders gender characterizations redundant. CLARISSA CAMPBELL ORR

Works: *The Wind Changes* (1938); *The Remarkable Expedition* (1947); *Growing Up* (1948); *The Dreaming Shore* (1950); *Artist among the Missing* (1950); *School for Love* (1951); *A Different Face* (1953); *The Doves of Venus* (1955); *My Husband*

Cartwright (1956); *The Levant Trilogy*, comprising *The Great Fortune* (1960), *The Spoilt City* (1962), *Friends and Heroes* (1965); *A Romantic Hero* (1967); *Extraordinary Cats* (1967); *The Play Room* (1969); *The Rain Forest* (1974); *The Balkan Trilogy*, comprising *The Danger Tree* (1977), *The Battle Lost and Won* (1978), *The Sum of Things* (1980).

References: Allen, W., *Tradition and Dreams* (1965); Binding, P., 'Tribute', *New Statesman* (1 August 1980); Burgess, A., *The Novel Now* (1967); Dick, K., *Friends and Friendship* (1974); English, I., 'Introductions' to *The Play Room* (1984) and *The Doves of Venus* (1984); Lee, H., 'The ultimate alien', *Observer* (12 November 1978); Mooney, H., Jr, 'Olivia Manning: witness to history,' in *Twentieth Century Women Novelists*, ed. T. Staley (1982); Salmon, M., 'Nowhere to belong: the fiction of Olivia Manning', *Linen Hall Review* (1986).

Mansfield, Katherine

b. 14 October 1888, Wellington, New Zealand; d. 9 January 1923, Fontainebleau, France

Short story writer, poet, critic

KM's father, Harold Beauchamp, was a successful banker in Wellington, New Zealand. When she was 5 the family moved from a wealthy suburb of Wellington to Karori, a little village in the country near Wellington. From 1895 to 1898 KM attended the Karori village school. The family moved back to Wellington in 1898, and after a short period at the Wellington Girls' High School, KM was sent to Miss Swainson's school in 1899, where she edited the school magazine. KM and her older sisters were sent to Queen's College, London, in 1903. There, KM met Ida Baker, who was to remain her lifelong companion. KM resented her parents' insistence that she return to New Zealand in 1906, and spent the next two years trying to persuade them to let her go back to London and write. Her first stories were published in October 1907, in *The Native Companion*. She became involved first with Maata Mahupuku, then with Edith Bendall, but she was always restless, and in November 1907, she joined a caravan trip through the New Zealand countryside. In July 1908, she had finally managed to persuade her parents to let her return to London, and she arrived in August. Here she began a love affair with the violinist Garnet Trowell, and abruptly in March 1909, married G. C. Bowden, after only a few weeks' acquaintance. She left him the same evening. Pregnant by Trowell, she went to Germany, where she miscarried her child in late June. After her return to London, in January 1910, she was rootless and unsettled. She became involved with John Middleton Murry in 1912, and they lived together on and off for the rest of her life, marrying in May 1918. Murry was editor of a magazine, *Rhythm*, which provided an outlet for KM's work, and in 1914–15, she was briefly associated with a new journal, *Signature*. In October 1915, she suffered a great loss with the death at the Front of her brother Leslie, and, in an effort to overcome her grief, she went with Murry to the South of France. The tuburculosis which was finally to kill her had already taken hold, and for the rest of her life she was to suffer increasing physical pain and weakness. However, during the winter of 1915–16 she and Murry were idyllically happy. It was followed by a turbulent summer spent in Cornwall with D. H. Lawrence and Frieda, whose incessant quarrels irritated KM and Murry. KM's first meeting with Virginia Woolf took place in November 1916, and in 1918 the Hogarth Press published *Prelude*. KM spent the remaining few years of her life writing, and wandering restlessly between England, France, Switzerland, and Italy in an attempt to recover her health, or at least alleviate her symptoms. Sometimes Murry accompanied her; more often it was Ida Baker. Very ill, and very frightened, she became absorbed in the teachings of the mystic Gurdjieff, who promised to cure her, and she joined his community at Fontainebleau in October 1922. By January she was dead.

Critics have often commented that KM's work changes dramatically after the death of her brother. She wrote a few months afterwards, 'I want to write about my own country till I simply exhaust my store.' She saw this writing as a 'debt of love' she owed to her brother: 'especially I want to write a long elegy to you . . . perhaps not in poetry. Nor perhaps in prose. Almost certainly in a kind of *special prose*.' Indeed, KM's posthumously published *Poems*, rarely read now, read almost like her prose. For the most part they are short lyrics, concerned with childhood, the landscape, and romantic love.

But it is for the 'special prose' of her short stories that she is famous. It has been said that her writing transformed the short story as Joyce's transformed the novel, and although critics have found Symbolist and Chekhovian tendencies in her work there is in her best writing a haunted sense of beauty and terror, and of the overwrought significance of the everyday, that is hers alone.

Her first collection of stories, *In a German Pension*, was published in 1911. Critics have found many of the pieces unattractive: they reflect her experiences, exiled and alone, in a German boarding house while she awaited the birth of Trowell's child. There is an embittered sarcasm about them, and an obsession with the claustrophobia particularly of women's lives which finds powerful expression in her adaptation of a story by Chekhov, 'The-Child-Who-Was-Tired', in which a young maidservant, driven mad by a baby's incessant howling, finally smothers it with a pillow. In April 1915, KM began work on a story called 'The Aloe,' later to be published as *Prelude*. This is the first of her great New Zealand stories (others include 'At the Bay' and 'The Garden Party') which rework experiences of her childhood in a new episodic form, concentrating on colour and detail to convey the world of each character in turn. The story's symbolism is centred upon the aloe tree on the lawn of the new house: to Kezia, the child, the tree is a source of amazement; to Linda, her mother, there is something simultaneously menacing and reassuring in its ugly infertility. The story has about it a vivid inconclusiveness: it closes with the childish vision of Kezia, who has dropped and almost broken the lid of one of her aunt's jars of cosmetics. Her shame ('for Kezia it had broken the moment it flew through the air') is an image for the intensity of all the private experiences described in the story.

Not all KM's stories use multiple perspectives, however. 'Je ne parle pas français', reprinted in *Bliss and Other Stories* (1920), is a monologue which explores the stream of consciousness technique which she had first used in 'Feuille d'Album' (1917). 'Bliss' describes the immature excitement of a young hostess who at the end of the story sees her husband kissing a woman to whom she has herself been powerfully drawn. Again the story is structured around the vision of a tree: the pear tree in the garden allows a moment of communion between the two women, and its image closes the story: 'but the pear tree was as lovely as ever and as full of flower and as still.' 'The Man without a Temperament', also in *Bliss and Other Stories*, describes a man caring for his invalid wife in a hotel abroad. The tyranny of her sickness and the weariness of both their lives is revealed in details such as her awareness that he is three minutes late. The claustrophobic pathos of her cheerfulness serves to emphasize her husband's loneliness. *The Garden Party and Other Stories*, published in 1922, includes 'At the Bay', another in the sequence of stories about Kezia and her family, and 'The Garden Party,' describing Laura's experience of death during the preparations for a party, and her shame carrying down the leftovers to the family of the labourer who has died.

Her other two volumes of stories, also published posthumously, contain a mixture of early and late work. 'The Doll's House,' in *The Doves' Nest and Other Stories*, is set almost exclusively within the imaginative world of children. Kezia is fascinated by the little lamp in her new doll's house, and her fascination, as well as her family's wealth, are used to accumulate a thouand associations around the image of the lamp. Shabby Else, a village child who comes to see the dolls' house, smiles her rare smile, having been hounded in disgrace from the house: ' "I seen the little lamp", she said softly.' It is for this kind of sympathetic delicacy that KM is remembered.   SUZANNE RAITT

Works: *In a German Pension* (1911); *Prelude* (1918); *Je ne parle pas français* (1920); *Bliss and Other Stories* (1920); *The Garden Party and Other Stories*, (1922); *The Doves' Nest and Other Stories*, ed. J. M. Murry (1923); *Poems*, ed. J. M. Murry (1923); *Something Childish and Other Stories*, ed. J. M. Murry (1924); *The Journal of Katherine Mansfield*, 2 vols, ed. J. M. Mury (1928); *The Aloe*, ed. J. M. Murry (1930); *Novels and Novelists*, ed. J. M. Murry (1930); *The Scrapbook of Katherine Mansfield*, ed. J. M. Murry (1937); *Katherine Mansfield's Letters to John Middleton Murry, 1913–1922*, ed. J. M. Murry (1937); *Undiscovered Country; The New Zealand Stories of Katherine Mansfield*, ed. I. A. Gordon (1974); *The Urewera Notebook*, ed. I. A. Gordon (1978); *Collected Letters of Katherine Mansfield 1903–1917*, ed. V. O'Sullivan and M. Scott (1984).

References: Aiken, C., 'The short story as poetry', in *Collected Criticism* (1968); Alpers, A., *The Life of Katherine Mansfield* (1982); Bateson, F. W. and Shahevitch, B., 'Katherine Mansfield's "The Fly": a critical exercise', *Essays in Criticism* 12, 1 (1962); Berkman, S., *Katherine Mansfield: A Critical Study* (1951); Bowen, E., 'Introduction' to *Thirty-Four Stories* (1957); Daly, S. R., *The Fiction of Katherine Mansfield* (1965); Gordon, I. A., *Katherine Mansfield* (1954); Hankin, C. A., *Katherine Mansfield and Her Confessional Stories* (1983); Hanson, C. and Gurr, A., *Katherine Mansfield* (1981); Mantz, R. E., *The Critical Bibliography of Katherine Mansfield* (1931); Meyers, J., *Katherine Mansfield: A Biography* (1978) *Modern Fiction Studies* 24, 3, issue on KM (1978–9); Moore, J., *Gurdjieff and Katherine Mansfield* (1980); Murry, J. M., *Katherine Mansfield and Other Literary Portraits* (1949); Porter, K. A., 'The art of Katherine Mansfield', *Nation* (23 October 1937); Pritchett, V. S., 'Review of *Collected Stories*', *New Statesman* (2 February 1946); Schneider, E., 'Katherine Mansfield and Chekhov', *Modern Language Notes*, 50 (June 1935); Stead, C. K., 'Katherine Mansfield and the art of fiction', *New Review* 4, 42 (September 1977).

Marryat, Florence

b. 9 July 1838, Brighton; d. 27 October 1899, St John's Wood, London
Novelist
FM was the youngest of the eleven children of Captain Frederick Marryat (also a novelist, best remembered for *The Children of the New Forest*) and Catherine Shairp. She was educated by governesses at home, but claimed to have gained more 'real learning' from her own voracious reading. In 1854, at the age of 16, she married T. Ross Church, afterwards a colonel in the Madras Staff Corps, and with him travelled extensively in India. (This was to lead to *'Gup': Sketches of Indian Life and Character*, 1868). They had eight children.

Her first novel, *Love's Conflict* (1865), was written in the intervals between nursing her children who were sick with scarlet fever. Between then and her death she published a vast number of novels, many of which were translated into several languages and became popular on both sides of the Atlantic. She was able to educate all her children through the profits. She also published, in 1872, the *Life and Letters of Captain Marryat* in two volumes, and from 1872 to 1876 edited the periodical *London Society*.

Her talents extended far beyond novel writing. She went on stage after a long illness, when doctors recommended a break from writing, and acted in a drama of her own, *Her World*, produced in London in 1881. She was in addition an operatic singer, lecturer, and light entertainer on both sides of the Atlantic (she gave a comic lecture entitled 'Women of the Future (1991), or, What Shall We Do Without Men?'), and manager of a school of journalism.

In 1890, after her husband's death, FM married Colonel Francis Lean of the Royal Marine Light Infantry. At around this time she became interested in spiritualism and, although a Roman Catholic, was granted permission by her director to pursue research into the subject. *There is No Death* (1891) is a detailed acount of the various mediums with whom she came into contact and of the seances she attended. It evoked a strong response and led to many conversions to spiritualism. Other books on the subject include *The Risen Dead* (1891) and *The Spirit World* (1894). FM continued to write prolifically until her death.

FM is remembered as a practitioner of the sensation novel, a form combining the melodrama and romance of the Gothic genre with a domestic setting and all its Victorian taboos, the invasion of the latter by the former often leading to tragedy. The plots centre upon mésalliances, loveless marriages, and crimes of passion, while the characters are stereotypes: glamorous and calculating anti-heroines like Lady Ethel Carr in *Her Lord and Master* (1871) provide an antidote to the prosaically respectable heroines, while heartless rakes subvert the moral and social order, allowing the novelist to deal with license, illicit sex, and violent crime under cover of pious moralizing. *A Crown of Shame* (1888) typifies this paradigm. Like many of FM's novels, it has a colonial setting, in this case a plantation in San Diego. The plantation owner's glamorous daughter Maraquita has an illegitimate child by the caddish and cruel overseer Henri de Courcelles, who is engaged to the stolid but morally impeccable Lizzie Fellows. Together, de Courcelles and Maraquita contrive to attribute their child to Lizzie, thus protecting Maraquita's reputation and giving de Courcelles an excuse for breaking off his engagement. Maraquita is, however, guilty of a double duplicity. Deeming de Courcelles to be socially beneath her, she aspires to a marriage with Sir Russell Johnstone, the Governor of San Diego. Once married to Sir Russell, she finds that her passion for de Courcelles increases, inducing her to confess her sin, thus losing her good name, a loss which, FM informs us, 'good women dread above everything'. De Courcelles, meanwhile, is murdered by a native woman whom he had seduced.

That FM's fictional world is one in which those who shirk their duty are severely punished is made particularly clear in *Love's Conflict* (1865), in which Elfrida Salisbury marries the heartless William Traherne in haste to repent at leisure, finding his brother far more companionable. Tellingly, the author's moralizing is directed at Elfrida for allowing her thoughts to stray, rather than at William for his brute selfishness. The authorial interventions have obvious parallels with those in Mrs Henry Wood's *East Lynne*: 'Her [Elfrida's] eyes were opened now – opened to the fact that her worse than folly – her sin, in marrying a man she did not care for – had brought upon her a trial which she should have to bear as best she might, to her deathbed, perhaps. . . .' Eventually, much to the narrator's approval, she 'takes up [her] cross patiently', and arrives at a muted reconciliation with her husband, living 'a life of duty, and therefore a life of peace', thus avoiding a fate like that of Mrs Wood's Lady Isabella Vane. A similar pattern is followed in the short story 'A Moment of Madness', where the glamorous and flirtatious Mabel Moore threatens an already precarious marriage in which Roland Tresham shows nothing but contempt for his overworked wife, but a brief infidelity is followed by penitence and resignation to the divine marriage bond.   ANNE FERNIHOUGH

Selected works: *Love's Conflict* (1865); *Woman Against Woman* (1865); *Too Good For Him* (1865); *For Ever and Ever: A Drama of Life* (1866); *'Gup': Sketches of Indian Life and Character* (1868); *Véronique* (1869); *The Girls of Feversham* (1869); *The Prey of the Gods* (1871) *Her Lord and Master* (1871); *Life and Letters of Captain Marryat* (1872); *Mad Dumaresq* (1873); *Sybil's Friend and How She Found Him* (1874); *Fighting the Air* (1875); *My Own Child* (1876); *Hidden Chains* (1876); *A Harvest of Wild Oats* (1877); *Written in Fire* (1878); *A Little Stepson* (1878); *A Scarlet Sin* (1880); *The Root of All Evil* (1880); *The Fair-Haired Alda* (1880); *With Cupid's Eyes* (1881); *Phyllida* (1882); *How They Loved Him* (1882); *Facing the Footlights* (with Sir C. L. Young) (1882); *A Moment of Madness and Other Stories* (1883); *The Heart of Jane Warner* (1885); *The Master Passion* (1886); *A Crown of Shame* (1888); *A Fatal Silence* (1891); *The Risen Dead* (1891); *There Is No Death* (1891); *How Like a Woman* (1892); *Parson Jones* (1893); *The Spirit World* (1894); *A Bankrupt Heart* (1894); *The Beautiful Soul* (1895); *The Strange Transfiguration of Hannah Stubbs* (1896); *A Rational Marriage* (1899); *The Folly of Alison* (1899).

References: Allibone; Black, H. C., *Notable Women Authors of the Day* (1893); *DNB*; Hamilton, C. J., 'Interview with Florence Marryat', *Womanhood III* (1899–1900); Hays, F., *Women of the Day* (1885); Plarr, V., *Men and Women of the Time* (1895); Showalter, E., *A Literature of Their Own* (1977).

Marsh, Ngaio

b. 23 April 1899, Christchurch, New Zealand; d. 18 February 1982, Christchurch

Detective novelist

In her autobiography NM described her experience as a director of amateur and student theatrical groups as her most fulfilling work, but it was the income from her detective novels that enabled her to do this, and it is these novels that have made her probably New Zealand's best-known writer after Katherine Mansfield.

Although an only child (of Henry Edmund and Rose Elizabeth (*née*) Seager Marsh) who never married, NM's many uncles, aunts, and cousins provided her with family in most parts of the British Commonwealth. Her second name (pronounced Ny-o) is Maori, its use indicating her strong identification with her native land. She was educated at Christchurch, first at a local school run by a Victorian gentlewoman, then at St Margaret's College, and finally at Canterbury University College School of Art. NM intended to be a professional painter, but she had also begun to write and, when she showed an original play to Allen Wilkie, the Shakespearean director/manager invited her to join his company for a tour of New Zealand and Australia from 1920 to 1923. In 1928 she travelled to England to visit friends and stayed on to run a gift and interior design shop. She had been writing articles for a paper in New Zealand and, having read a detective story, decided to try her own. *A Man Lay Dead* was published in 1934, and NM was launched on a career in crime fiction that continued for forty-eight years until her death.

Back in New Zealand she drove a Red Cross truck during the Second World War, continued to write detective novels, and began working with drama students at Canterbury University. From 1944 to 1952 she was a producer for the D. D. O'Connor Theatre Management, and in 1946 she became director of the Canterbury University College Student Players, the first all-New Zealand Shakespeare Company. Among the honours NM received – OBE (1948), CBE (1966), D. Litt. from Canterbury University (1963), The Mystery Writers of America Grand Master Award (1977) – perhaps none meant more than having the new University Theatre at Canterbury named after her in 1962. The last novel, *Light Thickens*, published after her death in 1982, focused on a production of *Macbeth*, a final statement of NM's love of Shakespearean drama.

One of the quartet of *grandes dames* of the Golden Age of detective writing (along with Christie, Sayers, and Allingham), NM saw her work as falling between that of Christie and Sayers. Like Sayers she tried to create realistic characters rather than the two-dimensional heroes of the classic puzzle tradition of Conan Doyle and Christie. But she criticized Sayers for becoming too interested in the complex psychology of her detective in her later books and allowing his personality to overwhelm her mystery. NM's detective, Roderick Alleyn, is more developed than Hercule Poirot, but he is never given the tortured humanity of Peter Wimsey. Alleyn may have aristocratic relatives, but he is also a professional policeman who has a team of investigators to collect data for him. The novels generally follow the same pattern. After a murder, which is often bizarre and sometimes brutal, Alleyn visits the scene of the crime, painstakingly searching for physical clues, reviews the evidence collected by his technical staff, interviews those associated with the victim, discusses the case with someone (usually the devoted Inspector Fox, but sometimes an amateur Watson), reveals that he knows the murderer, and calls all the suspects together, in some cases even reconstructing the crime. Not a particularly ingenious plotter, NM keeps readers' attention with her memorable characters, her fine ear for dialogue, and her ability to set scenes. Although she uses the traditional English country house setting in nine of the novels, most memorable are those with important scenes in theatres. Training in art made her especially sensitive to visual detail, and provided a realistic background for the novels in which the painter Agatha Troy (later Mrs Alleyn) appears.   FRANCES ARNDT

Works: *A Man Lay Dead* (1934); *Enter a Murderer* (1935); *The Nursing-Home Murder*, with Henry Jellett (1935); *Death in Ecstasy* (1936); *Vintage Murder* (1937); *Artists in Crime* (1938); *Death in a White Tie* (1938); *Overture to Death* (1939); *Death at the Bar* (1940); *Surfeit of Lampreys* (1940; published in the US as *Death of a Peer*); *Death and the Dancing Footman* (1941); *Colour Scheme* (1943); *Died in the Wool* (1945); *Final Curtain* (1947); *Swing, Brother, Swing* (1949; published in the US as *A Wreath for Rivera*); *Opening Night* (1951; published in the US as *Night at the Vulcan*; *Spinsters in Jeopardy* (1953); *Scales of Justice* (1955); *Off with His Head* (1956; published in the US as *Death of a Fool*); *Singing in the Shrouds* (1958); *False Scent* (1960); *Hand in Glove* (1962); *Dead Water* (1963); *Black Beech and Honeydew* (1965); *Death at the Dolphin* (1966; published in the US as *Killer Dolphin*); *A Clutch of Constables* (1968); *When in Rome* (1970); *Tied Up in Tinsel* (1972); *Black as He's Painted* (1974); *Last Ditch* (1977); *Grave Mistake* (1978); *Photo Finish* (1980); *Light Thickens* (1982); NM has also written several plays, and works on New Zealand and on drama.

References: Bargainnier, E. F., 'Ngaio Marsh', in *10 Women of Mystery*, ed. E. F. Bargainnier (1981); Bertram, M. A., article in *CMW*; Dooley, A. C. and Dooley, L. J., 'Rereading Ngaio Marsh', in *Art and Crime Writing: Essays on Detective Fiction*, ed. B. Benstock (1983); Haycraft, H., *Murder for Pleasure: The Life and Times of the Detective Story*; Hipolito, J., analytic review of *Tied Up in Tinsel* and *When in Rome*, in *The Mystery and Detection Annual*, ed. D. Adams (1972); Panet, L. L., *Watteau's Shepherd: The Detective Novel in Britain 1914–1940* (1979); Shadbolt, M., 'Ngaio Marsh', in *Love and Legend: Some 20th Century New Zealanders* (1976).

Marsh-Caldwell, Anne

b. 1791, Linley Wood, Staffordshire; d. 5 October 1834, Linley Wood
Novelist
(Also wrote under Anne Marsh, Mrs Marsh)
AM-C was the fourth child of the Staffordshire landowner and Deputy-Lieutenant of the county, James Caldwell and his wife, Elizabeth. She married a failed banker, Arthur Cuthbert Marsh, in 1817 and had seven children with him. When her brother James died in 1858, AM-C inherited the family estate at Linley Wood, and resumed her maiden name. She published anonymously because, as Harriet Martineau remarked, 'a father of many daughters did not wish their mother to be known as the author of what the world might consider second-rate novels.' Although Martineau considered inferior AM-C's works after *The Admiral's Daughter* (1834), which she admired, these novels were in fact very popular. In 1857 her collected works were published by Hodgson's 'Parlour Library' in fifteen volumes.

In the preface to *Emilia Wyndham* (1846), one of her most successful works, AM-C wrote that 'the object . . . of the novelist should be, not so much to illustrate a particular moral maxim as to point the tale of life – to bring actions and their consequences, passions, principles and their result into that sort of connexion, which, though it certainly and inevitably takes place in actual life, escapes the careless, or, perhaps, undiscerning eye of the reader'. AM-C's works follow the form of the fashionable novel of the 1820s and 1830s in contrasting the selfish indulgence in subversive passions with the need to follow duty selflessly in order to maintain the moral precepts on which the stability of society rests. The figure of the fallen woman, savagely punished for following her passions and neglecting her duty, was popular in the didactic novel, and she appears in *The Admiral's Daughter* as 'that penitent and broken Magdalene', Inêz. Married to a man she respects but does not love, Inêz has a passionate affair with his best friend, which destroys her family and causes the deaths of both men. Spiritual redemption comes through suffering; 'pain, humiliation, sorrow were not only the natural consequences of her fault, but the means of regeneration, the means of purifying her soul from the pollution into which it had fallen.' Social redemption, however, never occurs. Unfit to see her husband or her children, Inêz attends Harry disguised as a nurse, and lives with her children as their French governess.

Emilia Wyndham, written twelve years after *The Admiral's Daughter*, marks a shift in attitude towards the fallen woman. Lisa, neglected by her uncaring husband, nearly drifts into an affair with a philandering duke, but is fortunately prevented from doing so. She recovers her position in her family and in society because of the equal guilt of her husband who has neglected his duty to her. She is never condoned, but she is treated with a new sympathy. The heroine of the novel, Emilia, marries a seemingly cold-hearted lawyer, Mr Danby, in order to save her destitute father from a lunatic asylum, and herself from poverty. She suppresses her feelings for her childhood sweetheart, Colonel Lennox, who condemns society's morality in demanding this constant self-sacrifice from her, but who also blames Emilia for her apparently hypocritical devotion to her husband: 'You never had a heart – you never knew what it was to have a heart: you are a cold, calculating, conventional being – and you call *that* morality!' Yet Emilia is rewarded for her dutiful regard for Danby by a child and by a mutual and respectful love with her husband which is far more stable and lasting than her former passion for Lennox.

Women must do their duty, AM-C suggests in her later novels, but, since this is the case, men must be attentive to the needs of women. Without this reciprocity, social stability is ruined, and the individual's life becomes 'the slow, silent, death-struggle of the soul in solitude, darkness and obscurity, against the heavy, wearying, every-day evils of every-day actual life'.

CAROLINE COLEMAN

Works: *Two Old Men's Tales: The Deformed, and The Admiral's Daughter* (1834); *Tales of Woods and Fields* (1836); *The Triumphs of Time* (1844); *Mount Sorel, or, The Heiress of the de Veres* (1845); *Aubrey* (1846); *Father Darcy* (1846); *Emilia Wyndham* (1846); *Norman's Bridge, or, The Modern Midas* (1847); *The Protestant Revolution in France, or, The History of the Huguenots* (1847); *Angela, or, The Captain's Daughter* (1848); *Mordaunt Hall, or, A September Night* (1849); *Tales of the First French Revolution* (1849); *Lettice Arnold* (1850); *The Wilmingtons* (1850); *Ravenscliffe* (1851); *Time the Avenger* (1851); *Castle Avon* (1852); *The Longwoods of the Grange* (1853); *The Song of Roland as Chanted before the Battle of Hastings by the Minstrel Taillefer* (1854); *The Heiress of Houghton, or, The Mother's Secret* (1855); *Woman's Devotion* (1855); *Evelyn Marston* (1856); *Mr and Mrs Ashton* (1860); *The Valley of a Hundred Fires* (1861); *The Ladies of Lovel-Leigh* (1862); *Chronicles of Dartmoor* (1866); *Lords and Ladies* (1866); *The Rose of Ashurst* (1867); *A Book of Heroines* (1869).

References: Allibone; Colby, V., *Yesterday's Woman: Domestic Realism in the English Novel* (1974); Cruse, A., *The Victorians and Their Books* (1935); *DNB*; Martineau, H., *Autobiography* (1877); Mitchell, S., *The Fallen Angel: Chastity, Class and Women's Reading, 1835–1880* (1981).

Martineau, Harriet

b. 1802, Norwich, Norfolk; d. 1876, Ambleside, Cumberland

Journalist, historian, novelist, autobiographer, travel writer, writer for children

Termed the 'national instructor' for her zeal in popularizing information for the improvement of her compatriots, HM produced more than fifty books, manifold contributions to journals, and over 1,600 leaders in the *Daily News* (1851–66). A fighter for freedom, she wrote on behalf of the repeal of the Corn Laws, Forest and Game Laws, and Contagious Diseases Act, the breaking up of monopolies, the abolition of slavery in America, and equal opportunities for women. Her *Autobiography* (1877) throws light on a period of rapid change in its story of a penniless deaf girl's rise to international fame and her conversion from deep-rooted Christian faith to science as the world's panacea. She wrote one novel, *Deerbrook* (1839), much admired by Charlotte Brontë and a forerunner of George Eliot's *Middlemarch* (1870–1) in its analysis of provincial life, its doctor hero, and its awareness of unsung and frustrated women.

Described by Elizabeth Barrett as 'the most manlike woman in three kingdoms', HM owed much to her upbringing among tough-minded Dissenters. HM's father, Thomas Martineau, manufactured bombazine. His reversal of fortune and subsequent death after the crash of 1825–6 explains her early interest in economics and sometimes surprising sympathy for employers, as in her opposition to factory legislation urged by Dickens in the 1860s. HM was the third daughter, the sixth of eight children, born to Elizabeth Rankin Martineau, daughter of a Newcastle sugar refiner. She idolized her younger brother James, later a renowned Unitarian preacher and moral philosopher. Her comment that 'sisters can never be to brothers, what brothers are to sisters' had poignancy, for their relationship did not survive his harsh review of her book avowing atheism, *Letters on the Laws of Man's Nature and Development* (1851), co-authored by Henry Atkinson.

She described her childhood as 'wretched', and 'the winter' of her life. Pitifully anxious, she suffered from indigestion, had no sense of smell or taste, and became increasingly deaf in her teens. Not until 1830 did she adopt her ubiquitous ear-trumpet. She later advocated in *Household Education* (1849) that children be raised in an atmosphere of freedom and affection, for she had by then observed the beneficial effects of such an upbringing in America. Yet she grew very like her sensible and well-read mother, whose satirical eye saw through the pretensions of Norfolk society, and even shared her love of housekeeping and needlework. The Martineaus educated their children for independence. HM studied the classics at home and learnt French and English composition at the local boys' school from 1813 to 1815. She flowered intellectually in 1817–18 in the home of her cousins and aunt, who kept a school in Bristol. There she learnt German and was influenced by Lant Carpenter, a disciple of Priestley and Hartley, into believing that man and society were governed by discernible laws or principles and that it was her duty to act in accordance with them.

Life for HM thus became a matter of laying bare principles, illustrating them, and acting upon them in her own life. She made her reputation by illustrating the principles of political economy in a series of stories filling nine volumes – *Illustrations of Political Economy* (1832–4) – and was spelling out principles thirty years later in *Health, Husbandry, and Handicraft* (1861), on the management of her two-acre farm near Ambleside. Her Victorian sense of mission was so strong that she felt her career could not accommodate marriage. Thus she never regretted her abortive engagement in 1826 to John Worthington, a schoolfellow of James's, who died after a mental breakdown. Nevertheless, the confession of the spinster governess Maria in *Deerbrook*, of a devastating passion that took her unawares and of unrequited love, hints that HM knew what it was to love. She said she wrote the novel to relieve pent-up emotions.

Her literary bent, indicated early on by her love of *Paradise Lost* at the age of 7, became obvious with her anonymous first publication, 'Female Writers on Practical Divinity', in the Unitarian *Monthly Repository* (1822), which, ironically, her eldest brother read out to her as an example of fine writing. Her first books – *Devotional Exercises* (1823) and *Addresses with Prayers and with Original Hymns* (1826) – reflected her religious outlook. Under the tutelage of William Johnson Fox, editor of the *Repository* from 1827, she wrote poems, essays, reviews, and stories, all without pay until the failure of the family business in 1829; then he paid her £15 a year. To make a living, she had to write at night and ply her needle by day. She composed in lucid prose almost as fast as her pen could move, and the works poured forth: *Tradition of Palestine* (1830); three prize theological essays for the Unitarian Association in 1831–2; and before her thirtieth birthday, the first captivating monthly number of *Illustrations of Political Economy*, which made her a celebrity.

For the Shropshire publisher Houlston she had already written *The Rioters* (1827), about machine breaking, and *The Turn-out* (1829), about wage disputes. But it was her grand series of twenty-five numbers on political economy which showed her interpretative genius in learning up masses of material and feeding it to her readers in entertaining pictures of life. In her preface to the series, addressed to all classes, she argued that it was in everyone's interest to understand the science of political economy so that by mutual effort the nation could be brought under the same firm management as one's household. She proposed to illustrate basic principles through pictures of society from simple beginnings to the complexities resulting from the Industrial Revolution. For her organizational scheme, she was indebted to *Elements of Political Economy* (1821–2) by James Mill, father of John Stuart Mill. Her first number, *Life in the Wilds*, proved irresistible in its account of the survival of English settlers in South Africa left destitute by ravaging Bushmen, a survival made possible by division of labour and distribution of wealth, whether honey from a tree or firewood collected by children. The first 1,500 copies sold out and 5,000 more were demanded.

Her success secured, HM moved to London with her mother and aunt from 1833 to 1839. Under the urging of Brougham, the Lord Chancellor, she wrote *Poor Laws and Paupers Illustrated* (1833–4), and for Charles Fox, with information supplied by the Chancellor of the Exchequer, *Illustrations of Taxation* (1834). Malthus, Coleridge, Sidney Smith, Browning, and Macready were numbered among her friends.

Touring America in 1834 to 1836 she was lionized by both North and South until she attended an abolitionist meeting in Boston and reasserted the anti-slavery views she had expressed in *Demerara*, one of the *Illustrations of Political Economy* stories. Then she was deemed an 'incendiary foreigner' and had to avoid Ohio, where there was a plot to lynch her. But she made good friends, such as Maria Weston Chapman, whom she later entrusted with completing her autobiography. Books resulting from her trip were *Society in America* (1837), in which she measured the practices of a country suppressing the political freedom of women and allowing slavery against its proclaimed freedoms, and *Retrospect of Western Travel* (1838), a more anecdotal and popular account.

Deerbrook (1839), published in the year of *Nicholas Nickleby*, showed Dickensian concern in its depiction of the depressed conditions of the late 1820s and early 1830s, made worse by an epidemic, like the dreaded cholera, decimating the poor because of lack of sanitation. But she had modelled the novel on Jane Austen, with a pair of 'sense' and 'sensibility' sisters settling in gossipy Deerbrook and after various tribulations finding conjugal bliss with the local doctor and law student. The contrived plot, unalleviated by Austen's wit or dialogue, makes the enlightened middle class, HM's own class, the saviours of lawless Deerbrook. The novel's chief interest lies in its play of ideas, power struggles, and sensitivity to woman's lot – her vulnerable sexuality and restricted opportunities.

After the exertion of writing *Deerbrook*, she suffered from an ovarian cyst, and was an invalid in Tynemouth for five years. She caused a sensation when she announced herself cured by mesmerism, the rage in the 1840s. Recovery was followed by *Letters on Mesmerism* (1845), first published in the *Athenaeum*.

From her invalid couch, she had produced a romantic history of the black President of Haiti, Toussaint L'Ouverture, in *The Hour and the Man* (1840), as well as a popular series of children's stories, including *The Crofton Boys*, entitled *The Playfellow* (1841), and *Life in the Sickroom* (1843). During her illness friends raised £1,400 to be invested in annuities for her; she had twice refused a civil list pension, believing it would compromise her politically.

Recovered, HM enjoyed what she called 'the summer' of her life, the years 1845 to 1854. She revelled in domesticity at 'The Knoll'. There she managed her two-acre farm, set up a building society, and lectured the locals on American history, the Middle East, and sanitation. Many friends, including Emerson, Macready, Charlotte Brontë, and George Eliot, visited her there, and she remained as prolific as ever. *Eastern Life, Past and Present* (1848) resulted from her trip in 1847–8 to Egypt, Palestine, and the Sinai, and her consequent belief that the world's great religions had bubbled up from the same source. Such relativism undermined her faith and prepared the way for the atheism she endorsed under the influence of Henry Atkinson. Whatever credibility she lost by reference to Atkinson as her master, she regained with the publication of two remarkable works: her two-volume *History of England during the Thirty Years' Peace, 1816–1846* (1849–50), a valuable source for future historians, and her rendering of Comte's six-volume opus into two lucid volumes of English prose, *The Positive Philosophy of Auguste Comte* (1853), a text much admired that gave her contemporaries access to the scientific philosophy so popular in the 1840s and 1850s. As HM pointed out, he provided an anchor for intellectuals adrift, those 'alienated for ever from the kind of faith which sufficed for all in an organic period which has passed away'.

HM also contributed to periodicals, particularly the radical *Westminster Review* and the *Edinburgh Review*, and wrote regularly for Dickens's *Household Words* until she clashed with him over his anti-Catholicism and depiction of women. While translating Comte, she had begun writing leaders for the *Daily News* and she continued to contribute until 1866, sometimes as many as six articles a week.

In 1855 she wrote her *Autobiography* at breakneck speed in the belief that she was about to die. Though uneven in quality and defensive in tone, its two fat volumes provide a fascinating female success story, sharp if often uncharitable vignettes of her contemporaries, and insight into a period of radical reform.

TAMIE WATTERS

Selected works: *Devotional Exercises* (1823); *Addresses, with Prayers and Original Hymns* (1826); *Principle and Practice, or, The Orphan Family* (1827); *The Rioters* (1827); *The Turn-Out* (1829); *Traditions of Palestine* (1830); *Five Years of Youth, or, Sense and Sentiment* (1831); *Illustrations of Political Economy* (1832–4); *Poor Laws and Paupers Illustrated* (1833–4); *Illustrations of Taxation* (1834); *Miscellanies* (1836); *Society in America* (1837); *Retrospect of Western Travel* (1838); *How to Observe: Morals and Manners* (1838); *The Martyr Age of the United States* (1839); *Deerbrook* (1839); *The Hour and the Man* (1841); *Life in the Sick-Room* (1843); *Letters on Mesmerism* (1845); *Forest and Game-Law Tales* (1845); *Eastern Life, Past and Present* (1848); *Household Education* (1849); *History of England during the Thirty Years' Peace, 1816–1846* (1849–50); *Introduction to 'The History of the Peace', 1800–1815* (1851); *Letters on the Laws of Man's Nature and Development* (with H. G. Atkinson) (1851); *Letters from Ireland* (1852); (trans. and condensed), *The Positive Philosophy of Auguste Comte* (1853); *The Factory Controversy: A Warning against Meddling Legislation* (1855); *A History of the American Compromise* (1856); *British Rule in India* (1857); *The Manifest Destiny of the American Union* (1857); *England and her Soldiers* (1859); *Health, Husbandry, and Handicraft, or, Our Two-Acre Farm* (1861); *The History of England from the Commencement of the Nineteenth*

Century to the Crimean War (1864); *Autobiography, with Memorials by Maria Weston Chapman* (1877); *Harriet Martineau's Letters to Fanny Wedgwood*, ed. E. S. Arbuckle (1983); *Harriet Martineau on Women*, ed. C. G. Yates (1985).

References: *BA* (19); Bosanquet, T., *Harriet Martineau: An Essay in Comprehension* (1927); Miller, F. F., *Harriet Martineau* (1884); Pichanick, V. K., *Harriet Martineau: The Woman and Her Work* (1980); Rivlin, J. B., *Harriet Martineau: A Bibliography of Her Separately Printed Works* (1947); Sanders, V., *Reason over Passion: Harriet Martineau and the Victorian Novel* (1986); Spender, D., 'Harriet Martineau', in *Women of Ideas* (1982); Thomas, G., *Harriet Martineau* (1985); Walters, M., 'The rights and wrongs of women: Mary Wollstonecraft, Harriet Martineau, Simone de Beauvoir', in *The Rights and Wrongs of Women*, ed. J. Mitchell and A. Oakley (1976); Webb, R. K., *Harriet Martineau: A Radical Victorian* (1960); Weiner, G., 'Harriet Martineau: a reassessment', in *Feminist Theorists*, ed. D. Spender (1983); Weiner, G., 'Introductions' to *Deerbrook* (1983) and *Harriet Martineau's Autobiography* (1983); Wheatley, V., *The Life and Work of Harriet Martineau* (1957).

Marx, Eleanor

b. 16 January 1855, London; d. 31 March 1898, London
Political essayist and theorist, editor, translator
EM became, through her speaking, writing, and organizing, one of the foremost figures of British socialism. The third surviving daughter of Karl Marx and Julia (*née* von Westphalen) Marx, EM grew up in a household where concern for the international radical movement mixed easily with the domestic concerns of a close family. EM worked briefly as a tutor in French at a girls' school, later as a paid researcher in the British Museum. She translated from the French *History of the Commune of 1871* by Prosper Olivier Lissagary, to whom EM had been engaged, but her father's opposition led EM to end the relationship. She also translated from French Flaubert's *Madame Bovary*, and from German Georgii Plekhanov's *Anarchism and Socialism*, and she learned Norwegian in order to translate Ibsen's *An Enemy of the People*. EM trained as an actress and gave lectures on Shakespeare; although she never pursued a career in the theatre, her dramatic skill made her a popular political speaker. In 1883, the year of her father's death, EM began contributing essays to political journals and assisting Frederick Engels in the editing of her father's papers. In 1884, she formed a union with Edward Aveling, a trained scientist who became a political journalist, playwright, and critic. Aveling was married at the time but had been separated from his wife for ten years. EM's union with Aveling resulted in a literary partnership as well; *The Factory Hell* in 1885 was the first of their jointly authored publications about the conditions of working-class life. In 1886, EM and Aveling went to the United States on a fifteen-week speaking tour of the north-east and mid-west under the sponsorship of the Socialist Labour Party. Their meetings with the rank and file, as well as with the leaders of the trade union movement, resulted in EM's major work, *The Working Class Movement in America*. In this work, after surveying the intimate details of the domestic life of American workers, EM noted the absence of 'studies of factory hands and tenement dwellers' in American fiction. 'Yet these types will be, must be dealt with,' she predicted, 'and one of these days the Uncle Tom's Cabin of capitalism will be written.'

After returning to England, EM was active in the trade union movement, claiming membership in the working class because of her self-employment as a hired typist. She participated in several strikes, proving especially effective in organizing women factory workers, and agitated for the eight-hour workday. She served as translator for international conferences of workers and socialists, as well as performing countless behind-the-scenes tasks. In observance of May Day 1893, EM wrote her only historical, and most scholarly, work, *Der Böse Maitag*, an account of the night of 1 May 1517 when the London mobs attacked the homes of the hated foreigners living in the city. In 1896, EM edited Frederick Engel's *Revolution and Counter-Revolution, or, Germany in 1848*. Her father's letters on the Crimean War, *The Eastern Question*, which EM edited with Aveling, were published the following year. Her last editions of her father's work, Marx's *The Secret Diplomatic History of the Eighteenth Century* and *The Story of the Life of Lord Palmerston*, were published separately in 1899, the year following EM's death. In June 1897 Aveling, whose wife had died in 1892, secretly married a 22-year-old woman. Distraught when she learned the truth, EM committed suicide by taking prussic acid. Aveling, gravely ill, survived her by four months.

EM dealt with political issues in a straightforward and disarmingly down-to-earth way, a style that probably emerged from her experience as an organizer and lecturer to working-class audiences. In *The Working Class Movement in America* EM documents workers' lives in concrete ways; their hours and earnings are set beside the cost and price of the product. Wages are shown in the context of the cost of living. In Philadelphia, for example, 'the average wages paid to saleswomen and girls employed in clerical work does not exceed 5 dollars per week. On this they have to dress well in order to keep their position. Board and room at the lowest figure 3 dollars, not counting laundry work, which also has to come from the 5 dollars.' Argument is expressed in terms of dollars and cents, dialogue and anecdote. This vividness is also reflected in *The Woman Question*, where EM takes issue with contemporary feminists for 'agitating for woman suffrage, or admission to the universities and learned professions' and ignoring economics, for 'without that larger social change women will never be free'. Along with economic equality, EM here insisted upon sexual equality for women, an issue which suffragists avoided, fearful of the charge of promoting promiscuity. Under the double standard, EM argued passionately, an unmarried woman who gratified her 'sex instinct' was a pariah; after marriage, 'adultery for her is a crime, for him a venial offence.'

SANDRA ADICKES

Selected works: *The Factory Hell* (with E. Aveling) (1885); *The Chicago Anarchists* (with E. Aveling) (1887); *The Woman Question* (with E. Aveling) (1887); *The Working Class Movement in America* (with E. Aveling) (1887); *Shelley's Socialism* (with E. Aveling) (1888); *A Doll's House Repaired* (with Israel Zangwill) (1891); *Report from Great Britain and Ireland* (1891 Brussels Congress); *Der Böse Maitag* (1893); 'Stray Notes on Karl Marx' (n.d.); *The Working Class Movement in England* (1895).

References: Ellis, H., 'Eleanor Marx', *Modern Monthly* 9 (1935); Kapp, Y., *Eleanor Marx* (1972–6); Meier, O., (ed.), *The Daughters of Karl Marx: Family Correspondence 1866–1898*, trans. F. Evans (1982); Tsuzuki, C., *The Life of Eleanor Marx, 1855–98: A Socialist Tragedy* (1967).

Mavor, Elizabeth

b. 17 December 1927, Glasgow

Historian, novelist

EM was educated at St Leonard's School, St Andrews, and at Oxford University, where she read History and was the first woman to edit *Cherwell*. She is a distinguished historian of the eighteenth century, best known for her sympathetic and deeply researched study of *The Ladies of Llangollen* (1971), which illuminates the phenomenon of romantic friendship between women. She has also examined the life of another eighteenth-century woman who flouted convention, the bigamist Elizabeth Chudleigh. As suits the subject, her biography is written with bravura and zest, based on a scholarly grounding in the letters, literary personalities, and legal niceties of the period.

A writer from childhood, when she contributed to children's magazines, she was already a reviewer and occasional journalist when she made her debut as a novelist in the Hutchinson New Authors series. *Summer in the Greenhouse* (1959) takes the viewpoint of a determined and precocious 9-year-old who unwittingly engineers a reunion between her grandfather and an early sweetheart; it has both charm and ironic restraint. Coincidentally with her study of eighteenth-century romantic friendship she explored the same theme in a modern context in her novel *A Green Equinox* (1973), shortlisted for the Booker Prize in 1972. Her novels tend to be set among characters who have cultivated tastes as well as a passion for the past; their lyricism is balanced by an attractive astringency stemming undoubtedly from her admiration for the adroit clarity of Augustan models, and perhaps also from her descent from Congreve.

CLARISSA CAMPBELL ORR

Works: *Summer in the Greenhouse* (1959); *The Temple of Flora* (1961); *The Virgin Mistress: A Study in Survival: The Life of the Duchess of Kingston* (1964); *The Redoubt* (1967); *The Ladies of Llangollen: A Study in Romantic Friendship* (1971); *A Green Equinox* (1973); *A Year with the Ladies of Llangollen* (1984); (ed.), *The Grand Tour of William Beckford* (1986).

Mayor, F. M.

b. 20 October 1872, Kingston Hill; d. 28 January 1931, Hampstead

Novelist

(Also wrote under Mary Stafford)

FM was the twin daughter of two cultivated and highly intellectual parents, representative of the professional and clerical intelligentsia of the British Empire. Her father, the Rev. Joseph Mayor, was successively Professor of Classics and of Moral Philosophy at King's College, London, and two Mayor uncles were Cambridge fellows and distinguished scholars. On both sides of the family there was a tradition of respect for female intelligence and the provision of education for daughters. FM's mother Jessie came from the noted Grote family, whose brother George Grote was a leading Philosophic Radical, scholar, and co-founder of the University of London. Jessie Grote was a gifted linguist who had taught herself at least half a dozen modern languages, translating Icelandic sagas and, reputedly, a Zulu grammar from Danish; she was also very musical.

FM's upbringing fostered intellectual and cultural development. She and her twin sister Alice were among the first generation to attend the High Schools for Girls founded in this era; they went to Surbiton High School (motto: 'Be good, sweet maid, and let who will be clever'). But FM failed to fulfil her intellectual promise at Newnham College, achieving, to her chagrin, only a third-class honours degree; she had found social life too distracting. Her family would have encouraged professional aspirations, especially as they had become less well-off. Instead, like a growing number of genteel girls at this time such as Edith Olivier, FM dreamt of becoming an actress. She persisted in this, with no great success, but with dogged determination and without her family's approval, from 1896 to 1903. She also published a volume of stories, *Mrs Hammond's Children* (1901), under her stage name, Mary Stafford. These drew on her experience of the love, rivalry, and misery even among predominantly happy siblings. It identified with the child's point of view and was consistent with a literary trend to depict children less idealistically and more realistically.

FM's stage career came to an end with her engagement to Ernest Shepherd, a young architect, also active in the University Settlement Movement. He had been in love with FM for some time but until he had got 'prospects' through a position on the architectual survey of India he had refrained from proposing. Tragically he died of fever six months later. It was only then that her love for him really ripened. The bereavement weakened her health, already undermined by asthma, and precluded any further attempt to follow a full-time occupation. She had to fall back on the protracted daughterhood of the well-to-do middle classes. She shared her life for the most part with her parents – her mother died in 1927, aged 98; for a time with her brother Robin; then alternated with Alice in keeping house at Clifton School for their brother Henry. She finally settled in Hampstead with the devoted Alice.

FM's two best novels, *The Third Miss Symons* (1913) and *The Rector's Daughter* (1924), were both fuelled to an extent by the restrictions and frustrations of respectable spinsterhood, but both transcend what autobiographical elements they possess and also stand as studies of character. The rector's daughter of the latter title was modelled, probably, on a friend and a sister-in-law. The fictional Mary Jocelyn's unfulfilled love for a neighbouring clergyman is the keystone of the novel; the irony and intelligence of the narrator have rightly been likened to that of Jane Austen, whose *Persuasion* was an important source of inspiration. The marriage made by the Rev. Herbert to the brisk, horsey, vivacious, but sensitive Kathy Hollings is brilliantly portrayed, and there is great psychological penetration in the way FM shows how their very incompatibilities – 'They did not know what each other was going to say before the words were uttered, but presumably not one husband or wife in a million do' – was emotionally more healthy than the too-kindred sensibility of Mary and Herbert would have been. Equally telling is the portrait of the learned, controlled Canon Jocelyn, and Mary's devotion to him. There is an elegiac, meditative quality to the novel and it is perhaps insufficiently stressed that this is to a large degree an historical novel. FM sees the clerical intelligentsia and county families, who provide the main characters, as doomed by the *nouveaux riches* of the Jazz Age. Canon Jocelyn's mind, 'sumptuous in learning and luxury', contrasts with an age that has exchanged such learning for more education. In cherishing her passion, Mary permits herself desires impossible to her mother: 'The spirit of the times was moving in her.'

The Third Miss Symons is a considerable achievement in its economy and lucidity, going beyond portraying a superfluous spinster to anatomizing the tragic potential of self-absorption. In *The Squire's Daughter* (1929), FM tried to tell a story of changing manners and morals similar to that in *The Rector's Daughter*, set this time in county circles, but she was conspicuously less successful, being out of sympathy with her brittle heroine, Ron, less familiar with her material from first hand, and also failing in creative energy. In this territory, she is outclassed by Edith Olivier and Molly Keane. CLARISSA CAMPBELL ORR

Works: *Mrs Hammond's Children* (1901); *The Third Miss Symons* (1913); *The Rector's Daughter* (1924); *The Squire's Daughter* (1929); *The Room Opposite and Other Tales of Mystery and Imagination* (1935).

References: Masefield, J., 'Introduction' to *The Rector's Daughter* (1913); Morgan, J., 'Introduction' to *The Rector's Daughter* (1987) and *The Squire's Daughter* (1987); Hill, S., 'Introduction' to *The Third Miss Symons* (1980); *DLB*; Oldfield, S., *Spinsters of this Parish: The Life and Times of F. M. Mayor and Mary Sheepshank*, London (1984).

Meeke, Mary

fl. 1795–1823

Novelist

(Also wrote under 'Gabrielli')

Although MM was a popular writer of immense quantities of minor Gothic fiction, almost nothing is known about her life. She was probably the wife of the Rev. Francis Meeke, who graduated from Christ's College, Cambridge, in 1773, and this may have been the same Rev. Francis Meeke who is recorded as having died at Johnson Hall, Staffordshire, in 1816. Her writing career seems to have begun in 1795, with the publication of *Count St Blancard, or The Prejudiced Judge*, and ended in 1823 with the possibly posthumous publication of *What Shall Be, Shall Be*. It is difficult to ascertain the precise proportions of her output, for, in addition to writing seventeen novels and several translations under her own name, MM seems to have used a number of pseudonyms. In particular she adopted the rather Gothic name of 'Gabrielli', under which she brought out a further eight novels. There is no evidence, however, for the suggestion proposed from a number of quarters that this was her maiden name.

As a writer for the Minerva Press MM's career was probably fairly lucrative, and in the early nineteenth century her books were well-known, well-read and well-liked. A poem 'On Modern Female Writers' by Francisca Julia, published in *The Morning Post* of April 25 1807, opens with the lines: 'To beguile the dull hours, when for novels we seek,/We are charm'd by the well-told light fictions of Meeke', and Lady Trevelyan claimed that the historian Macaulay 'all but knew by heart' MM's romances. None the less she adds that 'he quite agreed in my criticism that they were one just like another, turning on the fortunes of some young man in a very low rank of life who eventually proves to be the son of a Duke' (Trevelyan, G. O., *The Life and Letters of Lord Macaulay*, 1876). In many respects this is an accurate account of the plot of the majority of MM's works. Her virtuous heroes are eventually granted a material reward for the sufferings they have endured, and the novels end with a misplaced aristocracy re-established at the head of a feudal society. As such they can be read, like the novels of Ann Radcliffe, as conservative political allegories, and this reading is endorsed by their explicit advocacy of the doctrine of passive obedience to the divine will. Indeed such is the passivity of many of her heroes that they are frequently characterized by ill-health, or a debilitating personal weakness. For much of the final volume of *The Count St Blancard*, for example, the eponymous hero is confined to bed, barely able to consume a light broth or to sip chocolate.

The basic inheritance plots of the novels are enlivened by elements of the Gothic and sentimental traditions. The heroes and heroines are endowed with exaggerated sensibilities, and the action is usually played out against a range of exotic locations, from the wilder regions of Italy and France to India, Smyrna, and Martinico. On the whole, however, the novels written under the name of Gabrielli tend to be more daring and lavish in their settings than those published under MM's own name.   LIZ BELLAMY

Selected works: *Count St Blancard, or, The Prejudiced Judge* (1795); *The Abbey of Clugny* (1795); *Palmira and Ermance* (1797); *The Mysterious Wife* (1797); *Ellesmere* (1799); *The Mysterious Husband* (1799); *Which is the Man?* (1801); *Independence* (1802); *Midnight Weddings* (1802); *A Tale of Mystery, or, Selina* (1803); *Amazement!* (1803); *The Old Wife and Young Husband* (1803); *Murray House* (1803); *The Nine Days' Wonder* (1804); (trans.), *Loberstein Village*, by A. la Fontaine (1804); *Ellen, Heiress of the Castle* (1807); (trans.), *Julian, or, My Father's House*, by D. Dumenial (1807); (trans.), *The Unpublished Correspondence of Madame du Deffand* (1810); *Matrimony the Height of Bliss or Extreme of Misery* (1811); *Laughton Priory: Stratagems Defeated* (1811); *Conscience* (1814); *Spanish Campaigns, or, The Jew* (1815); (trans.) *Elizabeth, or, The Exiles of Siberia*, by Madame de Cottin (1817); *The Veiled Protectress, or, The Mysterious Mother* (1818); *What Shall Be, Shall Be* (1823).

References: Blakey, D., *The Minerva Press, 1790–1820* (1939); *DNB*; Varma, D.P., *The Gothic Flame* (1957); Varma, D. P., *The Evergreen Tree of Diabolical Knowledge* (1972).

Melvill, Elizabeth

b. late sixteenth century, Halhil, Scotland; d. seventeenth century
Poet
(Also wrote under M.M., Gentlewoman in Culross)

EM's only extant work is a long poem in the Scottish dialect entitled *Ane Godlie Dreame* which was first published in 1603. Although Alexander Hume, who dedicated a book of hymns to her, wrote that EM took 'delight in Poesie', none of her other work has survived. Little is known of EM's life, although we know more about her father, Sir James Melvill, her husband, John Colville, third Lord of Culross, whom she married before 1603, and her son, Alexander Colville, who were all significant figures in Scottish life.

Ane Godlie Dreame is made up of fifty-five eight-line stanzas. It begins with a call to Christ to return and save the elect from the oppression inflicted upon them by the sinful. The speaker falls asleep and in a dream is led by Christ to a gold and silver castle which, however, the speaker is not permitted to enter before accompanying Christ to Hell. In the course of their descent into Hell the speaker apparently falls forward into the flames, but immediately wakes up. The speaker initially mistakes the inferno for a 'Papist' Purgatory but is soon set right by a staunchly Protestant Christ, who refutes the idea of purgatory by pointing out that 'My blude alone', rather than purchased indulgences, 'did saif thy saull from sin.' The poem ends with a long series of injunctions to those who may be wavering in their faith to follow Christ devotedly.

Aside from its narrative content, the poem also presents a drama of devotional feeling: at the beginning of the poem the speaker is tormented by her inability to pray, and finds relief in penitent weeping and in her subsequent lamentations over the hardships suffered by the just. But the poem repeatedly enforces the lesson that such religious emotion is neither in itself equivalent to, not sufficient for, salvation. Indeed, Christ explicitly rebukes the speaker for identifying devotional ecstasy with the kingdom of heaven: 'Thou thinks thee thair, thou art transportit so.' Despite Christ's warnings that heaven is only to be reached through hardship, the speaker believes such hardship to be complete after each individual trial ('I was sa neir, I thought my voyage endit'), only to discover that there are more difficulties to be faced ahead. This remains true at the end of the poem, where the speaker hopes to dream of heaven but remains frustratingly awake. She concludes, 'My dreame declaires, that we have far to go . . .'.

JAMES SMITH

Works: 'Ane Godlie Dreame' (1603).
References: *DNB*; Laing, D., *Early Metrical Tales* (1826); *Notes and Queries* 8 (1859).

Mew, Charlotte

b. 15 November 1869, London; d. 24 March 1928, London
Poet, short story writer

CM was the third child of Frederick Mew, an architect, and his wife, Anna Kendall, who was the daughter of his partner. CM was born in Mecklenburgh Square, where the family lived throughout her childhood and adolescence. Frederick and Anna had seven children in all: two of them died in infancy, another at the age of 5, and two of the remaining children became insane and were confined in asylums later in their lives. CM's attachment to her remaining sister Anne remained deep throughout her life. In 1888 the family moved to Gordon Square, and CM attended the Lucy Harrison School for Girls in Gower Street. Subsequently she attended lectures at University College; she also spent many hours in the Reading Room of the British Museum. As well as reading widely in French and English literature, she played the organ and the piano.

Her literary career began in 1894 when a story of hers, 'Passed', was published in *The Yellow Book*. She continued to publish stories until the eve of the Great War. The editor, Henry Harland, held literary evenings where CM met other contributors to *The Yellow Book* such as Max Beerbohm and George Moore. But she was slow to publish the work for which she is now best known, her poetry. It was not until 1916 that her first collection of poetry, *The Farmer's Bride*, appeared, under the auspices of Harold Monro's Poetry Bookshop, in an edition of 1,000 copies. The volume sold poorly: 850 copies remained unsold, despite the efforts of May Sinclair, then one of the most influential figures in the literary world, who sent out many copies for review to other influential figures. Although CM's work attracted high praise from several very well-known writers, including Thomas Hardy and Virginia Woolf, she never rose to prominence in her lifetime. After 1916 she wrote little; although she received a civil list pension of £75 annually (on the recommendation of John Masefield, Walter de la Mare, and Thomas Hardy), she later wished to resign it on the grounds that she was not writing enough to justify the award.

CM's personal life was in many ways a difficult one. The financial strain of supporting two children in private mental homes gradually impoverished the family and imposed a severe psychological burden on CM herself. Moreover, CM was extremely conscious of the contrast between her own comparative literary success and the total failure of Anne's artistic work to receive any recognition. After Pound accepted 'The Fête' for his journal *The Egoist* CM wrote, 'I hate telling [Anne] about these verses – because she's had no chance whatever, and has 100 times my pluck and patience – and her own very definite gift – all going to seed . . .'.

CM never married, and told Alida Monro that she and her sister had decided 'that they would never marry for fear of passing on the mental taint that was in their heredity'. There may also have been other reasons: soon after meeting May Sinclair CM fell in love with her. She attempted to win Sinclair's deeper friendship by carrying out tasks for her, such as looking for new houses when Sinclair was obliged to move, but her friend found this slightly intrusive. 'Of course I know you were angelic enough too,' she wrote to CM, 'perhaps – like running round to House Agents for me – but can't you see that your time ought to be given to poems, and not to lazy friends?' When CM eventually admitted the depth of her feelings to Sinclair, her friend was bewildered and upset, although later she was to treat the event, more hurtfully, with apparent amusement.

In 1922 when the lease of the house in Gordon Square expired CM, her mother, and her sister rented a house in Delancey Street, near Regent's Park. CM's mother died in May 1923 and CM and Anne moved into Anne's studio. But after 1925 Anne's health gradually worsened. When she died of cancer in June 1927 CM was devastated and in early 1928 she was herself admitted to a nursing home suffering from what was diagnosed as neurasthenia. On 24 March she killed herself by drinking lysol.

The major difficulties of CM's own life are the central themes of her poetry, although her work is rarely directly confessional. Instead her poems are often cast as dramatic monologues: the persona of the narrator offers CM a mask from behind which she can discuss difficult or disturbing subjects. Many of her poems present themselves as the reflections of a male speaker about a loved woman: characteristically there is some entirely insuperable obstacle to this love. In the title poem of the collection, *The Farmer's Bride*, the farmer's young wife becomes terrified of her husband, apparently inexplicably, as soon as they are married: 'When us was wed she turned afraid/ Of love and me and all things human.' The couple sleep apart, and the poem's measured rhymes are violently disrupted at its close by the farmer's frustration:

> 'Tis but a stair
> Betwixt us. Oh! my God! the down,
> The soft young down of her, the brown,
> The Brown of her – her eyes, her hair, her hair!

Many of her poems are concerned with mental illness. 'On the Asylum Road' shows how sanity is as incomprehensible to those who are called insane as that insanity itself is to the ostensibly rational. The asylum itself, 'that red brick barn upon the hill' in 'Ken', is a dominating presence in these poems. 'Ken' presents CM's ambivalent feelings about the asylum: the sense that Ken is part of a community when he lives in the village, a community for which there are no compensations in the asylum, is balanced by the narrator's inability to act to prevent him being taken there:

> So, when they took
> Ken to that place, I did not look
> After he called and turned on me
> His eyes. These I shall see –.

As remarkable as the subject matter of CM's poems are the technical innovations and resources of her work. The poems are generally written in a rhyming free verse which may owe something to such poems as 'Goblin Market' by Christina Rossetti. The freedom allows CM to use line length, stanza-length, and rhyme to express or hold back emotion. The repeated rhyme of 'down' and 'brown' in the last lines of 'The Farmer's Bride' is all the more effective for the moderation of the earlier stanzas. In 'Madeleine in Church', CM's longest poem, widely varying stanza lengths mark the ebb and flow of Madeleine's personal meditation. The combination of technical dexterity and psychological force in CM's small oeuvre make her one of the most interesting neglected poets of the early twentieth century. JAMES SMITH

Selected works: *The Farmer's Bride* (1916); *Saturday Market* (1921); *The Rambling Sailor* (1929); *Collected Poems* (1953); *Collected Poems and Prose*, ed. V. Warner (1981). **References:** *CP*; Meynell, V. (ed.), *Friends of a Lifetime: Letters to sydney Carlyle Cockerell* (1940); Monro, A., 'Charlotte Mew – a memoir', in *Collected Poems of Chrlotte Mew* (1953); Monro, H., *Some Contemporary Poets* (1920); Moore, V., *Distinguished Women Writers* (1934); Swinnerton, F., *The Georgian Literary Scene, 1910–1935: A Panorama* (1950); Untermeyer, L., *Modern British Poetry* (1962); Warner, V., 'Introduction' to *Charlotte Mew: Collected Poems and Prose* (1981); Williams-Ellis, A., *An Anatomy of Poetry* (1922).

Meynell, Alice

b. 17 August 1847, Barnes, Surrey; d. 27 November 1922, Greatham, Sussex
Poet, essayist

AM was highly regarded by the Victorian literary establishment, including, for example, Tennyson, Patmore, and Meredith. She combined the contemporary ideal of devout domesticity and maternity with the tough professionalism of a writer. Celebrated by a centenary in 1947, she has since been neglected though there has been some re-evaluation.

AM's early years were spent in a slightly bohemian family atmosphere in Italy, France, and Switzerland. Her mother, Christiana Weller, a concert pianist, was affectionate but engrossed in the arts, and AM and her sister Elizabeth (Lady Butler, a painter) were educated from an early age by their father, James Thompson, a graduate of Trinity College, Cambridge. The return to conventional London society in 1864 contributed to AM's sense of crisis, to her subsequent conversion to Roman Catholicism, and to her belief in the necessity for 'useful work' for a woman. *Preludes* (1875) brought her early recognition as a poet, and in 1877 she married Wilfred Meynell, a Catholic journalist, later editor of the *Weekly Register* and *Merry England*. In addition to bringing up seven children, she assisted Wilfred in his journalistic work, contributed regularly to the leading periodicals (*Spectator, Pall Mall Gazette, National Observer*) and published five further volumes of poetry.

The Meynells kept 'open house' for literary figures of the day and cared for the mystic poet Francis Thompson. In 1901–2, AM made a lecture tour of America, and in 1915 she was invited but failed to attend, the Panama Exposition, together with Madame Curie and Mr Sidney Webb. A woman of strong views, AM supported women's suffrage, but not militancy, and the First World War saw her feminism informed by pacifism. Her last years were spent on an estate in Sussex, where she continued to write and publish until her death.

Her early poetry, *Preludes* (1875) and *Poems* (1893), like her later work, is reminiscent of Christina Rossetti in its expression of intense personal and religious emotion in lyric form and in images drawn from nature. 'A Letter from a Girl to Her Own Old Age', however, already signals an individualistic feminist element, although here conventionally handled:

> What part of this wild heart of mine I know not
> Will follow with thee where the great winds blow not
> And where the young flowers of the mountain grow not.

Yet let my letter with my lost thoughts in it
Tell what the way was when thou didst begin it,
And win with thee the goal when thou shalt win it.

Other Poems (1896) marks a shift in style to greater economy and simplicity, and the appearance, in 'The Shepherdess', of a recurrent metaphor for poetic and emotional control:

She walks – the lady of my delight –
A shepherdess of sheep.
Her flocks are thoughts. She keeps them white;
She guards them from the steep;
She feeds them on the fragrant height,
And folds them in for sleep.

Later Poems (1902) and *Collected Poems* (1913) both include poems that represent direct observation and a recognizably modern sensibility, as in 'In Manchester Square':

The paralytic man has dropped in death
The crossing-sweeper's brush to which he clung,
One-handed, twisted, dwarfed, scanted of breath,
Although his hair was young.

I saw this year the winter vines of France,
Dwarfed, twisted goblins in the frosty drouth –
Gnarled, crippled, blackened little stems askance
On long hills to the South.

Great green and golden hands of leaves ere long
Shall proffer clusters in that vineyard wide.
And O his might, his sweet, his wine, his song,
His stature, since he died!

These same qualities find their strongest expression in the poems of 1916–17, collected in *Poems of War* (1916) and *A Father of Women* (1917), both of which were printed privately by her son Francis, a socialist journalist, conscientious objector, and the founder of the Pelican Press. 'Summer in England, 1914' juxtaposes English rural and urban calm with violence in Europe to create a sense of unease.

'A Father of Women' explains militarism through its patriarchal origins:

Like to him now are they,
The million living fathers of the War –
Mourning the crippled world, the bitter day –
Whose stripplings are no more.

The crippled world! Come then,
Fathers of women with your honour in trust,
Approve, accept, know them daughters of men,
Now that your sons are dust.

In contrast to her intermittent poetic output, AM's prose journalism was prolific. Written out of economic necessity and to deadlines, her essays are invariably intelligent, forceful, and stylish, as well as wide-ranging. Of particular interest are her essays on women and writing, collected in 1926 and 1947.

'Venetian Girls' and 'The Lady of the Lyrics' both identify a male-constructed ideal of femininity. 'Charlotte and Emily Brontë' defines the former's achievement as the creation of a feminine sentence in opposition to the dominant stylistic inheritance from Gibbon, while 'Mary Wollstonecraft's Letters' is a passionate identification with wronged womanhood. 'Mrs Johnson' is a spirited defence of Dr Johnson's wife against male critical prejudice; 'Mrs Dingley' is a similar defence, this time against omission since critics had preferred to believe that Swift's letters were addressed solely to the younger and more attractive 'Stella'.

AM's wit and irony, best characterized by the two above essays, are used, in 'Jane Austen', to attack the novelist, endorsing the established criticism of her 'narrowness of view', but on moral, not social grounds. Austen's novels are indicted for their 'triviality of relations' and 'observation without sympathy'. In general these essays form an interesting comparison with and contrast to the essays of Virginia Woolf.   JUDITH SKEELS

Selected works: Preludes (1875); *Poems* (1893); *The Rhythm of Life* (1893); *Other Poems* (1896); *The Colour of Life* (1896); *The Children* (1897); *London Impressions* (1898); *The Spirit of Place* (1899); *Later Poems* (1902); *Ceres Runaway* (1909); *Ten Poems* (1913–15); *Poems on the War* (1916); *A Father of Women* (1917); *Hearts of Controversy* (1917); *Second Person Singular* (1921); *Last Peoms* (1923).

References: Badeni, J., *Alice Meynell: A Life* (1981); Hamilton, G. R., *Poetry Review* 38 (1947); Kaplan, C., *Salt and Bitter and Good: English and American Women Poets* (1975); Meredith. G., *Letters* (1923); Meynell, W., (ed.), *Alice Meynell* (1926); Moore, V., *Distinguished Women Writers* (1934); Page, F., (ed.), *Prose and Poetry* (1947); Tuell, A. K., *Mrs Meynell and Her Literary Generation* (1925).

Mildmay, Grace

b. 1553, Laycock Abbey, Wiltshire; d. 1620, Apethorpe, Northamptonshire
Diarist
GM was the second of Sir Henry and Lady Sherrington's three daughters. Her only work, a diary, spans the greater part of her life, beginning at the age of 17 with a backward glance at her childhood and continuing until a few years before her death. The journal is interspersed with a series of Protestant meditations and with advice to her only child, Mary. She considered her childhood a strict one. Her account oscillates between respect for the two women who were responsible for her thorough education, her mother and her governess, Mrs Hamblyn, and awe of her father, who 'Lyked a woman well graced, with a constant and settled countenance, and a good behaviour throughout all her parts, which presenteth unto all men a good hope of stablished mynde and a virtuous disposition to be in her.'

At 14 GM married Sir Anthony Mildmay. The marriage did not begin well: 'His Father told him, if he did not marry me, he should never bring any other woman into his house.' Her husband's prolonged visits to the court meant 'he could not but be in debt, which he was', and when he was home their married life seems to have been coloured by 'the many afflictions and contrary occasions' that arose between them. GM seems then to have put her energy into studying the Bible and lute, educating her daughter and, on her succession to the title Lady Mildmay, the administration of the estate. 'Alsoe, every day I spent some time in the Herball and books of phisick.' These cures and recipes were copied and collected after her death by her daughter, Mary, in a volume entitled 'For

the Workhouse'. The journal offers insight into the lives of sixteenth-century women but remains unpublished, though extracts are available in R. Weigall's article (see below).   CATHERINE S. WEARING
Works: Journal and Papers (1570–1617); 'For the Workhouse: a Book of Prescriptions and Recommendations Collected and Copied by her Daughter' (unpublished).
References: Bush, D., *English Literature in the Earlier Seventeenth Century, 1600–1660* (1962); Warnicke, R., *Women of the English Renaissance and Reformation* (1983); Weigall, R., 'An English gentlewoman', *Quarterly Review* 215 (1911).

Mitchell, Gladys

b. 19 April 1901, Cowley, Oxford; d. 29 July 1983, Corfe Mullen, Dorset
Detective novelist, writer for children
(Also wrote under Stephen Hockaby and Malcolm Torre)
GM was the daughter of James Mitchell and Julia Maude Simmonds, both of Scottish ancestry. GM attended Goldsmith's College, London, from 1919 to 1921 and received a diploma in history from the University of London in 1926. From 1921 to 1961, she taught English and history in girls' boarding schools in or near London. She retired from teaching three times during her forty-year career in 1939, 1950, and finally in 1961. Her first published mystery novel, *Speedy Death* (1929), introduced her memorable main character, Beatrice LeStrange Bradley, to the world of detective fiction. Bradley, a psychiatrist with the Home Office and a sleuth, appeared in more than sixty of GM's seventy-seven novels. At various times between 1930 and 1950, GM published under the pseudonym Stephen Hockaby and between 1966 and 1971, some of her novels were written under the name Malcolm Torre. In addition to her mystery novels, GM also wrote eight children's books and contributed stories to *Fifty Famous Detectives of Fiction, Detective Stories of Today*, and *The Evening Standard Detective Book.*

GM's professional background as a literature and history teacher is evident in her novels which contain literary allusions and archaeological, architectural, and historical details. A careful craftswoman, she set her stories in or near actual places and was a student of the British Ordnance Survey maps. She is remarkable among detective fiction writers for her use of supernatural and folk elements. Sometimes she is criticized for improbabilities. For example, Dame Beatrice is acquitted of a murder she actually committed in *Speedy Death* (and confessed to) on the strength of the defence by her son who is also her Counsel, and the title character of *Here Lies Gloria Mundy* (1982) has black hair on one side of her head and red on the other – a condition inherited from an ancestor who was half burned at the stake! At other times she is praised for her eccentric plots with their necessary improbabilities, as well as for her ability to combine horror and humour.

GM was a member of the Society of Authors, the Crime Writers' Association, and the Detection Club. She was also a fellow of the Ancient Monuments Society. She received the Crime Writers' Association Silver Dagger Award in 1976.   B. E. SCHNELLER
Selected works: *Speedy Death* (1929); *The Mystery of the Butcher's Shop* (1929); *Printer's Error* (1939); *The Worsted Viper* (1943); *The Rising of the Moon* (1945); *The Dancing Druids* (1948); *Tom Brown's Body* (1949); *Merlin's Furlong* (1953); *Faintly Speaking* (1954); *On Your Marks* (1954); *The Twenty-Third Man* (1957); *Skeleton Island* (1967); *The Murder of Busy Lizzie* (1973); *Late, Late in the Evening*

(1976); *Fault in the Structure* (1977); *Mingled with Venom* (1978); *Lovers, Make Moan* (1981); *Here Lies Gloria Mundy* (1982); *The Greenstone Griffins* (1983); *Cold, Lone and Still* (1983); as Malcolm Torre: *Heavy as Lead* (1966); *Late and Cold* (1967); *Your Secret friend* (1968); *Churchyard Salad* (1969); *Shades of Darkness* (1970); as Stephen Hockaby: *March Hay* (1933); *Seven Stars and Orion* (1934); *Grabriel's Hold* (1935); *Shallow Brown* (1936); *Outlaws of the Border* (1936); *Grand Master* (1939).

References: *CA*; Reilly, J. M., (ed.), *Twentieth Century Crime and Mystery Writers* (1983); Obituary in *The Times* (July 1983).

Mitchison, Naomi

b. 1 November 1897, Edinburgh
Novelist, journalist, polemicist, writer for children
NM is the daughter of Louisa (*née* Trotter) and J. S. Haldane, physiologist. Her brother was J. B. S. Haldane, writer and scientist. She was brought up in Oxford, educated as one of the few girls at the Dragon School for boys. Formative summer holidays were spent at the family estate in Cloan, Auchterarder, where NM began to understand the Scottish element in her identity with which her birth and parentage had endowed her; her Haldane ancestors had always had a significant influence in Scottish affairs. A Home Student at St Anne's College, Oxford, her education was disrupted by the First World War. In 1915 she served as a VAD (Voluntary Aid Detachment) nurse in St Thomas's Hospital, London. In 1916 she married G. Richard Mitchison, Labour MP for Kettering, Northamptonshire from 1945 to 1964 when he was made Lord Mitchison. He died in 1970. NM had seven children, five of whom, three boys (Denny, Murdo, and Avrion) and two girls (Lois and Valentine) survived childhood. Geoff, her eldest son, died of meningitis in 1927 when he was 9, and a baby girl died in 1940 a few hours after birth.

NM's first novel, *The Conquered* (1923), established her as a writer of historical fiction, a genre she was to use often. At this time she became immersed in social and political issues, helping to establish early birth control clinics in London, and visiting Russia in 1932 and Austria, under Dolfuss, in 1934. *We Have Been Warned* (1935), a novel based on these experiences, contained a discussion of international socialism which showed signs of uneasiness about the direction of the Communist Party in the USSR. It was rejected, however, by Jonathan Cape, Victor Gollancz, and John Lane because its sexual explicitness and references to contraception were thought too radical. This experience upset NM who felt her publishers allowed her to write frankly about sexuality in an ancient context but not in a contemporary one. After this NM increased her involvement in Scottish politics, standing as the Labour candidate for the Scottish Universities in 1935. In 1937 the Mitchisons bought Carradale, an estate in Argyll. During the Second World War, NM ran the estate while her husband was involved in the Beveridge manpower survey in London. She took an active part in community affairs and in Scottish affairs generally, being closely associated with Scottish nationalism in the 1940s. She was a member of Argyll County Council from 1945 to 1946, of the Highland Panel from 1947 to 1964, and of the Highlands and Islands Advisory Council from 1966 to 1976. The Bakgatla people of Botswana made her their tribal mother (Mmarona) from 1963 to 1973. During the 1980s NM was based in Carradale, still writing and still actively involved in social issues.

NM's complex identity is reflected in her fiction. Her social class meant that she moved in the most powerful echelons of English society; yet, because she was a woman, positions of significance were not open to her. Meanwhile her Scottish background made her aware of an alternative society and culture. Her experience of cultural and sexual discrimination made NM sympathetic to people who suffered from varied forms of discrimination. In *The Corn King and the Spring Queen* (1931), an historical novel, she focuses on Marob, a small, pre-civilized state open to the influence of the Greek city states of Athens – which despises Marob's native culture – and Sparta, with its ambitious and imperialist king. At the Spartan court the Spring Queen of Marob, Erif Der, is perceived as a member of a 'barbaric' culture; yet the supposedly advanced Spartan court discriminates against women in a way which the Marob state does not, and female Spartan aristocrats can expect to be involved only in the domestic affairs of the palace. Erif Der, an equal in government with her husband, has mythical significance for she is a central figure in the agricultural rituals of Marob and essential to the maintenance of a healthy society. The analysis of the relative positions of women in the ancient world is only one of many issues dealt with in this epic novel which charts the political and religious mores of three different civilizations.

NM's preoccupation with the establishment of a just society, a preoccupation which had been hers since childhood, occasionally gives her writing a doctrinaire cast which sits uneasily with her liberal attitudes. *The Blood of the Martyrs* (1939) is set against the background of the Neronian persecution of the early Christians. Portrayed as proto-socialists, who share their possessions, trust each other and have a radical vision of how society ought to develop, this community of friends (similar groups appear in other novels) is in danger of becoming a law unto itself, implementing its policies for the 'good' of society, without taking sufficient account of dissenting opinions. In *The Bull Calves* (1947), which grew out of her participation in the Scottish Renaissance Movement, NM combines her desires for the reconstruction of Scottish society after the Second World War and for women's involvement in it. The story is set in the aftermath of the 1745 Jacobite Rebellion and concerns Kirstie, who finds a relationship which satisfies her emotionally and intellectually and who works to rebuild Scottish society but still within the context of male domination. NM continues to challenge unthinking male dominance in the short story 'Five Men and a Swan' (in a collection of that name, 1958) and the novella *Travel Light* (1952). Both these stories use a mixture of realistic and mythical styles. By using the animal myths of the swan girl and the girl who is raised by bears, NM seeks to understand human nature through its pre-human roots. Animal myths form an analogy for areas of the minds of her female characters which could be beneficial to society but which are disparaged or neglected. The otherness of the swan girl emphasizes the beautiful mystery of the sexual relation and her rape is a forceful plea for equality between men and women inside and outside marriage.

In recent decades NM's output has multiplied and diversified spectacularly; she wrote children's fiction in *The Land the Ravens Found* (1955), science fiction in *Memories of a Spacewoman* (1962), fiction dealing with the issues of race in *Images of Africa* (1980) and with nuclear war in *What Do You Think Yourself?* (1982). These later short stories often have a sombre, surreal, and sometimes post-apocalyptic atmosphere.   SUZANNE HALL

Selected works: The Conquered (1923); *When the Bough Breaks and Other Stories* (1924); *Cloud Cuckoo Land* (1925); *The Laburnum Branch* (1926); *Black Sparta: Greek Stories* (1928); *Anna Comnena* (1928); *Barbarian Stories* (1929); *Nix-Nought-*

Nothing: Four Plays for Children (1929); *The Hostages and Other Stories for Boys and Girls* (1930); *Comments on Birth Control* (1930); *The Corn King and the Spring Queen* (1931); *Boys and Girls and Gods* (1931); *The Powers of Light* (1931); *The Home and a Changing Civilization* (1934); *Beyond This Limit*, with Wyndham Lewis (1935); *We Have Been Warned* (1935); *Vienna Diary* (1935); *An End and a Beginning and Other Plays* (1937); *The Moral Basis of Politics* (1938); *Kingdom of Heaven* (1939); *As It Was in the Beginning* (with L. E. Gielgud) (1939); *The Blood of Martyrs* (1939); *The Bull Calves* (1947); *The Big House* (1950); *Lobsters on the Agenda* (1952); *Travel Light* (1952); *Graeme and the Dragon* (1954); *The Land the Ravens Found* (1955); *Little Boxes* (1956); *The Far Harbour* (1957); *Behold Your King* (1957); *Five Men and a Swan: Short Stories and Poems* (1958); *The Rib of the Green Umbrella* (1960); *Karensgaard: the Story of a Danish Farm* (1961); *Presenting Other People's Children* (1961); *Memories of a Spacewoman* (1962); *Henney and Crispies* (1964); *Return to the Fairy Hill* (1966); *Friends and Enemies* (1966); *Highland Holiday* (1967); *The Family at Ditlabeng* (1969); *The Africans: A History* (1970); *Sun and Moon* (1970); *Sunrise Tomorrow* (1973); *Small Talk* (1973); *Oil for the Highlands* (1974); *Snake!* (1976); *You May Well Ask* (1979); *Images of Africa* (1980); *What Do You Think Yourself?* (1982); *Endangered Species* (1983); *Among You Taking Notes: The Wartime Diary of Naomi Mitchison 1939–45*, ed. D. Sheridan; *Early in Orcadia* (1987).

References: Caldecott, L., *Women of our Century* (1984); Gish, N. K., *Images of Scotland and Africa* (1980); Hart, F. R., *The Scottish Novel: A Critical Survey* (1978); Lowry, S., 'No easy way', *Observer* Supplement (25 February 1979).

Mitford, Mary Russell

b. 16 December 1787, Alresford, Hampshire; d. 10 January 1855, Swallowfield, Berkshire

Essayist, playwright, novelist, poet

MRM's father, George Midford (as he originally spelled his name) had some medical training, but his life was ruled by a passion for gambling and speculation. Having at an early age squandered his own resources, he married Mary Russell, a descendant of the ducal house of Bedford, and proceeded to work his way through her substantial inheritance. Within a few years of his marriage, his financial affairs were again in disarray, and the family was eventually reduced to a penurious existence in what MRM described as a 'dingy, comfortless lodging' in the suburbs of London.

They had not been there long, however, when her father bought her, as a present for her tenth birthday, a lottery ticket which subsequently proved to have won her the then immense sum of £20,000. Yet she herself saw little of the money, which was rapidly swallowed up by her father's continued gambling and by extravagant expenditure on his estate at Grazely in Berkshire. In 1820 the family moved from Grazely to a humble cottage at nearby Three Mile Cross.

It was Three Mile Cross which provided the inspiration for *Our Village* (1824–32), the work for which she is best and most deservedly remembered. With their easy, conversational style and their sharp delineation of a rural world already under threat, the essays at once captivated the public and won the praise of critics, Charles Lamb among them. MRM claimed that she 'always wrote on the spot and at the moment and in nearly every instance with the closest and most resolute fidelity to the place and the people'; and she certainly creates a remarkable impression of immediacy as she guides the reader down the village street or out into the surrounding countryside in quest of the first primroses or a bonnetful of hazelnuts. She has an eye for evocative detail – the three village children 'dipping up water in their little homely cups shining with cleanliness', the weeds and gorse 'fixed and stiffened in the hoar-frost', the 'exquisitely tricksy' movement of water over pebbles; one senses throughout her own keen relish for the world she so vividly depicts.

If she seems at times to be presenting a somewhat idealized version of country life, she was nevertheless aware of its darker side, of the 'evils' of the condition of the rural poor; and while she does not develop this awareness in the manner of her older contemporary, George Crabbe, it clearly informs her work. Observing the fields 'lively . . . with troops of stooping bean-setters, women and children, in all varieties of costume and colour', she is struck not only by the superficially attractive aspect of the scene, but by the degradation involved in a form of labour which subverts 'the position assigned to man to distinguish him from the beasts of the field'. Perceptions of this kind serve at once to qualify and authenticate the celebratory impulse dominant in the essays.

MRM's most successful play, *Rienzi* (1828), opened in Drury Lane in October 1828, also to considerable public and critical acclaim, but neither this nor any of her other dramatic works can be said to have worn well. *Belford Regis* (1835), an attempt to do for the town of Reading what she had done in *Our Village* for Three Mile Cross, lacks the freshness and apparent spontaneity of its predecesor and bears the marks of hasty composition, while her late novel *Atherton* (1854) represents a venture into a genre to which her talents seem to have been little suited.

MRM's father lived until 1842, and the strain of caring for him in his old age undoubtedly weakened her health; the damp and dilapidated state of the cottage at Three Mile Cross may also have contributed to the crippling rheumatic condition which in her last years frequently made walking impossible. She retained into those years, however – as she herself noted in a letter written shortly before her death – her 'calmness of mind, clearness of intellect', and that 'enjoyment of little things' which so deeply colours her one enduringly popular work.   JEM POSTER

Works: *Miscellaneous Poems* (1810); *Christina, the Maid of the South Seas: A Poem* (1811); *Narrative Poems on the Female Character in the Various Relations of Life* (1813); *Our Village: Sketches of Rural Character and Scenery* (1824–32); *Foscari: A Tragedy* (1826); *Dramatic Scenes, Sonnets and Other Poems* (1827); *Rienzi: A Tragedy, in Five Acts* (1828); *Belford Regis, or, Sketches of a Country Town* (1835); *Recollections of a Literary Life, or, Books, Places, and People* (1852); *Atherton and Other Tales* (1854); *Dramatic Works* (1854).

References: Astin, M., *Mary Russell Mitford* (1930); Hill, C., *Mary Russell Mitford and Her Surroundings* (1920); Lee, E. (ed.), *Mary Russell Mitford: Correspondence with Charles Boner and John Ruskin* (1914); L'Estrange, A. G., *The Life of Mary Russell Mitford, Related in a Selection of Letters to Her Friends* (1870); Roberts, W. J., *The Life and Friendships of Mary Russell Mitford* (1913); Watson, V., *Mary Russell Mitford* (1949).

Mitford, Nancy

b. 18 November 1904, London; d. 30 June 1973, Versailles
Novelist, historian, journalist
The novels of NM's middle period (1945–51) were enthusiastically received by the general public, and her journalism was subsequently extremely popular,

but it lost favour with the change in the social climate which occurred during the late 1950s and early 1960s. From the viewpoint of the 1980s, her work has acquired a period charm and, though it tends always to be superficial, it captures the mood of its time with witty, stylish depiction of life among the English upper classes.

NM was the eldest of the seven children of David Mitford, later Lord Redesdale, and Sydney Gibson-Bowles. Her father was an impoverished, highly eccentric member of the English aristocracy; his children received little help from either parent in negotiating the emotional upheavals of childhood and their lack of integration was apparent in various ways throughout their lives.

NM's attempts to resolve some of the problems of a difficult adolescence led her to form close friends among the male homosexual community at Oxford, to which she was introduced by her only brother Tom, and she tended to develop intense relationships with men who did not return her affection significantly. Well able to be witty, charming, and socially acceptable, she was apparently without access to the deeper levels of her own emotional reality, a fact which not only dominated her life but also prevented her from achieving the expression needed to make her work other than superficial. Her first book, *Highland Fling* (1931), inspired by her experience of the new phenomenon of the generation gap in upper-class families of the 1920s, brings together a party of Bright Young Things and another of elderly philistines come to shoot grouse at a houseparty in a Scottish castle: like Edith Sitwell, NM found grouse-shooting a symbol of all that was most boring about the older generation. The book, light and amusing, contains dark references to the real strains of this conflict which might have been expected to form the basis for deeper reflection in later work, but *Christmas Pudding* (1932) goes no deeper, despite being written when NM was severely depressed and even attempted suicide, which suggests that she was unable to effect any personal catharsis through her work. In 1933 she married Peter Rodd, black sheep son of the diplomat Lord Rendell of Rodd (whom she later satirizes as Lord Mountdore in *Love in a Cold Climate*, describing him as 'wonderful old cardboard'). Rodd's personal and financial troubles caused her considerable difficulties in a relationship which apparently remained largely unfulfilling.

Wigs on the Green (1935) was planned as a spoof on the British Fascist Movement and its leader, Sir Oswald Mosley, inspired less by political fervour (NM had no strong political affiliations and was even briefly a member of the Fascist Movement herself) than by the desire to tease her sisters, Unity and Diana, who were both deeply committed to the party. For this reason it quite failed to be the penetrating satire for which there was undoubtedly a market and which NM was uniquely placed to write, yet it did upset her sisters, since she confined herself, as was her wont, to drawing characters from her immediate circle. (Diana afterwards married Mosley; Unity, on the declaration of war in 1939, shot herself; she was sent home from Germany brain-damaged, and died of meningitis in 1948).

During the 'phoney war' in 1939, NM, underemployed in hospital voluntary work, wrote *Pigeon Pie* (originally called *The Secret Weapon: A Wartime Receipt*), a comic tale about spies which, although the characters were still drawn exclusively from NM's acquaintance, was her most substantial story to date. But by the time the book was published in 1940, the real war had begun; there was no market for comic treatment.

Also in 1940, Peter Rodd was stationed abroad. The marriage, already irreparably damaged, steadily disintegrated from this time; NM suffered a second miscarriage. When Mosley was arrested and interned, NM apparently contacted the authorities to make sure that her sister Diana, now Lady Mosley, was imprisoned as well. At the end of this year another pregnancy, the result of a brief relationship with a Free French officer, was found to be ectopic and led to a complete hysterectomy.

In 1942 NM began work at Anne & Heywood Hill's fashionable bookshop, and became involved with Colonel Gaston Palewski, right-hand man of General de Gaulle, stationed in England. This entanglement lasted the rest of NM's life; despite an only partial commitment on the part of Palewski, it acted as a spur to her creativity and prefaced her most successful period. The fiction of the next years was also influenced by Evelyn Waugh, with whom she exchanged manuscripts. Though she expressed rather an obtuse view about *Brideshead Revisited*, claiming to be unaware of the 'Catholic propaganda' and saying that she did not understand his view about God, they remained close correspondents.

In 1944 Tom Mitford was killed in Burma. NM concealed even from close associates the grief she must have experienced at the loss of her much-loved only brother. Her relationship with Palewski failed to establish itself at any depth, and NM continued to 'play the mistress'. *The Pursuit of Love* (1945), as intensely autobiographical as earlier work but suffused with the champange-bubble atmosphere of the early days of her love affair, exactly suited the requirements of the post-war buying public. The characters, though still sketches of those known to her, are splendidly drawn, especially the caricature of her father as 'Matthew Alconleigh', and the essential Englishness of the upper classes is epitomized. The heroine's lover, Fabrice, based on Palewski, dies; this suggests that either NM was already feeling that the only fitting conclusion to a great love is death, or else that she was incapable of imagining what a mature relationship would be.

Earlier in 1945, NM's father gave her £3,000 to buy a partnership in Hill's bookshop; she chose to concentrate on French literature and on her first visit to Paris was captivated by it. She was never afterwards happy in England and used the contrast between the two cultures (French: charming, sophisticated, Mediterranean, witty; English: cold, grey, dull, morose) as material for subsequent work. Permanently established in Paris and part of the diplomatic social scene, she began *Love in a Cold Climate* and found that her fund of available characters was running low. She was obliged to use a family neighbouring to the 'Alconleighs' as protagonists so that she could recycle characters from the earlier book. Yet the figures in this book, created under duress, are her most original; Lady Mountdore and Cedric, though inspired by her usual source, are composites, and imaginatively enriched. Published in 1949, the book was also a remarkable success, but *The Blessing* (1951), which uses as its emotional source the contrast between England and France, is the most successful of her works in literary terms, and contains a child character who, though not like an actual child, is yet an original creation with a skill in manipulating the difference between his parents which is the closest NM ever comes to psychological acuity. The plot revolves around the necessity for the English wife, Grace, to come to terms with her French husband's promiscuity; NM's experience of this position in her relationship with Palewski may be what makes the book, though it is rather unconvincingly resolved. Despite its satiric attack on the boring pomposity of Americans, the book was well received in the United States.

During the 1950s NM wrote for *The Sunday Times* in a witty, malicious style about a miscellany of subjects, and commanded an immense readership. Her style was ideally suited to journalism, and she found it increasingly difficult to find material for fiction. As a result, she turned to history, with *Madame de Pompadour* (1954), *Voltaire in Love* (1957), *The Sun King* (1966), and *Frederick the Great* (1970). Unable to find the detachment necessary to research a character in any depth, she tended only to identify those characteristics familiar to her from her friends and family, so produced charming but superficial studies of these lives. *The Sun King*, lavishly illustrated, exemplified a new concept in publishing; *Madame de Pompadour* was reissued as a picture book in a companion volume, with resulting massive sales.

The article for which she is best remembered, 'The English Aristocracy', which details the foibles of speech and behaviour which separate 'U' (upper-class) from 'Non U', was published in Stephen Spender's magazine *Encounter* in 1955, appealing to the innate snobbery of the English public. It is extremely funny (though NM herself took it sufficiently seriously to eradicate all 'non U' usage in *Pigeon Pie* before it was reissued) and was republished in *Noblesse Oblige* in 1956; but the question of class distinction was becoming vexed. As the 'Angry Decade' took effect, the squawking upper-class accent rapidly became unfashionable in writing as in speech, and NM had little to offer as a writer but a style that owed its essence to that very voice. Her journalism remained popular for a while, as public tastes caught up with literary; *The Water Beetle*, a collection of essays, was published in 1962 and sold well enough but *Don't Tell Alfred*, the final novel (1960), was not well received critically.

In 1969 Palewski married and NM, already ill, was operated on for cancer of the liver. Not expected to live four months, she in fact recovered, but her health deteriorated again until in 1972 Hodgkins disease was diagnosed. She was nursed by her sisters and friends but despite various forms of treatment died at the age of 69.   JENNIFER PLASTOW

Selected works: *Highland Fling* (1931); *Christmas Pudding* (1932); *Wigs on the Green* (1935); (ed.), *The Ladies of Alderley* (1938); (ed.), *The Stanleys of Alderley* (1939); *Pigeon Pie* (1940); *The Pursuit of Love* (1945); *Love in a Cold Climate* (1949); (trans.), *La Princesse de Clèves*, by Madame de Lafayette (1950); *The Blessing* (1951); (trans.), *The Little Hut*, by A. Roussin. (1951); *Madame de Pompadour* (1954); *Voltaire in Love* (1957); *Don't Tell Alfred* (1960); *The Water Beetle* (1962); *The Sun King* (1966); *Frederick the Great* (1970).

References: Acton, H., *Nancy Mitford: A Memoir* (1975); Hastings, S., *Nancy Mitford* (1985); Mosley, C. (ed.), *A Talent to Annoy: Essays, Journalism, and Reviews* (1986).

Molesworth, Louisa
b. 29 May 1839, Rotterdam; d. 20 July 1921, London
Novelist, writer for children
(Also wrote under Ennis Graham)

LM was the daughter of Charles Stewart, a merchant shipper from Scotland. The family moved from Rotterdam to Manchester in 1841 and lived first in Rusholme and then in Whalley Range until, with increased wealth, they moved to West Hall in Cheshire when LM was already in her twenties. With the two brothers nearest her in age away at school she was a lonely child who amused herself making up stories about the things around her, like her mother's cotton reels. She did not go to school apart from one year in Lausanne, but she received some training in writing from the Rev. William Gaskell, the husband of Elizabeth Gaskell.

In 1861 she married Major Richard Molesworth; they had seven children, two dying young, but her marriage was not a happy one. He had been wounded in the Crimean War and became as a result short-tempered and unreliable in money matters. In 1878 she separated from her husband and went to live in France, visiting Germany several times, coming back to London in 1883 where she lived until her death.

Her earliest books, written for adults under the pseudonym 'Ennis Graham,' reflected the incompatibility of herself and Major Molesworth as marriage partners and, if not great novels, nevertheless highlighted the problems of Victorian women who felt they had lives of their own to protect. In the three-volume novel *Cecily* (1874), which ends with a happy wedding, the heroine avoids an earlier possible marriage where she would have been devalued. It is reminiscent of Jane Austen's fervent indignation in *Pride and Prejudice* over what happens to Charlotte when she marries Mr. Collins. Cecily Methvyn says to her mother, 'It is a pity when a girl has no future except marriage to look foward to: there is something undignified and lowering in the position.' Significantly, the last chapter is called 'Friend and Wife'. And if LM's writing contains too many phrases like 'dear primroses were nestling in the hedgerows', she is nevertheless capable of creating a character like Mrs. Crichton to be laughed at with something approaching the same ironic onslaught of writers like Jane Austen and Dickens.

Perhaps this undoubted feminism was one reason why Sir Noel Paton, illustrator of Charles Kingsley's *The Water Babies*, advised her to stop writing for adults and start writing for children. She took his advice and then remained as firmly on the side of the child (usually a girl) as she had been on the side of the woman in her earlier novels.

Out of her many books for young children, *Carrots* (1876) and *The Adventures of Herr Baby* (1881) are well worth reading although slightly marred by the irritating device of using baby-talk. These and other stories were based on incidents from her own life and on her own children. For older children the two books which have been often reprinted are *The Cuckoo Clock* (1877) and *The Carved Lions* (1895), where realism is mixed with magic in a way which places LM in a line of writers from Lewis Carroll though George Macdonald, Edith Nesbit, and C. S. Lewis to more recent writers like Russell Hoban. The cuckoo in the *The Cuckoo Clock* leads Griselda, who has come to stay with two old aunts, into a magic world where he helps her to learn to cope with growing up: their verbal exchanges are reminiscent of Alice's own encounters with many of the characters she meets in Wonderland. It is from these magic yet humourously human confrontations that LM creates what she herself called 'one of the most powerful levers for good' in writing for children.

Geraldine, in *The Carved Lions*, relates her own story of a childhood in a smoky town (LM's Rusholme in Manchester) and boarding school, followed by running away to find shelter in the shop with the carved lions. The magic dream episode at the end sets her free.

The characters in these and her other successful books are lively and appealing, so that we as readers, both adults and children, can join her in feeling 'as if somewhere the children [i.e. in her books] I have learnt to love are living, growing into men and women like my own real sons and daughters'. She wrote over 100 books altogether.

Marghanita Laski slated her for poor syntax; R. L. Green, following earlier critics, labelled her the Jane Austen of the nursery; and earlier still Swinburne wrote, 'Since the death of George Eliot there is none whose touch is so exquisite and masterly, whose love is so thoroughly according to knowledge, whose bright and sweet invention is so fruitful, so truthful or so delightful as Mrs Molesworth.' It seems that Marghanita Laski is unnecessarily severe, and that R. L. Green may have some right in his claim though for the wrong reasons. Since Mrs Gaskell called Jane Austen's books Chinese miniatures compared with Charlotte Brontë's full-size paintings, then R. L. Green's description of LM's writing as miniatures compared with Jane Austen's great painting would reduce LM to the size of microfilm! The irony, humour, and colossal moral indignation which Elizabeth Gaskell missed in Jane Austen, R. L. Green seems to have missed in LM. Swinburne perhaps comes nearest to appreciating her achievement, even if the expression of his approval is typically male in its patronizing tone.   LIZ CASHDAN

Selected works: *Lover and Husband* (1870); *She Was Young and He Was Old* (1872); *Cicely* (1874); *Carrots – Just a Little Boy* (1876); *The Cuckoo Clock* (1877); *Grandmother Dear* (1878); *The Tapestry Room* (1879); *The Adventures of Herr Baby* (1881); *Hoodie* (1882); *Two Little Waifs* (1883); *Lettice* (1884); *Us: An Old-fashioned Tale* (1885); *Four Ghost Stories* (1888); *The Rectory Children* (1889); *Twelve Tiny Tales* (1890); *Nurse Heatherdale's Story* (1891); *The Girls and I* (1892); *The Carved Lions* (1895); *The Oriel Window* (1896); *The Laurel Walk* (1898); *The House that Grew* (1900); *The Mystery of the Pinewood* (1904); *Fairies of Sorts* (1908); *Fairies Afield* (1911).

References: BA (19); Doyle, B., *Who's Who in Children's Literature* (1968); Green, R. L., *Mrs Molesworth* (1961); Green, R. L., *Tellers of Tales* (1969); Laski, M., *Mrs Ewing, Mrs Molesworth and Mrs Hodgson Burnett* (1950); OCCL.

Monk, Mary

b.1677 (?); d. 1715, Bath
Poet

Nothing is known oof the life of MM, second daughter of Robert, first Viscount Molesworth, except that she married George Monk of Dublin and died at Bath of a 'languishing Sickness'. In 1716 her father published a collection of her manuscripts under the title *Marinda: Poems and Translations Upon Several Occasions*. He explains, near the end of his rambling forty-seven-page preface, that the poems were found in MM's desk and that 'most of them are the Product of the leisure Hours of a Young Gentlewoman lately Dead, who in a Remote Country Retirement, without any Assistance but that of a good Library, and without omitting the daily Care due to a large Family, not only perfectly acquired the several Languages here made use of, but the good Morals and Principles contain'd in those Books'.

Two poems are identified as having been sent to MM by friends; eight others are addressed to MM as Marinda; and twenty-six are MM's translations of works by Italian and Spanish poets, including Tasso, Guarini, Petrarch, Della Casa, and Quevedo. The longest original work in the collection – 196 lines – is 'Moccoli: A Poem Address'd to Col. Richard Molesworth. At the Camp at Pratz del Rey in Catalonia. Anno. 1711'. Traditional odes, eclogues, songs and miscellaneous verse take up most of the remaining pages. MM's taste for satire and parody is seen in some of her epigrams and her burlesque translation of 'On a Lady's Statue in Marble'. She and her friends evidently enjoyed mocking the pastoral conventions, as in the series of three poems beginning with 'A Tale Sent by a Friend'. This is followed by 'Eclogue. In Return for the Foregoing Tale' and then by 'Answer to the Foregoing Eclogue', in which the writer ridicules 'the stale worn out Imagery,/Of Fields, Brooks and Shades'. One work not included in *Marinda* is 'Verses from a Lady at Bath, Dying with a Consumption, to her Husband'. This twenty-two-line poem was published in 1750 in *The Gentleman's Magazine* and, with some changes, in Theophilus Cibber's *The Lives of the Poets* (1753), in *Poems by Eminent Ladies* (1755), and in George Ballard's *Memoirs of Several Ladies of Great Britain* (1752).

JOYCE FULLARD

Works: *Marinda: Poems and Translations Upon Several Occasions* (1716); 'Verses from a Lady at Bath, Dying with a Consumption, to her Husband', *Gentleman's Magazine* 20 (1750).

References: Adams, H. G. (ed.), *Cyclopaedia of Female Biography* (1869); Allibone; Ballard; Cibber, T., *The Lives of the Poets of Great Britain and Ireland to the Time of Dean Swift* (1753); *DNB*; Reynolds, M., *The Learned Lady in England 1650–1760* (1920); Rowton, F. (ed.) *Cyclopaedia of Female Poets . . . With Additions by an American Editor* (1849); Todd; *The Works of Sir James Ware Concerning Ireland* (1739).

Montagu, Elizabeth

b. 2 October 1720, York; d. 25 August 1800, London

Scholar, critic, essayist, letter writer

Hailed by Dr Johnson as 'Queen of the Blues', EM reigned supreme in London for many years as a society hostess and patroness of the arts.

She was the fourth child and eldest daughter of Matthew Robinson, a wealthy landowner, and his wife Elizabeth (*née* Drake), who had been educated in the enlightened academic traditions of the famous Mrs Makin. EM herself spent several years at Cambridge with the family of her step-grandfather, the Rev. Dr Conyers Middleton, who taught her literature, history and theology.

She was a clever, lively, restless girl (nicknamed 'Fidget') and in August 1742 she married Edward Montagu, a rich MP, mathematician, and colliery owner, nearly thirty years her senior. In 1744, after the death of their only child in infancy, she turned more and more to literary and social activities, chiefly in London, her quiet, country-loving husband proving no obstacle to her ambitions. While her sister, Mrs Sarah Scott, became a successful novelist in the 1750s, EM was gaining fame through her lavish parties and receptions, where her conversation sparkled as brilliantly as her diamonds. Among her friends and guests were leading politicians, clergymen, scholars, actors, artists, writers, and a galaxy of *femmes savantes* from both sides of the Channel.

Her own ventures into authorship began in 1760, when she anonymously contributed three dialogues to her friend Lord Lyttelton's book *Dialogues of the Dead*, and in 1769 her essay on Shakespeare established her as a literary critic, in spite of Johnson's disapproval. Johnson always praised EM's conversational powers but not her writings, and this, together with her low opinion of Lyttelton and his dialogues, put a severe strain on their friendship.

Her husband died in 1775 and, far from retiring, EM, now very wealthy, had a palatial mansion built in Portman Square, complete with a Chinese Room, an Athenian Room, a Feather Room, a Room of Cupidons, and decorations by Angelica Kauffmann. There she entertained even more dazzlingly than before, sometimes with over 700 guests at a single reception, and occasionally graced by royalty (the Queen once came to breakfast with six princesses). Few could compete with such magnificence, although Hester Thrale, another affluent, fashionable, and learned hostess, vied with EM in the spendour of her dresses and the lustre of her jewels.

Extremely vain and often frivolous, EM was never 'fast' and expressed regret that 'the generality of women who have excelled in wit, have failed in chastity'. Respectable Bluestockings flocked to the salons of the 'Palais Portman'; heavy drinking, gambling, and card playing were discouraged, and coffee, tea, chocolate, and good food and conversation were substituted. Hannah More celebrated this transformation in her poem *The Bas Bleu*, and Elizabeth Carter marvelled at the refinement and 'elegant brilliancy' of these gatherings. Carter was a close friend and 'preceptress' to EM, and detractors claimed that most of EM's knowledge came secondhand from Carter.

EM also learned much from her continental friends. She visited France in 1776 and was invited to the salons of some of the most distinguished Parisian hostesses, where she carefully studied their houses and habits, their clothes, cosmetics and conversations. Back in London she became known as 'the Madame du Deffand of the English capital'.

Believing that 'gold is the principal ingredient in the composition of earthly happiness', EM enriched the lives of others by her considerable generosity. She gave pensions and presents to her friends (her gift of exquisite perfume to the blind Madame du Deffand is an instance of her thoughtful kindliness); she organized annual May Day feasts for the little chimney sweeps of London, and spent much time and money financing and promoting needy writers and artists. Through her salons she performed useful introductions, and her name appeared on dozens of subscription lists.

As well as a poetical shoemaker and a poetical milkwoman, the beneficiaries of this 'female Maecenas' included the poet and philosopher James Beattie (author of *The Minstrel*), who named his second son Montagu after her, the scholar Robert Potter, whose translation of Aeschylus became a standard work, the poet Cowper, and the painter James Barry. Many of her protégés rewarded her with extravagant praise and the most fulsome flattery, prompting Horace Walpole's sensible comment, 'There is nothing more foolish than the hyperboles of contemporaries on one another.'

EM of course flourished on hyperbole, and continued to hold court until her late seventies, when ill-health, with increasing 'spasms' and near-blindness, forced her to live more quietly, spending much of her time at Sandleford Priory, her Berkshire country home, where she had adopted a nephew and his family. Even there she was able to entertain regally on occasion, having converted the ruined priory chapel into a sumptuous banqueting hall. She died in her London home and was buried in Winchester Cathedral with her husband.

Her dialogues for Lyttelton are mediocre, except for a few flashes of satire, but her essay on Shakespeare attempts an interesting work of rehabilitation, stressing the poetical, sublime, and imaginative aspects of his genius, as well as his profound psychological insight, and hitting hard at Voltaire, Corneille, and the narrow dogmatism of classical pedantry. She is particularly perceptive in dealing with the characters of Lear and Falstaff, and, in praising the wilder side of Shakespeare's drama, she relates the horrors and terrors of *Macbeth* to Gothic mysteries and superstitions.

Such criticism from the pen of an Englishwoman was at that time an unusual event, and her romantic and enthusiastic approach (in contrast to the more cautious and conventional attitudes in Dr Johnson's *Preface*) ensured its popularity; it ran into several editions with translations into German, French and Italian.

Her extensive correspondence reveals her vivacious, versatile, and manipulative personality, and she deserves special credit for her success in developing the refining and civilizing influence of the salon, and for her notable achievements in raising the status of literary men and women during the second half of the eighteenth century.   MARGARET MAISON

Works: 'Dialogues XXVI, XXVII and XXVIII' (G. Lyttelton), *Dialogues of the Dead* (1760); *An Essay on the Writings and Genius of Shakespear, compared with the Greek and French Dramatic Poets. With Some Remarks upon the Misrepresentations of Mons. de Voltaire* (1769); Montagu, M. (ed.), *The Letters of Mrs Elizabeth Montagu, with some of the Letters of her Correspondents* (part 1 1809, part 2 1813); *Elizabeth Montagu, the Queen of the Bluestockings: Her Correspondence from 1720 to 1761*, ed. E. Climenson (1906); *Mrs Montagu, 'Queen of the Blues': Her Letters and Friendships from 1762 to 1800*, ed. R. Blunt (1923).

References: Balderston, K. (ed.), *Thraliana* (1942); Busse, J., *Mrs Montagu, Queen of the Blues* (1928); Doran, J., *A Lady of the Last Century* (1873); Elwood, A., *Memoirs of the Literary Ladies of England (1843)*; Freeman, A., 'Preface' to *An essay on the Writings and Genius of Shakespear etc.* (reprint) (1970); Hill, G. (ed.), *Boswell's Life of Johnson* (1934–50); Hornbeak, K., 'New light on Mrs Montagu' in *The Age of Johnson* (1949); Huchon, R., *Mrs Montagu and Her Friends* (1907); Johnson, R., *Bluestocking Letters* (1926); Jones, W., 'The romantic Bluestocking, Elizabeth Montagu', *Huntington Library Quarterly* 12, 1 (November 1948); Pennington, M., (ed.), *Letters from Mrs Elizabeth Carter to Mrs Montagu between the years 1755 and 1800. Chiefly upon Literary and Moral Subjects* (1817); Rogers, K., *Feminism in Eighteenth-Century England* (1982);Tinker, C., *The Salon and English Letters* (1915); Wheeler, E., *Famous Bluestockings* (1910).

Montagu, Lady Mary Wortley

christened 26 May 1689, London; d. 21 August 1762, London

Poet, essayist, letter writer

LM's sex, rank, and sense of decorum precluded publication in her own name during her lifetime, though a number of her compositions were pirated and she appears to have connived at the anonymous publication of others. She collaborated with Pope, Gay, and Lord Hervey on such equal terms that some of her poems were attributed to them. She published a number of essays anonymously but evidently intended her reputation as a writer to rest on her celebrated 'Turkish Letters' which she prepared for posthumous publication. Her other compositions took the form of verses and essays inscribed in private notebooks, and responses to topical events, for all of which the proposed audience consisted of close associates, so that their character is simultaneously public and intimate.

LM was the eldest of four children of Evelyn Pierrepont, fifth Earl and first Duke of Kingston, and Lady Mary Fielding, daughter of the Earl of Denbigh. After her mother's death in 1693 she lived for a time with her paternal grandmother near Salisbury and then in her father's sometimes negligent care in London and at Thoresby in Nottinghamshire. She compensated for the deficiencies of her governess ('one of the worst in the world') by reading avidly in her father's library and teaching herself Latin. Through her father she became acquainted early in her adult life with the intersecting worlds of Whig politics and contemporary literature. Her lively, topical verses began to be appreciated in fashionable circles and she became known for her intellect, wit, and, until she had smallpox in 1715, her beauty. After a long and emotionally complex courtship she eloped in 1712 with Edward Wortley, whose anxious and possessive wooing rapidly declined after marriage into cold indifference to her emotional needs. Her son, Edward, born in 1713, grew up to be a wastrel; her daughter Mary, born in Constantinople in 1718, married the Earl of Bute. In 1716 LM accompanied her husband on his appointment as ambassador to Turkey. She learned Turkish, explored Constantinople in disguise, used the advantage of gender to penetrate the exotic mysteries of the seraglio, and was sufficiently impressed by the practice of inoculation against smallpox to have the operation carried out on her litle son and to campaign for its introduction in England. On Wortley's recall in 1718, she settled in Twickenham. Her acquaintance spanned the *beau monde* and the world of letters, and her relations with both could be stormy: Pope's warm admiration degenerated into vindictive spite and they quarrelled spectacularly in print, to the entertainment of their associates and the detriment of her reputation. In 1736, at the age of 47, she fell passionately in love with Franceso Algarotti, a charming, unscrupulous, bisexual Venetian half her age, and three years later parted amicably from her family and left England for Venice, ostensibly for her health but actually in the unrealistic and unfulfilled hope that he would join her. For the next twenty-three years she lived variously in Italy and the South of France until, after Wortley's death in 1761, she became anxious about her financial position and her health and returned to London, where she died of cancer a few months later.

LM's juvenilia, carefully collected in two handwritten volumes in her teens, display an early pleasure in the role of author and a deft imitative capacity. Her allegory of a quest for love, in which Marriage is a place of discord, True Love is derelict and Coquetry a tangled thicket, witnesses to a precocious scepticism about the likelihood of attaining happiness which her adult experience tended to confirm. She developed her gift for witty parody in her mature poetry: her verse attacks on Pope and Swift capture precisely the characteristic manner of each victim. The expression of her poetic talent was restricted to the conventions of the Augustan tradition in terms of form, diction, and to some extent of content, though within these limitations she showed great versatility in a variety of modes. Her rhyming couplets can be both delicate and orotund and her diction is sometimes unexpectedly and attractively direct and concrete (as in 'The Lovers' when the clandestine pair 'meet with Champaign and a Chicken at last'). 'Constantinople', written in the 'kiosk' of the British Palace at Pera, is a pastoral meditation on the depredations of time and the pleasures of retirement. Her 'Eclogues', composed in close association with Pope and Gay, are a series of satirical vignettes of contemporary manners and morals, making pseudonymous reference to identifiable people. The eclogue on 'The Bassette Table' includes a convincing and possibly autobiographical account of 'Smilinda's' surrender to male charms, and 'The Smallpox' vividly expresses LM's own fear in her sickness. While her poetry sparkles with witty, rational observation of human behaviour and of the moral shortcomings of both public and private life, she also manifests a persistent pessimism about the power of love to endure. Her response to a sentimental epitaph by Pope on two lovers killed by lightning was to congratulate them on avoiding the inevitable decline of their passion. Elsewhere she observes that by dying three months after marriage a Mrs Bowes will never have to exchange the 'tender lover for the imperious Lord'. Her poetic manner can encompass moments of emotional desolation: in the fragment 'Ye soft ideas leave my tortur'd Breast', the anguish of her passion for Algarotti breaks through the formal structure.

LM's feminism was an aspect of her urbane, rational judgement on her society's failings. In 1714, in response to a satire by Addison on the conduct of widows, she contributed to the *Spectator* a lively analysis of women's experience of men in which the ironic tone extends to the representation of the shallow, selfish female narrator. Her poetic 'adaptation' of a satire by Boileau castigates both frivolous and intellectual women for foolishness and self-absorption. Her most ambitious effort in the journalistic mode, a pro-Walpole journal issued in nine parts in 1737–8, includes in issue no. 6 a defence of women in which she deplores the damage done to them by men's contemptuous devaluation of their abilities and urges recognition of their moral equality, but also represents the author as a 'Freind, tho' I do not aspire to be an admirer of the fair sex'. The careful distinction balances her respect for justice against her contempt for folly and hypocrisy in either sex.

Her prose writings testify to the range of her interests and information. In 1722 she contributed to the debate on inoculation an essay (by a 'Turkey Merchant') in which she describes the operation and attributes its occasional failure to medical incompetence. *The Nonsense of Commonsense*, a counterblast to the Opposition paper *Common Sense*, tackles a variety of social and political issues in vigorous and combative style. Among her prose pieces not intended for the public are a radical proposal to reform corruption in parliamentary elections by abolishing Parliament, and a gossipy, vivid, and incisive account of the court of George I. Her essay in response to a maxim of La Rochefoucauld seems entirely uncharacteristic in its, perhaps wishful, insistence that happiness can be found in marriage. Two prose pieces have a particularly personal character – an adolescent autobiographical fragment and a version in French of the tale of the Sleeping Beauty, in which the princess, whose misfortunes closely parallel LM's, is finally cursed with the gift of '*un grand fond de tendresse*'. Both essays convey a wry recognition of her emotional isolation.

LM was all her life a candid, entertaining letter writer, combining sharp-eyed observation with acute judgement. Her 'Turkish Letters', compiled from her correspondence with a number of recipients, form a narrative of sustained brilliance. As a traveller, she has little interest in topography: her attention is focused upon the human and the social. The energy and glitter of her style perfectly expresses her excitement at entering a world reminiscent at once of the Arabian Nights, Homer, and Ovid, while its balanced urbanity maintains an objective distance from what she describes. Her irony is reserved for her recognition that some Turkish practices show more civilization than those of Europe. Her accounts of the women's bath and of the seraglio are imbued with a sensuous appreciation of luxury refined by elegance to a condition of delicate beauty. She notes with relish the paradox of the Turkish women's greater emancipation than her own: while they regard her corset with pity and horror, she perceives that the Muslim veil liberates them into a life of undetected amours. Her later letters to her sister provide a scintillating and often malicious portrayal of London society. Those written in old age from Italy to her daughter contain some perceptive judgements of contemporary literature, some rather bitter reflections on the education of women and a memorable picture of the expatriate life of a rational, cultured, witty woman who seems always to have felt that she was 'born to be unfortunate, and I must fulfil my Destiny'.

ELIZABETH JOYCE

Works: 'Essay by Mrs President', *Spectator* (28 July 1714); *Town Eclogues* (1717); 'Constantinople' (1720); 'Virtue in Danger' (1721); *A Plain Account of the Innoculating of the Small Pox, by a Turkey Merchant* (1722); 'Verses Addressed to the Imitator of the First Satire of the Second Book of Horace' (1733); *The Nonsense of Common Sense* (nine issues) (1737–8); 'Epistle from Arthur G—Y to Mrs M— (1747); *Six Town Eclogues, with Some Other poems*, ed. H. Walpole (1747); verses in *A Collection of Poems*, printed for R. Dodsley (1748); 'Epistle to Lord Bathurst' (1748); 'The Eighth Ode of Horace Imitated' (1750); *Letters* (1763); *Poetical Works*, ed. I. Reed (1768); *Works*, ed. J. Dalloway (1803); *Letters and Works*, ed. Lord Wharnclife (1837); *Letters and Works*, ed. W. Moy Thomas (1861); *Letters 1709–1762*, ed. R. B. Johnson (1906); *Complete Letters*, ed. R. Halsband (1965–7); *Essays and Poems and Simplicity: A Comedy*, ed. R. Halsband and I. Grundy (1977).

References: Stuart, L., *Biographical Anecdotes* (1837); Halsband, R., *The Life of Lady Mary Wortley Montagu* (1957); Halsband, R., *The Lady of Letters in the Eighteenth Century* (1969); Halsband, R., 'Lady Mary Wortley Montagu as letter writer', *PMLA* (June 1965); Grundy, I., 'Ovid and eighteenth century divorce: an unpublished poem by Lady Mary Wortley Montagu', *Review of English Studies* (1972).

More, Hannah

b. 2 February 1745, Stapleton; d. September 1833, Clifton
Polemicist, poet, playwright, novelist
The combination of morally restrictive and politically reactionary teaching in HM's extensive writings invites a strong response from the reader. Her rejection of the rights of man – including those of woman – in favour of duty to God and King influenced the minds of her contemporaries and later generations. Her biographer's claim, in 1838, that her works were read 'from the Mississippi to the Ganges' is supported by evidence. *Practical Piety* was translated into Icelandic and Persian; her tracts were read with avidity in Sierra Leone. On the success of a royalist work in the republic, she declared, 'I have conquered America.' HM achieved the position of moral dictator, in spite of the handicaps of her sex and modest social rank, as a result of sound education, industry, and an evangelical sense of mission. Her persuasive use of language in the cause of 'the reformation of the British character' owes much to her early experience as a fashionable poet and playwright, before her withdrawal from the vanities of the world.

HM's father, Jacob More, was master of the Free School of Fishponds; her mother, Mary Grace, was the daughter of a respectable farmer. HM was the fourth of five daughters. The girls' talents were cultivated by the father, in order to enable them to earn their living by managing a school for young ladies. HM's mathematical abilities alarmed him; he curtailed these unfeminine studies, but allowed her to develop her Latin. At the age of 20 the eldest daughter opened a school in Bristol, where HM and her sisters were educated until they were old enough to take part in teaching and management. The school's emphasis on religious and moral education caused it to become nationally renowned.

HM gave up her share in the school at the age of 22, on acceptance of the proposal of William Turner, a middle-aged estate owner, who retreated twice from the marriage ceremony in the next six years. Friends persuaded her to break off the engagement and to accept – with reluctance – his compensatory offer of £200 per annum. This money gave her sufficient independence to rebuild her life. She resolved never to marry, in spite of proposals. Turner, with hindsight, said that Providence had intended her for higher things.

She went to London in 1773 or 1774, gaining entry to artistic and literary circles. Annual visits followed. Her social ease and wit ensured her popularity with the older women of the Bluestocking group, such as Elizabeth Montagu. Animated letters describe her response to the 'dissipation' of London life. Her sister reported that she was a great favourite of Dr Johnson. Although he objected to HM's excessive flattery, he admired her skill in versification; he contributed to her change from comparative levity to propriety by reprimanding her for a reference to *Tom Jones*, 'so vicious a book', that no modest lady should confess to having read it. Even in these 'few sunshiny days' of life, her conscience infused a 'tincture of wormwood' into her pleasures.

An introduction to Garrick and his wife led to warm friendship and useful advice on her experiments in drama. She had already developed an interest in the theatre in Bristol. The shortage of proper material for their private recitals led to her writing a sequence of pastoral dialogues – *A Search After Happiness* – at the age of 17. It was widely circulated in schools before publication in 1773. Four young ladies confess their typical follies to the wise shepherdess, Urania, who corrects them. The most interesting fault is that of Cleora who wants fame, in spite of her sex: 'I long'd to burst these female bonds.' However, this is no feminist tract. Urania teaches Cleora to unite humility with reading, as 'Learning for female minds was never made.' 'A meteor, not a star you would appear, / For woman shines but in her proper sphere.'

HM did not follow her own advice; with determination she set about achieving success as a dramatist. The enthusiastic public response to her plays is hard to understand today. They combine sentiment with moral rhetoric, lapsing into bathos in moments of passion. *The Inflexible Captive* (1774), a Roman tragedy based on Metastasio, was considered by the author to be insufficiently 'bustling and dramatic'; there is more plot in *Percy* (1778), a Gothic drama of thwarted love and revenge in which the meek Elwina, dragged to the altar, puts virtue and duty above emotion. Echoes of Shakespeare and Percy's *Reliques* can be heard. Garrick wrote the Prologue, citing precedents for female achievement – the Furies and Muses. Garrick's death, a deep personal loss, destroyed HM's interest in the theatre. Her last secular play, *The Fatal Falsehood* (1779), needed his revision. On its appearance, Hannah Cowley accused her of plagiarism; HM denied this charge, but she had drawn extensively on Shakespeare for her Elizabethan tragedy. An inflated speech in praise of England as the 'land of heroes' foreshadows her later preoccupation with national unity and character.

HM retired to Hampton with Mrs Garrick to mourn, meditate, and work. In 1782 her *Sacred Dramas* appeared, based on Old Testament subjects, intentionally didactic rather than dramatic. Moral discourse suits her talents better than the invention and interaction of character in the earlier plays. She understands the sin of pride in Belshazzar and presents it forcefully: 'What is empire?/ The privilege to punish and enjoy; / To feel our pow'r in making others fear it.' The time of her own exercise of power was soon to come, but during her retreat she analysed the experience of suffering. In *Sensibility*, her most ambitious poem, printed with the *Dramas*, she examines the fashionable cult of heightened emotion, distinguishing between the artificial ecstasies of a counterfeit response and the 'sacred rapture' of pain felt by finely fashioned nerves. *The Bas Bleu, or, Conversation*, celebrates the Bluestocking discussions at Mrs Vesey's house as reviving the art of talking, which had been threatened by pedantry, affectation, calumny, levity, and the tyranny of card-games:

> Long did Quadrille despotic sit,
> That Vandal of Colloquial wit
> And Conversation's setting light
> Lay half-obscured in Gothic night.

Slavery (1778) attacks injustice, in passionate and incisive verse. In a footnote, she records seeing a set of slave-chains and instruments for wrenching open jaws. This experience stirred her imagination to an unwonted degree; she attacks the lust for gold or conquest in the 'white savage' and the blindness of prejudice.

In *Thoughts on the Importance of the Manners of the Great* (1788), HM turns to correcting upper-class society, urging those whom 'the goodness of Providence has exempted from painful occupation' to act responsibly towards their social inferiors. The same privileged class is addressed in 1793, in *Remarks on the Speech of M. Dupont*, which appeals to British ladies to provide funds for the exiled French clergy. Her suggestion that retrenchment of costly dishes at table could provide the money reflects her awareness of the limited sphere of women's financial control. Her work in the next few years is expressly designed to overcome the infection of disorder in the body politic. She explains her shift in focus to the lower classes in a letter describing how the Bishop of London pleaded with her to write 'some little thing tending to open their eyes' to the dangers of Tom Paine's influence. She refused, but later wrote the pamphlet *Village Politics* (1793), which satirizes radical watchwords, encouraging submission to God and government, in a dialogue between Jack Anvil, the blacksmith, and Tom Hod, the mason:

Tom:. . . I want liberty.
Jack: Liberty! That's bad indeed! What! has anyone fetched a warrant for thee?
Come, man, cheer up, I'll be bound for thee. . . .
Tom:No, no, I want a new Constitution.
Jack: Indeed! why I thought thou hadst been a desperately healthy fellow.
Send for a doctor directly.

Jack explains that his friend's quarrel is with Providence, since it is ordained that 'the woman is below her husband, and the children are below their mother, and the servant is below his master'. Their argument is transposed into more popular verse in a ballad of 1795, 'The Riot', where Tom tries sedition:

> Come, neighbours, no longer be patient and quiet,
> Come let us go kick up a bit of a riot,
> I'm hungry, my lads, but I've little to eat . . .
> So we'll pull down the mills, and we'll seize all the meat.

Jack refuses to take part; he'd rather be hungry than hanged.

HM's successful imitation of popular ballads and tales owes much to careful research among chapbooks in which she identified best-selling narrative patterns which could be adapted to serve her political and moral purpose. *The Cheap Repository Tracts* of 1795–8 were designed for the edification of the poor. Two million sold in the first year, a tribute to the efficient system of distribution set up by philanthropic groups. Prices ranged from a halfpenny to twopence, but more expensive collected editions for families and boarding schools ensured a wider readership. In the political unrest of 1817 the tracts were reissued, with additions. The Tracts were produced as a collective enterprise; those written by HM herself are signed 'Z'. The best are strong in narrative, with lively touches of detail and shrewd insight into human folly and self-deception. HM's obvious pleasure in story telling is curbed by her sense of moral purpose; she insists on a serious reading. She also offers useful practical hints, sometimes under sub-headings, such as Advice to Young Tradesmen, or Rules for Retail Dealers. The most famous of the tracts was *The Shepherd of Salisbury Plain*. The shepherd, his wife, and eight children live in a damp cottage, fending off starvation by hard work, and giving thanks to God for merciful limitation of misfortune. In an attack of rheumatic paralysis, his wife rejoices that her hands were spared to patch the family's rags. A benefactor appoints the shepherd as Sunday School teacher, warning that 'I am not going to make you rich but useful.'

For some years, HM and her sister Martha (Patty) had been engaged in a project to educate the poor in the Mendip villages. In a heroic campaign, the sisters ventured into poor and hostile villages, some with absentee or drunken clergy and no supervising gentry. Over a period of years, many schools were built, and staff were employed to teach reading (for Bible study) and practical skills, such as spinning and knitting. HM declared, 'I allow of no writing for the poor,' perhaps remembering an earlier protégée – the milkwoman Ann Yearsley, who forgot to be deferential. As a pioneer, HM made enemies, who almost undermined her system during the Blagdon Controversy of 1800–4. According to her, two Jacobin and infidel curates accused her of supporting seminaries of vice and sedition. Pamphlet battles began. Apart from the familiar charge that she had leanings towards Methodism, the accusations against her included plotting the assassination of the king and instigating the war.

In 1802 she built Barley Wood, where her retired sisters later joined her. She returned to writing on the theme of education. In 1799 she published her major work: *Strictures on the Modern System of Female Education*. Although she completely accepts the inferior social status of women she advocates the development of a moral superiority based on the practice of religion and a more rigorous training of the mind at the expense of decorative accomplishments. She offers women a constructive approach to national crisis, calling on them to contribute towards 'the saving of their country' by trying 'to raise the depressed tone of public morals, and to awaken the drowsy spirit of religious principle'.

In *Hints Towards Forming the Character of a Young Princess* (1805), she avoids full discussion of the issues of female rule by resorting to the use of the masculine generic term 'the prince'; she advises a diet of history and religion to counteract any weakness that might allow revolution to uproot the British oak.

The theme of eduction dominates her best-known work, *Coelebs in Search of a Wife*, a treatise 'comprehending Observations on Domestic Habits in manners, religion and morals'. Coelebs inspects many women in his quest; all are unsuitable except the rationally educated but blushing and modest Lucilla, who combines self-denial with enterprise in the manner of the More sisters. The slight narrative presents some of the theories of *Strictures* in a more entertaining way.

HM devoted the rest of her long life to religious and political argument, anticipating the muscular Christianity of the Victorian public school. After *Christian Morals* (1813), her last important work was *Moral Sketches* (1819), in which she exhorts fathers to take responsibility for the education of their sons, warning against the 'base and grovelling pursuits of sensuality'. Her patriotism has become blatantly jingoistic. She praises divine wisdom for making her country an island, and she hopes that 'Britain . . . may still set an example to all the kingdoms of earth'.

HM survived her sisters by many years, giving audience to a stream of visitors – fifty were recorded in one week. The strain of illness, hospitality, and the dishonesty of servants forced her to move to Clifton, where she died.

CLARE MACDONALD SHAW

Selected works: *A Search after Happiness: A Pastoral Drama* (1773); *The Inflexible*

Captive: A Tragedy (1774); *Sir Eldred of the Bower and The Bleeding Rock: Two Legendary Tales* (1776); *Essays on Various Subjects, Principally Designed for Young Ladies* (1777); *Percy: A Tragedy* (1778); *Sacred Dramas* (1782); *Florio: A Tale for Fine Gentlemen and Fine Ladies, and The Bas Bleu, or, Conversation: Two Poems* (1786); *Slavery: A Poem* (1788); *Bishop Bonner's Ghost* (1789); *An Estimate of the Religion of the Fashionable World* (1791); *Remarks on the Speech of M. Dupont, Made in the National Convention of France* (1793); *Village Politics* (1793); *Questions and Answers for the Mendip and Sunday Schools* (1795); *Cheap Repository Tracts* (1795–8); *Strictures on the Modern System of Female Education* (1799); *Coelebs in Search of a Wife* (1808); *Practical Piety* (1811); *Christian Morals* (1813); *An Essay on the Character and Practical Writings of St Paul* (1815); *Stories for the Middle Ranks of Society, and Tales for the Common People* (1817); *Moral Sketches of Prevailing Opinions and Manners* (1819); *The Twelfth of August, or, The Feast of Freedom* (1819); *Bible Rhymes* (1821); *The Spirit of Prayer* (selections) (1825).
References: *DNB*; Drabble; Hopkins, M. A., *Hannah More and Her Circle* (1947); Jones, M. G., *Hannah More* (1952); Lewis, W. S., Smith, R. A., and Bennett, C. H., *Walpole: Correspondence*, vol. 31, *Correspondence with Hannah More* (1961); Roberts, A. (ed.), *Mendip Annals, or, A Narrative of the Charitable Labours of Hannah More and Martha More: Being the Journal of Martha More* (1859); Roberts, W., *Memoirs of the Life and Correspondence of Mrs Hannah More* (1834); Spinney, G. H., 'The Cheap Repository Tracts: Hazard and Marshall edition', *Transactions of the Bibliographical Society* (1940); Thompson, H., *Life of Hannah More, with Notices of Her Sisters* (1838); Todd; Weiss, H. B., *Hannah More's Cheap Repository Tracts in America* (1946); Yonge, C., *Hannah More* (1888).

Mortimer, Penelope

b. 19 September 1918, Rhyl, Flint
Novelist
(Also wrote under Penelope Dimont)

PM's father was a clergyman, A. F. G. Fletcher, who moved around the country from living to living. As a result PM's education was fragmented. Eventually she went to London University but left after one year. After starting work as a secretary she soon decided that she preferred marriage to a day-to-day outside job and she first married in 1937 and had four daughters. She continued to write on a freelance basis after her marriage, mainly for the *New Statesman*. She divorced, and then remarried in 1949. From this second marriage to the playwright and novelist John Mortimer she had a further two children. Her first novel, *Johanna* (written as Penelope Dimont) was published in 1947.

PM has said herself that the scope of her novels is narrow, dealing with universal situations: domestic relationships between adults and how these relationships affect children. Her novels are not unrelentingly serious and she uses humour for contrast. *A Villa in Summer* was published in 1955. It is a portrait of a relationship drifting apart, an examination of its breakdown and decay. The husband's feelings towards his wife are so bitter that he sees the world divided into two species of women: 'Emily and the others'. Emily sees the situation clearly but can do nothing to halt the disintegration.

Two more novels were published in the 1950s, *The Bright Prison* (1956) and *Daddy's Gone A-Hunting* (1959). *The Pumpkin Eater* appeared in 1962, PM's most widely known novel. It begins with the central character trying to be honest and finishes on the same note. She is a woman obsessed with procreating, a situation which must have been familiar to PM. Her house is packed full of

children, demanding her time, energy, and resources, and, in the process, she
alienates her (fourth) husband, Jake. He takes flight from this chaos to which,
of course, he has contributed, to other women. No one seems to escape this
domestic trap and the central couple in the novel continue the process of
destroying each other. Again PM is examining a relationship under a micro-
scope; its working jointly or separately. She has the knack of isolating her
characters from the chaos of their daily lives and subjecting them to a close
scrutiny, probing all the most sensitive areas.

PM is not concerned with the emancipated woman, in particular, nor society
in general. Her novels are peopled by servants – cooks, cleaners, nurses –
allowing her other women (for the servants are usually women) the freedom
to travel to the very edge of self-destruction, saved only by a need to record
and analyse the despair that has driven them to this state.

The Handyman (1983) is a novel of unrelenting tension with tragic consequences. Even the odd flashes of humour are black. The widowed Phyllis leaves
London after two years of trying to decide what to do with her life after her
husband's death, opting for what she imagines will be rural peace in the depths
of the country. A retired novelist looks like being a potential ally and friend.
Her plans are quickly thwarted. Her children bring their problems to disturb
the peace. The dream of friendship is not realized; rather she finds antagonism
in its place, and the handyman, Fred, proves to be the final horrific catalyst in
her rural idyll. Faced with this disarray, PM's readers are led back to a gentler
state where all looks as if it will be resolved. Not so. With a final twist she
reintroduces violence, which interrupts the smooth passage of her prose.

As a short story writer, PM does not stray far from the territory of her
novels. Children and parents vie for the stage. Children are bewildered by the
adult world which emphasizes their insecurity; a parson gropes his way through
life, unsatisfied with everything he does. PM allows no rest for her characters
– or her readers.   ALISON RIMMER

Works: (as Penelope Dimont) *Johanna* (1947); *A Villa in Summer* (1954); *The
Bright Prison* (1956); *With Love and Lizards* (with John Mortimer) (1957); *Daddy's
Gone A-Hunting* (1958; published in the US as *Cave of Ice*, 1959); *Saturday Lunch
with the Brownings* (1960); 'The Renegade' (1961); *Bunny Lake Is Missing* (with
John Mortimer) (1965); 'Ain't Afraid to Dance' (1966); *My Friend Says It's
Bullet-Proof* (1967); *The Home* (1967); 'Three's One' (1973); *Long Distance* (1974);
About Time: An Aspect of Autobiography (1979); *The Handyman* (1983); *Queen
Elizabeth: A Life of the Queen Mother* (1986).

References: *CA*; *CN*; Daiches, D., *The Penguin Series of Contemporary British
Novelists* (1973).

Muir, Willa

b. 13 March 1890, Montrose; d. 22 May 1970, London

Translator, novelist

(Also wrote under Agnes Neill Scott)

WM's interest in language began when as a child she spoke the Norse dialect
of her Shetland parents within the family, Scots with her friends in Montrose,
where her father ran a draper's shop, and a sort of English at school. She went
to Montrose Academy and then to the University of St Andrews where she
graduated in 1910 with a first-class degree in classics. During her degree course
she became engaged to a rugby-playing medical student, but the relationship
ended with his confession of infidelity and her throwing the engagement ring

into the sea. She wished to pursue a career in teaching and became a junior assistant in the Latin Department at St Andrews before teaching classics and educational psychology at the Gipsy Hill Training College in London where in 1918 she became Vice-Principal. In London she formed opinions on various contemporary issues, including feminism and the psychology of the unconscious, as well as keeping abreast of current ideas on education. She was involved in early Day Release projects. She met Edwin Muir in September 1918 and shortly before their marriage in June 1919, she had had to resign her post because her superiors objected to her marrying an 'atheist'. The next decade saw a series of European travels as Edwin, with WM's help, began to shed the disturbing effects of his time in Glasgow and discover his vocation as a poet. Translation work became a feature of the Muirs' lives. (When in the 1950s WM stopped translating, a factor in the decision was her annoyance with the tax burden Edwin incurred because of her earnings.) In 1932 WM and Edwin met A. S. Neill and agreed to assist him in setting up his International School at Hellerau. In 1925 WM miscarried and when she became pregnant in 1927 the couple returned to Britain; WM notes that this entailed returning to 'a patriarchally-minded country'. In October 1927 a son, Gavin, was born. The incompetent medical treatment WM received after the birth led to serious health problems from which she suffered for the rest of her life. In 1935 the Muirs moved to Scotland to provide a quieter environment for Gavin, who had been involved in a road accident. However the Muirs felt oppressed by the conservative conventions of St Andrews and were glad to move in 1942 to Edinburgh, where Edwin worked for the British Council. The stay was followed by stints in Prague from 1945 to 1948 and in Rome from 1949 to 1950. The unhappiness of the Prague years, overshadowed by the slow revelation of what Communist rule was to mean for the Czechs, was offset by the delight of being in Rome. The period 1950 to 1955 was spent at Newbattle Abbey, Edinburgh, the only Adult Education College in Scotland. Edwin was Warden and WM taught Latin to anyone interested. Then followed a year in America, where they met Robert Frost and Robert Lowell through Edwin's post as Norton Professor at Harvard. The couple returned to England where Edwin died in 1959. The Bollingen Award which he held was transferred to WM who completed a project he had begun, a book on ballads, from his notes. During the 1960s WM wrote an account of her relationship with Edwin. She was an extroverted and dynamic personality, a great conversationalist and mimic.

WM's versatile intelligence was not confined to a single genre but ranged through criticism, translation, the novel, and autobiography. She and Edwin translated together. Their method was to translate one half of a text each, then to revise each other's translation to minimize stylistic differences. According to P.H. Butter, Edwin's biographer, it is not possible to tell who translated what. Despite this equal workload, Edwin was often given sole credit for the translation. WM notes that it 'amused me, but irritated him'. It was through the Muirs' translations of Kafka in the 1930s that Kafka's work became more widely known. WM sometimes translated a text on her own, often under the pseudonym of Agnes Neill Scott.

In her autobiography, WM outlines one of the formative ideas of her life: belonging. As a child she felt she 'belonged' to the Universe but that sense of security and well-being was breached in later years by her awareness of discrimination against women. This experience is drawn on for the character of Elizabeth Shand in WM's first novel *Imagined Corners* (1931), where the deleterious effects of small-town Scottish life on women are discussed. Elizabeth escapes to Europe through the good offices of a friend, but WM is more convincing when she outlines the positions of the women who are left in Scotland when the novel closes. These themes are presaged in WM's monograph *Women: An Inquiry*, an essay which discusses women's attitudes to their emotions, and they are developed powerfully in *Mrs Ritchie* (1933), her last novel. As part of the resurgence of interest in Scottish culture during the 1920s and 1930s, WM published the cultural analysis *Mrs Grundy in Scotland* (1936), a companion work to her husband's *Scott and Scotland*. In her marriage to Edwin her sense of belonging, which had been damaged by circumstance, was healed and her autobiography records their creative and lasting partnership.

BETH DICKSON

Selected works: Women: An Inquiry (1925); (trans., under Agnes Neill Scott), *A Roumanian Diary* by Hans Carossa (1929); (trans., under Agnes Neill Scott), *Boyhood and Youth* by Hans Carossa (1931); *Imagined Corners* (1931); *Mrs Ritchie* (1933); *Mrs Grundy in Scotland* (1936); *Living with Ballads* (1965); *Belonging: A Memoir* (1968); selected translations by Willa and Edwin Muir: *Three Cities*, by Sholem Asch (1933); *Salvation*, by Sholem Asch (1936); *Mottke the Thief*, by Sholem Asch (1935); *The Sleepwalkers*, by Hermann Broch (1932); *The Unknown Quality*, by Hermann Broch (1935); *Richelieu*, by Carl J. Burckhardt (1940); *Jew Süss*, by Lion Feuchtwanger (1926); *The Ugly Duchess*, by Lion Feuchtwanger (1927); *Two Anglo-Saxon Plays: The Oil Islands and Warren Hastings* by Lion Feuchtwanger (1929); *Josephus*, by Lion Feuchtwanger (1932); *The False Nero*, by Lion Feuchtwanger (1937); *Class of 1902*, by Ernest Glaeser (1929); *Through the Eyes of a Woman*, by Zsolt de Harsányi (1941); *Dramatic Works*, vol. 7, by Gerhart Hauptmann (1925); *The Island of the Great Mother*, by Gerhart Hauptmann (1925); *The Inner Journey*, by Kurt Heuer (1932); *The Castle*, by Franz Kafka (1930); *The Trial*, by Franz Kafka (1937); *America*, by Franz Kafka (1938); *Parables in German and English*, by Franz Kafka (1947); *In the Penal Settlement*, by Franz Kafka (1948); 'Aphorisms' by Franz Kafka, *Modern Scot*, 3 (1932); *Little Friend*, by Ernest Lothar (1933); *The Mills of God*, by Ernest Lothar (1935); *The Hill of Lies*, by Heinrich Mann (1934); *The Queen's Doctor*, by Robert Neumann (1936); *A Woman Screamed*, by Robert Neumann (1938); *The Life of Eleonora Duse*, by E. A. Rheinhardt (1930).

Mulock, Dinah

b. 20 April 1826, Stoke on Trent, Staffordshire; d. 12 October 1887, Bromley, Kent

Novelist, essayist

Owing to the improvidence of her father, Thomas Mulock, DM led a difficult childhood, but by her energy she succeeded in supporting herself and her family through her writing. Her most famous novel, *John Halifax Gentleman* (1856), is a similar story of the efforts of a tanner's apprentice to rise in the world. The narrator of the novel, the crippled Phineas Fletcher, has feminine features, and his admiration for John Halifax seems to reflect, albeit with a concealment of gender, a conventionally Victorian view of the subservience of women. Other novels, notably *Agatha's Husband* (1853), have heroines who are a litle more strong-minded, although DM is rarely prepared to state, except in the most guarded terms, any opposition to the repression of women.

In her first novel, *The Ogilvies* (1849), her heroine Katherine marries her boring cousin Hugh although in love with the handsome Paul Lynedon. Katherine is discontented, but after Hugh's death there is no happy ending, since, after marrying Paul, Katherine soon dies. In *Christine's Mistake* (1865) Christine, a governess, who marries to escape a tedious life, is originally unhappy with her respectable husband, but eventually finds she loves him. In *A Brave Lady* (1870) Josephine Scanlon earns money, so that she is not dependent upon her husband, and eventually leaves his corrupting influence, but returns to him when he is dying. *Olive* (1850) appears to be a sober study of a single woman, but Olive's life ends in conventional married bliss. Rachel Armstrong, the heroine of *The Head of the Family* (1852), after being abandoned by her husband, tries to make a career as an actress, but finally ends up in a lunatic asylum. In all these novels we can see DM going some way towards a statement of a new role for women, but being eventually pulled back by conventional values. In her non-fictional writings like *A Woman's Thoughts About Women* (1858) DM speaks up against the view that women's only role is to marry, and even after her own marriage she continued to stress the need for feminine self-reliance. In *Plain Speaking* (1852) she speaks of the need for women to earn their living, and suggests ways of making this easier. Her own career, in which she kept up a constant stream of poetry, articles, and short stories as well as novels, seemed to suggest that women could be independent. After an earlier experience of unrequited love, in 1865 she married George Craik, who was much younger than herself, a marriage that seemed to defy convention. Nevertheless her works, with their careful historical setting, are more likely to be regarded as Victorian period pieces than as expressions of feminist revolt.

TOM WINNIFRITH

Selected works: *Michael the Miner* (1846); *How to Win Love* (1848); *The Ogilvies* (1849); *Cola Monti* (1849); *Olive* (1850); *The Half-Caste* (1851); *The Head of the Family* (1852); *Bread upon the Waters* (1852); *Alice Learmont* (1852); *A Hero* (1853); *Agatha's Husband* (1853); *The Little Lychetts* (1855); *John Halifax, Gentleman* (1856); *Nothing New* (1857); *A Woman's Thoughts about Women* (1858); *Poems* (1859); *Domestic Stories* (1859); *Romantic Tales* (1859); *Studies from Life* (1861); *Mistress and Maid* (1863); *The Fairy Book* (1863); *Christine's Mistake* (1865); *A New Year's Gift to Sick Children (1865);* *A Noble Life* (1866); *Two Marriages* (1867); (trans.), *A French Country Family*, by H. de Witt (1867); *The Woman's Kingdom* (1869); *The Unkind Word and Other Stories* (1870); *Fair France* (1871); *Little Sunshine's Holiday* (1871); *Hannah* (1872); *The Adventures of a Brownie* (1872); *My Mother and I* (1874); *Sermons out of Church* (1875); *Songs of Our Youth* (1875); *The Little Lame Prince and His Travelling Cloak* (1875); *A Legacy* (1878); *Young Mrs Jardine* (1879); *Thirty Years* (1880); *His Little Mother and Other Tales and Sketches* (1881); *Children's Poetry* (1881); *Plain Speaking* (1882); *An Unsentimental Journey through Cornwall* (1884); *Miss Tommy* (1884); *King Arthur* (1886); *About Money and Other Things* (1886); *Fifty Golden Years* (1887); *Poems* (1888); *Concerning Men and Other Papers* (1888).

References: BA (19); Brantlinger, P., *The Spirit of Reform: British Literature and Politics, 1832–1867* (1977); Calder, J., *Women and Marriage in Victorian Fiction* (1976); Foster, S., *Victorian Women's Fiction* (1985); Hickok, K., *Representations of Women: Nineteenth-Century Women's Poetry* (1984); Kunitz; Mitchell, S., *Dinah Mulock Craik* (1983); OCCL; Showalter, E., 'Dinah Mulock Craik and the tactics of sentiment', *Feminist Studies* (1975); *A Literature of Their Own* (1977).

Murdoch, Iris

b. 15 July 1919, Dublin, Ireland

Novelist, and writer on philosophy

Born of Anglo-Irish parents, Wills John Hughes and Irene Alice (*née* Richardson) Murdoch, IM grew up in London but frequently visited Ireland on holidays; her continuing interest in that country is reflected in her one historical novel, *The Red and The Green* (1965). She was raised as a Protestant, but now calls herself a 'Christian fellow-traveller'. She earned first-class honours at Somerville College, Oxford in 1942, where she studied classics, ancient history, and philosophy. Her studies interrupted by the war, she served as Assistant Principal in the Treasury from 1942 to 1944 and then became an administrative officer with the UN Relief and Rehabilitation Administration, aiding refugees in London, Belgium, and Austria from 1944 to 1946. She subsequently returned to Oxford to study philosophy and in 1948 became a fellow of St Anne's College. From 1963 to 1967 she was lecturer at the Royal College of Art. Her husband, John Bayley, whom she married in 1956, is a novelist, poet, literary critic, and a fellow of New College, Oxford.

IM had a considerable academic career in philosophy both as teacher and scholar; she is steeped in Platonism, existentialism, and analytic philosophy; she has produced three philosophical books, *Sartre, Romantic Rationalist* (1953), *The Sovereignty of Good* (1970), and *The Fire and the Sun: Why Plato Banished the Artists* (1977), as well as numerous philosophical articles, chiefly on ethics and aesthetics and the relation between the two.

She has also produced twenty-three novels in addition to several short stories and plays. IM has often insisted that her fiction and academic concerns are independent; however, her work belies her insistence. Anyone familiar with the twentieth-century philosophical scene immediately recognizes that IM's novels are replete with philosophical motifs, jokes, allusions, references, and concerns. But part of her intellectual system is the cardinal principle that human life and action is more complex than philosophical and ethical systems. And thus we can interpret her denial of philosophical influence on her fiction as a rejection of the reduction of her fiction to her philosophy. Such an interpretation would be an affirmation both of the richness of her fiction and of the truth of her philosophy.

In her first work, *Sartre, Romantic Rationalist*, IM traces Sartre's philosophy to Descartes and places it within a tradition which chooses as its starting place, as the place of certainty, the individual's thought and subjectivity. This concentration on self, according to IM, results in disregard of the world and others. Sartre's account of love focuses on the lover's speculation about his beloved's attitude towards him. In contrast, IM identifies as the salient characteristic of love the suppression of subjectivity and the recognition of the objective existence of others. IM believes not only in the importance of the acknowledgement of the independent status of others, but of the world and morals as well. In *The Sovereignty of Good* (1970), IM said that the ordinary person does not 'unless corrupted by philosophy believe that he creates values by his choices'. And in a recent interview she declared, 'It seems to me obvious that morality is connected with truth, with rejection of egoistic fantasy, and with apprehension of what's real; that the ability and the wish to tell the truth are a very fundamental part of morals.' These ideas of IM's about morality are woven through her fiction, both as concerns of her characters and as themes which emerge from their interaction.

In an important article, 'Against Dryness', IM develops her aesthetic theory, taking on the modern novel and criticizing it on much the same grounds as contemporary philosophy: it has too thin and circumscribed a view of human nature and life; it does not contain 'messy' characters. She emphasizes that, in literature, philosophy, and human modes of comprehension in general, we struggle between the brute facts of reality and the forms (stories, concepts, and words) that would make those understandable, and she believes that what we need now in this century is more attention to the former.

IM believes that the novel is inherently comic. And indeed, her novels are intensely funny. They often contain the stock features of burlesque – for instance, cars and other large objects fall into bodies of water and people pursue each other in madcap chases. But comedy results, too, from witty dialogue and self-conscious intellectual introspection. In *The Bell* (1954), a woman agonizes for a long time about the moral dilemma posed by whether or not to give her seat to someone. Full-scale dramatic events abound too – people drown or seem to, they fall from high places, they are kidnapped. But in spite of the often broad strokes on her large canvases, IM's novels treat everyday moral concerns such as marital infidelity and the betrayal of friends with the utmost serious attention and gravity. A chief concern of her novels is the exploration of the mythologies with which people understand themselves and the world. She has said, 'I think that people create myths about themselves and are then dominated by the myths. They feel trapped, and they elect other people to play roles in their lives, to be gods or destroyers or something, and I think that this mythology is often very deep and very influential and secretive, and a novelist is revealing secrets of this sort.' IM's novels reveal these secrets with wit and drama.

In her first novel, *Under the Net* (1954), and in some others like *A Severed Head* (1961), her own revered values of character development and contingency of plot are superseded by the development of philosophical ideas, patterned plotting, and mythological structures. Jake Donague, the hero of *Under the Net*, develops through the course of the novel in his understanding of the world. Throughout much of the book, he is like the Sartrean hero, self-involved, subjective, and more involved in applying concepts and essences than seeing anyone's particularity. Most of the novel deals with Jake's mistakes about people. He consistently misunderstands them; he misinterprets what they say, imposing his own theories and concepts on their actions. Wildly humorous scenes result from these misunderstandings. The image of the net comes from Wittgenstein who understands it as the concepts from which we construct reality and from which we cannot escape. In the end, Jake decides to become a creative writer, eschewing theory for particularity. *A Severed Head* tightly convolutes its characters in a web of Freudian and archetypal imagery and plays out existential philosophical concepts among them.

In contrast, to the symbolic and mythological elements are the realistic ones, the fully developed characters and fully realized human dilemmas. In *The Bell*, the story of a religious lay community, although traditional oppositions (self-centred neurosis and conventional morality) are embodied in pairs of characters, what is most striking about the novel is the detail in which individual characters, their relations, and their problems are portrayed, almost as if IM were heeding her own injunction to see the other. Against the background of this group is a community of cloistered nuns, among whom a wise and good nun leads each person along his/her own spiritual path. *Henry and Cato* (1976) has a similar structure. Two contrasting characters, one very worldly and the other conventionally spiritual, come to understand themselves and their ethical limitations more deeply through a series of dramatic occurrences.

In many ways *The Philosopher's Pupil* (1983) typifies IM's work and brings together many of her themes. It contains a dizzying number of characters and relationships; at its centre is the philosopher John Rozanoff, whom all the characters imbue with magical power. The philosopher himself is a tortured man who has become sexually obsessed with his granddaughter. The characters are in a mad whirl, following the dictates of their own mythological structures and reaching such resolutions as these will allow.

IM won the Booker Prize in 1978 for *The Sea, the Sea* (1978).

MARTHA SATZ

Works: *Sartre, Romantic Rationalist* (1953); *Under the Net* (1954); *The Flight from the Enchanter* (1955); *The Sandcastle* (1957); *The Bell* (1958); *A Severed Head* (1961, play 1963); *An Unofficial Rose* (1962); *The Unicorn* (1963); *The Italian Girl* (1964, play 1967); *The Red and the Green* (1965); *The Time of the Angels* (1966); *The Nice and the Good* (1968); *Bruno's Dream* (1969); *A Fairly Honourable Defeat* (1970); *The Sovereignty of Good* (1970); *The Servants and the Snow* (1970); *An Accidental Man* (1971); *The Three Arrows* (1972); *The Black Prince* (1973); *The Sacred and Profane Love Machine* (1974); *A Word Child* (1975); *Henry and Cato* (1976); *The Sea, the Sea* (1978); *The Fire and the Sun* (1978); *Nuns and Soldiers* (1980); *Art and Eros* (1980); *The Philosopher's Pupil* (1983); *The Book and the Brotherhood* (1987).

References: Baldanza, F., *Iris Murdoch* (1974); Bellamy, M., 'An interview with Iris Murdoch', *Contemporary Literature* 18 (1977); Biles, J.I., 'Interview with Iris Murdoch', *Studies in the Literary Imagination* 11, 2 (1978); Brans, J., 'Virtuous dogs and a unicorn: an interview with Iris Murdoch', *Southwest Review* 70, 1 (1985); Byatt, A. S., *Degrees of Freedom: The Novels of Iris Murdoch* (1965); Culley, A., 'Criticism of Iris Murdoch: a selected checklist', *Modern Fiction Studies* 15 (1969); Gerstenberger, D., *Iris Murdoch* (1975); Hague, A., *Iris Murdoch's Comic Vision* (1984); Scholes, R., 'Iris Murdoch's Unicorn', in *The Fabulators* (1967); Widman, R. L., 'An Iris Murdoch checklist', *Critique: Studies in Modern Fiction* 10 (1967); Wolfe, P., *The Disciplined Heart: Iris Murdoch and Her Novels* (1966).

Nairne, Carolina, Baroness

b. 16 August 1766, Gask, Perth; d. 27 October 1845, Gask, Perth
Songwriter
(Also wrote under Mrs Bogan of Bogan, BB)
Raised by ardent Jacobites, Laurence and Margaret Oliphant, and named after Prince Charles Stuart, CN spent her early life listening to tales of her Jacobite kin, the Robertsons, Murrays, Drummonds, and Graemes, and learning the music that was a particular pleasure to her aristocratic family. Both her grandfather and her father were veterans of the 1745 rebellion, and her maternal grandfather was Duncan Robertson, chief of the clan Donnochy. CN and her two sisters all played musical instruments and often entertained at social gatherings. This background provided the inspiration when 'pretty Miss Car' began writing Jacobite songs as a young woman. CN, her two sisters, and her two brothers were educated by a governess, while their religious instruction was provided by a non-juring clergyman. As a young belle, she supposedly had the pleasure of refusing a royal duke's marriage proposal. In 1804 CN married her kinsman William Nairne, who was heir to a peerage, but whose

lands and title were forfeit under an act of attainder. The couple had one son. Her husband was restored to the peerage by George IV in 1824, and CN became Baroness Nairne. He died in 1830, after which she took her ailing son to Ireland. But her son died in Brussels in 1837, and from that year onwards CN often remarked that she looked forward only to meeting her son and husband in the afterlife.

CN began writing songs before her marriage. She enthusiastically welcomed the poetry of Robert Burns and persuaded her brother, Laurence, to subscribe to the 1786 edition of his poems. CN was interested in Burns's method of providing new lyrics for old Scottish tunes because she felt that some of the old lyrics were too vulgar. In 1792, she persuaded her brother to present her own anonymous version of 'The Ploughman' or 'The Pleuchman' to a group of his tenants. It became very popular, and in succeeding years CN wrote a number of humorous and patriotic songs, among which were 'John Tod', 'Jamie the Laird', and 'The Laird o' Cockpen'. In 1798 she sent a copy of 'The Land o' the Leal' to her friend whose child had died. The song, a lament for a dead child that promises a better life in heaven, was for many years thought to be Burns's deathbed song because CN insisted on anonymity.

CN later continued to write lyrics as part of a committee of women dedicated to purifying the national minstrelsy. When the committee published *The Scottish Minstrel* (1821), CN contributed to the collection under the name of 'Mrs Bogan of Bogan'. Her songs were signed BB, and even the publisher did not know her true identity because she disguised herself as an old gentlewoman when she held interviews with him. Although she admired Burns, she believed that some of his songs 'tended to inflame the passions' and asked to have his 'Willie Brewed a Peck o' Maut', a drinking song, removed from *The Scottish Minstrel*. At this time, she was composing Jacobite songs for her aged uncle, the Chief of Strowan, and songs of the working classes for Nathaniel Gow, son of the famous Perthshire fiddler Neil Gow, among which was 'Caller Herrin' about a Newhaven fishwoman. The tune of the song represents the chimes of Iron Church in Edinburgh. Among the songs which she later wrote in Ireland, the best known is 'Wake, Irishmen, Wake', a political protest against the oppressive authority of the Catholic Church in Ireland.

CN's efforts to rewrite Scottish lyrics in a more modest vein, although welcomed in her own time, have been criticized by modern commentators as contributions to the sentimental and genteel falsifying of the Scottish working class in the early nineteenth century. Such a charge may be levelled at 'The Land o' the Leal' and perhaps 'Caller Herrin', but it is not fair to CN's patriotic airs. 'Will Ye No Come Back Again?' expresses the desolation of the Jacobites at the exile of their prince, and 'The Hundred Pipers', although apocryphal, is a rousing portrayal of the crossing of the Esk by Scottish troops.

CN agreed to have her songs published anonymously, and a book of them was in preparation at her death. With the approval of her sister, the songs were subsequently published in 1846 as *Lays from Strathearn* by Carolina Nairne, and CN's secret was at last revealed.   SUSAN WINN

Works: *The Scottish Minstrel* (1821); *Lays from Strathearn* (1846).

References: Allibone; *DNB*; Henderson, G., *Lady Nairne and Her Songs* (1900); Rogers, C., *The Life and Songs of the Baroness Nairne* (1869).

Nesbit, Edith

b. 15 August 1858, London; d. 4 May 1924, Dymchurch, Romney Marsh
Writer for children, novelist, poet
(Also wrote under Fabian Bland)

EN was the youngest of the four surviving children of John Collis Nesbit, the head of an agricultural college in Kennington, and Sarah Alderton. After her father's death when she was barely 4, her mother continued to run the college herself for a further six years. EN was educated in boarding schools in Brighton and Stamford, and at various schools in France and Germany, where Mrs Nesbit had taken the family in 1867 for the benefit of EN's tubercular sister Mary. She was persistently unhappy at school. After Mary's death in 1871, the family returned to England, settling in Halstead Hall in Kent, a setting which was to inspire many of EN's later stories. Three years later they ran out of money and were forced to move to Islington. At about 15 EN began to publish verse in magazines.

In 1877 she met Hubert Bland, a former bank clerk, now a partner in a small brush manufacturing business. They married in April 1880, and two months later EN gave birth to their first child. When shortly afterwards Hubert contracted smallpox, his partner absconded with the company funds, leaving the family penniless. EN, who had until now only published a small amount of verse, was forced to support her family by her poems, stories, and endless journalism. In addition to her own children, she was to bring up as her own the two children of Hubert (who proved an incurable philanderer) and the housekeeper, Alice Hoatson.

Both EN and her husband were socialists and founding members of the Fabian Society, and led a highly unconventional lifestyle, though on the issue of women's suffrage EN was surprisingly conservative. It was through the Fabians that EN met and fell in love with George Bernard Shaw, though this came to nothing. Her first novel, *The Prophet's Mantle* (1885), published by Henry Drane and written jointly with Hubert, took as its theme socialism in the 1880s; its hero was based on the Russian anarchist Prince Kropotkin.

EN continued to produce a stream of both adult and children's fiction, but only in her forties did she finally gain recognition with *The Story of the Treasure Seekers* (1899), a collection of short pieces about the Bastable family which had appeared in the *Pall Mall Gazette, Windsor*, and other periodicals. It was the first of a series of children's books about the Bastables, and the prosperity this brought enabled her to settle in Well Hall in Eltham, Kent, a moated sixteenth-century house. The second Bastable book, *The Wouldbegoods*, appeared in 1901.

EN continued to write prolifically, alone and with a variety of collaborators, though in 1900 she sustained the tragedy of the death under anaesthetic of her youngest son Fabian. Her husband died in 1914. In 1915 she was awarded a modest civil pension for her literary achievement, and in 1917 she married Thomas Terry Tucker, a retired marine engineer, settling with him on the Kent coast. She died of lung cancer in 1921.

The theme of the absent parent who is restored at the end of the tale was a recurring one in EN's children's fiction (depicted most memorably in *The Railway Children*, 1906), and bore an obvious relation to her own premature loss of her father. *The Story of the Treasure Seekers* presents a variation on this theme, in that the children's mother has died and their father is in financial difficulties. Each episode deals with a different child's ploy for making money, until a wealthy uncle takes the family under his wing at the end of the tale.

The hard-up middle-class family was a recurring feature of EN's fiction, though occasionally she dealt with real poverty and the horrors of industrialism, in a Dickensian vein: the hero of *Harding's Luck* (1909) is a crippled boy from the slums of Deptford. The criticism has been levelled against EN that her bourgeois background betrays itself in her handling of servants, who are always comic rather than sympathetic figures.

The child narrator of *The Treasure Seekers* shares the quixotic tendency of EN's child protagonists to allow their reading of other children's books to govern their expectations. The book alludes directly and frequently to other nineteenth-century children's literature. Fantasy, however, is always made to confront reality at the end of the day. This is true of the series of fantasy stories produced between 1902 and 1906 for which EN is perhaps best remembered (and which show the influence of the Victorian fantasist F. Anstey): in *Five Children and It* (1902), the Psammead or sand-fairy begrudgingly grants the children wishes every morning, but each of the wishes brings unforeseen trouble, a pattern which repeats itself in the sequel, *The Phoenix and the Carpet* (1904). In the third of the series, *The Story of the Amulet* (1906), the quest for the missing half of an amulet takes the children on a series of time travels to ancient civilizations. On finding the missing half, they gain their 'heart's desire', the return of their parents and younger brother.

EN's most popular work for adults was *The Red House* (1902), the setting of which is clearly based on Well Hall. The story, which centres on a newly married couple, is told by the infatuated husband, and clearly involves an element of wish-fulfilment on EN's part, since it was written in middle age during a period of considerable domestic hardship. In *The Secret of Kyriels* (1899), autobiographical elements are again incorporated in distorted form. Esther, the heroine, suspects her husband's infidelity and takes revenge by running away with an old suitor; later discovering her husband to be innocent, she goes mad and is shut away. The novel ends happily, however, when she is rescued from her imprisonment by a childhood sweetheart.

ANNE FERNIHOUGH

Works: *The Prophet's Mantle* (under Fabian Bland, with Hubert Bland) (1895); *The Secret of Kyriels* (1899); *The Story of the Treasure Seekers* (1899); *The Would-begoods* (1901); *Five Children and It* (1902); *The Red House* (1902); *The Phoenix and the Carpet* (1904); *The Story of the Five Rebellious Dolls* (1904); *The New Treasure Seekers* (1904); *Oswald Bastable and Others* (1905); *The Incomplete Amorist* (1906); *The Story of the Amulet* (1906); *The Railway Children* (1906); *The Enchanted Castle* (1907); *The House of Arden* (1908); *Daphne in Fitzroy Street* (1909); *Harding's Luck* (1909); *Salome and the Head: A Modern Melodrama* (1909); *The Magic City* (1910); *Dormant* (1911); *The Wonderful Garden* (1911); *The Magic World* (1912); *Wet Magic* (1913); *Wings and the Child, or, The Building of Magic Cities* (1913); *The Incredible Honeymoon* (1916); *The Lark* (1922); *Five of Us – And Madeline* (1925).

References: Bell, A., *E. Nesbit* (1960); Briggs, J., *A Woman of Passion: The Life of E. Nesbit 1858–1924* (1987); Crouch, M., *Treasure Seekers and Borrowers: Children's Books in Britain 1900–1960* (1962); Green, R. L., *Tellers of Tales: Children's Books and Authors from 1800 to 1968* (1969); *Junior Bookshelf* 22, 4, 'E. Nesbit centenary issue' (October 1958); Manlove, C., *The Impulse of Fantasy Literature* (1984); Moore, D. L., *E. Nesbit: A Biography* (1933); *OCCL*; Prickett, S., *Victorian Fantasy* (1979); Streatfeild, N., *Magic and the Magician: E. Nesbit and Her Children's Books* (1958).

Newcastle, Margaret Cavendish, Duchess of

b. 1623, St John's Abbey, Colchester, Essex; d. 15 December 1673, Welbeck Abbey, Nottinghamshire

Poet, playwright, biographer

Yearning for 'extraordinary fame', during her lifetime D of N wrote and published a dozen books of poetry, plays, romances, orations, letters, scientific speculations, Utopian fantasy, biography, and autobiography. Her daring, coupled with her extravagant manners and dress, brought her both praise and condemnation from her contemporaries.

Despite her meagre and undisciplined formal education, D of N began to write when she was quite young, filling sixteen 'baby books' with scraps which she later described as being 'as confused as the chaos'. As a child she lived an idyllic existence in pre-Civil War England, protected by her parents, Thomas Lucas and Elizabeth Leighton, and largely isolated from society. In 1642, after her home had been plundered and her mother attacked by an anti-Royalist mob, D of N went with her family to Oxford where she became an attendant to Queen Henrietta Maria, despite her social diffidence. She followed the court to St Germain in 1645 where she met William Cavendish, Marquis (later Duke) of Newcastle, thirty years older than she, and a commander in the Royalist forces. Their courtship was, uncharacteristically for D of N, conventional, guided as it was by the vogue of Platonic love among French and English courtiers. William's love of literature and philosophy, and his seventy love poems addressed to her, no doubt satisfied her ideals and aspirations as very little else could at the court where her bashfulness, her ignorance of French (or any other foreign language), and her distaste for the intrigues of the exiles, stood her in poor stead. After their marriage William maintained them with all the trappings of nobility in the face of enormous debt. He also encouraged her in her intellectual interests, introducing her to the new science through dinners with the most famous philosophers of the day and discussing with her and his brother Charles theories of literature.

By 1651, when D of N travelled back to England in an attempt to save her husband's estates, she had confidence enough in her own genius and 'singularity' to dare to write for publication. By the time her books appeared in print, however, D of N had ended her financially unsuccessful eighteen-month stay in England and was back on the continent with her husband, living far beyond their means in Rubens's Antwerp mansion.

Her first published volume, *Poems and Fancies* (1663), contains evidence of the free rein which her imagination was allowed in her early years, with its charming tales of fairies and animals. But the book also bears witness to the most obvious failings of her education: there is little discipline in D of N's spelling, grammar, metre, or rhyme. The book was written in the lodgings in Covent Garden, and composed in a great heat with little or no revision by herself or her printers. She later defended this haste, saying that in stopping to correct 'many fancies are lost, by reason they oftimes out-run the pen' – she preferred the 'free and noble style . . . it shows more courage than it does of fear'; her publishers would not fare so well later, when they were blamed for 'false printing' by the author, who had laid aside any consideration of the manuscripts' untrained handwriting and grammatical and spelling mistakes. *Poems and Fancies*, although greeted with much derision by Dorothy Osborne, who considered that there were 'many soberer People in Bedlam' than D of N, was followed within two months by *Philosophical Fancies* (1653), another book of poetry in which she elaborated upon the theory of nature she had advanced in the earlier volume.

On her return to the continent she compiled *The World's Olio* (1655), a collection of short prose essays which indulged her paradoxical love of the fantastic and the natural and ended with a spirited defence against the charges of plagiarism, so foreshadowing many later women writers. *The Philosophical and Physical Opinions* (1655), a greatly expanded version of her second book and D of N's personal favourite, continues the defence in its prefatory essays; in its dedication to the Universities of Oxford and Cambridge it unites her desire for individual fame with her growing feminist awareness: 'Thus by an Opinion, which I hope is but an Erroneous one in Men, we are Shut out of all Power and Authority, by reason we are never Imployed either in Civil or Martial Affairs . . .' *Natures Pictures Drawn by Fancies Pencil to the Life* (1656) is composed of wildly imaginative tales of heroines, usually projections of herself in their talents and aspirations, who triumph over all kinds of fantastic adversary by virtue of their rich inner resources.

Upon returning to England at the Restoration, D of N, already the most frequently published of women writers, retired to the peaceful countryside of Welbeck Abbey where she could devote all her time to her writing. The first book she published was *Playes* (1662), many of them modelled on her husband's. The fourteen unstaged plays, despite their desperately convoluted and unresolved plots, are unique in their presentation of extraordinary women, dramatic syntheses of the narcissistic heroines of the tales with women skilled in the arts of public debate. *Orations of Divers Sorts*, published within months of the plays, consists of rhetorical speeches; especially noteworthy is the systematic feminist debate of 'Female Orations', which, however, lacks the eccentric attraction of the more imaginative works. *CCXI Sociable Letters* (1664) recaptures the charm of intellect infused by personality in a literary form well suited to D of N's quick but unsustained wit, and in her following book, *Philosophical Letters* (1664), she adapts it to her never-ending interest in science. Science fiction, the last new genre she was to try, is not always a happy combination of her talents and interests. *The Description of the New Blazing World*, appended to the anti-experimental essays of *Observations upon Experimental Philosophy* (1666) and reprinted twice during the next two years, attempts in the manner of contemporary Utopian fantasies to tell the story of a voyage to another world where speculative science is the order of the day and the soul of D of N herself helps to maintain control over the arts, the army, and rulers alike.

In the remaining years of her life, D of N continued to write, revise, and publish new editions of her works. In 1667 she left the quiet retirement of Welbeck Abbey to travel to London where mobs of people, hoping to catch a glimpse of the already legendary author in her extravagant dress, thronged to satisfy her immediate vanity, and a visit to the Royal Academy fulfilled her ambition of being recognized for her intelligence. She was a curiosity to men like Samuel Pepys, but she was virtually unassailable owing to her high place in society and her own unshakable belief in her genius.

Throughout her career, D of N alternatively deplored and flaunted her lack of education, finally concluding that it was native wit that set her apart from the pedants and the unlearned alike. Yet her brief autobiography, 'A True Relation of my Birth, Breeding, and Life', is restrained and it is this work, together with her other attempt at 'writing history' – the appreciative *Life* of her husband published in 1667 – which represent to most critics, contemporary and modern, her most successful literary efforts, charming in the plainness of their style and historically valuable for the direct pictures which they present of the age.

Following her death, the Duke collected and published *Letters and Poems in Honour of the Incomparable Princess, Margaret, Dutchess of Newcastle* (1676), all adulatory tributes, but one of which (Walter Charleton's) comes close to honest criticism of her work: 'Your fancy is too generous to be strained, your invention too nimble to be fettered. . . . Hence it is that you do not always confine your sense to your verse, nor your verses to rhythm, nor your rhythm to the quantity and sounds of syllables.'   SUSAN HASTINGS

Works: *Poems and Fancies* (1653); *Philosophical Fancies* (1653); *The World's Olio* (1655); *The Philosophical and Physical Opinions* (1655); *Natures Pictures Drawn by Fancies Pencil to the Life* (1656); *Playes* (1662); *Orations of Divers Sorts, Accommodated to Divers Places* (1662); *CCXI Sociable Letters* (1664); *Philosophical Letters, or, Modest Reflections upon some Opinions in the Natural Philosophy, Maintained by Several Famous and Learned Authors of This Age, Expressed by Way of Letters* (1664); *Observations upon Experimental Philosophy. To Which Is Added the Description of a New Blazing World* (1666); *The Life of the Thrice Noble, High and Puissant Prince William Cavendishe, Duke, Marquess, and Earl of Newcastle . . .* (1667); *Playes, Never Before Printed* (1668).

References: Bickly, F., *The Cavendish Family* (1914); Firth, C. H. (ed.), *The Life of William Cavendish,Duke of Newcastle* (1906); Cotton, N., *Women Playwrights in England c. 1363–1751* (1980); Fraser, A., *The Weaker Vessel* (1984); Grant, D., *Margaret the First: A Biography of Margaret Cavendish, Duchess of Newcastle, 1623–1673* (1957); Goulding, R. W., *Margaret (Lucas) Duchess of Newcastle* (1925); Hobby, E., *Virtue of Necessity* (1988); Pearson, J., ' "Women may discourse . . . as well as men": speaking and silent women in the plays of Margaret Cavendish, Duchess of Newcastle', *Tulsa Studies in Women's Literature* (1985); Prasad, K., 'Margaret Cavendish's *Blazing World*; a seventeenth century Utopia', *Essays Presented to Amy G. Stock* (1951); Reynolds, M., *The Learned Lady in England from 1650 to 1760* (1920); Todd; Todd, J., *The Sign of Angellica* (1989); Turberville, A. S., *A History of Welbeck Abbey and Its Owners* (1938); Whibley, C., 'A princely woman', *Essays in Biography* (1913); Woolf, V., 'The Duchess of Newcastle', in *The Common Reader* (1925).

Nightingale, Florence

b. 12 May 1820, Florence, Italy; d. 13 August 1910, London
Polemical writer

FN was educated at home with her older sister Parthenope by their wealthy landowner father, the liberal William Edward Nightingale. The girls studied history, mathematics, Italian, and classical literature and philosophy, as well as reading widely in contemporary English authors from Mrs Gaskell to Swinburne. Encouraged by the classical scholar Benjamin Jowett, FN compiled an anthology of medieval mystical writing while declaring that reading was useful only as it prepared a person for work. She was heartily opposed to literature as escape and she poured considerable scorn on the romantic fiction enjoyed by other young ladies of her class. FN rejected marriage as unsatisfying to her morally active nature because of its emphasis on domesticity and she considered herself as one of those whom God 'had clearly marked out . . . to be single women'. Although her father took seriously her desire for a profession, he was unimpressed with her choice of nursing which had a very low social status at the time, the stereotypical nurse being drunken, coarse, and promiscuous. After experiencing this opposition, FN retreated into piety although she always felt that God was best served within the world. Early journals describe her anger and frustration at the conventional idleness prescribed for the English lady. 'Cassandra', an autobiographical fragment from her early adulthood, describes how women's ability is frittered away by social convention. John Stuart Mill used some of FN's criticism of female domestic life in *The Subjection of Women*. Rejecting sectarian religion, FN believed that the laws of God could be discovered by personal experience and reason and she felt that God had allowed evil in the world to provoke humanity to struggle and thought. Her ideas were presented in the massive, disorganized, and repetitive religious and philosophical work, *Suggestions for Thought*, of which 'Cassandra' formed a part. She sent the manuscript to Mill who wanted publication and to Jowett, who advocated considerable revision. Although FN had a few copies privately printed in 1860, she lost interest in rewriting the book for a general audience. She would continue to compose religious works throughout her life, ranging from meditations to apologies to God.

In 1851 FN spent three months at a hospital and orphanage in Germany, although receiving no regular training, and later, against family advice, worked in a hospital in Paris. Returning to London in 1853, she took unpaid work as superintendent of a hospital for 'gentlewomen'. She told her father, 'I hope now I have come into possession of myself.' In 1854 Britain entered the Crimean War and FN read descriptions of the British hospital without a single nurse. Her friend Sidney Herbert asked her to recruit some trained staff and, later in the year, she and thirty-eight nurses left for Turkey with backing from the British government and some support from a fund raised by *The Times*. Arriving on the day of the Battle of Inkerman to find the hospital filled with fleas and rats and its sewers loaded with filth, she set about fighting the obstructive military authorities to create orderly and sanitary conditions. Her personal attendance on the sick gave rise to the legend of the 'lady with a lamp' described by Longfellow in a poem of 1857. Within a few months of her reforms, the mortality rate had drastically dropped.

Returning to England in 1856, she was a national idol for a country demoralized by the war and eager to find examples of personal heroism. But she did not quietly enjoy her fame; instead she spent her enormous energies pushing for a commission to investigate medical care in the army in general. To persuade authorities she used statistics based on a new concept of mathematical probability which she helped to pioneer; with this method she promoted the idea of the objective measurement of social phenomena, in this case showing graphically how disease rather than wounds destroyed most soldiers. She brought her views to the attention of the Queen and Prince Albert and, despite a lack of co-operation from the War Office, gained an investigation in 1857 through a Royal Commission on the Health of the Army – on which as a woman she herself could not serve. To promote her views she wrote and had printed an 800-page work, *Notes on Matters Affecting the Health, Efficiency and Hospital Administration of the British Army* (1858). She had the statistical section of the report printed as a pamphlet and distributed to government and Parliament. Turning her attention to British soldiers in India, she also agitated for the establishment of another Royal Commission which in turn resulted in great improvement in sanitary conditions.

FN wanted to return to nursing but in her later years she became an invalid, possibly for neurotic reasons, possibly from a fever caught in the Crimea. She was not isolated, however, and she received a few visitors while confined in her bedroom and wrote an immense quantity of instructions and reports. She managed to raise money for the Nightingale Training School for nurses in 1860. Her most popular book was *Notes on Nursing: What It Is, and What It Is Not* (1859), which insisted on high professional standards for nursing; it sold 15,000 copies in a month and was enthusiastically reviewed. Fusing moral fervour with scientific authority, it aimed its opinions on domestic hygiene at a general readership since a nurse was defined as anyone responsible for another's health. In opposition to the germ theory, FN believed that disease was bred and was inhaled; consequently she stressed the need for a clean environment and good nursing, and the professional male doctor seemed almost superfluous. Nurses were to be a combination of the disciplined soldier or fighter against disease and difficult invalids, and the domestic, home-making lady who would make a hospital into a house and morally uplift the men to whom she ministered.

Although regarded by many as arrogant and overbearing, FN was concerned to promote her burgeoning image as the noble nurse of the Crimea, an heroic figure associated with Joan of Arc, Queen Victoria, the saints and even Christ. She popularized the figure of the nurse as both unthreatening in its non-professional status to medical men and as attractive to middle-class women who wished to work. To promote nursing she colluded in the mythical presentation of herself and helped to make other nursing women into heroic figures as well, for example Agnes Jones whom she did not especially admire but whose death while nursing in a workhouse allowed her glorification in the Spenserian 'Una and the Lion' (1868). But, although she eulogized the nurse and supported married women's property rights, FN felt uneasy at the suffrage campaign, asserting her own disenfranchised influence in the country. She disliked the idea of women's rights as well as the ideology of femininity that kept middle-class women idle.

Idealization of FN was almost universal, but there was debate over her suitability as a model for other women. In *Intellectual Education and Its Influences on the Character and Happiness of Women* (1858), Emily Shirreff summed up FN as a gifted woman who stepped forward at a time of national degradation to 'set the example of noble self-devotion to a lofty purpose. . . . She possesses all that is required in a leader'; yet Shirreff stressed that she was exceptional and could not provide an example for other refined and educated ladies. Harriet Martineau, who wrote an obituary of FN when in 1856 it was thought that she was dying, made her both heroic and domestic, a woman who carried the lamp 'through miles of sick soldiers in the middle of the night, noting every face, and answering the appeal of every eye as she passed', not a leader but instead 'a housewifely woman'.   JANET TODD

Works: *Notes on Matters Affecting the Health, Efficiency and Hospital Administration of the British Army* (1858); *Notes on Hospitals* (1859); *Notes on Nursing: What It Is and What It Is Not* (1859); *Suggestions for Thought* (1860); *Observations on the Evidence Contained in the Stational Reports Submitted to Her by the Royal Commission on the Sanitary State of the Army in India* (1863); 'How people may live and not die in India' (1863); *Suggestions on a System of Nursing for Hospitals in India* (1865); *Suggestions on the Subject of Providing, Training and Organizing Nurses for the Sick Poor in Workhouse Infirmaries* (1867); 'Una and the Lion' (1868); 'On trained nursing for the sick poor' (1876); *Florence Nightingale to Her Nurses* (1914); *Selected Writings of Florence Nightingale*, ed. L. R. Seymer (1954); *Cassandra* (1979).

References: Allibone; Bishop, W. J. and Goldie, S., *A Bio-Bibliography of Florence Nightingale* (1962); Boyd, N., *Three Victorian Women Who Changed Their World*

(1982); Bull, A., *Florence Nightingale* (1985); Cohen, I. B., 'Florence Nightingale', *Scientific American* (March 1984); Cook, E. T., *The Life of Florence Nightingale* (1913); Davis, J., *Florence Nightingale, or, The Heroine of the East: A Poem* (1856); *DNB*; Drabble; Forster, M., *Significant Sisters: The Grassroots of Active Feminism, 1839–1939* (1984); Goldsmith, M., *Florence Nightingale: The Woman and the Legend* (1937); Holton, S., 'Feminine authority and social care', *Social Analysis* 15 (1984); Keele, M. (ed.), *Florence Nightingale in Rome: Letters Written by Florence Nightingale . . . 1847–1848* (1981); Matheson, A., *Florence Nightingale* (1914); Pugh, E. L., 'Florence Nightingale and J. S. Mill debate women's rights', *Journal of British Studies* 21 (1982); Rosenberg, C. E., 'Florence Nightingale on contagion: the hospital as moral universe', in C. E. Rosenberg (ed.), *Healing and History* (1979); Showalter, E., 'Florence Nightingale's feminist complaint: women, religion, and *Suggestions for Thought*', *Signs* 6 (1981); Smith, F. B., *Florence Nightingale: Reputation and Power* (1982); Vicinus, M., *Independent Women: Work and Community for Single Women, 1850–1920* (1985); Whittaker, E. and Olesen, V., 'The faces of Florence Nightingale; functions of the heroine legend in an occupational sub-culture', in R. Dingwall and J. McIntosh (eds.), *Readings in the Sociology of Nursing* (1978); Woodham-Smith, C., *Florence Nightingale* (1950).

Norton, Caroline

b. 22 March 1808, London; d. 15 June 1877, London
Poet, novelist, editor, playwright, librettist, legal rights campaigner
(Also wrote under Pearce Stevenson)
An admired writer in fashionable circles in her own day, CN now attracts more interest for her writing in support of the legal rights of separated wives than for her poetry and prose.

CN was one of three granddaughters of Richard Brinsley Sheridan and Elizabeth Linley, known collectively as 'the three graces' for their charm, looks, and vivacity. Her great-grandmother, Frances Sheridan, had also written novels. The family were not well-off but were well-connected, and the girls, who were educated at home, were easily launched as debutantes, and expected to marry as well as dowry-less girls could. In 1827, CN married George Norton, heir to Lord Grantley, who proved to have neither the financial means nor the emotional capacity to cope with marriage to a woman of CN's talents and independent spirit.

The fundamental incompatibilities between CN and her husband were soon apparent, and included political differences, CN being a loyal Whig and her husband a Tory MP until 1830. However, CN successfully contacted Lord Melbourne, the new Home Secretary, requesting a post for her husband. With two children and a third on the way CN was already writing to support the family and she had made their modest home in Storey's Gate a centre for fashionable literary and political London. Lord Melbourne soon frequented her salon; a close friendship, but not, it seems, a love affair quickly developed between them. The gutter press of the day commented salaciously on their connection; but for five years CN's husband, the beneficiary of Lord Melbourne's patronage, made no objection to it. In 1836, however, Norton, encouraged by Tory opponents of Lord Melbourne and by relations who disliked his wife and disapproved of her, but above all with mercenary aims in mind, brought an action for adultery against Melbourne, claiming damages of £10,000.

The differences between CN and her husband were essentially temperamental. From the start George Norton had shown violence towards her, and CN, though forbearing and resilient, was not the woman to submit tamely to this. CN's inability to respect her boorish husband is projected through the heroine of an early poem, *Marriage and Love*, while George inevitably found his wife's talent and earning power an affront to his position, although it was financially necessary.

While Melbourne's reputation survived intact when the divorce case collapsed for lack of credible evidence, hers was permanently damaged in an age when a woman's 'good name' had to be preserved if she was to be received in society; the cloud of scandal never quite left her. But this was nothing compared with her six-year struggle to obtain access to and custody of her children. When CN realized she had no legal rights at all in this issue, she used her pen and her political contacts to obtain justice for women in such a position, and at her instigation in 1837 Thomas Talfourd MP introduced the Infant Custody Bill. This became law in 1839, aided by CN's two pamphlets in support of the reform (1837 and 1839). Tragically, when she and George Norton finally came to an agreement in 1842, the youngest child had died after a neglected riding injury.

It is however problematic to call CN a feminist. She definitely dissociated herself from any programmatic statements about the equality of the sexes and professed herself a believer in the natural superiority of men, and of woman's need for their protection. But she was ready to fight for justice for those individual cases where men failed to live up to this role. She indicted the male political elite she knew so well for its hypocritical willingness to pass humanitarian legislation, while preserving the legal rights of those men 'disposed to act despotically' to an entire sex. To the women's movement of her day she seemed too self-centred; to her family and friends she often seemed rash and indiscreet.

Moreover the spirit of the age was increasingly against her; the accession of Victoria meant that piety, domestic regularity, and earnestness were admired, not the frivolity and decadence of the Regency. CN's novels are evidence that she possessed a sincere belief in an essentially benign and merciful Providence, but some readers found this reflective seriousness sounded insincere coming from her.

The passing of the Infant Custody Bill did not close CN's contribution to the improvement of women's legal status; she also campaigned effectively for the property rights of divorced women when the law was reformed in the 1850s. Even without these two lawsuits CN's life was dogged by scandal, including the allegation that she had leaked to *The Times* knowledge obtained from Sidney Herbert of the impending repeal of the Corn Laws. The incident was used by George Meredith in his novel based on CN, *Diana of the Crossways* (1885), though her descendants forced him to disavow the connection between his novel and CN's life.

Throughout her life CN wrote professionally, out of financial necessity. Given this constant work she believed a woman had as much right to the recognition implicit in the Laureateship as a man; hence her petition to Peel in 1843 on Southey's death (Tennyson was awarded the role). She had a natural fluency and a good ear for poetic and prose rhythm. In her own day she attracted the greatest admiration for her poetry, and in 1840 Hartley Coleridge pronounced her 'the Byron of modern poetesses' and ranked her first in a group of ten, with Elizabeth Barrett Browning coming second. In both style and theme her oeuvre belongs to the school of Byron's imitators and followers.

Her two long poems on the 'Condition of England', *A Voice from the Factories* (1836) and *A Child of the Islands* (1845), are the poems most likely to attract the interest of a modern reader.

Her novels are emphatically worth attention today, since they are more overtly 'feminist' in theme than those of other professional women writers, even while using the fictional conventions of their day. Her first two novels, published together as *The Wife and Woman's Reward* (1835), belong in some degree to the 'Silver Fork' school of novels by contemporaries such as Mrs Gore, but take some unconventional positions on a woman's role.

In general her novels contain autobiographical elements; her third, *Stuart of Dunleath* (1851), which received the greatest critical acclaim, portrays a *mésalliance* not unlike CN's own.

CN's fourth novel, *Lost and Saved* (1863), is her most interesting. It takes as its theme the double standards not only between men and women, but also between women maintaining the façade of respectable married life while having extramarital affairs, and women who have 'fallen' by the standards of the day but have done so unintentionally and with a certain innocence and integrity. Beatrice Brooke, the daughter of a retired army officer, becomes entangled with a selfish dandy who has expectations of an earldom providing he complies with the complex provisions of a family will. After they elope she believes herself to be legally married after a mock-ceremony, taking place when she is ill with fever. Her lover persuades her to keep their 'marriage' a secret; her conduct estranges her from her family; and she finds herself bearing his child and living in apartments below his bachelor rooms, while he continues to live the life of a man about town, conducting an affair with a married woman which predates his romance with Beatrice. One of the points made by the narrator is Beatrice's ignorance of marital law. When their child dies and she breaks with her lover she decides to earn her own living rather than benefit from his financial settlement. Her efforts are woefully inadequate; accomplishments such as water-colouring have no market value, but she survives as a mender and laundress of valuable lace. In the denouement she is reconciled with her family, the circumstances of her mock-marriage are explained, and she finally receives her due by marrying a widower who has been deserted by an unworthy wife; but we are told that in spite of her return to respectability the shadow of disgrace never quite leaves her, as it is kept alive by female gossip. This novel had a mixed reception, because of its frankness in dealing with a 'fallen' woman who is shown to be essentially honest, and in portraying the mechanisms with which society women deceive their husbands. Today we are likely to appreciate the spiritedness of its heroine; as always CN's portraits of spoilt, fashionable young men are convincing, while children and servants are delineated with the same realism as the well-born characters. CN is in fact particularly good at portraying children, especially those who are casualties of their parents' fractured marriages.

Much of CN's literary work was for the magazine and fashionable keepsake books popular in the 1830s, and later for the Christmas annuals. Her husband's death in 1875 freed her to marry a friend of twenty-five years standing, the gentleman-scholar Sir William Stirling-Maxwell, but she died a few months later. Had she married as well as either of her sisters, respectively Lady Dufferin and the Duchess of Somerset, she might have found no need to exercise her literary gifts professionally; but her achievement was to surmount her personal difficulties and still write engagingly and attractively as financial necessity demanded.   CLARISSA CAMPBELL ORR

Selected works: The Sorrows of Rosalie and Other Poems (1829); The Undying One and Other Poems (1830); The Wife and Woman's Reward (1835); A Voice from the Factories (1836); The Separation of Mother and Child by the Law of Custody of Infants Considered (1837); (under Pearce Stevenson) A Plain Letter to the Lord Chancellor on the Infant Custody Bill (1839); The Dream and Other Poems (1840); The Child of the Islands (1845); Stuart of Dunleath (1851); English Laws for Women in the Nineteenth Century (1854); A Letter to the Queen on Lord Cranworth's Marriage and Divorce Bill (1855); Lost and Saved (1863); Old Sir Douglas (1868). *References:* Ackland, A., Caroline Norton (1948); Adburgham, A., Women in Print (1972); Cecil, D., The Young Melbourne (1939); Cecil, D., Lord Melbourne (1954); DLB; Forster, M., Significant Sisters (1984); Holcombe, L., Wives and Property (1983); Perkins, J. G., The Life of Mrs Norton (1909); Ziegler, P., Melbourne (1976).

Norton, Mary

b. 10 December 1903, London

Writer for children

MN, the daughter of Mary (*née* Hughes) and Reginald Spenser, a physician, was educated in a convent school. She has followed a varied career, working first as an actress until her marriage in 1927 to Robert Norton, a shipping magnate, with whom she has had four children. During the Second World War she worked in the War Office, then for the British Purchasing Commission in New York between 1940 and 1943, after which she returned to the stage, performing at the Old Vic until 1945. Her writing has received considerable critical acclaim; in 1952 she was awarded the Carnegie Medal, and in 1960 the Lewis Carroll Shelf Award.

MN's first two published books, *The Magic Bedknob* (1945) and *Bonfires and Broomsticks* (1947), were combined into the popular children's story, *Bedknob and Broomstick* (1957), which was later adapted for a Walt Disney film. It describes amusingly and imaginatively the adventures of four children who, while spending a dull summer holiday in the country at the home of a great-aunt, make the acquaintance of Miss Price, an eminently respectable music teacher and, in her spare time, a witch. She explains to the children, who discover her secret when she falls off her broomstick during a practice session, 'Well ever since I was a girl, I've had a bit of a gift for witchcraft, but somehow – what with piano lessons and looking after my mother – I never seemed to have the time to take it up seriously.' A number of adventures follow, none of which turns out quite as planned: when they try to visit their mother, they end up in the hands of the police, and a trip to a South Sea island culminates in a desperate competition between Miss Price and the local witchdoctor to save them all from the cannibals' cooking pot. Part of the zest in MN's stories comes from the presence of real evil and fear; the children always *do* escape from peril – just – but the reader is aware of the potential threat of magic, its uncontrollable power and unpredictability – and at moments even nice Miss Price is dangerous. MN's writing is as amusing for the adult reader as for the child; her acute social observation is always entertaining. 'If she paid her taxes, observed the English Sunday, and worked for the Red Cross, no one bothered what she did with the rest of her time. She could create a black cat as big as an elephant, and no one would molest her as long as she kept it off other people's property and did not ill treat it.'

In 1952 *The Borrowers* was published, the first in a series of books about a family of little people who live in humans' houses, unknown to the other occupants, and 'borrow' things the humans lay aside, ingeniously turning them to all sorts of uses. The books are all richly imaginative and refreshingly inventive, as MN pictures the world from the perspective of a Borrower. In *The Borrowers Aloft* (1961), MN describes the making of a hot air balloon. The Borrowers have been captured and imprisoned by a horrible human couple, the Platters, who want to keep them in a glass-fronted house in their model village, Ballyhoggin, to display them to the public. During the winter, however, the Borrowers are incarcerated in the attic. Like most attics, it is full of junk – under other circumstances a paradise for Borrowers – including a pile of old magazines, from which they learn about balloons. The Borrowers realize that this could provide a means of escape for them. They investigate the contents of the attic and construct their own miniature version filling a party balloon from the gas lamp (having scaled a tailor's dummy to reach it) and covering it with a shrimping net. Part of a fountain pen does for a valve, a strawberry basket is suspended below to travel in, and for ballast they use 'a tear-off roll of one-and-sixpenny entrance tickets to Ballyhoggin'. MN describes the whole episode in scientific detail, and creates tremendous suspense as parts of the plan fail and have to be reworked, while the Borrowers' strength, initiative, and patience are tried to the limits.

The human characters too are drawn with insight and humour; in contrast to the evil Platters are Mr Pott and Miss Menzies whose hobby of building a model village is copied and exploited for commercial ends by the Platters. As in *Bedknob and Broomstick*, MN is particularly sympathetic in her depiction of lonely, not-so-young, single women and describes sensitively Miss Menzies's difficulties. Her friendship with the utterly benevolent Mr Pott (a retired railwayman) is a source of gentle comedy. After years of practice with Mrs Pott (now dead), Mr Pott has learnt how to cope with a 'talker': 'Sometimes, to show his sympathy and disguise his lack of attention, Mr Pott would repeat the last word of Miss Menzies's last sentence; or sometimes anticipate Miss Menzies's last syllable. If Miss Menzies said: "King and Coun–", Mr Pott would chip in, in an understanding voice, with ". . . tree". Sometimes being far away in mind, Mr Pott would make a mistake and Miss Menzies, referring to "garden-produce", would find herself presented with ". . . roller" instead, and there would be bewilderment all round.'   LUCY SLOAN

Works: *The Magic Bedknob* (1945); *Bonfires and Broomsticks* (1947); *The Borrowers* (1952); *The Borrowers Afield* (1956); *Bedknob and Broomstick* (1957); *The Borrowers Afloat* (1959); *The Borrowers Aloft* (1961); 'Poor Stainless' in E. Farjeon (ed.), *The Eleanor Farjeon Book* (1966); *Are All the Giants Dead?* (1975); *The Borrowers Avenged* (1982).

References: *CA*; *OCCL*.

O'Brien, Edna
b. 15 December 1930, Tuamgraney, County Clare, Ireland
Novelist, short story writer, scriptwriter
A multi-faceted writer known primarily for her novels and short stories, EO'B, daughter of Michael and Lena Cleary O'Brien, was born and raised in the West of Ireland. She was educated at the National School in Scarriff and at the Convent of Mercy at Loughrea, County Galway (her convent days are most vividly recreated in her first novel, *The Country Girls*, 1960). She also attended the Pharmaceutical College in Dublin. In 1951 she married Ernest Gebler, by

whom she had two sons; they were divorced in 1964. Since 1959 she has lived in London, feeling like Joyce and other Irish writers before her, that she would 'have to leave Ireland in order to write about it'.

EO'B's work has been both celebrated and maligned. She has been praised for her lyrical prose, her sense of place, the vividness of her characterizations of women, and the honesty with which she deals with sex. This last element has also been the source of much of the adverse criticism. Especially in her homeland, she has been attacked for her obsession with sex and her alleged sensationalism; one critic described her novel *Night* (1972) as little more than 'lyrics of the loins'.

Three weeks after moving to London, EO'B completed her highly successful first novel, *The Country Girls*. She followed with *The Lonely Girl* (1962) and *Girls in Their Married Bliss* (1964). Employing a sometimes confessional first-person narrative in this trilogy, she traces the maturation of two Irish girls, one a reserved romantic, the other an engaging cynic. She treats many of the themes that recur in later work: the transition from romantic innocence to harsh experience, woman's sense of isolation in a man's world, and the ultimate failure of sexual love, despite its transient fulfilment. The vitality and *joie de vivre* of the first two novels are largely absent in the last more urbane novel, which documents the women's disillusionment with marriage and men. *The Country Girls Trilogy and Epilogue* (1986) included slightly edited versions of the novels and a brief epilogue, from one woman's point of view, which tells us of the other's mysterious death and brings us up to date with her life. Although the epilogue contains flashes of the brilliant prose found in the trilogy, on the whole it lacks the power of the early novels.

August Is a Wicked Month (1965) and *Casualties of Peace* (1967) describe the inability to find happiness in love of two women in their twenties who are the victims of failed marriages. These women possess a resilience which never allows them to forsake utterly the quest for love, a quality that is to reappear in many of EO'B's subsequent protagonists.

Although she is not regarded as a technical innovator, in *A Pagan Place* (1970) and *Night* (1972) she did experiment with narrative form, but with only moderate success. The first, told entirely from the second-person point of view, presents the recollections of a nun's Irish childhood and adolescence, recreating rural Ireland during the Second World War. The night-time reveries of Mary Hooligan, a middle-aged, divorced Irish émigrée living in England, that comprise *Night* have often been compared to Molly Bloom's soliloquy in *Ulysses*. Mary's lust for life and love, sense of humour, and firm grasp of reality combine to make her one of EO'B's most memorable characters. The free-associational reflections on her youth are enriched by a language reminiscent of the author's County Clare.

The novel *I Hardly Knew You* (1977) met with general disfavour. In the familiar confessional mode, it is narrated by a woman who has been imprisoned for killing her young lover. It has been criticized primarily for its lack of effective characterization and for its melodramatic climax.

EO'B's short stories have appeared regularly in such publications as *The New Yorker* and *Atlantic Monthly*. Reflecting similar concerns as those of her longer fiction, they have been collected in *The Love Object* (1968), *A Scandalous Woman and Other Stories* (1978), *A Rose in the Heart* (1979), and *Returning* (1982). The volume *A Fanatic Heart* (1984) includes the whole of *Returning*, stories from the earlier collections, and four previously uncollected pieces. While *A Fanatic Heart* has received favourable reviews, more than one critic notes the relative lack of new material.

EO'B has also written several successful screenplays, two of which are adaptations of her own works: *Girl With Green Eyes* (1964) of *The Lonely Girl*, and *Time Lost and Time Remembered* (1966) of the short story 'A Woman at the Seaside'. In addition she has written the screen version of Andrea Newman's novel *Three Into Two Won't Go* (1968) and an original screenplay, *Zee & Co.*, for the film *X, Y, and Zee*, starring Elizabeth Taylor (1971). Her plays, none of which has met with particular success, include *A Cheap Bunch of Nice Flowers* (1963) and *Virginia* (1981). EO'B also edited a collection of poems and short prose selections by Irish writers revolving around the theme of the volume's title, *Some Irish Loving* (1979).

EO'B has published three extended pieces of non-fiction. In *Mother Ireland* (1976), she explores the mystique of her native land, relying on personal responses, history, and mythology. *Arabian Days* (1978) studies the effect of sudden wealth on Abu Dhabi as a result of the town's discovery of oil. *James and Nora* (1981) offers an informal account of the relationship between Joyce and his wife.   PETER DREWNIANY

Selected works: *The Country Girls* (1960); *The Lonely Girl* (1962, reprinted as *Girl With Green Eyes*, 1964); *A Cheap Bunch of Nice Flowers*, in *Plays of the Year*, vol. 26, ed. J. C. Trewin (1963); *Girls in Their Married Bliss* (1964); *August Is a Wicked Month* (1965); *Casualties of Peace* (1966); *Time Lost and Time Remembered* (with D. Davis) (1966); *Three Into Two Won't Go* (1968); *The Love Object* (1969); *A Pagan Place* (1970); *Zee & Co.* (1971); *Night* (1972); *A Pagan Place: A Play* (1973); *The Gathering* (1974); *A Scandalous Woman and Other Stories* (1974); *Mother Ireland* (1976); *Johnny I Hardly Knew You* (1977); *Arabian Days* (1978); *Mrs Reinhardt and Other Stories* (1978); *A Rose in the Heart* (1979); (ed.), *Some Irish Loving* (1979); *Virginia: A Play* (1981); *James and Nora* (1981); *Returning* (1982); *A Fanatic Heart* (1984); *The Country Girls Trilogy and Epilogue* (1986); (ed.), *Tales for the Telling* (1986).

References: 'Dialogue with Edna O'Brien', in *Under Bow Bells: Dialogues with Joseph McCulloch* (1974); Drabble; Dunn, N. (ed.), 'Edna', in *Talking to Women* (1965); Eckley, G., *Edna O'Brien* (1974); Hogan; Kiely, B., 'The whores on the half-doors or an image of the Irish writer', in *Conor Cruise O'Brien Introduces Ireland*, ed. O. Edwards (1969); O'Brien, D., 'Edna O'Brien: a kind of Irish childhood', in *Twentieth Century Women Novelists*, ed. T. Staley (1982); Tuohy, F., 'Five fierce ladies', in *Irish Writers and Society at Large*, ed. M. Sekine (1985).

O'Brien, Kate

b. 3 December 1897, Limerick, Ireland; d. 13 August 1974, Canterbury, England

Novelist, playwright

The sixth of nine children of Thomas and Katherine (*née* Thornhill) O'Brien, KO'B was educated by French nuns at Laurel Hill Convent, Limerick, and in 1916 went to Dublin to continue her education at University College. After her graduation from UCD, she worked in London as a journalist and then as a teacher. Following a short stay in America, she became a governess during the winter of 1922–3 in Bilbao, Spain, where she began attempting to write plays and where she developed a lifelong interest in Spanish history and culture. In 1923 she married Gustav Renier, a Dutch journalist living in London. The marriage lasted less than a year. During her long life KO'B lived in England,

Spain, and Ireland. In 1961 she moved to a small village near Canterbury where she remained until her death.

KO'Bs first literary efforts were plays, notably *A Distinguished Villa* (1926), which ran in London for three months and won critical acclaim. But she is best known as a novelist. Indeed, in 1949 she declared that she had become 'addicted to novels', which 'you can carry on your back', and preferred the inward 'fuss and bother' involved in the writing of fiction to the collaborative chaos of theatrical productions.

Her first novel, *Without My Cloak* (1931), set in Mellick (KO'B's fictitious name for her native Limerick), is a chronicle of an Irish family of the prosperous merchant class through three generations. This work was a great success and won two leading literary prizes: the Hawthornden Prize (1932) and the James Tait Black Memorial Prize (1932). In *Without My Cloak* we encounter the themes which permeate KO'B's fiction. Her characters struggle against consuming parental love, societal constraints, and the dictates of Irish Catholicism. Tense dramas dealing with the conflict between, on the one hand, the individual's desire for love and intellectual liberty and, on the other, the suffocating responsibilities of family and Church are played out against the background of an accurately detailed depiction of late nineteenth- and early twentieth-century Ireland. KO'B's central interest lies in the reflective life of her characters rather than in any external incident. Her strengths are her expert dissection and analysis of human nature and the creation of atmosphere by acute observation of detail. It would be an oversight not to mention that, except for Mat Costello, the protagonist of *Pray for the Wanderer* (1938), all of KO'B's leading characters are women and that she is particularly adept at delineating the debates between desire and duty within the female mind.

The Ante-Room (1934), *The Land of Spices* (1941), and *That Lady* (1946) are generally recognized as KO'B's major works. The first of these deals with Agnes Mulqueen's agony in her adulterous desire for her brother-in-law and with her slow growth to the determination not to succumb to a forbidden passion. *That Lady* (published in the United States as *For One Sweet Grape*) is KO'B's best-known work; based on political and romantic intrigue in the court of Philip II of Spain, it dramatizes the clash between self-fulfilment and public duty. Because of her bold treatment of the monarch, KO'B was refused entry to Spain until the Irish ambassador intervened on her behalf. *That Lady* was adapted for the stage (1949) by KO'B herself and was also made into a motion picture in 1955, starring Olivia De Havilland.

The Land of Spices, a thoughtful examination of the interior life of the female mind, is perhaps KO'B's finest novel. It deals with the theme of woman's struggle for self-realization. A Reverend Mother, Helen Archer, and a school-girl, Anna Murphy, are the heroines. The novel traces Anna's development from her arrival at boarding school at the age of 6 until her graduation twelve years later. By the technique of flashback, we also follow Helen Archer's development down to the present from the age of 18 when she suffered the trauma of discovering her father's homosexuality, an event which 'would not leave the stretched canvas of her eyelids'. The impact of this discovery is skilfully reinforced by the use of alliteration and assonance: 'And suddenly its last scene, the last scene of youth, of innocence, filled the austere dim cell.' Her alienation and isolation are suggested through her own feelings as they are related by the omniscient narrator and by the attitudes of those around her. Helen Archer's psychological development is made possible by her concern and love for Anna. She sees her own younger self reflected in the bright pupil.

Having suffered in the hands of vindictive authority as a young girl and having lost her beloved younger brother in a drowning accident, Anna is encouraged to accept his death and to struggle for intellectual liberty. Finally Anna comes to appreciate the Reverend Mother's love and concern for her and, just before parting, she has her 'moment of insight', 'something understood' which leaves her 'emptied of grief' and peaceful.

Eschewing the techniques of the modernist novel, KO'B preferred straightforward, traditional narrative. She was a careful exponent of the novel of ideas, although some charged her with excessive character analysis and over-neat plots. KO'B once wrote of women in George Eliot's novels that they 'did emphatically go out to confront their destinies . . . forcing the whole moral conception of the novel forward to where it may be the vehicle of an active and unblinking conscience'. Much the same could be said of her own works.

In 1946 she won the Irish Women Writers Club prize for her novel *For One Sweet Grape*. In 1947 she was elected to membership of the Irish Academy of Letters and she became a Fellow of the Royal Society of Literature the same year. DEMETRES P. TRYPHONOPOULOS

Works: *Distinguished Villa* (1927); *The Bridge* (1927); *Without My Cloak* (1931); *The Ante-Room* (1934); *Mary Lavelle* (1936); *The Schoolroom Window* (1937); *Farewell Spain* (1937); *Pray for the Wanderer* (1938); *The Land of Spices* (1941); *English Diaries and Journals* (1943); *The Last Summer* (1944); *That Lady* (1946; published in the US as *For One Sweet Grape*); *That Lady* (1949); *Teresa of Avila* (1951); *The Flower of May* (1953); *As Music and Splendour* (1958); *My Ireland* (1962); *Presentation Parlour* (1963).

References: *DLB*; Hoehn, M. (ed.), *Catholic Authors* (1946); Jeffares, N. A., *Anglo-Irish Literature* (1982); Jordan, J., 'Kate O'Brien: a passionate talent', *Hibernia* (30 August 1974); Jordan, J., 'Some works of the month, Kate O'Brien – a note on her themes, being a consideration of the *Flower of May*', *The Bell*, 19 (7 January 1954); Lawrence, M., 'Matriarchs', in *The School of Femininity* (1936); Rivollan, A., *Littérature irlandaise contemporaine* (1939); Ryan, J., 'Women in the novels of Kate O'Brien: the Mellick novels', in *Studies in Anglo-Irish Literature*, ed. H. Kosok (1982); Ryan, J., 'Class and creed in Kate O'Brien', in *The Irish Writer and the City*, ed. M. Harmon (1984).

Oliphant, Margaret

b. 4 April 1828, Wallyford, near Musselburgh, Scotland; d. 25 June 1897, Wimbledon

Novelist, biographer, critic, travel writer

MO, one of the most prolific of Victorian novelists, was the youngest of the three surviving children of Francis Wilson and his cousin, Margaret Oliphant. She spent her early childhood in Lasswade, near Edinburgh, and in Glasgow, before moving to Liverpool, where her father worked in the custom-house, and later to Birkenhead. It is clear from her posthumously published *Autobiography* (1898) that, where her father was remembered only as 'a dim figure', her mother, uneducated but widely read and intellectually alert, exerted a profound influence over her. There is no evidence that Margaret received any formal education, though she could read by the age of 6, and wrote her first novel (*Christian Melville*, later published in her brother William's name) at the age of 16, while nursing her mother through sickness. Her first published work was a Scottish regional novel, *Passages in the Life of Mrs Margaret Maitland*, published in 1849 by Colburn. At about this time she was sent to London to tend to her brother Willie, a confirmed alcoholic. Throughout her life she was to channel her unflagging energies into the support of feckless male dependants.

In 1851 she made a trip to Edinburgh to meet her Wilson relatives, and through them came into contact with Blackwood's, beginning an association which was to last until her death. Not only did she contribute regularly to *Blackwood's Magazine*, but Blackwood's published a large proportion of her novels, beginning with *Katie Stewart* (1853). In 1852 she married her cousin, Francis Wilson Oliphant, an artist and stained-glass designer, and they settled in London. By 1856, when her first son, Cyril, was born, she had already lost two daughters. In 1859, on account of her husband's health, she moved with her family to Italy, settling first in Florence, and then in Rome, where her husband died of tuberculosis in the same year, leaving her pregnant, with two small children, and £1,000 in debt. There were more catastrophes to follow. In 1864, during a second visit to Rome, her only remaining daughter died of gastric fever, and, shortly after settling in Windsor in 1866 in order to educate her sons Cyril and 'Cecco' (Francis) at Eton, she heard of her brother Frank's financial ruin in Canada. When he returned, widowed with three children, it was she who supported him, financing her nephew Frank's training as an engineer as well as her sons' education at Oxford and frequent family holidays abroad; it was on holiday in Switzerland in 1875 that MO met Anne Thackeray, who was to be a lifelong friend. In spite of her immense efforts on behalf of her sons and nephew, all three died tragically young. Her autobiography ends on a note of bitter regret that she had outlived both her children and her literary reputation. None the less, with a resilience of spirit which she herself described as 'almost criminally elastic', she continued to write until her death in 1897, by which time she had worn a hole in her finger with her pen. For forty-nine years she had been enslaved to publishers, producing almost a hundred novels and a flood of non-fiction. She never enjoyed a regular salary.

MO's work is characterized by the unflinching realism that one might expect from a woman who had endured such emotional hardship; a 'happy ending', she believed, was simply 'a contemptible expedient'. Paradoxically, in spite of the fact that she explicitly denounced what she termed the 'Anti-Marriage League' of writers and was a reactionary with regard to sexual ethics (she deplored Hardy's *Tess of the D'Urbervilles*), matrimony rarely brings salvation in her own fiction. Her capable and enterprising heroines either shoulder the burdens imposed upon them by ineffectual brothers, fathers, and husbands, or, in defiance of the men around them, find fulfilment through their own careers. Catherine in *Hester* (1883) runs the family bank, while the heroine of *Kirsteen* (1890) escapes from home to set up a thriving dressmaker's establishment.

MO is best known, however, for her *Chronicles of Carlingford* (1863–76); they focus on the clashes of class, temperament, and ideology which enliven an otherwise unremarkable provincial town. These clashes are enacted around the three places of worship in Carlingford, the parish church, the Anglican chapel, and the Salem chapel for the Dissenters. MO, herself a Scottish Presbyterian who in adult life worshipped in the Church of England, remained detached from the religious sectarianism which she exploited primarily as a source of social comedy. A recurrent theme in the first *Chronicles* (*The Rector, and The Doctor's Family*, 1863; *Salem Chapel*, 1863; *The Perpetual Curate*, 1864) is that of the callow and optimistic young man whose life until now has been sheltered by academic institutions, and who finds himself pitifully ill-equipped for life in Carlingford. The heroine of *Miss Marjoribanks* (1866) has obvious affinities with Austen's Emma Woodhouse: she has 'that sublime confidence in herself which is the first necessity to a woman with a mission', and her ostensibly altruistic 'grand design of turning the chaotic elements of society into one grand unity' turns out to be her selfish quest for a husband. The heroine of *Phoebe Junior, A Last Chronicle of Carlingford* (1876) is another of MO's 'managing' women; as its title suggests, the book was influenced by Trollope's *Barsetshire Chronicles (The Last Chronicle of Barset* had appeared in 1867), most notably in its central episode which concerns a bill forged by the incumbent of St Roque's Chapel. Like so many of MO's works, it explores the problems of class feeling arising from the disintegration of the old social order. Phoebe is unable to reconcile her privileged education and her life in London with her parents' humble origins.

MO's other works include her *Tales of the Seen and the Unseen* (beginning with *A Beleaguered City*, 1880) which deal with the supernatural and the attempts at reunion between the dead and the living; biographies of the controversial Scottish clergyman Edward Irving (1862) and of MO's distant relation Laurence Oliphant (1891); and the first two volumes of the three-volume history of Blackwood's, *Annals of a Publishing House* (1897–8).   ANNE FERNIHOUGH

Selected works: Passages in the Life of Mrs Margaret Maitland (1849); Caleb Field (1851); Katie Stewart (1853); Harry Muir (1853); The Quiet Heart (1854); Magdalen Hepburn (1854); 'The Executor' (1861); The Life of Edward Irving (1862); The Rector, and The Doctor's Family (1863); Salem Chapel (1863); The Perpetual Curate (1864); Miss Marjoribanks (1866); A Son of the Soil (1866); The Curate in Charge (1876); Phoebe Junior, A Last Chronicle of Carlingford (1876); A Beleaguered City (1880); The Literary History of England (1882); A Little Pilgrim in the Unseen (1882); Hester (1883); The Ladies Lindores (1883); Sir Tom (1884); Two Stories of the Seen and the Unseen (1885); A House Divided Against Itself (1886); The Land of Darkness (1888); Lady Car (1889); Kirsteen (1890); A Memoir of the Life of Laurence Oliphant (1891); Sir Robert's Fortune (1895); The Ways of Life (1897); Annals of a Publishing House (1897–8); A Widow's Tale, and Other Stories (1898); The Autobiography and Letters of Mrs M. O. W. Oliphant (1899).

References: Clarke, I. C., Six Portraits (1935); Colby, V. and Colby, R. A., The Equivocal Virtue (1966); Moore, K., Victorian Wives (1974); Showalter, E., A Literature of Their Own (1977); Stebbins, L. P., A Victorian Album; Some Lady Novelists of the Period (1946); Terry, R. C., Victorian Popular Fiction (1983); Williams, M., Women Novelists of the Later Nineteenth Century (1984); Williams, M., Margaret Oliphant: A Critical Biography (1986); Wolff, R. L., Gains and Losses: Novels of Faith and Doubt in Victorian England (1977).

Olivier, Edith

b. 1875, Wilton, Wiltshire; d. 1948, Wilton, Wiltshire

Novelist, essayist, historian

EO was the daughter of Dacres Olivier, Rector of Wilton and chaplain to the Earls of Pembroke; her mother was a bishop's daughter and a relative of Bishop Wordsworth of Salisbury. Her father believed utterly in the Victorian patriarchal family and expected his family of ten to accept his conception of how life was to be lived; and such was his force of character, allied to a highly strung temperament reined in with utter dedication to his vocation, that two of the three daughters, Muriel and EO, lived at home until his death. Suitors who presented themselves were never deemed sufficiently suitable, although the eldest sister escaped after a four-year secret engagement. Their education was managed by governesses and their mother, who knew enough Latin to prepare her sons for public school. Later, EO's father consented to her sitting for a newly founded scholarship to St Hugh's College, Oxford, on the assumption that she would fail; to their joint surprise, she was awarded it and spent four non-consecutive terms at Oxford reading history, ill-health preventing her from wintering in Oxford.

Her schoolgirl ambitions were neither historical nor literary, but theatrical; but realizing that her father would never countenance his daughter's becoming a professional actress (though vicarage and country-house life was full of *amateur* dramatics), she accommodated herself, cheerfully enough it would seem, to her allotted role of active leisure. Her memoirs were later titled ironically *Without Knowing Mr Walkley*, Mr Walkley being drama critic of *The Times* when she still dreamed of life on the stage. In retrospect she defined her time as 'a happy life spent, not upon the stage or in any of the other professions which presented themselves, not as a wife, mother, mother-in-law, and grandmother (the fate of most of my friends), but as a lifelong inhabitant of Wiltshire, which is in my eyes, the most beautiful of English counties'. She had a deep feel for her part of 'Wessex' and chronicled affectionately and exactly its rural ways – the plebeian, aristocratic, and clerical mores, and the alterations made by compulsory education, the arrival of the military in 1899, and the mobility provided by cars and buses. Her last book was appropriately enough a volume on Wiltshire, in a series on English counties.

EO's connections with Wilton House and the Bishop's palace at Salisbury Cathedral meant that her horizons were far from provincial. In the First World War she helped to organize the Women's Land Army, and later was Mayor of Wilton four times. The catalyst for her career as a writer, which began when she was in her fifties, was in preparing a memorial volume for her sister Muriel who died in 1925. Her gift for anecdote and character analysis had been satisfied until then by conversing with her sister; now stories began forming and demanding written expression. At the same time the emotional centre of her life was filled by her friendship for the young Rex Whistler. She mothered his muse, was the confidante in his love affairs, helped find patronage from among her connections, and in general entered with surprising ease into the spirit of the aristocratic/bohemian circles of the 1920s and 1930s, with their interconnections among theatre, ballet, literature, and the visual arts. Indeed if the early part of her life could almost be found in the pages of Trollope or Charlotte Yonge, the latter decades would fit into Anthony Powell's *Dance to the Music of Time*. Her circle included Bryan Howard, Stephen Tennant, Siegfried Sassoon, Lord David Cecil, and William Walton, whose First Symphony was composed on the piano he chose for her *cottage ornée* in Wilton House grounds.

Her novels portray the psychological tensions generated by strong or obsessive personalities, through the medium of deft and ironic social comedies. She skilfully uses symbolism in incident, setting, and speech. She also gives a distilled panorama of changing manners and mores among the well-to-do before and after the First World War that is similar in theme to Molly Keane's work, though EO is undoubtedly the more accomplished craftsman. Her ironic wit bears comparison with the early Henry James and her sense of form has a classical assurance. It is not surprising she found such affinities with the rococo panache of Whistler, who often provided the decorations to her books.

EO's gifts as an historian equal hers as a novelist; her historical writings are in the genre of local history and antiquarianism in which the Victorians excelled, and they also belong to the style of critically scrupulous but elegant belles lettres. CLARISSA CAMPBELL ORR

Works: *The Love Child* (1927); *The Underground River* (1928); *As Far as Jane's Grandmother's* (1928); *The Triumphant Footman: A Farcical Fable* (1930); (ed.), *Mookraking: A Little Book of Wiltshire Stories Told by Members of the W. I.* (with M. K. S. Edwards) (1930); *Dwarf's Blood* (1931); 'Preface' to *An Adventure* (1931) by C. A. E. Moberly; *The Seraphim Room* (1932); *The Eccentric Life of Alexander Cruden* (1934); *Mary Magdalen* (1934); *Without Knowing Mr Walkley: Personal Memories* (1938); *Country Moods and Tenses: A Non-grammarian's Chapbook* (1941); *Night Thoughts of a Country Landlady* (1943); *Four Victorian Ladies of Wiltshire* (1945); *Wiltshire* (1951).

References: Cecil, D., 'Introduction' to *The Love Child* (1953); Green, M., *Children of the Sun* (1977); Lee, J., 'Introduction' to *The Love Child* (1981); Whistler, L., *The Laughter and the Urn* (1985).

Opie, Amelia

b. 12 November 1769, Norwich; d. 2 December 1853, Norwich
Novelist, poet

The only child of Amelia (*née* Briggs) and James Alderson, AO was born and brought up in Norwich, a city which, in the late eighteenth century, was still an important commercial, cultural, and social centre. Her father was a prosperous and respected medical practitioner and a stout Presbyterian, famed, according to his daughter, as much for his provision of free medical services for the poor as for his skills amongst the paying customers. He was also a man of literary and musical pretensions, and the Alderson house was frequented by the intellectual elite of eastern England. Following the death of her mother in 1784, AO took over as mistress of the household, and her precocious literary talents received considerable encouragement and direction from her contact with her father's distinguished friends. From an early age she began contributing pieces of verse and prose to the Norwich journal, *The Cabinet, The London Magazine,* and a number of other periodicals. Her first novel, *The Dangers of Coquetry,* was published anonymously in 1790, and in January 1791 her romantic play *Adelaide* was performed at a private Norwich theatre, with AO herself in the leading role.

During the early 1790s AO made regular visits to London, where she became intimate friends with the radical intellectuals William Godwin, Elizabeth Inchbald, and Thomas Holcroft. 'The report of the world is,' she wrote, 'that Mr Holcroft is in love with [Mrs Inchbald], *she* with Mr Godwin, Mr Godwin with *me,* and I in love with Mr Holcroft! A pretty story indeed.' It was, however, another member of the radical circle, the portrait painter John Opie, whom she finally married in May 1798. Opie, a Cornish carpenter's son, had formerly been lionized by fashionable society as a peasant genius, 'the Cornish wonder', but by the time of his marriage he had largely managed to free himself from this social role, and had established himself as a successful painter in his own right.

After their marriage Opie encouraged AO to write and publish, and her second novel was brought out under her own name in 1801. *The Father and Daughter* was an immediate success, going into a second edition within the year, and by 1844 it had reached its tenth edition. It was translated into French and Portuguese, and was used by Paër as the basis for his opera *Agnese.* The novel brought AO considerable fame. She was, according to her friend Mrs

Thomson Clarkson, 'amazingly noticed and courted by titled folk, and learned folk and rich folk'. In 1804 she followed up her achievement with the publication of *Adeline Mowbray, or, The Mother and Daughter.*

AO's career at centre of London literary society was fairly short-lived. In April 1807 John Opie died, having just completed a successful series of lectures as Professor of Painting at the Royal Academy. Almost immediately after his death AO retired to Norwich. She continued to write and publish, producing at least another thirteen works of poetry, prose, and fiction, but these did not enjoy the great popularity of her early novels. Her work became increasingly preoccupied with moral and religious didacticism, and in 1825 she finally became a member of the Society of Friends. Although her Quakerism did not prevent her enjoying regular visits to the decadent society of London and Paris, it did preclude the writing of novels. Her final works were two books of morality, and a volume of sacred poetry entitled *Lays for the Dead* (1833). Towards the end of her life, AO became active in the anti-slavery movement, and in 1851, at the age of 82, she made her final visit to London, to see the Great Exhibition. She died at her home in Castle Meadow, Norwich, having reached the age of 84.

Despite AO's personal connections with the radical circle around William Godwin and Mary Wollstonecraft, her novels cannot be seen as part of the 'Jacobin' tradition. They emphasize the importance of individual morality as a religious and social duty, rather than as part of a political system, and while the radicals sought to reintegrate political, economic, and ethical considerations, AO upheld the traditional separation of personal morality and social analysis. *The Father and Daughter*, described in the address to the reader as 'a SIMPLE MORAL TALE', represents a celebration of filial duty and self-sacrifice. It tells the story of Agnes Fitzhenry, who leaves her loving father for the sake of Captain Clifford, a villainous lover who subsequently seduces and refuses to marry her. When Agnes, overcome by guilt and repentance, returns to her home town, she finds that her elopement has driven her father insane. The novel describes how she expiates her original fault, by wholly devoting herself to her father's service. Fitzhenry recovers his reason on his death bed, so that he is able to forgive Agnes and give her his blessing. This done, both father and daughter expire and are buried together.

Several of AO's novels not only do not condone, but actually engage with the radical ideas of the 'Jacobin' writers. Like Mrs West's *A Tale of the Times* (1799) and the anonymous *The Citizen's Daughter* (1804), *Adeline Mowbray* is based around an attack on the Godwinian attitude to marriage. Loosely based on the life of Mary Wollstonecraft, it charts the unfortunate experiences of a young and innocent girl, who has imbibed the free-thinking antipathy to wedlock, and defies convention by openly living with her handsome young lover, Glenmurray. After a considerable amount of hardship and the death of Glenmurray, Adeline is finally persuaded of the fallaciousness of free thinking through the influence of a kindly Quaker, and dies reconciled to God and the ways of the world.

Although *Adeline Mowbray* has been interpreted by a few modern critics as an endorsement of the ideas of Mary Wollstonecraft, the novel is wholly unambiguous in its condemnation of this attitude, even though it is sympathetic in its portrayal of the character of Adeline. In *Valentine's Eve* AO dismisses revolutionary ideas by embodying them in the character of the unprepossessing Lucy Merle. Thus although AO's novels can be seen as 'novels of ideas' in that they deal with such issues as the role and position of women, and also with the rights of black people and the fight against slavery, they are characterized by a humanitarian religious ethos rather than a radical creed. Indeed, in many respects AO's novels hark back to the earlier tradition of the novel of sensibility. They dwell on the power of sympathy to alleviate suffering, and much of their appeal is located in the evocation of an intense pathos. Sir Walter Scott claimed to have wept buckets over *The Father and Daughter*, and AO wrote to William Hayley, 'I like to make people cry, indeed, if I do not do it, all my readers are disappointed.'

Like her novels, AO's poetry combined an invocation of the romantic melancholy of sensibility with an inculcation of moral precepts. She wrote in various forms, the ballad, the sonnet, the ode, the song, the elegy, but in all these genres the same pathetic motifs recur. Indeed, it was probably the widespread rejection of the philosophy of sensibility that led to the decline in the popularity of AO's poetry and fiction through the Victorian period, and ensured that nowadays she is largely remembered as the author of *Adeline Mowbray*, a novel which has a historical interest through its perspective on the life and ideas of Mary Wollstonecraft. LIZ BELLAMY

Selected works: The Dangers of Coquetry: A Novel (1790); The Father and Daughter: A Tale (1801); An Elegy to the Memory of the Duke of Bedford (1802); Miscellaneous Poems (1802); Adeline Mowbray, or, The Mother and Daughter: A Tale (1804); Simple Tales (1806); The Warrior's Return and Other Poems (1808); 'Memoir of John Opie', prefixed to his Lectures on Painting (1809); Temper, or, Domestic Scenes (1812); Tales of Real Life (1813); 'A Character of the Author', prefixed to Margaret Roberts's Duty (1814); Valentine's Eve: a Novel (1816); New Tales (1818); Tales of the Heart (1820); Madeline: A Tale (1822); Illustrations of Lying in all its Branches (1825); Detraction Displayed (1828); Lays for the Dead (1833).

References: Braithwaite, J. B. (ed.), Memoirs of Joseph John Gurney (1854); Brightwell, C. B., Memorials of the Life of Amelia Opie, Selected and Arranged from Her Letters, Diaries and Other Manuscripts (1854); Earland, A., John Opie and His Circle (1911); Jones, A. H., Best Sellers of Jane Austen's Age (1987); Kavanagh, J., English Women of Letters: Biographical Sketches (1863); Macgregor, M. E., 'Amelia Alderson Opie: worldling and friend', Smith College Studies in Modern Languages 14, 1–2 (October 1932–January 1933); Menzies-Wilson, J. and Lloyd, H., Amelia: The Tale of a Plain Friend (1937).

Orczy, Baroness

b. 23 September 1865, Tarna-Oss, Hungary; d. 12 November 1947, London
Writer of romance fiction, short detective stories, and plays
BO (Emma) was born into an aristocratic Hungarian family, but declared that England, where she lived most of her adult life, was her 'spiritual birthplace'. She spent her early childhood on large agricultural properties, first on her grandfather's, then her father's, Tisza-Abád. In her autobiography she recalls growing up in a lively extended family, which took every opportunity for pleasure, with great feasting always accompanied by gypsy music. This way of life for the family came to a dramatic end when BO was 3; during one such celebration, the local peasants burned the farm buildings and all the crops which were ready to harvest, in order to dissuade BO's father from continuing with his progressive farming techniques and mechanization. The financial difficulties following the fire forced the family to leave Tisza-Abád. Perhaps this event influenced BO's attitude to the working classes; in her novels she always stresses

the importance of remembering one's place. It must also have made the class conflict in the French Revolution particularly interesting to her, as is apparent in her most popular series of novels, about the Scarlet Pimpernel.

Through his friendship with Franz Liszt, BO's father, a talented amateur musician and composer, became *Intendant* (Supreme Administrator) of the National Theatres at Budapest. Though BO is very protective of him in her autobiography, she admits that she had gathered that he could be 'very difficult', and it seems that his lack of tact sent the family further on their travels, first to Brussels, then Paris, and eventually to England where they stayed for many years. The family was involved with the musical circle in London, and also included among their acquaintance noted actors like Henry Irving. But, despite this sociable and artistic upbringing, BO was very shy and introverted, and later when writing about the characters she created she said, 'I knew them all personally. They were more real and more vivid to me than the friends of this world.'

BO had a convent education; she recalled that the nuns in Brussels were 'more noted for their piety than their erudition', and that those in Paris taught her a version of history which as an adult she, typically, felt to be very unfair to the English. BO arrived in London, aged 15, speaking no English, but attended a day school for the 'daughters of gentlemen', where she rapidly progressed. However, her father considered female emancipation 'an anathema', so she could not go to university; instead she decided to pursue a career as a painter, and went to the West London School of Art, then the Heatherly School of Art, where she met Montague Barstow whom she married in 1898. They had one son, Jack, born in 1899. She soon abandoned painting and took up writing.

Although BO is now best known for her romantic fiction, early in her career she also worked as a translator, sometimes collaborating with her husband, and her first publishing success was in detective fiction. She took advantage of the current interest in detective stories created by Conan Doyle's Sherlock Holmes. BO's stories at first appeared only in *The Royal Magazine* (between 1901 and 1904), then in 1905 her third series was published in book form as *The Case of Miss Elliott*. This book was the first in her popular 'The Old Man in the Corner' series and marked an important development in the history of the modern detective novel, as the central character is the first 'armchair detective'. He sits in a cheap restaurant talking to a young newspaper woman about unsolved mysteries currently being reported in the press which have baffled the police. After analysing the situation and the characters involved, he reveals the solution. The formula is structurally significant because it throws the weight of activity on to the denouement, and only considers the crime and the period of detection retrospectively.

After initial disappointment in writing romantic fiction – *The Emperor's Candlesticks* (1899) sold only about ninety copies – BO returned to the genre with greater experience, and wrote *The Scarlet Pimpernel* which was completed in 1903, but not published until 1905, after the stage version had been a tremendous box-office success. BO recalls that the idea of the Scarlet Pimpernel stories came when she and her husband went to the Paris Exhibition in 1900. The anti-British feeling generated by French sympathy for the Boers, combined with the huge crowds on the streets, created a clear image of the French Revolution in her mind. In spite of her Hungarian birth, BO was deeply nationalistic about England, and her aim in the characterization of Sir Percy (the Scarlet Pimpernel) was to achieve 'the perfect presentation of an Englishman'. The perhaps inevitable result is a two-dimensional stereotype; and BO's frequent reference to the Englishness of certain qualities itself sounds distinctly un-English.

Interestingly, whereas the film and stage versions of *The Scarlet Pimpernel* concentrate on the adventures of Sir Percy and the League of the Scarlet Pimpernel as they perform impossible rescues, saving aristocrats from the clutches of the Republic, the novel usually focuses on the consciousness of Marguerite (Percy's French wife) making the romantic element of the story of paramount importance. After a whirlwind courtship, Percy and Marguerite marry, only to be estranged within hours owing to her Republican and his Royalist principles. Consequently he adopts a buffoonish persona, deceiving Marguerite and the world in order to conceal his work as the Scarlet Pimpernel. In the mode of most heroes of romances, unknown to Marguerite Percy is besotted with her: 'He was but a man madly, blindly, passionately in love, and as soon as her light footstep had died away within the house, he knelt down on the terrace steps, and in the very madness of his love he kissed one by one the places where her small foot had trodden, and the stone balustrade there where her tiny hand had rested last.' Marguerite is tricked by agents of the Republic into a situation where she must sacrifice either her brother or her husband in order to save the other. Fortunately, despite the emotional dilemma (there are frequent references to the confusions of 'a woman's heart'), both are saved, and husband and wife are reunited. Although the characterization is limited (Marguerite is frequently referred to as 'the most intelligent woman in Europe', but the claim is never substantiated by anything she does or says), the adventure is thoroughly entertaining, as is the deep, but very respectable, passion. BO never quite achieves the same excitement in the sequels, though they also incorporate romantic interest. BO is least interesting when she digresses from the storyline into lengthy generalizations about the history of the Revolution. For example, in *Lord Tony's Wife* (1917) the exciting story of the kidnapping by a vengeful revolutionary of an exiled French aristocrat who is married to one of the League, and her subsequent rescue by the Scarlet Pimpernel and friends, is swamped by BO's ponderous, biased relation of the history of Nantes.

Considering the immense and lasting popularity of the Scarlet Pimpernel in novels and on stage and screen, it was fortunate for BO that she did not, as a little-known writer, accept the tempting offer of a single payment of £30 for all the rights of the book, made by one of the first publishers she approached.

LUCY SLOAN

Selected works: (trans.), *Old Hungarian Fairy Tales* (with Montague Barstow) (1895); (trans.), *The Enchanted Cat* (1895); (trans.), *Fairyland's Beauty (The Suitors of Princess Fire-fly)* (1895); (trans.), *Vletka and the White Lizard* (1895); *The Emperor's Candlesticks* (1899); *The Case of Miss Elliott* (1905); *The Scarlet Pimpernel* (1905); *I Will Repay* (1906); *The Tangled Skein* (1907); *Beau Brocade* (1907); *The Elusive Pimpernel* (1908); *The Old Man in the Corner* (1909); *Lady Molly of Scotland Yard* (1910); *Petticoat Government* (1910); *A True Woman* (1911, published in the US as *The Heart of a Woman*); *Meadowsweet* (1912); *Unto Caesar* (1914); *The Laughing Cavalier* (1914); *The Bronze Eagle* (1915); *Leatherface: A Tale of Old Flanders* (1916); *Lord Tony's Wife: An Adventure of the Scarlet Pimpernel* (1917); *Flower o' the Lily* (1918); *The League of the Scarlet Pimpernel* (1919); *The First Sir Percy: An Adventure of the Laughing Cavalier* (1920); *Nicolette* (1922); *The Honourable Jim* (1924); *Pimpernel and Rosemary* (1924); *The Old Man in the Corner Unravels the Mystery of the Pearl Necklace, and The Tragedy in Bishop's Road* (1924); *A Question of Temptation* (1925); *The Old Man in the Corner Unravels the*

Mystery of the White Carnation, and The Montmartre Hat (1925); *The Miser of Maida Vale* (1925); *Unravelled Knots* (1925); *Sir Percy Hits Back: An Adventure of the Scarlet Pimpernel* (1927); *Marivosa* (1930); *A Child of the Revolution* (1932); *The Way of the Scarlet Pimpernel* (1933); *A Spy of Napoleon* (1934); *The Turbulent Duchess: HRH Madame la Duchesse de Berri* (1935); *The Divine Folly* (1937); *No Greater Love* (1938); *Mam'zelle Guillotine: An Adventure of the Scarlet Pimpernel* (1940); *Pride of Race* (1942); *Will-o'-the-Wisp* (1947); *Links in the Chain of Life* (1947).
References: *DNB*; *CA*; *CMW*; Drabble; *OCCL*; *RGW*.

Osborne, Dorothy

b. 1627, Chicksands Priory, Bedfordshire; d. 1695, Moor Park
Letter writer
DO was born into the royalist family of the Osbornes, the youngest of the eleven children of Lady Dorothy, daughter of Sir John Danvers, and Sir Peter Osborne. Her father defended Castle Cornet, Guernsey, for King Charles I, holding it gallantly for three years after the king's execution, until in 1651 he had to surrender it to the Commonwealth. Disappointed and impoverished, he retired to the family home of Chicksands, where soon after his return his wife died. DO cared for him there until his death in 1653. During this time, and for some years afterwards, she corresponded regularly with William Temple, and most of her letters have been preserved. She first met him while travelling to France with her brother, when she was 21 years old and William 20. They were all staying at an inn on the Isle of Wight, where DO's brother wrote some derogatory remarks about the government on a windowpane. As a result they were all three arrested, and only released because of DO's quick-wittedness in confessing to the crime herself and charming the officer in charge to overlook her womanly folly. William Temple was impressed, and there followed a friendship and courtship which lasted seven years.

It was a stormy courtship as neither family approved of the match. The letters, often conveyed in secret, show the many obstacles that had to be overcome. DO's family frequently promoted other suitors for her, including Henry Cromwell, the son of the Protector. Hope, despair, misunderstandings, and resignation are all reflected in the letters until at last the families capitulated, and in spite of the ravages of a recent dangerous attack of smallpox DO married William on Christmas Day 1655. As Lady Temple, she supported her husband in his diplomatic career, often travelling with him. Once when crossing the Channel with her children, she was involved in a sea-skirmish with the Dutch navy, and was later commended by Charles II for her courage. When apart, she would send her husband confidential information, and she shared in the confidential enquiries for William of Orange about the young Princess Mary who, as queen, became her close friend.

She had several children, most of whom died in infancy. Her daughter, Diana, died aged 14 in 1679, but almost certainly her greatest sorrow was the death of her son John in 1689, who drowned himself by filling his pockets with stones and throwing himself from a boat into the river below London Bridge. He had been Secretary at War for only one week and left a letter: 'My folly in undertaking what I was not able to perform has done the king and kingdom a great deal of prejudice.' DO, remembering John as 'the quietest and best little boy that ever was born', described the affliction of his death as 'truly great'. She died six years later, after forty years of marriage, and was buried in

Westminster Abbey. The young Jonathan Swift had recently become secretary to Sir William, and describes her approvingly in his 'Ode Occasioned by Sir William Temple's Late Illness and Recovery' (1693) as 'Mild Dorothea, peaceful, wise and great'.

DO's letters came to the public's attention almost by chance, published at first not in her own right, but her husband's. T. P. Courtenay published forty-two extracts in an appendix to his *Memoirs of the Life, Works and Correspondence of Sir William Temple* (1836), apologizing for including so many. Macaulay, reviewing the book, praised the extracts warmly. 'We only wish that there were twice as many. Very little indeed of diplomatic correspondence of that generation is so well worth reading.' This persuaded Edward Parry to edit the letters in 1888, with subsequent enlarged editions coming out over the next fifty years.

The many literary qualities in these private letters led Virginia Woolf to point out, 'Had she been born in 1827, Dorothy Osborne would have written novels; had she been born in 1527 she would never have written at all. But she was born in 1627, and, at that date, though writing books was ridiculous for a woman, there was nothing unseemly in writing a letter.' DO would have considered writing for publication ludicrous. She laughed at the Duchess of Newcastle: 'Sure the poor woman is a little distracted, she could never be so ridiculous else as to venture writing books . . . if I could not sleep this fortnight I should not come to that.'

She was a shrewd critic and avid reader. An admirer of French romances, she deplored the English translations of *Polexandre* and *L'Illustre Basse* which made them 'so disguised that I . . . hardly knew them'. Letter writing, she said, should be 'as free as one's discourse', and she laughed at grandiose style. She described a pompous suitor's letter as 'the most sublime nonsense that in my life I ever read, and yet . . . he descended as low as he could to come near my weak understanding'. Those who 'labour to find out terms that may obscure a plain sense' did not impress her.

Her own style is often graceful and rhythmic, emotional or dramatic: 'No, all the kindness I have or ever had is yours, nor shall I ever repent it so unless you shall ever repent yours.' Observant and witty, she could sum up a character in a few words: 'a travelled Monsieur, whose head is all feather inside and out', and she commented crisply on the behaviour of her acquaintances and relatives, some of whom inspired in her a desire to 'live in a hollow tree to avoid them'. Her life and letters continued against a background of change and political upheaval, like the new Marriage Act of 1653 'that sure will frighten the country people extremely', or the 'new discovered plot against the Protector'. Through the letters emerge, with immediate freshness, pictures of contemporary life: from games of shuttlecock and tennis, to a fireside discussion about whether people will ever learn to 'fly like birds and dispatch their journeys so'. Invaluable for giving a first-hand account of life during the Commonwealth, the letters have also intrinsic value in their lively charm, irony, descriptive powers, and wisdom. SHIRLEY EACHUS

Works: 'Appendix' to *Memoirs of the Life, Works and Correspondence of Sir William Temple* by T. P. Courtenay (1836); *Letters from Dorothy Osborne to Sir William Temple 1652–53*, ed. E. A. Parry (1888; revised and enlarged 1903).

References: Cecil, D., *Two Quiet Lives* (1948); *DLB*; *DNB* (under W. Temple); Irvine, L. L., *Ten Letter Writers* (1932); Longe, J. G., *Martha, Lady Gifford; Her Life and Correspondence* (1911); Woolf, V., 'The Letters of Dorothy Osborne', *The Second Common Reader* (1932).

'Ouida' (Marie Lousie de la Ramée)

b. 1 January 1839, Bury St Edmunds, England; d. 25 January 1908, Viareggio, Italy

Novelist, short-story writer, critic

The only child of Louis and Susan (*née* Sutton) Ramé, 'O' was left by the long and frequent absences of her French father to be raised almost entirely by her English mother and grandmother. The family liked to believe that the mysterious Ramé was involved in opposition politics in his native land and that he died during the days of the Commune. 'O's fierce pride in her French heritage soon combined with her fantasizing temperament to inflate her surname to de la Ramée.

Her fantasies having long outgrown the narrow provinciality of Bury St Edmunds, 'O' welcomed the move to London with her mother and grandmother in 1857. After being introduced to Harrison Ainsworth, then editor of *Bentley's Miscellany*, she began her writing career as 'Ouida' (her childhood mispronunciation of 'Louise'). She followed up the success of her 'Dashwood's Drag, or, The Derby and What Came of It', which appeared in *Bentley's* for April and May 1859, with a series of similar tales of high society and sporting life, many collected in *Cecil Castlemaine's Gage and Other Novelettes* (1867). *Granville de Vigne*, serialized in Ainsworth's *New Monthly Magazine* and reprinted as *Held in Bondage* (1863), typified her early fiction. The formula seen there – a combination of dashing military life, extravagant luxury, tortuous romantic intrigue, and a hero of almost impossible beauty, courage, and style – reached its epitome in *Under Two Flags* (1867). The public attention (and financial rewards) which such fiction attracted allowed 'O' to live out the fantasies otherwise denied by her lack of beauty and social status. Adorned in Worth gowns and surrounded by hothouse flowers, she held court to largely male audiences in the Langham Hotel during the 1870s; in later years she frequently dressed to resemble the heroine of her latest novel. Although essentially conventional in her own behaviour, she flouted Victorian codes of respectability by encouraging people to smoke throughout dinner and by remaining with the men over brandy and cigars, collecting material for her novels from their conversation. *Tricotrin* (1869) and *Folle-Farine* (1871) added a new element to her fictional formulas: the peasant heroine who becomes tragically enmeshed in the snares of high society, a device which she again exploited in *Two Little Wooden Shoes* (1874).

In 1871 'O' travelled to Europe, producing *A Dog of Flanders and Other Stories* (1872) from her observations of the Belgian peasantry and a series of novels set in Italy, among them *Pascarèl* (1873), *Signa* (1875), *In a Winter City* (1876), and *Ariadnê* (1877). She lived in the Villa Farinola outside Florence from 1871 to 1888. Of the several novels featuring fashionable members of Florentine society, the most notorious was *Friendship* (1878). Its main characters were recognized to represent 'O', the Marchese della Stuffa (a gentleman-in-waiting to the Italian court whom she had pursued with unrequited passion), and Mrs Janet Duff Gordon Ross, Stuffa's avowed mistress. 'O's insistence that the novel was based on absolute truth made its idealization of her own role and its vilification of her rival all the more outrageous. Her personal disappointments helped turn her attention from the glamour to the failings of polite society. *Moths* (1880), perhaps her most successful work, shows the social fabric being eaten away by the vice and hypocrisy of society's fashionable 'moths'. She was increasingly to lament the failure of the upper classes to live up to the ideals of taste and breeding she set for them, as well as their surrender to the values of the vulgar and encroaching middle classes whom she had all her life detested. She sentimentalized the Italian peasantry as victims abandoned by the aristocracy to the tyranny of the bourgeois bureaucracy in *A Village Commune and Other Stories* (1881). *The Massarenes* (1897) most directly condemns the *nouveaux riches* and the 'smart' set that collaborated with them.

As the 1880s waned, so too did 'O's popularity with an audience turning from three-decker romances to more realistic one-volume works. Her extravagant lifestyle continually outran her income, leaving unpaid bills and pending lawsuits behind her as she moved from place to place, her only companions after her mother's death being a servant or two and the pack of spoiled dogs on which she lavished her affection. In her final years only a civil list pension stood between her and real poverty. During the 1890s she turned increasingly to criticism and commentary: many of her analyses of British and European writers and her vendettas against publishers, plagiarists, cruelty to animals, female suffrage, Italian misgovernment, the Boer War, and the rising tide of vulgarity and ugliness brought on by the ascendancy of middle-class money and values were collected in *Views and Opinions* (1895) and *Critical Studies* (1900).

'O' owed her considerable success in the 1870s and 1880s partly to her abundant imagination for sensational plotting, vivid detail, and local colour, and partly to the expanding market for fiction created by lending libraries and railway bookstalls. Her eccentricity, her egotism, and her flamboyance were always straining against the prosaic and sometimes sordid reality of her life; her wish-fulfilling fictions fed her own and her audience's longing for the glamour, romance, and luxury which were beyond their reach.

ROSEMARY JANN

Works: *Held in Bondage* (1863); *Strathmore* (1865); *Chandos* (1866); *Cecil Castlemaine's Gage and Other Novelettes* (1867); *Under Two Flags* (1867); *Idalia* (1867); *Tricotrin* (1869); *Puck* (1870); *A Dog of Flanders and Other Stories* (1872); *Pascarèl* (1873); *Two Little Wooden Shoes* (1874); *Signa* (1875); *In a Winter City* (1876); *Ariadnê* (1877); *Friendship* (1878); *Moths* (1880); *Pipistrello and Other Stories* (1880); *A Village Commune and Other Stories* (1881); *Bimbi: Stories for Children* (1882); *In Maremma* (1882); *Wanda* (1883); *Frescoes: Dramatic Sketches* (1883); *Princess Napraxine* (1884); *Othmar* (1885); *Don Guesaldo* (1886); *A House Party* (1887); *Guilderoy* (1889); *Ruffino and Other Stories* (1890); *Syrlin* (1890); *The Tower of Taddeo* (1892); *The New Priesthood: A Protest against Vivisection* (1893); *Two Offenders and Other Tales* (1894); *The Silver Christ and A Lemon Tree* (1894); *Toxin* (1895); *Views and Opinions* (1895); *The Massarenes* (1897); *Dogs* (1897); *An Altruist* (1897); *La Strega and Other Stories* (1899); *The Waters of Edera* (1900); *Critical Studies* (1900); *Street Dust and Other Stories* (1901); *Helianthus* (1908).

References: *BA* (19); Bigland, E., *Ouida the Passionate Victorian* (1950); *DLB*; *DNB*; Elwin, M., *Victorian Wallflowers* (1934); Ffrench, Y., *Ouida: A Study in Ostentation* (1938); Garrison, D., ' "Immoral Fiction" in the late Victorian library', *American Quarterly* 28 (Spring, 1976); Lee, E., *Ouida: A Memoir* (1914); Stirling, M., *The Fine and the Wicked: The Life and Times of Ouida* (1958); Street, G. S., 'An appreciation of Ouida', *Yellow Book* 6 (1895); Van Vechten, C., *Excavations* (1926); Yates, E., *Celebrities at Home*, 1st series (1877).

Owenson, Sydney (Lady Morgan)

b. 25 December c. 1776 (often postdated) on board ship crossing the Irish sea;
d. 13 April 1859, London

Novelist, poet, biographer, travel writer

SO, an ardent champion of Ireland and the Irish, brought Celtic vivacity and
glamour to the literary scene of the early nineteenth century. Her father Robert
Owenson (formerly MacOwen) was a happy-go-lucky Irish comedian,
musician and actor-manager; her mother Jane Hill was a rather prim Methodist,
who died in 1789, leaving two daughters. SO and her younger sister Olivia
attended several Dublin schools but obtained their principal education backstage
among their father's various theatrical companies.

Paternal bankruptcy forced SO to work as a governess in 1798, first with
the Featherstones at Bracklin Castle, Westmeath, where she was extremely
happy and wrote romantic poems, and then with the Crawfords at Fort William,
Co. Tipperary, where she was even happier. Attractive, witty, and a gifted
raconteuse, she talked, danced, sang, and played the harp at their dinner parties,
enchanting family and guests alike. She also found time to begin her first novel,
St Clair (1802). After leaving Fort William, she took a trip to London in 1803
and charmed Richard Phillips into publishing her long second novel, *The Novice
of St Dominick* (1805).

Back in Ireland, she rejoined her father, and spent much time writing ballads,
pamphlets, and patriotic sketches, and gathering material for her best-selling
novel *The Wild Irish Girl*, which, appearing in 1806, made her a popular author,
gave her a new name, Glorvina (after the heroine), and promoted a brisk sale
in 'Glorvina' brooches and cloaks in both Dublin and London. SO then took
lodgings in Dublin with her sister, and there led a very liberated life. Her
flirtations and indiscretions became as famous as her books. She once attended
a Vice-Regal ball in a dress trimmed with pictures of her rejected lovers.

In 1809 she joined the household of the Marquis and Marchioness of Abercorn
in their palatial homes in Co. Tyrone and Stanmore, England. In the intervals
of writing she fulfilled her ambition of mixing in the highest social circles, with
introductions to royalty. Titles were important to her: her sister had married
a doctor who was subsequently knighted, and SO followed her example and
married the Abercorns' physician Sir Charles Morgan, a widower whose quiet,
steady temperament balanced her effervescent impulsive nature. The couple
took a house in Kildare Street, Dublin and resolved to work together for the
future of Ireland. SO's contribution to the cause was another best-seller, *O'Donnel* (1811), which pleaded eloquently for Ireland's greatness and glory. Her
books were cruelly savaged by one of her former suitors, John Wilson Croker,
a leading reviewer for *The Quarterly*, but the pornographic labels he affixed to
her writings only boosted the sales. SO caricatured him as a government toady
in her novel *Florence Macarthy* (1811).

She and her husband travelled widely on the continent, and SO wrote books
on France and Italy and a biography of Salvator Rosa. They settled in England
in 1834, and London came under her spell as rapidly as Dublin had done. Her
brilliant receptions and parties were the talk of the town, and continued after
the death of her husband in 1843 and of her sister in 1845. Failing eyesight
ended her career as an author, but never curtailed her social activities. On
St Patrick's day 1859, she gave a musical party at which, rouged, bewigged,
and bejewelled, she danced, sang songs, and caught a fatal cold. Estimates of

her age at the time of her death varied from 76 to 83. She had no children, and her not inconsiderable fortune went to her nieces.

She will be best remembered for her novels of Irish life, full of energy and sparkle. In particular, *The Wild Irish Girl* combines a delightful self-portrait with a glowing apologia for her native country. (The English hero, sent by his father to Ireland and expecting a nation of filthy savages in a state of 'primeval ferocity', is agreeably surprised by the courteous hospitality of the natives, the richness of the cultural heritage, the attraction and relevance of their Catholic faith and the breathtaking beauty of their countryside.)

SO's racy 'national tales' (especially *Florence Macarthy*, 1811 and *The O'Briens and the O'Flahertys*, 1827) stand the test of time better than her romantic fantasies of the Minerva school (*St Clair, The Novice*, 1805 and *The Missionary*, 1811), whose characters of profound sensibility throb with the palpitating rapture of ecstatic felicity or the feverish paroxysms of emotional crises. Her songs and ballads show her typical exuberance, *Kate Kearney* being the most celebrated.

As the historian and champion of her sex as well as of her native country, SO, 'The Irish de Staël', excited much controversy. *Woman, or, Ida of Athens* (1809) (the second title was usually preferred) is years ahead of its time in its educational theories, and *Woman and Her Master* (1840), asserting not only the equality of the sexes but also the superiority of woman in so many respects, forms a significant contribution to the history of feminist thought.

SO's accounts of her travels reveal an observant eye, a lively style and a talent for outspoken criticism. 'Fearless and excellent' was Byron's verdict on *Italy*. Her books, it is said, were battles. Often careless and outrageous, they provoked some of the most scurrilously abusive reviews ever printed in British journals. It is to SO's credit that she fought back and survived with undiminished zest and vitality. MARGARET MAISON

Selected works: *Poems* (1801); *St Clair* (1802); *The Novice of Saint Dominick* (1805); *Twelve Original Hibernian Melodies* (1805); *The Wild Irish Girl: A National Tale* (1806); *The Lay of an Irish Harp* (1807); *The First Attempt* (1807); *Patriotic Sketches of Ireland* (1807); *Woman* (1809); *O'Donnel: A National Tale* (1811); *France* (1817); *Florence Macarthy: An Irish Tale* (1811); *Italy* (1821); *The Life and Times of Salvator Rosa* (1824); *Absenteeism* (1825); *The O'Briens and the O'Flahertys: A National Tale* (1827); *France in 1829–30* (1830); *Dramatic Scenes from Real Life* (1833); *Woman and Her Master* (1840); *The Book without a Name* (in collaboration with T. C. Morgan) (1841); *Letter to Cardinal Wiseman* (1851); *Passages from My Autobiography* (1859); *Luxima, the Prophetess: A Tale of India* (revised version of *The Missionary*) (1859); *Lady Morgan's Memoirs*, ed. W. H. Dixon and G. Jewsbury (1862).

References: Chorley, H. F., *The Authors of England* (1838); Fitzpatrick, W. J., *The Friends, Foes and Adventures of Lady Morgan* (1859); Fitzpatrick, W. J., *Lady Morgan: Her Career, Literary and Personal* (1860); Jennings, L. J. (ed.), *The Croker Papers* (1884); Paston, G., *Little Memoirs of the Nineteenth Century* (1902); Plumptre, A., *Narrative of a Residence in Ireland during the Summer of 1814 and that of 1815* (1817); Redding, C., *Fifty years of Recollections* (1858); Stevenson, L., *The Wild Irish Girl* (1936); Suddaby, E. and Yarrow, P. J. (eds), *Lady Morgan in France* (1971).

Pankhurst, Christabel

b. 22 September 1880, Manchester; d. 13 February 1958, Los Angeles, California

Political and religious writer

CP was the charismatic leader of the militant woman suffrage campaign in Britain. She was the eldest daughter of Richard Marsden and Emmeline (*née* Gould) Pankhurst, and grew up in Manchester and in London. The family home was a centre for prominent radical politicians and intellectuals, and CP's father was known throughout Manchester for his work in popular politics. CP attended Manchester High School for Girls and graduated in law from the University of London (she was denied admission to Gray's Inn, her father's *alma mater*) at the top of her class.

In 1903 CP and her mother founded the Women's Social and Political Union (WSPU) in Manchester to promote the recently reviewed cause of female suffrage. The WSPU remained independent of any political party, even the Liberals as long as they refused to endorse woman suffrage. After two years of peaceful campaigning, CP and a factory worker named Annie Kenney took the first militant action at a Liberal political meeting and got themselves arrested. Both women went to London to organize, and the movement soon spread to other parts of Britain, owing in large part to the extraordinary public speaking ability of Emmeline and CP. After only three years a WSPU rally in Hyde Park drew half a million people. That same year, window smashing was adopted as a campaign tactic. CP and her mother were arrested for rushing the House of Commons, and CP used her legal expertise to defend them both at the trial.

Forcible feeding of imprisoned suffragettes raised a furore throughout the country. To avoid arrest, CP was forced into exile in Paris, from where she continued to inspire the movement and edit the WSPU journal. With the outbreak of war in 1914 the movement came to an abrupt halt, CP and Emmeline immediately going to work for the war effort, speaking at recruiting meetings and touring the US to encourage American entry into the war.

In 1918, after the anti-climactic wartime passage of female suffrage, CP stood (unsuccessfully) as coalition candidate for Smethwick. After the war CP, bereft of her former all-consuming passion, espoused radical religious beliefs and wrote books proclaiming the Second Coming. She went to Canada in 1920 (following her mother who had gone there to head the anti-venereal disease campaign), settled in California in 1940 and at the end of her life compiled her memoirs of the suffrage campaign. In 1936 she was made Dame of the British Empire.

CP's writing consists primarily of her articles contributed to the journal *Votes for Women* between 1906 and 1912, and her editing of *The Suffragette* from 1912 to 1920. Her political memoirs were published posthumously and, owing partly to their being written so long after the events and partly to the coolness of CP's character, their style is spare and their tone cut-and-dried. The chatty and intimate account of her sister Sylvia, published as *The Suffragette Movement*, is a far more readable and multidimensional history of the movement. CP's *Unshackled* is, however, valuable as the self-description of a brilliant and ruthless militant strategist, and for the eloquent quotations from lesser-known suffrage activists, whom CP cites at length.   AMY ERICKSON

Works: *The Lord Cometh* (1923); *Pressing Problems of the Coming Age* (1924); *The World's Unrest: Vision of the Dawn* (1926); *Seeing the Future* (1929); *The Uncur-*

tained Future (1940); *Unshackled: The Story of How We Won the Vote* (1959); *Suffrage and the Pankhursts*, ed. J. Marcus (1988).
References: Castle, B., *Sylvia and Christabel Pankhurst* (1987); *DNB*; Mitchell, D., *The Fighting Pankhursts: A Study in Tenacity* (1967); Mitchell, D., *Queen Christabel* (1977); Pankhurst, S., *Life of Emmeline Pankhurst* (1935).

Pankhurst, Sylvia

b. May 1882, Manchester; d. 27 September 1960, Addis Ababa, Ethiopia
Political writer, poet, biographer
Active in the woman suffrage campaign orchestrated by her mother Emmeline and elder sister Christabel, SP took a broader attitude to activism, vociferously espousing the causes of the working classes and of the newly independent Ethiopian people.

The second daughter of Richard Marsden and Emmeline (*née* Gould) Pankhurst, SP won a Free Studentship and then a scholarship to the Manchester Municipal School of Art. In 1902 she went to Venice to study mosaics on a Travelling Studentship, and returned to another scholarship at the Royal College of Art in London. While studying, SP organized for the Women's Social and Political Union (WSPU) in London's East End, and for eight years was frequently imprisoned and subjected to forcible feeding. Seemingly inexhaustible, in 1910 she made a three-month tour of North America, often speaking three times a day for the cause of woman suffrage.

In 1913 she severed the East End campaign from the WSPU, on the grounds that the WSPU's elitist feminism would still subordinate the working woman to the working man. SP (with her younger sister Adele in Australia) strongly opposed the war and was publicly condemned by her mother for doing so. SP attended socialist congresses in Russia, where she became disillusioned with the soviet cause, and in Italy, having crossed the Alps on foot to get there after her passport was confiscated. Meanwhile, she continued to work for the East End dwellers, particularly in a campaign for improved maternity services. She lived openly unmarried with Silvio Corio, the leader of Italian socialist exiles in London, by whom she bore Richard Keir Pethick Pankhurst, and until 1924 she continued editing the *Dreadnought*, which she had begun as a suffrage journal in 1912. (She subsequently edited *New Times* and *Ethiopian News*.) After the Second World War she took up the cause of Ethiopian independence and wrote extensively on the subject.

An intrepid and indefatigable activist, SP also found time to document her travels, exhort the English people on domestic and international issues, and describe her personal experience of the woman suffrage campaign and its leaders. Her style is straightforward: journalistic and totally without pretension. Just as her commitment to social justice never flagged, in over forty years of political writing her ringing tone of passionate urgency never mellowed. Two volumes of poems show an aesthetic sensitivity extraordinary in a political activist. The *Life of Emmeline Pankhurst* and *The Suffragette Movement* are highly detailed and full of the uncompromising honesty and human warmth which characterize her political appeals.   AMY ERICKSON
Works: *Soviet Russia as I Saw It* (1921); *Writ on Cold Slate* (1922); *India and the Earthly Paradise* (1926); *Delphos: The Future of International Language* (1927); (trans.), *Poems*, by M. Eminescu (in collaboration with I. O. Stefanovici) (1931); *The Suffragette Movement: An Intimate Account of Persons and Ideals* (1931); *The Home Front: A Mirror of Life in England During the World War* (1932); *Save the*

Mothers (1932); *The Life of Emmeline Pankhurst* (1935); *The Ethiopian People: their Rights and Progress* (1946); *Ex-Italian Somaliland* (1951); *Eritrea on the Eve: The Past and Future of Italy's 'First-born' Colony* (1952); *Ethiopia and Eritrea: The Last Phase of the Reunion Struggle, 1941–52* (with R. K. P. Pankhurst) (1953); *Ethiopia: a Cultural History* (1955).

References: Castle, B., *Sylvia and Christabel Pankhurst* (1987); *DNB*; Franchini, S., *Sylvia Pankhurst (1912–1914)* (1980); Fulford, R., *Votes for Women* (1957); Mitchell, D., *The Fighting Pankhursts* (1967); Pankhurst, R. K. P., *Sylvia Pankhurst: Artist and Crusader* (1979); Romero, P. W. E., *Sylvia Pankhurst: Portrait of a Radical* (1987).

Panter-Downes, Mollie

b. 25 August 1906, London

Novelist, journalist

MP-D is of Anglo-Irish descent. Her father, Edward Panter-Downes, came from a Cheshire family and her mother from Ireland. At the early age of 6, she began writing whilst convalescing in England without her parents who were in Africa at the time. Two years later, in 1914, her father, a major in the Royal Irish Infantry, was killed at the Battle of Mons. After his death MP-D lived with her mother in Brighton for four years, attending school at Winstons, Dyke Road. During this period she wrote extensively for amusement; her work included not only stories but also plays and poetry, some of which were printed in *Poetry Review* before she was 12 years old.

In 1918 she moved with her mother to a country town, Horsham, in Sussex where she attended Heathfield House School. Already obtaining high praise for her literary work, she began a novel that used four of her friends as heroines. She also helped to establish the school magazine before leaving, again for Brighton, two years later. The remainder of her education occurred at home under a French governess and a tutor. In 1927, at the age of 21, MP-D married Clare Robinson; the couple had three children. During the 1930s she travelled to the Far East and visited America. In 1939 she became London correspondent for *The New Yorker* and won considerable acclaim for her work, *Letter From England*, published between 1939 and 1941.

The Shoreless Sea, her first book, was written when MP-D was still a child. She had begun writing seriously in November 1922 and the novel was completed by March 1923. It was dedicated to her dead father and to the soldiers who had fought with him. The work is introduced in *Book Review Digest* (1924) as 'The novel which is the work of a girl of sixteen'. At first sight the clichéd plot – two young teenagers, Guy and Deirdre, fall in love only to part and meet again when it is too late – tends to encourage the reader to dismiss the book as simply a schoolgirl's romantic dream. But, although the style is innocent and young, it does hint at the future strength of MP-D; for example, Deirdre is a well-realized character whose real beauty is conveyed in contrast to the conventional goddess image of her mother: 'The mouth was large, but finely cut, with delicate, rather disdainfully arched red lips.' The book captures the attitudes and feelings of the young, obsessed with, for instance, 'This vile old dress. These heavy shoes.' Even the clichés seem refreshing in a Daisy Ashford sort of way when put into the context of childhood known to Deirdre.

Letter From England shows MP-D, sixteen years after her first novel, as an experienced and able writer. Originally the London letters were published weekly in *The New Yorker* and they covered the war events in England, especially in London, from 3 September 1939 to 14 September 1940. They proved to be very popular especially as an insight into the British 'wartime mood'. *London War Notes*, covering the period from 1939 to 1945, continues the reporting, noting major events but now concentrating on ordinary people. The combination gives the reader a sensitive insight into the tone and atmosphere of wartime London: 'Not only the allied armies but the stay at homes have had their tails up this last cheerful week.' The book is separated into chapters according to years, each chapter with a brief introduction of dates and main events; this organization gives the reader a sense of perspective on the 'ordinary' matters with which she deals, the rationing of food, fuel and clothing, shelter life, transport problems and morale. Leaders of the time who were often portrayed as superhuman are brought to life by MP-D's matter-of-fact style, while her jaunty, humorous approach captures both the communality and the tension of the times: 'A house next door to Anne Hathaway's cottage is today an uncomfortable liability, it seems, not a picturesque asset.'

The novel *One Fine Day* (1947) follows one day in the life of a woman, Laura. Again MP-D is concerned with war, but now with the effects of war in peacetime rather than the martial events themselves. The novel is not conventional in form, indeed it has very little plot or action. However, MP-D deals successfully with the difficult, emotive area of feelings through her vividly realized characters who suggest and reveal the emotional aftermath of war.

LISA BUCKBY

Works: *The Shoreless Sea* (1924); *The Chase* (1925); *Storm Bird* (1929); *My Husband Simon* (1931); *Nothing in Common But Sex* (1932); *Letter From England* (1940); *Watling Green* (1943); *One Fine Day* (1947); *Ooty Preserved* (1967); *At the Pines* (1971); *London War Notes* (1972).

References: Beauman, N., *A Very Great Profession* (1983).

Parr, Catharine

b. 1513, Kendal Castle; d. 1548, Sudeley, Wiltshire

Religious writer

Remembered primarily as the last surviving wife of Henry VIII, CP is a complex and controversial figure. The eldest child of Maud Green and Sir Thomas Parr, CP was brought up in close association with the king's court. There she received a thorough education from both her mother and Juan Vives, eventually leading to the accolade, 'eruditissima Regina.'

In 1525, aged 12, CP married the elderly widower Edward, Lord Borough of Gainsborough. This was to set a pattern for the rest of her life. By the age of 15 CP had become 'a king's widow', now officially needing Henry's permission to remarry. This she did in 1533, when she married Sir John Nevill, Lord Latimer. He died in 1542 and in 1543 she married Henry VIII.

Despite her precarious status as the sixth wife of the notorious king, CP exerted considerable influence in both the public and the private sphere. She became responsible for the education of Mary, Elizabeth, and Edward and was instrumental in persuading Henry to restore his daughters to the line of succession. From July 1544 to September of the same year CP successfully acted as Queen Regent while Henry campaigned in France.

Her practice and patronage of the arts was considerable; aside from her own writing, she commissioned Miles Coverdale's translation of the New Testament and, in 1545, printed Nicholas Uddal's translation of Erasmus's *Paraphrases* at her own expense. In 1546 Henry was planning to disinvest the universities as he had done the monasteries, and it was CP who ensured that this did not happen.

In his *Book of the Martyrs* Foxe recounts his version of the 1546 plot against her life. Condemned for heresy by Bishop Gardiner and Chancellor Wriothesley, CP is recorded to have skilfully negotiated her way out of a potentially fatal crisis. In 1548, soon after Henry's death, CP married Thomas Seymour. Later that same year she gave birth to a daughter, Mary, and died six days later, 'not without suspicion of poison', allegedly administered by her husband.

CP published two works, both of which enjoyed considerable popularity and were reprinted several times within the century. Her writing testifies to the importance of religion in her public and private life while displaying her learning and command of language. The *Prayers, or Meditations* (1545) form a series of her own religious exercises. The more striking work is however the *Lamentacion or Complaynt of a Sinner* (1547), a 'spiritual boke of the crucifix'. This moves from a narrative of confession to one of conversion and concludes with an affirmation of the tenets of the Reformist movement and a stinging attack on the Papists.   CATHERINE S. WEARING

Works: *Prayers, or Meditations, wherein the mynd is stirred, paciently to suffre all afflictions here, to set at nought the vaine prosperitie of this worlde, and always to longe for the everlasting felicitie: collected out of holy woorkes by the most vertuous and gracious Princess Katherine queene of Englaunde, France and Ireland* (1545); *The Lamentacion or Complaynt of a Sinner, made by the most vertuous Ladie, Quene Caterin, bewayling the ignoraunce of her blind life: set forth and put in print at the instaunt desire of the righte gracious ladie Caterin Duchesse of Suffolke, & the earnest requeste of the right honourable Lord, William Parre, Marquesse of North Hampton* (1547).

References: Ballard; *DNB*; Foxe, J., *Book of the Martyrs*, ed. G. A. Williamson (1965); Gordon, M. A., *The Life of Queen Katharine Parr* (1951); Haugaard, W. P., 'Katharine Parr: the religious convictions of a renaissance queen', *Renaissance Quarterly* 22 (1969); Hays, M., *Female Biography* (1807); Hogrefe, P., *Tudor Women* (1977); King, N., 'Patronage and piety: the influence of Catherine Parr', in *Silent But for the Word*, ed. M. P. Hannay (1985); Levin, C., 'Women in the *Book of Martyrs* as models of behaviour in Tudor England', *International Journal of Women's Studies* 4, 2 (1980); Martienssen, A., *Queen Katharine Parr* (1973); Strickland, A., *Lives of the Queens of England from the Norman Conquest* (1842); Strype, J., *Annals of the Reformation and Establishment of Religion* (1709); Travitsky, B. (ed.), *Paradise of Women* (1981); Warnicke, M., *Women of the English Renaissance and Reformation* (1983); Williams, J., *Literary Women of England* (1861).

Paston, Margaret

b. 1423, Reedham, Norfolk; d. 4 November (?) 1484, Mautby, Norfolk
Letter writer
Daughter and heiress of the wealthy Norfolk landowner John Mautby of Mautby and his wife Margery, MP married John Paston of Paston, Norfolk around 1440. They had eight children. MP was related to Sir John Fastolf on her mother's side, and Sir John made Paston an executor of his will in 1459. Although Paston took up residence on the Fastolf estates of Caister and Hellesdon, his right to do so was disputed because of the presence of an earlier will. This led to frequent attacks on the estates by the Duke of Suffolk, and the imprisonment of Paston in the Fleet in 1465. During the frequent periods in

which her husband was absent to deal with the Fastolf will, MP managed the property at Caister or Hellesdon. In an age when women surrendered all rights over their property on marriage, MP's position as Paston's active deputy was unusual. MP's letters are deferential to her husband and plead her inadequacy to act without male advice: 'I wolde fayn doo well yf I cowde, and as I canne I wol doo to youre pleasure and profet, and in such thyngys as I cannot skyle of I wylle take avyse of such as I know that be youre frendys, and doo as well as I canne' (11 June 1465), but her careful attention to the needs of her tenants and strength of will in the face of Suffolk's attacks led her husband and two elder sons to trust her decisions and seek her opinions. John III, MP's second son, wrote to his father concerning a conversation with the Duke of Norfolk: 'And then I answered my lord and said how that at that time I had my master within the manor of Cotton, which was my mother, and into that time that I had spoke with her I could give none answer' (3 October 1465).

Unlike the Paston men there is no evidence that MP could write; of the three Paston women whose letters survive only Margery could write her name. Sixty-nine of MP's 104 extant letters are addressed to her husband and dictated either to her scribes or one of her sons. This often gives them the appearance of an impersonal report, as they itemize events that have occurred on the estates during Paston's absence, and nearly always begin with the same deferential formula: 'Ryth worchepfull husbond, I recomand me to yow: Blest you to wet that. . . .' Yet the traditional formulae of letter writing are misleading, for they suggest that MP's role was far more subordinate and passive than it actually was. The direct and forceful language often ignores formal convention (recognizable formulae usually only appear at the beginning and end of the letter) and narrates events that show that MP took a very active role in Paston's interests and those of the estates. She asks his advice because he is lord of the manor, but when this advice is misguided she explains why she has ignored it: 'And as for kepying of any coorte for you at Drayton, I cannot wete how it cowde be brought a-bowte wythoute helpe of other but if ther shuld be grave gret inconvenyence of it' (7 August 1465), because she is in a better position to understand the situation than he is. She advises her husband on investments for the estates, treatment of tenants, and forcefully represents his interests against Suffolk at local courts. Husband and wife respected and trusted each other's abilities, and MP's letters, which are rarely concerned with the family, the traditional sphere of woman's influence, show the power Paston allowed her to exercise over the estate, and her thorough knowledge of its condition. After her husband's death MP remained a powerful figure, arranging John III's marriage and disinheriting Margery for marrying Richard Calle, the family steward. She continued to advise her children on the running of the estate, and bitterly condemned their neglect of it, for she expected them to show the same responsibility that had been invested in her. As 'captainess' at Caister she ensured that she was an effective and powerful deputy for her husband and adviser for her children in controlling a property of which she was intensely jealous.

CAROLINE COLEMAN

Works: *The Paston Letters* (1787–1823).
References: Bennett, H. S., *The Pastons and Their England* (1932); Gies, F. and Gies, G., *Women in the Middle Ages* (1978); Lucas, A., *Medieval Women – Religion, Marriage and Letters* (1983); Medcalf, S. (ed.), *The Later Middle Ages* (1981); Woolf, V., 'The Pastons and Chaucer', *Collected Essays*, vol. 3 (1925).

Pearce, Philippa

b. 1920, Great Shelford, Cambridgeshire

Novelist for children and short story writer

PP was educated at the Perse Girls' School, Cambridge from 1929 to 1939 and at Girton College, Cambridge where she gained an honours BA and MA in English and history in 1942. She married Martin Christie (now deceased) in 1963 and has one daughter.

From 1942 to 1945, PP was a civil servant; then she worked as a scriptwriter and producer until 1958. She became assistant editor for the education department of Oxford University Press for two years, before moving to André Deutsch as children's editor, a post she held until 1967. Between 1960 and 1962 she was also freelance producer for BBC Radio. Since 1967 she has continued as a freelance reviewer and lecturer as well as maintaining her career as a writer. She is a member of the Society of Authors.

In 1959, PP was awarded the Library Association's Carnegie Medal for *Tom's Midnight Garden* (1958) and in 1963 received the *Herald Tribune* Festival Award in New York. *Mrs Cockle's Cat* (1961), illustrated by Antony Maitland, was awarded the Kate Greenaway Medal for 1961.

PP's childhood environment provides the settings for her early novels and some of the short stories. In *Minnow on the Say* (1955), the river is the focus of events in an unusual treasure hunt; in *Tom's Midnight Garden* the most memorable description is of a skating expedition to Ely along the frozen river. In *A Dog So Small* (1962), the country cottage isolated in the fens, where Ben's grandparents live, makes an effective contrast with his cramped London home. All PP's writing shows an unerring choice of detail to bring places and atmospheres sharply alive to the reader. While such vivid description can be enjoyed for its own sake, it always serves to underline themes or emphasize qualities of characters within the stories.

PP is equally successful in the creation of interesting central characters, adult as well as juvenile, into whose experiences the reader is irresistibly drawn. She has an acute ear for the nuances of dialogue, especially for the differences between adult-child conversation and child-to-child talk. Characters are thereby presented with convincing immediacy. *Tom's Midnight Garden* and *A Dog So Small* focus on sensitive boys, isolated by distance or personality from their close relatives. Tom finds consolation through his encounters with Hatty in a now-vanished Victorian garden. Events lead to a powerful climax which provides a cogent and satisfying explanation of Tom's night-time experiences. The novel explores the nature of time and the power of human emotions to transcend it. In *A Dog So Small*, Ben finds consolation for his frustrated desire to own a dog in dangerous fantasizing. He matures to recognize that in real life 'if you didn't have the possible things, then you had nothing'. The conclusion of the novel properly evades tragedy by a hair's breadth and is deeply moving. In her best work, PP makes no concessions to 'childish' readers; her vision honestly faces the griefs and disappointments of life as well as its joys and satisfactions.

Other novels, and many of the short stories, are more concerned with the interplay of personalities within families or other groupings. *The Battle of Bubble and Squeak* (1978) appeals to younger readers with its plot of gerbils smuggled home despite the mother's abhorrence of pets. As the amusing but tense struggle develops, to keep or dispose of the animals, another battle becomes discernible to the perceptive reader: the striving of the children's stepfather to establish his place in the family. *The Elm Street Lot* (1969) concerns the activities of a gang of urban children, their shifting loyalties and enduring principles. In *The Children of the House* (1968), Edwardian childhood is stripped of its idyllic veneer, as parental incompetence and harshness drive the children into uneasy alliance with the servants. The result is a sombre but convincing story. PP's tales of the supernatural, including her most recent collection, *Who's Afraid?* (1986), satisfy the reader not only with taut narratives and effectively sinister or mysterious moods, but also with the way they draw attention to the strangeness of normality and encourage a fresh look at the familiar.

What the Neighbours Did (1972) is best described as a collection of childhood 'epiphanies', revelations about self, relationships or the possibilities of life. The topics are varied: the accidental felling of a tree, the overcoming of private fear, a girl's first quiet rebellion against a dominating father, and the sharing of an early morning adventure with a wheelchair-bound grandfather. Slight though the episodes may be, they linger in the mind by reason of their unusual viewpoints, the subtle accuracy of characterization, or the exquisite yet economical evocation of setting and atmosphere. Furthermore, although superficially these are stories for children about childhood, they embody perennial and universal themes: mutability and our responses to it, growing up, the search for stability.

JUDITH ALDRIDGE

Selected works: *Minnow on the Say* (1955; published in the US as *The Minnow Leads to Treasure*, 1958); *Tom's Midnight Garden* (1958); *Still Jim and Silent Jim* (1960); *Mrs Cockle's Cat* (1961); *A Dog So Small* (1962); *From Inside Scotland Yard* (with Sir Harold Scott) (1963); *The Strange Sunflower* (1966); *The Children of the House* (1968); *The Elm Street Lot* (1969); *What the Neighbours Did and Other Stories* (1972); *Beauty and the Beast: A Retelling* (1972); *The Shadow-Cage and Other Tales of the Supernatural* (1977); *The Battle of Bubble and Squeak* (1978); *On Sattin Shore* (1983); *Who's Afraid? And Other Strange Stories* (1986).

References: Aers, L., 'The treatment of time in four children's books', *Children's Literature in Education* 2 (1970); OCCL; Rees, D., 'The novels of Philippa Pearce', *Children's Literature in Education* 4 (1971); Townsend, J. R., *A Sense of Story* (1971).

Pembroke, Countess of (Mary Sidney)

b. 27 October 1561; d. 25 September 1621

Devotional writer and editor

C of P, daughter of Sir Henry Sidney and Lady Mary Dudley, was born into the Protestant alliance of the Dudley/Sidney family, an alliance begun by her grandfather, John Dudley, Duke of Northumberland, who had died for his attempt to place Lady Jane Grey on the English throne. Her uncles the Earls of Leicester, Warwick, and Huntingdon were primary patrons for Protestant writings in England, supported Elizabeth I against her Catholic rivals, and advocated military intervention on the continent on behalf of Protestants there. Her father, who had been educated with young King Edward VI, became Lord President of the Marches of Wales and Lord Deputy of Ireland. Among them, C of P's father and uncles administered approximately two-thirds of the land under Elizabeth's rule.

Her uncle Robert Dudley, Elizabeth's favourite and reputedly the most powerful man in England, arranged for her marriage to one of the great Protestant lords, Henry Herbert, Earl of Pembroke. At the age of 15 she became the third wife of the middle-aged Pembroke, and subsequently bore him four children: William (1580), Katherine (1581), Anne (1582/3), and Philip (1584).

Her brother, Philip Sidney, was the hope of Protestants on the continent. Banished from court because of his attempt to dissuade Elizabeth from marrying the Duc d'Alençon, Sidney spent his time of enforced idleness with the C of P at Wilton, her country estate. There he wrote *The Countess of Pembroke's Arcadia*, the most popular prose fiction for over a century. As he says in his dedication 'To My Dear Lady and Sister the Countess of Pembroke', it was written 'only for you, only to you'. After Sidney died of wounds incurred fighting under Leicester in the Netherlands, C of P published the *Arcadia* (1593), as well as his sonnet sequence *Astrophil and Stella* and other works (1598).

After her brother's death, C of P became the most important literary woman in England, serving not only as editor, but also as patron and writer. As patron she used her money and influence to encourage such writers as Edmund Spenser, Abraham Fraunce, Samuel Daniel, and possibly William Shakespeare. She also helped to create the hagiography which established Sir Philip as a Protestant martyr; she encouraged such commemorations as Edmund Spenser's 'The Ravine of Time' and 'Astrophel' and Thomas Moffett's *Nobilis, or, A View of the Life and Death of a Sidney*, a biography which presented Sir Philip's life as exemplar to her young son William Lord Herbert.

C of P wrote two original poems mourning his death, 'The Dolefull Lay of Clorinda', published with other elegies for Sidney in Spenser's *Colin Clouts Come Home Again*, and 'To the Angell Spirit of the Most Excellent Sir Philip Sidney', which exists in one manuscript copy of her *Psalmes*. Her authorship of 'The Dolefull Lay' has been questioned, but it appears to be an early and derivative piece by C of P, using the pastoral themes which had become synonymous with Sidney. The speaker is introduced by Spenser as 'Clorinda', who most resembles her brother 'both in shape and spright'. Sidney is portrayed as a 'mery maker', using his own word for poet, and is praised for his 'layes of loue' and his riddles. Using the flower imagery which also informs Spenser's accompanying poem 'Astrophel', she portrays his works as the 'flowre here left' which is 'but the shadow of his likenesse gone'. His immortal spirit is in heaven where he lives in 'euerlasting bliss' while we mourn below.

Her second poem mourning her brother was one of her last known works. 'To the Angell Spirit' eschews the pastoral for the Protestant plain style. Prefaced to their verse translation of the Hebrew psalms, it decorously begins by reference to 'this coupled worke, by double int'rest thine': he both began the work and inspired her completion of it. Asking his pardon for her presumption in finishing his work, she takes a humble place, comparing herself to the 'little streames' which run into his 'great sea'. Her suffering, she says, has been 'dissolu'd to Inke'. The work is signed with her habitual self-designation, 'By the Sister of that Incomparable Sidney'.

Her other two original poems praise the queen. 'A dialogue between two shepheards . . . in praise of Astrea' was written for Elizabeth's planned visit to Wilton, probably in 1599. A pastoral dialogue between two shepherds, it questions the adequacy of language. Piers, the Protestant spokesman, denies the truth of allegorical language while Thenot, a neo-Platonist, asserts that Astrea's divine nature can be apprehended and expressed through metaphor. 'Euen Now That Care' dedicates C of P's translation of the *Psalmes* to Queen Elizabeth, in an accompanying poem to 'The Angell Spirit'. In the tradition of those relegated to the margins of society, she uses flattery to instruct, but the relatively subdued compliments of the opening stanzas serve primarily as a reminder that the fate of Protestant Europe rests in Elizabeth's hands. After her opening salutation to the queen, C of P once again mourns for her co-author,

Philip. She reminds the queen that Sidney died wearing her livery and that, had she chosen rightly, he would have lived to wear it in her service. Now C of P must weave a web of words to create a livery with which to adorn Elizabeth, a livery which would emphasize the queen's own position as servant to God and to the Protestant cause.

In addition to these original poems, C of P translated four works in the 1590s: Robert Garnier's *Marc Antonie*, Philippe de Mornay's *Discours de la Vie et de la Mort*, Petrarch's *Trionfo della Morte*, and the Psalms of David. The first three works deal with the theme of death, which was particularly appropriate to her at that time: her 3-year-old daughter Katherine had died the same day her son Philip was born in 1584; her father, mother, and her brother Philip had all died in 1586; by 1595, her youngest brother Thomas and her powerful uncles had died as well.

Her major literary achievement was her translation of the psalms. Sir Philip had translated the first forty-three psalms into sophisticated English verse patterns; after his death C of P revised some of those psalms and translated many others. Rarely repeating a verse pattern, her work is a truimph of English prosody and consists more of meditations on the psalms than of literal translations. Although the work was unpublished, it circulated in manuscript and had considerable impact on seventeenth-century verse. John Donne praised these poems, saying 'They tell us *why*, and teach us *how* to sing.'

After her husband died in January 1601 C of P lacked the money, prestige, and, for a time, the leisure necessary to continue her literary endeavours. Her role as patron was assumed by her son William, third Earl of Pembroke, and C of P largely retired from court life after the accession festivities for James I. She administered her property, built Houghton House, continued her literary friendships, and spent much time taking the waters for her health in Spa. Her continued, although diminished, patronage is seen in Aemilia Lanyer's dedication of *Salve Devs Rex Judaeorum* to her and other women of her circle in 1611. MARGARET P. HANNAY

Works: (trans.), *A Discourse of Life and Death*, by Philippe de Mornay (1592); (trans.), *Antonius: A Tragoedie*, by Robert Garnier (1592); 'A Dialogve between two shepheards . . . in praise of *Astrea*', in *A Poetical Rhapsody*, ed. Francis Davison (1602); (trans.), *The Psalms of Sir Philip Sidney and the Countess of Pembroke*, ed. J. C. A. Rathmell (1963); *The Triumph of Death and Other Unpublished and Uncollected Poems by Mary Sidney, Countess of Pembroke (1561–1621)*, ed. G. F. Waller (1977).

References: Brennan, M. G., 'The date of the Countess of Pembroke's translation of the Psalms', *RES* 33 (1982); HTR, 'Mary Sidney and her writings', *Gentleman's Magazine* 24 (1845); Hannay, M. P. (ed.), *Silent but for the Word: Tudor Women as Patrons, Translators, and Writers of Religious Works* (1985); Hannay, M. P., 'Unpublished letters of Mary Sidney, Countess of Pembroke', *Spenser Studies* 6 (1986); Hogrefe, P., *Women of Action in Tudor England* (1977); Kinnamon, N., 'Emendations in G. F. Waller's Edition of the Countess of Pembroke's Psalms', *American Notes & Queries* 22 (1984); Lamb, M. E., 'The Countess of Pembroke's patronage', *ELR* 12 (Spring 1982); Lamb, M. E., 'The myth of the Countess of Pembroke: the dramatic circle', *Yearbook of English Studies* 11 (1981); Long, P. W., 'Spenseriana: The Lay of Clorinda', *MLN* 31 (1916); Osgood, C. W., 'The doleful lay of Clorinda', *MLN* 35 (1920); Rose, M. B. (ed.), *Women in the Middle Ages and the Renaissance: Literary and Historical Perspectives* (1986); Rowe, K. T., 'The Countess of Pembroke's editorship of the *Arcadia*', *PMLA* 54 (1939); Schanzer, E., '*Antony and Cleopatra* and the

Countess of Pembroke's *Antonius'*, *Notes and Queries* 201 (1956); Todd, R., ' "So Well Atyr'd Abroad": a background to the Sidney-Pembroke Psalter and its implications for the seventeenth-century religious lyric', *Texas Studies in Literature and Language* 29 (Spring 1987); Waller, G. F., *Mary Sidney, Countess of Pembroke: A Critical Study of Her Writings and Literary Milieu* (1979); Waller, G. F., 'A "matching of contraries": ideological ambiguity in the Sidney Psalms', *Wascana Review* 9 (1974); Waller, G. F., 'The text and manuscript variants of the Countess of Pembroke's Psalms', *RES* 26 (1975); Witherspoon, A. M., *The Influence of Robert Garnier on Elizabethan Drama* (1924); Woods, S., *Natural Emphasis: English Versification from Chaucer to Dryden* (1984); Young, F. B., *Mary Sidney, Countess of Pembroke* (1912).

Pfeiffer, Emily

b. 26 November 1827, Montgomeryshire, Wales; d. 23 January 1890, Putney
Poet, polemical writer
EP was the daughter of R. Davis, an army officer. Although her father recognized and encouraged her early talent as a painter and poet, his financial mismanagement prevented her from receiving a thorough and systematic education. When she married Jürgen Edward Pfeiffer, a prosperous German merchant who had settled in England, she acquired the financial means and leisure to educate herself. The result, despite constant bouts of ill-health and insomnia, was ten volumes of poetry and two of prose.

In general, EP wrote about the pressures on women, their victimization and the strategies they employed to escape it. She expressed solidarity with women unlike herself – single women, working-class women, 'fallen' women, and foreign women. She was conscious of being a woman artist and wrote often about the constraints on female aspiration and achievement in the nineteenth century, as well as the great social need she perceived for women's particular contributions to art, politics, and education.

Her first serious publication was *Gerard's Monument* (1873), a romantic poetic narrative of love and death set in medieval times. Here, as elsewhere, EP characteristically portrayed the sexual passion of lovers as both natural and spiritual. In *Poems* (1876), her religious inspiration is expressed in her hopes for an egalitarian future – for herself personally, for women in general, for the working poor, and indeed for the entire human race. 'The Winged Soul' – an image to which EP returns throughout her career – portrays the pain and frustration of the creative human spirit born into the captivity of class or gender.

EP's most successful poetry appeared in the 1880s: *Sonnets and Songs* (1880, revised and enlarged 1886), *Under the Aspens: Lyrical and Dramatic* (1882), *The Rhyme of the Lady of the Rock* (1884), and *Flowers of the Night* (1889). This work reveals a mature, feminist perspective on women's lives and problems. Sometimes EP speaks in her own voice (as in many of her sonnets) and sometimes she speaks in a metaphorical, dramatic, or historical/mythological mode. *The Wynnes of Wynhavod* (1881), although never staged, is a very readable full-length blank-verse drama of nineteenth-century life. Among the most interesting of EP's works is *The Rhyme of the Lady of the Rock* (1884), a complex narrative addressing various social issues, such as the marriage market, marital rape, domestic tyranny, and the nature of female heroism. In this piece, which is structurally similar to Tennyson's *The Princess* (1847), the heroine recites to an audience of mixed class, gender, education, and political perspectives her own poetic retelling of a local legend, pausing frequently to address their commentary on the morality of the action and the quality of the poetry. In the framing narrative, the poet heroine confides to her readers (though not her listening audience) the anxieties she experiences regarding her poetic authority and competence.

In many ways EP seems a 'modern' poet – she addressed issues still alive today and with a markedly female focus and tonality. Yet she is also very much a woman of her own times, bound by nineteenth-century artistic and social norms. Among the writers she most admired were Jane Austen, Charlotte Brontë, Elizabeth Barrett Browning, and George Eliot of whom she wrote a moving eulogy ('The Lost Light', 1880); she cited their literary achievements as evidence of women's equality with men in the area of creative thought and expression. In general, the ideals that emerge from EP's poetry are the Victorian ones of personal courage and integrity, faith, idealism, freedom, and achievement.

EP also wrote political essays. In 1885, after completing an extensive tour of Asia and America, she published *Flying Leaves from East and West*, a collection of political and artistic commentaries in travelogue form. In it she wrote, 'The lion has so long been the painter, that he is apt too wholly to ignore the aspect which his favourite subject may take from the point of view of the lioness. If the latter will sometimes tell the truth, and tell, not what she thinks she ought to see, but of what she really sees, many an intellectual picture which has hitherto satisfied the sense of mankind, may be found to be somewhat out of focus.' Among the political topics she addressed in this volume were class and race relations in the US and the degraded status of women in harems in Turkey.

Also during the 1880s EP wrote most of her numerous articles on women and education, work, suffrage, and trade unionism, published in periodicals such as the *Cornhill Magazine* and the *Contemporary Review*. Many of these essays were collected in *Women and Work* (1887), where she attacked the physiological, pseudoscientific theories that claimed that women were not strong enough to work and called for more occupational opportunities and more competitive wages for women.

When her husband died in 1889, EP was devastated; she did not survive him for much more than a year. In this year she made plans to found an orphanage, which was opened after her death, and she provided funds for a School of Dramatic Art for women. In addition to a fine collection of her paintings, which she bequeathed to her niece, she left £2,000 for higher education for women, which was used in 1895 to erect Aberdare Hall, the first dormitory for women students at University College, Cardiff, in South Wales.

KATHLEEN HICKOK

Works: *Valisneria, or, a Midsummer Night's Dream* (1857); *Margaret, or, the Motherless* (1861); *Gerard's Monument and Other Poems* (1873, enlarged 1878); *Poems* (1876); *Glân-Alarch: His Silence and Song* (1877); *Quarterman's Grace and Other Poems* (1879); *Sonnets and Songs* (1880, revised and enlarged 1886); *The Wynnes of Wynhavod: A Drama of Modern Life* (1881); *Under the Aspens: Lyrical and Dramatic* (1882); *The Rhyme of the Lady of the Rock and How It Grew* (1884); *Flying Leaves from East and West* (1885); *Women and Work: An Essay* (1887); *Flowers of the Night* (1889).

References: BA (19); *DNB*; Hickok, K., *Representations of Women: Nineteenth-Century British Women's Poetry* (1984); Robertson, E. S. (ed.), *English Poetesses* (1883); Miles, A. H. (ed.), *The Poets and the Poetry of the Century*, vol. 7 (1892); Sackville-West, V., 'The women poets of the seventies', in *The Eighteen Seventies*, ed. H. Granville-Barker (1929); Stedman, E. C. (ed.), *Victorian Poets* (1875).

Philips, Katherine

b. 1 January 1632, London; d. 22 June 1664, London

Poet

(Also wrote under 'Orinda')

Although KP was born in London to the middle-class family of John and Katherine Fowler and instructed nearby at Mrs Salmon's School for Girls, her life and poetic activities were centred in south-west Wales. About four years after her father died in 1642, her mother married Sir Richard Phillipps of Pembroke. KP herself, at the age of 16, married his kinsman and former son-in-law, the 54-year-old James Philips. They settled at Cardigan, but she travelled several times to London and once to Dublin. KP was writing in verse as early as 1650, and by the time of her death at the age of 32 from smallpox, she had gained a considerable literary reputation, built on the poems she had distributed among her acquaintances. Her two most intimate friends, often addressed in the poems by pseudo-classical names, were Mary Aubrey (Rosania) and Anne Owen (Lucasia). She herself was generally addressed by other writers as 'Orinda'. Other members of her circle included the Master of Ceremonies for Charles II, Sir Charles Cotterell (Poliarchus), her husband (Antenor), and at least peripherally, such admirers as the Earl of Orrery, the theologian Jeremy Taylor, and the poets Henry Vaughan and Abraham Cowley.

KP's extant literary works consist of approximately 120 original poems, five poems translated from French, and two translations of Corneille's dramas, *Pompey* and *Horace* (the latter incomplete). All of these, except for one poem that appeared in 1905 and three which were printed in 1977, were printed in her collected works in 1667. An edition of seventy-four poems had appeared without KP's consent in 1664, and a very few poems were printed earlier, the first prefixed to William Cartwright's works in 1651 and two in Henry Lawes's *Second Book of Ayres* (1655). Of her plays, *Pompey* had been published twice in 1663 after opening successfully at Dublin's Smock Alley during the 1662–3 season, and probably in London as well. *Horace*, completed by Denham, was performed at court in February 1668, and nearly a year later enjoyed a London theatre run. KP's letters also attracted interest: four of them were anthologized in 1697 and two editions of her letters to Cotterell appeared in the eighteenth century.

KP's reputation rests mainly on her poetry, but she is less original in style than in subject. Her verse is regular in metre and form, including heroic couplets, stanzas of tetrametres, and a few ballad stanzas. As a late Cavalier poet, she enjoys metaphysical conceits but usually avoids sharp incongruities and rough rhythms. Like Cartwright, who greatly influenced her, she gives most of her verse (although not necessarily her best) a smooth courtliness. KP's great theme, following the Cavalier poets' treatment of Platonic love, and adapted under the influence of the French *précieuse* society, is Platonic friendship between women. Her poems elevate her friends, particularly Rosania and Lucasia, to the heights of beauty and goodness and exclaim her own devotion to them. Men, she sometimes felt, could not possibly deserve such a sublime being as woman in marriage: 'She is a public deity, / And were't not very odd, / She should depose herself to be / A petty household god?' KP was much praised for her feminine chastity and propriety and frequently contrasted with the scandalously improper Aphra Behn.

When not praising or remonstrating with her friends, KP frequently lauds other acquaintances or, after the Restoration, other members of the court. If these verses are insipid, two Interregnum pieces that suggest Royalist leanings, one complaining of 'The dying Lion kick'd by every ass', have more power. In fact in one poem she angrily and wittily defends her husband, an official under Cromwell, from the taint of such verses. Although her upbringing and marriage might have been expected to put her in the Puritan camp, she had opposite political loyalties, perhaps because of her youthful association with Royalist literati.

Personal relationships and situations dominate KP's poetry, and her own isolation from London's literary and social scene may account for a minor strain of *contemptus mundi* verse. These poems, especially her translation of St Amant's 'Solitude', are often superior to her panegyrics. Occasionally, such subjects lead her away from personal verse to abstract philosophical poems, among the first instances of this genre in English. Although she is no master of the poetic essay, rare couplets like 'Mean sordid things, which by mistake we prize, /And absent covet, but enjoy'd despise' achieve considerable power of antithesis.

SAYRE GREENFIELD

Works: *Pompey* (1663); *Poems by the Incomparable Mrs KP* (1664); *Poems . . . To Which is added M. Corneille's Pompey and Horace, Tragedies . . .* (1667); *Letters from Orinda to Poliarchus* (1705); *Familiar Letters Written by John, Late Earl of Rochester . . . With Letters by . . . Mrs K. Philips*, ed. T. Brown (1699); work in *Minor Poets of the Caroline Period*, ed. G. Saintsbury (1905).

References: Allibone; Aubrey, J., *Brief Lives* (1895); Ballard; Drabble; Gosse, E., *Seventeenth Century Studies* (1897); Moers, E., *Literary Women* (1976); Morgan, F., *The Female Wits: Women Playwrights of the Restoration*; Souers, P., *The Matchless Orinda* (1931); Todd.

Pitter, Ruth

b. 7 November 1897, Ilford, Essex
Poet
The eldest child of East London school teachers, George and Louise (*née* Murrell) Pitter, RP began writing poetry at the age of 5. Having published a first poem in the *New Age* (later the *New English Weekly*) when only 14 years old, she served as a clerk in the War Office during the First World War before taking up lifelong pursuits as craftswoman and businesswoman, making furniture, household items and gift trays, and developing an abiding passion for gardening. She has written on gardening and religion for the mass-circulation magazine *Woman* and has made numerous radio and television appearances. She lives in retirement in Long Crendon, Buckinghamshire, seeking that peace for which, in her view, 'poetry, like all passion, seeks'.

RP's candid verse eschews contemporary fashions, drawing instead upon perennial themes, cultivating traditional, even archaic forms, combining a sense of the physical presence of nature with an intuition of the spiritual mysteries that may be sensed beyond. The range of her work is extensive. At one extreme are what she calls her 'grotesques' or 'babouineries', poems that display an earthy humour and celebrate the trivial joys of life, poems that, like Bill, the railwayman, of 'Gardeners All' in *The Rude Potato*, take on 'that stalwart form and ruddy face which make *simplicity a grace*'. Like the fabulists of old, RP is particularly adept at giving voice to animals or plants, for both a descriptive and an allegorical purpose, 'peopling' her poems with such creatures and creations as sparrows and swans, weeds and bats, as well as her favourite cats, in typically naturalist assimilations. Yet other poems, in reverential, elegiac or tragic modes, are more elevated in tone, like her typical 'Of Silence and the Air' in which the poet stands '*with* silence' on a winter night,

> void of desire, but full of contemplation
> both of these herds and of the gods above them:
> mindful of these, and offering submission
>   to those immortal.

The garden is indeed the true analogue of RP's poetry, teeming with life, yet a place for profound and silent meditation.

A strong sense of tradition informs RP's verse, the art of which lies in the almost deceptive impression of transparency that it conveys. With natural ease she captures the rhythms of ordinary speech. Her experimentation with verse is retrospective, resurrecting ancient forms and archaic styles, as in the mock-heroic 'Earwig's Complaint' or the epic manner of her account of 'Persephone in Hades'. In all her work she aspires to what she calls 'an ideal of simplicity'.

In 1937 RP won the Hawthornden Prize for *A Trophy of Arms*, then, in 1954, the Heinemann Foundation Award. A year later she became the first woman to receive the Queen's Gold Medal for Poetry. In 1979 she was awarded the CBE.   DAVID BAGULEY

Works: *First Poems* (1920); *First and Second Poems* (1927); *Persephone in Hades* (1931); *A Mad Lady's Garland* (1934); *A Trophy of Arms* (1936); *The Spirit Watches* (1939); *The Rude Potato* (1941); *The Bridge* (1945); *On Cats* (1947); *Urania* (1951); *The Ermine* (1953); *Still By Choice* (1966); *Poems 1926–1966* (1968; published in the US as *Collected Poems*); *End of Drought* (1975).

References: Bogan, L., 'A singular talent', *Poetry* (October 1937); *CA*; *DLB*; Gilbert, R., *Four Living Poets* (1944); Russell, A. (ed.), *Ruth Pitter: Homage to a Poet* (1969); Scott-James, R. A., 'Modern poets', in *Fifty Years of English Literature: 1900–1950* (1951); Swartz, R. T., 'The Spirit Watches', Poetry (September 1940); Wain, J., 'A note on Ruth Pitter's poetry', *Listener* (20 February 1969); Watkin, E. I., *Poets and Mystics* (1953); *Poetry Northwest* (special number, Winter 1960).

Pix, Mary

b. 1666, Nettlebed, Oxfordshire; d. 1709, London

Playwright

The daughter of an Oxfordshire vicar, MP married a London merchant tailor, George Pix, at the age of 18; her only child died in 1690. In 1696, at the age of 30, she became a professional writer, producing in one year a tragedy, *Ibrahim*, a successful comedy, *The Spanish Wives*, and a romantic novel, *The Inhumane Cardinal*, in which a cardinal disguises himself in order to seduce a young girl. Her initial success, together with her association with two other new women playwrights, Delarivier Manley and Catherine Trotter, led to her being satirized in an anonymous play, *The Female Wits* (1696), in which MP appears as Mrs Wellfed, 'a fat Female Author', unlearned but amiable and unpretentious. In 1697–98 MP was involved in dispute with George Powell, an actor and occasional playwright for the United Company at Drury Lane, who copied her play *The Deceiver Deceived* in his *The Imposture Defeated*. William Congreve and Thomas Betterton of the Lincoln's Inn Fields playhouse were supporters of MP. Except for these two occasions, her public and personal life was unremarkable.

A professional playwright of modest abilities and moderate success, MP wrote twelve plays – six comedies and six tragedies. Her tragedies, which were in the tradition of Fletcher, are written in what is effectively prose printed as blank verse. Her one overt attempt at stage reform, *The False Friend* (1699), was a combination of melodrama and moralizing. Her tragedies anticipate later developments in the drama in the increasing prominence of their heroines and of fatal accidents to love; their popularity probably rested on MP's knack for alternating scenes of ranting with love scenes in which a mighty hero languished at his lady's feet.

MP's comedies are her best work, especially *The Spanish Wives* (1696) and *The Adventures in Madrid* (1706). *The Spanish Wives* is a lively farce with a skilful double plot which contrasts the situations of two young wives. The lady of the old governor of Barcelona is given unusual liberty by her husband; touched by this goodness, she resists the advances of a young English colonel. Elenora, kept locked up by a jealous and avaricious husband, escapes to marry her former fiancé. In *The Adventures in Madrid* two English gentlemen intrigue with and eventually marry two Spanish ladies in spite of the machinations of the supposed husband of one of the ladies.

MP's comedies contain lively intrigues, much stage business, and some pleasant songs. Her encomium of the English merchant in *The Beau Defeated* (1700) anticipates the plays of Lillo and the bourgeois drama of the next generation. Forced or unhappy marriages also appear frequently and prominently in the comedies. MP is less concerned, however, with writing polemics against the forced marriage than with its uses as a plot device: the unhappily married person is often rescued and married more satisfactorily. Occasionally an unhappy wife or husband might seem erring whilst in reality being virtuous. MP's use of sentimental characters in intrigue comedies, while resulting in oddities of plotting, reflects the changing theatrical taste that called for less emphasis on adultery and more on virtuous love. MP's attempt to write a mixture of traditional and sentimental comedy is characteristic of turn-of-the-century drama.

NANCY COTTON

Works: *Ibrahim* (1696); *The Spanish Wives* (1696); *The Inhumane Cardinal* (1696); *The Innocent Mistress* (1697); *The Deceiver Deceived* (1697); *Queen Catherine* (1698); *The False Friend* (1699); *The Beau Defeated* (1700); *The Double Distress* (1701); *The Czar of Muscovy* (1701); *The Different Widows* (1703); *The Adventures in Madrid* (1706).

References: Allibone; Clark, C., 'Introduction' to *The Inhumane Cardinal* (1984); Clark, C., *Three Augustan Women Playwrights* (1986); Cotton, N., *Women Playwrights in England, c. 1363–1750* (1980); Hook, L. (ed.), *The Female Wits* (1967); Steeves, E. L., 'Introduction' to *The Plays of Mary Pix and Catherine Trotter* (1982); Todd.

Porter, Anna Maria

b. 1780, Durham; d. 21 September 1832, Montpellier, near Bristol
Novelist, poet

AMP was one of five children born to Jane Porter (*née* Blenkinsop) and William Porter, surgeon to the 6th Dragoons, who died in 1779. The family, which after William's death was impoverished and relied primarily on the support of his patrons in the army, moved to Edinburgh in 1780. AMP, the younger sister of Sir Robert Ker Porter, the painter and traveller, and Jane Porter, the novelist, was initially attracted by music and the visual arts, but decided, like her sister, to dedicate herself to literature. At the age of 13 she began to write a collection of stories which were published as *Artless Tales* in 1785, anonymously. Two more substantial stories followed: *Walsh Colville* (1797) and *Octavia* (1798). These too were published anonymously. At some time before 1803 the family settled in London, moving to Esher in Surrey by 1807. In this year her most successful novel, *The Hungarian Brothers*, appeared to general acclaim. Like most of her novels, it was translated into French later. When AMP's mother died in 1831 she moved to London. But in 1832 she suffered an attack of typhus while visiting her brother William in Bristol and shortly afterwards died there.

Walsh Colville, perhaps because it is an early work, written when AMP was still in her teens, presents in a conveniently schematic fashion topics which she was later to handle with greater subtlety and complexity. Subtitled *A Young Man's First Entrance Into Life*, it follows Walsh's fortunes as he is prevailed upon by his libertine friend Stanhope to join the Guards, a regiment renowned for its officers' extravagance, and is gradually drawn, first into suspected, and subsequently into outright, bad company. Stanhope cynically exploits his friend's trust and eventually betrays him into a compromised and indebted position from which only the somewhat improbably assiduous efforts of the virtuous set amongst the Guards can rescue him.

The influence of the sentimental male heroes portrayed in such novels as Mackenzie's *The Man of Feeling* is noticeable: Stanhope and Colville initially exchange affectionate glances and blushes, or communicate by squeezing each other's hands. Also remarkable are the seemingly limitless resources of patient forgiveness at the disposal of the virtuous characters. Lord Cantyre, who is repeatedly insulted by Colville, shows no inclination to stop approaching him in the most friendly manner. Even more surprisingly, Stanhope, who has lied viciously to every major character in the book in search of personal gain, is quickly forgiven by everyone after he is wounded in a duel. Such ready forgiveness is continually accompanied, moreover, by assertions that the crimes committed are ineradicable and unforgivable: Walsh Colville is consequently subjected to a double-bind which dissolves all the rational foundations of his conduct.

The Hungarian Brothers considers many of the same topics as *Walsh Colville*, and with many of the same devices, but in considerably more detail. Once more two young officers are the central characters, this time in the Imperial Austrian army opposing Napoleon, for whom both brothers betray a suitably aristocratic contempt. Here, however, one of the brothers, Charles, is unambiguously virtuous throughout, whilst the other, Demetrius, though often tempted, finally maintains his own virtue as well. Once more the heroes are creatures of sensibility: when Charles is delivering a monitory lecture to Demetrius before their arrival in Vienna, his brother's face is a barometer of emotion: 'The expressive colour in his attentive hearer's cheeks had varied rapidly during this address; he now bent his head over the hand of Leopolstat, to hide the sensibility which boyishly he blushed at . . .'

AMP's account of the relationship between Demetrius and his unsuitable beloved, Zaire de Fontainville, reveals an even deeper fear of the insidious advance of evil than does *Walsh Colville*. Zaire's 'habits relieved her from the necessity of reflection; and, conscious of no glaring offence in her life, she suspected not the hidden evil of the heart, which only waits an opportunity to surprise and overpower those who will not know that they have a bosom tempter to resist.' Once more the resources of human rationality in the face of the subtle self-rationalizations of desire are portrayed as perilously weak. This sense of weakness grew on AMP as her career advanced: and when, in 1831, she came to write a new introduction to *The Hungarian Brothers*, she had become anxious about the possible presence of temptation in her own work: 'I will frankly claim credit for a conscientious endeavour to expunge from it now, whatever false conclusion, or misleading sentiment, I was unqualified then to detect and erase.' AMP's work traces the path from a pragmatic, if emotionally complex, ethic of chastity, to a Victorian fear of undetectable and corrosive evil.   JAMES SMITH

Works: *Artless Tales* (1795); *Walsh Colville* (1797); *Octavia* (1798); *The Lake of Killarney* (1804); *A Soldier's Love* (1805); *The Hungarian Brothers* (1807); *Don Sebastian* (1809); *Ballad Romances* (1811); *The Recluse of Norway* (1814); *The Knight of St John* (1817); *The Fast of St Magdalen* (1819); *The Village of Mariendorpt* (1821); *Roche-Blanche* (1822); *Honor O'Hara* (1826); *Tales Round a Winter Hearth* (with Jane Porter) (1826); *Coming Out* (with Jane Porter) (1828); *The Field of the Forty Footsteps* (with Jane Porter) (1828); *The Barony* (1830).

References: Allibone; *DNB*; Luria, G., 'Introduction' to *Walsh Colville* (1974).

Porter, Jane

b. 1776, Durham; d. 24 May 1850, Bristol

Novelist

JP was the older sister of Anna Maria Porter, who began writing stories at the age of 13, and the younger sister of William, a naval surgeon, John, a colonel, and Robert, an artist. Her father William, from an old Irish family, was an army surgeon for twenty-three years to the 6th Dragoons; he died when she was 3. JP's mother Jane (*née* Blenkinsop) moved to Edinburgh with her five children; there the girls attended a school run by George Fulton. At an early age, JP read Spenser, Sidney, and many tales of chivalry. Her imagination was further stimulated by Scottish legends told to her by Walter Scott, and a woman named Luckie Forbes. She met John Sell Cotman, whose reminiscences suggested to her some of the incidents she later incorporated into her novel *Thaddeus* (1803). It was published after being shown in manuscript to an acquaintance, Owen Rees, who worked for the firm of Longman.

The family moved to London when Robert, under the patronage of Flora Macdonald and Benjamin West, obtained admission as an art student at Somerset House. They lived at 16 Great Newport Street, Leicester Square, subsisting on Robert's many commissions for altar pieces. When he was appointed historical painter to the tsar of Russia, the three women moved to a cottage at Esher, Surrey. JP's novel about the Polish exile Thaddeus, who fought the invading Russians with General Kosciuszko and Prince Poniatowski, had gone through nine editions by 1810, and had been translated into German. JP was given a gold ring with General Kosciuszko's portrait, and in recognition of this tribute, she dedicated the 10th edition, in 1819, to him. The ruler of Würtemberg made her a lady of the order of St Joachim in appreciation of her literary gifts. Four more editions testified to the immense popular success of *Thaddeus* in 1831, 1840, 1860, and 1868.

The Scottish Chiefs appeared in 1810, telling the fate of the Scottish patriot William Wallace, ending with the battle of Bannockburn. She had heard stories about this hero from Luckie Forbes, and had done research suggested by the poet, Campbell, to whom she dedicated the third edition (1816). It was translated into German and Russian, read in India, and so admired that it went through nine reprintings between 1816 and 1882.

The Pastor's Fireside (1815) about the later Stuarts went through five editions by 1880. *Duke Christian of Luneburg, or, Traditions From the Hartz* (1824) was dedicated to King George IV who had suggested to his librarian, Dr Adam Clarke, that he supply JP with information about this subject. In 1831 she published the fictionalized diary of a shipwrecked Caribbean explorer, *Sir Edward Seaward's Narrative*.

JP and her sister published three books collaboratively: *Tales Round a Winter Hearth* (1826), *Coming Out* (1828), and *The Field of the Forty Footsteps* (1828). In 1832, JP's sister died of typhoid while visiting their brother in Bristol, and in 1842, Robert, who had married a Russian princess, died suddenly of a stroke while JP was visiting them in St Petersburg.

Two of JP's dramas met with less success than the novels. *Egmont, or, The Eve of St Alyne* was never acted. *Switzerland* was performed at Drury Lane by Kean and Kemble in 1819, but was such a failure that the manager had to announce its withdrawal. JP also contributed to various periodicals such as *Amulet* and the *Gentleman's Magazine*. Several unpublished works of hers were sold by Sotheby in 1852 and some of her correspondence is kept in the library at Thirlestone House, Cheltenham.   RUTH ROSENBERG

Works: *The Two Princes of Persia: Addressed to Youth* (1801); *Thaddeus of Warsaw* (1803); *Sketch of the Campaign of Count A. Suwarrow Ryminski* (1804); *Aphorisms of Sir Philip Sidney with Remarks* (1807); *The Scottish Chiefs: A Romance* (1810); *Duke Christian of Luneburg, or, Traditions From the Hartz* (1824); *Tales Round a Winter Hearth* (with Anna Maria Porter) (1826); *Coming Out* (with Anna Maria Porter) (1828); *The Field of the Forty Footsteps* (with Anna Maria Porter) (1828); *Sir Edward Seaward's Narrative of his Shipwreck and Consequent Discovery of Certain Islands in the Caribbean Sea: With a Detail of many Extraordinary and Highly Interesting Events of His Life from 1733 to 1749 as Written in His Own Diary* (1831).

References: *BA*(19); *DNB*; Hall, A. M., 'Memoirs of Jane Porter', *Art Journal* 2 (1850); Helmons, R., 'Another source for Poe's *Arthur Gordon Pym*', *American Literature* 41 (January 1970); Maginn, W., *A Gallery of Illustrious Literary Characters* (1873); Todd; Wilson, M. A., *These Were the Muses* (1924).

Potter, Beatrix

b. 28 July 1866, South Kensington, London; d. 22 December 1943, Sawrey, Cumbria

Writer for children

BP was the only daughter of Helen Leech and Rupert Potter, a barrister; both her parents were well-connected, having inherited Lancashire cotton fortunes. Her paternal grandfather had been Liberal MP for Carlisle, a friend of Cobden and Bright, as well as of Mr and Mrs Gaskell, and her father, who had a passion for art and amateur photography, counted the painter Millais amongst his closest friends, sometimes taking BP with him to Millais's studio. She was educated by governesses at home in Bolton Gardens, South Kensington. As a child she was frequently ill (an attack of rheumatic fever in 1886 was to affect her heart permanently), and had few friends. Her chief companions were her younger brother, Bertram, and the menagerie they collected on their regular summer trips to Scotland and the Lake District. BP began drawing at an early age, copying the flowers and animals brought back from Dalguise, Perthshire, or the pets purchased in London petshops: dormice, bats, newts, snakes, frogs. Her love of drawing was equalled only by her keen interest in natural history. Her work on the germination of lichen spores was read to the Linnean Society in London in 1897.

BP's professional career began in 1890 when her uncle encouraged her to sell some of her drawings to Hildersheim and Faulkner as Christmas card designs and as illustrations for E. Weatherley's *A Happy Pair* (1890). In 1891 she submitted sketches and a booklet to Frederick Warne, which were, however, rejected. It was while holidaying in Eastwood, Dunkeld, in September 1893, that BP wrote her famous illustrated letter to her former governess's child, in which she told the story of her pet rabbit, Peter. This letter was, seven years later, to become the basis of *The Tale of Peter Rabbit*, initially printed and published by BP herself in 1901. A commercial publisher was eventually found in Frederick Warne & Co, a connection which was to last for most of BP's career. The Frederick Warne edition of *Peter Rabbit* was published in October 1902, shortly followed, in 1903, by *The Tale of Squirrel Nutkin* and *The Tailor of Gloucester*. These were the first of a whole series of 'little books' about woodland and farmyard creatures, written for young children and all illustrated by BP herself. They gained immediate popularity: by 1903 over 50,000 copies of *Peter Rabbit* had sold.

In the November of 1903 BP purchased a field in the village of Sawrey in the Lake District, an area with which she would ever afterwards be associated. In 1905 she bought Hilltop Farm and began to breed Herdwick sheep, and in the same year she became engaged to her publisher, Norman Warne, against the wishes of her repressive parents who objected to her marrying into 'trade'. Weeks later, however, Warne died suddenly. In 1909, BP became involved in politics, campaigning against the government's free trade policy, and writing leaflets on behalf of farmers and smallholders objecting to the plans to raise land taxes. In October 1913, she married the local solicitor who had handled all her property dealings, William Heelis. Her peak creative period was now past, and she devoted most of her energies to farming, continually expanding her estate, and in 1930 becoming the first woman president of the Herdwick Sheepbreeders Association. She also involved herself in the Lake District Defence Society (forerunner of the National Trust), and in 1919 she helped to set up a nursing trust in the Sawrey area, before the establishment of the National Health Service.

BP tried to avoid 'writing down' to her young readers, believing that they would grasp intuitively, or from the illustrations, what was meant by 'the effect of eating too much lettuce is soporific', or 'Tommy Brock snored conscientiously'. Her characters can be divided roughly into two social groups, those who are taken straight from the privileged upper-middle-class world into which BP was born, a world epitomized by the life at Bolton Gardens, and those who approximate to the status of domestic servants or assiduous country housewives. While Mr Jeremy Fisher and his pompous elderly gentlemen friends eat 'roasted grasshopper with ladybird sauce', and Tom Kitten is compelled by his mother to wear, like Beatrix as a child, 'all sorts of elegant uncomfortable clothes', we find that Mrs Tiggy-Winkle, by contrast, curtseys and addresses Lucy as 'Ma'am' and that her hand is 'very very wrinkly with the soapsuds'.

For all her tendency to anthropomorphize her fictional creatures, BP manages to find ways of making them reveal their own animal natures obliquely. We are never allowed to forget that they live in a brutal animal world in which everyone is a potential meal for everyone else. Graham Greene, in his well-known essay on BP's work, praised this freedom from sentimentality, writing of her 'selective realism, which takes emotion for granted and puts aside love and death with a gentle detachment'. Much to BP's indignation, he accounted for the violence of some of BP's stories in Freudian terms, asserting that 'At some time between 1907 and 1909 Miss Potter must have passed through an ordeal which changed the character of her genius'; this, he argued, explained the 'dark period of Miss Potter's art', expressed in Mr Drake Puddle-Duck, Mr Jackson, Samuel Whiskers and Mr Tod. BP retorted that, when writing *Mr Tod*, she had merely been suffering from a cold.

BP's books still sell in millions and have been translated into many languages including Japanese and Icelandic. In 1971 a full-length ballet film of the tales appeared. BP also kept a vast journal from her mid-teens until she was past thirty, written in a secret cipher understood by no one until Leslie Linder finally broke the code and published *The Journal of Beatrix Potter* (1966).

ANNE FERNIHOUGH

Works: *The Tale of Peter Rabbit* (1902); *The Tale of Squirrel Nutkin* (1903); *The Tailor of Gloucester* (1903); *The Tale of Benjamin Bunny* (1904); *The Tale of Two Bad Mice* (1904); *The Tale of Mrs Tiggy-Winkle* (1905); *The Pie and the Patty-Pan* (1905); *The Tale of Mr Jeremy Fisher* (1906); *The Story of a Fierce Bad Rabbit* (1906); *The Story of Miss Moppet* (1906); *The Tale of Tom Kitten* (1907); *The Tale of Jemima Puddle-Duck* (1908); *The Roly-Poly Pudding* (1908; republished as *The Tale of Samuel Whiskers*, 1926); *The Tale of the Flopsy Bunnies* (1909); *Ginger and Pickles* (1909); *The Tale of Mrs Tittlemouse* (1910); *The Tale of Timmy Tiptoes* (1911); *The Tale of Mr Tod* (1912); *The Tale of Pigling Bland* (1913); *Appley Dapply's Nursery Rhymes* (1917); *The Tale of Johnny Town-Mouse* (1918); *Cecily Parsley's Nursery Rhymes* (1922); *The Fairy Caravan* (1929); *The Tale of Little Pig Robinson* (1930); *Sister Anne* (1932); *Wag-by-Wall* (1944); *The Tale of the Faithful Dove* (1956); *The Journal of Beatrix Potter* (1966); *Dear Ivy, Dear June: Letters from Beatrix Potter* (1977).

References: Crouch, M., *Beatrix Potter* (1960); Godden, R., *The Tale of the Tales* (1971); Greene, G., 'Beatrix Potter', in *Collected Essays* (1969); Lane, M., *The Tale of Beatrix Potter* (1946); Lane, M., *The Magic Years of Beatrix Potter* (1978); Linder, L., *The Art of Beatrix Potter* (1955; revised edn 1972); Linder, L., *The History of the Writings of Beatrix Potter* (1971); Linder, L., *The History of the Tale of Peter Rabbit* (1976); OCCL; Parker, U. H., *Cousin Beatie* (1981); Taylor, J., *Beatrix Potter, Artist, Storyteller and Countrywoman* (1986).

Power, Eileen
b. 9 January 1889, Altrincham, Cheshire; d. 8 August 1940, London
Historian
EP was an eminent medievalist who specialized in women's economic position in the thirteenth and fourteenth centuries. She was the daughter of Philip Ernest Le Poer Power, a London stockbroker, and Mabel Grindley Clegg. Educated at Bournemouth and Oxford High Schools, EP took a first-class honours degree at Girton College, Cambridge in 1910. She won research fellowships at Girton and the London School of Economics, and studied in Paris for a year. As director of studies in history at Girton from 1913, she held two fellowships and spent a year in the Far East. She began lecturing at LSE in 1921 and became professor there ten years later.

EP's reputation as a teacher was outstanding. She revisited the Far East in 1929, lecturing on the modern history of both the Far East and Europe; the following year she taught at Barnard College in New York; and in 1938 was the first woman named Ford lecturer in English history at Oxford. (The Ford lectures were published posthumously as *The Wool Trade in English Medieval History*.) She was awarded an honorary D Litt by the University of Manchester and later made honorary fellow of Girton. In addition to her prodigious editing of medieval documents, EP served as secretary of the Economic History Society from its foundation in 1926 until her death, and helped found the *Economic History Review* in 1927. At the age of 48 she married a colleague at LSE, Michael Moissey Postan, son of Efim Postan of Bessarabia, and later professor of economic history at Cambridge. (EP is listed as 'Postan' in the *DNB*, although she never published under that name.)

EP thought that the past came alive better through personalities than through learned treatises on economic topics, and that history 'is valuable only insofar as it lives'. In her best-known work, *Medieval People* (1924), she reconstructs the lives of five 'ordinary people' between the ninth and the fifteenth centuries. One of these was the rather extraordinary Marco Polo, but for the other four EP brilliantly fleshes out the skeletal evidence for the lives of any one of them with her knowledge of documents relating to *other* ploughmen, abbesses, woolmerchants, and clothiers. EP intended *Medieval People* for a popular audience, and her attempts to convey a sense of the past to a modern layperson are occasionally patronizing, but more often her imagination illuminates a dry fact to reveal the human repercussions behind the record. For instance, it is attestable fact that in the ninth century Charlemagne was presented with an elephant named Alu-Lubabah, but EP imagines the ploughman's wife, whose name we know was Ermentrude, quelling her children with the threat, 'Abu-Lubabah will come with his long nose and carry you off!'

EP also wrote children's history books with her sister. It was her belief that human nature has changed little since the Middle Ages that allowed EP to represent that world in such an understandable and interesting way, a skill extremely rare among economic historians. In her work specifically on women (*Medieval Women* is a compilation of her lectures on the subject), EP was one of the first to make the crucial point that 'their position in theory and law is one thing, their practical position in everyday life another', and that 'the true position of women at any particular moment is an insidious blend of both'.

AMY ERICKSON

Selected works: The Paycockes of Coggeshall (1920); *The New World History Series*, vol. 1, ed. B. Manning (1920); 'Some women practitioners of medicine in the Middle Ages', *Proceedings of The Royal Society of Medicine* 15 (1921–2); *Medieval English Nunneries, c. 1275 to 1535* (1922); *Medieval People* (1924); (ed.), *Tudor Economic Documents* (with R. H. Tawney) (1924); *Boys and Girls of History* (with R. D. L. Power) (1926); *Twenty Centuries of Travel: A Simple Survey of British History* (with R. D. L. Power) (1926); 'The English wool trade in the reign of Edward IV', *Cambridge Historical Journal* (1926); 'The opening of the land routes to Cathay', in *Travel and Travellers of the Middle Ages*, ed. A. P. Newton (1926); 'The position of women', in *The Legacy of the Middle Ages*, ed. C. G. Crump and E. F. Jacob (1926); *Cities and Their Stories* (with R. D. L. Power) (1927); (ed.), *The Industrial Revolution, 1750–1850: A Select Bibliography; Poems from the Irish* (1927); (trans.), *Life and Work in Medieval Europe*, by Prosper Boissonnade (1927); (ed.), *Broadway Travellers* (with Sir E. D. Ross) (1926–33; some of these reprinted as *The Argonaut Series*, 1927–30); (ed.), *Broadway Medieval Library* (with G. G. Coulton) (1928); (ed.), *English Life in English Literature* (with A. W. Reed) (1928); (trans.), *The Goodman of Paris*, by Menagier de Paris (1928); (trans.), *Miracles of the Blessed Virgin Mary*, by Johannes Herolt (1928); *Europe Throughout the Ages: From the Coming of the Greeks to the End of the Middle Ages* (with N. H. Baynes) (1979); (ed.), *Studies in Economic and Social History* (with R. H. Tawney) (1929); (ed.), *Broadway Diaries, Memoirs and Letters*, 7 vols. (with E. Drew) (1929–31); 'Peasant life and rural conditions (c.1100 to c.1500)',

in *Cambridge Medieval History*, vol. 7 (1932); (ed.), *Studies in English Trade in the 15th Century* (with M. M. Postan) (1933); 'The wool trade in the 15th century', in *Studies in English Trade* (1933); *The Wool Trade in English Medieval History*, ed. M. M. Postan (1941); (ed.), *The Agrarian Life of the Middle Ages, Cambridge Economic History of Europe*, vol. 1 (with J. H. Clapham) (1941); *Medieval Women*, ed. M. M. Postan (1975); (ed.), *Holinshed's Chronicles* (with L. Miller) (1977).
References: DNB.

Procter, Adelaide Anne
b. 30 October 1825, London; d. 2 February 1864, London
Poet, reformer
(Also wrote under Mary Berwick)
AAP was the first child of Bryan Waller Procter, a poet known as 'Barry Cornwall', and Anne (*neé* Skepper) Procter. Considered extraordinary by her parents and their many literary friends, she studied geometry, piano, and drawing as well as French, German, and Italian. Her early poetry circulated in manuscript among friends. In 1853 she began submitting poems signed 'Mary Berwick' to Charles Dickens's *Household Words*. Over the next six years, a sixth of the poems that magazine published were AAP's. Her poetry also appeared in *All the Year Round, Cornwall*, and *Good Words*.

Her complementary interests in religion and social problems shaped her writing. She became a Roman Catholic in her mid-twenties, and some of her devotional lyrics have been used in Catholic and Protestant hymnals. *A Chaplet of Verse* (1862) was published as a benefit for England's first Catholic refuge for homeless women and children. With feminist friends she founded *The English Woman's Journal* in 1858 to encourage women to enter various occupations and professions; she contributed prose and poetry (including her most famous lyric, 'A Lost Chord') to the *Journal*. She also worked for women by founding clubs, publishing pamphlets, and circulating petitions. Her participation in efforts to educate and house the poor led in 1859 to her appointment by the National Association for the Promotion of Social Science to a committee to study ways of developing employment opportunities for women.

Contemporaries testifed that AAP shortened her life with overwork. Dickens could not forego ending his 1866 memoir of her with an inspirational deathbed scene, but he also recalled her 'honesty, independence, and quiet dignity' and complimented her for never displaying 'any of the conventional poetical qualities', such as the luxurious conviction that she was 'misunderstood and unappreciated'.

The moral idealism, piety, nostalgia, and pathos of her poems ensured the popularity Dickens had predicted. A number of them express values and concerns we now distance as 'Victorian'. The speaker in 'The Warrior of His Dead Bride' says, predictably enough, that his 'angel's' prayers protect him and that love and loss have made him more compassionate. The narrator of the often-anthologized 'A Legend of Provence' asserts, 'No star is ever lost we once have seen. / We always may be what we might have been.' Such poems had and have popular appeal precisely because they are touching but not disturbing. If many of AAP's works can fairly be described as conventional and lacking in vitality, they reveal much about the ideals approved by a large Anglo-American readership.

But AAP sometimes surprises. 'A New Mother' is related by a servant who, like Emily Brontë's Nelly Dean, plays a central role in a domestic competition for the loyalty of children. Protesting her love for their dead mother, this woman has deliberately, though perhaps unconsciously, alienated the children from a stepmother who longs for their confidence. Other dramatic monologues subtly question traditional and professed platitudes about altruism. Ostensibly addressing his niece, the obscure poet of 'True Honours' is actually persuading himself that a lifetime of self-sacrifice has been 'blest'. The poem apparently confirms received views, yet there is an undertone of doubt. The speaker and AAP (she never subverts the hope of heaven) are more confident that death will bring him 'light and rest'.

Some of the lyrics and third-person narratives directly state the dangers of passivity and dependency. The title characters of 'Philip and Mildred' are separated during a long engagement while he pursues his career. The narrator advises Mildred (and readers who stunt their growth by waiting or clinging), 'Live thy life: not a reflection or shadow of [the loved one's] own.' Mildred eventually realizes that Philip – 'beyond her now' – marries her only out of duty. The possibility that their youthful love will be restored in heaven is suggested in interrogative, not declarative, form. Several poems carry the sting of AAP's irony and experience of two unfortunate love affairs.

Literary distinction may have been a star AAP dreamed of. If it was, she defended herself against the sense of failure and guilt such ambition often engendered in nineteenth-century women. Her poem 'A False Genius' warns against the self-absorption and desire for praise that tempt the 'Soul' to neglect social responsibility. According to a friend, AAP was not pleased that her writings were more popular than Barry Cornwall's. 'Papa is a poet', she said. 'I only write verses.' Allowing for the modesty obligatory for her sex, one may still conclude that she valued her 'verses' as her means of sustaining the moral and spiritual ideals and thought conducive not only to endurance but also to constructive change.   MARY G. DE JONG

Selected Works: *Legends and Lyrics: A Book of Verses*, 1st series (1858); *Legends and Lyrics: A Book of Verses*, 2nd series (1861); (ed.), *The Victoria Regia: A Volume of Original Contributions in Poetry and Prose* (1861); *Chaplet of Verses* (1861); *The Poems of Adelaide Anne Procter* (1873); *Complete Works* (1905).

References: Belloc, B. R., *In a Walled Garden* (1895); *DNB*; Dickens, C., 'Introduction' to *The Poems of Adelaide Anne Procter* (1873); Drain, S., 'Adelaide Anne Procter', in *Victorian Poets Before 1850*, ed. W. E. Fredeman and I. B. Nadel (*DLB*, vol. 32)(1984); Hickok, K., *Representations of Women: Nineteenth-Century British Women's Poetry* (1984); Julian, J. (ed.), *A Dictionary of Hymnology*, 2nd revised edn (1907); Lohrli, A. (comp.), *Household Words: A Weekly Journal 1850–1859 Conducted by Charles Dickens* (1973); Maison, M., 'Queen Victoria's favourite poet', *Listener* 73 (29 April 1965).

Pym, Barbara

b. 2 June 1913, Oswestry, Shropshire; d. 11 January 1980, Oxford
Novelist
BP read English at St Hilda's College, Oxford. During the Second World War she served in the WRNS, and between 1946 and 1974 worked as editor and proofreader for the International African Institute. Her first novel, *Some Tame Gazelle* (1950), is a revised version of one started in 1935. It was followed by five others, concluding with *No Fond Return of Love* (1961). They portray the world of middle-aged, unmarried, middle-class people, the clergy, and scholarly

societies and institutions, a territory which BP made peculiarly her own. Her work then went out of fashion (with the publishers if not with the public) and it was another sixteen years before she published another novel. *Quartet in Autumn* (1977), however, coincided with her sudden return to critical favour, as the result of the simultaneous championship of her work by Philip Larkin and Lord David Cecil in a *Times Literary Supplement* questionnaire. Two more novels followed: *The Sweet Dove Died* (1978), which during the preceding decade had been rejected by over twenty publishers but which was now received with acclaim; and *A Few Green Leaves* (1980), completed a short while before the author's death. Since then three further books have appeared – *An Unsuitable Attachment* (1982, having been rejected in 1965), *Crampton Hodnet* (1985), an early work and the most high-spirited and purely comic of the novels, and *An Academic Affair* (1986), assembled from two unrevised drafts. *A Very Private Eye: The Diaries, Letters and Notebooks of Barbara Pym* appeared in 1984: it portrays a wryly humorous, romantically optimistic, yet wary personality of considerable charm.

While belonging to the tradition of satirical domestic novelists, exemplified in the inter-war years by such writers as E. H. Young and E. M. Delafield, and subsequently by Elizabeth Taylor, BP has a style and outlook peculiarly her own. She is a mistress of understatement, with a sharp eye for absurdities and trivia, and a meticulous sense of the niceties and inhibitions of middle-class behaviour. But the comedy is saved from superficiality by an underlying austerity of outlook, most obviously present in *Quartet in Autumn*. The frustrated love of women for men provides the subject of several of the novels, including two of the most successful, *A Glass of Blessings* (1958) and *The Sweet Dove Died*. *Some Tame Gazelle, Excellent Women* (1952) and *Jane and Prudence* (1953) focus on the world of the parish clergy, and are the most entertaining of the mature novels. *Less than Angels* (1955) casts an ironic eye on the behaviour of anthropologists, a subject of which the author had first-hand knowledge.

The implacably steady emphasis that BP places on the continual small disappointments of daily life does not allow for sentimental lapses into superficial optimism. Simply by virtue of subject matter she tends to subvert the conventions of popular fiction; but she achieves this through naturalistic means rather than through the arguably protective devices of symbol, fable or deliberate literary artifice. Her world may on the surface be a cosy one, but the implications it suggests are bleak.

BP's characters are usually resigned even to resignation itself, but there is only the faintest bitterness in her outlook; her compassion is sustained by an amused appreciation of human quirks and oddities and by a savouring of the lesser diurnal pleasures and compensations. In some ways her novels are a prose equivalent of certain poems by Philip Larkin, a writer whose admiration she reciprocated. Without being a feminist, she is intensely aware of the differences between men and women, her attitude towards the former being not so much caustic as protective. An unobtrusive but distinctive stylist, she is a novelist whose work should survive in its own right and not simply as an ironic chapter in twentieth-century literary history.   GLEN CAVALIERO

Works: *Some Tame Gazelle* (1950); *Excellent Women* (1952); *Jane and Prudence* (1953); *Less than Angels* (1955); *A Glass of Blessings* (1958); *No Fond Return of Love* (1961); *Quartet in Autumn* (1977); *The Sweet Dove Died* (1978); *A Few Green Leaves* (1980); *An Unsuitable Attachment* (1982); *A Very Private Eye* (1984); *Crampton Hodnet* (1985); *An Academic Affair* (1986).

References: Drabble; Holt, H., 'Preface', and Pym, H., 'The Early Life', *A Very Private Eye: The Diaries, Letters and Notebooks of Barbara Pym* (1984).

Radcliffe, Ann

b. 9 July 1764, London; d. 7 February 1823, London
Novelist

There was little extraordinary about AR's early life; in fact, when Christina Rossetti, an early admirer of AR, undertook to write her biography, she abandoned the project for lack of material. AR was the daughter of William and Ann Oates Ward. Her father first worked as a haberdasher, then as a representative of Wedgwood china, a firm established by his wife's relative and the latter's business partner. But as AR's husband emphasizes in the obituary notice that was to become the major source of material about her life, relatives on both sides of the family had higher status than that of her parents; her family included famous physicians and scholars. The obituary also attributes major importance to AR's childhood visits to her uncle Thomas Bentley. Bentley was a man of culture whose friends included scientists like Joseph Priestley and literary figures of the day. Also numbered among Bentley's friends were Joseph Banks and Dr Daniel Solander, who had accompanied Captain Cook on his famous journey around the world.

All sources indicate that AR's education was typical of young women of her time: she knew something of art and music, and she read widely. Her literary production was anticipated in her early reading preferences. Her favourite author was Shakespeare, her favourite plays *Macbeth* and Schiller's *The Robbers*, her favourite poet James Thomson. When AR lived in Bath, Sophia and Harriet Lee opened a school for young women there. It is not known whether AR was a student of the school, but in 1785, Sophia Lee published *The Recess*, an historical romance replete with sentiment, suspense, and sensibility, which had great impact on AR.

In 1787 AR married William Radcliffe, a law student at Oxford. Radcliffe never completed his legal education but instead turned to journalism, becoming the owner and editor of the *English Chronicle*. He strongly encouraged his wife in her writing, enthusiastically reading the manuscripts of her novels and travel diary as she produced them. By the time her fourth novel, *The Mysteries of Udolpho* (1794), appeared, she was the most popular author of her day, known in the press as the 'Great Enchantress'. Although AR's novels were filled with scenic descriptions of Italy and Sicily, she in fact travelled only once outside England – to France and Germany – and recorded that experience in a published travel diary. After the publication of her fifth novel, *The Italian*, in 1797, AR's husband became ill, her father died, and soon after, her mother. She was seized by melancholy. This change in her inner disposition, combined with a change in her external circumstances, made her less inclined to write for publication. Her mother's will rendered her financially independent so that she no longer had to rely on an income from writing. Thus her mood, her financial circumstances, the disgust she felt for her imitators, possibly combined with other circumstances of which we know nothing, led her to cease writing for publication. In these late years, she worked on one last novel, *Gaston de Blondeville*, a tale of the Middle Ages, which was published posthumously. Her long years of public silence led to rumours of her insanity and her death, rumours which she did nothing to contradict.

As the leading and best-known Gothic writer, AR and the names of her works have come to stand for Gothic writing in general. She is alluded to by, among others, Austen, Coleridge, Byron, Keats, Thackeray, and Scott. Her name has come to stand for a writer of terror, mystery, and suspense, for tales of the half-ruined medieval castle, reputedly Gothic, surrounded with striking, wild scenery and populated with a cast of characters made up of a lonely maiden, a middle-aged villain, a loyal servant, and a virtuous hero.

Yet AR's works differ from what her name summons in the popular imagination. She herself distinguished horror and terror, emphasizing the latter in her own work. And while AR's Gothic successors created heroines who were essentially defenceless, Emily, the heroine of The Mysteries of Udolpho, for example, meets each new disaster and challenge with strength and rationality, after momentarily succumbing to superstition and an excess of feeling. The literary tradition has represented AR's novels as replete with horror. Yet The Mysteries of Udolpho, as an instance, is not only a love story but a moral tale and one in which a young woman's struggle to recover her property predominates. We remember AR's novels not only for the introduction of isolated heart-stopping scenes but for the creation of a high level of suspense throughout the work which enthralls the reader. Indeed, many critics have claimed that it was AR who introduced suspense as a sustained technique in fiction.

The Mysteries of Udolpho, AR's most famous novel, begins as a pastorale. After her mother dies, Emily St Aubert lives alone with her father, the perfect man: noble in birth and mind. Emily undertakes a journey with her father, and when they meet Valancourt, the two young people fall in love. St Aubert dies soon after, entrusting Emily to his sister. Emily's aunt takes her away, forbids her marriage to Valancourt, and herself marries Montoni, an evil Italian. Montoni and her aunt remove Emily to Montoni's castle, Udolpho. Emily's aunt dies from Montoni's ill-treatment, and Montoni continues to try to get his wife's money from Emily. The rest of the story narrates Emily's adventures in the castle, her escape, and her reunion with Valancourt, whom she must initially reject because he has apparently gambled away his money and fallen into disgrace. The most famous incident in the novel is that of the black veil. Emily has been told of a mysterious picture concealed behind a black curtain. Finding such a veil, she curiously lifts the curtain and falls senseless to the floor. The image of the veil becomes a narrative refrain evoking all that is hidden and mysterious. When Emily eventually triumphs at the end, it is the triumph of rationality and strength.

The Italian, the final novel AR published in her lifetime, has perhaps the most dramatic plot of all. Vicentio di Vivaldi, seeing Ellena Rosalba at church, falls in love with her. His parents object to the match out of financial considerations. The monk, Schedoni, conspires with Vivaldi's mother, the Marchesa, to get Ellena out of the way. As they are about to be married, the couple are arrested in the name of the Inquisition. Vivaldi is imprisoned and Ellena taken to a lonely house on the seashore, where Schedoni, about to kill her, recognizes his own picture about her neck, and thinks that she is his daughter. At the end of the book, Schedoni poisons both himself and the monk who has betrayed him. Ellena finds her mother is the nun who has befriended her; she learns that she is the niece, not the daughter, of Schedoni, and she and Vivaldi are happily married. Suspense predominates throughout the novel. The narrator withholds information from the reader, and the monks appear and disappear mysteriously. The Italian contains AR's best writing and her best villain. Schedoni is a mixture of the implacable villainy of Montoni in Udolpho and a more human character.

Within AR's novels, heroines travel, encounter adventure, and take steps to resolve their own romantic and sexual fate.   MARTHA SATZ

Works: *The Castles of Athlin and Dunbayne* (1789); *A Sicilian Romance* (1790); *The Romance of the Forest* (1791); *The Mysteries of Udolpho* (1794); *A Journey Made in the Summer of 1794 through Holland and the Western Frontiers of Germany, with a Return down the Rhine, to Which are Added Observations during a Tour to the Lakes of Lancashire, Westmorland and Cumberland* (1795); *The Italian, or, The Confessional of the Black Penitents* (1797); *Gaston de Blondeville, or, The Court of Henry III Keeping Festival in Ardenne* (1826); *St Alban's Abbey* (1826).

References: Baker, E. A., 'The Gothic novel', in *The History of the English Novel: The Novel of Sentiment and the Gothic Romance* (1934); Durant, D., 'Ann Radcliffe and the conservative Gothic', *Studies in English Literature, 1500–1900* (Summer 1982); Grant, A., *Ann Radcliffe* (1920); Kiely, R., *The Romantic Novel in England* (1972); McIntyre, C., *Ann Radcliffe in Relation to Her Time* (1920); Murray, E. B., *Ann Radcliffe* (1872); Nichols, N. da V.,'Place and Eros in Radcliffe, Lewis, and Brontë', in *The Female Gothic*, ed. J. E. Fleenor (1983); Ruff, W., 'Ann Radcliffe, or, The Hand of Taste', *Essays to C. B. Tinker* (1949); Scott, W., 'Introduction' to *The Novels of Ann Radcliffe* (1824); Sedgwick, E. K., 'The characters in the veil: imagery of the surface in the Gothic novel', *PMLA* 96 (1981); Sypher, W., 'Social ambiguity in a Gothic novel', *Partisan Review* 12, 1 (1945); Todd, J., 'Posture and imposture: the Gothic manservant in Ann Radcliffe's *The Italian, Women and Literature* (1982); Todd, J., *The Sign of Angellica* (1989); Tompkins, J. M. S., *The Popular Novel in England: 1770–1800* (1932); Varma, D. P., 'Mrs Ann Radcliffe: the craft of terror', in *The Gothic Flame* (1957); Ware, M., *Sublimity in the Novels of Ann Radcliffe* (1963); Weiten, A. S. S., *Mrs Radcliffe, Her Relation towards Romanticism* (1926).

Radcliffe, Mary Ann

b. c. 1746, Scotland; d. after 1810, Edinburgh

Polemical writer, memoirist

MAR was the daughter of an elderly man who had acquired some property through trade. Her mother, forty years his junior, was a Roman Catholic. When MAR was 3, her father died and left her his estate under the management of two guardians, one Anglican like himself and the other Catholic. She was piously raised by nuns whose training seems to have been to little avail since, at the age of 14, she met a fortune hunter named Radcliffe whom she soon after married despite the strenuous efforts of her guardians. Neither she nor her rather naive mother appears to have had much notion of the seriousness of the step; later she would remark that the whole misery of her life stemmed from 'that one forenoon's frolick'. Over the next years she bore eight children and watched her property dwindle under the lazy mismanagement of her husband who proved 'inactive', kindly, and feckless rather than vicious. To provide for her family MAR gradually sold off the little land remaining to her, separated from her husband who found a position in a private family and tried almost every available method to make a living. At one time or another she was a governess, a teacher, a landlady, the keeper of a 'genteel' coffee shop, a milliner, a seamstress, and a seller of patent medicines, shoes, and pastries. She travelled backwards and forwards from Scotland to London to seek work, scouring the advertisements in newspapers. In due course her children, who had been placed in schools or left with her mother, died or grew up to begin adult lives of similar struggle and disappointment. From time to time MAR was buoyed up by a trust in providence directing her life, but of more constant help was what she described as an equable and cheerful temperament. In later years she tried but failed to find a place in an asylum in Edinburgh. She seems to have ended her days rheumatic and poor but not without a few friends.

In 1799 she published *The Female Advocate, or, An Attempt to Recover the Rights of Women from Male Usurpation*, written at Kennington Cross. Her desire to remain anonymous was overruled by the publisher's wish to capitalize on the closeness of her name to that of the famous Gothic novelist Ann Radcliffe. The title obviously harks back to Wollstonecraft's *A Vindication of the Rights of Woman*; yet in the conservative period at the end of the century, MAR is careful to distinguish herself from the 'Amazonian' spirit of her predecessor and she makes some apology for the political tone of her own work by insisting that she originally wrote it in 1792, the revolutionary time when Wollstonecraft's polemic was also written. MAR's work, more practical than Wollstonecraft's, concerns the misery of unprotected females not bred for any trade and increasingly barred by men from those few methods of making a living like mantua making and millinery once exclusively women's province. She tries to shame men out of these areas by referring to their effeminacy and to inspire wealthy women with female solidarity by urging them to accept service only from fellow women. She also pleads that the state should turn from its programme of prison building to consider the erection of asylums for women; she notes how little has been done for them, remarking that far more zeal has been directed towards slaves and even animals than towards women who remain without civic rights and with little share in the growing economic prosperity of the country. Although she is eloquent on the miseries of women who are reduced to prostitution and refused even the chance to beg by the Vagrant Act, her main concern is for women in her own situation, those of the middle class who have not been trained to keep themselves and who may have the added burden of whole families of children to support.

The source of MAR's bitterness and urgent tone becomes clear when *The Female Advocate* is read in conjunction with her next work which actually embeds the text in the story of her life. *The Memoirs of Mrs Mary Ann Radcliffe: in Familiar Letters to Her Female Friend* was printed for the author in 1810. The first letter was dated 1807 from Portobello but by letter 11 the address is simply Edinburgh in 1810. The story told is outlined above, the story of MAR's life, the sorry tale of a middle-class woman with some property and much energy who suffers from a mistaken marriage, a lazy husband, oppressive legal restrictions on women, and inadequate commercial or professional training. The letters are on the whole plainly written, although there are some rhetorical flights; the author insists that her plain style is a measure of her truthfulness for she is not writing a novel, but telling the facts of a life. Her attack is wide-ranging and not always entirely ordered; she blames men, female stupidity, and social conventions; 'it is the etiquette of the time for the daughters to be bred fine ladies, although it be without a fortune . . . to support it. As for trade, that is out of the question.' The letters were written when MAR was over 60, ill, poor, and still struggling; her only consolation was her sense of her own stamina and a glass of currant wine with a female friend.   JANET TODD

Works: *The Female Advocate, or, An Attempt to Recover the Rights of Women from Male Usurpation* (1799; *The Memoirs of Mrs Mary Ann Radcliffe: in Familiar Letters to Her Female Friend* (1810).
References: Todd.

Radcliffe, Mary Anne
fl. 1790–1809
Novelist

Almost nothing is known of MAR's life. In 1802 she compiled and issued *Radcliffe's New Novelist's Pocket Magazine*, a periodical specializing exclusively in Gothic fiction; her place of residence is there given as Wimbledon, Surrey. MAR is thought to have begun her career as a novelist for William Lane's Minerva Press and circulating library. *Radzivil* (1790) and *The Fate of Velina de Guidova* (1790), both published by Lane, are attributed to her. Lane's novelists typically imitated the novels of Ann Radcliffe rather than the more violent and sexually explicit Gothic of some German writers and, later, of Matthew Lewis's *The Monk*. It is significant that the only novel certainly known to be by MAR was not initially published by Lane, whose prospectus of 1794 boasts that his press would be 'open to such subjects as tend to public good – the pages shall never be stained with what will injure the mind or corrupt the heart'. *Manfroné, or, The One-Handed Monk*, owes as much to the luridity of Lewis as to Radcliffe, despite the author's name (which may have been chosen in an attempt to invite confusion with the more famous novelist). The book was only taken on to the Minerva list by Lane's successor ten years after its first publication.

MAR's apprenticeship as a writer for Lane, however, is perhaps to be seen in the narrative structure of her work: one of the rules of Lane's library was that new books could only be borrowed for four days at a time, and writers were thus encouraged to cram their books with sufficient incident to propel their readers through the entire book in the required time. *Manfroné* is no exception: in the short first chapter, a description of an attempt on the virtue of the heroine, Rosalina, is completed in time for her subsequent discovery of a severed hand in her bedroom. It has been suggested that MAR ineptly reveals one of the chief secrets of the book's plot in her subtitle: when Rosalina discovers that Grimaldi's arm is shorn at the wrist, she also realizes that he is 'the vile assailant of her honour, the intended assassin of Montalto, and the murderer of her parent', but these apparent discoveries must already have been evident to any reader bearing 'the one-handed monk' in mind. It seems more probable, however, that Grimaldi's identity is never intended as a secret to the reader, only to the heroine.

Many of the novel's gruesome incidents are anticipated in earlier Gothic novels and melodramas: a severed hand appears in Maturin's *Fatal Revenge* (1807), whilst the denouement is probably indebted to George Colman's *Blue Beard*, produced at Drury Lane in 1798. The novel's eventual happy ending, in which the noble Montalto knocks Manfroné to the ground from where he must watch the lovers embrace, casts a slightly spurious retrospective morality over the tale, allowing MAR to present it as a story of the rewards of virtue and the punishments of vice.   JAMES SMITH

Works: *Radzivil* (1790); *The Fate of Velina de Guidova* (1790); *Manfroné, or, The One-Handed Monk* (1809).

References: Adams, D K., 'The second Mrs Radcliffe', in *Mystery and Detection Annual* 1 (1962); Evans, B., *The Gothic Drama from Walpole to Shelley* (1947); Howells, C. A., *Love, Mystery, and Misery: Feeling in Gothic Fiction* (1979); Mayo, R. D., *The English Gothic Novel in the Magazines, 1740–1815* (1962); Todd.

Raine, Kathleen

b. 14 January 1908, Ilford, London

Poet, literary critic

KR's father was an English teacher at the County High School in Ilford; he was also a Methodist preacher active in the pacifist movement. But it was her mother, Jessie, who had the more enduring influence on her work: KR came to regard her mother's Scottish background and tales as essential to her own sense of poetic tradition. She later wrote in her autobiographical prose work *Farewell Happy Fields* (1973), by contrast, that 'Ilford, considered as a spiritual state, is the place of those who do not wish to (or who cannot be) fully conscious, because full consciousness would perhaps make life unendurable'.

KR was educated at schools in Ilford and then at the age of 18 won a scholarship to read natural sciences at Girton College, Cambridge. After graduating she married the poet Hugh Sykes Davies; later they were divorced and she married Charles Madge, the pioneer of mass observation, from whom she was subsequently separated. Despite KR's scientific training, her scholarly work (some of it completed outside any academic institution) was in the field of literary criticism; her first critical study, *William Blake*, was published in 1951, and her first volume of poetry had appeared eight years earlier. She has continued to write and publish in both fields since.

All KR's poetry bears witness to her strong preference for imagery that will represent what is permanent or archetypal in nature: she values such imagery for its potentially transcendental significance rather than for any descriptive precision. While her diction continually indicates her loyalty to the Romantic and symbolic literary tradition which she has defended in her criticism, her poetry displays a wide tonal and formal range. Her earliest volume, *Stone and Flower* (1943), is formally her most traditional and contains carefully patterned poems most of which make use either of rhyme or of assonance.

KR's work including and after *The Year One* (1952), which she regards as her first mature work, marks the advent of an increasingly hieratic voice, whose utterances range from deliberately repetitive 'invocations' and 'spells', such as a 'spell to bring lost creatures home' and a 'spell against sorrow', to poems narrated by first-person speakers presenting themselves as eternal and omnipresent. 'Northumbrian Sequence' begins, 'Pure I was before the world began, / I was the violence of wind and wave, / I was the bird before bird ever sang.' The small-scale crafted forms of KR's earlier volumes are more and more reminiscent of Blake or Whitman rather than Yeats. Such work often becomes a breathlessly unpunctuated deluge, as in 'Morning Image' from *The Hollow Hill* (1965): 'Inviolate spaces from infinite centre created at the opening of an eye/ World-wide into vision flow where on bright surfaces of light/ The mountain isles rest in a dream. . . .'

KR's critical work has principally concerned writers with a similarly strong interest in the mythological and has vigorously defended the continuing importance of mythology and symbolism to twentieth-century poetry. Myth is for KR a more important element of poetic tradition than verse forms and metres: thus she can regard the syntactically experimental work of the Welsh modernist David Jones as 'traditional' on the grounds of his strong interest in Welsh mythology. She is similarly sympathetic to writerrrrs with an antipathy to scientific materialism and an interest in the occult; much of her work has been on Yeats, whose mystical tract *A Vision* she regards, unlike many critics, as one of his central achievements.

Her critical *magnum opus*, however, is the two-volume study of Blake and his sources which she published in 1968, *Blake and Tradition*. The work is the first to demonstrate the depth and detail of Blake's indebtedness to the neo-Platonic philosophical tradition and to a range of associated mystical and magical traditions such as Orphism and Gnosticism. In her determination to demonstrate the cohesion of the poetic apparatus developed by Blake from these traditions, KR often comes close to regarding it as a single static system which, once decoded, offers an unproblematic method for the interpretation of all Blake's poems: she claims in her introduction that 'I know that the key for which many have sought is traditional metaphysics with its accompanying language of symbolic discourse'. At the same time KR seeks to underemphasize the political and historical significances of Blake's mythology, so that it appears primarily as a cosmology above, scarcely impinging upon history: 'mythology, not history, is Blake's cosmos.' But the thoroughness with which she investigates Blake's sources has made the book the standard work on the subject.

SIMON JARVIS

Works: *Stone and Flower* (1943); *Living in Time* (1946); *The Pythoness* (1949); *William Blake* (1951); *The Year One* (1952); *Coleridge* (1953); *Collected. Poems* (1956); *Poetry in Relation to Traditional Wisdom* (1958); *Blake and England* (1960); *The Hollow Hill* (1965); *Defending Ancient Springs* (1967); *The Written Word* (1967); *Six Dreams* (1968); *Blake and Tradition* (1968); *A Question of Poetry* (1969); *The Lost Country* (1971); *Yeats, the Tarot, and the Golden Dawn* (1972); *Hopkins and Human Nature* (1972); *Faces of Day and Night* (1972); *Farewell Happy Fields* (1973); *On a Deserted Shore* (1973); *David Jones* (1974); *The Land Unknown* (1975); *The Oval Portrait* (1977); *The Lion's Mouth* (1977); *David Jones and the Actually Loved and Known* (1978); *15 Short Poems* (1978); *Blake and the New Age* (1979); *From Blake to 'A Vision'* (1979); *Cecil Collins* (1979); *The Oracle in the Heart* (1980); *What is Man?* (1980); *The Human Face of God: William Blake and the Book of Job* (1982); *Blake and the Lily* (1984); *Poetry and the Frontiers of Consciousness* (1985).

References: *CA*; Deutsch, B., *Poetry in Our Time* (1963); Grubb, F., *A Vision of Reality* (1965); Mills, R. J., Jr, *Kathleen Raine* (1967); Stanford, D., *The Freedom of Poetry* (1947).

Reeve, Clara

b. 23 January 1729, Ipswich, Suffolk; d. 3 December 1807, Ipswich
Novelist, poet, critic

CR was the eldest daughter of Hannah and William Reeve's eight children. They had lived in Ipswich since her grandfather Thomas's time, when he had been rector of St Mary Stoke. William was rector of Freston and of Kerton, Suffolk, as well as curate of St Nicholas in Ipswich. CR's maternal grandfather had been jeweller to King George I. CR was educated by her father, who prescribed historical and biographical reading at an early age. While still very young, she studied Cato's speeches, Plutarch's *Lives*, and the parliamentary debates.

When CR's father died in 1755, three of the girls moved with their mother to Colchester, and CR began writing verse. These poems, dating from 1756 to 1769, were collected in *Original Poems on Several Occasions* (1769). CR showed facility in a range of genres: an epithalamion, an acrostic, a prologue, several elegies, lyrics paraphrased from French and German songs, and an oratorio based on the Book of Ruth. The interest in Latin evoked in CR by her father led her to a translation as her next work: the Latin allegory *Argenis* (1621), written by John Barclay, was published by her in 1771 as *The Phoenix*, in four volumes.

The Old English Baron was published in 1777 under the title *The Champion of Virtue*. The revisions for the second edition (1778) were made at the suggestion of Martha, one of Samuel Richardson's daughters, to whom it is dedicated. In the preface, CR wrote, 'this story is the literary offspring of the *Castle of Otranto*'. CR tried to lend credibility to the events of Walpole's 1765 Gothic novel. In order to make for more plausibility, she mitigated some horrors, like the skeleton wearing a hermit's cowl, and some improbabilities, like the sword so heavy that it required a hundred men to lift it. The story concerns a dispossessed heir, Edmond, whose title and castle have been usurped by Walter, his father's murderer. Edmond is forced to spend a night in the very room under whose floorboards his murdered father has been buried. In the circumstances, it seems natural that Edmond should dream and hear the groans and thuds of the fatal deed. Sir Walter is accused, and confesses his crime, restoring to Edmond his rightful property. So successful was CR's novel that it was reprinted thirteen times between 1778 and 1886. It was translated into both French and German. It was even adapted for the stage by John Broster, as *Edmond, Orphan of the Castle* (1779). Several abridged versions appeared in chapbooks.

In June 1778, two translations of CR's were published in the *Lady's Magazine*. These 'Letters to Aza' were an Inca love story of 1747 (*Lettres d'une Peruvienne*). The editors pleaded with CR to supply them with more, but she never complied. To satisfy the demands of readers for further instalments, the editors eventually translated them themselves.

The Two Mentors (1783) was an epistolary fiction. The hero, Edward Saville, is alternately torn between virtue and pleasure by his two mentors. The fashionable socialite, Richard Munded, urges Edward to indulge in a stylish life, and to let himself be polished by Lady Belmour. Instead, he rescues a young woman from Lady Belmour's house. The second mentor, the Rev. Jarvis Johnson, wins his pupil who marries the virtuous Sophia Melcombe, settling down to simple domestic contentment. CR considered such marriages spiritually important: 'An early attachment to a virtuous and amiable woman cultivates and ripens every noble quality.'

In 1785, CR published *The Progress of Romance*, in the form of conversations among friends about literature, about the history of prose fiction, and about contemporary novelists. CR included another of her translations, 'The History of Charoba, Queen of Egypt', which supposedly influenced Walter Savage Landor's epic poem, *Gebir* (1798).

In 1788 CR published *The Exiles*. It was much influenced by Baculard d'Arnaud. Again, it is narrated in a series of letters. Count de Cronstad had married a woman, who although she was both beautiful and virtuous, was only a peasant. His uncle forces him to marry a noblewoman; the peasant wife dies of grief, and the count, overcome by remorse, soon follows her to the grave.

CR's next two works, also epistolary in form, centre on Frances Darnford. *The School for Widows* (1791) tells of her unhappy marriage to an improvident husband. After his death, she befriends another widow, Mrs Strictland, whose husband denied her servants and society. A third widow, Donna Isabella, has become deranged because of the jealousy of Antonio, her former husband. The three widows console one another in sisterly friendship. In *Plans of Education with Remarks on the Systems of other Writers* (1792), Mrs Darnford advises Lady

A – on the education of her daughter, stressing the importance of discipline, of female seminaries, and of carefully studying the students' innate capacities before designing a course of study or determining a career.

In 1793, CR published the *Memoirs of Sir Roger de Clarendon*. This fictionalized the history of the natural son of Edward, Prince of Wales, and celebrated feudalism. Her praise of medieval times formed a conservative protest against the egalitarian French Revolution. The preface closes with a warning to England: 'Let Britain shudder at the scene before her, and grasp her blessings the closer.'

CR's last work was published in 1799. *Destination* is concerned with the education of the Bartlett children, and includes the firm advice that children should be guided in the directions of their natural aptitudes.

RUTH ROSENBERG

Works: *Original Poems on Several Occasions* (1769); *The Champion of Virtue: A Gothic Story* (1777; republished as *The Old English Baron*, 1778); *The Two Mentors: A Modern Story* (1783); *The Progress of Romance* (1785); *The Exiles, or, Memoirs of the Count de Cronstadt* (1788); *Plans of Education* (1792); *Memoirs of Sir Roger de Clarendon* (1793); *Destination, or, Memoirs of a Private Family* (1799).
References: Ashley-Montague, M. F., 'Imaginary conversations', *The Times Literary Supplement* (27 January 1940); Barbauld, A. L., 'Clara Reeve', *An Essay on the Origin and Progress of Novel Writing* (1820); *DNB*; Scott, Sir W., 'Clara Reeve', in *Sir Walter Scott on Novelists and Fiction*, ed. J. Williams (1968); Todd; Trainer, J., 'Introduction' to *The Old English Baron* (1969); Williams, S. T., 'The Story of Gebir', *PMLA* 36 (1921).

Renault, Mary

b. 4 September 1905, London; d. 13 December 1983, Cape Town, South Africa

Novelist

MR, one of the most popular historical novelists of her generation, was the eldest daughter of Frank and Mary Newsome Challans. At the time of her birth her father was a doctor in London's East End. MR was educated at Clifton High School in Bristol and at St Hugh's College, Oxford, where she took a degree in English. She made her decision to be a writer at an early age and for this reason rejected a career in teaching, the usual work for women graduates at the time, for fear that it would dig 'too deep into the sources of creation'. Instead, she trained as a nurse for three years at the Radcliffe Infirmary in Oxford and finished as an SRN in 1936. After her training, MR left nursing to write her first novel, *Purposes of Love* (1939), a hospital romance, and continued writing while she served as a nurse during the Second World War. Her early novels were all contemporary love stories. They had some success and one of them, *Return to Night* (1947), won an MGM prize of $150,000. Though the novel was never finished, the money gave MR her independence and in 1948 she emigrated to South Africa with her lifelong friend and companion, Julie Mullard, a fellow-nurse whom MR met during the war. They lived together in South Africa for the rest of MR's life. MR was politically active as a member of the Progressive Party and was a constant opponent of apartheid. While she served as the president of the South African PEN and was a Fellow of the Royal Society of Literature, she avoided publicity and objected strongly to the cult of the literary personality which she regarded as 'insidious'.

MR's most important fiction appeared after she left England. *The Charioteer*

(1953), which the author regarded as her first mature work, was the last of her six novels set in the modern period. It is an exceptionally acute and sympathetic study of a young British soldier coming to terms with the ethical implications of his homosexuality. MR's next novel, the highly praised *The Last of the Wine* (1956), was set in classical Greece and marked a turning point in her fiction which was, subsequently, all located in the ancient world. The novel is narrated by Alexis, a young man who lives through the turmoil of the Third Peloponnesian War, and features reconstructions of such historical figures as Socrates, Alcibiades, and Plato. MR pays great attention not only to detailed presentation of everyday life, but, more importantly, to a subtle analysis of her narrator's intimate response to issues of philosophy, loyalty, justice, war, and homosexuality as part of his experience. The combination of a highly crafted realist style, a close scrutiny of individual sensibilities emphasized by the use of first-person narrators, and attention to particularly contentious and dangerous twentieth-century issues, filtered through the distancing medium of the historical imagination, became the successful hallmarks of MR's novels.

The two books that follow *The Last of the Wine*, *The King Must Die* (1958) and *The Bull from the Sea* (1962), are probably MR's most popular productions. Both are narrated by Theseus, and MR, profoundly influenced by Robert Graves's theories regarding Greek mythology, is particularly concerned to chart the change from primitive matriarchy to modern patriarchy in religious and political practice in these novels. MR's detailed research provides a wealth of believable detail for a highly sophisticated analysis of a society undergoing a cultural revolution through changes in the status of the sexes.

The Mask of Apollo (1966) and *The Praise Singer* (1978) respectively give the life stories of an actor and a bard in ancient Greece and concentrate on the wide significance of aesthetic activity. MR's last major project, however, was the *Alexander Trilogy*, comprised of *Fire from Heaven* (1970), *The Persian Boy* (1972), and *Funeral Games* (1981). The trilogy follows the career of Alexander the Great and ranges from his boyhood in Macedonia to the aftermath of his wars of conquest. In these novels the historical canvas widens to encompass the whole of the ancient Near East, but MR's characteristic concerns with individual response to urgent social issues remains. Particularly impressive is the way in which these novels, especially *The Persian Boy*, deal with the subjects of racism and national identity in the context of a ramshackle empire held together by one individual's desire and will. To the end, MR's emphasis on the importance of tolerance combined with responsibility, together with an unflinching consciousness of the human capacity for cruelty, provided the basis for her intensely engaged and highly readable fiction.   KATE FULLBROOK

Works: *Purposes of Love* (1939); *Kind Are Her Answers* (1940); *The Friendly Young Ladies* (1944); *Return to Night* (1947); *North Face* (1948); *The Charioteer* (1953); *The Last of the Wine* (1956); *The King Must Die* (1958); *The Bull from the Sea* (1962); *The Lion in the Gateway: Heroic Battles of the Greeks and Persians at Marathon, Salamis, and Thermopylae* (1964); *The Mask of Apollo* (1966); *Fire From Heaven* (1970); *The Persian Boy* (1972); *The Nature of Alexander* (1975); *The Praise Singer* (1978); 'The fiction of history', *London Magazine* (18 March 1979); *Funeral Games* (1981).

References: Burns, L. C., 'Men are only men', *Critique*, 6, 3 (1964); Chambers, D. D. C., 'Mary Renault', in *Contemporary Novelists*, ed. J. Vinson (1976); Dick, B. F., *The Hellenism of Mary Renault* (1972); Heilbrun, C. G., 'Axiothea's grief: the disability of the female imagination', in *From Parnassus: Essays in Honour of Jacques Barzun*, ed. D. B. Wheeler and W. R. Keylor (1976); Sweetman, D., 'A novelist in the fight against sexual oppression', *Listener* (22 April 1982); Wolfe, P., *Mary Renault* (1969).

Rendell, Ruth
b. 17 February 1930, London
Novelist
(Also writes under Barbara Vine)
Although her work is often compared to that of other mystery writers as diverse as Agatha Christie and Georges Simenon, RR defies easy classification. However, her interest in both madness and the rational solution to crime link her to the originator of the detective genre, Edgar Allan Poe. Like Poe she writes two kinds of fiction: stories that follow the disintegration of a psychotic person and his or her destructive effect on others, and stories that follow the steps by which an analytic mind can assemble and reconstruct evidence to resolve mysteries and restore social order.

Born in London, the daughter of Arthur and Ebba Alise (*née* Kruse) Grasemann, RR attended Loughton High School in Essex. From 1948 to 1952 she worked as a reporter and editor of the *Essex Express* and *Independent*. In 1950 she married Donald John Rendell, whom she divorced in 1975 and remarried in 1977. They have one son. RR's first novel, *From Doon with Death*, was published in 1964 and introduced her series detective, Inspector Reg Wexford of Kingsmarkham in Sussex. Since then she has produced an average of one novel a year, alternating the Wexford books with novels focusing on neurotic and obsessed minds such as Arthur Johnson's in *A Demon in My View*, for which she received the Gold Dagger award from the Crime Writers Association in 1976. She has also been awarded the Edgar for *The Fallen Curtain* (1974), a collection of suspense stories, and the Silver Cup for Current Crime for her Wexford novel *Shake Hands Forever* (1975). In recent years she has received the Arts Council National Book Award (1981) and the Popular Culture Association Award (1983).

Using ironic juxtaposition to relate a psychotic killer to ordinary people, RR exposes the thin barrier between madness and sanity. Her murderers are often simple people, pathetically incomplete and isolated from normal life rhythms. Trapped by fears and shames they cannot define, they in turn trap and destroy others. For her readers terror grows from two sources: waiting for an inevitable convergence of killer and victim, and recognizing how closely the two are linked to each other – and to ourselves.

To balance the nightmare world of the suspense stories, RR offers a comforting father figure in Wexford (her son suggests that he is actually based on RR's own father), who brings to the investigation of murder intelligence, empathy, tolerance, and a dogged determination to discover the truth. Tensions between members of families – between husband and wife, parent and child – are often the source of violence. Wexford's own happy marriage and amicable relations with his grown daughters create a sense of order that contrasts with the disordered lives he explores professionally. Like Simenon's Maigret, whom he resembles in many ways, Wexford would like to be a 'mender of destinies', but too often lives are irreversibly distorted. To justice RR adds understanding: to the practice of analytic detection, a recognition of the dark regions of the human psyche.   FRANCES ARNDT
Selected works: From Doon with Death (1964); *To Fear a Painted Devil* (1965); *Vanity Dies Hard* (1965); *A New Lease of Death* (1967); *Wolf to the Slaughter*

(1967); *The Secret House of Death* (1968); *The Best Man to Die* (1969); *A Guilty Thing Surprised* (1970); *No More Dying Then* (1971); *One Across, Two Down* (1971); *Murder Being Once Done* (1972); *Some Lie and Some Die* (1973); *The Face of Trespass* (1974); *Shake Hands Forever* (1975); *The Fallen Curtain* (1976); *A Demon in My View* (1976); *A Judgement in Stone* (1977); *A Sleeping Life* (1978); *Make Death Love Me* (1979); *Means of Evil and Other Stories* (1979); *The Lake of Darkness* (1980); *Put on by Cunning* (1981); *Master of the Moor* (1982); *The Fever Tree and Other Stories* (1982); *The Speaker of Mandarin* (1983); *The Killing Doll* (1984); *The Tree of Hands* (1984); *The New Girl Friend and Other Stories* (1984); *An Unkindness of Ravens* (1985); *Heartstones* (1987); *Live Flesh* (1986); *A Dark-Adapted Eye* (1986); (ed.), *A Warning to the Curious: the Ghost Stories of M. R. James* (1987); *Talking to Strange Men* (1987); *The House of Stairs* (1988).

References: Bakerman, J. S., 'Ruth Rendell', in *10 Women of Mystery*, ed. E. F. Bargainnier (1981); Bakerman, J. S., 'Ruth Rendell', in *Twentieth-Century Crime and Mystery Writers*, 2nd edn, ed. J. M. Reilly (1985); Winn, D., 'The devious mind of Ruth Rendell', *Murderess Ink* (1979).

Rhys, Jean

b. 24 August 1890, Roseau, Dominica, British West Indies; d. 14 May 1979, Exeter.

Novelist, short story writer

The daughter of a Welsh doctor, William Rees Williams, and his Scottish-Dominican wife, Minna Lockhart. JR, who was born Ella Gwendolen Rees Williams, was educated at a convent in Roseau, Dominica, until she left the island to attend the Perse School in Cambridge, England. She later studied at the Royal Academy of Dramatic Art but left after her father's death. Over her family's objections, she remained in England and worked as a chorus girl in a musical comedy company touring the provinces. Some of her later jobs included modelling, tutoring, translating, and ghostwriting a book on furniture. She began to write after her marriage in 1919 to Jean Lenglet, a Dutch-French writer who was the father of her only child Maryvonne, born in 1922. JR's relationship with Lenglet was strained by his imprisonment in 1923 for illegal entry into France, and they were later divorced. JR's marriage in 1932 to Tilden-Smith, a literary agent, ended with his sudden death in 1945. In 1947, she married Max Hamer, a cousin of Tilden-Smith, who was jailed for embezzlement in 1952 and died in 1966 after a long illness. A member of the Royal Society of Literature, JR received the Arts Council of Great Britain Award for Writers in 1967, and the W. H. Smith Award for the publication of *Wide Sargasso Sea*, and she became a CBE in 1978.

JR wrote for many years before Ford Madox Ford encouraged her to publish her first work, *The Left Bank and Other Stories* (1927). These stories, and most of her later works as well, depict her experiences as a child growing up in Dominica and as a young woman living in London and Paris. Although life and art come close in her work, her prose transcends autobiography by capturing the impressions of an unrepresented class in literature. In his preface to *The Left Bank*, Ford characterized JR's innovation as 'an almost lurid! – [sic] passion for stating the case of the underdog'. Ford also praised her sensitive ear for dialogue and her careful eye for form in fiction, qualities that reveal JR's conviction that one must write from life in order to portray truth in fiction. As she stated in a 1968 interview, 'I am the only truth I know.'

In the four novels written in the 1920s and 1930s JR describes the same lonely female figure at different stages of life. In her first novel *Postures* (JR preferred the American title *Quartet*), she presents the *ménage à trois* of an English couple and Marya Zelli, a young married woman whose husband has been jailed. Seen by critics to be *roman à clef* of the difficult relationship of JR, Ford, and Ford's common-law wife Stella Bowen, the novel describes the cruel treatment of the unprotected single woman by 'respectable' people, a theme that recurs often in JR's works. In her second novel, *After Leaving Mr Mackenzie*, the former mistress of the title character has been pensioned off by her lover and ekes out a lonely existence in a Paris hotel room. The typical JR heroine ends up alone, friendless, and broke, without the protection of a man. JR's own favourite of the early novels, *Voyage in the Dark*, is the story of a chorus girl taken as mistress by an older man and then discarded when she asserts her independence. In JR's fictional world, women who abhor the hypocrisy of respectability are always at odds with those who have law and money on their side, usually men. Women of a certain type struggle desperately for money that provides them with security, but lose or spend money freely when they have it. Although the ageing Sasha Jansen in *Good Morning, Midnight* manages, through the generosity of a friend, to live well during a trip to Paris, she cannot let down her guard to trust a gigolo who reveals himself to be as vulnerable as she is. Sasha's experiences with love have scarred her and left her emotionally bankrupt. Reissued after the success of *Wide Sargasso Sea*, JR's early novels gained a wider audience in the 1960s and 1970s; critics pointed out that she had been a pioneer in addressing the difficulties faced by a single woman in a male-dominated society, although JR herself revealed in interviews that she opposed a strictly feminist reading of her fiction.

JR receded from public view in the 1940s and 1950s and lived in obscurity in Cornwall; she was rediscovered in 1957 when the BBC produced a radio version of *Good Morning, Midnight* and placed an advertisement in the *New Statesman* seeking its author. She had worked for years on a number of short stories and a novel based on the character of Antoinette Cosway, based on the mad wife of Rochester in Charlotte Brontë's *Jane Eyre*. Characteristically searching for the most appropriate words for her ideas, JR rewrote the novel many times with some chapters having as many as eleven versions. Her careful craftsmanship forbade her from publishing what she considered to be inferior work, and she continued to revise the manuscript of *Wide Sargasso Sea* until its publication in 1966, when it was much acclaimed. JR said she wrote the story of the Caribbean-born Antoinette in order to revise Brontë's nineteenth-century interpretation of the West Indian woman and to vindicate the madwoman in the attic. *Wide Sargasso Sea* is a painfully compelling story of violence and madness that questions the definition of the word 'primitive' in classifying English and Caribbean culture. While her earlier novels present the alienation of the foreigner in a European setting, the portrayal of Antoinette centres on the distorted view of Caribbean culture held by the English and the ambiguous status of the white West Indian who is not at home in either culture.

In the last years of her life, JR published two collections of short stories and worked on her autobiography. These collections of short stories are technically superior to her first book, which JR felt did not merit republication although she allowed selected stories to reappear in *Tigers Are Better-Looking*. The later stories in this collection are more developed and polished than the earlier sketches, but JR continued to focus on the themes of the struggling unmarried woman and the alienated West Indian in England subject to British prejudices.

In her last book, *Sleep It Off, Lady*, JR ordered the stories chronologically according to the stages of her life. Stories of the Caribbean are followed by those of England, and the collection ends with the story of an old woman reviled by the inhabitants of a small English village. In her unfinished autobiography, *Smile Please*, JR described the real-life versions of some of these stories and revealed how closely her work is tied to her life. She refused to have her biography written.

Called by A. Alvarez in 1974 'the best living English novelist', JR has been compared to Françoise Sagan in her ability to portray sadness. Although in her youth a voracious reader of Byron and Dickens, JR did not in later years keep up with other writers' work and she thus remained outside literary movements. Her contribution to literature bridges two traditions, the British and the Caribbean, but she does not rest securely in either. Her work is at its best when it treats those who do not belong anywhere and those who spit in the face of respectability.   CAROL COLATRELLA

Works: *The Left Bank and Other Stories* (1927); (trans.). *Perversity*, by Francis Carco (1928); *Postures* (1928; published in the US as *Quartet*, 1929); *After Leaving Mr Mackenzie* (1931); (trans.), *Barred*, by Edward de Nève (Jean Lenglet) (1932); *Voyage in the Dark* (1934); *Good Morning, Midnight* (1939); *Wide Sargasso Sea* (1966); *Tigers Are Better-Looking, with a Selection from The Left Bank* (1968); *Penguin Modern Stories I* (1969); *My Day* (1975); *Sleep It Off, Lady* (1976); *Smile Please: An Unfinished Autobiography* (1979); *The Letters of Jean Rhys*, ed. F. Wyndham and D. Athill Melly (1984); *Collected Short Stories* (1986).

References: Benstock, S., *Women of the Left Bank* (1987); *CA*; James, L., *Jean Rhys* (1978); O'Connor, T. F., *Jean Rhys: The West Indian Novels* (1986); Plante, D., *Difficult Women* (1983); Staley, T., *Jean Rhys* (1979); Wolfe, P., *Jean Rhys* (1980).

Richardson, Dorothy

b. 17 May 1873, Abingdon, Berkshire; d. 17 June 1957, Beckenham, Kent

Novelist, journalist, translator

DR was the third of the four daughters of Mary Miller Taylor and Charles Richardson, a grocer and wine-merchant who, on the death of his father, sold the family business to become a self-styled 'gentleman'. An aspiring intellectual, he joined the British Association for the Advancement of Science, and DR, to whom he referred as his 'son', accompanied him to the meetings. She attended private schools in Abingdon and Worthing, and when the family moved to Putney in 1883 she was taught for a year by a governess whose mode of 'female education', consisting of 'the minimum of knowledge and a smattering of various "accomplishments" ', she found to be 'torment unmitigated'. After this, however, she was sent to Southborough House (now Southwest London College), Putney, where the headmistress was a disciple of Ruskin, and the curriculum included logic and psychology.

In 1891, when her father's bankruptcy was imminent, DR left home to become a pupil-teacher at a finishing school in Hanover. Her experiences there were later to provide material for *Pointed Roofs* (1915), the first volume of her long autobiographical novel, *Pilgrimage*, published in its complete form in 1967. Returning to Britain after six months, she taught for a year and a half at the Miss Ayres' school in Finsbury Park, north London – the setting of *Backwater* (1916). In 1895 she gave up a post as governess to a wealthy family in order to tend to her mother who was suffering from acute depression. In November of that year she returned home to find that her mother had committed suicide by cutting her throat with a kitchen-knife.

In 1896, DR started a new life in London as secretary to a Harley Street dentist, taking an attic room in Endsleigh Street on the fringe of Bloomsbury. Here she met, among others, the Russian Jew Benjamin Grad, on whom was based Michael Shatov in *Deadlock* (1921), and the free-thinker Charles Daniels, and involved herself in diverse intellectual and religious activities, including those of the Fabians, the Anarchists, the Zionists, and the local women's club, the Arachne. Here, too, she made contact with her old schoolfriend Amy Robbins, then married to H. G. Wells. Thus began a lifelong friendship with Wells, who becomes Hypo G. Wilson in *Pilgrimage*, introduced in *The Trap* (1919).

By 1903 DR had begun to write in her spare time for Charles Daniels's unconventional monthly, *Ye Crank*. In 1904, she fell ill through stress and overwork, and her employer paid for her convalescence in the Swiss Alps (the setting of *Oberland*, 1927, which was nominated for the Femina-Vie-Heureuse prize). In 1906, she gave up her secretarial job for a journalistic career. An affair with Wells in the same year resulted in pregnancy and miscarriage, driving her to the edge of nervous collapse. A recuperative stay on a Quaker farm in Sussex was to be the source of her first imaginative writing, a series of descriptive sketches appearing in *The Saturday Review* in 1908; also, much later, it was to provide the setting of *Dimple Hill* (1938). The Quakers' search for a 'centre of being', and their recognition of a woman's 'spiritual identity', were to be central to the preoccupations of *Pilgrimage*.

Many of the reviews and polemical articles that DR wrote during this period were linked to Wells's scientific and political speculations – Wells dedicated *The Future in America* (1906) to DR. She also began, in 1911, to contribute to dental magazines. It was not until she was nearly 40, while staying with J. D. Beresford in St Ives, Cornwall, that she began *Pilgrimage*, the thirteen-volume novel which was to occupy her intermittently for the rest of her life. The manuscript of the first volume, *Pointed Roofs*, completed early in 1913, was initially rejected. Setting it aside, DR proceeded to publish two books on the Quakers and three translations from French and German. Eventually, *Pointed Roofs* was sent to Duckworth, whose reader Edward Garnett approved it as 'feminine impressionism'. It was published in September 1915, by which time Joyce had just begun to write *Ulysses* (1922). Proust's *Du Côté de Chez Swann* had appeared in France less than two years previously.

In the summer of 1915, DR settled at 32 Queen's Terrace, St John's Wood, where her fellow lodger was the young artist Alan Odle, whom she married in 1917 when she was 44. Throughout their married life they spent the summers in Queen's Terrace and the rest of the year in Cornwall. In 1939 DR was granted a civil list pension of £100. After the death of her husband in 1948, she continued to live and write in Cornwall until 1954, when she was taken to a nursing home in Beckenham, Kent.

Pilgrimage has been acclaimed as the first 'stream of consciousness' novel in English, its first volumes predating Joyce's *Ulysses* and Woolf's *Jacob's Room* (both published in 1922). It was May Sinclair who, in her reviews of DR's work, first adapted William James's term 'stream of consciousness' to literary criticism, but DR herself resented the term in that it neglected, in its emphasis on flux and dynamism, her belief that 'a literary work, for reader and writer alike, remains essentially an adventure of the stable contemplative human consciousness'. *Pilgrimage* is a quest for what DR calls 'the unchanging centre of being in our painfully evolving selves'.

All the events of *Pilgrimage* are filtered through the consciousness of Miriam Henderson, whose experiences correspond to those of DR's own life between 1891 and 1915. This is consonant with DR's belief that a novel is best understood as a 'psychological study of the author'. Yet at the same time *Pilgrimage* aspires to the status of an autonomous work of art; it centres around a protagonist who both is and is not her creator, in that Miriam is just one of the many 'selves' that DR might have created. In confining herself solely to Miriam's consciousness, DR acknowledged her debt to Henry James's use of 'point of view' in *The Ambassadors*, which she had read on its appearance in 1903. DR's own technique, however, is more radically experimental than James's, in that all Miriam's reflections are mediated through indirect and, increasingly in later volumes, direct monologue. Predictably, many of the early critics of *Pilgrimage* found DR's method unhealthily introspective: the *Saturday Review* called it 'fictional pathology', and D. H. Lawrence accused DR, together with Proust and Joyce, of a morbid self-consciousness, of 'stripping their smallest emotions to the finest threads'.

DR differentiated her own work from that of Proust, whom she read in 1922, by arguing that Proust wrote 'about consciousness'. She also denied any direct influence of Bergson on her experiences with time and consciousness, though she conceded that Bergson had succeeded in 'putting into words something then dawning within the human consciousness: an increased sense of inadequacy of the clock as a time measurer'. Throughout *Pilgrimage*, the external world is only meaningful in conjunction with subjective states, and the structuring principle of the novel is not so much chronology as the bringing into relationship of meaningful moments. DR explains how her work, in its merging of subject and object, is neither 'romance' nor 'realism' in the traditionally accepted senses.

The central encounter in *Pilgrimage* is that between Miriam and Hypo G. Wilson (based on Wells). The differences in their outlook mirror the differences between what DR sees as an essentially 'male' vision and the distinctively feminine consciousness which her own novel attempts to articulate. Hypo's world is a future-directed world of 'ceaseless "becoming" '; his ambition is such that he is caught in a stifling linearity, where Miriam is in search of the 'perfect present'. Further, where *Pilgrimage* attempts an investigation of the complexity of individual identity (Miriam's name suggests that she is constituted of a myriad of reflections and intuitions), Wilson/Wells's social visions make no distinction, as Miriam complains, between biological and spiritual categories: people are for Wells simply units, or members of a species. DR separates herself both from Wells's 'levelling' of humanity and from the Suffragettes' campaign for equal rights (represented in *Pilgrimage* by the character of Amabel, who is based on DR's militant Suffragette friend Veronica Leslie-Jones). She refuses to believe that women have ever been 'subject': 'Disabilities, imposed by law, are a stupid insult to women,' she concedes, 'but have never touched them as individuals.' Her feminism involves rather an affirmation of a specifically female experience and world-view. Miriam must make Hypo aware, as she tells us, of 'the reality that fell, all the time, in the surrounding silences, outside his shapes and classifications'. Such a quest for the ideational allies DR with other Modernist writers like Joyce and Virginia Woolf.

Further, Miriam argues that, where men think 'only one thing at a time', women 'have so much more to control . . . By seeing everything simultaneously'. If a woman becomes 'a partisan, a representative . . . of one only of the many sides of the question', she has 'abdicated' her sex. In general, a woman cannot help but respond to 'the human demand', which 'besieging her wherever she is', clamours for what DR calls an 'inclusive awareness'. DR investigates this problem in her polemical article 'Women in the Arts', which, four years before Woolf's *A Room of One's Own* (1929), argues that women require certain 'absolute conditions' in order to be able to write; unlike men, they do not have devoted wives or mistresses to minister to their needs.

Women can, however, turn their all-embracing vision to their advantage by making it the very material of a new kind of art. At a time when Joyce's *A Portrait of the Artist as a Young Man* (1914–15) was appearing in *The Egoist*, DR's parallel project was the portrait of a *woman* struggling towards artistic expression. Miriam's reflections constitute a pilgrimage both towards an 'inclusive awareness' and towards the act of writing, in that such an awareness is, for DR, the proper material of art. Towards the end of the last volume, *March Moonlight* (1967), Miriam embarks upon the novel which DR herself is about to renounce. In order to articulate her feminine aesthetic, DR evolves what Woolf has called 'the psychological sentence of the feminine gender', and DR herself explains in the Foreword to *Pilgrimage* that 'feminine prose . . . should properly be unpunctuated, moving from point to point without formal obstructions'. Many of the early readers of *Pilgrimage* found the text bewildering in its sudden shifts of tense and person – often within a single reflection – and in its unconventional syntax and punctuation.

Miriam's all-embracing receptivity conflicts, however, with an equally powerful desire for autonomy, a need to preserve an integrity of self threatened by unsatisfactory relationships, by the emotional claims of others. She asserts that 'The attainment of full womanhood was farewell, a lonely treading of a temple, surrounded by outcasts'. The events of *Pilgrimage* suggest that authenticity or internal freedom is at the price of withdrawal and isolation, in that a woman's identity is created in defiance of the categories and institutions built around her by men. ANNE FERNIHOUGH

Selected works: Pilgrimage: Pointed Roofs (1915); *Backwater* (1916); *Honeycomb* (1917); *The Tunnel* (1919); *Interim* (1919); *Deadlock* (1921); *Revolving Lights* (1923); *The Trap* (1925); *Oberland* (1927); *Dawn's Left Hand* (1931); *Clear Horizon* (1935); *Pilgrimage* (including *Dimple Hill*), 4 vols (1938); *Pilgrimage* (including *March Moonlight*), 4 vols (1967); *The Quakers Past and Present* (1914); *Gleanings from the Works of George Fox* (1914); *John Austen and the Inseparables* (1930); 'Women in the arts: some notes on the eternally conflicting demands of humanity and art', *Vanity Fair* 24 (May 1925); 'Beginnings: a brief sketch', in *Ten Contemporaries: Notes Towards Their Definitive Bibliography*, 2nd series (1933); 'Seven letters from Dorothy M. Richardson', *Yale University Library Gazette* 33 (January 1959); 'Data for a Spanish publisher', *London Magazine* 6 (June 1959).

References: Adam International Review 31 (issue devoted to Proust and DR) (1967); Blake, C.R., *Dorothy M. Richardson* (1960); Edel, L., *The Modern Psychological Novel 1900–1950* (1955); Fromm, G., *Dorothy Richardson: A Biography* (1977); Gregory, H., *Dorothy Richardson: An Adventure in Self-Discovery* (1967); Kaplan, S.J., *Feminine Consciousness in the Modern British Novel* (1975); Powys, J.C., *Dorothy M. Richardson* (1931); Rosenberg, J., *Dorothy Richardson: The Genius They Forgot* (1973); Sinclair, M., 'The novels of Dorothy Richardson', *Egoist* (April 1918); Sinclair, M., 'The novels of Dorothy Richardson', *Little*

Review 4 (April 1918); Staley,T.F., *Dorothy Richardson* (1976); Wells, H.G., *Experiment in Autobiography* (1934).

Richardson, Henry Handel

b. 1870, Melbourne, Australia; d. 1946, Fairlight, East Sussex

Novelist

HHR (Ethel Robertson) was the elder daughter of an Irish doctor and an English mother who had emigrated to Australia during the Victorian gold rush. In 1874, her mother worked as a postmistress in small gold-mining towns. HHR was educated at the Presbyterian Ladies College in Melbourne. In 1888 she went to study music in Leipzig, where she met George John Robertson, a philologist, whom she married in 1895. In 1904, on her husband's appointment as professor of German at London University, she moved to London where she lived (apart from one six-week visit to her native Australia in 1912) until his death in 1933. She then moved to Sussex with a companion, Olga Roncoroni.

HHR assumed her pen-name partly because she wanted her novels to be considered 'masculine'. Her first book, the experimental and often uneven *Bildunsgsroman, Maurice Guest* (1908), transmuted many of her own experiences into those of her male protagonist, a provincial English music student in Leipzig. It is a story of fatal passion and thwarted ambition and, in its insistent analysis of the degeneration of a personality, it reflects the uncertainties which had characterized HHR's early life. Its themes of provincialism, artistic development and sexual awakening are also explored in HHR's more controlled second novel, *The Getting of Wisdom* (1910). Based on her schooldays, the book portrays the assimilation into a conformist society of a young, imaginative girl who learns to direct her individualism into conventional channels. HHR's psychological insight is blended with a perceptive social commentary in this study of the tensions of adolescence and contemporary moral hypocrisy.

HHR's most ambitious work was her epic trilogy *The Fortunes of Richard Mahony* (1917–29) which used her family history, and in particular her parents' marriage, as a paradigm of the growth of Australia in the nineteenth century. Mahony's speculations, his material success and his sudden downfall are matched against the flowering and the deterioration of his marriage and his health, to form a penetrating analysis of the economic development of a society and its effects on personal values. Through her portrayal of Mahony, the restless spirit seeking elusive satisfaction, HHR created a powerful myth of the emergent society and its struggle for identity, investing local, domestic themes with wider historical and philosophical significance.

The Young Cosima (1939), HHR's last novel, sustained her abiding interest in the nature of ambition, the idea of the outsider and the tortured personality. She began but never completed her autobiography, *Myself When Young* (1948). HHR's Australian origins determined the direction of her literary career: an interest in provincialism, in rootlessness, and in the processes of history are the features which mark her work, as well as her refusal to be categorized as a writer with recognizably 'feminine' interests.   JUDY SIMONS

Works: *Maurice Guest* (1910); *The Getting of Wisdom* (1910); *The Fortunes of Richard Mahony*: vol. 1, *Australia Felix* (1917); vol. 2, *The Way Home* (1925); vol. 3, *Ultima Thule* (1929); *Two Studies* (1931); *The End of a Childhood and Other Stories* (1934); *The Young Cosima* (1939); *Myself When Young* (1948).

References: Buckley, V., *Henry Handel Richardson* (1973); Elliott, W. D., *Henry Handel Richardson* (1975); McLeod, K., *Henry Handel Richardson: A Critical Study*

(1985); Palmer, N., *Henry Handel Richardson: A Study* (1950); Roberston, J. G., 'The art of Henry Handel Richardson', in *Myself When Young* (1948); Walsh, W. (ed.), *Readings in Commonwealth Literature: Henry Handel Richardson* (1973); Wittrock, V. D., 'Henry Handel Richardson: an annotated bibliography of writings about her', *English Literature in Transition* 7 (1964).

Riddell, Mrs J. H.
b. 1832, Carrickfergus, near Belfast; d. 1906, Hounslow
Novelist, short story writer
(Also wrote under R. V. Sparling, Rainey Hawthorne, and F. G. Trafford)
CR's father James Cowan was High Sheriff of County Antrim and her early childhood was spent in affluence in a large house and grounds. The affluence vanished when her father suffered a breakdown and became an invalid; he died when CR (Charlotte) was 21. For a few years mother and daughter lived penuriously in Ireland; in 1855 they went to London where CR, who had been writing poetry and novels since childhood, hoped to earn a living as a writer. The winter that followed was severe and her miserable experiences tramping around editorial offices and writing through chilly nights are caught in her fourth novel, *The Rich Husband* (1858). Publishers' stinginess and pro-crastination were added to 'that unvarying urbanity which is enough to drive a rejected author out of his senses'. Despite her difficulties, she managed to publish her first novel under a pseudonym in 1856, *Zuriel's Grandchild*. After her mother died of cancer, she married Joseph Hadley Riddell in 1857. He was a civil engineer and inventor who seems to have lacked business sense and who possibly went to prison; his financial collapse is suggested in his wife's novel *Mortomley's Estate* (1874) which describes the disastrous workings of the Bank-ruptcy Act of 1866. Again CR was forced to provide the living and she wrote much to pay his debts about which she was extremely punctilious. Riddell aided her work by providing information from the world of technology and business unknown to most women writers, and the marriage itself no doubt fuelled the pictures of marital disasters and the numerous analyses of financial collapse. To earn her living, CR wrote at least forty-six novels, as well as numerous short stories and articles. In 1880 Joseph died leaving new debts and, after she had paid them off, CR was poor again. No longer in fashion, she made little in her final years and had to seek relief from the Society of Authors. She died of cancer.

In general CR made clear moral points and gave her plots and characters a thick texture of detail. She described the minutiae of crafts and trades such as greengrocery and dyeing, and the nuances of social status. Many of her fictional works were set in London – she was known as the Novelist of the City – and she had a major fictional success with *George Geith of Fen Court* (1864), a romantic Gothic novel that depicts the financial world of London; dramatized, it retained its popularity throughout the 1880s. CR also described the rapid material changes in the metropolis, the upheaval of the railways and the sprawl-ing growth of the suburbs. In her novels she created many memorable charac-ters, such as the naive musical country girl tugged in opposite directions by contrasting environments who narrates *Home, Sweet Home* (1873), the wife who has to run the family business and cope with legal sharks in *Mortomley's Estate*, the older woman who tries to buy the love of a young man in *Miss Gascoyne* (1887) (possibly there is some autobiographical resonance here since CR was at the time of writing associated with a young man, A. H. Norway), the foolish and selfish Connors who find that their characters are more of a curse than any family ghost in *The Nun's Curse* (1888), and the kindly embezzling lawyer in *The Head of the Firm* (1892). CR's four supernatural tales appeared in Routledge's *Christmas Annuals* for family amusement. She wrote many other short ghost stories; six of the best were collected as *Weird Stories* in 1882. The ghost story especially suited her writing temperament since the mid-Victorian version, not particulary fantastic, worked to set the supernatural within a detailed realistic framework and typically concentrated on the less flamboyant sorts of experience like prophetic dreams and extra-sensory perception which were under serious investigation at the time. An example is 'Nut Bush Farm' which appeared in *Weird Stories*; it tells the tale of a ghost drawing attention to a murder, but more insistently it concentrates on the situation of a commonsensical male narrator with a nervous wife and child who is made uneasy by his manly landlady without 'a single feminine belonging' and by the rumour that the dead man left his wife and children on the parish to run off with a young girl; immediately he thinks of his 'poor wife and the little lad' and wonders about his own capabilities. Again in 'Old Mrs Jones' there is a murder demanding justice, but much of the story concerns the stupidity of pointless and lazy charity and the need for wives to save money in good times, a point made intrusively and lengthily by the author who castigates weakness as much as greed and ambition since the domestic results may be worse. As in the previous tale, the horror of the parish equals the horror of the ghost.

As a novelist CR was less good, obviously writing in haste for deadlines, pulled into sensationalist and sentimental modes that did not suit her robust, realistic, and moralizing bent, as in *The Mystery in Palace Gardens* (1880) and *A Life's Assize* (1871) about an accidental murder that blights a clergyman's life. Consequently she is often more successful in minor characters than in the central stereotypical ones and at setting rather than plot. Her shorter tales are similarly a mixture of moralizing, realistic economic and psychological detail and predictable sensation, and in most of these works, as in the novels, she raises more questions than she settles. The extent to which she must sometimes have been writing against the grain of her literary talent and temperament is suggested by her attitude to Christmas: through the annuals she derived much income from the compulsory nature of the Victorian festive season; yet in 'The Miseries of Christmas' in *On the Cards, Routledge's Christmas Annual* (1867) she complained of the commercialization and coercion of a time when 'in the dull, dead, heavy Christmas weather every disagreeable [thing] which the close of a year can furnish is heaped together to make a cairn over the grave of merriment'.

JANET TODD

Selected works: *Zuriel's Grandchild* (1856; republished as *Joy after Sorrow*, 1873); *The Ruling Passion* (1857); *The Rich Husband* (1858); *The Moors and the Fens* (1858); *Too Much Alone* (1860); *City and Suburb* (1861); *The World in the Church* (1861); *George Geith of Fen Court* (1864); *Maxwell Drewitt* (1865); *Phemie Keller* (1866); *The Race for Wealth* (1866); *Far above Rubies* (1867); *Austin Friars* (1870); *A Life's Assize* (1871); *The Earl's Promise* (1873); *Home, Sweet Home* (1873); *Mortomley's Estate* (1874); *Frank Sinclair's Wife and Other Stories* (1874); *The Uninhabited House (Routledge's Christmas Annual,* 1875); *Her Mother's Darling* (1877); *The Disappearance of Mr Jeremiah Redworth (Routledge's Christmas Annual,* 1878); *The Mystery in Palace Gardens* (1880); *Alaric Spenceley, or, A High Ideal* (1881); *The Senior Partner* (1882); *Daisies and Buttercups* (1882); *The Prince of Wales's Garden Party and Other Stories* (1882); *Weird Stories* (1882); *Struggle for Fame* (1883); *Berna Boyle: A Love Story of the County Down* (1884); *Mitre Court:*

A Tale of the Great City (1885); *For Dick's Sake* (1886); *Miss Gascoyne* (1887); *Idle Tales* (1888); *The Nun's Curse* (1888); *Princess Sunshine and Other Stories* (1889); *A Mad Tour, or, A Journey Undertaken in an Insane Moment through Central Europe on Foot* (1891); *The Head of the Firm* (1892); *The Rusty Sword, or, Thereby Hangs a Tale* (1893); *A Silent Tragedy* (1893); *The Banshee's Warning and Other Tales* (1894); *Did He Deserve It?* (1897); *A Rich Man's Daughter* (1895); *Handsome Phil and Other Stories* (1899); *The Footfall of Fate* (1900); *Poor Fellow!* (1902). **References:** Bleiler, E. F., 'Introduction' to *The Collected Ghost Stories of Mrs J. H. Riddell* (1977); Cross, N., *The Common Writer: Life in Nineteenth-century Grub Street* (1985); Ellis, S. M., *Wilkie Collins, LeFanu and Others* (1931); Furniss, H., *Some Notable Women* (1923).

Ritchie, Lady (Anne Thackeray)

b. 9 June 1837, Kensington, London; d. 26 February 1919, Freshwater, Isle of Wight

Novelist, short story writer, essayist

One of AR's earliest recollections is of escaping the family residence to join other children dancing to music on the London streets: 'Someone walking by came and lifted me up bodily on to his shoulder, and carried me away from the charming organ to my home, which was close by.' This 'stranger' was her father, William Makepeace Thackeray, then 'writing for his life', as Thomas Carlyle reported. Her mother, Isabella Gethin Shawe, suffered acute mental illness, probably schizophrenia, and spent most of her life in care. 'Annie' and her younger sister 'Minnie' joined their grandparents in Paris in 1840, a removal of enduring cultural and political significance for the girls. In her *Chapters from Some Memoirs* (1894) AR counts among her formative experiences the funeral procession of Napoleon and her meetings with Chopin and the Provençal poet Jacques Boé. Her growth from childhood to womanhood was undoubtedly shaped by a sense of uprootedness but also by a maturing cosmopolitanism and a sympathy for the French people which set her apart from the francophobic, increasingly nationalistic Victorian English. 'Paris is all my youth,' she wrote in a letter of 1891.

When Thackeray was not lecturing in America, the children lived in Kensington, entertaining such eminent guests as Leigh Hunt and Charlotte Brontë, attending their father's lectures and sharing the happy prospect of Christmas with the Dickens family. After Thackeray's death in 1863, AR joined 'the green and sunshiny little republic' founded by Tennyson and Julia Margaret Cameron in Freshwater, Isle of Wight. Her story 'From an Island' is a fictional recreation of this artistic coterie, and a letter written to John Millais in Easter 1865 alludes to 'King Alfred' reading *Maud* ('it was like a harmonious thunder and lightning'). Other friends and correspondents included Swinburne, Ruskin, and the Brownings; ATR helped Browning to shape his *Red Cotton Night-Cap Country* (1873) and wrote the *DNB* entry for Elizabeth Barrett.

George Eliot was one of the few friends to welcome her marriage to Richmond Ritchie, her second cousin and godson, seventeen years her junior, in August 1877. Two children were born to the couple during their residence in Kensington: Hester Helena Thackeray and William Thackeray Denis. AR's most active years as a writer were those preceding her marriage; afterwards she produced mainly biographical sketches and reminiscences, including the essays on women writers in *A Book of Sibyls* (1883) and her study of Madame de Sévigné (1881). In the 1890s she contributed a series of memoirs to *Macmillan's*

Magazine and worked on the celebrated Biographical Edition of *The Works of William Makepeace Thackeray*. In 1903 she was elected a Fellow of the Royal Society of Literature and was the first woman to enjoy the distinction of being a member of the Academic Committee of the Society. From 1912 to 1913 she was President of the English Association, and in the summer of 1914 a group of her friends, including Henry James ('your stoutest and fondest old adherent'), commissioned a portrait of AR to be painted by John Singer Sargent. Her contribution to the war effort was tireless; she raised money for hospitals in Normandy, started clubs for soldiers' wives and organized the French Wounded Emergency Fund.

AR's early writings were largely determined by the stringent rules of propriety established in the pages of the *Cornhill Magazine*, under the editorship of her father and later of her brother-in-law Leslie Stephen. Not surprisingly, much of her serialized work was popular domestic fiction designed for the edification of the Victorian middle class, but her exposure to French ideas also had a profound impact on what she wrote. Her first novel, *The Story of Elizabeth* (1863), contrasts Victorian Anglicanism with the harsher French Protestantism of her own education in Paris. This concern with national, religious, and temperamental differences gives her writing a distinctive place in nineteenth-century fiction, but it seems likely that her stylistic tendencies owe something to the same continental ethos, as George Moore hinted when he praised *The Story of Elizabeth* in his *Confessions of a Young Man* (1888). Her second novel, *The Village on the Cliff* (1867), set in a small coastal area of Normandy, displays a more vivid impressionism in its landscape descriptions: 'The horizon is solemn dark blue, but a great streak of light crosses the sea; three white sails gleam, and so do the white caps of the peasant women, and the wings of the sea-gulls as they go swimming through the air.' *Old Kensington* (1873) looks forward to E. M. Forster's *Howards End* in its concern for an English culture which levels away 'a community of venerable elm trees and traditions' for a block of flats and a new generation of residents, but also in the 'yearning for a larger life' which its principal women characters feel. *Miss Angel* (1875), perhaps the least impressive of AR's five novels, embarks upon a strained historical reconstruction of the life of the artist Angelica Kauffmann. Her final novel, *Mrs Dymond* (1885), sets its story of love against the destructive passions of the Franco-Prussian war, which AR herself had witnessed in Paris, and introduces the admirable but misguided Jules Caron, whose revolutionary vision is betrayed by the 'wild bacchanalian crew'. Despite her early Republican sympathies, AR is finally unable to envisage a form of socialism which is not hopelessly utopian. The same compromising liberal humanism is evident in the philanthropic essays of *Toilers and Spinsters* (1874). The title essay of this collection represents what is probably her most direct contribution to the women's movement and calls attention to the plight of single, unemployed females in late Victorian England. Two 'fairy tales' – 'Cinderella' and 'The Sleeping Beauty' – in *Five Friends and a Young Prince* similarly highlight the neglect of children and the stifling of female creativity in a male-dominated world.

In her final years AR was the venerable 'Aunt Annie' of the Bloomsbury Group and provided her niece, Virginia Woolf, with the character of Mrs Hilbery in *Night and Day* (1919). In some ways AR was representative of those Victorian ideals and conventions which Bloomsbury rebelled against: 'she goes down the last, almost, of that nineteenth century Hyde Park Gate world,' Virginia Woolf reported in her diary. But she was, in many ways, a woman whose example as a writer deserved a more fitting tribute from the pen of the modernist: 'Her happiness was a domestic flame, tried by many sorrows. And the music to which she dances, frail and fantastic, but true and distinct, will sound on outside our formidable residences when all the brass bands of literature have (let us hope) blared themselves to perdition.'   STEPHEN REGAN

Works: *The Story of Elizabeth* (1863); *The Village on the Cliff* (1867); *Five Old Friends and a Young Prince* (1868); *To Esther and Other Sketches* (1869); *Old Kensington* (1873); *Bluebeard's Key and Other Stories* (1874); *Toilers and Spinsters* (1874); *Miss Angel* (1875); *Miss Williamson's Divagations* (1881); *Madame de Sévigné* (1881); *A Book of Sibyls* (1883); *Mrs Dymond* (1885); *Records of Tennyson, Ruskin and Browning* (1892); *Alfred Lord Tennyson and His Friends* (1893); *Chapters from Some Memoirs* (1894); *Blackstick Papers* (1908); *From the Porch* (1913); *Letters of Ann Thackeray Ritchie* (1924).

References: Fuller, H.T. and Hammersley, V., *Thackeray's Daughter* (1951); Gérin, W., *Ann Thackeray Ritchie: A Biography* (1981); Woolf, V., 'The enchanted organ: Anne Thackeray Ritchie', in *Collected Essays*, vol. 4 (1967).

Robertson, E. Arnot
b. 1903, Surrey; d. 1961, London
Novelist and reviewer

The daughter of a doctor, G. A. Robertson, EAR was brought up in Surrey and Notting Hill, London, and educated at Sherborne and in Paris and Switzerland. In 1927 she married Henry Turner (later knighted) who after fighting in the First World War had become General Secretary of the Empire Press Union, a position he retained until 1956. They had one son, and were an extremely close couple, with common interests in travel and sailing.

EAR's marriage was followed by the sequence of four novels in six years (1928–33) on which her reputation is largely based. *Cullum* (1928) and *Three Came Unarmed* (1929) received recognition as promising achievements from such a young author, but it was with *Four Frightened People* (1931) and *Ordinary Families* (1933) that she became a popular success. The first went into several editions and was made into a film; the second was a best-seller on both sides of the Atlantic, as well as gaining praise from critics like James Agate and Harold Nicolson.

The intervals were longer between EAR's five other novels, the last of which, *The Strangers on My Roof*, was published posthumously in 1964. She had extended the range of her activities, however, producing the children's story *Mr Cobbett and the Indians* (1942) and the illustrated *Thames Portrait* (1957) and becoming a film critic. The climax of the latter career came with a protracted and eventually unsuccessful lawsuit which she brought against MGM, who had banned her from screenings for 'hostile' reviews. She was also a regular radio broadcaster (contributing frequently to 'Woman's Hour') and lecturer.

Sir Henry Turner died in an accident on the river in April 1961. EAR committed suicide exactly five months later.

EAR's own social milieu is the English upper middle class, which she observes in her novels with a merciless eye for sentimentality and vulgarity, and a penchant for bookish men. The form of writing most natural to her is a mixture of social comedy and superior romantic fiction, with graceful descriptions of nature and pursuits like hunting and sailing. It is impressive, however, that she refuses to be satisfied with what gives her least difficulty, regularly departing from her favoured mode of the first-person female narrator, and trying out her ability to depict characters from other classes and other countries.

Her heroines tend to be young women with jobs, bright but not university-educated, emotionally wounded either at the start or the end of the novels. Their love stories provide EAR in the early work with the opportunity for a series of devastating portrayals of the courting habits of the inter-war male. The relative explicitness of the novels in sexual matters (she has been credited with the first mention of menstruation in English fiction) was one of the features that her reviewers found most striking.

Cullum, her debut, is the tale of a girl's affair with a writer who turns out to be a philanderer and a pathological liar. *Three Came Unarmed* is a variation on the myth of the innocent savage which shows three children who have been brought up in Borneo baffled and defeated by English ways. *Four Frightened People*, EAR's first best-seller, reverses the process by dropping English characters into Malaya. The narrator, Judy Corder, is a doctor travelling by sea to Singapore with her cousin Stewart. When they discover that plague is spreading through the ship they secretly escape, accompanied by Arnold Ainger, a linguist at the Foreign Office, and the intolerably loquacious Mrs Mardick. They are then forced to trek through the jungle to safety, facing threats from natural hazards and native hunters. Once the other three have coolly left Mrs Mardick behind, the novel divides its attention between the adventures of the journey and the 'Design for Living'-style romantic triangle which they form. It is the unlikely combination of a very English love story with an exotic backdrop which seems to explain the work's enormous success. The detachment with which Judy views her desires and choices made a strong impression on readers in the 1930s, as did the evocation of the jungle, which was based purely on research in the Reading Room of the British Museum.

Ordinary Families, generally regarded as EAR's finest achievement, is set in the imaginary village of Pin Mill near Ipswich on the Suffolk coast, shortly after the First World War. The narrator is Lallie (Lalage) Rush, one of four children resulting from the marriage of a well-bred beauty to an adventurer turned engineer and boat trader. The novel is a portrait of a middle-class family which is eccentric in its devotion to sailing, but ordinary, it suggests, in its private jokes and shifting interrelationships, and in 'the cross-currents that ran under the smooth surface'. Yet the title is perhaps misleading in giving the impression that it is dominated by the family theme. The centre of *Ordinary Families* is Lallie: her fluctuations of feeling towards the other Rushes over the course of her adolescence, her comic encounters with neighbouring families which are richer and more intellectual, her diminishing enjoyment of sailing, her pleasure in bird-watching, her one sphere of independence from the family, and her bewildered dealings with the opposite sex. Few studies of childhood render it so vividly without making it seem idyllic. Lallie relinquishes hers gradually, but with few regrets.

In her later work EAR continues to set herself challenges, while retaining conventional structure and the same basic style. She employs a male protagonist in two works written during the Second World War, *Summer's Lease* and *The Signpost*; and she explores other places and cultures, including Ireland, Greece, Hong Kong, and Zanzibar. But she never achieves again the integration of *Ordinary Families*, or the bizarre originality of *Four Frightened People*. And a vision which was advanced in the 1920s and 1930s appears dated by the time that its author overlaps with such figures as Muriel Spark and Iris Murdoch.

JOHN DUGDALE

Works: *Cullum* (1928); *Three Came Unarmed* (1929); *Four Frightened People* (1931); *Ordinary Families* (1933); *Thames Portrait* (1937); *Summer's Lease* (1940); *Mr*

Cobbett and the Indians (1942); *The Signpost* (1943); *Devices and Desires* (1954); *Justice of the Heart* (1958); *The Spanish Town Papers* (1959); *The Strangers on My Roof* (1964).
References: Devlin, P., 'Introductions' to *Four Frightened People* (1972) and *Ordinary Families* (1972).

Robins, Elizabeth
b. 1862, Louisville, Kentucky; d. 1952, Sussex
Novelist, essayist, actress
(Also wrote under C. E. Raimond)
ER was the eldest of the eight children of Charles E. Robins, a well-to-do New England banker, and Hannah, an artistic and emotionally unstable ex-opera singer who ended her days in an insane asylum. She spent her childhood in a country house on Staten Island, New York, until bankruptcy and her mother's illness resulted in the children being despatched to Zanesville, Ohio to live with their Southern grandmother. At the age of 16, after attending Putnam Female Seminary, she was sent to Vassar to study medicine but, rejecting this course, she ran away to New York and, using the names Claire Raymond and later Bessie Robins, she went on the stage.

Eventually she moved to Boston to become a member of the Boston Museum Company and, later, the Edwin Booth Company. In 1887 she married George Richmond Parkes, a leading man with the Boston Theater Company. They were seldom together and, after nine months of marriage, Parkes committed suicide by jumping into the Charles River in a suit of armour. It is possible that ER was pregnant and miscarried as a result of the suicide. In 1888 ER left for the London stage where she became famous for her roles in Ibsen, most notably, Hedda and Hilda. Leonard Woolf said of her, 'She was a great actress, the first, and almost certainly, the best actress of Ibsen in English.'

Together with Marion Lea, she took on the role of actress-manager, securing the performing rights of *Hedda Gabler* and *The Master Builder*, to escape the tyranny of actor-managers. During this period ER was putting her brothers through medical and law school and maintaining her mother. Pseudonymously she wrote four novels including, *George Mandeville's Husband* and the autobiographical *Open Question*. Her brother Raymond revealed her authorship, causing a rift with her family and outraging London society. She did not write another novel for eight years. In 1899 Raymond joined the Klondike Gold Rush and in 1900 was feared missing. ER, armed with a knife and a gun, travelled to Alaska to seek his whereabouts and there Raymond and ER made a pact of chastity, believing it to be vital to creativity.

On her return, still suffering from the typhoid fever she had contracted in the Klondike, she left the stage to concentrate on writing plays, articles, and novels under her own name and on her work in the suffrage movement. She was an accomplished orator and, as well as writing pamphlets and plays for the Suffragettes, she spoke at meetings, many women recording their 'conversion' to the suffrage cause after hearing her speak. In 1907 she wrote *Votes For Women*; produced at the Court Theatre, it was a great commercial success, and later that year she reworked the play into the equally successful novel, *The Convert*. The novel included the sensationalist notion of 'the woman with a secret' but the secret, once revealed, forms not her downfall, but a political lever used positively by the heroine to forward the cause of women.

ER also organized the Actresses Franchise League which worked with the suffrage movement, formed a union for actresses to write new contracts and settle disputes, ran competitions for plays on women's themes, and headed the Women Writers Suffrage League. She served on the board of the WSPU from 1907 to 1912, leaving when she became disturbed by the militancy and violence.

After the war, during which she worked as a nurse, she became a director and contributor to the newspaper *Time and Tide*. In 1924 she published *Ancilla's Share*, subtitled 'An indictment of sex-antagonism'. A comprehensive statement of feminist philosophy, which ER considered to be her most important work, it was published anonymously in order that it might get a fairer hearing. With the earnings from *Votes for Women* and *The Convert*, she and Octavia Wilberforce bought Backsettown Farm which they made into a rest home for suffragettes and women medical students. Here they brought up their adopted son, David Scott. The farm is still used today as a rest home for women. ER continued to write novels and articles, taking women's rights, race, and war as her subject matter up to her death in 1952.   SUE CORDWELL

Selected works: Alan's Wife (with Lady Bell) (1893); *George Mandeville's Husband* (1894); *Milly's Story, or, The New Moon* (1895); *Below the Salt* (1896); *The Magnetic North* (1904); *Votes for Women* (1907); *Under the Southern Cross* (1907); *Come and Find Me* (1907); *Where Are You Going To?* (1912); *Under His Roof* (1912); *Camilla* (1918); *The Mills of the Gods and Other Stories* (1920); *Ancilla's Share* (1924); *The Secret That Was Kept* (1926); *Ibsen and the Actress* (1928); *Theatre and Friendship* (1932); *Both Sides of the Curtain* (1940); *Portrait of a Lady, or, The English Spirit Old and New* (1941); *Raymond and I* (1956).

References: Drabble; Tomalin, C., *Katherine Mansfield* (1987).

Robinson, Mary

b. 27 November 1758, Bristol; d. 26 December 1800, Old Windsor

Novelist, poet, dramatist, essayist, pamphleteer

(Also wrote under Mary Darby, Tabitha Bramble, Daphne, Echo, A friend to Humanity, Julia, Horace Juvenal, Laura, Laura Maria, Louisa, Oberon, Ann Frances Randall, Sylphid)

MR is remembered chiefly for her triumphs as an actress and for her well-publicized romance with the young Prince of Wales (later George IV) rather than for her achievements as a best-selling author.

She was born Mary Darby, the third child of John Darby, an eccentric merchant, and his wife Maria Seys. Their home was near Bristol Cathedral, and as a child MR could often be found wandering down the aisles indulging in romantic melancholy among the tombs and monuments. She attended the famous school in Bristol run by Hannah More's elder sisters. Theatre trips were a feature of this excellent establishment and gave MR an early taste for the stage. Her father's desertion (to the Labrador Coast with a young woman) caused the family to move to London, where MR became a pupil of Meribah Lorington, a brilliant alcoholic, who, in her sober moments, taught MR to read widely and to write poetry. At 15 she still cherished theatrical ambitions, and was introduced to Garrick, who was enchanted by her beauty and star quality. Unfortunately she shortly afterwards met Thomas Robinson, a lecherous ne'er-do-well lawyer, and married him in April 1774. Their daughter Maria was born later that year.

Marriage placed no restraint on Robinson's gambling and womanizing; the couple were soon hopelessly in debt, and in an effort to raise money MR published her first book of poems in 1775. But it was too late to save Robinson from the debtors' prison, and MR loyally accompanied him there with the baby. She sent a copy of her verses to the Duchess of Devonshire, who generously befriended her. After the birth of a second daughter, who lived only six weeks, she concentrated on her acting career and, helped by Garrick and Sheridan, quickly rose to be one of the leading lights of Drury Lane. She excelled in Shakespearean parts, bringing to them all the fascinations of romantic sensibility. Her Ophelia never failed to move the audience to tears, and her performance as Juliet, in pink satin with silver spangles and a white feather headdress, gained thunderous applause and rave reviews.

But it was as Perdita, in the simple costume of a milkmaid, that, in 1779, she captivated the heart of the teenaged Prince of Wales, who pursued her with gifts of jewels, money, and paintings, together with vows of eternal constancy and letters signed in his own blood. MR fell deeply in love with him; fidelity, however, was not the prince's strong point: by the autumn of 1780 the royal roving eye had moved on and *The Winter's Tale* proved a gloomy tragedy for Perdita.

But 'the feeling heart must *love*, or it must *perish*', and MR soon became fatally involved with the dashing Colonel Banastre Tarleton, who boasted that he had killed more men and ruined more women than anyone else in Europe. His demolition work on MR was speedy and efficient: she became pregnant by him, and, while travelling in a coach to Dover, suffered a miscarriage that left her completely paralysed from the waist down. It was publicly stated that she had lost the use of her limbs after an attack of rheumatic fever, but the truth leaked out, causing much gossip in the press, where details of MR's affairs (with descriptions of her ravishing wardrobe) were regularly chronicled. Tarleton at first devoted himself to the helpless invalid; he took her abroad to sample steam baths, aromatic baths, and mud baths, but she remained a permanent cripple and, at 24, her acting career was finished.

The couple settled in London in 1788; Tarleton occupied himself with politics, becoming MP for Liverpool, and continued his leisure-time activities of drinking, gambling, and ruining more women. MR took to laudanum and literature, and penned plaintive love poems that became immensely popular, many being set to music. A volume of her verse appeared in 1791, beautifully presented, with the lovely Reynolds portrait of the author serving as the frontispiece. Not surprisingly, it was an instant best-seller.

MR then turned to fiction, and when her Gothic novel *Vancenza* appeared in 1792 the whole of the first edition sold out in a single day. She produced a succession of popular novels in the 1790s; many of them were translated into French and German, and most of them featured heroines of the most acute and exquisite sensibility, often hopelessly shattered by cruel men. But her masterpiece of sensibility was in fact a man, the hero of *Walsingham* (1797). By this time MR's popularity had reached such heights that publishers were competing for her work, and Longmans outbid all their rivals on this occasion. The newspapers too rushed to print extracts, and the *Morning Post* was first in the field, with poems and striking passages from the book. Never before had a novel written by a woman received such a rapturous reception.

Outstanding among her many admirers were Coleridge and Godwin, both agreeing that she had the most beautiful face of any woman they had ever met. Coleridge rhapsodized too over her 'fascinating metre', and Godwin introduced her to his future wife Mary Wollstonecraft. The two women became friends. They had much in common: both had been ill-used by men, both were considered whores by 'respectable' society, and both came to feminism through the agonies of sensibility. MR at that time was being doubly ill-used, Robinson and Tarleton continuing to spend her money as fast as she earned it. (Robinson refused to divorce her since she had proved such a lucrative source of income.)

Encouraged by Godwin and Wollstonecraft, in 1798 MR produced a pamphlet, *Thoughts on the Condition of Women, and on the Injustice of Mental Subordination*, emphasizing the degradation of the female mind resulting from matrimonial despotism. In the same year came her final break with Tarleton. Rumour had it that a rift had occurred because of his excessive interest in MR's attractive daughter. After a tearful scene of reconciliation, Tarleton left, and, just before MR's fortieth birthday, married a pretty young heiress, about half his age.

Shocked and in failing health, MR rallied for a last protest against 'the destroyer, man' and took her revenge on Tarleton in two novels, *The Natural Daughter*, publicizing his bride's illegitimate birth, and *The False Friend*, portraying him as a vicious monster, with the author paying a graceful tribute to Wollstonecraft, and the dying heroine lamenting the 'curse' of sensibility in women.

MR herself was now close to death. Deeply concerned, Coleridge consulted Humphry Davy about her condition and sent suggestions for medication (along with love poems and an early draft of *Kubla Khan*), but no cure could be found for her weak heart, her withered legs and her stiffening fingers. Dropsy and gallstones added to her miseries. Nursed by her devoted daughter, she died, penniless and in pain, bequeathing locks of her hair to Tarleton and the Prince of Wales. Today her face is more familiar than her writings, and we see her beauty in the works of Reynolds, Romney, Gainsborough, Zoffany, Stroehling, Hoppner, and a number of miniaturists.

Her verse shows considerable metrical skill and a delicate romantic charm (odes to the nightingale, to melancholy, to the snowdrop, a 'sublime' description of the Rhine, sonnets to sailors, shepherds, and peasants), and her love poetry exhibits varying moods of disillusion from sorrowful reproach (*Bounding Billow*) to passionate desolation and despair (*Sappho and Phaon*). In her verse too she explores the wider ranges of humanitarian sensibility, with sympathy for the mentally ill and the victims of violence, and enlightened protests against sexism, racism, slavery, and cruelty to animals.

Her plays lack distinction, and much of her fiction suffers from an excess of sentimentality and theatricality, with palpitating hearts, throbbing bosoms, torrential tears, and sudden swoons (the heroine of *Angelina* must surely hold the record for female fainting fits in eighteenth-century literature). But genuine feeling and intelligent reflection are not absent, and exhortations to fortitude (the traditional strengthener and controller of sensibility) are often accompanied by constructive feminist argument. MR's plea (in *Walsingham*) on behalf of prostitutes and seduced women is as courageous as her demand (in her pamphlet) for a women's university, with compulsory attendance for the daughters of the rich.

She also possesses a sharp talent for satire, targeting the artificiality of eighteenth-century London life, the 'tinsel' values of society, the follies of gambling and card-playing (particularly in faro clubs), and the eccentric theories of fashionable doctors.   MARGARET MAISON

Selected works: Poems (1775); *Elegiac Verses to a Young Lady, on the Death of her Brother* (1776); *The Songs, Chorusses [sic] in the Lucky Escape* (1778); *Ainsi Va Le Monde* (1790); *Poems* (1791); *Impartial Reflections on the Present Situation of the Queen of France* (1791); *A Monody to the Memory of Sir Joshua Reynolds* (1792); *Vancenza, or, The Dangers of Credulity* (1792); *Modern Manners* (1793); *A Monody* to the Memory of the Late Queen of France (1793); Sight, The Cavern of Woe, and Solitude (1793); Poems (1794); The Widow, or, A Picture of Modern Times (1794); Audley Fortescue (1795); Angelina: A Novel (1796); Hubert de Sevrac: A Romance, of the Eighteenth Century (1796); Sappho and Phaon: In a series of Legitimate Sonnets (1796); The Sicilian Lover: A Tragedy (1796); Walsingham, or, The Pupil of Nature (1797); Thoughts on the Condition of Women, and on the Injustice of Mental Subordination (1798; reprinted as A letter to the Women of England on the Injustice of Mental Subordination, 1799); The Natural Daughter (1799); Ellinda, or, The Abbey of St Aubert (1800); Lyrical Tales (1800); (trans.), Picture of Palermo, by Dr J. Hager (1800); Memoirs of the Late Mrs Robinson, Written by Herself (1801); Poetical Works (1806).

References: Adams, M., Studies in the Literary Background of English Radicalism (1947); Anon., Memoirs of Perdita (1784); Barrington, E., The Exquisite Perdita (1926); Bass, R., The Green Dragoon (1957); Brown, F., William Godwin (1926); Fothergill, B., Mrs Jordan (1965); Griggs, E., 'Coleridge and Mary Robinson', Modern Language Notes (February 1930); Huish, R., Memoirs of George IV (1831); Makower, S., Perdita (1908); Malloy, J., 'Introduction' to The Memoirs of Mary Robinson (1894); Mendenhall, J., 'Mary Robinson', University of Pennsylvania Library Chronicle 1,4 (March 1936); Paul, C.K., William Godwin: His Friends and Contemporaries (1876); Robins, E., Twelve Great Actresses (1900); Rogers, K., Feminism in Eighteenth-Century England (1982); Steen, M., The Lost One (1937); Tompkins, J., The Popular Novel in England 1770–1800 (1932).

Roche, Regina Maria

b. 1764, County Wexford, Ireland; d. 1845, Waterford, Ireland
Novelist
(Also wrote under Regina Maria Dalton)
The author of seventeen novels, RMR was extremely popular in her own time. She was in her teens when she wrote her first novel, The Vicar of Landsdowne, or, Country Quarters, published under her maiden name in 1789 and prefaced with an appeal to critics to 'disregard the humble tale' and not 'stifle my poor bantling on its first struggles into life'. This device gained her some attention, generally unsympathetic, although she was allowed to have shown more talent than the general run of first novelists. The Vicar, like most of her other novels, was immediately translated into French.

In 1796 RMR became famous with the publication of The Children of the Abbey, a Gothic novel with British settings. The heroine is orphaned, disinherited, and publicly defamed through the machinations of a greedy aunt and a wicked libertine, who are aided by the unwitting distrust of the hero.

Many of her novels were published by the Minerva Press, and their plots and morals were characteristic of popular fiction by and for women. RMR's Irish background seems to have inspired her to use provincial settings, which were made increasingly popular by Maria Edgeworth, Mary Brunton, and Walter Scott in the first two decades of the nineteenth century. Jane Austen refers twice to RMR's works. Clermont is one of the 'horrid' novels which feature in Northanger Abbey, and The Children of the Abbey is among the favourite reading of Harriet Smith in Emma.

RMR was a celebrity in the 1790s and seems to have received financial support, as well as patronage, from Queen Charlotte, but the new century inaugurated a 'long night of sickness and despair' for RMR. Her long illnesses and bouts of depression did not stem her literary production, but her work was either ignored or condemned by the reviewers. She seems to have spent some time living in London, but eventually returned to Waterford, where she lived at her residence on the Mall until her death at the age of 81. In her latter years she became devout and received consolation from religious practice, and, according to the Dedication to Princess Augusta of *Contrast* (1828), 'new friends have stepped forward, and ministered relief to wounds of long endurance'.

SIOBHAN KILFEATHER

Works: *The Vicar of Lansdowne* (1789); *The Maid of the Hamlet* (1793); *The Children of the Abbey* (1796); *Clermont* (1798); *The Nocturnal Visit* (1800); *Alvondown Vicarage* (1807); *The Discarded Son* (1807); *The House of Osma and Almeira* (1810); *LondonTales* (1814); *The Munster Cottage Boy* (1820); *The Bridal of Dunamore* (1823); *Lost and Won* (1823); *The Tradition of the Castle* (1824); *The Castle Chapel* (1825); *Contrast* (1828); *The Nun's Picture* (1836).

References: Allibone; *BA* (19); *DNB*; Schroeder, N. 'The anti-feminist reception of Regina Maria Roche', *Essays in Literature* 9, 1 (1982); Schroeder, N., 'Regina Maria Roche and the early nineteenth-century Irish novel', *Eire-Ireland* 19,2 (1983); Todd; Varma, D. P., 'Introduction' to *Clermont* (1967).

Roper, Margaret

b. 1505, Bucklersbury; d. 1544

Religious writer, translator, letter writer

Many writers from the sixteenth century onwards have portrayed MR as the 'virtuous' and 'learned' daughter of Sir Thomas More. The details of her life and extant works, however, do not rest easily within the confines of the image of the dutiful daughter.

She was the eldest child of Jane Colte and Sir Thomas More. She was brought up against a highly religious and intellectually stimulating background, in a household which was frequented by some of the leading humanist thinkers of the period. MR received a thorough education from an early age and by the time she was 18 wrote and spoke Latin and Greek fluently. In 1521 she married William Roper, with whom she had five children. Yet her study and writing did not cease with the advent of family life. In 1524 the *Deuout Treatise* was published. This piece is a free and creative translation of Erasmus's Latin meditations on the Lord's Prayer. It was widely read and ran into four editions in MR's lifetime.

By 1534 Henry VIII had cast off his queen, broken with Rome and set up his own Church of England with himself as its supreme head. Thomas More lay imprisoned in the Tower of London because he would not sign the oath of succession. His stand against the king was to lead to his eventual death and to change the life of his daughter beyond recognition. The More family were suddenly destitute and MR was faced with a public world of political intrigue and potential death. It was MR who consistently battled both with and for her father, who obtained the licence to visit the Tower and who was imprisoned after More's death because of her determination to publish his work.

The extant writing of MR consists of the *Deuout Treatise Upon The Pater Noster* and several letters written between herself and her father during the period of his imprisonment (April 1534 – July 1535). It is evident from contemporary sources, however, that her work did in fact have a far wider scope. The material that has not survived ranged from translations and imitations to original Latin and Greek compositions and a devotional treatise entitled *Die Quattuor Nouissimus*.

The intriguing series of letters written to and from the Tower have a cumulative effect which is both emotionally and intellectually powerful. As execution becomes imminent More's belief that 'Nothing can come but that that God will' is continually questioned by her sustained attempt to persuade him to save his own life: 'Father, what thinke you hath ben our comfort sins your departinge from us?' An urgent and sophisticated philosophical debate is conducted throughout the correspondence. The longest letter, an account of a dialogue which allegedly took place in the Tower, maintains a degree of authorial control which negotiates a delicate balance between the fervent and the dispassionate. Through the exploration of a series of popular fables and their political connotations MR produces a complex defence of her father's position.

MR's writing had some influence in the debate surrounding the question of women's education. Erasmus dedicated several works to her and, in a letter to G. Bude, cites MR's written work as the foundation for his new faith in female education. In his dedicatory letter to the *Deuout Treatise*, Richard Hyrde takes 'this boke, lyttel in quantite but bigge in value' as the starting point for a general defence of learning with particular reference to that of women, 'for he that had leuer have his wyfe a foole than a wyse woman I holde hyme worse than twyse frantyke.'   CATHERINE S. WEARING

Works: *A Deuout Treatise Upon the Pater Noster, made fyrst in latyn by the moost famous doctour mayster Erasmus Roterdamus and tourned into englisshe by a yong vertuous and well lerned gentyl woman of xix yere of age* (1524); 'Margaret Roper to Alice Alington' and other correspondence in Rogers, E.F. (ed.), *The Correspondence of Sir Thomas More* (1947).

References: Allibone; Ballard; *DNB*; Drabble; Erasmus, 'Precatio Dominica in Septem Portiones', in *Omnia Opera*, vol. 5 (1540); Lewis, C. S., *English Literature In The Sixteenth Century* (1954); Roper, W., *Life of Sir Thomas More* (1626); Stapleton, T., *The Life and Illustrious Martyrdom of Sir Thomas More* (1588); Verbrugge, R. M., 'Margaret More Roper's personal expression in the *Deuout Treatise Upon The Pater Noster*', in *Silent but for the Word*, ed. M. Hannay (1985).

Rossetti, Christina

b. 5 December 1830, London; d. 29 December 1894
Poet and writer for children

It is now a commonplace to see Christina Rossetti as the archetypal Victorian spinster writing morbid mystical sonnets from her sickbed. The testimony of her brother and editor, William Michael, gives credence to this view. In his memoir he reports that 'she was an almost constant and often sadly-smitten invalid, seeing at times the countenance of Death very close to her own' and that 'her life had two motive powers – religion and affection: hardly a third'. It would be foolish entirely to disregard her brother's evidence, but certainly before she was (wrongly) diagnosed with tuberculosis in 1865 she led a surprisingly active life. She was undoubtedly obsessed with death and was certainly deeply religious, but her brother did not tell the whole story.

Owing to the relative poverty of her family after her father retired from his post as professor of Italian at the University of London, she was forced to supplement its income in one way or another. In 1853 the Rossetti family moved to Frome in Somerset, where CR taught in a school run by the Anglo-Catholic W. J. E. Bennett. Unfortunately, her ever-demanding family decided to move back to London early in the next year and she was forced to abandon any teaching aspirations she may have had. Instead she applied to work as a nurse in the Crimean War, but was turned down on the grounds of age. It was during this period of frustration and personal disappointment that she wrote the lines,

> It is a weary life, it is, she said:-
> Doubly blank in a woman's lot:
> I wish and I wish I were a man:
> Or, better than any being, were not.

Despite her despondent mood she began to make some money from literary hack work. This brought her into contact with the scholar Charles Cayley, who, amongst other things, translated the Bible into Iriquois Indian. CR fell in love with him and remained devoted to him for the rest of her life, though they never married.

Around this time she began working at a refuge for single mothers and prostitutes in Highgate, 'The House of Charity'. She continued for ten years, and yet very little reference to her work there survives. CR herself wrote an article discussing the plight of the women she came across, but destroyed it because the conclusions she came to were too 'morally dangerous'. But what does survive from this highly active and (from what we have previously been led to believe) uncharacteristic period of her life is her poetry. Poems like 'Cousin Kate' ('The neighbours call you good and pure/ Call me an outcast thing') demonstrate a side of her unrepresented by her portrayal as insular and sterile.

In the early 1860s CR began to be published in *Macmillan's Magazine* and in 1862 Macmillan brought out her first collection, *Goblin Market and Other Poems*, a remarkably varied volume ranging from unrestrained Pre-Raphaelite moral fantasy to religious sonnets and love poetry. It was a great success and for two years she enjoyed an active social life in literary circles. But her increasing infirmity forced a move to Hastings and withdrawal. Yet even this did not halt her prolific poetic output. It is this period which gives us *The Prince's Progress and Other Poems* (1866), an understandably tense set of poems, filled with the urgency of one who knew her life could end at any moment: 'Life is sweet, love is sweet, use to-day while you may;/ Love is sweet and tomorrow may fail;/ Love is sweet, use to-day' (*The Prince's Progress*). Over the next year she discovered that she was not tubercular and celebrated by happily touring France and Italy from which she did not wish to return. Back in England, she initially managed to produce only a rather dreary set of short stories, *Commonplace* (1870).

Not until 1871 was CR's illness correctly diagnosed. By then she had fully developed the symptoms of Graves's disease: bulging eyes, darkening of the skin, loss of hair, and heart attacks. From this point on she was always threatened by total physical collapse. Over the next ten years she became increasingly obsessive about death, keeping a record of the funerals of her friends and relatives as they died around her. When *A Pageant and Other Poems* was published in 1881, she had already seen her sister Maria die of cancer. Within two years her brother Dante Gabriel and her great love Charles Cayley were both dead, and though she herself was to survive another ten years, she was in constant pain to the end.

It is impossible to impose a single vision on CR. For every poem intoning the spirit of the dead there is a fairy-tale; for every 'Love Lies Bleeding' there is a 'Goblin Market'. At her most assertive she was always ambiguous. But if one idea can be traced which informs her whole work, it is that she saw herself as speaking for the silent. This is most evident in her late 'Monna Innominata' sonnet sequence, a celebration of Dante's Beatrice and Petrarch's Laura, the 'donne innominate' of Italian poetry. CR gave them a voice:

> Youth gone and beauty gone, what doth remain?
> The longing of a heart pent up forlorn,
> A silent heart whose silence loves and longs;
> The silence of a heart which sang its songs
> While youth and beauty made a summer morn,
> Silence of a love which cannot sing again. (*Monna Innominata*, no 14)

It is these later poems, especially the sonnet sequences, which are her greatest testament, as they tentatively, politely scream into the silence: 'We lack yet cannot fix upon the lack:/ Nor this, nor that; yet somewhat certainly' (*Later Life*, no 6).   MARTIN BRIGHT

Works: *Verses by Christina G. Rossetti* (1847); *Goblin Market and Other Poems* (1862); *The Prince's Progress and Other Poems* (1866); *Commonplace and Other Short Stories* (1870); *Sing Song, a Nursery Rhyme Book* (1872); *Annus Domini: A Prayer for Each Day of the Year, Founded on a Text of Holy Scripture* (1874); *Speaking Likenesses* (1874); *Seek and Find* (1879); *A Pageant and Other Poems* (1881); *Called to Be Saints* (1881); *Letter and Spirit* (1883); *Time Flies* (1885); *Poems* (1880); *The Face of the Deep* (1892); *New Poems by Christina Rossetti Hitherto Unpublished or Uncollected*, ed. W. M. Rossetti (1896); *The Rossetti Birthday Book*, ed. O. Rossetti (1896); *Maude* (1897); *The Poetical Works of Christina Georgina Rossetti with Memoir and Notes*, ed. W. M. Rossetti (1904).

References: Battiscombe, G., *Christina Rossetti: A Divided Life* (1981); Bellas, R. A., *Christina Rossetti* (1977); Burnett, R. S., *Wonder and Whimsey: The Fantastic World of Christina Rossetti* (1960); Crump, R. W., *Christina Rossetti – A Reference Guide* (1976); *DNB*; Jimenez, N., *The Bible and the Poetry of Christina Rossetti* (1979); Sawtell, M., *Christina Rossetti: Her Life and Religion* (1955); Thomas, E. W., *Christina Georgina Rossetti* (1931).

Rowe, Elizabeth
b. 11 September 1674, Ilchester, Somerset; d. 20 February 1737, Frome, Somerset

Poet, translator, writer of epistolary fiction and devotional works
(Also wrote under Philomela)

ER was a highly influential writer, renowed for her piety, learning, and sensibility. She was the eldest of three daughters of Walter Singer, a clothier and Dissenting preacher (imprisoned for his beliefs during the reign of Charles II), and Elizabeth Portnell, an intensely religious woman, who met her husband while prison-visiting. ER was educated at a country boarding school, and was taught French and Italian by Henry Thynne, son of Lord Weymouth of Longleat. The Weymouths admired the Singers: their chaplain Bishop Ken and Henry's daughter Frances (later Countess of Hertford) both became valued friends of ER. She lost her mother at 16, but remained close to her father, who instructed her in religion, literature, art and music. He also encouraged a younger sister, who died at 20, to develop an interest in medicine, and both girls frequently studied together till midnight.

ER's favourite subject was poetry, which she composed from an early age, and in 1696 her *Poems on Several Occasions* appeared, written under the pseudonym of Philomela. This gained her instant fame, and she became widely known as 'the Heavenly Singer'.

Pretty, sweet-natured, tender-hearted, and mildly flirtatious, she attracted a number of 'desiring Swains', including Matthew Prior, Isaac Watts, the New England preacher Benjamin Coleman, and the eccentric bookseller John Dunton, whose wife was almost as gullible as ER. Dunton, having launched ER as a poet in his *Athenian Mercury* and published her first book of verse, proceeded to involve her in some dubious forms of 'Platonic Courtship' and 'Platonic Matrimony', from which she was rescued by her anxious father. She did not marry until 1710, when she fell deeply in love with Thomas Rowe, a poet and scholar, son of Isaac Watts's friend the Rev. Benoni Rowe, and thirteen years her junior. Five years later Rowe died of consumption.

A childless widow, ER returned to her father in Somerset, where she lived in rural tranquillity, occupying herself with charitable activities and the writing of hymns and scriptural paraphrases. Her father's death in 1719 increased her reclusive and introspective tendencies and her concern with life beyond the grave. In 1728 came her most famous work, *Friendship in Death*, a series of letters from the dead to the living. Its popularity lasted well into the nineteenth century. ER followed this by *Letters Moral and Entertaining*, full of lively anecdotes and warnings against worldly behaviour and unruly female passions. In later years she became less inclined to publish or to socialize: she cherished her solitude, communing with God and nature, and practising meditation and contemplation. 'My happiness is a sort of Quietism,' she wrote to Lady Hertford.

After her death from apoplexy at the age of 62, her devoted brother-in-law Theophilus published a collection of her work with a somewhat hagiographical memoir, and the ever-admiring Isaac Watts (his relationship with ER was satirized in verse by Edward Young) edited her *Devout Exercises of the Heart*, which proved to be another best-seller, joining the ranks of top 'sacred classics' in Britain and America.

Today ER is a neglected figure. Little of her early work is memorable, although her 1696 volume deserves recognition for its splendidly feminist preface. Probably her finest poem is her elegy on the death of her husband: pious, passionate, vivid with the anguish of personal recollection, and richly deserving of its publicization by Pope.

Ecstatic piety is blended with romantic imagination in *Friendship in Death*, an immensely charming and cheering book. The dead send a variety of loving messages to friends and relatives on earth, and rhapsodize over celestial glories. In one letter a child of 2 touchingly rebukes his mother for grieving too much, and explains the vast superiority of his heavenly happiness. As well as presenting a delightfully attractive view of death (a gentle liberator rather than the King of Terrors), ER here makes an unusual and significant contribution to epistolary prose fiction.

Her *Devout Exercises* (also in prose) continue the rapturous strain, as the soul longs, pants, and thirsts after God, with much self-abasement and a profound contempt for the world and all its vanities.

ER's achievements emboldened many women to take up their pens. Elizabeth Carter extolled her in verse as a shining example to female authors, and the fervency and beauty of her *Herzensreligion* remained a particular inspiration to women hymn writers throughout the eighteenth century.

MARGARET MAISON

Selected works: *Poems on Several Occasions, Written by Philomela* (1696); *Divine*

Hymns and Poems on Several Occasions by Philomela and Several Other Ingenious Persons (1704); elegy to her husband in *Eloisa to Abelard*, by A. Pope, 2nd edn (1720); *Friendship in Death, in Twenty Letters from the Dead to the Living* (1728); *Letters on Various Occasions* (1729); *Letters Moral and Entertaining, in Prose and Verse* (1729–33); *The History of Joseph* (1736); *Philomela; or, Poems by Mrs. Elizabeth Singer (now Rowe),* ed. E. C. Curll (1737); *Devout Exercises of the Heart, in Meditation and Soliloquy, Prayer and Praise,* ed. I. Watts (1737); *Select Translations from Tasso's Jerusalem* (1738); *The Miscellaneous Works, in Prose and Verse, of Mrs Elizabeth Rowe,* ed. T. Rowe (1739); *The Works of Mrs Elizabeth Rowe* (1796).

References: Chapman, C., 'Benjamin Coleman and Philomela', *New England Quarterly* 42 (June 1969); Gibbons, T., *Memoirs of Eminently Pious Women* (1777); Hughes, T., 'Elizabeth Rowe and the Countess of Hertford', *PMLA* 59, 3 (September 1944); Maison, M., 'Pope and two learned nymphs', *RES* 29,116 (November 1978); Reynolds, M., *The Learned Lady in England, 1650–1760* (1920); Richetti, J., 'Mrs Elizabeth Rowe: the novel as polemic', *PMLA* 82, 7 (December 1967); Rowe, T., 'The life of Mrs Rowe' (vol. 1 of *Miscellaneous Works*) (1739); Stetcher, H., *Elizabeth Singer Rowe, the Poetess of Frome* (1973); Toplady, A., 'Some account of Mrs Elizabeth Rowe', in his *Works* (1794); Wright, H., 'Matthew Prior and Elizabeth Singer', *Philological Quarterly* 24, 1 (January 1945).

Rubens, Bernice

b. 26 July 1928, Cardiff
Novelist, playwright

BR was born into a Jewish family of considerable musical talent, and educated at Cardiff High School for Girls and the University College of South Wales and Monmouth, gaining an Honours degree in English in 1947. She taught at a boys' school in Birmingham from 1948 to 1949, and since 1950 has worked as a documentary film writer and director for the United Nations and other organizations. She received the American Blue Ribbon award for film-making in 1968, the Booker Prize in 1970 (for *The Elected Member*), and a Welsh Arts Council award in 1976. She married Rudi Nassauer in 1947 and has two daughters.

BR's style is direct, plain, and virtually devoid of description. Her characters are mostly faceless and those on the periphery of the story are often sketched with the simple certainties of caricature, while those at the centre exist as voices and as sensibilities experiencing oppression. Although she employs a grand historical and geographical scale in *Brothers* (1983) and sets *The Ponsonby Post* (1977) in a developing country struggling for self-realization, her characteristic territory is domestic and her usual subject is the point of crisis in an individual spirit aspiring to fullness of life. Her novels resist categorization in terms of form or theme, ranging as they do from the tragi-comedies of Jewish family life in *Set on Edge* (1960), *Madame Sousatzka* (1962), *Mate in Three* (1965), and *The Elected Member* (1969), through the lonely monologues of the betrayed wife in *Go Tell the Lemming* (1973) and the mad isolate Luke in *Mr Wakefield's Crusade* (1985), the grotesque fantasy of *Spring Sonata* (1979) and the historical epic of *Brothers*. *The Ponsonby Post* has elements of the political thriller in its account of expatriate life in Java, where guerrillas lurk in the hills and a Kiplingesque shoeshine boy acts as go-between and spy. In *Birds of Passage* (1982) a cruise liner provides the setting for the journey into self-knowledge of a group of solitary people in late middle age, while *A Five Year Sentence* (1978) traces the descent into madness of a lonely spinster, cheated in her last pathetic grasp at

love. The vision of human experience expressed in these stories is consistent:
BR's characters are the victims of a terrible irony, in that life simultaneously
offers them the promise of fulfilment and frustrates their attempts to obtain it.
The musical genius of the child prodigy Marcus in *Madame Sousatzak* is stifled
first by the emotional needs of his mother and teacher, and eventually by the
commercial ambitions of a vulgar impresario. Norman's intellectual brilliance
in *The Elected Member* breaks down into drug-induced madness under the
suffocating pressure of his family's emotional disasters. The cruise liner seems
to offer Alice and Ellen a wider horizon than their suburban semis, but it is in
reality a confined and confining place where their last privacies are violated.

The forces which oppress the individual spirit are represented in several of
the novels by the figures of a monstrous mother whose remorseless devotion
to her children is fatally compromised by her insatiable desire to be loved in
return. Mrs Sperber in *Set on Edge* deforms her daughter's emotional nature:
Mrs Crominski creates in her son Marcus a numbing amalgam of pity and
revulsion. In *Spring Sonata* three generations of women pass on, like a relay
baton, the guilt of having failed to love sufficiently, until the foetus, Buster,
wise with the experience of his numerous previous incarnations, recognizes that
the cycle of maternal egotism and filial guilt can only be broken by his refusal
to be born. He thus maintains his relationship with his mother at a stage where
it is perpetually potential, and therefore perfect. For characters in other novels
the frustration of life's possibilities is represented differently. In *A Five Year
Sentence*, retirement offers Jean Hawkins unlimited leisure which she has no
means of filling. Luke's inheritance (*Mr Wakefield's Crusade*) likewise liberates
him from work, but in his solitary state his luxurious penthouse becomes a
prison, the outward sign of his inner isolation. Both characters compensate for
the meaninglessness of their existence by creating fantasies of another's need of
their championship and affection, which further insulate them from 'reality'.

Lonely, guilty, incompetent to communicate their longing to give and to
receive love, conscious of the dimensions of their failure, BR's characters experience life as pain. The pessimism of her vision is ameliorated by two factors,
however, one being the grimly farcical nature of the comic episodes which
rescue her novels from sentimentality, and the other, the occasional evidence
that redemption is a possibility, at any rate for some individuals. In *Brothers*, a
Jewish family survives through four generations and 150 years of anti-semitism.
In *The Ponsonby Post* Brownlow endures exposure and starvation and returns
from his sojourn in the guerrillas' cave with a personal, not merely a bureaucratic, commitment to humanity. In *Birds of Passage*, the waiter's sexual harassment has opposite but equally powerful effects on his victims: while it is
experienced as degradation and humiliation by Ellen, to both the older and the
younger Alice it brings full acceptance of their womanhood. Those with the
strength to confront the dark forces may survive and grow, but, for the majority
of BR's characters, the best that can be achieved is avoidance of pain through
a retreat into the self, like Buster's refusal to be born.   ELIZABETH JOYCE

Works: *Set on Edge* (1960); *Madame Sousatzka* (1962); *One of the Family* (1964);
Mate in Three (1965); *Call Us by Name* (1968); *The Elected Member* (1969); *Out
of the Mouths* (1970); *Sunday Best* (1971); *Third Party* (1972); *Go Tell the Lemming*
(1973); *I Sent a Letter to My Love* (1975); *The Ponsonby Post* (1977); *A Five Year
Sentence* (1978); *Spring Sonata* (1979); *Birds of Passage* (1981); *Brothers* (1983); *Mr
Wakefield's Crusade* (1985).
References: Nokes, D., 'Rules of the sea', *The Times Literary Supplement* (11
September 1981); Rumens, C., 'Dying generations', *The Times Literary Supple-*

ment (16 September 1983); Taylor, L., 'Suffering in W2', *The Times Literary Supplement* (23 July 1982).

Ruck, Berta
b. 1878, Murree, India; d. 1978
Novelist, short story writer

BR was born in India, the first of eight children of a British army officer who later became Chief Constable of Carnarvon. Most of her childhood was spent in Britain, usually the summer in England and the winter in Wales, where she stayed with her Welsh-speaking grandmother, 'a tall stately frigate in full sail, flying her cap of old lace'. She loved Wales, where, holidaying on Llanddwyn Island, 'all was a wonder and wild delight'; she cherished the Welsh legends and developed the passion for story telling which lasted all her life. Educated at St Winnifred's School, Bangor, she described affectionately how the girls 'wolfed the sodden vegetables with toughish meat, the ponderous jam roly-poly . . . and doorsteps of bread and butter' and 'slept on hard beds in icy dormitories riddled with draughts'. Afterwards, she studied art at the Slade School in London and at Colarossi's in Paris. In 1909 she married the writer Oliver Onions, who encouraged her in her writing.

Originally intending to illustrate books, she changed course and wrote her own, first in serial form for magazines. Her first novel to be published, *His Official Fiancée* (1914), had been previously serialized in *Home Chat*. It has the Cinderella motif of the hard-up heroine marrying her attractive and wealthy employer, and had very good reviews as a 'charming wholesome little love-story', although she herself described it as 'conventional, and stereotyped with but a flickering spark of originality'. This was followed by *The Courtship of Rosamund Fayre* (1914), *The Lad with Wings* (1915), *Miss Million's Maid* (1915), and in 1916 by *The Girls at his Billet* which she was told gave pleasure to readers 'in illness, people in prison and wounded soldiers in hospital'. Her next book, *Bridge of Kisses* (1917), was serialized first in the *Daily Mirror*, another war story which was popular with those at the front.

BR made good use of her own experiences and observations in her novels and created lively and credible characters. In 1919 she visited America to study her potential readers; half of *Sweet Stranger* (1919) occurs in the US. Several of her novels are set in Henley-on-Thames, including one of her own favourites, *Sir or Madam* (1923). Her novels almost always end happily – she described herself as a 'Happy Ender' – though one very successful short story, 'The Fan Dancer', ends with the dramatic death of the heroine at the end of her dance on stage. Instead of the dancer blowing the feathers away from her face at the end of her stage death, 'slowly, slowly from the dancer's breast there curled underneath the fan and down over the stage a slender trickle – blood-red'.

She continued writing prolifically until she was 96 years old, producing over fifty books. At 57 she wrote her first autobiography, *A Story-Teller Tells the Truth* (1935), in which she says, 'I feel as if I had lived on 3 separate planets, with late Victorians, bulgy, bumblesome, behaviour-conscious; Edwardians, all fluff over frills, all naughty-naughty (over nothing); and Georgians, pre-War, War and post-War Georgians.' The book is full of reminiscences, for example of the stage at the turn of the century, of Marie Lloyd, Shaw, the Gaiety girls and war shows, and of other writers whom she knew, like E. Nesbit and Alex Waugh, and it contains some helpful advice to new would-be writers. Several other novels followed, but, as she neared the end of her life, her books became largely autobiographical reminiscences of her long and interesting life, a series of flashbacks to the past with contrasts to the present day. She died in her hundredth year, having given much pleasure to countless readers over many decades.   SHIRLEY EACHUS

Selected works: His *Official Fiancée* (1914); *The Courtship of Rosamund Fayre* (1914); *The Lad with Wings* (1915); *Miss Million's Maid* (1915); *The Girls at his Billet* (1916); *The Bridge of Kisses* (1917); *The Girl who Proposed* (1918); *Sweet Stranger* (1919); *Sweethearts Unmet* (1919); *Arrant Rover* (1921); *The Wrong Mr Right* (1922); *Sir or Madam* (1923); *Kneel to the Prettiest* (1925); *Money for One* (1928); *To-day's Daughter* (1930); *A Story-teller Tells the Truth* (1935); *Mock-Honeymoon* (1937); *Money Isn't Everything* (1939); *Spinster's Progress* (1942); *Love and Apron Strings* (1949); *Fantastic Holiday* (1953); *A Wish a Day* (1956); *Romance of a Film Star* (1956); *Admirer Unknown* (1957); *Third Time Lucky* (1958); *Romantic Afterthought* (1959); *A Smile for the Past* (1959); *Love and a Rich Girl* (1960); *Sherry and Ghosts* (1961); *A Trickle of Welsh Blood* (1967); *An Asset to Wales* (1970); *Ancestral Voices* (1972).

References: Bell, Q., *Virginia Woolf: A Biography*, vol. 2 (1972); *DNB*; Drabble.

Russell, Dora

b. 1894, Thornton Heath, Surrey; d. 31 May 1986, Porthcurno, Cornwall
Polemical writer

DR, a leading campaigner for women's rights and world peace, was the second daughter of Sarah Isabella Davisson and Sir Frederick Black, KGB, a distinguished civil servant. She was educated at Sutton High School and a German finishing school before taking up a scholarship in modern languages at Girton College, Cambridge, in 1912. There she began her lifelong association with the organized free-thought movement, joining both the Cambridge Heretics and the Rationalist Press Association. Graduating with first-class honours in 1915, she subsequently obtained a research grant from Girton and continued her literary studies at University College, London, hoping, however, to give up academia in favour of a career on the stage.

She first became aware of politics through her father, a keen Liberal and progressive educationalist, but it was not until she accompanied him as secretary to the British War Mission in New York in 1917 (for which she was awarded the MBE) that she became 'almost overnight' a confirmed pacifist and socialist. In 1919 she became involved with Bertrand Russell, who asked her to accompany him on a trip to the USSR. In the event, however, he went without her and she made her own way there, smuggling herself across the border. Inspired by the Russian trip, she wrote the first chapter of a projected book on *The Religion of the Machine Age*, 'The Soul of Russia and the Body of America', in which she explained that the 'body' of America had appeared, during her 1917 visit, to be an 'immense, impressive mechanism in which producing goods, developing resources, and speeding transport were being mistaken for the goal of civilization'; in Russia, on the other hand, she thought she could see 'the creed which might civilize industrialism'. The book was not, however, completed until 1983; instead she contributed a chapter on 'Art and Education' to Bertrand Russell's *Practice and Theory of Bolshevism* (1920), in which she expressed misgivings about the future development of soviet education and saw in the growth of industrialism a concomitant regimentation of curriculum and conduct in schools.

In 1921 she gave up a Girton fellowship to spend a year in China with Russell who was teaching at the University of Peking. Returning to London, they married in November of that year, just before their son, John, was born. In 1923 they wrote jointly *The Prospects of Industrial Civilization*, and in 1924 DR stood unsuccessfully for Parliament, taking Russell's place as Labour candidate for Chelsea. Soon afterwards, the birth of a daughter, Kate, forced her to give up the beginnings of a promising acting career. This prompted her to form a Workers Birth Control Group which was run in co-operation with the Labour Party. She also began, in 1926, to contribute articles on controversial topics to the Spanish periodical *El Sol*, an assignment which was to last five years.

In 1927 the Russells founded the progressive Beacon Hill School near Petersfield, which was run along the lines laid out by such educational theorists as Margaret Macmillan, Maria Montessori and Friedrich Froebel. When Russell left her in 1932, DR ran the school alone for a further seven years. During her marriage with Russell, she had had two more children by an American journalist, Griffin Barry. Now a love affair with a young communist, Paul Gillard, was cut short by his sudden death under mysterious circumstances. This spelt, DR tells us, the end of her 'quest for liberty and love': 'From now on I lived for impersonal ends.' In 1940 she married a friend of Gillard's, Pat Grace, who had helped her with the running of the school.

From 1943 to 1950 DR worked for the Ministry of Information, chiefly in the Soviet Relations Division, and contributed regularly to the Moscow-published British paper *British Alley*. In 1958 she led the Women's Caravan for Peace across Europe, and later helped with the creation of the Campaign for Nuclear Disarmament. She was also actively involved in the National Council for Civil Liberties and in various women's organizations including the Married Women's Association and the Six Point Group. During this period her personal life was scarred by tragedy: in 1954 her son John had a nervous breakdown from which he never recovered, and shortly afterwards her son Roderick was confined to a wheelchair for life after a mining accident.

DR was still actively campaigning when living in Cornwall during her last years. In 1983, at the age of 89, she led the London CND rally in a wheelchair, and in 1986 took part in a demonstration outside the RAF base at St Mawgan in Cornwall.

DR's best-known works are the sociological treatises published during the 1920s and early 1930s. *Hypatia, or, Women and Knowledge* (1925) was written in reply to the anti-feminist *Lysistrata, or, Women's Future* by A. M. Ludovici. Hypatia, a lecturer at the University of Alexandria, had been torn to pieces by Christians. DR tells that she had expected the same fate for her book, which did in fact provoke a hostile response on account of its bold assertion of women's sexual freedom and of the right to safe and readily available forms of contraception. On the other hand, by warning her female readers against the dangers of 'living like men' and by demanding the right to motherhood, she alienated some women who thought her stance reactionary.

The Right to Be Happy (1927) looked at how the primary biological motives of human beings were suppressed and distorted by the highly intellectual concepts that dominated education and regulated an increasingly mechanical society. DR objected to the compartmentalization of thought into different disciplines, arguing that feelings should be made the basis of social organization. A later book, *In Defence of Children* (1932), deplored the low status accorded to children by society.

In the 1970s she embarked upon her three-volume autobiography, *The Tamarisk Tree*, the thesis of which, she claimed, was that 'it is not material circumstances that shape our ends, but human consciousness'. Spanning forty years, it is interspersed with the poems and plays produced by pupils of Beacon Hill School, as well as with DR's own poetry.   ANNE FERNIHOUGH

Works: *The Prospects of Industrial Civilization* (with Bertrand Russell) (1923); *Hypatia, or, Women and Knowledge* (1925); *The Right to Be Happy* (1927); *In Defence of Children* (1932); *The Religion of the Machine Age* (1983); *The Dora Russell Reader: 57 Years of Writing and Journalism* (1984); *The Tamarisk Tree* (1977, 1981, 1985).

References: Beauman, N., *A Very Great Profession* (1983); Uglow.

Sackville-West, Vita

b. 9 March 1892, Knole, Kent; d. 2 June 1962, Sissinghurst Castle
Novelist, poet, biographer, gardener

Until recently, VS-W was known mainly for her epic poem *The Land*, which won the Hawthornden Prize in 1927, for her weekly gardening notes that appeared in *The Observer* between 1946 and 1961, and for the beautiful and original garden created by her and her husband Harold Nicolson, at Sissinghurst Castle, near Cranbrook, Kent. More recently, however, her reputation as a novelist has begun to revive with the reissue of several of her more popular novels by feminist and other presses. But most of her work remains inaccessible and in the main unread. As well as novels, she published short stories, poetry, travel books, and biographies. She was, in other words, both versatile and prolific. She herself feared, however, that her work would date, and the decline in her reputation as a writer seems to bear this out. But there is much in her writing both to fascinate and to exasperate: her novels are compellingly gripping, and her later poems full of a strange, earthy mysticism.

VS-W's mother, Victoria, was the illegitimate eldest daughter of Lionel, 2nd Lord Sackville and a Spanish Flamenco dancer, Pepita de Oliva. Victoria married her cousin Lionel, who became 3rd Lord Sackville in 1910. VS-W was their only child, and she grew up at the family home of Knole, a vast estate with, supposedly, 365 rooms, fifty-two staircases and seven courtyards. VS-W loved Knole passionately, and never ceased to regret her sex, which barred her from inheriting it. In 1914 she married a young diplomat, Harold Nicolson, and spent the first few months of her marriage in Constantinople, where he was posted. Their two sons, Ben and Nigel, were born in 1914 and 1917 (VS-W had a stillborn son in 1915). Although the first years of her marriage were very happy, VS-W had always been attracted to women, and in 1918, she became passionately involved with a childhood friend, Violet Keppel. The story of their affair is told in VS-W's own words in *Portrait of a Marriage*. VS-W finally returned to Harold, after some months in France with Violet, and their marriage survived as a deep and stable friendship which lasted until VS-W's death. VS-W continued to fall in love with women throughout her life, among them Virginia Woolf, Mary Campbell, Evelyn Irons, and Hilda Matheson.

During the 1920s, her relationship with Virginia Woolf was at its height, culminating in the writing and publication of Woolf's *Orlando*.

VS-W's two main passions were writing and gardening. She wrote continually throughout her life and published an average of a book a year, sometimes more. In the late 1920s and the early 1930s, she became a well-known radio broadcaster on literary and other matters. She acquired Sissinghurst Castle in 1930, and during the 1930s and 1940s led an increasingly solitary life, writing and gardening during the week, and joined by Harold Nicolson at the weekends. Between 1958 and 1962 Harold Nicolson and VS-W took five winter cruises, and in the early summer of 1962, she died of cancer at Sissinghurst.

All of VS-W's work, whether poetry, novel, or biography, is characterized by an astonishingly vivid sense of place. She wrote to Harold Nicolson on 4 December 1956, 'I love places (Sissinghurst, the Dordogne, Florence) far more than I care for people.' Among her writings, she cared most about her poetry. Her early lyric poems, composed during her honeymoon in Constantinople, are haunted by nostalgic images of the East and a romantic sense of loss. Back in England in the 1920s, she turned with increasing confidence to epic, and her love of the English countryside and her sense of its peculiar Englishness led her to write her long and most famous poem, *The Land*, which combines a practical knowledge of farming with an intimate awareness of natural beauty. Her interest in religion and mysticism, and growing introspection in the 1930s and 1940s, produced the brooding monologue *Solitude*, whose anguished quest for faith and clinging to privacy are always rooted in the same passion for the rhythms and mystery of the countryside ('I take these verses out into a boat,/ On a lake, on a moat,/ Drifting on night-dark waters far removed . . .').

Her novels and short stories are all concerned with community, and with the relation of communities to their environments, whether that be an ancestral house like Chevron (Knole) in *The Edwardians*, or a rich agricultural valley, as in *Heritage*, her first novel. This is a tale of dark passion, with a claustrophobic sense of genetic determinism. Ruth, a farmer's daughter, is a throwback in her emotional intensity to her Spanish grandmother, and try as the mild narrator may, he cannot prise her apart from her equally intense, if more violent, cousin Rawdon. The tale of their ill-fated but irresistible passion is counterpointed by images of successive generations of a family of mice, which occasionally also experience reversion, and produce a throwback 'waltzing' mouse which whirls in the corner of its cage until it dies. Other novels that deal with working-class life include *The Dragon in Shallow Waters*, about a pair of brothers and their respective wives, who work in a soap factory, and *Grey Wethers*, a tale of the Kent Weald with unmistakable echoes of *Wuthering Heights*.

VS-W's most famous novels were those detailing the lives of the aristocracy, in particular *The Edwardians* and *All Passion Spent*. *The Edwardians* follows the fortunes of Sebastian, born to inherit Chevron, and his exploration of class difference through his affairs with a friend of his mother's, with a middle-class housewife, and with an artist. *All Passion Spent* has been hailed as a feminist classic, and depicts the independent widowhood of the once submissive Lady Slane.

VS-W's biographies are characterized mainly by their simultaneous interest in gender ambiguity and in female mysticism. In each work (apart from the early *Aphra Behn* and *Andrew Marvell*) she explores the relation of sexuality to the religious sense, and probes the motivation of women like St Teresa of Avila and St Thérèse of Lisieux. She also wrote a biography of her Spanish grandmother and her mother, *Pepita*, in which she explores her sense of her dual inheritance (Spanish/English) and attempts to come to terms with her anguished and ambivalent passion for her mother. 'If ever the phrase "turn one's heart to water" meant anything, it meant when my mother looked at you and smiled.'
SUZANNE RAITT

Selected works: *Constantinople: Eight Poems* (1915); *Poems of West and East* (1917); *Heritage* (1919); *Orchard and Vineyard* (1921); *The Heir* (1922); *Knole and the Sackvilles* (1922); *Challenge* (1923); *Grey Wethers* (1923); *Seducers in Ecuador* (1924); *The Land* (1926); *Passenger to Teheran* (1926); *Aphra Behn* (1927); *Twelve*

Days (1928); *King's Daughter* (1929); *Andrew Marvell* (1929); *Edwardians* (1930); *Sissinghurst* (1931); *Invitation to Cast Out Care* (1931); *All Passion Spent* (1931); *Vita Sackville-West's Poetry* (1931); *The Death of Noble Godavary and Gottfried Kunstler* (1932); *Family History* (1932); *Collected Poems* (1933); *Saint Joan of Arc* (1936); *Pepita* (1937); *Some Flowers* (1937); *Solitude* (1938); *Country Notes* (1939); *Country Notes in Wartime* (1940); *English Country Houses* (1941); *Grand Canyon* (1942); *The Eagle and the Dove: A Study in Contrasts, St Theresa of Avila and St Thérèse of Lisieux* (1943); *Nursery Rhymes* (1947); *Devil at Westease,* (1947); *In Your Garden* (1951); *The Easter Party* (1953); *More for Your Garden* (1955); *A Joy of Gardening* (1958); *Daughter of France: The Life of Anne Marie Louise d'Orléans* (1959); *No Signposts in the Sea* (1961); *Faces: Profiles of Dogs* (1961); *Dearest Andrew: Letters from V. Sackville-West to Andrew Reiber, 1951–1962,* ed. N. MacKnight (1980); *The Letters of Vita Sackville-West to Virginia Woolf,* ed. L. DeSalvo and M. Leaska (1984).

References: DeSalvo, L. A., 'Lighting the cave: the relationship between Vita Sackville-West and Virginia Woolf', *Signs* 8 (1982); Glendenning, V., *Vita: The Life of Vita Sackville-West* (1983); Hennegan, A., 'Introduction' to *Pepita* (1986); Nicolson, N. (ed.), *Portrait of a Marriage* (1973); Steven, M., *Vita Sackville-West: A Critical Biography* (1973); Trautmann, J., *The Jessamy Brides: The Friendship of Virginia Woolf and Victoria Sackville-West* (1980).

Sayers, Dorothy L.

b. 1893, Oxford; d. 1957, Witham
Detective writer, religious playwright, essayist, translator, poet

DLS was the only child of Helen Mary Leigh and the Rev. Henry Sayers. Her father moved from the Headship of Christchurch Cathedral Choir School to be Rector of Bluntisham in East Anglia in 1897. DLS was taught Latin by her father and learnt French from a governess. In 1909 she went to Godolphin School, Salisbury. After an illness she left school in 1911, but succeeded in winning a scholarship to Somerville College, Oxford. She was at Somerville from 1912 to 1915 and obtained first-class honours in modern languages.

After leaving university, unsure of what she wanted to do, DLS taught for two years in Hull. She then went to work as a reader for the publishing firm of Basil Blackwell. Blackwell's published two volumes of poetry by DLS. These volumes contain some interesting poems, which foreshadow her later interest in the relation between theological, aesthetic, and moral problems. Increasingly frustrated by the limitations of her work, DLS once more returned to teaching in 1920. In 1921 she joined Benson's advertising agency as a copywriter. She stayed there for about ten years, during which time she produced most of her detective writing.

DLS was committed to developing the potential of detective fiction as a genre. This commitment was expressed by her involvement, with G. K. Chesterton and others, in the Detection Club, which dedicated itself to improving the craft and the status of detective writing. DLS rejected the desire to know 'whodunnit' as the basis of detective fiction, and tried instead to explore in her novels the motivations for crime, its mechanisms, and the effect that murder has on an otherwise 'well-regulated' society. *Five Red Herrings,* the novel which sticks most closely to the 'whodunnit' model, offering us a number of plausible but uninteresting murderers, is also one of DLS's least successful.

All except one of DLS's detective novels feature the character of Lord Peter Wimsey. Wimsey is a wealthy aristocrat. He therefore has both the time and the resources to dedicate to detection. He is represented as a man of many talents: he is fluent in several languages, a talented musician, and amateur diplomat, a poet, a wine connoisseur. He is strong, courageous, and athletic, but also sensitive, intelligent, and gentlemanly. What he represents in DLS's writing changes as her novels develop. Initially his wealth and attainments seem to be merely devices to explain his successful involvement in detection. His social position guarantees him access to the best legal and forensic advice; it also, apparently, explains the sense of 'social responsibility' which leads him to become involved in detection at all. In the early novels, Wimsey is talented, but slightly foolish. By the time of *Strong Poison*, however, Wimsey is carrying a much greater symbolic weight. He represents the socially progressive nature of an enlightened aristocracy, the power of humanism, and a point of stability against the steady slide into trivialization.

These developments in the character of Wimsey are closely related to the introduction of the character of Harriet Vane. Harriet Vane appears in four novels, in the first of which, *Strong Poison*, Wimsey saves her from a wrongful conviction for the murder of her ex-lover. Wimsey declares his love for Harriet Vane in this novel, but has to wait for years before she finally agrees to marry him. The character of Harriet Vane produces the most interesting conflicts and tensions in DLS's work. She is the focus for explorations of the social and intellectual role of women. She initially rejects Wimsey's offer of marriage because she fears dependence. The marriage becomes possible only after Wimsey has shown himself capable of accepting the intellectual and moral contribution of women, and the autonomy of Harriet. It is at this point that Wimsey's status as the embodiment of the values of individualist humanism becomes so crucial. The real material difficulties and inequalities suffered by women writers are erased by an appeal to the universalizing power of poetry and philosophy. There is no doubt, however, about the power of Harriet Vane as a character, nor about the appeal of her ability to 'behave badly' and still get her man.

Many of the social and political attitudes expressed by characters in DLS's novels now seem either objectionable or implausible. The menace of 'socialism' recurs, to the extent of having a prominent Labour activist taking a pot-shot at Wimsey. The casual inclusion of racist remarks is inexcusable. The representation of members of the working class is unoriginal and uninteresting: they are either surly and dishonest or well-meaning and foolish.

As well as twelve novels, DLS wrote numerous short stories. Many of these also feature the character of Wimsey. Others involve Montague Egg, a travelling salesman, who solves crimes by careful observation and by application of the common sense embodied in his *Salesman's Handbook*. DLS also wrote several short stories which explore the supernatural or the grotesque.

In 1924, DLS had an illegitimate child. She had him brought up by a cousin, and did not admit her relation to him. In 1926, DLS married Oswald Arthur Fleming. The marriage was not particularly happy. Fleming was infrequently employed, and was therefore financially dependent on DLS. He died in 1950.

Busman's Honeymoon, published in 1937, was DLS's last detective novel. From then on she was much more interested in writing religious drama, in works of criticism, in translation, and in broadcasting. Her religious dramas vary hugely in quality. The most interesting is *The Zeal of Thy House*, which deals with the character of William of Sens, the architect responsible for the rebuilding of Canterbury Cathedral. The play, written in blank verse, is an exploration of the sin of pride, and of the divine element of creativity. DLS's best-known drama is *The Man Born to be King*, a radio drama which caused great controversy by its portrayal of the character of Jesus Christ, and its use of modern colloquial language.

DLS published numerous pamphlets and essays, and delivered many radio talks. These covered a range of topics including theology, aesthetics, mystery writing, the social position of women, and the nature of education. DLS's social pronouncements are generally fairly reactionary, although, in an attempt to understand the social transformations and divisions of the 1930s, in an essay such as 'Begin Here' she makes some surprisingly radical remarks. Her theological arguments are often unorthodox, but are always related to a project of making Christianity more pertinent to the moral dilemmas people face in the modern world. DLS's writing on women is based on a fundamentally humanist position. Thus, in *Are Women Human?*, she criticizes as nonsense, or as prejudice, arguments that women should not work, or should not be as fully educated as men. At the same time, she rejects the notion that, in matters of aesthetics, women have a specific point of view, or that, in matters of politics, women should work together for their own interests.

DLS revived the character of Wimsey in a series called the 'Wimsey Papers' which was published in the *Spectator* at the beginning of the war. The series was intended to comment on the war, and on social developments resulting from it, from the point of view of Wimsey and friends. During the Second World War, DLS left London and went to live in Witham.

In the 1940s, DLS began to work on a translation of Dante's *Divine Comedy*. Two volumes of this translation were published before her death. She was committed to producing a translation that would be lively, and would not be too dry, or too reverential. In this she was to some extent successful, but her translations were greeted with suspicion, or with hostility, by the academic community. As someone who had made her name through detective fiction, she was not to be treated seriously as a translator or as a poet.

MORAG SHIACH

Selected works: Op 1 (1916); *Catholic Tales and Christian Songs* (1918); *Whose Body?* (1923); *Clouds of Witness* (1926); *Unnatural Death* (1927); *The Unpleasantness at the Bellona Club* (1928); *Lord Peter Views the Body* (1928); *Strong Poison* (1930); *Five Red Herrings* (1931); *Have His Carcase* (1932); *Murder Must Advertise* (1933); *Hangman's Holiday* (1933); *The Nine Tailors* (1934); *Gaudy Night* (1935); *Busman's Honeymoon: A Love Story with Detective Interruptions* (1937); *In the Teeth of the Evidence* (1939); *Strong Meat* (1939); *Begin Here* (1940); *Unpopular Opinions* (1946); *The Poetry of Search and the Poetry of Statement* (1963); *Are Women Human?* (1971); *Striding Folly* (1972).

References: Brabazon, J., *Dorothy L. Sayers: A Biography* (1981); Gaillard, D., *Dorothy L. Sayers* (1981); Gilbert, C. B., *A Bibliography of the Works of Dorothy L. Sayers* (1978); Hannay, M. P. (ed.), *As Her Whimsey Took Her: Critical Works on the Work of Dorothy L. Sayers* (1979); Harman, R. B., and Burger, M. A., *An Annotated Guide to the Works of Dorothy L. Sayers* (1977); Hitchman, J., *Such a Strange Lady* (1975); Hone, R. E., *Dorothy L. Sayers: A Literary Biography* (1979); Youngberd, R. T., *Dorothy L. Sayers: A Reference Guide* (1982).

Schreiner, Olive

b. 1855, South Africa; d. December 1920, South Africa

Novelist and polemical writer

OS was born to missionary parents; her father Gottlob was of German, and her mother Rebecca Lyndall of English extraction. She had a troubled and often unhappy childhood, which included the death of a dearly loved infant sister and a later linked crisis of religious faith which led to conflict with her mother in particular. After her father's loss of employment, she lived with older siblings; then at the age of 15 in 1870 she began work with a series of mainly Boer farming families as resident governess to their children. Between posts she lived for some months of 1873 with two of her brothers and a sister in New Rush, later Kimberley, prospecting for diamonds.

During her time as a governess OS produced the draft manuscripts of her three novels, *Undine* (written first in 1873–4 but published posthumously in 1929), *The Story of an African Farm* (first written 1874–5 but published in 1883), and the unfinished *From Man To Man* (first drafted in about 1875 but published in 1924). *Undine* in particular uses her New Rush experience in both a literal and a symbolic sense. In the same period a chance meeting with 'a stranger' (a fictional version of which appears in *The Story . . .*) led OS to declare herself a 'free-thinker', then anathema within the narrow and inward-looking society in which she lived and against which she increasingly rebelled.

In 1880, with the help of Mary Brown (an active British liberal feminist and Co-operative Guildswoman) and her doctor husband John, OS left South Africa for medical training in England. This was abandoned with the onset of chronic asthma. However her brief work in hospitals and then, with her close friend Eleanor Marx, action in opposition to the Contagious Diseases Acts were later used in various of her periodic reworkings of *From Man To Man*. During this period in England (from 1881 to 1889) OS became close friends with Havelock Ellis, Edward Carpenter, and Karl Pearson (she had been emotionally involved with Ellis and unrequitedly and painfully in love with Pearson); and with Eleanor Marx, Charlotte Wilson, and then later Constance Lytton and Dora Montefiore, among many other feminist women.

Essentially OS eschewed all formally organized political groupings, although between 1885 and late 1886 she was a powerfully outspoken member of the Men and Women's Club and its only woman member who was necessarily respected as at least an intellectual equal by its male members. Throughout the rest of her life, both in England and in South Africa, she was a key influence on many individual feminist women, on the development of feminist ideas and analytic works, and thus on feminist organization of various kinds. Later questions of race and racism in South Africa increasingly came to preoccupy her. During the Boer War (1899–1901) OS had been a supporter of Boer homesteaders against English troops, not least because of her appreciation of the importance of Boer women in family and economic life. However, soon afterwards she analysed the essential unity of white interests in Africa as economic, capitalist, and imperialist, and became with her brother Will, an ex-prime minister of the Cape Colony, a leading and outspoken opponent of an apartheid constitution in South Africa. A very early supporter of the African National Congress, not long before her death OS said that if her life were given her over again she would devote it to anti-racist struggles.

The Story . . . was published in England in 1883 and quickly ran through edition after edition, making OS at one and the same time an admired celebrity and a notorious free-thinker, radical, and defender of 'immorality' (its central character Lyndall refused to marry the man she was pregnant by when she realized that her attraction to him had been only a physical one and that she could not respect him). In the same period the manuscript of *Undine* (which she never wanted to be published, as unreworked juvenilia) was given to Havelock Ellis and sat forgotten in a trunk until after her death, when conversation between Ellis and OS's estranged husband Samuel 'Cron' Cronwright-Schreiner (he took her name on marriage) revealed its existence. The manuscript of *From Man To Man* was reworked by OS periodically throughout her writing life, so that, although unfinished, it encapsulates her main political concerns: the sexual exploitation of women in prostitution and marriage, the 'new man' and the old, sisterhood, the often exploitative and violent relationship between adults and children, anti-racism as the 'moral duty' of whites towards black people, the presence and meaning of death within life. While thereby making it a fascinating although very uneven work, this continual reworking results in a difficult book to evaluate in terms of what it tells us about OS's political and other beliefs; within its pages jostle material written when she was 20 or so, when she was 65, and at various points between, and there is no indication of dating.

In 1894 OS married an ostrich farmer, Samuel 'Cron' Cronwright. In April 1895 she gave birth to a daughter who died some hours later and from whose death she never really recovered. She and Cronwright lived for increasing periods apart, he later working as a land dealer and estate agent. Following his 1902 election to the Cape Parliament, they moved further apart politically, particularly over questions of race and apartheid and pacifism and militarism. She later suspected a secret affair in his life, which Cronwright denied as a product of her unjustifiable paranoia. He remarried soon after her death.

She was en route for medical treatment in Italy for a heart condition brought on by many years of chronic asthma when the start of war in 1914 led to OS remaining in England until 1920. During this period she remained steadfastly pacifist and worked with other feminists on an internationalist pacifist platform. This occasioned major differences with old friends such as Ellis and Carpenter who, however reluctantly, supported British against German militarism, and Cronwright, who was an active and uncritical supporter of British militarism. In autumn 1920 OS returned to South Africa, sure that her death was imminent. A book-length manuscript examining pacifism as part of a developed feminist and socialist moral framework was left ready for publication with Cronwright; only an extract from it has ever appeared. OS died of a heart attack and was buried with her daughter and her dog in a stone tomb on a mountain in the South African karoo. Thousands of people lined the railway track when her body was taken there for burial.

Until the feminist renaissance of the 1970s and 1980s OS was remembered mainly as the author of *The Story of an African Farm*. However, to her contemporaries OS was a key feminist thinker and writer on an international scale. She was also well known and loved by people from all classes and many countries not only for *The Story* . . . but also for two collections of feminist and socialist allegories, *Dreams* (1890) and *Dream Life and Real Life* (1893), and for the extended anti-war allegory *Trooper Peter Halkett of Mashonaland* (1897), written in protest against the brutalities of the Jameson raid and the activities of Cecil Rhodes. In addition, to her own and then the succeeding generation of feminists she was known as a key feminist figure both for her fictional works and for the more overtly analytical *Woman and Labour* (1911), but also for the example of her attempts to live her life in a principled feminist way.

The stark oppression of children by adults, of women by men, of black people by white, of 'the masses' by 'the classes', of Africa by the capitalist nations, are made infinitely complex through her recognition of moral power in weakness, of the shifting distribution of personal power and influence in everyday relationships, and of the resistance enabled by sisterhood and comradeship. OS is one of the few feminist theorists to have dealt with the oppression of children by adults as a central theme in her work, seeing it as an exercise of power closely linked to men's sexual and other oppression of women. She still stands alone in her attempt to make sense in feminist terms of death and its relationship to life, seeing it as an end to conflict and suffering and a return not only to unity but also to life itself through the return of the body to the earth which gives us all life.

In OS's work 'social structure' and 'politics' are made concrete and everyday as she traces out her protagonists' life courses and the sometimes subtle and sometimes traumatic shifts and developments in their relationships with a range of others. She locates these events within graphically described and almost touchable settings: the warmth and familiar sights and smells of a farmhouse kitchen, a woman's own room where every item speaks of her inner and hidden self, a girl's face confronting itself in a mirror, a bird's wings catching the sunlight as it wheels and swoops in a clear sky. And in dealing with such things she uses the South African landscape itself, its beleaguered small farms, towering and awesome mountains, its wild expanses of the karoo or bushland, as a literal and solid backcloth, and as a symbolic representation of conflict within as well as of the basic unity of life and death.   LIZ STANLEY

Selected works: *The Story of an African Farm* (1883); *Dreams* (1890); *Dream Life and Real Life* (1893); *The Political Situation* (1896); *Trooper Peter Halkett of Mashonaland* (1897); *An English South African's View of the Situation* (1899); 'A letter on the Jew' (1906); *Woman and Labour* (1911); *Thoughts on South Africa* (1923); *Stories, Dreams and Allegories* (1923); *From Man To Man* (1926); *Undine* (1929).

References: Barash, C., 'Virile womanhood: Olive Schreiner's narratives of a "master race" ', *Women's Studies International Forum* 9 (1986); Barash, C., ed., *Olive Schreiner Reader* (1986); Carpenter, E., *My Days and Dreams* (1916); Cronwright-Schreiner, S. (ed.), *The Letters of Olive Schreiner* (1924); Cronwright-Schreiner, S., *The Life of Olive Schreiner* (1924); Ellis, H., *My Life* (1940); First, R. and Scott, A., *Olive Schreiner* (1980); Scott Winkler, B., *Victorian Daughters: The Lives and Feminism of Charlotte Perkins Gilman and Olive Schreiner* (1980); Stanley, L., 'Olive Schreiner: new women, free women, all women' in *Feminist Theorists*, ed. D. Spender (1983); Stanley, L., *Feminism and Friendship: Two Essays on Olive Schreiner* (1984); Woolf, V., 'Olive Schreiner', in *Virginia Woolf: Women and Writing*, ed. M. Barrett (1979).

Scott, Mary

fl. 1774–88

Poet

Few facts are known about the life of MS, author of *The Female Advocate*. Her father, a Church of England clergyman, apparently died much earlier than his wife. MS then delayed her own marriage to John Taylor, a Presbyterian minister, until after her mother's death. Whether this was because of parental opposition to the marriage or because MS felt an obligation to care for her elderly mother is unclear. MS converted to Taylor's faith, and after an engagement of almost fourteen years they married in May 1788. Their first child was born some time between February and May 1789; the second child, John Edward, born in September 1791, became a political journalist and founder of the *Manchester Guardian*; and comments in one of Anna Seward's letters seem to indicate that a third child had been born by 1793. In 1793 John Taylor became a member

of the Society of Friends and the family moved from Ilchester, Somerset, when
he accepted a teaching position in Bristol; they later moved to Manchester
where Taylor continued teaching.

In 1774 MS published *The Female Advocate: A Poem. Occasioned by Reading
Mr Duncombe's Feminead*. Inspired by Duncombe's poem and by the Rev.
Seward's 'The Female Right to Literature, in a Letter to a Young Lady from
Florence' (in J. Dodsley, *Collection of Poems by Several Hands*, vol. 2, 1766), MS
praises studious and accomplished women scholars and poets from Catherine
Parr, sixth wife of Henry VIII, to Laetitia Barbauld. She encourages women
to use their abilities despite male disapproval, stating in her preface, 'It is a duty
absolutely incumbent on every woman whom nature hath blest with talents,
of what kind soever they may be, to improve them.' The poem, 522 lines of
iambic pentameter, is accompanied by extensive notes on many of the women
mentioned in the verse.

As epigraph MS uses lines from 'The Female Right to Literature', changing
the *He* of line 2 to *Man*:

> Self prais'd, and grasping at despotic pow'r,
> Man looks on slav'ry as the female dow'r;
> To nature's boon ascribes what force has giv'n,
> And usurpation deems the gift of Heav'n.

At the end of her catalogue of accomplished women, she again emphasizes the
error of the common male view of women's intellectual abilities:

> Man, seated high on Learning's awful throne,
> Thinks the fair realms of knowledge his alone;
> But you, ye fair, his Salic Law disclaim:
> Supreme in Science shall the Tyrant reign!
> When every talent all-indulgent Heav'n
> In lavish bounty to your share hath giv'n?

After praising both Duncombe and Seward as the exceptions who resign 'their
sex's narrow views', MS adds further quotations from Seward's poem. The
Philander, to whom she addresses the closing lines as the individual who encouraged her to continue writing, is probably John Taylor.

MS evidently began corresponding with Anna Seward after the publication
of *The Female Advocate* with its praise of Seward's father, the Rev. Seward,
Canon of Lichfield. Writing to William Hayley in 1788, Anna Seward says she
and MS 'have been friends and correspondents more than ten years; though,
from the remoteness of our respective homes, we have been only once in each
other's company and that but for a single day.' In her last published letter to
MS, dated 10 September 1793, Seward refers to MS's complaints of ill-health,
which suggests the possibility that MS died soon after that date.

The BLC lists another edition of *The Female Advocate*. MS also published
Messiah: A Poem, in Two Parts for the benefit of the Royal Hospital at Bath.

JOYCE FULLARD

Works: *The Female Advocate: A Poem. Occasioned by Reading Mr Duncombe's
Feminead* (1774); *Messiah: A Poem, in Two Parts* (1788).
References: *DNB* (entry on Mary Scott's son, John Edward Taylor); Fullard,
J., 'Notes on Mary Whateley and Mary Scott's *The Female Advocate*', *The Papers
of the Bibliographical Society of America* 81 (1987); Holladay, G., 'Introduction'
to reprint of 1774 edn of *The Female Advocate* (1984); Todd.

Scott, Sarah

b. 1723, Yorkshire; d. 1795, Catton, Norfolk
Novelist, historian
(Also wrote under Henry Augustus Raymond)
The daughter of Matthew Robinson of West Layton, Yorkshire, and Elizabeth Drake, SS came from a long-established gentry family. Her elder sister was the distinguished Bluestocking Elizabeth Montagu, and the two girls were educated on an estate at Mount Morris in Kent which had been inherited by their mother. They also passed some time in Cambridge, at the home of their maternal grandmother, where their literary and intellectual pretensions received considerable encouragement from their grandmother's second husband, the classicist Professor Conyers Middleton.

After her sister's marriage in 1742, SS spent several years travelling around Britain, and while in Bath in 1748 she met Lady Barbara Montagu, the daughter of the first Earl of Halifax, who was to become her lifelong friend. Her first novel, *The History of Cornelia*, was published anonymously in 1750, and in 1752 she married George Lewis Scott, cyclopedist, mathematician, and sub-preceptor to the Prince of Wales. The marriage, of which her family strongly disapproved, soon turned out to be a disaster. Rumour had it that her husband had behaved very badly, although no one knew exactly what he had done, and in 1753 the marriage was dissolved. After a short period with her sister, SS moved to Bath with Lady Barbara Montagu (almost universally known as Lady Bab) and the two lived very happily together until Lady Bab's death in 1765. They had a house in the centre of Bath which they occupied during the winter 'season', and one in the nearby village of Bath Easton, for use during the summer months. They passed their time in a series of fashionable parties, charitable works, and acts of religious devotion.

It would appear, however, that the couple had some difficulty maintaining this lifestyle on their rather limited income, and financial necessity gave SS an added incentive to write. She had recovered only half her fortune after her abortive marriage, and had a settlement from her husband of £150 a year. In 1754 she published *Agreeable Ugliness*, which was loosely based on the French novel *La Laideur Aimable*, and explores the problems faced by ugly women in a sexist and unsympathetic society. This was followed by four more novels, and three historical works, including *The History of Gustavus Ericson, King of Sweden*, which was published under the pseudonym of Henry Augustus Raymond Esq. Even though her works were fairly popular, the emoluments were limited. She remarked that she received very little money for her most famous novel. *A Description of Millenium Hall* (1762), although, since the work had taken less than a month to write, it worked out at some rate of a guinea a day.

After Lady Bab's death, SS travelled for some time until in 1787 she settled in Catton, near Norwich, where she died in 1795. On her death she ordered that all her papers be destroyed, thereby ensuring that it is now possible to discover only sketchy details of what appears to have been an unusually interesting life. She has, however, left a series of fascinating novels. *Millenium Hall*, for instance (which Horace Walpole believed SS co-wrote with Lady Bab), tells the story of a group of wealthy women who have turned their backs on male-dominated society, in order to establish an ideal female community. By presenting the history of each of the characters, SS is able to explore the problems facing women in eighteenth-century Britain, but she also provides an alternative vision of a society organized around moral rather than economic principles. The women of *Millenium Hall* not only co-operate with one another, and live in the greatest amity, fulfilling themselves artistically and socially, but they also spread a reforming influence over the surrounding district. Their charitable work improves the material condition of the labouring class, while their example and their moral lectures encourage an ethos of contentment and self-help.

In many respects SS's social thinking was deeply conservative, derived from a celebration of a rigidly hierarchical feudal community based around the country estate. But this 'Merry England' ideology was framed within an often devastating critique of the moral failings of the commercial state. This juxtaposition is particularly striking in the sequel to *Millenium Hall*, *The History of Sir George Ellison* (1766). The first book of the novel is set in Jamaica, and is based around a lengthy exposition of the brutality of colonialism. The use of slaves is condemned as wholly inhuman, and SS attacks the bigotry and ignorance that have generated racial prejudice. The solution to this problem is, however, located in the construction of a kind of Jamaican version of Millenium Hall, a paternalistic dictatorship wherein the slaves are all well housed, well fed and well educated, and as a result work twice as hard for their master. Once George Ellison has returned to England, SS turns her attention to domestic organization, and condemns the administration of the poor law, and the inadequacy of welfare provision. But once again the solution to this political problem is identified in the charitable benevolence of a wealthy elite. Thus for all its social criticism, *Sir George Ellison*, like *Millenium Hall*, serves to celebrate the existence of a moral aristocracy which is associated with the values of old England.

SS's social vision, particularly as manifested in *Agreeable Ugliness* and *Millenium Hall*, has been identified by many modern readers as having a special relevance to the women's issues of the present day. Yet to read SS as a proto-feminist is to fail to appreciate the ideological direction of her writing. For SS's social thought and the popularity of her work were derived from that juxtaposition of radicalism and reaction that was so potent in the politics and above all in the literature of the second half of the eighteenth century.

LIZ BELLAMY

Works: *The History of Cornelia* (1750); *Agreeable Ugliness, or, The Trial of the Graces* (1754); *A Journey Through Every Stage of Life* (1754); *The History of Gustavus Ericson, King of Sweden* (1760); *A Description of Millenium Hall* (1762); *The History of Mecklenburgh* (1762); *The Man of Real Sensibility, or, The History of Sir George Ellison* (1766); *The Test of Filial Duty, In a Series of Letters between Miss Emilia Leonard and Miss Charlotte Arlington: A Novel* (1772); *The Life of Theodore Agrippa D'Aubigne* (1772).

References: Spencer, J., 'Introduction' to *Millenium Hall* (1986); Todd; Todd, J., *Women's Friendship in Literature* (1980).

Scovell, E. J.

b. 9 April 1907, Sharow, West Yorkshire

Poet

The daughter of a clergyman, EJS was educated at Casterton School, Westmorland, before going up to Oxford where she studied classics and then English at Somerville College. Graduating in 1930, she went to London where she took up secretarial work on a somewhat irregular basis, deliberately leaving herself enough free time for the writing of poetry; among her employers was Ellis

Roberts, literary editor of the weekly. *Time and Tide*, to which she sometimes contributed reviews. In December 1937 she married the ecologist Charles Elton, with whom she has two children.

Although she began to write at an early age, her first collection did not appear until she was 37. Since then her published output has been relatively small: preoccupied at times with motherhood, suffering at others from an apparent cessation of her creative powers, she has also adopted a stringently selective approach, withholding from publication work which she does not regard as 'viable'.

In the single brief paragraph which he devoted to EJS in *Poetry 1945–50*, Alan Ross patronizingly described her as writing 'essentially a woman's poetry; domestic, well-knit, circumstantial', and went on to characterize her work as being 'about family life, children and the small realities of contemporary living'. One suspects that the limited understanding implicit in Ross's assessment may be commonplace; certainly her subtle and complex talent has received nothing like the recognition it deserves.

If EJS's poetry is indeed about 'small realities', it is undoubtedly about much besides. Like Virginia Woolf, a writer whose work she admired and with whom she has a strong affinity, she engages lovingly with the surfaces of things – the yellow stamens of a single peony, the 'stiffening sheen' of freezing water, the pressure of a child's hand closing around her finger; but she also shares Woolf's visionary perception of the ways in which the small, the familiar, the domestic, may encapsulate or gesture towards a range of truths which are neither slender nor superficial. When she speaks of a newborn baby as one who 'of all on earth most/ Most stores in little substance' or of tables and chairs which, standing in a revelatory play of light, appear as 'witnesses to what they do not understand', she is simply making explicit an awareness which characteristically informs her poetry at the deepest level.

Similarly fundamental to her work is her awareness of the equivocal nature of life and of our understanding of it. In an early poem, 'The Swan's Feet', she emphasizes that the dark feet beneath the surface of the water – 'leaves of ridged and bitter ivy' – are inescapably 'part and plumage of the magnolia-flowering swan'; and again and again, whether in the recurrent representations of the interplay of light and shadow or in her tacit insistence on the interdependence of celebration and elegy, she reveals her sensitivity to the rich ambiguities of the perceived world.

Although EJS has spoken in her poetry of old age as a time of diminishing vigour and circumscribed achievement, her recent work is actually remarkable for its continuing vitality; she remains, in her unassertive, scrupulous way, a writer of considerable range and power. JEM POSTER

Works: *Shadows of Chrysanthemums and Other Poems* (1944); *The Midsummer Meadow* (1946); *The River Steamer* (1956); *The Space Between* (1982); *Listening to Collared Doves* (1986); *Collected Poems* (1988).

References: Mole, J., 'A visionary in sensible shoes: the poetry of E. J. Scovell', *Poetry Review* 76, 4 (December 1986).

Seward, Anna

b. 12 December 1742, Eyam, Derbyshire; d. 25 March 1809, Lichfield, Staffordshire

Poet

(Also wrote under Benvolio)

The daughter of the canon residentiary of Lichfield, Thomas Seward, and his wife Elizabeth Hunter, AS lived most of her life in the Bishop's Palace. She showed an early enthusiasm for poetry, which was encouraged by her father, who wrote verses, and by the poet and future naturalist Erasmus Darwin, whose mannered style greatly influenced her work. Later she was to defend strongly Darwin's style against his critics.

AS was avidly social; she was courted by many but never married, instead falling in love with a married vicar in Lichfield and involving herself in the romantic affairs of her sister Sarah and her adopted sister Honora. None of the affairs went well for her; her own love caused her much grief, Sarah died just before her wedding, and Honora married a man of whom she disapproved. AS expressed her sadness in her sentimentally melancholic poetry.

AS's first success was with the elegy. She published an *Elegy on Captain Cook* (1780), part of which may have been written by Darwin. The following year she published *Monody on the Death of Major André*, an elegy on the young Englishman whom she had known and who was hanged in the Benedict Arnold affair in the new USA. It was a considerable success and George Washington himself was eager to clear himself of the charge implied in it. Many epitaphs and occasional verses for her friends followed. In 1784 she published the extremely sentimental *Louisa*, a poetical novel in letter form concerning two virtuous lovers who are reunited. In 1786 she published a series of Horatian imitations in the *Gentleman's Magazine*; these were based on prose translations of Horace since she knew little Latin. At the same time she contributed a series of letters signed 'Benvolio', criticizing the character of Dr Samuel Johnson, Lichfield's most famous son who had recently died; he had been taught by AS's grandfather and was a distant relative of her mother. There followed an acrimonious public dispute over the character of the Doctor between AS and Johnson's biographer, James Boswell, who had already rejected her anecdotes about Johnson for his *Life*. AS especially disliked Johnson because of his criticism of poets whom she regarded as geniuses above criticism. In 1799 AS published *Sonnets*, a collection of one hundred rather repetitious poems, and in 1804, *Memoirs of the Life of Dr Darwin*, a muddled work which was poorly received.

The society of women was important to AS who was the centre of a network of visiting and letter-writing friends, who encouraged each other in poetry and other literary endeavours. She wrote about the Ladies of Llangollen, sentimentally admiring the rural retreat and their female friendship. The poet and novelist Helen Maria Williams was a close friend when the two women shared sentimental anti-slavery views, but AS could not follow Williams into continued support of French Revolutionary principles once the violent stage of the Revolution occurred.

AS belongs to the period of sensibility, disliking satire and seeking the emotional in poetry. She supported the early work of Walter Scott and Robert Southey, but had little sense of changing fashion in literature. To many the 'Swan of Lichfield', as she was called by admirers, was the epitome of the gushing, provincial, sentimental Bluestocking, but to many other women she represented a model of how a single life of literature could be lived in a circle

of friends. After her death her poetry was edited by Walter Scott, but was little regarded.   JANET JONES
Works: *Elegy on Captain Cook* (1780); *Monody on the Death of Major André* (1781); *Poem to the Memory of Lady Miller* (1782); *Louisa: A Poetical Novel in Four Epistles* (1784); *Variety: A Collection of Essays* (1788); *Llangollen Vale, with Other Poems* (1796); *Original Sonnets on Various Subjects and Odes Paraphrased from Horace* (1799); *Memoirs of the Life of Dr Darwin* (1804); *Poetical Works*, ed. W. Scott (1810); *Letters of Anna Seward Written Between the Years 1784 and 1807* (1811).
References: Ashmun, M., *The Singing Swan* (1931); *BA* (18); *DNB*; Lucas, E. V., *A Swan and Her Friends* (1907); Monk, S. H., 'Anna Seward and the Romantic poets', in *Wordsworth and Coleridge: Studies in Honor of George McLean Harper* (1939); Todd; Woolley, J. D., 'Johnson as despot: Anna Seward's rejected contribution to Boswell's *Life*', *Modern Philology* 70 (1972–3).

Sewell, Anna
b. 30 March 1820, Yarmouth; d. 25 April 1878, Old Catton, Norfolk
Novelist
Born into a devout Quaker family, AS was educated at a local day school until the age of 14 when she fell when running, injuring her ankles so badly that she was a semi-invalid for the rest of her life. She became dependent on horses for mobility, and her affection and respect for them later found literary expression in her only novel, *Black Beauty* (1877). AS and her mother Mary, also a writer, were concerned about the many social problems they saw around them, and became involved in philanthropic work. During the years they lived near Wick, a small village near Bath, they started a Temperance Society and a library, organized mothers' meetings and taught reading, writing, and natural history at an Evening Institute for Working Men. AS wrote verse and short stories for her own amusement and for her friends, but these were not published; it was only when ill-health forced her to give up riding at the age of 51 that she began to write concentratedly. Her intentions in writing were philanthropic and educational: the gratitude she felt to horses for the freedom they had given her made her want to improve the conditions in which they were kept. Apparently *Black Beauty* was initially intended for a readership of the working people who took care of horses (the novel contains clear and detailed information about the stabling of horses, correct feeding, and the treatment of common ailments, for example) but has long been considered a children's classic. It is still immensely popular, has been reprinted many times, and has been adapted for a much-repeated television series.
    The story is narrated by Black Beauty himself (not a very horse-like horse), although he also relates stories told to him by other horses of their different experiences (for example, an old war horse recalls the horrors of the Charge of the Light Brigade, and Ginger, an old friend, tells of her ill-treatment at the hands of a poverty-stricken cab driver). Black Beauty begins life very well as he is sold to a family who are particularly enlightened about the treatment of horses. However, bad luck sends him on a downward spiral. He experiences cruelty and neglect at the hands of rich and poor alike: a fashion-conscious aristocratic woman forces him to wear a bearing rein, pulling his head back unnaturally and painfully; a corrupt groom sells the food his master has given him for Black Beauty, and almost starves him; at the worst point, he is hired out to cab drivers whose only interest is short-term profit, even if it is at the expense of the horse's health. Ill-treatment does not come just from the lower

strata of society, for one of Black Beauty's happiest homes is with a caring, intelligent cab driver, Jerry, but AS makes it clear that extreme social inequality and poor education foster the sorts of problems she describes (though she supports whole-heartedly the class system: one must know one's place). Her message does not merely concern the welfare of horses, but her other philanthropic causes are brought in too. For example, Jerry says, 'If there's one devil I'd like to see in the bottomless pit more than any other, it's the drink devil.'

At last, however, Black Beauty's misfortunes come to an end, when his good breeding and kind temperament are recognized by a knowledgeable farmer at a sale of broken-down horses. He is cared for, and, when his health is restored, is sold to some ladies for a driving horse. By coincidence, their groom is the very one who looked after Black Beauty when he was young.   LUCY SLOAN
Works: *Black Beauty: His Grooms and Companions. The Autobiography of a Horse* (1877).
References: Baker, M. J., *Anna Sewell and Black Beauty* (1956); Bayly, M., *The Life and Letters of Mrs Sewell* (1889); *BA* (19); Chitty, S., *The Woman Who Wrote Black Beauty* (1971); Drabble; *OCCL*; Showalter, E., *A Literature of Their Own* (1977).

Sewell, Elizabeth

b. 18 February 1815, Newport, Isle of Wight; d. 17 August 1906, Bonchurch, Isle of Wight

Novelist, polemical writer

ES described herself, referring to the period 1840–80, as 'a successful popular authoress'. Her self-chosen audience was girls and women 'of the educated class', and she had a considerable following, in Great Britain and the United States. She is remembered now principally as a minor novelist of the Anglican revival and the Oxford Movement, a predecessor of her friend Charlotte M. Yonge.

One of a family of twelve children, she was the daughter of Thomas Sewell, solicitor, of Newport, and Jane Edwards, and spent her life in the Isle of Wight apart from occasional visits to Oxford, London, the Lakes (accompanying the boy Swinburne on a visit to Wordsworth), and the continent. She was sent to school early, first to a local school, Miss Crooke's, then to boarding school with the Misses Aldridge at Bath, but was summoned home at 15 to teach her two younger sisters. Thereafter she educated herself by wide reading, helped by her eldest brother, William, who also fostered her interest in religion and Church issues, and edited all of her earlier novels. She turned to writing partly to make money, the family having financial difficulties. In 1852 she established in her own house, Ashcliff at Bonchurch, a small school with a nucleus of her brothers' daughters and some outside girl pupils. A keen supporter of education, particularly Church schooling, for girls, she founded in 1866 St Boniface School for girls at Ventnor. Until her mind clouded over in extreme old age she continued to write and publish, her range extending from works of devotion, such as *Thoughts for Holy Week* (1857), to *A History of the Early Church* (1861), or *Grammar Made Easy* (1872), *Principles of Education* (1865), and an interesting if rather reserved *Autobiography* (1907).

Her purpose in all her writings was didactic and improving: *Laneton Parsonage* illustrates the precepts of the Catechism in scenes of practical life, *Margaret Percival* warns against flirting with Roman Catholicism. The interest in her novels comes from her constant focus upon the lives of women, usually single women, and their struggles with family duty, Church participation, and attempts to better the conditions of the poor. No feminist, she endorses home as the centre of a woman's life, taking precedence over any career or vocation – by 1880 this was already a burning question. Her best writing occurs when she draws directly, as in *Ursula* (1858), from her own experience.

ELIZABETH SEWELL

Selected works: Amy Herbert (1844); Gertrude (1845); Laneton Parsonage (1846); Margaret Percival (1847); The Earl's Daughter (1851); The Experience of Life (1853); Katherine Ashton (1854); Cleve Hall (1855); Ivors, or, The Two Cousins (1856); Ursula (1858); A Glimpse of the World (1863); Home Life (1867); After Life (1868); Autobiography (1907).

References: Baker, J. E., *The Novel and the Oxford Movement* (1932): Colby, R. A., *Fiction with a Purpose* (1967); Colby, V., *Yesterday's Woman: Domestic Realism in the English Novel* (1974); Cutt, M. N., *Ministering Angels: A Study of Nineteenth Century Evangelical Writing for Children* (1979); *DNB*; Maison, M., *The Victorian Vision* (1961); Showalter, E., *A Literature of Their Own* (1977).

Sharp, Marjory

b. 1905, Malta

Novelist, writer for children

MS is the third daughter of J. H. Sharp. Although she was raised on the island of Malta, she was educated in England at Streatham Hill High School and Bedford College, London, from which she received an honours degree in French. Her university career was devoted 'almost entirely to journalism and campus activities', and in 1929 she visited the US as a member of the first British Universities Women's Debating Team. MS married Geoffrey Lloyd Castle, a major in the Royal Army, in 1938. During the Second World War she worked for the Armed Forces Education Programme. As well as writing novels, short stories, and plays, MS has contributed to the *Encyclopedia Britannica* and to magazines in the US and England including *Punch, Ladies' Home Journal, Collier's, Saturday Evening Post, Strand,* and *Fiction Parade.*

MS's writings are best described as light entertainment, and her style is the episodic one of the 'situation' comedy. Well written, witty, and quaint, her novels and short stories have a penchant for nostalgia, harking back to a time when social conventions and niceties were clearly defined. Much of the humour, indeed, is derived from the transgression of acceptable social behaviour. In *Cluny Brown* (1944), for example, Cluny is a plumber's renegade daughter who refuses to conform to the stereotypes imposed on her either by her family or her class. She 'don't know her place' is a repeated refrain. Similarly in *The Nutmeg Tree* (1937), Julia Packett, a vaudeville entertainer of easy virtue who is also the daughter-in-law of a conservative country family, is called upon to rescue her prim daughter from the clutches of a young suitor whose nature is far too similar to Julia's own for the marriage to succeed. MS's idea for the novel came from a theory that 'people often aren't bad but circumstances make them so', and this is a recurring theme in her stories. Both of the above novels have been successfully adapted for the cinema, *Cluny Brown* in 1946 and *The Nutmeg Tree* as *Julia Misbehaves* in 1948.

Although there is some implied social criticism in MS's novels, their humour is based on ironic contrast which sometimes seems to reinstate rather than undermine social values. *The Faithful Servants* (1975) is the story of an old 'womaniser' who mischievously bequeaths his money to a trust for faithful female servants naming it after his own unpleasant housekeeper who has for years been quietly selling off his dinner service. The trustees of the Foundation, all respectable gentlemen, are faced over the years with a series of mostly comic women. The farce derives from the gentlemen's attempts to deal fairly with creatures from a world which is foreign to them. A more serious examination of social concerns is found in *Britannia Mews* (1946), the tale of the strong-willed Adelaide who marries beneath herself but nevertheless manages to survive a drunken husband and the criminal classes among whom she lives, albeit on a private income.

MS is a popular children's writer, and is best known for the Miss Bianca novels in which an aristocratic mouse and her somewhat rougher companion Bernard find themselves in the midst of unexpected and cleverly contrived adventures. The first of the series, *The Rescuers* (1959), involves the Mouse Prisoners' Aid Society's attempt to rescue a poet from the Black Castle. In 1977, Walt Disney Productions adapted the novel for an animated movie of the same name. Like her novels for adults, these children's stories reveal MS's inventiveness and her talent for story telling. She has said that children's stories allow her a 'complete release of the imagination', and that in all her novels she feels an obligation both to 'write good English' and, above all, 'to be interesting to the reader'.   ALISON M. LEE

Selected works: *Rhododendron Pie* (1930); *Fanfare for Tin Trumpets* (1932); *The Nymph and the Nobleman* (1932); *The Flowering Thorn* (1933); *Sophy Cassmajor* (1934); *Meeting at Night* (1934); *Four Gardens* (1935); *The Nutmeg Tree* (1937); *Harlequin House* (1939); *The Stone of Chastity* (1940); *Three Companion Pieces: Sophie Cassmajor, The Tigress on the Hearth, and The Nymph and the Nobleman* (1941); *Cluny Brown* (1944); *Britannia Mews* (1946); *The Foolish Gentlewoman* (1948); *Lise Lillywhite* (1951); *The Gipsy in the Parlour* (1953); *The Birdcage Room* (1954); *The Eye of Love* (1957); *Something Light* (1960); *Martha in Paris* (1962); *Miss Bianca* (1962); *The Turret* (1963); *Martha, Eric and George* (1964); *The Sun in Scorpio* (1965); *Miss Bianca in the Salt Mines* (1966); *In Pious Memory* (1967); *Rosa* (1969); *Miss Bianca in the Orient* (1970); *Miss Bianca in the Antarctic* (1970); *The Innocents* (1971); *Miss Bianca and the Bridesmaid* (1972); *The Lost Chapel Picnic and Other Stories* (1973); *The Magical Cockatoo* (1974); *The Children Next Door* (1974); *The Faithful Servants* (1975); *Summer Visits* (1978); *Bernard into Battle* (1979).

References: *CA*; *CN*; Newquist, R., *Counterpoint* (1964); *OCCL*; *Something About the Author 29*; *Twentieth Century Children's Writers* (1983).

Shelley, Mary

b. 30 August 1797, London; d. 1 February 1851, London
Novelist, biographer, editor

MS was the only child of the marriage of two of the most prominent English radical writers of the epoch of the French Revolution: philosopher and novelist William Godwin, author of *Enquiry Concerning Political Justice* (1793) and *Caleb Williams* (1794), and Mary Wollstonecraft, pioneer feminist and author of *A Vindication of the Rights of Woman* (1792). Her mother died of puerperal poisoning ten days after her birth and in 1801 Godwin married his widowed neighbour, Mrs Mary Jane Clairmont. MS grew up in a household consisting, besides herself, of her elder half-sister, Fanny (Mary Wollstonecraft's daughter by the American Gilbert Imlay), Mrs Clairmont's children, Charles and Jane, and William Godwin (born 1803). Her childhood was hardly unhappy, but she was frequently lonely and lacked a feeling of family identity: relations between her and her stepmother were poor, and though he gave her an excellent education Godwin was unresponsive to her emotional needs.

In the spring of 1814 she began a relationship with her father's new friend, Percy Bysshe Shelley, who, with his wife Harriet, had become a regular visitor to the Godwin house. In the summer they eloped, accompanied – apparently at Shelley's invitation – by Jane (later 'Claire') Clairmont. Their travels took them to France, Switzerland, Germany, and Holland and form the basis of the first part of *History of a Six Weeks' Tour*, written jointly by Shelley and MS, and published anonymously in 1817. Their return to England in the autumn marked the beginning of a difficult, almost vagrant, year in London, during which Shelley was frequently on the run from creditors. Godwin refused to communicate with his daughter in person and branded her action as a 'crime'. Socially isolated, already pregnant and only intermittently united with Shelley, MS none the less set about making herself 'worthy' of the poet by embarking upon an intensive course of reading in history, English literature, and the classics: 'I will be a good girl and never vex you any more. I will learn Greek.' Her first child, a girl, was born prematurely in February 1817 and died in early March. The improvement of Shelley's finances in the summer of 1815, and the temporary departure of Claire, the precise nature of whose relations with Shelley have been an inexhaustible topic of speculation, ushered in a quieter period. A house was rented near Windsor, and in January 1816 MS gave birth to a son, William, named after the still unforgiving Godwin. In May Claire, MS and Shelley travelled to Lake Geneva, where they spent the summer in the company of Byron and his friend and personal physician Polidori. It was here that MS began the story that grew into *Frankenstein, or, The Modern Prometheus*, her first, and still most celebrated, work of fiction.

In December 1816 Harriet Shelley was found drowned in the Serpentine. MS and Shelley married immediately, and a case was begun in Chancery for the custody of Shelley's children by Harriet which the Shelleys lost. Their daughter Clara was born in September 1817, shortly after the completion of *Frankenstein*, published anonymously in March 1818 and soon a best-seller. By the time the reviews appeared, the Shelleys, accompanied by Claire, had left England for Italy, and it was to be some years before it was generally realized that the book's author was a young woman of 19.

MS's 'hideous progeny', as she called it in later years, was initially intended as her contribution to a ghost story competition devised by Byron, though the work she completed almost a year later constitutes a break with the conventional Gothic paradigm of the supernatural and inexplicable: 'I have not considered myself as merely weaving a series of supernatural terrors.' With its solicitations of scientific credibility, *Frankenstein* crosses over into the modern genre of science fiction.

At the beginning of the story, Frankenstein is rescued from an ice floe and brought on board his ship by Walton, the leader of an expedition to the North Pole. Frankenstein narrates what is intended as the cautionary tale of his life: as a brilliant young scientist he animated a male 'creature' of gigantic proportions and superhuman strength. Instantly revolted by its grotesque appearance, he abandoned it to its fate. During a later, extraordinary encounter between Frankenstein and the monster on Mont Blanc, the monster tells his maker/father how he managed to learn language and the practice of 'benevolence' from the secret observation of a model family, only to be driven away when he believes he can risk showing himself. Learning from Frankenstein's papers of the appalling circumstances of his 'birth', he turns to revenge and strangles Frankenstein's younger brother. He now tries to strike a bargain with Frankenstein, demanding the creation of a wife for himself, in return for his removal from society. Frankenstein at first agrees but later abandons his work on the bride. The monster now murders Frankenstein's own bride and his remaining family and friends. Swearing revenge, Frankenstein pursues the monster to the icy wastes of the Arctic but dies before he can reach him. Recognizing that the death of his creator has cancelled the meaning of his life, the monster informs Walton of his intention of seeking 'the most northern extremity of the globe: I shall collect my funeral pile and consume to ashes this miserable frame, that its remains may afford no light to any curious or unhallowed wretch who would create such another as I have been.' Acknowledging the lethal potential of his own voyage, Walton turns his ship south and heads for more hospitable waters.

Written virtually on the eve of the incarnation of the eighteenth-century scientific *logos* in the technologies of the nineteenth century, *Frankenstein* is a negative fantasy of masculinist scientific enlightenment that has become part of the mythology of modernity. Its subject matter is the schizophrenic moral, libidinal, and aesthetic economy of the scientist in his increasingly prestigious role as Modern Prometheus. In an inspired dialectical reversal of the authorized (Romantic) version of Prometheus as humanity's God-defying 'benefactor', MS imaginatively submits him to the concrete reality of his 'Second Creation'. The moral of Frankenstein's life history is stated, for Walton's benefit, by Frankenstein himself in the course of his narrative: 'If the study to which you apply yourself has a tendency to weaken your affections, and to destroy your taste for those simple pleasures in which no alloy can possibly mix, then that study is certainly unlawful, that is to say, not befitting the human mind.' The monster is thus the material enactment of science as self-alienation; Frankenstein sacrifices his own (and others') identity, as a moral, social, and 'sentient' being, to the idol of rational technical self-sufficiency. The aesthetic 'monstrosity' of the composite body he creates, its failure to signify discrete human identity, nauseates (and at the same time 'rehumanizes') Frankenstein, as it will nauseate all to whom the monster shows himself in the course of his pathetic attempts to enter human society. Given that it is precisely the being's appearance that seals both his and his Creator's fate, the most catastrophic effect of Frankenstein's (science's) penetration of nature's secret would appear to be the withering of her beauty.

The monster is never unequivocally offered to the reader as an object of sympathy because he is indissociable from his creator's violation of an anthropologically grounded aesthetic taboo. In its transcendent ugliness, his patchwork body constitutes an absolute threat to the notion of a libidinally invested human and natural totality: manufactured in the charnel-house, it evokes fears of a living death of disintegrated identity, the emergent socio-historical sub-text of which is the division of labour under capitalism and the nineteenth-century industrial dismemberment of landscape.

In works such as *Queen Mab* ((1812) and *Prometheus Unbound*, published just two years after *Frankenstein*, Percy Shelley envisaged the future enlistment of science and technology in the re-aestheticization of nature and humankind, following a political revolution that included Mary Wollstonecraft's programme of equality between the sexes. Conceived and written during the period of MS's closest intellectual involvement with Shelley, *Frankenstein* may be seen as an unconscious reckoning with his and – less directly – her mother's radicalism.

MS's text is held in the gesture of horrified recoil from bourgeois patriarchal culture as an impending global disaster, to be mitigated, if at all, by the rejection of 'lawless devices' and the return (the possibility of which remains open to Walton, the narrator) to 'native town', the civilizing refinements of love, friendship, and 'domestic affection', and a harmonious, non-appropriative relationship to nature. However much she may have consciously identified with Shelley's radicalism during this period, the figuration, in *Frankenstein*, of the monster's ugliness as an absolute barrier to his socialization betrays an underlying attitude of mourning over the passing of pre-industrial and pre-technological society that has more in common with the Romantic conservatism of Burke, Wordsworth, and Coleridge than with the social, philosophical, and aesthetic progressivism of Godwin, Wollstonecraft, and Shelley. It is interesting to note that where *Queen Mab* was one of the canonical texts of the radical literary 'underground' of the 1820s and 1830s, acquiring the nickname of the 'Chartists' Bible', the 'Frankenstein Monster' image was repeatedly appropriated by the nineteenth-century English media, particularly during periods of agitation for political reform (1830s, 1848–9, 1860s), to signal the threat posed by 'revolting mobs' to the increasingly affluent bourgeoisie.

Although begun at Marlow in 1817, the composition of MS's second novel, the ambitious historical romance *Valperga* (1823), was interrupted by the bereavements and marital problems of the Shelleys' early years in Italy. Within months of their arrival they lost both of their children: Clara died in Venice in September 1818, and William in Rome the following June. These losses, particularly that of Clara, for which MS secretly considered Shelley to be partly to blame, seem to have precipitated a severe crisis in the Shelley marriage in 1818–19. MS's fourth child, Percy Florence, was born in November 1819, shortly after she completed *Mathilda*, a novella whose provocative theme, particularly for a woman writer, of a father's incestuous desire for his daughter probably ensured that it remained unpublished in her lifetime.

The quality of MS's writing rapidly deteriorates after *Frankenstein*. Critical studies of her development are invariably interwoven with the story of the enigmatic young Romantic widow (Shelley died in 1822) who, under the pressures of personal tragedy, circumstance, and the *Zeitgeist* of post-Regency England, came in out of the cold of social and literary scandal and controversy in the paradoxical pursuit – as author, woman, daughter of Godwin and Wollstonecraft and champion of Shelley's memory – of a kind of high-profile anonymity. In her own lifetime MS was much criticized for not speaking out plainly on the question of women's rights, as well as for her progressively ambiguous responses to class struggle and political reform. Considerable achievement though it was, her copiously annotated edition of Shelley's *Poetical Works* (1839, followed in the same year by the *Essays, Letters from Abroad, Translations and Fragments*) contained many distortions, suppressions, and manipulations, and has been widely blamed for its presentation of a spuriously harmonious, damagingly etherealized image of the poet and his work that was to remain dominant until well into the twentieth century.

What remains baffling is MS's failure, technically and intellectually, to build upon the distinctive achievement of *Frankenstein*. Her subsequent fictions are prolix and sentimental. *The Last Man* (1826) is perhaps her most significant work after the early tale. It is set in the late twenty-first century and portrays a republican England. The whole of the first volume and the early chapters of the second are occupied by a six-handed tale of love and ambition, set against the background of an apparently victorious parliamentary campaign by the republicans for the abolition of all remaining hereditary wealth, rank, and privilege. It is only after the death of one of these characters, Lord Raymond (a figure closely modelled on Byron), that the actual story of *The Last Man* – the gradual destruction of the human race by plague – properly begins. In a slow, pincer movement the disease spreads westwards from Asia and Europe and eastwards from the Americas, before fastening upon England. With the progressive extinction of the population civilization loses all its accreted meanings: 'Nature, our mother, and our friend . . . shewed us plainly, that, though she permitted us to assign her laws and subdue her apparent powers . . . she could take the ball in her hands, and cast it into space, where life would be drunk up, and man and all his efforts forever annihilated.' After a vain attempt to lead a small band of survivors across Europe to the supposed safety of the Swiss Alps, Verney, now the last surviving member of the human species, makes his way to Italy where, amidst the ruins of Rome, he begins to write the story that now ends.

The prolonged deferment of the tale of the plague in *The Last Man* creates a structural hiatus that is never satisfactorily bridged. Although some kind of symbolic connection between the plague as a universal levelling force and the republican dismantling of traditional social hierarchies seems intended, the linking political arguments are dispersed and naive. The weaknesses of MS's writing after *Frankenstein* have to do less with the melancholy conservatism of her world-view than with her failure to develop and organize the critical potential of that vision. Beneath the surface inconsistencies of *The Last Man*, a distinctively feminine, though hardly self-conscious, voice may be heard that is fundamentally at odds with masculinist culture as such, whether radical, liberal, or conservative; indeed, the work becomes a good deal more coherent when read as a fantasy of total patriarchal decay. In *Frankenstein* and again in *Valperga* and *The Last Man* the chain of moral self-destruction, tragedy, and cultural disaster leads back to male dereliction of an extra-territorial, feminine world of domestic affection, friendship, simple social pleasures: of life 'for each other'. Yet though the claims of this world are consistently advanced, they are just as consistently sacrificed. The feminine voice's seemingly compulsive repetition of messages of cultural despair in MS's more ambitious fictions can perhaps be explained in terms of a mystification of the private domain: unlike her mother, she was, in the end, unwilling to envisage the disengagement of the idea of the 'feminine' from its entanglements with marriage and the family, with the very bourgeois order, that is to say, whose modern dynamic she had so unerringly problematized in *Frankenstein*.

MS's last three novels, the historical novel *Perkin Warbeck* (1830) and the romances *Lodore* (1835), based on the early period of her life with Shelley, and often simply treated as a 'biographical source', and *Falkner* (1837), are rather lifeless, poorly constructed and, particularly the last two, acutely sentimental works by a writer now clearly contracted to mediocrity, and working well within the parameters of conventional feminine authorship. Indeed, the later MS did not baulk at producing well-turned escapist romances for periodicals such as the *Keepsake* which were targeted on the domestically incarcerated, though increasingly literate daughters of the new bourgeoisie.

In 1829–30 MS successfully headed off an attempt by E. J. Trelawny, an old friend from the Italian days, to write a full-scale biography of Shelley. This was a task she was reserving for herself after her father-in-law's death, though the closest she came to it, in the event, was in her *Notes* to the poems. Ironically, she had by this time already earned herself a reputation as a biographer with her two volumes of Italian *Lives* (1835) for Lardner's *Cabinet Cyclopedia*, a semi-popularizing yet prestigious publication which numbered Scott and Southey among its contributors. These were followed by a volume of Spanish and Portuguese *Lives* (1837), and two volumes of French *Lives* (1838–9). MS's literary career ended, as it had begun, with a travelogue: her two-volume *Rambles in Germany and Italy* (1844) is her account of her continental travels (with Percy Florence) in 1840, 1842 and 1843.

In 1844, Sir Timothy Shelley died. Percy Florence succeeded to the title and in 1848 was married to a young widow, Jane St John. After the multiple tragedies, exile, and social ostracism of her own early years, the survival, happiness, and prosperity of her only surviving child had, in a sense, become MS's life's work. MS never remarried and died in London in her fifty-third year. She was buried between the remains of her father and mother in St Peter's churchyard, Bournemouth, to be near Boscombe Manor, the Shelleys' new country home.

JAMES LYNN

Works: *History of Six Weeks' Tour through a Part of France, Switzerland, Germany and Holland* (with P. B. Shelley) (1817); *Frankenstein, or, The Modern Prometheus* (1818); *Valperga, or, The Life and Adventures of Castruccio, Prince of Lucca* (1823); *The Last Man* (1826); *The Fortunes of Perkin Warbeck* (1830); *Lodore* (1835); *Lives of the Most Eminent Literary and Scientific Men of Italy, Spain and Portugal* (1835–7); *Falkner* (1837); *Lives of the Most Eminent Literary and Scientific Men of France* (1838); 'Preface' and 'Notes' to *The Poetical Works of Percy Bysshe Shelley* (1839); 'Preface' to *Essays, Letters from Abroad, Translations and Fragments*, by Percy Bysshe Shelley (1840); *Rambles in Germany and Italy in 1840, 1842, and 1843* (1844); *Prosperine and Midas: Two Unpublished Mythological Dramas* (1922); 'The Choice', in *Mary Shelley*, by R. Glynn Grylls (1938); *The Letters of Mary Wollstonecraft Shelley* (1946; 1980–3); *Mary Shelley's Journal* (1947; 1985); *Mathilda* (1959); *Mary Shelley, Collected Tales and Stories* (1976).

References: *DNB*; Dunn, J., *Moon in Eclipse: A Life of Mary Shelley* (1978); Grylls, R. G., *Mary Shelley: A Biography* (1938); Levine, G. and Knoepflmacher, U. C. (eds), *The Endurance of Frankenstein: Essays on Mary Shelley's Novel* (1979); Nitchie, E., *Mary Shelley: Author of Frankenstein* (1953); Small, C., *Ariel Like a Harpy: Shelley, Mary and 'Frankenstein'* (1972); Spark, M., *Child of Light: A Reassessment of Mary Wollstonecraft Shelley* (1951).

Sheridan, Frances

b. 1724, Dublin; d. 1766, Blois, France

Novelist, playwright, poet

FS was the youngest daughter of the Rev. Dr Philip Chamberlaine and Anastasia Whyte. Her mother died soon after she was born, leaving her with three older brothers and a sister. Her father disapproved of educating girls, but her brothers secretly taught her to read and write. An intelligent pupil, she had displayed considerable ability by the time she was 20, writing two sermons and a prose romance in two volumes, *Eugenia and Adelaide*, which was published posthumously in 1791 and adapted for the stage as a comic opera by her daughter, Alicia. Lamed by an accident in early childhood and not physically very strong, she was none the less cheerful and energetic. Her granddaughter, Alicia Lefanu, writes of her 'playful gaiety . . . solid sense . . . and charm of conversation', which made her celebrated in society, apart from her literary talents, and James Boswell describes her as 'a most agreeable companion to an intellectual man . . . sensible, ingenious, unassuming yet communicative'.

She looked after her father in Dublin until his death, seizing the opportunity whenever possible to visit the theatre, where, in 1745, the disturbances leading to the Kelly riots began. FS took the side of the theatre manager, Thomas Sheridan, writing a pamphlet in his support, and some verses which appeared in Faulkner's *Journal: The Owls: A Fable Addressed to Mr Sheridan on his late Affair in the Theatre* (1746), where she attacked his enemies: 'Envy will Merit still pursue/ As shade succeeds to light.' Two years later, she and Thomas Sheridan were married. They had several talented children, the most famous being the second son, Richard Brinsley. In 1754 the family moved to London, where FS showed her unpublished novel to Samuel Richardson. He encouraged her to write a second one, and two years later she gave him the MS of *The Memoirs of Miss Sidney Bidulph, Extracted from Her Own Journal*, which he arranged to have published. It appeared in three volumes, anonymously, in 1761, with a dedication to Richardson. It was well received, winning the praise of statesmen like Lord North and Charles James Fox, and it wrung from Samuel Johnson the compliment, 'I know not, Madam, that you have a right upon moral principles to make your readers suffer so much.' In the following year it was adapted into French by the Abbé Prévost and translated again later by René Robinet, and also translated into German. In England it 'continued for a succession of years to be read and admired by all persons of true taste' (Lefanu).

With humour, pathos, and lively characterization, the novel tells the story of Sidney Bidulph, as if from her journal, with the inclusion of appropriate letters. Through her eyes we meet her well-meaning but domineering mother, Lady Bidulph, her heavy-handed brother, Sir George Bidulph, and the impetuous and imprudent hero, Orlando Faulkland. The novel begins with a reunion of Lady Bidulph, Sir George, and Sidney, who soon discuss the suitability of Faulkland as a husband for Sidney: ' "Good sense to be sure is requisite," said my mother, "but as for beauty it is but a fading flower . . . and in a man not at all necessary." ' As the financial advantages of the match are considered, Sidney is embarrassed: ' "Dear brother," I cried, "pray do not speak in that bargaining way." ' Faulkland arrives, Sidney admires his humanity and generosity, and a wedding date is fixed, but Sidney becomes ill with a fever and when she recovers finds that Faulkland has gone, his reputation blackened by a 'vile anonymous scrawl' which arrived while she was ill. Reluctantly she eventually marries a Mr Arnold instead, but all the time she is watched over from a distance by Faulkland, who comes to her rescue when her husband is persuaded to cast her off by the scheming Mrs Gerrard, who is contrasted savagely with Sidney: 'The woman is handsome 'tis true, but she is a silly toad and as fantastic as an ape'. Sidney, on the other hand, is 'that angel who deserved the first monarch of the universe'. The story continues with sudden turns of fortune 'so various and surprising that it is impossible for the reader to foresee them', until the closing scenes are reached. These, Mrs Lefanu advises, should be read 'in solitude and with the door locked to prevent interruption, for the mind hangs suspended in breathless anxiety upon the catastrophe'.

Two years afterwards, FS's first comedy, *The Discovery*, was performed in Drury Lane. She had shown it to Garrick, who said it was the best comedy he had ever read, and who took the part of the pedantic lover, Sir Anthony Branville. Thomas Sheridan also played a leading part, Lord Medway. The play, a mixture of comedy and sentiment with much freshness and charm, was a success, being performed to full houses for seventeen nights. It was followed some months later by a second comedy, *The Dupe*, which was unsuccessful on the stage, some of the audience objecting to the language, but copies sold well at the booksellers. FS refers to her disappointment in her 'Ode to Patience': 'Though by injurious foes borne down/ My fame, my toil, my hopes o'erthrown/ In one ill-fated hour. . . .' Hospitable and fond of society, the Sheridans were often in debt; it was left to FS to charm the creditors, as in her letter to Samuel Whyte: 'Mr Sheridan is obliged to you for the great delicacy with which you make your application. . . . He will not fail to send you the sum mentioned in about a month's time at the farthest.' Despite her efforts it was necessary for the Sheridans to move to France where living was cheaper. They settled in Blois, where FS wrote a second part to *Sidney Bidulph* (1767), another comedy *A Journey to Bath* (finally published in 1902), and *The History of Nourjahad* (1767), an oriental story which became very popular, and was later staged as a musical play, *Illusion* (1813). The plan, suggested to her 'one sleepless night', was to show that true happiness depends more on the 'due regulation of the passions' than on the outward signs of good fortune. Nourjahad was 'the rising star of the Persian court', favoured by the young sultan, Schemzed-din. Together they walk by moonlight in the exotic garden of the seraglio, and the sultan, sitting down on a bank of violets, asks Nourjahad what he values most in life. He is saddened by the answer: 'I should desire to be possessed of inexhaustible riches and . . . have my life prolonged to eternity.' For this he would exchange his future life in Paradise. He finds, however, that these do not give him true happiness after all. The story was intended to be the first of a series of 'instructive moral fictions', but shortly after it was written FS suffered a sudden and brief illness, and died, aged 42, unable to complete the writings that she had planned.   SHIRLEY EACHUS

Works: The Owls: A Fable Addressed to Mr Sheridan on His Late Affair in the Theatre (1746); The Memoirs of Miss Sidney Bidulph, Extracted from Her Own Journal (1761); The Discovery (1763); The Dupe (1763); The Memoirs of Miss Sidney Bidulph, Part 2 (1767); The History of Nourjahad (1767); Eugenia and Adelaide (1791, written 1739); A Journey to Bath (1902, written 1764); The Discovery, adapted for the modern stage by Aldous Huxley (1924).

References: BA (18); Birkhead, E., The Tale of Terror (1921); DNB; Drabble; Fitzgerald, P., The Lives of the Sheridans (1886); Lefanu, A., Memoirs of the Life and Writings of Mrs Frances Sheridan (1824); Todd; Todd, J., The Sign of Angellica (1989); Wilson, M., These Were Muses (1924).

Sherwood, Martha

b. 6 May 1775, Stanford, Worcestershire; d. 20 September 1851, Twickenham
Writer for children

Much is known about MS as she kept a diary for most of her life and edited it for her autobiography in 1854. It gives a lively and detailed account of a comfortable, cultured girlhood in a large social circle centred on vicarages and mansions in the Midlands, boarding school in Reading and later life in various regimental quarters in India. A clergyman's daughter, MS married her cousin, Captain Henry Sherwood, who also kept a diary and whose upbringing with a feckless father in Revolutionary France had been far less happy. They sailed for India in 1805 and remained there for eleven years. MS's diary gives detailed accounts of life in the barracks and the different postings they were sent to. It also shows her formidable energy. She began to write her books for children in India. The full extent of her work is still being explored but it is estimated that there are at least 400 titles. She was indefatigable in working for children, setting up schools for the children of the regiment wherever she went, and taking several orphans into her own home. The diary records the anguish of the deaths of several of her own children. Only two survived her, Sophia, who collaborated with her mother in her later writings, and Henry, who earned the distinction of serving his parish for more years than any other clergyman. In India MS came under the influence of the young missionary Henry Martyn, and began to put a heavy evangelical bias to her writings, though in later years she moved into a less orthodox religious position. Her return to England saw her as a famous author but still a tireless educator, running her own girls' school for several years and writing innumerable textbooks. Her marriage seems to have been a happy one and she survived her husband barely two years.

MS's most famous book for children, reprinted well into this century, was *The History of the Fairchild Family*. This has horrified modern readers with its account of a loving father taking his three young children (who have the same names as MS's own children) to see the body of their late gardener and, even worse, taking them to see a gibbet ('the face of the corpse was so shocking that the children could not look at it') as a warning against quarrelling which could lead ultimately to murdering one's brother. MS clearly did not turn aside from horror and her writing, particularly in this famous passage, has considerable power. She knew how to vary her prose rhythms, when to hint and when to give detail, and her conversations are lively and her children believable. As a girl she had told stories to younger children and a study of her work shows that she was a born story teller and a prose stylist of considerable sophistication. It is a pity that the work which shows these qualities best and which also illustrates her love for children should be impossible to reprint today because of its heavy warnings of hellfire and damnation.   MARY SHAKESHAFT

Selected works: The History of Susan Grey (1802); The History of Little Henry and his Bearer (1814); The Indian Pilgrim (1818); The History of the Fairchild Family (1818, 1842, 1847); The Story of Henry Milner, a Little Boy Who Was Not Brought up According to the Fashions of This World (1822).

References: BA (19); Cutt, M. N., *Mrs Sherwood and Her Books for Children* (1974); Darton, F. J. H., *The Life and Times of Mrs Sherwood* (1910); Smith, N. R., *The State of Mind of Mrs Sherwood* (1946); Wilson, M., *Jane Austen and Some Contemporaries* (1938).

Shuttle, Penelope

b. 12 May 1947, Staines, Middlesex
Poet, novelist

PS, daughter of Jack Frederick Shuttle, a salesman, and Joan Shepherdess Lipscombe Shuttle, a housewife, is an incantatory writer who invokes mythology and biological rhythms in her work. Educated at Staines Grammar School and Matthew Arnold County Secondary School, she forfeited her chance for higher education by not complying with examination regulations which she found stifling. In 1970, after a difficult adolescence during which she suffered from anorexia nervosa and agoraphobia, and after a short stint of secretarial work, she moved to Falmouth in Cornwall to live with the poet, Peter Redgrove, who worked as a lecturer at the Falmouth School of Art. They were married in 1980 and have one daughter, Zoe, born in 1976. The two authors have collaborated on a number of novels and books of poetry as well as working together for the Arvon Foundation. PS has won several prizes for her poetry, including the Greenwood Poetry Prize in 1972 and the Eric Gregory Award in 1974.

The Wise Wound (1978), written with Redgrove, has been PS's most popular book and its concern with the mystic and imaginative value of female biological cycles and with the importance of symbolic dream imagery point to continuing emphases in her poetry and novels. A divided writer, with great powers of invention and immense verbal facility, PS is noted for her spare, forceful, and direct writing as well as for a tendency to excess and loss of control in both her verse and her fiction.   KATE FULLBROOK

Selected works: *An Excusable Vengeance* (1967); *Nostalgia Neurosis* (1968); *All the Usual Hours of Sleeping* (1969); *Branch* (1971); *Wailing Monkey Embracing a Tree* (1973); *Midwinter Mandala* (1973); *The Hermaphrodite Album* (with Peter Redgrove) (1973); *Moon Meal* (1973); *The Terrors of Dr Treviles: A Romance* (with Peter Redgrove) (1974); *Autumn Piano and Other Poems* (1974); *Photographs of Persephone* (1974); *The Songbook of the Snow* (1974); *The Dream* (1975); *Webs on Fire* (1975); *Period* (1976); *Four American Sketches* (1976); *The Wise Wound* (with Peter Redgrove) (1978); *Rainsplitter in the Zodiac Garden* (1979); *Prognostica* (1980); *The Orchard Upstairs* (1981); *The Child-Stealer* (1983).

References: *CP*; *DLB*; Dix, C., 'The bloody cycle of the moon', *Sunday Times Magazine* (21 May 1978); Vincent, S., 'Such stuff as lives are made on', *Observer* (3 December 1978).

Sidgwick, Ethel

b. 1877, Rugby; d. 1970, Bromley, Kent
Novelist, playwright
ES was the only surviving daughter of Arthur and Charlotte Sidgwick of Oxford. She was educated at Oxford and lived much of her life in Paris. She never married.

The author of eleven novels published between 1910 and 1924, ES set most of her fiction in the refined homes of England and Ireland, treating her aristocratic characters with subtle humour and a certain amount of criticism of national and international traits. Her best-known novel, *Jamesie* (1918), a sequel to the earlier *Hatchways* (1916), follows the wartime fortunes of an aristocratic Irish family. The war forms a background to personal affairs in the novel and the title character is a symbol of new hope for a post-war England. According to a contemporary critic, Annie Marble, 'The war has left impress on her pages but in photographic not cynical reactions.'

ES spent her final years in a nursing home in Bromley.

                                                        JEAN HANFF KORELITZ
Selected works: *Promise* (1910); *Le Gentleman: An Idyll of the Quarter* (1911); *Herself* (1912); *Succession: A Comedy of the Generations* (1913); *Four Plays for Children* (1913); *A Lady of Leisure* (1914); *Duke Jones: A Sequel to 'A Lady of Leisure'* (1914); *The Accolade* (1915); *Hatchways* (1916); *Jamesie* (1918); *Madam* (1921); *Laura* (1924).
Reference: Marble, A. R., *A Study of the Modern Novel* (1928).

Simcox, Edith

b. 1844; d. 1901
Essayist, political activist
(Also wrote under H. Lawrenny)
ES was the only daughter of F. George Price Simcox, a merchant, and Jemima Haslope. Her mother, with whom she lived most of her life, was able to provide for herself and her daughter but ES sought economic independence to

support enterprises which brought her no personal remuneration. She knew the first editor of the *Academy* through her brothers and she was a contributor from its outset in October 1869 for more than twenty-five years. For the first two years she wrote under the pseudonym H. Lawrenny. She had taught herself Latin and the rudiments of Greek, and had learnt French and German at school, and in the early years wrote mainly reviews of foreign novels, some poetry, and biographies. Among the English novels she reviewed was *Middlemarch* (1 January 1873), a few weeks after having met George Eliot. G. H. Lewes later told her, 'I do not think you ought to review her books any more than I ought.'

ES recorded her passionate love and devotion to George Eliot in an unpublished journal, *Autobiography of a Shirt Maker*, begun in May 1876. Two-thirds of it relate to the period 1876–81, the last years of Eliot's life, and contain the statement, 'It is something known, lived through and unalterable, that my life has flung itself at her feet – and not been picked up – only told to rise and make itself a serviceable place elsewhere. – So be it – so it is.'

From 1875 to 1884, in support of starving women workers from one of the worst sweated trades, she ran a successful company in Soho with her friend Mary Hamilton and told the story of the enterprise in 'Eight years of co-operative shirtmaking' (*Nineteenth Century*, June 1884). She took an active part in the trade union movement, as representative of the Shirt and Collar Makers, being one of the first women delegates at the annual conference in Glasgow in 1875. She visited the workshops of stocking makers and tailors to study the conditions of employment, particularly of women, helped organize and spoke at meetings, several times attending International Labour Congresses on the continent, which she reported for the *Manchester Guardian*, and for which she learned Flemish and Italian. When the trade unions were blamed for the severe trade depression she wrote a closely reasoned defence (which was assumed to be by a man) in *The Times* (8 January 1878). Articles in *Fraser's Magazine* on 'Unremunerative industry' (November 1878) and 'The industrial employment of women' (February 1879) urged that ladies of leisure and means should act as 'civilised managers' of co-operative enterprises, instead of abandoning working women to the 'lowest class of speculators'.

Meanwhile she brought out her first book, *Natural Law: An Essay in Ethics* (1877), an attempt to formulate a moral code given that 'there is no prospect of the wrongs of earth being righted in heaven', and dedicated a personal copy to George Eliot 'with idolatrous love'. In 1879 ES was elected as a Radical member of the London School Board and for three years inspected and worked to reform London schools. An article on 'Ideals of feminine usefulness' (*Fortnightly Review*, May 1880) emphasized the personal sadness and waste in women's lives caused by social disapproval.

Her plan for the 'vignettes', five being first published anonymously in *Fraser's Magazine* (June–November 1881), which were to make up *Episodes in the Lives of Men, Women and Lovers* (1882), arose out of the emotional stresses caused by the death of G. H. Lewes, Eliot's grief, her marriage to J. W. Cross and her death in December 1880. Although disguised and set in a fictional framework, they express intense love for George Eliot, 'the one great joy and blessing of my life', and grief at her death. For ES they were confessional reminiscences which she hoped would not be too obvious. Her only other major work, *Primitive Civilisations, or, Outlines of the History of Ownership in Archaic Communities* (1894), was prepared over a long period partly as 'opium for the growing pain' and partly in order to produce a worthy monument to her beloved.

CHRISTINE DEVONSHIRE

Works: *Natural Law: An Essay in Ethics* (1877); *Episodes in the Lives of Men, Women and Lovers* (1882); *Primitive Civilisations, or, Outlines of the History of Ownership in Archaic Communities* (1894).
Reference: McKenzie, K. A., *Edith Simcox and George Eliot* (1961).

Sinclair, Catherine

b. 17 April 1800, Edinburgh; d. 16 August 1864, Kensington
Novelist, writer for children
CS was the fourth daughter of Sir John Sinclair, the first President of the Board of Agriculture, of whom the *DNB* says, 'Owing to a lack of humour and unbounded self-conceit, he viewed all his achievements with a somewhat ludicrous complacency.' CS, who did not inherit his lack of humour, acted as her father's secretary until his death in 1835, when she began writing. She did much philanthropic work among the poor in Edinburgh where she lived for most of her life, setting up drinking fountains, seats in public places, and soup kitchens. Her adult novels were frequently reprinted with variations in their titles, as for example *Jane Bouverie, or, Prosperity and Adversity*, which on its reissue in 1855 became the more daunting *Jane Bouverie, and How She Became an Old Maid*. It is interesting to note that she continued to write novels which have, as their titles indicate, a moralistic tone, after the publication of her most famous and liveliest work, *Holiday House*, written for children, in 1839. She even published a tract in 1852 entitled *A Letter on the Principles of the Christian Faith*.

This earnestness is perhaps surprising because of the manifesto which forms the introduction to *Holiday House*, whose very title implies pleasure. After stating that 'Every infant is born with a character as peculiar to himself as the features on his countenance', she complains that modern education does not allow this individuality to develop and the brain is stuffed 'like a cricket ball' with 'well-known facts and ready-made opinions' so that feelings do not have their full expression. She recalls Sir Walter Scott's lament that in the coming generation there would be no poets because 'all play of the imagination is now carefully discouraged'. In splendid defiance of the prevailing fashion, CS concludes, 'In these pages the author has endeavoured to paint that species of noisy, frolicsome, mischievous children, now almost extinct, wishing to preserve a sort of fabulous remembrance of days long past, when young people were like wild horses on the prairies, rather than well-broken hacks on the road; when amidst many faults and eccentricities, there was still some individuality of character and feeling allowed to remain.' Although there is the almost inevitable deathbed, the book largely fulfilled the writer's intentions. Harry and Laura are entertained by an ideal Uncle David whose only advice is practical – 'Never crack nuts with your teeth' – and who tells tales of a giant so tall he has to climb a ladder to comb his hair. Like many lasting children's books, this was designed for a specific child, a favourite nephew. CS's only other work for children was a series of picture letters which, though lacking the wit of *Holiday House*, proved even more popular. Without *Holiday House* perhaps nonsense to entertain 'noisy, frolicsome, mischievous children' would have taken longer to enter children's literature.   MARY SHAKESHAFT
Selected works: *Modern Accomplishments, or, The March of Intellect* (1836); *Holiday House* (1839); *Scotland and the Scotch* (1841); *Jane Bouverie, or, Prosperity and Adversity* (1846); *A Letter on the Principles of the Christian Faith* (1852); *Picture Letters* (1861–4).
References: Avery, G., *Childhood's Pattern* (1975); Avery, G., *Nineteenth Century*

Children (1965); Darton, F. J. H., *Children's Books in England* (1932), *DNB*; Green, R. L., *Tellers of Tales* (1946); Muir, P., *English Children's Books* (1954); Thwaite, M. F., *From Primer to Pleasure* (1963); Townsend, J. R., *Written for Children* (1965).

Sinclair, May

b. 24 August 1863, Cheshire; d. 14 November 1946, Aylesbury
Novelist
MS was the only daughter and youngest of Amelia and William Sinclair's six children. Her father was a third-generation shipowner in Liverpool, where MS spent her early years. Her father's business went bankrupt and the family moved from Liverpool to Gloucester, then to Devon. Her parents separated while she was still a child. Her father, an intermittent alcoholic, died in 1881. MS lived with her mother in lodgings under reduced circumstances, often dependent on financial assistance from relatives, until her mother's death in 1901. Four of her brothers were stricken by heart disease, most of them nursed by their sister, dying while MS was in her twenties and thirties. Apart from one important year at Cheltenham Ladies College, where she was taught by the influential educator Dorothea Beale, MS was educated at home. Under Beale's aegis, she began to read philosophy, psychology, and classical literature. Her essays first appeared in the *Cheltenham Ladies College Magazine*, and Beale showed them to a number of her influential friends. Although her mother withdrew her from the college after one year, this year was obviously a decisive one in her growth as a writer. Even after MS left Cheltenham, Beale continued to support MS in her writings and encourage her to attend Oxford to study philosophy. Despite her mentor's belief that fiction was not worthy of her talents, she began to write poetry and fiction along with her philosophical treatises.

She lived in genteel poverty with her mother, earning money by translating into English a German work on church history. She developed her own writing, moving from poetry to fiction. She published two volumes of verse in 1887 to mild reaction. In 1897 she published her first novel, *Audrey Craven*, about a young woman who assumes successively different identities relating to her pursuit of a number of young men. This book, and her next, *Mr and Mrs Nevill Tyson* (1898), about a loveless marriage, received favourable reviews and modest sales. In 1901 her novella *The Cosmopolitan* was published, the central character of which MS described in a letter as 'very Henry Jamesy', thereby acknowledging one of her sources of influence. The work gives a fictional rendering to MS's commitment to philosophical idealism.

In 1904, with the publication of *The Divine Fire*, MS was brought to the attention of the general public. *The Divine Fire* traces the moral and intellectual progress of a London poet called Rickman who must renounce profit for conscience and easy success for intellectual integrity. Through self-denial, or what MS calls 'perfect self-sacrifice', he achieves self-realization and, as a result, recognition of the worth of his poetry. He also wins the hand of the beautiful and good Lucia. Not surprisingly, Ford Maddox Ford called the book 'a fairy-tale', and perhaps this very element had something to do with its remarkable popularity. The book was a best-seller. MS did a promotional tour in America and was invited to the White House to meet one of her admirers, President Theodore Roosevelt. Despite the widespread popularity of her novel, MS did not seem to enjoy the public nature of the attention she received. Mark Twain sat next to her at a literary dinner and thanked her for 'a remarkably interesting silence'. Her reticence was no doubt due to a natural shyness, but might also reflect her own dissatisfaction with the novel; she herself came to doubt the quality of the work that defined her as one of the leading literary figures of the day.

Simultaneous with her growing success as an author, MS continued to pursue her independent study of philosophy and psychology. She was an active worker and voice for the suffragist cause and worked with other writers such as Violet Hunt and Cicely Hamilton to secure women's right to vote. She wrote a pamphlet entitled *Feminism* for the Women Writers Suffrage League in 1912. She became an admirer of the works of Freud and Jung and is often regarded by critics as one of the earliest writers to employ consciously and systematically the images and ideas suggested by psychoanalysis in order to repudiate what she called 'Victorian Puritanism'. Her books, especially those written after 1913, deal with the psychological tension between determinism and free will; she chronicles the importance of childhood and family influences on the development of personality and the struggle, particularly a woman's struggle, to free herself from the inherited and prescribed roles of her culture.

From the years 1907 to 1913, MS published widely. Her novels *The Helpmate* (1907), *The Judgement of Eve* (1907), *Kitty Tailleur* (1908), and *The Creators* (1910) once again deal with the plight of women involved in relationships, sexual, domestic, and intellectual, which they gradually find unacceptable. *The Combined Maze*, a novel realistic in tone and concerned with the sordid existence of a Gissing-like character called Rannie, reflects MS's drive towards dealing with social conditions. In 1912 MS wrote a biography of the Brontës called *The Three Brontës*, and in 1914 published what was to be one of her most important works, *The Three Sisters*. The Brontës were important influences on MS; she described them as creating 'the first presentiment of that Feminist novel we all know'. In her novel, MS creates the three Cartaret girls, daughters of a domineering and manipulative clergyman, the Vicar of Garth. The three, who represent different psychological types, are all drawn towards the eligible young doctor, Rowcliffe. The novel is a study in women's confrontation of the unspoken but all-pervasive patriarchal code and is a revolutionary 'modern' work, therefore indicative of a breakthrough in MS's own abilities as a writer. By exploring the tensions between repression and desire, between subconscious and conscious action, and between a will towards independence and the desire for sexual union, MS confirms her position as a truly remarkable voice for her time.

During the First World War MS dealt with issues particular to the movements of the day in *Tasker Jevons* (1916) and *The Tree of Heaven* (1917), both of which have the war as a central focus. She also published a number of essays, including 'On Imagism', and a review article of T. S. Eliot's work called 'Prufrock: and Other Observations' (1917). In 1918 she wrote an assessment of the novels of Dorothy Richardson, where she made the much-quoted remark concerning Richardson's use of 'stream of consciousness'. MS is often cited as the first literary critic to make use of the term, although it had been used earlier by French, British, and American philosophers.

Mary Oliver: A Life (1919) is often grouped with *The Three Sisters* as one of MS's important psychological novels. Dealing with a woman who sublimates all her desires in order to look after her domineering mother, it is regarded as nearly autobiographical. Mary's mother continually attempts to suppress any active desires in her daughter and thwart any impulse towards independence. Mary grows up wishing to be like her brothers, busying herself by knocking down their towers in a rather ill-concealed Freudian gesture. But she learns to act passively as she gets older, seeking only a sort of negative attention. In the end she has a mystical experience proceeding from her rigorous self-denial. The novel moves from the second to the third person, from 'you' to 'she', at particular moments of psychological crisis or understanding. While some of her reviewers felt the novel to be overly concerned with sex, E. M. Forster wrote that 'All who care for literature should read *Mary Oliver*'.

The Life and Death of Harriet Frean (1920) is the third in the trio of psychological novels. Described in a letter by MS as 'an experiment', it covers seventy years of a woman's life. In its bleak and unrelentingly spare style, the short novel was praised for its exploration of the 'crippling and binding powers of living by acquired catchword standards'. The *TLS*, however, reduced the novel to 'a mother complex' and dismissed it as too clinical an account. Two other novels, *The Romantic* (1920) and *Anne Severn and the Fieldings* (1922), continue to illustrate psychological concepts. In contrast, a novel published in 1921, *Mr Waddington of Wyck*, is a highly convincing comic portrait of a pretentious, sexist, Conservative bureaucrat. A similar novel, *A Cure of Souls* (1924), deals with a fleshy, narcissistic clergyman, made comic by his pretensions towards spirituality. The deflation of male pretensions in these novels reflects MS's continuing subtle feminist revolt against the conventions of her day.

MS's later novels, *Arnold Waterlow* (1924), *The Dark Night* (1924), *The Rector of Wyck* (1925), *Far End* (1926), *The Allinghams* (1927), and *History of Anthony Waring* (1927), are often regarded as of little interest to scholars of Modernism because of their apparent return to the conventions of early fiction in their lack of experimentation and their concern with the advancement of the plot. However, they are of interest to scholars of feminist Modernism in their portraits of relationships in the early years of the century. The swift publication of the final six novels reflects the declining health of MS, who suffered from Parkinson's disease. She spent the last years of her life in Buckinghamshire.

GINA BARRECA

Works: *Nakiketas and Other Poems* (1887); *Essays in Verse* (1892); *Audrey Craven* (1897); *Mr and Mrs Nevill Tyson* (1898); *Two Signs of a Question* (1901); *The Divine Fire* (1904); *The Helpmate* (1907); *The Judgement of Eve* (1907); *Kitty Tailleur* (1908); *The Creators* (1909–10); *The Flaw in the Crystal* (1912); *The Three Brontës* (1912); *The Combined Maze* (1913); *The Three Sisters* (1914); *The Return of the Prodigal and Other Stories* (1914); *The Judgement of Eve and Other Stories* (1914); *A Journal of Impressions in Belgium* (1915); *Tasker Jevons* (1916); *The Tree of Heaven* (1917); *Mary Oliver: A Life* (1919); *The Romantic* (1920); *The Life and Death of Harriet Frean* (1920–1); *Mr Waddington of Wyck* (1921); *Anne Severn and the Fieldings* (1922); *A Cure of Souls* (1924); *The Dark Night* (1924); *The Rector of Wyck* (1925); *Far End* (1926); *The Allinghams* (1927); *History of Anthony Waring* (1927); *Tales Told by Simpson* (1930); *The Intercessor and Other Stories* (1931).

References: Boll, T. E. M., *Miss May Sinclair, Novelist* (1973); Robb, K., 'May Sinclair: an annotated bibliography of writings about her', *English Literature in Transition* 16, 3 (1973); Zegger, H. D., *May Sinclair* (1976).

Sitwell, Edith

b. 7 September 1887, Scarborough; d. 8 December 1964, London
Poet, literary critic
The eldest child of Sir George and Lady Ida Sitwell of Renishaw Hall, ES re-examined her unhappy childhood throughout her life, attributing her feelings

of rejection largely to her mother. Unhappily married, Lady Ida was a young, spendthrift beauty, while George Sitwell became increasingly self-centred and eccentric, preoccupied with genealogy, family architecture, his ancestry, and his illnesses. ES was educated at home by governesses, unlike her younger brothers Osbert and Sacheverell. Nevertheless, in antagonism to their parents, the trio of siblings developed a deep common loyalty, which survived for most of their lives. In her autobiography, *Taken Care Of*, published posthumously in 1964, she still remembered with bitterness the rejection of her childhood and youth: 'My childhood, when I was not being bullied by my mother, resembled, before the birth of my two much-loved brothers, that of the child in Rimbaud's "Enfance" – I was an arrogant young being – who had "neither family nor courtiers. . . ." "On the forest-verge, where dream-flowers tinkle, glitter, and shine, sits the young girl, clothed by the passing shadows of the rainbows, by the shadows of the flowers and sea." '

Not conventionally pretty or ladylike, the young ES escaped into an inner world of imagination, music, and poetry. In 1903 Helen Rootham, an accomplished pianist, translator, and a great lover of poetry, became her governess. She provided ES with spiritual comradeship, and shared her knowledge of French poetry. Already an admirer of Yeats, Pope, and Swinburne, ES was now greatly influenced by the French Symbolist poets, especially Rimbaud. About this time she began a lifelong habit of copying favourite passages and remarks in large folio notebooks; when she died, more than a hundred of these existed. In 1914, finally independent, ES moved into a Bayswater flat, with Helen, on a small yearly income. She distanced herself from the family scandal when, in 1915, Lady Ida served a three-month sentence in Holloway prison, her huge debts and careless dealings with fraudulent debtors the result of her extravagant lifestyle.

ES herself was plagued throughout her life by money and health problems. Until the start of the Second World War she often stayed in Paris, where life was cheaper, but also frequently travelled to Spain, or the family castle in Italy. In the public eye, she became notorious for her self-advertisement, her homeric literary quarrels, and her eccentric clothes, as well as famous for her poetry. Painfully aware of her tall, gawky figure, she dressed in long, baroque clothes in elaborate fabrics. This mysterious fantasy image was enthusiastically captured in the photographs of the young Cecil Beaton, and the paintings of Wyndham Lewis, Albaro Guevara, and Pavel Tchetlichew. Throughout her career she generously championed young struggling artists like Tchetlichew, or later Dylan Thomas. During a second period of great popular interest after the Second World War, she was awarded many public honours, was made Dame of the British Empire in 1954, and on her seventy-fifth birthday was offered a public celebration in the Albert Memorial Hall. She had great success with two lecturing and reading tours of the US. In 1955 she joined the Catholic Church.

ES published a first volume of poetry, *The Mother* (1915), at her own expense, and a compilation of her own and Osbert's poems, *Twentieth-Century Harlequinade* (1916). The literary fame of the three Sitwells, aristocratic, eccentric, and gifted, rose fast. As the editor of a controversial literary anthology, *Wheels*, a periodical venture which involved Nancy Cunard, ES became one of the most famous and notorious exponents of English literary Modernism. *Wheels* was a determined attack on the contemporary poetic scene, notably the commonsensical, colloquial, but limited poetics of the Georgian poets. To this, the six issues or 'cycles' of *Wheels* opposed formal experiments, the imaginative play with rhythms, and opaque images. ES made her name as editor and poet with *Wheels*, and in 1916 published *Clowns' Houses*, the first volume of poetry not self-funded. Here, too, her Modernist verse, the use of new, unexpected, and shocking imagery, her imaginative sometimes obscure play with language, and the use of children's rhymes provided her with vigorous detractors and supporters.

Façade (1922) was another milestone in poetic innovation – and in poetic scandal. Its separate poems originated in ES's interest in modern dance rhythms and in the effects of assonance and alliteration, as in 'Fox Trot'.

> OLD
> Sir
> Faulk,
> Tall as a stork,
> Before the honeyed fruits of dawn were ripe, would walk,
> And stalk with a gun
> The renard-coloured sun,
> Among the pheasant-feathered corn the unicorn has torn,
>   forlorn the
>   Smock-faced sheep
> Sit
>   And
>   Sleep;
> Periwigged as William and Mary, weep. . . .

The poems were set to music by the young Sir William Walton and performed by the author herself through a megaphone. The disastrous first public performance resulted in a satiric take-off by Noel Coward of the literary 'Shufflebottom' trio. Only slowly would the inherent qualities and innovative power of the poetry become obvious. Here, as often in her early poetry, nursery rhymes, nonsense verse, and the memory of the Renishaw gardens and interiors accompanied the rhythm, and the mood of light-heartedness overhung a deeper, darker centre.

From the 1930s, however, the rise of a new poetic style advanced by the Auden generation, growing up after the First World War in a grimmer social situation, uprooted the atmosphere of formal experiment and ES's poetry became at once dated and isolated. For a period of roughly ten years she wrote no major poetry and, partially to supplement a feeble income, took to prose. A huge number of lightweight articles for popular papers, historical works, and many laboriously undertaken anthologies followed. A commissioned work, *Bath* (1932), preceded *Fanfare for Elizabeth* (1946), a first best-seller, *Victoria of England* (1936), and *The Queens and the Hive* (1962). Unschooled in academic work, she was found lacking in historical accuracy, but compensated for this by a rich, imaginative evocation of life during the Tudor period or of the streets of Bath. Her only novel, *I Live under a Black Sun* (1937), followed a similar imaginative technique, recreating the lives of Jonathan Swift, Vanessa and Stella in a setting of the First World War. It proved a difficult, opaque book which offered a rich portrayal of Swift's complex character and sudden flashes of prophetic prose poetry. 'All winter long, the mountainous seas, now livid white with passion and roaring like a universe of lions, now swollen immense and black, thundering and boiling like a hell of lava-pouring volcanoes, vast as the maelstrom of madness that will burst the roaring, cracking world of a brain, the unavailing hell that had been a human heart, rushed onwards to uproot the universe of man, the civilization founded upon a beast-world.' ES also wrote several works of literary criticism, like *Aspects of Modern Poetry* (1934) and a sensitive representation of the character and work of *Alexander Pope* (1930).

A second poetic period revealed a new, darker poetic mode during and after the Second World War. Her perception of the cold, inhuman side of life inspired a social-minded, compassionate, human poetic attitude already to some extent present in the earlier *Gold Coast Customs* (1929), which compared the uncaring, artificial, cold lifestyle of the wealthy London scene with the bloody rituals of the Ashanti tribe. A dark, surrealistic atmosphere is present in the combination with a hectic, jazz-age rhythm. When ES published 'Still Falls the Rain'(1942), about the air-raids on London, or *The Song of the Cold* (1945), formal experiments made way for a more balanced, cerebral verse, and darker, visionary poems. An intense compassion for those suffering from poverty, human coldness and egotism, or the violence of war, was now expressed in the incantatory rhythm of prophetic poetry. ES constantly featured the same symbols and metaphors – the cold, rain, warmth, growth, or biblical imagery such as the second fall, the crucifixion, Lazarus and Dives. In their totality these repeated symbols form a sustained cosmic vision, a philosophical and religious worldview which made sense of the suffering, presenting the bombs on London ('the Rain') as the 'nineteen hundred and forty nails/ Upon the Cross' and referring to an eternal re-creation, as in the last lines of 'The Shadow of Cain' (1947):

> When the last Judas-kiss
> Has died upon the cheek of the Starved Man Christ,
>   those ashes that were men
> Will rise again
> To be our Fires upon the Judgment Day!
> And yet – who dreamed that Christ has died in vain?
> He walks again on the Seas of Blood, He comes in the
>   terrible Rain.   SABINE VANACKER

Selected works: *The Mother and Other Poems* (1915); *Twentieth-Century Harlequinade and Other Poems* (with Osbert Sitwell) (1916); *Clowns' Houses* (1918); *The Wooden Pegasus* (1920); *Façade* (1922); *The Sleeping Beauty* (1924); *Troy Park* (1925); *Poetry and Criticism* (1925); *Elegy on Dead Fashion* (1926); *Poem for a Christmas Card* (1926); *Popular Song* (1928); *Five Poems* (1928); *Gold Coast Customs* (1929); *Alexander Pope* (1930); *Jane Barston* (1931); *Epithalamium* (1931); *Bath* (1932); *The English Eccentrics* (1933); *Aspects of Modern Poetry* (1934); *Victoria of England* (1936); *I Live under a Black Sun* (1937); *Trio* (with Osbert and Sacheverell Sitwell) (1938); *Poems New and Old* (1940); *Street Songs* (1942); *A Poet's Notebook* (1943); *Green Song and Other Poems* (1944); *The Song of the Cold* (1945); *Fanfare for Elizabeth* (1946); *The Shadow of Cain* (1947); *A Notebook on William Shakespeare* (1948); *The Canticle of the Rose: Selected Poems 1920–1947* (1949); *Façade and Other Poems 1920–1935* (1950); *A Poet's Notebook* (1950); *Collected Poems* (1954); *The Outcasts* (1962); *Music and Ceremonies* (1963); *Taken Care Of: An Autobiography* (1965); *Selected Poems* (1965).

References: Brophy, J. D., *Edith Sitwell: The Symbolist Order* (1968); Fifoot, R., *A Bibliography of Edith, Osbert and Sacheverell Sitwell* (1963); Glendinning, V., *Edith Sitwell: A Unicorn Among Lions* (1981); Lehman, J., *Volume VII: Sean O'Casey to Poets of World War II*, in *British Writers*, ed. I. Scott-Kilvert (1984); Macvean, J., 'Another look at Edith Sitwell', *Agenda* 21, 3 (1983–4); Ower, B. J., 'Cosmic aristocracy and cosmic democracy in Edith Sitwell', *Contemporary Literature* 12 (1971); Pearson, J., *Façades: Edith, Osbert and Sacheverell Sitwell* (1978); Salter, E., *The Last Years of a Rebel: A Memoir of Edith Sitwell* (1967).

Smith, Charlotte

b. 4 May 1749, St James's, London; d. 28 October 1806, Tilford, near Farnham, Surrey

Novelist, poet

CS was the eldest daughter of Anna Towers and Nicholas Turner, a landed gentleman of considerable standing. Her life was marked by misfortunes. The first occurred when she was 3: her mother died giving birth to her brother. Her father temporarily abandoned his children to the care of his wife's sister, who supervised her niece's education. Disapproving of 'Bluestockings', her concern was with the cultivation of the necessary graces to fit CS for society and to attract a suitable husband. She was taught to dance and draw and was sent to an elementary school at Chichester. Before she was 8, she went to a finishing school at Kensington.

When CS was 10 or 11, her father made Bignor Park in the South Downs, Sussex, her permanent residence. Situated in an area rich in history and natural beauty, it proved a permanent source of inspiration for CS, who had already started to write poetry. Her father approved of her literary interests. She read, and remembered, the classics of literature and would pour scorn on the trivial romantic novels provided for young ladies by the circulating libraries. Physically as well as intellectually precocious, she received a proposal of marriage between the ages of 13 and 14. Although rejected by her father on the grounds of her age, marriage was soon in the air again, for it offered him a solution to a problem. He was contemplating remarrying a wealthy lady whose dowry would help him out of financial difficulties. But CS was very fond of her father and, as a girl of some spirit, was unlikely to accept her stepmother with equanimity. The callous solution was to marry her off. A marriage was quickly arranged in February, 1766, to Benjamin Smith, second son of Richard Smith, a West Indian merchant and director of the East India Company.

Benjamin Smith was wealthy but he moved in less refined circles than his wife. The couple took up residence over his father's shop in London. CS was only relieved of her mother-in-law's harassment by her death in 1767. Her widowed father-in-law, although genuinely fond of her, was not the best of company and she had to dissimulate to hide her husband's spendthrift ways. CS had had by now the first of many children and when her first child died a few days after the birth of a second, Richard Smith, concerned at her faltering health, moved her to Southgate, on the outskirts of the metropolis. CS found herself alone for the first time since her marriage. According to her only sister, Catherine Anne, as CS reflected on her situation she came to regard herself as 'a pearl that had been basely thrown away'. She found solace in her library and her children.

About this time, CS defended her father-in-law against libel so effectively that he tried to persuade her to reside in the city and assist him in his business. Instead, she persuaded him to take her husband out of business and set him up as a gentleman at Lys Farm, Hampshire. They lived there for nine years, CS's longest continuous residence. The location was beautiful, the move disastrous. Benjamin threw himself into playing the squire. He was a man of crazes. These were satirized in CS's first novel *Emmeline* (1788), when, as Mr Stafford, he tries a scheme for fertilizing land with spent wigs. In October 1776 the death of Mr Smith deprived her of a source of support against her husband's waywardness. He left a complicated will which was the cause of many subsequent difficulties and was at the root of CS's dislike of lawyers. His aim had been to ensure that his grandchildren should receive equal legacies. CS was one of the executors of the will, but the main burden fell on her husband, and he was unequal to it. It was only a matter of time before disaster struck.

Benjamin's position was temporarily relieved by a lucrative government contract, but when the legatees of his father's will went to law to procure settlement, he was thrown into the King's Bench prison. CS stood by her husband. Her brother looked after her children, while she spent most of her time living in prison with Benjamin. She received a rough schooling. She witnessed two attempts at escape made by prisoners blowing holes in the walls. It was the beginning, too, of another schooling, in the baroque complexities of law and their manipulation by the rich and powerful. These were noted in *Emmeline*, where she wrote of the 'dirty chicane of law'; by the time she wrote her last novel, *The Young Philosopher* (1798), her exasperation knew no bounds and detracted from the work. Yet, despite her trials, she maintained a degree of detachment. At the time she was writing her splenetic last novel, she was penning a charming work of moral instruction for children.

After seven months in prison, her husband was released in July 1784. His estate was broken up and sold, and he was displaced as executor of his father's will. The new executors would take well over a decade to release her children's property. CS, looking back, suggested that had she known what was in store for her she would have been wiser 'to have descended at once into the inferior walk of life'. This was wishful thinking; she had no training in domestic skills and she was quite unused to making economies. Her reaction at the time was to publish the poems which she had been writing since her youth. Unperturbed by the refusals of publishers, she sought the assistance of her Sussex neighbour, the poet William Hayley. With his recommendation, Dodsley published them, though at her expense. Her confidence proved justified. Within a year of the publication of her *Elegaic Sonnets* (1784), a second edition was called for; it was the first of many. Of these, the fifth edition (1789) is particularly noteworthy. Published by subscription, the list formed a galaxy of the eminent in politics, society, and literature. Her fame led to the promotion of her eldest son in the civil service in Bengal. The sonnets, too, gave CS the first indications of the likely success of her efforts at self-help.

Within three months of his release, her husband was in trouble again. He fled to France. CS spent the cold winter of 1785 in a decaying château near Dieppe, where she gave birth to another son. In the spring, CS pacified her husband's creditors and they returned to England. While in Normandy, CS had translated *Manon Lescaut* which she published on her return. When criticized for translating another immoral work, she immediately withdrew it. She published one other translation, stories entitled *The Romance of Real Life* (1787).

In 1787 CS left her husband. It was an amicable but not a full legal separation. She continued to try to settle the family legal difficulties and occasionally would send her husband money. She had a small income, irregularly paid. It was quite insufficient for her own and her family needs. She took to writing novels to raise money. She began *Emmeline* in the summer of 1787 and finished it in the spring of 1788. It was an instant success; it soon went into a second edition and her publisher, Cadell, voluntarily increased his payment. CS was now set fair on her novelistic career. In the next ten years, she was to write ten novels. By her efforts, she succeeded in maintaining herself and her family at the station in life to which she was accustomed. She was fortunate in her ability to write in an easy, natural prose, to compose quickly and, ironically, to draw on a rich set of experiences which gave her novels character. William Cowper knew of no one 'who could compose so rapidly and so well'. Her masterpiece, *The Old Manor House* (1793), was written while she enjoyed his and George Romney's company at Hayley's home. By the time CS had written her last novel, she was in poor health. She wrote a series of stories, *The Letters of a Solitary Wanderer* (1799), but her main attention was now focused on the less lucrative but more enjoyable moralistic work for children and on a rather more arduous task, a history of England for the young.

As the 1790s progressed, personal success hardly served to mitigate her growing ill-health and the continuance of family tragedies. Her third son, Charles Dyer, a reluctant soldier, had to have his leg amputated after taking part in the siege of Dunkirk in 1793. A year later her favourite daughter, Anna Augusta, died. Earlier in the year, her publisher was ungracious enough to blame her publicly for the delay in publishing *The Wanderings of Warwick* (1794). While writing it, her fingers were distorted with arthritis. In it, she wrote of how 'the unhappy almost always fancy that a change of place will relieve them'. She was unable to resist such imaginings and the closing years of her life were increasingly restless. She lived in a variety of places including London, Oxford, Weymouth, Exmouth, and Bath. The legacies for the grandchildren were belatedly completed, by about 1801. But not everything was settled. Charles Dyer went to the West Indies to sort out his grandfather's bequests. He succeeded at the cost of his life; he died of yellow fever. The final legal settlement was not complete until six months after CS's death. CS's restlessness continued to the end. Her last move was in 1805 to Tilford, near Farnham, where she died the following year. She had survived her husband by a few months, and was survived by eight of her twelve children.

CS's experiences gave her work an authenticity unusual in contemporary novels. Her characters are well drawn apart from the stereotypical heroes and heroines, and the dialogue lively except when virtue is on display. Her plots tend to race madly for home in the final furlong. Although predominantly melancholy, her poetry displays that truth to nature which she sought and felt. She was no *enragée*, but was profoundly critical of existing society. Like many reformers of the time, her aspiration was that everyone should act virtuously. Her novels are Christian parables in secular dress.   MARTIN FITZPATRICK

Selected works: *Elegaic Sonnets and Other Essays* (1784); (trans.), *Manon Lescaut*, by Abbé Prévost (1785); *Emmeline, or, The Orphan of the Castle: A Novel* (1788); *Ethelinda, or, The Recluse of the Lake* (1789); *Celestina: A Novel* (1791); *Desmond: A Novel* (1792); *The Emigrants: A Poem, in Two Books* (1793); *The Old Manor House: A Novel* (1793); *The Wanderings of Warwick* (1794); *The Banished Man: A Novel* (1794); *Rural Walks: In Dialogues: Intended for the Use of Young Persons* (1795); *Montalbert: A Novel* (1795); *Rambles Farther: A Continuation of Rural Walks: In Dialogues Intended for the Use of Young Persons* (1796); *Marchmont: A Novel* (1796); *Elegaic Sonnets*, vol. 2 (1797); *Minor Morals, Interspersed with Sketches of Natural History, Historical Anecdotes, and Original Stories* (1798); *The Young Philosopher: A Novel* (1798); *Letters of a Solitary Wander, Containing Narratives of Various Descriptions* (1799); *Conversations, Introducing Poetry: Chiefly on Subjects of Natural History for the Use of Children and Young Persons* (1804); *History of England, from the Earliest Records to the Peace of Amiens: In a Series of Letters to a Young Lady at School* (1806); *Beachy Head, with Other Poems* (unfinished) (1806); *The Natural History of Birds: Intended Chiefly for Young Persons* (1807).

References: Allen, W., *The English Novel* (1954); Baker, E. A., *The History of the English Novel* (1931); Brydges, Sir, E., *Censura Literaria* (1815); *DNB*; Ehrenpreis, A. H., 'Introduction' to *The Old Manor House* (1969); Ehrenpreis,

A. H., 'Introduction' to *Emmeline: The Orphan of the Castle* (1971); Foster, J. R., *History of the Pre-Romantic Novel in England* (1949); Foster, J. R., 'Charlotte Smith, pre-romantic novelist', *PMLA* 48 (June 1928); Hilbish, F. M. A., *Charlotte Smith, Poet and Novelist (1749–1806)* (1941); Kavanagh, J., *English Women of Letters* (1863); Kelly, G., *The English Jacobin Novel, 1780–1805* (1976); Magee, W. H., 'The happy marriage: the influence of Charlotte Smith on Jane Austen', *Studies in the Novel* 5 (1975); Rogers, K. M., 'Inhibitions on eighteenth-century women novelists: Elizabeth Inchbald and Charlotte Smith', *Eighteenth-Century Studies* 11 (1978); Schofield, M. S. and Macheski, C. (eds), *Fetter'd or Free? British Women Novelists 1670–1815* (1986); Scott, Sir W., *Biographical Memoirs of Eminent Novelists* (1834); Todd; Todd, J., *Women's Friendship in Literature* (1980); Todd, J., *Sensibility: An Introduction* (1986); Tompkins, J. M. S., *The Popular Novel in England 1770–1800* (1932).

Smith, Stevie

b. 1902, Hull; d. 7 March 1971, London

Poet, novelist

Of SS's life there is little to tell. At the age of 3 she moved with her mother from Yorkshire to Palmer's Green in north London, where she lived for the rest of her life, her father having gone to sea shortly after she was born. She attended North London Collegiate School for Girls and later worked as secretary to the publishers Newnes & Pearson, the office typing paper providing the title and the substance of her first novel. When she was 16 her mother died and her 'Lion Aunt' moved in. She was to remain SS's constant companion until she died in 1968. Palmer's Green and its inhabitants provided much of the material for SS's work and her portraits sometimes made her enemies, as 'The Story of a Story' (in '*Me Again*': *The Uncollected Writings of Stevie Smith*) reports. But too much time has been spent attempting to align her characters with 'real' people, and perhaps we should read the stories the sinners write and leave their private lives to heaven.

When SS took her first collection of poems to Jonathan Cape she was told to go away and write a novel. This rejection resulted in *Novel on Yellow Paper* (1936), which mischievously contained many of the poems intended for her book of poetry, either thinly disguised as prose or inserted into the text as whole poems. The effect is unsettling and demands a slow, concentrated read. As the writer Ian Hamilton Finlay advised, 'You must read *one* SS novel every five years – very slowly at that.' These melancholy books demand perseverance, especially *Over the Frontier* (1938), a tale of international espionage in the style of John Buchan. Her last novel, *The Holiday* (1949), is disappointing, amounting to little more than an overgrown autobiographical sketch, but it was her favourite and as such it has a certain interest. Unfortunately, she chose not to include in it the heroine of the first two novels Pompey Casmilus, one of her most endearing characters. Without her the novel flounders in tender but irritating nostalgia.

SS's apparent flippancy annoyed many a reviewer of her poetry – Philip Larkin described her poem 'Nourish Me on an Egg, Nanny' as 'facetious bosh'. Poet-critics do not like their art demeaned and SS had no time for their posturing. Consequently she is a 'minor' poet. This is not to say that she was untouched by the opinions of reviewers. Her poem 'They Killed' explains her predicament:

> They killed a poet by neglect
> And treating him worse than an insect
> They said what he wrote was feeble
> And should never be read by serious people.
>
> Serious people, serious people.
> I should think it were serious to be such people.

Categories and hierarchies were anathema to SS and she refused to be classed
either as a 'serious' or 'comic' writer. She attempted to rescue language from
'serious people', allowing the sounds of utterance to fuse in a kind of playground
babel. Her style remained remarkably constant from *A Good Time Was Had By
All* (1937) to *Scorpion and Other Poems* (1971). She does not mature; she would
have thought the idea foolish. Her little rhymes were portable myths of primarily therapeutic importance and, apart from her aunt, her characters were her
only love. 'The absolute dearth of companionship in Palmer's Green drives one
into writing,' she once admitted, though she always underplayed her talent.

SS's poetry tends to derive from three main sources: classical literature,
religion, or fairy-tale, but it is her childlike voice which pleases most readers.
Her nursery rhymes and fairy-tales dwell in the transitional world somewhere
between blissful dependence and respectable behaviour. It is a world which
adults cannot enter because it makes no sense. 'What are we looking for over
the wall?' you ask. 'We are not looking for anything at all,' comes the reply.
SS appreciated fully the destructive nature of a reality constructed by adults
and she learnt from children a way of disrupting that reality. Without ever
overestimating the power of illusion, she saw that children and adults alike
could use rhythm and rhyme to play out the contradictory messages they
received from the outside world. For her the role of the poet was to stare
outside her prison-room with the eye of an anarchist.

Reading SS's poetry is a game rather than a chore and is aided by her line
drawings which illustrate her work. All of her work, from her book reviews
and essays to her novels and poetry, contains a little of herself. All of her
characters were created out of the necessity of loneliness. But her greatest
creation was 'Stevie Smith', and she constantly warned 'The Reader' against
taking the game outside the confines of illusion: 'Now Reader don't go making
trouble fixing up names to all this. I say there's not a person or a thing in this
book [*Novel on Yellow Paper*] that ever stepped outside of this book. It's all just
out of my head.'   MARTIN BRIGHT
Works: *Novel on Yellow Paper* (1936); *Over the Frontier* (1938); *The Holiday*
(1949); *The Collected Poems of Stevie Smith* (1975); *'Me Again'* – *The Uncollected
Writings of Stevie Smith* (1981).
References: Dick, K., *Ivy and Stevie* (1971); Rankin, A. C., *The Poetry of Stevie
Smith 'Little Girl Lost'* (1985).

Smyth, Ethel
b. 22 April 1858, Sidcup; d. 9 May 1944, Woking
Composer, autobiographical writer
ES was the daughter of Lieutenant-Colonel (later Major-General) John Hall
Smyth CB and Nina (*née* Struth) Smyth. One of eight children, she lived in
Sidcup until 1867 when her father's promotion to the command of the Royal
Artillery at Aldershot occasioned the family's move to Frimley which remained
ES's home until her father's death in 1894. Although she was educated mostly

by governesses, in 1872 ES was sent, with her sister Mary, to boarding school in Putney. Leaving school in 1875, she was given musical instruction by a neighbour, Alexander Ewing, an officer in the Army Service Corps and the composer of the hymn 'Jerusalem the Golden'. ES was passionately interested in music and, aspiring to be a composer, convinced her reluctant father to allow her to enrol in the Leipzig Conservatorium at the age of 19. She was taught by Reineke, Jadassohn, and Maas, but found a prevailing attitude of indifference among her masters not to her liking. She was offered tuition by Heinrich von Herzogenburg, whose wife, Elizabeth, was one of her closest friends, and in 1878 ES withdrew from the Conservatorium. Through the Herzogenburgs she came to know Brahms, Greig, Dvořák, Clara Schumann, and Joachim, and to gain a limited audience for her own compositions. ES never married, although she was engaged for three weeks to William Wilde (Oscar's brother). Her twenty-year love affair with Henry Bennet Brewster was never formalized in marriage.

ES's writings are largely autobiographical, following her contention that 'I am by far the most interesting person I know.' In the later years of her life, she spent much of her time writing rather than composing. Her two-volume *Impressions That Remained* (1919) was both a popular and a critical success. It contains her recollections of her life in Leipzig, and is remarkable for the vivid and entertaining portraits of her many friends. ES was an inveterate collector of people, particularly of those who shared her passion for music and, latterly, for women's suffrage. Her witty, anecdotal reminiscences include character sketches of her neighbour Empress Eugénie, Tchaikovsky, and Brahms. From her writings emerges an eccentric and vigorous personality. She was militant, not only in her fight for recognition in a field dominated and controlled by men, and for women's emancipation in general, but also in her demands on herself, her friends, and family. Once told by Sir Henry Wood that she should not move her body while conducting, ES rehearsed for a forthcoming performance tied to a tree so as to concentrate her energies on her baton.

Eight volumes of autobiographical writings followed *Impressions That Remained*, among them *Inordinate (?) Affection* (1936), a history of the dogs she owned between 1888 and 1928, and *Female Pipings in Eden* (1933) which contains the texts of essays and lectures on the plight of women composers and musicians, as well as an affectionate portrait of Emmeline Pankhurst and a discussion of ES's own membership in the Women's Social and Political Union. ES joined the WSPU in 1910 and composed their marching song, 'March of the Women'. Briefly imprisoned for her activities with the WSPU, she once conducted the March with her toothbrush from the window of her Holloway cell.

ES's battle to secure performances for her music, and her suspicion that it was denied 'fair play' because it was the work of a woman, was perhaps one of the reasons for her involvement with the WSPU. Her *Mass in D*, performed at the Albert Hall in 1893, surprised the music world with its power and scope. Its revival in 1924 prompted G. B. Shaw to write that it had cured him forever 'of the old delusion that women could not do men's work in art and other things'. ES is best known for her operatic works, among which *The Wreckers*, with a libretto by Brewster, is considered her greatest artistic achievement and popular success. ES's music is perhaps too eclectic for its own durability, with its difficult blend of originality and convention. She was one of the first women, however, to work with the large forms of opera, oratorio, and concerto. Although she had to fight for acceptance by critics and fellow musicians, often resorting to bullying and cajoling in order to get her works performed at all, she was accorded recognition. In 1910 she was awarded an honorary doctorate of music by Durham University, by Oxford in 1926, and by Manchester in 1930. She received an honorary LLD from St Andrews in 1928, and in 1922 she was created Dame of the British Empire.   ALISON M. LEE

Works: *Impressions That Remained* (1919); *Streaks of Life* (1921); *A Three-legged Tour in Greece* (1927); *A Final Burning of Boats* (1928); *Female Pipings in Eden* (1933); *Beecham and Pharaoh* (1935); *As Time Went On* (1935); *Inordinate (?) Affection* (1936); *What Happened Next* (1940).

References: Beecham, T., 'Dame Ethel Smyth (1858–1944)', *Music Times* 99 (1958); Dale, K., 'Dame Ethel Smyth', *Music and Letters* 35 (1944); Howes, F., *The English Musical Renaissance* (1966); McNaught, W., 'Dame Ethel Smyth', *Music Times* 85 (1944); St John, C., *Ethel Smyth* (1959); White, E. W., *The Rise of English Opera* (1951).

Somerville and Ross
Somerville, Edith

b. 2 May 1858, Corfu; d. 8 October 1949, Castle Townsend, Ireland
(Also wrote under Geilles Herring, Viva Graham)

Martin, Violet

b. 11 June 1862, Ross House, County Galway, Ireland; d. 21 December 1915, Cork, Ireland

Novelists

S and R (Violet Martin) formed one of the most notable literary partnerships of the late nineteenth and early twentieth centuries. S, daughter of Thomas and Adelaide Coghill Somerville, was educated primarily by governesses, and for a short time at Alexandra College, Dublin. She also studied art in England and eventually became a student of Délécluse and Colarossi in Paris. In addition to her writing, she illustrated numerous serial publications and many of the works on which she collaborated with R.

R, the daughter of James and Anna Fox Martin, lived in her family's 'Big House' until she was 10, when her mother took the children to Dublin. Her nostalgia for her childhood at Ross House permeates much of the writers' work.

Second cousins, S and R met in 1886, became fast friends, and shortly after began their collaborative efforts. The degree to which each writer contributed to their joint works cannot be fully ascertained. The diffuseness of the novels that S wrote after her cousin's death, however, suggests that R was far more concerned with matters of form and style than S. The first two novels of S and R point to the major strengths and limitations of their work in general. *An Irish Cousin* (1889), their first attempt to delineate the milieu of Anglo-Irish Ascendancy, is flawed by its Gothic trappings, but vividly recreates its social setting. The subject of *Naboth's Vineyard* (1891) is Irish Catholic village life, of which the authors had perhaps too little experience to create fully realized characters or convincing situations. Their later forays outside the restricted environs of the Ascendancy were marred by a similar superficiality.

From 1890 to 1893 S and R travelled to Connemara, Bordeaux, north Wales and Denmark, recounting their journeys in *Through Connemara in a Governess Cart* (1893), *In the Vine Country* (1893), *Beggars on Horseback* (1895), and *Stray-Aways* (1920; originally entitled *In the State of Denmark*). Some of the light, charming pieces in these collections first appeared in genteel periodicals such as *The Lady's Pictorial*.

The Real Charlotte (1894) is S and R's fullest fictional exploration of the Anglo-Irish Ascendancy. The outstanding achievement of the novel is the characterization of Charlotte Mullen, a social climber of middle-class origins, whose success in her ruthless business deals contrasts with her failure in personal relationships. In Charlotte, S and R subtly create a character who arouses hatred and pity. While the authors present their own social background sympathetically they also view it objectively, especially in their depiction of the decaying Dysart family.

S and R's next novel, *The Silver Fox* (1897), is concerned with the plight of the English in an unfamiliar Ireland. Clearly inferior to *The Real Charlotte*, the work is marred by improbabilities in plot and multiple climaxes, the latter necessitated by its serial form.

The first of S and R's stories about an Irish magistrate appeared in the *Badminton Magazine* in October 1898. The publication of the collection *Some Experiences of an Irish RM* in 1889 quickly brought the writers international fame. In this first of three volumes of the Irish RM stories, S and R concentrate on the lighter side of life of the Anglo-Irish Ascendancy and the Irish Catholics who surrounded them. They follow the adventures and misadventures of the Resident Magistrate, Major Sinclair Yeates, as he attempts to bring order to the eccentric peasantry and aristocracy in and around Skebaun. Much of the humour of the stories derives from the victimization of the hapless major by the clever Irish peasants and by his crafty landlord, Flurry Knox, one of the writers' most memorable comic creations. The success of the first volume of the Irish RM stories led to the publication of two more collections, *Further Experiences of an Irish RM* (1908) and *In Mr Knox's Country* (1915). The latter of these is weaker than the first two volumes chiefly because of its looser organization and its repetition of familiar themes and situations. Some of the stories take a more sombre look at the decline of the Big House tradition.

Except for the Irish RM stories, S and R produced little work between 1899 and 1915. In order to satisfy the publishers' and reading public's demands they collected hunting stories in *All on the Irish Shore* (1903), articles and occasional pieces in *Some Irish Yesterdays* (1906), and wrote one additional novel, *Dan Russel the Fox* (1911) – all undistinguished.

After R's death in 1915, S wrote five novels and published ten other works, including volumes of reminiscences and sketches, and a biography. She continued to sign many of these books 'Somerville and Ross', claiming that her spiritual communications with R kept their partnership alive. *Irish Memories* (1917) sheds light on the writers' younger days. Two of these later novels were S's most considerable solo achievements: in *Mount Music* (1919) she treats the subject of intermarriage between Irish Protestants and Catholics, and in *The Big House of Inver* (1925), a work in the tradition of *Castle Rackrent*, she explores the corruption and deterioration of an Ascendancy family.

PETER DREWNIANY

Selected works: (ed. Somerville), *The Mark Twain Birthday Book* (1885); *An Irish Cousin* (1889); *Naboth's Vineyard* (1891); *In the Vine Country* (1893); *Through Connemara in a Governess Cart* (1893); *The Real Charlotte* (1894); *Beggars on Horseback* (1895); *The Silver Fox* (1898); *Some Experiences of an Irish RM* (1899); *A Patrick's Day Hunt* (1902); *All on the Irish Shore* (1903); *Some Irish Yesterdays* (1906); *Further Experiences of an Irish RM* (1908); *In Mr Knox's Country* (1915); *Irish Memories* (1917); *Mount Music* (1919); *Stray-Aways* (1920); *Wheel-Tracks*

(1923); *The Big House of Inver* (1925); *French Leave* (1928); *The States Through Irish Eyes* (1930); *An Incorruptible Irishman* (1932); *The Smile and the Tear* (1933); (ed. Somerville), *Notes of the Horn: Hunting Verse, Old and New* (1934); *The Sweet Cry of Hounds* (1936); *Sarah's Youth* (1938); *Notions in Garrison* (1941); *Happy Days!* (1946); *Maria and Some Other Dogs* (1949).
References: Collis, M., *Somerville and Ross: A Biography* (1968); Cronin, J., *Somerville and Ross* (1972); Cummins, G., *Dr E. O. Somerville: A Biography* (1952); Drabble; Hudson, E. (ed.), *A Bibliography of the First Editions of the Works of E. OE Somerville and Martin Ross* (1942); Institute of Irish Studies, Queen's University, Belfast, *Somerville and Ross: A Symposium* (1969); Lucas, E. V., 'Two Ladies', in *Cloud and Silver* (1916); O'Brien, C. C., 'Somerville and Ross', in *Writers and Politics* (1965); Powell, V., *The Irish Cousins* (1970); Pritchett, V. S., 'The Irish RM', in *The Living Novel* (1946); Robinson, H., *Somerville and Ross: A Critical Appreciation* (1980); Williams, O., 'A Little Classic', in *Some Great English Novels* (1926).

Southcott, Joanna

b. April 1750, Gittisham, East Devon; d. 27 December 1814, London
Religious writer
The leader of the most popular millenarian movement of the early nineteenth century, JS was the fourth daughter of an impoverished farmer, William Southcott, and his wife Hannah. On Easter Monday 1792, when employed as an upholstress and domestic in Exeter and shortly after joining the Wesleyans, JS began to hear voices from the Spirit of God. She went to her sister's house in Plymtree, Devon, and began to prophesy in doggerel verse and prose. A sealed box of her prophecies, which foretold bad harvests and wars until the clergy heeded her warnings, was left with her sister when she returned to Exeter. The Spirit commanded her to publish the messages, and in 1801 *The Strange Effects of Faith* appeared. Her followers by then included the clergymen Stanhope Bruce, Thomas Philip Foley, and Thomas Webster, and the engraver William Sharp, who persuaded JS to move to London where she began to 'seal' the faithful for the Millennium. In 1794 JS had identified herself with 'the woman clothed with sun' in *Revelation* 12, and in October 1802 foretold that the ambiguities of her earlier prophecies had been explained to her and that she had been chosen to fulfil the passage in *Genesis* 49 which prophesied the birth of Shiloh, the second Christ. In March 1814 she became ill, and although six of the nine doctors consulted diagnosed symptoms of pregnancy, JS died on the date of the expected birth, disillusioned with her prophecies. An autopsy revealed no sign of pregnancy.

Southcottianism continued as a powerful religious force after her death; one of her followers, George Turner, a prosperous Leeds merchant, prophesied the exact date of Shiloh's birth in 1817, and the movement reflected many people's need to find a non-revolutionary form of resistance to the social conditions resulting from government policy. This need was strong during the time of the Napoleonic wars; JS had been involved with the Methodists, although they later denounced her, and her predecessors included Anne Lee, who founded the Shaker sect in America, and Richard Brothers, a prophet who claimed to be the nephew of God, and who was imprisoned in Islington Lunatic Asylum in 1795. JS's movement contained a large number of Brothers's supporters, and although she claimed to be religiously orthodox her sect soon set up its own chapels and organized its own services. At the height of the movement, the

Southcottians, or 'Joannas' numbered about 100,000 country wide; the major strongholds of members were in London, the West Country and the industrial Midlands and North. Southcottianism appealed to women, who comprised about two-thirds of the members, and men of all classes, from scholars and businessmen to priests and workers. JS's many published pamphlets were mostly uncensored because they did not advocate active political opposition. The only revolution demanded was that against personal sin, and although JS's Spirit condemned the social distress inflicted upon the working class it warned that the reason for this was that the Church refused to examine the truth of JS's writings. Instead of looking for political causes of distress, JS blamed the religious state of the nation, and demanded that her followers should blame their own personal inadequacies: 'when will these sorrows have an end? I am told, never; till ministers do awake, as men do out of sleep, to search out the cause; which, I am told, in my writings, is men's unbelief of what I have written; and ministers' neglect of not trying the Spirit, whether it came from God, or not. If men will not try the Spirit, God will prove the Spirit, by sending a heavier curse on the land, than is already sent.'

Although they were primarily popular because of their wide circulation in newspapers, JS's works could be easily understood by all because the biblical passages are translated into more concrete and accessible language and imagery. God's Spirit, in a confiding and intimate relationship with JS, makes his images very visual: He explains that bad weather at New Year symbolizes the state of her own soul and the spiritual condition of the country, and JS writes, 'my sins must be of the blackest die.' God's presence, like that of sin, becomes a very real, visible force. In the prophecies concerning Shiloh, verbal ambiguities of the possibility of extending grace to the socially oppressed are clarified and made into physical fact, as JS perceives in herself qualities that will fulfil the prophecies and declare the truth of her words: 'for so the WOMAN was in the creation; and being taken from the MAN, she was his SISTER; but as bearing him children, she was a WIFE and a MOTHER. Thus was the WOMAN made at first, and *this must be the state of the woman at last*, now I am come to free the fall of woman.' CAROLINE COLEMAN

Selected works: *The Strange Effects of Faith* (1801); *A Continuation of the Prophecies* (1802); *Dispute Between the Woman and the Powers of Darkness* (1802); *Answer of the Lord to the Powers of Darkness* (1802); *Second Book of Visions* (1803); *A Word in Season* (1803); *A Word to the Wise* (1803); *Divine and Spiritual Communications* (1803); *Sound an Alarm in My Holy Mountain* (1804); *A Warning to the World* (1804); *On the Prayers for the Fast Day* (1804); *Copies and Parts of Copies* (1804); *The Trial of Joanna Southcott* (1804); *Answer to the Five Charges in the Leeds' Mercury* (1805); *True Explanation of the Bible* (1805); *Explanations of the Parables* (1805); *Kingdom of Christ is at Hand* (n. d.); *Full Assurance That the Kingdom of Heaven Is at Hand* (1806); *The Long Wished for Revolution* (1806); *Caution and Instruction to the Sealed* (1807); *An Account of the Trials of the Bills of Exchange* (1807); *Answer to False Doctrines* (1808); *True Explanation of the Bible* part 7 (1809); *True Picture of the World* (1809); *Controversy of the Spirit* (1811); *An Answer to Thomas Paine* (1812); *The Books of Wonders* (1813–14); *Prophecies Announcing the Birth of the Prince of Peace* (1814).

References: Balleine, G. R., *Past Finding Out – The Tragic Story of Joanna Southcott and Her Successors* (1956); *DNB*; Harrison, J. F. C., *Robert Owen and the Owenites in Britain and Ireland* (1969); Harrison, J. F. C., *The Second Coming* (1979); Hopkins, J. K., *A Woman to Deliver Her People* (1982); Johnson, D. A., *Women in English Religion* (1983); Thompson, E. P., *The Making of the English*

Working Class (1963); Todd; Wright, E. P. (ed.), *Catalogue of the Joanna Southcott Collection of the University of Texas* (1969).

Spain, Nancy

b. September 1917, Newcastle-upon-Tyne; d. 21 March 1964 in plane crash near Aintree
Journalist, novelist, biographer, broadcaster
The daughter of George and Norah Spain, NS grew up in Newcastle-upon-Tyne: 'My main root is there, drawing strength from my rebellion against middle-class provincial society, against the giving and taking of merchandise in marriage, the petty routine of bridge party and back-biting, jealousy and "keeping up with the Joneses".' In *A Funny Thing Happened on the Way* (1964) NS describes the comic results of well-meaning attempts to impose a conformist gloss on her unvarnished individualism. She was sent to Roedean, where she excelled at lacrosse and won the school prize for verse speaking, but failed to assume the 'feminine' qualities she felt were expected of her: 'I looked simply appalling in the coffee-coloured lace that mother had in mind . . . the role of young lady from the provinces was not for me.' She never married.

Other roles proved more congenial. NS shared her mother's enthusiasm for sport, although she suggests that Norah's commitment to the social benefits of tennis sometimes outweighed her devotion to the fine points of the game: 'I went creeping off to join less socially acceptable clubs where the people actually managed to hit the ball over the net.' Her father helped to foster her love of poetry and prose, and introduced her, through his contributions to *Punch* and other periodicals, to the idea that publication is the natural consequence of writing. By the time she was 17 NS had found a readership through her sports column, syndicated in newspapers in the north of England, and an audience for her performances in BBC radio drama.

NS's talent for bringing a light touch to serious subjects is well illustrated in *Thank You – Nelson* (1945) an account of her wartime experience with the WRNS. The narrative hurtles forward, like a requisitioned lorry NS is commissioned to drive, carrying everything from 'cabbages to corpses'. When she stops to talk to Dunkirk survivors, their understated comments, like snapshots, reflect the confusion, mess, and waste of war.

After the war NS settled in London and began to write biographies and detective fiction. She researched *Mrs Beeton and Her Husband* (1948) with meticulous care, following the route described in her great-aunt's diary around the lakes of Killarney. The plane trip to Dublin was the first of many flights combining the pleasure of travel with the business of trailing a story.

Miriam Birdseye and Natasha Nevkorina, NS's memorable detective partners, share a penchant for solving bizarre crimes. The conventions of the murder mystery are thoroughly flouted; there is no pretence to serious investigation. The real enemy is boredom, the odd murder an amusing diversion. As the women rip through their series of highly-coloured adventures, assuming and discarding disguises at a whim, the casualties left in their wake include one or two comfortable assumptions. 'Kiddies are fiends', concludes Natasha in *Out, Damned Tot* (1952). Worse, the women discover that cosy families harbour vice, marriage induces murderous impulses and exclusive girls' schools (particularly one called Radcliff Hall) seem to encourage antisocial tendencies. 'It is all,' says Miriam Birdseye, 'most unsettling.'

In the last decade of her life, NS enjoyed popular acclaim; critical recognition proved more elusive. When the second volume of her autobiography, *Why I'm Not a Millionaire*, appeared in 1956, she was already something of a celebrity. She lived with Jonnie, Joan Werner Laurie, editor of *She* magazine. They shared a family life with Jonnie's two sons, entertained friends generously, and worked together. As NS expanded her career as a communicator she moved from the *Daily Express* to the *News of the World*; her columns and features for *She* and *Elle* ranged over current affairs, the arts, and travel. She gained a wider audience as a panelist on radio and television. In *My Word!*, *Twenty Questions* and *Juke Box Jury* her distinctive voice and figure, her intelligence and vivacity combined to create a lasting impressions on listeners and viewers.

NS was able to articulate the confident optimism of post-war Britain. She celebrated the emergence of popular culture as a participant, without contempt or condescension. She was a warm, sometimes sharp but never sour observer of the human comedy. In 1964, NS was flying to cover the Grand National. The plane crashed; Jonnie died with her. Among the many tributes, Clement Freud wrote 'she might well have picked her own death; dramatically, in harness, at an occasion and among people.' ELFRIDA LAUGHARNE

Works: *Thank You – Nelson* (1945); *Poison in Play* (1946); *Death Before Wicket* (1946); *Mrs Beeton and Her Husband* (1948); *Murder, Bless It* (1948); *Death Goes On Skis* (1949); *Poison for Teacher* (1949); *Cinderella Goes to the Morgue* (1950); *'R' in the Month* (1950); *Not Wanted on Voyage* (1951); *Out, Damned Tot* (1952); *'Teach' Tennant: The Story of Eleanor Tennant* (1953); *The Tiger Who Couldn't Eat Meat* (1954); *The Kat Strikes* (1955); *The Tiger Who Went to the Moon* (1956); *Why I'm Not A Millionaire* (1956); *The Tiger Who Won His Star* (1957); *My Boy Mo* (1959); *The Tiger Who Saved the Train* (1960); *Nancy Spain's Tiger Annual* (1961); *The Tiger Who Found the Treasure* (1961); *The Beaver Annual* (1962); *The Nancy Spain Colour Cookery Book* (1963); *A Funny Thing Happened on the Way* (1964).

References: Craig, P. and Cadogan, M., *The Lady Investigates: Women Detectives and Spies in Fiction* (1981); Ward, A. C., *Longman Companion to Twentieth Century Literature* (1970).

Spark, Muriel

b. 1918, Edinburgh

Novelist, poet

MS was brought up in Edinburgh, where her Jewish father, Bernard Camberg, was employed as an engineer; her mother, Sarah Elizabeth Maud (*née* Uezelli), from Hertfordshire, was of Italian descent. She was educated at James Gillespie's School for Girls which she fictionalized as the Marcia Blaine School in *The Prime of Miss Jean Brodie* (1961). From the age of 19, she spent some years in Rhodesia which inspired poems such as 'Like Africa' and several short stories including 'The Portobello Road', 'The Go-Away Bird', 'Bang Bang You're Dead', and 'The Seraph and the Zambesi'. The last of these won a national short story competition run by the *The Observer* in 1951 which established her reputation as a creative writer. On returning to Britain in 1944, MS worked in the Political Intelligence Department of the Foreign Office on anti-Nazi propaganda. She utilized her knowledge of psychological warfare in her novel set in New York, *The Hothouse by the East River* (1973). The techniques acquired at the Foreign Office of camouflaging facts served her with an apprenticeship for the experiments in her novels relating to the truths of fiction.

Though widely renowned as a novelist, MS has regarded herself primarily as a poet, having written poetry from the age of 9. In 1947 she was appointed secretary of the Poetry Society, shortly afterwards becoming the editor of the Society's *Poetry Review*. Her advocacy of Modernism antagonized members of the Poetry Society who eventually called for her dismissal. She left in 1948 to found the poetry magazine *Forum*, and continued writing her own poetry which she published in 1952 as *The Fanfario and Other Verse*. Her *Collected Poems 1* were not published until 1967. Some of these have been reprinted in *Sotheby's and Other Poems* (1982).

Apart from writing poetry, MS has also published works of literary criticism. In 1950, she edited with Derek Stanford a *Tribute to Wordsworth* on the centenary of the poet's death. The following year, MS produced a critical biography of Mary Shelley called *Child of Light* and then an edition of the life and work of Emily Brontë in 1953. In the same year, she published selections of the letters of the Brontës and Mary Shelley.

Her conversion to Catholicism in 1954 had a profound influence on her life and work. During this period. Macmillans commissioned her to write her first novel, *The Comforters* (1957), the title of which was taken from the Book of Job. A few years later, she wrote an article for the *Church of England Newspaper* on 'The mystery of Job's suffering'. MS was later to revive her fascination with Job in her novel *The Only Problem* (1984), in which Harvey Gotham retires to France in order to write a monogram on the Book of Job. Catholic characters appear frequently in her novels, such as Jean Taylor in *Memento Mori* (1959), a macabre comedy about death, and the nuns in *The Abbess of Crewe* (1974), a witty political satire set in a convent. MS was later to insist that she had not been able to write novels until becoming a Catholic. She claimed that since entering the Church she had begun to see life in its totality rather than as a series of disconnected occurrences. Underlying this is her belief that life is not composed of chaos but is built up on an order which the novelist can delineate. Furthermore, the analogue between the writer and God generated a frame of reference for her art.

The Comforters is an experimental foray into the relationship between the author and her characters through which she was able to explore her own role as a novelist. Such self-consciousness is reflected in her heroine, Caroline Rose, who realizes that she is a character in a novel. Her resistance to the plot imposed upon her by the invisible author turns on the problems relating to the exercise of free will from within a pre-ordained existence. MS uses this technique in her drama, *Doctors of Philosophy*, performed in October 1962 at the New Arts Theatre, London, where some characters are aware that they are taking part in a play.

In her second novel, *Robinson* (1958), MS allegorically explores Robinson the island and the man as a 'landscape of the mind'. *Memento Mori*, published the following year, confronts the metaphysical mystery of death. The novel concerns itself with a community of elderly people who become the recipients of anonymous telephone calls, presumably from death itself, reminding them that they are going to die. MS employs the supernatural to a greater extent in her next novel, *The Ballad of Peckham Rye* (1960), inspired by her stay in neighbouring Camberwell in 1956. In this satanic ballad, the demonic figure, Dougal Douglas, assumes the power to change his appearance. The characters in *The Bachelors* (1960) are caught up, likewise, in a web of spurious beliefs, spiritualism and demonology. A more compelling study of misguided and even dangerous ideologies may be found in *The Prime of Miss Jean Brodie* where a fascistic school teacher attempts to subvert a schoolgirl elite of her own creation. The character of Jean Brodie is believed to have been based upon one of MS's own teachers, Miss Christine Kay. For her next novel, MS again drew upon her own life when in 1947, finding herself short of money, she took up residence at a hostel in Lancaster Gate called the Helena Club. It was this period which formed the basis of her novel set in the post-war years, *The Girls of Slender Means* (1963). *The Mandelbaum Gate* (1965) is even more autobiographical. Two of its characters are modelled on MS's mother and grandmother while the heroine, Barbara Vaughan, like the author, is a Jewish Catholic convert who goes to Israel in order to attend the trial of the Nazi war criminal Adolph Eichmann. In 1961, the year of Barbara's visit to Jerusalem, the city was divided by the Mandelbaum Gate.

A sense of place is evoked again in *The Public Image* (1968) which is set in Rome where MS settled in 1966. Here she explores the relationship between fiction and reality through the image-building machinery of the film industry. Frederick Christopher, who becomes resentful of his wife's success as an actress, tries to destroy her public image through his own suicide. *The Take-Over* (1976) also takes place in Italy and concerns the intrigues of fraud in the art world. The heroine, Maggie Radcliffe, takes on the persona of the goddess Diana in the pagan setting of her country villa. Another Italian novel is *Territorial Rights* (1979), focusing this time on Venice amidst the blackmail and corruption of big business interests.

MS's earlier thriller set in a stately home is *Not to Disturb* (1971), which, in places, parodies the Gothic novel. MS's delight in parody may be seen in *The Driver's Seat* (1970) which inverts the conventional murder story formula. The twist in the tale is that Lise, the victim, seeks out her own killer! The title of the novel begs the question, who is in the driver's seat, the novelist or the main character? In this pastiche on Catholic teleology, Lise appears to take over from the novelist by offering herself as an alternative plotmaker, thus generating the substance of her own creative fiction. In *Loitering with Intent* (1981) MS returns to the interplay between fiction and fact that she introduced in *The Comforters*. Her autobiographical heroine, the novelist Fleur Talbot, is a self-conscious celebration of woman as artist during the twentieth century.

MS's novels document her struggle with and against her own characters to find her authorial voice through the exploration of her role as a writer. For MS, the role of novelist lies in a transformation of the commonplace which she believed could also be realized through religious faith. Describing her books as a pack of lies, MS regards her novels as poetic fictions out of which some valuable truth emerges. She has received critical acclaim and recognition for her achievements in fiction, having been awarded the Italia Prize, the James Tait Black Memorial Prize, and, in 1967, the OBE. MS now lives in Italy.

MARIE ROBERTS

Works: *Tribute to Wordsworth* (1950); *Child of Light* (1951); *A Selection of Poems by Emily Brontë* (1952); *Emily Brontë* (1953); *The Brontë Letters* (1953); *My Best Mary* (1953); *The Comforters* (1957); *Robinson* (1958); *The Go-Away Bird and Other Stories* (1958); *Memento Mori* (1959); *The Ballad of Peckham Rye* (1960); *The Bachelors* (1960); *Voices at Play* (1961); *The Prime of Miss Jean Brodie* (1961); *Doctors of Philosophy* (1963); *The Girls of Slender Means* (1963); *The Mandelbaum Gate* (1965); *Collected Poems 1* (1967); *Collected Stories 1* (1967); *The Public Image* (1968); *The Very Fine Clock* (1968); *The Driver's Seat* (1970); *Not to Disturb* (1971); *The Hothouse by the East River* (1973); *The Abbess of Crewe* (1974); *The Takeover* (1976); *Territorial Rights* (1979); *Loitering with Intent* (1981); *Sothebys*

and Other Poems (1982); *Bang-Bang You're Dead and Other Stories* (1982); *The Only Problem* (1984).
References: Bold, A., *Muriel Spark* (1986); Kemp, P., *Muriel Spark* (1974); Stanford, D., *Muriel Spark: A Biographical and Literary Study* (1963); Stubbs, P., *Muriel Spark* (1973); Whittaker, R., *The Faith and Fiction of Muriel Spark* (1982).

Speght, Rachel
b. c.1597, London; d. ?
Polemicistt, pamphleteer
RS was the daughter of a minister, James Speght. In 1616 she wrote *A Mouzell for Melastomus*, an answer to Joseph Swetnam's *Arraignment of Lewd, Idle, Forward and Unconstant women* (1615) ['Melastomus' means black mouth, or slanderer: Swetnam's attack is seen to be like that of a dog in bear-baiting, hence the need for a muzzle]. RS was perhaps the first woman in this period to answer under her own name the regular (and commercially successful) attacks on women. Her pamphlet is serious and religious; it goes beyond satiric controversy in its use of the Bible to demonstrate the dignity of woman and her rights in marriage: 'For man was created of the dust of the earth . . . but woman was made of a part of man after that he was a living soul. Yet was she not produced from Adam's foot, to be his too low inferior; nor from his head to be his superior; but from his side, near his heart, to be his equal: that where he is lord, she may be lady.' In her second work, *Mortality's Memorandum*, RS writes an allegorical *Dream* which recounts her intellectual autobiography. Furthermore, in her Epistle to that work she claims her rights as a woman author by condeming those who attributed authorship of her first work to her father. By contrast, it is the women relatives who are important: *Mortality's Memorandum* is a poem written partly in response to her mother's death; it is dedicated to her godmother Mary Moundford, wife of the sometime Bursar of King's College, Cambridge. In August 1621 RS married William Procter, both being resident in St Botolph's Aldersgate. There were at least two children, a girl and a boy (born 1626 and 1630), the first being given RS's own name Rachel.
SIMON SHEPHERD

Works: *A Mouzell for Melastomus* (1617); *Mortality's Memorandum* (1621).
References: Dusinberre, J., *Shakespeare and the Nature of Women* (1975); Shepherd, S., *Amazons and Warrior Women* (1981); Shepherd, S., *The Women's Sharp Revenge* (1985).

Stanhope, Lady Hester
b. 12 March 1776, Chevening, Kent; d. 23 June 1839, Mount Lebanon, Lebanon
Memoirist
(Also wrote under Hester Lucy Stanhope, Lady Esther Stanhope, Hester Stanhope, Isteir Istanheub, Histir Leusei Steanheub)
HS was first of all famous for her birth; her father was Viscount Mahon, later 3rd Earl of Stanhope, heir to the richest peerage in Kent, and her mother was the elder daughter of the Earl of Chatham and the sister of William Pitt. Her father was an eccentric, often single-minded, scientist, and her mother was celebrated for her cleverness. HS was especially famous when she served her uncle, the prime minister, until his death in 1806. She was also singular because of her arrogance and her height, being six feet tall.

Much of HS's posthumous fame has come to her through others' accounts. A popular topic for many European visitors and journalists when she lived in Syria after 1810, HS has enjoyed her most lasting fame through her doctor, Charles Lewis Meryon, who published her *Memoirs* and *Travels*. Through those works and the other briefer studies and reports, she came to be known by the end of the nineteenth century as an eccentric, not as a writer. Neither Thomas Seccombe in the *DNB* nor Lytton Strachey in his witty biographical sketches mentions her writing skills. Seccombe concentrates his account on her travels, and Strachey on the 'Pitt nose'. Since 1919, when Strachey published his essay, HS has been the subject for historical novels because of her unusual life, not her literary achievement.

HS's life, like her literary reputation, defied convention from its beginnings. She was 4 when her mother died, leaving HS and two younger sisters with their father. Within six months he remarried, shifting the care of his daughters to his second wife, by whom he had three sons. Both parents were distant and casual about their children, and HS's younger sister, Lucy, claimed that she would not have recognized her stepmother were they to meet on the street.

In 1800 HS escaped her eccentric father's arbitrary rule at Chevening to live with her grandmother Chatham in Somerset. When she helped one of her half-brothers escape, her selfless gesture attracted the attention of her uncle, William Pitt, and she soon became one of his most trusted friends. By 1803 she was his housekeeper. Until Pitt's death in 1806, she dispensed official patronage, arranged the Treasury banquets, and enjoyed her uncle's protection. On his deathbed, Pitt left her his blessing and an annuity, which she later declared was not enough to keep a carriage. Her disappointment and isolation deepened two years later when her favourite brother, Major Stanhope, and a good friend, Sir John Moore, died at Corunna.

In 1808 she again tried to escape from a society that had now no place for her, this time to Wales, where she remained until 1810 when she began the great adventure of her life. In February she set sail from England for the Levant, taking with her a Welsh companion, Miss Williams, and Meryon. The small entourage steadily grew as she travelled east and encountered adventures and hardships. At Malta she met Michael Bruce, eleven years her junior, who none the less became the love of her life. The son of a titled Scot, he was on a lengthy foreign, educational tour. Evidently HS was reluctantly accepted by Bruce's father as an important part of his education, until October 1813, when Bruce finally returned to England.

On the initial trip HS was shipwrecked off Rhodes, conducted a pilgrimage to Jerusalem, and crossed the desert. From January 1813 until the summer of 1814, she held court over a Bedouin encampment in Syria. Later in 1814, she settled on the slopes of Mount Lebanon in the ruins of a convent on land ceded to her by the pasha of Acre. Nearby was Dahar-June, a village of Druses.

On her land, HS built a medieval fortress with houses set in a garden surrounded by an outer wall. There she spent her life plotting against the British Consul, managing her slaves, inciting the Druses to rebel against the pasha, and undermining the central power of the sultan. While in Lebanon she ruled as a despot and a prophetess. Gradually she isolated herself from England and adopted eastern dress, manners, and customs. By 1828 none of her thirty personal attendants was European. She kept an assortment of animals, especially cats and horses, treating them with great care because she believed in the transmigration of souls. Although she limited her contacts with Europeans, in October 1827 she took into her compound those who sought her protection after the Battle of Navarino. Occasionally she received distinguished guests who requested an audience, among them the French poet Lamartine and Prince Maximilian of Bavaria.

HS's accounts of her life and travels, published posthumously and edited by Meryon, ostensibly give us her words. However, Meryon does not let her letters, speeches, or lectures speak for themselves. For example, in one letter, we find that HS has strong views on maids and education: she wants 'no boarding-school miss – for education of all things is most odious'. In another letter, she explains she is blind and must dictate her letters; she tells Meryon, 'The books I cannot read, and I have nobody to read them to me'. More informative than her words, Meryon soon becomes our authority. He tells us that HS would find her greatest happiness haranguing her visitors – talking to them for more than an hour at a time without stopping, usually in the early hours of the morning. He tells us some of her favourite topics: the superiority of the vices of the high-born to the virtues of the low-born or the superiority of a concubine to a wife. He explains that during the lectures, listeners could not sit, and slaves were to kneel in postures of oriental humility that suited her position as eastern princess. Meryon insists that her greatest fear was being alone and that she would summon him to fill the void.

As we read Meryon's descriptions of HS and her outrageous behaviour, we wonder why he was there. He *chose* to find her; he *elected* to abide by her absurd demands. At first driven by self-interest, he was soon spellbound. He became HS's protector, behaving in chivalrous ways, insisting that he was indispensible to her. Yet, she abused him, not just by haranguing him for hours, but also by refusing to receive his wife. In one letter to Meryon, she wrote, 'Salute Mrs M., and say I hope no childish feeling will prevent her allowing you to be absent a little while'. So prompted, Meryon left his wife to be with HS during the spring of 1831 and the summers of 1837 and 1838.

When HS died, she was without Meryon or any other European. She had by then sent abusive letters to the queen and to Lord Palmerston concerning her pension. Even though she had refused to receive visitors for almost a year, she had become famous enough that newspapers took up her grievances. By the time Niven Moore, the British consul at Beirut, reached her, she had died. Her compound was deserted, the servants had gone, and only her body with the jewels she had been wearing remained. William McClure Thomson, an American missionary, buried HS by torchlight at midnight in the garden. A sketch of her compound and her grave appeared in Thomson's book.

SOPHIA B. BLAYDES

Works: *Memoirs of the Lady Hester Stanhope, As Related by Herself in Conversations with Her Physician [Charles Lewis Meryon]: Comprising Her Opinions and Anecdotes of Some of the Most Remarkable Persons of Her Time* (1845); *Travels of Lady Hester Stanhope: Forming the Completion of Her Memoirs. Narrated by Her Physician [Charles Lewis Meryon]* (1846); *The Nun of Lebanon: The Love Affair of Lady Hester Stanhope and Michael Bruce: Their Newly Discovered Letters*, by I. Bruce (1951).

References: Armstrong, M. D., *Lady Hester Stanhope* (1928); Bordeaux, P. H. *Lady Stanhope en Orient* (c. 1924); Bordeaux, P. H., *The Circle of the Deserts* (1925); Cleveland, C. L. W. [Stanhope] Powlett, Duchess of, *The Life and Letters of Lady Hester Stanhope* (1914); *DNB*; Haslip, J., *Lady Hester Stanhope: A Biography* (1934); Haslip, J, *Lady Hester Stanhope* (1945); Hughes, J. G., *Queen of the Desert: The Story of Lady Hester Stanhope* (1967); Leslie, D., *The Desert Queen* (1972); Mattingly, G., 'Two queens of Regency society', *Saturday Review*

14 (27 June 1936); Simmons, J. C., *Passionate Pilgrims: English Travelers to the World of the Desert Arabs* (1987); Strachey, L., 'Curious History of Lady Hester Stanhope', *Golden Book* 22 (July 1935); Strachey, L., 'Lady Hester Stanhope', in *Books and Characters: French and English* (1922); Strachey, L., 'Un-Victorian Victorian', *Living Age* 301 (17 May 1919); Watney, J. B., *Travels in Araby of Lady Hester Stanhope* (1975).

Stark, Freya

b. 31 January 1893, Paris

Travel writer

FS, travel writer and explorer, was born 'in the middle of Bohemia', in her parents' studio in Montmartre, as the first surviving child of Robert Start, painter and sculptor, and Flora Stark (Robert's first cousin), an accomplished pianist and portrait painter. Her travels began at the age of 2½ when, together with her younger sister Vera, she was carried across the Alps, in a basket, to Cortina. She had a cosmopolitan upbringing, dividing her time between Italy, where her mother had grown up, and her father's home in the Devonshire moors. By the age of 5, she was fluent in three languages.

In 1901, she settled with her mother in Italy, her father remaining in Devon. They set up house first in Asolo, a village in the foothills of the Dolomites, and, two years later, in Dronero. Having been educated thus far by German and Italian governesses, FS and her sister were now sent to the Sacré Coeur Convent to learn French and embroidery. For a time, FS also worked in the carpet factory belonging to Count Mario di Roascio, her mother's lover. It was here that in 1906 she was nearly killed, when her hair was caught in one of the looms and half her scalp torn away.

In 1908 she was allowed to stay with friends in London, attending lectures in English at the University (Professor Ker became a close friend), and by 1912 she had enrolled for a degree course at Bedford College, returning periodically to Italy to keep house for her mother. With the outbreak of the First World War she had completed most stages of an honours degree in history, but abandoned her studies to train as a nurse at the clinic of St Ursula in Bologna. At the age of 22 she received a marriage proposal from bacteriologist Guido Rueta, but he later broke off the engagement in favour of an earlier lover. Returning to England, FS worked in the Censor's Office for a time, but in the autumn of 1917 was dispatched to Italy again, to the ambulance unit set up ten miles from Gorizia by G. M. Trevelyan.

After the war she settled at Ventimiglia near the French border, and became involved in the near-smuggling of paintings. Persistently troubled by ill-health, she convalesced during this period by learning Arabic. At 33, inspired by Charles Montagu Doughty's *Travels in Arabia Deserta*, her own travels began in earnest. Before she departed, Herbert Young, a student friend of her father's, left his Asolo house to her; it became known as Casa Freia. In November 1927, having been baptized a Presbyterian so as not to die 'outside the Christian brotherhood', she embarked for Beirut.

She journeyed to Brummana in the Lebanon and to Damascus. Seven months later, having spent the £200 she had saved, she left for Europe, 'with a feeling dim but insistent, that the whole of my future must be rearranged'. Her next destination was Baghdad, leading to a series of articles for *The Baghdad Times*, and later to *Baghdad Sketches* (1932). Here in 1929 she journeyed with the

Bedouin into the desert and was on terms of intimacy with the natives, shocking the British whose unthinking orthodoxy she despised.

In 1930 and 1931 she made two journeys into Persia, planning a history of the fortresses of the Assassins between Aleppo and the Persian border, which was to become her first full-length travel book, *The Valleys of the Assassins*, published in 1934 by Murray. As a tribute to her travels in Luristan she was presented with the Royal Geographical Society's Back Grant, and became the first woman to hold the Burton Medal of the Royal Asiatic Society.

In the mid-1930's travels in the Hadramaut were to lead to *The Southern Gates of Arabia* (1936) and the Royal Scottish Geographical Society's Mungo Park Medal. An archaeological dig in the Hadramaut in conjunction with Gertrude Caton Thompson and Elinor Gardner led to *A Winter in Arabia* (1940). During the Second World War, FS worked as a South Arabia expert for the Ministry of Information, assisting the spread of propaganda. She helped to found the Brothers and Sisters of Freedom, a Middle East network of pro-Ally committees, helping to enlist Arab support for the Allied Cause. In 1940 she received the Royal Geographical Society's Founder's medal.

At the end of the war, FS worked in India for several months as personal assistant to the Vicereine, Lady Wavell, after which she returned to Asolo. Two years later she married Stewart Perowne who had been a colleague in Aden and Baghdad. After six months they separated, and once again FS established herself in Asolo. She continued to travel extensively, riding a pony in the footsteps of Alexander the Great (*Alexander's Path*, 1958), and negotiating the remote Hakkiari Mountains of Eastern Turkey (*Riding to the Tigris*, 1959). At the age of 77, she embarked on the first of three mounted treks into the Himalayan foothills. Having received the CBE in 1953, she was awarded the DBE in 1972. In 1984, she was presented with the keys to Asolo. In her late eighties she was still to be seen trekking around Annapurna in the Himalayas.

FS was a conscientious letter writer, both to her family and to a distinguished group of friends including Bernard Berenson, Sir Sydney Cockerell, Field Marshall Wavell, and her lifelong publisher, Jock Murray. She was also an indefatigable photographer, amassing over 6,000 prints of a world which has now for the most part vanished.

FS's long career as a travel writer never inured her to a sense of the world as a continual revelation and a daily challenge which must be met. She deplored the encouragement of reticence and restraint in women's education, believing that 'the beckoning counts and not the clicking of the latch behind you: and all through life, the actual moment of emancipation still holds that delight, of the whole world coming to meet you like a wave'.

Her writings are characterized by a complete absence of patriotism, an emotion which, in its dependence on geographical boundaries, FS considered to be entirely arbitrary. Her complete openness towards people and places, and her acceptance of native hospitality wherever she went, provided her with a rich human material to which she could respond on many different levels, interspersing tough-minded practical hints with metaphysical speculation and an extravagant lyricism. What she termed her 'own Everywoman philosophy' pervades all her travel writings. It was based on lessons she had learnt from her wide reading in history, especially Roman history, and the classics. It is to be found in a distilled form in *Perseus in the Wind* (1948), written during a summer spent in the mountains of Elburz, with the constellation of Perseus overhead, and dealing with perennial themes 'beyond our grasp, yet visible to all, dear to our hearts and far from our understanding as the constellations, a comfort for the frail light they shed'. ANNE FERNIHOUGH

Works: *Baghdad Sketches* (1932); *The Valleys of the Assassins* (1934); *The Southern Gates of Arabia* (1936); *Seen in the Hadramaut* (1938); *A Winter in Arabia* (1940); *Letters from Syria* (1942); *The Arab Island: The Middle East 1939–1943* (1943); *East is West* (1943); *Perseus in the Wind* (1948); *Traveller's Prelude: Autobiography, 1893–1927* (1950); *Beyond Euphrates: Autobiography, 1928–1933* (1951); *The Coast of Incense: Autobiography, 1933–1939* (1953); *Ionia: A Quest* (1954); *The Lycian Shore* (1956); *Alexander's Path* (1958); *Riding to the Tigris* (1959); *Dust in the Lion's Paw: Autobiography, 1939–1946* (1961); *The Journey's Echo* (1963); *Rome on the Euphrates* (1966); *The Zodiac Arch* (1968); *The Minnaret of Djam: An Excursion in Afghanistan* (1970); *Gateways and Caravans: A Portrait of Turkey* (1971); *A Peak in Darien* (1976); *Letters*, 8 vols (1974–82).

References: Maitland, A. (ed.), *A Tower in a Wall: Conversations with Dame Freya Stark* (1982); Moorhead, C., *Freya Stark, Travel Writer and Explorer* (1984).

Steel, Flora Annie

b. 2 April 1847, Harrow, Middlesex; d. 12 April 1929, Talgarth, Wales
Novelist, short story writer

FAS was the sixth of the ten children surviving beyond infancy of Isabella MacCallum, the heiress to a Jamaican plantation, and George Webster. Her father was Scottish Parliamentary Agent and, later, Sheriff-Clerk of Forfar, necessitating a family move to Scotland. Except for six months at school in Brussels, FAS was largely self-educated.

In December 1867 she married Henry William Steel who worked for the Indian civil service, and they sailed immediately for India, settling in the Punjab. Apart from home leaves, they lived there for the next twenty-two years. Within a year of the marriage, FAS gave birth to a stillborn daughter; another daughter, Mabel, was born in December 1870.

In spite of repeated attacks of 'Punjab fever', FAS led a highly energetic life, participating whenever possible in her husband's duties as school inspector in Kasur, acting as medical advisor to local villagers, producing plays and musical events, and assisting in the revival of traditional handicrafts. Shocked by the low standards in schools, she instituted her own reading classes, and, impressed by her methods, the Chief Native Administrator suggested that a girls' school be set up in Kasur. In 1884 she became a member of the Provincial Educational Board with John Lockwood Kipling (Rudyard Kipling's father), and was eventually appointed the first Inspectress of Girls' Schools.

Her first literary attempts were poems based on the tales from Indian folklore which she gleaned from the local villagers, having taught herself Punjabi. She eventually produced a collection of such tales, *Wide-Awake Stories* (1884), initially published in India and subsequently reissued in England as *Tales of the Punjab* (1894), illustrated by J. L. Kipling.

On her husband's retirement in 1889 she returned to Britain, settling first in Scotland and then in Talgarth, in mid-Wales. It was now that she began writing in earnest. Her first original work was a short story published in *Macmillan's Magazine*, entitled 'Lâl', in which the male narrator arrives in India on his first ICS appointment and gives an account of his initial inspection. Uncertainty surrounds the figure of Lâl himself, an elusive inhabitant of the riverlands, obliquely connected to fertility and harvest. FAS's first novel was *Miss Stuart's Legacy* (1893), published by Macmillan. It centres upon the scheming and mercenary John Raby who marries the gullible heroine for her inheritance. His hard-heartedness backfires on him when his attempts to erect a dam which will ruin the fields of the neighbouring village are sabotaged, killing him in the process.

FAS made two subsequent visits to India in 1894 and 1898, one of which was to research for *On the Face of the Waters*, the novel of the Indian Mutiny which established her literary reputation. Rejected by Macmillan, it was published by Heinemann in 1896. FAS continued to write prolifically, producing around twenty full-length novels and several collections of short stories, which in their day were compared favourably with those of Kipling. Among these were four historical novels dealing with the lives of the Moghul Emperors: *A Prince of Dreamers* (1908); *King Errant* (1912); *Mistress of Men* (1917); and *The Builder* (1928). These are written in a romantic vein, treating of disguises, murders, semi-magical jewels and victorious campaigns. FAS claimed that several of her tales had been told her by a mysterious apparition, Nathaniel James Craddock.

After her husband's death in 1923, she began to study what she termed 'philosophy and metaphysics' and became increasingly convinced that sex was at the root of all human problems, a theme she was to explore in her last novel, *The Curse of Eve*. The novel is set in contemporary Britain in the slums of Chelsea, and was published posthumously in 1929. During the 1920s she also set down her thoughts on the causes of the subjection of women, in a pamphlet published at her own expense, *The Fruit of the Tree* (she had been a supporter of votes for women). Even in her eighties she was indefatigable, sailing to Jamaica to visit relatives, and joining her grandson in his rooms in Oxford in order to read in the Bodleian. Her unfinished autobiography, *The Garden of Fidelity*, was published in the year of her death.

Although FAS prided herself on her so-called 'knowledge' of India, her writings reveal that this does not so much involve an open-minded responsiveness towards the country as the seeking of a *practical* kind of knowledge, a way of dealing with Indian life and people and, by extension, of facilitating British rule. This is particularly evident in *On the Face of the Waters*, for which she is best remembered, in which the British are not seen to be *morally* culpable (General John Nicholson, whose violent excesses have since been well documented, is hagiographized in the novel), but only *practically*, in their complacent dismissal of reports of discontent among the Indians. The title of the novel comes from the mystified answer which Indians would give to enquiries as to how the Mutiny had started: 'God knows. He sent a breath into the world.' This view of Indian violence as irrational and lacking in political content was one which pervaded all her work. In her autobiography, FAS accounts for the immense success of the novel in terms of its subject, one which was guaranteed to evoke imperial pride: 'The Indian Mutiny was then the epic of the race. It held all possible emotion, all possible triumph.'

In most of her novels of colonial life, FAS reveals her inability to transcend the racist orthodoxies of the period. The British are seen to be 'natural leaders' in a role of paternal protection, and Indians are viewed in rather clichéd terms as slaves to sexual passion and religious fanaticism. Several stories are devoted to the theme of the passionate Indian woman who has been wronged (in 'Fire and Ice' (*In the Guardianship of God*, 1900), Lazizan burns down the house of her rival in love), or to the more gruesome aspects of the Hindu religion, particularly those connected with the bloodthirsty goddess Kali (*The Law of the Treshold*, 1924). East and west are defined in terms of inborn, unchanging, and antipathetic racial characteristics, and many of the novels illustrate what is seen to be the absurdity of trying to mix two incompatible cultures. It is a theme most clearly articulated through the dual personality of Chris Davenant, alias Krish Devenund, the London-educated Brahmin who has married an English girl to his peril in *Voices of the Night* (1900).

Such conformities are, however, tempered by formal assertions of tolerance and frequent attempts to defend Indian culture and, in particular, Indian spirituality. FAS's eagerness to do justice to the complexity of India is brought out in her autobiography, where she describes setting sail from Bombay: looking back at the harbour from the deck of the ship, 'All things seemed to merge in that blue mist. Even the distant hills were lost in it. So India looked homogeneous, and so looked a lie. For India is as multitudinous as the sands of the sea.'   ANNE FERNIHOUGH

Selected works: Wide-Awake Stories (1884); From the Five Rivers (1893); Miss Stuart's Legacy (1893); The Flower of Forgiveness (1894); The Potter's Thumb (1894); Red Rowans (1895); On the Face of the Waters (1896); In the Permanent Way and Other Stories (1897); In the Tideway (1897); The Complete Indian Housekeeper and Cook (1899); Voices in the Night (1900); The Hosts of the Lord (1900); In the Guardianship of God (1900); A Book of Mortals (1905); India (1905); A Sovereign Remedy (1906); India Through the Ages (1908); A Prince of Dreamers (1908); The Gift of the Gods (1911); King Errant (1912); The Adventures of Akbar (1913); The Mercy of the Lord (1914); Marmaduke (1917); Mistress of Men (1917); English Fairy Tales (1918); A Tale of Indian Heroes (1923); A Tale of the Tides (1923); The Law of the Threshold (1924); The Builder (1928); The Curse of Eve (1929); The Garden of Fidelity (1929); The Indian Scene (1933).

References: Greenberger, A. J., *The British Image of India* (1969); Parry, B., *Delusions and Discoveries: Studies on India in the British Imagination 1880–1930* (1972); Patwardhan, D., *A Star of India* (1963); Powell, V., *Flora Annie Steel* (1981); Webster, M., 'Biographical introduction' to *The Indian Scene* (1933).

Steen, Marguerite

b. 1894, Liverpool; d. 4 August 1975

Novelist, playwright

(Also wrote under Jane Nicholson)

MS was the adopted daughter of Joseph and Margaret Steen. As a child she was educated in Liverpool, then at a private boarding school, where she was not happy, and then at Kendal High School. At an early age she showed a keen interest in literature and by the age of 8 had written her first novel. During the First World War, when she was 19, she went, albeit reluctantly, into school teaching. She was never really happy in this profession and, after three years, she left for London to try to make her career on the stage. Later she once again found herself in teaching after she was offered a position as an instructor in dancing and eurhythmics in Halifax. She became discontented once more and willingly accepted an offer of £3 a week to tour with the Fred Terry–Julia Neilson company, with which she stayed from 1921 until 1923. In 1926, a time of scarcity and unemployment, the famous actress Ellen Terry (Fred Terry's sister) first advised her to think seriously about writing. She took the advice and produced *The Gilt Cage* (1927). In her autobiography, *Looking-Glass*, MS writes, 'It was no use offering a novel in manuscript to any publisher: it had got to be type written. I didn't have a typewriter and I couldn't type. Wandering down St. Martin's Lane one morning, with my basket of sandwiches and my thermos of coffee, I saw a shop window displaying typewriters. I went in and asked for the manager. "I want a typewriter. I can't pay very much . . . ." ' In the following years her writing career became firmly established. She never married but shared many years of happiness with William Nicholson to whom the second part of her autobiography, *Pier Glass*, is dedicated.

Matador (1934), the choice of the Book Society in England and of the Book of the Month Club in the US, is set in Granada, where MS spent much of her time after the First World War. The story deals with a family's tragic life in Spain and in its depiction of a conflict of personality pits the old against the emerging Spain: the traditional mysticism and brutality and the revolt against it. Don José, an ex-bullfighter, part of the tradition of Spain, moulds his son, Pepe, into his own image to become a bullfighter too; he arranges Pepe's marriage to Pilar, a girl who he believes has money and a good reputation: 'He himself had arranged the matter, on the lines of his own experience.' Things go wrong when Pepe acts in ways belonging to the new youth of Spain. His brothers, Miguel and Juan, are also expressions of the changes taking place: Miguel is a young priest rejecting the old religious order for a belief in communism, while Juan, a sensitive-minded poet, reverses the Spanish ideal of the courageous young man – the bullfighter. Set against these expressions of rebellion is the character of the traditional Pilar who has lived with her old grandmother all her life: 'But it was a part of being betrothed; it was part of one's martyrdom . . . .' *Matador* depicts a Spain in transition. The bullfighter's arena is perhaps the best place to highlight this. MS seems to be sympathetic to both sides of the debate, but later, in her autobiography, *Looking Glass*, she writes, 'the bull fight in *Matador* is an obvious fake and I never wrote a line about the bulls of which I was not inwardly ashamed until 1954' (when she wrote *Bulls of Parral*).

The Sun is My Undoing (1941) was the Literary Guild Selection in England and a best-seller in both England and the US. MS put much time and effort into this immensely long novel, noting of it, 'it was five years before I completed the research for *The Sun is My Undoing*; three before I roughed out the first chapter, which was written eleven times before I felt free to get on with the rest' (*Looking Glass*). The book deals with the slave trade during the eighteenth century and shows both the evils of the system and the work of the English abolitionists. MS uses her characters, especially Matthew Flood, to highlight the cruelty of the slavers and their reaction to abolitionists. Matthew is to be married to an English girl, Pallas, but when he finds that she is a serious abolitionist he leaves England and enters the slave trade. From then on the novel is picaresque. Attention moves from England to the sea and the West Indies where there are adventures, storms, piracies, abductions, murder, and romance. Melodrama mingles with serious drama that focuses on conflicts of social and political ideals.

At about the same time MS published the very different book *Shelter* (1941), written under the pseudonym Jane Nicholson. This is set in the August and September of 1940 and deals mainly with the people of London and their reactions to the bombardment of the city at the beginning of the war. MS shows the mixture of fear and excitement, which she herself had experienced, through the story of the Masons and their associates, interrupted at intervals by a 'West End Newsreel' in which MS, in diary form, writes down snippets of people's conversations, newspaper reports, and observations. The first newsreel in August is filled with bravado and ignorance: 'Air-raid warning. Three parts of London goes on jay walking staring hopefully at the sky. Waiting for the show to start.' But the last, in October, expresses despair and fright: 'They've not got the church? Yes they have. It's blazing away. You can't breathe in Jermyn Street.' In this book MS attempts to show what matters to 'ordinary' people and she uses dialect to express their concerns: 'Reminds you of the coloured postcards when you was a kid – you remember? we use' to c'lect them in a album.' The closeness of her own life to what she described is revealed in a comment in her second autobiography, *Pier Glass*: 'In the original typescript of *The Sun is My Undoing* a cross in the margin showed each time a bomb came down close enough to shake my typewriter.'   LISA BUCKBY

Works: *Gilt Cage* (1927); *Duel in the Dark* (1928); *The Reluctant Madonna* (1929); *They That Go Down* (1930); *When the Wind Blows* (1931); *Unicorn* (1931); *The Wise and the Foolish Virgins* (1932); *Oakfield Plays* (1932); *Stallion* (1933); *Spider* (1933); *Hugh Walpole: A Study* (1933); *Peepshow* (1933); *The Spanish Trilogy: Matador* (1934): *The Tavern* (1935): *The One Eyed Moon* (1935); *Return of a Heroine* (1936); *Matador* (with M. Lang) (1936); *The Lost One* (1937); *Who Would Have Daughters?* (1937); *The Marriage Will Not Take Place* (1938); *Family Ties* (1939); *French for Love* (with D. Patmore) (1939); *A Kind of Insolence and Other Stories* (1940); *The Sun is My Undoing* (1941); (under Jane Nicholson) *Shelter* (1941); *William Nicholson; A biography* (1943); *Rose Timpson* (1946); *Granada Window* (1949); *Twilight on the Floods* (1949); *The Swan* (1951); *Phoenix Rising* (1952); *Anna Fitzalan* (1953); *Bulls of Parral* (1954); *The Unquiet Spirit* (1955); *Little White King* (1956); *The Woman in the Back Seat* (1959); *The Tower* (1959); *A Pride of Terrys* (1962); *A Candle in the Sun* (1964); *Looking Glass* (1966); *Pier Glass* (1968).

References: *Current Biography* (1941); *Wilson Library Bulletin* (February 1937).

Stern, G. B.

b. 17 June 1890, London; d. 19 September 1973, Wallingford, Berkshire
Novelist

GBS, who gained considerable popularity with a series of novels about a family dominated by a matriarch, was the second daughter of Albert Stern and Elizabeth Schwabacher. She attended Notting Hill High School until she was 16, when she left to travel with her parents in Germany and Switzerland. Her education continued at a day school in Wiesbaden and, as she put it in *Monogram*, was 'finished and given a lick and a high polish' at Montreux. Although GBS is best known for her novels and autobiographies, until she was 20 she seemed destined for the stage. She began writing plays and acting in them when she was 7 and her favourite early reminiscences, sprinkled throughout her autobiographies, are of Coronet Theatre productions. After studying at the Academy of Dramatic Art in London for nearly two years, GBS remembers looking at the beginning of her novelistic career 'as no better than marking time' before she would become, if not an actress, then at least a dramatist. In 1919, she married Geoffrey Lisle Holdsworth, a New Zealand journalist, whom she met through Noel Coward and from whom she was later divorced. She lived for some periods of time in Cornwall, Italy, France, New York, and Hollywood, but she always regarded London as her home. Her London flat and all her possessions were destroyed by an incendiary bomb in 1940, an incident which resurfaced in her later fiction and memoirs. In 1947 GBS was converted to Roman Catholicism, an event which she describes in *All in Good Time* (1954).

GBS published her first novel, *Pantomime*, in 1914. She is best known for her chronicles that explore the extended family tree of the Rakonitz and Czelo-

var families of Vienna, Paris and London. *Children of No Man's Land* (1919) is
the first volume of five in the largely autobiographical Matriarch series. Many
of the central characters were based directly on members of GBS's own Jewish
family. The Matriarch herself was modelled on GBS's great-aunt, Anastasia
Schwabacher, whom GBS professed not to like: 'I was not very deeply attached
to the Matriarch. She was too despotic.' The saga begins with the violation of
family law when the first Matriarch marries her own first cousin. Although
Anastasia dominates the family in the domestic sphere, like all the Czelovar
and Rakonitz women of the first and second generations, she remains dependent
financially upon men. After a financial crisis, which is based upon the Vaal
River diamond smash in which GBS's own family lost most of its money, the
Rakonitz women go into business themselves. Taken collectively, the five
novels show the increasing dominance of women in a single family, and, by
implication, in the world.

The Matriarch novels best demonstrate GBS's energetic flair for creating
characters. The boundless and engaging Rakonitz women are involved in a
constant frenzy of activities and schemes, from planning dinner parties to
rescuing refugees from occupied countries. GBS traces this energy and interest
in life through many of the women, exploring the cycles of humanity through
the medium of a single family. Although she has been criticized for her disregard
of the literary fashions of her time, she preferred to examine 'universal life
reduced to a scale where it is easy to see what is going on and what it is all
about'. The reasons behind a world war could be conveyed through a family
squabble, she thought.

GBS also wrote several autobiographies. In these informal memoirs, she
allowed herself to be guided by coincidence and personal whim. As in her
novels, her associative speculations often led her to broach much larger issues.
She wrote three plays (two of which were based on her novels), film scripts,
book reviews, and short stories. She also wrote criticism on Jane Austen and
Robert Louis Stevenson.   CHARMAINE EDDY

Selected works: Pantomime (1914); *See-saw* (1914); *Twos and Threes* (1916); *Grand
Chain* (1917); *A Marrying Man* (1918); *Children of No Man's Land* (1919; published
in the US as *Debatable Ground*); *Larry Munro* (1920; published in the US as *The
China Shop*); *The Room* (1922); *The Back Seat* (1923); *Tents of Israel: A Chronicle*
(1924; published in the US as *The Matriarch*); *Thunderstorm* (1925); *A Deputy
was King* (1926); *The Happy Meddler* (with Geoffrey Holdsworth) (1926); *The
Dark Gentleman* (1927); *Bouquet* (1927); *Debonair: The Story of Persephone* (1928);
Petruchio (1929; published in the US as *Modesta*); *Mosaic* (1930); *The Shortest
Night* (1931); *Little Red Horses* (1932; published in the US as *The Rueful Mating*);
Long-lost Father: a Comedy (1932); *The Rakonitz Chronicles* (includes *Tents of
Israel, A Deputy Was King,* and *Mosaic*) (1932); *The Augs: An Exaggeration* (1933;
published in the US as *Summer's Play*); *Shining and Free* (1935); *Monogram* (1936);
Oleander River (1937); *The Ugly Dachshund* (1938); *The Woman in the Hall* (1939);
A Lion in the Garden (1940); *Another Part of the Forest* (1941); *The Young Matriarch*
(1942); *Talking of Jane Austen* (with S. Kaye-Smith) (1943); *Trumpet Voluntary*
(1944); *The Reasonable Shores* (1946); *A Duck to Water* (1949); *Benefits Forgot*
(1949); *Ten Days of Christmas* (1950); *The Donkey Shoe* (1952); *Robert Louis
Stevenson* (1952); *A Name to Conjure With* (1953); *Johnny Forsaken* (1954); *All in
Good Time* (1954); *For All We Know* (1956); *The Way it Worked Out* (1956);
Seventy Times Seven (1957); *The Patience of a Saint* (1958); *Unless I Marry* (1959);
Bernadette (1960); *Dolphin Cottage* (1962); *Promise Not to Tell* (1964).

References: Boileau, H. T., *Italy in the Post-Victorian Novel* (1931); Kunitz, S. J., *Living Authors: A Book of Biographies* (1931); Lawrence, M., *The School of Femininity* (1936); Millett, F. B., *Contemporary British Literature* (1935).

Stewart, Mary

b. 17 September 1916, Sunderland, County Durham
Novelist, writer for children

MS is the daughter of Mary (*née* Matthews) and Frederick Rainbow, a clergyman. She read English at Durham University, gaining first-class honours, and worked there as a lecturer full-time between 1941 and 1945 and part-time from 1948 until 1955. During the Second World War she was in the Royal Observer Corps, then in 1945 she married Frederick Stewart. Since 1954 she has been a writer; she has achieved tremendous international success commercially and has received a number of awards, including the British Crime Writers Award (1960), the Mystery Writers Award (1964), and the Frederick Niven Award (1971). She is best known for her romantic thrillers, but has also written radio plays and children's stories, among other genres. In 1968 she became a Fellow of the Royal Society of Arts.

Her first novel, *Madam Will You Talk?* (1955), is a romantic thriller set in the South of France where the heroine and narrator, Charity, is on holiday. She befriends a 13-year-old boy, and through him unwittingly gets caught up in the dealings of a gang of murderers led by an escaped Nazi war criminal who fears exposure by the boy's father. MS tells an exciting story full of suspense and action, as Charity hurtles round Provence in her own sports car and another she wrests from one of the criminals while he is trying to seduce her. The romantic element is provided by the boy's father, Richard, but it departs somewhat from the usual formula. Charity is, at 28, older than most romantic heroines and is a widow, her husband Johnny having been killed in the Second World War. Her feeling of loss is as important in the novel as her falling in love; but finally the former is overcome: 'I would never again miss Johnny, with that deep dull aching, as if part of me had been wrenched away, and the scar left wincing with the cold; but paradoxically enough, now that I was whole again, Johnny was nearer to me than he had ever been since the last time we had been together, the night before he went away. I was whole again, and Johnny was there for ever, part of me always. Because I had found Richard, I would never lose Johnny.'

A number of other romantic thrillers have followed *Madam Will You Talk?* which, while they contain some similar features (a gripping story played out in a closely described, atmospheric setting, accompanied by romance that is persuasive without being slushy or coy), show also MS's growing sophistication as a writer. Whereas the action of her first novel, though exciting, centres on large coincidences, in her later work (dating perhaps from *My Brother Michael*, 1959) the storyline is more tightly written and convincing. Her heroines' response to romance also changes over the years in tune with each contemporary setting: whereas Charity, in the 1950s, rather likes Richard being dictatorial, by the 1970s, in *Touch Not the Cat* (1976), Bryony is amused that the hero refuses to have sex before marriage, and is more overt about sexuality than her predecessors: 'The mixture of strangeness, tenderness and sheer sexual excitement took away the power of coherent thought and struck me silent.'

Touch Not the Cat is perhaps MS's best romantic thriller to date. In it she juxtaposes a century-old family tragedy with contemporary action, until at the end of the novel the intimate connection between the two stories becomes apparent. Bryony's father has died in unusual circumstances, leaving a dilapidated, ancient estate which is entailed on the male heir, his brother. In his last moments, he left Bryony a confused message, warning her of danger and giving her certain instructions. She is faced with a double problem: not only has she to unravel this mystery and find the source of danger, but she has also to discover the identity of her 'lover'. Ever since she can remember, she has been telepathically linked with some male of about her own age, but he has never allowed her to know who he is. She presumes he is one of her twin cousins (this kind of communication has been known in her family before); however they turn out to be greedy and scheming, short of money, prepared to kill to get more, and involved in her father's death. She at last discovers that her 'lover' is the estate gardener, with whom she grew up, and who, in fact (when the true story behind the old tragedy emerges) turns out to be an Ashley descendant and the rightful heir to the estate, though he has no desire to claim it.

In 1970 *The Crystal Cave* was published, a novel which marked MS's move into a new field of writing. It is the first of a trilogy about Merlin set in fifth-century Britain, and was followed by *The Hollow Hills* (1973) and *The Last Enchantment* (1979). MS's interest in unusual powers of the mind is apparent (as in *Touch Not the Cat*), and her characterization of Merlin departs from the traditional one of a magician attached to a chivalric court; instead he is gifted with prophecy. As in her romantic thrillers, the story is told retrospectively by the central character. He begins with his childhood in the royal palace in Carmarthen, where his position as the illegitimate son of a princess was not easy. His early ability of knowing more than seemed possible had nothing to do with magic, but was a result of frequent secret visits to the hypocaust system beneath the palace where he overheard many things. Later, however, his powers became more mystical, and far stronger, only to be lost eventually because of his seduction by an enchantress. In all of her novels, to one degree or another, MS's literary and intellectual background is apparent; in the romantic thrillers, there is, for instance, her apt and often witty choice of quotation to introduce each chapter; and in the Merlin trilogy, she calls on the language of Geoffrey of Monmouth's *Historia Regum Britanniae*, on which she bases her interpretation.

LUCY SLOAN

Selected Works *Madam, Will You Talk?* (1955); *Wildfire at Midnight* (1956); *Thunder on the Right* (1957); *Nine Coaches Waiting* (1958); *My Brother Michael* (1959); *The Ivy Tree* (1961); *This Rough Magic* (1964); *Airs Above the Ground* (1965); *The Gabriel Hounds* (1967); *The Wind Off the Small Isles* (1968); *The Crystal Cave* (1970); *The Little Broomstick* (1971); *The Hollow Hills* (1973); *Ludo and the Star Horse* (1974); *Touch Not the Cat* (1976); *The Last Enchantment* (1979); *A Walk in Wolf Wood* (1980); *The Wicked Day* (1983).
References: *CA; CMW; RGW.*

Stopes, Marie

b. 15 October 1880, Edinburgh; d. 2 October 1958, Norbury Park, Surrey
Polemical writer, campaigner for birth control
(Also wrote under Mark Arundel, Marie Carmichael, Erica Fay, G.N. Mortlake)
MS was the eldest daughter of Henry Stopes, a prosperous architect specializing in the building of breweries but regarding himself more as a leisured scholar

of archaeology, and his wife Charlotte Carmichael, a passionate advocate of female suffrage and a pioneer in higher education for women. The mrriage was not a close one – Charlotte was uninterested in the sexual side of the relationship – and MS and her father became very attached to each other. MS was raised in London and educated at home until the age of 12 when she went to St George's School and then North London Collegiate School. She proceeded to University College, London, where she took degrees in geology, botany, and geography. After a year of research she went to Munich, obtaining a doctorate in 1904; in the same year she became the first woman on the science faculty in Manchester University where she was an expert in fossil plants. Later she became a fellow of University College, London and published *Ancient Plants* in 1910 and a catalogue of *Cretaceous Flora* from 1913 to 1915.

In 1907 and 1908, while pursuing research in Japan, she became involved with a Japanese professor, Fujii; in 1911, two years after the affair, from which Fujii seems to have retreated, she published her correspondence, using the publication as a kind of therapy. She entered a marriage with a Canadian, Reginald Ruggles Gates, which was annulled four years later in 1916 owing to her husband's impotence. An involvement with Aylmer Maude was followed in 1918 by another rather unsuccessful marriage to Humphrey Verdon Roe, an aircraft manufacturer, with whom she campaigned for birth control. Her first child died at birth and her second was born in 1924. In 1926 she exposed the failure of her first marriage in a play *Vectia* (1926) which she claimed to have been 'almost unadulterated autobiography'. With her second husband she started a clinic in Islington much opposed both by the medical establishment and the Roman Catholic Church. Libel suits and other legal battles ensued. After the Second World War she continued to advocate birth control in the Far East and she developed an interest in mystical literature.

With her books *Married Love* (1918), beginning 'Every heart desires a mate', and *Wise Parenthood* (1918), MS became a best-selling author, and her works were translated into thirteen languages. Her later books on motherhood had similar success. She also wrote a film script, *Maisie's Marriage*, a rather melodramatic publicizing of her views. She regarded birth control as an aid to sexual fulfilment, unlike Margaret Sanger and Aletta Jacobs who saw it as necessary in the fight against poverty. *Married Love* argued that women could enjoy sex and, sensationally, showed how this might occur, while *Wise Parenthood* declared it was wrong to have unwanted children. As a result of these works MS received thousands of confessional letters. Other of her ideas seem less attractive now. She was fascinated with eugenic theories which might improve the race through selective breeding and she was horrified at what she considered the low intelligence of blacks and at the overbreeding of the thriftless poor. Despite her advocacy of sexual fulfilment, she seems to have had a rather ambivalent attitude to sexuality; obviously attracted to other women, she totally rejected homosexuality.

JANET JONES

Works: *Ancient Plants* (1910); *Love Letters of a Japanese* (1911); *Man, Other Poems and a Preface* (1914); *Cretaceous Flora* (1913–15); *Conquest, or, a Piece of Jade* (1917); *The Constitution of Coal* (1918); *Married Love* (1918); *Wise Parenthood* (1918); *Radiant Motherhood* (1920); *A Letter to Working Mothers* (1919); *The Truth About Venereal Disease* (1921); *A New Gospel to All Peoples* (1922); *Contraception: Its History, Theory and Practice* (1923); *The Human Body* (1926); *Enduring Passion* (1928); *Love's Creation* (1928); *Fuel* (1935); *Change of Life in Men and Women*

(1936); *Oriri* (1940); *Wartime Harvest* (1944); *The Bathe, an Ecstasy* (1946); *Sleep* (1956).
References: Box, M., *The Trial of Marie Stopes* (1967); Briant, K., *Marie Stopes* (1962); Fryer, P., *The Birth Controllers* (1966); Hall, R., *Marie Stopes* (1977); Hall, R., (ed.), *Dear Dr Stopes: Sex in the 1920s* (1978); Maude, A., *The Authorized Life of Marie C. Stopes* (1924); Stopes-Roe, H. V., with J. Scott, *Marie Stopes and Birth Control* (1974).

Stretton, Hesba
b. 27 July 1832, Wellington, Shropshire; d. 8 October 1911, Richmond, Surrey
Novelist, writer of short stories and tracts, writer for children
HS was the third daughter of a bookseller, Benjamin Smith, and his fervently Evangelical wife Anne Bakewell, who died when HS (Sarah) was 8 years old. She proved a bright pupil at a local day school and wrote 'improving' stories from an early age. Dickens encouraged her to contribute to *Household Words* and *All the Year Round*, and the Religious Tract Society published much of her work. *Jessica's First Prayer* (1866) brought her international fame; it was translated into over a dozen languages and made compulsory reading in Russian schools by Tsar Alexander II.

HS lived a long life of Puritan austerity with her sister Elizabeth, devoted to the cause of Evangelical Christianity through unwearying philanthropy and prolific writing. Childless, she wrote many books for children and helped to found the London Society for the Prevention of Cruelty to Children in 1884.

As an author she followed the fashion of combining religious propaganda with sensationalism. Some of her novels resemble lengthy tracts, but her shorter works have a simplicity, charm, and pathos that touched the heart of millions. She moralizes effectively over a variety of lifestyles and frailties (suburban materialism is neatly dealt with in *Mrs Burton's Best Bedroom*, 1878) but she excels in stories of city waifs and urchins brought to Christ (Charlotte Yonge called them her 'Street Arab Tales'), and *Jessica's First Prayer*, *Little Meg's Children* (1868), *Alone in London* (1869), and *Pilgrim Street* (1872) are among her most engaging productions.   MARGARET MAISON
Selected Works: 'The Lucky Leg', *Household Words* (19 March 1859); *Fern's Hollow* (1864); 'The Travelling Post Office' in 'Mugby Junction', *All the Year Round* (December 1866); *The Clives of Burcot* (1867); *Jessica's First Prayer* (1867); *Paul's Courtship* (1867); *Little Meg's Children* (1868); *Alone in London* (1869); *David Lloyd's Last Will* (1869); *The Doctor's Dilemma* (1872); *Max Crömer* (1872); *Pilgrim Street* (1872); *The King's Servants* (1873); *Lost Gip* (1873); *Friends till Death* (1875); *Mrs Burton's Best Bedroom* (1878); *Through a Needle's Eye* (1878); *A Thorny Path* (1879); *Cobwebs and Cables* (1881); *No Place Like Home* (1881); *Only a Dog* (1889); *The Soul of Honour* (1898).
References: Maison, M., *Search Your Soul, Eustace* (1961); OCCL; Wolff, R., *Gains and Losses* (1977).

Strickland, Agnes
b. 19 August 1796, London; d. 13 July 1874, Southwold, Suffolk
Historian, poet, writer for children
AS was the second of six daughters of Thomas Strickland, a landed gentleman of Suffolk. Although four of her sisters also published, AS was the most renowned. She and her older sister Elizabeth were educated by their father who

forbade their reading plays or novels; instead they studied history and poetry in English, Latin, Greek, French, and later Italian. He also taught them mathematics. Strickland died in 1818 having lost most of his fortune; the daughters, who had already begun to write, turned more seriously to this means of increasing their income.

AS's first published work was *Monody on the Death of the Princess Charlotte* which appeared anonymously in the *Norwich Mercury* in 1817. She and her sisters Elizabeth, Jane, Margaret, and Susanna produced several short works for children. AS contributed to various magazines and in 1827 published two volumes in verse, *Worcester Field, or, The Cavalier* and *The Seven Ages of Woman*. Elizabeth, who was editor of the *Court Magazine*, and AS collaborated on several volumes of historical tales for children in the 1830s, and AS alone wrote another volume of tales, *The Pilgrims of Walsingham* (1835). The attractions of history and royal biography led the sisters to write *The Lives of the Queens of England*, of which the first two volumes appeared in 1840. Although they shared the authorship nearly equally, only AS's name appeared on the title page. AS also wrote a brief biography of Queen Victoria in 1840, based on inaccurate gossip; the queen was not at all pleased with it. AS was most attracted to earlier times and especially to the Stuarts. She published *Letters of Mary Stuart* in 1842–3 and *Lives of the Queens of Scotland*, again with Elizabeth, in 1850–9. In addition the sisters published volumes on the bachelor kings of England, the seven bishops, and the Tudor and Stuart princesses. The sisters lived and worked together in London and after 1864 in Southwold. Elizabeth died in 1875.

AS seems to have been responsible for most of the research for the works on the queens and other royal personages. Although in no way sympathetic to the usual feminist aims, she felt she herself should have access similar to men's to public, royal, and private archives. After some initial resistance to the idea of a woman historian, various collections were opened to AS both in Britain and on the continent. The success of the first volumes of the *Queens* made work on later publications easier. The methods and results of the sisters' research were typical of history at the time. They relied as much as possible on manuscript material and contemporary records. The volumes of biography went through a number of editions, but by the end of the nineteenth century they were not regarded seriously, perhaps in part because they were by and about women.   BARBARA BRANDON SCHNORRENBERG

Works: *Monody on the Death of the Princess Charlotte* (1817); *Guthred: The Widow's Slave* (1821); *The Tell-Tale* (1823); *Prejudice Reproved, or, The Young Emigrants* (1825); *The Juvenile Forget-Me-Not* (1827); *Worcester Field, or, The Cavalier* (1827); *The Seven Ages of Woman* (1827); *Historical Tales of Illustrious British Children* (with Elizabeth Strickland) (1833); *The Pilgrims of Walsingham* (1835); *Tales and Stories From History* (with Elizabeth Strickland) (1836); *Queen Victoria from her Birth to her Bridal* (1840); *Alda: The British Captive* (1841); *Letters of Mary Stuart* (1842–3); *Lives of the Queens of England* (with Elizabeth Strickland) (1840–8); *The Royal Sisters* (1849); *Historic Scenes and Poetic Fancies* (1850); *Lives of the Queens of Scotland* (with Elizabeth Strickland) (1850–9); *Old Friends and New Acquaintances* (1860); *Lives of the Bachelor Kings of England* (with Elizabeth Strickland) (1861); *Lives of the Seven Bishops* (with Elizabeth Strickland) (1863); *Althea Woodville, or, How Will it End?* (1864); *Lives of the Tudor Princesses* (with Elizabeth Strickland) (1867); *Lives of the Last Four Princess of the House of Stuart* (1870); *St Edmund, the Last King of East Anglia* (1871).

References: Smith, B. G., 'The contribution of women to modern historiography in Great Britain, France, and the United States, 1750–1940', *American*

Historical Review 89 (June 1984); Strickland, J. M., *Life of Agnes Strickland* (1887); Pope-Hennessy, U., *Agnes Strickland: Biographer of the Queens of England 1796–1874* (1940).

Sutcliff, Rosemary

b. 1920, West Clandon, Surrey
Historical novelist, writer for children

RS's father was a British naval officer and for her first ten years she travelled with her parents to various postings throughout the world. The family settled in Devon and because RS at the age of 2 had contracted Still's Disease (a polio-arthritic condition which has confined her to a wheelchair for many years), she was taught mainly at home by her mother. She went to school briefly but left at 14 to attend Bideford Art School, where she became a competent miniaturist; she is a Member of the Royal Society of Miniature Painters. She now lives and writes at Arundel, Sussex. From an early age she was fascinated by stories of men of action, listening to her father's naval tales and legends her mother told her. Her greatest influence, she has said, was Kipling who reinforced her early feeling for history. Her first attempt to put this on paper was rejected by the publishers but they recognized her quality and invited her to write *Chronicles of Robin Hood* (1950). This was followed by a number of novels for younger children, but her first characteristic work was *Simon* (1953), followed by *The Eagle of the Ninth* (1954) which reached a wide audience when it was serialized on radio's Children's Hour. After composing a number of similarly complex novels she had a gap in her writing for ten years, but in 1979 she published *The Light Beyond the Forest* about King Arthur, whom she had first written about in 1963 in *Sword at Sunset*. In 1983 she wrote her autobiography, *Blue Remembered Hills*, giving an account of her early years.

Her work is marked by seriousness and a fascination with history being made, as the values of one kind of society are challenged and changes in attitude lead to the evolution of a new form of civilization. For this reason her favourite periods are the Bronze Age and Roman, Viking, or Norman Britain. The Dark Ages are to her a period of change similar to our own and this is frequently expressed in the novels in terms of the symbolism of light and darkness. She undertakes careful research but her main characters tend to be fictional rather than historically significant figures. They are usually boys and the periods are those when fighting and violence were commonplace, and masculine and heroic virtues clear. It is significant that she loads the dice against her heroes succeeding in this kind of world. They are either physically maimed like Drem in *Warrior Scarlet* or Marcus in *The Eagle of the Ninth*, or radically at a disadvantage like Randal the Saxon dog-boy in *Knight's Fee*, or socially outcast like the ex-gladiator hero of *Mark of the Horse-Lord*. The books are about learning, particularly the hard learning loosely called 'growing up', and therefore her stories in their accurate historical setting have a universal application. Her style is carefully solemn, free from modern colloquialisms and whimsical 'gadzookery'. It frequently uses periphrases and inversion and occasionally archaism, while the sentences are lengthy and move with a semi-Biblical rhythm. The influence of the Kipling of *Puck of Pook's Hill* is seen here, as much as in her sense of the breadth and relevance of far-off times. In making few concessions to the younger reader she has found an adult audience as well, and for many teenagers must help to move their imaginative responses on to complex and ambiguous situations dealt with in complex and ambiguous ways.   MARY SHAKESHAFT

Works: *Chronicles of Robin Hood* (1950); *The Queen Elizabeth Story* (1950); *The Armourer's House* (1951); *Brother Dusty-Feet* (1952); *Simon* (1953); *The Eagle of the Ninth* (1954); *Warrior Scarlet* (1958); *Knight's Fee* (1960); *Sword at Sunset* (1963); *The Light Beyond the Forest* (1979); *Blue Remembered Hills* (1983). **References:** Crouch, M., *The Nesbit Tradition* (1972); Meek, M., *Rosemary Sutcliff* (1962); OCCL.

Talbot, Catherine
b. May 1721, Berkshire; d. 9 January 1770, London
Poet, essayist
Descended on both sides from clerical families, CT was born five months after her father's death. In 1725 she and her mother joined the household of Thomas Secker and his wife Catherine, who was a family friend. Secker became Bishop of Oxford, Dean of St Paul's, and, in 1758, Archbishop of Canterbury. Childless himself, he virtually adopted CT and superintended her education, especially in scripture and modern languages. Through him she became acquainted with many of the leading literary figures of the day. In 1741 she met Elizabeth Carter; their friendship enhanced CT's reputation in her own time and later. The two women corresponded continually and each encouraged the other's literary efforts. Archbishop Secker left CT and her mother a large legacy on his death in 1768. CT suffered from ill-health for most of her life. Her mother survived her and gave her manuscripts to Carter, who published some of them in 1770 and 1772. Carter's nephew, Montagu Pennington, published CT's complete works in 1809.

CT's reputation in her own day for talent and learning rested on the regard of her friends. A reader with no personal involvement can find little merit or interest in her poems and essays and they have been deservedly neglected; the subject matter is generally trivial and the style unoriginal. Her letters are, however, far more lively and engaging although they suffer in comparison with those of Carter or Elizabeth Montagu.   BARBARA BRANDON SCHNORRENBERG
Works: *The Rambler* (30 June 1750); *The Works of the Late Miss Catherine Talbot*, ed. M. Pennington (1809); *A Series of Letters between Mrs Elizabeth Carter and Miss Catherine Talbot*, ed. M. Pennington (1809). **References:** Faderman, L., *Surpassing the Love of Men* (1981); Ferguson, M., *The First Feminists* (1985); Scott, W. S., *The Bluestocking Ladies* (1947); Todd.

Taylor, Ann
b. 1782, London; d. 1866, Nottingham
Poet, writer for children, reviewer

Taylor, Jane
b. 1783, London; d. 1824, Ongar, Essex
Poet, writer for children, essayist
(also wrote under QQ)
The Taylor family moved from London to Lavenham, Suffolk, for reasons of health and economy, in 1786. A developing religious commitment led to Isaac Taylor's acceptance of a Nonconformist ministry at Colchester in 1796; he later became a writer and illustrator of popular children's books, but his daughters' fame preceded his own. With his wife, Ann, who also wrote improving works, he devised an intensive system of moral and intellectual education for their large family. AT and JT were taught the rudiments of mechanics, anatomy,

and astronomy, as well as more conventional subjects and household skills. Their father trained them as engravers, his original craft, to enable them to become self-supporting, but their preferred activity was scribbling; the drafts of their poems were written on the margins of engraved fortification systems.

A Quaker publishing firm which had printed some of their plates for children's books, as well as a few rhymes in the annual *Minor's Pocket Book*, asked them for 'some specimens of easy Poetry for young children' and they responded with anonymous verses for *Original Poems* (1804–5), with contributions from other 'young persons', including thirty-four by Adelaide O'Keeffe. The success of this work was remarkable; it was published in America and translated into German. The equally popular *Rhymes for the Nursery* (1806) includes JT's 'The Star' ('Twinkle, twinkle, little star').

The sisters jointly wrote *Lime Twigs to Catch Young Birds* (1808), a simple reading primer ('Why is the bee on the bud?'); *Signor Topsy-Turvy's Wonderful Magic Lantern* (1808), and a sequence of moral fables with grotesque illustrations ('The Horse turned Driver', 'The Cook Cooked'), but their next major work was the influential *Hymns for Infant Minds* (1810), in which the freshness of their earlier songs has been replaced by sombre moralizing on sin and death. The poems were revised in later editions. A Russian prose translation of selected hymns was published in 1831. Many American editions appeared. The values expressed in 'A Child's Hymn of Praise', by AT, suggest that Christian humility is compatible with cultural superiority – a useful lesson for future empire-builders:

> I was not born as thousands are
> Where GOD was never known;
> And taught to pray a useless prayer,
> To blocks of wood and stone. . . .

Apart from other hymns and a late work, *The Linnet's Life* (1822), a handbook in verse on the compassionate treatment of a caged bird, the sisters developed separate careers in writing.

AT wrote a pastiche of Roscoe, *The Wedding among the Flowers* (1809, dated 1808). Fancy replaces the imagination of her earlier poems in the tripping metre of this animated gardening catalogue. She turned to writing articles: her criticism of Hannah More's *Christian Morals* appeared in the *Eclectic Review* in 1813. This year marked her curtailment of a literary career on her marriage to the Rev. Joseph Gilbert. He had offered himself as a suitor before they met, partly on the evidence of her writing. After living in Rotherham and Hull, they settled in Nottingham in 1825, where he became minister of an Independent Chapel. AT involved herself in good causes: she attacked slavery and supported a Blind Asylum and a refuge for Unfortunate Women. However, she refused to join campaigners for women's rights, preferring to develop the maternal role which she had celebrated in her most famous poem, 'My Mother' ('Who fed me from her gentle breast . . . ?'), which played a significant part in the developing nineteenth-century sentimentalization of woman's role as domestic angel. She wrote occasionally on social and religious issues, continued to compose hymns, and produced a biography of her husband in 1853, after his death. Her 'Domestic Recollections' of early years, published with a memoir by her son in 1874, provide a detailed account of Dissenting family life.

JT did not marry. She began to write under her own name, and soon acquired a literary reputation denied to AT until her later years. The Taylors moved to Ongar, Essex in 1811. The involvement of her parents and of her brothers Isaac junior and Jefferys in the business of writing and illustrating books explains the family's reputation as a literary collective: 'The Taylors of Ongar'. JT left the family in 1812 to live with Isaac in Devon and Cornwall and concentrate on her writing. She attributed the continuing success of the *Original Hymns* to her sister's verses, but the public response to *Display* in 1815 gave her confidence. Subtitled 'A Tale for Young People' to distance it from the frivolity of a novel, the book records the reformation of a foolish young woman who judges by appearances; she falls in love with a military uniform, and learns wisdom, appropriately, behind a linen drapery counter. Didacticism stifles JT's promisingly perceptive insight into character and manners. Her denunciation of dancing was regarded as extreme by some readers. In 1816 her satirical and polemical *Essays in Rhyme* appeared, to critical acclaim. Her brother records her spiritual crisis in 1817, the year after her return to Ongar. Its resolution led her to make a public commitment to religion. Eager to use her gifts for the salvation of the young, she regularly contributed moral essays to the evangelical *Youth's Magazine* under the pseudonym 'QQ', in spite of illness, until her death from cancer in 1824.

The originality of the sisters' early verse can be underestimated by modern readers, but it contrasted with conventional stiff verse addressed to children; realizing that adult images are 'terrible stumbling blocks to children', they try to discourage raids on nests by putting the child in the young bird's place: 'Suppose that some monster, a dozen yards high, / Should stalk up at night to your bed . . .'(AT). The poems relate to the everyday experiences of children.

Keats, writing to his sister in 1817, refers to her former enjoyment of 'those pleasant little things, the Original Poems'. He recommends to her JT's *Essays in Rhyme* as 'the more mature production' of the same hand, which includes her mocking attack, in 'Poetry and Reality', on the self-indulgent poet who worships nature:

> Nay, let him slumber in luxurious ease,
> Beneath the umbrage of his idol trees,
> Pluck a wild daisy, moralize on that
> And drop a tear for an expiring gnat,
> Watch the light clouds o'er distant hills that pass,
> Or, write a sonnet to a blade of grass.

CLARE MACDONALD SHAW

Selected works: jointly written by AT and JT: *Original Poems for Infant Minds* (1804–5); *Rhymes for the Nursery* (1806); *Limed Twigs to Catch Young Birds* (1808); *Signor Topsy-Turvy's Wonderful Magic Lantern* (1808); *Hymns for Infant Minds* (1810); *Original Hymns for Sunday School* (1812); *The Linnet's Life* (1822); by AT: *The Wedding among the Flowers* (1809); *Original Anniversary Hymns* (1827); *The Convalescent* (1839); *Seven Blessings for Little Children* (1844); 'Sixty years ago', *Sunday School Magazine* (1848); *A Biographical Sketch of the Rev. Joseph Gilbert*, (1853); *Autobiography and Other Memorials of Mrs Gilbert*, ed. J. Gilbert (1874); by JT: *Display* (1815); *Essays in Rhyme* (1816); *Poetical Remains*, vol. 2 of *Memoirs and Poetical Remains of the late Jane Taylor*, ed. I. Taylor (1825); by Mrs Ann Taylor (1757–1830) and JT: *Correspondence between a Mother and her Daughter* (1817).

References: Armitage, D. M., *The Taylors of Ongar* (1939); Gilbert, J., 'Memoir' in *Autobiography and Other Memorials of Mrs Gilbert*, (1874); Darton, F. J. H., *Children's Books in England: Five Centuries of Social Life* (1932); Stewart, C. D., *The Taylors of Ongar: An Analytical Bio-Bibliography* (1975); Taylor, I., 'Memoir' in *Memoirs and Poetical Remains of the late Jane Taylor*, vol. 1 (1825); Woolf, V., 'The Lives of the Obscure: I: Taylors and Edgeworths', *The Common Reader* (1925).

Taylor, Elizabeth

b. 3 July 1912, Reading, Berkshire; d. 19 November 1975, Penn, Buckinghamshire

Novelist, short story writer

ET was the daughter of Oliver and Elise (*neé* Fewtrell) Coles. Educated at the famous local Abbey School, she subsequently worked as a governess and a librarian. In 1936 she married John William Kendall Taylor, a director in the confectionery business, and with her two children, Renny and Joanna, lived in the Buckinghamshire village of Penn. Although she had been writing since childhood, ET only published her first novel, *At Mrs Lippincote's*, in 1946.

She knew Rebecca West and maintained a long friendship with Ivy Compton-Burnett. The story of this friendship in her letters to a common friend, the writer Robert Liddell, has recently been published as *Ivy and Elizabeth* (1986). ET visited Greece several times before the Generals' coup blacklisted her, and also travelled to Morocco. During her final illness from cancer in 1974, she completed her last novel, *Blaming*, posthumously published in 1976.

Although generally considered a gifted author, ET has not received major critical attention. For this a review by Kingsley Amis suggested a possible reason: 'Mrs Taylor's work bears a superficial resemblance to the "library novel" or "women's novel" frequently vilified (though rarely read) in literary circles.' Characteristically her writing has been called 'feminine', because of the domestic settings, often in the wealthy suburbs of the Thames Valley. Her understated, untragic, ironic style is matched by plots equally undramatic, centring on marriage, friendship, or the slow processes of life within several households. *A View of the Harbour* (1947) is typical, describing the lives and relationships of neighbours, a deserted wife, a widow, and a writing doctor's wife, who all live around a small harbour. Similarly, *A Wreath of Roses* (1949) focuses on the friendship between the painter Francis Rutherford and her two guests, Liz and Camilla, which is temporarily endangered by Camilla's affair with a fugitive murderer. With its violent shattering of romance, this novel was ET's first attempt to widen her scope beyond the domestic plot.

The viewpoint in her novels is usually that of women characters locked into and accepting a middle-class gentility which determines their lives and precludes dramatic action. In the sensitive but formal household of *In a Summer Season* (1961), social obligations hinder Kate from dealing with her uncertain second husband Dermot, her adolescent, doting daughter, and a mature son in love: an uncongenial mother-in-law must be visited and the cook humoured, while a self-effacing but ever-watchful spinster cousin, an ex-suffragette with a Freudian interest in Kate's sexual and emotional life, has to be faced. The tone of the writing remains cool, even though it explores the loneliness of a civilized, wealthy wife whose widowing during the novel is revealed as only an extension of her previous emotional isolation within marriage.

These feminine social roles and their dangerous attraction are bitingly analyzed in the character of Flora, who self-deludingly believes herself to be *The Soul of Kindness* (1964). Her intermeddling forces her father-in-law and his mistress out of a comfortable arrangement into a restrictive marriage and causes a near-suicide. In *The Wedding Group* (1968) social roles and manipulation are again the theme, as Cressida rebels against her grandfather's domination, only to succumb to the subtle, if half-conscious machinations of yet another self-negating woman, her mother-in-law Madge. By indulging Cressy in her domestic incompetence and her childish addiction to Wimpey bars and television, Madge tries to retain her son and the eventual grandson.

Frequently in ET's later novels, the writers or painters are the most ruthless and manipulative of the characters. *The Wedding Group* features the eccentric Catholic painter, Harry Bretton, founder and 'Master' of the self-supporting archaic community Quayne. When Cressida's cousin becomes pregnant, she is cold-shouldered but her grandfather nevertheless exploits her pregnancy in a religious painting of the meeting between Mary and Elizabeth. Using her for both saints, he is said to achieve an uncanny 'family likeness'. The ruthless, self-deceiving and manipulative author has pride of place in *Angel* (1957), an untypical, harder novel presenting a sensation novelist who egotistically uses her writing to acquire the great house she wanted to own as a child.

ET's penultimate novel, *Mrs Palfrey at the Claremont* (1971), is a portrait of brave, impoverished old age. Mrs Palfrey, a widow with a colonial background, moves permanently to a cheaper residential London hotel. Here, the elderly guests while away the boredom between meals until illness, or incontinence, forces them out. Mrs Palfrey, however, lives and dies with dignity. As visitors bestow prestige, she passes off a young man as the nephew who never comes and, significantly, he writes her character into his novel.   SABINE VANACKER

Works: *At Mrs Lippincote's* (1945); *Palladian* (1946); *A View of the Harbour* (1947); *A Game of Hide-and-Seek* (1951); *The Sleeping Beauty* (1953); *Hester Lilly and Other Stories* (1954); *Angel* (1957); *The Blush and Other Stories* (1958); *In a Summer Season* (1961); *The Soul of Kindness* (1964); *A Dedicated Man and Other Stories* (1965); *Mossy Trotter* (1967); *The Wedding Group* (1968); *Mrs Palfrey at the Claremont* (1971); *The Devastating Boys and Other Stories* (1972); *Blaming* (1976).

References: Amis, K., 'At Mrs Taylor's', *Spectator* 14 (June 1957); *CN*; Kunitz; Liddell, R., 'The novels of Elizabeth Taylor', *Review of English Literature* 1 (April 1960); Liddell, R., *Ivy and Elizabeth* (1986); Sudrann, J., 'The necessary illusion: a letter from London', *Antioch Review* 18 (1958–9); Toulson, M., 'The sensibility angle', *Isis* 28 (January 1959).

Taylor, Harriet
b. 1807, Walworth, London; d. 1858, Avignon, France
Essayist

HT was one of seven children born to Harriet (*née* Hurst) and Thomas Hardy, a London surgeon. The Hardys were well-connected Unitarians, the intellectual elite among Dissenters. Nothing is known of her schooling, but she had a good grasp of French and German. She was probably cleverer than her five brothers, for she was boldly confident and never doubted the equality of the sexes in brainpower. She felt little attachment to her family, except for a younger brother who emigrated to Australia. Marriage in 1826 to John Taylor, a wholesale druggist, provided an escape from emotional scenes with her mother and sister and the miserly ways of her father.

Eleven years her senior, Taylor was an original member of the Reform Club. He doted on his wife and she at first returned his love. They had two sons and a daughter, Helen, who served Mill as collaborator and companion after the death of HT. Near their home in Finsbury was the South Place Chapel where the radical Unitarian William Johnson Fox preached his advanced views including the intellectual development of women: in his feminist essay 'A Political and Social Anomaly' (*Monthly Repository*, September 1832), Fox maintained that properly educated women might shame 'men into something like intellectual progress', and that in training a dependant, man had lost a companion. Since HT espouses similar ideas in her 1832 essay for Mill on 'Marriage and Divorce', it is questionable who was the original thinker.

Fox introduced HT to Mill in 1830. Mill had formed the Utilitarian Society in 1823 and belonged to a group known as the Philosophic Radicals. Each learned the other had turned to the Romantic poets for solace, he from a feeling of dejection over the dry rationalism of his father's Benthamism and she from frustrated ambitions. They soon turned to each other. Taylor tried to bring a halt to the relationship in 1833 when Mill was a constant visitor at their new home in Kent Terrace, but after HT threatened a permanent separation, he conceded to their seeing each other whenever they wished, even to their travelling abroad together. Both praised the character of Taylor.

Like many high-minded Victorians, HT and Mill were elitist in regard to sex, thinking it a matter for lower natures. Nevertheless, even the Unitarian Radicals gossiped about them, and Carlyle noted the strain upon Mill. John Taylor died in 1849. Marrying in 1851, the Mills had seven and a half years together before she died. They had two main objects in life: to regain their health, and to write their books for the improvement of society. Mill never ceased to pay tribute to his wife and the role she had played as joint author of his greatest books, but after her death he resumed his connections with family and friends and became an MP for Westminster (1865–8). In 1866 he presented a petition to Parliament for women's suffrage. He died in 1873 at Avignon where he had lived in a cottage near his wife's grave.

Mill, who had been influenced by the Saint-Simonians and Owenites, was already a confirmed supporter of sexual equality before he met his future wife. But she gave context to his abstract ideas and the impetus to press them forward. In the essays they wrote for each other in 1832 on 'Marriage and Divorce', her views are far bolder than his – advanced even for the later twentieth century. Not only does she advocate divorce on request, after a suitable length of time, but speculates that if women obtain equal rights and are educated along with men so as to enter public offices and take an equal share of the occupations, all laws concerning marriage may be abolished. Women would then maintain their own children and be free from the patronage of men, a circumstance that would bring about a Malthusian check on population growth and thereby create higher employment. In the 'Enfranchisement of Women' HT again declares that women can be truly independent only when they take financial responsibility for themselves and their children. In this essay she also airs her socialist view of a future society in which rewards are no longer dictated by supply and demand and the division between capitalists and labourers ceases. Mill, who had reservations about socialism, never seemed convinced of the possibility or desirability of the Utopian society she envisioned. But at her insistence he wrote the chapter 'The probable future of the labouring classes', often 'in words taken from her own lips', for *Principles of Political Economy* (1848), and wrote more positively about socialism in later editions.

Nothing much came of HT's early attempts to write, though at Mill's urging she produced a few poems, essays, and reviews of mixed quality for Fox's respected *Monthly Repository* in 1832. Perhaps to assuage their mutual disappointment over this, he enlisted her help on his manuscripts. But there can be no doubt that over the years she influenced his mode of thought with her impassioned sense of how to put the world right. A fragment of an early essay she wrote in 1832 sets forth the same views that critics have found most controversial in Mill's *On Liberty* – the sovereignty of the individual, the relativism of good and evil, disdain for authority, even the importance of eccentrics in a society. Regarding authorship, Mill said that in the years 1856–8 he and HT worked over every sentence of *On Liberty* together and 'that it was more directly and literally our joint production than anything else which bears my name' (*Autobiography*). The paranoid attitude to society's phantom power over the individual in both it and her 1832 essay can be traced to HT's sense of persecution at failing to conform, and further back to her Dissenter roots and Fox's anarchic radicalism. A reviewer wrote that *On Liberty* sounded as if it had come from 'the prison cell of some persecuted thinker rather than from the study of the most influential and respected writer of his generation'.

The exaltation of freedom above all other values links *On Liberty* to the Mills's essays on sexual equality ('The Enfranchisement of Women' and *The Subjection of Women*) and sets these writings apart from John Stuart Mill's other works which evince no such single-minded approach. 'The Enfranchisement of Women', which appeared anonymously in the *Westminster Review*, but (according to Mill) was publicly known to be by his wife, was inspired by the 1850 women's movement in the United States demanding the rights promised in the Declaration of Independence. But the startling point in both this essay and *The Subjection of Women* (Mill's last work) is that 'What is now called the nature of women is an eminently artificial thing'. No one will know what women are really like until they are freed from the yoke of their male masters and the tyranny of custom and tradition. Because it was composed after HT's death, he could attribute to her only its innovative ideas and not its composition. A landmark in feminist literature, *The Subjection of Women* was not only hostilely received by Victorians but ignored until the women's suffrage movement gained momentum just before the First World War.

To feminists, John Stuart Mill, for all his lavish eulogies, failed to give HT her due by not printing her name with his as co-author of some of his most significant works. Literature on HT will continue to mount as scholars debate whether her abilities and contributions were largely the fancy of a man besotted with love. But without her he might never have written *The Subjection of Women* nor given *On Liberty* and the *Autobiography* their present shape and thrust.   TAMIE WATTERS

Works: unpublished 1832 essays, 'Essay Fragment' and 'On Marriage and Divorce' in Hayek, F. A., *John Stuart Mill and Harriet Taylor Mill: Their Friendship and Subsequent Marriage* (1951); reviews and poetry in the *Monthly Repository* (1832); *Principles of Political Economy* (with J. S. Mill) (1848); 'The Enfranchisement of Women', *Westminster Review* (July 1851); *On Liberty* (with J. S. Mill) (1859); *Subjection of Women* (with J. S. Mill) (1869); *Autobiography* (with J. S. Mill) (1873); *The Earlier Letters of John Stuart Mill, 1812–1848*, ed. F. Mineka, in *Collected Works* (1963); *Essays on Sex Equality by Harriet Taylor Mill and John Stuart Mill*, ed. A. Rossi (1970); *Later Letters of John Stuart Mill, 1849–1873*, ed. D. Lindley and F. Mineka, in *Collected Works* (1972).

References: Bain, A., *John Stuart Mill* (1882); Hayek, F. A., *John Stuart Mill and Harriet Taylor* (1951); Himmelfarb, G., *On Liberty and Liberalism: The Case of John Stuart Mill* (1974); Kamm, J., *John Stuart Mill in Love* (1977); Packe, M., *The Life of John Stuart Mill* (1954); Pappe, H. O., *John Stuart Mill and the Harriet Taylor Myth* (1960); Pugh, E. L., 'John Stuart Mill and Harriet Taylor, and women's rights in America, 1850–1873', *Canadian Journal of History* 13 (1978); Rossi, A., 'Sentiment and intellect: the story of John Stuart Mill and Harriet Taylor', 'Introduction' to *Essays on Sex Equality* (1970); Spender, D., 'Harriet Taylor', in *Women of Ideas* (1982); Stillinger, J., 'Introduction', *The Early Draft of J. S. Mill's 'Autobiography'* (1961).

Tey, Josephine

b. 1896 or 1897, Inverness; d. 13 February 1952
Detective novelist, playwright
(Also wrote under Gordon Daviot)

Most readers of JT's eight detective novels have never heard of Gordon Daviot, who wrote historical dramas, nor of Elizabeth Mackintosh, the very private Scottish woman whose own life remains her greatest mystery. The exact date of her birth is unknown. The daughter of Colin and Josephine (*née* Horne) Mackintosh, she grew up in Inverness where she attended the Royal Academy, then studied at Anstey Physical Training College in Birmingham. She taught physical education for eight years until her mother's death when she returned to Inverness to care for her father. JT never gave interviews, so little is known about her personal life, but she was part of that generation who came of age during the First World War. Her friend John Gielgud always believed that she had experienced personal loss connected with the war. She never married and had few close friends.

By the late 1920s JT had begun to write for literary magazines, and in 1929 Methuen brought out her first detective novel, the winner of a national competition. Although *The Man in the Queue* was published under the name Gordon Daviot, it was later reissued under the more familiar pseudonym Josephine Tey, the name of JT's maternal grandmother. It was as a mystery writer that she gained recognition, but she always preferred the works she wrote as Daviot, novels such as *Kif* and *The Expensive Halo* and the dramas based on historical or biblical characters. The most famous of these, *Richard of Bordeaux*, which ran for fourteen weeks in London in 1932, brought fame to both the playwright and the young actor/director John Gielgud.

In 1936 *A Shilling for Candles* introduced readers to the name Josephine Tey, but marked a return for Alan Grant, her serial detective. After writing a biography, *Claverhouse*, and a drama about the Old Testament hero Joseph, *The Stars Bow Down*, JT returned to mysteries. At the end of the 1940s she published the three mysteries that do not feature Grant: *Miss Pym Disposes*, *The Franchise Affair*, and *Brat Farrar*. She brought Grant back in *To Love and Be Wise* and *The Daughter of Time*, the last work to be published in her lifetime.

JT began writing detective stories at the time when Christie, Sayers, Allingham, and Marsh were breathing new life into Conan Doyle's eccentric gentleman sleuth and proving that women could play the game with consummate skill. Her hero, like Marsh's, is a professional policeman of independent means and exceptional polish, but, unlike the other detectives, he is essentially a loner. Yet the reader knows him better than Hercule Poirot, Roderick Alleyn, or even the early Peter Wimsey. Because Grant functions without a Watson, without a family or intimate friends, his mind provides the focus, his reactions, the emotional and moral filter for the novels. Like the late novels of Dorothy Sayers, JT's detective fiction goes beyond the 'whodunnit' formulas to present sensitive psychological studies. This is true also of the three novels that do not feature Grant. For example, the heroine of *Miss Pym Disposes* becomes so emotionally involved in her experiences that she conceals evidence. Forced to play God, Lucy Pym discovers that final justice is neither final nor just.

The Daughter of Time, JT's most famous novel, combines her love of history with detection as Alan Grant turns armchair detective to vindicate Richard III. The year after it was published, JT was dead. She had told no one about her terminal cancer, but she left two completed manuscripts to be published posthumously. One was a fictionalized biography of Harry Morgan, *The Privateer*; the other was her last detective story. In *The Singing Sands* Grant has suffered a nervous breakdown and gone to Scotland to try to recover by fishing. However, it is his interest in solving the mystery of a dead boy he sees on a train that cures him. Written when JT knew she was dying, this last detective story is a curious reflection of its author. Faced with illness, Grant does not need the help of sympathetic relatives, the love of a beautiful woman, nor even the friendship of those he helps. Instead he turns to what he knows; he works, hard – and alone.   FRANCES ARNDT

Works: *The Man in the Queue* (1929); *Kif: An Unvarnished History* (1929); *The Expensive Halo* (1931); *Richard of Bordeaux* (1933); *Queen of Scots* (1934); *The Laughing Woman* (1934); *A Shilling for Candles* (1936); *Claverhouse* (1937); *The Stars Bow Down* (1939); *Leith Sands and Other Short Plays* (1946); *Miss Pym Disposes* (1947); *The Franchise Affair* (1948); *Brat Farrar* (1949); *To Love and Be Wise* (1950); *The Daughter of Time* (1951); *The Privateer* (1952); *The Singing Sands* (1952); *Plays by Gordon Daviot* (1953–54).

References: *DNB*; Kunitz; Roy, S., *Josephine Tey* (1980); Steinbrunner, C. and Penzler, O., eds., *The Encyclopedia of Mystery and Detection* (1976); Talburt, N. E., 'Josephine Tey' in *10 Women of Mystery* ed. E. F. Bargainnier.

Thirkell, Angela

b. 30 January 1890, London; d. 29 January 1961, Bramley, Surrey
Novelist
(Also wrote under Leslie Parker)
Born into a milieu of learning, culture, and creativity, AT was the daughter of the classicist and Oxford professor of poetry, J. W. Mackail, and of Margaret Burne-Jones, the daughter of Edward Burne-Jones. The Burne-Jones household, where AT and her sister Clare spent much of their early lives, was often visited by such late-nineteenth-century literary figures as Beatrix Potter, Henry James, John Ruskin, and William Morris, and was the subject of her first book, *Three Houses* (1931). She was educated at home by a succession of French and German governesses and later at the newly founded St Paul's School, Hammersmith. At home she read Trollope, Gaskell, George Eliot, and Charles and Henry Kingsley, all of whom influenced her work.

In 1911 she married James Campbell McInnes, a concert baritone, with whom she had two sons, Graham, born in 1912, and Colin, who later became a novelist, born in 1914, and a daughter, Mary, who died in infancy. She divorced McInnes in 1917 and in 1918 married George Thirkell, an Australian, with whom she had a son, Lance, who was the inspiration for her character Tony Morland. The Thirkells left England for Australia in 1920 aboard a troopship, a harrowing adventure which was the subject of *Trooper to the Southern Cross* (1934), written under the name of Leslie Parker. The troopship was crowded with army prisoners, many deserters, and some hardened criminals, who caused a near-mutiny when the failure of the refrigeration system early in the long hot voyage resulted in passengers and prisoners alike being served spoiled food.

This experience, the first of its kind in AT's sheltered life, may have contributed to the lack of confidence in the lower classes which she continually expressed in her novels, at first with Dickensian humour, but later with bitterness.

AT was always homesick for England, and after a long visit in 1928 she returned permanently, her marriage having failed. AT began to write for English magazines, as she had for Australian ones, on literary topics, drawing on her family contacts and her own interests. Her first novel, *Ankle Deep* (1933), was largely autobiographical. During this period she was also reader for a British publisher, using her French and German professionally for the first time.

The first of the 'Barsetshire' novels (although not intended as such) was *High Rising* (1933) whose heroine is Laura Morland, a valiant lady novelist who writes in order to support her family. The book was dismissed as mere 'feminism' by *The Times* but led to *Demon in the House* (1934) in which Barsetshire was first mentioned as AT's imaginary county modelled on that of Trollope (who was enjoying a revival in the mid-1930s). After a break in the following year, when she published another autobiographical novel, *O These Men, These Men!* (1935), and a children's book, *The Grateful Sparrow* (1935), the 'Barsetshire' novels continued yearly until 1960. AT died of a rare blood disease in 1961.

The Barsetshire novels have been called both social history by Elizabeth Bowen and social documentary by Richard Church, and have given rise to controversy as to whether they are valuable as descriptions of a lost middle class or are to be condemned for false values. A good deal of the interest in her work is due to her unabashed debt to Trollope (and also to the Kingsleys, Meredith, and Dickens). These nineteenth-century writers provided not only the allusive texture of AT's work, but plots and parts of plots as well. *Miss Bunting* (1945), for example, has heroines and a plot which are very similar to those in Trollope's *The Two Heroines of Plumpington*. Such procedures worked well until the last, tired novels, which are essentially pastiches. Her point of view was almost that of an upper-middle-class observer of a decade or so before her birth and owed much to her early exposure to the Burne-Jones milieu as well as to her academic home. Her perspective was a nostalgic one: she regretted the passing of a world which had never been hers except by hearsay.

Other notable works by AT include *The Fortunes of Harriette* (1936) and *Coronation Summer* (1937). The first is a biography of Harriette Wilson, the intellectually liberated eighteenth-century courtesan, and the second a fictional account of the coronation festivities of 1837. She wrote short stories and novelettes for various magazines which she deprecated and which have never been collected. In the 1950s she wrote two articles on Henry Kingsley for *Nineteenth Century Fiction* and introductions to Thackeray's *The Newcomes* and Trollope's *The Warden* for The Limited Editions Club: these are appreciations from the perspective of a working novelist.   ELEANOR LANGSTAFF

Works: *Three Houses* (1931); *Ankle Deep* (1933); *High Rising* (1933); *The Demon in the House* (1934); *Wild Strawberries* (1935); *Trooper to the Southern Cross* (1935); *The Grateful Sparrow and Other Stories* (1935); *O These Men, These Men!* (1935); *August Folly* (1936); *The Fortunes of Harriette* (1936); *Coronation Summer* (1937); *Summer Half* (1937); *Pomfret Towers* (1938); *Before Lunch* (1939); *The Brandons* (1939); *Cheerfulness Breaks In* (1940); *Northbridge Rectory* (1941); *Marling Hall* (1942); *Growing Up* (1943); *The Headmistress* (1944); *Miss Bunting* (1945); *Peace Breaks Out* (1946); *Private Enterprise* (1947); *Love Among the Ruins* (1948); *The Old Bank House* (1949); *County Chronicle* (1950); 'Henry Kingsley, 1830–1876', *Nineteenth Century Fiction* 5 (1950); 'The works of Henry Kingsley', *Nineteenth Century Fiction* 5 (1951); *The Duke's Daughter* (1951); *Happy Returns* (1952);

Jutland Cottage (1953); *What Did It Mean?* (1954); *Enter Sir Robert* (1955); *Never Too Late* (1956); *A Double Affair* (1957); *Close Quarters* (1958); *Love At All Ages* (1959); *Three Score and Ten* (with C. A. Lejeune) (1961).
References: Bowen, E., 'Introduction' to *An Angela Thirkell Omnibus* (1966); McInnes, G., *The Road to Gundagai* (1965); Strickland, M., *Angela Thirkell* (1977).

Thompson, Flora
b. 5 December 1877, Juniper Hill, Oxfordshire; d. 21 May 1947, Brixham, Devon
Fictional autobiographer, essayist, poet
FT was the eldest of the ten children of Albert Timms, a stonemason, and Emma Lapper, a former housemaid. She was brought up in Juniper Hill, a hamlet near Brackley in Oxfordshire, and educated at home by her father and at school in Cottisford, a nearby village. Instead of going into service at the age of 12, as the other village girls did, FT was encouraged by her mother to take a job as junior assistant to the postmistress at Fringford, Mrs Whitton. Well-read and well-educated, Mrs Whitton (the Miss Lane of *Lark Rise to Candleford*) had, wrote FT, 'more influence than anyone else in shaping the course of my life'. After six years in Fringford, FT worked as a holiday relief worker in several post offices, before applying in 1897 for the job of post office assistant at Grayshott in Hampshire. Residing with the postmaster's family at first, she later moved into lodgings on account of the postmaster's mental instability (he later murdered his wife and child). In Grayshott she was able to pursue her literary education through free libraries and penny readings. Grayshott was, moreover, a centre for literary celebrities like Bernard Shaw, Conan Doyle, and Grant Allen.
At 24, FT married another post office clerk, John Thompson, and settled with him first in Bournemouth, and later in Liphook. Her interest in writing increased, in spite of her husband's discouragement. Her first serious effort, an essay on Jane Austen, won a prize in a women's magazine competition. She went on to write what she called 'sugared love stories' and trivial verses to help support her growing family (she had three children in all). In 1912, she met Dr Ronald McFie after winning a competition for the best criticism of one of his poems; he encouraged her to continue writing, and became a lifelong friend. In 1916 FT's brother Edwin, her closest childhood companion, was killed in the war. After a period of silence, she resumed writing. For eight years, she contributed to the *Catholic Fireside* (though not a Catholic herself), writing nature essays. She also 'ghosted' for a big game hunter's autobiography. In 1921, a collection of verse, *Bog Myrtle and Peat*, appeared, but met with little success, confirming FT's suspicions that verse was not her ideal medium. In 1924 she founded 'The Peverel Society', a literary association.
Her first serious work was *Lark Rise* (1939), a portrait of an Oxfordshire hamlet in the 1880s. It began as a short essay published in *The Lady* in 1937, depicting Old Queenie the lacemaker and her eccentric husband 'the Twister', who died from pneumonia after digging a horse and cart out of a snow drift. Equally successful essays followed, and she was encouraged to send a collection of them to the Oxford University Press, where Sir Humphrey Milford suggested she expand them into a book. *Lark Rise* was followed by *Over to Candleford* (1941) and *Candleford Green* (1943), the three volumes being published together in 1945 as *Lark Rise to Candleford*, now an acknowledged classic. In

1941, on her husband's retirement, the family moved to Dartmouth. At around the same time their youngest son Peter was killed in an Atlantic convoy, and FT never fully recovered from the shock. She developed pneumonia, and died in 1947.

Lark Rise to Candleford is essentially autobiographical: 'Lark Rise' is Juniper Hill, and 'Laura' is based on FT herself. The three books constitute a pioneering account of a social revolution, of a rural society just beginning to abandon its old customs and values under the onslaught of urban invasion. In particular, FT focuses on the 'survivals', those who remember the hamlet in its pre-enclosure and pre-industrialization prosperity, contrasting it with present poverty. The land labourers have lost their economic independence, and are paid starvation wages. The trilogy does not have a 'plot': instead, it combines the chronological sequence of autobiography with the seasonal cycle and the slow but irrevocable change from a rural to an urban society. The final volume in particular focuses on the social and demographical changes affecting country life, on the newly expanding lower middle class, and the 'mass standardization of a new civilization'. Modern suburbia is foreshadowed in the appearance of a row of villas linking Candleford Green to Candleford town. Laura herself, disappearing from the country scene, unconsciously heralds such changes, unaware of their darker implications. Towards the end of the trilogy she rejects the stability of marriage offered by Philip White preferring the challenge of a new post away from her native county.

FT's ear for the language of the village people, 'stiff with similes', and her feeling for the old country customs and craftsmanship, represented by characters like Queenie the lacemaker and Uncle Tom the cobbler, are evident throughout the trilogy. But although she laments 'an older, sweeter country civilization', her account is not sentimental: she evokes a stifling atmosphere in which reading and education are distrusted, and she faces up to the cruelty and suffering which are seen to be a necessary part of survival. Further, some of the changes initiated by the new 'standardization' (the arrival of contraception and of the old age pension) are seen to be of obvious benefit.

Her last book, *Still Glides the Stream*, published posthumously in 1948, is set in fictional form but is more directly autobiographical than *Lark Rise to Candleford*. It, too, celebrates in a mass of concrete detail the surviving pockets of a relatively unchanged rural tradition (a tradition of Christmas mummers and May Day garlands). Charity Finch revisits the village of her youth: 'now, looking back upon it over the vortex of war upon war, the simple life of that time was seen to be in all but actual time nearer to the bow-and-arrow age than to that of the bombing aeroplane'. Another book, *Heatherly*, remained unpublished until 1979 when it appeared in *A Country Calendar and Other Writings*. Keith Dewhurst has written two plays based on *Lark Rise to Candleford*.

ANNE FERNIHOUGH

Works: *Bog Myrtle and Peat* (1921); *Lark Rise* (1939); *Over to Candleford* (1942); *Candleford Green* (1943); *Lark Rise to Candleford* (1945); *Still Glides the Stream* (1948); *A Country Calendar and other Writings* (1979).

References: Lane, M., *Flora Thompson* (1976); Massingham, H. J., 'Introduction' to *Lark Rise to Candleford* (1944); Sambrook, H., *Notes on Lark Rise to Candleford* (1984).

Thrale, Hester

b. 27 January 1741, near Pwllheli, Caernarvonshire; d. 2 May 1821, Clifton, Bristol

Letter writer, diarist, poet

HT was the daughter of John and Hester Maria (*née* Cotton) Salusbury. She was educated by her mother and aunt, and soon became something of an intellectual prodigy: by the age of 22 she had published poems and short articles in newspapers, and spoke competently four languages. But after the death of her father in 1786 her mother arranged her unwilling marriage to Henry Thrale, a prosperous brewer. The marriage left her with little time for writing: in the course of fourteen years she became pregnant thirteen times, although only four of her children survived infancy. In spite of the demands of her family, she became one of the most celebrated hostesses of her time. The popular actor and playwright Arthur Murphy introduced the Thrales to Samuel Johnson in 1765. Johnson began to come to dinner every Thursday, moved in with them at their Streatham home in 1766, and soon people like Oliver Goldsmith, Sir Joshua Reynolds, Edmund Burke, James Boswell, and Guiseppe Baretti joined her husband's political friends around her table. She had a lively interest in politics and worked eagerly for Thrale in all his election campaigns. Later she knew the most celebrated literary women of her time: Fanny Burney, Elizabeth Montagu, Hester Chapone, Hannah More, and Elizabeth Carter.

HT's literary career was a diverse one: she published numerous poems throughout her life, once translated Boethius with Johnson, wrote a two-act comedy, and composed a masque 'in the manner of Milton's *Comus*'. She always kept diaries and journals; when she was bringing up her children she wrote *The Children's Book* (a record of family events), travel journals (of visits to Wales in 1774 and to France in 1775), account books, and collections of anecdotes as well as a diary of daily events. In 1776 she began her most famous notebook, *Thraliana*, in one of the quarto books given her by Thrale, which fills over 800 folio manuscript pages. Like the French collections with similar titles upon which it is modelled, it contains quotations, original and transcribed poems, aphorisms, curious facts, reflections, and anecdotes about people both living and dead. The earlier volumes have sections of grouped material; for example her second volume brings together a sizeable amount of description of Johnson. The later volumes are more autobiographical but continue to display her lively cosmopolitan mind. *Thraliana* has long been read for its picture of famous people in eighteenth-century society, but it is also an important key to understanding HT's mind and published work. It includes over 150 of her poems, entries on word usage and etymology, and observations about history and politics.

After her husband died in 1781, she married Gabriel Piozzi, an Italian musician, a marriage which she made to please herself but which antagonized her eldest daughter and Johnson, neither of whom ever forgave her. But her literary career flourished during her second marriage, and she was able to complete a number of ambitious projects including a popular universal history. HT travelled extensively and happily during the mid-1780s. In the subsequent decade, however, her life was made more difficult by protracted disputes with her daughters arising from her first husband's will, and by her second husband's sickness. Her sadness at his death, together with the failure of her history of the world, virtually brought to an end her career as a publishing author, but she continued to be a prolific writer of notebooks and letters until her death after a fall in 1821.

HT's *Anecdotes of the Late Samuel Johnson, LL.D., during the Last Twenty Years of His Life* was published in 1786. She had collected anecdotes and *bons mots* from the time they first met with the intention of publishing them. At an early stage of the collection she wrote, 'These Anecdotes are put down in a wild way just as I received or could catch 'em from Dr. Johnson's Conversation, but I mean one day or another to digest and place them in some order . . . .' When Johnson died, HT was travelling on the continent with her husband. Urged by her husband and others to publish her material while interest in Johnson was at its peak, she composed the *Anecdotes* based on *Thraliana* and other sources. Two years later she published a two-volume collection, *Letters to and from the Late Samuel Johnson, LL.D. to Which are Added Some Poems Never Before Printed.* HT worked diligently at selecting and editing these letters. Although modern readers may be distressed by her omissions and especially by her obliterations of names mentioned in Johnson's letters, she was following the standard practice of the time and reacting to the harsh criticism which the blunt *Anecdotes* had drawn. In order to fill two volumes, she included some of her own letters which she edited and expanded extensively.

Her subsequent publications demonstrate her considerable ambition: they include a travel book, a synonymy, and a universal history. *Observations and Reflections Made in the Course of a Journey through France, Italy, and Germany* can still be enjoyed and appreciated today. Offering 'observations' (specific descriptions) and accompanying 'reflections' (short sections on the thoughts aroused and which, therefore, give the significance of the descriptions), as did most of the popular travel books of the time, HT's book is full of clear narrative of sights seen, shrewd observations about people, and honest enjoyment. The book pursues certain topics persistently: she gives a steady stream of comments, for instance, on language, speech, intonation, and gesture, together with comparisons from country to country and class to class. It is full of apt quotations from poets such as Milton, Dryden, Swift, and Pope and has perceptive references to appropriate passages from other travel books, notably Addison's *Remarks on Several Parts of Italy* (1705). HT did break with eighteenth-century generic expectations by including more autobiographical incidents and reactions and by writing in a familiar, idiomatic style, and she was criticized for this. HT had always recorded amusing blunders in word usage in her journals, many of which are included in her *British Synonymy: An Attempt at Regulating the Choice of Words in Familiar Conversation.* The book groups words of similar meaning, defines them, and illustrates their correct usage in sentences. The value of the work might be gauged by its popularity: portions of it continued to be reprinted for a dozen years in England and abroad.

Her universal history, *Retrospection, or, A Review of the Most Striking and Important Events, Characters, Situations, and Their Consequences Which the Last Eighteen Hundred Years Have Presented to the Views of Mankind,* was written to appear at the beginning of the new century. Her ambition and her political interests were combined in this huge project, which she described as an 'abridgement' for a 'busy' and 'disturbed' age.

HT selected 'our redemption' by the Crucifixion as the moment from which she would begin her history, a choice which caused her many problems; moreover, she failed to make illuminating historical connections and comparisons. The style she chose also acted against the purposes of such a history. Allying herself with the *Rambler* and beginning with an anecdote about three different people's reactions to a 'stag-horned tree', apparently in order to persuade her readers to accept her choices of events, she trapped herself in a leisurely mode at odds with both her subject matter and her purpose. *Retrospection*, however, has some interest as a key to her conservative political opinions and is strengthened by her gift for selecting an individual incident which captures the experience of a nation, as does the anecdote of the woman who finds her son's bloody stockings in prison in Revolutionary France.

But the vogue for universal histories was past by the time of *Retrospection*'s appearance in print, and critics in any case viewed the writing of such a work by a woman with considerable disfavour. The work was both a critical and a commercial failure.

HT's political interests found expression in two works written in the 1790s. *Una and Duessa*, an unpublished 'dialogue essay', considers many of the political and philosophical ideas sparked by the French Revolution. *Three Warnings to John Bull before He Dies* puts these ideas in the form of a political pamphlet like thousands written throughout the eighteenth century and gives the conservative warnings about the preservation of Church, Constitution, and English morality familiar since the Restoration. In publishing this tract, HT contributed to a genre employed by the greatest writers of the age and joined a substantial list of distinguished women 'propagandists'. PAULA BACKSCHEIDER

Works: *Florence Miscellany* (1785); *Anecdotes of the Late Samuel Johnson* (1786); *Letters to and from the Late Samuel Johnson* (1788); *Observations and Reflections Made in the Course of a Journey through France, Italy, and Germany* (1789); *The Three Warnings* (1792; originally appeared in Williams's *Miscellanies* in 1766); *British Synonymy* (1794); *Three Warnings to John Bull before He Dies* (1798); *Retrospection* (1801); *Thraliana: The Diary of Mrs Hester Lynch Thrale (Later Mrs Piozzi), 1776–1809*, ed. K. C. Balderston (1942).

References: Clifford, J. L., *Hester Lynch Piozza* (1941); Clifford, J. L., *From Puzzles to Portraits* (1970); Esdaile, A., 'Hester Thrale', *Quarterly Review* 284 (1946); Hyde, M., *The Impossible Friendship: Boswell and Mrs Thrale* (1972); Lustig, I., 'Boswell at work: the "Animadversions" on Mrs Piozzi', *Modern Language Review* 67 (1972); Spacks, P. M., 'Scrapbooks of a self: Mrs Piozzi's late journals', *Harvard Library Bulletin* 18 (1970).

Tonks, Rosemary

b. 1932, London
Poet, novelist

RT's father died in Africa shortly before her birth. Her early life was spent in boarding homes and schools; later she was sent to Wentworth School. Despite her academic success she was expelled at the age of 16 for stealing tomatoes. Her writing career began almost immediately afterwards: in the same year she published a book for children, and several of her stories were accepted for broadcast by the BBC. When she was 19 she married a civil engineer and later travelled with him to Pakistan. She fell ill with typhoid; after recovering from her illness in England, she returned to Pakistan, only to contract polio. On this occasion she recovered whilst staying in Paris.

Once recuperated, RT returned to England, where in 1963 she published a volume of poetry and two novels, to moderately favourable critical response. Five further novels and another volume of poetry appeared in the 1960s and early 1970s. But at some stage after the appearance of *The Halt during the Chase*

(1972) RT became a convert to evangelical Christianity, burnt the manuscript of the long novel on which she had been working for five years, and withdrew permission to anthologize her poems.

RT's two volumes of poetry stand entirely outside any of the main or even marginal currents of post-war English writing. They are more recognizably influenced, both in their content and in their range of techniques, by French poetry of the last two centuries. RT's habitual territory is, as the title of her first collection, *Notes on Cafés and Bedrooms* (1963) suggests, metropolitan; but her city landscape is one which owes as much to the extravagantly decaying cities of nineteenth-century literary description as to direct observation of the more sanitized modern city. Whilst some of the poems explicitly refer to London, the 'narrow alleys' and ever-present cafés of her cities more often suggest continental settings.

The 'cafés and bedrooms' of RT's first collection do indeed provide the background for many of her poems, but these 'notes' are less concerned to record the external features of the surroundings than to analyse their inhabitants. These protagonists and narrators also show signs of their French origin. RT's most typical human figure is the *flâneur* or urban wanderer for whom the city represents not a place of work but an infinitely various spectacle. Such a figure is easily conflated or confused with the figure of the poet; and on occasion RT's interest in these literary personages betrays her into an endorsement of their poses. 'April and the Ideas-Merchant' ends portentously: 'Poets are only at work . . . / When they live, dream, *bleed* – within an inch of giving in to art.' But RT more frequently qualifies or undercuts such gestures. In 'Rome' an atmosphere of leisured *ennui* is painstakingly built up, only to be confronted with its dependence on an aristocratic freedom from, and aversion to, work: 'It's the jade breath of the waterjar . . . that is mortality/ For the blood that is too insolent for work.' Elsewhere RT proceeds by oblique qualification rather than blunt irony: in the last stanza of 'Poet as Gambler', the self-aggrandizement of the first two lines veers off into a more muted conclusion:

> I went with nothing but the shirt on my back,
> To cast lots with the Infinite,
> And my bid was the blouse that rocks
> On gamblers with a linen sail all night.

These lines give some idea of the equivocality of the first person in RT's work. Whilst the first two are easily imagined as being spoken, the latter two are not. Such shifts allow RT a subtle play with the distance or lack of it which she keeps from her personae. In rare poems such as 'The Little Cardboard Suitcase', from RT's second volume, *Iliad of Broken Sentences* (1967), a whole poem is made up of ironic ventriloquism, in this case of the fulminations of an outmoded intellectual and xenophobic misogynist. More often, as in 'The Sofas, Fogs and Cinemas' from the same collection, RT's tone varies from outright satire to apparent sincerity.

RT has always regarded her fiction as less significant than her poetry. Her novels often share the landscape and themes of her poems but, unlike them, deploy these features primarily to comic effect. *Opium Fogs* and *Emir*, both published in 1963, are set in a London reminiscent of RT's poetic metropolis and harbouring equally Bohemian inhabitants. One of the central characters of *Opium Fogs* displays his enervated decadence in his 'strong pale features of a malefactor – features which respond only to the highest forms of excitement', whilst RT's own note on the book describes its setting as 'a wintry London,

in one of those intense companionable villages of it where intellectuals congre-
gate on foggy evenings to drink cheap wines in one another's workrooms'.
But RT's fiction has subsequently developed an ability to deal with broader
societies and questions. *The Halt during the Chase* (1972), the last novel which
RT completed before her conversion, centres, for example, on the complex
pattern of dependence set up between the heroine and her mother.

SIMON JARVIS

Works: *On Wooden Wings: The Adventures of Webster* (1948); *Wild Sea Goose*
(1951); *Notes on Cafés and Bedrooms* (1963); *Emir* (1963); *Opium Fogs* (1963); *Iliad
of Broken Sentences* (1967); *The Bloater* (1968); *Businessmen as Lovers* (1969); *The
Way out of Berkeley Square* (1970); *The Halt during the Chase* (1972).
Reference: *DLB*.

Tonna, Charlotte Elizabeth

b. 1 October 1790, Norwich; d. July 1846, Ramsgate
Novelist, poet, short story writer, writer of religious tracts
(Also wrote under Charlotte Elizabeth)
CET, daughter of a clergyman, Michael Browne, grew up in Norwich. She
apparently studied hard in her childhood, although from the age of 10 she was
handicapped by deafness. At a young age she married Captain Phelan with
whom she travelled to Canada for two years, returning to live on Phelan's
small estate in Kilkenny, Ireland. This seems to have been an extremely influential period in CET's life. She was converted to Evangelicalism and became
deeply involved in the Irish people, preoccupations which remained dominant
in both her life and work until her death. Also at this time CET began to write,
mainly religious tracts, published under the name of Charlotte Elizabeth in
order to prevent her husband from claiming the money she earned; clearly the
marriage was deteriorating. In 1824 CET and her husband separated, and from
this time until 1841 she lived with her brother, in Sandhurst and in London.
In London she campaigned to improve the living conditions of the impoverished
Irish community, despite her fierce anti-Catholic fervour. Captain Phelan died
in 1837 and in 1841 CET married Lewis Hippolytus Joseph Tonna, also an
ultra-Protestant author. Five years later she died of cancer.

Most of CET's works are novels, although she also wrote poems, short
stories, and tracts, and edited the *Christian Lady's Magazine* (1836–46), the
Protestant Magazine (1841–6) and the *Protestant Annual* (1841). She was widely
read in Britain and published in the United States. Much of CET's work
combines preaching with dull narrative, but in her novel *Helen Fleetwood*, she
produces interesting developments in social fiction. Serialized in the *Christian
Lady's Magazine* between 1839 and 1840, it was one of the first novels to devote
itself wholly to the life and experiences of a working-class family in the northern
industrial factories. Not only did this novel set a precedent for writers such as
Disraeli, Charles Kingsley, and Mrs Gaskell, but it also suggested the ability
of a woman writer to treat the subject of industry both accurately and effectively. In order to achieve accuracy, CET dramatized factual government
reports known as the *Blue Books*, combining fact with fiction as a form of social
propaganda. She wrote 'The abstract idea of a suffering family does not strongly
affect the mind, but let its particles be known to us, let their names call some
familiar images to our view . . . we are enabled much more feelingly to enter
into their trial.'

VIRGINIA CROMPTON

Selected works: *A Friendly Address to Converts from the Roman Catholic Church*

(1827); *The System: A Tale of the West Indies* (1827); *The Rockite: An Irish Story* (1829); *Derry: A Tale of Revolution* (1833); *The Museum* (1833); *Chapters on Flowers* (1836); *Alice Benden, or, The Bowed Shilling* (1838); *Glimpses of the Past* (1839); *Falsehood and Truth* (1841); *Personal Reflections* (1841); *Helen Fleetwood* (1841); *Judah's Lion* (1843); *The Wrongs of Woman* (1843); *Tales and Illustrations, Chiefly Intended for Young Persons* (1844); *The Church Visible in All Ages* (1844) *Judaea Capta* (1845); *Posthumous and Other Poems* (1846); *War with the Saints* (1848); *Memoir of John Britt, the Happy Mute* (1850).

References: Brantlinger, P., *The Spirit of Reform* (1977); Cazaman, L., *The Social Novel* (1973); Kestnor, J., 'Men in female condition of England novels,' in *Men by Women*, ed. J. Todd (1982); Kovacevic, I. and Kanna, B. S., 'Blue Book into novel: the forgotten industrial fiction of C. E. Tonna,' *Nineteenth Century Fiction* 25 (September 1970); Moers, E., *Literary Women* (1976); Skilton, D., *The English Novel: Defoe to the Victorians* (1977); Stowe, H. B., 'Introduction' to *The Works of Charlotte Elizabeth Tonna* (1845).

Tracy, Honor

b.19 October 1913, Bury St Edmunds, Suffolk

Novelist, travel writer

HT was educated at Grove School, Highgate, London, from 1925 to 1929. She began her career in publishing, then became a foreign reader for a film company. She worked at the Ministry of Information, specializing in Japan, from 1942 to 1945. From 1946 to 1950 she was a journalist in Dublin, and later a foreign correspondent for London papers, before settling to the life of a full-time writer, generally spending summers in Ireland and winters in Spain.

HT's gift is for comedy, arising from an incongruity in her perception of the world: between a respect for morality and common sense and simultaneous delight in absurdity and amoral charm. In possibly her best books, this opposition is associated (fairly or not) with Protestantism and Catholicism, and particularly with Englishness and Irishness. Three books of the 1950s illustrate this: a travel book, *Mind You, I've Said Nothing* (1953) and two novels, *The Straight and Narrow Path* (1956) and *The Prospects Are Pleasing* (1958). In the former of the novels, a bewildered anthropologist is set down amidst Irish customs, religion, and love of litigation; in the latter, an Irishman confounds English notions of legality by deciding he has a moral right to steal an 'Irish' painting. More recently the same theme appears, with *The Man From Next Door* (1977) (a beguiling Irishman gets dull English woman put in prison) and *The Ballad of Castle Reef* (1979), in which British huntin' and shootin' types are helpless against the vagaries of Irish police and terrorists.

Silk Hats and No Breakfast (1957) rejoices in the same duality, while revealing a love of Spain. In fact, in most of HT's writings, groups or cultures are sympathetically observed by a sane mind which relishes the amusement and challenge of folly.   R. F. LOBEL

Works: *Kakemono: A Sketch Book of Post-War Japan* (1950); *Mind You, I've Said Nothing: Forays in the Irish Republic* (1953); *The Deserters* (1954); *The Straight and Narrow Path* (1956); *Silk Hats and No Breakfast: Notes on a Spanish Journey* (1957); *The Prospects Are Pleasing* (1958); *A Number of Things* (1960); *A Season of Mists* (1961); *The First Day of Friday* (1963); *Spanish Leaves* (1964); *Men at Work* (1966); *The Beauty of the World* (1967; published in the US as *Settled in Chambers*); (1968); *The Butterflies of the Province* (1970); *The Quiet End of the Evening* (1972);

Winter in Castille (1973); *In a Year of Grace* (1975); *The Man From Next Door* (1977); *The Ballad of Castle Reef* (1979).
References: Hogan.

Trefusis, Violet

b. 6 June 1894, London; d. 1 March 1972, Florence, Italy
Novelist, autobiographer

VT was the elder daughter of the Hon. George Keppel (son of the 7th Earl of Albemarle) and Alice Edmonstone. She grew up in a strict Edwardian household: her mother was a famous hostess, and mistress of Edward VII. VT's childhood and adolescence were spent moving among London and various country houses, and later from country to country – France, Italy, Sri Lanka, and Germany. She met Vita Sackville-West in 1904, and in 1918 the two women became lovers. VT's marriage to Denys Trefusis in 1919 complicated but did not end the women's involvement, and their passionate affair lasted until 1921. In that year VT and Denys moved to France, which VT had always loved, and in Paris she gradually became acquainted with such figures as the Princesse de Polignac, Anna de Noailles, Colette, Marcel Proust, and Poulenc. Colette, on meeting VT, is supposed to have said 'Violette? Je vous appelerai Géranium.' VT published her first book in 1929, and in the same year, in September, Denys died of tuberculosis. VT continued to write for the rest of her life. She had bought a house with a tower at St Loup in France in 1927, and after Denys's death, she divided her time between St Loup and the family Villa L'Ombrellino in Florence. She spent the war years in England, but returned to France in 1945. She died in Florence in 1972. Her epitaph, at her own request, was 'She withdrew'.

VT published in both French and English, and three of her French novels remain untranslated. Her prose style is confusing and erratic, but at its best it has a rococo charm and her description of places that she loved can be vivid and compelling. In Paris, 'pink and white tapers ascended the sky; revolving sprays like the tails of whirling birds of paradise watered the plushy turf; excited children rode demure little donkeys; there was even an ostrich harnessed to a tiny cart' (*Don't Look Round*). Her first two novels, *Sortie de Secours* and *Echo*, both in French, are love stories: the first concerns Laure's choice of her independence over life with Oradour, with whom she is passionately in love (there are bitter echoes here of VT's experience with Vita Sackville-West), and the second is a tragic tale of two sisters' rival loves for their glamorous French cousin, ending with the suicide of one of the sisters. *Tandem, Broderie Anglaise,* and *Pirates at Play* all describe illicit love affairs, and the translator of *Broderie Anglaise,* Barbara Bray, sees in the novel VT's version of the affair between Vita Sackville-West and Virginia Woolf, in which the Vita figure (a man in the novel) is obsessed with his love for a woman bearing suspicious resemblance to VT. *Tandem* and *Hunt the Slipper* are both preoccupied with the contrast between England and France: Irène in *Tandem* and Vica in *Pirates at Play* both come to England when they marry. Irène loves England and is fittingly killed while riding to hounds; Vica's brother Guido persuades Vica to come back to Italy (hints of an incestuous relationship here) and Vica finally becomes involved with Gigi, whom she has really loved all along, and ends her marriage. *Hunt the Slipper* describes the obsessional love affair of Nigel and Caroline, and Caroline's attempts to persuade Nigel to marry her. The novel comes to a poignant and tantalizing close when Nigel, by delaying opening a letter, loses

Caroline for ever. *Prelude to Misadventure* and *Don't Look Round* are both autobiographical works. *Prelude to Misadventure* is in more episodic, fragmentary form and describes, among other things, VT's interview with Mussolini in 1937. *Don't Look Round* develops the sketches of the earlier work into a full-length autobiographical narrative which omits any reference to the depth of her intimacy with Vita Sackville-West, mentioning her simply as a close friend. *From Dusk till Dawn*, published posthumously, is a comic account of family and sexual skirmishes in and around the castle of Gloaming in the valley of Ghast.

SUZANNE RAITT

Works: *Sortie de Secours* (1929); *Echo* (1931); *Tandem* (1933); *Broderie Anglaise* (1935); *Hunt the Slipper* (1937); *Les Causes Perdues* (1941); 'The Carillon', *Horizon* (June 1943); *Prelude to Misadventure* (1942); 'Triptych', *Horizon* (November 1943); *Pirates at Play* (1950); *Don't Look Round* (1952); *Memoirs of an Armchair* (with Philippe Jullian) (1960); *From Dusk till Dawn* (1972).

References: Jullian, P. and Phillips J., *Violet Trefusis: A Biography* (1976); Nicolson, N., *Portrait of a Marriage* (1973); Sharpe, H., *A Solitary Woman: A Life of Violet Trefusis* (1981).

Trimmer, Sarah
b. 6 January 1741, Ipswich; d. 15 December 1810, Brentford
Educator, writer for children

ST was the daughter of Sarah and John Joshua Kirby, an architectural draftsman. Educated at a girl's school in Ipswich, she was a precocious reader of French and English literature. When she was 15, her father was appointed instructor in perspective drawing to the Prince of Wales (later George III), so the family moved to London in 1756. The Kirbys were friendly with Hogarth, Gainsborough, and Reynolds. ST met Dr Samuel Johnson at a party in Reynolds's home and discussed Milton with him, drawing a copy of *Paradise Lost* from her pocket to settle a dispute. In 1759 ST's father was appointed Clerk of the Works at Kew. There ST met her future husband, James Trimmer, whom she married at 18 in 1762. In Brentford, she spent the next twenty-three years raising and educating her twelve children. ST taught them herself, except for Greek and Latin, for which her sons were sent to a nearby cleric. In 1780, she was persuaded to publish some of this instructional material which proved popular enough to go through eleven editions in the next twenty years. ST's lessons were called *An Easy Introduction to the Knowledge of Nature and Reading the Holy Scriptures, Adapted to the Capacities of Children*. A devout evangelical Anglican, ST also published *Abridgements of the Old and New Testaments* (1793) which was used for seventy-seven years by the Society for Promoting Christian Knowledge, as well as another religious book for children, *Sacred History, Selected from the Scriptures, with Annotations and Reflections Adapted to the Comprehension of Young Persons* (1782–4). In order to find the time to write without neglecting the instruction of her six sons and six daughters, it was her custom to rise at four.

She also worked diligently for the education of the poor. She opened Sunday schools in Brentford in May 1786. By August, she had an enrolment of 159, which increased to 300 by June 1788. In November 1786, Queen Charlotte consulted her for two hours on the procedure for setting up similar institutions at Windsor. *The Oeconomy of Charity* (1786) resulted from that meeting, detailing the management of charity schools. it was reprinted in three editions, and expanded in the 1801 version. In 1787, ST set up a trade school where girls might learn to spin flax.

It was also in 1787 that she devised the idea of using copperplate engravings to hang in nurseries. She prepared explanatory chapters to accompany each illustration. These *New and Comprehensive Lessons* were republished five times between 1814 and 1830.

From 1788 to 1789, ST wrote a monthly for lower-class readers, the *Family Magazine*, which contained housekeeping and gardening advice as well as hymns, meditations, and abridged sermons. A volume culled from that magazine was printed in 1810 as *Instructive Tales*. From 1802 to 1806, ST reviewed children's books in her periodical *The Guardian of Education*, addressed to parents and teachers. In it, ST severely condemned fairy-tales. The book for which she is best known is *The Robins*, first published (as *Fabulous Histories*) in 1786, and dedicated to the Princess Sophia; it is still in print.   RUTH ROSENBERG

Works: *Easy Introduction to the Knowledge of Nature* (1782); *Sacred History, Selected from the Scriptures* (vol. 1, 1782; vols 2, 3 and 4, 1783; vols 5 and 6, 1784); *Fabulous Histories. Designed for the Instruction of Children, Respecting Their Treatment of Animals* (1786); *The Oeconomy of Charity, or, An Address to Ladies Concerning Sunday Schools* (1787); *The Family Magazine, or, A Repository of Religious Instruction and Rational Amusement* (1788–9); *Reflections Upon the education of Children in Charity Schools* (1792); *The Charity School Spelling Book* (1798–9); *A Comparative View of the New Plan of Education Promulgated by Mr Lancaster* (1805); *An Essay on Christian Education* (1812); *Some Account of the Life and Writings of Mrs Trimmer* (1814).

References: *DNB*; *OCCL*; Todd; Yarde, D. M., *The Life and Works of Sarah Trimmer, a Lady of Brentford* (1972).

Trollope, Frances

b. 10 March 1779, Stapleton, near Bristol; d. 6 October 1863, Florence, Italy
Travel writer, novelist

FT was the second surviving daughter of the Rev. William Milton and Mary Gresley Milton. After her mother's death and her father's remarriage, FT, not disliking her stepmother but wanting more independence, moved to London to keep house for her brother, Henry, who held an appointment at the War Office. She married a barrister, Thomas Anthony Trollope, in 1809 and settled with him first in London, later on a farm in Harrow. FT had seven children, including the novelist Anthony Trollope. Until she was nearly 50, FT was a devoted wife and mother, creating a happy family life despite her husband's financial difficulties, illnesses, and difficult moods. However, when her husband's failure in farming, property investments, and law practice brought the family to ruin, FT sought other means to support them. In 1827, with three of her children and the artist Auguste Hervieu, FT accompanied Frances Wright to America to investigate Wright's settlement designed to advance the emancipation of slaves in Nashoba, Tennessee. Repelled by the settlement's wilderness, desolation and poor management, FT soon departed for Cincinatti, where she opened a department store which quickly failed. Back in England and desperate for money, FT set down her impressions of the country in *Domestic Manners of the Americans* (1832), for which Hervieu supplied comic illustrations. Her unflattering individual and group portraits, her criticisms of the 'most vile and universal habit of chewing tobacco' among men, and 'the lamentable insignificance of the American women', her declaration about the population generally, 'I do not like them. I do not like their principles, I do not like their manners, I do not like their opinions', dismayed her American subjects but pleased her English readers. The book's immediate success launched FT's career; thereafter her prodigious writing relieved her family of further financial difficulties and, eventually, placed them in comfortable circumstances. FT's discipline – she rose at four each morning – resulted in five more travel books and thirty-four novels. After the death of her husband in 1834, she travelled on the continent, resided for periods in England and eventually settled in Florence. The illnesses and deaths of five children had brought sorrow, but she was consoled by her own success and by the domestic happiness and professional success of her surviving sons, Thomas and Anthony, who also became writers. Although FT declined into senility in her final years, she had until her death the devoted care of her son Thomas.

FT's first book is the one by which she is best known. Her novels, though popular, were not held in critical esteem and are now largely unknown. However, FT deserves reconsideration not only for her productivity but also for the diversity and boldness of her fiction. FT wrote the first anti-slavery novel, *The Life and Adventures of Jonathan Jefferson Whitlaw* (1836), whose central character is a prototype for Harriet Beecher Stowe's villainous Simon Legree. Whitlaw, a Mississippi squatter's son, becomes 'confidential clerk' to Colonel Dart, owner of Paradise Plantation in Louisiana. Whitlaw deems slavery 'a most righteous and Christian-like doctrine', and oversees the Paradise workforce of 500 slaves with the conviction that 'there's nothing so despisible in my mind as a man what's afraid to kick the life out of his own nigger if he sees good'. In contrast to Whitlaw are the Steinmarks, who refuse to use slave labour, but who nevertheless prosper as farmers. Whitlaw tries to increase his fortunes through marriage to Selena Crofts, who rejects him. He learns that Selena has 'black blood', then threatens to expose her ancestry unless she gives him part of her estate. Selena commits suicide. In time Whitlaw inherits Paradise, but prosperity does not mellow him and he continues feuding and exploiting. Finally he is brought down through the vengeance of an old female slave, Juno, Selena's grandmother, who lures him to a forest where her fellow slaves are waiting to assassinate him. Juno hides Whitlaw's body; 'It was my child he killed,' she says, 'and it was my hands that hollowed out his grave.'

Throughout the novel, FT depicted the contrasting aspects of slave-owning Southern society: the sale of slaves in open markets; the brutal treatment of plantation slaves; the quadroon balls in New Orleans; the luxurious homes of slave-owning gentlemen; the petty cruelty of the slave-owning, powerless wives. FT is especially sympathetic to sexually exploited slave women; a woman may weep in secret when her children are taken from her, or when her own daughter is subject to the rapacious pursuits of an owner or overseer, but otherwise she 'cannot show that she is a mother.' Yet her slave hero is not passive; unlike *Uncle Tom's Cabin*, where the denouement is brought about by the martyrdom of a Christian man, the conclusion of Trollope's *Whitlaw* comes through the unpunished violence of an unconciliatory, vengeful woman.

FT's concern with exploited child labour led her to investigate the factory system, and incorporate her findings into another remarkable novel of social reform, *The Life and Adventures of Michael Armstrong, the Factory Boy*. Michael, a child of 7 at the novel's beginning, is befriended by a wealthy manufacturer, Sir Matthew Dowling, who uses him to defuse the anger aroused by the death of a young girl in an accident in one of his factories. After tiring of helping Michael, Sir Matthew sends him away as an apprentice in Deep Valley Mills.

However, an heiress, Mary Brotherton, has taken an interest in Michael and goes in search of him. Through the quest, FT enlightened her readers on the destructive effects of the factory system on children, whose 'lean and distorted limbs, sallow and sunken cheeks, dim hollow eyes' give them a look of 'hideous premature old age'. During a factory visit, a 'dirty, ragged crew' is seen 'in active performance of their various tasks; the overlookers, strap in hand, on the alert; the whirling spindles urging the little slaves who waited on them to movements as unceasing as their own; and the whole monstrous chamber redolent of all the various impurities that . . . are converted for the rich, after passing in the shape of certain poison through the lungs of the poor'. Mary's investigations, paralleling FT's own, lead to the recommendation that an Act of Parliament should render factory labour illegal for longer than ten hours, with no loss of wages to the workers. At the end of the novel, Sir Matthew is bankrupt and ill, haunted by a vision of factory children with smashed limbs. Michael, who is involved in labour reform, is reunited with his brother and friends in a contrived conclusion that undermines the authenticity of the industrial settings and, like the conclusion of *Whitlaw*, the good go off to live far from the scene of their sufferings in Germany.

FT's novels with reformist themes include *The Vicar of Wrexhill*, which deals with the abuses of Evangelicism, and *Jessie Phillips: A Tale of Today*, a sympathetic portrait of a 'fallen woman' and the first of a series of novels about the problems of women in English society. FT avoided the stereotype of the Victorian heroine – patient, virtuous, young, beautiful, submissive, and destined for marriage – and preferred to create central female characters who were, like their author, strong, aggressive, resourceful, and successful in making their own way in the world. Her heroines include plain, middle-aged women (*Mrs Matthews*), roguish women (*The Widow Barnaby*), and downright wicked women (*The Ward of Thorpe Combe*).

FT's travel books also reflect her intense interest in the condition of women. In *Paris and the Parisians in 1835*, FT reported that, while in England the most popular dance partners are pretty young girls, 'on entering a French ball-room, instead of seeing the youngest and loveliest part of the company occupying the most conspicuous places, surrounded by the gayest men and dressed with the most studied and becoming elegance, you must look for the young things quite in the background, soberly and quietly attired, and almost wholly eclipsed behind the more fully-blown beauties of their married friends'. FT gave the explanation for this contrast with English culture through her frequently used device of a reported conversation, in this case allowing a French woman to tell FT's readers that, since French women marry early, they must be allowed to have the pleasures normal to their age. FT concluded that, despite their seeming confinement, French women 'have more power and more important influence than the women of England'. FT's travel books are marked by strong narrative structure, vivid characters and settings, and descriptions of the sights, sounds and smells of everyday life. In *Belgium and Western Germany*, she described radical students with hair 'long and exquisitely dishevelled', their foreheads bared 'à la Byron', and their wild eyes rolling 'à la Juan'. In another vivid sketch, she described the Jews of Vienna in *Vienna and the Austrians* as people 'clothed in sable fine linen', who 'fare sumptuously every day', but who, despite their wealth, 'are not, perhaps, the better loved for this by their Christian fellow-subjects'.

A distinguishing feature of FT was her political conservatism, masked by compassion for the oppressed in her reformist novels, but explicit in the travel books. In *Paris and the Parisians*, she opposed 'any further trial of a republican form of government' and considered freedom of the press 'the most awful engine that Providence has permitted the hand of man to wield'. In *Belgium and Western Germany*, she expressed her liking for Germany because 'everyone knows his place, and keeps it'. In *Vienna and the Austrians* her bias in favour of the Austrian system of government angered her English critics.

SANDRA ADICKES

Selected works: *Domestic Manners of the Americans* (1832); *The Refugee in America* (1833); *The Mother's Manual* (1833); *The Abbess: A Romance* (1833); *Belgium and Western Germany* (1834); *Tremordyn Cliff* (1835); *Paris and the Parisians in 1835* (1836); *The Life and Adventures of Jonathan Jefferson Whitlaw* (1836); *The Vicar of Wrexhill* (1837); *A Romance of Vienna* (1838); *The Widow Barnaby* (1839); *The Widow Married: A Sequel to the Widow Barnaby* (1840); *One Fault* (1840); *The Life and Adventures of Michael Armstrong, the Factory Boy* (1840); *The Ward of Thorpe Combe* (1841); *The Blue Belles of England* (1842); *A Visit to Italy* (1842); *The Barnabys in America, or, The Adventures of the Widow Married* (1843); *Jessie Phillips: A Tale of the Present Day* (1843); *The Laurringtons* (1844); *Travel and Travellers* (1846); *The Robertsons on Their Travels* (1846); *The Three Cousins* (1847); *Father Eustace: A Tale of the Jesuits* (1847); *Town and Country* (1848); *The Old World and the New* (1849); *Petticoat Government* (1850); *Second Love, or, Beauty and Intellect* (1851); *The Young Heiress* (1853); *The Life and Adventures of a Clever Woman* (1854); *Fashionable Life, or, Paris and London* (1856).

References: Bigland, E., *The Indomitable Mrs Trollope* (1953); Heineman, H., *Mrs Trollope: The Triumphant Feminine in the 19th Century* (1979); Heineman, H., *Frances Trollope* (1984); Johnston, J., *The Life, Manners, and Travels of Fanny Trollope* (1978); Mitchell, S., 'Lost women: feminist implications of the fallen in forgotten women writers of the 1840s', *University of Michigan Papers in Women's Studies* 2 (June 1974); Pope-Hennessy, U., *Three English Women in America* (1929); Trollope, F. E., *Mrs Trollope: Her Life and Literary Work from George III to Victoria* (1895); Trollope, T. A., *What I Remember* (1888); Trollope, J., 'Introduction' to *Domestic Manners of the Americans* (1984).

Trotter, Catherine

b. 16 August 1679; d. 11 May 1749, Northumberland
Philosophical writer, poet, playwright
(Also wrote under Catherine Cockburn)

CT was born into a genteel London family. Her father, a Scotsman, David Trotter, was a naval commander under King Charles II. Her mother, Sarah Ballenden, was a relation of several noble Scottish families. CT had one sister. In 1683, Captain Trotter contracted the plague and died during naval operations against the Turks near Tangiers. His death reduced his family to penury, forcing them to live off meagre pensions at the pleasure of the crown until CT's mother's death during the reign of Queen Anne.

CT taught herself French and writing in English. She also learned Latin with the help of a tutor and wrote an unpublished guide to learning the language. Her career began with tragic dramas based on romantic stories. In 1695 her first play, *Agnes de Castro*, was performed at the Theatre Royal in Drury Lane, adapted from Aphra Behn's story, in which the beautiful, but ill-fated Agnes, a pawn in the power struggle between a prince and his discarded mistress, is killed by one of her suitors during a duel over her fate.

In 1697, CT came to the attention of the dramatist William Congreve, to whom she sent verses on his *Mourning Bride*. In these laudatory heroic couplets, CT compares Congreve to Dryden and praises his talent as a playwright:

> Sublime thy thoughts, easy thy numbers flow,
> Yet to comport with them, majestic too!
> But to express how thou our souls do'st move
> How at thy will, we rage, we grieve, we love. . . .

Congreve, who was pleased by such unsolicited adulation, sent CT a copy of his play and in a letter of 15 March 1697 regretted that her verses had arrived too late to be included in the published version of the text.

Her second tragedy, *The Fatal Friendship*, was performed at Lincoln's Inn Fields in 1698. This domestic tragedy was judged her best play well into the nineteenth century and is the only play in Dr Birch's edition of her works. It is the story of four noble lovers whose lives end variously in death and sorrow. Gramont is secretly married to Felicia. To get his friend, Castalio, out of jail, Gramont is induced by Felicia's brother, Bellgard, to marry a young widow, Lamira. Gramont does so, but does not consummate the marriage. Castalio, who is secretly in love with Lamira, misunderstands Gramont's motives and is ignorant of the secret marriage, so he seeks revenge on Bellgard for destroying his chances of marrying Lamira. Gramont interferes in the duel between Castalio and Bellgard and mortally but accidentally wounds Castalio. Gramont then kills himself. Felicia and her child are taken in by Gramont's father and Lamira enters a convent. The story, though complicated, is told in clear but unexceptional dialogue. Most of the speeches do not exceed seven lines, except in Act II, when the arranged marriage is taking place. The characters are not well developed and the unperformed text does not provoke much sympathy from the reader. For example, Gramont's defence for not wanting to marrying Lamira begins: 'Marriage, I hold a sacred bond, /Which should be made for nobler ends than interest; /Hearts should first be joined (II, I).' And in Act V Felicia, fearing that Gramont is dead, begins her speech; 'Love will supply my strength'. The printed version of the play is preceded by five laudatory poems and the epilogue was spoken by Mrs Barry.

In 1700, CT was a contributor to the *Nine Muses, or, Poems written by many Ladies upon the death of the late Famous John Dryden*. Her piece 'Calliope's Directions how to Deserve and Distinguish the Muses' Inspiration' begins with the quatrain:

> Attend, ye numerous daring throng, who strive
> To gain the dangerous hill, where few arrive;
> Learn, how the sacred height you may attain,
> And shine among the Muses sacred train.

The poem describes various aspects of inspiration and concludes by urging dramatic poets to study Shakespeare, Dryden, Vanbrugh and Samuel Garth. That same year, she wrote her only comic play, *Love at a Loss*, which was not performed, but was published in 1701. The play was later revised for performance as *The Honorable Deceivers, or, All Right at the Last*, but it was never staged.

CT's next play was *The Unhappy Penitent*, performed at Drury Lane in 1701. Its plot is similar to that of both *Agnes de Castro* and *The Fatal Friendship*. The heroine is induced to separate from her secret husband in order to vindicate herself from the treachery of a forged letter which intimated she was having an affair with the King of France. Again, the heroine is a pawn in a power struggle between a noble person and a jilted lover which ends in the heroine's sacrifice of her own happiness.

For her final play, CT sought the advice and approval of Congreve before it was printed. In a letter that contains little criticism of her manuscript, Congreve yet warned her to reduce the action in the fifth act, in order to focus more on the *pathos* of the play's conclusion. Set in Sweden, *The Revolution in Sweden* is based on a story in Swedish history. It was first performed at the Haymarket Theatre and ran for six nights, in 1707. In this play of love, sacrifice, deceit, and death, Arwide has been tricked into signing a treasonous letter by the evil Beron. Arwide's wife, Constantia, learns of the deceit and tells the king, Gustavus, who attempts to secure a pardon for Arwide from the Senate. Simultaneously, Beron stabs his wife, Christina (who is disguised as Fredage, Beron's nephew), when she tries to tell Gustavus of her husband's guilt. She recovers long enough to tell her story and to see Beron sent to prison, then she dies.

CT was also the author of several poems on topical subjects, including two on the Duke of Marlborough's successes at Blenheim in 1702, a paraphrase of a religious poem on Christ's crucifixion by Francis Xavier, a poem to Bevil Higgins on his illness and recovery from smallpox, a poem to Queen Anne urging better education for women, and assorted songs, two of which are included in Frederic Rowton's collection, *The Female Poets of Great Britain* (1853). With the exclusion of the songs, her poems take the form of competently crafted heroic couplets of around fifty lines each.

Celebrated for her beauty, CT was offered marriage several times before she married the Rev. Patrick Cockburn in 1708. He was a scholarly writer himself, best known for a treatise on Mosaic law. The couple had four children, three of whom survived to adulthood. They lived in Long Horseley near Morpeth, Northumberland after 1726 until their deaths in 1749. Prior to her marriage, CT returned to the Anglican faith, having spent her early years as a converted Roman Catholic.

From her youth, CT had a keen interest in religion (she parted with Catholicism over logical inconsistencies in its doctrine) and philosophy, and she read with keen interest John Locke's *Essay Concerning Human Understanding* (1690). In this controversial work, Locke investigated the growth of knowledge; especially radical were his ideas that knowledge, to be useful in daily life, must come from simple sensory experiences (or affirmations), and that an individual entered the world with a clean mental slate.

In May 1702, CT published *A Defense of Mr Locke's Essay Concerning Human Understanding* in which she defended the philosopher from charges of materialism made by Bishop Burnet who corresponded with CT. She taxed Burnet with not understanding what he attempted to criticize, quotes both Burnet and Locke with facility and shows excellent analytical skills in her confident prose style. When Locke was shown her defence, he was so pleased that he sent his thanks in books. Again in 1726 and 1727, CT defended Locke against criticism although she had given up regular writing and had to pay for the publication of the second part of the pamphlet herself. Another essay on moral obligation and moral virtue was written in 1737, but not published until 1743 in *The History of the Works of the Learned*; in it CT argues: 'It seems clear to me, that if the *nature* and *reason* of things is the foundation of moral virtue, it must be the foundation of *moral obligation* likewise to reasonable beings. . . . The moral sense, and the will of God are both grounds of obligation to moral agents.'

Her *Remarks upon Dr Rutherford's Essay on the Nature and Obligation of Virtues*

(1747) is another systematic refutation, but in its support of the ethical theories of Samuel Clarke CT is actually contradicting Locke. Published anonymously, this forty-nine-page tract contains a four-page preface by William Warburton, to whom her philosophical writings must have been known.

Shortly before her death, CT proposed the publication of her collected works, which was accomplished posthumously and edited by Dr Thomas Birch. *The Works of Mrs Catherine Cockburn, Theological, Moral, Dramatic and Poetical* (1751) contained a detailed life of the author, all her philosophical writings, *The Fatal Friendship*, poetry, and letters of advice to her son and a niece. 'A Letter of Advice to my Son' (reprinted in the *Monthly Review* August 1751) advises the young man to be modest in the practice of his religion, seek a profession carefully, to read widely and form his own opinions and to respect women: 'But do not imagine, that women are to be considered only as objects of your pleasure, as the fine gentlemen of the world seem, by their conduct to do. There is nothing more unjust, more base, and barbarous, than is often practised towards them, under the specious names of love and gallantry; as if they had not an equal right, with those of the other sex, to be treated with justice and honour.' Among the subscribers to the volume were the major bishops of England, led by the Archbishop of Canterbury and many political and literary figures such as Ralph Allen, Alexander Pope's lifelong friend from Bath, Charles Churchill, the poet, and Thomas Pelham Hollis, Duke of Newcastle.

As early as 1704, CT was lampooned along with two other women dramatists, Mrs Manley and Mrs Pix, as 'Calista' in the satirical play, *The Female Wits*. In 1752, George Ballard wrote about her in his *Memoirs of Several Learned Ladies in Great Britain* and in 1755 Bonnell Thornton and George Coleman included CT in *Poems by Eminent Ladies*. B. E. SCHNELLER

Works: *Agnes de Castro: A Tragedy* (1696); *The Fatal Friendship: A Tragedy* (1698); *Love at a Loss, or, Most Votes Carry It: A Comedy* (1701); *The Unhappy Penitent* (1701); *Philosophical Works: A Defense of Mr Locke's Essay Concerning Human Understanding* (1702); *The Revolution in Sweden* (1706); *A Discourse Concerning a Guide* (1707); *A Letter to Dr Holdsworth* (1726); *Remarks upon the Principles and Reasonings of Dr Rutherford's Essay on the Nature and Obligation of Virtue* (1747); *Olinda's Adventures* (attrib.) (1718); *The Works of Mrs Catherine Cockburn*, ed. Thomas Birch (1751).

References: Ballard; *Biographica Dramatica* I, II; Clarke, C., *Three Augustan Women Playwrights* (1986); Congreve, W., *Letters and Documents*, ed. John C. Hodges (1964); *DNB*; Doran, *Annals of the Stage* I (1835); Duncombe, J., *The Feminiad: A Poem* (1754); Genest, *Some Account of the English Stage* II (1832); Greer, G., *et al* (eds) *Kissing the Rod* (1988); Hale, Mrs, *Woman's Record, or, Sketches of all Distinguished Women* (1870); Hook, L., (ed.), *The Female Wits* (1967); Rowton, F., *The Female Poets of Great Britain* (1853); Thornton, B. and Coleman, G., *Poems by Eminent Ladies* (1755); Todd.

Tyler, Margaret
(fl. 1578)

Translator, polemical writer

MT's remarks in a prefatory 'Epistle to the reader' constitute the earliest known defence by an Englishwoman of a woman's right to take up the pen. In 1578 MT brought out her translation of a chivalric romance, *The First Part of the Mirrour of Princely Deedes and Knyghthood*, by the Spanish-Portuguese author Diego Ortunez de Calahorra. What is known of the translator is based primarily upon the internal evidence found in the dedication and epistle which she affixed to this translation. In the dedication, addressed to Lord Howard Thomas, she praises the young lord while referring, in particular, to the good will which she bore his parents while they lived. It is very likely that MT was herself either of noble birth or a member of a prominent family that espoused humanist concepts of learning, for few Renaissance women outside the aristocracy would have received an education, let alone one liberal enough to include scholarly familiarity with a romance language. Moreover, the general tone of both the dedication and the 'Epistle to the Reader' suggests a great deal of self-confidence on the part of their author; there is, indeed, surprisingly little of the servile attitude that one might expect to find in such an early attempt by a woman to enter male-dominated literature. Furthermore, it is clear from MT's frequent references to friends who have encouraged her in undertaking this translation, and who apparently saw to the actual publication of her book, that she moved in circles of well-educated people and felt herself their social equal. And, finally, we have MT's use in the epistle of the phrase 'Ladyes and Gentlewomen', followed by a reference to herself as a 'Gentlewoman'. Beyond these speculations, there is little else that one can infer, except that MT was of mature age when she made the translation, for she refers to her 'staid age' and 'aged yeares'. She also writes that undertaking this project meant having to reacquaint herself with her 'olde reading', so we can assume that it was some years earlier when she first read Ortunez in the original Spanish.

The significance of MT's contribution lies in her arguments for the right of women to enter intellectual life and write whatever a man might write. Her epistle begins with an appeal to the reader to accept the tale of war and adventure that she has translated, 'rather for that it is a womans worke, though in a storye prophane, and a matter more manlike then becometh my sexe'. Though the story may be masculine in nature, she maintains, it can inspire others to courage and patriotism, so that her efforts at translation will be worthwhile. MT knew, however, that she was taking a bold step, for there is more than a tinge of irony in her anticipation of criticism for not 'penning matters of great weight and sadnesse in divinitie, or other studies', as might be expected of a woman. Attempting through polemic means to dispel the myth of female superficiality, she contends that if men dedicate their writings to women, women may then read them, and in their reading, search deeply for truth. Therefore, she asserts, a woman may 'discourse in learning' with as much right as any man, for men are not, as some may claim, the 'sole possessioners of knowledge'.

For her forthright defence of the intellectual rights of women, MT might justly be considered perhaps the first true English feminist.

BARBARA MCGOVERN

Works: 'Dedication and Epistle to the Reader', in (trans. MT), *The First Part of the Mirrour of Princely Deedes and Knyghthood: Wherein is Shewed the Worthinesse of the Knight of the Sunne, and His Brother Rosicleer, Sonnes to the Great Emperour Trebatio, with the Straunge Love of the Beautiful Princesse Briana, the Valiant Acts of Other Noble Princes and Knights*, by Diego Ortunez de Calahorra (1578).

References: Ferguson, M., 'Introduction' to *First Feminists: British Women Writers. 1578–1799* (1985); Mackerness, E. D., 'Margaret Tyler: an Elizabethan feminist', *Notes and Queries* (23 March 1946).

Tynan, Katharine

b. 23 January 1859, Clondalkin, Dublin; d. 2 April 1931, Wimbledon
Poet, novelist, critic

KT was the fifth of twelve children born to Elizabeth O'Reilly and Andrew Tynan. In 1868 her father, a prospering livestock farmer, acquired the house and lands of Whitehall, Clondalkin, where she spent her later childhood and youth amidst the deeply formative influences of Irish politics, folklore, and religion. It was impossible, she said in her reminiscences, 'for a child of the imagination to grow up there anything but a patriot'. Her father was profoundly nationalistic and her early memories of Fenian heroes found a place alongside the colourful local stories of the Irish peasantry. Her mother became an invalid at an early age and it was her father who exerted the primary influences in her life, encouraging her artistic interests in a period when the Catholic Church in Ireland was prohibiting dancing, theatre, and even reading. For almost two years KT was without full vision, the result of a severe chill following a bout of measles. In 1872, however, she attended the Dominican Convent of St Catherine of Siena in Drogheda and developed strong literary aspirations. Her poem 'Dreamland' appeared in *Young Ireland* in 1875 and further work was printed in *United Ireland*, the *Spectator* and *Merry England*.

The 1880s were years of intense political activity when KT, as she later confessed, was 'crammed to the lips with patriotic ardours'. She joined Anna Parnell (the sister of Charles Stewart Parnell) in the Ladies Land League, which, among other things, campaigned for the rights of evicted tenant farmers. Like her father, she supported Parnell throughout 'the split' when the Irish leader was castigated for his relationship with a divorced woman, Katherine O'Shea. Looking back on Parnell's funeral, she wrote; 'I have never been able to look at white chrysanthemums since without seeing a grave.' Like W. B. Yeats, she was also deeply influenced by the political ideals of John O'Leary, 'the old Fenian chief'.

The 1880s were a time, too, of ascending literary fortunes and KT's first book, *Louise de la Vallière*, was published in 1885. In the same year she received letters from William Michael and Christina Rossetti, and later visited them in Torrington Square. Having already visited London in 1880 and 1884, she had made the acquaintance of Oscar and Constance Wilde and Alice and Wilfred Meynell. She contributed a series of articles to *Woman's World* under Wilde's editorship and in critical writings elsewhere helped to establish the reputations of such poets as Lionel Johnson and Richard Le Gallienne. She was herself one of the poets whose work was later published at John Lane's celebrated Sign of the Bodley Head. 1885 was also the year of her first meeting with W. B. Yeats; the friendship is vividly portrayed in the early Yeats letters and in KT's autobiographical writings. She sat for a portrait by Jack Butler Yeats in 1886 and developed strong ties with the family. While never sharing the enthusiasm of Yeats and George Russell ('AE') for theosophy, she made a significant contribution to the Celtic literary revival, encouraging Yeats to produce a play about Ireland and writing two books of her own, *Shamrocks* (1887) and *Ballads and Poems* (1891) in support of the Irish cause.

In May 1893 KT married Henry Hinkson, a former classics scholar of Trinity College, Dublin, a barrister and *littérateur*. For sectarian reasons (Hinkson was presumably a Protestant) the marriage took place in London and the couple settled in Ealing. Under difficult financial constraints, KT increased her literary output enormously, publishing her first book of prose sketches in 1894, two volumes of short stories in 1895 and her first novel in 1896; a host of reviews by KT appeared in the *Pall Mall Gazette*, the *Irish Daily Independent*, the *Westminster Review*, the *National Observer*, the *Speaker*, the *Sketch*, and the *Illustrated London News*. In 1911 the family returned to Ireland, and in 1914 Hinkson was appointed magistrate for Castlebar, County Mayo, where they remained until his death in 1919. During the war years KT was involved in philanthropic work, while her two sons served in Palestine and France. Her poem 'Flowers of Youth' had a tremendous impact after it appeared in the *Spectator* in the autumn of 1914 and, like Rupert Brooke's sonnet 'The Soldier', was declaimed from the pulpit. KT's account of the Easter Rebellion in Dublin during these years is one of the most vivid and memorable passages in *The Years of the Shadow*. After 1916 she could no longer believe that affection for England and love of Ireland might go quietly hand in hand. *The Wandering Years* describes her flitting between England, Ireland, and the continent in the post-war period. Her daughter, Pamela Hinkson, followed her mother to become a novelist. KT died in Wimbledon and is buried in St Mary's Churchyard, Kensal Green.

The early poems of KT are clearly the work of a woman 'born to the country pursuits', but a strong idealizing tendency leads the imagination away from any sustained engagement with the landscape into light-hearted pastorals and rural idylls. Stylistically, too, the early poems are very much conventional exercises composed in unvarying rhymed quatrains. Her most significant work draws on a distinctively Irish blend of Catholic mysticism and rural sentiment, while ballards like 'The Children of Lir' represent an important contribution to the Irish literary renaissance. There is some truth in Yeats's opinion that at her best KT could transform emotion into legend, while at her worst she was 'merely a poet of the picturesque'. Not a single poem by KT was included in *The Oxford Book of Modern Verse* which Yeats edited in 1936. Motherhood is the abiding theme in her poetic writings; independence of thought and action is characteristically muted by religious ideals of womanhood. As Marilyn Rose suggests, 'Her poems are assertions turning into prayers.'

In her work as a novelist KT was prone to 'a good deal of necessary pot-boiling', though the novels of the 1920s depict some of the most urgent social issues in contemporary Ireland. *The Lover of Women* (1928) and *Grayson's Girl* (1930) expose the miserable working conditions of Irish shop girls, while *The Golden Rose* (1924) examines class prejudice in war-time Ireland, and *The Playground* (1930) insists on improved conditions for Dublin slum children. By this time, however, KT's youthful idealism had given way to a cautious philanthropy, and her exploration of social and political dilemmas are generally disappointing. The best introduction to KT's prose writing is to be found in the five autobiographical volumes which chronicle the crucial transitional period in English and Irish literary history from 1890 to 1920 with unflagging energy and verse.   STEPHEN REGAN

Selected works: *A Cluster of Nuts* (1894); *An Isle in the Water* (1895); *The Land of Mist and Mountains* (1895); *Oh, What a Plague is Love!* (1896); *Dear Irish Girl* (1899); *Daughter of the Fields* (1900); *Twenty-Five Years* (1913); *The Middle Years* (1916); *Lord Edward: A Study in Romance* (1916); *Love of Brothers* (1919); *The Years of the Shadow* (1919); *The Wandering Years* (1922); *Memories* (1924); *The Golden Rose* (1924); *Life in the Occupied Area* (1925); *The Lover of Women* (1928); *The Playground* (1930); *Grayson's Girl* (1930); *Collected Poems* (1930).

References: Kelly, J. and Domville, E., *The Collected Letters of W. B. Yeats*, vol 1 (1986); Rose, M. G., *Katharine Tynan* (1974).

Uttley, Alison

b. 17 December 1884, Cromford, Derbyshire; d. 7 May 1976, High Wycombe
Writer for children

AU was the elder child of Henry Taylor, a tenant farmer, and Hannah Dickens, a former lady's maid. She grew up at Castle Top Farm near Cromford in the Derbyshire Peak District. Educated initially by her strictly Evangelical mother, she was sent at the age of 7 to Lea Board School, where she spent the next five years. At 12 she won a scholarship to the Lady Manners School at Bakewell, where she excelled academically. In 1903 she won a Major County Scholarship from Derbyshire to Owens College in Manchester, then part of the federal Victoria University, to read physics. Here she began to write poems for *Yggdrasill*, the student magazine of Ashburne House, the all-female hall of residence where she lived. After receiving her degree she went on to train as a teacher at the Ladies' Training College in Cambridge, and in 1908 became junior science mistress at the London County Council Secondary School in Fulham. Here she became interested in socialism, and developed a close friendship with the Ramsay MacDonalds, though in later life she was to become a staunch Conservative.

In 1911 she married James Uttley, a civil engineer, settling in Knutsford, Cheshire, and in 1914 they had a son, John. In the late 1920s AU began to take up writing seriously, but her husband was discouraging about her first completed manuscript, the largely autobiographical *The Country Child*, which she put aside and did not publish until 1931. In 1928 she published her first article in the August edition of *Homes and Gardens*, entitled 'What should children read?' Her first published book, *The Squirrel, the Hare and the Little Grey Rabbit* (1929), was published by Heinemann under the name of Alison (rather than Alice, her actual name) Uttley. This was the first of what was to be a whole series of children's books featuring Little Grey Rabbit, for which AU is best remembered. The earlier books in the series were illustrated by Margaret Tempest, and the later ones by Katherine Wigglesworth, while many of AU's books for adults were to be illustrated by C. F. Tunnicliffe.

In 1930 her husband commited suicide, perhaps as a result of financial worries which were placing stress on the marriage. AU now began to develop an unhealthily close and possessive relationship with her son, and was to react badly to his marriage in 1947. He was later to suffer psychological collapse, committing suicide shortly after his mother's death. Now she was faced with the difficulty of financing his education at Sedburgh School, and began to increase her literary output. In 1931 she published *The Country Child*, which had a warm reception. The following year she began to keep a detailed diary, which she continued until 1971 and which ran to forty volumes.

She went on to publish a large number of stories and articles for journals, as well as children's books and books of country life. Among the most successful (apart from the Little Grey Rabbit tales and the Sam Pig tales) was *A Traveller in Time* (1939), which fuses the present day on a Derbyshire farm with sixteenth-century history, that of Mary Queen of Scots and the Babington plot. She also wrote several autobiographical works in addition to *The Country Child*: these included *Ambush of Young Days* (1937) and *Country Hoard* (1943). In 1970 she received the honorary degree of Doctor of Letters from Manchester University. She continued to write well into old age, but in 1976 suffered a bad fall which eventually led to her death.

AU worked with great assiduity on her series of Little Grey Rabbit books.

She was sensitive to charges of derivativeness, especially from Beatrix Potter, and irritated by the assumption of some readers that she had simply created human characters in fancy dress, insisting that she wrote of real animals. Believing that 'they have such a raw deal' and ascribing to human arrogance the notion that they cannot feel, she wrote in *A Ten O'Clock Scholar* (1970), 'Animals are mysteries, a race apart. . . . They are too noble to be humanised in story and fable . . . and yet only by a humanisation shall we know them and learn to love them.' The three characters in the central household of her stories certainly have human touches and may even relate to facets of her own character: the motherly domestic Grey Rabbit, the intellectually conceited Hare, and the vain Squirrel.

In later editions of the Grey Rabbit books a foreword places the tales in a past before electricity and tap water, when country dwellers had to depend only on themselves. AU tried 'to give some specially English touch of country life', Modern readers might find some of this in the class structure of her fictional society in which the Grey Rabbit family is clearly above that of the plebeian Hedgehog. But at all levels the animals are decorous in prose and picture; when Grey Rabbit falls down a crevice the illustration shows her skirts entirely in place.

AU's stories all 'have truth in the background', an implicit moral or 'scrap of wisdom'. In *Little Grey Rabbit Goes to the North Pole* (1970), for example, the animals travel on only to discover the Pole in their own village maypole, for the snow and frost have transformed the world and made everything magical. Sometimes the threatening sentimentality of the stories is curbed by a detail, as when in *Little Grey Rabbit's Birthday* (1944) young hedgehog Fuzzypeg comes in the night to be the first to wish her a happy birthday and falls asleep in her bed while Grey Rabbit ruefully realizes that she can get no rest next to a bundle of prickles. The physical details throughout are precise and appealing: the sop-wort with which the animals wash, Sam Pig's trousers dyed with hips and borage, or Grey Rabbit's washing, which takes in Wise Owl's night cap, Speckledy Hen's sunbonnet, a spider's silken web, and a fly's black suit. ANNE FERNIHOUGH AND JANET TODD

Selected works: The Squirrel, the Hare and the Little Grey Rabbit (1929); The Country Child (1931); The Story of Fuzzypeg the Hedgehog (1932); Little Grey Rabbit's Party (1936); The Knot Squirrel Tied (1937); Ambush of Young Days (1937); Fuzzypeg Goes to School (1938); Little Grey Rabbit's Christmas (1939); Moldy Warp, The Mole (1940); The Adventures of Sam Pig (1940); Hare Joins the Home Guard (1942); Country Hoard (1943); Little Grey Rabbit's Birthday (1944); The Adventures of Tim Rabbit (1945); Country Things (1946); Little Grey Rabbit and the Wandering Hedgehog (1948); Carts and Candlesticks (1948); Little Grey Rabbit Makes Lace (1950); Little Grey Rabbit Goes to Sea (1954); A Year in the Country (1957); Little Red Fox and the Magic Moon (1958); Grey Rabbit and the Circus (1961); Little Grey Rabbit's Pancake Day (1967); The Button Box and Other Essays (1968); The Ten O'Clock Scholar and Other Essays (1970); Little Grey Rabbit Goes to the North Pole (1970); Little Grey Rabbit and the Snow-Baby (1973).

References: Judd, D., Alison Uttley: The Life of a Country Child 1884–1976 (1986); Saintsbury, E., The World of Alison Uttley (1980).

Voynich, E. L.

b. 1864, Cork, Ireland; d. 1960, New York

Novelist, translator

ELV's reputation rests chiefly upon her achievement in her first novel, *The Gadfly* (1897). This novel enjoyed considerable popularity at the time of its publication, being reprinted eight times in the first four years after its initial appearance. Today the novel and its author are probably best known in eastern Europe; *The Gadfly* has been translated into Russian and several other eastern European languages, and a film based upon the novel, with a score written by Shostakovich, was made in the Soviet Union in 1955. Two biographical studies of ELV have also been published in the Soviet Union.

ELV was the daughter of Mary Everest Boole, a feminist philosopher, and George Boole, a mathematician. She was educated in Ireland and Berlin and later worked as a governess and music teacher. In 1891 she married a Polish political exile named Habdank-Woynicz (who adopted the Anglicized name Wilfred Michael Voynich). Her husband had come to England the previous year after escaping from Siberia where he had been sent as a political prisoner as punishment for his part in the Polish nationalist movement. Her own experience and that of her husband are clearly reflected in the plots of ELV's novels.

Jack Raymond (1901) is the story of a boy scarred by the cruelty of his family who is saved from his bitterness through the sympathetic understanding of a friend's mother, Helen Mirski. Mrs Mirski is the widow of a Polish patriot who died in Siberia, and her understanding is derived from her own experience. We are told that 'she had heard other stories told long ago in Siberia . . . she had lived outside the pale of men's mercy, and her unsheltered eyes had seen the naked sores of the world'. ELV's next novel, *Olive Latham* (1904), is the story of an English nurse who becomes involved with Russian anarchists, nihilists and Polish revolutionaries. She marries Vladimir Damarov, an anarchist, who dies in a tsarist prison. After his death, Olive drifts towards madness but her sanity is finally restored by Karol, a doctor and Polish revolutionary who has himself been imprisoned in Siberia.

The Gadfly also deals with the politics of national liberation, but it is set in Italy at the time of the nationalist revolt against Austrian domination. The central characters are all involved in the political agitation of the period and are supporters of Mazzini, but, although the politics are sympathetically presented, as in her later novels, ELV is also interested in exploring personal relationships. The novel's hero, Arthur Burton, is imprisoned at a very early stage in his revolutionary career as a result of betrayal; on his release he discovers that the girl he was in love with, Gemma, has married one of his comrades and that the Catholic priest, Montanelli, who had been his friend and spiritual adviser, is in fact his father. Bitterly disillusioned with humanity, Arthur feigns his death and escapes to South America. He returns thirteen years later and, under the *nom de plume* 'The Gadfly', resumes his rôle as a political agitator working with the now widowed Gemma Bolla. He is finally captured and the novel culminates in a confrontation between the Gadfly and his father, now Cardinal Montanelli, in which the cardinal agrees to the execution of the son he loves. In these personal confrontations ELV achieves real dramatic power and intensity. In his book *Ace of Spies* Robert Bruce Lockhart claims that ELV had an affair with the spy Sidney Reilly in 1895 and that the character of the Gadfly is based on Reilly's experiences. ELV herself claimed that she based the character of Gemma on Charlotte Wilson, who was the lover of the Russian anarchist Kropotkin.

ELV's other novels, *The Interrupted Friendship* (1910) and *Put Off Thy Shoes* (1946), are not as intense as her earlier work. In 1916 ELV and her husband went to live in the USA.   JUDITH VINCENT

Selected works: (trans.), *Stories from Garshin* (1892); (trans.), *Nihilism as It Is*, by Stepniak (1895); *The Gadfly* (1897); *Jack Raymond* (1901); *Olive Latham* (1904); *The Interrupted Friendship* (1910); (trans.), *Six Lyrics from the Rutherian of Tarás Schevchenko* (1911); (trans.), *Chopin's Letters* (1931); *Put Off Thy Shoes* (1946).

References: Courtney, W. L., *The Feminine Note in Fiction* (1904); Kettle, A., 'E. L. Voynich: a forgotten English novelist', *Essays in Criticism* 7 (1957); Lockhart, R. B., *Ace of Spies* (1967).

Waddell, Helen

b. 31 May 1889, Tokyo; d. 5 March 1965, London

Translator, scholar

HW was the daughter of an Anglo-Irish Presbyterian missionary, the Rev. Hugh Waddell, and his wife Jane Martin. She lived in Japan for some of her early life and there visited Shinto temples. She was much influenced by the experience of another culture and by her father who quoted Greek poetry to her when she was a child. Later she attended Victoria College and Queen's University in Belfast, receiving a BA degree in 1911 and an MA in 1912. For seven years she interrupted what was promising to be a brilliant academic career to care for her ailing and dominating stepmother in Ulster; during this period she wrote *Lyrics from the Chinese* (1913), articles, children's stories, and a play entitled *The Spoilt Buddha* (1919). In 1920 she entered Somerville College, Oxford, where she gave a series of lectures on medieval mime. She taught briefly at Bedford College, London, from 1922 to 1923, and then, from 1923 to 1925, studied in Paris with a scholarship from Lady Margaret Hall, Oxford. In Paris she became friendly with Enid Starkie and finished her study of medieval Latin poets which she had begun at Oxford. She published the results of her study as *The Wandering Scholars* (1927) and *Mediaeval Latin Lyrics* (1929), which, remarkably, won immediate recognition and became best-sellers. In 1933 she published a novel, *Peter Abelard*, a work that finely expressed and conveyed to the reader her enthusiasm for the twelfth-century world. While working on this novel, she published *A Book of Mediaeval Latin for Schools* (1931), an edition of Cole's *Paris Journal* (1931), a play entitled *The Abbé Prévost* (1931), and a translation of *Manon Lescaut* (1931). A translation of Rosweyd's *Vitae Patrum* of 1615 appeared as *The Desert Fathers* (1936). A brilliant conversationalist, HW was courted socially and was received by Queen Mary. She gave many lectures and was awarded a series of honorary degrees. He friends included 'AE', George Saintsbury, Max Beerbohm, George Bernard Shaw, Siegfried Sassoon, W. B. Yeats, and Maude Clark, a close friend since her undergraduate days despite forty-four years' difference in age.

HW began a study of John of Salisbury, but interrupted herself by taking on a large house which brought problems and demanded her energy. The Second World War impacted greatly on her and she expressed her patriotism by writing and translating poems about the British struggle. She became actively involved with the publishing house of Constable and she took over the assistant editorship of *The Nineteenth Century*. She continued translating, her translations from this period being collected by Dame Felicitas Corrigan in *More Latin Lyrics from*

Virgil to Milton (1976). After the war she suffered some form of mental and physical collapse and experienced periods of amnesia. One of her last public activities was the W. P. Ker Lecture at the University of Glasgow in 1947; it was published as *Poetry in the Dark Ages* (1948).

HW was a devout Christian, with a strong mystical bent. She was impressed with a deep sense of the redemption and of the power of suffering. She delighted in natural beauty which she regarded as part of the working of God in the world. Both this devotion and her appreciation of nature find expression in her novel and translations. Her scholarship helped bring medieval Latin poetry into the mainstream of intellectual life connecting academic and popular audiences; none the less she herself remained ambiguous about her relationship to institutionalized scholarship. JANET JONES

Works: *Lyrics from the Chinese* (1913); *The Spoiled Buddha* (1919); *The Wandering Scholars* (1927); *Mediaeval Latin Lyrics* (1929); *A Book of Mediaeval Latin for Schools* (1931); (ed.), *Paris Journal* by Cole (1931); (trans.), *Manon Lescaut*, by Abbé Prévost (1931); *The Abbé Prévost* (1931); *Peter Abelard* (1933; published in the US in 1935); *Beasts and Saints (1934); The Desert Fathers* (1936); *Poetry in the Dark Ages* (1948); *More Latin Lyrics*, ed. F. Corrigan (1976); *Papers of Helen Waddell*, ed. M. T. Kelly (1981).

References: Blackett, M., *The Mark of the Maker: A Portrait of Helen Waddell* (1973); *CA*; Corrigan, F., 'Introduction' to *More Latin Lyrics* (1976); Corrigan, F., *Helen Waddell: A Biography* (1986); *DNB*; Drabble.

Wakefield, Priscilla

b. 31 January 1750/1, Tottenham, Middlesex; d. 12 September 1832, Ipswich, Suffolk

Writer of natural philosophy and travel books for children

Daughter of Daniel Bell and Catherine Barclay, PW was born into a well-connected Quaker family, learning from her religious heritage a concern for improving the quality of human life. In January 1771 she married Edward Wakefield, a London merchant, with whom she raised three children. She initiated several philanthropic projects in Tottenham, such as a lying-in charity (1790) and several of England's earliest savings or 'frugality' banks (1798).

When her family fell on hard times in the early 1790s, she started writing successful textbooks suitable for both girls and boys, but aimed at girls being taught at home. Several of her books remained in print for over forty years, and seven of her seventeen works reached at least seven editions. The most successful were two of her educational travelogues: *The Juvenile Travellers* (1801), a prose expedition through Europe, reached nineteen editions by 1850, and *A Family Tour through the British Empire* (1804) saw fifteen editions by 1840. Several books were also published in the United States.

Her earliest books primarily teach natural history, an emphasis upon science characteristic of Quaker educational interests. These books as well as the later travelogues sweeten the instruction by blending fiction with fact. PW often invents a family or group of friends that converses or corresponds on a vast array of scientific, anthropological, and geographical subjects. For example, *An Introduction to Botany* (1796), one of the first in English, teaches Linnaeus's system of taxonomy (with the sections about sexual characteristics bowdlerized), but it presents itself as a series of instructive letters from Felicia to her sister, Constance. The epistolary style makes a rigorous scientific subject (and its Greek and Latin terminology) more approachable by presenting role models who admit to the difficulties of the subject but learn to overcome them.

PW aims at improving the general education of young women, calling the usual mode of education 'effeminate' in her one book for adults, *Reflections on the Present Condition of the Female Sex* (1798). She recommends strengthening both the female body and mind, the one with vigorous outdoor exercise in sensible clothing, the other with a vigorous course of study led by properly trained instructors. No radical, she outlines courses of instruction 'appropriate' for the various social classes and suggests productive professions for which women of each class may train.

She also argues that a proper education will make women better companions for men, not wilful harridans: 'an increase of real knowledge will conduce to give them a just estimate of what they owe to themselves and what is due to their husbands . . . it will promote a diffidence of their own judgment in concerns of moment, and an habitual reference, on such occasions, to the more enlarged experience of mankind in their husbands.'

In general, she recommends that all women, whether married or single, learn to support themselves and encourage other women in their entrepreneurial ventures, especially those related to women but on which men have encroached. PW mentions the following suitable occupations: writing, painting, engraving, landscaping, teaching, stay-making, hairdressing, farming, and preparing female corpses for burial. She also cites the importance of establishing seminaries for training governesses, hoping that, in time, all the instructors in the seminaries would be female.

Her own writings provide not just the theory but also the means to develop the intellect of women. Her texts address a wide range of scientific and social subjects, thereby giving the many young women who had not learned Latin or seen much of the world the chance to acquire mental discipline and a broad understanding of the society in which they lived.   LINDA V. TROOST

Works: *Mental Improvement* (1794); *Leisure Hours* (1794); *Juvenile Anecdotes* (1795); *An Introduction to Botany* (1796); *Reflections on the Present Condition of the Female Sex* (1798); *The Juvenile Travellers* (1801); *A Family Tour through the British Empire* (1804); *Domestic Recreation* (1805); *Excursions in North America* (1806); *Sketches of Human Manners* (1807); *Variety* (1809); *Instinct Displayed* (1811); *The Traveller in Africa* (1814); *An Introduction to the Natural History and Classification of Insects* (1816); *A Brief Memoir of the Life of William Penn* (1816); *The Traveller in Asia* (1817).

References: *Gentleman's Magazine* 2 (1832); *Ipswich Journal* (15 September 1832); Riddenhough, G., 'Priscilla Wakefield', *The Dalhousie Review* 37 (1958); Todd.

Walford, Lucy

b. 17 April 1845, Portobello, Scotland; d. 11 May 1915, London
Novelist

LW was born Lucy Colquhoun in 1845 in Portobello, near Edinburgh. Her father, John Colquhoun, was the author of *The Moor and the Loch*, a contemporary classic among sportsmen. Her grandfather, Sir James Colquhoun, was 10th Baronet of Colquhoun and Luss. LW was educated at home with foreign governesses and in 1869 married Alfred Launders Walford, a magistrate from Essex. The Walfords had two sons and five daughters.

LW started writing novels after her marriage when poor health prevented her from pursuing outdoor interests. Her first book, *Mr Smith: A Part of His*

Life, was published in 1874 and Queen Victoria so enjoyed it that she asked to meet its author. LW was duly presented.

During the next years she wrote well over thirty novels and volumes of stories and, for four years, she worked as the London correspondent for the *New York Critic*. Shortly before her death in 1915, she published two memoirs: *Recollections of a Scottish Novelist* (1910) and *Memoirs of Victorian London* (1912).

JEAN HANFF KORELITZ

Selected works: *Mr Smith* (1874); *Nan and Other Tales* (1875); *Pauline* (1877); *Troublesome Daughters* (1880); *The Baby's Grandmother* (1885); *A Stiffnecked Generation* (1888); *A Mere Child* (1889); *The Havoc of a Smile* (1890); *A Pinch of Experience* (1891); *A Question of Penmanship* (1893); *The Matchmaker* (1894); *A Bubble: A Story* (1895); *Successors to the Title* (1896); *Leddy Margaret* (1898); *The Archdeacon* (1899); *One of Ourselves* (1900); *A Dream's Fulfillment* (1902); *The Enlightenment of Olivia* (1907); *Celia: And the Parents* (1910); *Recollections of a Scottish Novelist* (1910); *Memories of Victorian London* (1912); *David and Jonathan on the Riviera* (1914).
Reference: *NWAD*.

Ward, Mrs Humphry (Mary Ward)

b. 11 June 1851, Tasmania, Australia; d. 24 March 1920, London
Novelist

MW's life continued a family tradition of intellectual enquiry, service, and leadership. The granddaughter of Thomas Arnold, headmaster of Rugby, and the niece of Matthew Arnold, MW shared their interest in conservative reform. She came to accept religious doubt, but never surrendered her faith in unchanging moral laws and inflexible moral duties.

MW's most famous novel, *Robert Elsmere* (1888), was shaped in part by her experience of a Victorian religious crisis. Her father, Thomas Arnold's second son, showed no sign of wavering from his father's Broad Church Christianity when he went out to homestead in New Zealand in 1847 and married the staunchly Protestant Julia Sorell in 1850. But in 1856 his conversion to Roman Catholicism shocked his family and cost him his job as a school inspector. The family returned to Britain and faced a life of relative privation for the next ten years, despite John Henry Newman's help in finding MW's father employment in Catholic schools. As was usual with interfaith marriages, the daughters remained Protestant like their mother and the sons were raised as Catholics. When MW was 15, her father returned to the Church of England. His new position as a tutor took him and his family to Oxford, where MW was able to repair the large gaps left in her education by concentrated study at the Bodleian Library. She married Thomas Humphry Ward, a fellow of Brasenose College, in 1872. The second of their three children had just been born when Thomas Arnold returned to Roman Catholicism in 1876. Despite her lifelong loyalty to her father, MW keenly sympathized with the sufferings of her mother, who this time refused to follow her husband to the Catholic University in Dublin.

MW's literary career began when the *Churchman's Companion* accepted 'A Westmoreland Story' in 1870. Her inclination for more serious work was soon evident in the many articles by her on literature and history published in such periodicals as *Macmillan's*, the *Saturday Review*, the *Oxford Spectator, The Times*, the *Fortnightly*, and the *Pall Mall Gazette*. In 1877 she began to contribute entries based on her early studies in Spanish history to the *Dictionary of Christian Biography*. She published *Miss Bretherton*, her first novel, in 1884, and a translation of Frederic Henri Amiel's *Journal Intime* in 1885. She had long been devoted to the novels of the Brontë sisters, and wrote a series of introductions to the Haworth edition of their works between 1899 and 1900.

When MW began work on *Robert Elsmere* in 1885, she had already been thinking for many years about the religious issues it raised. Her own historical studies had convinced her that the Bible was a fallible cultural and historical document. She was confirmed in a liberal, antidogmatic theology by such Oxford intellectuals as Benjamin Jowett, Mark Pattison, and T. H. Green. After she had heard the Rev. John Wordsworth attack such liberal theology as sinful in 1881, she responded with *Unbelief and Sin*, a pamphlet arguing that intellectual honesty, not weak morality, led to the questioning of dogmatic faith. *Robert Elsmere* recounts the 'deconversion' of an intellectual. An Oxford philosopher modelled on T. H. Green introduces the first doubts about Christian dogma into the mind of its eponymous hero, a young Anglican clergyman, and his reading (of *The Origin of Species* and of contradictory Church histories) further erodes his orthodoxy. Sceptical continental scholarship completes the task, and Elsmere, much to the distress of his strictly Evangelical wife, leaves the ministry. He continues to serve his fellow man as a social worker and teacher, however, carrying his secularized Christianity into the London slums where he ultimately dies of tuberculosis. The tremendous success of *Robert Elsmere*, which by 1889 had sold over 300,000 copies in England and 200,000 in the US, suggests how topical were the issues it raised. Its combination of serious intellectual questions, uplifting didacticism, and human interest was typical of MW's later fiction. The suffering caused by religious doubt was again her subject in *The History of David Grieve* (1892) and in *Robert Elsmere*'s sequel, *The Case of Richard Meynell* (1911). The Roman Catholic hero of *Helbeck of Bannisdale* (1898), torn between his faith and the nonbeliever he loves, offers the closest analogy in MW's fiction with her own father.

MW's essential conservatism is apparent in her social and political novels, in which the most effective form of social conscience is always that allied with a respect for wealth and tradition. She embodied her ideals in women characters who fulfilled themselves through subordination to duty, such as the self-sacrificing heroine of *Eleanor* (1900), and in aristocratic reformers such as Aldous Raeburn in *Marcella* (1894) and the title character of its sequel, *Sir George Tressady* (1896). Women who transgressed the bounds of traditional wifely duty, no matter what the provocation, were routinely punished: Lady Rose in *Lady Rose's Daughter* (1903), Kitty Ashe in *The Marriage of William Ashe* (1905), and Daphne in *Marriage à la Mode* (1909) are cases in point. Believing that direct involvement in political life would 'blunt the special moral qualities of women', she steadfastly opposed the vote for women. In 1908 she organized the Women's Anti-Suffrage League, dedicated to 'bringing the views of women to bear on the legislature without the aid of the vote'. MW's fear of feminism's subversive potential is evident in *Delia Blanchflower* (1915), in which MW describes a neurasthenic and fanatical suffragette who burns down a country home to dramatize her cause. Despite MW's skill in combining melodrama with bracing moral lessons, her attempts to adapt works like *Eleanor* and *The Marriage of William Ashe* for the stage were neither financially nor artistically successful.

MW herself was a tireless if traditional worker for social reform. She was involved in the earliest efforts to open higher education to women in Oxford. After she and her family moved to London in 1881, she became active in planning the Passmore Edwards Settlement; the Settlement House later named after her opened in 1897 to serve the poor of the Bloomsbury community. In later years she was instrumental in winning government support for childcare centres and schools for handicapped children. At the request of the US President, Theodore Roosevelt, she undertook several works dramatizing the British war effort for American audiences: *England's Effort* (1916), *Towards the Goal* (1917), and *Fields of Victory* (1919). The British War Ministry allowed her to visit the Front and other military installations as a war correspondent. Her unfinished autobiography, *A Writer's Recollections*, appeared in 1918.

MW's writing remains essentially Victorian in its peculiar blend of moral seriousness and sentimentality. Her life and work, whilst limited by Victorian conceptions of woman's proper sphere, were animated by high standards of intellectual and social responsibility. ROSEMARY JANN

Selected works: *Milly and Olly, or, A Holiday among the Mountains* (1881); *Miss Bretherton* (1884); *Robert Elsmere* (1888); *The History of David Grieve* (1892); *Marcella* (1894); *The Story of Bessie Costrell* (1895); *Sir George Tressady* (1896); *Helbeck of Bannisdale* (1898); *Eleanor* (1900); *Lady Rose's Daughter* (1903); *The Marriage of William Ashe* (1905); *Fenwick's Career* (1906); *The Playtime of the Poor* (1906); *The Testing of Diana Mallory* (1908); *Daphne, or, Marriage à la Mode* (1909); *Canadian Born* (1910); *The Case of Richard Meynell* (1911); *The Mating of Lydia* (1913); *The Coryston Family* (1913); *Delia Blanchflower* (1915); *Eltham House* (1915); *A Great Success* (1916); *England's Effort* (1916); *Lady Connie* (1916); *Towards the Goal* (1917); *Missing* (1917); *A Writer's Recollections* (1918); *The War and Elizabeth* (1918); *Fields of Victory* (1919); *Cousin Philip* (1919); *Harvest* (1920).

References: Allibone; Colby, V., *The Singular Anomaly* (1970); *DLB*; *DNB*; Drabble; Gwynn, S., *Mrs Humphry Ward* (1917); Huws Jones, E., *Mrs Humphry Ward* (1973); Moers, E., *Literary Women* (1976); Peterson, S., *Victorian Heretic* (1976); Phelps, W. L., *Essays on Modern Novelists* (1921); Showalter, E., *A Literature of Their Own* (1977); Smith, E. M., *Mrs Humphry Ward* (1980); Trevelyan, J. P., *The Life of Mrs Humphry Ward* (1923); Walters, J. S., *Mrs Humphry Ward, Her Work and Influence* (1912).

Warner, Sylvia Townsend
b. 6 December 1893, Harrow on the Hill; d. 1 May 1978, Frome Vauchurch, Dorset
Novelist, poet
STW was the only child of George Townsend Warner, a housemaster at Harrow, and was educated privately, a situation in which she felt herself to be in competition with the school boys for her father's attention and intellectually deprived. Her mother, Nora Hudleston, who had been brought up in India, was a glamorous but rather oppressive presence. STW left home at an early age to live on a small allowance in a flat in Bayswater. She intended to study musical composition in Vienna with Arnold Schoenberg but the outbreak of the First World War made this impossible and for a time she worked in a munitions factory. Music remained an abiding interest however: she had an expert knowledge of the music of the fifteenth and sixteenth centuries and was one of four editors of *Tudor Church Music* (1922–29). She claimed that it was the 'beautiful smooth white' paper that she used in her editorial work that first inspired her to write and that she 'discovered that it was possible to write poetry' during a month's exploration of the Essex marshes in 1922. On the suggestion of David Garnett she submitted some of her poems to Charles Prentice at Chatto and Windus who published her first collection, *The Espalier*, in 1925. Though she continued to produce poetry at intervals throughout her

life, her reputation both in her lifetime and since has been founded more securely upon her prose. She wrote numerous short stories, the majority of which first appeared in *The New Yorker*, seven novels, and biographical and critical works on T. H. White and Jane Austen.

Through Theodore Powys and his wife, in 1926 STW met Valentine Ackland who became her life-long companion. The two women lived at various addresses in southern England until they settled in Dorset. In 1935 they both joined the Communist Party of Great Britain in reaction to the spread of European Fascism, and in 1936 they went to Spain to support the Government and to work for the Red Cross.

STW's enjoyment of the paradox inherent in her way of life, which combined the tranquil retirement of a country gentlewoman with political and sexual unorthodoxy, is evident in her exuberant and witty letters, a selection of which was published in 1982 edited by William Maxwell. In these, as in her stories, she combines a fascination with the eccentricities of human behaviour with clear-eyed, though compassionate, detachment and a joy in the natural world.

As a poet, STW bears some resemblance to Thomas Hardy, both in her choice of forms and in her meticulous concern with her craft. Some of her early poems are overloaded with elaborate conceits, while others attempt to signal profundity of thought by simplicity of utterance. In her later poems, particularly those published in *King Duffus* (1968) and *Twelve Poems* (1980), she used the dramatic monologue to challenge conventional judgements, as in the case of the leper who resents the cure that has reawakened him to sensation. This device of subverting the conventional viewpoint recurs throughout her poetic work. Her own admiration was for Emily Dickinson, Emily Brontë and Christina Rossetti, poets whose work she felt exemplified 'immediacy'. This quality is found most strikingly in her own poetry and prose in the representation of the material or natural world through the perceptions of another being: when she approaches the autobiographical mode the effect is often evasive and whimsical. The stories which draw upon the eccentricities of her own upbringing in an upper-middle-class Edwardian family, *Scenes of Childhood* (1981), preserve the vitality of her most successful work by maintaining a distance between the child involved in the events and the adult who recollects them with ironic detachment. In addition to their sociological interest and sharp humour, these stories provide an insight into the origins of some of her recurrent topics: the constraints on individual expression imposed by social class, the means by which an individual seeks personal liberation, the indifference to others of the privileged, and the minor but recurrent motif of the mysterious autonomy of domesticated animals. Several of the 'Scenes' deal with the intrusion into the family life of some alien but powerful object (an electric fire alarm, a haunted chair, an oak bedstead, a grapefruit), with disturbing, comic and sometimes liberating results. This device both echoes and parodies the central action of her novels, in which she explores the interaction in an individual life of a repressive, formal code of behaviour and the disruptive influence of some external force or power.

This is the theme of *Lolly Willowes* (1926). Possibly her recent discovery of her own creative identity underlies the novel which is both a pastoral romance and a feminist parable in which the masculine, sterile and conventional values of the town are challenged by the feminine, fecund, and subversive countryside. After years of subjection to her apparently affectionate but actually exploitative family, Lolly insists on her right to an austere rural existence. Responding with sensuous and aesthetic delight to the countryside, she is initiated into her vocation as a witch. This gives her power as well as knowledge: in fealty to Satan she is able to determine the conditions for her own way of life and to enjoy the solitude in nature which is often found in STW's work as the condition of greatest happiness.

Mr Fortune's Maggot (1927) is a pastoral idyll which explores the theme of self-liberation. Devout and inhibited, Mr Fortune follows what he believes to be his call to convert the natives of the island of Fanua to Christianity. He is received hospitably by the islanders without having any noticeable effect upon them, while their influence upon him is profound. Through his love for his single convert, Lueli, Mr Fortune undergoes an emotional and moral education, loses his faith, and comes to understand he is capable only of love which is flawed in its desire to 'convert', alter and possess.

Summer Will Show (1936) reflects both the increasingly radical nature of STW's thinking and her capacity for meticulous historical research. Set in 1848 the novel is concerned with the development of Sophia Willoughby from a haughty and emotionally frigid social parasite to a revolutionary communist. Her complacent, sterile existence is shattered first by the death of her children and then by her passionate feeling for her husband's mistress, Minoa, through whom she becomes involved with a revolutionary group in Paris. While working for their cause, she sheds material and class security and is liberated into real self-reliance and responsibility. The early chapters are reminiscent of George Eliot in their feeling for the moral significance of the ordinary events of daily life. *After the Death of Don Juan* (1938) continues the theme of awakening to political realities.

The Corner that Held Them (1948) also recreates a historical period with scrupulous attention to detail and without resorting to pastiche. In language which achieves a balance between the archaic and the colloquial, a sharp, ironic narrative voice records with wry detachment the life of the fourteenth-century convent of Oby through about forty years. Throughout this period the spiritual life of the convent is rooted in an undetected deception: their 'priest' is a clerk in minor orders and their sacraments therefore invalid. The lives of the nuns are chronicles of non-fulfilments, their desires, all frustrated by mischance and incompetence. Hidebound by its social as well as religious rituals, the convent stultifies creativity and self-expression as the price for the security it offers. Only the very few who take the chance to leave and the surrounding peasantry achieve a glimpse of larger possibilities as well as dangers in the secular world.

STW's 'Elfin' stories (the majority of which are collected in *Kingdoms of Elfin* (1977) are witty, elegant and occasionally chilling variations upon a similar theme. In the elfin world, which coexists and sometimes interacts with human arrangements, the leisured classes lead lives of exquisite boredom circumscribed by the absolute demands of etiquette and good form. To maintain caste status, they eschew the use of wings. Working fairies, who may fly and are unencumbered with the requirements of social ritual, are freer in effect than their superiors. This perception of the paradoxes inherent in a class society echoes the ironic treatment of the Edwardian household in *Scenes of Childhood*. STW also published two novels with an East Anglian setting, *The True Heart* (1929) which retells the story of Cupid and Psyche, and *The Flint Anchor* (1954). Her short stories, published in eight volumes, illustrate her versatility of both manner and subject matter, ranging from the farcical to the macabre. Recurrent themes are the struggle of an overlooked person for recognition, the painful effects of mutual incomprehension, and moments of sharp insight into obscure lives. Her feeling for the marginalized and emotionally derelict, which is expressed in many of her stories, also informs her sympathetic and revealing biography of T. H. White (1967). STW is most successful on her own social territory: her attempts to represent working-class people are sometimes disconcertingly stereotyped.

In describing Jane Austen as 'a completely worldly artist' STW made a judgment equally applicable to herself. The conventions of behaviour and expression inherited from her class and family perhaps influenced the elegant authorial detachment of her style, while her political convictions determined her characteristic theme: analysis of the forces which suppress and inhibit development into full expression of the self.   ELIZABETH JOYCE

Selected works: *The Espalier* (1925); *Lolly Willowes* (1926); *Mr Fortune's Maggot* (1927); *The True Heart* (1929); *Some World Far From Ours & Stay Corydon* (1929); *A Moral Ending* (1931); *The Salutation* (1932); *Whether a Dove or a Seagull* (1934); *More Joy in Heaven* (1939); *Summer Will Show* (1936); *After the Death of Don Juan* (1938); *The Portrait of a Tortoise, extracted from the Journals and Letters of Gilbert White,* Introduction and Notes by STW (1946); *The Museum of Cheats* (1947); *The Corner That Held Them* (1948); *Jane Austen* (1951); *The Flint Anchor* (1954); *Winter in the Air* (1955); *The Cat's Cradle Book* (1960); *A Spirit Rises* (1962); *A Stranger With a Bag* (1966); *T. H. White: A Biography* (1967); *King Duffus and Other Poems* (1968); *The Innocent and the Guilty* (1971); *Kingdoms of Elfin* (1977); *Azrael and Other Poems* (1978); *Twelve Poems* (1980); *Scenes of Childhood and Other Stories* (1981); *Collected Poems,* ed. C. Harman (1982); *One Thing Leading to Another,* ed. S. Pinney (1984); *Selected Poems,* (1985).

References: Harman, C. (ed.), 'Sylvia Townsend Warner 1893–1978: A Celebration', *Poetry Nation Review* 23, Vol. 8, No. 3 (1981); Morgan, L., *Writers at Work* (1931); Mulford, W., *This Narrow Place: Sylvia Townsend Warner and Valentine Ackland: Life, Letters and Politics 1930–51* (1988).

Warwick, Mary Rich, Countess of

b. November 1624, Youghal, Ireland; d. April 1678, Essex

Diarist, autobiographer

C of W was the seventh of eight daughters of Richard Boyle, later first Earl of Cork, and his second wife, Catherine Fenton, who died in 1629. With two of her sisters she was cared for in the family of Sir Randall and Lady Cleyton, 'a prudent and virtuous lady' who looked after her 'as if she had been an own mother to me'. She learned the foundations 'of religion and civility' but had little formal education, although she did study French. In 1638 she was taken to her father's new estate of Stalbridge in Dorset near Bristol where she was approached for marriage by a suitor of her father's choosing – his daughters were mostly married off to further his own political and economic interests – but C of W disliked his choice intensely, 'though I could give my father no satisfactory account why it was so'. Much wrangling followed during which the earl cut off his daughter's allowance, although it was later restored and backdated. In the winter of 1639–40 the family went to London where C of W met Charles Rich, a younger son of the Earl of Warwick with inadequate financial prospects for her father's liking. The couple fell in love or, as she put it, he 'did insensibly steal away my heart'. The courtship was carried on in secret but in due course her father agreed to the match. The wedding took place in 1641. The young couple moved in with the Earl of Warwick at the Warwick estate at Leighs and she soon bore a daughter, who died in infancy, and a son. The couple then appear to have practised some sort of birth control about which she later felt guilty.

The household was a Puritan one and C of W gradually became influenced by this atmosphere, coming much under the sway of Anthony Walker, her 'soul father', the Warwick household chaplain. She was also influenced in her piety by external events; in the mid-1640s her husband began to suffer from gout which made him increasingly moody and difficult, and in 1647 her son became ill which she took as a punishment for her own 'backsliding'. On his recovery she was confirmed in her religious tendency. In 1648 she was alone at Leighs when Royalist soldiers arrived, but they did not plunder the house. In 1658 her husband unexpectedly became Earl of Warwick. Although he had backed the Parliamentarians, he was one of the six peers deputed to invite Charles II to return, but any political ambitions were cut short by the worsening of his health. In 1664, shortly after his marriage, their son contracted smallpox and, despite her doing 'everything I could both for his soul and body', he died a few days later. C of W was grief-stricken: 'I confess I loved him at a rate that, if my heart did not deceive me, I could, with all the willingness in the world, have died either for him or with him, if God had only seen fit, yet I was dumb and held my peace, because God did it.' After her son's death, she spent her days in piety and philanthropy, bringing up her three nieces, and bearing with the ill-humour of her afflicted husband, whose affection she seems to have retained since he made her his sole executrix when he died in 1673.

In 1666 she began a spiritual diary which she kept until her death; it was used to record her religious exercises and meditations. The early years are dominated by the earl's declining health and his blasphemous railings against his wife, whose pious devotions he resented. Towards the end of his life she used a symbol of a cross to refer to him and she often records her repression of her anger against him: 'He fell violently passionate against me, which made me, wicked wretch that I was! speak passionate words softly to myself, unadvisedly with my lips.' After his death, which grieved her a great deal, the diary is less emotionally intense and religiously rapturous, more concerned with worldly matters; consequently she often accuses herself of backsliding. External events like the Great Fire and the plague are interpreted in providential terms, as are the many deaths and illnesses that punctuate the years. In her Meditations she effusively describes her religious sensations, but also notes trivial domestic events and natural details: 'Upon observing a snail, that where so ever it crept, it left some skin.'

In 1672 she decided to write her autobiography, primarily as another religious duty, but it much concerns the secular events of her life, especially her struggle with her father and her courtship, and it may well have been inspired by the published autobiography of the Duchess of Newcastle. The rest of her life was spent in good works; at her death she was described by Anthony Walker as 'the most Illustrious Pattern of Sincere Piety, and Solid Goodness this Age hath produced'.   JANET TODD

Works: Selections from the Diary and 'Pious and Useful Meditations', in *Eureka, or, The Virtuous Woman Found*, by A. Walker (1678); *Memoirs of Lady Warwick: Also Her Diary, from 1666 to 1672* (1848).

References: *DNB*; Mendelson, S. H., *The Mental World of Stuart Women* (1987); Smith, C. F., *Mary Rich, Countess of Warwick* (1901); Todd; Walker, A., *Eureka, or, The Virtuous Woman Found* (1678).

Webb, Beatrice

b. 22 January 1858, Standish, Gloucestershire; d. 20 April 1943, Passfield
Corner, nr Liphook, Hampshire

Diarist, political writer, social reformer
BW was the eighth of nine daughters of Richard Potter who added to his
already considerable wealth by involvement in Britain's expanding railway
network of the late 1800s. She was, therefore, born to comfort, security, and
Britain's new ruling classes. She was not, as a consequence, sheltered from the
wider world and, although she was educated privately at home, she soon began
travelling overseas, a pattern which she was to follow for the rest of her active
life. She was an observant traveller and absorbed what she saw.

Initially, her life followed a predictable pattern and at 18 she 'came out'; the
next six years were spent in the customary social round. Then, in 1882, her
mother died and BW assumed the role of mistress of her father's house and
became his business partner. This involvement in her father's business entailed
BW in rent collecting in the East End of London, exposing her to the misery,
acute poverty and disease, and it provided her with the impetus to learn the
task of social investigation. At the same time she was reading voraciously in
mathematics and philosophy, and studying biology with her brother-in-law,
William Harrison Cripps. In the East End she began a friendship with Mary
and Charles Booth, who were influential in BW's development as a social
investigator, and she was involved in gathering information for Booth's *Life
and Labour of the People of London*. BW's background was political. Both her
grandfathers were Liberal MPs and her final decision to work for social reform
was instinctive as well as achieved through long hours of constructive thought.
Her work in the East End provided material for a series of articles on the social
conditions she encountered. Her first book, *The Co-operative Movement in Great
Britain*, appeared in 1891.

BW's socio-political books gained her the reputation of being a dry, pas-
sionless writer. These books were, however, concerned with facts and statistics
and left little room for expression. With the publication of extracts from her
diary, *My Apprenticeship*, in 1926, BW's reputation altered; the character to
emerge from this book was one full of life and emotion, a person who was
also brave enough to write about the most sensitive periods in her history.
Her honesty in tackling the subject of her four-year infatuation with Joseph
Chamberlain is an example of her forthrightness. A woman as strong and
independent as BW could only have felt humiliation in recording the events of
these years but she had the courage to do so.

In the 1880s BW was still caught in the dilemma of a decision between a
career and the idea of marriage. 'What is there in the life [of ladies in society]
which is so attractive? How can intelligent women wish to marry into the set
where this is the social régime?' she wrote in March 1883. But in 1889 she
could say, 'God knows celibacy is painful to a woman.' In a letter to Beatrice
Chamberlain, Joseph Chamberlain's daughter, she further said, 'a working life
has its attractions. It is full of interest and sympathy, and it has its own peculiar
charm of an impersonal way of life.' On the subject of women's emancipation,
political and social, BW was, in the same decade, also ambiguous. She rejected
Charles Booth's invitation to make the state of female labour her special subject
for investigation after she had completed her study of the immigrant Jewish
community in the East End. She was a signatory to Mrs. Humphry Ward's
manifesto against the enfranchisement of women. Twenty years later she pub-

licly withdrew her support from this position and she wrote, 'At the root of my anti-feminism lay the fact that I had never myself suffered the disabilities assumed to rise from my sex.'

In 1890 BW's dilemma over marriage was brought closer to a solution. While researching her book on the co-operative movement she was introduced to Sidney Webb. They were a strange couple; BW tall, handsome and wealthy, Sidney a product of the poorer side of London, his family supported by his mother's meagre earnings as a hairdresser. It took two years for BW to decide to marry Sidney but when she did there began a unique partnership of social and professional harmony which became the 'firm of Webb', as BW called it. Their first joint book, *A History of Trade Unionism*, was published in 1894. Their home in Grosvenor Road, London, became a centre for reforming activity. In 1895 they launched an idea which was to be realized in the formation of the London School of Economics. Until 1906 Sidney was the 'public' half of the partnership, but in 1905 Beatrice became a member of the Royal Commission on the Poor Law and she was once again in a prominent position. The Webbs founded the *New Statesman* in 1913. During this period they were 'absorbed into' the Labour Party, with Sidney eventually becoming MP for Durham. 'The partnership' did not always have a smooth passage and people who at one time had been friends, like H. G. Wells, were swift to criticize, and in public. But the Webbs were magnanimous and responded to criticism with understanding rather than alienation and rejection.

My Apprenticeship covers the period from 1873 up until BW's marriage to Sidney. As well as a social record, it is a history of her family and the travels which she undertook with her father, travelling remaining her one luxury in a life basically austere and devoted to social reform. Although BW's political books remain as a testimony to her major contribution to this work of social reform at the beginning of the century, it is the book born of her diaries which will ensure that she is long-remembered. They are more than just well-written diaries; they are the record of Britain at a time of great and swift change.

ALISON RIMMER

Selected works: *The Co-operative Movement in Britain* (1891); *My Apprenticeship* (1926); *Our Partnership* (1948); *The Diary of Beatrice Webb:* vol.1, *Glitter Around and Darkness Within* (1982); vol.2, *All the Good Things of Life* (1983); vol.3, *The Power to Alter Things* (1984); vol.4, *The Wheel of Life* (1985); with Sidney Webb: *The History of Trade Unionism* (1894); *Industrial Democracy* (1897); *English Local Government* (1906–29); *A Constitution for the Social Commonwealth of Great Britain* (1920); *The Consumers Co-operative Movement* (1920); *The Decay of Capitalist Civilisation* (1923); *Methods of Social Study* (1932); *Soviet Communism: A New Civilisation?* (1935).

References: Caine, B., *Destined to Be Wives: The Sisters of Beatrice Webb* (1986); Cole, M., *Beatrice Webb* (1946); Cole, M., *The Webbs and Their Work* (1974); MacKenzie, J., *A Victorian Courtship: The Story of Beatrice Potter and Sidney Webb* (1979); MacKenzie, N. (ed.), *The Letters of Sidney and Beatrice Webb* (1978); MacKenzie, N. and J., *The First Fabians* (1977); Muggeridge, K. and Adam, R., *Beatrice Webb 1888–1943* (1967); Nord, D.E., *The Apprenticeship of Beatrice Webb* (1985).

Webb, Mary

b. 25 March 1881, Leighton, Shropshire; d.8 October 1927, St Leonards,
Sussex

Novelist

MW was the eldest of the six children of George Edward Meredith, the head
of a boarding school in Leighton, Shropshire, and Sarah Alice Scott, the
daughter of an Edinburgh surgeon. In 1882 the family moved to The Grange
in Much Wenlock, where Mr Meredith became a gentleman farmer, and when
MW was 12 they moved again to Stanton-on-Hine-Heath near Shrewsbury. In
1895 Mrs Meredith was injured in a hunting accident, making her an invalid
for the next five years, and MW became responsible for the running of the
household. She was educated at home, by her father and governesses, and from
1895 to 1897 attended Mrs Walmsley's Finishing School in Southport, where
she excelled academically. Her first writings were poems for the parish magazine, written in the late 1890s.

Soon after her twentieth birthday she began to suffer from Graves' disease,
a severe thyroid malfunction, the symptoms of which gave her a deep sense of
physical inadequacy. The disease was to recur throughout her life. In convalescence she began to write essays, nine of which were later published as *The Spring
of Joy* (1917), sharing a central theme of 'the healing power of nature'. Her first
published poem was 'The Railway Accident', submitted to the *Shrewsbury
Chronicle* in October 1907, without her knowledge. After her father's death
early in 1909 she suffered a period of intense grief. In 1910 she tried to publish
a collection of essays as *The Scallop Shell*, but failed.

In 1910 she met Henry Webb, a Cambridge graduate who had taken up a
teaching post at a preparatory school near Meole Brace where the Merediths
now lived. Like MW, he was an animist rather than an orthodox Christian.
They married in 1912, and the wedding guests included seventy inmates of the
women's ward of the local workhouse. After the marriage they settled in
Weston-super-Mare for two years, then returned to their native Shropshire,
working as market gardeners to supplement their income. Here MW embarked
on her first novel, *The Golden Arrow*, written in the space of three weeks, and
containing a strong autobiographical element. John Arden is, like MW, a
pantheist, and his visionary experiences are central to the novel. It was published
by Constable in 1916. By this time MW had become book reviewer for the
Liverpool Post.

In 1921 the Webbs moved to London, and MW began reviewing for the
Spectator and later for the *Bookman*. She went on to write a further five novels,
of which *Precious Bane* (1924) is the most highly regarded; it received the Prix
Femina Vie Heureuse of 1924–25. *Seven for a Secret* (1922) was dedicated to
Thomas Hardy, to whom MW has been compared. In 1926 she received a letter
from Stanley Baldwin praising her work, but it was not until shortly after her
death that she gained full recognition. The last two years of her life were
unhappy, with her failing marriage and rapidly deteriorating health, and she
abandoned the manuscript of her last novel, *Armour Wherein He Trusted* (1928),
before finishing it.

All MW's novels are set in her native Shropshire and inspired by a pantheistic
response to its landscape: 'For the personality of a man reacting upon the spirit
of a place produces something which is neither the man nor the place, but
fiercer or more beautiful than either' (*The Golden Arrow*). This nature mysticism
subsumes a more orthodox Christianity: in nature MW sees an 'occult script',

'a writing not in fire upon tablets of stone, but in subtle traceries on young leaves and buds, . . . For the thought . . . that all fine contours are a direct message from God, is rooted deep in the minds of the simple-hearted, who are the Magi of the World.' Many of her short stories and some of the novels are told from the point of view of these 'simple-hearted' people, the rural poor, the alienated, the victimized.

The novels as a whole deal with human passion in all its aspects, and in particular with adolescent female sexuality. The lesson of *The Golden Arrow*, borne out by later novels, is that finding love is like finding the golden arrow which brings great happiness by wounding. Love (both spiritual and sexual) is seen to be life's greatest gift, but MW makes clear that it is inextricably bound up with suffering: the lover is 'forever martyred and forever gladsome'. This is a lesson which also has to be learned by the women in *Gone to Earth* (1917), *The House in Dormer Forest* (1920), and especially in *Seven for a Secret*, a *Bildungsroman* centred upon the callow and selfish Gillian Lovekin.

Often love can be won only through the transgression of social codes. This is the case in *The House in Dormer Forest*, where rigid adherence to convention is seen to suffocate the body and spirit. In the short story 'Caercariad: A Story of the Marches', Dinah Tudor, after forty-five stifling years of marriage to the pious Zedekiah, abandons him for a former lover and finds fulfilment in old age. But such transgression does not always bring its reward. Hazel Woodus in *Gone to Earth* is such a child of nature that she can never adjust herself to 'the strait orbit of human life', and she is literally hounded to death by hunters, choosing to die with the pet fox who is her alter ego. *Precious Bane* tells the tragic tale of Gideon Sarn whose mad lust for the 'precious bane' of money drives his sweetheart, and eventually himself, to suicide. The tale is narrated in Shropshire dialect by his gentle sister, Prue. Prue speaks for the women of the rural poor who normally lead 'such lost-and-forgotten lives'. Her 'precious bane' is her harelip, thought to be the Devil's curse by the pious, superstitious, and ignorant people among whom she lives. This, coupled with the fact that she can read and write, having been taught by Beguildy, an atheist locally known as the wizard, makes her the object of a witch-hunt. Her love for the Shropshire landscape is rivalled only by her passion for Kester Woodseaves the weaver, who rescues her from the witch-ducking and chooses his 'bit of Paradise' on her breast.

MW's last novel, *Armour Wherein He Trusted*, marks a new departure. It is the only one written from a man's point of view, in the archaic language of Norman Shropshire. Where earlier novels had advocated a union of carnal and spiritual love, Sir Gilbert finds salvation in the renunciation of earthly love. MW's earlier mysticism has been replaced by a more orthodox Christianity.

MW also wrote critical essays, the first of which was 'The Love of Poetry' published in the *English Review* in 1920. Here she argues that 'the love of poetry is akin to the animal world, so that the poet of genius is more in tune with the bee than he is with the poet of talent'.   ANNE FERNIHOUGH

Works: *The Golden Arrow* (1916); *The Spring of Joy* (1917); *Gone to Earth* (1917); *The House in Dormer Forest* (1920); *Seven for a Secret* (1922); *Precious Bane* (1924); *Armour Wherein He Trusted* (1928); *Fifty-One Poems* (1946); *Collected Prose and Poems* (1977).

References: Addison, H., *Mary Webb: A Short Study of Her Life and Work* (1931); Barale, M. A., *Daughters and Lovers: The Life and Writing of Mary Webb* (1986); Cavaliero, G., *The Rural Tradition in the English Novel, 1900–1939* (1977); Coles, G. M., *The Flower of Light: A Biography of Mary Webb* (1978); Dickins, G.,

Mary Webb: A Narrative Bibliography of Her Life and Works (1981); Hannah, B., *Striving Towards Wholeness* (1971); Moult, T., *Mary Webb: Her Life and Works* (1932); Wrenn, D., *Goodbye to Morning* (1964).

Webster, Augusta

b. 30 January 1837, Poole, Dorset; d. 5 September 1894, Kew

Poet, playwright, essayist
(Also wrote under Cecil Home)
AW was the daughter of Vice-Admiral George Davies, who held several coast-guard commands; as a consequence she spent her girlhood on various islands and ships. In her youth she studied classical authors, particularly the Greek dramatists, and in her twenties she published translations of Aeschylus and Euripides. At the age of 26 she married Thomas Webster, fellow of Trinity College, Cambridge, and a practising solicitor. From 1860 until her death she wrote plays, poems, and essays on both contemporary and classical themes.

In *A Housewife's Opinions* (1878), she collected essays on issues related to the lives of married women like herself. She considered seriously the consequences of expecting housewives to do their own housework, anticipating that women's time for study, art, or music would be drastically curtailed hereby, as would their time with their husbands. Co-operative housekeeping she ruled out, because of the English ideal of private home life. An ardent feminist, AW believed that women's achievement of the suffrage was inevitable despite the six parliamentary defeats she witnessed in her lifetime. She had a strong commitment to advancing women's educational opportunities and was twice elected to the London School Board, in 1879 and 1885.

AW's dramas – *The Auspicious Day* (1872), *Disguises* (1879), *In a Day* (1882), and *The Sentence* (1887) – were praised by contemporaries for their 'concentrated strength'. William Michael Rossetti pronounced *The Sentence* (about Caligula) to be 'one of the masterpieces of European drama'. *In a Day* was produced at a matinée in 1890, with AW's adult daughter appearing as the heroine; it was the only one of her dramas to be staged. Also in the dramatic vein, AW composed numerous studies of Christian saints, addressing the glory and the difficulty of asceticism and submission to God, for instance, 'Jeanne d'Arc' and 'Sister Annunciata' (1866). In 1864, she published a three-volume novel, *Lesley's Guardians*, under the pseudonym Cecil Home.

AW's most lasting work is her poetry, beginning with the 1866 volume *Dramatic Studies*, which included the widely admired poem 'Snow-Waste', and culminating in the unfinished sonnet sequence *Mother and Daughter*, published the year after her death. Showing the influence of her acknowledged mentor, Robert Browning, she wrote dramatic monologues in blank verse, often on sociological themes related especially to women. These pieces are interesting for their rendering of female consciousness, and are much more psychologically convincing than most contemporary poems on similar subjects. Outstanding examples include 'By the Looking-Glass' (1866) about spinsterhood, and 'The Heiress's Wooer' and 'A Mother's Cry' (both 1867) about the marriage market and parental matchmaking. 'A Castaway' (1870), a 600-line poem ranging widely over the whole complicated issue of the fallen woman and prostitution in the nineteenth century, compares favourably with Dante Gabriel Rossetti's 'Jenny', which appeared in the same year. The poem went into three editions and was greatly admired by both Browning and Rossetti, although some contemporary critics complained that the subject matter was unsuitable for a woman poet.

'Circe' (1870) is a psychological character study of the mythological figure, marked by sexual imagery and an erotic tone, and its persuasive representation of the heroine's inner life. In *A Book of Rhyme* (1881), AW introduced into English poetry an Italian form of peasant song known as 'rispetti' or 'stornelli'. Her last volume of poetry, *Mother and Daughter* (1895), is at once a personal expression of maternal love and a commentary on the varying moods and experiences of motherhood.

AW's moral leadership was widely recognized in her lifetime. In 1880 Theodore Watts placed her in the company of George Eliot and Frances Power Cobbe, 'who, in virtue of lofty purpose, purity of soul, and deep sympathy with suffering humanity, are just now ahead of the men'. Yet Victorian commentators were often made uneasy by the realism and directness of her poetry. Some complained of AW's eccentricity in printing her blank verse without capitals at the beginning of the lines; others found her diction inadmissibly vulgar, particularly for a woman writer. Mackenzie Bell, while comparing AW favourably with Elizabeth Barrett Browning, Christina Rossetti, and Jean Ingelow, nevertheless remarked, 'the other women poets of England must yield to her [W.] in that quality which, as it is generally deemed the specially masculine quality, is called virility.' KATHLEEN HICKOK

Works: *Blanche Lisle and Other Poems* (1860); *Lilian Gray* (1864); *Lesley's Guardians* (1864); *Dramatic Studies* (1866); *A Woman Sold and Other Poems* (1867); *Portraits* (1870, enlarged 1893); *The Auspicious Day* (1872); *Yu-Pe-Ya's Lute* (1874); *A Housewife's Opinions* (1878); *Disguises* (1879); *A Book of Rhyme* (1881); *In a Day* (1882); *Daffodil and the Croäxaxicans: A Romance from History* (1884); *The Sentence* (1887); *Selections from the Verse of Augusta Webster* (1893); *Mother and Daughter* (1895).

References: BA (19); Bell, M., 'Augusta Webster', in *The Poets and the Poetry of the Century*, ed. A. H. Miles (1892); Evans, B. I., *English Poetry in the Later Nineteenth Century* (1933); Forman, H. B., *Our Living Poets* (1871); Hickok, K., *Representations of Women: Nineteenth Century British Women's Poetry* (1984); Robertson, E. S. (ed.), *English Poetesses* (1883); Sackville-West, V., 'The women poets of the seventies', in *The Eighteen Seventies*, ed. H. Granville-Barker (1929); Watts, T., Obituary in *Athenaeum* (15 September 1894).

Wedgwood, C. V.

b. 20 July 1910, Stocksfield, Northumberland
Historian, translator
CVW is a widely respected historian of seventeenth-century England and France. She was born Cicely Veronica to Ralph Lewis and Iris (*née* Pawson) Wedgwood. Ralph was a younger son of the famous china manufacturing family and became chairman of British Railways in the Second World War; Iris wrote several books on history and topography. CVW grew up in London and took first-class honours at Lady Margaret Hall, Oxford, in 1931. She has worked as director of the weekly *Time and Tide*, been a member of many organizations, including the Institute for Advanced Study at Princeton, and served for many years as trustee of the National Gallery. Although a special lecturer at many universities, CVW declines to take a regular teaching post because she wishes to maintain her independence. She was made an honorary fellow of LMH in 1962, of University College, London in 1965, and several

universities in the UK and the US have awarded her honorary doctorates. CVW has won the James Tait Black Memorial Prize for *William the Silent* (1944) and the Goethe medal for her translations from the German.

CVW's narrative historical style has been influenced by G. M. Trevelyan (a friend of her father) and A. L. Rowse. Her work on the seventeenth century is largely biographical – it is the personalities of the past she is interested in. Her writing reverberates with the sheer delight she takes in primary sources. She introduces the collection of essays *Velvet Studies* (1946) with, 'If I was not born a historian, I was an aspirant at six and a practitioner at twelve.'

Her best-known work is the two-volume *Great Rebellion* (1958), recounting the events of Charles I's reign and restoring the immediacy of the experience for the people involved, and so for the reader as well. The highly detailed nature of her work makes it eminently readable and novelistic, but her narrative style and lack of theoretical interpretation have been criticized by other historians and her works are no longer standard academic reading. CVW has responded with her accustomed eloquence that she prefers to emphasize the individual characters of history rather than adopt the method of her critics 'which treats developments as though they were the massive anonymous waves of an inhuman sea or pulverizes the fallible surviving records of human life into the grey dust of statistics'. And again, 'it is not lack of prejudice which makes for dull history, but lack of passion.' CVW has made it clear in her historiographical lectures that it is important to combine serious historical enquiry with an imaginative leap, and that the elements of literary style are the natural concomitants of the clear, enquiring, disciplined, and imaginative mind which is needed for historical research.

CVW's most recent work, *The Spoils of Time* (1984), a short history of the world planned for two volumes, is a unique attempt by a specialist historian to make sense of the 'vast and confused record of world history' up to her own period and in different parts of the world. Despite the silliness inevitable when modern sensibilities are applied to prehistoric existence – such as CVW's reference to the 'cheerless region of Tierra del Fuego' c. 8,000 BC, or the assurance that 20,000 years ago man's life may have been pretty unpleasant, but 'there are compensations: he had a sense of awe and a sense of beauty' – this volume is laudable in its intent and as entertaining and elegantly written as all of CVW's prose.   AMY ERICKSON

Works: *Strafford, 1593–1641* (1935); *The Thirty Years War* (1938); (trans.), *The Emperor Charles V*, by K. Brandt (1939); *Oliver Cromwell* (1939); *Battlefields in Britain* (1944); *William the Silent: William of Nassau, Prince of Orange, 1533–84* (1944); *Velvet Studies* (1946); (trans.), *Auto da Fé*, by Elias Canetti (1946); *Seventeen-Century English Literature* (1950); *The Last of the Radicals: Josiah Wedgwood* (1951); *Montrose* (1952); *The Great Rebellion: The King's Peace* (1955); *The Great Rebellion: The King's War* (1958); *Poetry and Politics under the Stuarts* (1960); *Truth and Opinion: Historical Essays* (1960); *The Trial of Charles I* (1964); *Richelieu and the Frenchy Monarchy* (1974); *The Spoils of Time: A Short History of the World*, vol. 1, *From the Earliest Times to the Sixteenth Century* (1984).

References: *CA*; Ollard R. and Tudor Craigs, P., 'Preface' to *For Veronica Wedgewood These* (1986).

Weldon, Fay

b. 22 September 1933, Alvechurch, Worcestershire

Novelist, playwright, critic

FW, daughter of Margaret Jepson and Frank Birkinshaw, grew up in an all-female household in London following her parents' divorce when she was 10. She was educated at Hampstead Girls' High School and St Andrews University, Fife, where she gained an MA in economics and psychology in 1954. She is married to Ron Weldon. They have four sons. She lives in London and the West Country.

FW has written many novels, most of which tend to have a married or unmarried mother at their centre. Her work takes up some of the issues that are of concern to the women's movement, such as friendship and rivalry between women, motherhood, women and work, the oppressive nature of heterosexual relationships, patriarchial attitudes towards women, etc., but suggests that, while women can do something to alter their situation, such activity will ultimately tend towards greater accommodation within existent expectations of how women are to fulfil their patriarchally determined roles. There seems little hope for attitudinal changes towards women in society at large in FW's work. Her first novel, *The Fat Woman's Joke* (1967), describes the effects of going on a diet on a greedy couple. Towards the end of the book Esther Sussman, the heroine, says, 'I am finished. I am over. It's very simple, really. I am a woman and so I am an animal. All women are animals. They have no control over themselves. They feel compelled to have children – there is no merit in it, there is no cause for self-congratulation, it is blind instinct.' This statement, which can be seen as pessimistic and/or realistic, seems to express FW's view of women's lot. In her novels many of her female characters experience lack of control, the 'blindness' of having children, the no-win situation that society places them in. FW's second novel, *Down Among the Women*, follows the lives and explores the survival instincts of a group of women of whom FW says, 'Men are irrelevant. Women are happy or unhappy, fulfilled or unfulfilled, and it has nothing to do with men.' Alternating between blaming women and blaming men for women's lot, FW is clear-sighted enough to see the shortcomings of both sexes and exploit these for her comic representations of life in twentieth-century Britain. *Female Friends* (1975) gives an account of the enduring friendship of Marjorie, Chloe, and Grace through the various stages of their lives. Stylistically this novel is interesting because much of the dialogue is set apart from the rest of the text by being written in play form with the name of the character speaking appearing before each bit of speech. The result is a curious sense of stagedness of the conversations which points to the artificiality of individuals' preoccupations. It also betrays the fact that FW has a parallel interest in play writing. In *Remember Me* (1976) the same stylistic device is employed; not only is dialogue set out as if in a play, the reader is also offered a second version of the conversations in which what people 'really mean' is revealed. *Little Sisters* (1978) changes the scenario from 'ordinary' people to the ultra-rich. Elsa and her lover spend a weekend with his wealthy friends Hamish and Gemma who is wheelchair-bound. Embedded in the story of that weekend, which turns into a disaster, is Gemma's story. This story-within-story device, used also in *Praxis* (1978), allows FW to present different time sequences within one work, thus giving the impression of the repetition of women's experience through time. *Puffball* (1980) describes the interactions of Liffey, a pregnant woman, with the rural community in Somerset where she stays while her husband continues to work in London and joins her for weekends. Liffey finds herself at the mercy of various members of the community. FW in this novel invokes the supernatural and witchcraft to express Liffey's uneasiness at her situation, and suggests similar forces in the title of *The Life and Loves of a She-Devil* (1984). Here a large woman uses her abilities, supernatural or otherwise, to revenge herself upon her unfaithful accountant husband by gradually breaking down the popular woman novelist with whom he has been having an affair. In the end the 'she-devil', through a number of means such as ensuring that her husband is in prison for a prolonged period of time during which she undergoes extensive plastic surgery, manages to change her exterior to match that of her husband's ex-lover, and, in effect, takes over completely that lover's role and life, including her home and her professional career. She becomes that other woman. On one level the book vividly illustrates the extent to which women will go to accommodate themselves to the demands of their men. Other novels include *The President's Child* (1982) and *The Shrapnel Academy* (1986), which uses an intrusive narrator to distance the reader from the awful and violent events.

FW has become known to a wider audience both through the publication of short stories in magazines such as *Cosmopolitan, Company*, and *Woman's Own*, and through numerous adaptations and plays she has written both for radio and television. Her most recent television work was *The Heart of the Country* (1987), her first original television serial. This is a black comedy that probes marital relationships and the myth of rural living through the experiences of a middle-class wife who lives through the destruction of her cosy, affluent world. FW's stories were collected in the two volumes *Watching Me, Watching You* (1981) and *Polaris and Other Stories* (1985). She won the SFTA Award for the Best Series for Episode 1 of *Upstairs, Downstairs* (1971), and the Giles Cooper Award for Best Radio Play for *Polaris* (1978). FW was Chairwoman of the Booker Prize in 1983, and of the Sinclair Prize in 1986. She is on the Video Censorship Appeals Committee, and was a member of the Arts Council literary panel.   GABRIELE GRIFFIN

Selected works: The Fat Woman's Joke (1967); *Permanence* (1969); *Down among the Women* (1971); *Time Hurries On* (1972); *Words of Advice* (1974); *Female Friends* (1975); *Remember Me* (1976); *Moving House* (1976); *Little Sisters* (1978); *Praxis* (1978); *Friends* (1978); *Mr Director* (1978); *Action Replay* (1978) *Puffball* (1980); *Watching Me, Watching You* (1981); *I Love My Love* (1981); *Woodworm* (1981); *The President's Child* (1982); *After The Prize* (1983); *The Life and Loves of a She-Devil* (1984); *Letters to Alice* (1984); *Polaris and Other Stories* (1985); *The Shrapnel Academy* (1986); *The Heart of the Country* (1987).

References: Drabble; Krouse, A. N., 'Feminism and art in Fay Weldon's novels', *Critique* 20, 2 (1978); Svane-Mikkelsen, L., 'Forfatter eller feminist? Om Fay Weldon og hendes forfatterskab' ('Author or feminist? On Fay Weldon and her work'), *Kritik* 61 (1982).

West, Jane

b. 30 April 1758, London; d. 25 March 1852, Little Bowden, Northamptonshire
Novelist, poet, playwright, educational writer
(Also wrote under Prudentia Homespun)
The only child of Jane and John Iliffe, JW was born in the building which subsequently became St Paul's Coffee House in London. Her family moved to

Desborough in Northamptonshire in 1769. She was apparently self-educated, and claimed to have begun writing poetry at the age of 13. She married Thomas West, a yeoman farmer of Northamptonshire related to the poet Gilbert West, and they had three sons, Thomas (born 1783), John (born 1787), and Edward (born 1794). A successful and prolific writer, she chose, however, to present herself rather as a humble farmer's wife writing to help support her children; her poem addressed 'To the Hon. Mrs C—e' offers the following self-portrait:

> You said the author was a charmer,
> Self-taught, and married to a farmer;
> Who wrote all kinds of verse with ease,
> Made pies and puddings, frocks and cheese.
> Her situation, tho' obscure,
> Was not contemptible or poor.
> Her conversation spoke a mind
> Studious to please, but unrefin'd.
> (*Misc. Poms*, 1791)

Her social and economic position, however, was a matter for debate even at the time (see *Gentleman's Magazine* 91, January 1802, *Gentleman's Magazine* 91, February 1802). Despite this publicized self-effacement, she was a protégée of Bishop Percy after 1800 and a correspondent of the educationist Sarah Trimmer after 1801. Very little other information is available on her life. Her husband died in January 1823. On her death in 1852, she was buried in the family plot in St Nicholas's Church, Little Bowden.

Although JW published a number of volumes of poetry and plays, her reputation rested and still rests primarily upon her novels. Her first two titles, *The Advantages of Education* (1793) and *A Gossip's Story* (1797), are classic examples of the anti-sensibility plot, common to Edgeworth's *Letters for Literary Ladies* and Austen's *Sense and Sensibility*, in which the heroine of sensibility is subjected to eventual ruin as a consequence of her overblown notions of romantic love, whereas the heroine of sense makes a happy and judicious marriage. Under the alias of Prudentia Homespun, JW proclaimed a new anti-romantic aesthetic and set her heroines in a rural middle-class society to which they are forced to accommodate their desires and expectations. *A Tale of the Times* (1799) was acclaimed as a major anti-Jacobin novel (that is to say, a polemic against Godwin's *Political Justice*) and was ranked alongside Elizabeth Hamilton's *Memoirs of Modern Philosophers* by contemporary critics. It deals with the break-up of the idealized Montalbert marriage through the abduction and rape of Geraldine Montalbert by a philosopher-villain whose seductive discourse is modelled on Godwin's rhetoric. This break-up functions as a figure for a threat of larger social disintegration, even more violently portrayed in JW's next novel, *The Infidel Father* (1802). This novel's unusually convoluted plot is designed to anatomize the baleful effects of atheistic tenets on the part of Lord Glanville. The denouement, in which his daughter by a second marriage who has been educated in his system is proved illegitimate and commits suicide, enabling his virtuous and legitimate, but hitherto unacknowledged son by a first, secret marriage to take her place as heir, powerfully figures the expulsion of disruptive ideology (and of the self-willed insubordinate woman who comes to epitomize it) from the legitimate social order sanctioned by divine patriarchy.

The Loyalists (1812), JW's first historical novel, tells the story of the triumph of legitimacy in the Civil War a century earlier. The politically conservative implications of this are clearly in line with the concerns of her earlier work, and foreshadow Scott's treatment of a similar theme in *Waverley*. JW's 'historical romance', *Alicia de Lacey* (1814), seems to be something of an attempt to capitalize on Scott's success in this new genre.

Her last novel, *Ringrove* (1827), published late on in her life when she had faded into obscurity, is of interest mainly because of its structural and thematic affinity with the school of Evangelical fiction which originated with Hannah More's *Coelebs In Search of a Wife*. JW's relationship to mainstream conservative Evangelicalism is manifested as early as 1806 in her *Letters to a Young Lady*, an influential conduct manual which, in its advocacy of education for women in order to fit them for the task of regenerating society, is in many respects similar to More's *Strictures on the Modern System of Female Education*.

NICOLA WATSON

Selected Works: *Miscellaneous Poems, Translations, and Imitations* (1780); *Miscellaneous Poetry* (1786); *The Humours of Brighthelmstone: A Poem* (1788); *Miscellaneous Poems* (1791); *The Advantages of Education, or, The History of Maria Williams* (1793); *The Gossip's Story* (1797); *A Tale of the Times* (1799); *Poems and Plays* (1799–1805); *Letters . . . to a Young Man* (1801); *The Infidel Father* (1802); *The Sorrows of Selfishness: A Story for Children* (1802); *Letters . . . to a Young Lady* (1806); *The Mother: A Poem in Five Books* (1809); *The Refusal* (1810); *The Loyalists: An Historical Novel* (1812); *Select Translation of the Beauties of Massillon* (1812); *Alicia de Lacey: An Historical Romance* (1814); *The Vicissitudes of Life* (1815); *Scriptural Essays* (1816); *Ringrove, or, Old Fashioned Notions* (1827). (Of these attributions, Pamela Lloyd (see below) suggests that *Miscellaneous Poems, Translations, and Imitations* should properly be attributed to Benjamin West. In addition the attribution by the Bodleian Library of *The Vicissitudes of Life* seems highly suspect, as it is a lurid epistolary romance, the very genre against which JW was writing.)

References: Butler, M., *Jane Austen and the War of Ideas* (1975); Lloyd, P., 'Some new information on Jane West', *Notes & Queries* 31, 229 (December 1984); Rendall, J., *The Origins of Modern Feminism . . . 1780–1860* (1985); Todd; Tompkins, J. M. S., *The Popular Novel in England* (1932).

West, Rebecca

b. 21 December 1892, London; d. 15 March 1983

Novelist, reviewer

(Also wrote under Rachel East)

RW's mother, Isabella Campbell Mackenzie, had travelled from Edinburgh to Australia for the benefit of her health; there she met the Anglo-Irish Charles Fairfield who was working for the Melbourne *Argus*. They were married in 1883 and had three daughters; the first two, Letitia and Winifred, were born in Australia. RW (Cicely) was born in London.

On his return to Britain, after a brief period with the *Glasgow Herald*, Charles Fairfield moved his family to London, but he had no steady career and no steady income, and tension between husband and wife began to mount. While the family was relatively impoverished, there was no shortage of cultural contributions; from 'Cissie's' mother came musical education and appreciation, and from her father, exposure to ideas, politics, books. But marital difficulties increased and in 1901 Charles Fairfield left his family, going first to West Africa. The 8-year-old Cissie wrote two of her first poems, 'He' and 'She' – on the end of love. She was distressed by her father's departure; he died in 1906 without seeing his family again. Isabella returned, with her three daughters, to her mother's home in Edinburgh; then she moved to 2 Hope Park Square (later the setting for Ellen Melville in the novel, *The Judge*). The young RW had many unhappy memories of this impoverished period.

A bursary enabled RW to become a pupil at George Watson's Ladies' College. She had no gift for modern languages, but already displayed considerable literary talents. At the age of 14 she won the school Best Essay prize for juniors, and then in October 1907 she had a letter to *The Scotsman* published, in her own name, displaying some of the features which were to characterize her writing over the next seventy years. The letter was radical and witty, adamant and amusing. Entitled 'Women's Electoral Claims', it supported the creation of an independent women's party – the National Women's Social and Political Union – and it denounced the degradation that *manhood* suffrage meant for women.

For a 15-year-old pupil to be the object of such public attention was in itself a breach of convention; when to this were added other suffrage activities – selling *Votes for Women*, attending gatherings, meeting and emulating leaders like Mary Gawthorpe – it was not surprising that Isabella Fairfield should have thought it necessary to rescue her wilful daughter and direct her to more positive pursuits. RW's schooling was discontinued. But by then the three Fairfield daughters were aware that they had to earn their own livings; Letitia graduated from Edinburgh Medical College for Women in 1907, and Winifred embarked on a teaching career. Nothing so sedate seemed to appeal to the youngest sister who rejected Letitia's advice to try office work. The theatre was what she was interested in. In April 1910, she was accepted at the Academy of Dramatic Art in London and the family moved to Hampstead Garden Suburb.

For three terms she attended the Academy, though it did not engage her imagination or affection. She also started to write, as a 'natural' activity. Her first published piece was a theatre review for the London *Evening Standard*. She then began to look for regular work in journalism; when in November 1911 the feminist weekly *Freewoman* made its appearance, she found her platform. It was edited by Dora Marsden and co-edited by the much-admired Mary Gawthorpe; in the second issue, on 30 November, there was a review by RW of *The Position of Women in Indian Life*. The opening sentence was striking and came to typify her stock in trade: 'There are two kinds of imperialists – imperialists and bloody imperialists.' Such sensationalism, however, did not find favour with her mother and it was to allay *her* fears about reputation and respectability that RW elected to use a pseudonym. When she picked the name *Rebecca West* (a character in Ibsen's play *Rosmersholm*) she was not aware of the significance that would later be attached to her choice (Rebecca West was the mistress of a married man); on occasion she also wrote under the name Rachel East.

Her career in journalism flourished. Articles and reviews such as 'The Gospel according to Mrs Humphry Ward' (*Freewoman*, 15 February 1912) and '*Views and Vagabonds* by Rose Macaulay' (*Freewoman*, 21 March 1912) helped to establish her reputation as a shrewd literary critic as well as a wickedly amusing writer. Her review of H. G. Wells's novel *Marriage* prompted much merriment in many circles: 'he is the old maid among novelists,' she wrote of this eminent and ostensibly progressive man, 'even the sex obsession that lay clotted on *Ann Veronica* and *The New Machiavell* like cold white sauce was merely old maid's mania' (*Freewoman*, 21 March 1912).

Nothing was sacred. RW burst upon the scene and challenged convention to the core. She was the *enfant terrible*, an energizing and irreverent writer. George Bernard Shaw said of her that she could 'handle a pen as brilliantly as ever I could, and much more savagely'. She supported the suffragettes in the most outrageous fashion, reserving the right to be critical of their campaigns ('The poor dears are weak at metaphysics but they are doing their best to revolt.'). She supported Christabel Pankhurst's exposé of venereal disease and endorsed her slogan, 'Votes for Women – and Chastity for Men.' She aroused the wrath of the patriots when she wrote, 'We have asked men for votes, they have given us advice. At present they are also giving us abuse. I am tired of this running comment on the war like conduct of my sex, delivered with such insolent assurance and such self-satisfaction. So I am going to do it too. Men are poor stuff' (*Clarion*, 18 April 1913).

When the *Freewoman* collapsed, RW was distressed; when the *New Freewoman* made its appearance in June 1913, she was delighted and became assistant editor at £52 a year. Not that the euphoria lasted for long. She and Dora Marsden disagreed, mainly about the literary quality and content of the journal, and RW withdrew after four months – without taking any remuneration: 'As Miss Marsden has let me go, I think the least I can do is to go without looting the till.' But by this time she also had other sources of support. She was writing regularly for the *Clarion* and contributing book reviews for the *Daily News*. By the age of 21 she was a well-known, well-respected and well-paid social/political and literary commentator.

RW made the acquaintance of many of the leading figures of the period, H. G. Wells among them. A man of many mistresses, he was at first reluctant to become involved with the brilliant young woman who had so effectively mocked his work and who so admired him. RW was depressed; she and her mother went to Spain for a holiday, she wrote a story, 'At Vallodolid', about a young woman who attempted suicide. But in 1913 she and H. G. Wells (1866–1946) became lovers; their son Anthony was born in 1914.

This marked an extraordinarily difficult period for RW. She had no illusions about the way society treated unmarried mothers and illegitimate children and she did her best to protect her private life. This meant that she had to leave London, and she was psychologically as well as physically isolated. Despite the difficulties, personal and professional, she persevered with her writing. Though she had done extremely well in journalism, the genre did not satisfy her; she determined to do some serious writing. 1916 saw the publication of her study of Henry James and, although it did not sell well, it reinforced her reputation for dazzling defiance as she mocked the recently deceased master in wryly amusing terms. Then in 1918 her first novel, *The Return of the Soldier*, was published and was a considerable success in Britain and America; RW often encoded messages to H. G. Wells in her work (in this case there is even a character, 'Bert Wells'), and *The Return of the Soldier* has much to say about the nature of love, and parenthood.

Dissatisfied with the patchy nature of her relationship with H. G. Wells and her rural existence, she returned to London in 1919 to a more satisfying and satisfactory life. She worked on her second novel, *The Judge* (1922). It drew on her experiences of Edinburgh. Not only does the heroine deal with many of the problems that the author had encountered during this often painful period, she is also a young suffragette; much of the psychological force of the novel lies in the meeting between the older and the younger generation. She dedicated the novel to her mother.

At this time RW's relationship with H. G. Wells was difficult and often destructive. She portrayed much of the manipulative nature of their attachment in *Sunflower*, the novel that she worked on during the 1920s but which was not published until after her death. With its characterization of H. G. Wells as the ageing lover Essington, and with Lord Beaverbrook cast as the heroine's new lover, Francis Pitt (and with both readily identifiable), this was the sort of fiction that it was not politic to print. Apart from the insights it provides into the West-Wells affair – and the RW and Lord Beaverbrook relationship – the novel is a powerful and impressive study of some of the cruelties of love.

RW distanced herself from H. G. Wells. During the 1920s she led a very active social and literary life. Her witty, epigrammatical style was widely recognized and her perspicacious judgement widely appreciated on both sides of the Atlantic. In the United States she undertook lecture tours and had an arrangement with the New York *Herald Tribune* whereby she stayed for two months of the year in America writing book reviews; she also wrote for the *Bookman, Good Housekeeping,* and *Vanity Fair.* She was extremely well paid for her efforts.

Violet Hunt, Marie Belloc-Lowndes, Violet Trefusis, Fannie Hurst, Naomi Mitchison, and Anais Nin were among some of her friends, though she and Virginia Woolf were not particularly enamoured of each other. She gave enormous support to Emma Goldman when she left Russia. RW claimed to be a socialist and a feminist writer. She was a regular contributor to the feminist political periodical *Time and Tide* and it was at the home of fellow-contributors Vera Brittain and Winifred Holtby that she met her future husband Henry Andrews, whom she married in 1930.

Held up as a model of the new independent woman, RW was a prolific as well as an outspoken writer. *The Strange Necessity,* a book of essays, was published in 1928, and in 1929 a novel, *Harriet Hume,* which RW referred to as a fantasy rather than a novel; sometimes regarded as one of her lesser achievements by her critics, it was acknowledged as her favourite fictional work by the author. But it was *Black Lamb and Gray Falcon* (1941), her study of Yugoslavia, which put RW at the forefront of political commentary. *Ending in Earnest: A Literary Log* (1931), *St Augustine* (1933), and *The Thinking Reed* (1936) all helped to consolidate her reputation and to attest to her prodigious and talented efforts across genres. But the publications associated with war, with loyalty, law, and treason were the ones which placed her at the centre of the world of letters in the mid-twentieth century. There was some criticism of her imaginative leaps in *The Meaning of Treason* (1947) but it was partly because she took them that her work went beyond political reporting and became a literary exploration of the human condition.

In 1956 the novel *The Fountain Overflows* was published and proved to be her most popular work of fiction. Drawing again on some of her family experiences, the novel was a source of deep distress to Letitia Fairfield on whom it appears the talentless and torturous Cordelia was based. In *The Birds Fall Down* (1966), the last of her novels to be published before she died, RW returned to a representation of her father. *1900* was a book of reminiscences and the last that she published in her lifetime. Three novels were published posthumously, *This Real Night* (1984), *Cousin Rosamund* (1985), and the unfinished *Sunflower* (1986).

Few writers have written across so many genres and with such outstanding success. Yet despite the recognition, fame and fortune, little serious scholarly attention has been paid to RW's work. In comparison with some of her male peers of comparable achievement (such as Evelyn Waugh or Graham Greene) she has been accorded little significance in the modern world of letters, and this cannot be fully explained by reference to the quality of her literary contribution. The few studies there are tend to concentrate on her relationship with H. G. Wells rather than her writing; she is rarely included in contemporary literature courses in Britain or the United States. Yet much of her work is in print.

DALE SPENDER

Selected works: Henry James (1916); *The Return of the Soldier* (1918); *The Judge* (1922); *The Strange Necessity* (1928); *Harriet Hume* (1929); *War Nurse* (1930); *Ending in Earnest: A Literary Log* (1931); *St Augustine* (1933); *The Thinking Reed* (1936); *Black Lamb and Gray Falcon* (1941); *The Meaning of Treason* (1947); *A Train of Powder* (1955); *The Fountain Overflows* (1956); *The Court and the Castle* (1957); *The New Meaning of Treason* (1964); *Birds Fall Down* (1966); *1900* (1982); *This Real Night* (1984); *Cousin Rosamund* (1985); *Sunflower* (1986).
References: Glendinning, V., *Rebecca West: A Life* (1987); Ray, G. N., *H. G. Wells and Rebecca West* (1974).

Wharton, Anne
b. 1659, Ditchley(?), Oxfordshire; d. 29 October 1685, Adderbury, Oxfordshire
Poet, translator
During her brief life and for a few years following her death. AW was one of the most publicly honoured women poets of the Restoration. Her high position in society may have been partially responsible for the poems which Aphra Behn, Edmund Waller, Gilbert Burnet, and other prominent poets wrote in her honour, but her own poetry, scattered throughout the miscellanies of the day, merited the praises given to it.

Orphaned at birth, AW, the daughter of Sir Henry Lee and Anne Danvers, was co-heiress with her sister (Dryden's 'Eleanora') to extensive properties in Oxfordshire and around London. She was raised at Ditchley in Oxfordshire by her pious grandmother, Anne Wilmot, who was also the mother of the poet John Wilmot, Earl of Rochester. As a result of complex political and financial manoeuvres, AW was married at the age of 14 to the future Whig leader Thomas Wharton. By 1682, childless, ill, and unhappy, she appears to have devoted her life to her poetry and to the memory of her uncle Rochester. Edmund Waller and Bishop Gilbert Burnet were her most important poetic advisers after Rochester, but she also carried on literary correspondences with Aphra Behn, Robert Wolseley, and William Atwood. She also had the friendship and support of two other women poets in her own family, Rochester's wife Elizabeth and his daughter Anne. AW died, according to her grandmother, of a 'pox' contracted from her husband at Rochester's home at Adderbury when she was only 26 years old. Aphra Behn, John Dryden, and Nahum Tate were among the influential poets and editors who included her works in volumes published after her death.

Honoured for her piety, AW wrote at least four biblical paraphrases, and many contemporary readers considered her a pious version of Rochester. Her poems frequently display the agonized religious uncertainty typical of Rochester's work. Bishop Burnet scolded AW for writing the line 'In death's dark mists the working soul's dissolved'; the poem is now lost, and it is possible that AW suppressed it in response to his criticism. Although she could be gently satirical, AW's poetry is rarely inspired purely by social circumstances and it rarely sets a pastoral mood. 'To Melpomene Against Complaint' speaks openly against the contemporary style: 'Romantic Heroes may their Fancy please/ In telling of their Griefs to senseless trees. . . .' Most frequently she writes of her personal disillusionment and loneliness. In the progressive, dignified, rhetorical accumulations of the long paraphrases and the one 'translation' (of Ovid's 'Epistle of Penelope to Ulysses'), as well as in the short poems and songs, she appears to make an effort to control the desperate tedium of life by putting frames around the various unhappy elements of it. Her moral reaction to unjustified 'scorn', whether public or private, is apparent not only in her famous 'Elegy on the Earl of Rochester', but also in poems written to Behn and Wolseley in which she speaks of the special dangers that women face if their reputations do not meet the public's standards. Her poem 'Upon the Duke of Buckingham's Retirement' brings the problem of reputation into the political sphere.

AW's longest work, 'Love's Martyr, or Witt above Crowns', a blank verse tragedy withheld from publication in 1686, and indeed never published, combines love with political intrigue in the court of Augustus. Dedicated to Mary Howe, 'who alone makes the happiness of [her] life', the play takes a poet for its hero and appears to be ironically autobiographical, carrying its bitter tone from the first scene (where 'the rudest untaught things women and fools/ Will poets turn') through to the last where any tradition of poetic justice remains unsatisfied. SUSAN HASTINGS

Works: *Poems by Several Hands, And on Several Occasions. Collected by N. Tate* (1685); *Vinculum Societatis* (1687); *The Idea of Christian Love* (1688); *Lycidus, or, The Lover in Fashion* (1688); *Miscellany Poems on Several Occasions* (1692); *The Gentleman's Journal, or, The Monthly Miscellany* (1692); *A Collection of Poems by Several Hands Most of them Written by Persons of Eminent Quality* (1693); *The Temple of Death* (1695); *Examen Miscellaneum* (1702); (trans.), *Ovid's Epistles, Translated by Several Hands* (1712); *Whartoniana, or, Miscellanies in Verse and Prose by the Wharton family and Several Other Persons* (1727).

References: Anon., *The Life of Thomas, Marquess of Wharton* (1716); Carswell, J., *The Old Cause: Three Biographical Studies in Whiggism* (1954); *DNB*; Farley-Hills, D. (ed.), *Rochester: The Critical Heritage* (1972); Malcolm, J. P. (ed.), *Letters of the Reverend James Granger* (1805); Todd.

White, Antonia

b. 31 March 1889, Kensington; d. 10 April 1980, Sussex
Novelist

The most significant event of AW's childhood and perhaps of her life was the conversion to Catholicism of her father, Cecil George Botting when AW was 7, followed by the conversion of AW and her mother, Christina. At the age of 9 AW was sent to boarding school at the Convent of the Sacred Heart at Roehampton, Surrey. Although successful academically, AW felt uncomfortable both as a middle-class child among her social superiors, and as a convert among born Catholics. At the age of 15 she decided to write a novel chiefly designed to please her father by exemplifying his religious beliefs. The projected plot would have shown the novel's sinful characters experiencing a revelation and repentence. As AW recalled, 'I made everybody as wicked as possible. As I couldn't think of anything bad enough for them to do, I said they indulged in "nameless vices".' However the nuns discovered the novel after only five chapters had been written and expelled AW. Her father was enraged, and to the end of his life refused to discuss the incident. All these events are chronicled in her first published novel, *Frost in May* (1933). AW attributes her inability to write for some twenty years, until after her father's death, to his reaction to the event. She often remarked that she could never again write original work without feelings of guilt and anxiety.

From 1914 to 1916 she attended St Paul's Girls' School, and then became first a governess, then a teacher at a boys' school, and a civil servant, while working as a freelance writer of magazine stories and advertising copy. In 1919 she attended what is now the Royal School of Dramatic Art, and the following year toured playing ingenue roles. Her first marriage in 1921 ended in annulment in 1924; during this period she spent nine months in an asylum, and her mental breakdown is vividly described in *Beyond the Glass* (1954). Her second, more successful marriage, in 1924, was nevertheless annulled in 1929. During these years she became head woman copywriter in an advertising agency, and then spent six months as assistant to Desmond MacCarthy, the editor of *Life and Letters*. After the end of her second marriage, AW married the journalist, Tom Hopkinson, who encouraged her to write again, after he heard the first two chapters of a manuscript written when she was young. The completed novel was *Frost in May* and was published in 1933. In the same year AW became fashion editor of the *Daily Mirror* and drama critic of *Time and Tide*; she wrote no more novels until 1950. In 1937 she divorced Tom Hopkinson, and fifteen years elapsed between the first and last chapters of her second novel, *The Lost Traveller* (1950). She suffered from recurrent bouts of mental illness, and attributed her ultimate recovery to a prolonged Freudian analysis. At this time she lapsed from the Catholic Church, although she reconverted in 1940. *The Hound and the Falcon* is a collection of letters written in 1940 and 1941 to a fellow Catholic in which AW discusses her attitude to Catholicism. During the Second World War she worked for the BBC and then for the Political Intelligence Department of the Foreign Office. After the war, when she was experiencing financial difficulties, she was commissioned to translate a number of works from French, producing them at the rate of two or three a year. She soon found herself able to write original work again, and a trilogy based on her life after leaving the convent was published; *The Lost Traveller* (1950) took longest to write; *The Sugar House* (1952) and *Beyond The Glass* (1954) followed quickly.

It would be inaccurate to say that Catholicism is a major 'theme' of AW's; rather, it constitutes her world-view, her native language, and the lens through which she experiences love, sexuality, grief, her career, or her madness. *Frost in May* is an account of Nanda Gray's experience in a Catholic school from the ages of 9 to 13, and remains AW's best-known work. Elizabeth Bowen has remarked that it is both a girls' school story and a work of art. AW's writing is characteristically objective in its tone: it gives equal weight to school ceremonies and emotional upheavals. AW shows, through Nanda's eyes, how the ritual of the school creates an hermetically sealed atmosphere within which the young girls experience their own growing sense of the world. She also records the cruelties and inconsistencies of the nuns. The Mother Superior, who believes that Nanda's will must be broken, is pleased when Nanda's literary efforts are discovered, causing the girl to lose both her father's love and the school which has become of paramount value to her. It is apparent that even while Nanda questions and criticizes the details of her Catholic school environment, she loves it and accepts it as the only reality.

In her subsequent trilogy, AW changes the name of her heroine to Clara Batchelor, but the novels are clearly a continuation of *Frost in May*. The first of them, quoting Augustine, announces human separation as a central theme of this and AW's subsequent works. The book deals with Clara's confused ideas about sexuality and her longing for love. The novel portrays scenes from her parents' point of view as well as from Clara's, and both her father and her mother are seen as sexual beings. Clara adores her father but feels contempt for her mother. But it is her mother, sensitive to the subtleties of feeling, who understands the dangers of Clara's proposed marriage; her father, obsessed with his religion and his ideals, is blind to them. The novel also deals with Clara's love for the 10 year-old boy who is her charge. AW portrays the relationship of teenager to child with unusual complexity, and eventually, when the boy dies, poignancy. *The Sugar House* (1952) recounts Clara's unhappy romantic involvement with an actor, and then her unhappy marriage to Archie, the man she almost married in *The Lost Traveller*. Infantile and psychologically damaged by the war, he is an alcoholic, and the novel details the gradual disintegration of both Clara and Archie as well as of their marriage. *Beyond the Glass* (1954), perhaps her finest novel, deals with a perfect love affair, and then describes Clara's mental breakdown. Her visions, perceptions, the blanks in her memory, and her parents' emotional reactions are starkly and straightforwardly recounted. Like all her experiences, Clara's madness is subsumed in Catholicism; her hallucinatory visions and her fears are specifically Catholic. Her eventual recovery occurs with as little explanation as her original madness. The novel concludes AW's account of a young woman's development through a course of destruction and dissolution, having had all that she relied on stripped away.

MARTHA SATZ

Works: *Frost in May* (1933); *Three in a Room* (1947); *The Lost Traveller* (1950); *The Sugar House* (1952); *Beyond the Glass* (1954); *Strangers* (1954); *Minka and Curdy* (1957); *The Hound and the Falcon: The Story of a Reconversion to the Catholic Faith* (1965); *Living With Minka and Curdy: A Marmalade Cat and His Siamese Wife* (1970).

References: Bowen, E., 'Introduction' to *Frost in May* (1948); Callil, C., 'Introduction' to *The Lost Traveller, The Sugar House,* and *Beyond the Glass* (1979); *CA*; Drabble; Hynes, S., 'Reputations: Antonia White', *Times Literary Supplement,* (3 July 1969); Showalter, E., *A Literature of Their Own* (1977).

Whitney, Isabella

b. (probably) Cheshire; fl. 1567–73

Poet

Daughter of Geoffrey Whitney of Coole Pilate in Cheshire and sister of the Protestant poet Geoffrey Whitney whose *Choice of Emblems* was published in Antwerp in 1568, IW is the author of two books of poems, published in 1567 and 1573 by the London printer Richard Jones. Nine poems in Jones' collections *A Gorgeous Gallery of Gallant Inventions* (1578) and *A Handful of Pleasant Delights* (1566?, 1584) may also be by IW. In her poems we are told that IW's parents lived, at least for some time, in Smithfield in London; that she herself was 'bred' there (though her description of herself as George Mainwaring's 'Countrywoman' suggests she moved to London with her parents after having been born in Cheshire); and that she suffered some distress which caused her to leave London in 1573. Her not being named in her brother's will, written in 1600, may indicate that she was no longer living or that, as a result of marriage, she had assumed the name 'Eldershae' by that date.

Both of IW's books of poems consist of carefully crafted pieces the author of which intends to comment on – even subvert – London poetic and social mores. An introductory poem from 'The Printer to the Reader' of the 1567 *Copy of a letter* says 'this Treatise is, / both false and also true': 'the matter' (content, meaning), he explains, 'is true as many know: / And in the same, some fained tales, the Auctor doth bestow'. The explanation confuses, rather than clarifies, however, for it calls into question the issue of 'truth' in the volume. (Is the young gentlewoman who writes to her inconstant lover the 'real' IW or a persona whose story is as artificial as the poems her verses override? Or are the 'fained tales' to which the printer alludes the legends of figures like Helen, Cleopatra, and Penelope to which IW compares and contrasts her own story?) In the volume proper are two poems written in the person of IW paired with two poems in the same four-line stanza form by two male writers. 'W. G' and 'R. Witc'. The latter two poems are conventional in their complaints against women's inconstancy; IW's verses undermine that convention in witty and subtle ways.

The sweet Nosgay (1573) opens with 110 'Phylosophicall flowers' which, IW says in her introductory prose letter to George Mainwaring, 'be of anothers growing' but of her 'owne gathering and makeing vp'. In a verse letter, 'The Author to the Reader', IW names her source – '*Plat* his Plot' she says is the ground from which her nosegay comes; and she recommends that her readers 'repayre' themselves 'to Master *Plat* his ground' to find more flowers they might want to use for their own purposes. An examination of Hugh Plat's *Flouers of Philosophie* (1572) reveals IW's playful method here, for Plat had printed 883 maxims which were 'once most carefully planted in Rome by Seneca'. As Plat had rewritten Seneca's 'flowers', so IW transforms Plat's novel sentences into verse and arranges them in the coherent collection she calls her 'nosgay'. Completing the collection is, first, a series of verse letters to relatives and friends, answers to three of those epistles by T. B., and C. B., and G. W., and, finally, a witty 'Will and Testament' in which IW declares that even though she writes in a moment of distress, she has power over even London, for *she* will 'leave' to *it* 'Brave buildyngs', 'fayre streats', active commerce, houses for its residents, 'portions' for its prisoners, and money for its book binders and her own printer; she wishes 'good Fortune' to her city; and she concludes by dating her poem 'this, xx, of October' – the same date as the one on the introductory epistle written to Mainwaring from his 'welwillyng Countri-woman'. *A sweet Nosgay* is thus presented as a single day's work by an active poet with wide-ranging interests and abilities.   ELIZABETH H. HAGEMAN

Works: *The Copy of a letter, lately written in meeter, by a younge Gentilwoman: to her vnconstant Louer* (1567); *A Sweet Nosgay, Or pleasant posye: contayning a hundred and ten Phylosophicall flowers* (1573).

References: Beilin, E. V., *Redeeming Eve: Women Writers of the English Renaissance* (1987); *DNB*; Fehrenbach, R. J., 'Isabella Whitney (f. 1565–75) and the popular Miscellanies of Richard Jones', *Cahiers Elizabethains* 19 (1981) and 'Isabella Whitney, Sir Hugh Plat, Geoffrey Whitney, and "Sister Eldershae"', *English Language Notes* 21 (1983); Jones, A. R., 'Nets and bridles; early modern conduct books and sixteenth-century women's lyrics', in *The Ideology of Conduct: Essays in Literature and the History of Sexuality*, ed. N. Armstrong and L. Tennenhouse (1987); Travitsky, B., 'The Lady Doth Protest: Protest in the Popular Writings of Renaissance Englishwomen', *English Literary Renaissance* 14 (1984), 255–83, and 'The "Wyll and Testament" of Isabella Whitney', *English Literary Renaissance* 10 (Winter 1980), 76–95.

Wickham, Anna

b. 1884, Wimbledon, Surrey; d. April 1947, Hempstead

Poet

(Also wrote under Edith Harper, John Oland)

AW was born Edith Alice Mary Harper, the only daughter of a self-educated piano repairman, Geoffrey Harper, and his wife Alice Whelan. AW spent most of her girlhood in Australia, where she went to a convent school. At 10, she promised her father she would some day be a poet; later, she took her *nom de plume* after Wickham Terrace, Brisbane, where that 'curious and very emotional pact' was made. As a young woman, she taught elocution in Sydney. When she was 21, she studied drama at the Tree Academy of Acting in London; the following year, at the Paris Conservatoire, she took voice lessons in de Reszke's master-class. Privately, she wrote verse, as she had done since she was 6. According to her friend and editor R. D. Smith (whose 1984 Virago edition of AW's *Writings* adds approximately 100 previously unpublished poems to the total now in print), AW 'wrote compulsively, producing over 1,400 poems in her lifetime.' Of these, some 1,100 are extant, in print, manuscript, or type-script. While many recent reviewers of the expanded canon consider the greater part of her poetry slapdash, even 'appallingly amateurish' or 'wretchedly bad', they nearly unanimously assert that as a feminist voice she definitely com-manded and still deserves deep respect.

When her first volume of poetry, *Songs of John Oland*, was published (pseudo-nymously) in 1911 by a feminist vanity press, AW was 27, the mother of two small boys, and married to Patrick Hepburn, a lawyer and astronomer, whom she loved but who violently and jealously opposed her art. In 1914, after their 'bitterest clash' – caused by AW's insistence on writing to purge her intolerable feelings of oppression – and against Patrick's determined efforts to kill her poetic career, Harold Monro and Alida Klemantaski (owners of the highly regarded poetry Bookshop) printed nine of AW's poems in their collection *Poetry and Drama*; in the following year, the Poetry Bookshop published her second volume of verse, *The Contemplative Quarry*; and the year after that, Grant Richards brought out *The Man with a Hammer*. But it was not until 1921 that AW, at 37, achieved any recognition. That year AW published *The Little Old House*; and, in New York, Louis Untermeyer, recognizing a rare integrity in her poetry, arranged the joint publication of *Contemplative Quarry* and *Man with a Hammer*. Untermeyer compared AW to May Sinclair, Virginia Woolf, Rebecca West, Willa Cather, and Dorothy Richardson, admiring AW's 'vigor-ous self-examination'. In the same year AW's 4-year-old son died of scarlet fever; AW blamed herself, and temporarily stopped attempting to publish her work although she continued to write. By this time AW was moving in the literary circles of Rilke, Valéry, d'Annunzio, Colette, Pound, Proust, and Stein. D. H. Lawrence, Malcolm Lowry, and Dylan Thomas came often to visit. She was acquiring a firm reputation as a feminist symbol for daring to versify her often self-contradictory and nearly always iconoclastic views. Indeed, Humbert Wolfe paid AW the high compliment of including her name in his 1932 *Encyclo-pedia Britannica* (14th edn) article on British poetry, saying that her poems 'should be lived with like a great picture rather than caught like the colour of flowers'. John Gawsworth published a volume of her latest poetry in 1936 and included her work in two of his most important collections, *Edwardian Poetry* and *Neo-Georgian Poetry*, both published in 1937.

AW's best poetry is about a desire for freedom of expression. She wanted to create, spontaneously, a poetry as perfect as that for which others laboured. In 'Examination', AW wrote:

> If my work is to be good,
> I must transcend skill, I must master mood.
> For the expression of the rare thing in me
> Is not in *to do*, but deeper, in *to be*.

Her use of what one reviewer called 'plonking' rhythms is deceptive; she breaks all prosodic patterns at will and defends the practice in poems like 'The Egoist', where she writes, 'Of the dead poets I can make a synthesis,/ . . . But I will use the figure that is real/ For me, the figure that I feel'. Some of her best poems are metrically free, like 'Comment' ('Tone/ Is utterly my own . . .') and 'The Mill', a daringly original love poem; but the spontaneity she hoped for seems most fully achieved in short satirical pieces like 'The Housemaid', in lightly defiant lyrics like 'The Little Love', and in caustic verses such as 'The Tigress', 'Nervous Prostration', and 'The Boor's Wooing'.

AW's posthumously published *Fragment of An Autobiography: Prelude to a Spring Clean* (written in 1935) was probably not meant for public consumption, but it may prove in the long run her most enduring work. Here, her trenchant eye is perhaps in greatest evidence. In an equally incisive shorter prose piece, 'The Spirit of the Lawrence Women', AW draws as much from her insights into D. H. Lawrence's relations with real women as she does on her own psychoanalysis of his fictional ones.

Eccentric, fearless in her criticism of cant and repression, socially unruly, colourfully bohemian, given to loud, extemporaneous expressions of passionate intelligence, AW sometimes thought of herself as the prototypical woman. At one point, she said she wanted the following lines at the beginning of all her books:

> Here is no sacrificial I,
> Here are more I's than yet were in one human,
> Here I reveal our common mystery:
> I give you *woman*. (*Writings*)

At the end of her autobiography, she summed up another, less positive if more revealing sense of self: 'As I look back over this long and melancholy road, I am ashamed. I try to think why I endured so much futile pain, and the truth is that I believed in pain . . . that I was working out some salvation. Nearly all the relationships of my life had been tawdry, insincere and unsatisfactory. Many people were attracted to me, but I was intimate with nobody. I was not sufficiently like anyone to invite that self-identification which is the essence of true friendship and love' (*Writings*). In such dark moods, AW was fiercely self-critical, capable of seeing her own writings as 'bunk' and 'rubbish', fully and prophetically aware that she would not be deemed a major poet, for as she put it:

> The tumult of my fretted mind
> Gives me expression of a kind;
> But it is faulty, harsh, not plain –
> My work has the incompetence of pain. (Self Analysis)

In 1947, having ministered to her three grown sons all through their partici-pation in the war, she hanged herself.   R. VICTORIA ARANA
Works: *The Seasons – Speaking Tableaux for Girls (100 Performers) (1901?)*; *Wonder*

Eyes – A Journey to Slumbertown (For 80 Little People) 1901?); *Songs of John Oland*
(1911); *The Contemplative Quarry* (1915); *The Man with a Hammer* (1915); *The
Contemplative Quarry and The Man with a Hammer* (1921); *The Little Old House*
(1921); *Thirty-Six New Poems*, ed. J. Gawsworth (1936); *Selected Poems* (1971);
The Writings of Anna Wickham: Free Woman and Poet, ed. R. D. Smith (1984);
'I and my Genius', *Women's Review* 5 (March 1986).
References: Dehn, P., Interview in *Sunday Referee* (12 June 1935); Enright, D.
J., 'Pride of ink', *Listener* (17 May 1984); Fullbrook, K., article in *British Book
News* (December 1984); Garnett, D., 'Introduction' to *Selected Poems* (1971);
Hill, F., article in *The Times Educational Supplement* (30 November 1984);
Kunitz; Smith, R. D., memoir in *The Writings of Anna Wickham* (1984); Unter-
meyer, L., 'Introduction' to *The Contemplative Quarry and The Man with the
Hammer* (1921); Untermeyer, L., *Lives of the Poets* (1959).

Willard, Barbara
b. 12 March 1909, Brighton, Sussex
Novelist, writer for children
BW was born into a theatrical family. Her father was an actor by profession,
her mother a keen amateur actress, and an uncle on her father's side was
an actor-manager. BW was educated at the Convent of La Sainte Union in
Southampton and then took up acting as a career. She worked for literary
agents as a play reader and also for 20th Century Fox in their European story
department before becoming a full-time writer. She lives in the Ashdown
Forest, scene of many of her most successful books. In 1974 she received the
Guardian Award for her novel *The Iron Lily* (1973), one of the much acclaimed
Mantlemass series.

BW has reversed the pattern of a number of contemporary novelists, for
example Penelope Lively and Jane Gardam, who served their apprenticeship
writing for children and then successfully expanded into the adult field. Her
apprentice-output from 1930 to 1954 she describes as 'just novels' for adults,
and expresses satisfaction that they are no longer available. Once BW recognized
that she had found her true métier, she quickly developed into a versatile writer.
She has successfully written for young readers who need simple though stylishly
told stories which are emotionally and imaginatively satisfying despite their
small compass, such as *The Penny Pony* (1961), *The Reindeer Slippers* (1970),
and *The Dragon Box* (1972). For older readers, there are family adventures
or sensitive studies of intergeneration relationships with either contemporary
settings, such as *Charity at Home* (1965), or historical ones, such as *A Grove of
Green Holly* (1967). This last is tautly plotted and vividly conveys the hazards
of an actor's life in the years of Puritan theatre closures.

It is with the Mantlemass series of historical novels that BW has reached full
maturity as a writer. These novels have been rightly hailed as a land-mark in
historical fiction and have removed the barrier between adult and juvenile
fiction. The first of the series, *The Lark and the Laurels* (1970), is still clearly a
children's book, in the directness of its themes and its narrative stance. Set in
the time of Henry VII, it describes how Cecily, uprooted from her London
home and sent to live with relatives, the Mallerys, in Ashdown Forest, learns
to be herself rather than a pawn in her father's ambitious moves. As the
series has continued, tracing the developments of the family, its intermarriages,
dealings in horse breeding and iron foundries, with both losses and successes,
the scope and depth of the books has increased too. From *A Cold Wind Blowing*

(1972) onwards, the novels combine intriguing plots, and subtle characterizations of both young and adult figures, set against a beautifully observed forest
background. As well as tracing how family traits are handed on, modified, or
exaggerated through the generations, BW also explores deftly and sometimes
passionately the effects of major social or political events on the lives of ordinary
people. Abiding themes of perennial interest are the need for roots and the
importance of family, whether for creative or destructive ends.

The novels, though not written in chronological order, cover the years up
to 1660. In *Harrow and Harvest* (1974), Mantlemass, the central family home,
is burnt down. Internal divisions and disloyalties, triggered by the Civil War,
have finally broken the family and its last direct descendants leave for the New
World. The mood of the series changes with each novel. *A Cold Wind Blowing*,
set in the time of the dissolution of the monasteries, has as its centre the growing
love between the son of the family, Piers, and a refugee from a sacked nunnery,
forbidden to renounce her vows, though no longer able to be a nun. The tragic
conclusion of the couple's love, poignantly though unsentimentally depicted,
highlights how easily fanaticism can warp or destroy people. *The Iron Lily* ends
on a buoyant note, with the discovery by the central figure, Lilias, of her true
links with the Mallery family. During the course of events, BW provides a
fascinating picture of Elizabethan iron working, and in Lilias herself creates a
powerful, entirely credible woman, proud yet caring, sometimes hard and
unlovable.

BW has avoided the twin hazards of historical writing, presenting modern
characters in fancy dress, or quaint puppet-like figures. Her descriptions are
vivid, yet economical, so the reader grows to know the forest, an important
element in all the novels, intimately yet unobtrusively. The mood and pace of
the narrative fluctuates easily with the nature of the events portrayed. Dialect
is discreetly employed to add colour and conviction. BW's stage-experience
may have aided the skill with which she matches conversational manner to
personality. A more recent novel, *The Queen of Pharisees' Children* (1983), shows
the same talents used to create a very different work. Still set in the past, it
charts the experiences of a family living wild in the forest, and what happens
when their father is imprisoned for vagrancy.   JUDITH ALDRIDGE

Selected works: *Love in Ambush* (with E. H. Devas) (1930); *Ballerina* (1931);
Candle Flame (1932); *As Far as in Me Lies* (1936); *Set Piece* (1938); *Portraits of
Philip* (1950); *He Fought for His Queen* (1954); *Son of Charlemagne* (1959); *The
Penny Pony* (1961); *Stop the Train!* (1961); *The Summer with Spike* (1961); *Duck
on a Pond* (1962); *The Dippers and the High-Flying Kite* (1963); *Three and One to
Carry* (1964); *Charity at Home* (1965); *The Grove of Green Holly* (1967); *My Pet
Club* (1967); *Hurrah for Rosie!* (1968); *The Toppling Towers* (1969); *Priscilla
Pentecost* (1970); *The Reindeer Slippers* (1970); *The Lark and the Laurel* (1970);
The Dragon Box (1972); *A Cold Wind Blowing* (1972); *The Iron Lily* (1973);
Bridesmaid (1976); *The Convent Cat* (1976); *The Gardner's Grandchildren* (1978);
Spell Me a Witch (1979); *Queen of the Pharisees' Children* (1983); *Ned Only* (1984).
References: Moss, E. (ed.), *Children's Books of the Year* (1972, 1973, 1974, 1977,
1978, 1981).

Williams, Helen Maria
b. 1762(?) London; d. 1827, Paris
Chronicler, poet, novelist
HMW was the daughter of a Welsh army officer and a Scottish mother, Helen
Hay. Her father died when she was young and the mother and two daughters
moved from London to Berwick-on-Tweed, where HMW was educated at
home. From an early age she must have been a voracious reader of sentimental
writing, for her first literary efforts display its influence in their fluent, conventional diction, their parade of feminine sensibility and their pathetic tableaux of
family distress. With her long poem *Edwin and Eltruda* completed in 1781, she
set out for London, where her mother and sister later joined her. Andrew
Kippis, a well-known Dissenting minister, helped her to publish her poem,
which was pleasantly received by London literary society, Gregarious and
sociable, HMW made many acquaintances, some of whom, like Fanny Burney,
thought her insufferably affected, while others, like Mrs Montagu and Samuel
Johnson, found her warm and charming. She also acquired literary correspondents, for example Anna Seward and Robert Burps. At this stage her liberal
Dissenting views agreed with those of her readership; idealizing the figures of
the slave and political victim, she lamented slavery and colonial exploitation in
such poems as *Peru* (1784), and she imagined social progress in terms of individual benevolence. In 1786 she published a collection of poems which included
her 'Sonnet to Twilight', much admired by the young Wordsworth, who
addressed a sonnet of praise to her as the epitome of the genteel and sensitive
female poet. Throughout her life she wrote sentimental, occasional and
devotional poems, two examples of which – 'Whilst Thee I See' and 'My
God! All Nature Owns Thy Sway' – became well-known hymns. In 1790 her
sentimental novel *Julia* appeared; although showing some formal skill, it was
condemned in a review by Mary Wollstonecraft as too simple in its characterization of the incorruptibly virtuous heroine.

Julia was interrupted by a poetic piece called 'The Bastille' which extends
HMW's libertarian enthusiasm to the French Revolution. But her praise is given
resonance by her acquaintance with an actual French political victim, Madame
du Fossé, the wife of a French aristocrat imprisoned by his father. When the
father died at the beginning of the Revolution, the du Fossés invited the
Williams sisters to France; except for a few short absences, HMW was to spend
the remainder of her life there. Immediately she began her series of accounts
of political and social events, the first volume, *Letters Written from France in the
Summer of 1790*, including the dramatic story of the suffering du Fossés. The
work, much read in England, made the early Revolution into a sentimental
event in which the nation experienced a change of heart expressed in its great
communal festivals. Over the next three decades HMW would treat in her
sometimes over-gushing, sometimes astute way the political events of Revolutionary and imperial France as she experienced them. At first she was
acquainted with both Jacobins and Girondists, but, as their positions hardened,
she sided with the latter, whose leader, Madame Roland, became her friend
and a noble character in her chronicles. Her death at the hands of the Jacobins
is movingly recorded by HMW who visited her in prison. In 1793 HMW and
her family were imprisoned after the general arrest of British subjects; they
were freed through Madame du Fossé's nephew, Athanase Coquerel, who
later married HMW's sister. Although HMW met and entertained English
Revolutionary sympathizers such as Paine and Wollstonecraft, more radical

thinkers than the Bluestockings and Dissenters with whom she had mixed in England, she continued to see political events in sentimental and personal terms, and there is no effort to comprehend the economic basis of the Revolution or the Jacobin Terror, for which she was unprepared and which filled her with extreme horror. Her judgements remained spontaneous and emotional, and she sought in the atrocities she related for examples of individual distress and heroism, especially in female victims. Jacobin cruelty formed the main subject of the four volumes of *Letters from France 1792–6*, which were published like most of her letters first in single volumes and then in a collected edition. In 1794, fearing reprisals for her anti-Jacobin writings, she went to Switzerland where she arrived just before the French intervention, prompting some speculation, fuelled by the French surveillance of her during the Jacobin and Napoleonic regimes, that she might have been a spy for England. Her six months in Switzerland were described in *A Tour of Switzerland* (1798).

HMW's failure to retreat from the libertarian principles of the Revolution despite the Terror alienated many of her liberal English friends like Anna Seward and Mrs Piozzi. Her readership was further outraged by her association with John Hurford Stone, her literary collaborator in a military account in one of her volumes and possibly, later, her husband. Her long association with Stone, a divorced man who was considered a traitor in England, provoked much abuse; the conservative *Anti-Jacobin* portrayed HMW as Lechery personified, while Horace Walpole dismissed her as a scribbling trollop.

After the fall of Robespierre HMW returned to Paris where she continued entertaining and publishing letters. She translated *Paul et Virginie* and later the seven volumes of Humboldt's travels. Her sister died in 1798, leaving two sons whom HMW raised according to her own Dissenting views; both became noted French Protestants. In her later volumes, far less popular in England than her earlier ones, HMW portrayed life under the inefficient Directory and described her initially favourable and subsequently unfavourable impressions of Napoleon, who detained her and her family for a day because of a complimentary reference to British sea power in an ode on the Peace of Amiens. In 1801 she returned to fiction with *Perourou, the Bellows-Mender*, a lively story of a mismatched pair, later adapted for the stage by Edward Bulwer Lytton. During 1803 she edited the forged correspondence of Louis XVI, which she accepted as authentic, and was much abused in England for her republican observations. By 1815 she could be wry about her earlier enthusiasm for liberty but she continued to hold her liberal principles and she welcomed the end of empire. She was still a determined hostess, despite financial difficulties brought about by her own falling sales and by Stone's ill-judged publishing ventures. In 1819 her last work, *Letters on Events Which Have Passed in France since the Restoration in 1815*, completed her account of nearly three decades of French history. In 1818 Stone died and after a short period in Amsterdam, HMW spent her last years in Paris on a small pension from her nephew.   JANET TODD

Works: *Edwin and Eltruda* (1782); *An Ode on the Peace* (1783); *Peru* (1784); *Poems* (1786); *Julia* (1790); *Letters from France 1792–6: Letters Written from France in the Summer of 1790*; *Letters from France Containing Many New Anecdotes*; *Letters from France Containing a Great Variety of Interesting and Original Information*; *Letters from France 1795–6: Letters Containing a Sketch of the Politics of France 1794*; *Letters Containing a Sketch of the Scenes*; a further vol. was added to the 2nd edn; *A Tour of Switzerland* (1798); *Sketches of the State of Manners and Opinions in the French Republic towards the Close of the Eighteenth Century* (1801); *Perourou, the Bellows-Mender* (1801); (ed.), *The Political and Confidential Correspondence of Louis*

XVI (1803); *A Narrative of Events Which Have Taken Place in France from the Landing of Napoleon Bonaparte . . . till the Restoration of Louis XVIII* (1815); *On the Late Persecution of the Protestants in the South of France* (1816); *Letters on Events Which Have passed in France since the Restoration in 1815* (1819); *Souvenirs de la Révolution Française*, trans., C. A. Coquerel from Williams's manuscripts. *A Residence in France during the Years 1792, 1793, 1794, and 1795; Described in a Series of Letters from an English Lady . . .* (1797) is attributed to HMW but is unlikely to be hers.

References: Adams, M. R., 'Helen Maria Williams and the French Revolution', in *Wordsworth and Coleridge Studies in Honor of G. M. Harper* (1939); Allibone; *DNB*; Funck-Brentano, F., 'Introduction' to *La Regne de Robespierre* (1909); *Memoirs of the Reign of Robespierre* (1929); Kurtz, B. P. and Autrey C. C. (eds), *Four New Letters of Mary Wollstonecraft and Helen Maria Williams* (1937); Todd, J., 'Introduction' to *Letters from France 1790–95* (1976); Todd J., *Sensibility: An Introduction* (1986); Woodward, L. D., *Une anglaise amie de la révolution française: Hélène-Maria Williams et ses amies* (1930).

Winchilsea, Anne Finch, Countess of

b. April 1661; d. 5 August 1720, London
Poet

C of W, born to an aristocratic family in 1661, lost her father, William Kingsmill, when she was an infant, her mother, Anne, when she was 3, and her stepfather when she was 10. By 1683, she was living at court as maid of honour to Mary of Modena, the wife of James, Duke of York, where she met Heneage Finch, gentleman of the bedchamber to James, and married him in 1684; the marriage proved happy, although childless. The Finches remained at court although C of W resigned her position. After the deposition and exile of James II in 1688, refusing to take the oath of allegiance to the new sovereigns, William and Mary, the Finches were obliged to retire from public life. In 1690 they found a permanent home when the young Earl of Winchilsea, Heneage Finch's nephew, invited them to his family seat in Kent, where they spent the rest of their lives, the C of W taking walks in the countryside and writing, whilst Heneage pursued his scholarly interests. They were surrounded by a congenial social group, including many intelligent women to whom C of W wrote poems expressing warm affection or thanks for wise guidance. Others of her poems show her appreciative awareness of the work of contemporary women poets such as Aphra Behn, Katherine Philips, and Elizabeth Rowe. In 1712, when the young earl died, Heneage succeeded to the title and Anne Finch thus became Countess of Winchilsea.

The Finches spent their winters in London and knew the leading Augustan wits. Gay included C of W among Pope's friends in 'Mr Pope's Welcome from Greece'; Swift complimented her in 'Apollo Outwitted' and mentioned her in his *Journal to Stella*. She exchanged verses with Pope about his belittlement of women in 'The Rape of the Lock'. She was a friend of the playwright Nicholas Rowe and wrote a humorous epilogue to his *Jane Shore*. C of W began writing poems in the 1680s, but kept them private, as she noted in the preface to her manuscript volume of poems, lest she be ridiculed as 'a Versifying Maid of Honour.' Several traditional songs and religious pieces by her appeared, anonymously, in various anthologies during the 1690s and early 1700s; her Pindaric ode 'The Spleen' was published in 1701 and often reprinted. In 1713 she published her *Miscellany Poems*, some copies of which bear her name, while others are simply ascribed to 'a lady'. She also left a carefully arranged manuscript volume of poems, evidently hoping that it would be published after her death; but it remained unpublished until 1903. C of W generally published those of her poems which voiced conventionally acceptable attitudes, while she withheld those which were concerned with personal feeling or contained feminist protest against the contemporary disparagement of women and women poets. 'Mercury and the Elephant', which prefaces *Miscellany Poems*, is characterized by urbane self-disparagement. 'The Introduction' to her manuscript volume, on the other hand, bitterly complains of critics who automatically sneer at poems 'by a woman writt' because they believe that woman's duty is primarily to please and accommodate men. The poem goes on to protest that women are made foolish by poor education rather than nature, but concludes with regret that it is safer for an imaginative woman to conceal her talent. Her poem 'To Mr F., Now Earl of W', which artfully presents her love for her husband through a playful classical allegory, was published; but her more direct expression of love in 'A Letter to Dafnis' remained in manuscript.

C of W was encouraged to write, and even to publish, by her husband and friends; and her social position protected her from the criticisms levelled at women who wrote for their living. Nevertheless, even her unpublished works reveal a tormenting ambivalence about her poetic vocation. She would declare that writing poetry was her only escape from the depression that recurrently afflicted her (as in 'Ardelia to Melancholy'), and would ask indignantly why women poets should be denied pen and ink, like state prisoners (as in 'Ardelia's Answer to Ephelia'). Yet in 'The Preface' and 'The Apology' she described her writing as a foolish weakness. She was, however, consistently scornful of the trivial activities in which eighteenth-century ladies were expected to find fulfilment. C of W wrote in a wide variety of favoured Augustan genres, including love lyrics, fables, satires, Miltonic burlesques, odes, dramas, and meditations on religion and nature. Many of these poems show a poetic sensibility which distinguishes her from her contemporaries. Her most famous poem, 'A Nocturnal Reverie' (admired by Wordsworth), delicately evokes the sights, sounds, and smells of a serene moonlit night; unlike much Augustan nature poetry, it has little recourse to formal moralizing or conventional diction. Her love poems, unusually, are written to her husband rather than the casual lover addressed by most of her male contemporaries. Some of these poems make artful use of classical convention ('To Mr Finch') or elaborate metaphor ('An Invitation to Dafnis'), while others express feeling plainly and simply ('A Letter to Dafnis'). Her graceful songs range from witty exercises on conventional themes to light feminist protest: in 'The Unequal Fetters' she points out that marriage, stereotypically a constraint on men, is in fact more destructive to the natural freedom of women. 'The Spleen' stands out among other eighteenth-century treatments of the subject for its depth and seriousness: instead of merely deriding those who suffer from 'the spleen' (depression without apparent cause, producing hypochondria, ill-temper, and despondency), she distinguishes genuine from affected spleen and describes its symptoms with the understanding of one afflicted by them.

C of W often satirized women (as well as men), but recognized that women's failings were often socially induced. Unlike most of her contemporaries, she measured women against a human rather than a narrowly sexual ideal. In her most sustained satire, 'Ardelia's Answer to Ephelia', she contrasts Almeria, a typical fashionable lady, who spends her life flirting, shopping, criticizing other women, and devising creative new ways to place her facial patches, with Ardelia, a rational and moral woman.   KATHARINE ROGERS

Works: *The Spleen: A Pindarique Ode* (1709); *The Poems of Anne Countess of Winchilsea*, ed. M. Reynolds (1903); 'Poems by Anne Finch', ed. E. Hampsten, *Women's Studies* 7 (1980).

References: Allibone; Ballard; Brower, R. A., 'Lady Winchilsea and the poetic tradition of the seventeenth century', *Studies in Philology* 42 (1945); *DNB*; Drabble; Messenger, A., 'Publishing without perishing: Lady Winchilsea's *Miscellany Poems* of 1713', *Restoration: Studies in English Literary Culture, 1660–1700* 5 (1981); Messenger, A., 'Selected nightingales and an "Augustan" sensibility', *English Studies in Canada* 6 (1980); Murry, J. M., 'Introduction' to *Poems (Selected)* (1928); Rogers, K. M., 'Anne Finch, Countess of Winchilsea: An Augustan woman poet', in *Shakespeare's Sisters*, ed. S. Gilbert and S. Gubar (1979); Todd.

Wingfield, Sheila

b. 23 May 1906, Hampshire

Poet

(Also writes under Sheila Powerscourt)

The daughter of a landowner who fought in both the Boer War and the First World War, SW was educated at home in London in her early childhood by a succession of governesses. As a child she was harshly treated by her mother: she commented in her volume of autobiographical sketches, *Sun Too Fast* (1974), that 'My chief objection to the theory of an afterlife is the prospect of meeting my mother.' Later she was sent to Roedean School, in Sussex, and subsequently to a finishing school in Paris. On her return she describes herself as 'acting a triple role to please my father. This was, first, wife-surrogate in the form of hostess and housekeeper in his London house; second, fashionable daughter; and, third, substitute son. . . .' Even as a child SW was compelled to conceal her interest in reading and writing poetry from her parents, who disapproved of it, and as an adult she remained isolated from the literary movements and personalities of her time. This isolation continued after her marriage to the Hon. Mervyn Wingfield in 1932, for her husband also disliked her meeting literary acquaintances. Nevertheless, SW's first volume of poetry appeared in 1938. She has continued to publish since, despite the serious illness with which she has struggled for the last thirty years.

SW's best-known yet nevertheless little-known poem, *Beat Drum, Beat Heart* (1946), is an extended meditation divided into four linked and contrasted sections: 'Men in War', 'Men at Peace', 'Women in Love', and 'Women at Peace'. The function of this division by gender is not to offer any feminine consolation for the masculine experience of war. Rather, the familiar prayer for an end to all war which appears at the close of 'Men in War', 'I swear, I pray, never again', is startlingly and directly paralleled by the request for an end to 'love' with which 'Women in Love' culminates: 'For pity's sake, no more.' This is only one of a series of analogies between military and psychological violence. 'Women in Love' compares a group of apparently domestic or private experiences to military disasters: 'These are my Flanders, Valley Forge, Carthage.' The corresponding sections 'Men at Peace' and 'Women at Peace' argue the impossibility of making reparation for the violence done in love and war: the prayer at the end of 'Women in Love' to 'Renew me, make me whole' appears desperately tentative beside the description of:

> How we hate each other
> In a narrow room,
> We terrible knitters
> Under the lamp.

SW's narrative voice varies through the poem from a first-person singular which is on occasion sharply individualized to, in 'Men in War', a collective subject which acts as a transhistorical essence manifesting itself in violent phenomena:

> We are the men who pulled Lorca
> Between shrubs, beyond night-shadowed houses;
> We are a man dragged and killed on the outskirts
> Of a town in Spain.

At other times SW uses collective historical experience less experimentally: the narrator of 'Women in Love' invokes a catalogue of famous predecessors, whilst 'Men in War' juxtaposes narratives of military experience since the Alexandrian wars of conquest.

An interest in a long historical, and occasionally prehistorical or archaeological, perspective is a feature of much of SW's work. This perspective is rarely a nostalgic one: instead it is used to indicate the permanence of suffering. 'Sonnet' from *The Leaves Darken* (1964) is written in explicit justification of her historical and mythological figures: their sufferings are 'never outdated,/ But horrible as streets of slated/ Victorian grime . . .'. Her conception of history throughout her work is one in which evil and pain are ineradicable elements for which any remedy can only be transcendental. Her interest in the natural world is an equally anti-Romantic one: her nature is more often a source of emblems or similes for moral qualities than the scene of more generalized meditation.

SW's poetry is markedly traditional in form. She rarely dispenses with either rhyme or metre, but employs an unusual variety of formal and metrical schemes. Many of these indicate the influence of seventeenth-century models upon her work: one of her most favoured forms is the Jonsonian or Marvellian octosyllabic couplet, whilst other poems, like 'Janus' from *A Kite's Dinner* (1954), employ the multiple short-rhymed lines characteristic of much seventeenth-century devotional poetry. A regard for such poetry might be thought to link her with Eliot and other early twentieth-century admirers of metaphysical verses; but, whilst some of her early work has an imagist brevity, she is generally uninterested in twentieth-century experiments with syntax and punctuation. Her occasional departures from this practice are the more effective for being sparing: the several entirely unpunctuated lyrics in *Her Storms* (1977) form a striking contrast with the rest of the volume.   SIMON JARVIS

Works: *Poems* (1938); *Beat Drum, Beat Heart* (1946); *A Cloud Across The Sun* (1949); *Real People* (1952); *A Kite's Dinner* (1954); *Sun Too Fast* (1974); *Admissions* (1977); *Her Storms* (1977); *Collected Poems* (1983).

References: Fraser, G. S., 'Preface' to *Collected Poems* (1983); *The Times Literary Supplement* (2 June 1978).

Winter, John Strange

b. 13 January 1856, York; d. 13 December 1911, Putney, London
Novelist
(Also wrote under Violet Whyte)

JSW (Henrietta), was the only daughter of Emily Catherine Cowling and Henry Vaughan Palmer, rector of St Margaret's, York. Her father belonged to three generations of military men and before entering the Church had served as an officer in the Royal Artillery. She referred to herself as 'a restless, impatient sort of child, who tired of everything before it was half done', but she had a voracious appetite for books and, unusual among Victorian children, enjoyed unrestricted reading. From the age of 11 she was educated at Bootham House School in York, and in her late teens began to contribute sketches to the *Family Herald* under the pseudonym of 'Violet Whyte'. Her father died when she was 21, after which she began a writing career in earnest. 'John Strange Winter', the name of one of her own fictional characters, was adopted at the advice of her publishers who insisted that works so military as *Cavalry Life* (1881) and *Regimental Legends* (1883) should be presented to readers as the work of a man.

In February 1884, at Fulford, York, she married Arthur Stannard, a civil engineer who had once served under General Gordon. After settling in London JSW began to write prolifically. Her first commercial success was *Bootles' Baby: A Story of the Scarlet Lancers* (1885), serialized in the *Graphic* and then released in the popular One Shilling Volume series. The novel was dramatized and performed at the Globe Theatre in London in 1889 and the play later went on tour. The characters of Bootles (Captain Algernon Ferrers) and his adopted child Mignon were to reappear in later stories. In a letter to *The Daily Telegraph* John Ruskin complimented JSW as 'The author to whom we owe the most finished and faithful rendering ever yet given of the character of the British soldier'. She visited Ruskin in Sandgate in 1888 and became a close correspondent. In 1891 she founded the *Golden Gates* magazine (subsequently *Winter's Weekly*), the first weekly periodical to be exclusively owned, edited and published by a popular novelist. She was the first president of the Writers Club (1892) and president of the Society of Women Journalists (1901–3). The later years of her life were spent in Dieppe.

An intimate knowledge of army life and ways gleaned from her own upbringing in the garrison town of York pervades almost every published work by JSW. Not surprisingly, her fiction is frequently preoccupied with the wives and children of military heroes. Her stories undoubtedly served to reify the patriotic and militaristic cravings of a nation of which John Ruskin asked, 'Are we ceasing to be English?', and in which one publisher boldly presented the stories as 'portraits from Life of our British-born sons of Mars'. Indirectly, too, her stories served a social purpose: her indignant comments on overloaded hackney carriages with broken-down horses (*He Went for a Soldier*, 1890) led to the passing of by-laws to bring such vehicles under effective police supervision. Her novel *A Soldier's Children* (1892) was sold for the benefit of the Victoria Hospital for Children. Part of her popularity must, however, be attributed to the light-hearted simplicity and tender pathos of her writing. She expressed a preference for Anglo-Saxon over Latinate diction and told an interviewer from the *Young Woman*, 'My plots are not intricate, and, as far as possible, I use colloquial and modern English.' In more ambitious moods, as in chronicling the Sepoy Mutiny of 1857 in *A Siege Baby* (1887), she was able to combine a sweeping imaginative reconstruction of historical events with an acute observation of the familiar and the commonplace. In her view of women's rights she was far from radical, and those novels which detail the matrimonial incidents of a military career have a strong tendency to subordinate the cultural aspirations of women to their husbands' less desirable interests and activities. The result, as one cautious publisher announced, 'may not altogether please the more ultramontane members of the Pioneer Club.'   STEPHEN REGAN

Selected Works: *Cavalry Life* (1881); *Regimental Legends* (1883); *Bootles' Baby: A Story of the Scarlet Lancers* (1885); *Mignon's Secret* (1885); *A Siege Baby* (1887); *That Imp* (1887); *He Went for a Soldier* (1890); *A Blameless Woman* (1895); *The Strange Story of My Life* (1896); *A Summer Jaunt* (1899).

References: Capes, B. and Eglinton, C. (eds.), *Men and Women of the Day*, vol. 3 (1890); *NWAD*; Parker, P. L., 'The author of *Bootles' Baby* at home: an interview with John Strange Winter', *Young Woman*, 3 (1894).

Wollstonecraft, Mary
b. 27 April 1759, London; d. 10 September 1797, London
Polemical writer, novelist

MW was the second of seven children. Her grandfather had been a wealthy weaver and her father was eager to rise in the world as a gentleman farmer. But he had little talent for farming or business, and his fortunes and status declined; he and his family moved back and forth across England and Wales trying to halt the decline. Between the ages of 9 and 15 MW lived in Beverley in Yorkshire where she formed a close female friendship and gained some education. In later life she would be bitter about her family, deeply resenting her mother's favouritism of the eldest son, buttressed by the social custom that 'the first-born son is in all Christian countries the head of the house, and that the rest must scramble through the world as well as they can'. When she was 16 living in Hoxton near London she met Fanny Blood, a genteel but poor young lady with whom she contracted a close friendship. The two girls planned to live and work together, and it was with this idea in mind that MW at 19 left her family to begin earning her living. Her first position was as a companion to a wealthy widow in Bath, a position which gave her a chance to survey the frivolous life of the more privileged classes. She was recalled home by the ill-health of her mother who died shortly afterwards. For the rest of her life MW was to feel a mother's responsibility for the younger children whose lives she carefully but sometimes tactlessly tried to manage.

After her mother's death she moved in with Fanny Blood and saw real poverty at close quarters. Her life with the family was interrupted by the depression of her sister Eliza after the birth of her first child. MW resolutely interpreted the situation in political terms and abducted her sister from the husband's house, knowing, she said, that she would be accused of being the 'shameful incendiary' in the affair. With her sisters and Fanny Blood she opened a school in 1784. She chose Newington Green, the centre of an intellectual Dissenting community, which included the famous polemicist Richard Price with whom she became acquainted. The school foundered when MW decided to rush to Portugal where her friend Fanny, who had recently married, was about to have a child. Knowing her friend to be consumptive, MW feared the worst; she arrived just in time to witness Fanny's death. Returning to England, she speedily wrote a book on the education of girls, *Thoughts on the Education of Daughters* (1787). It earned her ten guineas which she gave to Fanny's impoverished parents. She herself took a post as a governess in Ireland in the home of Lord and Lady Kingsborough and began the sort of dependent life that she had already described as 'disagreeable'. During her time in Ireland she wrote *Mary: A Fiction* (1788), a novel about her friendship with Fanny, giving a self-pitying account of her own childhood and revealing her resentment of trivial aristocratic women.

Dismissed by Lady Kingsborough in 1787, she excitedly determined to be a writer and she moved to London to work as a reviewer and editorial assistant on the new liberal journal, the *Analytical Review*, started by Joseph Johnson, who had published her books. Over the years she was to contribute a large number of reviews to this periodical, predominantly on fiction and educational works, but also on books concerning religion, philosophy, and aesthetics. Absolute certainty about what she wrote is however impossible since reviews were signed only by cryptic initials. Through Johnson MW was introduced to the liberal and radical circle which included Blake, Paine, Godwin, Hays, and Fuseli. Between 1787 and 1790 she also wrote two books designed for children, *Original Stories from Real Life*, a set of cautionary tales connected through an exemplary older lady Mrs Mason, and *The Female Reader*, a book of reading passages for girls. She also translated from the French Necker's *Of the Importance of Religious Opinions* and from the German Salzmann's *Elements of Morality*.

Her speedy political education in Newington Green and London made her a suitable person to enter the pamphlet war begun by Burke's *Reflections on the Revolution in France* which attacked her friend Richard Price. Wollstonecraft's *A Vindication of the Rights of Men* (1790) was the first of many replies disputing Burke's conservative assumptions. It denied that all was well with the British constitution and state and urged the need for much reform; at the same time it drew attention to the trivialization of women in British society, the main topic of her next work, *A Vindication of the Rights of Woman* (1792). This drew on her own experiences as an independent woman trying to earn a living in the few ways open to her, on her feelings of bitterness at her skimpy education, and on her observations on the frivolous lives of the upper classes; it took issue with male writers on women, especially Rousseau in *Emile*, and drew on arguments of the recently dead Catherine Macaulay whose book on female education MW had glowingly reviewed. The work was a powerful statement of rationalist feminism, demanding that women give up the privileged and degrading position of weakness which they could embrace because of society's association of them with emotionality and vulnerability. Instead it urged women to use reason and engage in strenuous mental activity, taking on new roles in society, although it accepted women's central function of motherhood. MW desired to restore to women their 'lost dignity' and to persuade them to eschew the role of helpless sentimental being. Her stance was rigidly moral and there was no room for sexual passion in her ideal, although she did appeal for a decent treatment of fallen women who, quite ridiculously, had to bear the whole punishment for sexual activity involving both sexes. In the beginning *The Rights of Woman* was immensely influential, inspiring many women to a new outspokenness, but in the conservative backlash at the end of the 1790s it became notorious, and in novels of these years a perusal of it by a fictional character often suggested wrong-headedness and, ironically, readiness for seduction.

During the writing of *The Rights of Woman* MW became infatuated with the married painter and philosopher Henry Fuseli; rejected by him she left for France in 1792 to witness the progress of the Revolution. She arrived in time to see the king passing to his trial and her immediate response to this event and to the alien city of Paris was a revulsion from her earlier idealism. This mood produced 'Letter on the Present Character of the French Nation', in which she poured out her disillusion with liberal philosophy and expressed the idea that vice and evil were the springs of action. In time, however, she worked out a more balanced view and her history of the early Revolution, *An Historical and Moral View of the Origin and Progress of the French Revolution* (1794), while still critical of many facets of French character and Revolutionary activities, held to the basic principles of the Revolution which she saw as inevitable and desirable.

During her time in Paris she began or renewed acquaintance with many of the English liberals and radicals such as Helen Maria Williams and Tom Paine. She also met and fell in love with an American speculator, Gilbert Imlay. In the rather desolate months that followed the expulsion of the British from Paris she nurtured her love for Imlay whose child, named after her early friend Fanny, she bore in 1794. By that time MW was living with Imlay in Le Havre, and it is clear from her passionate letters to him, later published in *Posthumous Works* (1798), that she knew his love to be waning. In 1795 she followed him to England; discovering his infidelity she attempted suicide.

Activity seemed to be a way forward and it was decided that she, her baby, and a nursemaid should travel to Scandinavia to help sort out a lawsuit in which Imlay was involved owing to the loss of a ship carrying silver. During her travels in Scandinavia she wrote descriptions of the scenery and people, as well as of her own melancholy mood, many of which formed the basis of *Letters Written during a Short Residence in Sweden, Norway, and Denmark* (1796). Returning to England, having been disappointed in a promised meeting with Imlay, she tried suicide a second time by plunging into the Thames in late 1795. She was dragged from the water unconscious. Over the next months she tried to conquer her infatuation with Imlay and begin a new life.

One element in her new life was William Godwin, author of *Political Justice*, whom she remet through her friend Mary Hays. Godwin had not been impressed with the younger strident MW but had been much moved by her recent *Letters*. As he put it in his *Memoirs* of her, it was 'friendship melting into love'. At this time MW began but did not finish a novel, *The Wrongs of Woman, or, Maria*, in which, through the life stories of two female characters, she described the economic, legal, and emotional oppression of middle- and lower-class women. The middle-class Maria makes many of the mistakes that MW had made with Imlay and the ambivalent message of the book seems to be the power of conditioning on women as well as their political oppression; the lower-class Jemima, a unique character in women's fiction of the time, is a downtrodden servant, prostitute, and thief.

Soon MW was pregnant, and despite their opposition to patriarchal marriage, she and Godwin thought it prudent to marry. Paradoxically the action shocked many friends who now understood that MW had not been married to Imlay. In 1797 she gave birth to a daughter, Mary: the birth went wrong and eleven days later she died in considerable pain. Godwin assuaged his grief by publishing fragments of her works, as well as a memoir of her, in which he freely described her affair with Imlay. The times were not propitious for such revelations and MW was much attacked as a corrupter of youth and an 'unsex'd female', whose books aimed at the propagation of whores. None the less her *Rights of Woman* continued to be read and she remained inspirational for feminists of both the nineteenth and twentieth centuries.   JANET TODD

Works: *Thoughts on the Education of Daughters* (1787); *Mary: A Fiction* (1788); *Original Stories from Real Life: With Conversations Calculated To Regulate the Affections and Form the Mind to Truth and Goodness* (1788); (trans.), *Of the Importance of Religious Opinions*, by J. Necker (1788); *The Female Reader, or, Miscellaneous Pieces, in Prose and Verse; Selected from the Best Writers, and Disposed under Proper Heads* (1789); *A Vindication of the Rights of Men, in a Letter to the Right Honourable Edmund Burke* (1790); (trans.), *Elements of Morality, for the Use of Children*, by C. G. Salzman (1790–1); *A Vindication of the Rights of Woman with Strictures on Political and Moral Subjects* (1792); *An Historical and Moral View of the Origin and Progress of the French Revolution, and the Effect It Has Produced in Europe* (1794); *Letters Written during a Short Residence in Sweden, Norway, and Denmark* (1796); *Posthumous Works of the Author of A Vindication of the Rights of Woman* (1798); *A Wollstonecraft Anthology* (includes some reviews) (1977); *Collected Letters* (1979).

References: BA (18); Butler, M., *Jane Austen and the War of Ideas* (1975); Drabble; DNB; Eliot, G., 'Margaret Fuller and Mary Wollstonecraft', *Essays of George Eliot* (1963); Flexner, E., *Mary Wollstonecraft: A Biography* (1972); Godwin, W., *Memoirs of the Author of A Vindication of the Rights of Woman* (1798); Jacobus, M., 'The difference of view', in *Women Writing and Writing about Women* (1979); Nystrom, P., *Mary Wollstonecraft's Scandinavian Journey*, Acta Regiae Societatis Scientiarum et Litterarum Gothoburgensis (1980); Poovey, M., *The Proper Lady and the Woman Writer* (1984); Sunstein, E., *A Different Face* (1975); Todd; Todd, J., *Women's Friendship in Literature* (1980); *Mary Wollstonecraft: A Bibliography* (1976); *The Sign of Angellica* (1989); Tomalin, C., *The Life and Death of Mary Wollstonecraft* (1974); Wardle, R., *Mary Wollstonecraft: A Critical Biography* (1951).

Wolstenholme-Elmy, Elizabeth
b. 1834; d. 1913
Essayist, poet
(Also wrote under E. Ellis, Ellis Ethelmer, Ignota)

Little is known of the early years of EW-E, who was orphaned as a child. Her father was a Methodist minister from Eccles and her brother a professor of mathematics at Cambridge. EW-E had a domestic education in which reading for pleasure was forbidden and which was deemed complete when she was 14, knowing 'as much as any woman needed to know'. A change in her guardianship allowed her to attend the Moravian School at Fulneck near Leeds for two years, but a request to attend the Bedford College for Women was vetoed and she studied for three years at home. She was then advised at the age of 19 to invest in, and manage, a boarding school. By 1865 she had set up the Manchester Schoolmistresses Association, her first act in a life of feminist commitment characterized by the breadth of her interests and concerns. She campaigned vigorously for women's suffrage, reform of the laws relating to marriage and the custody of children, and abolition of the Contagious Diseases Act. She became honorary secretary of the Manchester Women's Suffrage Society (1865) and secretary of the Married Women's Property Committee (1867–82), was a founding member of the Women's Franchise League (1899), formed the Women's Emancipation Union (1891), and then joined the Women's Social and Political Union.

Her belief that bodily integrity for women was a fundamental right and her anger at women's reduction to a sexual object as a consequence of men's obsession with physical love was the theme of much of her writing. In 'Judicial

Bias' (*Westminster Review* 1898), written under the pseudonym Ignota, EW-E argues against the definition of rape as possible only outside the confines of marriage, stating that this reduced the wife to 'bodily slavery'. As Ellis Ethelmer, EW-E wrote two sex education manuals for children and parents, *The Human Flower* and *Baby Buds*, containing clear and simple descriptions of human reproduction, in an attempt to dispel the state of ignorance of most women entering marriage.

In 1893 EW-E published a long poem, *Woman Free*, interesting for its verse and notes, which dealt with the history of woman's subordination to man. In it her anger is particularly vehement when she is considering man's brutality and sexual aggression, and she asserts that women must necessarily remain slaves until 'Free from all uninvited touch of man'. *Phases of Love* (1897) discusses the ideal sex relationship between men and women, that of psychic love, which promotes sexual self-control, thus releasing women from a role defined only by their sexual function. Her last work was a pamphlet issued by the Independent Labour Party in 1907, entitled *Woman's Franchise: The Need of the Hour*. SU CARDELL

Works: A collection of pamphlets relating to the guardianship of infants (1883–8); *A Woman's Plea to Women* (1886); *The Enfranchisement of Women* (1892); *Woman Free* (1893); *The Human Flower* (1894); *Baby Buds* (1895); *Life to Woman* (1896); *Phases of Love* (1897); *Woman's Franchise: The Need of the Hour* (1907).

References: Strachey, R., *The Cause* (1928).

Wood, Mrs Henry (Ellen Wood)

b. 17 January 1814, Worcester; d. 10 February 1887, Hampstead, London
Novelist
(Also wrote under Johnny Ludlow)

EW was the daughter of Thomas Price, a prosperous Worcester glove manufacturer, and Elizabeth Evans. Until she was 7 she lived with her grandmother in the shadow of Worcester Cathedral (Worcester was to provide the setting of many of her tales). With the death of her grandfather she was returned to her parents. Her father, who was passionately fond of music and the classics, supplemented the teaching offered by EW's governess. At the age of 13 she began to show signs of curvature of the spine; she was bedridden for four years, and left permanently handicapped, so that she always wrote in a reclining chair.

In 1836 she married Henry Wood, the head of a large banking and shipping firm, and settled with him in the South of France, where they lived for the next twenty years. They had several children, at least one of whom died of scarlet fever. In 1856 some undisclosed event caused Henry Wood, in the words of his son's memoir, to 'retire young from business life', and the family returned to England, taking furnished lodgings in Norwood. By then, EW had been writing short stories for about ten years, presumably to alleviate straitening financial circumstances; she published them in the *New Monthly Magazine* and, from 1854, in *Bentley's Miscellany*. Her first novel was *Danesbury House* (1860), written in response to the Scottish Temperance League's advertisement for a prize of £100 for the best story treating the theme of intemperance. The Scottish sales of this tale of a manufacturing family's fight against alcoholism exceeded those of any earlier novel. Shortly after this came *East Lynne*, which was written during a period of illness, and which brought EW almost immediate fame. Though initially rejected by two publishers, including Chapman and Hall whose reader, George Meredith, denounced it as 'foul' sentimentalism, it was finally accepted by Richard Bentley. It appeared in 1861 and, largely owing to a favourable review in *The Times*, sold over half a million copies within a short time. By 1900 over two and a half million copies had been sold. It was translated into numerous languages, including Hindi, and became a popular stage melo-drama both in England and America.

In 1866 Henry Wood died, and EW, suffering from nervous stress, went to France for four months to recuperate. Returning to London, she settled in St John's Wood and became the proprietor and editor (with her son's assistance) of the *Argosy*. At least half of the material for the periodical was contributed by EW herself, much of it anonymously, including a series of stories about Worcestershire life narrated by 'Johnny Ludlow'. By the end of her life, EW had written over thirty full-length novels and over 300 short stories. Having suffered from bronchitis for many years, she died of heart failure in 1887.

All EW's novels are firmly grounded in an extreme conservatism, found in its most overtly political form in *A Life's Secret* (1867), which provoked a workers' demonstration outside the publishing house on account of its hostility towards strikers. *Mrs Halliburton's Troubles* (1862) also has scenes of industrial dispute drawn from EW's background as a manufacturer's daughter. This conservatism is closely bound up with a repressive Victorian morality. An unrelenting retributive pattern is traced out for those who err according to the moral code of the patriarchal Victorian family, the code upheld by the Channing family (*The Channings*, 1862), who are shaken by false accusations directed at their favourite son. EW's first novel, in which the younger sons of Mr and Mrs Danesbury either die of *delirium tremens* or repent at the eleventh hour after a deathbed appeal by their father, sets the tone for the later novels, where submission to the passions always leads to expulsion from the Eden of Victorian society: home and family life. George Godolphin in *The Shadow of Ashlydyat* (1863) loses his wife through callous neglect of her, only to repent when it is too late.

EW's plots, which were always tightly constructed before she embarked on the main writing of the novels, have all the ingredients of the sensation novel of the period: murder, adultery, illegitimacy, disguise, and supernatural elements (though melodrama is combined with a realistic rendering of middle-class life). It is a formula epitomized by *East Lynne*, in which the anti-heroine, Lady Isabel Vane, mistakenly believing her husband, the kind-hearted Archibald Carlyle, to be having midnight assignations with another woman, is induced to run away with the 'false and heartless' rake, Frank Levison. Here she sets into motion one of the most sadistic retributive patterns of Victorian literature: she bears Levison a child, is deserted, reported killed in a train crash (which cripples and disfigures her), and returns in disguise to East Lynne as governess to her own children, to find that her husband has replaced her with her former rival, now the stereotype of the Victorian model wife, adoring and dutiful. Isabel has to preside at the deathbed of her own son, unable to reveal her identity, so that in the famous dramatized version, he dies without addressing her as mother. EW reinforces her already blatant message in a celebrated exhortation to the reader, in which the institution of marriage is seen to be inviolate: 'Lady – wife – mother! Should you ever be attempted to abandon your home . . . bear unto death, rather than forfeit your fair name and your fair conscience.' Adeline Sergeant, a contemporary, remarked that *East Lynne* owed half its popularity to the reaction against 'inane and impossible goodness' as the only suitable characteristic for a heroine. Although on the surface it presents a classic statement of the Victorian sexual code for women, there is a covert sympathy implicit in the close examination of Isabel's motives and feelings. Beneath this 'safe' and highly 'moral' tale there is a sub-text treating of female fantasies of escape from the patriarchal home.   ANNE FERNIHOUGH

Works: *Danesbury House* (1860); *East Lynne* (1861); *Mrs Halliburton's Troubles* (1862); *The Channings* (1862); *The Shadow of Ashlydyat* (1863); *The Foggy Night at Offord* (1863); *Verner's Pride* (1863); *William Allair, or, Running Away to Sea* (1864); *Lord Oakburn's Daughters (1864); Oswald Cray* (1864); *Trevlyn Hold, or, Squire Trevlyn's Heir* (1864); *Mildred Arkell* (1865); *St Martin's Eve* (1866); *Elster's Folly* (1866); *Lady Adelaide's Oath* (1867); *A Life's Secret* (1867); *Orville College* (1867); *The Red Court Farm* (1868); *Anne Hereford* (1868); *Roland Yorke* (1869); *Bessy Rane* (1870); *George Canterbury's Will* (1870); *Dene Hollow* (1871); *Within the Maze* (1872); *The Master of Greylands* (1873); *Johnny Ludlow*, 6 series of short stories (1874–89); *Told in the Twilight* (1875); *Bessy Wells* (1875); *Adam Grainger* (1876); *Edina* (1876); *Our Children* (1876); *Pomeroy Abbey* (1878); *Court Netherleigh* (1881); *About Ourselves* (1883); *Lady Grace and Other Stories* (1887); *The Story of Charles Strange* (1888); *Featherston's Story* (1889); *The Unholy Wish and Other Stories* (1890); *The House of Halliwell* (1890); *Ashley and Other Stories* (1897).

References: Auerbach, N., *Woman and the Demon: The Life of a Victorian Myth* (1982); Burgauer, R., *Mrs Henry Wood: Persönlichkeit und Werk* (1950); Elliott, J. B., 'A lady to the end: the case of Isabel Vane', *Victorian Studies* 19 (1976); Elwin, M., *Victorian Wallflowers* (1934); Hughes, W., *The Maniac in the Cellar: Sensation Novels of the 1860s* (1980); Maison, M. M., 'Adulteresses in agony', *Listener* (19 January 1961); Sergeant, A., *Women Novelists of Queen Victoria's Reign* (1897); Showalter, E., *A Literature of Their Own* (1977); Wood, C. W., *Memorials of Mrs Henry Wood* (1894).

Woolf, Virginia

b. 25 January 1882, Kensington, London; d. 28 March 1941, Lewes, Sussex
Novelist, essayist, reviewer

Now widely recognized as one of the great innovative novelists of the twentieth century, and a leading figure in feminist literature, VW was the daughter of the biographer and critic Sir Leslie Stephen and Julia Jackson Duckworth. From an early age she was immersed in literature, having access to her father's library and coming into frequent contact with his many distinguished literary friends (Meredith, Hardy, James, etc.). To her lifelong regret, however, she did not attend university.

Shortly after her mother's death in 1895, she experienced the first of a series of mental breakdowns which were to plague her for the rest of her life, leading to her eventual suicide in·1941. On the death of her father in 1904, she set up house at 46 Gordon Square, Bloomsbury, with her sister Vanessa (the painter, later to marry the art critic Clive Bell), and her two brothers Thoby and Adrian. Here, the Stephens' entertainment of Thoby's Cambridge friends, who included Lytton Strachey, Maynard Keynes, and E. M. Forster, marked the beginning of the cultural phenomenon which came to be known as Bloomsbury. In the same year VW wrote her first critical review for *The Times Literary Supplement*, and was to be a regular contributor almost until her death.

In 1912 she married the journalist and political theorist Leonard Woolf. By this time, she was close to finishing her first novel, *The Voyage Out*, which was not, however, published until 1915. Centring upon Rachel Vinrace, who leaves her sheltered home in Richmond to travel to South America on her father's steamer, the novel is essentially a *Bildungsroman*, conventional in form, charting a voyage of self-discovery.

In 1917 the Woolfs founded the Hogarth Press, which was to include among its early publications Katherine Mansfield's *Prelude* (1918) and T. S. Eliot's *Poems* (1919). *Two Stories* by Leonard and Virginia Woolf was Hogarth's first publication. VWs contribution, 'The Mark on the Wall', embodied in microcosm the techniques of her more experimental novels. The story opens with the narrator focusing her attention on a mark on the wall across the room and wondering what it might be. The stable world of referentiality dissolves as the mark, at the mercy of the subjective interpretations of the narrator, undergoes several transformations.

Although her second novel, *Night and Day* (1919), was still rooted in the positivistic 'realism' of Edwardian fiction, VW produced in the same year the essay 'Modern Fiction', in which she condemned Wells, Galsworthy, and Bennett as 'materialists', and which established her as one of the leading figures in the Modernist movement. References in the essay indicate that Joyce's *Ulysses* (1922) had begun to appear in serial form, and VW clearly recognized the implications of Joyce's narrative methods, and in particular of his rendering of the 'stream of consciousness'. In this essay we find her often-quoted description of life as 'a luminous halo, a semi-transparent envelope surrounding us from the beginning of consciousness to the end'. This new conception of reality, she argued, required a correspondingly new fictional technique, which would dispense with the teleological plot of the traditional novel.

Jacob's Room (1922), in which Jacob's death is clearly related to that of VW's brother Thoby in 1906, was the first of a series of experimental works in which VW put her fictional theories into practice. In it, the omniscient narrator and objective 'reality' disappear; instead, the world is filtered through one or more streams of consciousness. Such a technique necessarily involved a new approach to characterization. Her bold declaration in her celebrated essay 'Mr Bennett and Mrs Brown' (written in its original form in December 1923) that 'in or about December 1910, human character changed' made it clear that she was embarking upon a new epistemological quest. Since no single, external evaluation of a person's identity could be valid, the presentation in *Jacob's Room* of multiple consciousnesses – overlapping, complementary, and contradictory – yielded a synthesized view of Jacob which, the author implied, was the closest we could ever come to 'reality'. In this way, VW was fostering the open-mindedness and suspension of judgement characteristic of Modernism.

Whether or not Woolf found philosophical support for her theories in the Bergsonian concepts of time as duration (*durée*) and consciousness as an indivisible flux is still a matter for debate. Certainly she became increasingly preoccupied with the concept of time as her career progressed, and in particular, like many of the Modernists, with what she termed 'moments of being', the points at which temporality and eternity intersect. In *Mrs Dalloway* (1925) she exploits the tension between the clock-time of Big Ben (an essentially spatial concept, lending itself to mathematical measurement) and what would seem to be Bergson's 'real duration', 'a duration in which the past, always in motion, enlarges itself ceaselessly into a present that is absolutely new' (*L'Evolution Créatrice*). This in turn points to a further tension in the novel, that between man as a unique individual consciousness and man as a representative of common humanity. As in Joyce's *Ulysses*, the whole of the 'action' in *Mrs Dalloway* takes place in a single day, yet VW makes it clear (by the way in which the diverse characters scattered about London respond simultaneously to common stimuli) that Mrs Dalloway's day in London is all days everywhere for everybody.

In *To the Lighthouse* (1927), she draws heavily on her recollection of her parents, whom she recreates as Mr and Mrs Ramsay. Through the Ramsays, she sets two ways of knowing in opposition to each other, Mrs Ramsay's intuitive apprehension of 'truth' and Mr Ramsay's uncompromising adherence to 'fact'. The first section of the novel is dominated by the eagerness of the Ramsays' youngest son James to sail out to the lighthouse visible from the window of their summer home. On account of the weather, however, Mr Ramsay forbids it, and it is not until several years later, in the third section of the novel, that the lighthouse is finally reached. In the interim period (section 2), Mrs Ramsay has died and one of her sons been killed in the war. VW mentions these deaths parenthetically, thus illustrating the way in which such 'catastrophes' are necessarily absorbed into, and frequently submerged by, the flux of consciousness. The arrival at the lighthouse at the end of the novel, with its concomitant shedding of all personal grudges, coincides with Lily the artist's achievement of her vision, as she puts the final brushstroke to the painting begun several years previously. This climactic moment reveals the novel to be a metaphor for the coherence achieved by aesthetic composition, for the need to 'frame' reality and thus escape from the tyranny of immediacy. Significantly, Lily is a post-impressionist painter: on her canvas, Mrs Ramsay becomes a purple triangle, an implicit acknowledgement on VW's part that art can only hope to represent, and not to reproduce, life. For VW, as for Roger Fry whose biography she wrote in 1940, art does not concern dates, likenesses, and names; in short, it has nothing to do with the 'realism' of the preceding generation.

After *Orlando* (1928), a prose-fantasy in which the androgynous hero-heroine (inspired by VW's friend Vita Sackville-West) careers through the centuries, came *The Waves* (1931), her most experimental novel. Here, the lives of six human beings are glimpsed in a succession of interior monologues taking them from childhood to old age. Intermittently, descriptions of the sea, covering a day from dawn to dark, set the march of the sun in opposition to the true movement of reality as charted by these six lives. The novel raises questions of identity: are all identities really one, and does the individual identity remain constant in time and space? *The Waves*, too, through its spokesman, Bernard, a writer, is VW's most extensive exploration of language, and in particular of its boundaries, its failure to encompass experience in its entirety.

The Years (1937) marks a return to the 'realism' of the first two novels, taking us from the bleak and oppressive patriarchal home of the 1880s to the even bleaker 'Present Day' and the threat of dictatorship from abroad. In marked contrast to this essentially conventional handling of time, *Between the Acts*, VW's last novel, written shortly before her death, centres upon a village pageant which telescopes hundreds of years into a single July day. It is a last effort to reconcile the disordered and fragmentary experience of living with the sense of order or unity achieved through art, and to disentangle life's permanent significance from its apparent mutability. Further, it is the culmination of VW's exploration of continuity: ' "The Victorians", Mrs Swithin mused, "I don't believe that there ever were such people. Only you and me and William dressed differently." '

Woolf's critical reputation has been subject to dramatic fluctuations over the years. The emergence of the Leavises' *Scrutiny* as an arbiter of literary taste in the 1930s and 1940s had a powerful impact on the critical opinion of her work.

She was charged with sheltered hypersensitivity, moral inertia, and cultural snobbery. F. R. Leavis connected these deficiencies with Bloomsbury, 'her congenial and applauding socio-cultural milieu'. Such allegations received a powerful impetus both from the contemporary socio-political scene and from the impact of Marxist ideology, and led to the decline of VW's reputation after 1945, in spite of the counter-argument that, in her preoccupation with the isolation of the individual consciousness in a fragmented world, she was dealing with a major problem of modern life.

Ironically, however, it was from a sociological standpoint that interest in VW's work revived from the 1960s onwards, with the emergence of the feminist school of criticism. She is now seen to have repudiated rather than absorbed the Bloomsbury ethos, and an understanding of her two feminist tracts, *A Room of One's Own* (1929) and *Three Guineas* (1938), has become central to an understanding of her work as a whole, and to her vision of life. In these works, she sets out to create the uncreated model of her sex, uncreated because of the way in which women have, through the centuries, been judged by male standards and forced to adhere to alien modes of thought and expression; now they are 'outsiders', exiles within their own country.

A Room of One's Own is not only a plea for the privacy and financial independence implicit in its title; it is an investigation of the whole question of women and writing. In it, VW is seen to be deeply conscious of a tradition of female writing in which she herself is immersed, a tradition of novel writing, for when woman began to write, 'the novel alone was young enough to be soft in her hands.' Using an imaginary sister of Shakespeare whose literary aspirations end in suicide as an illustration of the difficulties women have had to encounter, VW looks forward to the day when women will become poets as well as novelists, and literature will explore the feminine areas of experience with which, hitherto, it has never dealt. Until now women have only been shown in relation to men. History must be rewritten, with a new emphasis on women's friendship: 'For if Chloe likes Olivia and Mary Carmichael knows how to express it, she will light a torch in that vast chamber where nobody has yet been.' In the last chapter, VW examines the concept of the androgynous mind: 'Perhaps a mind that is purely masculine cannot create, any more than a mind that is purely feminine'. She does not attempt to minimize the difference between the sexes; rather, her feminism involves both an assertion and a transcendence or reconciliation of sexual difference, in terms of co-operation between the sexes as well as within the individual mind. In the light of this, a new emphasis has been placed on *Orlando* as a celebration of androgyny: only when individuals learn to cultivate both masculine and feminine sides of their mind, can they approach wholeness of being.

This argument is carried through into *Three Guineas*, where the subjugation of women is seen as both cause and symptom of a fundamental imbalance, an 'excessive virility', in society. Here, VW's polemic rests upon the assertion 'that the public and the private worlds are inseparably connected; that the tyrannies and servilities of the one are the tyrannies and servilities of the other'. In particular, she links the tyrannous hypocrisy of the Victorian patriarchal home with the evils of fascism. The text manages, however, to transcend its own bitterness by pointing towards an androgynous dream, 'the dream of peace, the dream of freedom', based on 'the capacity of the human spirit to overflow boundaries and make unity out of multiplicity'.

This comparatively recent emphasis on VW as a sociological writer has led to a re-evaluation of those novels previously passed over as dull works of unredeemed fact. Paradigms of oppression and female inability to achieve fulfilment have been brought to the surface of *The Voyage Out, Night and Day,* and *The Years*; the last in particular has been accorded a new status as the fictional embodiment of the themes of *A Room of One's Own* and *Three Guineas,* and is a novel deeply subversive of patriarchal and capitalist British culture.

In addition to being a fiction writer and polemicist, VW was a prolific diarist, letter writer and literary critic. Two collections of critical essays were published during her lifetime (*The Common Reader*, 1925 and *The Common Reader: Second Series*, 1932), and there have been numerous posthumous collections. In these essays, VW frequently focuses her attention on minor writers, as if in conscious defiance of a patriarchal 'canon' of literature, and her tone is deliberately anti-authoritarian, abjuring omniscience.   ANNE FERNIHOUGH

Selected works: *The Voyage Out* (1915); *Night and Day* (1919); *Jacob's Room* (1922); *The Common Reader* (1925); *Mrs Dalloway* (1925); *To the Lighthouse* (1927); *Orlando* (1928); *A Room of One's Own* (1929); *The Waves* (1931); *The Common Reader: Second Series* (1932); *Flush: A Biography* (1933); *The Years* (1937); *Three Guineas* (1938); *Roger Fry: A Biography* (1940); *Between the Acts* (1941); *The Death of the Moth and Other Essays* (1942); *A Haunted House and Other Short Stories* (1943); *The Moment and Other Essays* (1947); *The Captain's Death Bed and Other Essays* (1950); *Granite and Rainbow* (1958); *Contemporary Writers* (1965); *Collected Essays* (1966–7); *Letters*, ed. N. Nicolson and J. Trautmann (1975–80); *Books and Portraits* (1977); *Diaries*, ed. A. Olivier Bell and A. McNeillie (1977–84); *The Complete Shorter Fiction of Virginia Woolf* (1985); *Essays*, ed. A. McNeillie (1987).

References: Bazin, N. T., *Virginia Woolf and the Androgynous Vision* (1973); Bell, Q., *Virginia Woolf: A Biography* (1972); Bennet, J., *Virginia Woolf: Her Art as a Novelist* (1945); Clements, P. and Grundy, I. (eds), *Virginia Woolf: New Critical Essays* (1983); Daiches, D., *Virginia Woolf* (1942); Delattre, F., *Le Roman Psychologique de Virginia Woolf* (1932); Dibattista, M., *Virginia Woolf's Major Novels: The Fables of Anon* (1980); Forster, E. M., *Virginia Woolf* (1942); Freedman, R. (ed.), *Virginia Woolf: Revaluation and Continuity: A Collection of Critical Essays* (1980); Gordon, L., *Virginia Woolf: A Writer's Life* (1984); Guiguet, J., *Virginia Woolf and Her Works*, trans. J. Stewart (1965); Hafley, J., *The Glass Roof: Virginia Woolf as Novelist* (1954); Harper, H., *Between Language and Silence: The Novels of Virginia Woolf* (1982); McLaurin, A., *Virginia Woolf: The Echoes Enslaved* (1973); Majumdar, R. and McLaurin, A. (eds), *Virginia Woolf: The Critical Heritage* (1975); Marcus, J., *New Feminist Essays on Virginia Woolf* (1981); Marcus, J., *Virginia Woolf: A Feminist Slant* (1983); Marder, H., *Feminism and Art: A Study of Virginia Woolf* (1968); Naremore, J., *The World without a Self: Virginia Woolf and the Novel* (1974); Rantavaara. I., *Virginia Woolf and Bloomsbury* (1953); Richter, H., *Virginia Woolf: The Inward Voyage* (1970); Rose, P., *Woman of Letters: A Life of Virginia Woolf* (1978); Schaefer, J. O., *The Three-Fold Nature of Reality in the Novels of Virginia Woolf* (1965); Spilka, M., *Virginia Woolf's Quarrel with Grieving* (1980); Sprague, C. (ed.), *Virginia Woolf: A Collection of Critical Essays* (1971); Trautmann, J., *The Jessamy Brides: The Friendship of Virginia Woolf and Victoria Sackville-West* (1980); Warner, E. (ed.), *Virginia Woolf: A Centenary Perspective* (1984).

Wordsworth, Dorothy

b. 25 December 1771, Cockermouth, Cumberland; d. 25 January 1855, Rydal

Diarist, travel writer

DW's first biographer, Ernest de Selincourt, described her as 'probably the most remarkable and the most distinguished of English writers who never wrote a line for the general public'. Apart from short extracts from her journals and letters which her brother, William Wordsworth, adapted for inclusion in his *Guide to the Lakes*, and a poem addressed 'To a Child' which he included in his *Poems* of 1815, nothing she wrote was published in her lifetime. Her vigorous assertion that she 'should detest the idea of setting [herself] up as an author', her lack of confidence when publication was urged by admiring friends, and the nature of her productions, indicate that for her the act of writing was a means of confirming her relationship with those she loved, not of communicating with others unknown.

DW was the third child and only daughter of Ann and John Wordsworth. Her father, who was agent to the Lowther family in Cockermouth, died intestate in 1783, leaving his affairs in disarray and his estate complicated by a large debt owed to him by his employer which was not settled until 1803. The children therefore grew up largely dependent upon the charity of their relations. Even before this disaster however, DW had experienced the sudden disintegration of her family when, on the death of her mother in 1778, she was sent to live with her mother's cousin in Halifax. Here she received her formal education, briefly at a boarding school and then at a day school until 1787. There followed a short unhappy period with her maternal grandparents in Penrith, and then six pleasant years in Norfolk with her uncle and his wife, assisting with the care of their young family. In 1795 a small legacy enabled William Wordsworth to offer his sister a home with him at Racedown in Dorset, where they became close associates of Coleridge, moving to Alfoxton House in Somerset in 1797 to be near him. In a misguided attempt at economizing and in order to learn the language, the Wordsworths spent a dispiriting winter in Germany, and then returned to the Lake District in 1797 to settle at Dove Cottage in Grasmere. DW dedicated the rest of her active life to the concerns of her brother and his family, living with them at various houses in Grasmere and finally at Rydal where she died in 1855. In 1803 she visited Scotland with Wordsworth and Coleridge; in 1820 she accompanied her brother, sister-in-law, a cousin and his bride on a six months' tour in Europe; in 1822 she made a second Scottish journey; in 1828 she stayed on the Isle of Man. These, and regular visits to relatives and friends, represent the only interruptions in a life of devoted service to the objects of her affection, lived in surroundings whose familiar beauty stirred her to passionate response. While keeping house for her recently ordained and lonely nephew in Leicestershire in 1828 she suffered an acute attack of gallstones from which her physical strength never fully recovered, and in 1835 she began to show signs of the onset of Alzheimer's disease. The last twenty years of her life were passed in a state of senile confusion, lovingly cared for by her brother and his wife.

DW's acute sensibility and power of living intensely in the moment were celebrated in her brother's poetry and acknowledged by Coleridge, who called her Wordsworth's 'exquisite sister'. In his memoir of Wordsworth, de Quincey included a detailed, perceptive, and sympathetic portrait of her as a woman 'so artless and fervent in her feelings, and so embarrassed in their utterance' that she seemed 'ungraceful' and even 'unsexual', 'the creature of impulse' burning with a 'self consuming style of thought'. This quality of ardent response, particularly to the natural world, is apparent in her writings, though it is almost entirely reserved for scenes and events which are already imbued with emotional meaning for her, and for contexts, such as journals and letters, where her relationship with her audience is one of confident intimacy. Her accounts of her 'tours' in Scotland and on the continent, written for a slightly larger group than her immediate family, while they contain much sharp observation, lack the spontaneity and visionary power of the journals which were intended to be shared only with her brother and Coleridge. The inter-relationship between their poetry and her prose indicates how productive this sharing was.

The *Alfoxton Journal* covers the first four months of 1798, a period of intense creative activity for Wordsworth and Coleridge, and the *Grasmere Journal*, begun in May 1800, 'because I shall give Wm pleasure by it', breaks off in January 1803, a few weeks after Wordsworth's marriage to DW's friend Mary Hutchinson. After a slight sense of strain in the first few entries, as if experimenting to find an appropriate style, DW relaxes into an informal, impressionistic record in which events of widely differing emotional significance are juxtaposed. The effect is not incongrous but integrated: domestic details included to identify the day provide a living context for moments of vision and delight. DW's imaginative response is particularly sensitive when some loved and familiar feature presents itself in a new guise through a change of light, weather, or season, as when the 'Island house' of Rydal Water, seen in fitful moonlight 'among the dark and lofty hills, with that bright soft light upon it', made her 'half a poet'. The journals are a record both of the landscape and of her imaginative delight in it. Her vivid, concrete, and particular observations of the colours, forms, and sounds of nature are a recreation of moments when she has felt, or shared, an intensity of response to the mysterious spiritual identity of natural objects. The same absorption in what she sees is evident in her compassionate but unsentimental accounts of vagrants met on the roads. She rarely comments or reflects, but catches the passing moment with fresh immediacy.

DW kept journals of all her 'tours', so that those from whom she was absent could share in her experiences. *Recollections of a Tour Made in Scotland* (1803) was written in its entirety after the event for 'a few friends who, it seemed, ought to have been with us', and who admired it sufficiently for publication to have been twice considered in DW's lifetime. It represents an impressive feat of memory, with its precise and minute recollection of places, encounters, and adventures, and it includes some vivid topographical writing, but the manner of its composition and its comparatively public nature inhibit the spontaneity and directness of expression found in earlier journals. *The Journal of a Tour on the Continent* (1820) DW herself accurately described as 'all written about the outside of things hastily viewed'. Her failure to respond imaginatively to Swiss and Italian scenery is evidenced by her habitual comparisons with the Lake District, which function partly to assist the imagination of her readers and partly to stimulate her own relatively unengaged feelings, so much less powerful than when she 'first visited the Wye, and all the world was fresh and new'. Her occasional use of erudite references, a formal, self-conscious style modelled on the conventions of travel literature, and some hitherto uncharacteristic moralizing are pointers to the fact that on this occasion the act of composition is a more pressing reality to her than the total engagement with experience recorded in the early journals.

DW's only attempt at a narrative of the experience of others is her moving account of the deaths in 1808 of the Grasmere couple, George and Sarah Green, and of the stoical courage of their children, which was circulated in manuscript to raise money for the orphans. She was an assiduous letter writer, and while her correspondence provides evidence of the increasing conventionality of her religious and social views from her thirties onwards, her letters to close friends also reveal something of the same clarity and intensity of vision as her early journals. In a letter written to the Rev. William Johnson in 1818, her description of an ascent of Scafell Pike, the panoramic views, and a brief but violent storm which 'came boiling over the mountains' manifests the same joy and imaginative immersion in the power and beauty of nature as she had felt in the Alfoxton days. She wrote 'nothing for the general public' because her sensibility depended for its expression upon an auditor, such as her brother, who was in complete sympathy with it, and with whom, therefore, her writing was not an act of communication, but of communion.   ELIZABETH JOYCE

Works: De Selincourt, E. (ed.), *Journals of Dorothy Wordsworth* (1941); Hill, A.G. (ed.), *Letters of William and Dorothy Wordsworth* (1967); Knight, W. (ed.), *Journals of Dorothy Wordsworth* (1897).

References: De Quincey, T., *Recollections of the Lakes and the Lake Poets*, ed. D. Wright (1970); De Selincourt, E., *Dorothy Wordsworth* (1933); Gittings R. and Manton, J., *Dorothy Wordsworth* (1985); Maclean, R., *Dorothy Wordsworth: The Early Years* (1932).

Wroth, Lady Mary

b. 1586 or 1587, Penshurst Place, Kent; d. 1651 or 1653
Poet, fiction writer

Born into a literary family MW had as models her uncle Philip Sidney, her father Robert Sidney, author of *Rosis and Lysa*, and her aunt and godmother Mary [Sidney] Herbert, Countess of Pembroke. MW herself was well known in Jacobean literary circles. Her poetry was circulated in manuscript and was praised by such contemporary writers as Nathaniel Baxter, Joshua Sylvester, George Chapman, and Ben Jonson, who said that he had become 'a better lover and much better Poet' after reading her sonnets. Jonson dedicated *The Alchemist* to her and praised her as 'a Sydney' (Epigram 103) who incorporated the virtues of all the goddesses (Epigram 105); in 'To Sir Robert Wroth' Jonson praised MW's husband and estate much as he had praised her parents in 'To Penshurst'.

Her extravagant husband, whom she married in 1604, died in 1614, leaving the young widow with an infant son (James, who died in 1616) and a staggering debt of some £23,000. She undertook to pay off the debt herself and, despite King James's repeated pardoning of various debts, by 1624 she had paid off just half of the total. She was in financial difficulties for the rest of her life. It may have been the need for money that prompted her to publish *The Countesse of Mountgomeries URANIA. Written by the right Honorable the Lady MARY WROATH. Daughter to the right Noble Robert Earle of Leicester. And Neece to the ever famous, and renowned Sr Phillips Sidney knight. And to ye most exelet Lady Mary Countesse of Pembroke late deceased* (1621).

Urania, the first known full-length work of fiction by an Englishwoman, is modelled on *The Countess of Pembroke's Arcadia* by Philip Sidney. Although published in the seventeenth century, it is in Elizabethan mode. Like the *Arcadia*, the narrative is polyphonic; each event leads to the telling of several more stories, forming an intricate web. Whereas the *Arcadia* follows the adventures of two princes and their wooing of two princesses, the *Urania* has a female protagonist and focuses on the love of Pamphilia, the image of Constancy, for her cousin Amphilanthus, 'Lover-of-two'. Pamphilia is condemned to passive suffering more often than active redress, reflecting gender roles. Love is usually false, and the romance has a disillusioned, even cynical, tone. Inconstancy appears an almost inevitable male attribute that is sometimes presented comically: Pamphilia reads of 'the affection of a Lady to a braue Gentleman, who equally loued, but being a man, it was necessary for him to exceede a woman in all things, so much as inconstancie was found fit for him to excell her in, hee left her for a new'. Thinking herself 'safe in the happinesse of her loue', Pamphilia throws away the book. Her subsequent adventures challenge the traditional feminine virtues of obedience, silence, and chastity. She refuses to marry the man her father proposes, choosing instead to marry her kingdom. Unlike the silent Stella, Pamphilia is an accomplished poet. Although she was 'the discreetest fashiond woman', she allows Amphilanthus to come into her Cabinet to fetch some verses. From her verses and her blushes, Amphilanthus realizes that she loves him and embraces her. Disdaining the part of the disdainful mistress, she 'chid him not, nor did so much as frowne, which shewed she was betrayd'. Amphilanthus unfortunately is 'matchlesse in all vertues, except . . . loue'. Inconstancy is his only fault: yet 'thou art constant to loue; for neuer art thou out of loue, but variety is thy staine'. Reverting to the feminine virtue of patient suffering, Pamphilia resolves to remain true despite his unfaithfulness for 'to leaue him for being false, would shew my loue was not for his sake, but mine owne'. Her friend Urania wryly says, 'tis pitie . . . that euer that fruitlesse thing Constancy was taught you as a vertue'. Virtue is eventually rewarded, however, for after many wanderings Amphilanthus returns to his forgiving Pamphilia. Like the *Arcadia, Urania* stops in the middle of a sentence: 'Pamphilia is the Queene of all content; Amphilanthus ioying worthily in her; And'. The 'and' is supplied in the second, unpublished, section of the *Urania*, wherein Pamphilia and Amphilanthus each marry someone else.

Since it supposedly satirized various court intrigues, including those of Lord Hay, *Urania* caused such a scandal that MW was forced to withdraw the book from sale; it has never been reprinted. Sadly, the example of the Countess of Pembroke was used as a weapon to silence her goddaughter. Lord Denny, father of Lady Hay, admonished MW to imitate her 'vertuous and learned Aunt, who translated so many godly bokes, and especially the holy Psalms of David' rather than creating 'lascivious tales and amarous toyes'; translation, not creation, was the province of a learned woman. MW gave a spirited reply to Denny, but she was apparently forced to learn the womanly virtue of silence; none of her other work was published. Denny's admonition is particularly ironic, since it was undoubtedly her 'vertuous and learned Aunt' who encouraged her to imitate the model of Philip Sidney's works, as her father Robert had done. Until her marriage MW was often with her aunt at Wilton or Baynards Castle, or at the Sidney home of Penshurst. She was about 12 years old when the countess brought out the 1598 collected edition of Philip's works, including the *Arcadia* and *Astrophil and Stella*, the models for MW's own work. In addition to poems scattered through the text in the manner of the *Arcadia*, a series of over 100 love songs and sonnets entitled *Pamphilia to Amphilanthus* is appended to *Urania*; these may not refer to a specific person, but there are hints that Amphilanthus may be MW's cousin, William Herbert, Earl of Pembroke, father of her two illegitimate children. MW includes in *Urania* a poem elsewhere attributed to Pembroke, beginning, 'Had I loved butt att that rate/Which hath binn ordain'ed by fate'.

In addition to the *Urania*, MW also wrote an unpublished pastoral romance, 'Loues Victorie', wherein the vagaries of love are presented with interspersed poems to Venus. Like *Urania*, this drama has topical references, including Philisses (Philip Sidney), his sister Simena (the Countess of Pembroke), and Lissius (the Countess's friend Dr Mathew Lister). Simena loves Lissius. He has scorned love but, as is typical for pastoral romance, is punished by falling desperately in love. Simena overhears him confess, 'O sweet Simena looke butt on my paine I . . . curse my selfe for my disdaine.' At first she rejects his profession as insincere, but he convinces her that he offers 'a Vertuous loue'. Although they vow eternal love, their subsequent relationship is tempestuous because Simena listens to rumours which turn out to be unfounded. After they are reconciled, they vow to abjure jealousy, thereby becoming 'the couple Cupid best doth loue'. Probably an early work, 'Loues Victorie' is light-hearted pastoral, without the darker tones of the *Urania*.

In her younger days MW acted in masques, including Jonson's *The Masque of Blacknesse*. As a widow, she withdrew from court and went abroad; Anne Clifford mentioned that she saw her at Penshurst, and she brought 'news from beyond the sea'. Like her godmother, she developed literary friendships and circulated her manuscripts, as evidenced by her letters to Dudley Carleton in 1619. Although she must have written other works besides the *Urania* and 'Loues Victorie', they have been lost to us. Through these two works, however, we hear a woman's voice speaking of the cost of courtly love.

MARGARET P. HANNAY

Works: *The Countesse of Mountgomeries URANIA. Written by the right Honorable the Lady MARY WROATH. Daughter to the right Noble Robert Earle of Leicester. And Neece to the ever famous, and renowned Sr Phillips Sidney knight. And to ye most exelet Lady Mary Countesse of Pembroke late deceased.* (1621); 'Loues Victorie' (unpublished, n.d.); *The Poems of Lady Mary Wroath* (1983).

References: Beilin, E. V., ' "The onely perfect vertue": constancy in Mary Wroth's *Pamphilia to Amphilanthus*', *Spenser Studies* 2 (1981); Parry, G., 'Lady Mary Wroth's *Urania*', *Proceedings of the Leeds Philosophical and Literary Society* 16 (1975); Paulissen, M. N., *The Love Sonnets of Lady Mary Wroth: A Critical Introduction* (1982); Paulinssen, M. N., 'Forgotten love sonnets of the court of King James: the sonnets of Mary Wroth', *Publications of the Missouri Philological Association* 3 (1978); Roberts, J. A., 'Lady Mary Wroth's sonnets: a labyrinth of the mind', *Journal of Women's Studies in Literature* 1 (1979); Salzman, P., 'Contemporary references in Mary Wroth's *Urania*', *Review of English Studies* 29 (1978); Swift, C. R., 'Feminine identity in Lady Mary Wroth's romance *Urania*', *ELR* 14 (Autumn 1984).

Yates, Frances

b. 28 November 1899, Portsmouth; d. 29 September 1981, London
Historian, literary critic
FY was the daughter of a naval architect in the service of the Royal Corps of Naval Constructors, James Alfred Yates, and his wife, Hannah Malpas. Her father's work in dockyards around Britain meant that FY's education was unsettled, and, although she attended the Laurel Bank School in Glasgow and Birkenhead High School at various periods, she was mostly educated at home, where her family, particularly her two elder sisters, assisted her efforts. She read French at the University of London, graduating with a BA in 1924; she obtained her MA two years later. For the next thirteen years FY, whilst not

officially attached to any academic institution, continued with her research; she also did some teaching at the North London Collegiate School. It was during this period, in 1934, that her first book, *John Florio: The Life of an Italian in Shakespeare's England*, appeared.

The dominating intellectual interest of FY's life, the work of Giordano Bruno, the Italian magus and philosopher, led to a decisive step forward in her academic career. In 1936 she advertised her intention of making a translation of Bruno's *The Ash Wednesday Supper* in *The Times Literary Supplement* and received a response from Dorothea Walbank Singer, who introduced her to Edgar Wind, one of the circle of German-Jewish scholars associated with the Warburg Institute which had fled Germany in 1933. After working as an ambulance attendant for two years at the beginning of the war, FY became a part-time research assistant at the Institute in 1941. Three years later she was appointed Lecturer in Renaissance Culture and Editor of Publications there. She remained at the Institute for the rest of her life, becoming Reader in the History of the Renaissance in 1956, and an honorary fellow in 1967. She continued to write until the end of her life and was working on an autobiography when she died.

FY's many books combine a remarkable continuity of interest with an unusual breadth and depth of learning in a way characteristic of the work of the Warburg Institute. Her informal education and initial independence from any official post, however, meant that even before joining the Institute she had little respect for the arbitrary boundaries separating academic disciplines. Even where, as in *Giordano Bruno and the Hermetic Tradition* (1964), FY investigates a discrete strand of intellectual history, the implications for areas of culture apparently untouched by hermetic and magical thinking are many and fruitful. A chapter dealing with Ficino's hermeticism ends with a suggestion that Botticelli's *Primavera* may be a magical object concerned with the attraction of the favourable planets and the warding-off of Saturn; a section considering ecclesiastical and humanist responses to hermeticism argues that the 'disapproval of the use of force in religious matters' displayed by More's Utopians is distinctively hermeticist.

More substantially, *The Art of Memory* (1966) moves from a demonstration of the Renaissance use of metaphorical 'memory theatres' as mnemonic devices to the dramatic claim that Robert Fludd's Theatre Memory System contains factual information about the second Globe Theatre, and even that the Globe can itself be understood as a memory theatre. A later and even more thoroughly interdisciplinary example of FY's approach is *Astraea: The Imperial Theme*, in which contemporary poetry, paintings, and collections of madrigals, amongst other sources, are used to elucidate the cult of Queen Elizabeth I as 'Astraea'. Such a breadth of approach is matched by the chronological span of FY's work: both her book on Bruno and *The Art of Memory* begin their investigations in classical antiquity and pursue them through the Middle Ages to the Renaissance.

These qualities put FY in a position to untangle the complex syncretism of Renaissance thought in a way which has proved influential for all branches of Renaissance studies. But FY's work is not of merely antiquarian interest, for its unifying emphasis is on the recovery of lost discourses and practices hitherto regarded as 'occult', and their relation to those apparently established as definitively rational. *Giordano Bruno and the Hermetic Tradition* indicates the importance of those like John Dee who were simultaneously magi and mathematicians to the scientific revolution of the seventeenth century; at the same time FY carefully distinguishes between Bruno's magical and philosophical, and Kepler's more purely mathematical, interest in Copernicus. Such care adds force to the book's

closing suggestion that much philosophical resonance has been lost in the transition from magical to scientific rationality.   SIMON JARVIS
Works: *John Florio: The Life of an Italian in Shakespeare's England* (1934); *A Study of* Love's Labour's Lost (1936); *The French Academies of the Sixteenth Centuries* (1947); *The Valois Tapestries* (1959); *Giordano Bruno and the Hermetic Tradition* (1964); *The Art of Memory* (1966); *Theatre of the World* (1969); *The Rosicrucian Enlightenment* (1972); *Astraea: The Imperial Theme* (1975); *Shakespeare's Last Plays* (1975); *The Occult Philosophy of the Elizabethan Age* (1979); *Collected Essays* (1982–4); *Frances A. Yates, 1899–1981* (1983).
References: *CA*.

Yearsley, Ann
b. 1756, Clifton, near Bristol; d. 8 May 1806, Melksham, Wiltshire
Poet, novelist
AY's mother delivered milk to houses and AY took the same job in her turn. She was later to be known in literary circles as 'Lactilla' or 'the poetical milkwoman', taking her place in a series of working-class poets habitually known to the public by their trades, including Stephen Duck, 'the thresher poet', and Robert Burns, 'the poetical ploughboy'. AY was taught to write by her brother, and read voraciously such books as she could obtain, including Shakespeare, Milton, and Young's *Night Thoughts*. She married a young illiterate man called Yearsley in 1774 and gave birth to six children over the next seven years. The family fell into severe financial distress, and AY's plight, as well as her poetry, were brought to the notice of Hannah More by her cook in 1784.

More's first response was to lend AY a grammar, a spelling book, and a dictionary, but her assistance later took more generous forms: she spent much of the following year obtaining subscribers for an edition (with corrections by herself) of AY's *Poems on Several Occasions* (1784). The first edition earned £350, whilst subsequent editions brought in a further £250. However, More and her friend Elizabeth Montagu invested the money in funds and made themselves joint trustees, refusing to allow AY access to the money. Not surprisingly, AY was furious and a public dispute followed between 'Lactilla' and her patrons, in which AY not only demanded that she be paid for her work but also accused More of having spoiled her poems by 'correcting' them. AY eventually regained control of her money, but without More's patronage she had few prospects of literary success, and her subsequent tragedy *Earl Goodwin*, performed in 1789, and novel *The Royal Captives* (1795) made little critical impression. She opened an unsuccessful circulating library in Bristol Hot Wells and in 1793 was obliged to accept financial help from Joseph Cottle. She died almost entirely forgotten.

AY was encouraged by her patrons to think of herself as an unlearned, inspirational poet. A letter from More to Montagu prefixed to AY's poems promised, 'By the next post I will send you some of her wild wood notes. You will find her, like all unlettered poets, abounding in imagery, metaphor, and personification.' The later preface by AY to *The Royal Captives* shows that even after her breach with More and Montagu AY continued to regard herself in this light: 'None may condemn me; Nature herself drew delusion in the desart where I was beloved by Fancy, before I was alive to Fame. . . .' But the evidence of AY's poetry itself often contradicted her patrons' preconceptions: More was compelled to confess herself 'surprised at the justness of her taste, the faculty I least expected to find in her'. Although More was at pains to point out that 'it has been denied her to drink at the *pure well-head* of Pagan Poesy', AY's poems are frequently adorned with classical allusions, which More occasionally criticizes in footnotes. 'It is supposed this word ["Croesean"] is derived, although not very legitimately, from CROESUS.' But such critical footnotes were less prevalent in the volume than outright correction.

AY's poetry sometimes casts her as the untaught rustic in the most conventional way possible. Her first collection of poems includes an 'artless song' addressed as a Valentine to 'Strephon'. Her poems could also cater for her patrons' taste in a more direct way, as in 'To Mr R—, on his Benevolent Scheme for rescuing Poor Children from Vice and Misery, by promoting Sunday Schools': as an authentic representative of the poor, AY was ideally placed to sponsor this personal interest of More's. Other poems occasionally verge on sycophancy: 'On Mrs Montagu' portrays its subject in flight: 'Lo! where she mounting spurns the steadfast earth,/ And, sailing on the cloud of science, bears/ The banner of perfection.' Such praise betrays a slight uncertainty of register: whilst James Thomson, for example, could decorously portray the deceased Sir Isaac Newton on the wing, his addresses to living patrons were cast in more sober terms.

The reader expecting 'wild wood notes' in AY's work is likely to be surprised by the extent to which it recalls particular earlier eighteenth-century poems. 'Night – to Stella' is strongly reminiscent both in style and content of Edward Young's *Night Thoughts*: its title immediately recalls his, its blank verse includes, like Young's, a high proportion of end-stopped lines, whilst its unruly personifications, emblems, and apostrophes, far from being the indications of noble savagery that More thought them, are closely modelled upon the older poet's. However, AY could also write with a refreshing disrespect for the rules of poetic genre: 'Clifton Hill', whose title would appear to announce it as a topographical poem along the lines of, for example, Richard Jago's *Edge Hill*, in fact veers between being a georgic and being a meditative soliloquy.

                                                                           JAMES SMITH

Works: *Poems on Several Occasions* (1784); *Poems on Various Subjects* (1787); *Stanzas of Woe* (1790); *Earl Goodwin* (1791); *The Royal Captives* (1795); *The Rural Lyre* (1796).

References: Allibone; *DNB*; Lewis, W. S. *et al.* (eds), *Horace Walpole's Correspondence* (1974); Roberts, W. (ed.), *Memoirs of the Life and Correspondence of Hannah More* (1834); Southey, R., *The Lives and Works of the Uneducated Poets* (1925); Tinker, C. B., *Nature's Simple Plan* (1922); Todd; Tompkins, J. M. S., *The Polite Marriage* (1938); Unwin, R., *The Rural Muse* (1954).

Yonge, Charlotte Mary

b. 1823, Otterbourne, Hampshire; d. 1901, Otterbourne

Novelist, writer for children

One of the most prolific writers in a period of prolific writers, CMY led an outwardly uneventful life. Her father was an army officer and she had only one brother, seven years younger than herself. She was educated at home and her great delight was her annual visit to her large family of cousins in Devonshire about whom she must have thought a great deal in her solitary days. She writes of this in the preface to the first of her family chronicles, *Scenes and Characters*, when it was reprinted in 1886: 'An almost solitary child, with periodical visits to the Elysium of a large family, it was natural to dream of other children and their ways and sports till they became almost realities.' In the same preface she tells us how her writing came about. A French master set her the task of writing letters which developed into narrative about a family; 'the tale was actually printed for private sale, as a link between translations of short stories.' The family remained in her mind and were 'my companions in many a solitary walk'. They were to form the first of the families, mostly very large indeed, who people the lively linked novels she wrote in the next fifty years. The greatest influences in her life were her father and the vicar who came to nearby Hursley in 1838, the great Tractarian, John Keble. It was he who gave her a mission, to use her writing to help girls in their formative years: 'to help [you] to perceive how to bring your religious principles to bear upon your daily life . . . show you the examples, both good and evil, of historical persons, and . . . tell you of the workings of God's providence both here and in other lands' (Introductory Letter to the first volume of *The Monthly Packet*, 1851). She never swerved in her devotion to the High Church teachings of her youth, a devotion which all her good characters share. Her earnings, as well as her enthusiasm, went to support many Anglican charities and missions.

For forty-three years she edited a bulky magazine for adolescent girls, *The Monthly Packet*, writing much of it herself. Many of her family novels were first serialized in it. Her working methods were extraordinary in that she usually had three things on the go at once, all lying on her desk – perhaps a family novel, a historical story, and a work of religious instruction – and she wrote a page at a time while waiting for the ink to dry. As her biographer, Christabel Coleridge, says, it 'could only be watched with awe.' Her books were very popular with girls all over the world but one in particular won her critical acclaim from several of the great literary figures of her day. *The Heir of Redclyffe* (1853) is one of the finest expressions of the Tractarian spirit and was admired by Tennyson, Kingsley, Rossetti, and Morris. In Ethel May in *The Daisy Chain* (1856) she created a bookish, untidy, unladylike heroine twelve years before Jo March appeared across the Atlantic in *Little Women*. Her historical stories engaged her in research, especially of early French history, but they are, with the exception of *The Little Duke* (1854), not as highly regarded by devotees of her work as the family stories, particularly those involving the May family of *The Daisy Chain* and the Underwoods of *The Pillars of the House*. These novels are remarkable for their insight into family relationships and their convincing studies of child development. The incidents in which the moral growth of these children is so engagingly revealed give the books the same fascination as Hawthorne detected in the linked novels of Trollope: 'just as real as if some giant had hewn a great lump out of the earth and put it under a glass case, with all its inhabitants going about their daily business, and not suspecting that they were being made a show of.' She was good at conversation, often racy, really colloquial child's speech, and the openings of her novels are arresting. She had an amazing facility with Christian names, usually giving her characters two and frequently a nickname as well, and she published a scholarly *History of Christian Names* in 1863. Edith Sichel wrote in her obituary, 'she plucks the heart out of the obvious' and pointed to the nature of her realism: 'She knew in their essence all the little things that affect family life, even to the frictions that exist, without fault on any side, between differing temperaments in the same circle. That is why we do not so much read her stories as live next door to her characters, embracing all the worry and tedium as well as the pleasure which identification with a family must mean.' As she wrote for so many years her novels are a mine of information about social life and its changes in the Victorian period: church life and worship, manners, reading, education, illness, dress, taste in furnishings, houses, meals and the times of them – all the minutiae which make the reading of her novels enthralling. In her critical writings she had some valuable things to say about writing for children.

MARY SHAKESHAFT

Selected Works: Scenes and Characters (1847); The Heir of Redclyffe (1853); Hearts-ease (1854); The Daisy Chain (1856); Dynevor Terrace (1857); Hopes and Fears (1860); The Young Stepmother (1861); Countess Kate (1862); The Clever Woman of the Family (1865); The Pillars of the House (1873); Magnum Bonum (1879).

References: BA (19); Battiscombe, G., *Charlotte Mary Yonge* (1943); Battiscombe, G. and Laski, M. (eds), *A Chaplet for Charlotte Mary Yonge* (1965); Coleridge, C., *Charlotte Mary Yonge: Her Life and Letters* (1903); Mare, M. and Percival, A. C., *Victorian Bestseller: The World of Charlotte Mary Yonge* (1947); Romanes, E., *Charlotte Mary Yonge: An Appreciation* (1908).

Index